The Wiley-Blackwell Handbook of Addiction Psychopharmacology

The Wiley-Blackwell Handbook of Addiction Psychopharmacology

Edited by James MacKillop and Harriet de Wit

A John Wiley & Sons, Ltd., Publication

This edition first published 2013
© 2013 John Wiley & Sons, Ltd.

Wiley-Blackwell is an imprint of John Wiley & Sons, formed by the merger of Wiley's global
Scientific, Technical and Medical business with Blackwell Publishing.

Registered Office
John Wiley & Sons Ltd, The Atrium, Southern Gate, Chichester, West Sussex,
PO19 8SQ, UK

Editorial Offices
350 Main Street, Malden, MA 02148-5020, USA
9600 Garsington Road, Oxford, OX4 2DQ, UK
The Atrium, Southern Gate, Chichester, West Sussex, PO19 8SQ, UK

For details of our global editorial offices, for customer services, and for information about how
to apply for permission to reuse the copyright material in this book please see our website at
www.wiley.com/wiley-blackwell.

The right of James MacKillop and Harriet de Wit to be identified as the authors of the
editorial material in this work has been asserted in accordance with the UK Copyright,
Designs and Patents Act 1988.

Library of Congress Cataloging-in-Publication Data

The Wiley-Blackwell handbook of addiction psychopharmacology / edited by
James MacKillop, Harriet De Wit.
     p. cm.
  Includes index.
  ISBN 978-1-119-97826-8 (hardback)
1. Substance abuse–Chemotherapy–Handbooks, manuals, etc.   2. Psychopharmacology–
Handbooks, manuals, etc.   I. MacKillop, James, 1975–   II. De Wit, Harriet.
  RC564.15.W53 2013
  616.89′18–dc23

                                                                    2012030907

A catalogue record for this book is available from the British Library.

Cover image: © FotograficaBasica / iStockphoto
Cover design by Cyan Design

Set in 10/12.5 pt Galliard by Aptara Inc., New Delhi, India
Printed and bound in Singapore by Markono Print Media Pte Ltd

1   2013

To Emily
–JM

Contents

Plate section between 688 and 689

About the Editors

James MacKillop

Dr MacKillop received his PhD in clinical psychology at the State University of New York at Binghamton, completing his predoctoral internship in clinical psychology at the Brown University Clinical Psychology Consortium. He subsequently completed a postdoctoral fellowship in addiction research at the Brown University Center for Alcohol and Addiction Studies, where he remains as an adjunct faculty member. His primary appointment is as an Associate Professor of Psychology at the University of Georgia, where he directs the Experimental and Clinical Psychopharmacology Laboratory. Dr MacKillop's research uses diverse research strategies to study addictive behavior, from cognitive neuroscience and molecular genetics to human laboratory and clinical approaches. Dr MacKillop's research has been supported by the National Institutes of Health, the Robert Wood Johnson Foundation, and the Alcoholic Medical Research Foundation, among other granting agencies, and he has published over 90 peer-reviewed articles and book chapters in this area.

Harriet de Wit

Dr de Wit obtained her PhD in experimental psychology from Concordia University in Canada, and has conducted extensive research on the behavioral effects of drugs of abuse in human volunteers. She has published over 200 empirical papers and she has editorial roles with two journals, *Psychopharmacology* and *Alcoholism: Clinical and Experimental Research*. Dr de Wit has conducted research on individual differences in responses to drugs, including differences related to genetic variation. She has also studied the role of impulsivity, stress, and sex hormones in acute responses to drugs. She is a Professor of Psychiatry and Behavioral Neuroscience at the University of Chicago.

About the Contributors

Bina Ali, MPH, Department of Behavioral and Community Health, University of Maryland, College Park

Michael T. Amlung, MS, Graduate Student, Department of Psychology, University of Georgia

James (Jim) C. Anthony, PhD, Professor, Department of Epidemiology and Biostatistics, College of Human Medicine, Michigan State University

Guadalupe Bacio, MA, Doctoral Student, Department of Psychology, University of California, Los Angeles

Amy Bacon, PhD, Department of Psychology, Bradley University

Marian R. Beasley, MA, Doctoral Student, Counseling and Human Development Services, University of Georgia

Warren K. Bickel, PhD, Professor and Director, Addiction Recovery Research Center, Virginia Tech Carilion Research Institute

James Robert Brašić, MD, MPH, Assistant Professor, Department of Radiology and Radiological Science, The Johns Hopkins University School of Medicine

Ashley Braun, MA, Doctoral Student, Department of Psychology, University of Illinois at Chicago

Anne E. Carter, PhD, Research Associate, Addiction Recovery Research Center, Virginia Tech Carilion Research Institute

Laurie Chassin, PhD, Regents Professor of Psychology, Arizona State University

Young-Il Cho, PhD, Assistant Professor, Sungshin Women's University

Paul Christiansen, School of Psychology, University of Liverpool

Kelly E. Courtney, MA, Doctoral Student, Department of Psychology, University of California, Los Angeles

Jennifer Dahne, BA, Department of Psychology, University of Maryland, College Park

Stacey B. Daughters, PhD, Department of Behavioral and Community Health, University of Maryland, College Park

Harriet de Wit, PhD, Professor, Department of Psychiatry and Behavioral Neuroscience, University of Chicago

Herman A. Diggs, MA, Department of Psychology, Southern Illinois University

Monique Ernst, MD, National Institute of Mental Health, National Institutes of Health

Matt Field, PhD, Reader in Experimental Addiction Research, School of Psychology, University of Liverpool

Mark Fillmore, PhD, Professor, Department of Psychology, University of Kentucky

Kirstin M. Gatchalian, PhD, Research Associate, Addiction Recovery Research Center, Virginia Tech Carilion Research Institute

Emily Gean, PhD, Senior Research Assistant, Department of Radiology, Division of Nuclear Medicine, Johns Hopkins Medical Institutions

David Gilbert, PhD, Professor, Department of Psychology, Southern Illinois University

Adrienne J. Heinz, PhD, San Francisco Veteran Affairs Medical Center

Jokae Ingram, MS, Doctoral Student, Counseling and Human Development Services, University of Georgia

David P. Jarmolowicz, PhD, Post-doctoral Associate, Addiction Recovery Research Center, Virginia Tech Carilion Research Institute

Jon D. Kassel, PhD, Professor of Psychology, Department of Psychology, University of Illinois at Chicago

Thomas R. Kirchner, Research Investigator, Schroeder Institute for Tobacco Research and Policy Studies, The American Legacy Foundation

Matthew Kirkpatrick, PhD, Post-doctoral scholar, Department of Psychiatry and Behavioral Neuroscience, University of Chicago

Mikhail N. Koffarnus, PhD, Research Assistant Professor, Addiction Recovery Research Center, Virginia Tech Carilion Research Institute

Matthew R. Lee, Doctoral Candidate in Psychology, Arizona State University

Carl W. Lejuez, PhD, Professor, Department of Psychology, University of Maryland, College Park

Alyson Listhaus, BS, University of Maryland, College Park

Donald R. Lynam, PhD, Professor, Department of Psychological Sciences, Purdue University

In Kyoon Lyoo MD, PhD, Department of Psychiatry and Interdisciplinary Program for Neuroscience, Seoul National University, The Brain Institute, University of Utah

James MacKillop, PhD, Associate Professor, Department of Psychology, University of Georgia

Laura MacPherson, PhD, Department of Psychology, University of Maryland, College Park

Jonathan Macy, PhD, Assistant Professor of Applied Health Sciences, Indiana University

Gregory J. Madden, PhD, Professor, Department of Psychology, Utah State University

Jessica F. Magidson, MS, University of Maryland, College Park

Jeffrey C. Meehan, Center for Alcohol and Addiction Studies, Brown University

Jane Metrik, PhD, Assistant Professor (Research), Center for Alcohol and Addiction Studies, Department of Behavioral and Social Sciences, Alpert Medical School, Brown University

Joshua D. Miller, PhD, Associate Professor, Department of Psychology, University of Georgia

Robert Miranda, PhD, Associate Professor (Research), Center for Alcohol and Addiction Studies, Brown University

Peter M. Monti, PhD, Director, Center for Alcohol and Addiction Studies, Donald G. Millar Distinguished Professor of Alcohol and Addiction Studies, Brown University

E. Terry Mueller, PhD, Post-doctoral Associate, Addiction Recovery Research Center, Virginia Tech Carilion Research Institute

Cara Murphy, MS, Graduate Student, Department of Psychology, University of Georgia

Ayon Nandi, MS, Senior Research Assistant, Department of Radiology and Radiological Science, The Johns Hopkins University School of Medicine

Ezemenari M. Obasi, PhD, Associate Professor, Counseling and Human Development Services, University of Georgia

Delishia M. Pittman, MA, Doctoral Student, Counseling and Human Development Services, University of Georgia

Clark C. Presson, PhD, Professor of Psychology, Arizona State University

Kristen L. Ratliff, MS, Doctoral Student, Counseling and Human Development Services, University of Georgia

Lara Ray, PhD, Assistant Professor, Department of Psychology, University of California, Los Angeles

Perry F. Renshaw, MD, PhD, Director of Magnetic Resonance Imaging, Brain Institute of the University of Utah, Professor, Department of Psychiatry, College of Medicine, University of Utah

Elizabeth K. Reynolds, PhD, Department of Psychiatry and Behavioral Sciences, Johns Hopkins School of Medicine

Jaime L. Richards, MEd, Doctoral Student, Counseling and Human Development Services, University of Georgia

Jessica M. Richards, MA, Department of Psychology, University of Maryland, College Park

Damaris J. Rohsenow, PhD, Professor (Research), Center for Alcohol and Addiction Studies, Department of Behavioral and Social Sciences, Brown University

Abigail Rose, PhD, Lecturer, School of Psychology, University of Liverpool

Saul Shiffman, PhD, Research Professor of Psychology, Psychiatry, Pharmaceutical Sciences, and Clinical Translational Research, University of Pittsburgh

Jeffrey S. Stein, MS, Department of Psychology, Utah State University

Lawrence H. Sweet, PhD, Gary R. Sperduto Professor of Psychology, Department of Psychology, University of Georgia

Suzanne Thomas, PhD, Associate Professor, Department of Psychiatry and Behavioral Sciences, Medical University of South Carolina

Jennifer C. Veilleux, PhD, Assistant Professor, Department of Psychology, University of Arkansas

Margaret C. Wardle, PhD, Post-doctoral Fellow, University of Chicago

Jessica Weafer, MA, Department of Psychology, University of Kentucky

Stephanie Weber, BA, Project Manager, Department of Psychology, University of Illinois at Chicago

Dean F. Wong, MD, PhD, Professor of Radiology, Neurosciences, Psychiatry and Environmental Health Sciences, Johns Hopkins University

Sujung Yoon MD, PhD, Department of Psychiatry, The Catholic University of Korea College of Medicine, Department of Psychiatry, University of Utah

Introduction:
The Science of Addiction
Psychopharmacology

The scope of the problem of alcohol, tobacco, and other drug addiction is massive. In the United States, tobacco is the single largest cause of overall mortality – above all other causes of death, including poor diet and accidents – and alcohol and illicit drug use are the third and ninth largest causes (Mokdad, Marks, Stroup, and Gerberding, 2004). Together, use of licit and illicit drugs is estimated to cause over 500,000 deaths annually, resulting from diverse forms of morbidity. Nicotine dependence is the most prevalent substance use disorder, with a US prevalence of around 13% (Grant *et al.*, 2004), and tobacco use is a major contributor to chronic illnesses, such as cardiovascular disease, pulmonary disease, and cancer (Centers for Disease Control and Prevention, 2008). Alcohol is the most commonly used psychoactive drug and excessive consumption is associated with acute risks, such as motor vehicle crashes, physical and sexual assault, and suicide, as well as chronic health problems such as cardiovascular disease and an array of cancers (Hingson *et al.*, 2002; Hingson, Zha, and Weitzman, 2009; Room and Rehm, 2011). Similarly, illicit drug use is associated with both acute and chronic health risks (Degenhardt *et al.*, 2011; Maraj, Figueredo, and Lynn Morris, 2010). Translated into economic terms, the estimated annual costs to society are onerous: for tobacco, $167 billion (Centers for Disease Control and Prevention, 2008); for alcohol, $223.5 billion (Bouchery *et al.*, 2011); and, for illicit drug use, $193 billion (National Drug Intelligence Center, 2011). Although the preceding data pertain to the US, drug addiction is as pressing a public health problem worldwide (World Health Organization, 2011; Rehm *et al.*, 2007; Rehm *et al.*, 2009; Rehm, Taylor, and Room, 2006).

This devastating public health problem can be directly addressed via prevention and treatment, but these solutions require a full understanding of the determinants and mechanisms underlying addiction. To achieve this goal, carefully designed and experimentally rigorous research is essential. The current volume provides a comprehensive review of the methods developed to study addiction in humans. Historically,

The Wiley-Blackwell Handbook of Addiction Psychopharmacology, First Edition. Edited by James MacKillop and Harriet de Wit.
© 2013 John Wiley & Sons, Ltd. Published 2013 by John Wiley & Sons, Ltd.

drug addiction has been attributed purely to the pharmacological properties of a drug or to the moral failing of the user. More recently, the science of addiction psychophar-macology has provided multidisciplinary tools to study the complex interplay between the drug, the user, and the surrounding context. Drug use can be studied within a single experience, across episodes, and across the lifespan. It can be studied in relation to macro-level factors, such as personality and developmental experiences, as well as micro-level factors, such as the physical, psychological, and physiological contexts in which drug use takes place. Moreover, new technologies from cognitive neuroscience can now provide unique insights into addiction by revealing heretofore unobserv-able dimensions of the brain. Thus, contemporary researchers have a rich array of techniques at their disposal to study the complex phenomenon of addiction.

Nonetheless, many challenges remain to understand and treat drug addiction. One challenge is the multifactorial nature of the problem and the fact that research efforts tend to take a single perspective that reflects the disciplinary background of the researchers themselves. Addiction researchers include experts from many backgrounds, including basic scientists, such as behavioral pharmacologists or neuroscientists; clin-ical scientists, such as clinical psychologists or psychiatrists; and social scientists, such as sociologists or anthropologists. These disciplines reflect "silos" which stand in the way of truly interdisciplinary research that integrates methodologies across disciplinary boundaries. These silos have their own established literatures, set of validated experi-mental tools, and jargon, creating barriers to understanding and collaboration across fields.

We hope that the current volume will address this challenge and facilitate inter-disciplinary exchanges in addiction psychopharmacology. Each chapter provides an overview of a domain, a review of its associated methods, and some directed insights into the causes and results of drug addiction. The authors describe methods that can be used in various contexts, and make "best practice" recommendations for different approaches. Finally, each chapter briefly characterizes priorities and future directions for the domain and methodology. Taken together, the goal of the volume is to provide current and future addiction researchers with a broad and deep grounding in diverse experimental methods to foster increased collaboration and transdisciplinary research on addiction.

The book is organized according to the methods used. The first section takes a macrocosmic approach and focuses on stable factors that may function across the lifespan. These include developmental influences, cognitive factors, and personality traits. Each of these influences is multifaceted. For example, impulsivity is a trait that has been consistently associated with drug addiction, but it is now thought to be comprised of multiple, distinct facets (Cyders and Coskunpinar, 2011; de Wit, 2009). Therefore, one chapter focuses on personality-based assessments of impulsivity while the following three chapters each individually focus on different dimensions of impul-sivity and risk taking. The second section takes a microcosmic approach and focuses on studying the individual under experimental conditions. This includes essential methods for measuring the psychoactive and physiological effects of addictive drugs and how individuals self-administer drugs, as well as the influence of environmental cues, priming doses, or stress. The third section focuses on insights gleaned from cognitive neuroscience. Technical advances in electrophysiology, magnetic resonance imaging, positron emission tomography, and magnetic resonance spectroscopy offer an unprecedented opportunity to study brain and behavior concurrently, and to study the neurobiological dimensions of addiction in humans.

Despite extensive research to date and substantial advances, the complexity of drug addiction is clear and the prospects for easy solutions or "silver bullets" are extremely low. Rather, via systematic scientific study from an array of fields, we believe a greater understanding of addiction is possible and this understanding, in turn, can be applied to improve treatment and prevention. In this sprit, we hope this volume ultimately contributes to alleviating the burden of addiction by assembling the "tools of the trade" and expanding the perspectives and research programs of the addiction scientists of today and tomorrow.

References

Bouchery EE, Harwood HJ, Sacks JJ, Simon CJ, and Brewer RD (2011) Economic costs of excessive alcohol consumption in the US, 2006. *American Journal of Preventive Medicine* 41(5): 516–524.

Centers for Disease Control and Prevention (2008) Smoking-attributable mortality, years of potential life lost, and productivity losses – United States, 2000–2004. *Morbidity and Mortality Weekly Report* 57(45): 1226–1228.

Cyders MA and Coskunpinar A (2011) Measurement of constructs using self-report and behavioral lab tasks: Is there overlap in nomothetic span and construct representation for impulsivity? *Clinical Psychology Review* 31(6): 965–982.

de Wit H (2009) Impulsivity as a determinant and consequence of drug use: a review of underlying processes. *Addiction Biology* 14(1): 22–31.

Degenhardt L, Bucello C, Mathers B, Briegleb C, Ali H, Hickman M, *et al.* (2011) Mortality among regular or dependent users of heroin and other opioids: a systematic review and meta-analysis of cohort studies. *Addiction* 106(1): 32–51.

Grant BF, Hasin DS, Chou SP, Stinson FS, and Dawson DA (2004) Nicotine dependence and psychiatric disorders in the United States: results from the national epidemiologic survey on alcohol and related conditions. *Archives of General Psychiatry* 61(11): 1107–1115.

Hingson RW, Heeren T, Zakocs RC, Kopstein A, and Wechsler H. (2002) Magnitude of alcohol-related mortality and morbidity among US college students ages 18–24. *Journal of Studies on Alcohol* 63(2): 136–144.

Hingson RW, Zha W, and Weitzman ER (2009) Magnitude of and trends in alcohol-related mortality and morbidity among US college students ages 18–24, 1998–2005. *Journal of Studies on Alcohol and Drugs Supplement* 16, 12–20.

Maraj S, Figueredo VM, and Lynn Morris D (2010) Cocaine and the heart. *Clinical Cardiology* 33(5): 264–269.

Mokdad AH, Marks JS, Stroup DF, and Gerberding JL (2004) Actual causes of death in the United States, 2000. *Journal of the American Medical Association* 291(10): 1238–1245.

National Drug Intelligence Center (2011) *The Economic Impact of Illicit Drug Use on American Society*. Washington, DC: Department of Justice.

Rehm J, Gnam W, Popova S, Baliunas D, Brochu S, Fischer B, *et al.* (2007) The costs of alcohol, illegal drugs, and tobacco in Canada, 2002. *Journal of Studies on Alcohol and Drugs* 68(6): 886–895.

Rehm J, Mathers C, Popova S, Thavorncharoensap M, Teerawattananon Y, and Patra J (2009) Global burden of disease and injury and economic cost attributable to alcohol use and alcohol-use disorders. *Lancet* 373(9682): 2223–2233.

Rehm J, Taylor B, and Room R (2006) Global burden of disease from alcohol, illicit drugs and tobacco. *Drug and Alcohol Review* 25(6): 503–513.

Room R and Rehm J (2011) Alcohol and non-communicable diseases-cancer, heart disease and more. *Addiction* 106(1): 1–2.

World Health Organization (2011) *WHO Report on the Global Tobacco Epidemic 2011: Warning about the Dangers of Tobacco.* Washington, DC: World Health Organization.

Part I

Distal Determinants of Drug Use

1

Developmental Factors in Addiction: Methodological Considerations[1]

Laurie Chassin, Clark Presson, Young Il-Cho, Matthew Lee, and Jonathan Macy

1 Introduction

Epidemiological data show that substance use and substance use disorders follow characteristic age-related trajectories, such that the onset of substance use typically occurs in adolescence, peaks in rates of substance use (and in rates of clinical substance use disorders) occur during emerging adulthood (ages 18–25), and rates of both substance use and substance use disorders decline later in adulthood (Bachman *et al.*, 2002; Masten, Faden, Zucker, and Spear, 2008). Moreover, adult substance use outcomes and substance use disorders are predictable from early childhood factors (Caspi, Moffitt, Newman, and Silva, 1996; Masten, Faden, Zucker, and Spear, 2008). These age-related patterns of substance use and their association with early childhood predictors suggest the value of applying a developmental perspective to the study of addiction. Accordingly, this chapter focuses on methodological issues in research on developmental factors in addiction. We focus on methodological issues in studies of substance use among children and adolescents, and particularly on longitudinal studies, which are well suited for examining developmental trajectories and prospective predictors of addiction outcomes. However, it is also important to recognize that each of the topics that are covered in the other chapters of this volume also present methodological challenges when the particular domain of interest is studied in childhood and adolescence. Thus, studies of drug administration, psychophysiology, imaging, genetics, intellectual functioning, psychiatric comorbidities, impulsive and risky behavior, distress tolerance, expectancies, social context, implicit cognition, ecological momentary assessment, etc. each present both opportunities and methodological challenges when applied to child and adolescent samples and studied in a developmental context.

[1] Preparation of this chapter was supported by Grants AA016213 from the National Institute of Alcohol Abuse and Alcoholism and DA013555 from the National Institute on Drug Abuse.

Clearly, no single chapter could cover the numerous methodological issues involved in studying developmental factors in each of those many different domains. Therefore, instead we focus on more general methodological and conceptual issues involved in studying substance use (and risk factors for substance use) during childhood and adolescence, and we illustrate some of the unique methodological challenges in this research.

2   Empirical Relevance of Developmental Factors for Substance Use Research

Research on developmental factors is critical to an understanding of substance use disorders for multiple reasons. First, these studies are needed to inform etiology by identifying prospective predictors of substance use outcomes and testing the multivariate and multilevel etiological mechanisms that are hypothesized to underlie addiction. Second, these studies inform the design and targeting of preventive intervention. They identify the risk and age groups who are the target audiences for preventive intervention and, to the extent that malleable risk and protective factors can be identified, these studies pinpoint the factors to be targeted for modification in prevention programs. Third, studies of developmental factors are needed to understand the impact and consequences of substance use. Cross-sectional comparisons of individuals with and without substance use disorders cannot disentangle the causes of substance use disorders from their consequences. Thus, studies of children and adolescents before the onset of substance use are needed to separate the antecedents from the consequences of substance use.

Another sense in which developmental factors are critical to addiction research is that substance use involvement itself can be conceptualized as a series of stages or developmental milestones ranging from initial exposure to experimental use, regular and/or heavy use, substance use-related problems, and diagnosable clinical substance use disorders (e.g., Jackson, 2010; Mayhew, Flay, and Mott, 2000). The time that it takes to pass through these stages varies for different individuals and substances and is predictable by factors such as gender and family history of substance use disorder (Hussong, Bauer, and Chassin, 2008; Ridenour, Lanza, Donny, and Clark, 2006; Sartor *et al.*, 2008). Such predictable variability in the speed of transition from first exposure to addiction suggests that the speed of progression may itself be an important phenotype to study in order to understand the etiology of addiction.

Importantly, particular etiological factors may not only determine the speed of progression but may show unique prediction of specific transitions such that different factors may influence substance use initiation than influence substance use progression (e.g., Sartor *et al.*, 2007). For example, Fowler *et al.* (2007) found that common environment influences were more important for initiation whereas genetic influences were more important for progression. Methodologically, this suggests the need for researchers to disaggregate predictors of different developmental milestones in the development of addiction.

Moreover, developmental progressions may be important not only within "stages" of the use of a single substance but across different substances. It has been suggested that individuals progress from involvement with "gateway" drugs such as alcohol, tobacco, and marijuana to the use of other illicit drugs (Kandel, Yamaguchi, and Chen, 1992). This progression might reflect a common propensity to use drugs, an affiliation with a drug-using social network that promotes the use of multiple substances, or a causal effect in which the use of one drug sensitizes an individual to the use of other substances (Kandel, Yamaguchi, and Klein, 2006; MacCoun, 2006). Methodologically, the notion of developmental progressions across the use of different substances implies that researchers who study the use of any one particular substance should measure and consider the co-occurring use of other substances.

Another developmental milestone that is important for the study of addiction is the age at which an individual first begins to use substances. Early onset of use is associated with a greater likelihood of developing dependence, and this has been reported for cigarette smoking (Breslau and Peterson, 1996), alcohol use (Dawson *et al.*, 1998) and illicit drug use (Grant and Dawson, 2008). There have been multiple interpretations of these findings, including the idea that they are spurious and caused by correlated "3rd" variables that are associated both with early onset and with risk for addiction (Prescott and Kendler, 1999). Other studies that have considered various hypothesized confounding variables have still supported a relation between early onset and greater likelihood of dependence or heavy use in adulthood. This pattern was found by Buchmann *et al.* (2009) for alcohol use and by King and Chassin (2007) for drug dependence. It has also been suggested that age of onset is a feature that might distinguish different subtypes of substance disorder. For example, Zucker (1986) distinguished among different forms of alcoholism with early-onset forms being either antisocial or developmentally limited (compared to older-onset negative affect forms of alcoholism). Other disorders have similarly considered age of onset in formulating subtypes. For example, Moffitt (1993) distinguished between adolescent-limited and child-onset life course persistent forms of conduct disorder. Methodologically, the possibility that age of onset is a marker for a particularly high-risk group for addiction suggests that age of onset is a useful phenotype for study. For example, Schmid *et al.* (2009) found effects of DAT1 on tobacco and alcohol use for individuals who started daily smoking or drinking to intoxication at a young age. Finally, it is possible that the relation between early onset of use and elevated risk of developing dependence occurs not because of particular subtypes of substance disorder or particular high-risk phenotypes, but rather because the central nervous system, early in development, is particularly vulnerable to substance use effects. For example, Levin *et al.* (2003) found that female rats who were randomly assigned to begin self-administration of nicotine in adolescence showed higher levels of later adult self-administration than did those whose self-administration began in adulthood.

These findings thus suggest that both age of onset of substance use and the speed of progression from initiation to heavy use or to clinical substance use disorder might be important developmental factors to study in order to better understand addiction. Some researchers have built on these findings by attempting to identify heterogeneity in longitudinal trajectories of substance use that consider multiple features, including age of onset, steepness of acceleration in use, peaks of use, and stability of use over time. These studies have often used mixture modeling techniques to identify clusters of trajectories, and have suggested that such dynamic trajectories might be better

phenotypes for the study of addiction than static features of the addictive behavior
(see Chassin *et al.*, 2009 for a review). For example, Chassin *et al.* (2008) reported
that parents' smoking trajectories had a unique effect on their adolescents' cigarette
smoking over and above parents' current smoking. Parents whose smoking showed
early onset, steep acceleration, high levels, and greater persistence were more likely to
have adolescent children who smoked. That is, over and above parents' current smoking, their different smoking trajectories showed different levels of intergenerational
transmission.

The potential value of developmental trajectories as phenotypes for addiction
research raises important methodological issues. Measuring these trajectories is challenging because it requires either a reliance on retrospective data, which are limited
by recall biases, or longitudinal studies, which are expensive and difficult to implement. Moreover, statistical methods for identifying and clustering trajectories (such
as mixture modeling) have limitations (Bauer and Curran, 2003; Chassin *et al.*, 2009;
Jackson and Sher, 2006; Sher *et al.*, 2011; Sterba and Bauer, 2010), requiring that
researchers interpret their findings cautiously and follow recommended practices for
establishing the validity of the findings (see Ialongo, 2010), including making decisions about competing models based on theoretical considerations in addition to
empirical means of comparison (Sher *et al.*, 2011) .

Finally, given the evidence reviewed to this point concerning the etiological significance of age of onset, speed of progression, and developmental milestones or
"stages" of substance use both within and across substances, it is not surprising that
different findings are produced by studying addiction among participants of different
ages and stages of use. For example, behavioral genetic studies often report that the
heritability of substance use phenotypes is lower in adolescence than in adulthood
(Dick *et al.*, 2007; Kendler, Schmitt, Aggen, and Prescott, 2008). One interpretation
of this finding is that developmentally limited, peer-driven forms of substance use in
adolescence may mask the effects of genetic risk, which are then more clearly detected
in adulthood when developmentally limited forms of use have remitted. In addition,
adults probably have greater control to select their own social environments than do
adolescents. Thus, there is probably greater gene–environment covariation in adult
peer social environments than adolescent peer social environments because of greater
adult "niche picking." Methodologically, this suggests that researchers should carefully consider the effects of age and "stage" of substance use in sample selection and
data analysis.

3   Methodological Issues in Sampling Child and Adolescent Populations

Many studies of child and adolescent populations use school-based samples because of
their relative ease of access, cost-effectiveness, and ability to accrue large sample sizes.
However, although school-based samples contain quite diverse samples of children
and adolescents, there are also limits to their representativeness. School-based samples
may under-represent pathology, because truant, homeless, runaway, and institution-
alized children are unlikely to be accessed. Moreover, because of school drop-out, the

representativeness of school-based samples in terms of including high-risk individuals is likely to diminish with the age of the participants, particularly after the age of legal school drop-out. The need for active parent consent also limits sample representativeness in school-based settings (e.g., Anderman *et al.*, 1995; Esbensen, Miller, Taylor, and Freng, 1999) as well as other settings (Rojas, Sherrit, Harris, and Knight, 2008), and active parental consent has been found to under-represent higher-risk and lower-socioeconomic-status participants.

Recruiting community-based samples of children and families using techniques like random digit dialing or birth records has the potential to achieve greater representativeness, but is expensive and labor intensive. Moreover, recruitment using telephone screening has become more difficult with changes in telecommunications and declining participation rates. Recruiting community samples may require mixed methods including using address-based sampling frames to mail surveys or to send advance invitation letters followed up by phone contacts (Mokdad, 2009).

Methods for improving recruitment rates (and parent consent rates) include mailing parent consent forms directly to parents (with telephone follow-up for non-responders) rather than attempting to obtain parental consent by going through the adolescent, and also stressing that participants include both users and non-users of substances so that the adolescent's privacy is protected (Kealey *et al.*, 2007). The use of incentives also improves recruitment, within the ethical constraint that the incentive cannot be large enough to create coercion (Moolchan and Mermelstein, 2002). Of course, sampling methods and selection criteria will necessarily vary with the specific research questions of interest. For example, if clinical substance use disorders are outcome variables of interest, then researchers must weigh the time it takes for these outcomes to develop, given various initial ages as well as the sample size required to produce sufficient "cases." It might be necessary to over-sample high-risk groups, older participants, or initial users in order to produce sufficient prevalence of clinical substance use disorder outcomes. Accelerated longitudinal designs (i.e., cohort sequential designs) can also be used to reduce the time that is required for observation of substance use outcomes (Collins, 2005).

4   Age, Cohort, and Time of Measurement Effects in Studying Development

Although we noted earlier that substance use outcomes show clear age-related patterns, age, per se, is rarely an important theoretical construct in understanding these phenomena. Rather, "age" is a proxy for complex developmental processes. These processes might include maturational changes (e.g., the onset of puberty, maturation of top-down central nervous system pathways for cognitive control) or age-graded social change (e.g., the transitions to middle school or to high school). When these proxies are known, studies can test them directly. For example, the onset of puberty has been studied with respect to increases in reward seeking (particularly peer reward), which, in combination with incompletely developed central nervous system top-down control systems, are believed to contribute to making adolescence a particularly high-risk period for substance use (Casey, Jones, and Somerville, 2011; Forbes and Dahl,

2010; Steinberg, 2010). Social transitions such as the transitions to middle school and then high school environments are particularly important periods to consider, as they are periods in which adolescents' social networks expand or change, and adolescents are potentially exposed to new contextual opportunities and influences. These transitions are periods of sensitivity to and openness to change in the new contexts to which adolescents must adapt. Finally, the greater time spent out of parent supervision, which accompanies normal development, contributes to risk during the adolescent years.

In examining age effects as proxies for complex developmental processes, an interpretational problem is that intertwined within any developmental data set are potential effects of age, time of measurement (period), and cohort (typically, year of birth). The problem is that these parameters have a linear dependency, such that they are non-independent in any specific data set. This problem has been long recognized (Baltes, 1968; Schaie, 1965; Nesselroade and Baltes, 1979), and various strategies have been proposed to address it.

The most typical designs used to examine developmental factors are cross-sectional studies (comparisons of different age groups at a single point in time) and longitudinal studies (observations of a single birth cohort over multiple times of measurement). The problem with these simple designs is that in focusing on one factor, they confound others. Cross-sectional studies are the most efficient in identifying age differences, but they do so for different groups, so that observed age differences are confounded with cohort differences. Similarly, in longitudinal studies, the observed differences are again typically interpreted as general age effects, but the design confounds age and the period effects, so that it is unclear if they would generalize to other cohorts.

Period effects (i.e., effects of the particular time/historical period of measurement) include things ranging from disease epidemics, war, or secular changes in the social context. For example, changes in laws, access, or price of a substance might influence the development of addiction. One relevant example is the introduction of the Surgeon General's report on smoking in 1964, which was an historical event that began a long and profound social change in the way that people thought about cigarettes and smoking in the United States. It is important to realize that period effects can influence different birth cohorts in different ways. For example, significant social change regarding the perceived negative effects of cigarette smoking might have greater effects on later birth cohorts (i.e., younger people) who have grown up in a social climate with a lowered prevalence of smoking, more stringent tobacco control policy, and more awareness of the negative health consequences of smoking. Indeed, cohort effects have been reported for adolescent cigarette smoking, with each successive cohort (i.e., 12th-grade class) smoking less between the years of 1976 and 1982 (O'Malley, Bachman, and Johnson, 1984).

Thus, a general goal of developmental research in addiction would be to know whether particular age-related effects generalize across different birth cohorts or historical periods. For example, Little *et al.* (2008) found that the relation between "deviance proneness" and marijuana use for adolescent boys was weakest at the cohort in which there was the lowest population prevalence of marijuana use. However, just because there are secular changes in the prevalence of a substance use behavior does not automatically mean that the etiological influences on that substance use behavior will also change (Donovan, Jessor, and Costa, 1999). Thus, it is important to know whether the etiological factors or predictors of substance use outcomes vary over birth cohorts or historical periods.

The proposed strategies to achieve these goals have a common thread of combining features of longitudinal and cross-sectional designs. Schaie (1965) proposed various cohort sequential designs that combined features of longitudinal and cross-sectional studies to study several cohorts of individuals across time. Although these designs cannot realistically fully disentangle age, period, and cohort effects empirically (Masche and van Dulmen, 2004), they do provide replications of the critical comparisons of age differences (at differing time points) and, most importantly, of longitudinal sequences across separate birth cohorts. Moreover, compared to studying a single cohort, a further advantage of the cohort sequential design is that it collapses the time required to gather longitudinal data over a broader range of ages.

5   Methodological Issues in Measuring Adolescent Substance Use and Substance Use Disorders

Fundamentally, addiction research depends on the measurement of substance use behaviors, which are most often assessed by self-reports. Questions have been raised about the validity of self-reported substance use, given concerns about social desirability in reporting a behavior that is often illegal and socially stigmatized. These concerns may be particularly important when there are motivations to under-report, such as treatment outcome studies when treated participants may wish to portray themselves as improved or "cured." Although these concerns apply to both adolescents and adults, they may be magnified for adolescent reports because more behaviors are illegal for adolescents than for adults (i.e., alcohol and tobacco use are illegal for adolescents but legal for adults), and because parents and other authority figures have more control over adolescents than over adults. Thus, adolescents may be more motivated than adults to hide their substance use from others. It has also been suggested that adolescents may be particularly confused by the terminology that is applied to drug classes in research studies and that allowing adolescents to write in the substances that they use might improve measurement (Morral, McCaffrey, and Chien, 2003). Finally, adolescents' reports of substance use may be also influenced by situational constraints that limit their opportunity for use, and thus provide mistakenly low estimates of substance use behavior. For example, the presence of parental supervision, school attendance, and time spent in supervised settings such as juvenile correctional settings will limit opportunities for use and thus possibly produce misleading reports (Piquero *et al.*, 2001).

One method for validating self-reported substance use is to compare self-reports with biological measures. Of course, biological measures themselves have limitations, including often being limited to the assessment of relatively recent substance use, varying rates of false positives and negatives, and substantial expense. Adolescent self-reports of substance use (including both calendar methods such as the Time Line Follow-Back and quantity-frequency items) show significant correlations with biological measures, both for non-Hispanic Caucasians and for ethnic minority adolescents

(Dillon, Turner, Robbins, and Szapocznik, 2005; Dolcini, Adler, Lee, and Bauman, 2003), although under-reporting has also been demonstrated (e.g., Delaney-Black *et al.*, 2010). Research with adults (Lennox, Dennis, Scott, and Funk, 2006) suggests that combining data from biological assays and self-reports can be useful in overcoming the limitations of each individual method.

Although adolescent self-reported substance use correlates with biological methods, there are systematic influences that affect the rates of substance use that are obtained. Higher self-reported use rates are obtained in contexts that maximize privacy and minimize risk of disclosure, particularly to parents. For example, self-reported substance use is lower when it is measured in household settings than in school settings (e.g., Griesler *et al.*, 2008) and lower in interviews than in self-administered questionnaires or computer-administered surveys (Turner *et al.*, 1998). Of course, these differences may reflect either under-reporting in household and interview contexts or over-reporting in school contexts and self-administered surveys. Inconsistent reporters tend to be younger, lighter substance users, more conventional (i.e., less delinquent) and members of ethnic minority groups (see Griesler *et al.*, 2008 for a review). Similar characteristics predict recanting of earlier-disclosed substance use in longitudinal studies of adolescents (Fendrich and Rosenbaum, 2003; Percy *et al.*, 2005). Light-using and socially conventional adolescents may recant because they re-consider their self-definitions as "users" and/or because they are more sensitive to social norms and adult disapproval. Even more worrisome, inconsistent reporting by adolescents who were receiving substance use treatment was associated with self-reports of improvement over time, suggesting that reporting biases might inflate findings of treatment success (Harris, Griffin, McCaffrey, and Morral, 2008). These problems dictate that researchers collect data on self-reported adolescent substance use in conditions that reinforce confidentiality and privacy and that minimize motivations for false reporting. Federal Certificates of Confidentiality may be useful for achieving this goal, although they do not necessarily eliminate under-reporting (Delaney-Black *et al.*, 2010).

In addition to using biological measures, one useful method of compensating for limitations of any single report (including self-report) is to use multiple informants. For research on children and adolescents, these are typically parents and teachers (Achenbach, McConaughy, and Howell, 1987). Indeed, such multiple reporter data are important in studies of the development of addictive behaviors not only as a way to compensate for individual biases and measurement error, but as a way to capture variability in behavior across contexts, which are differentially observable by different informants (Achenbach, 2011). However, for reports of substance use as outcome variables, parents may lack awareness of the extent of their child's use and thus under-report, and parent–adolescent agreement in reports of use and disorders is typically small to moderate (e.g., Fisher *et al.*, 2006; Green *et al.*, 2011).

Thus, in terms of assessing adolescent substance use, it is recommended that researchers assess self-reports under conditions that reinforce privacy and confidentiality and minimize demand characteristics and social desirability concerns, including the use of a Certificate of Confidentiality when possible. Situational constraints that misleadingly suppress reports of use (e.g., time spent incarcerated) should be assessed. If resources allow, self-reports can be supplemented with biological measures (Lennox, Dennis, Scott, and Funk, 2006) and other informant reports.

There are also methodological complexities in assessing adolescents' substance-use related social consequences and dependence symptoms, resulting in dilemmas for diagnosing adolescent substance use disorders. Adolescents report more substance use-related symptoms than do adults even at comparable levels of use (Chen and Anthony, 2003; Kandel and Chen, 2000). There are multiple interpretations of this finding. One interpretation draws on developmental differences in substance use effects that are shown in animal studies (Spear, 2000; Torres, Tejeda, Natividad, and O'Dell, 2008) and argues that adolescents are more vulnerable to developing dependence than are adults even at low levels of use. In fact, some researchers have suggested that adolescents develop indications of dependence quite quickly after the onset of use (DiFranza, 2007). However, although animal data show greater rewarding effects of substances for adolescents than for adults, this does not necessarily translate into greater intake for adolescents. Moreover, animal studies suggest that adolescents are less sensitive to withdrawal effects than are adults (Schramm-Sapyta *et al.*, 2009). Thus, the animal data do not clearly and consistently point to greater vulnerability to substance dependence among adolescents than among adults. Moreover, there are other possible interpretations of age differences in symptom reporting. Chen and Anthony (2003) point out that age and duration of use are confounded in cross-sectional studies and that there may be cohort effects. For example, more potent forms of cannabis have been introduced in recent years, and thus younger individuals' initial exposure to cannabis probably constituted a different dose than did older individuals' initial exposure.

It is also possible that age differences in the reporting of symptoms are due to problems in the diagnostic criteria, which are identical for adolescents and adults, at least in the *Diagnostic and Statistical Manual of the American Psychiatric Association* (American Psychiatric Association, 2000). For example, Chung *et al.* (2004) note that tolerance, rather than being a symptom of dependence, might represent a relatively normal part of adolescent substance use as adolescents move from experimentation to regular use. Thus, tolerance may not have the same clinical significance for adolescents that it does for adults. Chung and Martin (2005) conducted focus groups and interviews with substance-disordered adolescents and found that the diagnostic criterion of "impaired control" may also be problematic because adolescents rarely reported any intention to limit their use. Without such an intended limit on use, it is not possible to assess failed attempts to control. These findings suggest that simply applying adult diagnostic criteria to adolescent substance use disorders may not be optimal. Finally, there is some evidence that adolescents over-report symptoms. Chen and Anthony (2003) found that adolescents reported more symptoms than adults even with just 1–2 days of cannabis use. MIMIC models which compared adolescents and adults at equal overall levels of cannabis dependence found that adolescents over-reported the symptoms of tolerance and inability to cut down on use, which have also been identified as possibly problematic in Chung and Martin's studies (described above). Moreover, these same two symptoms of tolerance and an inability to limit use were also found to be early appearing symptoms of tobacco dependence in adolescents (Kandel, Hu, and Yamaguchi, 2009). Thus, tolerance and failed attempts at control may be problematic as symptoms for assessing adolescents' alcohol, tobacco, and cannabis disorders. If these symptoms are over-reported, then using the same symptom thresholds for diagnosis for both adolescents and adults will also be problematic (Winters, Martin, and Chung, 2011).

As evident from the above discussion, the possibility that measures and constructs have different meanings at different ages means that researchers need to examine the extent to which their measures demonstrate invariance over age. If measures do not demonstrate age invariance, then this needs to be considered within longitudinal statistical models. For example, Item Response Theory (IRT) methods provide one approach to accommodating non-invariance within longitudinal models (Flora, Curran, Hussong, and Edwards, 2008).

Finally, a methodological challenge in analyzing substance use data that is particularly acute for child and adolescent populations is the large percentage of non-users who are typically sampled. This results in a non-normal, zero-inflated distribution of substance use outcomes, violating the normality assumption of most of the statistical models used in analyzing longitudinal data. Moreover, as discussed earlier, a large number of non-users in these analyses also risks blurring distinctions between "stages" of substance use, since the predictors of abstinence versus use may differ from the predictors of gradations of use among users. To address this problem, analyses can use a zero-inflated model (Liu and Powers, 2007) or a two-part random-effects model (Blozis, Feldman, and Conger, 2007). These models separate the frequency of substance use into two parts (i.e., log-odds of substance use and frequencies of substance use). Thus, these models provide prediction of two separate outcomes within a single model – the propensity to initiate substance use and the extent of substance use.

6   Creating Multilevel, Probabilistic Models of the Development of Addiction: Methodological Issues in a Developmental Psychopathology Approach

As reflected in the many domains covered in this volume, the development of addiction is considered to be the result of multiple, interacting processes that occur at different levels of analysis. It is beyond the scope of any individual chapter to exhaustively review all of these determinants. Here we provide a brief discussion of some of the major risk pathways that have been proposed and illustrate their conceptual and methodological implications when studying addiction from a developmental perspective.

Sher (1991) identified three interrelated biopsychosocial pathways to substance use disorders, which are not mutually exclusive. They are termed the deviance proneness pathway, the stress and negative affect pathway, and the enhanced reinforcement pathway. Although these pathways were developed to specifically understand the increased risk of substance use among children of substance users, the same processes are hypothesized to increase risk for substance use disorders more broadly, regardless of family history. Briefly summarized, the deviance proneness pathway suggests that adolescents who are temperamentally poorly regulated, and have poor executive functioning, and who are also exposed to poor parenting will be at elevated risk for later school failure and affiliation with deviant peers, who model, encourage, and provide opportunities for substance use behavior. The stress–negative affect pathway hypothesizes that adolescents who have poor emotion regulation and coping skills and who are exposed to high levels of environmental stress will be more likely to use substances to self-medicate the resulting negative affect. The enhanced reinforcement pathway focuses on individual differences in substance use effects, suggesting that individuals who derive either stronger positive reinforcement or less negative effects from ingesting a substance will be at greater risk for substance use disorder. All of these pathways view substance use as more likely when individuals have positive expectancies about substance use. For example, individuals will be more likely to use substances to self-medicate negative affect if they believe that the substance use will successfully change their mood.

Sher's models are an excellent illustration of some of the key features of a developmental psychopathology approach to understanding substance use disorders (Cicchetti, 2006; Sroufe, 1997). Some of these features are that a developmental psychopathology perspective: (a) recognizes the interplay of genetic and environmental risk and protective factors and, more generally, of factors that operate on multiple levels of analysis; (b) recognizes that the same outcome (i.e., substance use disorder) can be the result of different pathways for different people (a principle termed "equifinality"); (c) posits probabilistic models recognizing that individuals at the same level of initial risk may not all develop a clinical disorder (a principle termed "multifinality"; (d) recognizes that early (distal) risk can be "re-modeled" by exposure to later (more proximal) influences but that, conversely, early risk exposure may constrain an individual's ability to adapt to later challenges; (e) recognizes that risk processes can cascade over domains, creating deeper and broader levels of problems (Haller, Handley, Chassin, and Bountress, 2010; Rogosch, Oshri, and Cicchetti, 2010); and (f) recognizes that individuals actively participate in creating and selecting their own environments.

These features of a developmental psychopathology approach to addiction have several methodological implications. Longitudinal designs or validly measured retrospective data are needed to test the ways in which early risk factors may constrain later adaptation. Moreover, in terms of longitudinal study design, researchers must match the timing of the measurement lags to the theoretical lags of effect that are hypothesized for the variables in question (Collins, 2005). This becomes increasingly challenging when studying complex meditational processes (e.g., developmental cascades; MacKinnon, 2008). For example, consider the effects of life stress. Life stress can have acute (i.e., time-specific) effects on substance use through self-medication mechanisms in which individuals use substances to reduce the levels of negative affect that are created by the stressor. To test these acute self-medication effects in a longitudinal study would require closely spaced measurements, such as those used in ecological momentary sampling (see Chapter 7, this volume). However, the effects of stress exposure early in development on risk for substance use disorders may operate in quite different ways and with a quite different lag of effect. Early exposure to adversity may create long-term lingering risk for substance use disorders through multiple mechanisms and complex, cascading influences. Early adversity can sensitize the hypothalamic–pituitary–adrenal axis, such that individuals who are exposed to high levels of adversity early in development may be more sensitized to respond to stress (Sinha, 2008). Early adversity also affects the development of the prefrontal cortex, influencing self-regulation, executive functioning, and behavioral control (Sinha, 2008; Andersen and Teicher, 2009), and early adversity can affect the accumbens dopamine system, producing anhedonia, with the possibility of enhanced reinforcement from substance use (Andersen and Teicher, 2009). Moreover, the full effects of these changes may not be manifest until adolescence, when stress influences maturation of the prefrontal cortex, influencing vulnerability to drug-associated cues (Andersen and Teicher, 2009). These mechanisms have been tested mostly with animal models. To do so in humans requires carefully constructed long-term longitudinal designs in order to establish temporal precedence between exposure to early adversity and later magnitude of stress response or carefully validated retrospective measures of exposure to early adversity.

Moreover, the example of early adversity effects on addiction also nicely illustrates the methodological challenges associated with establishing causal inference in passive, observational, longitudinal studies. Although animals can be randomly assigned to conditions that vary in early adversity, in human studies, individuals who are exposed to high levels of early adversity are also likely to be exposed to other risk factors as well. Thus, there are many potentially confounding "third variables", which may be responsible for what appears to be effects of early adversity. For instance, parental substance use disorder may drive a spurious (i.e., non-causal) relationship by increasing both exposure to early adversity and heritable risk for later substance problems. Further, other early risk factors such as behavioral under-control may operate as third variables by evoking the experience of early stressful events and also producing later risk for substance problems.

In terms of solutions to address the methodological challenge of establishing causal inference in passive, observational, longitudinal studies, there are multiple strategies that can be used. In general, they can be conceptualized as attempts to equate individuals on potential third variables (Morgan and Winship, 2007; Rubin, 1974). Using the example of early adversity as the predictor of interest, the most common approach uses conditional models where the effect of early adversity on later substance use is estimated while including potential third variables as covariates. A less commonly used alternative is propensity score matching (Rosenbaum, 2002; Rosenbaum and Rubin, 1983) where, for example, a preliminary model could predict early adversity from a set of potential third variables, thereby producing predicted scores representing each participant's propensity to experience early adversity. Then, participants with and without early adversity can be matched on propensity scores, and the resulting matched (i.e., equated) groups can be compared on later substance use. A propensity scores approach holds several advantages over conditional models, including (a) greater statistical power and stability of estimates, particularly when considering many potential third variables, and (b) more straightforward confirmation that groups were successfully equated and that key assumptions of accounting for third variables were met (e.g., adequate third variable overlap between groups; Little and Rubin, 2000; Morgan and Winship, 2007; West and Thoemmes, 2008). However, both approaches are limited in that it cannot be determined whether there are other important third variables that were unmeasured and whose effects are therefore not considered. Thus, to effectively employ these approaches, design and theoretical considerations are critically important to increase the likelihood that all important third variables are appropriately measured (Rubin, 2008).

In addition to the importance of considering the appropriate time lag of effect and potential third variables, another methodological challenge to testing these multivariate risk pathways is that they are characterized by reciprocal directions of influence. For example, to this point, we have been discussing risk factors for adolescent substance use, such as poor parenting, substance-using peers, or life stress. However, substance use itself is likely to affect these variables. Adolescents who use drugs are likely to seek out similar substance-using peers. They may also evoke poor parenting and create life stress – for example, being more likely to lose a job because of their poor performance. These effects of adolescent characteristics in creating their environments must be considered in testing etiological models. The effects of substance use itself on these risk factors is particularly important because substance use exposure may change reward pathways and self-regulatory abilities in addition to cognitive functioning (Volkow, Baler, and Goldstein, 2011). As can be seen from this discussion, testing these probabilistic risk models requires appropriate statistical tests of reciprocal influences, of mediation, and of moderated mediation within longitudinal data.

As noted earlier, a developmental psychopathology approach as exemplified in Sher's models also incorporates interactions among etiological factors that operate at multiple levels, including genetic risk, individual dispositions, and parent and peer relationship contexts. Moreover, although not a major focus of Sher's models, higher-level macro social determinants of adolescent substance use, such as schools and neighborhoods, and social policy also play important roles and interact with individual and more proximal social context factors (Siegel *et al.*, 2005; Thomson *et al.*, 2004; Brook, Nomura, and Cohen, 1989; Perry, Kelder, and Komro, 1993; Petraitis, Flay, and Miller, 1995). Bronfenbrenner's Ecology of Human Development Theory (Bronfenbrenner, 1979) provides a theoretical framework to guide research to explore these multiple layers of influence within a developmental perspective. Bronfenbrenner described three higher levels of environmental influences that interact with individual variables to influence behavior. The microsystem refers to interpersonal interactions in specific settings, such as within the family and peer networks. The mesosystem stems from the interrelations among the microsystems (e.g., the family competing with an adolescent's peer influence). Finally, the exosystem is the larger social system that can affect individuals and includes neighborhoods, cultural beliefs and values, and policy.

From a methodological standpoint, testing the effect of multiple levels of influence on adolescent substance use requires multilevel modeling approaches (Raudenbush and Bryk, 2002) due to the nesting of data (e.g., adolescents nested within families, schools, and neighborhoods). For example, Ennett *et al.* (2008) used multilevel modeling to apply Bronfennbrenner's theory to characterize multiple levels of influence on adolescent alcohol use. Their microsystem model included variables describing family, peer, and school contexts. Their mesosystem models included interactions among the family, peer, and school influences. Their exosystem model added the variables representing the influence of the neighborhood. Ennett *et al.*'s (2008) findings showed that attributes of family, peer, school, and neighborhood contexts all uniquely predicted adolescent alcohol use. As these multilevel models show, studies of developmental factors in addiction have become multidisciplinary because they span levels ranging from the cellular to the macro social policy environment and historical context.

In addition to the multilevel nature of the data, studying these models, which attempt to capture the interplay and reciprocal influence among multiple factors, and which also change over time, requires complex statistical approaches. These include the need to test longitudinal multiple mediator processes and moderated mediation (MacKinnon and Fairchild, 2009) and to accommodate the non-normal, often zero-inflated distribution of the outcome variable (Liu and Powers, 2007). Such meditational models require large sample sizes (Fritz and MacKinnon, 2007).

7   Summary, Limitations, and Future Directions

Given evidence of age-related patterns of substance use disorders as well as evidence of their predictability from early childhood risk, the study of developmental factors is clearly important to research aimed at understanding addiction. Moreover, the study of developmental factors is critical for the design of preventive intervention programs. However, as described in this chapter, there are also significant methodological challenges to this research. These challenges include the difficulties of recruiting and retaining large, representative child and adolescent samples, choosing appropriate ages and measurement lags to evaluate the effects of interest, obtaining valid reports of adolescent substance use and substance-use related symptoms, creating valid diagnoses of clinical substance use disorders for adolescent populations, creating phenotypes that reflect developmental milestones both within the course of use of an individual substance and across different substances, obtaining multiple informant reports of risk and protective factors, establishing invariance of measures across age ranges, and testing complex longitudinal, multilevel, meditation and moderated mediation models, including reciprocal effects. In addition, of course, each specific domain of addiction research (discussed in the other chapters in this volume) presents its own specific methodological dilemmas when applied to child and adolescent populations.

Given these challenges, there are several relevant newly emerging research directions. As might be expected, research on developmental factors in addiction is becoming increasingly multidisciplinary, in order to be able to capture the influence of etiological factors that operate on multiple biopsychosocial levels of influence. Moreover, the need for very large samples has created an interest in data sharing and in methods that allow researchers to combine data across different studies. For example, Curran and Hussong (2009; Curran *et al.*, 2008) used IRT methods to combine data from different longitudinal studies. These methods allowed them to reconstruct trajectories and test hypotheses about the effects of parent alcoholism across a broader age range than would be possible using any of the individual studies taken alone (see e.g., Hussong *et al.*, 2007). Moreover, these methods allow the identification of study-specific effects compared to findings that generalize across multiple studies. The use of IRT methods helps to harmonize data from multiple studies that use different measures of key constructs. However, another approach is to encourage studies to use consensus measures, making it easier to combine studies and/or compare results across different studies. A current example of this approach is the PhenX project, which is reviewing and recommending consensus measures for the integration of genetics and epidemiological research, including applications to substance use outcomes.

Because most of the impact of addictions occurs in adulthood, it is possible to overlook the fact that the roots of substance use are typically established in adolescence. It is important to study the precursors and the process of onset of drug use and the emergence of dependence in order to fully understand those processes and to successfully prevent or intervene to reduce the problems of addiction. Whether one studies the developmental progression of use of a single drug, or the co-relations among the use of several drugs, researchers need to take into account developmental issues in the onset of addition. As we have seen, these factors affect the conceptualization of the phenomena, the measurement of the behaviors themselves (as well their predictors), and the issues of unraveling the entwined causal factors involving time and change across development. Some of these issues are complex, but they are of both practical and theoretical importance to our understanding of addiction and are central for its prevention.

References

Achenbach TM (2011) Commentary: Definitely more than measurement error: But how should we understand and deal with informant discrepancies? *Journal of Clinical Child and Adolescent Psychology* 40: 80–86. doi: 10.1080/15374416.2011.533416.

Achenbach TM, McConaughy SH, and Howell CT (1987) Child/adolescent behavioral and emotional problems: Implications of cross-informant correlations for situational specificity. *Psychological Bulletin* 101: 213–232.

American Psychiatric Association (2000) *Diagnostic and Statistical Manual of Mental Disorders* (4th edn, Test Revision). Washington, DC: American Psychiatric Association.

Anderman C, Cheadle A, Curry S, Diehr P, Schultz L, and Wagner E (1995) Selection bias related to parental consent in school-based survey research. *Evaluation Review* 19: 633–674.

Andersen S and Teicher M. (2009) Desperately driven and no brakes: Developmental stress exposure and subsequent risk for substance abuse. *Neuroscience and Biobehavioral Reviews* 33: 516–534.

Bachman JG, O'Malley PM, Schulenberg JE, Johnston LD, Bryant AL, and Merline AG (2002) The decline of substance use in young adulthood: Changes in social activities roles and beliefs. *Research Monographs in Adolescence*. Mahwah, NJ: Erlbaum.

Baltes PB (1968) Longitudinal and cross-sectional sequences in the study of age and generation effects. *Human Development* 11: 145–171.

Bauer DJ and Curran PJ (2003) Distributional assumptions of growth mixture models: Implications for overextraction of latent trajectory classes. *Psychological Methods* 8: 338–363.

Blozis SA, Feldman B, and Conger RD (2007) Adolescent alcohol use and adult alcohol disorders: A two-part random-effects model with diagnostic outcomes. *Drug and Alcohol Dependence* 88: S85–S96.

Breslau N and Peterson EL (1996) Smoking cessation in young adults: Age at initiation of smoking and other suspected influences. *American Journal of Public Heathl* 86: 214–220.

Bronfenbrenner U (1979) *The Ecology of Human Development: Experiments by Nature and Design*. Cambridge, MA: Harvard University Press.

Brook JS, Nomura C, and Cohen P (1989) A network of influences on adolescent drug involvement: Neighborhood school peer and family. *Genetic, Social and General Psychology Monographs* 115: 125–145.

Buchmann AF, Schnid B, Blomeyer D, Becker K, Treutlein J, Zimmermann US, Jennen-Steinmetz C, Schmidt MH, Esser G, Banaschewski T, Rietschel M, Schumann G, and Laught M (2009) Impact of age at first drink on vulnerability to alcohol-related problems: Testing the marker hypothesis in a prospective study of young adults. *Journal of Psychiatric Research* 43: 1205–1212.

Casey BJ, Jones RM, and Somerville LH (2011) Braking and accelerating of the adolescent brain. *Journal of Research on Adolescence* 21: 21–33.

Caspi A, Moffitt T, Newman D, and Silva P (1996) Behavioral observations at age 3 years predict adult psychiatric disorders: Longitudinal evidence from a birth cohort. *Archives of General Psychiatry* 53: 1033–1039.

Chassin L, Curran P, Presson C, Wirth RJ, and Sherman SJ (2009) Trajectories of adolescent smoking: Conceptual issues and an empirical example. *Phenotypes and Endophenotypes: Foundations for Genetic Studies of Nicotine Use and Dependence Tobacco Control Monographs* 20. Bethesda MD: US Department of Health and Human Services National Institutes of Health National Cancer Institute NIH Publication No. 08-6366.

Chassin L, Presson C, Sherman SJ, Seo D-C, Macy J, Wirth RJ, and Curran P (2008) Multiple trajectories of smoking and the intergenerational transmission of smoking: A multigenerational longitudinal study of a Midwestern community sample. *Health Psychology* 27: 819–828.

Chen C-Y and Anthony C. (2003) Possible age-associated bias in reporting of clinical features of drug dependence: Epidemiological evidence on adolescent-onset marijuana use. *Addiction* 98: 71–82.

Chung T and Martin C (2005) What were they thinking? Adolescents' interpretations of DSM-IV alcohol dependence symptom queries and implications for diagnostic validity. *Drug and Alcohol Dependence* 80: 191–200.

Chung T, Martin C, Winters K, Cornelius J, and Langenbucher J (2004) Limitations in the assessment of DSM-IV cannabis tolerance as an indicator of dependence in adolescents. *Experimental and Clinical Psychopharmacology* 12: 36–46.

Cicchetti D (2006) Development and psychopathology. In D Cicchetti and DJ Cohen (eds), *Developmental Psychopathology*, Vol. 1: *Theory and Method* (2nd edn, pp. 1–24). Hoboken, NJ: John Wiley & Sons, Inc.

Collins LM (2005) Analysis of longitudinal data: The integration of the theoretical model temporal design and statistical model. *Annual Review of Psychology* 57: 505–528.

Curran P and Hussong A (2009) Integrative data analysis: The simultaneous analysis of multiple data sets. *Psychological Methods* 14: 81–100.

Curran P, Hussong A, Cai L, Huang W, Chassin L, Sher K, and Zucker R (2008) Pooling data from multiple longitudinal studies: The role of item response theory in integrative data analysis. *Developmental Psychology* 44: 365–380.

Dawson DA, Goldstein RB, Chou SP, Ruan WJ, and Grant BF (2008) Age at first drink and the first incidence of adult-onset DSM-IV alcohol use disorders. *Alcoholism: Clinical and Experimental Research* 32: 2149–2160.

Delaney-Black V, Chiodo LM, Hannigan JH, Greenwald MK, Janisse J, Patterson G, Huestis MA, Ager J, and Sokol RJ (2010) Just say "I don't": Lack of concordance between teen report and biological measures of drug use. *Pediatrics* 126(5): 887–893.

Dick DM, Pagan JL, Viken R, Purcell S, Kaprio J, Pulkkinen L, and Rose RJ (2007) Changing environmental influences on substance use across development. *Twin Research and Human Genetics* 10: 315–326.

DiFranza JR (2007) Hooked from the first cigarette. *The Journal of Family Practice* 56: 1017–1022.

Dillon F, Turner C, Robbins M, and Szapocznik J (2005) Concordance among biological interview and self-report measures of drug use among African American and Hispanic adolescents referred for drug abuse treatment. *Psychology of Addictive Behaviors* 19: 404–413.

Dolcini N, Adler N, Lee P, Bauman KE (2003) An assessment of the validity of adolescent self-reported smoking using three biological indicators. *Nicotine & Tobacco Research* 5: 473–483.

Donovan J, Jessor R, and Costa F (1999) Adolescent problem drinking: Stability of psychosocial and behavioral correlates across a generation. *Journal of Studies on Alcohol and Drugs* 60: 352–361.

Ennett ST, Foshee VA, Bauman KE, Hussong A, Cai L, McNaughton Reyes HL, *et al.* (2008) The social ecology of adolescent alcohol misuse. *Child Development* 79: 1777–1791.

Esbensen F-A, Miller M, Taylor T, Hi N, and Freng A. (1999) Differential attrition rates and active parental consent. *Evaluation Review* 23: 316–335.

Fendrich M and Rosenbaum D (2003) Recanting of substance use reports in a longitudinal prevention study. *Drug and Alcohol Dependence* 5: 241–253.

Fisher S, Bucholz K, Reich W, Fox L, Kuperman S, Kramer J, Hesselbrock V, Dick D, Nurnberger J, Edenberg H, and Bierut L (2006) Teenagers are right – parents do not know much: An analysis of adolescent–parent agreement on reports of adolescent substance use abuse and dependence. *Alcoholism: Clinical and Experimental Research* 30: 1699–1710.

Flora D, Curran PJ, Hussong A, and Edwards M. (2008) Incorporating measurement non-equivalence in a cross-study latent growth curve analysis. *Structural Equation Modeling* 15: 676–704.

Forbes EE and Dahl RE (2010) Pubertal development and behavior: Hormonal activation of social and motivational tendencies. *Brain and Cognition* 72: 66–72.

Fowler T, Lifford K, Shelton K, Rice F, Thapar A, Neale M, McBride A, Van den Bree M (2007) Exploring the relationship between genetic and environmental influences on initiation and progression of substance use. *Addiction* 103: 413–422. doi: 10.1111/j.1360-0443.2006.01694.x.

Fritz, MS and MacKinnon DP (2007) Required sample size to detect the mediated effect. *Psychological Science* 233–239.

Grant BF and Dawson DA (1998) Age of onset of drug use and its association with DSM-IV drug abuse and dependence: Results from the National Longitudinal Alcohol Epidemiologic Survey. *Journal of Substance Abuse Treatment* 10: 163–173.

Green AE, Bekman N, Miller E, Perrott J, Brown S, and Aarons G (2011) Parental awareness of substance use among youths in public service sectors. *Journal of Studies on Alcohol and Drugs* 77: 44–52.

Griesler PC, Kandel DB, Schaffran C, Hu M-C, and Davies M (2008) Adolescents' inconsistency in self-reported smoking: A comparison of reports in school and in household settings. *Public Opinion Quarterly* 72: 260–290. doi: 10.1093/poq/nfn016.

Haller M, Handley E, Chassin L, and Bountress K (2010) Developmental cascades: Linking adolescent substance use affiliation with substance use promoting peers and academic achievement to adult substance use disorders. *Development and Psychopathology* 22: 899–916.

Harris K, Griffin B, McCaffrey D, and Morral A (2008) Inconsistencies in self-reported drug use by adolescents in substance use treatment: Implications for outcomes and performance measurement. *Journal of Substance Abuse Treatment* 34: 347–355. doi:10.1016/jsat.2007.05.004.

Hussong A, Bauer D, and Chassin L (2008) Telescoped trajectories from initiation to disorder in children of alcoholic parents. *Journal of Abnormal Psychology* 117: 63–78.

Hussong A, Wirth R, Edwards M, Curran P, Chassin L, and Zucker R (2007) Externalizing symptoms among children of alcoholic parents: Entry points for an antisocial pathway to alcoholism. *Journal of Abnormal Psychology* 116: 529–542.

Ialongo N (2010) Steps substantive researchers can take to build a scientifically strong case for the existence of trajectory groups. *Development and Psychopathology* 22: 273–275.

Jackson KM (2010) Progression through early drinking milestones in an adolescent treatment sample. *Addiction* 105: 438–449.

Jackson KM and Sher KJ (2006) Comparison of longitudinal phenotypes based on number and timing of assessments: A systematic comparison of trajectory approaches. *Psychology of Addictive Behavior* 20: 373–384.

Kandel DB and Chen K (2000) Extent of smoking and nicotine dependence in the United States: 1991–1993. *Nicotine & Tobacco Research* 2: 263–274.

Kandel DB, Hu M, and Yamaguchi K (2009) Sequencing of DSM-IV criteria of nicotine dependence. *Addiction* 104: 1393–1402.

Kandel DB, Yamaguchi K, and Chen K (1992) Stages of progression in drug involvement from adolescence to adulthood: Further evidence for the gateway theory. *Journal of Studies on Alcohol and Drugs* 53: 447–457.

Kandel DB, Yamaguchi K, and Klein L (2006) Testing the gateway hypothesis. *Addiction* 101: 470–476.

Kealey K, Ludman E, Mann S, Marek P, Phares M, Riggs K, and Petreson A (2007) Overcoming barriers to recruitment and retention in adolescent smoking cessation. *Nicotine & Tobacco Research* 9: 257–270.

Kendler KS, Schmitt E, Aggen SH, and Prescott CA (2008) Genetic and environmental influences on alcohol, caffeine, cannabis, and nicotine use from early adolescence to middle adulthood. *Archives of General Psychiatry* 65: 674–682.

King KM and Chassin L (2007) A prospective study of the effects of age of initiation of alcohol and drug use on young adult substance dependence. *Journal of Studies on Alcohol and Drugs* 68: 256–265.

Lennox R, Dennis M, Scott C, and Funk R (2006) Combining psychometric and biometric measures of substance use. *Drug and Alcohol Dependence* 28: 95–103.

Levin ED, Rezvani AH, Montoya D, Rose JE, and Swartzwelder HS (2003) Adolescent-onset nicotine self-administration modeled in female rats. *Journal of Psychopharmacology* 169: 141–149.

Little M, Weaver SR, King KM, Liu F, and Chassin L (2008) Historical change in the link between adolescent deviance proneness and marijuana use, 1979–2004. *Prevention Science* 9: 4–16.

Little RJA and Rubin DB (2000) Causal effects in clinical and epidemiological studies via potential outcomes: Concepts and analytical approaches. *Annual Review of Public Health* 21: 121–145.

Liu H and Powers DA (2007) Growth curve models for zero-inflated count data: An application to smoking behavior. *Structural Equation Modeling* 14: 247–279.

MacCoun R (2006) Competing accounts of the gateway effect: The field thins but still no clear winner. *Addiction* 101: 470–471.

MacKinnon DP (2008) *Introduction to Statistical Mediation Analysis*. Mahwah, NJ: Erlbaum.

MacKinnon DP and Fairchild A (2009) Current directions in mediation analysis. *Current Directions in Psychological Science* 18: 16–20.

Masche JG and van Dulmen MHM (2004) Advances in disentangling age cohort and time effects: No quadrature of the circle but a help. *Developmental Review* 24: 322–342. doi: 10.1016/j.dr.2004.04.002.

Masten A, Faden V, Zucker R, and Spear L (2008) Underage drinking: A developmental framework. *Pediatrics* 121(S4): 5235–5251.

Mayhew K, Flay B, and Mott J (2000) Stages in the development of adolescent smoking. *Drug and Alcohol Dependence* 59(S1): 61–81.

Moffitt TE (1993) Adolescence-limited and life-course-persistent antisocial behavior: A developmental taxonomy. *Psychological Review* 100: 674–701.

Mokdad A (2009) The behavioral risk factors surveillance system: Past present and future. *Annual Review of Public Health* 30: 43–54.

Moolchan ET and Mermelstein R (2002) Research on tobacco use among teenagers: Ethical challenges. *Journal of Adolescent Health* 30: 409–417.

Morgan SL and Winship C (2007) *Counterfactuals and Causal Inference: Methods and Principles for Social Research.* Cambridge: Cambridge University Press.

Morral A, McCaffrey D, and Chien S (2003) Measurement of adolescent drug use. *Journal of Psychoactive Drugs* 35: 303–309.

Nesselroade JR and Baltes PB (1979) *Longitudinal Research in the Study of Behavior and Development.* San Diego, CA: Academic Press.

O'Malley P, Bachman J, and Johnson L (1984) Period age and cohort effects on substance use among American youth: 1976–1982. *American Journal of Public Health* 74: 682–688.

Percy A, McAlister S, Higgins K, McCrystal P, and Thornton M (2005) Response consistency in young adolescents' drug self-reports: A recanting rate analysis. *Addiction* 100: 189–196.

Perry CL, Kelder SH, and Komro K (1993) A world of adolescents: Family peers schools and the community. In SG Millstein, AC Peterson, and EO Nightingale (eds), *Promoting the Health of Adolescents: New Directions for the Twenty-First Century* (pp. 73–96). New York: Oxford University Press.

Petraitis J, Flay BR, and Miller TQ (1995) Reviewing theories of adolescent substance use: Organizing pieces of the puzzle. *Psychological Bulletin* 117: 67–86.

Piquero AR, Blumstein A, Brame R, Haapanen R, Mulvey EP, and Nagin DS (2001) Assessing the impact of exposure time and incapacitation on longitudinal trajectories of criminal offending. *Journal of Adolescent Research* 16: 54–74. doi: 10.1177/0743558401161005.

Prescott CA and Kendler KS (1999) Age at first drink and risk for alcoholism: A noncausal association. *Alcoholism: Clinical and Experimental Research* 23: 101–107.

Raudenbush SW and Bryk AS (2002) *Hierarchical Linear Models: Applications and Data Analysis Methods* (2nd edn). London: Sage.

Ridenour TA, Lanza ST, Donny E, and Clark DB (2006) Different lengths of time for progressions in adolescent substance involvement. *Addictive Behaviors* 31: 962–983.

Rogosch FA, Oshri A, and Cicchetti D, (2010) From child maltreatment to adolescent cannabis abuse and dependence: A developmental cascade model. *Development and Psychopathology* 22: 883–897.

Rojas N, Sherrit L, Harris S, and Knight J (2008) The role of parental consent in adolescent substance use research. *Journal of Adolescent Health* 42: 192–197.

Rosenbaum PR (2002) *Observational Studies* (2nd edn). New York: Springer.

Rosenbaum PR and Rubin DB (1983) Assessing sensitivity to an unobserved binary covariate in an observational study with binary outcome. *Journal of the Royal Statistical Society*, Series B 45: 212–218.

Rubin D (1974) Estimating causal effects of treatments in randomized and nonrandomized studies. *Journal of Educational Psychology* 66: 688–701.

Rubin D (2008) For objective causal inference, design trumps analysis. *Annals of Applied Statistics* 2: 808–840.

Sartor C, Lynskey M, Heath A, Jacob T, and True W (2007) The role of childhood risk factors in initiation of alcohol use and progression to alcohol dependence. *Addiction* 102: 216–225.

Sartor C, Xian H, Scherrer J, Lynskey M, Duncan A, Haber J, Grant J, Bucholz KK, and Jacob T (2008) Psychiatric and familial predictors of transition times between smoking stages: Results from an offspring-of-twins study. *Addictive Behaviors* 33: 235–251.

Schaie KW (1965) A general model for the study of developmental problems. *Psychological Bulletin* 64: 92–107. doi: 10.1037/h0022371.

Schmid B, Blomeyer D, Becker K, Treutlein J, Zimmermann US, Buchmann AF, Schmidt MJ, Esser G, Banaschewski T, Rietschel M, and Laucht M (2009) The interaction between the dopamine transporter gene and age at onset in relation to tobacco and alcohol use among 19-year-olds. *Addiction Biology* 14: 489–499.

Schramm-Sapyta N, Walker QD, Caster J, Levin E, and Kuhn C (2009) Are adolescents more vulnerable to drug addiction than adults? Evidence from animal models. *Psychopharmacology* 206: 1–21. doi: 10.1007/s00213-009-1585-5.

Sher K J (1991) *Children of Alcoholics: A Critical Appraisal of Theory and Research.* Chicago: University of Chicago Press.

Sher KJ, Jackson KM, and Steinley D (2011) Alcohol use trajectories and the ubiquitous cat's cradle: Cause for concern? *Journal of Abnormal Psychology* 120: 322–335.

Siegel M, Albers AB, Cheng DM, Biener L, and Rigotti NA (2005) Effect of local restaurant smoking regulations on progression to established smoking among youths. *Tobacco Control* 14: 300–306.

Sinha R (2008) Chronic stress drug use and vulnerability to addiction. *Annals of the New York Academy of Sciences* 1141: 105–130.

Spear LP (2000) The adolescent brain and age-related behavioral manifestations. *Neuroscience & Biobehavioral Review* 24: 417–463.

Sroufe LA (1997) Psychopathology as an outcome of development. *Development and Psychopathology* 9: 251–268.

Steinberg L (2010) A dual systems model of adolescent risk taking. *Developmental Psychobiology* 52: 216–224.

Sterba SK and Bauer DJ (2010) Matching method with theory in person-oriented developmental psychopathology. *Development and Psychopathology* 22: 239–254.

Thomson CC, Fisher LB, Winickoff JP, Colditz GA, Camargo CA, King C, *et al.* (2004) State tobacco excise taxes and adolescent smoking behaviors in the United States. *Journal of Public Health Management and Practice* 10: 490–496.

Torres O, Tejeda H, Natividad L, and O'Dell L (2008) Enhanced vulnerability to the rewarding effects of nicotine during the adolescent period of development. *Pharmacology Biochemistry and Behavior* 90: 658–663. doi 10 10161.

Turner CF, Ku L, Rogers SM, Lindberg L, Pleck JH, and Sonenstein FL (1998) Adolescent sexual behavior drug use and violence: Increased reporting with computer survey technology. *Science* 280: 867–873.

Volkow ND, Baler RD, and Goldstein RZ (2011) Addiction: Pulling at the neural threads of social behaviors. *Neuron* 69: 599–602.

West SG and Thoemmes F (2008) Equating groups. In P. Alasuutari, J Brannen, and L Bickman (eds), *The Sage Handbook of Social Research Methods* (pp. 414–430). London: Sage.

Winters K, Martin C, and Chung T (2011) Substance use disorders in DSM-V when applied to adolescents. *Addiction* 106: 882–884.

Zucker, RA (1986) The four alcoholisms: A developmental account of the etiologic process. *Nebraska Symposium on Motivation* 34: 27–83.

2

Executive Dysfunction in Addiction

David P. Jarmolowicz, E. Terry Mueller,
Mikhail N. Koffarnus, Anne E. Carter,
Kirstin M. Gatchalian, and Warren K. Bickel

1 Introduction

Executive dysfunction has been increasingly recognized in addiction. In fact, it has been estimated that 50–80% of individuals suffering from addiction exhibit some type of executive dysfunction (Bates, Pawlak, Tonigan, and Buckman, 2006). These patterns of impairment, which will be discussed below, may interfere with many therapeutic approaches to addiction. For example, basic planning, inhibition, flexibility and memory skills may be prerequisites to successful cognitive behavior therapy (Verdejo-Garcia, Lopez-Torrecillas, Gimenez, and Perez-Garcia, 2004). As such, understanding these skills, the ways that they may be impaired in addicted individuals, and the neurobiological mechanisms responsible for their execution may be an important step towards improving addiction treatment.

In our view, the patterns of executive dysfunction seen in addiction result from a disruption in the regulatory balance between two competing neurobehavioral decision systems (CNDS). Specifically, effective executive function requires a balance in activation between the impulsive system (i.e., limbic and paralimbic areas), which preferentially values immediate rewards, and the executive system (i.e., the prefrontal cortex [PFC]), which performs the operations necessary to value and work for temporally distant events (Bickel *et al.*, 2012; Bickel *et al.*, 2007). Delay discounting rates (see Chapter 7) may reflect the relative activation in the two decision systems (McClure *et al.*, 2007b; McClure, Laibson, Loewenstein, and Cohen, 2004), with CNDS dysregulation (i.e., executive dysfunction) manifesting as higher than normal discounting rates (Bickel, Jarmalowicz, Mueller, and Gatchalian, 2011). As such, the elevated discounting rates widely seen in those suffering from addiction (see Madden and Bickel, 2009, for a review) suggest that CNDS dysregulation may be a frequent, if not general, characteristic of addiction.

The Wiley-Blackwell Handbook of Addiction Psychopharmacology, First Edition. Edited by James MacKillop and Harriet de Wit.
© 2013 John Wiley & Sons, Ltd. Published 2013 by John Wiley & Sons, Ltd.

The CNDS approach places cognitive performance on a continuum defined by the balance of activation between the impulsive and executive systems. Intact executive function and executive dysfunction are on opposite ends of this continuum (Bickel *et al.*, 2012). This approach is consistent with a number of other accounts. For example, Bechara (2005) noted that decision making reflects the balance between the separate yet interacting impulsive and reflective (i.e., executive) systems. Similarly, Jentsch and Taylor (1999) posited that addiction results from the inability of prefrontal brain regions to inhibit the impulsive system's drive to use drugs. Also, this sort of disruption in CNDS regulatory balance is one of Redish, Jensen, and Johnson (2008) ten key vulnerabilities to addiction.

In the current chapter we will review executive dysfunction in addiction (i.e., drug addiction, pathological gambling, and obesity). First, prevalent approaches to executive function from both outside and within the addiction research literature will be examined. Second, a comprehensive approach to executive function, which accounts for the skills emphasized in previous conceptualizations and for the patterns of dysfunction seen in addiction, will be synthesized (Bickel *et al.*, 2012). Third, these executive functions and their prevalence in addiction will be considered. In doing so, the approaches to measuring these skills, and their neurobiological underpinning, will be considered. Lastly, some directions for future research will be discussed.

2   Theoretical Status of Executive Function

Although many agree that individuals suffering from addiction show deficits in executive function, there is far less consensus on what constitutes executive function. As such, many differing accounts of executive function exist. Some of these accounts emphasize one particular cognitive faculty whereas others emphasize an array of cognitive skills. This theoretical diversity may make it difficult to understand what executive function is, and how it may be deficient in the addicted. Because of the sheer volume of theoretical accounts, a comprehensive exposition of all approaches is beyond the scope of the current chapter. Instead, we will briefly and selectively review notable features of prominent theories of executive/cognitive function.

2.1   Accounts emphasizing one cognitive faculty

Many classic accounts of executive function focus on one particular cognitive skill, such as attention or working memory. For example, Posner and Peterson (1990) posit that attention is a fundamentally important system that is separate from the systems that process data. Deficits in this attention system – which is made up of separate anatomical systems responsible for orienting, signal detection, and vigilance – are said to underlie many disorders of higher-level cognition (e.g., schizophrenia, ADHD, etc.). Similarly, Stuss and Alexander's (2007) approach also emphasizes attention. This account, which they arrived at via an analysis of brain lesion data, divides attention into three distinct domains (i.e., energizing, task setting, and monitoring).

According to Stuss and Alexander, the flexible use of energizing (i.e., initiating and sustaining responding), task setting (i.e., setting of stimulus–response relations), and monitoring (i.e., ongoing checking and adjusting of responding) can account for executive function, without the appeal to unobserved entities such as a central executive (Baddeley, 2003; Baddeley and Hitch, 1974) or a supervisory system (Norman and Shallice, 1986). This account mentions, but does not discuss, higher-order processes such as metacognition.

Other accounts emphasize the pivotal role of working memory in executive function. For example, Baddeley (2003) posits that working memory underlies human thought. Baddeley's conceptualization divides working memory into three components, namely the central executive and two peripheral systems – the phonological loop and the visuospatial sketchpad. According to Baddeley, the phonological loop is a temporary storage and sub-vocal rehearsal system that enables language/verbal learning. The phonological loop is functionally mirrored by the visuospatial sketchpad, which enables visual and spatial learning. The central executive is an attention-limited supervisory system that acts as an episodic buffer to integrate information from the two peripheral systems, switches attention between the peripheral systems, performs non-routine tasks, and integrates working memory with long-term memory.

2.2   Comprehensive accounts of executive function

Other researchers have forgone emphasis on a singular cognitive faculty to form accounts that emphasize a range of executive functions. For example, Robbins (1996) proposed that executive function consists of numerous empirically dissociable cognitive skills. These executive functions – which include planning, working memory, and inhibitory control/response shifting – account for many of the unique deficits seen in individuals with various types of prefrontal cortex damage (e.g., Owen *et al.*, 1990; Owen *et al.*, 1991; Owen *et al.*, 1995).

Similarly, Miller and Cohen's (2001) account focuses on the roles of the prefrontal cortex (PFC) in executive control. Their theory posits that the PFC actively works to achieve planned goals by sending biasing signals that control other cognitive skills such as emotional processing, monitoring and control of behavior, sustained activity, and planning. Failures to provide appropriate top-down signals can result in various cognitive impairments, sometimes called executive dysfunction.

Barkley's (1997) comprehensive account differs from those of Robbins (1996) and Miller and Cohen (2001). In Barkley's account, many executive functions are built upon behavioral inhibition. Specifically, behavioral inhibition prevents automatic prepotent responses, providing an opportunity for executive functions to influence responding. As a result, behavioral inhibition is seen as fundamental to (a) working memory, (b) self-regulation of affect, motivation, and arousal, (c) the use of self-directed speech, rules, or plans, and (d) reconstitution (i.e., response analysis and synthesis). Importantly, from Barkley's perspective, improving behavioral inhibition should result in improvements in each of these inhibition-dependent executive functions. As such, Barkley's view suggests a path beyond understanding executive dysfunction to the amelioration of these deficits.

2.3   Accounts of executive dysfunction in addiction

Although general approaches to executive function may be informative, accounts focused on addiction may be more directly relevant. Many researchers have developed such accounts to explain addiction-related phenomena. As with the accounts described above, considerable heterogeneity exists within these approaches, making an exhaustive delineation of these accounts beyond the scope of the present review.

Hester, Lubman, and Yucel (2010) articulated one of these approaches. According to them, "executive control processes are fundamental for successfully inhibiting the immediate pursuit of pleasurable stimuli, and for the development of adaptive patterns of behavior – both key factors in drug addiction" (p. 302). Accordingly, Hester, Lubman, and Yucel's account focuses on attentional bias (i.e., difficulty directing attention away from drug-related stimuli), response inhibition, and, to a lesser extent, the ability to switch from one task to another. Hester, Lubman, and Yucel provide evidence that these skills are deficient in the addicted, and suggest that these deficits may be central to addiction.

George and Koob (2010) offer an alternative approach to executive dysfunction in addiction that emphasizes top-down self-regulation of various cognitive modules. These cognitive modules include incentive salience, stress reactivity, habitual responding, emotional processing, pain tolerance, and decision making. The decision-making module's involvement in working memory, attention, emotion, outcome expectation, and planning may make it particularly relevant to our discussion of executive dysfunction. According to George and Koob (2010), these modules act independently, and insufficient self-regulation of any of these modules can result in an elevated risk of addiction.

Lastly, we will consider the dual-systems approach to the cognitive skill deficits seen in addiction (e.g., Bechara, 2005; Bickel *et al.*, 2007; Jentsch and Taylor, 1999). These approaches were briefly considered above. Although a number of such approaches exist, the similarities among them would make comprehensive coverage of each of them redundant. Instead, we will focus on Bickel *et al.*'s (2007) CNDS theory as its development was informed by the other approaches to the topic (e.g., Bechara, 2005; Jentsch and Taylor, 1999). The CNDS posits that executive function is observed behaviorally in individuals' choices, and is neurobiologically subserved by competition between two independent and competing brain systems. The impulsive system, made up of the evolutionarily older limbic and paralimbic areas, biases responding towards immediate gratification; whereas the executive system, made up of more recently evolved areas of the PFC, is involved in the valuation of longer-term goals and rewards. Regulatory balance between these systems allows individuals to value future rewards, plan for the future, sustain attention, flexibly move from task to task, and engage in higher-order cognition (Bickel *et al.*, 2012). By contrast, dysregulation in the CNDS may lead to executive dysfunction (entailing impulsivity) and an elevated risk of addiction.

Importantly, many response patterns associated with CNDS dysregulation could be viewed as manifestations of impulsivity. For example, an inability to value future events can manifest as excessive rates of delay discounting (see Chapter 7). This may be because, like executive dysfunction and effective executive function, impulsivity and effective executive function sit on opposite ends of the CNDS's regulatory continuum. As such, it is possible that impulsivity and executive dysfunction may be analogous manifestations of CNDS dysfunction. This view is supported by a recent analysis by Bickel *et al.* (2012) which found that executive dysfunction and impulsivity have considerable definitional overlap, are similarly measured, are present in the same populations, and are subserved by the same neurobiological systems. Given the present evidence, we conceptualize impulsivity as, like executive dysfunction, the antipode of executive function.

2.4   Our synthesis-based approach

The above review reveals that there are many ways of conceptualizing executive function, each emphasizing different cognitive faculties. Exclusive focus on any one approach will surely neglect skills emphasized by other approaches. For this reason, our approach will not directly mirror any of the approaches outlined above. Instead, we will present a conception of executive function that we feel capitalizes on the strengths of the approaches reviewed above (Bickel *et al.*, 2012).

Our account will focus on eight cognitive faculties that are emphasized in previous approaches to executive function: (1) attention (Baddeley, 2003; Hester, Lubman, and Yucel, 2010; Posner and Petersen, 1990; Robbins, 1996; Stuss and Alexander, 2007); (2) working memory (Baddeley, 2003; Barkley, 1997; Miller and Cohen, 2001; Robbins, 1996); (3) behavioral/cognitive flexibility (Hester, Lubman, and Yucel, 2010; Robbins, 1996); (4) inhibition (Barkley, 1997; George and Koob, 2010; Hester, Lubman, and Yucel, 2010; Robbins, 1996); (5) valuing future events (Bechara, 2005; Bickel *et al.*, 2007; George and Koob, 2010); (6) planning (Miller and Cohen, 2001; Robbins, 1996); (7) regulation of arousal and emotional reactions (Barkley, 1997; Bechara, 2005; George and Koob, 2010; Miller and Cohen, 2001; Stuss and Alexander, 2007); and (8) higher-order cognitive skills such as social cognition and metacognition.

We believe that this synthesis-based approach accounts for most executive-dysfunction-related addiction phenomena. For example, failures of behavioral inhibition and/or an inability to value future events may account for the loss of control over drug use and relapse (Bickel, Jarmolowicz, Mueller, and Gatchalian, 2011; George and Koob, 2010; Monterosso and Ainslie, 2007).

3   Eight Executive Functions, and Evidence of their Dysfunction in Addiction

Remediation of the cognitive deficits observed in addiction may require an understanding of how these deficits are measured, as well as which brain regions are associated. Thus, for each executive function implicated in our synthesis-based account we will review (1) how the executive function is defined, (2) how it is measured, (3) evidence of its dysfunction in addiction, and (4) the associated brain areas.

3.1 Attention

Attention entails concentrating on one aspect of the environment while ignoring other aspects of the environment (Barkley, 1997). In addiction, two features of attention may be relevant: sustained attention (Levine *et al.*, 2006) and attentional bias (Sinclair, Nausheen, Garner, and Bladwin, 2010). *Sustained attention* is "the ability to maintain a certain level of performance, especially in the ability to detect the occurrence of infrequent or unpredictable events over extended periods of time" (Levine *et al.*, 2006, p. 30). By contrast, *attentional bias* is "the tendency to selectively attend to disorder-specific as compared to neutral stimuli" (Sinclair, Nausheen, Garner, and Bladwin, 2010, p. 515).

Persons with sufficient attentional skills can continually attend to stimuli corresponding to healthy behavioral goals without distraction (e.g., actively participating in therapy sessions, concentrating on post-therapy assignments such as journaling or job searching in the presence of non-therapeutic stimuli). Attentional skills contribute to addiction therapy by enabling continued participation in therapeutic activities or learning of coping skills, in spite of distraction from environmental or internal stimulation.

Sustained attention typically is measured via performance on tasks that require vigilance, such as continuous performance tasks, part A of the trail-making task (Bowie and Harvey, 2006), or the digit span forward task (Miller, 1956). The Conners continuous performance task (CCPT; Conners, 2000), for example, briefly displays various letters and requires participants to quickly respond to any letter other than a specific target letter. Sustained attention is inferred from participants' ability to quickly respond to non-target letters. By contrast, attentional bias is often measured by the disproportionate propensity of disorder-related stimuli to disrupt performance on a task involving neutral stimuli. For example, the addiction Stroop requires participants to suppress their prepotent response (i.e., word reading) in order to report the display-color of the word. Drug-related words typically disrupt performance (i.e., lengthen reaction times) more than neutral words, suggesting an attentional bias toward drug-related stimuli (Hester *et al.*, 2010). Alternatively, the visual-probe task assesses attentional bias in the absence of an ongoing task. In these assessments, disorder-specific versus neutral stimuli are replaced by a stimulus to which the subject is required to respond, and differences in response times after disorder-specific versus neutral stimuli are used to assess the attention-capturing effect (i.e., bias) of disorder-specific stimuli (Chanonours, and Boettiger, 2010).

Poor sustained attention is seen in many substance-abusing or using populations. For example, Levine *et al.* (2006) compared sustained attention in HIV patients who used cocaine and/or methamphetamine to HIV patients that did not. Both groups completed the CCPT (Conners, 2000), as well as other measures of attention, global neuropsychological functioning, and mood. Levine *et al.* found that the stimulant-using group performed significantly worse on the sustained attention task than the non-drug-using group, whereas the other measures did not distinguish the two groups. Moreover, poorer-than-normal sustained attention has been observed in cigarette smokers (Spilich, June, and Renner, 1992; Tong, Leigh, Campbell, and Smith, 1977; Yakir *et al.*, 2007), alcohol dependent patients (Schellekens *et al.*, 2009), methadone-maintained opioid addicts (Mintzer and Stitzer, 2002; Prosser *et al.*, 2008; but see

Appel, 1982; Rothernberg *et al.*, 1977), former opioid addicts (Prosser, London, and Galynker, 2009), recently abstinent methamphetamine users (Johanson *et al.*, 2006; Levine *et al.*, 2006; London *et al.*, 2005), cocaine users (Goldstein *et al.*, 2007; Gooding, Burroughs, and Boutros, 2008; Kalapatapu *et al.*, 2011; Levine *et al.*, 2006; Moeller *et al.*, 2005), cannabis users (Bahri and Amir, 1994; Croft, Mackay, Mills, and Gruzelier, 2001; Ehrenreich *et al.*, 1999; Ilan, Smith, and Gevins, 2004; Moskowitz and McGlothlin, 1974; Pope and Yurgelun-Todd, 1996; Scholes and Martin-Iverson, 2009; but see Grant, Chamberlain, Schreiber, and Odlaug, 2011 for exceptions), and the obese (e.g., Cserjesi, Luminet, Poncelet, and Lenard, 2009). Although studies have examined sustained attention in pathological gamblers (e.g., Rodriguez-Jimenez *et al.*, 2006) there is no evidence that pathological gamblers suffer from deficits in sustained attention.

Addicted individuals also tend to show attentional bias for addiction-related stimuli. For example, Chanon, Sours, and Boettiger (2010) had cigarette smokers complete a visual probe task wherein two pictures – one smoking-related, the other neutral – were briefly displayed (i.e., for 150 or 500 milliseconds) prior to both disappearing and one being replaced by a small checkerboard. The participant's task was to report the location of the checkerboard. Reaction times were shorter when the checkerboard replaced the smoking-related pictures, suggesting a bias towards the smoking-related stimuli. This attentional bias for addiction-related stimuli has been demonstrated in smokers (Bradley, Field, Mogg, and De Houwer, 2004; Cane, Sharma, and Albery, 2009; Chanon, Sours, and Boettiger, 2010; Drobes, Elibero, and Evans, 2006; Ehrman *et al.*, 2002; Mogg, Bradley, Field, and de Houwer, 2003; Munafo *et al.*, 2003; Waters *et al.*, 2003), alcohol abusers (Cox, Blount, and Rozak, 2000; Johnsen *et al.*, 1994; Jones, Bruce, Livingstone, and Reid, 2006; Lusher, Chandler, and Ball, 2004; Stetter *et al.*, 1995; Stormark, Field, Hugdahl, and Horowitz, 1997), problem drinkers (Sharma, Albery, and Cook, 2001), cocaine addicts (Copersino *et al.*, 2004), cocaine users (Hester, Dixon, and Garavan, 2006; but see Montgomery *et al.*, 2010), opioid addicts (Franken, Kroon, Wiers, and Jansen, 2000; Lubman *et al.*, 2000), and cannabis users (Cane, Sharma, and Albery, 2009; Field, Eastwood, Bradley and Mogg, 2006). Additionally, greater attentional bias towards food-related stimuli has been found in obese children (Braet and Crombez, 2003), obese adult females (Castellanos *et al.*, 2009; Nijs, Muris, Euser, and Franken, 2010; Werthmann *et al.*, 2011), and formerly obese individuals (Phelan *et al.*, 2011) relative to healthy weight controls (see Soetens and Braet, 2007, for an exception).

Results from functional magnetic resonance imaging (fMRI) studies suggest that sustained attention is modulated by the PFC. For example, cocaine addicts exhibit less attention-task-oriented activation in the thalamus and more activation in the occipital lobe and PFC than do non-using controls (Tomasi *et al.*, 2007). Thus, the thalamus may be impaired in this population, and consequently the occipital lobe and PFC are more highly activated to compensate. Such elevated levels of PFC activation may have the result of taxing the PFC to the extent that it is unable to contribute to other demanding PFC activities, such as working memory.

Research using the visual probe task (Vollstadt-Klein *et al.*, 2011) and the drug Stroop task (Goldstein *et al.*, 2007) suggests that attentional bias towards substance-related stimuli is related to hyperactivation of the anterior cingulate cortex (ACC) and thalamus, areas of the cortico-striatal circuit (prefrontal areas, ventral and dorsal striatum) and to the insula. The hyperactivation of the ACC is suggested to modulate the cognitive effort involved in processing conflicting cues in the assessments of attentional bias. The lack of success in regulating the emotional reactions to substance-related cues (i.e., the poorer scores for those stimuli) might be modulated by hypoactivation of rostral anterior cingulate cortex/medial orbitofrontal cortex (rACC/mOFC) (Goldstein *et al.*, 2007).

3.2   Inhibitory control

"Behavioral inhibition refers to three inter-related processes (a) inhibition of the initial prepotent response to an event; (b) stopping of an ongoing response which thereby permits a delay in the decision to respond; and (c) the protection of this period of delay and the self-directed responses that occur within it from disruption by competing events and responses (interference control)" (Barkley, 1997, p. 67). For individuals with drinking problems, for example, inhibiting the initial impulse to go to a bar, or terminating the ongoing behavior of going to a bar may be skills learned en route to overcoming the problem.

Inhibition of an initial prepotent response is typically measured by tasks that have individuals inhibit a response rendered prepotent by experimental procedures. For example, in the stop sign reaction time task (SSRT) a "go signal" is presented on every trial, making the required "go response" prepotent. A "stop signal" follows the "go signal" in a small proportion of trials, requiring the individual to omit the "go response." By titrating the interval between the stop and go signals, the shortest interval at which a participant can inhibit responding is determined. This interval, referred to as the SSRT, measures inhibitory control, with shorter SSRTs representing greater inhibition. By contrast, the Stroop task (Stroop, 1935) has been used to measure participants' interference control.

Addicted individuals often show poor inhibition of prepotent responding. For example, Fillmore and Rush (2002) used the SSRT task to examine the inhibitory control of chronic cocaine users and non-using controls. Control participants had significantly shorter SSRTs and exhibited a higher probability of inhibiting responses. Similarly, smokers (Dinn, Aycicegi, and Harris, 2004; Spinella, 2002), alcohol-dependent individuals (Goudriaan, Oosterlaan, de Beurs, and van den Brink, 2006a; Kamarajan *et al.*, 2005), heroin addicts (Pau, Lee, and Chan, 2002), chronic and dependent cocaine users (Fillmore and Rush, 2002; Kaufman, Ross, Stein, and Garavan, 2003; Lane *et al.*, 2007b; Verdejo-Garcia, Perales, and Perez-Garcia, 2007b), and chronic and dependent methamphetamine users (Monterosso *et al.*, 2005; Salo *et al.*, 2005) all show poorer inhibition than non-using controls. Moreover, recreational cocaine users (Colzato, van den Wildenberg, and Hommel, 2007) and drinkers (Colder and O'Connor, 2002), problem gamblers (Goudriaan, Oosterlaan, de Beurs, and van den Brink, 2005; Goudriaan, Oosterlaan, de Beurs, and van den Brink, 2006b; Kertzman *et al.*, 2008; Roca *et al.*, 2008; but see Leiserson and Pihl, 2007 for an exception), and obese individuals (Nederkoorn *et al.*, 2006a; Nederkoorn *et al.*, 2006b) show poorer inhibition than healthy controls.

Drug-dependent individuals also have difficulties with interference control. For example, Salo *et al.* (2009) administered the Stroop color–word task to a group of methamphetamine abusers who recently initiated abstinence, a group who had been abstinent from methamphetamine for a year, and a group of non-substance-using controls. The recently abstinent users performed worse on the Stroop task than the other two groups, suggesting that interference control is negatively impacted by regular drug use and that this cognitive function may improve with protracted abstinence. Compared to non-substance-using controls, interference control is deficient in alcoholics (Cordovil De Sousa Uva *et al.*, 2010; Fishbein *et al.*, 2007; Jang *et al.*, 2007; Tedstone and Coyle, 2004), heroin addicts (Fishbein *et al.*, 2007), former opioid addicts (Aniskin *et al.*, 2011), methadone-maintained patients (Mintzer and Stitzer, 2002), cocaine-dependent individuals (Fernandez-Serrano *et al.*, 2011; Verdejo-Garcia and Perez-Garcia, 2007), regular methamphetamine users (King, Alicata, Cloak, and Chang, 2010; Simon *et al.*, 2000), recently abstinent methamphetamine abusers (Salo *et al.*, 2009; Salo *et al.*, 2007), cannabis users (Battisti *et al.*, 2010; Croft, Mackay, Mills, and Gruzelier, 2001), pathological gamblers (Brand *et al.*, 2005; Kertzman *et al.*, 2011; Potenza *et al.*, 2003; Regard, Knoch, Gutling, and Landis, 2003; Rugle and Melamed, 1993), and obese individuals (Maayan, Hoogendoorn, Sweat, and Convit, 2011; Verdejo-Garcia *et al.*, 2010; Waldstein and Katzel, 2006).

Many brain regions are associated with inhibition of prepotent responding. Stopping an initial prepotent behavior is associated with activity in the inferior frontal cortex (Aron, Robbins, and Poldrack, 2004; Cai and Leung, 2011). Moreover, studies have revealed deficits in regional brain activation associated with deficits in inhibitory control. For example, Norman *et al.* (2011) found teenagers' transitions from moderate to heavy drug use were predicted by decreases in activation of the left dorso-lateral prefrontal cortex (dlPFC), the right frontal gyrus, right medial gyrus, left cingulate, left putamen, medial temporal, and inferior parietal cortex during behavioral inhibition tasks. Similarly, Hendrick, Luo, Zhang, and Li (2011) found that, compared to healthy controls, obese females exhibited lower levels of activation in the inferior parietal cortex and the cuneus during inhibition tasks.

Theoretical accounts of interference control posit that the anterior cingulate cortex (ACC) detects interference, in the form of response conflict, and that the dlPFC subserves processes that reduce that conflict (Carter and van Veen, 2007). This view is supported by Nestor, Ghahremani, Monterosso, and London's (2011) finding that methamphetamine-dependent individuals' poorer-than-control performance on the Stroop color–word task was associated with relatively low levels of activation in the right inferior frontal gyrus, the supplementary motor cortex/anterior cingulate gyrus, and the ACC.

3.3   Valuing future events

Valuing future events entails a pattern of behavior characterized by the influence of future reinforcers on current responding. In drug addiction, "staying clean" involves a sustained preference for the large but delayed reinforcers of drug-free living (e.g. medical, material, and social health and well-being) and eschewing the small immediate reinforcing effects of drug use (Bickel, Odum, and Madden, 1999). Moreover, the strategies learned in substance abuse therapy emphasize reinforcers obtainable in the future rather than the present.

Individuals' valuation of future events is often reflected in the rate at which they discount delayed rewards. For example, Madden, Petry, Badger, and Bickel (1997) administered delay-discounting assessments for (hypothetical) $1,000 and $1,000 worth of heroin to opioid-dependent patients and healthy controls. The procedure presented a series of choices between the $1,000 reward to be received after a delay and a smaller amount to be received immediately. Within the series the value of the immediate amount was titrated to determine the value at which the participant was indifferent between receiving the two rewards (i.e., the indifference point). These indifference points were determined at seven different delays, and non-linear regression was used to estimate the delay-discounting rates. Madden, Petry, Badger, and Bickel (1997) found that opioid-dependent participants discounted monetary rewards more than non-drug-using participants and they discounted delayed heroin rewards more than delayed monetary rewards. Studies have shown that persons who abuse or are addicted to cigarettes (Baker, Johnson, and Bickel, 2003; Bickel, Odum, and Madden, 1999; Johnson, Bickel, and Baker, 2007; Mitchell, 1999), alcohol (Petry, 2001a; 2002; Vuchinich and Simpson, 1998), cocaine (Bickel *et al.*, 2011a; Coffey, Gudleski, Saladin, and Brady, 2003; Heil, Johnson, Higgins, and Bickel, 2006; Monterosso *et al.*, 2001), heroin (Kirby, Petry, and Bickel, 1999; Madden, Petry, Badger, and Bickel, 1997; Odum, Madden, Badger, and Bickel, 2000), and methamphetamine (Hoffman *et al.*, 2006; Monterosso *et al.*, 2007) discount future rewards more rapidly than do non-using control participants. Additionally, pathological gamblers (Dixon, Marley, and Jacobs, 2003; MacKillop *et al.*, 2006; Petry, 2001b) and obese individuals (Davis, Patte, Curtis, and Reid, 2010; Weller, Cook, Avsar, and Cox, 2008; Zhang and Rashad, 2008) exhibit higher discounting rates than controls.

Multiple brain regions may subserve the valuing of future events. McClure, Laibson, Lowenstein, and Cohen (2004) found preferential activation in limbic and paralimbic regions (i.e., ventral striatum, medial orbitofrontal cortex, medial prefrontal cortex, posterior cingulate cortex, left posterior hippocampus) during selection of alternatives when money was available immediately. During all trials, areas of the right and left intraparietal cortex, right dorsolateral prefrontal cortex (DLPFC), right ventrolateral prefrontal cortex and right lateral orbitofrontal cortex were activated (see also Bickel, Pitcock, Yi, and Angtuaco, 2009; Kable and Glimcher, 2007; 2010; McClure *et al.*, 2007a). This correlational evidence is strengthened by the observation that manipulating activation in these prefrontal areas alters discounting rates. For example, Cho *et al.* (2010) used transcranial magnetic stimulation (TMS) to alter dlPFC activation and found that this manipulation decreases rates of delay discounting (i.e., increased valuation of future events; also see Figner *et al.*, 2010).

3.4   Cognitive (behavioral) flexibility

Behavioral flexibility is the ability to appropriately adjust behavior in response to changing environmental contingencies (Hanna-Pladdy, 2007). Therapeutically, flexible behavior allows those in recovery to switch from one coping strategy to another as they encounter situations that put them at risk of relapse.

Commonly used measures of cognitive flexibility are the Wisconsin Card Sorting Task (WCST), and part B of the trail-making task. For example, Lane *et al.* (2007a) administered the WCST to a group of adolescent heavy cannabis users and a group of matched non-drug-using controls. They found that heavy cannabis users committed more perseverative errors on the WCST. Studies of behavioral flexibility in various populations show that cannabis users (Bolla *et al.*, 2002a; Lane *et al.*, 2007a), chronic amphetamine users (Ornstein *et al.*, 2000), chronic cocaine users (Bolla, Rothman, and Cadet, 1999; Ersche *et al.*, 2008; Fillmore and Rush, 2006), smokers (Kalmijn *et al.*, 2002; Razani, Boone, Lesser, and Weiss, 2004), pathological gamblers (Forbush *et al.*, 2008; Goudriaan, Oosterlaan, de Beurs, and van den Brink, 2006a; Marazziti *et al.*, 2008), and the obese (Cserjesi, Luminet, Poncelet, and Lenard, 2009; Maayan, Hoogendoorn, Sweat, and Convit, 2011; Verdejo-García *et al.*, 2010) are significantly less flexible in the face of changing contingencies than control participants.

Many brain areas are associated with cognitive flexibility. For example, Moser *et al.* (2002) used TMS to inhibit the activity of the medial frontal gyrus (MFG) and found that this diminished behavioral flexibility. Moreover, studies of patients with lesions in the ventromedial frontal cortex and dlPFC revealed impaired behavioral flexibility (Bechara, Damasio, Damasio, and Anderson, 1994; Bechara, Damasio, Tranel, and Damsaio, 1997; Fellows and Farah, 2005), suggesting that flexible behavior may depend upon proper functioning of these regions.

3.5 Working memory

Working memory refers to "the ability to retain some information active for further use, and to do so in a flexible way allowing information to be prioritized, added or removed" (Bledowski, Kaiser, and Rahm, 2010, p. 172). Working memory may be particularly important in addiction, due to its role in the learning and the execution of skills for resisting the short-term compulsion to use. Working memory is measured by tasks, such as the n-back task (Kirchner, 1958), digit span task (Miller, 1956), and digit span forward task (King, Alicata, Cloak, and Chang, 2010), which require the participant to process, retain, and subsequently report back information.

Working memory is often deficient in addiction. For example, Patterson *et al.* (2010) found that performance on the Letter n-Back Test during a 3-day mandatory (biochemically confirmed) abstinence period predicted the rate at which individuals resumed smoking (i.e., lower working memory scores were associated with more rapid resumption of smoking). Similar deficits have been seen across a range of populations, including cannabis users (Block and Ghoneim, 1993; Bolla *et al.*, 2002b), methamphetamine users (McKetin and Mattick, 1997; Rippeth *et al.*, 2004; Simon *et al.*, 2000), amphetamine users (Ersche *et al.*, 2006; Ornstein *et al.*, 2000), opioid users (Ersche *et al.*, 2006; Ornstein *et al.*, 2000), cocaine users (Beatty, Katzung, Moreland, and Nixon, 1995; Berry *et al.*, 1993; Di Sclafani, Tolou-Shams, Price, and Fein, 2002; Hoff *et al.*, 1996; Kalapatapu *et al.*, 2011; Kubler, Murphy, and Garavan, 2005; Mittenberg and Motta, 1993; Verdejo-Garcia, Bechara, Recknor, and Perez-Garcia, 2006), alcoholics (Beatty, Katzung, Moreland, and Nixon, 1995; Thoma *et al.*, 2011), cigarette smokers (Ernst, Heishman, Spurgeon, and London, 2001; Jacobsen *et al.*, 2005), pathological or problem gamblers (e.g., Leiserson and Pihl, 2007; Roca *et al.*,

2008), and the obese (Gunstad *et al.*, 2007; Maayan, Hoogendoorn, Sweat, and Convit, 2011).

Various studies point to the neural substrates of working memory. For example, fMRI brain imaging studies have observed that regions such as the dlPFC, ventro-medial PFC, dorsal cingulate, frontal poles, medial inferior parietal cortex, frontal gyrus, medial frontal gyrus, and precentral gyrus are activated during working memory tasks (de Fockert, Rees, Frith, and Lavie, 2001; Glahn *et al.*, 2002). Also, studies implementing TMS and transcranial direct current stimulation (tDCS) have suggested that the dlPFC (Mottaghy *et al.*, 2000; Mulquiney, Hoy, Daskalakis, and Fitzgerald, 2011) and inferior frontal junction (Zanto, Rubens, Thangavel, and Gazzaley, 2011) are causally related to working memory.

3.6   Planning

Reflecting the colloquial understanding of planning, Hanna-Pladdy (2007) noted that "planning requires the ability to identify and organize the necessary steps required to achieve a goal. These steps can include the ability to conceptualize (look ahead), view one-self and the environment in an objective fashion, generate alternatives, make decisions, and consider sequential and hierarchical ideas" (Hanna-Pladdy, 2007, p. 120). These planning skills may be necessary to the effective therapeutic process. For example, treating addiction with cognitive behavioral therapy will often require identifying desirable outcomes and developing plans to obtain them. The lack of planning associated with addiction works against successful therapy, and therefore it must be overcome on the path to recovery. Planning is typically assessed via tasks in which successful outcomes are dependent on developing and implementing plans. The Tower of Hanoi Task and the Tower of London (Kaller, Rahm, Kostering, and Unterrainer, 2011) task are commonly used examples (Kaller, Rahm, Kostering, and Unterrainer, 2011; Sullivan, Riccio, and Castillo, 2009).

Planning is frequently deficient in drug users. For example, Ersche *et al.* (2006) administered a version of the Tower of London task in separate groups of current chronic heroin users and amphetamine users, non-drug-taking controls, and a group of former heroin and/or amphetamine users (at least 1 year of abstinence). They found that the substance-using groups exhibited significantly impaired planning compared to the control group. The amphetamine users were significantly more impaired in this function than the heroin users. Also, there were no group differences between current and former drug users. Deficits in planning have been observed in studies comparing planning-task performance of non-drug-using controls to cigarette smokers (Yakir *et al.*, 2007), and also chronic users of amphetamine (Ersche *et al.*, 2006) and heroin (Davydov and Polunina, 2004; Ersche *et al.*, 2006). Additionally, planning deficits have also been seen in pathological gamblers (Goudriaan, Oosterlaan, de Beurs, and van den Brink, 2006b) and the obese (Lokken *et al.*, 2010) relative to healthy controls.

The dlPFC may be the primary substrate of planning. This association was first noticed when Shallice and Burgess (1991) observed that patients with damage to the dlPFC were unable to perform basic planning activities such as shopping for the items on a small list. Brain imaging studies have since supported this association. They suggest that the dlPFC has a role in coordinating activity in brain regions that may underlie the motivational and attentional aspects of creating and maintaining a plan. In addition to the dlPFC, de Ruiter *et al.* (2009) implicated the ventromedial PFC, parietal cortex, and striatum as brain regions underlying planning. Dockery, Hueckel-Weng, Birbaumer, and Plewnia (2009) measured the effect that applying trans-cranial direct current stimulation (tDCS) to the dlPFC would have on tower task performance. They found that it improved performance, giving further support to the suggestion that the dlPFC plays a causal role in planning.

3.7 Emotional and activation self-regulation (EASR)

Here, two skill-sets are grouped into a single executive function because they both apply to interrelated aspects of behavior that are commonly referred to as "hot" – emotion and motivation (Bechara, 2005; Metcalfe and Mischel, 1999; Miller and Cohen, 2001; Steinberg, 2010; Urcelay and Dalley, 2011). EASR is defined as the behavioral processes involved in controlling affective states. "The self-regulatory role of the executive system is stressed here in that emotions, once elicited, come to be moderated or regulated by self-directed, executive actions. Included in the component is also the self-generation of drive or motivational arousal states that support the execution of goal-directed actions and persistence towards the goal" (Barkley, 1997, p. 74).

Addictions are manifest as highly motivated patterns of behavior that evoke emotion when prematurely terminated. This absence of calmness in the face of unattained reinforcement distinguishes persons lacking in EASR – addicted persons, in particular – from those proficient in it. The "loss of control" that occurs in persons with diminished EASR is a characteristic of addiction and must be transcended to "beat" addiction. Importantly, however, this diminution of self-regulation may also be an impediment to overcoming addiction because it is closely related to the diminution of other executive functions. EASR is strongly related to valuation of future events and to planning because all three are directed toward the receipt of future rather than imminent rewards. Similar to planning and valuation of future rewards, deficits in EASR may entail negative consequences to personal development, such as the inability to learn, remember, and plan for coping strategies that could be used in the battle against addiction.

The Iowa Gambling Task (IGT) and/or the Cambridge Gamble Task are often used to measure EASR. These tasks entail choosing from decks that contain cards, some of which result in gaining money, others resulting in losing money. The decks differ in their overall payout, with some decks being "winning" decks (i.e., net gain if all cards chosen) and some decks being "losing" decks (i.e., net loss if all cards chosen). These tasks measure EASR in two ways: (1) experimenters can infer levels of emotional regulation from participants' reactions (e.g., continuing or changing course) to negative consequences of choices between probabilistic outcomes; and (2) while healthy control subjects perform the task they typically develop physiological responses (e.g., galvanic skin response and/or heart rate) in anticipation of choosing response options associated with reward and punishment (Bechara, Damasio, Damasio, and Anderson, 1994; Bechara, Damasio, Tranel, and Damasio, 1997; Bechara, Tranel, Damasio, and Damasio, 1996). The absence of these signals can be seen as EASR dysfunction.

EASR is often deficient in the addicted. For example, Passetti *et al.* (2008) administered the Iowa and Cambridge Gambling Tasks and other neuropsychological assessments (Tower of London; delay discounting; go/no go task) prior to initiating opioid replacement therapy. Three months into treatment, Passetti *et al.* observed that individuals with sub-standard scores on the gambling tasks were significantly more likely to have reverted to illicit drug use, while similar predictive relations were not obtained for the other neuropsychological assessments. Moreover, polysubstance abusers (Grant, Contoreggi, and London, 2000) and chronic or heavy users of alcohol (Bechara *et al.*, 2001; Fein, Klein, and Finn, 2004), cannabis (Verdejo-Garcia *et al.*, 2007; Whitlow *et al.*, 2004), cocaine (Verdejo-Garcia *et al.*, 2007), opioids (Rogers *et al.*, 1999), methamphetamine (Bechara *et al.*, 2001), amphetamine (Rogers *et al.*, 1999), MDMA (Quednow *et al.*, 2007), and opiates (Rogers *et al.*, 1999), all show poorer EASR than healthy controls, as also do pathological gamblers (Forbush *et al.*, 2008; Goudriaan, Oosterlaan, de Beurs, and van den Brink, 2005; Lakey *et al.*, 2007; Roca *et al.*, 2008) and the obese (Horstmann *et al.*, 2011; Verdejo-García *et al.*, 2010).

Performance of EASR tasks such as the IGT is associated with activation in the medial PFC (Fukui *et al.*, 2005) and lateral PFC (Hartstra *et al.*, 2010), the ACC, and the orbitofrontal cortex (Hartstra *et al.*, 2010). Moreover, individuals with ventromedial PFC lesions perform poorly on the IGT (e.g., Bechara, Damasio, and Damasio, 2003), and tDCS applied to the dlPFC disrupts IGT performance in older adults (Boggio *et al.*, 2010).

3.8 Metacognitive processes

The executive functions described above are relatively simple classes of behavior that facilitate appropriate choices. Decisions, however, are often made in complex social contexts. As such, individuals must choose courses of action that are appropriate from both their own and others' perspectives. Metacognitive processes (MP) are the processes whereby we discriminate our and others' perspectives, and act accordingly. We will discuss two pertinent MPs, namely social cognition and metacognition.

Social cognition, sometimes called "theory of mind," or empathy, is the ability to utilize cues in others' behavior (e.g., facial expression, posture, etc.) to correctly attribute their intentions, thoughts and beliefs (see Pickup, 2008; Uekermann and Daum, 2008, for a discussion). Individuals with these skills are aware when things that they have said upset others, whereas those without these skills may be surprised to hear that they have offended someone. By contrast, *metacognition* (sometimes called insight or self-awareness; see Goldstein *et al.*, 2009a, for a review) is "awareness, beliefs, and knowledge about one's self, including abilities, weaknesses, knowledge, skills and personal history" (Wasserstein and Lynn, 2001, p. 379). For example, individuals with strong metacognitive repertoires can understand that their behavior (e.g., excessive drinking or drug use) may be problematic. By contrast, individuals that lack such insight may not see such behavior as problematic. This lack of insight has been likened to denial (Goldstein *et al.*, 2009a).

Social cognition is measured in many ways. Some social cognition tasks require participants to identify the intensity (Oscar-Berman *et al.*, 1990) or valance (Philippot *et al.*, 1999) of emotion expressed in photographs of faces. Other social cognition tasks have participants identify the emotional valance of spoken language (Oscar-Berman *et al.*, 1990). Theory-of-mind assessments ask participants to infer and report the perspective or intention of individuals from within a story (see Uekermann and Daum, 2008, for a discussion), or to predict the behavior of a character who has a false belief about where an item is located (Wimmer and Perner, 1983). There are also many ways to measure metacognition/insight. The Meta-Cognitions Questionnaire (Cartwright-Hatton and Wells, 1997) asks participants subjective questions about their beliefs and their ability to monitor their thinking. Other metacognition/insight measures, however, are less subjective. For example, awareness of one's errors on cognitive tasks such as a modified go/no go task is used as a proxy for one's level of insight (e.g., Hester, Nestor, and Garavan, 2009).

Substance-dependent individuals often have deficits in social cognition (Uekermann and Daum, 2008) or metacognitive insight (Goldstein *et al.*, 2009b). For example, alcoholics have social cognition deficits, manifest as overestimation of the emotions in facial expressions (Clark, Oscar-Berman, Shagrin, and Pencina, 2007; Foisy *et al.*, 2007; Oscar-Berman *et al.*, 1990; Philippot *et al.*, 1999; Salloum *et al.*, 2007) or poor identification of the perspective of cartoon characters (Uekermann *et al.*, 2007). Moreover, it has been proposed that the impairments in social functioning seen in methamphetamine addiction are related to a social cognition deficit (Homer *et al.*, 2008). Although interesting, further research is needed to shed light on the relation between addiction and social cognition.

Insight also appears to be impaired in the addicted. For example, Moeller *et al.* (2010) found that cocaine-dependent individuals performed at chance levels on a task that required them to report which type of picture they most frequently viewed (i.e., they were unaware of their own responses). Similar deficits in insight are also seen in users of other drugs such as cannabis (Hester, Nestor, and Garavan, 2009). Poor scores on the Meta-Cognitions Questionnaire are associated with elevated levels of alcohol consumption (Moneta, 2011; Spada and Wells, 2005) and cigarette smoking (Spada, Moneta, and Wells, 2007) in college students.

Although these metacognitive processes (i.e., social cognition and insight) appear similar, they can be dissociated via fMRI. Specifically, insight is associated with activation in the insula and ACC (Craig, 2009; Hester, Nestor, and Garavan, 2009). By contrast, social cognition is associated with activation in the medial PFC, right superior temporal gyrus, left temporal parietal junction, left somatosensory cortex and right dlPFC (e.g., Germine, Garrido, Bruce, and Hooker, in press; van den Bos *et al.*, 2011), and impaired social cognition is seen in individuals with ventromedial PFC lesions (Bechara, 2004).

4   Novel Conceptual and Empirical Findings

The conceptualization of executive functions outlined above provides a framework that has spawned novel approaches to studying, understanding, and treating the range of executive dysfunctions associated with addiction. As novel findings come to light, future research directions, with the potential to further our understanding and treatment of addiction, become apparent. Some of these findings, and the research directions they suggest, are reviewed below.

4.1   Executive function training

Over time, numerous studies have examined the effects of cognitive remediation on the executive function, primarily working memory. For example, Butterfield and Wambold (1973) improved learning-disabled individuals' short-term memory by teaching them sub-vocal rehearsal strategies. Although these skills did not generalize to other untrained executive function tasks, Butterfield's demonstration of training-related working memory improvement inspired the development of training tasks with more generalizable effects.

Subsequent studies have demonstrated generalized improvements in executive function following working memory training. For example, Klingberg, Forssberg, and Westerberg (2002) compared performance on working memory tasks, a complex reasoning task (i.e., Raven Progressive Matrices), and motor activity of seven children who underwent a computerized battery of working memory training to seven other children who underwent a sham control condition. The participants who underwent working memory training decreased their rate of motor movements and improved their performance on both trained and untrained working memory tasks, as well as on the Raven Progressive Matrices. No such improvement was obtained in the control group. This finding, which has been systematically replicated in individuals with ADHD (Mezzacappa and Buckner, 2010) and stroke (Westerberg *et al.*, 2007), demonstrates that working memory training can yield generalized improvements in executive function (see Morrison and Chein, 2011, for a review). The training of executive function may help remediate some of the executive dysfunction seen in addiction (Vocci, 2008). For example, Bickel *et al.* (2011b) recently extended Klingberg, Forssberg, and Westerberg (2002)'s findings to stimulant addicts. Specifically, Bickel and colleagues exposed a group of 14 stimulant addicts to 4–15 one-hour sessions of a commercially available working-memory-training battery (PSSCogReHab), and a control group of 13 stimulant addicts to a yoked control condition wherein the same task stimuli were presented along with other stimuli (i.e., correct answers) that eliminated the need to exercise working memory in order to respond correctly. Delay discounting rates decreased in the working-memory-training group, but not in the control group, suggesting that the effects of working memory training generalized to the valuation of future events. Demonstrating improvement in future event valuation may be particularly important given that elevated rates of discounting are associated with a wide range of behavioral maladies such drug addiction, gambling, obesity, and poor health behaviors (for review and discussion, see Bickel *et al.*, 2012b; Bickel and Mueller, 2009).

4.2   Brain stimulation

As noted above, executive functions are associated with activation in frontal brain regions, such as the PFC. The success of working memory training, which indirectly exercises areas of the PFC, suggests that direct stimulation of prefrontal areas via technologies such as TMS or trans-cranial direct current stimulation (tDCS) may impact executive function. Studies using these brain stimulation techniques may be important for two reasons: (1) they can pinpoint the brain regions for which there are causal relations to specific executive functions, and (2) they may yield a way to remediate the various forms of executive dysfunction associated with addiction (Miniussi *et al.*, 2008).

TMS uses magnetic fields to increase or decrease brain activation in the areas stimulated. Because TMS directly manipulates brain activation, TMS studies identify the brain mechanisms causally linked to performance on executive function tasks. For example, Mottaghy and colleagues (2000) compared 14 subjects' performance on the n-back task after repetitive TMS (rTMS) to the left dlPFC, the right dlPFC or the midline frontal cortex to n-back performance without brain stimulation. Performance was impaired temporarily after stimulation to either lobe of the dlPFC, but not to the midline frontal cortex, indicating that the dlPFC plays a causal role in working memory (Feredoes *et al.*, 2011). Similar studies have determined that the inferior frontal junction (IFJ) (Zanto, Rubens, Thangavel, and Gazzaley, 2011), the posterior middle frontal gyrus (Kaminski, Korb, Villringer, and Ott, 2011), and the superior fontal gyrus (Soto *et al.*, 2011) also play causal roles in working memory. Beyond working memory, TMS studies have highlighted brain regions responsible for other executive functions. For example, Moser *et al.* (2002) demonstrated the functional role of the middle frontal gyrus in cognitive flexibility, and Heinen *et al.* (2011) highlighted the role of the angular gyrus in attention. Further research may map the brain regions responsible for each of the executive functions that we have discussed above.

Although the long-term impact of TMS on executive function remains unknown, data suggest that rTMS could develop into a therapeutic intervention to remediate the executive dysfunction associated with a range of addictions. Few studies have examined this possibility directly, but studies addressed to the treatment of depression using rTMS have reported modest improvement in executive functions such as working memory (Martis *et al.*, 2003). Effects of TMS are subject to highly specific parameters such as frequency, intensity, timing, and location of the stimulation (Wagner, Valero-Cabre, and Pascual-Leone, 2007). In light of that specificity, it is encouraging that improved executive function was observed while using TMS to treat depression (i.e., a protocol not intended to impact executive function).

Other forms of brain stimulation also show promise for the remediation of the executive dysfunction associated with addiction. For instance, tDCS, a technology that sends low frequency electrical currents through the brain, shows promise as a research and therapeutic tool (Miniussi *et al.*, 2008). For example, Mulquiney, Hoy, Daskalakis, and Fitzgerald (2011) had ten volunteers do the Sternberg working memory task (Sternberg, 1966) while receiving 10 minutes of tDCS, or a sham tDCS control condition. Sessions were spaced at least one week apart and each participant experienced each condition. Performance on the Sternberg working memory task improved with tDCS, but not in the other condition. This working memory improvement, however, did not generalize to untrained working memory tasks (i.e., one card learning, 1-back or 2-back memory tasks) administered after the stimulation, suggesting that the effect is short lived or task specific. Future studies will further explore the use of tDCS in the context of other executive functions.

4.3   Real-time fMRI

Recent advances in brain imaging have facilitated the real-time analysis of fMRI images. This new technology has enabled a different type of manipulation of brain activity – real-time fMRI (rtfMRI) biofeedback. For example, Magland, Tjoa, and Childress (2011) trained participants to make an on-screen marker move up by thinking about hitting a tennis ball (i.e., repetitive motor thoughts) or to go down by thinking about moving from room to room in a familiar building (i.e., spatial navigation thoughts). Similarly, LeConte, Peltier, and Hu (2007) trained healthy subjects to move an on-screen arrow using brain activation associated with tapping the index finger of their right or left hands.

Although use of this technology to improve executive function is forthcoming, rtfMRI biofeedback has yielded clinically relevant improvements in other brain dysfunctions. For example, Haller, Birbaumer, and Veit (2010) trained individuals suffering from tinnitus (i.e., the presence of a constant aversive tone associated with excessive auditory activation) to decrease activation in the auditory cortex by presenting a thermometer image that depicted the current level of auditory cortex activation. Not only were participants able to control the level of activation during feedback sessions, but self-reports of tinnitus decreased as a result of the training. This study shows the therapeutic promise of rtfMRI neurofeedback.

4.4   Cognitive enhancers

Drugs that facilitate the improvement in executive function (i.e., cognitive enhancers) may be helpful in remediating the executive dysfunction associated with drug addiction. Because recent reviews (e.g., Brady, Gray, and Tolliver, 2011) have provided detailed descriptions of the varied pharmacological mechanisms underlying the effects of these drugs, we direct readers interested in the pharmacology of cognitive enhancers to those works.

A number of cognitive enhancers have improved the cognitive function of addicted individuals. For example, acute nicotine administration is associated with improvements in attention and working memory in both smokers and non-smokers (see Heishman, Kleykamp, and Singleton, 2010, for a meta analysis), and varenicline (a nicotinic acetylcholine receptor partial agonist) improves working memory and sustained attention in abstinent nicotine-dependent individuals (Patterson *et al.*, 2010; see also Loughead *et al.*, 2009). Similarly, modafinil (a non-amphetamine stimulant) improved working memory in treatment-seeking methamphetamine users with poor baseline working memory scores (Kalechstein, De La Garza, and Newton, 2010). Lastly, the anticonvulsant tiagabine improved performance on the Stroop test in recently abstinent smokers (Sofuoglu *et al.*, 2005).

Other cognitive enhancers may also improve executive function in addicted individuals. For example, the success of the partial glutamate N-Methyl-D-aspartate (NMDA) receptor agonist D-Cycloserine in facilitating fear extinction in clinical populations such as those with anxiety disorders (see Norberg, Krystal, and Tolin, 2008, for a review) suggests that it may be helpful in remediating dysfunctional EASR or valuation of future events. Similarly, the success of the selective nonepinephrine transporter inhibitor atomoxetine in improving attention in children with ADHD, and inhibition in healthy individuals (see Bidwell, McClernon, and Kollins, 2011, for a review), combined with its low abuse liability (e.g., Jasinski *et al.*, 2008), suggests that this drug may successfully remediate attention and inhibition deficits in drug-dependent individuals.

Some studies, however, have failed to show an effect of these and other cognitive enhancers (see Brady, Gray, and Tolliver, 2011, for a review). This may be due to the fact that most studies provide the drugs without concurrent neurocognitive rehabilitation. Thus, analogous to an individual who takes steroids and sits on the couch instead of working out, it is not surprising that executive function does not improve in these studies.

5   Conclusions and Directions

As outlined above, there are many basic cognitive processes that are often deficient in the addicted. Research on these patterns of executive dysfunction, however, is primarily in its early, descriptive, phase. As such, there is still much to learn. For example, why does executive dysfunction occur across so many addictive patterns of behavior? It is possible that these deficits are trans-disease processes that elevate one's risk of developing addiction. Few longitudinal studies have evaluated this possibility (Bickel *et al.*, 2012b; Bickel and Mueller, 2009). In a notable example, however, Audrain-McGovern *et al.* (2009) found that teenagers' delay-discounting rates predicted if they would become smokers. Thus, it appears that poor valuation of future events may predispose one to cigarette smoking. The extent to which this observation generalizes to the other executive dysfunctions, or other addictions, however, awaits future longitudinal research.

Similarly puzzling is why each population of addicted individuals (e.g., alcoholics, cocaine addicts, etc.) tends to show deficits across most of these executive functions. Previous accounts (Baddeley, 2003; Barkley, 1997; 2004; Posner and Petersen, 1990) have posited that some executive functions are necessary for the development/execution of other executive functions, but the structure of these relations varies widely from author to author. If some executive functions build upon others, impairment in the foundational executive function may result in widespread patterns of executive dysfunction. Future research may clarify these relations, and the observed patterns of co-impairment across executive functions.

As this area of study advances from description, to prediction, and then to therapeutic manipulation, additional questions remain. For example, will improvement in executive function improve treatment outcome for therapeutic approaches that depend on thinking skills (e.g., cognitive behavioral therapy)? Will improvement in executive function alone be sufficient to impact addiction-oriented phenomena such as relapse? Are there means (e.g., cognitive enhancers, tDCS) to improve the outcomes of treatments that build executive functions? As these questions are answered, they may be replaced by additional, practical questions. For example, how much training is needed to improve executive function? Is training one executive function more effective than training another? Are there ways to make these treatments more accessible and/or affordable? This progression, of course, is not unique to this approach, and can lead to improved outcomes only for the 50–80% of all addicted individuals suffering from this dysfunction (Aharonovich *et al.*, 2006; Bates, Pawlak, Tonigan, and Buckman, 2006). As such, we eagerly await additional information on these approaches, with the expectation that future developments will help better the human condition.

References

Aharonovich E, Hasin DS, Brooks AC, Liu X, Bisaga A, and Nunes EV (2006) Cognitive deficits predict low treatment retention in cocaine dependent patients. *Drug and Alcohol Dependence* 81: 313–322.

Aniskin DB, Fink E, Prosser J, Cohen LJ, Boda N, Steinfeld M, and Galynker, II (2011) The effect of pain on Stroop performance in patients with opiate dependence in sustained remission. *Journal of Addiction Medicine* 5: 50–56.

Appel PW (1982) Sustained attention in methadone patients. *International Journal of the Addictions* 17: 1313–1327.

Aron A, Robbins T, and Poldrack R (2004) Inhibition and the right inferior frontal cortex. *Trends in Cognitive Sciences* 8: 170–177.

Audrain-McGovern J, Rodriguez D, Epstein LH, Cuevas J, Rodgers K, and Wileyto EP (2009) Does delay discounting play an etiological role in smoking or is it a consequence of smoking? *Drug and Alcohol Dependence* 103: 99–106.

Baddeley A (2003) Working memory: Looking back and looking forward. *Nature Reviews Neuroscience* 4: 829–839.

Baddeley AD and Hitch GJ (1974) The psychology of learning and motivation. In GH Bower (ed.), *Psychology of Learning and Motivation* (pp. 47–89). New York: Academic Press.

Bahri T and Amir T (1994) Effect of hashish on vigilance performance. *Perceptual and Motor Skills* 78: 11–16.

Baker F, Johnson MW, and Bickel WK (2003) Delay discounting in current and never-before cigarette smokers: Similarities and differences across commodity, sign, and magnitude. *Journal of Abnormal Psychology* 112: 382–392.

Barkley RA (1997) Behavioral inhibition, sustained attention, and executive functions: Constructing a unifying theory of ADHD. *Psychological Bulletin* 121: 65–94.

Barkley RA (2004) Adolescents with attention-deficit/hyperactivity disorder: An overview of empirically based treatments. *Journal of Psychiatric Practice* 10: 39–56.

Bates ME, Pawlak AP, Tonigan JS, and Buckman JF (2006) Cognitive impairment influences drinking outcome by altering therapeutic mechanisms of change. *Psychology of Addictive Behaviors* 20: 241–253.

Battisti RA, Roodenrys S, Johnstone SJ, Pesa N, Hermens DF, and Solowij N (2010) Chronic cannabis users show altered neurophysiological functioning on Stroop task conflict resolution. *Psychopharmacology* (Berlin) 212: 613–624.

Beatty WW, Katzung VM, Moreland VJ and Nixon SJ (1995) Neuropsychological performance of recently abstinent alcoholics and cocaine abusers. *Drug and Alcohol Dependence* 37: 247–253.

Bechara A (2004) Disturbances of emotional regulation after focal brain lesions. *International Review of Neurobiology* 62: 159–193.

Bechara A (2005) Decision making, impulse control and loss of willpower to resist drugs: A neurocognitive perspective. *Nature Neuroscience* 8: 1458–1463.

Bechara A, Damasio H, and Damasio AR (2003) Role of the amygdala in decision-making. *Annals of The New York Academy of Sciences* 985: 356–369.

Bechara A, Damasio AR, Damasio H, and Anderson SW (1994) Insensitivity to future consequences following damage to human prefrontal cortex. *Cognition* 50: 7–15.

Bechara A, Damasio H, Tranel D, and Damasio AR (1997) Deciding advantageously before knowing the advantageous strategy. *Science* 275: 1293–1295.

Bechara A, Dolan S, Denburg N, Hindes A, Anderson SW, and Nathan PE (2001) Decision-making deficits, linked to a dysfunctional ventromedial prefrontal cortex, revealed in alcohol and stimulant abusers. *Neuropsychologia* 39: 376–389.

Bechara A, Tranel D, Damasio H, and Damasio AR (1996) Failure to respond autonomically to anticipated future outcomes following damage to prefrontal cortex. *Cerebral Cortex* 6: 215–225.

Berry J, van Gorp WG, Herzberg DS, Hinkin C, Boone K, Steinman L, and Wilkins JN (1993) Neuropsychological deficits in abstinent cocaine abusers: Preliminary findings after two weeks of abstinence. *Drug and Alcohol Dependence* 32: 231–237.

Bickel WK and Mueller ET (2009) Toward the study of trans-disease processes: A novel approach with special reference to the study of co-morbidity. *Journal of Dual Diagnosis* 5: 131–138.

Bickel WK, Jarmolowicz DP, Mueller ET, and Gatchalian KM (2011) The behavioral economics and neuroeconomics of reinforcer pathologies: Implications for etiology and treatment of addiction. *Current Psychiatry Report* 13: 406–415.

Bickel WK, Jarmolowicz DP, Mueller ET, Gatchalian KM, and McClure SM (2012) Are executive function and impulsivity antipodes? A conceptual reconstruction with special reference to addiction. *Psychopharmacology* 221(3): 361–387.

Bickel WK, Jarmolowicz DP, Mueller ET, Koffarnus MN, and Gatchalian KM (2012b) Excessive discounting of delayed reinforcers as a trans-disease process contributing to addiction and other disease-related vulnerabilities: Emerging evidence. *Pharmacology and Therapeutics* 134(3): 287–297

Bickel WK, Landes RD, Christensen DR, Jackson L, Jones BA, Kurth-Nelson Z, and Redish AD (2011a) Single- and cross-commodity discounting among cocaine addicts: The commodity and its temporal location determine discounting rate. *Psychopharmacology* (Berlin) 217: 177–187.

Bickel WK, Miller ML, Yi R, Kowal BP, Lindquist DM, and Pitcock JA (2007) Behavioral and neuroeconomics of drug addiction: Competing neural systems and temporal discounting processes. *Drug and Alcohol Dependence* 90S: S85–S91.

Bickel WK, Odum AL, and Madden GJ (1999) Impulsivity and cigarette smoking: Delay discounting in current, never, and ex-smokers. *Psychopharmacology* (Berlin) 146: 447–454.

Bickel WK, Pitcock JA, Yi R, and Angtuaco EJ (2009) Equivalent neural correlates across intertemporal choice conditions. *Neuroimage* 47: S39–S41.

Bickel WK, Yi R, Landes RD, Hill PF, and Baxter C (2011b) Remember the future: Working memory training decreases delay discounting among stimulant addicts. *Biological Psychiatry* 69: 260–265.

Bidwell LC, McClernon FJ, and Kollins SH (2011) Cognitive enhancers for the treatment of ADHD. *Pharmacology Biochemistry and Behavior* 99: 262–274.

Bledowski C, Kaiser J, and Rahm B (2010) Basic operations in working memory: Contributions from functional imaging studies. *Behavioural Brain Research* 214: 172–179.

Block RI and Ghoneim MM (1993) Effects of chronic marijuana use on human cognition. *Psychopharmacology* (Berlin) 110: 219–28.

Boggio PS, Campanha C, Valasek CA, Fecteau S, Pascual-Leone A, and Fregni F (2010) Modulation of decision-making in a gambling task in older adults with transcranial direct current stimulation. *European Journal of Neuroscience* 31: 593–597.

Bolla KI, Brown K, Eldreth D, Tate K, and Cadet JL (2002a) Dose-related neurocognitive effects of marijuana use. *Neurology* 59: 1337–1343.

Bolla KI, Brown K, Eldreth D, Tate K, and Cadet JL (2002b) Dose-related neurocognitive effects of marijuana use. *Neurology* 59: 1337–1343.

Bolla KI, Rothman R, and Cadet JL (1999) Dose-related neurobehavioral effects of chronic cocaine use. *The Journal of Neuropsychiatry and Clinical Neuroscience* 11: 361–369.

Bowie CR and Harvey PD (2006) Administration and interpretation of the Trail Making Test. *Nature Protocols* 1: 2277–2781.

Bradley B, Field M, Mogg K, and De Houwer J (2004) Attentional and evaluative biases for smoking cues in nicotine dependence: Component processes of biases in visual orienting. *Behavioural Pharmacology* 15: 29–36.

Brady KT, Gray KM, and Tolliver BK (2011) Cognitive enhancers in the treatment of substance use disorders: clinical evidence. *Pharmacology Biochemistry and Behavior* 99: 285–294.

Braet C and Crombez G (2003) Cognitive interference due to food cues in childhood obesity. *Journal of Clinical Child and Adolescent Psychology* 32: 32–39.

Brand M, Kalbe E, Labudda K, Fujiwara E, Kessler J, and Markowitsch HJ (2005) Decision-making impairments in patients with pathological gambling. *Psychiatry Research* 133: 91–99.

Butterfield EC and Wambold C (1973) On the theory and practice of improving short-term memory. *American Journal of Mental Deficiency* 77: 654–659.

Cai W and Leung HC (2011) Rule-guided executive control of response inhibition: Functional topography of the inferior frontal cortex. *PLoS One* 6: e20840.

Cane JE, Sharma D, and Albery IP (2009) The addiction Stroop task: Examining the fast and slow effects of smoking and marijuana-related cues. *Journal of Psychopharmacology* 23: 510–519.

Carter CS and van Veen V (2007) Anterior cingulate cortex and conflict detection: An update of theory and data. *Cognitive, Affective, and Behavioral Neuroscience* 7: 367–379.

Cartwright-Hatton S and Wells A (1997) Beliefs about worry and intrusions: The Meta-Cognitions Questionnaire and its correlates. *Journal of Anxiety Disorders* 11: 279–296.

Castellanos EH, Charboneau E, Dietrich MS, Park S, Bradley BP, Mogg K, and Cowan RL (2009) Obese adults have visual attention bias for food cue images: Evidence for altered reward system function. *International Journal of Obesity* 33: 1063–1073.

Chanon VW, Sours CR, and Boettiger CA (2010) Attentional bias toward cigarette cues in active smokers. *Psychopharmacology* (Berlin) 212: 309–320.

Cho SS, Ko JH, Pellecchia G, Van Eimeren T, Cilia R, and Strafella AP (2010) Continuous theta burst stimulation of right dorsolateral prefrontal cortex induces changes in impulsivity level. *Brain Stimulation* 3: 170–176.

Clark US, Oscar-Berman M, Shagrin B, and Pencina M (2007) Alcoholism and judgments of affective stimuli. *Neuropsychology* 21: 346–362.

Coffey SF, Gudleski GD, Saladin ME, and Brady KT (2003) Impulsivity and rapid discounting of delayed hypothetical rewards in cocaine-dependent individuals. *Experimental and Clinical Psychopharmacology* 11: 18–25.

Colder CR and O'Connor R (2002) Attention biases and disinhibited behavior as predictors of alcohol use and enhancement reasons for drinking. *Psychology of Addictive Behaviors* 16: 325–332.

Colzato LS, van den Wildenberg WP, and Hommel B (2007) Impaired inhibitory control in recreational cocaine users. *PLoS One* 2: e1143.

Conners C (2000) *Conners' Continuous Performance Test II: Computer Program for Windows Technical Guide and Software Manual.* North Tonawanda, NY: Multi-Health Systems.

Copersino ML, Serper MR, Vadhan N, Goldberg BR, Richarme D, Chou JC, Stitzer M, and Cancro R (2004) Cocaine craving and attentional bias in cocaine-dependent schizophrenic patients. *Psychiatry Research* 128: 209–218.

Cordovil De Sousa Uva M, Luminet O, Cortesi M, Constant E, Derely M, and De Timary P (2010) Distinct effects of protracted withdrawal on affect, craving, selective attention and executive functions among alcohol-dependent patients. *Alcohol and Alcoholism* 45: 241–246.

Cox WM, Blount JP, and Rozak AM (2000) Alcohol abusers' and nonabusers' distraction by alcohol and concern-related stimuli. *American Journal of Drug and Alcohol Abuse* 26: 489–495.

Craig AD (2009) How do you feel now? The anterior insula and human awareness. *Nature Reviews Neuroscience* 10: 59–70.

Croft RJ, Mackay AJ, Mills AT, and Gruzelier JG (2001) The relative contributions of ecstasy and cannabis to cognitive impairment. *Psychopharmacology* (Berlin) 153: 373–379.

Cserjesi R, Luminet O, Poncelet AS, and Lenard L (2009) Altered executive function in obesity: Exploration of the role of affective states on cognitive abilities. *Appetite* 52: 535–539.

Davis C, Patte K, Curtis C, and Reid C (2010) Immediate pleasures and future consequences: A neuropsychological study of binge eating and obesity. *Appetite* 54: 208–213.

Davydov DM and Polunina AG (2004) Heroin abusers' performance on the Tower of London Test relates to the baseline EEG alpha2 mean frequency shifts. *Progress in Neuropsychopharmacol and Biological Psychiatry* 28: 1143–1152.

de Fockert JW, Rees G, Frith CD, and Lavie N (2001) The role of working memory in visual selective attention. *Science* 291: 1803–1806.

de Ruiter MD, Veltman DJ, Goudriaan AE, Oosterlaan J, Sjoerds Z, and van den Brink W (2009) Response perseveration and ventral prefrontal sensitivity to reward and punishment in male problem gamblers and smokers. *Neuropsychopharmacology* 34: 1027–1038.

Di Sclafani V, Tolou-Shams M, Price LJ, and Fein G (2002) Neuropsychological performance of individuals dependent on crack-cocaine, or crack-cocaine and alcohol, at 6 weeks and 6 months of abstinence. *Drug and Alcohol Dependence* 66: 161–171.

Dinn WM, Aycicegi A, and Harris CL (2004) Cigarette smoking in a student sample: Neurocognitive and clinical correlates. *Addictive Behaviors* 29: 107–126.

Dixon MR, Marley J, and Jacobs EA (2003) Delay discounting by pathological gamblers. *Journal of Applied Behavior Analysis* 36: 449–458.

Dockery CA, Hueckel-Weng R, Birbaumer N, and Plewnia C (2009) Enhancement of planning ability by transcranial direct current stimulation. *Journal of Neuroscience* 29: 7271–7277.

Drobes DJ, Elibero A, and Evans DE (2006) Attentional bias for smoking and affective stimuli: A Stroop task study. *Psychology of Addictive Behaviors* 20: 490–495.

Ehrenreich H, Rinn T, Kunert HJ, Moeller MR, Poser W, Schilling L, Gigerenzer G, and Hoehe MR (1999) Specific attentional dysfunction in adults following early start of cannabis use. *Psychopharmacology* (Berlin) 142: 295–301.

Ehrman RN, Robbins SJ, Bromwell MA, Lankford ME, Monterosso JR, and O'Brien CP (2002) Comparing attentional bias to smoking cues in current smokers, former smokers, and non-smokers using a dot-probe task. *Drug and Alcohol Dependence* 67: 185–191.

Ernst M, Heishman SJ, Spurgeon L, and London ED (2001) Smoking history and nicotine effects on cognitive performance. *Neuropsychopharmacology* 25: 313–319.

Ersche KD, Clark L, London M, Robbins TW, and Sahakian BJ (2006) Profile of executive and memory function associated with amphetamine and opiate dependence. *Neuropsychopharmacology* 31: 1036.

Ersche KD, Roiser JP, Robbins TW, and Sahakian BJ (2008) Chronic cocaine but not chronic amphetamine use is associated with perseverative responding in humans. *Psychopharmacology* (Berlin) 197: 421–431.

Fein G, Klein L, and Finn P (2004) Impairment on a simulated gambling task in long-term abstinent alcoholics. *Alcoholism: Clinical and Experimental Research* 28: 1487–1491.

Fellows LK and Farah MJ (2005) Different underlying impairments in decision-making following ventromedial and dorsolateral frontal lobe damage in humans. *Cerebral Cortex* 15: 58–63.

Feredoes E, Heinen K, Weiskopf N, Ruff C, and Driver J (2011) Causal evidence for frontal involvement in memory target maintenance by posterior brain areas during distracter interference of visual working memory. *Proceedings of the National Academy of Sciences USA* 108: 17510–17515.

Fernandez-Serrano MJ, Perales JC, Moreno-Lopez L, Perez-Garcia M, and Verdejo-Garcia A (2011) Neuropsychological profiling of impulsivity and compulsivity in cocaine dependent individuals. *Psychopharmacology* (Berlin), in press. Epub ahead of print.

Field M, Eastwood B, Bradley BP, and Mogg K (2006) Selective processing of cannabis cues in regular cannabis users. *Drug and Alcohol Dependence* 85: 75–82.

Figner B, Knoch D, Johnson EJ, Krosch AR, Lisanby SH, Fehr E, and Weber EU (2010) Lateral prefrontal cortex and self-control in intertemporal choice. *Nature Neuroscience* 13: 538–539.

Fillmore MT and Rush CR (2002) Impaired inhibitory control of behavior in chronic cocaine users. *Drug and Alcohol Dependence* 66: 265–273.

Fillmore MT and Rush CR (2006) Polydrug abusers display impaired discrimination-reversal learning in a model of behavioural control. *Journal of Psychopharmacology* 20: 24–32.

Fishbein DH, Krupitsky E, Flannery BA, Langevin DJ, Bobashev G, Verbitskaya E, Augustine CB, Bolla KI, Zvartau E, Schech B, Egorova V, Bushara N, and Tsoy M (2007) Neurocognitive characterizations of Russian heroin addicts without a significant history of other drug use. *Drug and Alcohol Dependence* 90: 25–38.

Foisy ML, Kornreich C, Fobe A, D'Hondt L, Pelc I, Hanak C, Verbanck P, and Philippot P (2007) Impaired emotional facial expression recognition in alcohol dependence: Do these deficits persist with midterm abstinence? *Alcoholism: Clinical and Experimental Research* 31: 404–410.

Forbush KT, Shaw M, Graeber MA, Hovick L, Meyer VJ, Moser DJ, Bayless J, Watson D, and Black DW (2008) Neuropsychological characteristics and personality traits in pathological gambling. *CNS Spectrums* 13: 306–315.

Franken IH, Kroon LY, Wiers RW, and Jansen A (2000) Selective cognitive processing of drug cues in heroin dependence. *Journal of Psychopharmacology* 14: 395–400.

Fukui H, Murai T, Fukuyama H, Hayashi T, and Hanakawa T (2005) Functional activity related to risk anticipation during performance of the Iowa Gambling Task. *NeuroImage* 24: 253–259.

George O and Koob GF (2010) Individual differences in prefrontal cortex function and the transition from drug use to drug dependence. *Neuroscience and Biobehavioral Reviews* 35: 232–247.

Germine L, Garrido L, Bruce L, and Hooker C (in press) Social anhedonia is associated with neural abnormalities during face emotion processing. *NeuroImage*.

Glahn DC, Kim J, Cohen MS, Poutanen VP, Therman S, Bava S, Van Erp TG, Manninen M, Huttunen M, Lonnqvist J, Standertskjold-Nordenstam CG, and Cannon TD (2002) Maintenance and manipulation in spatial working memory: Dissociations in the prefrontal cortex. *NeuroImage* 17: 201–213.

Goldstein RZ, Alia-Klein N, Tomasi D, Zhang L, Cottone LA, Maloney T, Telang F, Caparelli EC, Chang L, Ernst T, Samaras D, Squires NK, and Volkow ND (2007) Is decreased prefrontal cortical sensitivity to monetary reward associated with impaired motivation and self-control in cocaine addiction? *American Journal of Psychiatry* 164: 43–51.

Goldstein RZ, Craig AD, Bechara A, Garavan H, Childress AR, Paulus MP, and Volkow ND (2009a) The neurocircuitry of impaired insight in drug addiction. *Trends in Cognitive Science* 13: 372–380.

Goldstein RZ, Craig AD, Bechara A, Garavan H, Childress AR, Paulus MP, and Volkow ND (2009b) The neurocircuitry of impaired insight in drug addiction. *Trends in Cognitive Science* 13: 372–380.

Gooding DC, Burroughs S, and Boutros NN (2008) Attentional deficits in cocaine-dependent patients: converging behavioral and electrophysiological evidence. *Psychiatry Research* 160: 145–154.

Goudriaan A, Oosterlaan J, de Beurs E, and van den Brink W (2005) Decision making in pathological gambling: A comparison between pathological gamblers, alcohol dependents, persons with Tourette syndrome, and normal controls. *Cognitive Brain Research* 23: 137–151.

Goudriaan AE, Oosterlaan J, de Beurs E, and van den Brink W (2006a) Neurocognitive functions in pathological gambling: A comparison with alcohol dependence, Tourette syndrome and normal controls. *Addiction* 101: 534–547.

Goudriaan AE, Oosterlaan J, de Beurs E, and van den Brink W (2006b) Psychophysiological determinants and concomitants of deficient decision making in pathological gamblers. *Drug and Alcohol Dependence* 84: 231–239.

Grant JE, Chamberlain SR, Schreiber L, and Odlaug BL (2011) Neuropsychological deficits associated with cannabis use in young adults. *Drug and Alcohol Dependence*, in press. Epub ahead of print.

Grant S, Contoreggi C, and London ED (2000) Drug abusers show impaired performance in a laboratory test of decision making. *Neuropsychologia* 38: 1180–1187.

Gunstad J, Paul RH, Cohen RA, Tate DF, Spitznagel MB, and Gordon E (2007) Elevated body mass index is associated with executive dysfunction in otherwise healthy adults. *Comprehensive Psychiatry* 48: 57–61.

Haller S, Birbaumer N, and Veit R (2010) Real-time fMRI feedback training may improve chronic tinnitus. *European Radiology* 20: 696–703.

Hanna-Pladdy B (2007) Dysexecutive syndromes in neurologic disease. *Journal of Neurologic Physical Therapy* 31: 119–127.

Hartstra E, Oldenburg JF, Van Leijenhorst L, Rombouts SA, and Crone EA (2010) Brain regions involved in the learning and application of reward rules in a two-deck gambling task. *Neuropsychologia* 48: 1438–4146.

Heil SH, Johnson MW, Higgins ST, and Bickel WK (2006) Delay discounting in currently using and currently abstinent cocaine-dependent outpatients and non-drug-using matched controls. *Addictive Behaviors* 31: 1290–1294.

Heinen K, Ruff CC, Bjoertomt O, Schenkluhn B, Bestmann S, Blankenburg F, Driver J, and Chambers CD (2011) Concurrent TMS-fMRI reveals dynamic interhemispheric influences of the right parietal cortex exogenously cued visuospacial attention. *European Journal of Neuroscience* 33: 991–1000.

Heishman SJ, Kleykamp BA, and Singleton EG (2010) Meta-analysis of the acute effects of nicotine and smoking on human performance. *Psychopharmacology* (Berlin) 210: 453–469.

Hendrick OM, Luo X, Zhang S, and Li CS (2011) Saliency processing and obesity: A preliminary imaging study of the Stop Signal Task. *Obesity* (Silver Spring), in press. Epub ahead of print.

Hester RK, Dixon V, and Garavan H (2006) A consistent attentional bias for drug-related material in active cocaine users across word and picture versions of the emotional Stroop task. *Drug and Alcohol Dependence* 81: 251–257.

Hester R, Lee N, Pennay A, Nielsen S, and Ferris J (2010) The effects of modafinil treatment on neuropsychological and attentional bias performance during 7-day inpatient withdrawal from methamphetamine dependence. *Experimental and Clinical Psychopharmacology* 18: 489–497.

Hester RK, Lubman DI, and Yucel M (2010) The role of executive control in human drug addiction. *Current Topics in Behavioral Neuroscience* 3: 301–318.

Hester R, Nestor L, and Garavan H (2009) Impaired error awareness and anterior cingulate cortex hypoactivity in chronic cannabis users. *Neuropsychopharmacology* 34: 2450–2458.

Hoff AL, Riordan H, Morris L, Cestaro V, Wieneke M, Alpert R, Wang GJ, and Volkow N (1996) Effects of crack cocaine on neurocognitive function. *Psychiatry Research* 60: 167–176.

Hoffman WF, Moore M, Templin R, McFarland B, Hitzemann RJ, and Mitchell SH (2006) Neuropsychological function and delay discounting in methamphetamine-dependent individuals. *Psychopharmacology* (Berlin) 188: 162–170.

Homer BD, Solomon TM, Moeller RW, Mascia A, DeRaleau L, and Halkitis PN (2008) Methamphetamine abuse and impairment of social functioning: A review of the underlying neurophysiological causes and behavioral implications. *Psychological Bulletin* 134: 301–310.

Horstmann A, Busse FP, Mathar D, Muller K, Lepsien J, Schlogl H, Kabisch S, Kratzsch J, Neumann J, Stumvoll M, Villringer A, and Pleger B (2011) Obesity-related differences between women and men in brain structure and goal-directed behavior. *Frontiers in Human Neuroscience* 5: 58.

Ilan AB, Smith ME, and Gevins A (2004) Effects of marijuana on neurophysiological signals of working and episodic memory. *Psychopharmacology* (Berlin) 176: 214–222.

Jacobsen LK, Krystal JH, Mencl WE, Westerveld M, Frost SJ, and Pugh KR (2005) Effects of smoking and smoking abstinence on cognition in adolescent tobacco smokers. *Biological Psychiatry* 57: 56–66.

Jang DP, Namkoong K, Kim JJ, Park S, Kim IY, Kim SI, Kim YB, Cho ZH, and Lee E (2007) The relationship between brain morphometry and neuropsychological performance in alcohol dependence. *Neuroscience Letters* 428: 21–26.

Jasinski DR, Faries DE, Moore RJ, Schuh LM, and Allen AJ (2008) Abuse liability assessment of atomoxetine in a drug-abusing population. *Drug and Alcohol Dependence* 95: 140–146.

Jentsch JD and Taylor JR (1999) Impulsivity resulting from frontostriatal dysfunction in drug abuse: Implications for the control of behavior by reward-related stimuli. *Psychopharmacology* (Berlin) 146: 373–390.

Johanson CE, Frey KA, Lundahl LH, Keenan P, Lockhart N, Roll J, Galloway GP, Koeppe RA, Kilbourn MR, Robbins T, and Schuster CR (2006) Cognitive function and nigrostriatal markers in abstinent methamphetamine abusers. *Psychopharmacology* (Berlin) 185: 327–338.

Johnsen BH, Laberg JC, Cox WM, Vaksdal A, and Hugdahl K (1994) Alcoholics' attentional bias in the processing of alcohol-related words. *Psychology of Addictive Behaviors* 8: 111–115.

Johnson MW, Bickel WK, and Baker F (2007) Moderate drug use and delay discounting: A comparison of heavy, light, and never smokers. *Experimental and Clinical Psychopharmacology* 15: 187–194.

Jones BT, Bruce G, Livingstone S, and Reed E (2006) Alcohol-related attentional bias in problem drinkers with the flicker change blindness paradigm. *Psychology of Addictive Behaviors* 20: 171–177.

Kable JW and Glimcher PW (2007) The neural correlates of subjective value during intertemporal choice. *Nature Neuroscience* 10: 1625–1633.

Kable JW and Glimcher PW (2010) An "as soon as possible" effect in human intertemporal decision making: Behavioral evidence and neural mechanisms. *Journal of Neurophysiology* 103: 2513–2531.

Kalapatapu RK, Vadhan NP, Rubin E, Bedi G, Cheng WY, Sullivan MA, and Foltin RW (2011) A pilot study of neurocognitive function in older and younger cocaine abusers and controls. *The American Journal on Addictions* 20: 228–239.

Kalechstein AD, De La Garza R, 2nd, and Newton TF (2010) Modafinil administration improves working memory in methamphetamine-dependent individuals who demonstrate baseline impairment. *American Journal on Addictions* 19: 340–344.

Kaller CP, Rahm B, Kostering L, and Unterrainer JM (2011) Reviewing the impact of problem structure on planning: A software tool for analyzing tower tasks. *Behavioural Brain Research* 216: 1–8.

Kalmijn S, van Boxtel MP, Verschuren MW, Jolles J, and Launer LJ (2002) Cigarette smoking and alcohol consumption in relation to cognitive performance in middle age. *American Journal of Epidemiology* 156: 936–944.

Kamarajan C, Porjesz B, Jones KA, Choi K, Chorlian DB, Padmanabhapillai A, Rangaswamy M, Stimus AT, and Begleiter H (2005) Alcoholism is a disinhibitory disorder: Neurophysiological evidence from a Go/No-Go task. *Biological Psychology* 69: 353–373.

Kaminski JA, Korb FM, Villringer A, and Ott DV (2011) Transcranial magnetic stimulation intensities in cognitive paradigms. *PLoS One* 6: e24836, in press. Epub ahead of print.

Kaufman JN, Ross TJ, Stein EA, and Garavan H (2003) Cingulate hypoactivity in cocaine users during a GO–NOGO task as revealed by event-related functional magnetic resonance imaging. *Journal of Neuroscience* 23: 7839–7843.

Kertzman S, Lidogoster H, Aizer A, Kotler M, and Dannon PN (2011) Risk-taking decisions in pathological gamblers is not a result of their impaired inhibition ability. *Psychiatry Research* 188: 71–77.

Kertzman S, Lowengrub K, Aizer A, Vainder M, Kotler M, and Dannon PN (2008) Go–no-go performance in pathological gamblers. *Psychiatry Research* 161: 1–10.

King G, Alicata D, Cloak C, and Chang L (2010) Neuropsychological deficits in adolescent methamphetamine abusers. *Psychopharmacology* (Berlin) 212: 243–249.

Kirby KN, Petry NM, and Bickel WK (1999) Heroin addicts have higher discount rates for delayed rewards than non-drug using controls. *Journal of Experimental Psychology: General* 128: 78–87.

Kirchner WK (1958) Age differences in short-term retention of rapidly changing information. *Journal of Experimental Psychology* 55: 352–358.

Klingberg T, Forssberg H, and Westerberg H (2002) Training of working memory in children with ADHD. *Journal of Clinical and Experimental Neuropsychology* 24: 781–791.

Kubler A, Murphy K, and Garavan H (2005) Cocaine dependence and attention switching within and between verbal and visuospatial working memory. *European Journal of Neuroscience* 21: 1984–1992.

LaConte SM, Peltier SJ, and Hu XP (2007) Real-time fMRI using brain-state classification. *Human Brain Mapping* 28: 1033–1044.

Lakey CE, Goodie AS, Lance CE, Stinchfield R, and Winters KC (2007) Examining DSM-IV criteria for pathological gambling: Psychometric properties and evidence from cognitive biases. *Journal of Gambling Studies* 23: 479–498.

Lane SD, Cherek DR, Tcheremissine OV, Steinberg JL, and Sharon JL (2007a) Response perseveration and adaptation in heavy marijuana-smoking adolescents. *Addictive Behaviors* 32: 977–990.

Lane SD, Moeller FG, Steinberg JL, Buzby M, and Kosten TR (2007b) Performance of cocaine dependent individuals and controls on a response inhibition task with varying levels of difficulty. *American Journal of Drug and Alcohol Abuse* 33: 717–726.

Leiserson V and Pihl R (2007) Reward-sensitivity, inhibition of reward-seeking, and dorsolateral prefrontal working memory function in problem gamblers not in treatment. *Journal of Gambling Studies* 23: 435–455.

Levine AJ, Hardy DJ, Miller E, Castellon SA, Longshore D, and Hinkin CH (2006) The effect of recent stimulant use on sustained attention in HIV-infected adults. *Journal of Clinical and Experimental Neuropsychology* 28: 29–42.

Lokken KL, Boeka AG, Yellumahanthi K, Wesley M, and Clements RH (2010) Cognitive performance of morbidly obese patients seeking bariatric surgery. *American Journal of Surgery* 76: 55–59.

London ED, Berman SM, Voytek B, Simon SL, Mandelkern MA, Monterosso J, Thompson PM, Brody AL, Geaga JA, Hong MS, Hayashi KM, Rawson RA, and Ling W (2005) Cerebral metabolic dysfunction and impaired vigilance in recently abstinent methamphetamine abusers. *Biological Psychiatry* 58: 770–778.

Loughead J, Wileyto EP, Valdez JN, Sanborn P, Tang K, Strasser AA, Ruparel K, Ray R, Gur RC, and Lerman C (2009) Effect of abstinence challenge on brain function and cognition in smokers differs by COMT genotype. *Molecular Psychiatry* 14: 820–826.

Lubman DI, Peters LA, Mogg K, Bradley BP, and Deakin JF (2000) Attentional bias for drug cues in opiate dependence. *Psychological Medicine* 30: 169–175.

Lusher J, Chandler C, and Ball D (2004) Alcohol dependence and the alcohol Stroop paradigm: Evidence and issues. *Drug and Alcohol Dependence* 75: 225–231.

Maayan L, Hoogendoorn C, Sweat V, and Convit A (2011) Disinhibited eating in obese adolescents is associated with orbitofrontal volume reductions and executive dysfunction. *Obesity*, July: 1382–1387.

MacKillop J, Anderson EJ, Castelda BA, Mattson RE, and Donovick PJ (2006) Divergent validity of measures of cognitive distortions, impulsivity, and time perspective in pathological gambling. *Journal of Gambling Studies* 22: 339–354.

Madden GJ and Bickel WK (2009) *Impulsivity: The Behavioral and Neurological Science of Discounting.* Washington, DC: American Psychological Association.

Madden GJ, Petry NM, Badger GJ, and Bickel WK (1997) Impulsive and self-control choices in opioid-dependent patients and non-drug-using control participants: Drug and monetary rewards. *Experimental and Clinical Psychopharmacology* 5: 256–262.

Magland JF, Tjoa CW, and Childress AR (2011) Spatio-temporal activity in real time (STAR): Optimization of regional fMRI feedback. *NeuroImage* 55: 1044–1053.

Marazziti D, Catena Dell'osso M, Conversano C, Consoli G, Vivarelli L, Mungai F, Di Nasso E, and Golia F (2008) Executive function abnormalities in pathological gamblers. *Clinical Practice and Epidemiology in Mental Health* 4: 7.

Martis B, Alam D, Dowd SM, Hill SK, Sharma RP, Rosen C, Pliskin N, Martin E, Carson V, and Janicak PG (2003) Neurocognitive effects of repetitive transcranial magnetic stimulation in severe major depression. *Clinical Neurophysiology* 114: 1125–1132.

McClure MM, Romero MJ, Bowie CR, Reichenberg A, Harvey PD, and Siever LJ (2007a) Visual-spatial learning and memory in schizotypal personality disorder: Continued evidence for the importance of working memory in the schizophrenia spectrum. *Archives of Clinical Neuropsychology* 22: 109–116.

McClure SM, Ericson KM, Laibson DI, Loewenstein G, and Cohen JD (2007b) Time discounting for primary rewards. *Journal of Neuroscience* 27: 5796–5804.

McClure SM, Laibson DI, Loewenstein G, and Cohen JD (2004) Separate neural systems value immediate and delayed monetary rewards. *Science* 306: 503–507.

McKetin R and Mattick RP (1997) Attention and memory in illicit amphetamine users. *Drug and Alcohol Dependence* 48: 235–242.

Metcalfe J and Mischel W (1999) A hot/cold-system analysis of delay of gratification: Dynamics of willpower. *Psychological Review* 106: 3–19.

Mezzacappa E and Buckner B (2010) Working memory training for children with attention problems or hyperactivity: A school-based pilot study. *School Mental Health*, in press. Epub ahead of print.

Miller EK and Cohen JD (2001) An integrative theory of prefrontal cortex function. *Annual Review of Neuroscience* 24: 167–202.

Miller GA (1956) The magical number seven plus or minus two: Some limits on our capacity for processing information. *Psychological Review* 63: 81–97.

Miniussi C, Cappa SF, Cohen LG, Floel A, Fregni F, Nitsche MA, Oliveri M, Pascual-Leone A, Paulus W, Priori A, and Walsh V (2008) Efficacy of repetitive transcranial magnetic stimulation/transcranial direct current stimulation in cognitive neurorehabilitation. *Brain Stimulation* 1: 326–336.

Mintzer MZ and Stitzer ML (2002) Cognitive impairment in methadone maintenance patients. *Drug and Alcohol Dependence* 67: 41–51.

Mitchell SH (1999) Measures of impulsivity in cigarette smokers and nonsmokers. *Psychopharmacology* (Berlin) 146: 455–464.

Mittenberg W and Motta S (1993) Effects of chronic cocaine abuse on memory and learning. *Archives of Clinical Neuropsychology* 8: 477–483.

Moeller FG, Hasan KM, Steinberg JL, Kramer LA, Dougherty DM, Santos RM, Valdes I, Swann AC, Barratt ES, and Narayana PA (2005) Reduced anterior corpus callosum white matter integrity is related to increased impulsivity and reduced discriminability in cocaine-dependent subjects: Diffusion tensor imaging. *Neuropsychopharmacology* 30: 610–617.

Moeller FG, Steinberg JL, Schmitz JM, Ma L, Liu S, Kjome KL, Rathnayaka N, Kramer LA, and Narayana PA (2010) Working memory fMRI activation in cocaine-dependent subjects: Association with treatment response. *Psychiatry Research* 181: 174–182.

Mogg K, Bradley BP, Field M, and De Houwer J (2003) Eye movements to smoking-related pictures in smokers: Relationship between attentional biases and implicit and explicit measures of stimulus valence. *Addiction* 98: 825–836.

Moneta GB (2011) Metacognition, emotion, and alcohol dependence in college students: A moderated mediation model. *Addictive Behaviors* 36: 781–784.

Monterosso J and Ainslie G (2007) The behavioral economics of will in recovery from addiction. *Drug and Alcohol Dependence* 90(Suppl. 1): S100–111.

Monterosso JR, Ainslie G, Xu J, Cordova X, Domier CP, and London ED (2007) Frontoparietal cortical activity of methamphetamine-dependent and comparison subjects performing a delay discounting task. *Human Brain Mapping* 28: 383–393.

Monterosso JR, Aron AR, Cordova X, Xu J, and London ED (2005) Deficits in response inhibition associated with chronic methamphetamine abuse. *Drug and Alcohol Dependence* 79: 273–277.

Monterosso J, Ehrman R, Napier KL, O'Brien CP, and Childress AR (2001) Three decision-making tasks in cocaine-dependent patients: Do they measure the same construct? *Addiction* 96: 1825.

Montgomery C, Field M, Atkinson AM, Cole JC, Goudie AJ, and Sumnall HR (2010) Effects of alcohol preload on attentional bias towards cocaine-related cues. *Psychopharmacology* (Berlin) 210: 365–375.

Morrison AB and Chein JM (2011) Does working memory training work? The promise and challenges of enhancing cognition by training working memory. *Psychonomic Bulletin and Review* 18: 46–60.

Moser DJ, Jorge RE, Manes F, Paradiso S, Benjamin ML, and Robinson RG (2002) Improved executive functioning following repetitive transcranial magnetic stimulation. *Neurology* 58: 1288–1290.

Moskowitz H and McGlothlin W (1974) Effects of marihuana on auditory signal detection. *Psychopharmacology* (Berlin) 40: 137–145.

Mottaghy FM, Krause BJ, Kemna LJ, Topper R, Tellmann L, Beu M, Pascual-Leone A, and Muller-Gartner HW (2000) Modulation of the neuronal circuitry subserving working memory in healthy human subjects by repetitive transcranial magnetic stimulation. *Neuroscience Letters* 280: 167–170.

Mulquiney PG, Hoy KE, Daskalakis ZJ, and Fitzgerald PB (2011) Improving working memory: Exploring the effect of transcranial random noise stimulation and transcranial direct current stimulation on the dorsolateral prefrontal cortex. *Clinical Neurophysiology* 122: 2384–2389.

Munafo M, Mogg K, Roberts S, Bradley BP, and Murphy M (2003) Selective processing of smoking-related cues in current smokers, ex-smokers and never-smokers on the modified Stroop task. *Journal of Psychopharmacology* 17: 310–316.

Nederkoorn C, Braet C, Van Eijs Y, Tanghe A, and Jansen A (2006a) Why obese children cannot resist food: The role of impulsivity. *Eating Behaviors* 7: 315–322.

Nederkoorn C, Smulders FTY, Havermans RC, Roefs A, and Jansen A (2006b) Impulsivity in obese women. *Appetite* 47: 253–256.

Nestor LJ, Ghahremani DG, Monterosso J, and London ED (2011) Prefrontal hypoactivation during cognitive control in early abstinent methamphetamine-dependent subjects. *Psychiatry Research* 194: 287–295.

Nijs IM, Muris P, Euser AS, and Franken IH (2010) Differences in attention to food and food intake between overweight/obese and normal-weight females under conditions of hunger and satiety. *Appetite* 54: 243–254.

Norberg MM, Krystal JH, and Tolin DF (2008) A meta-analysis of D-cycloserine and the facilitation of fear extinction and exposure therapy. *Biological Psychiatry* 63: 1118–1126.

Norman AL, Pulido C, Squeglia LM, Spadoni AD, Paulus MP, and Tapert SF (2011) Neural activation during inhibition predicts initiation of substance use in adolescence. *Drug and Alcohol Dependence*, in press. Epub ahead of print.

Norman W and Shallice T (1986) Attention to action. In: RJ Davidson, GE Schwartz, D Shapiro (eds), *Consciousness and Self Regulation: Advances in Research and Theory* (pp. 1–18). New York: Plenum.

Odum AL, Madden GJ, Badger GJ, and Bickel WK (2000) Needle sharing in opioid-dependent outpatients: Psychological processes underlying risk. *Drug and Alcohol Dependence* 60: 259–266.

Ornstein TJ, Iddon JL, Baldacchino AM, Sahakian BJ, London M, Everitt BJ, and Robbins TW (2000) Profiles of cognitive dysfunction in chronic amphetamine and heroin abusers. *Neuropsychopharmacology* 23: 113–126.

Oscar-Berman M, Hancock M, Mildworf B, Hutner N, and Weber DA (1990) Emotional perception and memory in alcoholism and aging. *Alcoholism: Clinical and Experimental Research* 14: 383–393.

Owen AM, Downes JJ, Sahakian BJ, Polkey CE, and Robbins TW (1990) Planning and spatial working memory following frontal lobe lesions in man. *Neuropsychologia* 28: 1021–1034.

Owen AM, Roberts AC, Polkey CE, Sahakian BJ, and Robbins TW (1991) Extra-dimensional versus intra-dimensional set shifting performance following frontal lobe excisions, temporal lobe excisions or amygdalo-hippocampectomy in man. *Neuropsychologia* 29: 993–1006.

Owen AM, Sahakian BJ, Semple J, Polkey CE, and Robbins TW (1995) Visuo-spatial short-term recognition memory and learning after temporal lobe excisions, frontal lobe excisions or amygdalo-hippocampectomy in man. *Neuropsychologia* 33: 1–24.

Passetti F, Clark L, Mehta MA, Joyce E, and King M (2008) Neuropsychological predictors of clinical outcome in opiate addiction. *Drug and Alcohol Dependence* 94: 82–91.

Patterson F, Jepson C, Loughead J, Perkins K, Strasser AA, Siegel S, Frey J, Gur R, and Lerman C (2010) Working memory deficits predict short-term smoking resumption following brief abstinence. *Drug and Alcohol Dependence* 106: 61–64.

Pau CW, Lee TM, and Chan SF (2002) The impact of heroin on frontal executive functions. *Archives of Clinical Neuropsychology* 17: 663–670.

Petry NM (2001a) Delay discounting of money and alcohol in actively using alcoholics, currently abstinent alcoholics, and controls. *Psychopharmacology* (Berlin) 154: 243–250.

Petry NM (2001b) Pathological gamblers, with and without substance use disorders, discount delayed rewards at high rates. *Journal of Abnormal Psychology* 110: 482–487.

Petry NM (2002) Discounting of delayed rewards in substance abusers: Relationship to antisocial personality disorder. *Psychopharmacology (Berlin)* 162: 425–432.

Phelan S, Hassenstab J, McCaffery JM, Sweet L, Raynor HA, Cohen RA, and Wing RR (2011) Cognitive interference from food cues in weight loss maintainers, normal weight, and obese individuals. *Obesity* 19: 69–73.

Philippot P, Kornreich C, Blairy S, Baert I, Den Dulk A, Le Bon O, Streel E, Hess U, Pelc I, and Verbanck P (1999) Alcoholics' deficits in the decoding of emotional facial expression. *Alcoholism: Clinical and Experimental Research* 23: 1031–1038.

Pickup GJ (2008) Relationship between Theory of Mind and executive function in schizophrenia: A systematic review. *Psychopathology* 41: 206–213.

Pope HG, Jr, and Yurgelun-Todd D (1996) The residual cognitive effects of heavy marijuana use in college students. *Journal of the American Medical Association* 275: 521–527.

Posner MI and Petersen SE (1990) The attention system of the human brain. *Annual Review of Neuroscience* 13: 25–42.

Potenza MN, Leung HC, Blumberg HP, Peterson Bs, Fulbright RK, Lacadie CM, Skudlarski P, and Gore JC (2003) An fMRI Stroop task study of ventromedial prefrontal cortical function in pathological gamblers. *American Journal of Psychiatry* 160: 1990–1994.

Prosser J, Eisenberg D, Davey E, Steinfeld M, Cohen L, London E, and Galynker I (2008) Character pathology and neuropsychological test performance in remitted opiate dependence. *Substance Abuse Treatment, Prevention, and Policy* 3: 23.

Prosser J, London ED, and Galynker, II (2009) Sustained attention in patients receiving and abstinent following methadone maintenance treatment for opiate dependence: Performance and neuroimaging results. *Drug and Alcohol Dependence* 104: 228–240.

Quednow BB, Kuhn KU, Hoppe C, Westheide J, Maier W, Daum I, and Wagner M (2007) Elevated impulsivity and impaired decision-making cognition in heavy users of MDMA ("Ecstasy"). *Psychopharmacology* (Berlin) 189: 517–530.

Razani J, Boone K, Lesser I, and Weiss D (2004) Effects of cigarette smoking history on cognitive functioning in healthy older adults. *American Journal of Geriatric Psychiatry* 12: 404–411.

Redish AD, Jensen S, and Johnson A (2008) Addiction as vulnerabilities in a decision process. *Behavioral and Brain Science* 31: 461–487.

Regard M, Knoch D, Gutling E, and Landis T (2003) Brain damage and addictive behavior: A neuropsychological and electroencephalogram investigation with pathologic gamblers. *Cognitive and Behavioral Neurology* 16: 47–53.

Rippeth JD, Heaton RK, Carey CL, Marcotte TD, Moore DJ, Gonzalez R, Wolfson T, and Grant I (2004) Methamphetamine dependence increases risk of neuropsychological impairment in HIV infected persons. *Journal of the International Neuropsychology Society* 10: 1–14.

Robbins TW (1996) Dissociating executive functions of the prefrontal cortex. *Philosophical Transactions of the Royal Society B: Biological Sciences* 351: 1463–1471.

Roca M, Torralva T, Lopez P, Cetkovich M, Clark L, and Manes F (2008) Executive functions in pathologic gamblers selected in an ecologic setting. *Cognitive and Behavioral Neurology* 21: 1–4.

Rodriguez-Jimenez R, Avila C, Jimenez-Arriero MA, Ponce G, Monasor R, Jimenez M, Aragues M, Hoenicka J, Rubio G, and Palomo T (2006) Impulsivity and sustained attention in pathological gamblers: Influence of childhood ADHD history. *Journal of Gambling Studies* 22: 451–461.

Rogers RD, Everitt BJ, Baldacchino A, Blackshaw AJ, Swainson R, Wynne K, Baker NB, Hunter J, Carthy T, Booker E, London M, Deakin JF, Sahakian BJ, and Robbins TW (1999) Dissociable deficits in the decision-making cognition of chronic amphetamine abusers, opiate abusers, patients with focal damage to prefrontal cortex, and tryptophan-depleted normal volunteers: evidence for monoaminergic mechanisms. *Neuropsychopharmacology* 20: 322–339.

Rothernberg S, Schottenfeld S, Meyer RE, Krauss B, and Gross K (1977) Performance differences between addicts and non-addicts. *Psychopharmacology* (Berlin) 52: 299–306.

Rugle L and Melamed L (1993) Neuropsychological assessment of attention problems in pathological gamblers. *Journal of Nervous and Mental Disease* 181: 107–112.

Salloum JB, Ramchandani VA, Bodurka J, Rawlings R, Momenan R, George D, and Hommer DW (2007) Blunted rostral anterior cingulate response during a simplified decoding task of negative emotional facial expressions in alcoholic patients. *Alcoholism: Clinical and Experimental Research* 31: 1490–1504.

Salo R, Nordahl TE, Galloway GP, Moore CD, Waters C, and Leamon MH (2009) Drug abstinence and cognitive control in methamphetamine-dependent individuals. *Journal of Substance Abuse Treatment* 37: 292–297.

Salo R, Nordahl TE, Moore C, Waters C, Natsuaki Y, Galloway GP, Kile S, and Sullivan EV (2005) A dissociation in attentional control: Evidence from methamphetamine dependence. *Biological Psychiatry* 57: 310–313.

Salo R, Nordahl TE, Natsuaki Y, Leamon MH, Galloway GP, Waters C, Moore CD, and Buonocore MH (2007) Attentional control and brain metabolite levels in methamphetamine abusers. *Biological Psychiatry* 61: 1272–1280.

Schellekens AF, van Oosterwijck AW, Ellenbroek B, de Jong CA, Buitelaar JK, Cools L, and Verkes RJ (2009) The dopamine agonist apomorphine differentially affects cognitive performance in alcohol dependent patients and healthy controls. *European Neuropsychopharmacology* 19: 68–73.

Scholes KE and Martin-Iverson MT (2009) Alterations to pre-pulse inhibition (PPI) in chronic cannabis users are secondary to sustained attention deficits. *Psychopharmacology* (Berlin) 207: 469–484.

Shallice T and Burgess PW (1991) Deficits in strategy application following frontal lobe damage in man. *Brain* 114(Pt 2): 727–741.

Sharma D, Albery IP, and Cook C (2001) Selective attentional bias to alcohol related stimuli in problem drinkers and non-problem drinkers. *Addiction* 96: 285–295.

Simon SL, Domier C, Carnell J, Brethen P, Rawson R, and Ling W (2000) Cognitive impairment in individuals currently using methamphetamine. *American Journal of Addictions* 9: 222–231.

Sinclair JM, Nausheen B, Garner MJ, and Baldwin DS (2010) Attentional biases in clinical populations with alcohol use disorders: Is co-morbidity ignored? *Human Psychopharmacology* 25: 515–524.

Soetens B and Braet C (2007) Information processing of food cues in overweight and normal weight adolescents. *Brittish Journal of Health Psychology* 12: 285–304.

Sofuoglu M, Mouratidis M, Yoo S, Culligan K, and Kosten T (2005) Effects of tiagabine in combination with intravenous nicotine in overnight abstinent smokers. *Psychopharmacology* (Berlin) 181: 504–510.

Soto D, Rotshtein P, Hodsoll J, Mevorach C, and Humphreys GW (2011) Common and distinct neural regions for the guidance of selection by visuoverbal information held in memory: Converging evidence from fMRI and rTMS. *Human Brain Mapping*, in press. Epub ahead of print.

Spada MM and Wells A (2005) Metacognitions, emotion and alcohol use. *Clinical Psychology and Psychotherapy* 12: 150–155.

Spada MM, Moneta GB, and Wells A (2007) The relative contribution of metacognitive beliefs and expectancies to drinking behaviour. *Alcohol and Alcoholism* 42: 567–574.

Spilich GJ, June L, and Renner J (1992) Cigarette smoking and cognitive performance. *British Journal of Addiction* 87: 1313–1326.

Spinella M (2002) Correlations between orbitofrontal dysfunction and tobacco smoking. *Addiction Biology* 7: 381–384.

Steinberg L (2010) A dual systems model of adolescent risk-taking. *Developmental Psychobiology* 52: 216–224.

Sternberg S (1966) High-speed scanning in human memory. *Science* 153: 652–654.

Stetter F, Ackermann K, Bizer A, Straube ER, and Mann K (1995) Effects of disease-related cues in alcoholic inpatients: Results of a controlled "Alcohol Stroop" study. *Alcoholism: Clinical and Experimental Research* 19: 593–599.

Stormark KM, Field NP, Hugdahl K, and Horowitz M (1997) Selective processing of visual alcohol cues in abstinent alcoholics: An approach-avoidance conflict? *Addictive Behaviors* 22: 509–519.

Stroop JR (1935) Studies of interference in serial verbal reactions. *Journal of Experimental Psychology* 18: 643–662.

Stuss DT and Alexander MP (2007) Is there a dysexecutive syndrome? *Philosophical Translations of the Royal Society B: Biological Sciences* 1481: 901–915.

Sullivan JR, Riccio CA, and Castillo CL (2009) Concurrent validity of the tower tasks as measures of executive function in adults: A meta-analysis. *Applied Neuropsychology* 16: 62–75.

Tedstone D and Coyle K (2004) Cognitive impairments in sober alcoholics: Performance on selective and divided attention tasks. *Drug and Alcohol Dependence* 75: 277–286.

Thoma RJ, Monnig MA, Lysne PA, Ruhl DA, Pommy JA, Bogenschutz M, Tonigan JS, and Yeo RA (2011) Adolescent substance abuse: The effects of alcohol and marijuana on neuropsychological performance. *Alcoholism: Clinical and Experimental Research* 35: 39–46.

Tomasi D, Goldstein RZ, Telang F, Maloney T, Alia-Klein N, Caparelli EC, and Volkow ND (2007) Thalamo-cortical dysfunction in cocaine abusers: implications in attention and perception. *Psychiatry Research* 155: 189–201.

Tong JE, Leigh G, Campbell J, and Smith D (1977) Tobacco smoking, personality and sex factors in auditory vigilance performance. *British Journal of Psychology* 68: 365–370.

Uekermann J, Channon S, Winkel K, Schlebusch P, and Daum I (2007) Theory of mind, humour processing and executive functioning in alcoholism. *Addiction* 102: 232–240.

Uekermann J and Daum I (2008) Social cognition in alcoholism: A link to prefrontal cortex dysfunction? *Addiction* 103: 726–735.

Urcelay GP and Dalley JW (2011) Linking ADHD, impulsivity, and drug abuse: A neuropsychological perspective. *Current Topics in Behavioral Neurosciences*, in press. Epub ahead of print.

van den Bos W, van Dijk E, Westenberg M, Rombouts SA, and Crone EA (2011) Changing brains, changing perspectives: The neurocognitive development of reciprocity. *Psycholgical Science* 22: 60–70.

Verdejo-Garcia A and Perez-Garcia M (2007) Profile of executive deficits in cocaine and heroin polysubstance users: Common and differential effects on separate executive components. *Psychopharmacology* (Berlin) 190: 517–530.

Verdejo-Garcia AJ, Bechara A, Recknor EC, and Perez-Garcia M (2006) Executive dysfunction in substance abuse dependent individuals during drug use and abstinence: An examination of the behavioral, cognitive and emotional correlates of addiction. *Journal of the International Neuropsychological Society* 12: 405–415.

Verdejo-Garcia A, Benbrook A, Funderburk F, David P, Cadet JL, and Bolla KI (2007) The differential relationship between cocaine use and marijuana use on decision-making performance over repeat testing with the Iowa Gambling Task. *Drug and Alcohol Dependence* 90: 2–11.

Verdejo-Garcia AJ, Lopez-Torrecillas F, Gimenez CO, and Perez-Garcia M (2004) Clinical implications and methodological challenges in the study of the neuropsychological correlates of cannabis, stimulant, and opioid abuse. *Neuropsychology Review* 14: 1–41.

Verdejo-Garcia AJ, Perales JC, and Perez-Garcia M (2007) Cognitive impulsivity in cocaine and heroin polysubstance abusers. *Addictive Behaviors* 32: 950–966.

Verdejo-Garcia A, Perez-Exposito M, Schmidt-Rio-Valle J, Fernandez-Serrano MJ, Cruz F, Perez-Garcia M, Lopez-Belmonte G, Martin-Matillas M, Martin-Lagos JA, Marcos A, and Campoy C (2010) Selective alterations within executive functions in adolescents with excess weight. *Obesity* 18: 1572–1578.

Vocci FJ (2008) Cognitive remediation in the treatment of stimulant abuse disorders: A research agenda. *Experimental and Clinical Psychopharmacology* 16: 484–497.

Vollstadt-Klein S, Loeber S, Richter A, Kirsch M, Bach P, von der Goltz C, Hermann D, Mann K, and Kiefer F (2011) Validating incentive salience with functional magnetic resonance imaging: Association between mesolimbic cue reactivity and attentional bias in alcohol-dependent patients. *Addiction Biology*, in press. Epub ahead of print.

Vuchinich RE and Simpson CA (1998) Hyperbolic temporal discounting in social drinkers and problem drinkers. *Experimental and Clinical Psychopharmacology* 6: 292–305.

Wagner T, Valero-Cabre A, and Pascual-Leone A (2007) Noninvasive human brain stimulation. *Annual Review of Biomedical Engineering* 9: 527–565.

Waldstein SR and Katzel LI (2006) Interactive relations of central versus total obesity and blood pressure to cognitive function. *International Journal of Obesity* 30: 201–207.

Wasserstein J and Lynn A (2001) Metacognitive remediation in adult ADHD: Treating executive function deficits via executive functions. *Annals of the New York Academy of Sciences* 931: 376–384.

Waters AJ, Shiffman S, Sayette MA, Paty JA, Gwaltney CJ, and Balabanis MH (2003) Attentional bias predicts outcome in smoking cessation. *Health Psychology* 22: 378–387.

Weller RE, Cook III EW, Avsar KB, and Cox JE (2008) Obese women show greater delay discounting than healthy-weight women. *Appetite* 51: 563–569.

Werthmann J, Roefs A, Nederkoorn C, Mogg K, Bradley BP, and Jansen A (2011) Can (not) take my eyes off it: Attention bias for food in overweight participants. *Health Psychology*: 561–569.

Westerberg H, Jacobaeus H, Hirvikoski T, Clevberger P, Osternsson M, Bartfai A, and Klingberg T (2007) Computerized working memory training after stroke – a pilot study. *Brain Injury* 21: 21–29.

Whitlow CT, Liguori A, Livengood LB, Hart SL, Mussat-Whitlow BJ, Lamborn CM, Laurienti PJ, and Porrino LJ (2004) Long-term heavy marijuana users make costly decisions on a gambling task. *Drug and Alcohol Dependence* 76: 107–111.

Wimmer H and Perner J (1983) Beliefs about beliefs: Represntation and constraining function of wrong beliefs in young children's understanding of deception. *Cognition* 13: 103–128.

Yakir A, Rigbi A, Kanyas K, Pollak Y, Kahana G, Karni O, Eitan R, Kertzman S, and Lerer B (2007) Why do young women smoke? III. Attention and impulsivity as neurocognitive predisposing factors. *European Neuropsychopharmacology* 17: 339–351.

Zanto T, Rubens M, Thangavel A, and Gazzaley A (2011) Casual role of the prefrontal cortex in top-down modulation of visual processing and working memory. *Nature Neuroscience* 14: 656–661.

Zhang L and Rashad I (2008) Obesity and time preference: The health consequences of discounting the future. *Journal of Biosocial Science* 40: 97–113.

3

The Roles of Race and Sex in Addiction Research[1]

Ezemenari M. Obasi, Jaime L. Richards,
Delishia M. Pittman, Jokae Ingram,
Marian R. Beasley, and Kristen L. Ratliff

1 Introduction

Scientific research in the United States has been plagued with a turbulent history when it comes to the inclusion of non-White participants and women (Guthrie, 1976). Whether it is the use of unsophisticated research methods to pursue an ideology of racial superiority, the use of deception to further science at the cost of human life (Belmont Report, 1978), or the blatant exclusion of marginalized racial groups (i.e., Blacks, Latinos/as, and Native Americans) and women in scientific studies, there continues to be a need to think through culturally competent best practices regarding the inclusion, reporting, and translation of scientific research into prevention and intervention efforts. The inclusion of all segments of society in the pursuit of knowledge is not only the ethical thing to do, such findings could also be used as a tool for social change. Despite efforts to address health disparities via national reports (Institute of Medicine, 2003; US Department of Health and Human Services, 2001) and large endowments of private and federal funding, there remains a dearth in the amount of experimental literature examining the etiology of known disparities that disproportionately affect marginalized racial groups and women.

The purpose of this chapter is to provide some best practices regarding how race and sex might be included and acknowledged in addictions research. More specifically, this chapter will provide definitions of key constructs (i.e., race, ethnicity, sex, and gender), investigate group-specific prevalence rates, known risk factors, and measurement issues, and provide best practices for including race and sex in the scientific literature. It is imperative that scientists acknowledge who participated in their research with precision and sensitivity. Without this step, it will remain

[1] This manuscript was supported in part by grants from the National Institute of Health: R03-DA027481 (EO); P30-DA027827 (EO).

The Wiley-Blackwell Handbook of Addiction Psychopharmacology, First Edition. Edited by James MacKillop and Harriet de Wit.

difficult – if not impossible – to generalize research findings to the appropriate populations and design empirically driven prevention and intervention strategies that have the capacity to improve the health of all people struggling with addictions.

1.1   Defining race

According to biologists, race is a construct that describes an inbreeding subspecies or geographically isolated population that differs in distinguishable physical traits from other members of the species (Lieberman and Jackson, 1995; Zuckerman, 1990). Such a biological conceptualization of race suggests that a species can easily be subdivided into discrete homogeneous groups; however, the subdivision of *Homo sapiens* into descendants of Africa (Negroid), Europe (Caucasoid), and Asia (Mongoloid) – based on phenotypic differences in skin pigmentation, facial features, and the distribution and texture of body hair – is largely unsupported by biological research. For example, African samples tend to show the highest mtDNA heterozygosity (having two different alleles – one from each parent) and phenotypic variation (e.g., craniometrics and skin color) relative to European and Asian samples (Relethford, 2001). To further complicate matters, European and Asian populations have a smaller genetic distance with each other in comparison to both of their relation to African populations (Relethford, 2001). While such findings support the hypothesis of an African origin of *Homo sapiens* and the effect of geographic distance on gene flow, the genetic difference between human populations across the world is small in comparison to other species (Relethford, 2001).

Extensive research on the racial paradigm tends to support the idea that roughly 10% of the total genetic variation in the human species occurs between geographic regions (e.g., race), 5% occurs between populations within regions, and 85% occurs within local populations (Relethford, 2001). Biological characteristics impacted by natural selection, migration, and genetic drift occur in geographical gradations – or clines (the frequency that a biological trait changes in a geographical gradient) – and are not categorical phenomena (Lieberman and Jackson, 1995). Such gradations cross alleged racial lines as if they are nonexistent (Lieberman and Jackson, 1995). This would suggest that there are no races – only clines (Livingstone, 1962).

The construct of race is a dubious construct when applied to human beings since anthropologists do not acknowledge *Homo sapiens* to have evolved since their conception some 200,000 years ago in East Africa (Zuckerman, 1990). In the field of physical anthropology, the validity of race as a construct is currently being challenged. In fact, its usage is sharply declining in the anthropological literature and is approaching conceptual extinction (Lieberman and Jackson, 1995). While there is nothing gained by using the construct of race that the term "population," "cline," or "ethnicity" cannot serve equally well (Lieberman and Jackson, 1995), the racial paradigm continues to be used by psychologists as a categorical way of organizing the world and reducing complexity.

A racial level of analysis is incapable of capturing complex constructs like worldview, personality, "self", etiology of health, spirituality, and so on, when larger within-group (versus between-group) variance is probable on the level of race. It is important to note that in the United States, some constructs based on race (racism, racialism, stereotypes, race-related stress, discrimination, prejudice, etc.) have meaning when addressing the stimulus value that physical features might have on attitude formulation and its subsequent impact on health (Obasi, Flores, and James-Myers, 2009). However, a racial level of analysis will have little to no utility in describing cultural phenomena that may have larger between-group (versus within-group) differences (Obasi, Flores, and James-Myers, 2009; Obasi and Leong, 2010).

A meaningful alternative to the racial level of analysis might be an ethnic level of analysis. Ethnicity stems from the Greek word *ethnos* which refers to a nation or tribe (Bentancourt and López, 1993). Given the impact of migration and globalization, it is more probable that a nation would consist of multiple ethnic groups as opposed to one homogeneous ethnic group. Ethnicity can be summarized as the self-definition of any human social unit that has a shared culture that is generally linked to a common ancestral origin, history, worldview, language, tradition, religion and/or spiritual system (Gordon, 1964; Shiraev and Levy, 2004). Moreover, an ethnic level of analysis would allow scientist to provide a greater level of specificity to the widely used racial construct: Whites (i.e., European American, British, French, German, Italian, etc.), Blacks (i.e., African American, Haitian, Ghanaian, Nigerian, Kenyan, etc.), Latinos/as (i.e., Mexican American, Brazilian, Columbian, Cuban, Guatemalan, etc.), Asians (i.e., Chinese American, Japanese, Korean, Pilipino, Vietnamese, etc.), and Native Americans (i.e., Cherokee, Navajo, Choctaw, Sioux, Apache, etc.).

An ethnic level of analysis permits scientists to identify the mutual influences of biological traits and cultural variables, to distinguish genetically based characteristics from learned characteristics, and to base the social identity of the group upon the latter of these traits (Jackson, 1992; Lieberman and Jackson, 1995). Since each ethnic group has a culture that provides a general design for living and pattern for interpreting reality, cultural phenomena should be investigated on an ethnic level of analysis as opposed to a racial level of analysis. Scientists must appreciate contextual factors that may inform the cultural variables being examined.

In summary, there are three primary options when applying the construct of race to human beings: (1) acknowledging that there is only one race (i.e., human race), (2) acknowledging that there are three global races from which all ethnic groups are derived (i.e., people of African, Asian, and European descent), or (3) focusing on the five racial categorizations that are often used in the United States (i.e., Whites, Blacks, Latinos/as, Asians, and Native Americans). It is important to reemphasize that the biological bases for the last two options are largely unsubstantiated by the data. Moreover, the racial construct may not be sensitive enough to simultaneously capture the complexity of within-group variation and between-group differences despite the advancement of high-density single nucleotide polymorphism (SNP) chips aimed at identifying ancestry-informative genetic markers that could be used for the purpose of categorizing populations. That being said, race is a social construct that can be used to explore group differences as it relates to experiences to racism, prejudice, and discrimination; social injustices that are predicated on phenotypic observations independent of biological confirmation.

1.2 Defining sex

In the case of human beings, the construct of sex is largely determined by biological characteristics. According to Wizemann and Pardue (2001), sex represents a categorical system where females are represented by an XX sex chromosome and males are represented by an XY chromosome. Furthermore, such a biological distinction is typically manifested in differences in reproductive organs (i.e., genitalia, gonads, etc.) and quantity of steroid sex hormones (i.e., estrogen, testosterone) that are produced (Lewin, 2008). To this end, many of these biological characteristics are largely unchangeable. That being said, a sexual revolution with the help of medical advances has also forged a third sex where transsexual individuals have undergone medical procedures to change many aspects of their sex-based phenotype. While sex is widely reported in the scientific literature, some social scientists might argue that research should extend beyond the construct of sex and investigate gender, or the socially constructed roles, expectations, and psychological characteristics that are ascribed to men and women by individual cultures and social institutions.

These concepts of gender roles and identity are thought to be multidimensional (i.e., masculine, feminine, etc.), measured on a continuum, and amendable across time and place (Phillips, 2005; Wizemann and Pardue, 2001). While gender is rooted in a person's biologically determined sex, it is largely shaped by environmental factors (i.e., parenting, friends, media, etc.) and personal experiences (Phillips, 2005; Wizemann and Pardue, 2001). It is important to note that gender identification may not always match one's biological characteristics. More specifically, transgendered individuals represent – for example – males that self-identify as women and females that self-identify as men. Similar to the distinction between race, ethnicity, and culture (see section 1.1), the combined assessment of sex and gender would allow scientists to disentangle genetically based characteristics related to being a female or male from learned psychological characteristics and associated risks and benefits of being a woman or man in a specific society.

2 Race and Substance Abuse

2.1 Substance use prevalence rates by race

Racial differences in the prevalence rates of substance use are well established (Center for Disease Control and Prevention, 2005; Substance Abuse and Mental Health Services Administration, 2006). Whites often report greater incidence of substance abuse in comparison to other racial groups in the USA (Caldwell, Silver, and Strada, 2010). According to the results from the 2009 National Survey on Drug Use and Health (2010) among persons aged 12 or older in the United States, Whites were more likely to report current alcohol use (56.7%) than any other racial group (i.e., Blacks: 42.8%; Latinos/as: 41.7%; Asians: 37.6%; and Native Americans: 37.1%). Furthermore, Latinos/as (19.8%) reported the highest binge use rates (Whites: 16.9%; Blacks: 15.3%; Native Americans: 13.9%; and Asians: 9.6%), while Native Americans (8.3%) reported the highest heavy alcohol use rates (Whites: 7.9%; Latinos/as: 5.2%; Blacks: 4.5%; and Asians: 1.5%). Native Americans (41.8% and 18.3% respectively) were the most likely to report current use of tobacco (Whites: 29.6%; Blacks: 26.5%; Latinos/as: 23.2%; and Asians: 11.9%) and illicit drugs (Blacks: 9.6%; Whites: 8.8%; Latinos/as: 7.9%; and Asians: 3.7%). Finally, the rate of substance dependence or abuse was found to be lowest among Asians (3.5%) in comparison to any other racial group (Native Americans: 15.5%; Latinos/as: 10.1%; Whites: 9.0%; and Blacks: 8.8%).

The potential for missing within-group variation is a serious limitation when substance use, abuse, and dependence prevalence rates are provided at the racial level of analysis. Amongst people of Latino/a descent, Mexicans (6.9%) report a relatively high heavy alcohol use rate in comparison to ethnic groups residing in Central America (2.2%) and South America (3.0%) (Substance Abuse and Mental Health Services Administration, 2011). Additionally, Puerto Ricans (28.8% and 12.0%) are relatively high in past-month cigarette use and heavy smoking in comparison to Mexicans (21.6% and 4.7%) and Central Americans (18.9% and 2.3%) aged 12 or older (Substance Abuse and Mental Health Services Administration, 2006b). While Asians reported the lowest current use of tobacco (Substance Abuse and Mental Health Services Administration, 2010), Koreans (24.9%) and Vietnamese (16.4%) reported much higher past-month cigarette use than Chinese (7.5%) aged 12 or older (Substance Abuse and Mental Health Services Administration, 2006b). Furthermore, age patterns of substance use behaviors are also important to acknowledge. For example, Blacks report one of the lowest rates of tobacco use at ages 12–17 (9.3%), but are among the highest users at ages 35 and older (34%) (Substance Abuse and Mental Health Services Administration, 2011). This trend of peak substance use prevalence rates taking place at later ages in Blacks can also be found with marijuana and cocaine use (Substance Abuse and Mental Health Services Administration, 2011).

Blacks, Latinos/as, Asians, and Native Americans make up nearly one-third of the US population (Humes, Jones, and Ramirez, 2011). However, they account for significantly more substance abuse treatment admittances in any given year (African Americans: 17.8%; Native Americans: 12.4%; Latinos/as: 11.3; and Asians: 5.5%) when compared to their White counterparts (Substance Abuse and Mental Health Services Administration, 2009d). Despite comprising the largest segment of substance abuse treatment admittance, Blacks have one of the lowest rates of substance abuse or dependence. While prevalence rates for Blacks are consistently lower than for Whites, Blacks and Native Americans experience greater chronicity rates, disability burden, and substance-related problem behaviors in comparison to Whites (Kip, Peters, and Morrison-Rodriguez, 2002).

2.2 Race and substance use risk factors in the USA

While race seems to have undue influence on substance use, abuse, and dependence behaviors, race alone fails to adequately encapsulate these phenomena due to the interaction of genetic, environmental, psychological, and cultural factors. Differential exposure to risk factors may account for racial/ethnic differences in substance use over the life course (Akins, Smith, and Mosher, 2010). The extant literature highlights the confluence of socioeconomic status and disenfranchisement, personality, age of initiation, level of education, and unemployment in exacerbating the incidences of substance use behavior. Therefore, it is difficult to assert that race or ethnicity are sufficient predictors of substance use behavior when there is overrepresentation of Blacks, Latinos/as, and Native Americans living in poverty, incarcerated, unemployed, and suffering from known health disparities without adequate access to quality education and comprehensive healthcare.

While problematic substance use is not limited to any one race, ethnicity, age group, or socioeconomic status, it is overrepresented in low-income populations (Diala, Muntaner, and Walrath, 2004; Fothergill and Ensminger, 2006; Wu *et al.*, 2010) and young adults aged 18–25 (Substance Abuse and Mental Health Services Administration, 2006; 2009c), and is often believed to be a problem plaguing marginalized racial groups. For example, problematic substance use has long been known to be greater in impoverished Black neighborhoods (Freedman, 2009). The rate of poverty for Blacks (25.8%) is nearly twice the national average (14.3%). The median wealth of Whites is ten times greater than that of Blacks (Institute for Research on Poverty, 2009), with Blacks being consistently more likely to live in poverty (Center for Disease Control and Prevention, 2009). Asians have the highest median income ($64,308) in the USA, while Blacks have the lowest median income ($32,068) (DeNavas-Walt, Proctor, and Smith, 2011). Although Asians have the highest median household income of any racial group, they have a higher rate of poverty (12.5%) than Whites (9.4%), but still lower than other marginalized racial groups.

Unemployment rates in a given community are a strong predictor of poverty. In the USA, Blacks maintain the highest unemployment rates (14.8%) of all major racial groups; and it has generally been twice that of Whites (US Bureau of Labor Statistics, 2010). Similarly, the unemployment rates for Latinos/as exceed 12%. Black teenagers (aged 16–19) are particularly vulnerable to poverty with an unemployment rate of 39.5% – compared with 30.2% for Latinos/as, 26.4% for Asians, and 21.8% for Whites. Further, Blacks tend to be jobless longer (19.7 weeks) and earn considerably less than Whites and Asians. Educational obtainment is also a significant predictor of poverty. According to data compiled by the US Department of Education, Native Americans (~16%), Blacks (~11%), and Latinos/as (~11%) are more likely to drop out of high school than their White classmates (~6%) (Aud *et al.*, 2010). As a result, an overrepresentation of poverty rates by marginalized racial communities is to be expected.

Substance use disorders are highly heritable illnesses (Kendler, Jacobsen, Prescott, and Neale, 2003). Specifically, studies have repeatedly linked genetic predispositions to alcohol use and dependence (Cotton, 1979; Hill *et al.*, 2004; Kaufman *et al.*, 2007; Lappalainen *et al.*, 2004; Sartor *et al.*, 2009) and tobacco use and dependence (Kendler *et al.*, 1999; Niu *et al.*, 2000) in human and animal models. However, few of these studies have explored racial/ethnic variation as it relates to gene expression in the development of these disorders (Prescott, Madden, and Stallings, 2006). Some researchers have indicated that approximately half of the variance in alcohol dependence is accounted for by genetic factors (Heath *et al.*, 1997; Knopik *et al.*, 2004; Reed *et al.*, 1994; True *et al.*, 1996; van den Bree, Svikis, and Pickens, 1998). Researchers have also demonstrated that the initiation of substance use at earlier ages was generally a risk factor for later drug use (Wu *et al.*, 2010). More specifically, early alcohol and marijuana use increases the risk of cocaine and heroin use later in life (National Center on Addiction and Substance Abuse, 1994). In addition, early initiation of substance use has also been linked to low educational achievement and delinquent behavior (Ellickson, Tucker, and Klein, 2003; Kandel and Chen, 2000). However, Bassuk, Buckner, Perloff, and Bassuk (1998) found that traditional drug use progressions do not hold for all racial groups. More specifically, Blacks and Latinos/as often initiate marijuana use prior to tobacco or alcohol use; a pattern that is inconsistent with other racial groups. Furthermore, White youth typically report earlier onset and higher levels of substance use, while Black adults frequently experience more serious long-term health outcomes as a result of substance use (Griffin, Scheier, Botvin, and Diaz, 2000; Watt, 2008).

Race has also been found to be an important factor in service utilization (Aarons, Brown, Garland, and Hough, 2004; Novins *et al.*, 1999). Blacks, Latinos/as, and Native Americans may be less likely to receive specialty care in comparison to their White counterparts (Aarons, Brown, Garland, and Hough, 2004). That being said, the extent to which this relationship is a conflation between race, socioeconomic status, and access to healthcare remains unclear (McCabe *et al.*, 1999; Pumariega, Glover, Holzer, and Nguyen, 1998). These disparities in service provision and utilization probably prolong the course of substance use disorders, thus reducing the efficacy of future treatment efforts while increasing the likelihood of relapse.

3 Measuring Race

The vast majority of empirical research studies measure the construct of race via self-report. That being said, there seems to be two primary inconsistencies that are worth noting. First, race is often used interchangeably with ethnicity even though the two constructs are designed to measure two different things (see section 1.1). Furthermore, a significant proportion of research papers fail to assess and/or report the racial/ethnic composition of their sample. For example, we reviewed how race/ethnicity was measured in three peer-reviewed addiction journals (i.e., *Alcohol and Alcoholism*, *Alcoholism: Clinical and Experimental Research* [*ACER*], and *Addiction*) over the past 5 years (2006–2010). We found that race/ethnicity was only reported in ~61% of the manuscripts in *ACER*, ~49% of the manuscripts in *Addiction*, and ~29% of the manuscripts in *Alcohol and Alcoholism* that utilized human participants from 2006 to 2010 (see Table 3.1). Furthermore, Blacks were the most included marginalized group, while Native Americans were the least included. While it is unclear if the readership is to assume that the sample is White unless otherwise noted, we find it unethical not to characterize the racial/ethnic composition of any research sample, especially as it relates to the generalizability of each study's findings. Unfortunately, this content analysis failed to illustrate any trends that such reporting is getting better across time.

3.1 Recommendations

All empirical studies should describe the racial and ethnic makeup of the sample that was studied with the greatest level of precision as possible. To this end, we offer the

Table 3.1 The reporting of race and sex from 2006 to 2010 in research papers published in *Alcohol and Alcoholism*; *Alcoholism: Clinical and Experimental Research*, and *Addiction* (%)

Year	Reported race	Blacks	Asians	Latinos/ as	Native Americans	Reported sex	Sex	Gender
Alcohol and Alcoholism								
2006	19.7	5.6	7.0	5.6	1.4	91.6	63.4	33.8
2007	35.8	16.4	11.9	10.5	3.0	92.5	59.7	34.3
2008	22.7	5.3	6.7	5.3	2.7	86.7	62.7	33.3
2009	32.1	10.7	7.1	8.9	3.6	89.3	51.8	46.4
2010	35.6	10.2	8.5	10.2	6.8	93.2	64.4	44.1
Total	**28.7**	**9.5**	**8.2**	**7.9**	**3.4**	**90.6**	**60.7**	**37.8**
Alcoholism: Clinical and Experimental Research								
2006	54.6	29.6	13.0	18.5	11.1	93.5	63.9	30.6
2007	60.0	33.6	12.0	22.4	5.6	91.2	68.0	22.4
2008	69.2	35.0	9.2	20.0	8.3	94.2	68.3	25.8
2009	61.5	29.1	20.5	25.6	7.7	95.7	74.4	22.2
2010	57.4	27.0	15.7	20.9	5.2	94.8	58.3	37.4
Total	**60.7**	**30.9**	**14.0**	**21.5**	**7.5**	**93.9**	**56.9**	**23.9**
Addiction								
2006	36.7	15.4	5.9	10.3	3.7	98.2	72.1	30.9
2007	45.9	28.0	10.4	16.8	5.6	99.2	79.4	28.0
2008	46.6	21.6	6.8	17.1	5.7	99.2	73.9	27.3
2009	41.8	17.7	10.1	12.7	6.3	100.0	78.5	21.5
2010	43.5	24.4	10.7	16.8	5.3	100.0	84.0	17.6
Total	**48.5**	**21.3**	**8.6**	**14.5**	**5.1**	**99.3**	**76.4**	**24.9**

Note: Reported race and reported sex represent the percentage of articles that characterized the race and sex of their sample. The percentage of articles that reported the inclusion of Blacks, Asians, Latinos/as, Native Americans are included in their respective columns. Sex and gender represent the percentage of articles that reported the sex or gender of the included sample even if sex was incorrectly labeled as gender. That being said, there were a few articles that characterized their sample using sex and gender. As a result, these columns are not mutually exclusive.

following recommendations: (1) Measure the construct of race using a forced-choice format. Examples of races might include White, Black, Latino/a, Asian, and Native American. If options like biracial or multiracial are included, the participations should have the opportunity to specify the specific races that they self-identify with. It is imperative that the researchers have an *a priori* assessment of what their target sample will be so as to minimize the reporting of racial groups as being "non-White," "racial minorities," "other," or any other non-descriptive terminology. (2) In addition to race, the construct of ethnicity should be measured using an open-ended format that will allow the research participant to identify their ethnicity without any constraints. Researchers may want to consider the possibility of providing examples of various ethnic groups, so the research participant is clear about how ethnicity is being conceptualized in the research study. (3) Finally, it is time for researchers to go beyond the simple identification of racial or ethnic differences in research findings. It is imperative that researchers advance the scientific literature by measuring variables that have the capacity to explain such differences (i.e., genes, environment, culture, world-view, acculturation, etc.) as opposed to inferring ethnocultural explanations without concurrent empirical support. Moreover, an assessment of socioeconomic indicators should also be included so researchers can attempt to disentangle race from social status when making causal inferences in addictions research.

4   Sex and Substance Abuse

4.1   Substance use prevalence rates by sex

Studies using animal models have posited that sex differences are evident in the acquisition, maintenance, escalation, dysregulation, and withdrawal of drug use (see Carroll *et al.*, 2004, for a review). Based on epidemiological data, males are at greater risk to use and abuse alcohol and other drugs in comparison to their female counterparts. For adults ages 18 and over, 54.2% of males and 44.6% of females engage in illicit drug use within their lifetime (Substance Abuse and Mental Health Services Administration, 2009a). The number of persons aged 12 or older with substance use or dependence in 2008 was estimated to be about 22 million, of which approximately 3 million were shown to be abusing or dependent upon both illicit drugs and alcohol (Substance Abuse and Mental Health Services Administration, 2009a). Specifically, in 2008, males were twice as likely as females (11.5% versus 6.4%) to be classified with dependence and abuse of illicit drugs and alcohol. Furthermore, across a range of illicit substances, males used drugs at higher rates than females with regard to marijuana (45.2% versus 36.2%), hallucinogens (i.e., LSD, PCP, and Ecstasy) (17.2% versus 10.6%), inhalants (11.9% versus 6.4%), heroin (2.3% versus 0.8%), cocaine (17.8% versus 11.3%), methamphetamine (6.3% versus 4.3%), and non-medical use of prescription-type drugs (i.e., pain relievers, tranquilizers, stimulants, or sedatives) (22% versus 18.8%) (Substance Abuse and Mental Health Services Administration, 2009a).

Overall, the lifetime prevalence rate of using illicit drugs (54.2% versus 44.6%), past-year use (16.4% versus 12.2%), and past-month use (9.9% versus 6.3%) is greater in adult males aged 18 and older in comparison to their female counterparts (Substance Abuse and Mental Health Services Administration, 2009a). Interestingly, this discrepancy is not nearly as evident among adolescents aged 12 to 17 years old, as illicit drug use within this age range is nearly identical for males and females (26.0% versus 26.3% respectively) (Substance Abuse and Mental Health Services Administration, 2009a). The trends in alcohol use, binge drinking, and heavy alcohol use for adolescent and young adult populations (aged 12–20 years old) reveal interesting results as well. While the prevalence of alcohol use in this age group for males and females is nearly identical (52.0% versus 52.4%), males exhibit greater patterns of risky drinking behavior than females, including binge alcohol use (19.2% versus 15.5%) and heavy alcohol use (7.0% versus 4.0% respectively) (Substance Abuse and Mental Health Services Administration, 2009a). This pattern of risky drinking is also seen with males aged 12 and older. More specifically, males engage in alcohol use (57.7%

versus 45.9%) as well as binge drinking behavior about twice as much as females (31.6% versus 15.4%). In addition to illicit drug use, males aged 12 and older utilize tobacco products including cigarettes, smokeless tobacco, cigars, and pipe tobacco at a higher rate than their female (34.5% versus 22.5%) counterparts (Substance Abuse and Mental Health Services Administration, 2009a).

4.2   Sex and substance use risk factors in the USA

Utilization of epidemiological data can help researchers in understanding general developing trends and can aid in assessing proximal and distal risk factors toward engaging in drug use. While many factors have been theorized to explain sex differences in the initiation, effects, and prevalence rates associated with licit and illicit substances, it is clear that researchers have largely focused on biological explanations while essentially ignoring environmental forces that influence gender roles and expectations in specific communities. Carroll and colleagues (2004) assert that the biological bases of sex differences may be responsible for differences in drug abuse in males and females. First, there may be peripheral sex differences that relate to the pharmacokinetics of using licit and illicit substances. More specifically, the process of absorption, distribution, biotransformation, and excretion is affected by the percentage of body fat and metabolic differences that often occur between males and females. Secondly, there may be sex differences in the neurocircuitry involved in the mesolimbic reward system. Finally, sex hormones probably play a significant role in facilitating or inhibiting the process of drug use.

Turner and de Wit (2006) conducted a comprehensive review of the literature to examine the potential influence of menstrual cycle phases on female responses to a wide range of licit and illicit substances. Findings suggested that circulating levels of ovarian hormones had modest to no effect on female responses to alcohol, benzodiazepines, caffeine, marijuana, nicotine, and opioids. However, reactivity to psychomotor stimulants like amphetamines and cocaine were found to be greater during the follicular – in comparison to the luteal – phase of the menstrual cycle. Results from cocaine studies have found females to indicate feeling more "nervous" than males during intranasal cocaine use; as well as reporting less euphoric and more dysphoric feelings with regard to the subjective effects of the drug (Kosten *et al.*, 1996; Lukas *et al.*, 1996). Sofuoglu and colleagues (1999) found that males rated subjective effects from cocaine higher than females in both single and repeated cocaine delivery. However, females in the luteal phase of their cycle exhibited a decreased subjective response to cocaine, while females in the follicular phase of their menstrual cycle as well as the males in the study had increased positive subjective responses to the delivery of cocaine. Lukas and colleagues (1996) found that male participants reached the highest peak plasma cocaine levels and were able to detect cocaine effects faster than females. Among females who were menstruating, those who were studied during the follicular phase of their cycle exhibited a higher peak plasma cocaine level in comparison to women who were studied during the luteal phase of their menstrual cycle. However, Lukas and colleagues (1996) found no effects of the menstrual cycle on the actual subjective ratings of cocaine.

Examination of the biological basis of sex differences in males and females also focuses on the pharmacokinetics of drugs. Some studies support the notion that females are at a higher risk of being more vulnerable to the effects of alcohol because of their physiological and hormonal differences than their male counterparts. For example, females become more impaired by alcohol and demonstrate higher blood alcohol concentrations levels in comparison to males even when similar quantities of alcohol are consumed. The extant literature suggests that females have a slower alcohol elimination rate than males: that is, it takes their body longer to metabolize ethanol. Since ethanol is distributed across water compartments of the human body, a person's blood alcohol concentration is largely dependent on their body composition (Ferreira and Willoughby, 2008). For example, Baraona and colleagues (2001) found that women exhibited a decreased volume of ethanol distribution, contributing to higher blood alcohol levels, a higher rate of ethanol oxidation in the liver, and a slower rate of gastric emptying of alcohol. In sum, this occurs as a result of a decreased amount of tissue mass in females as well as a lower amount of total body water, which inhibits alcohol from being diffused away from the bloodstream (Ferreira and Willoughby, 2008; Mancinelli, Binetti, and Ceccanti, 2006; Ramchandani, Bosron, and Li, 2001).

Findings suggest that sex hormones interact with alcohol to produce reproductive dysfunction in both men and women. Specifically, males exhibit signs of sexual dysfunction associated with alcohol abuse, including testicular atrophy, sterility, impotence, loss of libido, reduction in the size of the prostate gland, and decreased sperm production (Wright and Gavaler, 1991). The use of alcohol for females has been found to also have detrimental consequences, as their lower amount of tissue mass and total body water causes a larger amount of alcohol to reach the liver directly. Subsequently, this can cause a faster and more pronounced degree of liver damage (Mancinelli, Binetti, and Ceccanti, 2006) and other alcohol-induced diseases that may be accelerated in women, such as cardiomyopathy and cognitive deficits (Urbano-Márquez *et al.*, 1995; Ashley *et al.*, 1977; Nixon, 1994). Similarly, Ashley and colleagues (1977) found that while female inpatients had not been drinking as long as male inpatients (14.2 years versus 20.2 years respectively), the female rate of physical disease was akin to their male counterparts.

Some researchers have suggested that the sex differences regarding the prevalence rates of drug use can be partially explained by the thesis that males have more access to and opportunities to try drugs in comparison to females. Van Etten and Anthony (2001) found that males and females were strikingly similar regarding drug use when both were presented with the same opportunities to use. Importantly, variability in subjective responses to drugs may have an impact on how a person views their initial experience as well as future use. Davidson, Finch, and Schenk (1993) found that the initial global positive score was correlated with latency of the next use of cocaine as well as with the lifetime prevalence of use. More specifically, those with higher global positive scores on their initial use indicated a shorter interval lapse before using cocaine a second time as well as a higher lifetime use score (Davidson, Finch, and Schenk, 1993). Therefore, positive initial encounters are probably related to subsequent abuse.

Sociocultural factors may play a role in the sex differences with regard to substance use. Westermeyer and Boedicker (2000) examined retrospective data and found that females who were being treated for substance abuse were more likely to have a sibling or spouse who also abused substances. In addition, while the use of licit drugs (i.e., alcohol, caffeine, and tobacco) did not differ with regard to males and females, females were less likely to have ever used an illicit substance, and as such, displayed less deviant drug usage, a phenomenon that has been mirrored in epidemiological studies (Westermeyer and Boedicker, 2000). Consistent with previous research studies, females used substances for a significantly shorter period of time in comparison to males prior to entering treatment. Females also displayed fewer legal problems related to substances (e.g., driving while intoxicated). With regard to the treatment history of individuals who had ever been treated for substance abuse in an outpatient or day program setting, females had fewer previous and lifetime admissions for all types of substance abuse treatments. In total, females spent less time in treatment facilities and had a lower lifetime cost of substance treatment overall than their male counterparts (Westermeyer and Boedicker, 2000).

Historically, drug abuse treatment centers have focused on the needs of males, largely due to the proportion of males within the facilities. Males and females are typically housed within the same programs and facilities, thus limiting the amount we know about targeting sex-specific issues that may be important to consider during treatment (Brady and Randall, 1999). As prevalence and subjective effects of alcohol and drug use vary, so do treatment outcomes for many males and females. On average, females seek treatment for all medical problems at a greater rate than their male counterparts. The Services Research Outcomes Study (SROS) found that the overall use of illicit drugs decreases after substance abuse treatment. However, females were more likely than males to exhibit a decrease in post-treatment usage, which was confirmed through self-report and urine toxicology tests (Substance Abuse and Mental Health Services Administration, 1998). The Treatment Episode Data Set (Substance Abuse and Mental Health Services Administration, 2009b) suggests that males were more likely than females to actually complete intensive outpatient substance abuse treatment or to be transferred for additional treatment in a subsequent program or treatment facility. Conversely, among those clients discharged from long-term residential substance abuse treatment, females were more likely than males to complete treatment or to be transferred to another treatment program or facility (Substance Abuse and Mental Health Services Administration, 2009b).

Not only does substance use significantly reduce one's quality of life, but substance abuse has been linked to problem behaviors such as unsafe sexual practices (Hingson, Heeren, Winter and Wechsler, 2005), intimate partner violence (Hines and Straus, 2007), and suicide attempts (Kung, Liu and Juon, 1998; Shiang *et al.*, 1997). Negative health problems are a significant consequence as well, as the use of illicit drugs presents varying issues such as cardiovascular disease, neurological deficits, psychiatric comorbidity, and pulmonary issues (Cornish and O'Brien, 1996).

5 Measuring Sex

The vast majority of empirical research studies measured the construct of sex via self-report. We found that sex was reported in ~99% of the manuscripts in *Addiction*, ~94% of the manuscripts in *ACER*, and ~91% of the manuscripts in *Alcohol and Alcoholism* from 2006 to 2010 (see Table 3.1). In contrast to race/ethnicity, researchers tended to do a good job of noting the percentage of males and females in their sample. Unfortunately, sex (i.e., male, female) was often used interchangeably with gender (i.e., men, women) even though these constructs have very different meanings (see section 1.2). In our content analyses, we found that sex was reported more often than gender (see Table 3.1). Furthermore, there were numerous instances where sex was measured, but reported with gendered terminology. It is our interpretation that gender was typically used as a synonym to sex as opposed to the assessment of learned psychological characteristics or role expectations in a specific cultural and societal context. This bias follows the assumption that all males would self-identify as men and all females would self-identify as women; and negates the possibility of a transgendered identity.

5.1   Recommendations

It is imperative that researchers investigate biological (i.e., sex) and social (i.e., gender) determinants of health. To this end, we offer the following recommendations: (1) Sex should be measured using a forced-choice response format that includes female and male. (2) In addition to the assessment of sex, gender should be measured using a forced-choice response format that includes woman, man, and transgendered. (3) Finally, we recommend that social, cultural, and psychological variables that may influence gender role identification be included in the research design so that potential gender differences can be explained while minimizing stereotype-based inferences.

6   Summary, Limitations, and Future Directions

It is imperative that scientists who are studying addictions accurately characterize the sample that participated in their research studies. At a minimum, all empirical articles should detail the ethnicity, sex, age, and indicators of the socioeconomic status (i.e., educational obtainment, occupational status, household income, etc.) of the sample being studied. When appropriate, constructs like race, gender, and cultural variables should be included to investigate sociological factors (i.e., racism, discrimination, gender roles, ethnic identity, acculturation, worldviews, values, etc.) that may account for between-group and within-group variation. In this chapter we have made recommendations regarding how race, ethnicity, sex, and gender could be measured with accuracy and sensitivity. That being said, it is important to recognize that the self-report of these constructs will probably have some measurement error associated with it. For example, it is not uncommon for Whites – who happen to be born in America – to identify as being native to America, or Native American. Some of this error in measurement can be minimized by offering brief definitions and examples of the group identifiers being measured. It is important to note that there should be some consistency between a person's self-identified ethnic (i.e., African American) and racial (i.e., Black) group. Furthermore, there could be experimenter/institutional variables that cause some individuals from marginalized communities (i.e., Blacks,

Latinos/as, Native Americans, transsexuals, and transgendered) to not feel comfortable self-reporting their race, ethnicity, sex, or gender. As the technology for genotyping the human genome advances, population markers become more precise, and assay cost becomes more economical, researchers will soon have the capacity to confirm many of these constructs with genetic-based data. Ultimately, it is essential that researchers abandon research designs that focus on simple group differences and begin to grapple with the complexity associated with how genetics, race, ethnicity, sex, gender, and psychological characteristics interact with one's culture and environmental context when understanding the pathogenesis to addictions and designing best practices for empirically based prevention and intervention strategies.

References

Aarons GA, Brown SA, Garland AF, and Hough RL (2004) Race/ethnic disparity and correlates of substance abuse service utilization and juvenile justice involvement among adolescents with substance use disorders. *Journal of Ethnicity in Substance Abuse* 3(1): 47–64. doi: 10.1300/j233v03n01_04.

Akins S, Smith CL, and Mosher C (2010) Pathways to adult alcohol abuse across racial/ethnic groups: An application of general strain and social learning theories. *Journal of Drug Issues* 40(2): 321–351.

Ashley M, Olin J, le Riche W, Kornaczewski A, Schmidt W, and Rankin J (1977) Morbidity in alcoholics: Evidence for accelerated development of physical disease in women. *Archives of Internal Medicine* 137(7): 883–887.

Aud S, Hussar W, Planty M, Snyder T, Bianco K, Fox M, Frohlich L, Kemp J, and Drake L (2010) *The Condition of Education 2010* (NCES 2010-028). Washington, DC: National Center for Education Statistics, Institute of Education Sciences, US Department of Education.

Baraona E, Abittan C, Dohmen K, Moretti M, Pozzato G, Chayes Z, Schaefer C, and Lieber CS (2001) Gender differences in pharmacokinetics of alcohol. *Alcoholism, Clinical and Experimental Research* 25(4): 502–507.

Bassuk EL, Buckner JC, Perloff JN, and Bassuk SS (1998) Prevalence of mental health and substance use disorders among homeless and low-income housed mothers. *American Journal of Psychiatry* 155(11): 1561–1564.

Belmont Report (1978) *Ethical Principles and Guidelines for the Protection of Human Subjects of Research*. Report of the National Commission for the Protection of Human Subjects of Biomedical and Behavioral Research.

Betancourt H and Lopez SR (1993) The study of culture, ethnicity, and race in American psychology. *American Psychologist* 48(6): 629–637.

Brady K and Randall C (1999) Gender differences in substance use disorders. *Psychiatric Clinics of North America* 22(2): 241–252.

Caldwell RM, Silver NC, and Strada M (2010) Substance abuse, familial factors, and mental health: Exploring racial and ethnic group differences among African American, Caucasian, and Hispanic juvenile offenders. *American Journal of Family Therapy* 38(4): 310–321. doi: 10.1080/01926187.2010.493438.

Carroll ME, Lynch WJ, Roth ME, Morgan AD, and Cosgrove KP (2004) Sex and estrogen influence drug abuse. *Trends in Pharmacological Sciences* 25(5): 273–279.

Center for Disease Control and Prevention (2005) Health disparities experienced by black or African Americans – United States. *MMWR* 54(1): 1–3.

Cornish JW and O'Brien CP (1996) Crack cocaine abuse: An epidemic with many public health consequences. *Annual Review of Public Health* 17: 259–73.

Cotton NS (1979) The familial incidence of alcoholism: A review. *Journal of Studies on Alcohol* 40(1): 89–116.

Davidson ES, Finch JF, and Schenk S (1993) Variability in subjective responses to cocaine: Initial experiences of college students. *Addictive Behaviors* 18(4): 445–453. doi: 10.1016/0306 4603(93)90062.

DeNavas-Walt C, Proctor BD, and Smith JC (2011) US Census Bureau, Current Population Reports, P60-238, *Income, Poverty, and Health Insurance Coverage in the United States: 2010.* Washington, DC: US Government Printing Office.

Diala CC, Muntaner C, and Walrath C (2004) Gender, occupational, and socioeconomic correlates of alcohol and drug abuse among US rural, metropolitan, and urban residents. *American Journal of Drug and Alcohol Abuse* 30(2): 409–428. doi: 10.1081/ADA-120037385.

Ellickson PL, Tucker JS, and Klein DJ (2003) Ten-year prospective study of public health problems associated with early drinking. *Pediatrics* 111(5): 949–955.

Ferreira MP and Willoughby D (2008) Alcohol consumption: The good, the bad, and the indifferent. *Applied Physiology, Nutrition and Metabolism* 33(1): 12–20.

Fothergill KE and Ensminger ME (2006) Childhood and adolescent antecedents of drug and alcohol problems: A longitudinal study. *Drug and Alcohol Dependence* 82(1): 61–76. doi: 10.1016/j.drugalcdep.2005.08.009.

Freedman R (2009) Genetic investigation of race and addiction. *American Journal of Psychiatry* 166(9): 967–968. doi: 10.1176/appi.ajp.2009.09071018.

Gordon MM (1964) *Assimilation in American Life: The Role of Race, Religion, and Natural Origins.* New York: Oxford University Press.

Griffin KW, Scheier LM, Botvin GJ, and Diaz T (2000) Ethnic and gender differences in psychosocial risk, protection, and adolescent alcohol use. *Prevention Science* 1(4): 199–212. doi: 10.1023/A:1026599112279.

Guthrie RV (1976) *Even the Rat was White: A Historical View of Psychology* (2nd edn). New York: Harper & Row.

Heath AC, Bucholz KK, Madden PAF, Dinwiddie SH, Slutske WS, Bierut LJ, *et al.* (1997) Genetic and environmental contributions to alcohol dependence risk in a national twin sample: Consistency of findings in women and men. *Psychological Medicine: A Journal of Research in Psychiatry and the Allied Sciences* 27(6): 1381–1396. doi: 10.1017/S0033291797005643.

Hill SY, Shen S, Zezza N, Hoffman EK, Perlin M, and Allan W (2004) A genome wide search for alcoholism susceptibility genes. *American Journal of Medical Genetics Part B: Neuropsychiatric Genetics* 128B(1): 102–113. doi: 10.1002/ajmg.b.30013.

Hines DA and Straus MA (2007) Binge drinking and violence against dating partners: The mediating effect of antisocial traits and behaviors in a multinational perspective. *Aggressive Behavior* 33: 441–457. doi: 10.1002/ab.20196.

Hingson R, Heeren T, Winter M, and Wechsler H (2005) Magnitude of alcohol-related mortality and morbidity among US college students ages 18–24: Changes from 1998 to 2001. *Annual Review of Public Health* 26: 259–279. doi: 10.1146/annurev. publhealth.26.021304.144652.

Humes KR, Jones NA, and Ramirez RR (2011) Overview of race and Hispanic origin 2010: 2010 Census Briefs. US Department of Commerce Economics and Statistics Administration.

Institute for Research on Poverty (2009) *Frequently asked questions about poverty: Who is poor?* Retrieved March 21, 2011, from http://www.irp.wisc.edu/faqs/faq3.htm

Institute of Medicine (2003) *Unequal Treatment: Confronting Racial and Ethnic Disparities in Health Care.* Washington, DC: National Academies Press.

Jackson FLC (1992) Race and ethnicity as biological constructs. *Ethnicity and Disease* 2: 120–125.

Kandel DB and Chen K (2000) Types of marijuana users by longitudinal course. *Journal of Studies on Alcohol* 61(3): 367–378.

Kaufman J, Yang B, Douglas-Palumberi H, Crouse-Artus M, Lipschitz D, Krystal JH, and Gelernter J (2007) Genetic and environmental predictors of early alcohol use. *Biological Psychiatry* 61(11): 1228–1234. doi:10.1016/j.biopsych.2006.06.039.

Kendler KS and Heath AC (1992) A population-based twin study of alcoholism in women. *JAMA: Journal of the American Medical Association* 268(14): 1877.

Kendler KS, Neale MC, Sullivan PF, Corey LA, Gardner CO, and Prescott CA (1999) A population-based twin study in women of smoking initiation and nicotine dependence. *Psychological Medicine* 29: 299–308.

Kendler KS, Jacobson KC, Prescott CA, and Neale MC (2003) Specificity of genetic and environmental risk factors for use and abuse/dependence of cannabis, cocaine, hallucinogens, sedatives, stimulants, and opiates in male twins. *American Journal of Psychiatry* 160(4): 687.

Kip KE, Peters RH, and Morrison-Rodriguez B (2002) Commentary on why national epidemiological estimates of substance abuse by race should not be used to estimate prevalence and need for substance abuse services at community and local levels. *American Journal of Drug and Alcohol Abuse* 28(3): 545.

Knopik VS, Heath AC, Madden PA, Bucholz KK, Slutske WS, Nelson EC, Statham D, Whitfield JB, and Martin NG (2004) Genetic effects on alcohol dependence risk: Re-evaluating the importance of psychiatric and other heritable risk factors. *Psychological Medicine* 34: 1519–1530.

Kosten TR, Kosten TA, McDougle CJ, Hameedi FA, McCance EF, Rosen MI, Oliveto AH, and Price LH (1996) Gender differences in response to intranasal cocaine administration to humans. *Biological Psychiatry* 39: 147–148. doi: 10.1016/0006-3223(95)00386-X.

Kung HC, Liu X, and Juon HS (1998) Risk factors for suicide in Caucasians and in African Americans: A matched case-control study. *Social Psychiatry and Psychiatry Epidemiology* 33: 155–161. doi: 10.1007/s001270050038.

Lappalainen J, Kranzler HR, Petrakis I, Somberg LK, Page G, Krystal JH, and Gelernter J (2004) Confirmation and fine mapping of the chromosome 1 alcohol dependence risk locus. *Molecular Psychiatry* 9(3): 312–319. doi:10.1038/sj.mp.4001429.

Lewin B (2008) *Genes IX.* Sudbury, MA: Jones and Barlett.

Lieberman L and Jackson FLC (1995) Race and three models of human origin. *American Anthropologist* 97(2): 231–242.

Livingstone FB (1962) On the non-existence of human races. *Current Anthropology* 3(3): 279–281.

Lukas S, Sholar M, Lundahl L, Lamas X, Kouri E, Wines J, Kragie L, and Mendelson J (1996) Sex differences in plasma cocaine levels and subjective effects after acute cocaine administration in human volunteers. *Psychopharmacology* 125(4): 346–354. doi: 10.1007/BF02246017.

Mancinelli RR, Binetti RR, and Ceccanti MM (2006) Female drinking, environment and biological markers. *Annali dell'Istituto Superiore di Sanità* 42(1): 31–38.

McCabe K, Yeh M, Hough RL, Landsverk J, Hurlburt MS, Wellss Culver S, and Reynolds B (1999) Racial/ethnic representation across five public sectors of care for youth. *Journal of Emotional and Behavioral Disorders* 7(2): 72–82. doi: 10.1177/106342669900700202.

National Center on Addiction and Substance Abuse (1994) *Cigarettes, Alcohol, Marijuana: Gateways to Illicit Drug Use*. New York: National Center on Addiction and Substance Abuse at Columbia University.

Niu T, Chen C, Ni J, Wang B, Fang Z, Shao H, and Xu X (2000) Nicotine dependence and its familial aggregation in Chinese. *International Journal of Epidemiology* 29(2): 248–252. doi: 10.1093/ije/29.2.248.

Nixon S (1994) Cognitive deficits in alcoholic women. *Alcohol Health and Research World* 18(3): 228.

Novins DK, Duclos CW, Martin C, Jewett CS, and Manson SM (1999) Utilization of alcohol, drug, and mental health treatment services among American Indian adolescent detainees. *Journal of the American Academy of Child and Adolescent Psychiatry* 38(9): 1102–1108. doi: 10.1097/00004583-199909000-00013.

Obasi EM and Leong FTL (2010) Construction and validation of the Measurement of Acculturation Strategies for People of African Descent (MASPAD). *Cultural Diversity and Ethnic Minority Psychology* 16(4): 526–539.

Obasi EM, Flores LY, and James-Myers L (2009) Construction and initial validation of the Worldview Analysis Scale. *Journal of Black Studies* 39(6): 937–961.

Phillips SP (2005) Defining and measuring gender: A social determinant of health whose time has come. *International Journal for Equity in Health* 4(11): 1–4.

Prescott CA, Madden PAF, and Stallings MC (2006) Challenges in genetic studies of the etiology of substance use and substance use disorders: Introduction to the special issue. *Behavior Genetics* 36(4): 473–482. doi: 10.1007/s10519-006-9072-9.

Pumariega AJ, Glover S, Holzer I, and Nguyen H (1998) Utilization of mental health services in a tri-ethnic sample of adolescents. *Community Mental Health Journal* 34(2): 145.

Ramchandani VA, Bosron WF, and Li TK (2001) Research advances in ethanol metabolism. *Pathologie Biologie* 49(9): 676–682. doi: 10.1016/S0369-8114(01)00232-2.

Reed T, Slemenda CW, Viken RJ, Christian JC, Carmelli D, and Fabsitz RR (1994) Correlations of alcohol consumption with related covariates and heritability estimates in older adult males over a 14- to 18-year period: The NHLBI twin study. *Alcoholism: Clinical and Experimental Research* 18(3): 702–710. doi: 10.1111/j.1530-0277.1994.tb00934.x.

Relethford JH (2001) *Genetics and the Search for Modern Human Origins*. New York: John Wiley & Sons, Inc.

Sartor CE, Agrawal A, Lynskey MT, Bucholz KK, Madden PAF, and Heath AC (2009) Common genetic influences on the timing of first use for alcohol, cigarettes, and cannabis in young African-American women. *Drug and Alcohol Dependence* 102(1–3): 49–55. doi: 10.1016/j.drugalcdep.2008.12.013.

Shiang J, Blinn R, Bongar B, Stephens B, Allison D, and Schatzberg A (1997) Suicide in San Francisco, CA: A comparison of Caucasian and Asian groups, 1987–1994. *Suicide and Life-Threatening Behavior* 27(1): 80–91. doi: 10.1111/j.1943-278X.1997.tb00505.x.

Shiraev E and Levy D (2004) *Cross-Cultural psychology: Critical Thinking and Contemporary Applications*. Boston: Allyn & Bacon.

Sofuoglu M, Dudish-Poulsen S, Nelson D, Pentel PR, and Hatsukami DK (1999) Sex and menstrual cycle differences in the subjective effects from smoked cocaine in humans. *Experimental and Clinical Psychopharmacology* 7(3): 274–283. doi: 10.1037/1064-1297.7.3.274.

Substance Abuse and Mental Health Services Administration, Office of Applied Studies (1998) Services Research Outcomes Study, DHHS Publication No. (SMA) 98-3177.

Substance Abuse and Mental Health Services Administration (2006a) *Results from the 2005 National Survey on Drug Use and Health: National Findings* (NSDUH Series H-30, DHHS Publication No. SMA 06-4194). Rockville, MD: Office of Applied Studies.

Substance Abuse and Mental Health Services Administration (2006b) *The NSDUH Report: Past Month Cigarette Use among Racial and Ethnic Groups.* Rockville, MD: Office of Applied Studies.

Substance Abuse and Mental Health Services Administration (2007) *Results from the 2006 National Survey on Drug Use and Health: National Findings* (NSDUH Series H-32, DHHS Publication No. SMA 07-4293). Rockville, MD: Office of Applied Studies.

Substance Abuse and Mental Health Services Administration (2009a) *Results from the 2008 National Survey on Drug Use and Health: National Findings* (NSDUH Series H-36, DHHS Publication No. SMA 09-4434). Rockville, MD: Office of Applied Studies.

Substance Abuse and Mental Health Services Administration (2009b) *The TEDS Report: Predictors of Substance Abuse Treatment Completion or Transfer to Further Treatment, by Service Type.* Rockville, MD: Office of Applied Studies.

Substance Abuse and Mental Health Services Administration (2009c) *The NSDUH Report: Concurrent Illicit Drug and Alcohol Use.* Rockville, MD: Office of Applied Studies.

Substance Abuse and Mental Health Services Administration (2009d) *The NSDUH Report: Treatment for Substance Use and Depression among Adults, by Race/Ethnicity.* Rockville, MD: Office of Applied Studies.

Substance Abuse and Mental Health Services Administration (2010) *Results from the 2009 National Survey on Drug Use and Health: Volume I. Summary of National Findings* (NSDUH Series H-38A, DHHS Publication No. SMA 10-4586 Findings). Rockville, MD: Office of Applied Studies.

Substance Abuse and Mental Health Services Administration (2011) *Results from the 2010 National Survey on Drug Use and Health: Summary of National Findings* (NSDUH Series H-41, DHHS Publication No. SMA 11-4658). Rockville, MD: Office of Applied Studies.

True WR, Heath AC, Bucholz KK, Slutske W, Romeis JC, Schemer JF, *et al.* (1996) Models of treatment seeking for alcoholism: The role of genes and environment. *Alcoholism: Clinical and Experimental Research* 20(9): 1577–1581. doi: 10.1111/j.1530-0277.1996.tb01702.x.

Turner JM and de Wit H (2006) Menstrual cycle phase and responses to drugs of abuse in humans. *Drug and Alcohol Dependence* 84: 1–13.

Urbano-Marquez A, Estruch R, Fernandez-Sola J, Nicolas J, Pare J, and Rubin E (1995) The greater risk of alcoholic cardiomyopathy and myopathy in women compared with men. *Journal of the American Medical Association* 274(2): 149–154. doi: 10.1001/jama.1995.03530020067034.

US Bureau of Labor Statistics (2010) *Labor Force Statistics from the Current Population Survey.* Retrieved September 1, 2011, from http://www.bls.gov/cps/earnings.htm#demographics.

US Department of Health and Human Services (2001) *Mental Health: Culture, Race, and Ethnicity – A Supplement to Mental Health: A Report of the Surgeon General.* Rockville, MD: US Department of Health and Human Services.

van den Bree MB, Svikis DS, and Pickens RW (1998) Genetic influences in antisocial personality and drug use disorders. *Drug and Alcohol Dependence* 49(3): 177–187. doi: 10.1016/S0376-8716(98)00012-X.

Van Etten ML and Anthony JC (2001) Male–female differences in transitions from first drug opportunity to first use: Searching for subgroup variation by age, race, region, and urban status. *Journal of Women's Health and Gender-Based Medicine* 10(8): 797–804. doi: 10.1089/15246090152636550.

Watt TT (2008) The race/ethnicity age crossover effect in drug use and heavy drinking. *Journal of Ethnicity and Substance Abuse* 7(1): 93–114. doi: 10.1080/15332640802083303.

Westermeyer J and Boedicker AE (2000) Course, severity, and treatment of substance abuse among women versus men. *American Journal of Drug and Alcohol Abuse* 26: 523–535.

Wizemann TM and Pardue ML (2001) *Exploring the Biological Contributions to Human Health: Does Sex Matter?* Washington, DC: National Academy Press.

Wright HI and Gavaler JS (1991) Effects of alcohol on the male reproductive system. *Alcohol Health and Research World* 15(2): 110.

Wu ZH, Temple JR, Shokar NK, Nguyen-Oghalai TU, and Grady JJ (2010) Differential racial/ethnic patterns in substance use initiation among young, low-income women. *American Journal of Drug and Alcohol Abuse* 36: 123–129. doi: 10.3109/00952991003718072.

Zuckerman M (1990) Some dubious premises in research and theory on racial differences. *American Psychologist* 45(12): 1297–1303.

4

Understanding Psychiatric Comorbidities and Addictions[1]

James C. (Jim) Anthony

1 Introduction

This chapter's point of departure is a question, pertinent to comorbidity, as it was asked 160 years ago: "How can one decide with certainty which of two coexistent phenomena is the cause and which the effect, whether one of them is the cause at all instead of both being effects of a third cause, or even whether both are effects of two entirely unrelated causes?" (Virchow, 1847). Forty years ago, Alvan Feinstein offered a more general description: "In a patient with a particular index disease, the term co-morbidity refers to any additional co-existing ailment." Feinstein broadened "ailment" to include "non-disease" clinical entities: pregnancy; deliberate dieting for weight loss; nausea and other responses to therapeutic maneuvers (Feinstein, 1970, pp. 456–457, 467). Feinstein's general definition of comorbidity is used in this chapter and in psychiatric comorbidity research reviews generally (e.g., Angold, Costello, and Erkanli, 1999; Costello, Erkanli, Federman, and Angold, 1999; Schuckit, 2006; Angold and Costello, 2009; Cerdá, Sagdeo, Johnson, and Galea, 2010). In keeping with the overall theme of this volume, the chapter's examples generally concern neuropsychiatric and behavioral comorbidities, focusing on those related to use of tobacco, alcohol, inhalants, and the internationally regulated drugs (IRD) such as cannabis and cocaine.

Little numeracy is required when comorbidity is studied in an individual case or patient; there might never be another case or patient with the two observed conditions. If so, the term "dual diagnosis" tends to be more appropriate than "comorbidity."

[1]The preparation of this chapter was supported, in part, by a NIDA research project grant award (R01DA016558) and a NIDA senior scientist career award (K05DA015799). There are no other conflicts of interest to disclose. The content is the sole responsibility of the author and does not necessarily represent the official views of MSU, the National Institute on Drug Abuse, or the National Institutes of Health.

More numeracy is required when a comorbidity syndrome is studied as a clinical or population research construct, defined below as the "greater than chance co-occurrence of two or more clinical features, signs, or symptoms" of disease processes. Both Cohen's "kappa" and the "odds ratio" (OR) can be used to quantify greater than chance co-occurrence in this context, but kappa is a margin-sensitive statistic that depends upon the actual frequency of each condition under study, whereas the OR is not margin-sensitive and is preferred for that reason (e.g., see Anthony *et al.*, 1985). In an example created for this chapter, the co-occurrence of diagnosed depression and tobacco dependence has been estimated (Table 4.1). The OR will be used to convey whether the odds of diagnosed depression as observed among cases of tobacco dependence is the same as, or is different from, the expected odds of diagnosed depression as observed among those without tobacco dependence (non-cases). The OR estimate equals 1.0 when these odds are the same; OR < 1.0 is "inverse," with observed odds lower than expected. When there is a comorbid association, OR > 1.

Concerning comorbidity and syndromes in general, during 1965, the late A. L. Cochrane (1909–1988), now known mainly as the progenitor of the "Cochrane Collaboration" for evidence-based medicine, wrote as follows:

> PHYSICIANS appear to have a special love for syndromes. They enjoy diagnosing, demonstrating and discussing them. The syndrome seems to have a snob value denied the simple symptom. The reasons for this are possibly concerned with the cult of the rare, or even with that widespread human weakness of "namedropping". Some of the names associated with syndromes do trip off the tongue in an attractive way. The reason for their popularity is unlikely to be scientific as no one seems to have pointed out how closely a medical syndrome in its description and investigation typifies the scientific method in its simplest form. This, as everyone knows, consists of, first, the idea, then the translation of the idea into a hypothesis, and finally the critical testing of the hypothesis. A syndrome fits this pattern perfectly. The idea connects two medical phenomena (signs and/or symptoms) that have not previously been connected; the hypothesis in these cases is simply a restatement of the idea, i.e., that the two phenomena occur more frequently together than can be accounted for by chance association and the testing of the hypothesis is, theoretically, relatively straightforward – or so it would seem. The physician's interest unfortunately seems to stop short at discussion and does not extend, in all cases, to detailed investigation. (Cochrane, 1965, p. 440)

In comorbidity research, the co-occurrence may be cross-sectional, but the time dimension and the passage of time remain crucial. One important subtype of comorbidity in clinical research involves the presence of two entities at some observed time point. These two entities might be jointly determined by a common underlying cause originating at some prior point in time, as in a genetic vulnerability trait formed at conception, later expressing itself in the co-occurring clinical entities (e.g., a clear pleiotrophy) or in concurrent failure of multiple systems. In another important subtype, the two clinical entities are observed in sequence, one followed by the other, possibly jointly determined by a common prior underlying cause, as we see with clinical chickenpox during primary school and then clinical shingles in late life, both caused by pre-chickenpox infection by the varicella zoster virus, which can be conceptualized as a necessary cause of both clinical entities. In a third important subtype, one

Table 4.1 The estimated cross-sectional association linking presence of tobacco dependence with presence of depression. Panel A, data from individuals in a treatment program for alcohol or drug use [problems] as of October 1 in the survey year. Panel B, data from individuals not in a treatment program for alcohol or drug use [problems] on that date. Panel C, data from all individuals.

Panel A. Estimated cross-sectional association linking presence of tobacco dependence with presence of depression. Data from individuals in a treatment program for alcohol or drug use [problems] as of October 1 in the survey year ($n = 340$).

	Unweighted sample data cell counts			Weighted population estimates for cell proportions			Weighted population estimate for the association
	D+	D−		D+	D−		
T+	37	110	T+	0.075	0.319		Estimated
T−	40	153	T−	0.131	0.474		OR = 0.8
							$p = 0.718$

Panel B. Estimated cross-sectional association linking presence of tobacco dependence with presence of depression. Data from individuals not in a treatment program for alcohol or drug use [problems] as of October 1 in the survey year ($n = 55,432$).

	Unweighted sample data cell counts			Weighted population estimates for cell proportions			Weighted population estimate for the association
	D+	D−		D+	D−		
T+	698	4,896	T+	0.014	0.096		Estimated
T−	2,603	47,235	T−	0.055	0.835		OR = 2.2
							$p = 0.001$

Panel C. Estimated cross-sectional association linking presence of tobacco dependence with presence of depression. Data from all individuals in the survey year ($n = 55,772$).

	Unweighted sample data cell counts			Weighted population estimates for cell proportions			Weighted population estimate for the association
	D+	D−		D+	D−		
T+	735	5,006	T+	0.014	0.097		Estimated
T−	2,643	47,388	T−	0.055	0.833		OR = 2.2
							$p = 0.001$

clinical entity might cause the other, as in a drug intoxication causing a later psychiatric disturbance.

Scientific strategies for disentangling these alternative pathways are the focal points of this chapter and are addressed in the following sections. Section 2 of this chapter addresses empirical relevance of research on these three comorbidity subtypes. Section 3 covers standardized and validated methods in more detail, and is based on a general outline that begins with a consideration of alternative research designs (section 3.1) and the population under study in comorbidity research (section 3.2). The section then moves on to drawing the sample for comorbidity research (section 3.3). Thereafter, issues pertinent to measurement are covered in section 3.4. Finally, the topic of analysis is addressed in brief (section 3.5), prior to a general concluding section that recaps major limitations with a sketch of future directions (section 4).

2 Empirical Relevance of the Topic

Whether one's research is about drug use or drug self-administration *per se*, or whether the research concerns drug dependence, drug addiction, or some other drug use disorder, the idea of psychiatric comorbidity has general empirical relevance. An exception is seen in the extreme "lumping" perspective: all drug use disorders and psychiatric disturbances are regarded as essentially exchangeable manifestations of a unitary "neuro-psychiatric-behavioral illness" construct, akin to the undifferentiated "mental illness" construct advanced with much influence by Menninger and colleagues some 50 years ago (1958). According to the Menninger school of psychopathology, mental illness was one thing only:

> Suppose that instead of putting so much emphasis on different kinds of illness we tried to think of all mental illness as being essentially the same in quality, and differing, rather, quantitatively. This is what we mean when we say that we all have mental illness of different degrees at different times, and that sometimes some of us are much worse or much better. (Menninger, Ellenberger, Pruyser, and Mayman, 1958, p. 10)

This mid-twentieth-century expression of Menninger's school of thought was not idiosyncratic in the field of psychopathology. Menninger traced his ideas back to the influential nineteenth-century clinical psychiatrist Heinrich Neumann, and provided this translation of Neumann's original treatise in German:

> We consider any classification of mental illness to be artificial, and therefore unsatisfactory, (and) we do not believe that one can make progress in psychiatry until one has resolved to throw overboard all classifications and to declare with us: *there is only one kind of mental illness* ... (Menninger, Ellenberger, Pruyser, and Mayman, 1958, p. 6)

When the point of departure is this extreme unitary concept of one mental illness, psychiatric comorbidities cannot occur. Psychiatric comorbidity research blossomed from 1960 onward, due to a very clear articulation of non-hierarchical, non-unitary diagnostic categories in both international and American diagnostic nomenclatures for psychiatry and in the statistical classifications of the time (e.g., see Robins and Helzer, 1986; Mezzich, Honda, and Kastrup, 1994).

Based on searches using bibliographic tools such as JSTOR and Web of Science, it seems that the first published papers on these psychiatric comorbidities and the most influential papers in terms of citation impact started with questions about comorbidities observed in general medical or neurological clinics of the general medical sector (e.g., diabetes, stroke), which were thought to be important determinants of quality of care. Brook and colleagues (1977) were the first to take into account comorbidities that encompassed "adult psychiatric disorders" and "drug abuse" (e.g., see Table 2 of that article). Soon thereafter, Young (1984) identified comorbidity in a list of the three most critical issues for patient classification systems intended to control healthcare costs, payments to hospitals and physicians for patient care, hospital management, and utilization monitoring.

Goodwin (1988) was an early clinical researcher who noted "comorbidity" in depression–alcoholism associations, which had been neglected due to non-integration of depression–alcoholism services; however, Goodwin presented no empirical estimates. Empirical comorbidity estimates started to appear in reports from National Institute of Mental Health Epidemiologic Catchment Area (ECA) program of research. Leaf and colleagues (1988) were the first ECA investigators to report healthcare utilization estimates for cases with drug use disorders comorbid with other psychiatric disorders. Wells, Golding, and Burnam (1989) extended this line of ECA comorbidity research, investigating eight chronic medical conditions comorbid with drug use disorders and other psychiatric disorders.

This is not to say that there was no pertinent work at this intersection before 1988. The idea that drug use might cause psychiatric disorders surfaced before the twentieth century, as did the idea that psychiatric conditions or features of personality might foster drug self-administration (e.g., see Anthony, 2012). Erlenmeyer was one of the many clinicians of the late nineteenth century who were well informed about manias and other mood disturbances that followed onset of cocaine self-administration (e.g., see Anthony, Tien, and Petronis, 1989; Tien and Anthony, 1990; Anthony and Petronis, 1991; Crum and Anthony, 1993; Alvarado, Storr, and Anthony, 2010). Early-twentieth-century arguments favoring international regulation of cannabis included assertions such as "[Use of] … hashish is the principal cause of most of the cases of insanity occurring in Egypt" (quoted in Willoughby, 1925; Anthony, 2012).

Since 1990, an abundance of epidemiological and clinical research on the psychiatric comorbidities and drug use disorders has been published. The most highly cited articles at this intersection now seem to be from the National Comorbidity Survey (NCS), which was commissioned to provide a national perspective on lines of comorbid associations disclosed in the five-site ECA program (Kessler, McGonagle, and Zhao, 1994; cited 6338 times as of October 2011). Based on a nationally representative cross-sectional sample, the NCS found that roughly one-sixth of non-institutionalized 15–54-year-old community residents in the United States (USA) had been affected by more than one psychiatric condition; roughly 90% of cases with the most severe mental disorders had experienced three or more separately diagnosed disorders. Among these cases, only one-third had received any form of recent professional mental health care;

an estimated 8% had received services in an alcohol or other drug treatment program (Kessler, McGonagle, and Zhao, 1994).

Empirical relevance of psychiatric comorbidities linked with the drug use disorders also is seen in genetic research, progressing from an early blueprint stage toward increasingly complex investigations, mainly in the behavioral genetics tradition of twin research, and a small handful of studies tightly focused on hypotheses about 1–10 single nucleotide polymorphisms (candidate SNP loci) or with the broad spectrum view of genome-wide association studies (GWAS). The most highly cited twin research on comorbidity now is from Kendler and colleagues, who found evidence that drug use disorders seem to have disorder-specific genetic risks, whereas externalizing disorders (e.g., conduct disorder; adult antisocial behavior) are more subject to influences of shared environment. Overall, lifetime comorbidity patterns are judged to arise largely due to background genetic influences (Kendler, Prescott, Myers, and Neale, 2003); Cerdá, Sagdeo, Johnson, and Galea (2010) recently have drawn attention to exceptions. Methodological concerns will be discussed in later sections of the chapter.

3   Standardized and Validated Methods Used in the Field, Including Methodological Recommendations

3.1   Research designs

A standard design in early health services research on comorbidities involved medical records abstracting with dates of diagnosis used to manage the important time dimension mentioned in the introductory section, and to clarify which diagnosis was logged first, and which came later (e.g., Brook *et al.*, 1977; Young, 1984). Concerns about measurement qualities of psychiatric diagnoses in standard clinical records combined with uncertainties about highly selected clinical case samples have made ECA- and NCS-like cross-sectional snapshot surveys a design of choice for recent research on psychiatric comorbidities. Especially prominent twenty-first-century examples are the World Mental Health Surveys (using NCS-like methods to survey inhabitants of more than 20 different countries of the world, WMHS), the United States National Survey on Alcohol and Related Conditions (NESARC), and the US National Survey on Drug Use and Health (NSDUH). Nonetheless, the ECA and NCS reports continue to be the most highly cited source materials for comorbidity estimates, possibly due to the rigor of their predefined study populations, with removal or control of biases via careful sampling of cases and non-cases, and with sound recruitment, assessment, and analysis plans.

In theory, longitudinal elaborations of the cross-sectional survey snapshot can illuminate the time sequencing questions faced in comorbidity research. ECA, NCS, NESARC, and NSDUH follow-up surveys have been completed. Nonetheless, major methodological threats to validity in this context are (1) differential sample attrition over time (i.e., loss of comorbid participants during the follow-up interval), and (2) "reactive" measurements such that responses to follow-up assessments depend upon responses to similar assessments taken previously.

Readers interested in alternatives to the cross-sectional snapshot survey approach should consult Feinstein's textbooks (1967; 1970; 1985). A recent article by Weissman, Brown, and Talati (2011) is quite comprehensive in its coverage. Nonetheless, the essence of study design in comorbidity research can be reduced to that of a comparative study with a time axis. When the goal is to describe or to estimate a comorbidity association at some point in time, without sorting out of temporal sequencing, a strictly cross-sectional survey is appropriate, irrespective of the population, sampling, or measurement choices.

When the task requires knowing temporal sequences, the cross-sectional snapshot must assess background history and temporal sequencing of conditions. One elaboration involves use of trustworthy medical histories observed at cross-section – the appearance of each condition in the medical history lines up the temporal sequencing. Another elaboration is longitudinal and prospective, but the above-mentioned problems such as differential losses to follow-up and reactivity in repeated follow-up assessments can make the prospective design even more vexing than the cross-sectional design (e.g., see Richard, Abbacchi, Przybeck, and Gfroerer, 2007; Anthony, 2010).

A noteworthy example of a temporal sequencing research design for comorbidity studies is the epidemiologic case-crossover design. Here, the subject is used as his or her own control, and the outcome of interest is the second condition hypothesized to be triggered in a fairly rapid causal temporal sequence that runs from the first condition almost immediately to the second condition. This design requires specification of a "hazard" interval just before onset of the outcome condition in the series, and a "control" interval typically is chosen from among prior alternatives (i.e., preceding the "hazard" interval in the life of the affected case). The design logic can be understood in relation to the clinician's question, "What were you doing that was different or atypical just prior to the first appearance of this symptom?" (e.g., where the symptom often might be a feeling of numbness, pain or other discomfort). For example, we might consider the hypothesis that first onset of cocaine use triggers first onset of a panic attack. Making use of the epidemiologic case-crossover design, we sample from a predefined population, asking participants to report the month and year of the outcome condition (first onset of panic attack), with independent questions about the month and year of the first onset of cocaine use, and with both the participants and the field staff members kept blind to the hypothesis under study. If cocaine use is *not* kindling a panic attack (i.e., the null hypothesis), then the evidence favoring the null is the number of cases with onset of cocaine use in the control month, but not in the month just prior to the onset of panic attack. In contrast, evidence to reject the null hypothesis is found in the number of cases with onsets of cocaine use occurring in the month just prior to the panic attack onset, but not in the control interval. The relative risk of cocaine-attributable panic attack is estimated as the ratio of these two numbers, with the number of cases favoring the null hypothesis in the denominator. As noted elsewhere, this design is superior to co-twin research in that the subject serves as his/her own control, effectively matching all characteristics and experiences up to the point of the intervals under study, including genetic influences as well as gene–environment interactional influences, reducing "omitted variable bias" to a minimum. In contrast, the co-twin research design leaves uncertainty about "omitted variable bias". For example, whether the co-twin discordance for one clinical entity might signify some other fundamental unmeasured between-twin difference that accounts for the second entity (Wu and Anthony, 2000; O'Brien, Wu, and Anthony, 2005; O'Brien, Comment, Liang, and Anthony, 2012).

When non-participation bias, selective follow-up losses ("attrition bias"), and reactive measurement biases can be prevented, longitudinal research designs with co-twins help reduce omitted variable biases (e.g., by matching on zygosity). Multi-wave longitudinal research designs with community samples of individuals can constrain omitted variable biases in the analysis stage (e.g., via difference-of-difference and fixed effects modeling), prompting Weissman, Brown, and Talati (2011) to outline strengths of such research. These designs, twin or otherwise, are especially informative when there is prospective elaboration of the follow-up process from conception or from birth. The conception cohort prospective design has strengths due to its control over differential survivorship and losses to follow-up during gestation (e.g., as when a prenatal cocaine exposure might cause an abrupted placenta and other origins of premature fetal losses, leaving an imbalanced comparison when incidence of later psychiatric or behavioral disturbances is studied in the cocaine-exposed newborn survivors versus non-exposed newborns).

The birth cohort prospective design suffers from potential differential attrition between conception and birth, but can bring the advantage of a developmental trace from the time of delivery (e.g., see Jaffee *et al.*, 2002; Fergusson, Boden, and Horwood, 2009). Most co-twin prospective studies of comorbidity patterns have not been started at birth of the twins, and suffer from threats to validity in the form of differential survivorship until the time of recruitment and initial observation. Some noteworthy prospective co-twin research projects of newborns deserve continuing attention in relation to potential contributions in psychiatry comorbidity research (e.g., see Kim-Cohen *et al.*, 2005).

Before closing this section on research design, opportunities for experimentation should be noted. At first blush, experimentation and randomized assignment of interventions might seem to be out of reach for comorbidity researchers. Upon reflection, it seems that the leverage of random assignment of conditions and experimentation can be achieved in comorbidity research when there is an effective intervention, such as might be directed toward the first-occurring condition in order to reduce the risk of seeing the second condition in the comorbidity's temporal sequence. For example, based on population-level research designs, it is possible to make a convincing argument *against* the idea that cannabis smoking precipitates new onsets of schizophrenia that otherwise would not occur. The argument is based on the absence of observational evidence of any increases in first admissions or new treatment of incipient schizophrenia during decades when cannabis smoking was showing dramatic increases (e.g., see Degenhardt, Hall, and Lynskey, 2003). In the evidence from between-individual research designs, including discordant co-twin studies, the current evidence is not convincing because cannabis smoking in one individual versus another does not occur at random. To illustrate in the discordant co-twin context, one twin has started to smoke cannabis and has developed a psychosis, whereas the other co-twin is discordant, has not started to smoke cannabis, and has not developed a psychosis. Regrettably, this design does not account for how it happens that one twin smoked cannabis and the other co-twin has not smoked cannabis. The "omitted variable" explanation for that discordance in cannabis experience might also be the explanation for the discordance in the psychosis outcome.

These currently unresolved issues might be brought into focus in an experiment on the many co-twins who jointly have become cannabis smokers, with a cannabis smoking cessation intervention assigned at random to one twin but not the co-twin. If it is persistence of cannabis smoking that accounts for an excess risk of psychosis or psychosis-like experiences, then the post-experiment observed level or risk of these experiences should differ across the two co-twins, to the extent that the randomly assigned intervention has been effective. Even when this type of experimentation is not possible, long-term studies can be conducted on the cannabis–psychosis hypothesis, as was done to produce evidence that tobacco smoking cessation eventually is followed by a return to baseline levels of mortality risk. Nonetheless, the agentry of random assignment in a cessation intervention helps to constrain threats to validity that otherwise cannot be constrained in the observational research context. In section 4, the chapter returns to this topic.

3.2 The "population" in comorbidity research

Prior sections of the chapter have alluded to the importance of a predefined population in the standardization of methods for comorbidity research at the intersection of the psychiatric disturbances and the drug use disorders. The general concept of population was introduced in section 3.1, where several prospective research design alternatives were compared and contrasted. In particular, the study of a conception cohort was described as superior to the study of a birth cohort of newborns. For example, with respect to a hypothesized effect of a prenatal drug exposure on subsequent psychiatric disturbances, that same prenatal drug exposure might cause selective attrition (e.g., fetal death), with resulting crucial imbalances observed among newborns. In an extreme case, the drug-exposed newborns might be healthier than the non-exposed newborns, when drug exposure culls via fetal loss, and the drug-exposed newborns qualify as hardy survivors after challenge.

Can useful comorbidity research be done without a predefined population? Some observers would count lack of a predefined population as a major weakness in a comorbidity research design. This author's perspective is that a predefined population is an important strength, and without it, the research team cannot look into the possibility of threats to validity in the form of selection biases. Nonetheless, some of the most highly cited psychiatric comorbidity research is based upon clinical case samples where there was no predefined population under study (e.g., see Sheline, Wang, and Gado, 1996; cited 897 times). Cerdá, Sagdeo, Johnson, and Galea (2010) recently produced a systematic review of methods used in almost 100 recent studies of the genetic and environmental influences on psychiatric comorbidity, and provided a useful table that describes all of the various types of study population that have been predefined in this domain of research.

The time concept comes into play when we consider the idea of comorbidity research with predefined and specified populations. To provide an empirical illustration, the three panels presented in Table 4.1 introduce an attempt to bring the time concept into our thoughts about the population or populations under study in comorbidity research, with a focus on a hypothesized comorbidity association that links recent depression and recent tobacco dependence. The data are from audio-enhanced computerized self-interview (ACASI) assessments in one of the most recent cross-sectional surveys of the US non-institutionalized civilian population aged 12 years and older, completed for the National Survey on Drug Use and Health. The ACASI variable depicted in each column of each panel table is a 0/1 binary indicator of whether any doctor, within the year prior to the date of assessment, had told the individual that he or she had depression. One might think of this variable as pertaining to "diagnosed depression." The ACASI variable depicted in each row of each panel table is a 0/1 binary indicator of whether the individual had smoked tobacco within the year prior to the date of assessment *and* had said "Within 30 minutes after waking up" in response to the following standardized survey question: "On the days that you smoke, how soon after you wake up do you have your first cigarette?" One might think of this independently assessed variable as an indicator for the presence of tobacco dependence, at least with respect to the neuroadaptive changes that occur after sustained tobacco cigarette smoking. (There was "blinding" in this study: neither the participant nor the field staff member knew that the depression–tobacco association would be estimated.)

The "time" variable is pertinent. First, the time frame of the questions references the year prior to the assessment date. Different estimates can be obtained by shifting the time frame (e.g., to the lifetime history), and may be biased if the sample excludes all persons who died after onset of drug use, depression, or both. Second, there is no assertion that tobacco dependence precedes depression in these tables, or that depression precedes tobacco in these tables. Here, we have two "coexistent phenomena" of the comorbid type noted by Virchow, and we cannot be confident about the causal processes at play, given these data. The "insidious" onset of both tobacco dependence and depression introduces complexity. Temporal sequencing and drawing causal inferences are easier when there is an abrupt onset of one event followed by another abrupt onset of the second event, as is illustrated in the epidemiologic case-crossover research design as applied to newly incident cocaine use and the first onset of a panic attack, as described in section 3.1.

A third reason why the time dimension is pertinent involves the fact that the Table 4.1 data entries are from a single year of the NSDUH, which now is repeated each year. Can the observed comorbidity associations be replicated? Will they ever be replicated in other years, or in other populations? This is an external generalizability issue that deserves greater attention in comorbidity research. In section 4 of this chapter, this issue will be revisited in the form of a general recommendation to ask comorbidity researchers about inference beyond the observed sample space and about the external generalizability of their observed comorbidity estimates.

Even though the data from Table 4.1 come from a single NSDUH survey year, the observed variation in the estimated tobacco–depression associations across the panels of the table serves to illustrate the value of a predefined population. In Panel A, akin to what one might specify in a clinical trials network or other multi-clinic study of national scope, the predefined population is limited to all US non-institutionalized civilians aged 12 years or older who had been in detoxification or other treatment programs for alcohol and/or other drug problems (excluding tobacco) during the month of October in 2008. This is a perfectly respectable predefined population, nested within the overall NSDUH sample, and assessed using the standardized ACASI approach. The resulting estimated odds ratio, OR = 0.8, indicates essentially no depression–tobacco association in this predefined population ($p = 0.712$; unweighted sample $n = 340$). If this evidence from Panel A, or from similar studies of predefined clinical populations in treatment, were to be published in a clinical research article, the lines of comorbidity research might well come to a halt – given absence of the foundational evidence required for more probing research on a depression–tobacco syndrome, and the potential causal origins of the syndrome (i.e., greater than chance co-occurrence).

As for Table 4.1's Panel B, the predefined study population is the complement of the Panel A study population. It was predefined to consist of all individuals *not* in alcohol or other drug treatment services in October 2008, as sampled and assessed for the NSDUH. With the study population predefined and studied in this fashion, there is evidence of a moderately strong association that links diagnosed depression with this indicator of tobacco dependence (OR = 2.2; $p < 0.001$; unweighted sample $n = 55,432$). That is, with the study population predefined to encompass individuals not in treatment, the resulting tangible association might well provoke new research on the tobacco–depression association.

Of course, the union of the non-intersecting Panel A and Panel B study populations also can be specified as a predefined study population. Defined so as to encompass all non-institutionalized civilians, irrespective of receipt of alcohol or other drug treatment services in October 2008, the resulting estimate for the US non-institutionalized population is depicted in Table 4.1's Panel C, which appropriately applies the survey analysis weights to individuals in treatment programs and those not in treatment programs. The result is not appreciably different from the estimate obtained for the Panel B study population (i.e., OR = 2.2; $p < 0.001$; $n = 55,772$). That is, the evidence lends some support to the idea that diagnosed depression and tobacco dependence are associated in the population at large, in the survey year represented here. Nonetheless, if the population had been restricted to patients in treatment, as often is true in clinical sample comorbidity research, the different conclusion described above would have been reached. The observed point estimate for the treatment segment of this nationally representative population sample actually was inverse at 0.8, on the opposite side of the null odds ratio value of 1.0, when compared to the observed population-level point estimate of 2.2. As for whether an unweighted sample of size $n = 340$ might not have sufficient power to detect an OR = 2.2, a rough power calculation suggests otherwise, given observed distributions of the depression and tobacco dependence variables under study in the treatment segment of this nationally representative sample (http://sampsize.sourceforge.net/iface/s3.html).

The reader can decide which panel of Table 4.1 represents the most compelling source of evidence about the tobacco–depression association, and may wish to judge whether we should be satisfied with evidence from comorbidity research that is based solely upon predefined populations of patients in treatment, or whether decisions about the potential clinical or causal significance of observed comorbidities require more definitive evidence from epidemiological population samples. Cochrane's perspective, from 1965, is clearly articulated in his statement of what he thought would be required to evaluate a then-prevailing hypothesis about a dysphagia–anemia comorbidity: "This hypothesis of association can, of course, only be adequately tested by comparing an unselected group of people with this particular type of dysphagia with a group of the same age and sex, chosen *at random from people without dysphagia living in the same area* as the former" (emphasis added; Cochrane, 1965). The information chosen by Cochrane as definitive evidence on this topic was from a community survey that had just been completed in a coal-mining district of Wales known as Rhondda Fach, with ascertainment of all dysphagia cases in the population, and Cochrane noted:

> ... to everyone's surprise no difference as regards anemia was found between the two groups [community members with and without dysphagia] ... No evidence in support of the existence of the syndrome could be found. Although this finding needs confirming in another area, it looks as if Paterson and Kelly's day as a syndrome is over; they must be content with being a symptom in the future. (Cochrane, 1965, p. 441)

In the conclusion of his article, Cochrane offered some advice: "Probably the best advice to give those who are nursing new syndromes in the back of their minds is to arrange a critical test with the help of an epidemiologist before anything is published at all" (Cochrane, 1965, p. 442).

Cochrane's advice may be extreme, but in the comorbidity research domain, there are more than negligible or minor weaknesses when the population of interest is specified after the fact, in place of a pre-specification of a defined population from which unselected cases and unselected non-cases can be recruited for observation. Definitive evidence about comorbidity relationships may not require the involvement of an epidemiologist and may not require an epidemiological sample, but it does require a pre-specification of a defined population from which unselected cases and unselected non-cases will be sampled, recruited, and assessed. Otherwise, one important form of selection bias will remain hidden from view.

3.3   "Drawing the sample" for comorbidity research

Within the domain of research on neuropsychiatric disturbances, the top six most highly cited empirical research reports are based upon large sample epidemiological studies such as the National Comorbidity Survey in the United States, akin to the nationally representative sample survey upon which Table 4.1 entries are based (e.g., see Kessler, McGonagle, and Zhao, 1994; cited 6338 times as of October 2011). The next most highly cited article in the list concerns hippocampal atrophy and depression, and is based upon ten depressed patients and ten matched controls recruited for a neuropsychiatric research project with material from clinics affiliated with a single university-based center at the University of Washington in Seattle (Sheline, Wang, and Gado, 1996; cited 897 times).

Notwithstanding the seven-fold ratio of citations for these two articles, clinicians studying small clinic-based samples and laboratory scientists studying small laboratory-based samples should take some encouragement from the fact that the sample of ten patients and ten matched controls assembled by Sheline and colleagues in a single university medical setting can achieve almost 1000 citations within 15 years of publication of the results. A concept of "particularistic" research is pertinent here (Miettinen, 1985). It is almost certain that Sheline and colleagues, working in the mid-1990s, did not have the local area population of Seattle, Washington, in mind when they recruited the sample for their study. Reading the Sheline comorbidity research article, one will see a reach in the direction of Avogadro's number – that is, estimation of a relationship such as might hold for all persons in all times in the "universal" research approach that Miettinen contrasts with the "particularistic" approach.

In contrast, the US senators and congressional representatives almost certainly had a "particularistic" research agenda in mind when they authorized the National Institute on Mental Health (NIMH) to commission the National Comorbidity Survey. Egged on by reports from the NIMH ECA surveys in five metropolitan areas of the USA, they wanted to know whether the NIMH, National Institute on Drug Abuse (NIDA), and National Institute on Alcohol Abuse and Alcoholism (NIAAA), and Substance Abuse and Mental Health Services Administration (SAMHSA) might be double-dipping, each agency making its case for federal support for a large number of cases who concurrently suffered from alcohol, drug, and other neuropsychiatric or behavioral disorders (i.e., the ADM disorders). If they had anything other than "particularistic" public health research in mind, these notions of research findings such as might apply to all persons in all times were not expressed in the legislative history of the NCS appropriations bill.

What of the NCS research team? What did they have in mind? Based on the experience of reading the NCS research reports (and being an NCS-affiliated investigator), the chapter author can assert that the research team has made no systematic attempt to ground the NCS estimates in the particularistic experiences of the United States population. Instead, there was an attempt to draw inferences from the sample under study to a much larger context. Indeed, in my own NCS research about the transition from drug use to drug dependence, it was my goal to provide an empirical basis for regularities such as might be applicable for the long term and over the long haul. To illustrate, we had a large population concept in mind when we harnessed the NCS data to estimate that roughly 1 in 3 tobacco smokers developed a tobacco dependence syndrome, that roughly 1 in 6 cocaine users developed a cocaine dependence syndrome, that roughly 1 in 8–9 alcohol users developed an alcohol dependence syndrome, and that roughly 1 in 9–11 cannabis smokers developed a cannabis dependence syndrome (Anthony, Warner, and Kessler, 1994).

To be sure, we expected challenges in subsequent empirical evidence from other sources in other parts of the world and at other times, as in the NESARC project and in the NCS analogue projects in the World Mental Health Surveys. Nonetheless, we published these estimates not simply to characterize the public health situation in the United States in the early 1990s, such as one might disseminate through the Morbidity and Mortality Weekly Reports (MMWR) of the US Centers on Disease Control and Prevention, but rather to create some benchmark values that might be challenged in future research (or confirmed).

There are alternatives to ECA- and NCS-like community-based sampling, such as sampling from driving license records or from random-digit dialing telephone surveys, but for the most part these sampling "frames" are regarded as inferior to the sampling frames devised for multi-stage area probability sampling for reasons that probably are obvious to the chapter reader. For example, those who apply for and obtain driving licenses are not apt to constitute a representative sample of the total population of interest, when the goal is to estimate comorbidity associations. Moreover, those who now have telephone numbers included in random-digit dialing surveys no longer are likely to constitute a representative sample of the total study population for the purposes of comorbidity research. As such, here, even when the predefined study population of interest might be exactly the same, variations in the approach to drawing the sample may introduce biases (e.g., via use of non-standard sampling frames).

At this point, it may be instructive to compare the quite large estimates for prevalence of Major Depressive Episode and of Drug Use Disorders, as obtained in the recent Internet-Based MGS2 Control Sample project (Sanders *et al.*, 2010), with the much smaller estimates obtained from the NCS – even though the study population for these surveys was predefined to be roughly identical. Estimated disorder prevalence proportions in the MGS2 project were some 1.5 to 3 times larger than were observed in other more conventionally derived study estimates such as those from the NCS. For example, the NCS prevalence estimates for alcohol dependence and for dependence on internationally regulated drugs were roughly 14% and 7–8%, respectively; the NCS prevalence estimate for major depression was 17%. Corresponding MGS2 prevalence estimates were 23% for alcohol dependence, 12% for other drug dependence, and 40% for major depression. It is not possible to pinpoint the exact source of the variation in these survey estimates, but the two projects used completely different approaches to drawing and recruiting the samples. The NCS project used a standard multi-stage area probability sampling approach of the type that also had been used in the ECA project, whereas the Internet-Based MGS2 Control Sample was drawn primarily via random-digit dialing of the type used in political science and consumer preference surveys. The NCS project was able to secure participation of more than 70% of the designated respondents in the community sample; the corresponding value for the Internet-Based MGS2 Control Sample seems to have been well under 50%. In addition, the NCS project included rigorous sub-studies to probe into biases that might have been created by differential non-participation. This type of sub-study represents "best practice" in this type of comorbidity research (e.g., see Kessler *et al.*, 1997; Kessler *et al.*, 2004).

Whereas most population-based comorbidity research projects have not yet applied costly measurement approaches based on "in silica" technology, it is possible to yoke community survey sampling of predefined populations with "in silica" technology required for brain mapping and gene sequencing in comorbidity research. For example, decades ago, our Johns Hopkins-based research groups showed how it was possible to harness local area probability sampling with MRI brain imaging, neurocognitive testing, and diagnostic assessments (e.g., see Folstein, Anthony, and Parhad, 1985; Schretlen, Pearlson, and Anthony, 2000). Nonetheless, this is not an approach to be recommended for nationally representative sample survey research at present, due to logistics and cost issues.

Even so, it may be stated that the most definitive comorbidity research will include a reach from the sample in hand out to a larger predefined population, and an effort to seek results that apply beyond the sample in hand to the larger human condition, working toward such estimates as might hold for all peoples in all times, and not constrained by the geopolitical or time boundaries of the sample in hand. Nonetheless, it is possible to craft highly influential comorbidity research by drawing samples that fall short of the standards of nationally representative research survey samples.

For some useful comorbidity research, one might define "population" in a circumscribed fashion. To illustrate, the directors of a large corporation's employee health service might wish to know how often alcohol dependence, nicotine dependence, and major depression are co-occurring so as to re-organize the corporation's service delivery plans accordingly. Alternatively, a unit that uses newspaper ads to recruit young people for medication development trials or behavioral psychopharmacology research might wish to know the probability that a study recruit from this source might be excluded due to a serious neuropsychiatric syndrome such as psychosis or mood disorder with recent suicidal intent or ideation. A large university health program director might wish to know how many students visiting the health clinics are affected by neuropsychiatric comorbidities, again with service planning in mind. These illustrations exemplify "particularistic" research or a special kind of "operations research" of utility within the specific "population under study," but not necessarily with generalizability beyond the time and space boundaries of each population from which recruits are drawn.

One reason why the United States National Institutes of Health continue to make or to plan investments in neuropsychiatric and behavioral research on the populations of Denmark, Iceland, and other Scandinavian countries is that these countries have universal health coverage with fairly generous benefits that cover neuropsychiatric and behavioral disturbances, and have organized population record-keeping systems and diagnoses of reasonable reliability and validity. In these contexts, basic comorbidity research requires no survey sampling and assessment protocols for individuals. Instead, newly incident cases of each of two or more comorbid disorders can be identified via record review, and controls without the disorder, as recorded, can be sampled from among non-cases alive at the time each newly incident case is detected. Because temporal sequencing of disorders can be studied on the basis of dates of first admissions or first diagnoses, this population research context makes it possible to manage the time dimension and to estimate the degree to which the risk of developing disorder A might depend upon a prior history of disorder B, or vice versa. When family history data are in the records, along with data on season of birth, birth complications, socioeconomic status of the index cases and controls and the family members, the result is a fairly rich set of data for probing population-level comorbidity research. Here, the predefined population is one and the same as the sample under study in the research project (e.g., see Flensborg-Madsen *et al.*, 2009).

In sum, it is not enough to specify a predefined population under study for comorbidity research. It also is necessary to have a sampling approach that provides protection against sampling biases. These biases can be introduced at the stage of specifying the "sampling frame" according to which the sample is drawn (e.g., multi-stage area probability sampling versus random-digit dialing versus driving license sampling), or during the recruitment process (e.g., yielding participation levels so low as to call the validity of the observed sample-based estimates into question). "Best practice" in this aspect of comorbidity research methods continues to be multi-stage area probability sampling where the 100% census lists, citizenship (voting) rosters, or population registers are not available, with a sound plan to achieve designated respondent participation levels of 70% or better, and with deliberate study of participants versus non-participants, as described in Kessler *et al.* (2004), whenever participation levels fall below optimized values approaching 100% participation. At present, in psychiatric epidemiology, the substitution of sampling and recruitment approaches found suitable for market research or political science seems to yield contrived estimates that lack credibility when compared to other research approaches (e.g., as in the Internet-Based MGS2 Control Sample of Sanders *et al.*, 2010). Until careful probes for the sources of variation in estimates have been conducted, it will be difficult to recommend internet-based sampling and recruitment approaches in comorbidity research, which might represent major weaknesses in approach.

4   Measurement

For the purposes of this chapter, the "measurement" of comorbidity encompasses (1) how comorbidity is defined, (2) how the comorbidity definitions are made operational in empirical research constructs, and (3) the specific ratings or items used to measure the constructs. Cerda, Sagdeo, Johnson, and Galea (2010) present a comprehensive list of specific ratings, items, and interview schedules or questionnaires that were used in almost 100 publications about psychiatric comorbidity. Other useful reviews at a conceptual level are available, not only for adult psychiatry, but also for child and adolescent psychiatry (e.g., Schuckit, 2006; Angold, Costello, and Erkanli, 1999; Costello, Erkanli, Federman, and Angold, 1999; Angold and Costello, 2009).

Standardization of comorbidity definitions is required, especially with many scientific and professional disciplines involved. To illustrate, at first blush, distinctions between a "primary" condition and a "secondary" condition in psychiatric comorbidity research might seem to be a straightforward issue for resolution, requiring little more than a simple definition. Nonetheless, sometimes "primary" may refer to the first-occurring of two conditions. Alternatively, "primary" might be the more fundamental condition, as in the conventional pre-emption of the major depression diagnosis in the presence of psychosis or an acute intoxication state.

Once conceptual definitions are set, the task is to make the definitions operational. For example, consider a generally dysthymic patient, possibly with persistent subsyndromal low mood as a generalized response set irrespective of day-to-day happenings, but for whom the first episode of Major Depression does not occur until age 17 years, in an example of a "double depression" comorbidity (e.g., see Wells *et al.*, 1992). Thereafter, tobacco cigarette smoking starts, and within 1 year the patient has developed dependence on tobacco cigarette smoking. In this example, Major Depression would seem to be primary and tobacco dependence secondary, but let us consider an alternative patient, also with a persistent subsyndromal dysthymic mood, with onset of tobacco smoking at age 14 years followed by tobacco dependence within 1 year. Thereafter, the first episode of Major Depression occurs at age 17 years. In this case, the tobacco dependence might seem to be primary with respect to Major Depressive Episode (MDE), in that tobacco dependence (TD) appears first in the TD–MDE sequence of syndromes. Nonetheless, in both cases, there is the background of persistent subsyndromal dysthymic mood that might be regarded as a primary liability trait or diathesis substrate fostering later co-occurrence of both MDE and TD. Here, the chickenpox–shingles example might be useful. In any effort to understand the chickenpox–shingles comorbidity, the comorbidity research team would ignore the underlying varicella zoster virus (VZV) infection at its peril. Similarly, if we were to ignore the dysthymic mood substrate from which both MDE and TD emerge, a threat to validity would be faced, analogous to designating chickenpox as primary because it occurs first, with shingles seen as secondary to chickenpox – with VZV infection as truly causal "omitted variable." Examples of "omitted variables" are apt to surface more rapidly as neuroscience, genetics, and basic pathophysiological pathways are brought into play in the psychiatric comorbidity research setting (e.g., see Brenner and Beauchaine, 2011; Johnson and Shorvon, 2011).

Diagnostic hierarchies also must be made operational. To illustrate, in the ECA survey research generally, the NIMH Diagnostic Interview Schedule (DIS) tried to implement the MDE hierarchy by asking participants whether depression symptoms and episodes ever occurred at times other than when they were using alcohol or other drugs; a similar approach of asking the participants to account for these sources of variation in their depression experiences has been taken in the NCS, NESARC, and World Mental Health Surveys. Needless to say, this approach places a lot of reliance upon the participant's own capacity to make individual-level causal inferences about the origins of his or her symptom experiences. An alternative approach harnesses the power of multiple regression modeling. In this approach, the participant is not asked to explain the sources of variation in his or her psychiatric experiences. Instead, the multiple regression model incorporates covariate terms for onset of drug use, as well as other potentially influential covariates, and seeks estimates of the comorbidity associations under these constraints, without reliance upon self-reports of what causes this or that (e.g., see Clarke *et al.*, 2010).

Back in the early 1980s, as part of the work of the Baltimore ECA site, our research team designed a Clinical Reappraisal Study, with board-eligible psychiatrists completing standardized diagnostic assessments of 810 of the community sample survey participants (almost 25% of the total sample). The examiners were blind to DIS status, and made use of the Present State Examination with adaptation for evaluation of the DSM-III criteria. What we found was considerable disagreement between the DIS diagnoses of Major Depression and the psychiatrist-diagnosed Major Depression, with many of the disagreements traced back to diagnostic hierarchy issues. For example, when the psychiatrists found heavy drinking or other drug use among the examinees, they were hesitant to make the diagnosis of active Major Depressive Episode because they could not be certain that the mood disturbances were independent of the concurrent drinking or drug use. The participants often said that their clinical features of depression were not due to drinking or drug use, but the clinicians could not be certain that this was true; the DIS approach is one that accepts the participants' reports and causal inferences at face value (Anthony *et al.*, 1985). In this instance, the clinicians approached the diagnostic challenge as it often is faced in the practice of psychiatry, as stated here by the two main developers of the DIS: "if an alcohol abuser becomes depressed, one cannot know whether the depression is only a side effect of his alcohol abuse unless he stops drinking so that it can be observed whether the depression lifts" (Robins and Helzer, 1986, p. 416).

Be that as it may, at present, the most highly standardized diagnostic assessments in comorbidity research involve the use of audio-enhanced computer-assisted personal assessment approaches in the context of community surveys of dwelling unit residents, more akin to a self-rated questionnaire with laptop display of the questions and key-board input of the participant's responses. A field staff member completes sampling, recruitment, and consent process task, introduces the participant to the laptop computer approach and provides basic instructions, and then leaves the participant alone. This is not an "interview" in the sense of an interaction "between" two people. Instead, if it is an "interview" at all, it is the computer program interviewing the participant, with pre-programmed branching to gather details about experiences (e.g., episodes of depressed mood when they have occurred), and with skip or "gating" patterns when it seems that the details are not essential to the assessment. The process has become highly standardized with anticipated increases in diagnostic reliability, and there is some evidence that this approach may yield more complete and accurate reporting of sensitive behaviors. Nonetheless, the best research of this type also will include a clinical reappraisal study of the type conducted in the Baltimore ECA project, with at least a subsample of the participants, in order to probe validity assumptions, as can be seen in the more recent clinical reappraisal for the National Comorbidity Survey Replication survey of adolescents in the USA (Green *et al.*, 2011). There continues to be considerable controversy about variations induced in relation to aspects of assessment such as the use of computers versus field interviewers, the skip or "gating" algorithms, and the prominence of government sponsorship of the survey work (e.g., see Grucza, Abbacchi, Przybeck, and Gfroerer, 2007; Degenhardt, Bohnert, and Anthony, 2007; 2008; Degenhardt, Cheng, and Anthony, 2007).

As regards the specific items or ratings used in psychiatric comorbidity research, there is not yet a sufficient level of standardization to permit a specific recommendation beyond some pragmatic considerations. For research in the United States, an argument can be made in favor of using the depression and drug dependence assessments of the National Survey on Drug Use and Health because this is a large-sample national survey repeated annually, with estimates and public use datasets that can help comorbidity researchers calibrate their own local area sample findings with those of a concurrent nationwide survey – that is, in a check on external generalizability. Nonetheless, there are some features of the NSDUH assessments that might not be satisfactory for all purposes, including a general focus on the past 12 months in the life of the participant, and without the details in lifetime history that a comorbidity researcher might like to have when gauging primary versus secondary disorders along the time dimension. For investigators outside the USA, the corresponding advantage would be to make use of diagnostic assessments being used in other national or regional surveys at least roughly contemporaneous with one's own comorbidity research project (e.g., the most recently devised WMHS assessment protocols, which are based on the US NCS protocol).

Cerdá, Sagdeo, Johnson, and Galea (2010) have produced a comprehensive list of potential measurement tools for comorbidity research in this area, based on their systematic review of published comorbidity studies. Neale and colleagues (2006) have addressed methodological issues that cover such decisions as must be made about whether dimensional approaches might be preferred over categorical approaches. Krueger and Piasecki (2002), among others, provide examples of the value to be gained in the use of dimensional approaches, which have become especially popular in research on psychiatric comorbidities observed in children and adolescents (e.g., see Youngstrom, Findling, and Calabrese, 2003; Hudziak, Achenbach, Althoff, and Pine, 2007).

Finally, readers with a background in psychopharmacology and drug treatment services research may wish to know that familiar standardized measurement tools such as the Profile of Mood States (POMS), the Addiction Severity Index (ASI) subscales, and the SF-36 have not yet become widely adopted for comorbidity research, as gauged by science citation impact. To illustrate, summed across the handful of published journal articles on psychiatric and drug use comorbidity studies that used the POMS, the aggregate number of science citations as of October 2011 is only 15. The comorbidity research articles using the ASI and the SF-36 have done much better, but neither of these measurement tools appears to have achieved comorbidity research prominence levels achieved by DSM-focused measurements. Of course, the tool must be chosen with a specific task in mind, and for some tasks, the POMS, the ASI, and the SF-36 will provide the best possible measurement tool for comorbidity research at the intersection of the psychiatric disturbances and drug use research.

In order to reinforce points made in prior sections, it should be noted that strong measurement does not ensure valid findings. The Internet-Based MGS2 Control Sample project apparently used a sound measurement approach involving standardized online self-report questionnaires designed to tap DSM constructs, akin to those used in the US NCS and NSDUH assessments. One might surmise that it was the MGS2 project's unorthodox approach to population predefinition and community sampling that produced the anomalous findings described above, although the validity of the MGS2 online measurement approaches deserves clinical reappraisal and validity studies of the type completed in the ECA and NCS programs of research.

5 Analysis

The introduction to this chapter provided an initial orientation to the odds ratio (OR), the "workhorse" statistic for psychiatric comorbidity research for a variety of reasons. A more direct alternative to the odds ratio is the prevalence ratio, which now can be estimated with covariate adjustments under a multiple regression model, but it requires an adaptation of specifications for the generalized linear model (e.g., Poisson regression; see Barros and Hirataka, 2003). As such, estimation of the odds ratio cannot be described as "best practice" in comorbidity research, but it certainly has become highly conventional and standardized in such research (e.g., see de Graaf *et al.*, 2010).

Availability of public use datasets with online analysis options now makes it relatively easy to investigate comorbidities in large-sample field survey data (e.g., NSDUH), but many published analyses of these data do not meet standards of the field. Drawn with multi-stage area probability sampling, with selection probabilities varying across population subgroups, the samples virtually always require use of sampling weights, and analysis methods appropriate for area-clustered observations. There are very clear instructions about these facets of analysis, available not only in monograph form (e.g., Heeringa, West, and Berglund, 2010), but also in online publications (e.g., see http://www.ats.ucla.edu/stat/stata/seminars/svy_stata_8/default.htm). However, some comorbidity researchers choose to ignore these instructions, and make the assumption of simple random sampling with no "survey design effects," which often introduces serious errors in relation to correct estimation of variances and tests of statistical significance.

Several advanced analysis developments deserve attention because they generally have been neglected in comorbidity research. For example, in anticipation of comorbidity research at the intersection of depression and drinking of alcoholic beverages, Gallo, Anthony, and Muthén (1994) started a line of research on the possibility that conventional standardized diagnostic assessments of depression of the type implemented in the Diagnostic Interview Schedule (DIS) or Composite International Diagnostic Interview (CIDI) might not meet such "measurement equivalence" assumptions as would be required to make valid comparisons of depression across population subgroups. Using latent structure models with simultaneous estimation of measurement parameters (e.g., "factor loadings") and structural parameters (e.g., regression slopes), they found evidence of measurement non-equivalence with respect to the age subgroups under study. Chen and Anthony (2003), studying cannabis dependence, also found evidence of measurement non-equivalence in cannabis dependence assessments for earlier-onset versus later-onset cannabis smokers. More recently, Neale and colleagues (2006) formalized these problems of measurement non-equivalence in an article about methodological issues in measurement of drug-related constructs, including coverage of the general topic of "differential item functioning" such that the utility of a standardized questionnaire or scale item in one subgroup might differ from the utility of that same standardized item in another subgroup. In the research by Chen and Anthony (2003), there clearly was a problem of differential item functioning in the assessment of the "tolerance" criterion of cannabis dependence: some of the earlier-onset cannabis smokers described pharmacological tolerance to cannabis after no more than 1–3 occasions of cannabis smoking, whereas this was not the case for older-onset cannabis smokers.

These lines of methodological research create uncertainties that should be examined more completely in comorbidity studies. For example, it is quite possible that standardized drug dependence items function differently across subgroups defined by presence or absence of psychiatric disturbances. To date, most comorbidity research teams have assumed measurement equivalence in their analyses.

To close this section, several analysis advances in comorbidity research have been made in recent years, and they deserve the attention of the more numerate members of the comorbidity research community. Some especially interesting contributions on the mediation of comorbid relationships have been prepared by members of the World Mental Health Surveys research project (e.g., see Kessler *et al.*, 2011a; 2011b). In addition to more conventional latent structure analysis approaches, the research group has devised novel analysis approaches that integrate survival or time-to-event analyses with the latent structure approaches. These novel approaches will require additional methodological research, but at present they represent innovations of potential significance and utility in the field of psychiatric comorbidity research.

6 Conclusions, Including Directions for Future Research

This concluding section of the chapter is intended to provide a brief synopsis of limitations in past research as a guide to recommendations and directions for future research projects where drug use or drug use disorders intersect with other neuropsychiatric disturbances and disorders. One limitation is that the domain of published articles on these comorbidities is heavily populated by particularistic projects of the type described above, with little or no guidance by advance hypotheses, and with no reach toward the larger "universal" context of inquiry in public health research.

In many published studies, a decision has been made to administer a broad spectrum of diagnostic assessments to patients being seen in clinics or hospitals, and a sizeable number of assessments have been secured. Thereafter, data management and analysis tasks required to disclose patterns of comorbid associations in these practice settings. By most of the standards covered in this chapter, this type of research project is first rate. Nonetheless, the study population has not been predefined so as to clarify the significance of the completed research beyond the domain of "particularistic" research about a specific practice setting. What is required is advance specification of a predefined study population for the research, without which the sample-based evidence remains particularistic, potentially publishable in a government report, or in a newsletter or periodical such as the CDC Morbidity and Mortality Weekly Reports, but not necessarily suitable for publication as a refereed journal article.

This commonly encountered situation provokes a clear recommendation to reviewers of submitted articles and proposals in the domain of psychiatric comorbidity research. Namely, it is recommended that the reviewer should ask about the predefined population under study, and to look into whether the goal of the research is limited to the "particularistic" form of empirical studies that might best be published in newsletters and MMWR-type venues, or whether the goal is more universal and deserving of publication in the best science or clinical practice journals. Ultimately, this is a question about the "sample space" and external generalizability of the empirical estimates.

The limitation that comes next in priority involves sampling and recruitment of participants, labeled as "drawing the sample" in this chapter's sectional organization, but encompassing not only the sampling operations but also the experimental control over participation levels. Where there is no specification of a predefined population, it is difficult and sometimes impossible to report levels of participation or non-response. In a multi-stage area probability sample, the participation level takes the differing stages into account, as in the Baltimore ECA studies, where the probability of participation of sampled dwelling units had to be multiplied by the probability of participation of a designated respondent within the dwelling unit, yielding an 82% participation level. In longitudinal or prospective research on comorbidity associations, the initial participation level must be chain-multiplied through successive follow-up assessment participation levels, and the initial cross-sectional 82% can become compromised, even when only 10% is lost from one follow-up to the next. To illustrate, a four-wave longitudinal study with 82% participation at cross-section, followed by only 10% loss in three waves, ultimately yields a sample participation level below 60% (= 0.82 × 0.9 × 0.9 × 0.9). Clearly, a strong recommendation for future comorbidity research projects involves more careful consideration of non-participation, particularly when non-participation might be related to the combination of comorbid conditions under study, and sub-studies of non-participation to probe for influential differences in participation, as illustrated in the NCS project (e.g., see Kessler *et al.*, 2004).

A comorbidity research team's choices about measurements taken and analyses completed are somewhat more difficult to critique in relation to established methodological standards. Whether the research design is cross-sectional or prospective and longitudinal in nature, there will be issues that involve the research team's choice among options for specifying when each condition starts. In research involving drug use, there is advantage to specifying the onset of the drug use disorder from the date of the onset of the drug use, with an assumption that a subsequent drug dependence process is driven forward in a sequence of repetitive drug taking and formation of a drug dependence syndrome (e.g., see Anthony, 2002; Anthony, 2010). By the same token, in research on depression–drugs comorbid associations, one might wish to specify the date of the first-experienced 2-week interval of depressed mood as the onset date for a depression syndrome, even when the major depressive episode does not coalesce into a syndrome for many months or even years. Judgments are required here, and one recommendation for future research may involve increased expert consensus in judgments about these aspects of measurement.

The best analysis plans for comorbidity research will include probes into assumptions of measurement equivalence. If measurement equivalence cannot be assumed, then it is difficult to interpret comorbidity relationships. A major threat to validity in this context involves shared methods covariation such that response tendencies create larger associations than otherwise would be present or induce smaller associations than otherwise would be present. An example of "constructive" shared methods covariation can be imagined quite readily in self-reports on conduct problems, antisocial behavior, and socially maladaptive drug taking. A young person who is willing to self-report one facet of conduct problems (e.g., teasing animals, setting fires, starting fights) may be more likely to self-report another facet of conduct problems (e.g., onset of tobacco or cannabis smoking). All else being equal, the resulting shared methods covariation will yield an artifactual influence on the comorbidity association that links conduct problems with socially maladaptive drug use.

In the opposite direction, a study participant unwilling to disclose a risk-taking behavior of lower sensitivity, such as eating raw oysters, may also be unwilling to disclose a risk-taking behavior of higher sensitivity, such as smoking cannabis. As such, in the odds ratio estimation of the strength of association that links the one risk-taking behavior with the other risk-taking behavior, the odds ratio becomes artifactually elevated by the shared methods covariation.

Given an increased sophistication in statistical modeling of measurement challenges, as well as modeling of causal structures, one might expect the future of comorbidity research to be enhanced by progress and application of novel analysis approaches. The recent articles by Neale and colleagues (2006) and by Kessler and colleagues (2011a; 2011b) represent some of the vanguard developments in this field.

Finally, the chapter has included ideas about using randomized assignment and experimentation in comorbidity research projects. Regrettably, in research where psychiatric disturbances intersect with the drug use disorders, there are no good examples. This gap in the evidence constitutes an area for future inquiry, and prompts a recommendation in favor of more experimentation in the comorbidity research setting.

References

Alvarado GF, Storr CL, and Anthony JC (2010) Suspected causal association between cocaine use and occurrence of panic. *Substance Use and Misuse* 45(7–8): 1019–1032.

Angold A and Costello EJ (2009) Nosology and measurement in child and adolescent psychiatry. *Journal of Child Psychology and Psychiatry* 50(1–2): 9–15.

Angold A, Costello EJ, and Erkanli A (1999) Comorbidity. *Journal of Child Psychology and Psychiatry* 40(1): 57–87.

Anthony JC (2002) Epidemiology of drug dependence. In KL Davis, DS Charney, JT Coyle, and CB Nemeroff (eds), *Neuropsychopharmacology: The Fifth Generation of Progress* (pp. 1557–1573). Philadelphia: Lippincott Williams & Wilkins.

Anthony JC (2010) Novel phenotype issues raised in cross-national epidemiological research on drug dependence. *Annals of the New York Academy of Sciences* 1187: 353–369.

Anthony JC and Petronis KR (1991) Epidemiologic evidence on suspected associations between cocaine use and psychiatric disturbances. *NIDA Research Monograph* 110: 71–94.

Anthony JC, Folstein M, Romanoski AJ, Von Korff MR, Nestadt GR, Chahal R, Merchant A, Brown CH, Shapiro S, and Kramer M (1985) Comparison of the lay Diagnostic Interview Schedule and a standardized psychiatric diagnosis: Experience in eastern Baltimore. *Archives of General Psychiatry* 42(7): 667–675.

Anthony JC, Tien AY, and Petronis KR (1989) Epidemiologic evidence on cocaine use and panic attacks. *American Journal of Epidemiology* 129(3): 543–549.

Anthony JC, Warner LA, and Kessler RC (1994) Comparative epidemiology of dependence on tobacco, alcohol, controlled substances, and inhalants: Basic findings from the National Comorbidity Survey. *Experimental and Clinical Psychopharmacology* 2: 244–268.

Anthony JC (2012) Steppingstone and gateway ideas: A discussion of origins, research challenges, and promising lines of research for the future. *Drug and Alcohol Dependence* 123(Suppl. 1): S99–S104.

Barros AJ and Hirakata VN (2003) Alternatives for logistic regression in cross-sectional studies: An empirical comparison of models that directly estimate the prevalence ratio. *BMC Medical Research Methodology* 20: 3–21.

Brenner SL and Beauchaine TP (2011) Pre-ejection period reactivity and psychiatric comorbidity prospectively predict substance use initiation among middle-schoolers: A pilot study. *Psychophysiology* 48(11): 1588–1596.

Brook RH, Avery AD, Greenfield S, Harris LJ, Lelah T, Solomon NE, and Ware JE (1977) Assessing quality of medical-care using outcome measures – overview of method. *Medical Care* 15(9): 1–165.

Cerdá M, Sagdeo A, Johnson J, and Galea S (2010) Genetic and environmental influences on psychiatric comorbidity: A systematic review. *Journal of Affective Disorders* 126(1–2): 14–38.

Chen CY and Anthony JC (2003) Possible age-associated bias in reporting of clinical features of drug dependence: Epidemiological evidence on adolescent-onset marijuana use. *Addiction* 98(1): 71–82.

Clarke DE, Eaton WW, Petronis KR, Ko JY, Chatterjee A, and Anthony JC (2010) Increased risk of suicidal ideation in smokers and former smokers compared to never smokers: Evidence from the Baltimore ECA follow-up study. *Suicide and Life-Threatening Behavior* 40(4): 307–318.

Cochrane AL (1965) Science and syndromes. *Postgraduate Medical Journal* 41: 440–442.

Costello EJ, Erkanli A, Federman E, and Angold A (1999) Development of psychiatric comorbidity with substance abuse in adolescents: Effects of timing and sex. *Journal of Clinical Child and Adolescent Psychology* 28(3): 298–311.

Crum RM and Anthony JC (1993) Cocaine use and other suspected risk factors for obsessive-compulsive disorder: A prospective study with data from the Epidemiologic Catchment Area surveys. *Drug and Alcohol Dependence* 31(3): 281–295.

De Graaf R, Radovanovic M, Van Laar M, Fairman B, Degenhardt L, Aguilar-Gaxiola S, Bruffaerts R, de Girolamo G, Fayyad J, Gureje O, Haro JM, Huang Y, Kostychenko S, Lépine JP, Matschinger H, Mora ME, Neumark Y, Ormel J, Posada-Villa J, Stein DJ, Tachimori H, Wells JE, and Anthony JC (2010) Early cannabis use and estimated risk of later onset of depression spells: Epidemiologic evidence from the population-based World Health Organization World Mental Health Survey Initiative. *American Journal of Epidemiology American Journal of Epidemiology* 172(2): 149–159.

Degenhardt L, Bohnert KM, and Anthony JC (2007) Case ascertainment of alcohol dependence in general population surveys: "Gated" versus "ungated" approaches. *International Journal of Methods in Psychiatric Research* 16(3): 111–123.

Degenhardt L, Bohnert KM, and Anthony JC (2008) Assessment of cocaine and other drug dependence in the general population: "Gated" versus "ungated" approaches. *Drug and Alcohol Dependence* 93(3): 227–232.

Degenhardt L, Cheng H, and Anthony JC (2007) Assessing cannabis dependence in community surveys: Methodological issues. *International Journal of Methods in Psychiatric Research* 16(2): 43–51.

Degenhardt L, Hall W, and Lynskey M (2003) Testing hypotheses about the relationship between cannabis use and psychosis. *Drug and Alcohol Dependence* 71(1): 37–48.

Feinstein AR (1967) *Clinical Judgment*. Baltimore: Williams & Wilkins.

Feinstein AR (1970) The pre-therapeutic classification of co-morbidity in chronic disease. *Journal of Chronic Diseases* 23(7): 455–468.

Feinstein AR (1985) *Clinical Epidemiology: The Architecture of Clinical Research*. New York: WB Saunders.

Fergusson DM, Boden JM, and Horwood LJ (2009) Tests of causal links between alcohol abuse or dependence and major depression. *Archives of General Psychiatry* 66(3): 260–266.

Flensborg-Madsen T, Mortensen EL, Knop J, Becker U, Sher L, and Grønbaek M (2009) Comorbidity and temporal ordering of alcohol use disorders and other psychiatric disorders: Results from a Danish register-based study. *Comprehensive Psychiatry* 50(4): 307–314.

Folstein M, Anthony JC, and Parhad I (1985) The meaning of cognitive impairment in the elderly. *Journal of the American Geriatrics Society* 33(4): 228–235.

Gallo JJ, Anthony JC, and Muthén BO (1994) Age differences in the symptoms of depression: A latent trait analysis. *The Journals of Gerontology* 49(6): 251–264.

Goodwin FK (1988) Alcoholism research: Delivering on the promise. *Public Health Reports* 103(6): 569–574.

Green JG, Avenevoli S, Finkelman M, Gruber MJ, Kessler RC, Merikangas KR, Sampson NA, and Zaslavsky AM (2011) Validation of the diagnoses of panic disorder and phobic disorders in the US National Comorbidity Survey Replication Adolescent (NCS-A) supplement. *International Journal of Methods in Psychiatric Research* 20(2): 105–115.

Grucza RA, Abbacchi AM, Przybeck TR, and Gfroerer JC (2007) Discrepancies in estimates of prevalence and correlates of substance use and disorders between two national surveys. *Addiction* 102(4): 623–629.

Heeringa SG, West BT, and Berglund PA (2010) *Applied Survey Data Analysis*. Boca Raton, Florida: CRC Press.

Hudziak JJ, Achenbach TM, Althoff RR, Pine DS (2007) A dimensional approach to developmental psychopathology. *International Journal of Methods in Psychiatric Research* 16(1): 16–23.

Jaffee SR, Moffitt TE, Caspi A, Fombonne E, Poulton R, and Martin J (2002) Differences in early childhood risk factors for juvenile-onset and adult-onset depression. *Archives of General Psychiatry* 59(3): 215–222.

Johnson MR and Shorvon SD (2011) Heredity in epilepsy: Neurodevelopment, comorbidity, and the neurological trait. *Epilepsy and Behavior* 22(3): 421–427.

Kendler KS, Prescott CA, Myers J, and Neale M C (2003) The structure of genetic and environmental risk factors for common psychiatric and substance use disorders in men and women. *Archives of General Psychiatry* 60(9): 929–937.

Kessler RC, Anthony JC, Blazer DG, Bromet E, Eaton WW, Kendler K, Swartz M, Wittchen H U, and Zhao S (1997) The US National Comorbidity Survey: Overview and future directions. *Epidemiologia e Psichiatria Sociale* 6(1): 4–16.

Kessler RC, Berglund P, Chiu WT, Demler O, Heeringa S, Hiripi E, Jin R, Pennell BE, Walters EE, Zaslavsky A, and Zheng H (2004) The US National Comorbidity Survey Replication (NCS-R): Design and field procedures. *International Journal of Methods in Psychiatric Research* 13(2): 69–92.

Kessler RC, Cox BJ, Green JG, Ormel J, McLaughlin KA, Merikangas KR, Petukhova M, Pine DS, Russo LJ, Swendsen J, Wittchen HU, and Zaslavsky AM (2011a) The effects of latent variables in the development of comorbidity among common mental disorders. *Depression and Anxiety* 28(1): 29–39.

Kessler RC, McGonagle KA, and Zhao SY (1994) Lifetime and 12-month prevalence of DSM-III-R psychiatric-disorders in the United States – results from the National Comorbidity Survey. *Archives of General Psychiatry* 51(1): 8–19.

Kessler RC, Cox BJ, Green JG, Ormel J, McLaughlin KA, Merikangas KR, Petukhova M, Pine DS, Russo LJ, Swendsen J, Wittchen HU, and Zaslavsky AM (2011a) The effects of latent variables in the development of comorbidity among common mental disorders. *Depression and Anxiety* 28(1): 29–39.

Kessler RC, Ormel J, Petukhova M, McLaughlin KA, Green JG, Russo LJ, Stein DJ, Zaslavsky AM, Aguilar-Gaxiola S, Alonso J, Andrade L, Benjet C, de Girolamo G, de Graaf R, Demyttenaere K, Fayyad J, Haro JM, Hu C, Karam A, Lee S, Lepine JP, Matchsinger H, Mihaescu-Pintia C, Posada-Villa J, Sagar R, and Ustün TB (2011b) Development of lifetime comorbidity in the World Health Organization world mental health surveys. *Archives of General Psychiatry* 68(1): 90–100.

Kim-Cohen J, Arseneault L, Caspi A, Tomás MP, Taylor A, and Moffitt TE (2005) Validity of DSM-IV conduct disorder in $4^1/_2$–5-year-old children: a longitudinal epidemiological study. *The American Journal of Psychiatry* 162(6): 1108–1117.

Krueger RF and Piasecki TM (2002) Toward a dimensional and psychometrically-informed approach to conceptualizing psychopathology. *Behavior Research and Therapy* 40(5): 485–499.

Leaf PL, Bruce ML, Tischler GL, Freeman DH, Weissman MM, and Myers JK (1998) Factors affecting the utilization of specialty and general medical mental health services. *Medical Care* 26(1): 9–26.

Menninger K, Ellenberger H, Pruyser P, and Mayman M (1958) The unitary concept of mental-illness. *Bulletin of the Menninger Clinic* 22(1): 4–12.

Mezzich JE, Honda Y and Kastrup M (1994) *Psychiatric Diagnosis: A World Perspective*. New York: Springer.

Miettinen OS (1985) *Theoretical Epidemiology: Principles of Occurrence Research in Medicine*. New York: John Wiley & Sons, Inc.

Neale MC, Aggen SH, Maes HH, Kubarych TS, and Schmitt JE (2006) Methodological issues in the assessment of substance use phenotypes. *Addictive Behaviors* 31(6): 1010–1034.

O'Brien MS, Comment LA, Liang KY, and Anthony JC (2012) Does cannabis onset trigger cocaine onset? An epidemiologic case-crossover approach. *International Journal of Methods in Psychiatric Research*, Jan. 8. doi: 10.1002/mpr.359.

O'Brien MS, Wu LT, and Anthony JC (2005) Cocaine use and the occurrence of panic attacks in the community: A case-crossover approach. *Substance Use and Misuse* 40(3): 285–297.

Richard G, Abbacchi AM, Przybeck TR, and Gfroerer JC (2007) Discrepancies in estimates of prevalence and correlates of substance use and disorders between two national surveys. *Addiction* 102(4): 623–629.

Robins LN and Helzer JE (1986) Diagnosis and clinical assessment: The current state of psychiatric diagnosis. *Annual Review of Psychology* 37: 409–432.

Sanders AR, Levinson DF, Duan J, Dennis JM, Li R, Kendler KS, Rice JP, Shi J, Mowry BJ, Amin F, Silverman JM, Buccola NG, Byerley WF, Black DW, Freedman R, Cloninger CR, and Gejman PV (2010) The Internet-Based MGS2 control sample: Self report of mental illness. *The American Journal of Psychiatry* 167(7): 854–865.

Schretlen D, Pearlson GD, and Anthony, JC (2000) Elucidating the contributions of processing speed, executive ability, and frontal lobe volume to normal age-related differences in fluid intelligence. *Journal of the International Neuropsychological Society* 6(1): 52–61.

Schuckit MA (2006) Comorbidity between substance use disorders and psychiatric conditions. *Addiction* 101(1): 76–88.

Sheline YI, Wang PW, and Gado MH (1996) Hippocampal atrophy in recurrent major depression. *Proceedings of the National Academy of Sciences of the United States of America* 93(9): 3908–3913.

Tien AY and Anthony JC (1990) Epidemiological analysis of alcohol and drug use as risk factors for psychotic experiences. *Journal of Nervous and Mental Disease* 178(8): 473–480.

Virchow R (1847) Standpoints in scientific medicine. As translated by Rather LJ (1956) Rudolf Virchow: Standpoints in scientific medicine. *Bulletin of the History of Medicine* 30: 436–449.

Weissman MM, Brown AS, and Talati A (2011) Translational epidemiology in psychiatry: Linking population to clinical and basic sciences. *Archives of General Psychiatry* 68(6): 600–608.

Wells KB, Burnam MA, Rogers W, Hays R, and Camp P (1992) The course of depression in adult outpatients: Results from the Medical Outcomes Study. *Archives of General Psychiatry* 49(10): 788–794.

Wells KB, Golding JM, and Burnam MA (1989) Chronic medical conditions in a sample of the general population with anxiety, affective, and substance use disorders. *American Journal of Psychiatry* 146(11): 1440–1446.

Willoughby WW (1925) Opium as an international problem. *The Geneva Conferences.* Baltimore: Johns Hopkins University Press.

Wu LT and Anthony JC (2000) The use of the case-crossover design in studying illicit drug use. *Substance Use and Misuse* 35(6–8): 1035–1050.

Young DW (1984) Medical audit using a computer-based medical record system. *Journal of the Royal College of Physicians of London* 18(4): 244–247.

Youngstrom EA, Findling RL, and Calabrese JR (2003) Who are the comorbid adolescents? Agreement between psychiatric diagnoses, youth, parent, and teacher report. *Journal of Abnormal Child Psychology* 31(3): 231–245.

5

Personality and Addiction: A Critical Review of Assessment Approaches

Joshua D. Miller and Donald R. Lynam

1 Introduction

Personality represents an individual's longstanding patterns of thinking, feeling, and behaving that tend to be stable over time and situations. Discernible personality traits, in the form of temperament, arise early in life and become increasingly stable over time with meaningful change occurring in mid-life (e.g., Roberts and DelVecchio, 2000). Personality traits have proven to be reliable correlates of a variety of externalizing behaviors such as antisocial behavior (Miller and Lynam, 2001; Jones, Miller, and Lynam, 2011), risky sexual behavior (Hoyle, Fejfar, and Miller, 2000), pathological gambling (MacLaren, Fugelsang, Harrigan, and Dixon, 2011), and substance use (e.g., smoking: Malouff, Thorsteinsson, and Schutte, 2006; alcohol: Malouff, Thorsteinsson, Rooke, and Schutte, 2007).

Before reviewing the personality correlates of substance use and providing recommendations for the assessment of personality in relation to substance use, it is helpful to provide an organizing framework. There is increasing consensus that individual differences in personality can be represented with five broad domains. Despite some differences in the development of these models, the Big Five (Goldberg, 1993) and Five Factor Model (FFM; e.g., Costa and McCrae, 1992) are quite convergent. Research suggests that a five-factor model structure can successfully encompass different models of normal (Markon, Krueger, and Watson, 2005) and pathological personality traits (O'Connor, 2005; O'Connor and Dyce, 1998). Given the comprehensiveness and popularity of this model, as well as its ability to organize findings from other personality models and related assessments, we use the FFM as an organizing framework for the current chapter. Neuroticism reflects individual differences in the proclivity to experience a wide array of negative emotional states such as depression, anxiety, anger, and shame. Extraversion reflects individual differences in both sociability (e.g., outgoingness, interpersonal warmth) and agency (e.g., assertiveness). Agreeableness refers

The Wiley-Blackwell Handbook of Addiction Psychopharmacology, First Edition. Edited by James MacKillop and Harriet de Wit.
© 2013 John Wiley & Sons, Ltd. Published 2013 by John Wiley & Sons, Ltd.

to individuals' interpersonal strategies and orientations; agreeable individuals tend to be honest, compliant, empathic, and concerned with the plights of others, whereas antagonistic individuals may view interactions with others from a more instrumental and less empathic perspective. Conscientiousness reflects an individual's ability to delay gratification, persist at tasks in the face of boredom or fatigue, consider consequences before acting, and engage in the world in an efficacious manner. Finally, openness to experience is the smallest and most controversial (and inconsistently titled) of the five major domains and refers to interest in engaging in new activities and considering intellectual, emotional, and perceptual experiences from different perspectives.

There are several reasons to use the FFM as an organizing structure for the current chapter. First, the FFM was originally derived from the natural language ensuring that the most important aspects of personality are represented (Ashton and Lee, 2001; John and Srivastava, 1999). Second, the FFM, as measured by the NEO PI-R, provides both breadth and depth via overall factor indices and a reasonably extensive and comprehensive lexicon of 30 lower-order facets. Third, the FFM enjoys considerable empirical support in the form of convergent and discriminant validation across self, peer, and spouse ratings (Costa and McCrae, 1988), temporal stability across the life span (Roberts and DelVecchio, 2000), etic and emic cross-cultural support (Ashton and Lee, 2001; Church, 2001; McCrae *et al.*, 2005), behavioral genetic support for the FFM structure (Yamagata *et al.*, 2006), and relations to important outcomes. In particular, measures of the FFM (i.e., Revised NEO Personality Inventory: NEO PI-R; Costa and McCrae, 1992) have been used in empirical studies of externalizing behaviors such as substance use and abuse (Flory *et al.*, 2002; Ruiz, Pincus, and Dickinson, 2003), antisocial behavior (Miller, Lynam, and Leukefeld, 2003), and risky sexual behavior (Miller *et al.*, 2004). In addition, the FFM has been used as an organizing framework for meta-analysis of studies of the personality correlates of antisocial behavior (Miller and Lynam, 2001; Jones, Miller, and Lynam, 2011), aggression (Bettencourt, Talley, Benjamin, and Valentine, 2006), and risky sexual behavior (Hoyle, Fejfar, and Miller, 2000).

2   Empirical Relevance to Addiction

Meta-analytic reviews of the FFM-based personality correlates of both smoking (Malouff, Thorsteinsson, and Schutte, 2006) and alcohol use (Malouff, Thorsteinsson, Rooke, and Schutte, 2007) suggest that conscientiousness (negative effect size), agreeableness (negative effect size), and neuroticism (positive effect size) are the key personality domains in relation to substance use. For alcohol use, several of the effect sizes were moderated by sample type, such that these effect sizes (e.g., neuroticism; conscientiousness) were even larger in treatment seeking samples. The pattern of personality correlates associated with substance use is quite similar to the meta-analytic profiles identified for other externalizing behaviors such as antisocial behavior (Miller and Lynam, 2001), aggression (Bettencourt, Talley, Benjamin, and Valentine, 2006; Jones, Miller, and Lynam, 2011), risky sexual behavior (Hoyle, Fejfar, and Miller, 2000), and gambling (MacLaren, Fugelsang, Harrigan, and Dixon, 2011). Findings of these types have led many to speculate that these personality traits may be partially responsible for the comorbidity found among these behaviors and disorders (Miller and Lynam, 2001; Krueger *et al.*, 2002; Lynam, Leukefeld, and Clayton, 2003).

Although substantial attention has been paid to the examination of the personality correlates of substance use and misuse, researchers have also begun to examine these associations in a variety of other ways. For example, recent work suggests that developmental changes in personality are associated with changes in alcohol use. More specifically, Littlefield, Sher, and Wood (2009) found that changes in neuroticism and impulsivity (i.e., decreases) from age 18 to 35 were associated with decreased levels of problematic alcohol use.

In addition, the majority of trait-based models of substance use see personality as a risk factor for the development of substance use problems (or moderators of the course of said problems), and there is some evidence that substance use also predicts personality change. Quinn, Stappenbeck, and Fromme (2011) found that while traits of impulsivity and sensation seeking predicted heavy drinking during college, heavy drinking also predicted changes (i.e., increases) in these two traits. The authors argue that these findings are consistent with Caspi's "corresponsive principle" (Caspi, Roberts, and Shiner, 2005), which suggests that "life experiences do not impinge themselves on people in a random fashion causing widespread personality transformations; rather, the traits that people already possess are changed (i.e., deepened and elaborated) by trait-correlated experiences that they create" (p. 470). Similarly, Hicks and colleagues (2012) found that alcohol use dependence affected the rates of change for both negative emotionality and behavioral disinhibition. These fascinating findings require replication, however, and further study to identify the mechanism underlying such change (see Quinn, Stappenbeck, and Fromme, 2011, for a thoughtful discussion of two potential explanations for these findings, one of which is more substantive and one of which suggests that these changes could be an artifact based on how the experience of heavy drinking affects research participants' "self-perceptions" and subsequent ratings on these traits). More generally, these studies illustrate that that personality traits appear to play a recursive etiological role in substance misuse, serving both as predisposing factors and also characteristics that are further modified by persistent overconsumption.

There is also increasing evidence that personality traits are related to alcohol use by affecting the context in which one operates. For instance, with regard to alcohol use in college, Park, Sher, Wood, and Krull (2009) found that "individuals high in impulsivity/novelty seeking appear to select into the Greek system because of its drinking-centered atmosphere" and that these individuals "increase their drinking through selection into a high-risk environment, which then exerts further influence on drinking" (p. 251). Finally, personality factors may be helpful in identifying individuals who are most at risk for relapse following treatment (e.g., Cannon, Keefe, and Clark, 1997; Fisher, Elias, and Ritz, 1998; Muller, Weijers, Boning, and Wiesbeck, 2008). For instance, Bottlender and Soyka (2005) found that alcohol-dependent patients with higher scores on the trait of neuroticism and lower scores on conscientiousness were significantly more likely to relapse following treatment.

In sum, it is clear that personality has much to offer to the study of substance use and that the literature has begun to move away from a basic review of the correlates to more sophisticated examinations of the reciprocal manner in which personality and substance use may be related. Similarly, there is ample evidence to suggest that personality factors should be taken into consideration with regard to treatment-related prognosis.

3   Standardized and Validated Methods Used in the Field of Personality Assessment

As noted above, the FFM appears to be an excellent framework for organizing various personality measures and constructs into a larger overarching model. In what follows, we review a number of prominent measures of personality that are thought to be reliable and valid measures of personality. We focus first on structural models of personality that identify and organize a relatively small number of basic traits in order to provide comprehensive descriptions of personality. These measures correspond to 2, 3, 5, 6, and 7-factor models of personality. Second, we review a few narrower measures designed to specifically assess impulsivity and impulsivity-related traits as these are often of significant interest to individuals researching substance use and addiction. Although some of the measures included here were designed to assess both normal and maladaptive personality traits, we do not include those whose primary or sole focus is on pathological personality traits.

It is important to note that the underlying theories behind these approaches often differ substantially. For instance, the development of the Big Five/FFM was atheoretical, guided by the lexical hypothesis, which suggests that traits of fundamental importance to human behavior are encoded in our natural language as single trait terms. If this is true then the basic elements of personality can be uncovered via exploration of the natural language or what has been called "sedimentary deposits of the observations of persons" (e.g., Widiger and Mullins-Sweatt, 2010). Other models reviewed here are based on attempts to link core personality domains to underlying biological mechanisms. For instance, Cloninger's seven-factor model of temperament and character is based on hypothesized links between the key temperament dimensions (e.g., harm avoidance; novelty seeking) and certain neurotransmitter systems (e.g., serotonin; dopamine). Empirical support for the biological claims of several of these models, however, is mixed at best (see Farmer and Goldberg, 2008, for a review); nonetheless, the various measures tend to cover much of the same personality "ground."

3.1   Two-factor measures

3.1.1   Behavioral Inhibition System/Behavioral Activation System Scales (BIS/BAS).
The BIS/BAS scales (Carver and White, 1994) are assessed via 20-self-report items answered on a 1 (Strongly Agree) to 4 (Strongly Disagree) scale. Seven items are used to score the BIS scale, whereas BAS is measured using three short subscales including Reward Responsiveness (5 items), Drive (4 items), and Fun Seeking (4 items). Carver and White developed these self-report scales to assess Gray's (e.g., 1972) constructs

of the Behavioral Inhibition System (BIS) and Behavioral Activation System (BAS). Carver and White suggested that the BIS "inhibits behavior that may lead to negative or painful outcomes" (1994, p. 319). Alternatively, the BAS responds to environmental cues for reward and nonpunishment by initiating approach and active avoidance. BAS appears to be a relatively consistent positive correlate of alcohol and drug use but this relation appears to be driven primarily by the BAS subscale of Fun Seeking, whereas BIS tends to be either nonsignificantly or negatively related to substance use (Feil and Hasking, 2008; Johnson, Turner, and Iwata, 2003; Loxton and Hawe, 2001; Voight *et al.*, 2009). For instance, van Leeuwen and colleagues (2011) found that BAS scores in early adolescence predicted greater use of tobacco and marijuana in mid-adolescence, whereas BIS scores were negatively related to repeated marijuana use. Concerns have been raised, however, about the structural validity of this measure, as neither a two- nor a four-factor model proved a good fit to the data (Cogswell, Alloy, van Dulmen, and Fresco, 2006).

3.1.2   Sensitivity to Punishment and Sensitivity to Reward Questionnaire (SPSRQ). The SPSRQ (Torrubia, Avila, Molto, and Caseras, 2001) is a 48-item self-report measure of sensitivity to reward and punishment (24 items are used for each domain) answered using a yes/no format. Similar to the BIS/BAS scales (Caci, Deschaux, and Bayle, 2007; Cogswell, Alloy, van Dulmen, and Fresco, 2006), the sensitivity to reward scale appears to be the stronger and more reliable correlate of substance use (Loxton, Nguyen, Casey, and Dawe, 2008). Some data even suggest that sensitivity to reward, but not punishment, is related to greater risk for alcohol problems, with risk being defined as manifesting an increased heart rate following intoxication (Brunelle *et al.*, 2004). There is other research that suggests that the combination of high sensitivity to reward and low sensitivity to punishment may be particularly relevant to substance abuse (Genovese and Wallace, 2007). Finally, sensitivity to punishment and reward may operate in other ways that affect substance use; for example, Wray, Simons, and Dvorak (2011) found that sensitivity to reward was related to experiencing alcohol-related infractions among heavy drinking college students (e.g., being caught in possession of alcohol while underage) and that these infractions led to decreased drinking at a later time point. Of note, individuals with greater sensitivity to punishment responded to these infractions with a greater decrease in alcohol use. Like Carver and White's (1994) BIS/BAS scales, concerns have been raised regarding the structural validity of the SPSRQ (Cogswell, Alloy, van Dulmen, and Fresco, 2006; O'Connor, Colder, and Hawk, 2004).

3.2   Three-factor measures

3.2.1   Eysenck Personality Questionnaire (EPQ; EPQ-Revised).   The EPQ-R (Eysenck, Eysenck, and Barrett, 1985) is a 100-item self-report inventory that contains scales assessing the domains of Extraversion, Neuroticism, and Psychoticism, as well as a Lie scale; items are assessed using a yes/no format. While the first two factors are consistent in name and content with other similarly titled constructs (e.g.,

Neuroticism; Negative Emotionality; Extraversion; Positive Emotionality), Psychoticism (e.g., "Do you stop to think things over before doing anything?"; "Would it upset you a lot to see a child or an animal suffer?") requires further explication as this dimension is thought to be a blend of both agreeableness and conscientiousness from five-factor models and does not represent a proclivity towards psychosis. In general, psychoticism appears to be the most consistent and robust correlate of substance use, although extraversion and neuroticism sometimes manifest significant positive relations as well (e.g., Anderson, Barnes, and Murray, 2011; Conrod, Petersen, and Pihl, 1997; George, Connor, Gullo, and Young, 2010; Newbury-Birch, White, and Kamali, 2000).

3.2.2   Multidimensional Personality Questionnaire (MPQ). The MPQ (Tellegen, 1985; Tellegen and Waller, 2008) is a 276-item, self-report inventory that uses a true/false format to assess 11 personality trait scales and three broad personality domains (i.e., Positive Emotionality, Negative Emotionality, and Constraint) included in Tellegen's model. Positive Emotionality can be further split into two subfactors: communal and agentic positive emotionality. Communal positive emotionality reflects positive emotional responsiveness and interpersonal connectedness; agentic positive emotionality reflects positive emotional responsiveness and interpersonal effectiveness (Tellegen and Waller, 2008). Only one of the subscales, Absorption, is a stand-alone subscale; it does not feed into the scoring of any of the higher-order domains. A recent briefer version of the MPQ (155 items; Patrick, Curtin, and Tellegen, 2002) has been developed that appears to be a promising method for assessing these traits using significantly fewer items.

McGue and colleagues (1997; 1999) reported that alcohol-related disorders, when controlling for drug disorders, were most strongly related (positively) to Negative Emotionality, whereas drug-related disorders, when controlling for alcohol disorders, were most strongly associated (negatively) with Constraint. These personality domains are also associated with an earlier onset (Negative Emotionality) and more persistent course of alcohol use disorders (Constraint; Hicks, Iacono, McGue, 2010).

3.2.3   Schedule of Nonadaptive and Adaptive Personality (SNAP). The SNAP (Clark, 1993; Clark, Simms, Wu, and Casillas, in press) is a 390-item, true/false format, self-report inventory designed to assess both normal and pathological personality traits (i.e., 12 lower-order primary traits and 3 higher-order temperament dimensions) associated with personality pathology. The SNAP was developed by compiling personality disorder (PD) criteria as well as characteristics based on non-DSM conceptualizations of personality disorders. Clark also included criteria for DSM-III Axis I disorders which resemble PD constructs (e.g., dysthymia). At this time, little work has been done to examine the relations between the SNAP traits and substance use. Pryor, Miller, Hoffman, and Harding (2009) found that latent factors representative of content related to negative emotionality, disagreeableness, and disinhibition were the strongest correlates of a latent externalizing variable that comprised, in part, lifetime reports of substance use.

3.3   Five-factor measures

The majority of five-factor measures of personality were designed to assess the Big Five/Five Factor Model (FFM) of personality, which includes the traits of neuroticism (or emotional stability), extraversion, openness to experience (or intellect, culture), agreeableness, and conscientiousness. A number of measures have been created to assess these traits; we review some of the more popular ones here. The five-factor measures have received a significant amount of empirical attention in terms of the relations between personality and substance use. As a result, meta-analyses are available which summarize the relations between the five domains and various substance use outcomes. In general, the evidence suggests that agreeableness and conscientiousness (negatively) and neuroticism (positively) are the most reliable Big Five/FFM-based correlates of substance use including smoking (Malouff, Thorsteinsson, and Schutte, 2006), alcohol use (Malouff, Thorsteinsson, Rooke, and Schutte, 2007), substance use disorders (Kotov, Gamez, Schmidt, and Watson, 2010; Ruiz, Pincus, and Schinka, 2008) and relapse (Bottlender and Soyka, 2005). Extraversion and openness to experience are generally unrelated to these outcomes.

3.3.1   Revised NEO Personality Inventory (NEO PI-R).   The NEO PI-R (Costa and McCrae, 1992) is a 240-item self-report inventory (informant report variants are also available) of the FFM in which answers are scored on a 5-point scale with answers ranging from 0 (Disagree Strongly) to 4 (Agree Strongly). The NEO PI-R yields scores on the five primary domains as well as 30 specific traits (called facets; each domain is composed of six specific facets). For instance, the domain of neuroticism is underlain by scores on the following facets: anxiety, angry hostility, depression, self-consciousness, impulsiveness, and vulnerability. The NEO PI-R is among the most popular personality instruments for use in studying both Axis I and II disorders.

3.3.2   NEO-Five Factor Inventory (NEO-FFI).   The NEO-FFI (Costa and McCrae, 1992) is a 60-item short report version of the NEO PI-R that provides scores solely for the five primary domains. It is worth noting that not all facets of the NEO PI-R are equally represented in the NEO-FFI domains, so one cannot assume that the content of the domains are identical. For instance, within agreeableness, there is little representation of content related to immodesty and deceitfulness (facets of agreeableness when assessed using the NEO PI-R), facets which may be correlated with alcohol use (e.g., Ruiz, Pincus, and Dickinson, 2003) and are substantial correlates of other externalizing behaviors such as antisocial behavior and aggression (Jones, Miller, and Lynam, 2011), as well risky sexual behavior (Miller *et al.*, 2004). As such, researchers should be cautious in assuming that the shortened version of the NEO PI-R will provide identical information to that provided by the full-length test (e.g., Miller, Gaughan, Maples, and Price, 2011).

3.3.3   Big Five Inventory (BFI).   The BFI (John, Donahue, and Kentle, 1991) is a 44-item self-report measure of the Big Five domains that uses a 1 (Strongly Disagree) to 5 (Strongly Agree) response format. Unlike the NEO PI-R and FFI, the BFI does not use full sentences to assess the Big Five/FFM domains but instead uses "short phrases based on the trait adjectives known to be prototypical markers of the Big Five" (John and Srivastava, 1999, p. 115). Like the concerns noted for the NEO-FFI, there is evidence that the BFI's assessment of agreeableness may miss important content related to immodesty and deceitfulness (to an even greater extent than the NEO-FFI), which may be important in the study of substance use and personality disorders related to substance use such as psychopathy (Miller, Gaughan, Maples, and Price, 2011).

3.3.4 International Personality Item Pool (IPIP).

The IPIP (Goldberg *et al.*, 2006) is a large set of personality items that can be used to assess a wide variety of traits and models, including the Big Five and Five Factor Model, but which are free to use and have no restrictions regarding modifications. A number of IPIP-based scales have been created to assess the Big Five and FFM, and preliminary evidence suggests that these scales manifest reasonable convergent and discriminant validity (Gow, Whiteman, Pattie, and Deary, 2004; Zheng *et al.*, 2008), and manifest expected relations with substance use (Raynor and Levine, 2009; Walton and Roberts, 2004).

3.3.5 Zuckerman–Kuhlman Personality Questionnaire (ZKPQ-III-R).

The ZKPQ-III-R (Zuckerman *et al.*, 1993) is a 99-item self-report measure (true/false format) designed to capture the "alternative five-factor model" (Zuckerman, Kuhlman, Thornquist, and Kiers, 1991) which includes the following traits: neuroticism-anxiety, sociability, activity, impulsive sensation seeking, and aggression-hostility. Despite substantive differences surrounding the theoretical underpinnings of this alternative five-factor model from the Big Five/FFM, these domains from the ZKPQ map fairly cleanly on four of the five domains from the "traditional" Big Five/FFM, with the exception that domains from the ZKPQ do not include content related to openness to experience (Garcia, Aluja, Garcia, and Cuevas, 2005; Zuckerman *et al.*, 1993). The ZKPQ has received relatively limited attention in addiction research. Nonetheless the empirical data to date suggest that the ZKPQ domain of impulsive sensation seeking is correlated with drinking, smoking (cigarettes), and drug use, whereas aggression-hostility and sociability manifest significant but less consistent relations with substance use scales (Zuckerman and Kuhlman, 2000).

3.4 Six-factor measures (HEXACO-PI-R)

The HEXACO-PI-R (Lee and Ashton, 2006) is a 200-item self-report measure of the HEXACO model of personality that uses a 1 (Strongly Disagree) to 5 (Strongly Agree) scale to assess six broad domains of honesty-humility, emotionality, extraversion, agreeableness, conscientiousness, and openness to experience. Each of these six domains is subserved by four facets. Five of the HEXACO dimensions are thought to represent variants of the broad factors of the Big Five/FFM whereas the sixth (i.e., honesty-humility) is argued to be absent from the Big Five but not from certain measures of the FFM such as the NEO PI-R. Measures of the Big Five/FFM and measures of the HEXACO tend to manifest reasonable convergent validity (e.g., Gaughan, Miller, and Lynam, 2012; Lee, Ogunfowora, and Ashton, 2005), although there are some differences across the models and their respective measures, particularly with regard to the conceptualizations of the domains of neuroticism/emotionality and agreeableness (e.g., Lee and Ashton, 2004). At this time there are no studies examining measures related to this model of personality and substance use, although one might expect a similar pattern of correlation as manifested by measures of the Big Five/FFM.

3.5   Seven-factor measures

3.5.1   Temperament and Character Inventory (TCI).   The TCI (Cloninger, Przybeck, Svrakic, and Wetzel, 1994) is a 226-item self-report inventory (using a true/false format) that provides scores on four temperament domains (novelty seeking; reward dependence; harm avoidance; persistence) and three "character" domains (cooperativeness; self-directedness; self-transcendence). Cloninger suggests that the temperament domains are more genetically mediated, whereas the character domains are most environmentally mediated, although evidence for these hypotheses is sparse. A more recent and less empirically validated revision is now available (TCI-Revised; Cloninger, 1999) which uses 240 items measured using a 1 to 5 response format. A number of studies have raised significant concerns regarding the psychometric qualities of the TCI (see Farmer and Goldberg, 2008, for a review of the TCI and test of the TCI-R), as well as some of the underlying assumptions including the hypothesized differences in heritability between the temperament and character dimensions, and the relations between the temperament scores are specified neurotransmitters.

Despite the many concerns that surround both the theory and operationalization of Cloninger's model, the TCI has been used in a number of studies relevant to substance use and abuse. With regard to the temperament dimensions, there is some evidence to suggest that novelty seeking (positively) and harm avoidance (negatively) are related to alcohol use (Koposov, Ruchkin, Eisemann, and Sidorov, 2005; Skeel, Pilarski, Pytlak, and Neudecker, 2008). Of the character dimensions, both cooperativeness and self-directness may be related to alcohol use (Egger *et al.*, 2007). There is some work that suggests that these dimensions may help differentiate among individuals with drug use problems, alcohol problems, and polysubstance problems. For example, Evren, Evren, Yancar, and Erkiran (2007) reported that the polysubstance users scored the highest on novelty seeking and the lowest on reward dependence, self-directedness, and cooperativeness.

4   Focal measures of impulsivity-related traits

Acting without thinking, disregard for consequences, and a preference for engaging in risky behavior, often lumped together under the term "impulsivity," is one of the most ubiquitous personality traits found in the fields of psychology and psychiatry. It can be found in one form or another in each of the structural personality models described previously. It appears in the criterion sets for at least 18 separate disorders in the fourth version of the *Diagnostic and Statistical Manual for Mental Disorders* (DSM-IV; American Psychiatric Association, 1994). Most important to the present review, it serves as a centerpiece in many etiologic theories of substance use and abuse (e.g., Bechara, 2005; Iacono, Malone, and McGue, 2010; Verdejo-Garcia, Lawrence, and Clark, 2008; Wills, Vaccaro, and McNamara, 1994).

A number of studies have demonstrated that the personality characteristics lumped together under the term "impulsivity" are associated with alcohol and drug use. High scorers on scales assessing these dimensions use substances at earlier ages, use more substance of any type, and use more substance types than low scorers (e.g., Ball, Carroll, and Rounsaville, 1994; Chassin, Flora, and King, 2004; de Wit and Bodker, 1994; Finn, Sharkansky, Brandt, and Turcotte, 2000; King and Chassin, 2004; Lynam and Miller, 2004; Milich *et al.*, 2000; Zuckerman and Como, 1983). Additionally, impulsivity-related traits dimensions are related to the development of substance abuse/dependence (e.g., Gelernter *et al.*, 1997; Kosten, Ball, and Rounsaville, 1994; Wills and Stoolmiller, 2002; Zuckerman and Neeb, 1980). In fact, impulsivity appears to be one of the most robust individual difference correlates of substance use.

Although it is straightforward to say that impulsivity is robustly related to substance use and abuse, it is more difficult to say exactly what impulsivity is. The area suffers from both the "jingle" and "jangle" fallacies (Block, 1995). The jingle fallacy refers to instances in which equivalently labeled scales assess different constructs, whereas jangle fallacy refers to situations in which differently labeled traits assess the same construct. Depue and Collins (1999) have argued that "impulsivity comprises a heterogeneous cluster of lower-order traits that includes terms such as impulsivity, sensation seeking, risk-taking, novelty seeking, boldness, adventuresomeness, boredom susceptibility, unreliability, and unorderliness" (p. 6). For their part, Whiteside and Lynam (2001) have called impulsivity "an artificial umbrella term" that encompasses distinct and separable aspects of personality that give rise to impulsive behavior (p. 687). With this in mind, we review five assessments focused on impulsivity. Most conceptualize impulsivity as a unitary trait comprised of several facets; one, the UPPS model by Whiteside and Lynam (2001), proposed that several, separable, and distinct traits give rise to impulsive behavior. In the subsequent sections, we review each conception, spending more time on the UPPS model, which we believe can help to organize the various conceptions. Interestingly and importantly, a number of behavioral measures of impulsivity are also frequently used in addiction research, but are reviewed separately in this volume (Chapters 6 and 7), but also contribute to heterogeneity in the literature, as these measures have only very modest associations with personality-based measures (Cyders and Coskunpinar, 2011).

4.1   Barratt Impulsiveness Scale-11 (BIS-11)

The BIS (Patton, Stanford, and Barratt, 1995) represents the latest effort by Barratt and colleagues to measure an impulsivity construct that is orthogonal to anxiety and is related to similar personality traits, such as extraversion and sensation seeking. The BIS-11 consists of 30 items responded to on a 4-point scale and provides a total score as well as scores on three subscales: attentional impulsiveness (e.g. "I get easily bored when solving thought problems"), motor impulsiveness (e.g. "I do things without thinking"), and non-planning impulsiveness (e.g. "I am more interested in the present than the future"). A number of studies examining substance use have been conducted with the BIS-11; most have found positive relations between the BIS-11 Total Score and substance use and abuse (for a recent listing, see Stanford *et al.*, 2009). However, there are few, if any, substantive differential relations observed for the subscales.

4.2   Sensation Seeking Scale-Form V (SSS-V)

The SSS-V (Zuckerman, 1994) represents an attempt by Zuckerman and colleagues to operationalize "the construct of optimal level of stimulation" (p. 139). The scale contains 40 items with each item consisting of two options from which a respondent must choose one. The SSS-V yields a total score and four subscale scores, each consisting of 10 items: thrill and adventure seeking (TAS), experience seeking (ES), disinhibition (DIS), and boredom susceptibility (BS). Many studies have examined the relations between scores on the SSS-V and substance use. These studies have generally supported the hypothesized relations between total scores and substance use; higher total scores have been associated with greater quantity and frequency of use and earlier ages of onset across a variety of drug use categories. For example, in their meta-analysis of SSS-V scores and alcohol use, Hittner and Swickert (2006) report a mean weighted correlation across 55 studies of 0.26. Importantly, the four subscales of the SSS-V do not behave identically; the TAS and DIS subscales appear to have the most divergent relations. Hittner and Swickert (2006) reported significant differences among the subscales in their overall relations to alcohol use, with DIS showing the largest effect (mean weighted $r = 0.37$) and TAS showing the smallest (mean weighted $r = 0.14$).

4.3   Functional and Dysfunctional Impulsivity Scales (F/D-IS)

The F/D-IS (Dickman, 1990) consists of 23 items answered in a true/false format. The scales are based on an information-processing approach to personality and are predicated on the assumption that impulsivity can have positive as well as negative consequences. Dickman differentiates between functional (i.e., the tendency to act with relatively little forethought when such a trait is optimal) and dysfunctional impulsivity (i.e., the tendency to act with less forethought than most people of equal ability when this is a source of difficulty). In line with the theory, the instrument assesses both functional impulsivity (11 items; e.g. "Most of the time I can put my thoughts into words very rapidly") and dysfunctional impulsivity (12 items; e.g. "Often I don't spend enough time thinking over a situation before I act"). Very few studies have examined the relations between these scales and substance use.

4.4   Impulsiveness–Venturesomeness–Empathy Questionnaire (I-7)

The I-7 (Eysenck, Pearson, Easting, and Allsopp, 1985) is a 54-item, true/false response inventory designed to measure impulsiveness (e.g., "I generally do and say things without stopping to think"), venturesomeness (e.g. "I quite enjoy taking risks"), and empathy. The scale grew out of work by Eysenck and colleagues to identify to which higher-order personality dimension impulsivity belonged. Ultimately, they identified two variants of a broad impulsiveness construct, and placed venturesomeness on extraversion and impulsiveness on psychoticism. A few studies have examined the relations between impulsiveness and venturesomeness and substance use, primarily alcohol use (e.g., Allsopp, 1986; MacKillop *et al.*, 2007; Morgan, 1998; Nagoshi, Wilson, and Rodriguez, 1991). Most studies have found consistent positive relations between impulsiveness and substance use, but less consistent relations for venturesomeness.

4.5   A multiple trait model of impulsivity – the UPPS-P

In an effort to bring some clarity to the field, Whiteside and Lynam (2001) administered the most widely used measures of impulsivity/disinhibition, including those discussed above, along with the scales from the NEO PI-R, to a large sample of students and then factor analyzed the results. This approach was meant to yield a summary and taxonomy of current perspectives on impulsivity-related traits. The factor analysis produced four factors. Urgency, referenced as negative urgency (NU) hereafter, reflects the tendency to act rashly under conditions of negative affect (e.g., anger, distress). Perseverance (PSV), or lack thereof, reflects the inability to remain focused on a task in the face of boredom and/or distraction. (Lack of) Premeditation (PMD) reflects the tendency to act without thinking. Sensation seeking (SS) reflects the tendency to enjoy and pursue activities that are exciting or novel. Based on the results of the factor analyses, Whiteside and Lynam developed the UPPS Impulsive Behavior Scale, which independently assesses each of these four personality pathways to impulsive behavior. Cyders *et al.* (2007) have recently made a compelling case for the addition of a fifth personality pathway to impulsive behavior – positive urgency (PU), which reflects the tendency to act rashly when experiencing extremely positive emotion. In its current version, the UPPS-P consists of 59 items answered from "Agree Strongly" (1) to "Disagree Strongly" (4). It yields five subscales scores; consistent with the underlying theory, no total score is provided. A number of studies, including those conducted using French and German translations, have supported the original UPPS and UPPS-P factor structures (e.g., Van der Linden *et al.*, 2006; Kampfe and Mitte, 2009; Lynam and Miller, 2004).

In addition to the research on the internal structure (i.e., factor structure) of the UPPS-P scales, approximately 50 studies have examined the relations between the UPPS-P constructs and various forms of deviance including substance use and abuse. There are several general conclusions that can be drawn from this body of research. First, lack of perseverance typically bears the weakest relation to the negative outcomes. Its only consistent correlates appear to be inattention and poor school performance (Miller, Flory, Lynam, and Leukefeld, 2003; Smith *et al.*, 2007). Second, sensation seeking, the tendency to enjoy and pursue activities that are exciting and/or novel, seems more strongly related to sampling deviant behaviors than to long-term acquisition of those behaviors. For example, across two samples of undergraduates, Smith and colleagues (Cyders, Flory, Rainer, and Smith, 2009; Spillane, Smith, and Kahler, 2010) examined the relations between the UPPS-P and cigarette smoking and alcohol use. In terms of cigarette use, SS distinguished between smokers and non-smokers but did not predict level of nicotine dependence. Similarly, SS was related to frequency of drinking but not to the quantity or the number of problems experienced. These results underscore the narrower view of SS in the UPPS-P relative to the broader conception contained in Zuckerman's (1994) early formulations, in which sensation seeking was defined as "the seeking of varied, novel, complex, and intense sensations and experiences" *and* "the willingness to take physical, social, legal, and financial risks for the sake of such experience" (p. 27).

Third, both negative and positive urgency relate consistently to problematic levels of deviant behavior. Several studies have found that NU and/or PU are related to substance abuse (e.g., Fischer and Smith, 2008; Smith *et al.*, 2007; Whiteside and Lynam, 2003). Verdejo-Garcia, Bechara, Recknor, and Perez-Garcia (2007) compared a group of substance-dependent individuals to a group of healthy controls on the four original UPPS scales. Negative urgency showed the largest difference between groups (Cohen *d* = 1.96) and, in a discriminant function analysis, was able to correctly classify 83.3 and 80.6% of the substance-dependent and control groups respectively. Moreover, NU was the strongest predictor of addiction severity. Fourth and finally, lack of premeditation, one of the most robust correlates of antisocial behavior and antisocial personality (Lynam and Miller, 2004; Whiteside and Lynam, 2003), has also been found to relate to alcohol, marijuana, and other illicit drug use (e.g., Lynam and Miller, 2004).

In addition to being a useful assessment tool for studying the contribution of "impulsivity" to substance use, we believe the UPPS-P model has the potential of making several important contributions to our understanding of impulsive behavior. First, it serves to demonstrate that the term "impulsivity" lacks specificity and references not a single dimension or process, but rather a collection of separable traits. Second, particularly with the work of Cyders, Smith, and colleagues, the UPPS-P model has drawn attention to affect-related traits that were relatively neglected by the field previously. Third, and perhaps most importantly, the UPPS-P offers a framework or taxonomy that may help bring clarity to extant research and guide future research. An example of this latter contribution can be seen in a meta-analysis by Fischer, Smith, and Cyders (2008) on the relation between bulimic symptoms and impulsivity/inhibition. These authors identified 50 studies with relevant effect sizes and coded effect sizes based on which of the four original UPPS dimensions was assessed; these decisions were based on the original factor analyses reported by Whiteside and Lynam (2001) and on content analysis. Although previous studies on these relations had yielded mixed results, results from the meta-analysis indicated that the effect size varied as a function of which UPPS construct was being examined. NU had the largest mean effect size (mean weighted *r* of 0.38), whereas PSV had the smallest (mean weighted *r* of 0.08). SS and PMD showed mean weighted effect sizes of 0.16; PU was not included in this particular study. Studies such as this suggest that the UPPS offers substantial promise in organizing results from disparate studies using different impulsivity measures in relation to a dependent variable of interest (e.g., substance use).

In an effort to facilitate future organizations of extant research, Table 5.1 provides the aggregated correlations between the UPPS-P scales and measures of impulsivity discussed earlier; results are from several samples of undergraduates with the number of subjects for each correlation ranging from slightly over 300 to slightly over 1,000. There are several important findings in the table. First, one can see that the five

Table 5.1   Correlations between UPPS-P scales and other commonly used measures

	NU	PSV	PMD	SS	PU
Negative Urgency (NU)					
Perseverance (PSV)	0.31				
Premeditation (PMD)	0.36	0.44			
Sensation Seeking (SS)	0.11	−0.10	0.31		
Positive Urgency (PU)	−0.60	−0.29	−0.44	−0.23	
BIS 11 Total	0.54	0.51	0.64	0.25	
BIS Nonplanning	0.29	0.61	0.63	0.04	
BIS Motor Impulsiveness	0.58	0.18	0.47	0.43	
BIS Attentional Impulsiveness	0.43	0.46	0.42	0.11	
Dickman Dysfunctional Impulsivity	0.51	0.41	0.67	0.14	
Dickman Functional Impulsivity	0.07	−0.09	0.23	0.46	
I-7 Impulsiveness	0.63	0.35	0.58	0.41	
I-7 Venturesome	0.13	−0.08	0.13	0.93	
SSS total	0.32	0.08	0.52	0.60	0.44
SSS Thrill and Adventure Seeking	−0.11	−0.08	0.20	0.80	0.12
SSS Experience Seeking	0.23	0.11	0.47	0.33	0.25
SSS Disinhibition	0.45	0.08	0.41	0.28	0.49
SSS Boredom Susceptibility	0.27	0.13	0.30	0.14	0.27

BIS = Barratt Impulsiveness Scale; SSS = Sensation Seeking Scale. Ns = 1105 for intercorrelations among NU, PSV, PMD, and SS; and 290 for those involving PU. N = 389 for correlations with BIS, Dickman, and I-7 scales. N = 308 for correlations with SSS scales.

dimensions of the UPPS-P, with one notable exception, are not highly intercorrelated, supporting the argument that these represent relatively distinct traits. Second, given its provenance, there are several scales with predictably high and specific relations to UPPS-P SS. For example, the correlations between UPPS-P SS and I-7 venturesomeness ($r = 0.93$) and SSS V Thrill and Adventure Seeking ($r = 0.80$) are among the highest correlations in the table. Third, neither NU nor PU has many strong, unique relations with other scales, suggesting a general underrepresentation in the field of these two personality pathways to impulsive behavior. Further, the high correlation between the two suggests a general characteristic of sensitivity to both positive and negative mood states, or affective reactivity. Fourth, beyond the specific correlations already noted, most other impulsivity measures manifest strong correlations with more than one of the UPPS-P scales. Perhaps explaining their relations to substance use outcomes, many traits represent blends of NU and PMD – BIS 11 Total, Motor, and Attentional scales, SSS V Total and Disinhibition scales; Dickman Dysfunctional Impulsivity; and I-7 Impulsiveness.

5   Limitations, Shortcomings, and Future Directions

The current review provides a number of options for the assessment of personality that may prove useful in the broader context of research on substance use. These options range from relatively narrow, focused assessments that attempt to measure only one or two basic personality dimensions (e.g., Barratt Impulsiveness Scale) to more comprehensive assessments that are aimed at providing a broad assessment of the major personality domains thought to be most robust, replicable, and important to psychological functioning. Although these latter measures can be more time-intensive, especially those that provide lower-order "facet-level" data, they do not have to be. For instance, a number of relatively brief measures of five- and six-factor models exist that will provide scores on the primary domains. We recommend the regular inclusion of such comprehensive personality measures in research protocols, as the cost–benefit ratio seems to weigh heavily in favor of their inclusion. If personality is to be a prominent component of the research design, then it makes sense to use an instrument that provides both higher-order domain scores as well as lower-order facet-level scores (e.g., NEO PI-R), as these lower-order facets may have greater predictive utility (Paunonen and Ashton, 2001). If time concerns outweigh a more secondary interest in personality, then researchers could consider including a briefer measure (e.g., 44 items: BFI; 60 items: NEO-FFI) that would take little time but would yield valuable data on several prominent personality domains. There are also much briefer versions that can be used, such as the Ten-Item Personality Inventory (TIPI; Gosling, Rentfrow, and Swann, 2003), although we suggest that researchers be cautious in their use, as their brevity (i.e., two items used per domain) may result in attenuated reliability and validity.

The assessment tools reviewed here are most commonly used as self-report instruments. It is important to note, however, that some of these have informant versions (e.g., NEO PI-R) that can be used and all can be fairly easily converted for use with informants. There is no clear "gold standard" for the assessment of personality, but agreement among self and informant reports of personality tends to be reasonably good with average correlations of around 0.50 (e.g., Connolly, Kavanagh, and Viswesvaran, 2007) and both sources tend to provide useful information with regard to external criteria. We agree with Vazire (2006), who suggested that informant reports of personality can be a "cheap, fast, and easy method for personality assessment" that can "increase the validity of . . . personality assessments" (p. 479). There are even interesting new data to suggest that another valuable technique for potentially improving the validity of self-report personality data is to ask individuals to fill these assessments out not as they see themselves but how they believe others see them – a term called "meta-perception" or "meta-insight" (e.g., Carlson, Vazire, and Furr, 2011). Finally, there is even a semi-structured interview aligned with the FFM of personality that can be used (i.e., Structured Interview for the Five-Factor Model; Trull and Widiger, 1997). These alternative techniques have received relatively little, if any, attention from scientists interested in the role of personality in understanding substance use and represent an area ripe for investigation.

In conclusion, it is clear that personality is related to substance use, particularly traits related to behavioral disinhibition/impulsivity, increased neuroticism/negative emotionality, and aggressive/antagonistic interpersonal styles. Some of these factors have proven to be genetically related to substance use and other externalizing behaviors (e.g., Krueger *et al.*, 2002; Young *et al.*, 2009). New research suggests that personality change may lead to change in alcohol use and vice versa – that changes in alcohol use may result in later personality change. We believe that research into the etiology, prevention, and treatment of substance use disorder would benefit from more regular inclusion of valid and broad personality assessments. Such an effort can be done at little cost to the researchers and participants, and is likely to yield important information as to the complex relations between personality and substance use and abuse.

References

Allsopp JF (1986) Personality as a determinant of beer and cider consumption among young men. *Personality and Individual Differences* 7: 341–347.

American Psychiatric Association (1994) *Diagnostic and Statistical Manual of Mental Disorders* (4th edn). Washington, DC: American Psychiatric Association.

Anderson RE, Barnes GE, and Murray RP (2011) Psychometric properties and long-term predictive validity of the Addiction-Prone Personality (APP) scale. *Personality and Individual Differences* 50: 651–656.

Ashton MC and Lee K (2001) A theoretical basis for the major dimensions of personality. *European Journal of Personality* 15: 327–353.

Ball SA, Carroll KM, and Rounsaville BJ (1994) Sensation seeking, substance abuse, and psychopathology in treatment-seeking and community cocaine abusers. *Journal of Consulting and Clinical Psychology* 62: 1053–1057.

Bechara A (2005) Decision making, impulse control and loss of willpower to resist drugs: A neurocognitive perspective. *Nature Neuroscience* 8: 1458–1463.

Bettencourt B, Talley A, Benjamin A, and Valentine J (2006) Personality and aggressive behavior under provoking and neutral conditions: A meta-analytic review. *Psychological Bulletin* 132: 751–777.

Block J (1995) A contrarian view of the five-factor approach to personality description. *Psychological Bulletin* 117: 187–215.

Bottlender M and Soyka M (2005) Impact of different personality dimensions (NEO Five-Factor Inventory) on the outcome of alcohol-dependent patients 6 and 12 months after treatment. *Psychiatry Research* 136: 61–67.

Brunelle C, Assaad J-M, Barrett SP, Avila C, Conrod PJ, Tremblay RE, and Pihl RO (2004) Heightened heart rate response to alcohol intoxication is associated with a reward-seeking personality profile. *Alcoholism: Clinical and Experimental Research* 28: 394–401.

Caci H, Deschaux O, and Bayle FJ (2007) Psychometric properties of the French versions of the BIS/BAS scales and the SPSRQ. *Personality and Individual Differences* 42: 987–998.

Cannon DS, Keefe CK, and Clark LA (1997) Persistence predicts latency to relapse following inpatient treatment for alcohol dependence. *Addictive Behaviors* 22: 535–543.

Carlson EN, Vazire S, and Furr RM (2011) Meta-insight: Do people really know how others see them? *Journal of Personality and Social Psychology* 101: 831–846.

Carver CS and White TL (1994) Behavioral inhibition, behavioral activation, and affective responses to impending reward and punishment: The BIS/BAS scales. *Journal of Personality and Social Psychology* 67: 319–333.

Caspi A, Roberts BW, and Shiner RL (2005) Personality development: Stability and change. *Annual Review of Psychology* 56: 453–484.

Chassin L, Flora DB, and King KM (2004) Trajectories of alcohol and drug use and dependence from adolescence to adulthood: The effects of familial alcoholism and personality. *Journal of Abnormal Psychology* 113: 483–498.

Church AT (2001) Personality measurement in cross-cultural perspective. *Journal of Personality* 69: 979–1006.

Clark LA (1993) *Manual for the Schedule for Nonadaptive and Adaptive Personality (SNAP).* Minneapolis: University of Minnesota Press.

Clark LA, Simms LJ, Wu KD, and Casillas A (in press) *Manual for the Schedule for Nonadaptive and Adaptive Personality (SNAP-2).* Minneapolis: University of Minnesota Press.

Cloninger CR (1999) *The Temperament and Character Inventory – Revised.* St Louis: Washington University, Center for Psychobiology of Personality.

Cloninger CR, Przybeck TR, Svrakic DM, and Wetzel RD (1994) *The Temperament and Character Inventory (TCI): A Guide to Its Development and Use.* St Louis: Washington University, Center for Psychobiology of Personality.

Cogswell A, Alloy LB, van Dulmen MHM, and Fresco DM (2006) A psychometric evaluation of behavioral inhibition and approach self-report measures. *Personality and Individual Differences* 40: 1649–1658.

Connolly JJ, Kavanagh EJ, and Viswesvaran C (2007) The convergent validity between self and observer ratings of personality: A meta-analytic review. *International Journal of Selection and Assessment* 15: 110–117.

Conrod PJ, Petersen JB, and Pihl RO (1997) Disinhibited personality and sensitivity to alcohol reinforcement: Independent correlates of drinking behavior in sons of alcoholics. *Alcoholism: Clinical and Experimental Research* 21: 1320–1332.

Costa PT and McCrae RR (1988) Personality in adulthood: A six-year longitudinal study of self-reports and spouse ratings on the NEO Personality Inventory. *Journal of Personality and Social Psychology* 54: 853–863.

Costa PT and McCrae RR (1992) *Revised NEO Personality Inventory (NEO-PI-R) and NEO Five-Factor Inventory (NEO-FFI) Professional Manual.* Odessa: Psychological Assessment Resources, Inc.

Cyders MA and Coskunpinar A (2011) Measurement of constructs using self-report and behavioral lab tasks: Is there overlap in nomothetic span and construct representation for impulsivity? *Clinical Psychology Review* 31: 965–982.

Cyders MA, Flory K, Rainer S, and Smith GT (2009) The role of personality dispositions to risky behavior in predicting first-year college drinking. *Addiction* 104: 193–202.

Cyders MA, Smith GT, Spillane NS, Fischer S, and Annus AM (2007) Integration of impulsivity and positive mood to predict risky behavior: Development and validation of a measure of positive urgency. *Psychological Assessment* 19: 107–118.

Depue RA and Collins PF (1999) Neurobiology of the structure of personality: Dopamine, facilitation of incentive motivation, and extraversion. *Behavioral and Brain Sciences* 22: 491–569.

de Wit H and Bodker B (1994) Personality and drug preferences in normal volunteers. *International Journal of the Addictions* 29: 1617–1630.

Dickman SJ (1990) Functional and dysfunctional impulsivity: Personality and cognitive correlates. *Journal of Personality and Social Psychology* 58: 95–102.

Egger JIM, Gringhuis M, Breteler MA, De Mey, H, Wingbermuhle E, Derksen J, and Hilberink S (2007) MMPI-2 clusters of alcohol-dependent patients and the relation to Cloninger's temperament–character inventory. *Acta Neuropsychiatrica* 19: 238–243.

Evren C, Evren B, Yancar C, and Erkiran M (2007) Temperament and character model of personality profile of alcohol-and drug-dependent inpatients. *Comprehensive Psychiatry* 48: 283–288.

Eysenck SBG, Eysenck HJ, and Barrett P (1985) A revised version of the psychoticism scale. *Personality and Individual Differences* 6: 21–29.

Eysenck SBG, Pearson PR, Easting G, and Allsopp JF (1985) Age norms for impulsiveness, venturesomeness, and empathy in adults. *Personality and Individual Differences* 6: 613–619.

Farmer RF and Goldberg LR (2008) A psychometric evaluation of the Revised Temperament and Character Inventory (TCI-R) and TCI-140. *Psychological Assessment* 20: 281–291.

Feil J and Hasking P (2008) The relationship between personality, coping strategies, and alcohol use. *Addiction Research and Theory* 16: 526–537.

Finn PR, Sharkansky EJ, Brandt KM, and Turcotte N (2000) The effects of familial risk, personality, and expectancies on alcohol use and abuse. *Journal of Abnormal Psychology* 109: 122–133.

Fischer S and Smith GT (2008) Binge eating, problem drinking, and pathological gambling: Linking behavior to shared traits and social learning. *Personality and Individual Differences* 44: 789–800.

Fischer S, Smith GT, and Cyders M (2008) Another look at impulsivity: A meta-analytic review comparing specific dispositions to rash action in their relationship to bulimic symptoms. *Clinical Psychology Review* 28: 1413–1425.

Fisher LA, Elias JW, and Ritz K (1998) Predicting relapse to substance abuse as a function of personality dimensions. *Alcoholism: Clinical and Experimental Research* 22: 1041–1047.

Flory K, Lynam D, Milich R, Leukefeld C, and Clayton R (2002) The relations among personality, symptoms of alcohol and marijuana abuse, and symptoms of comorbid psychopathology: Results from a community sample. *Experimental and Clinical Psychopharmacology* 10: 425–434.

Garcia LF, Aluja A, Garcia O, and Cuevas L (2005) Is openness to experience an independent personality dimension? Convergent and discriminant validity of the openness domain and its NEO PI-R facets. *Journal of Individual Differences* 26: 132–138.

Gaughan ET, Miller JD, and Lynam DR (2012) Examining the utility of general models of personality in the study of psychopathy: Comparing the HEXACO-PI-R and NEO PI-R. *Journal of Personality Disorders* 26: 513–523.

Gelernter J, Kranzler H, Coccaro E, Siever L, New A, and Mulgrew CL (1997) D4 dopamine-receptor (DRD4) alleles and novelty seeking in substance-dependent, personality-disorder, and control subjects. *The American Journal of Human Genetics* 61: 1144–1152.

Genovese JEC and Wallace D (2007) Reward sensitivity and substance abuse in middle school and high school students. *Journal of Genetic Psychology* 168: 465–469.

George SM, Connor JP, Gullo MJ, and Young R (2010) A prospective study of personality features predictive of early adolescent alcohol misuse. *Personality and Individual Differences* 49: 204–209.

Goldberg LR (1993) The structure of phenotypic personality traits. *American Psychologist* 48: 26–34.

Goldberg LR, Johnson JA, Eber HW, Hogan R, Ashton MC, Cloninger CR, and Gough HG (2006) The international personality item pool and the future of public-domain personality measures. *Journal of Research in Personality* 40: 84–96.

Gosling SD, Rentfrow PJ, and Swann, WB (2003) A very brief measure of the Big-Five personality domains. *Journal of Research in Personality* 37: 504–528.

Gow AJ, Whiteman MC, Pattie A, and Deary IJ (2005) Goldberg's "IPIP" Big-Five factor markers: Internal consistency and concurrent validation in Scotland. *Personality and Individual Differences* 39: 317–329.

Gray JA (1972) The psychophysiological basis of Introversion–Extraversion: A modification of Eysenck's theory. In VD Nebylitsyn and JA Gray (eds), *The Biological Bases of Individual Behavior* (pp. 182–205). San Diego: Academic Press.

Hicks BM, Durbin CE, Blonigen DM, Iacono WG, and McGue M (2012) Relationship between personality change and the onset and course of alcohol dependence in young adulthood. *Addiction* 107: 540–548.

Hicks BM, Iacono WG, and McGue, M (2010) Consequences of an adolescent onset and persistent course of alcohol dependence in men: Adolescent risk factors and adult outcomes. *Alcoholism: Clinical and Experimental Research* 34: 819–833.

Hittner JB and Swickert R (2006) Sensation seeking and alcohol use: A meta-analytic review. *Addictive Behaviors* 31: 1383–1401.

Hoyle RH, Fejfar MC, and Miller JD (2000) Personality and sexual risk taking: A quantitative review. *Journal of Personality* 68: 1203–1231.

Iacano WG, Malone SM, and McGue M (2008) Behavioral disinhibition and the development of early-onset addiction: Common and specific influences. *Annual Review of Clinical Psychology* 4: 325–348.

John OP and Srivastava S (1999) The Big Five trait taxonomy: History, measurement, and theoretical perspectives. In LA Pervin and OP John (eds), *Handbook of Personality: Theory and Research* (2nd edn, pp. 102–138). New York: Guilford.

John OP, Donahue EM, and Kentle RL (1991) *The Big Five Inventory – Versions 4a and 54*. Berkeley, CA: University of California, Berkeley, Institute of Personality and Social Research.

Johnson SL, Turner RJ, and Iwata, N (2003) BIS/BAS levels and psychiatric disorder: An epidemiological study. *Journal of Psychopathology and Behavioral Assessment* 25: 25–36.

Jones SE, Miller JD, and Lynam DR (2011) Personality, antisocial behavior, and aggression: A meta-analytic review. *Journal of Criminal Justice* 39: 329–337.

Kampfe N and Mitte K (2009) A German validation of the UPPS impulsive behavior scale: Further evidence for a four-dimensional model of impulsivity. *European Journal of Psychological Assessment* 25: 252–259.

King KM and Chassin L (2004) Mediating and moderated effects of adolescent behavioral undercontrol and parenting in the prediction of drug use disorders in emerging adulthood. *Psychology of Addictive Behaviors* 18: 239–249.

Koposov RA, Ruchkin VV, Eisemann M and Sidorov PI (2005) Alcohol abuse in Russian delinquent adolescents: Associations with comorbid psychopathology, personality and parenting. *European Child and Adolescent Psychiatry* 14: 254–261.

Kosten TA, Ball SA, and Rounsaville BJ (1994) A sibling study of sensation seeking and opiate addiction. *Journal of Nervous and Mental Disease* 182: 284–289.

Kotov R, Gamez W, Schmidt F, and Watson D (2010) Linking "big" personality traits to anxiety, depressive, and substance use disorders: A meta-analysis. *Psychological Bulletin* 136: 768–821.

Krueger RF, Hicks BM, Patrick CJ, Carlson SR, Iacono WG, and McGue M (2002) Etiologic connections among substance dependence, antisocial behavior, and personality: Modeling the externalizing spectrum. *Journal of Abnormal Psychology* 111: 411–424.

Lee K and Ashton MC (2004) Psychometric properties of the HEXACO Personality Inventory. *Multivariate Behavioral Research* 39: 329–358.

Lee K and Ashton MC (2006) Further assessment of the HEXACO Personality Inventory: Two new facet scales and an observer report form. *Psychological Assessment* 18: 182–191.

Lee K, Ogunfowora B, and Ashton MC (2005) Personality traits beyond the Big Five: Are they within the HEXACO space? *Journal of Personality* 73: 1437–1463.

Littlefield AK, Sher KJ, and Wood PK (2009) Is "maturing out" of problematic alcohol involvement related to personality change? *Journal of Abnormal Psychology* 118: 360–374.

Loxton NJ and Dawe S (2001) Alcohol abuse and dysfunctional eating in adolescent girls: The influence of individual differences in sensitivity to reward and punishment. *International Journal of Eating Disorders* 29: 455–462.

Loxton NJ, Nguyen D, Casey L, and Dawe S (2008) Reward drive, rash impulsivity, and punishment sensitivity in problem gamblers. *Personality and Individual Differences* 45: 167–173.

Lynam DR and Miller JD (2004) Personality pathways to impulsive behavior and their relations to deviance: Results from three samples. *Journal of Quantitative Criminology* 20: 319–341.

Lynam DR, Leukefeld C, and Clayton RR (2003) The contribution of personality to the overlap between antisocial behavior and substance use/misuse. *Aggressive Behavior* 29: 316–331.

MacKillop J, Mattson RE, MacKillop EJA, Castelda BA, and Donovick PJ (2007) Multidimensional assessment of impulsivity in undergraduate hazardous drinkers and controls. *Journal of Studies on Alcohol and Drugs* 68: 785–788.

MacLaren VV, Fugelsang JA, Harrigan KA, and Dixon MJ (2011) The personality of pathological gamblers: A meta-analysis. *Clinical Psychology Review* 31: 1057–1067.

Malouff JM, Thorsteinsson EB, Rooke S, and Schutte NS (2007) Alcohol involvement and the five factor model of personality: A meta-analysis. *Journal of Drug Education* 37: 277–294.

Malouff JM, Thorsteinsson EB, and Schutte NS (2006) The five-factor model of personality and smoking: a meta-analysis. *Journal of Drug Education* 36: 47–58.

Markon KE, Krueger RF, and Watson D (2005) Delineating the structure of normal and abnormal personality: An integrative hierarchical approach. *Journal of Personality and Social Psychology* 88: 139–157.

McCrae RR, Terracciano A, and 78 members of the Personality Profiles of Cultures Project (2005) Universal features of personality traits from the observer's perspective: Data from 50 cultures. *Journal of Personality and Social Psychology* 88: 547–561.

McGue M, Slutske W, and Iacono WG (1999) Personality and substance use disorders: II. Alcoholism versus drug use disorders. *Journal of Consulting and Clinical Psychology* 67: 394–404.

McGue M, Slutske W, Taylor J, and Iacono WG (1997) Personality and substance use disorders: I. Effects of gender and alcoholism subtype. *Alcoholism: Clinical and Experimental Research* 21: 513–530.

Milich R, Lynam DR, Zimmerman R, Logan TK, Martin C, Leukefeld C, and Clayton R (2000) Differences in young adult psychopathology among drug abstainers, experimenters, and frequent users. *Journal of Substance Abuse* 11: 69–88.

Miller JD, Flory K, Lynam DR, and Leukefeld C (2003) A test of the four-factor model of impulsivity-related traits. *Personality and Individual Differences* 34: 1403–1418.

Miller JD, Gaughan ET, Maples J, and Price J (2011) A comparison of Agreeableness scores from the Big Five Inventory and the NEO PI-R: Consequences for the study of narcissism and psychopathy. *Assess* 18: 335–339.

Miller JD and Lynam DR (2001) Structural models of personality and their relation to antisocial behavior: A meta-analysis. *Criminology* 39: 765–798.

Miller JD, Lynam DR, and Leukefeld C (2003) Examining antisocial behavior through the use of the Five Factor Model facets. *Aggressive Behavior* 29: 497–514.

Miller JD, Lynam DR, Zimmerman R, Logan T, Leukefeld C, and Clayton R (2004) The utility of the five-factor model in understanding risky sexual behavior. *Personality and Individual Differences* 36: 1611–1626.

Morgan MJ (1998) Recreational use of "ecstasy" (MDMA) is associated with elevated impulsivity. *Neuropsychopharmacology* 19: 252–264.

Muller S, Weijers H-G, Boning J, and Wiesbeck GA (2008) Personality traits predict treatment outcome in alcohol-dependent patients. *Neuropsychobiology* 57: 159–164.

Nagoshi CT, Wilson JR, and Rodriguez LA (1991) Impulsivity, sensation seeking, and behavioral and emotional responses to alcohol. *Alcoholism: Clinical and Experimental Research* 15: 661–667.

Newbury-Birch D, White M, and Kamali F (2000) Factors influencing alcohol and illicit drug use amongst medical students. *Drug and Alcohol Dependence* 59: 125–130.

O'Connor BP (2005) A search for consensus on the dimensional structure of personality disorders. *Journal of Clinical Psychology* 61: 323–345.

O'Connor BP and Dyce JA (1998) A test of models of personality disorder configuration. *Journal of Abnormal Psychology* 107: 3–16.

O'Connor RM, Colder CR, and Hawk LW (2004) Confirmatory factor analysis of the Sensitivity to Punishment and Sensitivity to Reward Questionnaire. *Personality and Individual Differences* 37: 985–1002.

Park A, Sher KJ, Wood PH, and Krull JL (2009) Dual mechanisms underlying accentuation of risky drinking via fraternity/sorority affiliation: The role of personality, peer norms, and alcohol availability. *Journal of Abnormal Psychology* 118: 241–255.

Patrick CJ, Curtin JJ, and Tellegen A (2002) Development and validation of a brief form of the Multidimensional Personality Questionnaire. *Psychological Assessment* 14: 150–163.

Patton JH, Stanford MS, and Barratt ES (1995) Factor structure of the Barratt Impulsiveness Scale. *Journal of Clinical Psychology* 51: 768–774.

Paunonen SV and Ashton MS (2001) Big Five factors and facets and the prediction of behavior. *Journal of Personality and Social Psychology* 81: 524–539.

Pryor LR, Miller JD, Hoffman BJ, and Harding H (2009) Pathological personality traits and externalizing behavior. *Personality and Mental Health* 3: 26–40.

Quinn PD, Stappenbeck CA, and Fromme K (2011) Collegiate heavy drinking prospectively predicts change in sensation seeking and impulsivity. *Journal of Abnormal Psychology* 120: 543–556.

Raynor DA and Levine H (2009) Associations between the five-factor model of personality and health behaviors among college students. *Journal of American College Health* 58: 73–81.

Roberts BW and DelVecchio WF (2000) The rank-order consistency of personality traits from childhood to old age: A quantitative review of longitudinal studies. *Psychological Bulletin* 126: 3–25.

Ruiz MA, Pincus AL, and Dickinson KA (2003) NEO PI-R predictors of alcohol use and alcohol-related problems. *Journal of Personality Assessment* 81: 226–236.

Ruiz MA, Pincus AL, and Schinka JA (2008) Externalizing pathology and the five-factor model: A meta-analysis of personality traits associated with antisocial personality disorder, substance use disorder, and their co-occurrence. *Journal of Personality Disorders* 22: 365–388.

Skeel RL, Pilarski C, Pytlak K, and Neudecker J (2008) Personality and performance-based measures in the prediction of alcohol use. *Psychology of Addictive Behaviors* 22: 402–409.

Smith GT, Fischer S, Cyders MA, Annus AM, Spillane NS, and McCarthy DM (2007) On the validity and utility of discriminating among impulsivity-like traits. *Assessment* 14: 155–170.

Spillane NS, Smith GT, and Kahler CW (2010) Impulsivity-like traits and smoking behavior in college students. *Addictive Behaviors* 35: 700–705.

Stanford MS, Mathias CW, Dougherty DM, Lake SL, Anderson NE, and Patton JH (2009) Fifty years of the Barratt Impulsiveness Scale: An update and review. *Personality and Individual Differences* 47: 385–395.

Tellegen A (1985) Structures of mood and personality and their relevance to assessing anxiety, with an emphasis on self-report. In AH Tuma and JD Maser (eds), *Anxiety and the Anxiety Disorders* (pp. 681–706). Hillsdale: Lawrence Erlbaum Associates, Inc.

Tellegen A and Waller NG (2008) Exploring personality through test construction: Development of the Multidimensional Personality Questionnaire. In GJ Boyle, G Matthews, and DH Saklofske (eds), *The Sage Handbook of Personality Theory and Assessment* (pp. 261–292). Los Angeles: Sage.

Torrubia R, Avila C, Molto J, and Caseras X (2001) The sensitivity to punishment and sensitivity to reward questionnaire (SPSRQ) as a measure of Gray's anxiety and impulsivity dimensions. *Personality and Individual Differences* 31: 837–862.

Trull TJ and Widiger TA (1997) *Structured Interview for the Five-Factor Model of Personality.* Odessa: Psychological Assessment Resources.

van der Linden M, d'Acremont M, Zermatten A, Jermann F, Laroi F, Willems S, Juillerat A, and Bechara A (2006) A French adaptation of the UPPS Impulsive Behavior Scale: Confirmatory factor analysis in a sample of undergraduate students. *European Journal of Psychological Assessment* 22: 38–42.

van Leeuwen AP, Creemers, HE, Verhulst FC, Ormel J, and Huizink AC (2011) Are adolescents gambling with cannabis use? A longitudinal study of impulsivity measures and adolescent substance use: The TRAILS study. *Journal of Studies on Alcohol and Drugs* 72: 70–78.

Vazire S (2006) Informant reports: A cheap, fast, and easy method for personality assessment. *Journal of Research in Personality* 40: 472–481.

Verdejo-Garcia A, Bechara A, Recknor EC, and Perez-Garcia M (2007) Negative emotion-driven impulsivity predicts substance dependence problems. *Drug and Alcohol Dependence* 91: 213–219.

Verdejo-Garcia A, Lawrence AJ, and Clark L (2008) Impulsivity as a vulnerability marker for substance use disorders: Review of findings from high-risk research, problem gamblers and genetic association studies. *Neuroscience and Biobehavioral Reviews* 32: 777–810.

Voight DC, Dillard JP, Braddock KH, Anderson JW, Sopory P, and Stephenson MT (2009) Carver and White's (1994) BIS/BAS scales and their relationship to risky health behaviours. *Personality and Individual Differences* 47: 89–93.

Walton KE and Roberts BW (2004) On the relationship between substance use and personality traits: Abstainers are not maladjusted. *Journal of Research in Personality* 38: 515–535.

Whiteside SP and Lynam DR (2001) The Five Factor Model and impulsivity: Using a structural model of personality to understand impulsivity. *Personality and Individual Differences* 30: 669–689.

Whiteside SP and Lynam DR (2003) Understanding the role of impulsivity and externalizing psychopathology in alcohol abuse: Application of the UPPS Impulsive Behavior Scale. *Experimental and Clinical Psychopharmacology* 11: 210–217.

Widiger TA and Mullins-Sweatt SN (2010) Clinical utility of a dimensional model of personality disorder. *Professional Psychology: Research and Practice* 41: 488–494.

Wills TA, Vaccaro D, and McNamara G (1994) Novelty seeking, risk taking, and related constructs as predictors of adolescent substance use: An application of Cloninger's theory. *Journal of Substance Abuse* 6: 1–20.

Wills T and Stoolmiller M (2002) The role of self-control in early escalation of substance use: A time-varying analysis. *Journal of Consulting and Clinical Psychology* 70: 986–997.

Wray TB, Simons JS, and Dvorak RD (2011) Alcohol-related infractions among college students: Associations with subsequent drinking as a function of sensitivity to punishment. *Psychology of Addictive Behaviors* 25: 352–357.

Yamagata S, Suzuki A, Ando J, One Y, Kijima N, Yoshimura K., *et al.* (2006) Is the genetic structure of human personality universal? A cross-cultural twin study from North America, Europe, and Asia. *Journal of Personality and Social Psychology* 90: 987–998.

Young SE, Friedman NP, Miyake A, Willcutt EK, Corley RP, Haberstick BC, and Hewitt JK (2009) Behavioral disinhibition: Liability for externalizing spectrum disorders and its genetic and environmental relation to response inhibition across adolescence. *Journal of Abnormal Psychology* 118: 117–130.

Zheng L, Goldberg LR, Zheng Y, Zhao Y, Tang Y, and Lui L (2008) Reliability and concurrent validation of the IPIP Big-Five factor markers in China: Consistencies in factor structure between internet-obtained heterosexual and homosexual samples. *Personality and Individual Differences* 45: 649–654.

Zuckerman M (1994) *Behavioral Expressions and Biosocial Bases of Sensation Seeking.* New York: Cambridge University Press.

Zuckerman M and Como P (1983) Sensation seeking and arousal systems. *Personality and Individual Differences* 4: 381–386.

Zuckerman M and Kuhlman DM (2000) Personality and risk taking: Common biosocial factors. *Journal of Personality* 68: 999–1029.

Zuckerman M and Neeb M (1980) Demographic influences in sensation seeking and expressions of sensation seeking in religion, smoking, and driving habits. *Personality and Individual Differences* 1: 197–206.

Zuckerman M, Kuhlman DM, Joireman J, Teta P, and Kraft M (1993) A comparison of three structural models for personality: The big three, the big five, and the alternative five. *Journal of Personality and Social Psychology* 65: 757–768.

Zuckerman M, Kuhlman DM, Thornquist M, and Kiers H (1991) Five (or three) robust questionnaire scale factors of personality without culture. *Personality and Individual Differences* 12: 929–941.

6

Behavioral Inhibition and Addiction[1]

Mark T. Fillmore and Jessica Weafer

1 Introduction

The idea that drug addiction is characterized by the addict's inability to suppress behavioral impulses to use drugs is widely accepted among researchers and practitioners in the addiction field. Impulsivity is considered to be an important risk factor for the onset of drug abuse and has been the focus of considerable research attention in recent years. Broadly defined, impulsivity refers to a pattern of under-controlled behavior in which the individual is unable to delay gratification and acts without forethought or consideration of potential consequences. Its role as a risk factor for drug abuse is based on findings from studies examining drug abuse in relation to impulsivity as a central characteristic of psychopathology and as a dimension of normal personality. It is well recognized that substance abuse disorders have a high comorbidity with antisocial, borderline, histrionic, and externalizing disorders, which are all characterized by under-controlled, impulsive patterns of behavior (e.g., Grekin, Sher, and Wood, 2006; Trull, Waudby, and Sher, 2004). Studies also show that impulsivity, as a dimension of normal personality, is associated with increased risk for alcohol and other drug abuse (Bjork, Hommer, Grant, and Danube, 2004; Dom, D'Haene, Hulstijn, and Sabbe, 2006; Soloff, Lynch, and Moss, 2000). In addition to characterizing the behavior of substance abusers, impulsivity also appears to play an etiological role in the development of drug addiction. Genetic studies implicate the transmission of impulsivity in the heritability of substance abuse disorders (for a review, see Lejuez *et al.*, 2010) and longitudinal studies have shown that impulsivity often precedes the onset of drug abuse (Caspi, Moffitt, Newman, and Silva, 1998; Littlefield, Sher, and Steinley, 2010; Shuckit, 1998).

[1] The research in this chapter was supported by National Institute on Alcohol Abuse and Alcoholism Grants R01 AA018274, R01 AA012895, and F31 AA018584.

Growing evidence for the involvement of impulsivity in drug addiction has prompted questions concerning the specific behavioral mechanisms through which impulsivity operates to promote drug abuse. One fundamental aspect of impulsivity that appears particularly relevant to drug abuse is the failure to inhibit inappropriate actions or behaviors. Behaviors are instigated or motivated by a host of factors, including internal states, such as hunger, and external events, such as the rich array of environmental cues that signal biologically relevant stimuli (e.g., primary and secondary reinforcers). Without any means to suppress or delay reactions to these signals, an organism's behavior would be immediately responsive and completely determined by such events. However, it is widely recognized that higher organisms, such as humans and other mammals, can exert control over behavioral output to delay, alter, or completely inhibit environmentally instigated responses. The ability to inhibit or suppress an action enhances the organism's behavioral repertoire by affording it control over when and where responses are expressed. As such, behavioral inhibition serves several important functions, such as allowing time to process information in working memory before initiating the next action; in short, giving the individual time to think before acting. Not surprisingly then, deficient or impaired inhibitory control has been implicated in the display of impulsivity and in substance disorders.

This chapter describes tasks that have been developed to measure behavioral inhibition in the laboratory. The chapter examines how these measures add to our understanding of drug addiction as a problem of deficient inhibitory control. Measures of behavioral inhibition are described in the context of studies that seek to characterize drug abusers in terms of deficits in their ability to inhibit specific actions, and in studies that test the direct effects of abused drugs on inhibitory control over these actions. The measures of behavioral inhibition are examined with a focus on methodological issues concerning their use in experimental research and on their psychometric properties, including reliability, validity, and standardization. The chapter concludes with a discussion of the limitations of laboratory measures of behavioral inhibition in addiction research and future directions for increasing their utility.

2 Behavioral Inhibition as a Multi-process Function

The concept of behavioral inhibition has played an important role in theories of behavior and psychopathology for many years. Inhibition was central to Freud's theory of repression (Freud, 1910) and in early theories of verbal learning (McGeoch, 1932). Today it has become well recognized that behavioral inhibition is not a unitary concept but refers to a set of various cognitive mechanisms designed to serve goal-directed behavior (Dempster, 1993; Nigg, 2000). Various methods of classifying common forms of behavioral inhibition have been proposed based on a variety of criteria. For example, in some situations the inhibition of behavior is intentional, as a conscious effortful action of the individual, as when an individual deliberately suppresses a response to a particular stimulus. However, in other cases inhibitory influences occur reactively without conscious effort. For example, we take longer to respond to stimuli that we recently ignored as being irrelevant compared with stimuli that we did not previously ignore (Houghton and Tipper, 1994). Such response biases against recently ignored stimuli are not intentional but reflect the lingering effects of having previously inhibited their influence. In addition to intentional-versus-reactive distinctions, behavioral inhibition also can be classified on the basis of the response modality or output that is being inhibited. In many cases the action being inhibited is an overt behavioral response, such as uttering a word or pressing a button in a reaction time task. However, in other cases it is the allocation of our attention that is controlled by inhibitory mechanisms, as when we inhibit the direction of our gaze towards irrelevant objects in the environment in an effort to maintain goal direction.

Although such classification schemes are important because they drive theory and research, they also invite the notion that the tasks are in fact measures of distinct types of behavioral inhibition. However, it should be recognized that no task provides a "process-pure" assessment of any specific form of behavioral inhibition. Indeed, these tasks at best represent specially constructed stimulus–response environments that require some degree of response inhibition as part of successful performance. In this chapter, we focus our examination on behavioral tasks that measure inhibition as intentional acts of the individual, and we separate behavioral inhibition tasks into two categories: (1) inhibition as control of manual action; and (2) inhibition as control of attention. It is important to recognize that this dichotomy does not assume that manual action and attention are necessarily controlled by different underlying inhibitory processes or neural substrates. Rather, the categorization is used for didactic purposes and is particularly appropriate for a review focused on measurement and methodological issues. Within each category, behavioral tasks are of similar design and employ similar methodology, allowing for potential generalization of methodological principles and issues within each category, and important comparisons across categories.

3   Inhibition in the Control of Manual Action

Despite the complexity of the central nervous system, much of its influence can be reduced to the summed effects of opposing inhibitory and excitatory neural activity, and studies in neurophysiology have identified distinct neural systems that implicate separate inhibitory and activational mechanisms in the control of behavior (Feil *et al.*, 2010; Goldstein and Volkow, 2002; Jentsch and Taylor, 1999; Leigh and Zee, 1999; Lyvers, 2000). These opposing influences have been modeled at the behavioral level using reaction time tasks that measure the countervailing influences of inhibitory and activational mechanisms. Individuals are required to quickly activate a response to a "go" stimulus and to inhibit a response when a "stop" stimulus is presented. Activation is typically measured as the speed of responding to go stimuli and inhibition is assessed by the probability of suppressing the response to stop stimuli or by the time needed to suppress the response. The inhibitory response in these models is a sudden, intentional and brief act of control that is usually required in a context in which there is a strong tendency to respond to a stimulus (i.e., a pre-potency), thus making inhibition difficult. Common examples of these inhibition tasks are continuous performance tasks, go/no-go tasks, and stop-signal tasks.

3.1   Laboratory measures of manual inhibition

3.1.1   Continuous performance tasks.   These tasks, first developed by Rosvold *et al.* (1956), are used as measures of inhibition and as measures of inattention. Subjects continuously monitor a series of letters that are presented individually on a computer screen in random order. Subjects are required to respond to a target letter (e.g., X) but only when this target immediately follows a specific pre-target letter (e.g., A). These A–X target sequences occur randomly and infrequently during a test. Test duration is lengthy (e.g., 10–20 minutes), requiring sustained attention over a prolonged period of time. Performance measures include targets missed (omission errors; e.g., failing to respond to "X" after an "A") and responses to non-targets (commission errors). Commission errors are common to non-target letters that are preceded by the pre-target letter, as the pre-target letter can instigate a premature response to the next letter, suggesting disinhibition. Commission errors are also common to targets that are not preceded by the specific pre-target letter, suggesting lapses of attention to the pre-targets. Signal detection measures of discrimination and response bias are commonly calculated and used to estimate levels of inattention and disinhibition. Inattention is inferred by low discrimination and disinhibition is inferred by a liberal response bias. Several variations of continuous performance tasks have been developed, many that manipulate the level of difficulty for target detection. For example, some versions require detecting a multi-digit number where only one of the digits differentiates a target from a non-target (Dougherty *et al.*, 2000; 2005). Figure 6.1 illustrates a multi-digit version of a continuous performance task.

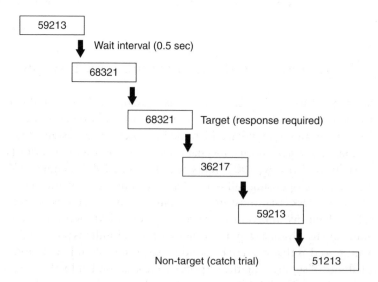

Figure 6.1   Schematic of a multi-digit version of a continuous performance task. Five-digit numbers are presented sequentially at 0.5 second intervals. Participants respond to target stimuli that are identical to the five-digit number presented immediately prior. Catch trials are occasionally presented in which the stimulus differs from a target stimulus by only one digit. Commission errors on these catch trials provide a measure of disinhibition

3.1.2 Go/no-go tasks. Go/no-go tasks measure behavioral control by the ability to quickly execute a response or inhibit a response to a single stimulus. In the basic go/no-go task, the subject is presented with stimuli designated as "go" stimuli and stimuli designated as "no-go" stimuli. For example, a go/no-go task might require a subject to respond quickly to the letter "X" (the go stimulus) and withhold the response to the letter "O" (the no-go stimulus). Several variations of this basic model have been developed and are widely used in substance abuse research. One commonly used variation, developed by Newman and colleagues (1985), employs go and no-go stimuli, and the subject must learn which stimuli signal a response and which signal inhibition. The task presents subjects with a set of numbers, some "correct" and others "incorrect." The numbers are repeatedly presented in random order. Subjects receive monetary rewards (e.g., 10 cents) for responding to correct numbers and are punished by equal monetary loss for responding to incorrect numbers. Feedback about money gained/lost is presented after each trial, and based on this information subjects learn over trials which numbers signal a response and which signal inhibition. The task measures the ability to associate response inhibition with specific stimuli based on memory of punishment for previously responding to such stimuli.

Another commonly used variation is the cued go/no-go task that manipulates response prepotency by presenting a preliminary go or no-go cue before the actual go or no-go target is displayed (Fillmore, 2003). The cues provide information concerning the probability that a go or no-go target will be presented. The cue–target relationship is manipulated so that cues have a high probability of correctly signaling a go or no-go target (valid cues), and a low probability of incorrectly signaling a target (invalid cues). Correct (i.e., valid) cues tend to facilitate response execution and response inhibition. For example, responses to go targets are faster when they are preceded by a go cue. Similarly, the likelihood of suppressing a response to a no-go target is greater when it is preceded by a no-go cue. Figure 6.2 presents a schematic of the cue–target probabilities and the trial procedure for the cued go/no-go task.

3.1.3 Stop-signal tasks. Originally developed by Gordon Logan and colleagues, stop-signal tasks are reaction time scenarios in which individuals are required to quickly activate a response to a go-signal and to inhibit a response when a stop-signal occasionally occurs (Logan and Cowan, 1984; Logan, 1985). Much of this research has been influenced by a "stop-signal" model of behavioral control (Logan, 1985). According to the model, go- and stop-signals elicit respective activating and inhibitory processes, and the time in which each process is completed determines the behavioral outcome. If the inhibiting processes are completed first, the response is withheld, but if the activating processes finish first, the response is executed. Activation is typically measured by the speed of responding to go-signals and inhibition to stop-signals is assessed by the probability of suppressing the response or by the time needed to suppress the response, referred to as the stop-signal reaction time. Stop-signal reaction time is defined as the difference between the time the stop signal is presented and the end of the inhibitory process, and can be estimated mathematically based on the probability of successfully inhibiting a response when the stop-signal is presented at various delays following the go-signal (see Logan, 1994). Longer stop-signal reaction times indicate weaker inhibitory control over behavior, perhaps due to a slow inhibitory process.

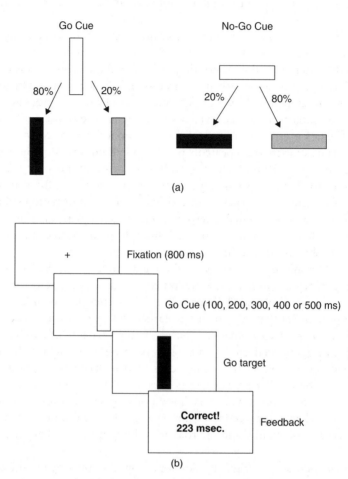

Figure 6.2 (a) Cue–target combination probabilities on the cued go/no-go task. Left panel: Go cues precede go targets (black boxes) on 80% of trials (valid go cue condition) and no-go targets (gray boxes) on 20% of trials (invalid go cue condition). Inhibitory failures are most common in the invalid go cue condition, when the response is prepotent. Right panel: No-go cues precede no-go targets (gray boxes) on 80% of trials (valid no-go cue condition) and go targets (black boxes) on 20% of trials (invalid no-go cue condition). (b) Schematic of the trial procedure in the valid go cue condition. Following the fixation, a go cue is presented at one of five SOAs, signaling participants to prepare to respond to the expected go target. The go target is then presented, and the computer provides feedback regarding accuracy and speed of response

Stop-signal tasks are rather unique among measures of behavioral inhibition because they provide this estimation of the time needed to inhibit a response.

Stop-signal tasks often present go-signals as visual stimuli, such as letters (e.g., O versus X) that require a simple choice response by pressing one of two keys on a keyboard. Subjects are required to inhibit the response when stop-signals (e.g., brief

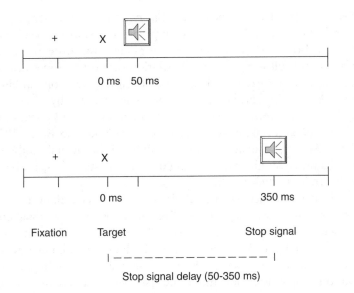

Figure 6.3 Schematic of the trial procedure of a stop trial on the stop-signal task. A fixation is briefly presented, followed by presentation of the target stimulus (X), which signals a response. The stop-signal is presented at variable delays (top panel: 50 ms; bottom panel: 350 ms) following target presentation. Probability of inhibiting the response is greatest when the stop-signal delay is short (i.e., when the stop-signal occurs soon after target presentation), and probability of inhibition decreases with longer duration of stop-signal delay

auditory tones) occasionally accompany go-signal presentations. The presentation of a go-target on every trial produces a prepotency (i.e., instigation) to respond. Subjects must overcome the prepotent tendency in order to suppress responses when stop-signals occur. Although all stop-signal tasks share the same basic stimulus arrangement of go- and stop-signals, the go- and stop-signals can differ considerably across tasks. For example, stop-signals can be auditory tones or a secondary visual stimulus that accompanies the go-signal, or the stop-signal might be indicated by change in the stimulus property of the go-signal itself, such as a color change from green to red. Figure 6.3 illustrates the sequence of events for a stop-signal task in which a visual target serves as the go-target and an auditory tone serves as the stop-signal.

3.2 Relevance to substance abuse

Use of behavioral inhibition tasks in substance abuse research has been prompted by the general theory that substance abuse should be associated with poor behavioral inhibition, and therefore substance abusers should show less behavioral inhibition on these tasks (Fillmore and Weafer, 2011; Jentsch and Taylor, 1999; Lyvers, 2000). The association between poor inhibition and substance use could be the result of neuro-toxic effects from prolonged, excessive drug use or could also suggest a pre-existing deficit of inhibitory control that puts the individual at heightened risk for substance abuse. Regardless of causal direction, validity for these tasks can be demonstrated by showing that they can detect deficient inhibitory control in substance abusers that are not observed in other healthy control samples with no history of substance abuse. Task validity can also be assessed by studies that examine the acute, transitory changes in inhibitory control following the administration of a drug. Some drugs of abuse, such as alcohol, are recognized for their acute impairing effects on inhibitory control over behavior. Alcohol intoxication is commonly characterized by reduced inhibition, possibly leading to hazardous behaviors such as aggression, risky sex, driving while intoxicated, and binge drinking (e.g., Giancola, Godlaski, and Roth, 2012; Weafer and Fillmore, 2012b). As such, assessing the ability of behavioral inhibition tasks to detect acute changes in inhibition following drug administration is another important method of determining their validity.

Below we review evidence for the validity of these tasks as indicators of deficient inhibitory control from two major lines of research: (1) cross-sectional comparisons between substance abusers and healthy control samples; and (2) examination of the acute effects of the abused drugs on behavioral inhibition. A comprehensive review is beyond the scope of the chapter. Rather, our goal is to highlight some typical findings and some inconsistencies among the tasks when they are used to characterize substance abusers and the acute responses to the drugs that they abuse.

3.2.1 Cross-sectional comparisons. There are a growing number of studies that have compared substance abusers to healthy control samples in terms of their ability to intentionally inhibit action. Much of this research has focused on alcohol use. Some research using continuous performance tasks shows that detoxified alcoholics commit more commission errors compared with controls (e.g., Bjork, Hommer, Grant, and Danube, 2004). That is, alcoholics respond to non-targets instead of inhibiting reactions to these stimuli. Heavy drinkers who are not in treatment also show similar deficits on these tasks. For example, Rubio *et al.* (2008) showed that heavy drinkers displayed slower response inhibition on a stop-signal task compared with moderate drinking controls. Some research using these tasks suggests that the inhibitory deficits might actually precede the onset of abusive drinking. For example, Acheson and colleagues (2011) found that adults with a positive family history of alcohol abuse showed poorer levels of response inhibition as measured by more commission errors on a continuous performance task and by more inhibitory failures on a stop-signal task. Despite reports of poorer response inhibition among problem drinkers, the evidence is not entirely consistent. Some research has failed to observe increased commission errors in binge drinkers on a go/no-go task (e.g., Marczinski, Combs, and Fillmore, 2007). Also, there is not always agreement between different measures of response inhibition. A recent study by Castellanos-Ryan, Rubia, and Conrod (2011) examined adolescents and found that levels of binge drinking were predicted by greater commission errors on a go/no-go task, but not by their response inhibition as measured by the stop-signal task.

Other cross-sectional studies using these tasks have examined stimulant abusers, such as cocaine users. On the stop-signal task, compared with controls cocaine users display slower inhibition to stop-signals and increased failures to inhibit responses to stop-signals (Fillmore and Rush, 2002; Li *et al.*, 2006). Figure 6.4 illustrates the findings by Fillmore and Rush (2002). The figure plots the mean probability of inhibiting

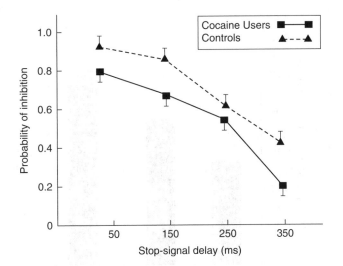

Figure 6.4 Mean probability of inhibiting a response at each of four stop-signal delays (50, 150, 250, 350 ms) for cocaine users ($N = 20$) and controls ($N = 20$). Vertical capped lines indicate standard error of the mean. Adapted from Fillmore and Rush (2002)

a response at each of four stop-signal delays and shows that the probability of inhibiting a response to a stop-signal diminishes as the stop-signal delay increases because less time is available to inhibit the pre-potent response. The figure also shows that the cocaine users displayed a consistently lower probability of successfully inhibiting to stop-signals than controls at all stop-signal delays.

Other behavioral inhibition tasks used to study cocaine users also find deficits of inhibition. For example, cocaine users are slower to learn to associate no-go cues with response inhibition on a cued go/no-go task (Fillmore and Rush, 2006). Compared with control samples, cocaine users have been shown to display greater commission errors on the continuous performance task (Gooding, Burroughs, and Boutros, 2008) and on a go/no-go task (Lane *et al.*, 2007; Verdejo-García and Perez-Garcia, 2007). Abusers of other stimulant drugs, such as methamphetamine (Monterosso *et al.*, 2005), also show inhibitory deficits on these tasks, such as slower response inhibition on the stop-signal task and more commission errors on a go/no-go task compared with control samples. Some research also has used these tasks to examine inhibitory control in smokers, but the results have not been consistent. Mitchell (2004) found that smokers made more commission errors on a go/no-go task compared with non-smokers, and that this indicator of behavioral disinhibition might be a risk factor, evident prior to the onset of smoking. However, Dawkins *et al.* (2009) compared abstinent smokers to continuing smokers and found that abstinence led to poorer performance on measures of attention but not on the measures from a continuous performance task. Although to date the majority of cross-sectional studies have examined alcohol and stimulant abuse, there is some evidence that these tasks can detect inhibitory deficits in opiate abusers as well. For example, a study using the go/no-go task showed that heroin users displayed increased commission errors compared with a control sample (Verdejo-García and Perez-Garcia, 2007).

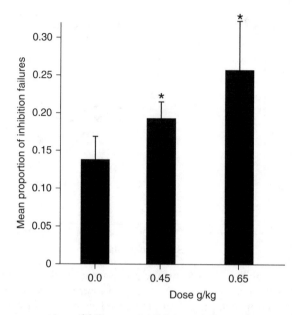

Figure 6.5 Mean proportion of failures to inhibit responses to no-go targets after go cues under three alcohol dose conditions: 0.0 g/kg (placebo), 0.45 g/kg, and 0.65 g/kg ($N = 12$). Vertical bars show standard errors of the mean. * indicates significant difference from placebo ($p < 0.05$). Adapted from Marczinski and Fillmore (2003)

3.2.2 Examination of acute drug effects. Several studies also have used these tasks to examine the acute effects of drugs on the intentional inhibition of actions. Generally speaking, these studies demonstrate considerable methodological rigor, such as employment of placebo-controls, and multiple dose determinations based on within-subjects, randomized designs. Like cross-sectional work, the majority of these dose challenge studies examined the acute effects of alcohol and stimulants. With respect to alcohol, these tasks have provided remarkably consistent evidence for the acute disinhibiting effects of the drug. Go/no-go and continuous performance tasks have been used in many studies of the acute effects of alcohol and have shown that alcohol increases commission errors in a dose-dependent manner (Dougherty *et al.*, 1999; Marczinski and Fillmore, 2003). The findings by Marczinski and Fillmore (2003) are presented in Figure 6.5. The figure shows that probability of failing to inhibit responses to no-go targets increased as a function of alcohol dose. The lowest active dose (0.45 g/kg abs. alcohol) produces a blood alcohol concentration (BAC) of approximately 50 mg/100 ml. This BAC can be achieved by as few as two to three drinks. Based on several subsequent studies in our laboratory, it appears that this BAC is the threshold concentration for observing reduced response inhibition on the cued go/no-go task (Fillmore, 2007). This is particularly significant as it demonstrates the sensitivity of the task to detect behavioral impairments from moderate BACs that are below the legal driving limit of 80 mg/100 ml.

Stop-signal tasks also show that alcohol produces acute impairments of inhibitory control, as evidenced by slower response inhibition and by increased failures to inhibit responses (de Wit, Crean, and Richards, 2000; Fillmore and Vogel-Sprott, 1999). However, although rare, there are some reports in which tasks, such as the go/no-go task, have failed to demonstrate alcohol effects (Rose and Duka, 2007). Studies using these tasks have shown that other central nervous system (CNS) depressants, such as benzodiazepines, can impair inhibitory control. Triazolam slowed response inhibition on a stop-signal task (Fillmore, Rush, Kelly, and Hays, 2001), and diazepam was found to increase commission errors on a go/no-go task (Acheson, Reynolds, Richards, and de Wit, 2006).

Use of behavioral inhibition tasks has provided less consistent evidence with respect to the acute effects of stimulants on inhibitory control. These tasks have shown that stimulants can enhance the ability to inhibit behavioral responses (de Wit, Engasser, and Richards, 2002; Tannock, Schachar, and Logan, 1995). Much of this evidence is based on stop-signal and cued go/no-go tasks. Studies using these tasks have found that the stimulants methylphenidate and *d*-amphetamine can improve inhibitory control in children with attention deficit hyperactivity disorder (ADHD) and in healthy adults (de Wit, Engasser, and Richards, 2002; Tannock, Schachar, and Logan, 1995). However, some studies of cocaine and *d*-amphetamine have failed to demonstrate facilitating effects on inhibitory control. For example, our group found that orally administered doses of cocaine HCl (50–150 mg) and *d*-amphetamine (5–20 mg) produced slight impairments of inhibitory control in stimulant abusers, as evidenced by a decreased ability to inhibit responses on stop-signal and go/no-go tasks (Fillmore, Rush, and Hays, 2002; Fillmore, Rush, and Marczinski, 2003). However, in a study of adults with no history of stimulant abuse, we found that *d*-amphetamine (5–20 mg) improved working memory but had no effect on inhibitory control (Fillmore, Kelly, and Martin, 2005). In addition, there is not always agreement between different measures of response inhibition. Fillmore, Rush, and Hays (2006) compared inhibition measures from stop-signal and go/no-go tasks following higher cocaine HCl doses (100–300 mg). At this dose range, both tasks showed some cocaine-induced facilitation of inhibitory control; however, the dose-response functions differed depending on the task.

Although few, there are some recent studies that have used these tasks to examine the effects of other classes of drugs, including hallucinogens, such as marijuana (Ramaekers *et al.*, 2009), and opioid-based analgesics, such as oxycodone (Zacny and de Wit, 2009). Possible disinhibiting effects of opioids are of clinical interest not only because of the abuse potential of opioids, but also because such disinhibition would indicate a potentially serious negative side-effect in the pharmacotherapy of pain management. To test such a possibility, a recent study used the go/no-go and stop-signal tasks to examine the acute effects of oxycodone on inhibitory control across a range of therapeutic (5–10 mg) and supra-therapeutic (20 mg) doses and found no effect of the drug on commission errors (Zacny and de Wit, 2009).

4 Inhibition in the Control of Attention

A separate component of behavioral inhibition that has been implicated in addiction involves inhibitory control of attentional mechanisms. Attentional control refers to

the ability to ignore distracting stimuli in the environment in order to focus attention on relevant information. As such, individuals with poor attentional control are
characterized by increased distractibility and failure to ignore irrelevant information.
Control models have identified distinct inhibitory mechanisms that facilitate selective
attention by directing cognitive resources away from irrelevant stimuli and toward
relevant stimuli (Houghton and Tipper, 1994). The neurological substrates thought
to govern these attentional control mechanisms include frontal brain regions, specifically the dorsolateral prefrontal cortex and the anterior cingulate cortex (Everling and
Fisher, 1998; Iacono, Carlson, and Malone, 2000; Chung *et al.*, 2011). Researchers
have utilized behavioral tasks to assess the inhibitory control of attention, particularly
through the examination of ocular response (i.e., saccade) with eye-tracking technology. Tasks, such as the antisaccade and memory-guided saccade task, involve the
inhibition of a reflexive saccade to the sudden appearance of a distracter object. As
such, individuals must utilize inhibitory mechanisms of attention to overcome the
prepotent impulse to look at the distracter stimulus.

4.1   Laboratory measures of attentional inhibition

4.1.1   Antisaccade tasks.   These tasks have been used for several decades to examine
the ability to inhibit oculomotor responses (Everling and Fischer, 1998). A typical
antisaccade task involves the inhibition of a prosaccade (i.e., a reflexive saccade toward
an object), followed by the execution of an antisaccade (i.e., a saccade in the mirror
opposite location). Participants are instructed to focus on a fixation point presented
on a computer screen. An object is then briefly presented in the periphery, eliciting
a reflexive impulse to look at the object. However, participants are instructed to
inhibit this reflexive response, and instead to move their eyes to look in the mirror
opposite the direction of the stimulus as quickly as possible. Thus, participants must
inhibit the reflexive saccade, while simultaneously executing a saccade in the opposite
direction (i.e., the antisaccade). Figure 6.6 presents a schematic illustration of the
antisaccade task. The dependent measure of attentional inhibition for these tasks is
the number of errors committed on the antisaccade trials (i.e., the number of trials
in which participants fail to inhibit the prosaccade or fail to execute the antisaccade).
Latency to execute saccades, peak velocity of saccades, and accuracy of saccades are
also measured.

There are several versions of the task that vary in difficulty. In the simplest version
of this task, only antisaccade trials are presented. Thus, participants are told to execute
an antisaccade for every trial (i.e., for all targets presented onscreen). Alternately,
prosaccade trials can also be included in the task. In this case, participants are told
to respond to targets by making a saccade towards the target (i.e., a prosaccade) as
quickly as possible. However, on some trials a signal is presented (e.g., an auditory
tone or a change in fixation point color), indicating for that specific trial that an
antisaccade should be executed. There is an increased prepotency to execute the
reflexive orienting response towards the stimulus in this situation, as the participant
is executing the prosaccade as quickly as possible on the majority of trials. Thus,
inhibition of the prepotent saccadic response is more difficult in this version of the
task. An additional variant of the antisaccade task involves the inclusion of 'overlap'

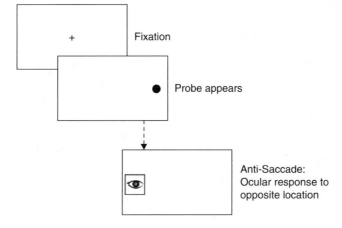

Figure 6.6 Schematic of the trial procedure in an antisaccade task. A fixation is presented for a brief period, followed by a probe stimulus (black dot). The probe typically elicits a reflexive response to look in the direction of the probe (i.e., a prosaccade). However, participants must inhibit that reflexive response, and instead execute a saccade in the mirror opposite the location of the probe as quickly as possible following onset of the probe. Inhibitory deficits are measured by the number of errors committed (i.e., failures to inhibit a prosaccade in the direction of the target)

and 'gap' trials. In these conditions, all trials call for the execution of an antisaccade; however, the onset of the target stimulus is varied in specific ways. In the overlap condition, the fixation remains on the screen throughout the entire trial. By contrast, in the gap condition, the fixation point disappears for a short interval (e.g., 200 ms) before the presentation of the target, causing the inhibition of the prosaccade to be more difficult.

4.1.2   Memory-guided saccade tasks.   As with antisaccade tasks, memory-guided saccade tasks also require the inhibition of a prepotent eye movement towards the sudden appearance of a salient target stimulus that normally elicits a reflexive saccade towards the stimulus (Peterson, Kramer, and Irwin, 2004; Theeuwes *et al.*, 1999). However, instead of executing an antisaccade, participants must instead remember where the target stimulus was located, and, after a signal is presented, move their eyes to the previous location of the target as quickly as possible. Speed of responding is emphasized in order to create a greater prepotency of the eye movement (consequently causing inhibition to be more difficult). The delayed ocular return task is an example of a memory-guided saccade task (Ross *et al.*, 1994; 2000; 2005). Here, subjects are instructed to 'delay' looking at the stimulus (i.e., intentionally inhibit the reflexive saccade) until the signal is given to make a saccade to the location in which the target stimulus had appeared. Figure 6.7 illustrates the trial procedure for this task. The primary measure of a memory-guided saccade task is the number of trials in which a subject fails to inhibit the reflexive saccade (i.e., premature saccades), indicating failure of attentional inhibition. Saccadic reaction time and accuracy are also measured.

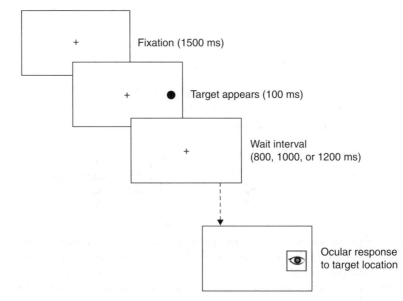

Figure 6.7 Schematic of the trial procedure in the delayed ocular return task. A fixation point is presented, and the participant is instructed to focus on the fixation the entire time it is on the screen. After 1500 ms, a target briefly appears (100 ms) in the periphery. The target presentation typically elicits a reflexive saccade in the direction of the target (i.e., a prosaccade). However, the participant must inhibit the saccade, and instead maintain focus on the fixation point during a wait interval (800, 1000, or 1200 ms). After the wait interval, the fixation disappears, and the participant executes the 'delayed' ocular response to the prior location of the target as quickly as possible. Inhibitory failures are measured as the number of trials in which a participant fails to wait and executes the "premature" prosaccade to the target during the wait interval

4.1.3 Countermanding tasks. These tasks are direct modifications of stop-signal tasks developed by Logan and colleagues (Logan and Cowan, 1984; Logan and Irwin, 2000). As with stop-signal tasks, countermanding tasks require subjects to execute quick responses to go-signals and inhibit the response when a stop-signal is occasionally presented. However, instead of a manual response (e.g., a key press), the countermanding task requires the subject to execute a saccade following a go-signal. A trial involves the presentation of a fixation point on screen for a short duration, followed by the presentation of a target stimulus in the periphery. Subjects execute a saccade toward the target as quickly as possible. Occasionally a stop-signal is presented, such as an auditory tone, or a visual signal, such as a change in color of the fixation point. Subjects are to inhibit the saccade when the stop-signal is presented. As with the manual stop signal task, the delay between presentation of the go-signal and stop-signal is varied between trials, thus allowing for a measurement of the time needed to inhibit a response, the stop-signal reaction time. Both the stop-signal reaction time and number of inhibitory failures serve as dependent measures in this task. Saccadic latency on go trials is also recorded.

4.2   Relevance to substance abuse

Deficits in inhibitory control of attention could potentially confer a specific risk for substance abuse. A growing body of research has shown that alcohol abusers and other drug abusers display a biased attention towards drug-related stimuli, and that such stimuli could elicit craving and drug self-administration in these individuals (Field and Cox, 2008; Field, Munafo, and Franken, 2009; Robinson and Berridge, 1993; 2000). Thus, it is important for individuals attempting to control substance use to be able to ignore drug-related stimuli when they are encountered, and instead to focus attention towards stimuli that encourage restraint or abstinence. As individuals with poor attentional control might have difficulty inhibiting attention towards such drug-related stimuli, this could increase their risk for drug abuse. Some studies have used tasks that measure inhibitory control of attention in order to test this general hypothesis. Research has employed cross-sectional designs to compare substance abusers to healthy comparison groups, and also dose-challenge methods to test the effects of acute drug administration on inhibitory control of attention.

4.2.1   Cross-sectional comparisons.   Campanella and colleagues (2009) compared chronic alcoholics to a group of controls on an antisaccade task, and found that the chronic alcoholics exhibited deficits in attentional inhibition. Weafer, Milich, and Fillmore (2011) used a delayed ocular return task to test the hypothesis that poor inhibition of attention could predict alcohol abuse, particularly in individuals with attentional deficits. Poor inhibitory control on the task predicted greater self-reported alcohol consumption in those with ADHD, but not in controls.

These tasks have shown that poor inhibitory control of attention is related to other drug use as well. In a study examining antisaccade performance in smokers, Spinella (2002) found that smokers commit more inhibition errors than do non-smokers. Further, Chung *et al.* (2011) found that adolescents diagnosed with substance use disorder committed more inhibition errors in a rewarded antisaccade task than did those without a history of substance abuse. By contrast, no difference in inhibition errors on this task was found between a group of heavy cannabis users and non-users (Huestegge, Radach, and Kunert, 2009). These tasks have also been used to measure potential deficits in attentional control in adolescents at risk for substance abuse, and there is some evidence to suggest that children with a family history of alcoholism show deficits in attentional inhibition (e.g., Habeych, Folan, Luna, and Tarter, 2006; Iacono *et al.*, 1999). Although these findings suggest that impaired mechanisms of attentional control might predate and thus play an influential role in the development of substance abuse and dependence, the lack of longitudinal studies examining this question prevents any conclusions being drawn regarding whether impaired attentional control is a cause or consequence (or both) of substance abuse.

4.2.2   Examination of acute drug effects.   In addition to cross-sectional research, these tasks also have been used to examine acute drug effects on mechanisms of attentional inhibition. Similar to studies examining drug effects on inhibition of manual action, the majority of this research involves the acute administration of moderate doses of alcohol or stimulants. Regarding alcohol effects, results have been mixed. For

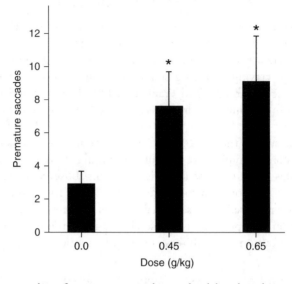

Figure 6.8   Mean number of premature saccades on the delayed ocular return task in response to 0.0, 0.45, and 0.65 g/kg alcohol ($N = 12$). Capped vertical lines indicate standard error of the mean. * indicates significantly different from placebo ($p < 0.05$). Adapted from Abroms *et al.* (2006)

instance, alcohol has been shown to dose-dependently increase premature saccades on the delayed ocular return task (Abroms, Gottlob, and Fillmore, 2006). In this study, task performance was examined following placebo and two active doses of alcohol (0.45 g/kg and 0.65 g/kg). Results showed that both doses of alcohol significantly increased premature saccades, and these are presented in Figure 6.8. These results have been replicated in subsequent studies in our lab (e.g., Weafer and Fillmore, 2012a), providing further support for the sensitivity of this task to detect impairment of attentional inhibition at low to moderate doses of alcohol.

Alcohol has also been shown to increase inhibition errors on the antisaccade task, but only in individuals with no family history of alcoholism (Ramchandani *et al.*, 1999). By contrast, several studies have found no effect of alcohol on antisaccade errors (e.g., Blekher *et al.*, 2002; Vorstius, Radach, Lang, and Riccardi, 2008), and some studies have reported that alcohol actually *decreases* inhibitory errors on these tasks (Khan, Ford, Timney, and Everling, 2003; Roche and King, 2010; Vassallo and Abel, 2002). Although these latter studies appear to provide evidence for a facilitating effect of alcohol on attentional inhibition, it is more likely that these results are due to a speed–accuracy trade-off in task performance. Alcohol slows saccadic response latency of both prosaccades and antisaccades. Thus, intoxicated individuals are slower to execute saccades in general, and this slowing decreases the prepotency of the reflexive saccade, allowing more time for inhibitory mechanisms to suppress the saccade.

With respect to stimulant drug effects, studies typically report acute increases in attentional control following administration of these substances. For example, nicotine has been shown to decrease inhibitory failures on the antisaccade task compared to placebo (Larrison, Briand, and Sereno, 2004), especially in regular smokers following a period of abstinence (Dawkins *et al.*, 2007; 2009; Powell, Dawkins, and Davis, 2002). Similarly, amphetamine decreased inhibition errors on the antisaccade task in a group of healthy controls (Allman, 2010), and methylphenidate did the same in a sample of young adults with ADHD (Klein, Fischer, Fischer, and Hartnegg, 2002). Improved inhibitory control in response to stimulants in these studies is probably not an artifact of a speed–accuracy trade-off, as overall saccadic response times tended to become faster in response to the active drug. Thus, similar to manual control of inhibition, attentional control appears to improve in response to moderate doses of stimulant drugs.

These tasks also have been used to examine the effects of other classes of drugs on attentional control. For instance, cannabis has been found to increase errors on both an antisaccade and a memory-guided saccade task (Ploner *et al.*, 2002). Further, countermanding tasks have been used to measure effects of anesthetics on attentional inhibition. Findings show that both isoflurane and sevoflurane increase stop-signal reaction time, indicating impairment of inhibitory mechanisms of attention (Khan *et al.*, 1999; Nouraei, De Pennington, Jones, and Carpenter, 2003).

5 Psychometrics

5.1 Task reliability

Given the widespread use of behavioral inhibition tasks in addiction research, the lack of attention to psychometric issues, such as reliability, is somewhat surprising. Few studies that employ these measures in substance abuse research have reported on the reliability of the tasks. For tasks that measure inhibition of manual actions, most reliability studies concern their use in the assessment of inhibitory impairments among children with ADHD. Reliability studies of continuous performance tasks typically involve Conners' version of the task, which is widely used in the assessment of ADHD (Conners, 2004). These tasks show high test–retest reliability (>0.85) of commission errors in child and adult samples over short time intervals, from 1 to 2 weeks (e.g., Halperin, Sharma, Greenblatt, and Schwartz, 1991; Soreni, Crosbie, Ickowicz, and Schachar, 2009), and modest reliabilities (0.62 to 0.82) over longer intervals from 3 to 8 months (e.g., Kaminski, Groff, and Glutting, 2009; Zabel *et al.*, 2009). Other more complex versions, such as the immediate and delayed memory task, typically used in adults, also demonstrate high test–retest reliability across consecutive testing days (Mathias, Marsh, and Dougherty, 2002).

Like continuous performance tasks, the reliability of the stop-signal task is almost exclusively studied by ADHD researchers and is based on child samples. In general, the stop-signal task demonstrates good test–retest reliability in children with and without ADHD. Studies even report good consistency in children's response inhibition on the task over fairly lengthy intervals of 2 to 5 months (Kindlon, Mezzacappa, and Earls, 1995; Soreni, Crosbie, Ickowicz, and Schachar, 2009). One of the few studies that examined the reliability of response inhibition in healthy adults tested individuals on a stop-signal task six times over a 3-week period (Fillmore, Kelly, and Martin, 2005).

The intraclass correlation of inhibition scores across tests yielded a coefficient alpha of 0.98, indicating a high degree of consistency in inhibitory control over this time period. Although few, there are also some reports on the test–retest reliability of the go/no-task. Kuntsi *et al.* (2005) reported moderate to good reliability of commission errors in children over a 2-week period.

For tasks that measure inhibition in the control of attention, there is also limited information concerning their reliability in substance abuse research. Rather, the majority of evidence for their reliability comes from investigations of attentional impairments in schizophrenia. Schizophrenia is associated with "eye movement dysfunction" which could be an endophenotypic marker of the underlying genetic predisposition for the disorder. As such, there is considerable interest in the psychometrics of tasks that assess eye movement dysfunction in this population, and chief among them is the antisaccade task. Studies of schizophrenic populations and healthy control groups show moderate reliability (>0.65) of inhibition errors on the antisaccade task at intervals from 2 months to 2 years (Calkins, Iacono, and Curtis, 2003; Klein and Fischer, 2005). Evidence of adequate reliability of this measure also has been reported over longer intervals, ranging from 3 to 5 years (Gooding, Shea, and Matts, 2005).

5.2   Task validity

As mentioned earlier, it is widely assumed that a lack of behavioral inhibition is a key feature of impulsivity. As such, it is reasonable to expect that measures of response inhibition obtained from tasks measuring both manual and attentional control should bear some relationship to impulsivity. This section examines three distinct approaches to validity assessment of the behavioral inhibition tasks described in this chapter: (1) examination of differences in inhibitory control between clinical versus control samples; (2) examination of task performance in relation to individual differences in trait measures of impulsivity; and (3) examination of the interrelations among task measures.

5.2.1   Clinical versus control comparisons.   Some research has demonstrated validity of behavioral inhibition tasks by assessing the response inhibition of clinical samples characterized by impulsive, under-controlled behavior. Such groups should demonstrate poorer inhibitory control on these tasks compared with healthy "control" samples. The manual and attentional inhibition tasks described above have been shown effective in detecting deficits of inhibitory control in clinical populations, including schizophrenic patients, brain-injury patients, and those with ADHD (Cremona-Meteyard and Geffen, 1994; Malloy, Bihrle, Duffy, and Cimino, 1993; Oosterlaan and Sergeant, 1996; Schachar, Tannock, Marriott, and Logan, 1995; Tannock, 1998; Thakkar *et al.*, 2011; Turetsky *et al.*, 2007).

The majority of evidence demonstrating poor inhibitory control in clinical populations with these tasks comes from studies of children and young adults with ADHD (for a review, see Quay, 1997). In addition to attentional deficits, ADHD is characterized by impulsivity. As such, these individuals should display poorer inhibitory control compared with control samples. Indeed, a growing number of studies using stop-signal, continuous performance, and go/no-go tasks find that those with ADHD typically display more commission errors and slower response inhibition compared with controls (Alderson, Rapport, and Kofler, 2007; Barkley, 1997; Derefinko *et al.*, 2008; Murphy, Barkley, and Bush, 2001). Additionally, children and adults with ADHD show deficits in attentional inhibition compared to controls, as evidenced by more inhibition errors on antisaccade, memory-guided saccade, and countermanding tasks (Adams, Roberts, Milich, and Fillmore, 2011; Aman, Roberts, and Pennington, 1998; Nigg, Butler, Huang-Pollock, and Henderson, 2002; Roberts, Fillmore, and Milich, 2011; Ross, Harris, Olincy, and Radant, 2000; Weafer, Milich, and Fillmore, 2011).

Other clinical populations also provide evidence for the validity of these tasks. For instance, patients diagnosed with schizophrenia, often characterized by disinhibited and impulsive behavior, have been shown to exhibit deficits on response inhibition tasks. The majority of this research has examined mechanisms of attentional inhibition, and schizophrenic patients have consistently been shown to commit more inhibitory failures on antisaccade and countermanding tasks (e.g., Holahan and O'Driscoll, 2005; Radant *et al.*, 2007; Thakkar *et al.*, 2011; Turetsky *et al.*, 2007). Studies examining inhibitory control in patients with frontal brain injury have also demonstrated marked impairment on these tasks. Specifically, frontal lobe degeneration has been associated with increased errors on the antisaccade task (Boxer *et al.*, 2006; Fukushima, Fukushima, Miyasaka, and Yamashita, 1994) and increased stop-signal reaction time on the stop-signal task (Floden and Stuss, 2006; Rieger, Gauggel, and Burmeister, 2003).

5.2.2   Task performance in relation to trait impulsivity.   Another approach to validating behavioral inhibition tasks as measures of impulsivity is to examine the degree to which these tasks actually relate to impulsivity when measured as a trait dimension of normal personality. As a trait, impulsivity is measured using self-report inventories, such as the Barratt Impulsivity Scale (BIS; Patton, Stanford, and Barratt, 1995), Eysenck Impulsiveness Questionnaire (I-7; Eysenck, Pearson, Easting, and Allsopp, 1985), and the UPPS Impulsive Behavior Scale (UPPS; Whiteside and Lynam, 2001). The inventories provide an overall trait measure of impulsivity and can provide domain-specific measures of impulsivity. For example, the BIS and UPPS are comprised of individual scales that assess specific behavioral domains or general characteristics of impulsive behavior such as lack of motor control, lack of perseverance, and sensation seeking. Using these instruments, validity for behavioral inhibition tasks is demonstrated by their correlation with scores on the impulsivity inventories.

Compared with the clinical-control comparison studies described above, these correlational studies provide less clear evidence for the association between behavioral inhibition tasks and measures of impulsivity. Some studies have reported correlations between measures from behavioral tasks involving manual inhibition and impulsivity inventories. Logan, Schachar, and Tannock (1997) reported that adults who were slower to inhibit responses on the stop-signal task also self-reported higher levels of impulsivity on the Eysenck Impulsiveness Questionnaire. Castellanos-Ryan, Rubia, and Conrod (2011) showed that poor response inhibition on the stop-signal task was associated with greater self-reported impulsivity in adolescents, and Swann, Bjork,

Moeller, and Dougherty (2002) found that subjects who displayed greater commis-sion errors on continuous performance tasks self-reported greater levels of impulsivity on the BIS. However, Enticott, Ogloff, and Bradshaw (2006) found no correlation between response inhibition on the stop-signal task and self-reported impulsivity using the BIS. Gay *et al.* (2008) found that subjects who displayed more commission errors on go/no-go tasks reported higher scores on the Urgency subscale of the UPPS. However, Horn *et al.* (2003) and Reynolds, Ortengren, Richards, and de Wit (2006) found no correlation between commission errors on go/no-go tasks and self-reported levels of impulsivity. In regard to attentional measures of inhibition, few studies have examined correlations between these tasks and trait measures of impulsivity. However, significant associations have been reported between errors on the antisaccade task and greater impulsivity scores on subscales of both the BIS and the UPPS (Spinella, 2004; Jacob *et al.*, 2010).

5.2.3   Interrelationships among tasks.   To the extent that behavioral inhibition tasks all measure the ability to inhibit prepotent actions, individual differences in measures of response inhibition should be correlated among the tasks. For example, subjects who are slower to inhibit responses on a stop-signal task (i.e., longer SSRTs) should also demonstrate more commission errors on a go/no-go or continuous performance task. However, such congruence across tasks has not been generally observed. For example, in a group of stimulant abusers, Fillmore, Rush, and Hays (2006) found no relationship between their response inhibition as measured by a stop-signal task and their response inhibition as measured by a cued go/no-go task. Similarly, other studies have reported no association between response inhibition on stop-signal tasks and inhibition errors on go/no-go and continuous performance tasks in healthy adults (Enticott, Ogloff, and Bradshaw, 2006; Reynolds, Ortengren, Richards, and de Wit, 2006). By contrast, some studies have shown correlations between slow response inhibition on stop-signal tasks and commission errors on continuous performance and go/no-go tasks in control populations (Marsh *et al.*, 2002; Reynolds, Ortengren, Richards, and de Wit, 2006) and children with ADHD (Rubia, Smith, and Taylor, 2007). As with tasks of manual inhibition, individual differences in measures of attentional inhibition among antisaccade, memory-guided saccade, and countermanding tasks are also expected to be correlated. However, to date studies have not yet examined associations between these measures.

Some research has examined relationships among tasks that measure inhibitory con-trol of manual action and those that measure inhibition of attention. Two studies from our laboratory (Adams, Milich, and Fillmore, 2010; Weafer, Milich, and Fillmore, 2011) used a multitask assessment to examine inhibitory control in individuals with ADHD and healthy controls. The tasks included the cued go/no-go, the stop-signal, and a delayed ocular response task. Subjects' inhibitory control over their manual action showed no relation to their inhibitory control of attention in either study. Similarly, Jacob *et al.* (2010) found no association between antisaccade errors and response inhibition on a stop-signal task in a sample of adults with borderline personality disorder and controls. By contrast, Spinella (2004) showed a positive association between antisaccade and go/no-go errors in a non-clinical sample. Finally, a small number of studies have directly compared inhibition of manual and attentional responses on comparable versions of the stop-signal task. Findings showed that less time is needed to inhibit saccades compared to manual responses, but that both forms of inhibition operate under the same overriding response inhibition principles (Boucher, Palmeri, Logan, and Schall, 2007; Logan and Irwin, 2000).

6 Limitations and Future Directions

In recent years, behavioral inhibition tasks have received wide application in substance abuse research, driven in large part by theory implicating deficits of impulse control in the etiology of drug addiction. Much has been learned from these tasks. Generally speaking, these tasks have been useful in identifying inhibitory deficits in substance abusers who abuse alcohol, stimulant drugs (e.g., cocaine), and opiates. Moreover, the inhibitory deficits observed in these groups are not behavior-specific, but appear to be general deficits that are evident in the control of manual actions and in the control of attention. Further, these tasks have been useful tools to examine the acute effects of different drug classes on inhibitory control. Studies using tasks measuring inhibition of manual responses provide remarkably consistent evidence for the disinhibiting effects of alcohol and other CNS-depressant drugs. However, evidence regarding the acute effects of alcohol on inhibition of attentional responses is equivocal. It has been suggested that the overall slowing of the visual system in response to alcohol could preclude the ability to detect impairment of inhibitory control, and for this reason tasks measuring attentional inhibition might not be the best choice for this type of study. In terms of acute effects of stimulants, tasks measuring inhibition of both manual and attentional control generally show an increase in inhibitory control in response to these drugs. However, it is important to consider dose effects in this research, as higher doses of stimulants could produce opposite (i.e., disinhibiting) effects. With regard to other drug classes (i.e., opiates, hallucinogens), studies are just beginning to employ these tasks to measure their effects on inhibitory control, and should provide important new information concerning their actions on the control of behavior and attention.

Although these tasks do show utility in identifying drug abusers and in evaluating their acute reactions to drugs of abuse, findings from these tasks are by no means universally consistent, and there are several methodological and psychometric limitations that need to be considered in order to increase the utility of these measures for future research. More attention needs to be allocated towards determining reliability estimates for these tasks. To date, most of the information on task reliability, standardization, and norms comes from clinical research in areas other than substance abuse. The extent to which information on psychometrics, such as task reliability, might be generalizable from these clinical populations to substance abusers is as yet unknown.

The research to date also raises questions about the validity of these tasks as measures of trait impulsivity. The measures of response inhibition obtained from behavioral inhibition tasks generally demonstrate poor relationships with common trait measures of impulsivity. However, the use of trait impulsivity as a criterion for validation of these tasks might not be entirely appropriate. Trait measures examine impulsivity as patterns of under-controlled behaviors that are context-laden and are evident by social behaviors, interpersonal interactions, and affective responses to situations. In contrast with such molar examinations, behavioral inhibition tasks provide a microanalysis of inhibitory control as the ability to exert brief, momentary suppression over a simple action (e.g., key press, eye movement). When considering the divergence in the scope of analysis between these approaches, the lack of correlation between laboratory assessments of response inhibition and self-report measures of trait impulsivity is not so surprising. It is also important to note that such correlational approaches typically examine the extent to which inhibitory control covaries with individual differences within a "normal range" of impulsivity in non-clinical samples. This excludes the higher end of the spectrum that is typically associated with clinical populations who are characterized by under-controlled behavior. Indeed, approaches based on clinical versus control group comparisons do support the notion that impulsivity is associated with deficient inhibitory control. For example, groups characterized by impulsivity, such as those with ADHD and schizophrenia, reliably display poorer inhibitory control of manual action and attention as measured by laboratory tasks.

Regarding the assumption that measures of response inhibition should be correlated among these tasks, the research is limited and the evidence is equivocal. Any failure to observe correlations between tasks could be due to low task reliability. However, given the strong evidence for the reliability and stability of these measures from clinical studies, this explanation seems unlikely. Others suggest that lack of correlation between these tasks could be due to differences in task stimuli (Friedman and Miyake, 2004). Tasks differ greatly in terms of the stimuli used to signal the execution and inhibition of responses. Tasks also differ in behavioral responses to be controlled (manual actions, ocular saccades). There are also differences in test duration, practice effects (learning), performance feedback, and performance-based rewards. All of these factors could account for failures to observe relationships between various laboratory tasks. In an effort to detect some common neural basis for inhibitory control in behavioral inhibition tasks, Rubia *et al.* (2001) used fMRI to identify brain regions that are activated by response inhibition as subjects performed several different stop-signal and go/no-go tasks. Their analysis revealed a shared inhibitory neurocognitive network common to go/no-go and stop-signal tasks that involved mesial, medial, and inferior frontal and parietal cortices. Thus, there is reason to assume that these various tasks might tap some common inhibitory process or set of processes, despite the lack of correlation observed between individual tasks.

In summary, there is evidence for the reliability and sensitivity of these tasks in detecting inhibitory deficits among substance abusers and for detecting acute changes in inhibitory control in response to drugs of abuse. Their continued use in addiction research is well justified as these tasks bring unique assessments of behaviors that are of special relevance to addiction. Specifically, these laboratory tasks can provide assessments of momentary changes in the drug abuser's inhibitory control in response to a drug or drug-related "conditioned" stimuli. The stability of these measures over time allows their use in the examination of long-term changes in substance abusers, such as potential recovery of cognitive functions following treatment and periods of drug abstinence. Finally, these tasks might offer new insight into research on the genetic basis of drug addiction, which often relies on identification of endophenotypes. These are typically simple behavioral markers that are easy to assess and could reflect the actions of genes associated with drug addiction. As such, the use of laboratory tasks to measure inhibitory control at the level of simple behavioral mechanisms fits well with this emerging interest.

References

Abroms BD, Gottlob LR, and Fillmore MT (2006) Alcohol effects on inhibitory control of attention: Distinguishing between intentional and automatic mechanisms. *Psychopharmacology* 188: 324–334.

Acheson A, Reynolds B, Richards JB, and de Wit H (2006) Diazepam impairs behavioral inhibition but not delay discounting or risk taking in healthy adults. *Experimental and Clinical Psychopharmacology* 14: 190–198.

Acheson A, Richard DM, Mathias CW, and Dougherty DM (2011) Adults with a family history of alcohol related problems are more impulsive on measures of response initiation and response inhibition. *Drug and Alcohol Dependence* 117: 198–203.

Adams ZW, Milich R, and Fillmore MT (2010) Examining manual and visual response inhibition among ADHD subtypes. *Journal of Abnormal Child Psychology* 38: 971–983.

Adams ZW, Roberts WM, Milich R, and Fillmore MT (2011) Does response variability predict distractibility among adults with attention-deficit/hyperactivity disorder? *Psychological Assessment* 2: 427–436.

Alderson RM, Rapport MD, and Kofler MJ (2007) Attention-deficit/hyperactivity disorder and behavioral inhibition: A meta-analytic review of the stop-signal paradigm. *Journal of Abnormal Child Psychology* 35: 745–758.

Allman AA, Benkelfat C, Durand F, Sibon I, Dagher A, Leyton M, Baker GB, and O'Driscoll GA (2010) Effect of d-amphetamine on inhibition and motor planning as a function of baseline performance. *Psychopharmacology* 211: 423–433.

Aman CJ, Roberts, Jr. RJ, and Pennington BF (1998) A neuropsychological examination of the underlying deficit in attention deficit hyperactivity disorder: Frontal lobe versus right parietal lobe theories. *Developmental Psychology* 34: 956–969.

Barkley RA (1997) Behavioral inhibition, sustained attention, and executive functions: Constructing a unifying theory of ADHD. *Psychological Bulletin* 121: 65–94.

Bjork JM, Hommer DW, Grant SJ, and Danube C (2004) Impulsivity in abstinent alcohol-dependent patients: relation to control subjects and type 1-/type 2-like traits. *Alcohol* 34: 133–150.

Blekher T, Ramchandani VA, Flury L, Foroud T, Kareken D, Yee RD, Li TK, and O'Connor S (2002) Saccadic eye movements are associated with a family history of alcoholism at baseline and after exposure to alcohol. *Alcoholism: Clinical and Experimental Research* 26: 1568–1573.

Boucher L, Palmeri TJ, Logan GD, and Schall JD (2007) Inhibitory control in mind and brain: An interactive race model of countermanding saccades. *Psychological Review* 114: 376–397.

Boxer AL, Garbutt S, Rankin KP, Hellmuth J, Neuhaus J, Miller BL, and Lisberger SG (2006) Medial versus lateral frontal lobe contributions to voluntary saccade control as revealed by the study of patients with frontal lobe degeneration. *Journal of Neuroscience* 26: 6354–6363.

Calkins ME, Iacono WG, and Curtis CE (2003) Smooth pursuit and antisaccade performance evidence trait stability in schizophrenia patients and their relatives. *International Journal of Psychophysiology* 49: 139–146.

Campanella S, Petit G, Maurage P, Kornreich C, Verbanck P, and Noel X (2009) Chronic alcoholism: insights from neurophysiology. *Neurophysiologie Clinique* 39: 191–207.

Caspi A, Moffitt TE, Newman DL, and Silva PA (1996) Behavioral observations at age 3 years predict adult psychiatric disorders: Longitudinal evidence from a birth cohort. *Archives of General Psychiatry* 53: 1033–1039.

Castellanos-Ryan N, Rubia K, and Conrod PJ (2011) Response inhibition and reward response bias mediate the predictive relationships between impulsivity and sensation seeking and common and unique variance in conduct disorder and substance misuse. *Alcoholism: Clinical and Experimental Research* 35: 140–155.

Chung T, Geier C, Luna B, Pajtek S, Terwilliger R, Thatcher D, and Clark D (2011) Enhancing response inhibition by incentive: Comparison of adolescents with and without substance use disorder. *Drug and Alcohol Dependence* 115: 43–50.

Conners KC (2004) Conners continuous performance test (2nd edition). *Multi Health Systems*. Toronto: Western Psychological Services.

Cremona-Meteyard SL and Geffen GM (1994) Event-related potential indices of visual attention following moderate to severe closed head injury. *Brain Injury* 8: 541–558.

Dawkins L, Powell JH, Pickering A, Powell J, and West R (2009) Patterns of change in withdrawal symptoms, desire to smoke, reward motivation and response inhibition across 3 months of smoking abstinence. *Addiction* 104: 850–858.

Dawkins L, Powell JH, West R, Powell J, and Pickering A (2007) A double-blind placebo-controlled experimental study of nicotine: II – Effects on response inhibition and executive functioning. *Psychopharmacology* 190: 457–467.

de Wit H, Crean J, and Richards JB (2000) Effects of d-amphetamine and ethanol on a measure of behavioral inhibition in humans. *Behavioral Neuroscience* 114: 830–837.

de Wit H, Enggasser JL, and Richards JB (2002) Acute administration of d-amphetamine decreases impulsivity in healthy volunteers. *Neuropsychopharmacology* 27: 813–825.

Dempster FN (1993) Resistance to interference: Developmental changes in a basic processing dimension. In ML Howe and R Pasnak (eds), *Emerging Themes in Cognitive Development, vol. 1: Foundations* (pp. 3–27). New York: Springer.

Derefinko KJ, Adams ZW, Milich R, Fillmore MT, Lorch EP, and Lynam DR (2008) Response style differences in the inattentive and combined subtypes of attention-deficit/hyperactivity disorder. *Journal of Abnormal Child Psycholology* 36: 745–758.

Dom G, D'Haene P, Hulstijn W, and Sabbe B (2006) Impulsivity in abstinent early- and late-onset alcoholics: Differences in self-report measures and a discounting task. *Addiction* 101: 50–59.

Dougherty DM, Marsh DM, Moeller FG, Chokshi RV, and Rosen VC (2000) Effects of moderate and high doses of alcohol on attention, impulsivity, discriminability, and response bias in immediate and delayed memory task performance. *Alcoholism: Clinical and Experimental Research* 24: 1702–1711.

Dougherty DM, Mathias CW, Marsh DM, and Jagar AA (2005) Laboratory behavioral measures of impulsivity. *Behavior Research Methods* 37: 82–90.

Dougherty DM, Moeller FG, Steinberg JL, Marsh DM, Hines SE, and Bjork JM (1999) Alcohol increases commission error rates for a continuous performance test. *Alcoholism: Clinical and Experimental Research* 23: 1342–1351.

Enticott P, Ogloff J, and Bradshaw J (2006) Associations between laboratory measures of executive inhibitory control and self-reported impulsivity. *Pers Individ Dif* 41: 285–294.

Everling S and Fischer B (1998) The antisaccade: A review of basic research and clinical studies. *Neuropsychologia* 36: 885–899.

Eysenck SBG, Pearson PR, Easting G, and Allsopp JF (1985) Age norms for impulsiveness, venturesomeness and empathy in adults. *Personality and Individual Differences* 6: 613–619.

Feil J, Sheppard D, Fitzgerald PB, Yucel M, Lubman DI, and Bradshaw JL (2010) Addiction, compulsive drug seeking, and the role of frontostriatal mechanisms in regulating inhibitory control. *Neuroscience & Biobehavioral Reviews* 35: 248–275.

Field M and Cox WM (2008) Attentional bias in addictive behaviors: A review of its development, causes, and consequences. *Drug and Alcohol Dependence* 97: 1–20.

Field M, Munafo MR, and Franken IH (2009) A meta-analytic investigation of the relationship between attentional bias and subjective craving in substance abuse. *Psychological Bulletin* 135: 589–607.

Fillmore MT (2003) Drug abuse as a problem of impaired control: Current approaches and findings. *Behavioral and Cognitive Neuroscience Reviews* 2: 179–197.

Fillmore MT (2007) Acute alcohol-induced impairment of cognitive functions: Past and present findings. *International Journal of Disability and Human Development* 6: 115–125.

Fillmore MT and Rush CR (2002) Impaired inhibitory control of behavior in chronic cocaine users. *Drug and Alcohol Dependence* 66: 265–273.

Fillmore MT and Rush CR (2006) Polydrug abusers display impaired discrimination-reversal learning in a model of behavioural control. *Journal of Psychopharmacology* 20: 24–32.

Fillmore MT and Vogel-Sprott M (1999) An alcohol model of impaired inhibitory control and its treatment in humans. *Experimental and Clinical Psychopharmacology* 7: 49–55.

Fillmore MT and Weafer J (2011) Impaired inhibitory control as a mechanism of drug addiction. In M. Bardo, D. Fishbein, and R Milich (eds), *Inhibitory Control and Drug Abuse Prevention: From Research to Translation* (pp. 85–100). New York: Springer.

Fillmore MT, Kelly TH, and Martin CA (2005) Effects of d-amphetamine in human models of information processing and inhibitory control. *Drug and Alcohol Dependence* 77: 151–159.

Fillmore MT, Rush CR, and Hays L (2002) Acute effects of oral cocaine on inhibitory control of behavior in humans. *Drug and Alcohol Dependence* 67: 157–167.

Fillmore MT, Rush CR, and Hays L (2006) Acute effects of cocaine in two models of inhibitory control: Implications of non-linear dose effects. *Addiction* 101: 1323–1332.

Fillmore MT, Rush CR, and Marczinski CA (2003) Effects of d-amphetamine on behavioral control in stimulant abusers: The role of prepotent response tendencies. *Drug and Alcohol Dependence* 71: 143–152.

Fillmore MT, Rush CR, Kelly TH, and Hays L (2001) Triazolam impairs inhibitory control of behavior in humans. *Experimental and Clinical Psychopharmacology* 9: 363–371.

Floden D and Stuss DT (2006) Inhibitory control is slowed in patients with right superior medial frontal damage. *Journal of Cognitive Neuroscience* 18: 1843–1849.

Freud S (1910) The origin and development of psychoanalysis. *The American Journal of Psychiatry* 21: 196–218.

Friedman NP and Miyake A (2004) The relations among inhibition and interference control functions: A latent-variable analysis. *Journal of Experimental Psychology: General* 133: 101–135.

Fukushima J, Fukushima K, Miyasaka K, and Yamashita I (1994) Voluntary control of saccadic eye movement in patients with frontal cortical lesions and parkinsonian patients in comparison with that in schizophrenics. *Biological Psychiatry* 36: 21–30.

Gay P, Rochat L, Billieux J, D'Acremont M and Van Der Linden M (2008) Heterogeneous inhibition processes involved in different facets of self-reported impulsivity: Evidence from a community sample. *Acta Psychologica* 129: 332–339.

Giancola PR, Godlaski AJ and Roth RM (2012) Identifying component-processes of executive functioning that serve as risk factors for the alcohol–agression relation. *Psychology of Addictive Behaviors* 26: 201–211.

Goldstein RZ and Volkow ND (2002) Drug addiction and its underlying neurobiological basis: Neuroimaging evidence for the involvement of the frontal cortex. *The American Journal of Psychiatry* 159: 1642–1652.

Gooding DC, Burroughs S, and Boutros NN (2008) Attentional deficits in cocaine-dependent patients: Converging behavioral and electrophysiological evidence. *Psychiatry Research* 160: 145–154.

Gooding DC, Shea HB, and Matts CW (2005) Saccadic performance in questionnaire-identified schizotypes over time. *Psychiatry Research* 133: 173–186.

Grekin ER, Sher KJ, and Wood PK (2006) Personality and substance dependence symptoms: Modeling substance-specific traits. *Psychology of Addictive Behaviors* 20: 415–424.

Habeych ME, Folan MM, Luna B, and Tarter RE (2006) Impaired oculomotor response inhibition in children of alcoholics: The role of attention deficit hyperactivity disorder. *Drug and Alcohol Dependence* 82: 11–17.

Halperin JM, Sharma V, Greenblatt E, and Schwartz S (1991) Assessment of the continous performance test: Reliability and validity in a nonreferred sample. *Psychological Assessment* 3: 603–608.

Holahan AL and O'Driscoll GA (2005) Antisaccade and smooth pursuit performance in positive- and negative-symptom schizotypy. *Schizophrenia Research* 76: 43–54.

Horn NR, Dolan M, Elliott R, Deakin JF, and Woodruff PW (2003) Response inhibition and impulsivity: An fmri study. *Neuropsychologia* 41: 1959–1966.

Houghton G and Tipper SP (1994) A model of inhibitory mechanisms in selective attention. In D. Dagenback and TH Carr (eds), *Inhibitory Processes in Attention, Memory and Language* (pp. 53–112). San Diego: Academic Press.

Huestegge L, Radach R, and Kunert HJ (2009) Long-term effects of cannabis on oculomotor function in humans. *Journal of Psychopharmacology* 23: 714–722.

Iacono W, Carlson S, and Malone S (2000) Identifying a multivariate endophenotype for substance use disorders using psychophysiological measures. *International Journal of Psychophysiology* 38: 81–96.

Iacono W, Carlson S, Taylor J, Elkins I, and McGue M (1999) Behavioral disinhibition and the development of substance-use disorders: Findings from the Minnesota Twin Family Study. *Development and Psychopathology* 11: 869–900.

Jacob GA, Gutz L, Bader K, Lieb K, Tuscher O, and Stahl C (2010) Impulsivity in borderline personality disorder: Impairment in self-report measures, but not behavioral inhibition. *Psychopathology* 43: 180–188.

Jentsch JD and Taylor JR (1999) Impulsivity resulting from frontostriatal dysfunction in drug abuse: Implications for the control of behavior by reward-related stimuli. *Psychopharmacology* 146: 373–390.

Kaminski TW, Groff RM, and Glutting JJ (2009) Examining the stability of automated neuropsychological assessment metric (Anam) Baseline Test Scores. *Journal of Clinical and Experimental Neuropsychology* 31: 689–697.

Khan O, Taylor SJ, Jones JG, Swart M, Hanes DP, and Carpenter RH (1999) Effects of low-dose isoflurane on saccadic eye movement generation. *Anaesthesia* 54: 142–145.

Khan S, Ford K, Timney B, and Everling S (2003) Effects of ethanol on anti-saccade task performance. *Experimental Brain Research* 150: 68–74.

Kindlon D, Mezzacappa E, and Earls F (1995) Psychometric properties of impulsivity measures: Temporal stability, validity and factor structure. *Journal of Child Psychology and Psychiatry* 35: 645–661.

Klein C and Fischer B (2005) Instrumental and test-retest reliability of saccadic measures. *Biological Psychology* 68: 201–213.

Klein C, Fischer, Jr B, Fischer B, and Hartnegg K (2002) Effects of methylphenidate on saccadic responses in patients with adhd. *Experimental Brain Research* 145: 121–125.

Kuntsi J, Andreou P, Ma J, Borger NA, and Van Der Meere JJ (2005) Testing sssumptions for endophenotype studies in ADHD: Reliability and validity of tasks in a general population sample. *BMC Psychiatry* 5: 40.

Lane SD, Moeller FG, Steinberg JL, Buzby M, and Kosten TR (2007) Performance of cocaine dependent individuals and controls on a response inhibition task with varying levels of difficulty. *The American Journal of Drug and Alcohol Abuse* 33: 717–726.

Larrison AL, Briand KA, and Sereno AB (2004) Nicotine improves antisaccade task performance without affecting prosaccades. *Human Psychopharmacology* 19: 409–419.

Leigh RJ and Zee DS (1999) *The Neurology of Eye Movements.* Oxford: Oxford University Press.

Lejuez CW, Magidson JF, Mitchell SH, Sinha R, Stevens MC, and de Wit H (2010) Behavioral and biological indicators of impulsivity in the development of alcohol use, problems, and disorders. *Alcoholism: Clinical and Experimental Research* 34: 1334–1345.

Li CS, Milivojevic V, Kemp K, Hong K, and Sinha R (2006) Performance monitoring and stop signal inhibition in abstinent patients with cocaine dependence. *Drug and Alcohol Dependence* 85: 205–212.

Littlefield AK, Sher KJ, and Steinley D (2010) Developmental trajectories of impulsivity and their association with alcohol use and related outcomes during emerging and young adulthood I. *Alcoholism: Clinical and Experimental Research* 34: 1409–1416.

Logan GD (1985) On the ability to inhibit simple thoughts and actions: II. Stop-signal studies of repetition priming. *Journal of Experimental Psychology: Learning, Memory, and Cognition* 11: 675–691.

Logan GD (1994) On the ability to inhibit thought and action: A user's guide to the stop-signal paradigm. In D Dagenbach and TH Carr (eds), *Inhibitory Processes in Attention, Memory, and Language* (pp. 189–239). San Diego: Academic Press.

Logan GD and Cowan WB (1984) On the ability to inhibit thought and action: A theory of an act of control. *Psychological Review* 91: 295–327.

Logan GD and Irwin DE (2000) Don't look! Don't touch! Inhibitory control of eye and hand movements. *Psychonomic Bulletin & Review* 7: 107–112.

Logan GD, Schachar R, and Tannock R (1997) Impulsivity and inhibitory control. *Psychological Science* 8: 60–64.

Lyvers M (2000) "Loss of control" in alcoholism and drug addiction: A neuroscientific interpretation. *Experimental and Clinical Psychopharmacology* 8: 225–249.

Malloy P, Bihrle A, Duffy J, and Cimino C (1993) The orbitomedial frontal syndrome. *Archives of Clinical Neuropsychology* 8: 185–201.

Marczinski CA and Fillmore MT (2003) Preresponse cues reduce the impairing effects of alcohol on the execution and suppression of responses. *Experimental and Clinical Psychopharmacology* 11: 110–117.

Marczinski CA, Combs SW, and Fillmore MT (2007) Increased sensitivity to the disinhibiting effects of alcohol in binge drinkers. *Psychology of Addictive Behaviors* 21: 346–354.

Marsh D, Dougherty DM, Mathias C, Moeller F, and Hicks L (2002) Comparisons of women with high and low trait impulsivity using behavioral models of response-disinhibition and reward-choice. *Personality and Individual Differences* 33: 1291–1310.

Mathias CW, Marsh DM, and Dougherty DM (2002) Reliability estimates for the immediate and delayed memory tasks. *Perceptual & Motor Skills* 95: 559–569.

McGeoch J (1932) Forgetting and the law of disuse. *Psychological Review* 39: 352–370.

Mitchell SH (2004) Measuring impulsivity and modeling its association with cigarette smoking. *Behavioral and Cognitive Neuroscience Reviews* 3: 261–275.

Monterosso J, Aronb A, Cordova X, Xua J, and London E (2005) Deficits in response inhibition associated with chronic methamphetamine abuse. *Drug and Alcohol Dependence* 79: 273–277.

Murphy KR, Barkley RA, and Bush, T (2001) Executive functioning and olfactory identification in young adults with attention deficit-hyperactivity disorder. *Neuropsychology* 15: 211–220.

Newman JP, Wisdom CS, and Nathan S (1985) Passive avoidance in syndromes of disinhibition, psychopathy, and extraversion. *Journal of Personality and Social Psychology* 48: 1316–1327.

Nigg JT (2000) On inhibition/disinhibition in developmental psychopathology: Views from cognitive and personality psychology and a working inhibition taxonomy. *Psychological Bulletin* 126: 220–246.

Nigg JT, Butler KM, Huang-Pollock CL, and Henderson JM (2002) Inhibitory processes in adults with persistent childhood onset adhd. *Journal of Consulting and Clinical Psychology* 70: 153–157.

Nouraei SA, De Pennington N, Jones JG, and Carpenter RH (2003) Dose-related effect of sevoflurane sedation on higher control of eye movements and decision making. *British Journal of Anaesthesia* 91: 175–183.

Oosterlaan J and Sergeant JA (1996) Inhibition in ADHD, aggressive, and anxious children: A biologically based model of child psychopathology. *Journal of Abnormal Child Psychology* 24: 19–36.

Patton JH, Stanford MS, and Barratt ES (1995) Factor structure of the barratt impulsiveness scale. *Journal of Clinical Psychology* 51: 768–774.

Peterson MS, Kramer AF, and Irwin DE (2004) Covert shifts of attention precede involuntary eye movements. *Perception & Psychophysics* 66: 398–405.

Ploner CJ, Tschirch A, Ostendorf F, Dick S, Gaymard BM, Rivaud-Pechoux S, *et al.* (2002) Oculomotor effects of delta-9-tetrahydrocannabinol in humans: Implications for the functional neuroanatomy of the brain cannabinoid system. *Cerebral Cortex* 12: 1016–1023.

Powell J, Dawkins L, and Davis RE (2002) Smoking, reward responsiveness, and response inhibition: Tests of an incentive motivational model. *Biological Psychiatry* 51: 151–163.

Quay HC (1997) Inhibition and attention deficit hyperactivity disorder. *Journal of Abnormal Child Psychology* 25: 7–13.

Radant AD, Dobie DJ, Calkins ME, Olincy A, Braff DL, Cadenhead KS, *et al.* (2007) Successful multi-site measurement of antisaccade performance deficits in schizophrenia. *Schizophrenia Research* 89: 320–329.

Ramaekers JG, Kauert G, Theunissen EL, Toennes SW, and Moeller MR (2009) Neurocognitive performance during acute THC intoxication in heavy and occasional cannabis users. *Journal of Psychopharmacology* 23: 266–277.

Ramchandani VA, O'Connor S, Blekher T, Kareken D, Morzorati S, Nurnberger Jr. J, *et al.* (1999) A preliminary study of acute responses to clamped alcohol concentration and family history of alcoholism. *Alcoholism: Clinical and Experimental Research* 23: 1320–1330.

Reynolds B, Ortengren A, Richards JB, and de Wit H (2006) Dimensions of impulsive behavior: Personality and behavioral measures. *Personality and Individual Differences* 40: 305–315.

Rieger M, Gauggel S, and Burmeister K (2003) Inhibition of ongoing responses following frontal, nonfrontal, and basal ganglia lesions. *Neuropsychology* 17: 272–282.

Roberts W, Fillmore MT, and Milich R (2011) Separating automatic and intentional inhibitory mechanisms of attention in adults with attention-deficit/hyperactivity disorder. *Journal of Abnormal Psychology* 120: 223–233.

Robinson TE and Berridge KC (1993) The neural basis of drug craving: An incentive-sensitization theory of addiction. *Brain Research Reviews* 18: 247–291.

Robinson TE and Berridge KC (2000) The psychology and neurobiology of addiction: An incentive-sensitization view. *Addiction* 95 Suppl. 2: S91–117.

Roche DJ and King AC (2010) Alcohol impairment of saccadic and smooth pursuit eye movements: Impact of risk factors for alcohol dependence. *Psychopharmacology* 212: 33–44.

Rose AK and Duka T (2007) The influence of alcohol on basic motoric and cognitive disinhibition. *Alcohol and Alcoholism* 42: 544–551.

Ross RG, Harris JG, Olincy A, and Radant A (2000) Eye movement task measures inhibition and spatial working memory in adults with schizophrenia, adhd, and a normal comparison group. *Psychiatry Research* 95: 35–42.

Ross RG, Heinlein S, Zerbe GO, and Radant A (2005) Saccadic eye movement task identifies cognitive deficits in children with schizophrenia, but not in unaffected child relatives. *Journal of Child Psychology and Psychiatry* 46: 1354–1362.

Ross RG, Hommer D, Breiger D, Varley C, and Radant A (1994) Eye movement task related to frontal lobe functioning in children with attention deficit disorder. *Journal of the American Academy of Child and Adolescent Psychiatry* 33: 869–874.

Rosvold HE, Mirsky AF, Sarason I, Bransome, Jr ED, and Beck LH (1956) A continuous performance test of brain damage. *Journal of Consulting Psychology* 20: 343–350.

Rubia K, Smith A, and Taylor E (2007) Performance of children with attention deficit hyperactivity disorder (ADHD) on a test battery of impulsiveness. *Child Neuropsychology* 13: 276–304 .

Rubia K, Taylor E, Smith AB, Oksanen H, Overmeyer S, and Newman S (2001) Neuropsychological analyses of impulsiveness in childhood hyperactivity. *The British Journal of Psychiatry* 179: 138–143.

Rubio G, Jimenez M, Rodriguez-Jimenez R, Martinez I, Avila C, Ferre F, *et al.* (2008) The role of behavioral impulsivity in the development of alcohol dependence: A 4-year follow-up study. *Alcoholism: Clinical and Experimental Research* 32: 1681–1687.

Schachar R, Tannock R, Marriott M, and Logan GD (1995) Deficient inhibitory control in attention deficit hyperactivity disorder. *Journal of Abnormal Child Psychology* 23: 411–437.

Shuckit MA (1998) Biological, psychological and environmental predictors of the alcoholism risk: A longitudinal study. *Journal of Studies on Alcohol and Drugs* 59: 485–494.

Soloff PH, Lynch KG, and Moss HB (2000) Serotonin, impulsivity, and alcohol use disorders in the older adolescent: A psychobiological study. *Alcoholism: Clinical and Experimental Research* 24: 1609–1619.

Soreni N, Crosbie J, Ickowicz A, and Schachar R (2009) Stop signal and Conners' continuous performance tasks: Test–retest reliability of two inhibition measures in ADHD children. *Journal of Attention Disorders* 13: 137–143.

Spinella M (2002) Correlations between orbitofrontal dysfunction and tobacco smoking. *Addiction Biology* 7: 381–384.

Spinella M (2004) Neurobehavioral correlates of impulsivity: Evidence of prefrontal involvement. *International Journal of Neuroscience* 114: 95–104.

Swann AC, Bjork JM, Moeller FG, and Dougherty DM (2002) Two models of impulsivity: Relationship to personality traits and psychopathology. *Biological Psychiatry* 51: 988–994.

Tannock R (1998) Attention deficit hyperactivity disorder: Advances in cognitive, neurobiological, and genetic research. *Journal of Child Psychology and Psychiatry* 39: 65–99.

Tannock R, Schachar R, and Logan G (1995) Methylphenidate and cognitive flexibility: Dissociated dose effects in hyperactive children. *Journal of Abnormal Child Psychology* 23: 235–266.

Thakkar KN, Schall JD, Boucher L, Logan GD, and Park S (2011) Response inhibition and response monitoring in a saccadic countermanding task in schizophrenia. *Biological Psychiatry* 69: 55–62.

Theeuwes J, Kramer AF, Hahn S, Irwin DE, and Zelinsky GJ (1999) Influence of attentional capture on oculomotor control. *Journal of Experimental Psychology: Human Perception and Performance* 25: 1595–1608.

Trull TJ, Waudby CJ, and Sher KJ (2004) Alcohol, tobacco, and drug use disorders and personality disorder symptoms. *Experimental and Clinical Psychopharmacology* 12: 65–75.

Turetsky BI, Calkins ME, Light GA, Olincy A, Radant AD, and Swerdlow NR (2007) Neurophysiological endophenotypes of schizophrenia: The viability of selected candidate measures. *Schizophrenia Bulletin* 33: 69–94.

Vassallo S and Abel LA (2002) Ethanol effects on volitional versus reflexive saccades. *Clinical and Experimental Ophthalmology* 30: 208–212.

Verdejo-García A and Perez-Garcia M (2007) Profile of executive deficits in cocaine and heroin polysubstance users: Common and differential effects on separate executive components. *Psychopharmacology* 190: 517–530.

Vorstius C, Radach R, Lang AR, and Riccardi CJ (2008) Specific visuomotor deficits due to alcohol intoxication: Evidence from the pro- and antisaccade paradigms. *Psychopharmacology* 196: 201–210.

Weafer J and Fillmore MT (2012a) Comparison of alcohol impairment of behavioral and attentional inhibition. *Drug and Alcohol Dependence* June 4 [Epub ahead of print].

Weafer J and Fillmore MT (2012b) Acute tolerance to alcohol impairment of behavioral and cognitive mechanisms related to driving: Drinking and driving on the descending limb. *Psychopharmacology* 220: 697–706.

Weafer J, Milich R, and Fillmore MT (2011) Behavioral components of impulsivity predict alcohol consumption in adults with ADHD and healthy controls. *Drug and Alcohol Dependence* 113: 139–146.

Whiteside S and Lynam D (2001) The five factor model and impulsivity: Using a structural model of personality to understand impulsivity. *Personality and Individual Differences* 30: 669–689.

Zabel TA, Von Thomsen C, Cole C, Martin R, and Mahone EM (2009) Reliability concerns in the repeated computerized assessment of attention in children. *The Clinical Neuropsychologist* 23: 1213–1231.

Zacny JP and de Wit H (2009) The prescription opioid, oxycodone, does not alter behavioral measures of impulsivity in healthy volunteers. *Pharmacology Biochemistry and Behavior* 94: 108–113.

7

Delay Discounting and Drug Abuse: Empirical, Conceptual, and Methodological Considerations[1]

Jeffrey S. Stein and Gregory J. Madden

1 Introduction

The drug abuser makes irrational choices. She or he sacrifices substantial, long-term gains (e.g., physical and psychological health) for the sake of short-term drug effects. This temporal myopia has long been of interest to those wishing to understand and treat addiction. As early as the 1960s, researchers began to reason that drug abuse[2] may arise from, or be exacerbated by, a diminished capacity to consider future outcomes. Using a variety of subjective instruments, early investigations demonstrated more present-oriented time perspectives (i.e., diminished concern for future events) among abusers of alcohol and opioid drugs when compared to controls (e.g., Alvos, Gregson, and Ross, 1993; Foulks and Webb, 1970; Imber, Miller, Faillace, and Liberman, 1971; Manganiello, 1978; Petry, Bickel, and Arnet, 1998; Roos and Albers, 1965; Sattler and Pflugrath, 1970; Smart, 1968). Among the questionnaires used in these early studies was the Time Reference Inventory (Roos, 1964), in which participants are asked to complete a priming sentence (e.g., *Most of my fantasies are about the* ...) with the answers *past*, *present*, or *future*. A participant's distribution of answers provides a measure of past-, present-, or future-oriented time perspective.

Over the next several decades, standardized procedures were developed (e.g., the Zimbardo Time Perspective Inventory, ZTPI; Zimbardo and Boyd, 1999) which continued to support the relation between drug abuse and present-orientation (e.g., Apostolidis, Fieulaine, Simonin, and Rolland, 2006). Importantly, this relation was observed even when controlling for covariates of drug abuse such as depression, risk taking, and sensation seeking (Keough, Zimbardo, and Boyd, 1999).

[1] Preparation of this chapter was supported by NIH grant 1R01DA029605, awarded to the second author (G. J. Madden).

[2] Throughout this chapter, we use the term *drug abuse* to refer generally to substance abuse and dependence.

The Wiley-Blackwell Handbook of Addiction Psychopharmacology, First Edition. Edited by James MacKillop and Harriet de Wit.
© 2013 John Wiley & Sons, Ltd. Published 2013 by John Wiley & Sons, Ltd.

Questionnaires like the ZTPI ask participants to reflect on temporally extended patterns of their previous behavior and indicate whether certain statements describe these patterns (e.g., *I believe that getting together with friends to party is one of life's important pleasures*, ZTPI-short form). Such questionnaires provide information about general tendencies to act in a way suggestive of future- or present-oriented time perspectives, but they do not allow understanding of predictable exceptions to these general tendencies. For example, one of the criteria used in diagnosing drug dependence is a persistent desire to reduce or control drug use (presumably an orientation toward future events) but repeated failure to do so (American Psychiatric Association, 2000; Hogue, Dauber, and Morganstern, 2010). This alternation between stated future orientation (treatment-seeking activities) and present hedonistic action (relapse) is common in drug abuse (for a review, see McKay, Franklin, Patapis, and Lynch, 2006) and requires a systematic, theoretical account. Within a behavioral economic framework, the study of *delay discounting* may provide such an account. We begin with a general outline of the model.

1.1   Delay discounting

Delay discounting is an inductive theory of intertemporal choice (e.g., Chung and Herrnstein, 1967). In Mazur's (1987) seminal experiments, pigeons were given simple choices between smaller-sooner (SS) and larger-later (LL) food outcomes. The pattern of choice observed as food amounts and delays were experimentally manipulated in these and subsequent experiments suggested that the value of a delayed outcome is discounted according to the hyperbolic decay function,

$$V_d = \frac{A}{1 + kD} \tag{1}$$

where V_d is the discounted value of food amount A, delivered after delay D. Procedural details are considered in depth later in the chapter. For now, we note that when the pigeon chooses the SS outcome, its choice reveals that the subjective value of the LL has decayed. When the pigeon is indifferent between the two outcomes, they have the same subjective value (despite the delayed outcome being objectively larger). The objective amount of the SS outcome at this point of indifference provides a measure of the discounted value (V_d) of the LL. When indifference points are obtained across a wide range of delays, the discounting function fit to these points most often takes a hyperbolic shape (equation 1), as illustrated in the top panel of Figure 7.1 (for reviews, see Green and Myerson, 2004; Mazur, 1997).[3] The two discounting curves in this panel illustrate the role of equation 1's single free parameter, k: it allows the

---

[3]Alternative forms of the discounting function have been proposed, such as the hyperboloid (for a review, see Green and Myerson, 2004), exponential-power (Ebert and Prelec, 2007), and additive-utility (Killeen, 2009) models, each of which can theoretically account for predictable anomalies of choice (see below) due to a hyperbola-like, non-constant rate of decay. We present only Mazur's (1987) simple hyperbola here for the sake of parsimony.

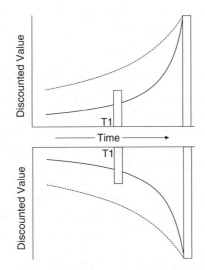

Figure 7.1 Depictions of steep (solid curves) and shallow (dashed curves) delay-discounting functions. Top and bottom panels reflect positively and negatively valued outcomes, respectively. Bars represent the undiscounted value of the outcome when available immediately, while curves represent the outcome's discounted value

discounting curve to vary in steepness. Thus, k quantifies between-subject or between-commodity differences in how outcome value decays with increasing delay.

Consider the top panel of Figure 7.1, in which the bars depict the undiscounted (objective) value of both SS and LL outcomes, whereas the curve depicts the LL outcome's discounted value. The solid discounting curve illustrates steep discounting of the LL outcome (the larger bar on the right of the x-axis). When the decision maker is situated in time at T1, the discounted value of the LL outcome falls below the undiscounted value of the immediately available SS (the smaller bar on the left). Assuming that the outcome with greater subjective value is chosen, the steep discounting function (solid curve) describes a tendency toward impulsive choices. The shallower discounting function (dashed curve) illustrates a tendency toward "self-controlled" choices, as the discounted value of the LL outcome exceeds that of the SS at time T1.

As illustrated in the lower panel of Figure 7.1, this analysis may also be applied to the discounting of delayed aversive outcomes (costs). When situated in time at T1 in the lower panel, the individual must choose between SS and LL aversive events (represented in the negative values of both bars). For example, Deluty (1978) arranged for rats to choose between a small electric shock delivered in 2 seconds and a larger shock delivered after a 12-second delay. Here, selecting the LL shock is impulsive because, all else being equal, this choice exposes the organism to more aversive stimulation than would have been experienced if the SS had been chosen. Consistent with the steeper delay-discounting function in the lower panel of Figure 7.1 (solid curve), Deluty's rats preferred the LL shock, suggesting that at time T1 the negative value of the SS shock was subjectively more aversive than the discounted negative value of the LL shock. In a similar manner, humans hyperbolically discount the negative value of delayed monetary (e.g., Murphy, Vuchinich, and Simpson, 2001) and health (e.g., Odum, Madden, and Bickel, 2002) costs.

1.2   Delay discounting and predictable anomalies of choice

As suggested earlier, theoretical accounts focusing on present- or future-oriented time perspectives run into difficulties when the individual behaves inconsistently (i.e., future-oriented at times, present-oriented at others). Between meals, for example, one may speak of the benefits of healthy eating and vow to eat more vegetables and whole grains. However, when ordering a meal later that day, the same individual passes over the salad, fruit, and granola option as he instead orders the selection featuring red meat, cheese, and white bread. Such *preference reversals* are common in our everyday lives and are one example of what Loewenstein and Thaler (1989) referred to as anomalies of intertemporal choice – reliable deviations from rationality. Some of these anomalies, including the preference reversal, are predicted by equation 1.

Here we note just two of Loewenstein and Thaler's (1989) anomalies. First, the rate at which delayed outcomes are discounted is not constant over time, as it should be if we were rational economic agents (defined, in part, as consistent preference over time). Instead, rats, pigeons, monkeys, and humans discount behavioral outcomes at a higher rate when the delays are short and at a slower rate when these delays are long (e.g., Benzion, Rapoport, and Yagil, 1989; Green *et al.*, 2004; Freeman, Green, Myerson, and Woolverton, 2009; Murphy, Vuchinich, and Simpson, 2001). This, of course, describes the deeply bowed, hyperbolic discounting functions (equation 1) observed in members of these species.

Second, Loewenstein and Thaler (1989) discussed the tendency for humans (e.g., Green *et al.*, 1994) and nonhumans (e.g., Green and Estle, 2003) to reverse their preferences between self-control and impulsivity. This is illustrated in Figure 7.2, which retains the formatting of Figure 7.1, but now a hyperbolic discounting function accompanies both SS and LL outcomes. When situated in time at T2 (temporally distant from both SS and LL outcomes), the discounted value of the LL outcome exceeds that of the SS; hence, from this temporal vantage point, one can clearly see the delayed benefits of, say, eating a sensible diet (e.g., weight loss and improved health). However, at a subsequent meal time (T1), the discounted values of the two

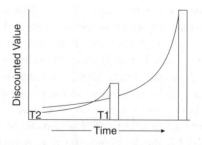

Figure 7.2   Examples of steep delay-discounting functions at varying choice points (T1 and T2)

outcomes have reversed and so has preference. After the meal, one returns to T2 and, in many cases, a period of self-loathing. These preference reversals are, to some degree, common to all of us and demonstrate recurrent and predictable alternations between present and future orientations.

1.3   Empirical relevance of delay discounting to drug abuse

In the last two decades, a large body of research demonstrates steeper delay discounting in drug-abusing populations compared to matched controls. This relation is robust across users of opioids (e.g., Madden, Petry, Badger, and Bickel, 1997), cocaine (e.g., Coffey, Gudleski, Saladin, and Brady, 2003), methamphetamine (e.g., Hoffman *et al.*, 2006), tobacco (e.g., Reynolds, Richards, Horn, and Karraker, 2004), and alcohol (e.g., Vuchinich and Simpson, 1998). This relation was not observed, however, in two studies of delay discounting in marijuana users (Johnson *et al.*, 2010; Romer, Duckworth, Sznitman, and Park, 2010).

The most comprehensive review of the relation between delay discounting and human addictive disorders was conducted by MacKillop *et al.* (2011). In their meta-analysis, MacKillop *et al.* reviewed 46 peer-reviewed journal articles that provided comparisons of delay discounting between a control group and a group meeting clinical or subclinical criteria of addiction. Analysis of all effect-size comparisons (Cohen's *d*) within this sample yielded a moderate aggregate effect size ($d = 0.58$), with no significant differences across addiction type (e.g., tobacco, alcohol, or stimulant abuse). However, severity of drug abuse appeared to moderate the positive relation between delay discounting and addictive behavior. That is, comparisons between *clinical* populations and controls yielded a larger aggregate effect size ($d = 0.61$) than comparisons between *subclinical* populations and controls ($d = 0.45$). From MacKillop *et al.*'s analysis, one can be reasonably confident that the relation between steep delay discounting and drug abuse is a real and clinically relevant phenomenon.

A predominant account of this relation is that steep delay discounting *directly* predisposes individuals toward drug abuse. That is, if the delayed and objectively larger benefits of drug abstinence (e.g., vocational success, good psychological and physical health) are steeply discounted, these prospects will have little subjective value and, therefore, will be unable to compete with immediately rewarding (or nearly so) drug effects. Figure 7.3 provides an illustration of this hypothesis, in which steep and shallow discounters, situated in time at T1, each face a choice between two options: drug use or abstinence. Considering only the positively valued outcomes (top panel), steeply discounting the delayed benefits of drug abstinence (solid curve) renders these consequences small relative to the immediate benefits of drug use. Shallow discounting (dashed curve) reverses these relative values and is said to be one factor underlying abstinence.

When framed as negative outcomes (bottom panel of Figure 7.3), the choice is between the immediate costs of abstinence (e.g., physiological withdrawal, peer disapproval) and the delayed, but objectively larger costs of prolonged drug abuse (e.g., deteriorating psychological and physical health). For the steep discounter, the immediate costs of abstinence are functionally more aversive than the delayed costs of sustained drug use.

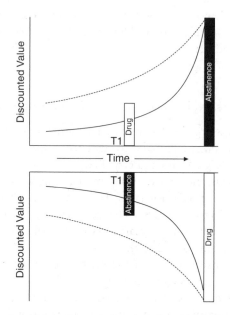

Figure 7.3 Examples of a steep (solid curves) and shallow (dashed curves) delay-discounting functions fit to hypothetical values of drug use and abstinence. Top and bottom panels reflect positively and negatively valued outcomes, respectively

This analysis may be extended to the tendency for alternations between abstinence and relapse in those attempting to abstain from drug use. This is illustrated in Figure 7.4. Assuming steep discounting, the discounted benefits of drug abstinence should be regarded as more worthwhile than drug intoxication across the time span labeled "Vows to Abstain." Across this same span, the delayed negative effects of sustained drug use should be regarded as a more aversive prospect than the immediate costs associated with drug abstinence. However, when moving closer in time to a point at which the drug is available (moving right along the *x*-axis toward T1), the hyperbolic discounting curves intersect and equation 1 predicts ambivalence between abstinence and drug use. When the drug becomes even more immediately available, equation 1 predicts relapse given that the immediate benefits of drug use now outweigh the discounted LL outcomes associated with abstinence. As noted above in the discussion of preference reversals, this account of temporally inconsistent choice has been documented in the laboratory (albeit with non-drug outcomes) in both humans (e.g., Green, Fristoe, and Myerson, 1994) and nonhumans (e.g., Green and Estle, 2003).

The discussion thus far has focused on the hypothesis that steep delay discounting directly predisposes individuals toward drug abuse (illustrated in Figure 7.5, panel (a)). Given the robust relation between steep delay discounting and drug abuse (MacKillop *et al.*), and the ubiquity of studies demonstrating that discounting functions take a hyperbolic form (for a review, see Green and Myerson, 2004), this hypothesis is conceptually appealing and has been widely discussed. However, variables that may moderate this putative causal relation have gone unexplored. Assuming steep discounting, such moderator variables would serve as risk or protective factors that

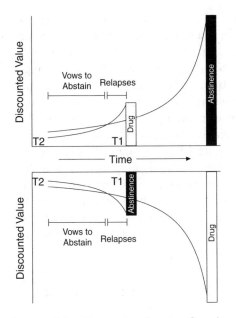

Figure 7.4 Examples of a steep delay-discounting function fit to hypothetical values of drug use and abstinence at varying choice points (T1 and T2). Top and bottom panels reflect positively and negatively valued outcomes, respectively

increase or decrease, respectively, the likelihood of drug abuse, and may serve as potential targets for applied intervention.

In addition, the empirical support for this account is limited. The cross-sectional design of the studies reviewed by MacKillop *et al.* (2011) does not address the etiology of either steep discounting or drug abuse. As illustrated in panels (b) and (c) of Figure 7.5, at least two other hypotheses can economically account for the differences in delay discounting between drug abusers and controls (for a complementary discussion, see Perry and Carroll, 2008). First, steep delay discounting could also be a *consequence*, rather than a cause, of drug abuse (panel (b)). In this account, drug abuse

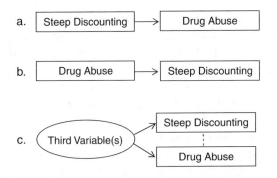

Figure 7.5 Potential relations between delay discounting and drug abuse. Arrows represent causal relations. The dashed line represents a non-causal relation

could initiate a cascade of behavioral effects, beginning with early, state-dependent increases in discounting and terminating, due to the long-term sequelae of abuse, in a generalized, trait-like pattern of steep delay discounting, even in the absence of drug intoxication or deprivation. Second, steep delay discounting may be neither cause nor consequence of drug abuse; rather, a *third variable* (e.g., pre-existing neurochemical dysfunction) may simultaneously govern both variables panel (c). In this case, the relation between delay discounting and drug abuse could be explained, in whole or part, by their mutual relation to this third variable.

The hypotheses in Figure 7.5 are not mutually exclusive; each may interact contemporaneously or sequentially in the development of drug abuse. Further, a complete account of drug abuse will undoubtedly be multivariate. Thus, in suggesting that steep delay discounting plays an etiological role in drug abuse, we mean only that it may serve as one among many causal factors. In the sections that follow, we consider the empirical evidence for and against each of these accounts.

2   Cause–Effect Relations

2.1   Steep delay discounting as a cause of drug abuse

2.1.1   Human studies.   Verifying a potential etiological role of delay discounting in drug abuse (like that depicted in Figures 7.3 and 7.4) has proven difficult because researchers have almost exclusively had to rely on cross-sectional, correlational research designs. However, not all correlational methods are cut from the same statistical cloth, as some better distinguish between the hypotheses in Figure 7.5 than others. Particularly useful in delay-discounting research is the use of longitudinal designs, in which an experimenter assesses delay discounting in a sample of participants prior to the adoption of drug use. Subsequent differences in drug abuse at varying time points may be evaluated against pre-existing differences in discounting.

At present, we are aware of only two relevant longitudinal studies. In the first, Ayduk *et al.* (2000) followed 550 participants who had previously been screened under a *delay-of-gratification* (DG) task in early childhood (see Mischel, Shoda, and Rodriquez, 1989). The DG task quantifies a construct that is formally similar to delay discounting (i.e., a willingness to tolerate a delay to obtain a preferred outcome). Ayduk *et al.* reported that inability to wait in the DG task significantly predicted self-reported cocaine use, but not marijuana use, up to 20 years later. More recently, Audrain-McGovern *et al.* (2009) reported that steeply discounting delayed monetary rewards in late adolescence significantly predicted cigarette smoking in early adulthood. Further evidence comes from studies that have assessed delay discounting before drug-treatment trials that offer modest monetary incentives for continued drug abstinence (see Higgins, Heil, and Lussier, 2004). In these studies, steep delay discounting appears to predict failure in treatment or treatment analogues for alcohol, cocaine, and tobacco use (Dallery and Raiff, 2007; Krishnan-Sarin *et al.*, 2007; MacKillop and Kahler, 2009; Washio *et al.*, 2011; Yoon *et al.*, 2007). These studies offer provisional support for delay discounting as a causal variable; additional longitudinal studies are clearly warranted.

A potential moderator variable was identified in two of the longitudinal studies. Mischel, Shoda, and Peake (1988) reported that an inability to wait in the DG task predicted poor academic performance and behavioral problems in elementary school. Similarly, Audrain-McGovern *et al.* (2009) reported that steep delay discounting was related to poor academic performance. If steep delay discounting serves to isolate the adolescent from positive academic and social behavioral outcomes, then this may increase the *relative* attractiveness of drug outcomes. According to Herrnstein's (1970) quantitative model of choice (matching theory), scarcity of socially acceptable behavioral alternatives will drive behavior toward available substitutes, such as drugs of abuse – an analysis with some empirical support (Correia and Carrey, 1999; Correia, Simons, Carey, and Borsari, 1998; Correia, Carey, and Borsari, 2002). Such environmental restriction may serve to moderate the influence of steep delay discounting in drug abuse. If this moderator analysis holds, then drug-abuse prevention efforts might target children identified as steep delay discounters for academic assistance *before* they develop academic difficulties.

2.1.2 Nonhuman studies. In an effort to further illuminate the relation between steep delay discounting and drug abuse, some researchers have begun to investigate these phenomena in nonhuman models. The general strategy of the researchers in this area has been to assess delay discounting (or impulsive choice; i.e., preference for SS over LL food) among a large number of animals, split the subjects into two or more groups reflecting distinct levels of the dependent measure, and then evaluate if this behavioral outcome predicts drug self-administration (SA) across experimental phases that are potentially analogous to human drug abuse (e.g., acquisition, maintenance, and escalation of drug SA). For ease of discussion (and reference to Table 7.1), we adopt the verbal convention of this literature and refer to steep delay discounting and frequent impulsive choice as *high-impulsive* (HiI), and shallow discounting and infrequent impulsive choice as *low-impulsive* (LoI). Like the human longitudinal studies, measures of delay discounting predate drug exposure, thereby eliminating the possibility that prior drug exposure is responsible for individual differences in discounting. Table 7.1 provides a summary of all studies to our knowledge that have examined delay discounting as a predictor of drug SA in rats.

2.1.2.1 ACQUISITION. Resolving the role of delay discounting in acquisition of drug SA is important because subjective experience (positive or negative) upon initial drug exposure may determine the trajectory of subsequent drug use. Thus far, only two studies have been designed to determine if steep delay discounting predicts acquisition of cocaine SA.[4] In the first of these, Perry *et al.* (2005) used an autoshaping procedure

---

[4]We note that three other studies reporting on acquisition of cocaine SA in HiI and LoI rats used procedures designed to facilitate rapid acquisition of drug SA (e.g., a larger cocaine dose; 0.8 mg/kg; Anker, Perry, Gliddon, and Carroll, 2009; Koffarnus and Woods, 2011; Perry, Nelson, and Carroll, 2008, Experiment 3) and "to eliminate group differences in acquisition … " (Perry, Nelson, and Carroll, 2008, p. 171). Such procedures were arranged so that other aspects of cocaine SA (e.g., response to extinction) could be investigated. Nonetheless, Perry *et al.* reported that HiI rats still acquired cocaine SA faster than LoI rats, and our analysis of the Anker *et al.* data revealed a trend-level difference across HiI and LoI acquisition ($p = 0.08$).

Table 7.1 Delay discounting as a predictor of drug SA in rats

Drug	Authors	Delay-discounting procedure	EGA comparison	SA phase	Dose (mg/kg, except where noted)	Group differences in drug SA
ALC	Diergaarde et al. (2011)	Increasing delay	Quartile split (upper/lower)	ACQ	12% w/v	HiI = LoI
				DMND	12% w/v	HiI = LoI
ALC	Poulos, Le, and Parker (1995)	Fixed delay (T-maze)	Tertile split (upper/middle/ lower) and full range	N/A	3%, 6%, 12% w/v	HiI > MedI > LoI[‡]
AMPH	Marusich et al. (2011)	Adjusting delay	Full range	ACQ	0.03	HiI = MedI = LoI[#]
				MAINT	0.0056, 0.01, 0.056, 0.1	HiI = MedI = LoI[#]
COC	Anker, Perry, Gliddon, and Parker (2009)	Adjusting delay	Median split (upper/lower)	ACQ	0.8	HiI = LoI
				MAINT	0.4	HiI = LoI
				DMND	0.2, 0.8, 3.2	HiI = LoI
				ESC	0.4	HiI > LoI
COC	Koffarnus and Woods (2011)	Increasing delay	Tertile split (upper/middle/lower)	ACQ	0.56	HiI = LoI[§]
COC	Perry et al. (2005)	Adjusting delay	Approximate median split[©] (upper/lower)	DMND	0.1	HiI > MedI/LoI
				ACQ	0.2	HiI > LoI[Δ]
COC	Perry, Nelson, and Carroll (2008) Exp. 2	Adjusting delay	Approximate median split[©] (upper/lower)	ACQ	0.2	HiI > LoI[Δ]
COC	Perry, Nelson, and Carroll (2008) Exp. 3	Adjusting delay	Approximate median split[©] (upper/lower)	ACQ	0.8	HiI > LoI
				MAINT	0.4	HiI = LoI
				EXT	0.0	HiI < LoI
				RST (D)	10	HiI = LoI
				RST (D)	15	HiI > LoI

MPH	Marusich and Bardo (2009)	Adjusting delay	Median split (upper/lower)	ACQ	0.56	HiI = LoI
				DMND	0.1, 0.3, 1.0	HiI = LoI
				MAINT	0.1, 0.3, 1.0	HiI > LoI
HER	Schippers, Binnekade, Schoffelmeer, and de Vries (2011)	Increasing delay	Quartile split (upper/lower)	ACQ	0.1	HiI = LoI
				DMND	0.1	HiI = LoI
				EXT	0.0	HiI = LoI
				RST (C)	0.0	HiI = LoI
				RST (D)	0.25	HiI = LoI
NIC	Diergaarde et al. (2008)	Increasing delay	Quartile split (upper/lower)	ACQ	0.04	HiI = LoI
				MAINT	0.04	HiI = LoI
				DMND	0.04	HiI > LoI
				EXT	0.0	HiI > LoI
				RST (C)	0.0	HiI > LoI
NIC	Sweitzer (2008)	Adjusting delay	Tertile Split (Upper/Lower)	ACQ	0.03	HiI = LoI
				DMND	0.03	HiI = LoI
				MAINT	0.015, 0.03, 0.09	HiI = LoI

*Both the between-groups and continuous, full-range data were statistically significant at the 12% w/v solution. #Only continuous, full-range data analyzed. ©A small proportion of intermediate discounting scores (~5–10%) were excluded from HiI/LoI categorization and were not assessed in subsequent SA phases. ∆Autoshaping procedure used during acquisition. §Data obtained through personal communication. ALC = alcohol; AMPH = amphetamine; COC = cocaine; HER = heroin; MPH = methylphenidate; NIC = nicotine; ACQ = acquisition; DMND = demand; ESC = escalation; EXT = resistance to extinction; MAINT = maintenance; RST = reinstatement; C = cue-primed reinstatement; D = drug-primed reinstatement.

in which 0.2 mg/kg cocaine infusions were delivered at irregular intervals in the absence of responding, or more immediately by pressing a lever. During a subsequent 6-hour SA portion of these sessions, HiI female rats were significantly more likely to acquire cocaine SA, and to do so more rapidly, than female LoI rats; a finding replicated with both male and female rats by Perry, Nelson, and Carroll (2008). In both studies, control measures of novelty seeking (locomotor activity in a novel environment) did not differ between groups – an important finding because previous research demonstrates that novelty seeking is also a predictor of cocaine SA (e.g., Piazza, Deminére, and Simon, 1989). Further removing the possibility that locomotor differences across groups might affect the dependent measure, Yates *et al.* (2011) reported that HiI rats demonstrated greater conditioned place preference in response to amphetamine (a measure of the drug's rewarding efficacy) than LoI rats.

Comparisons between inbred rat strains in the acquisition of drug SA yield findings similar to those of Perry *et al.* (2005) and Perry, Nelson, and Carroll (2008). Across studies, the Lewis (LEW) strain exhibits both (a) greater impulsive choice/delay discounting (Anderson and Woolverton, 2005; Anderson and Diller, 2010; García-Lecumberri *et al.*, 2011; Madden *et al.*, 2008; Stein, Pinkston, Brewer, Francisco, and Madden, 2012; but see also Wilhelm and Mitchell, 2009), and (b) more robust acquisition of drug SA than their histocompatible Fischer 344 (F344) comparison strain. This acquisition strain difference has been observed across multiple drugs of abuse, including cocaine (Kosten *et al.*, 1997), opioids (Ambrosio, Goldberg, and Elmer, 1995; Martín *et al.*, 1997; Suzuki, Otani, Koike, and Misawa, 1988), and alcohol (Suzuki, George, and Meisch, 1988). Further, impulsive LEW rats show greater acquisition of conditioned place preference than F344 rats for cocaine (Kosten, Miserendino, Chi, and Nestler, 1994), opioids (Guitart *et al.*, 1992) and nicotine (Horan *et al.*, 1997). However, LEW rats also exhibit greater novelty seeking (Gulley, Everett, and Zahniser, 2007; another apparent predictor of drug SA acquisition) and LEW rats also appear to acquire instrumental food responding more quickly than F344 rats (Martín *et al.*, 1997; but see also Martín *et al.*, 1999). These latter findings suggest behavioral differences may not be specific to acquisition of drug SA and suggest a role for the known neurochemical and neuroendocrine differences between these strains. By extension, these findings suggest the possibility of similar differences across HiI and LoI rats in studies like those of Perry *et al.* (2005, 2008).

In a related set of findings, Perry *et al.* (2007) reported that rats selectively bred for high saccharin intake (HiS) made more impulsive choices than rats bred for low saccharin intake (LoS). This is of interest because, relative to LoS rats, HiS rats more quickly acquire cocaine SA (Carroll *et al.*, 2002), show greater escalation (Perry *et al.*, 2006) and dysregulation of cocaine intake (Carroll, Anderson, and Morgan, 2007), and are more likely to reinstate cocaine-seeking activities following a period of extinction (Perry *et al.*, 2006).

A clear relation between delay discounting and acquisition of drug SA has not been universally observed. One peer-reviewed paper (Diergaarde *et al.*, 2008) and one unpublished thesis (Sweitzer, 2008) reported no differences between HiI and LoI rats in acquisition of nicotine SA. Similarly, Schippers, Binnekade, Schoffelmeer, and De Vries (2011) reported no such relation in the acquisition of heroin SA. Marusich and Bardo (2009) reported a similar null finding in the acquisition of methylphenidate

SA. However, not noted by the latter authors, during the initial seven acquisition sessions in which a single lever press produced a 0.56 mg/kg drug infusion, HiI rats discriminated better, and more often favored the active (drug) lever over the inactive lever when compared with LoI rats (Mann–Whitney U = 8, $p < 0.05$). A second study from the same lab (Marusich *et al.*, 2011) evaluated the correlation between impulsivity and acquisition of *d*-amphetamine SA. Although the correlation coefficient between impulsivity scores and *d*-amphetamine intake during acquisition was higher than other predictor variables (e.g., novelty seeking), the correlation (0.30) did not achieve traditional levels of significance.

Recently, Diergaarde *et al.* (2011) reported that HiI and LoI rats self-administered equivalent amount of alcohol during acquisition sessions. However, Poulos, Le, and Parker (1995) reported that HiI rats consumed more alcohol in a two-bottle test (Richter and Campbell, 1940) than LoI rats. Differences emerged at 6% w/v alcohol and were most evident at 12% w/v. Percent impulsive choice was correlated with alcohol consumption even when rats were declassified from their LoI, "medium impulsive" (MedI), or HiI groups.[5] Further, the relation between steep delay discounting and alcohol consumption is bolstered by findings that at least two rat strains selectively bred for high alcohol consumption discount delayed food more steeply than their respective non-alcohol-preferring comparison strains (Oberlin and Grahame, 2009; Wilhelm and Mitchell, 2008). However, this relation was not observed in two mouse strains selectively bred for high and low alcohol consumption (Wilhelm, Reeves, Phillips, and Mitchell, 2007). This discrepancy may relate to the fact that selectively bred rat strains in the former studies were stable over multiple generations, whereas mice in the latter study were only in their second generation of breeding.

Inconsistencies across these acquisition studies underscore the need for further research. Perhaps steep delay discounting is predictive only of cocaine SA, but procedural differences across studies should be systematically investigated before any conclusions are reached. In the cocaine studies of Perry *et al.* (2005) and Perry, Nelson, and Carroll (2008, Experiment 2) the arrangement of the experimental chamber was altered between the delay-discounting assessment (using food rewards) and the drug SA conditions; other studies left the chamber unaltered (e.g., Diergaarde *et al.*, 2008; 2011). This may be important if some of the instrumental responding in the drug acquisition sessions occurs either because lever pressing has been reinforced with food in this chamber arrangement in the past, or because pressing the drug lever produces stimulus changes previously associated with food reinforcers. In studies that left the experimental chamber unchanged, HiI and LoI rats tend to respond at terminal rates (e.g., Diergaarde *et al.*) or higher (Marusich and Bardo, 2009) in the first session of acquisition. When this happens, preference for the drug over the inactive lever may be an important measure of acquisition.

A second approach to future research would be to investigate the possibility that response acquisition differences between HiI and LoI rats would also be observed

---

[5] Despite enormous interest in this area (e.g., nearly 100 citations of this article in the literature, to date), there are no published studies which have replicated Poulos *et al.*'s finding that degree of impulsivity predicts subsequent alcohol consumption within a single rat strain. This is suggestive of the file-drawer problem, wherein nonsignificant findings go unpublished (Rosenthal, 1979).

when a non-drug reward is employed. In at least one study, "HiI" rats purportedly acquired operant food responding more quickly than "LoI" rats in an autoshaping paradigm (Tomie, Aguado, Pohorecky, and Benjamin, 1998). A shortcoming of this study is that rats classified as LoI tended to poorly discriminate between large and small food outcomes. Thus, these rats may have acquired food "SA" more slowly than HiI rats because of a general insensitivity to procedural contingencies. Future drug SA studies comparing HiI and LoI rats should empirically evaluate the possibility that HiI rats are likely to acquire Pavlovian or instrumental responding more rapidly than LoI rats regardless of the unconditioned stimulus employed.

2.1.2.2 MAINTENANCE.   Six published studies have compared HiI and LoI rats in drug SA during a maintenance phase (see Table 7.1). Of these, only two have shown a difference between HiI and LoI rats. Marusich and Bardo (2009) reported that HiI rats consumed more methylphenidate than LoI rats at the lowest of three doses (0.1 mg/kg). Perry, Nelson, and Carroll (2008) reported no differences in cocaine SA across HiI and LoI rats, but in some sessions either the LoI females or HiI males responded at higher rates on the cocaine lever. This appears to have been due to responding during the infusion period.

Carroll *et al.* (2010) have suggested that the lack of a systematic difference between HiI and LoI rats during maintenance may be due to constrained session durations or ceiling effects produced by high drug doses. That being said, the preparation used by Diergaarde *et al.* (2008) to study maintenance of nicotine SA was adequately sensitive to detect differences between groups of rats differentiated on a separate measure of impulsivity (i.e., response inhibition, measured by the 5-choice serial reaction time task), but the same SA procedure revealed no difference in maintenance of nicotine SA between HiI and LoI rats.

Comparisons between inbred LEW and F344 rats in drug SA provide an interesting, but paradoxical, complement to those between outbred HiI and LoI rats. While LEW rats show greater acquisition of drug SA compared to F344 rats, this strain difference during maintenance either erodes (i.e., LEW = F344; Kosten *et al.*, 1997), or more typically reverses (i.e., F344 > LEW; Haile, Zhang, Carroll, and Kosten, 2005; Haile and Kosten, 2001; Kosten, Zhang, and Haile, 2007). These findings led Kosten, Zhang, and Haile (2007) to suggest that maintenance, and not acquisition, provides the more relevant model of human drug abuse as it typifies the transition from initial drug exposure to regular use. Such an assertion, if valid, complicates interpretation of the relation between steep delay discounting and drug SA in nonhuman models.

2.1.2.3 ESCALATION AND INELASTIC DEMAND.   To date, only one study has examined if HiI rats are more likely to escalate their drug intake when given the opportunity to do so in long-duration sessions. Anker, Perry, Gliddon, and Carroll (2009) reported that HiI rats increased their cocaine intake over a 21-day period, whereas LoI rats did not. One caveat to this finding is that LoI rats self-administered more cocaine during the first three long-duration sessions than did HiI rats; however, during the final six sessions of this condition, HiI rats' cocaine intake was higher than that of LoI rats. The difference in drug intake escalation was not due to differences in acquisition or prior drug intake, as high doses ensured approximately equal rates of acquisition and no differences were observed in an earlier cocaine maintenance condition.

Inelastic demand for a drug is observed when instrumental responding continues to increase in the face of price increases (for a review, see Madden, 2000). Drug prices are usually increased by increasing fixed-ratio (FR) response requirement between sessions. Using this procedure, Diergaarde *et al.* (2008) reported that HiI rats' demand for nicotine was more inelastic than LoI rats. Koffarnus and Woods (2011) used the same general procedure and reported the same outcome for cocaine SA. Importantly, Koffarnus and Woods found that demand for sucrose pellets was equivalent across HiI and LoI rats; thus, the difference in delay discounting was specific to demand for cocaine.

No relation between impulsivity and elasticity of demand for methylphenidate (Marusich and Bardo, 2009) or heroin (Schippers, Binnekade, Schoffelmeer, and De Vries, 2011) has been observed. In these studies FR values were increased more slowly (i.e., incremented by one or two responses every few sessions) and the range of FR values explored was smaller (FR 1–5) than in the studies just summarized (Diergaarde *et al.*, 2008: FR 2–25; Koffarnus and Woods, 2011: FR 1–32). Across this low range of FR values, neither Diergaarde *et al.* nor Koffarnus and Woods observed differences in elasticity between HiI and LoI rats; the difference emerged only at higher drug prices. Finally, Diergaarde *et al.* (2011) reported no differences in elasticity of demand for alcohol between HiI and LoI rats, despite the use of relatively high drug prices (FR 25).

An approximation of this elasticity-assessment procedure is a progressive ratio (PR) schedule of reinforcement, in which the FR requirement increases following each drug infusion and the session ends when a predetermined period of time elapses without responding. The final FR value reached (the PR breakpoint) provides a measure of the highest price the animal will pay for drug infusions. Three studies have used this procedure with cocaine (Anker, Perry, Gliddon, and Carroll, 2009), nicotine (Sweitzer, 2008), or heroin (Schippers, Binnekade, Schoffelmeer, and De Vries, 2011) and none of these has reported a significant difference between HiI and LoI rats. One possible reason for this is that all three studies terminated the session before the PR breakpoint was reached if the programmed session duration expired. In the Sweitzer (2008) study the PR breakpoint was not obtained in >20% of the 4-hour sessions; comparable measures were not reported by Anker *et al.* (2-hour sessions) and Schippers *et al.* (4-hour sessions).

Finally, and counter to the hypothesis that steep delay discounting is predictive of drug abuse, the less impulsive F344 inbred strain demonstrates greater escalation of cocaine intake (Freeman, Kearns, Kohut, and Riley, 2009) and more inelastic demand for cocaine (Christensen *et al.*, 2009; Kosten, Zhang, and Haile, 2007) than the more impulsive LEW strain. These mixed findings underscore, once again, the need for additional studies taking a systematic approach to the procedural differences noted above.

2.1.2.4 RESISTANCE TO EXTINCTION AND REINSTATEMENT. Continued responding following termination of the response-outcome contingency (extinction) is thought to provide a measure of the efficacy of the previously available outcome (e.g., Nevin and Grace, 2005). Reinstatement tasks have been used after drug SA extinction to model some components of cue- or drug-induced relapse in humans. Three studies have thus far examined the relation between delay discounting and these outcome measures. Diergaarde *et al.* (2008) reported that HiI rats continued to respond at higher rates than LoI rats across the first 7 days of extinction from nicotine SA. In the final five sessions of extinction there were no significant differences across groups but this changed when pressing the active lever produced stimuli that were previously correlated with nicotine. In these cue-reinstatement sessions, HiI rats responded at higher rates than LoI rats.

By contrast, Perry, Nelson, and Carroll (2008; Experiment 3) reported that among female rats, the *LoI* group emitted more responses during cocaine extinction than HiI rats; no difference was observed among males. However, consistent with Diergaarde *et al.*'s (2008) finding, a 15 mg/kg priming dose induced more reinstatement responding among HiI than LoI rats. This difference was not observed, however, at lower priming doses.

Finally, Schippers, Binnekade, Schoffelmeer, and De Vries (2011) reported no difference between HiI and LoI rats in either resistance to extinction or cue- or drug-induced reinstatement of heroin SA. That these authors observed no relation between impulsive choice and heroin SA in these or any other SA phase investigated (acquisition or demand) suggests that group differences observed with psychostimulants (e.g., cocaine, nicotine) do not generalize to opioid drugs. More work is needed to elucidate this possibility.

2.2   Steep delay discounting as a consequence of drug abuse

In contrast to the hypothesis that steep delay discounting predisposes individuals toward drug abuse, the robust correlation between drug abuse and steep delay discounting in humans may also be explained as a *consequence* of drug abuse. Over the last two decades, several investigators have examined the effects of acute and chronic drug exposure on subsequent delay discounting in humans and nonhumans. Several recent reviews of this literature are available elsewhere (de Wit, 2009; de Wit and Mitchell, 2010; Setlow, Mendez, Mitchell, and Simon, 2009; Perry and Carroll, 2008).

2.2.1   Nonhuman studies.   Nonhuman studies of acute drug effects on delay discounting are inconsistent. Most studies conducted to date have examined the effects of psychomotor stimulants on delay discounting. In some of these, stimulants produced shallower discounting, others have shown the opposite effect, and others no effect at all (for reviews, see de Wit and Mitchell, 2010; Perry and Carroll, 2008). Similar inconsistencies have been observed with other drugs of abuse.

However, if nonhuman drug effects are to shed light on the relation between steep delay discounting and human drug abuse, chronic or daily drug administration may provide a more valid model than acute drug manipulations. The majority of research on delay discounting and drug abuse in humans features clinically dependent populations (MacKillop *et al.*, 2011) for whom patterns of drug use are chronic, not acute. A number of studies have examined the effects of chronic or daily drug dosing on delay discounting in rats, with the majority of these studies investigating psychomotor stimulants. In a review of this literature, Setlow, Mendez, Mitchell, and Simon (2009) suggested that the immediate effects of chronic/daily exposure to stimulants on delay discounting were inconsistent. Some studies (e.g., Simon, Mendez, and Setlow, 2007) suggested that high doses of cocaine could increase impulsive choice, but other studies employing similar (e.g., Winstanley *et al.*, 2007) or higher (Paine, Dringenberg, and Olmstead, 2003) cumulative daily doses reported no consistent effect. Setlow *et al.* suggested that the effects of cocaine on delay discounting may be most evident following an "incubation" period extending several months after cocaine withdrawal (see Grimm, Hope, Wise, and Shaham, 2001). Consistent with this hypothesis, two studies examining delay discounting 3 or more months after cocaine withdrawal reported either more impulsive choices (Simon, Mendez, and Setlow, 2007) or enhanced sensitivity to delays (Roesch *et al.*, 2007) in cocaine-exposed rats.

Details of the studies summarized by Setlow, Mendez, Mitchell, and Simon (2009), and those published since, may be found in Table 7.2. The conclusions of Setlow *et al.* are supported by these data with one important caveat. Interpreting the effects of stimulant and other drugs on delay discounting is difficult when the drug produces effects nonspecific to impulsive choice. If these nonspecific effects are difficult to discriminate from a change in impulsive choice, then erroneous conclusions may be reached. Specifically, the most commonly used technique for evaluating chronic drug effects on discounting is the *increasing-delay* procedure developed by Evenden and Ryan (1996). In this procedure, the delay to the larger food reward increases from 0 to usually 60 seconds over several blocks of discrete trials. Typically, choice of the larger option decreases with increasing delays and the delay at which interpolated percent choice crosses indifference is often taken as a summary measure of delay discounting. The difficulty with these interpretations occurs when the drug disrupts choice in the initial block of trials when the animal is choosing between two immediate food rewards – one small and one large. In baseline sessions, rats (on average) choose the larger option more than 80% of the time. A common effect of chronic/daily drug injections is a decrease in this preference for the larger option in this trial block. This reflects either decreased sensitivity to food amounts (given that no delays are arranged in this initial block of trials) or a nonspecific disruption of response allocation (e.g., disorientation). Failure to take this insensitivity/disruption into consideration when interpreting the remainder of the choice data is potentially important.

Consider, for example, the results of an experiment conducted by Dandy and Gatch (2009). The upper panel of Figure 7.6 shows the effects of two doses of daily cocaine on choices made in the increasing-delay procedure. Based on these data, the researchers concluded that cocaine significantly increased impulsive choice. However, it is clear from the choices made in the 0-second delay trial block that cocaine either decreased sensitivity to food amount or produced a nonspecific disruption of choice. In the lower panel of Figure 7.6, the choices made by rats in the cocaine groups are normalized to those made by rats given daily injections of deionized water. When the amount-insensitivity or nonspecific effects of the drug are removed in this way, it is clear that cocaine did not increase impulsive choice. We applied this normalization procedure to the studies in Table 7.2 that used the increasing-delay procedure and

Table 7.2 Effects of chronic/daily drug administration on delay discounting in nonhuman subjects

Drug	Authors	Subjects	Dose (mg/kg, except where noted)	Frequency	Duration (days)	Pre-drug task training	Procedure	Chronic drug effects on discounting	Post-chronic tests of discounting	Post-chronic drug effects on discounting
ALC	Bañuelos et al. (2012)	Rat (infant)	5.25 g/kg	Daily	7	No	Increasing delay	–	~42 days' withdrawal; 40 sessions (no drug)	ALC < SAL
ALC	Pupe, Brys, Asherton, and Bizarro (2011)	Rat (prenatal)	Liquid diet; 10% or 35% of mother's calories	Daily	Throughout gestation	No	Increasing delay	–	60 days' withdrawal; 45 sessions (no drug)	ALC = SAL
d-AMPH	Gipson and Bardo (2009)	Rat	0.03, 0.1 (SA)	Daily	15	Yes	Adjusting delay	AMPH = SAL	–	–
d-AMPH	Stanis, Burns, Sherrill, and Gulley (2008)	Rat	3	Every other day	20	No	Increasing delay	**AMPH = SAL**	Acute AMPH (0.1, 2 mg/kg)	**AMPH = SAL**
Meth-AMPH	Richards, Sabol, and de Wit (1999)	Rat	4	Daily	14	Yes	Adjusting amount	AMPH > SAL	–	–
ATX	Sun, Cocker, Zeeb, and Winstanley (2012)	Rat (adolescent)	1	Daily	14	No	Increasing delay	–	14 days' withdrawal; X sessions (no drug)	**ATX < SAL**
CAF	Diller, Saunders, and Anderson (2008)	Rat	30	Daily	15 +	Yes	Increasing delay	**CAF < SAL**	10 sessions (no drug)	**CAF = SAL**
COC	Dandy and Gatch (2009)	Rat	3, 7.5, 15	Daily	9	Yes	Adjusting delay	7.5/15 > SAL	14 sessions (no drug)	Transient 15 > SAL/3/7.5
COC	Hamilton, Czoty, and Nader (2011)	Monkey (prenatal)	1–8.5 (escalating)	3 × Daily	Throughout gestation	No	Increasing delay (b/w sessions)	–	14 years' withdrawal; variable # of sessions (no drug)	**COC > CONT**
COC	Logue et al. (1992)	Rat	15	Daily	10 +	Yes	Adjusting delay	COC > SAL	–	–
COC	Mendez et al. (2010)	Rat	0.5 (SA)	Daily	14	No	Increasing delay	**COC > SAL**[52]	–	–
COC	Paine, Dringenberg, and Olmstead (2003)	Rat	15	3 × Daily	14	Yes	Increasing delay	**COC = SAL***	–	–

Drug	Citation	Species	Dose	N	Schedule	Sensitivity	Ho et al. (1999)	Procedure	Withdrawal	Result
COC	Roesch et al. (2007)	Rat	30	14	Daily	No	Increasing delay	–	21 days' withdrawal; 1–6 sessions (no drug)	‡
COC	Simon, Mendez, and Setlow (2007)	Rat	30	14	Daily	No	Increasing delay	–	21 days' withdrawal; 40 sessions (no drug)	**COC > SAL**
COC	Winstanley et al. (2007)	Rat	15	21	2 × Daily	Yes	Increasing delay	COC = SAL	Acute COC (7.5–15 mg/kg)	COC = SAL
FLU	Eppolito, Fance, and Gerak (2011)	Pigeon	0.32, 1, 3.2	6	Every other day	Yes	Increasing delay	**FLU < SAL**	3 sessions (no drug)	FLU = SAL
HER	Harry, Whaley, Halperin, and Ranaldi (2011)	Rat	2	9	Daily	Yes	Increasing delay	HER = SAL	–	–
HER	Schippers, Binnekade, Schoffelmeer, and De Vries (2011)	Rat	0.1, 0.25 (SA)	25	Daily	Yes	Increasing delay	HER > SAL	35 days' withdrawal; # sessions undefined	HER = SAL
MPH	Adriani, Canese, Podo, and Laviola (2007)	Rat (adolescent)	2	14	Daily	No	Increasing delay (b/w sessions)	–	16 days' withdrawal; 7 sessions (no drug)	**MPH < SAL**
NIC	Anderson and Diller (2010)	Rat (LEW)	1	30+	Daily	Yes	Increasing delay	**NIC = SAL**	10 sessions (no drug)	NIC > CONT
NIC	Anderson and Diller (2010)	Rat (F344)	1	30+	Daily	Yes	Increasing delay	**NIC = SAL**	10 sessions	**NIC = CONT**
NIC	Dallery and Locey (2005)	Rat	0.3, 1	65	Daily	Yes	Adjusting delay	NIC > SAL	65 sessions (no drug)	Transient NIC > SAL
NIC	Mitchell et al. (2012)	Rat (infant)	6	7	Daily	No	Increasing delay	–	~130 days' withdrawal; 30 sessions (no drug)	**NIC = CONT**

SA indicates that rats self-administered the drug. Dose per SA infusion is presented; total daily intake varied. Bolded findings indicate examinations of psychostimulants in the increasing-delay procedure that remained unchanged following normalization (see text). ΩApproached significance (p = 0.07) *Small and transient significant difference (COC > SAL) on 1 of 14 days of testing. ‡Cocaine increased rats' sensitivity to both reward delay *and* amount. How this translates to impulsive choice is unclear because these sensitivity enhancements pull choice in opposite directions when choosing between SS and LL options. ATX = atomoxetine; CAF = caffeine; FLU = flunitrazepam; SAL = saline. All other abbreviations are as in Table 7.1.

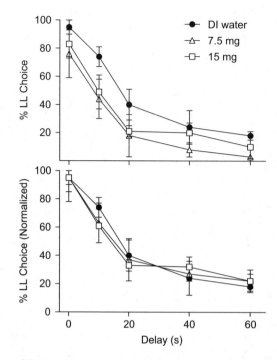

Figure 7.6   Effects of daily doses of cocaine in rats on percent choice for the LL food option in the increasing-delay procedure. Top panel depicts data originally reported by the authors, whereas the bottom panel depicts these data normalized to choice in the 0-second delay trial block. Data reprinted from Dandy and Gatch (2009)

reported a significant or near-significant effect. The bolded results indicate those effects that were unchanged by the normalization process. These provide little evidence that chronic drugs increase impulsive choice under the increasing-delay procedure.

In their review, Setlow, Mendez, Mitchell, and Simon (2009) also suggested that pre-training on the discounting procedure prior to drug administration may attenuate chronic/daily drug effects on delay discounting. The studies in Table 7.2 accord with this hypothesis. Further substantiation, however, awaits explicit experimental manipulation of this variable, as other covariates of drug effects may be identified (e.g., drug administration during adolescence or the presence of an incubation period).

Nonspecific drug effects may also be difficult to discriminate from changes in delay discounting when other procedures are used. For example, Perry and Carroll (2008) briefly described the results of an unpublished study of the effects of chronic *d*-amphetamine on delay discounting. The effect depended on baseline level of delay discounting. That is, *d*-amphetamine shifted the choices of LoI rats toward steeper discounting, but the opposite effect was observed in HiI rats. Such a "rate-dependent" effect may simply have been a non-specific regression toward less-extreme discounting. Finally, two studies using alternative procedures suggest that chronic nicotine (Dallery and Locey, 2005) and methamphetamine (Richards, Sabol, and de Wit, 1999) increase delay discounting. Systematic replications of these findings would be useful.

To summarize, our analysis of the available empirical evidence suggests that when the increasing-delay procedure is used, reported increases in impulsive choice appear more often than not to be a product of either diminished sensitivity to reward amount or a nonspecific disruption in choice. Future studies must consider how the latter two may be disentangled, as diminished sensitivity to reward amount is a second mechanism that may produce impulsive choice.

2.2.2 Human studies. In the human lab, examination of chronic or repeated drug effects on delay discounting has relied on correlational findings. Some evidence suggests that daily cigarette smokers discount delayed monetary rewards more steeply than either of two demographically matched groups of ex-smokers or non-smokers (Bickel, Odum, and Madden, 1999); further, current alcoholics discount more steeply than currently abstinent alcoholics, who in turn discount more steeply than matched controls (Petry, 2001). These findings might suggest that discontinuation of drug exposure (e.g., in ex-smokers) produces a return to more normative levels of delay discounting. However, another interpretation is that drug users who demonstrate shallower discounting are more likely to succeed in achieving sustained drug abstinence. As noted earlier, that steep delay discounting predicts failure in drug treatment programs (e.g., MacKillop and Kahler, 2009) supports this alternative explanation. A perhaps more interpretable data set was provided by Audrain-McGovern *et al.* (2009). In their longitudinal assessment of delay discounting and cigarette smoking in teenagers, these authors observed no apparent effects of cigarette smoking on delay discounting (pre- versus post-tests). Whether this would also be observed with other drugs of abuse awaits further evidence.

2.3 Are steep delay discounting and drug abuse the product of a third variable?

In many respects, the discussion thus far has focused on the hypothesis that steep delay discounting plays a causal role in drug abuse. However, at present, the paucity of longitudinal human studies restricts interpretation to the nonhuman data reviewed thus far. This, in turn, raises the question of cross-species generalization. For instance, the top panels of Figures 7.3 and 7.4 frame human decisions regarding drug use as a competition between immediate drug effects and the delayed, but more beneficial, outcomes associated with abstinence. The nonhuman findings challenge this assumption because analogous delayed benefits of abstinence for the rat are presumably nonexistent at the ontogenic level.

Theorists may salvage this account by presuming instead that the HiI rat, compared to the LoI, more steeply discounts the delayed *aversive* state of acute drug withdrawal (e.g., depressant effects of "coming down") – an outcome with which the rat has commerce (bottom panels of Figures 7.3 and 7.4). Some evidence suggests that acute doses of numerous drugs of abuse (including cocaine) have aversive properties, as these drugs elicit conditioned taste aversion (CTA) in drug-naïve rats (for a review, see Cappell and Le Blanc, 1975). That is, pairing a highly palatable food (e.g., sucrose solution) with experimenter-administered drug doses suppresses subsequent approach and consumption of that food. However, the range of cocaine doses sufficient to elicit CTA (e.g., 10–36 mg/kg; Goudie, Dickins, and Thornton, 1978) extends well beyond the low cumulative daily doses shown to produce acquisition differences in HiI and LoI rats (Perry *et al.*, 2005; Perry, Nelson, and Carroll, 2008). In addition, some authors suggest that drugs of abuse produce CTA not because they are aversive, but because their more salient rewarding properties overshadow those of the food with which they are paired (Grigson, 1997). These considerations cast doubt on the conceptual underpinnings of how steep delay discounting may predispose individuals toward drug abuse.

A more parsimonious account of the relation between delay discounting and drug abuse – one that requires little need for complex cross-species generalization – may be that both steep delay discounting and drug abuse are the mutual products of a third variable. Supporting this possibility, steep delay discounting has been shown to predict locomotoric sensitization to repeated doses of ethanol in mice (Mitchell, Reeves, Li, and Phillips, 2006) and *d*-amphetamine in rats (Perry and Carroll, 2008), and rats' responsiveness to the locomotor-inducing effects of cocaine is correlated with subsequent delay discounting (Stanis, Burns, Sherrill, and Gulley, 2008). More recently, Yates *et al.* (2011) reported that steep delay discounting in rats predicted greater conditioned place preference for a compartment previously paired with amphetamine – a measure of the rewarding efficacy of a drug. Because greater sensitization and conditioned place preference in these studies occurred outside the context of instrumental responding, steep delay discounting seems to reflect a vulnerability to drugs of abuse independent of the outcome-valuation hypotheses depicted in Figures 7.3 and 7.4.

As a result, those looking for a third variable may wish to examine the neural substrates of drug action – particularly, ventral striatal areas of the brain. Because striatal dopamine is recruited by both drugs of abuse (Nicoll, 1989; Nicola and Deadwyler, 2000; Ritz, Lamb, Goldberg, and Kuhar, 1987) and decisions involving immediacy (e.g., Kobayashi and Schultz, 2008; for a review, see Winstanley, 2010), dopaminergic dysfunction in these areas may simultaneously induce (a) greater subjective experience of drug reward (hence, greater drug seeking) and (b) steeper delay discounting.

Regarding vulnerability to drug reward, drug abusers exhibit fewer D_2/D_3 receptors in several brain regions, including the nucleus accumbens (Dackis and Gold, 1985; Gill *et al.*, 1991; Volkow, Ding, Fowler, and Wang, 1996). Fewer accumbal D_2 receptors have also been reported in high-alcohol-preferring rat and mouse strains (McBride *et al.*, 1997; Thanos *et al.*, 2004). In addition, some evidence suggests that increasing D_2 receptor availability in rats decreases cocaine self-administration and alcohol consumption (Thanos *et al.*, 2001; 2004; 2008).

Regarding delay discounting, Diergaarde *et al.* (2008) showed that a drug-naïve cohort of HiI rats, compared to LoI rats, later showed lower levels of electrically induced in vitro dopamine release in the nucleus accumbens. Likewise, the LEW inbred rat strain, prone to steeper delay discounting, greater acquisition of drug SA, and greater conditioned place preference for a number of drugs of abuse, also exhibits fewer accumbal dopamine D_2/D_3 receptors and dopamine transporters compared to the F344 strain (for a review, see Kosten and Ambrosio, 2002). Despite lower tonic dopamine levels, LEW rats exhibit greater phasic increases in extracellular dopamine in the nucleus accumbens in response to several drugs of abuse, including cocaine, codeine, morphine, and nicotine (Cadoni and Di Chiara, 2007; Cadoni, Muto, and Di Chiara, 2009). Lower tonic dopamine levels, yet greater phasic firing in response to drugs of abuse increases the ratio of signal to noise and suggests a mechanism that enhances a drug's rewarding efficacy.

Thus, combining data across studies, dopaminergic dysfunction/dysregulation may be a third variable that governs both delay discounting and vulnerability to drug reward. In this case, deficits in the valuation of delayed outcomes as depicted in Figures 7.3 and 7.4 would not initially cause, but could perhaps exacerbate, drug abuse. Substantiation of this hypothesis awaits further investigation.

3 Methodology for the Study of Delay Discounting and Drug Abuse

The majority of procedures used to assess delay discounting in humans and non-humans are based on methods of psychophysical titration. In these procedures, the researcher arranges initial choices between SS and LL outcomes and then titrates an outcome parameter (e.g., amount of the SS reward) until indifference is reached. The titrated parameter at indifference provides a measure of the discounted value of the LL outcome. In the following sections, we discuss procedures used most widely to assess delay discounting in both human and nonhuman subjects.

3.1 Assessment of delay discounting in humans

3.1.1 Hypothetical monetary gains and costs. The majority of the procedures used to assess delay discounting in humans are derived from one pioneered by Rachlin, Raineri, and Cross (1991), in which participants initially choose between a hypothetical $1,000 reward delivered either immediately or after a range of delays (1 month to 50 years). Across a series of choices at each prospective delay, the amount of the immediate option is decreased in a fixed sequence (e.g., $1,000, $980, $960, etc.) until reaching $1. This procedure is repeated in an ascending order with the indifference point defined as the average amount of the SS option when preference switches to the LL.

More recently, researchers have used dynamic titration methods in which the direction of the adjustment is based on previous choices (e.g., Johnson and Bickel, 2002). One of the most efficient of these (Du, Green, and Myerson, 2002) asks participants to make only six choices at each delay (e.g., $100 now or $200 after a delay). Choosing the SS option decreases this amount on the subsequent trial, while choosing the LL option produces the opposite adjustment. The size of the adjustment is cut in half with each choice, allowing one to identify quickly an indifference point. This procedure yields orderly hyperbolic discounting functions at the group and individual level with no systematic differences in estimates of discounting when compared to those obtained using the Rachlin, Raineri, and Cross (1991) procedure (Rodzon, Berry, and Odum, 2011).

Other procedures ask the participant to fill in a blank with either the present value of the delayed monetary gain (e.g., Rossow, 2008) or the amount of a delayed gain at which the participant would be indifferent. From the information provided, a single discounting rate may be derived. MacKillop *et al.* (2011) reported that comparisons between drug abusers and controls using these fill-in-the-blank methods yielded significantly smaller aggregate effect sizes (Cohen's $d = 0.13$) than did the other methods reviewed thus far (Cohen's $d = 0.56$).

The procedures discussed above may also be used with delayed monetary costs. Although the discounting of delayed monetary gains in these procedures tends to correlate positively with the discounting of delayed monetary costs (Mitchell and Wilson, 2010; Murphy, Vuchinich, and Simpson, 2001; Ohmura, Takahashi, and Kitamura, 2005), costs are discounted less steeply than gains (the *sign effect*). This effect has been demonstrated with the use of all procedures discussed in this section (e.g., Benzion, Rapoport, and Yagil, 1989; Chapman, 1996; Estle, Green, Myerson, and Holt, 2006; Loewenstein, 1988; Shelley, 1993).

3.1.2 Hypothetical health gains and costs.

The procedures described above may also be used with delayed health outcomes (e.g., Chapman, 1996). Two studies have examined delay discounting of delayed health outcomes as it relates to cigarette smoking. In the first of these, Odum, Madden, and Bickel (2002) reported that current and former cigarette smokers discounted both gains *and* costs more steeply than never-smokers. These authors framed health gains as an immediate or delayed escape from a present illness, while specifying relevant symptoms (e.g., frequent colds, hospitalization, weight loss, lethargy, decreased sexual desire) to be relieved by the health gain. Using Rachlin, Raineri, and Cross's (1991) procedure, participants chose between shorter periods of immediate health (SS gain) or a 10-year period of health after a delay (LL gain). In the costs condition, health outcomes were framed as a transition from good to bad health that could, upon the participant's choice, be induced for a shorter period now (SS cost) or put off but experienced for a longer duration later (LL cost). As with the studies of monetary gains and costs, the magnitude (i.e., duration) of the immediate health outcome at indifference provided a measure of the discounted value of the delayed health outcome. Similar framing was used by Baker, Johnson, and Bickel (2003) using another dynamic titration procedure (Richards, Sabol, and de Wit, 1999). However, these latter authors reported no differences in delay discounting between smokers and non-smokers.[6]

At present, little is known about the discounting of hypothetical health outcomes in other drug abusing populations. Because health outcomes are arguably more relevant to choices between abstinence and drug use than are monetary outcomes, more work is needed in this area to elucidate the role of delay discounting in drug abuse.

3.1.3 Potentially real monetary gains and costs.

Although these procedures using hypothetical outcomes yield orderly data and consistently distinguish between drug abusing populations and controls, many researchers have expressed concerns about the hypothetical nature of the outcomes (e.g., Bickel and Marsch, 2001). These concerns led some researchers to instruct their participants that one of their choices

---

[6]Only a trend-level difference between smokers and non-smokers was observed ($p = 0.09$).

would be selected at random and that the monetary outcome selected on that trial would be awarded at the end of the session (e.g., Kirby and Maraković, 1995; 1996). However, a large number of studies have looked for differences in delay discounting across hypothetical, potentially real, and all real rewards, but no significant differences have been found (Johnson and Bickel, 2002; Lagorio and Madden, 2005; Madden, Begotka, Raiff, and Kastern, 2003; Madden *et al.*, 2004).

3.1.4   Real non-monetary gains.   Recently a handful of investigators have assessed delay discounting in humans using real consumable outcomes (e.g., McClure *et al.*, 2007). For example, Jimura *et al.* (2009; 2011) used the Du, Green, and Myerson (2002) dynamic titration method to examine discounting of delayed juice. Use of real consumables has at least two advantages over traditional methods. First, the experimenter can control precisely when the outcome is delivered and consumed, a useful feature when one is interested in the neurobiological correlates of choice, real delays, and real rewards (e.g., McClure *et al.*). Second, when real rewards and delays are arranged, one can control events during the delay. In traditional delay discounting methods used with humans, the hypothetical delays stretch beyond the experimental session and the participant is free to imagine the many activities that they might pursue during the delay. Substantial individual differences may characterize these inter-delay activities (e.g., a wealthy participant may have a better time of waiting for a monetary reward than an impoverished participant) and these individual differences may underlie differences in delay discounting that might not be apparent if brief delays to consumables are used.

Consistent with this possibility, Jimura *et al.* (2011) reported that measures of delay discounting for juice and hypothetical monetary outcomes were not significantly correlated within participants. This finding might suggest distinct discounting processes across different time spans, but a more parsimonious account may be that the delay to juice is procedurally different from the delay to money because, as mentioned above, other rewards may be pursued during the latter delay but not during the former.

Because monetary outcomes differ in many respects from non-monetary outcomes such as juice, it is perhaps not surprising that the discounting of these two outcome types is dissociable. Among the properties not shared by monetary and non-monetary outcomes, SS monetary rewards may be invested in a way that yields more than the LL amount (e.g., Frederick, Loewenstein, and O'Donoghue, 2003); the same is not true of juice. Additionally, the value of LL monetary rewards may be affected by rates of inflation that affect the buying power of the LL reward when it is eventually delivered (Ostaszewski, Green, and Myerson, 1998); a factor that does not affect the value of an LL juice reward. Finally, the marginal utility function of fungible monetary rewards and nonfungible consumable rewards (particularly in the range of juice rewards arranged by Jimura *et al.*, 2009; 2011; and McClure *et al.*, 2007) may be different and, as a result, produce differences in discounting.

These, and many other, uncontrolled intra-delay variables in human discounting studies of delayed monetary and hypothetical consumable rewards suggest that procedures arranging brief delays to real consumable rewards are most likely to reflect the "pure" delay discounting process. To our knowledge, no study has compared drug-abusing populations and controls in the discounting of real consumable outcomes.

If a between-group difference is observed, it would expand the scope of outcomes across which steeper discounting is observed among addicted populations. If no difference is observed, it may point to between-group differences in any of the extraneous variables discussed above; variables that, if experimentally manipulated, might affect drug-related decision making.

3.1.5   Non-systematic data.   In studies with human participants, it is not uncommon for some participants to make unsystematic choices. These may arise from poor attention, demand characteristics, or a host of other reasons not presently understood. Many researchers use a predetermined criterion for excluding such data; most often this is based on the variance accounted for (R^2) by the discounting model (e.g., equation 1). However, Johnson and Bickel (2008) demonstrated empirically that excluding participants with low R^2 values can result in disproportionate exclusion of those with shallow delay discounting functions. As an alternative, these authors proposed a set of exclusion criteria that does not make any assumption regarding model fit, but assumes only a monotonically decreasing discounting function (regardless of steepness). A complementary approach is to set a criterion value for the sum of squared deviations between indifference points and the discounting curve. Finally, a method recently introduced in our lab is to ask participants to anonymously rate their level of engagement with the discounting task after they complete it. The rating scale ranges from "I paid close attention and made my choices as if the rewards were real" to "I paid little attention and made my choices haphazardly." Data from participants in the latter category are excluded before they are analyzed.

3.1.6   Choosing between dependent measures.   When fitting equation 1 to an individual's or group's indifference points, experimenters often use values of the equation's single free parameter (k) as their measure of delay discounting. The appropriateness of this depends on the fit of the hyperbolic model. While discounting curves are overwhelmingly better described as hyperbolic rather than exponential, there are systematic departures from the strict hyperbola. For example, Green, Fristoe, and Myerson (1994) proposed the hyperbola-*like* discounting model, in which the denominator in equation 1 is raised to a power, s, to represent the nonlinear scaling of outcome amount or delay (for a review, see Green and Myerson, 2004). The addition of a second free parameter (s) provides better fits but complicates interpretation of k as a measure of discounting because it interacts with s. As an alternative, Myerson, Green, and Warusawitharana (2001) proposed that area under the discounting curve (AUC) provides a theory-free measure of delay discounting that is not dependent on how well a particular curve fits the indifference points. Unlike k-values, measures of AUC (which can vary from 0 to 1) are most often normally distributed, allowing the use of parametric statistics. When using AUC, it is important to look for nonsystematic data (as discussed above) before quantifying delay discounting.

3.2   Assessment of delay discounting in nonhumans

In nonhuman experiments, subjects (typically rats or pigeons) choose between SS and LL food or liquid options (e.g., food pellets or sucrose solution). Four general procedures are common to virtually all of the specific procedures discussed below. First, an inter-trial interval (ITI) is used to hold constant the time between trials, regardless of which option is chosen. In the absence of an ITI, repeated selection of the SS option would increase the local rate of food delivery and end the session sooner – thus failing to isolate delay as the independent variable. Second, subjects make their choices by emitting a single instrumental response; requiring more introduces an additional delay (and effort) to the programmed delay and this may complicate interpretation of the results (e.g., Hamilton, Czoty, and Nader, 2011).

Third, at the beginning of each trial, an instrumental response is made at a location equidistant from the locations at which they will subsequently make choices. This "centering" response increases the likelihood that choice is controlled by the experimental contingencies rather than by location when the trial starts. Finally, forced-exposure trials (in which only one option is available) are distributed among the choice trials, in which subjects are allowed to choose freely between options. The purpose of these forced-exposure trials is to ensure continued contact with the contingencies arranged on both options. Loosely speaking, forced-exposure trials ensure subjects are making "informed" choices.

In the sections that follow, we provide a brief overview of the specific procedures used in the nonhuman literature. A weakness of this literature is that very few studies have provided systematic comparisons between measures of delay discounting that these procedures yield (but see Green *et al.*, 2007; Stein *et al.*, 2012). Thus, evaluating the robustness of findings (e.g., delay discounting as a predictor of drug SA) is difficult. For example, Diergaarde *et al.* (2008) and Sweitzer (2008) both examined delay discounting as a predictor of subsequent nicotine SA, but did so using different delay-discounting procedures. Because choice in the former study predicted subsequent nicotine SA but in the latter study did not, one must wonder if the first study represents a Type 1 error or if a procedural variable separating the studies can systematically account for the difference. The internal validity of a delay discounting procedure must be well established against known measures of the construct under investigation. Unfortunately, this is an area of investigation that gets little attention in the delay discounting literature, but it may underlie many of the unsystematic findings summarized in Tables 7.1 and 7.2.

3.2.1 *Fixed-delay procedure.*

In the simplest procedure, the experimenter arranges repeated choice between SS and LL food options with no change in reward magnitude or delay (e.g., Rachlin and Green 1972). A similar procedure, although less frequently used, allows rats to choose between SS and LL food options in one of two goal arms in a T-maze (e.g., Poulos, Le, and Poulos, 1995). Percent impulsive choice serves most often as the dependent measure. One problem with fixed-delay procedures is that, given the fixed contingencies, exclusive preference most often emerges (Mazur, 1987); thus, fine distinctions between the value of the SS and LL options are lost. A second problem is that if one wishes to investigate choice across a wide range of delays, especially in response to acute or chronic drug administration, then the large number of sessions required to reach steady state at each delay may introduce testing or maturational variables into data collection.

3.2.2 Increasing-delay procedure. The increasing-delay procedure (Evenden and Ryan, 1996) also arranges repeated choices between SS and LL food outcomes. However, within each session, delay to the LL option increases across trial blocks (e.g. 0, 10, 20, 40, 60 seconds), while the SS option remains available immediately. Forced-exposure trials are included at the beginning of each trial block to ensure adequate contact with the contingencies. When choice stabilizes across sessions, this procedure yields a baseline from which the experimenter can quickly and efficiently assess the effects of acute and chronic experimental variables across a range of delays.

The increasing-delay procedure is not designed to obtain indifference points across the programmed delays. However, linear interpolation is often used to estimate the delay at which indifference should be obtained (e.g., Evenden and Ryan, 1996). The validity of this technique has, to our knowledge, not been established by comparing interpolated indifference points to those obtained empirically using one of the procedures described below. Because rats typically prefer the LL option at much longer delays under the increasing-delay procedure than under the fixed-delay procedure, there is reason to question the quantitative accuracy of these interpolated indifference points.

Madden and Johnson (2010) summarized evidence suggesting that the increasing-delay procedure is prone to carryover effects between trial blocks within a session. That is, choice in a given trial block may be influenced by delay contingencies in the previous block. Because delay strictly ascends across trial blocks, insensitivity to rapid within-session changes in *any* experimental parameter could be mistaken for shallow discounting. Unfortunately, no other experimental parameter is typically varied in these studies to evaluate this possibility. This is of particular concern when the effects of drugs or lesions are investigated, if little is known about these manipulations on sensitivity to changing contingencies of reinforcement.

A related concern is that, following drug administration or brain lesions, rats often display substantial deviations from exclusive preference for the larger reward in the first trial block, when that reward is not delayed (e.g., Cardinal, Robbins, and Everitt, 2000; Cardinal *et al.*, 2001; Dandy and Gatch, 2009). As discussed previously (and illustrated in Figure 7.6), interpreting these effects as an increase in impulsivity is problematic because they more likely reflect either insensitivity to reward amount or nonspecific effects of the experimental manipulation. Figure 7.7 illustrates the latter effect. In this study, Madden, Johnson, Brewer, and Pinkston (2010) examined the effects of acute pramipexole (a dopamine D_2/D_3 agonist) on preference in the increasing-delay procedure. As illustrated, the 0.3 mg/kg dose decreased LL preference at the two shortest delays (0 and 10 seconds) relative to saline, but *increased* LL preference at the longest delay (30 seconds). This shift toward indifference suggests a nonspecific, disruptive effect of the drug. Such subtle aspects of performance may be missed if one attends solely to more global dependent measures, such as *AUC* or interpolated indifference points.

3.2.2.1 BETWEEN-SESSION INCREASING DELAYS. Researchers have occasionally used a procedure in which the LL delay increases *between*, rather than within, sessions (e.g., Adriani, Canese, Podo, and Laviola, 2007; Hamilton, Czoty, and Nader, 2011). As in the within-session increasing-delay procedure, the delay at which indifference is

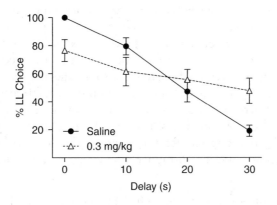

Figure 7.7 Effects of acute doses of pramipexole in rats on percent choice for the LL option in the increasing-delay procedure. Data points represent mean percent choice ($\pm$ *SEM*) at each delay. Data reprinted from Madden, Johnson, Brewer, and Pinkston (2010)

interpolated may serve as a measure of delay discounting. The concerns discussed in the preceding section apply to this procedure as well.

3.2.3 Adjusting-delay procedure. Mazur (1987) devised the first titrating procedure to directly quantify indifference points in nonhumans. In this procedure, the subject chooses between SS and LL food options. Across trial blocks (four trials each), the LL delay is titrated based on previous choices until an indifference point is reached. Each trial block contains two forced-exposure trials (one on each option) and two choice trials. If the SS is selected on both choice trials, the LL delay is decreased in the subsequent trial block (typically by 1 second, although percentage-based increments are sometimes used), whereas exclusively choosing the LL option increases the delay to that option in the subsequent trial block. Split preference (i.e., one choice for each) results in no titration. In each subsequent session, the titrated LL delay is carried over from the end of the previous session. Over multiple sessions, variability in subjects' adjustments is constrained and a quantitative stability criterion may be met (typically within 20–40 sessions). The average adjusted delay over this stable window serves as the indifference point. Indifference at brief delays reflects steeper discounting.

This procedure may be repeated across a range of SS delays to yield a discounting function. However, it is more common to assess the indifference delay only when the SS reward is available immediately. This procedure is often used when evaluating animals as HiI and LoI (e.g., Perry *et al.*, 2005; Perry, Nelson, and Carroll, 2008) and, because it may be completed quickly, it avoids maturational confounds (Pinkston and Lamb, 2011; Simon *et al.*, 2008). A concern with this procedure was raised by Cardinal, Daw, Robbins, and Everitt (2002). They reported that most of their rats, despite completing thousands of forced-exposure and free-choice trials, failed to constrain their delay adjustments to a range from which stable indifference points could be reasonably derived. Computer simulations in which choices were random could not be differentiated from their obtained data. To our knowledge, the concerns raised in this study have not been empirically addressed beyond demonstrating that the adjusting-delay procedure yields orderly discounting functions that conform well to the predictions of equation 1.

A second potential shortcoming of this procedure is that assessing choice at only a single SS delay does not rule out nonspecific drug effects. Such effects would probably produce indifference between choice alternatives regardless of the delay and amount parameters used. In the absence of control conditions, such effects may often be mistaken for an effect (increase or decrease) on delay discounting. If possible, researchers should examine drug choice in at least two SS delay conditions (e.g., 0 seconds and 10 seconds). If the resulting indifference points appear sensitive to this parametric manipulation, then non-specific, disruptive drug effects may be ruled out.

3.2.4   Adjusting-amount procedures.   Of all the procedures used in nonhumans, the adjusting-amount procedure (Mazur, 2000; Richards, Mitchell, de Wit, and Seiden, 1997) most closely resembles the titrating procedures used with humans. As in other nonhuman procedures, the subject chooses between SS and LL rewards (food or water). The SS option is always delivered immediately. Across trials, SS food amount is titrated based on previous choices until an indifference point is reached. The indifference point quantifies the value of the delayed option in terms of the *amount* of the SS option.

There exist at least two versions of the adjusting-amount procedure: the *rapid-determination* (Richards, Mitchell, de Wit, and Seiden, 1997) and *steady-state* (Mazur, 2000) procedures. These versions differ most saliently in how they quantify indifference points. In the rapid-determination version, measures of delay discounting are calculated from a fixed number of sessions in which delay changes daily, while measures from the steady state are calculated from discrete delay conditions in which choice is allowed to stabilize across many consecutive sessions.

3.2.4.1   RAPID-DETERMINATION ADJUSTING-AMOUNT PROCEDURE.   In the rapid-determination procedure, choosing the LL reward increases the amount of the SS option by a fixed percentage (e.g., 10% more or less of the liquid reward) on the subsequent trial; choosing the SS has the opposite effect. To ensure contact with both outcomes, forced-exposure trials occur each time the subject chooses the same reward on two consecutive trials. The SS amount is reset to the same value at the beginning of each session. The delay to the LL is changed daily in a pseudo-random order. Terminal indifference points within each session are calculated as the average adjusted amount over the last half of the session (typically 60 trials). Initial training typically takes 50–70 sessions with indifference points averaged over an additional 25 sessions. Although delay changes daily under this procedure, Richards, Mitchell, de Wit, and Seiden (1997) observed no systematic carryover effects on indifference points, suggesting the procedure provides an unambiguous measure of delay discounting.

To evaluate the effects of drugs or brain lesions on delay discounting, some have implemented this procedure at a single LL delay (e.g., 4 seconds; Wade, de Wit, and Richards, 2000). Wade *et al.* set the starting amount of the SS reward at a low value in some sessions and a high value in others. When the adjusting amount obtained in the last half of the session converged on the same indifference point, good evidence was provided that the drug affected delay discounting, rather than having a nonspecific effect such as response perseveration.

Some researchers using the rapid-determination adjusting-amount procedure have provided subjects with less initial training before assessing discounting (e.g., 5 sessions, instead of 50–70; Wilhelm and Mitchell, 2008; 2009). At present it is unknown if this abbreviated training produces the same indifference points that would be obtained had a longer period of initial training been completed.

3.2.4.2 STEADY-STATE ADJUSTING-AMOUNT PROCEDURE. In the steady-state version of the adjusting-amount procedure (Mazur, 2000), the LL delay remains fixed within experimental conditions until the adjusting amount of the SS stabilizes. Adjustment of the SS proceeds as described for the rapid-determination procedure, with the following exceptions: (1) two forced-exposure and two choice trials are completed between adjustments to the SS, (2) fixed, rather than percentage-based, adjustments are most commonly used (e.g., 1 pellet), (3) the amount of the SS reward is carried over between sessions, and (4) each condition is continued until the adjusted amount stabilizes (typically within 10–40 sessions). Indifference points are calculated as the average adjusted amount over this stable window. Obtaining indifference points across a range of steady-state delay conditions yields the discounting function.

A drawback of this procedure is the large number of sessions required to obtain a complete discounting curve. For example, pigeons and rats in a study by Green *et al.* (2004) required more than 6 and 8 months, respectively. In rats, this meant that the last obtained indifference point followed the first by approximately 200 days, raising the possibility of maturation effects that are not of concern with the rapid-assessment adjusting-amount procedure (in which delays vary between sessions rather than between conditions). The time required to complete the steady-state adjusting-amount procedure may be the reason that no published studies have used it when evaluation the effects of drugs or lesions on delay discounting. However, the effects of acute or chronic/daily drug administration on a pre-drug, steady-state discounting could be efficiently evaluated at a single LL delay. To identify non-specific drug effects, a second condition in which both the small and large rewards are delivered immediately would need to be included.

3.3 Population sampling

As noted previously, the majority of research examining the relation between steep delay discounting and drug abuse (or drug SA in nonhumans) has featured cross-sectional, correlational research designs (e.g., cigarette smokers versus never-smokers, or HiI versus LoI rats). In the following sections, we discuss the procedures researchers have used to obtain cross-sectional samples.

3.3.1 Human studies. In studies of delay discounting and substance abuse, common practices are to recruit participants either from outpatient treatment programs (e.g., Kirby, Petry, and Bickell, 1999) or, in the case of licit drugs such as tobacco and alcohol, by posting newspaper advertisements or fliers in the community (e.g.,

Odum, Madden, and Bickel, 2002). The latter technique is most often used in recruiting non-drug-using control participants matched on potentially relevant demographic variables (e.g., age, education, gender, IQ). While these sampling methods have been useful in demonstrating a clear relation between delay discounting and drug abuse (see MacKillop *et al.*, 2011), they have proven less useful in resolving the precise role of delay discounting in drug abuse. Demographic matching, while important in exploring the primary relation of interest, impedes the discovery of variables that may moderate the relation between delay discounting and drug abuse (e.g., education, socioeconomic status). Identifying moderators will require significantly larger *N*s than have been arranged in the cross-sectional studies reviewed earlier. It will also likely require an emphasis on full-range data as an alternative to the cross-sectional methods that dominate the literature. However, we do not believe the cost of the research would be prohibitive, considering that hypothetical monetary outcomes may be used to confidently obtain estimates of delay discounting (e.g., Madden *et al.*, 2004).

3.3.2 Nonhuman studies.   Studies examining group differences in delay discounting as a predictor of subsequent drug SA (e.g., among HiI and LoI rats) are variants of the *extreme groups approach* (EGA), a quasi-experimental design ostensibly similar to those used in the human cross-sectional studies. With EGA, the experimenter obtains measures of delay discounting across a full sample of subjects, identifies sample-dependent quantiles, and then retains for further drug SA testing only rats falling above and below some predetermined cutoff. When using EGA, the relation between extreme *x* scores and *y* is typically examined using correlational techniques (see Preacher, Rucker, MacCallum, and Nicewander, 2005). However, most of the nonhuman studies reviewed in Table 7.1 dichotomize rats into HiI and LoI groups, with subsequent drug SA compared using two-sample statistical methods. Alternatively, some have employed tertile splits and retained *all* groups for further testing (i.e., HiI, MedI, and LoI; Koffarnus and Woods, 2011; Poulos, Le, and Parker, 1995; Sweitzer, 2008). Likewise, some researchers supplement or eschew the use of EGA by examining the continuous, full-range data using standard regression methods (Poulos, Le, and Parker, 1995; Marusich *et al.*, 2011).

The use of EGA-like methods is a long-standing tradition in psychological research as it increases statistical power (e.g., Kelley, 1939) and reduces costs of obtaining full-range data (e.g., Peters and Van Voorhis, 1940). However, using EGA in studies of delay discounting and drug SA poses a number of potential methodological problems. First, dichotimization of subjects into supposedly homogeneous groups assumes a linear relation between delay discounting and drug SA and prevents discovery of systematic nonlinear relations. Evidence for nonlinearity was reported by Koffarnus and Woods (2011), who observed greater cocaine demand in HiI rats compared to cohorts, but no difference between MedI and LoI rats. Such a finding would not have been apparent had the authors dichotomized their discounting data using quartile or median splits.

A second problem with dichotimization is that under many conditions it may sacrifice statistical power when compared to full-range methods. Specifically, dichotimization in EGA maximizes power in *t* tests only if one retains for further testing approximately the upper and lower quartiles of the original distribution (i.e., the 27% rule; D'Agostino and Cureton, 1975; Feldt, 1961; Garg, 1983; McCabe, 1980) – a finding later extended to use of ANOVA (Preacher, Rucker, MacCallum, and Nicewander, 2005). Dichotimization of the full-range data with the use of median splits probably sacrifices power when compared to obtaining and testing the sample correlation (r_{xy}) using the quartile-split or even the non-EGA, full-range data (Alf and Abrahams, 1975).

4   Conclusions and Future Directions

Despite the ubiquity of the correlation between delay discounting and drug abuse, more research is required to resolve the nature of this relation – specifically, whether steep delay discounting serves as cause or consequence of drug abuse, or whether both are the products of a third variable. In this chapter we have provided evidence supporting all three possibilities, although the evidence suggesting that steep delay discounting precedes the acquisition of drug taking in nonhumans is stronger than the opposite relation. That being said, we have noted several concerns with the evidence currently available (e.g., the possibility that HiI rats are more likely than LoI rats to "self-administer" *any* reward); concerns that we hope will be addressed empirically in the coming years.

We also hope to see human delay discounting preparations expanded so as to capture some of the characteristics of choices between drug use and abstinence. Choices faced by drug abusers are more complex than those that have thus far been arranged in the laboratory. For example, LL outcomes are rarely delivered in a single lump sum as they are in the lab. Instead, delayed costs such as deterioration of health and social relationships are gradual over the course of many months or years. Likewise, the benefits accrued by drug abstinence are not discrete events. If they were, abstinence might be more easily maintained. Instead, these benefits accrue slowly over time and may not be discriminated (in much the same way that one does not discriminate the growth of one's own children). At present, nothing is known about the discounting of gradually accruing outcomes, gradual decrements of current holdings, or individual differences in the ability to discriminate such changes. Our understanding of the relation between delay discounting and drug abuse may benefit from human and animal studies conceived along these lines.

Critical to resolving the role of delay discounting in drug abuse will be to experimentally manipulate discounting and examine its effects on subsequent drug abuse (or SA). Bickel *et al.* (2010) reported significant reductions in delay discounting in stimulant abusers following training designed to improve working memory. This technique might be used in designing an experiment in which one group of non-smokers is provided with this executive-function training and another group is given sham training. Following the groups over time and documenting incidents of licit and illicit drug use (in addition to periodic checks to ensure that changes in delay discounting remain) may prove useful.

A similar approach may be pursued in nonhuman models and the ability to control extraneous factors in the laboratory strongly supports this direction. Our laboratory is currently exploring the effects of executive-function training in rats on subsequent delay discounting. Another promising experimental manipulation is the use of delay-fading procedures (Dixon and Holcomb, 2000; Mazur and Logue, 1978; Schweitzer and Sulzer-Azaroff, 1988), in which the disparity in delays between SS and LL options is introduced gradually over the course of many days, weeks, or months. Likewise, preliminary data from our own lab indicate significant reductions in impulsive choice in rats following 120-day exposure to response-contingent delayed reinforcement (Stein and Madden, unpublished data). If these experimentally produced "delay-tolerant" rats are less susceptible to drug taking than their "delay-intolerant" counterparts, this would provide clearer evidence that delay discounting plays an etiological role in drug abuse (see Oberlin, Bristow, Heighton, and Grahame, 2010, for an approximation of this research strategy). Should future research establish a clearer relation between delay discounting and drug abuse, then the experimental procedures that reliably impact discounting may prove useful as a component of drug-abuse treatment or prevention efforts.

References

Adriani W, Canese R, Podo F, and Laviola G (2007) 1H MRS-detectable metabolic brain changes and reduced impulsive behavior in adult rats exposed to methylphenidate during adolescence. *Neurotoxicology and Teratology* 29: 116–125.

Alf EF and Abrahams NM (1975) The use of extreme groups in assessing relationships. *Psychometrika* 40: 563–572.

Alvos L, Gregson RA, and Ross MW (1993) Future time perspective in current and previous injecting drug users. *Drug and Alcohol Dependence* 31(2): 193–197.

American Psychiatric Association (2000) *Diagnostic and Statistical Manual of Mental Disorders* (4th edition, text revision; DSM-IV-TR). Arlington: American Psychiatric Association.

Ambrosio E, Goldberg SR, and Elmer GI (1995) Behavior genetic investigation of the relationship between spontaneous locomotor activity and the acquisition of morphine self-administration behavior. *Behavioural Pharmacology* 6: 229–237.

Anderson KG and Diller JW (2010) Effects of acute and repeated nicotine administration on delay discounting in Lewis and Fischer 344 rats. *Behavioural Pharmacology* 21: 754–764.

Anderson KG and Woolverton WL (2005) Effects of clomipramine on self-control choice in Lewis and Fischer 344 rats. *Pharmacology Biochemistry and Behavior* 80: 387–393.

Anker JJ, Perry JL, Gliddon LA, and Carroll ME (2009) Impulsivity predicts the escalation of cocaine self-administration in rats. *Pharmacology Biochemistry and Behavior* 93: 343–348.

Apostolidis T, Fieulaine N, Simonin L, and Rolland G (2006) Cannabis use, time perspective and risk perception: Evidence of a moderating effect. *Psychology and Health* 21: 571–592.

Audrain-McGovern J, Rodriguez D, Epstein LH, Cuevas J, Rodgers K, and Wileyto EP (2009) Does delay discounting play an etiological role in smoking or is it a consequence of smoking? *Drug and Alcohol Dependence* 103: 99–106.

Ayduk O, Mendoza-Denton R, Mischel W, Downey G, Peake PK, and Rodriguez M (2000) Regulating the interpersonal self: Strategic self-regulation for coping with rejection sensitivity. *Journal of Personality and Social Psychology* 79: 776–792.

Baker F, Johnson MW, and Bickel WK (2003) Delay discounting in current and never-before cigarette smokers: Similarities and differences across commodity, sign, and magnitude. *Journal of Abnormal Psychology* 112: 382–392.

Bañuelos C, Gilbert RJ, Montgomery KS, Fincher AS, Wang H, Frye GD, Setlow B, and Bizon JL (2012) Altered spatial learning and delay discounting in a rat model of human third trimester binge ethanol exposure. *Behavioural Pharmacology* 23: 54–65.

Benzion U, Rapoport A, and Yagil J (1989) Discount rates inferred from decisions: An experimental study. *Management Science* 35: 270–284.

Bickel WK and Marsch LA (2001) Toward a behavioral economic understanding of drug dependence: delay discounting processes. *Addiction* 96: 73–86.

Bickel WK, Odum AL, and Madden GJ (1999) Impulsivity and cigarette smoking delay discounting in current, never, and ex-smokers. *Psychopharmacology* 146: 447–454.

Bickel WK, Yi R, Landes RD, Hill PF, and Bazter C (2010) Remember the future: Working memory training decreases delay discounting among stimulant addicts. *Biological Psychiatry* 69: 260–5.

Cadoni C and Di Chiara G (2007) Differences in dopamine responsiveness to drugs of abuse in the nucleus accumbens shell and core of Lewis and Fischer 344 rats. *Journal of Neurochemistry* 103: 487–499.

Cadoni C, Muto T, and Di Chiara G (2009) Nicotine differentially affects dopamine transmission in the nucleus accumbens shell and core of Lewis and Fischer 344 rats. *Neuropharmacology* 57: 496–501.

Cappell H and Le Blanc AE (1975) Conditioned aversion by psychoactive drugs: Does it have significance for an understanding of drug dependence? *Addictive Behaviors* 1: 55–64.

Cardinal RN, Daw N, Robbins TW, and Everitt BJ (2002) Local analysis of behavior in the adjusting-delay task for assessing choice of delayed reinforcement. *Neural Networks* 15: 617–634.

Cardinal RN, Robbins TW, and Everitt BJ (2000) The effects of D-amphetamine, chlordiazepoxide, alpha-flupenthixol and behavioural manipulations on choice of signalled and unsignalled delayed reinforcement in rats. *Psychopharmacology* 152: 362–375.

Cardinal RN, Pennicott DR, Sugathapala CL, Robbins TW, and Everitt BJ (2001) Impulsive choice induced in rats by lesions of the nucleus accumbens core. *Science* 292: 2499–2501.

Carroll ME, Anderson MM, and Morgan AD (2007) Regulation of intravenous cocaine self-administration in rats selectively bred for high (HiS) and low (LoS) saccharin intake. *Psychopharmacology* 190: 331–341.

Carroll ME, Anker JJ, Mach JL, Newman JL, and Perry JL (2010) Delay discounting as a predictor of drug abuse. In GJ Madden and WK Bickel (eds), *Impulsivity: The Behavioral and Neurological Science of Discounting* (pp. 243–271). Washington, DC: American Psychological Association.

Carroll ME, Morgan AD, Lynch WJ, Campbell UC, and Dess NK (2002) Intravenous cocaine and heroin self-administration in rats selectively bred for differential saccharin intake: Phenotype and sex differences. *Psychopharmacology* 161: 304–313.

Chapman GB (1996) Temporal discounting and utility for health and money. *Journal of Experimental Psychology: Learning, Memory, and Cognition* 22: 771–791.

Christensen CJ, Kohut SJ, Handler S, Silberberg A, and Riley A (2009) Demand for food and cocaine in Fischer and Lewis rats. *Behavioral Neuroscience* 123: 165–171.

Chung SH and Herrnstein RJ (1967) Choice and delay of reinforcement. *Journal of the Experimental Analysis of Behavior* 10: 67–74.

Coffey SF, Gudleski GD, Saladin ME, and Brady KT (2003) Impulsivity and rapid discounting of delayed hypothetical rewards in cocaine-dependent individuals. *Experimental and Clinical Psychopharmacology* 11: 18–25.

Correia CJ and Carey KB (1999) Applying behavioral theories of choice to substance use in a sample of psychiatric outpatients. *Pscyhology of Addictive Behaviors* 13: 207–212.

Correia CJ, Carey KB, and Borsari B (2002) Measuring substance-free and substance-related reinforcement in the natural environment. *Psychology of Addictive Behaviors* 16: 28–34.

Correia CJ, Simons J, Carey KB, and Borsari BE (1998) Predicting drug use: Application of behavioral theories of choice. *Addictive Behaviors* 23: 705–709.

D'Agostino RB and Cureton EE (1975) The 27 percent rule revisited. *Educational and Psychological Measurements* 35: 47–50.

Dackis C and Gold MS (1985) Neurotransmitter and neuroendocrine abnormalities associated with cocaine use. *Psychiatric Medicine* 3: 461–483.

Dallery J and Locey ML (2005) Effects of acute and chronic nicotine on impulsive choice in rats. *Behavioural Pharmacology* 16: 15–23.

Dallery J and Raiff BR (2007) Delay discounting predicts cigarette smoking in a laboratory model of abstinence reinforcement. *Psychopharmacology* 190: 485–496.

Dandy JL and Gatch MB (2009) The effects of chronic cocaine exposure on impulsivity in rats. *Behavioural Pharmacology* 20: 400–405.

de Wit H (2009) Impulsivity as a determinant and consequence of drug use: A review of underlying processes. *Addiction Biology* 14: 22–31.

de Wit H and Mitchell S (2010) Drug effects on delay discounting. In GJ Madden and WK Bickel (eds), *Impulsivity: The Behavioral and Neurological Science of Discounting* (pp. 213–241). Washington, DC: American Psychological Association.

Deluty, MZ (1978) Self-control and impulsiveness involving aversive events. *Journal of Experimental Psychology: Animal Behavior Processes* 4: 250–266.

Diergaarde L, Pattij T, Poortvliet I, Hogenboom F, de Vries W, Schoffelmeer ANM, and de Vries TJ (2008) Impulsive choice and impulsive action predict vulnerability to distinct stages of nicotine seeking in rats. *Biological Psychiatry* 63: 301–308.

Diergaarde L, van Mourik Y, Pattij T, Schoffelmeer AN, and De Vries TJ (2012) Poor impulse control predicts inelastic demand for nicotine but not alcohol in rats. *Addiction Biology* 17: 576-587.

Diller JW, Saunders BT, and Anderson KG (2008) Effects of acute and repeated administration of caffeine on temporal discounting in rats. *Pharmacology Biochemistry and Behavior* 89: 546–555.

Dixon MR and Holcomb S (2000) Teaching self-control to small groups of dually diagnosed adults. *Journal of Applied Behavior Analysis* 33: 611–614.

Du W, Green L, and Myerson J (2002) Cross-cultural comparisons of discounting delayed and probabilistic rewards. *The Psychological Record* 52: 479–492.

Ebert JEJ and Prelec D (2007) The fragility of time: Time-insensitivity and valuations of the near and far future. *Management Science* 53: 1423–1438.

Eppolito AK, Fance CP, and Gerak LR (2011) Effects of acute and chronic flunitrazepam on delay discounting in pigeons. *Journal of the Experimental Analysis of Behavior* 95: 163–174.

Estle SJ, Green L Myerson J, and Holt DD (2006) Differential effects of amount on temporal and probability discounting of gains and losses. *Memory and Cognition* 34: 914–928.

Evenden JL and Ryan CN (1996) The pharmacology of impulsive behaviour in rats: The effects of drugs on response choice with varying delays of reinforcement. *Psychopharmacology* 128: 161–170.

Feldt LS (1961) The use of extreme groups to test for the presence of a relationship. *Psychometrika* 26: 307–316.

Foulks JD and Webb JT (1970) Temporal orientation of diagnostic groups. *Journal of Clinical Psychology* 26: 155–159.

Frederick S, Loewenstein G, and O'Donoghue T (2002) Time discounting and time preference: A critical review. *Journal of Economic Literature* 40: 351–401.

Freeman KB, Green L, Myerson J, and Woolverton WL (2009) Delay discounting of saccharin in rhesus monkeys. *Behavioural Processes* 82: 214–218.

Freeman KB, Kearns DN, Kohut S, and Riley AL (2009) Strain differences in patterns of drug-intake during prolonged access to cocaine self-administration. *Behavioral Neuroscience* 123: 156–164.

García-Lecumberri C, Torres I, Martín S, Crespo JA, Miguéns M, Nicanor C, Higuera-Matas A, and Ambrosio E (2011) Strain differences in the dose-response relationship for morphine selfadministration and impulsive choice between Lewis and Fischer 344 rats. *Journal of Psychopharmacology* 25: 783–791.

Garg R (1983) An empirical comparison of three strategies used in extreme groups designs. *Educational and Psychological Measurements* 43: 359–371.

Gill K, Gillespie HK, Hollister LE, Davis CM, and Peabody CA (1991) Dopamine depletion hypothesis of cocaine dependence: A test. *Human Psychopharmacology: Clinical and Experimental* 6: 25–29.

Gipson CD and Bardo MT (2009) Extended access to amphetamine selfadministration increases impulsive choice in a delay discounting task in rats. *Psychopharmacology* 207: 391–400.

Goudie AJ, Dickins DW, and Thornton EW (1978) Cocaine-induced taste aversion in rats. *Pharmacology Biochemistry and Behavior* 8: 757–761.

Green L and Estle SJ (2003) Preference reversals with food and water reinforcers in rats. *Journal of the Experimental Analysis of Behavior* 79: 233–242.

Green L and Myerson J (2004) A discounting framework for choice with delayed and probabilistic rewards. *Psychological Bulletin* 130: 769–792.

Green L, Fristoe N, and Myerson J (1994) Temporal discounting and preference reversals in choice between delayed outcomes. *Psychonomic Bulletin and Review* 1: 383–389.

Green L, Myerson J, Holt DD, Slevin JR and Estle SJ (2004) Discounting of delayed food rewards in pigeons and rats: is there a magnitude effect? *Journal of the Experimental Analysis of Behavior* 81: 39–50.

Green L, Myerson J, Shah AK, Estle SJ and Holt DD (2007) Do adjusting-amount and adjusting-delay procedures produce equivalent estimates of subjective value in pigeons? *Journal of the Experimental Analysis Behavior* 87: 337–347.

Grigson PS (1997) Conditioned taste aversions and drugs of abuse: a reinterpretation. *Behavioral Neuroscience* 111: 129–136.

Grimm JW, Hope BT, Wise RA, and Shaham Y (2001) Incubation of cocaine craving after withdrawal. *Nature* 412: 141–142.

Guitart X, Beitner-Johnson D, Marby DW, Kosten TA, and Nestler EJ (1992) Fischer and Lewis rats differ in basal levels of neurofilament proteins and their regulation by chronic morphine in the mesolimbic dopamine system. *Synapse* 12: 242–253.

Gulley JM, Everett CV, and Zahniser NR (2007) Inbred Lewis and Fischer 344 rat strains differ not only in novelty- and amphetamine-induced behaviors, but also in dopamine transporter activity in vivo. *Brain Research* 1151: 32–45.

Haile CN and Kosten TA (2001) Differential effects of D1- and D2-like compounds on cocaine self-administration in Lewis and Fischer 344 inbred rats. *Journal of Pharmacology and Experimental Therapeutics* 299: 509–518.

Haile CN, Zhang XY, Carroll FI, and Kosten TA (2005) Cocaine self-administration and locomotor activity are altered in Lewis and F344 inbred rats by RTI 336, a 3-phenyltropane analog that binds to the dopamine transporter. *Brain Research* 1055: 186–195.

Hamilton LR, Czoty PW, and Nader MA (2011) Behavioral characterization of adult male and female rhesus monkeys exposed to cocaine throughout gestation. *Psychopharmacology* 213: 799–808.

Harty SC, Whaley JE, Halperin JM, and Ranaldi R (2011) Impulsive choice, as measured in a delay discounting paradigm, remains stable after chronic heroin administration. *Pharmacology Biochemistry and Behavior* 98: 337–340.

Herrnstein RJ (1970) On the law of effect. *Journal of the Experimental Analysis of Behavior* 13: 243–266.

Higgins ST, Heil SH, and Lussier JP (2004) Clinical implications of reinforcement as a determinant of substance use disorders. *Annual Review of Psychology* 55: 431–461.

Ho MY, Mobini S, Chiang TJ, Bradshaw CM, and Szabadi E (1999) Theory and method in the quantitative analysis of "impulsive choice" behaviour: Implications for psychopharmacology. *Psychopharmacology* 146: 362–372.

Hoffman WF, Moore M, Templin R, McFarland B, Hitzemann RJ, and Mitchell SH (2006) Neuropsychological function and delay discounting in methamphetamine-dependent individuals. *Psychopharmacology* 188: 162–170.

Hogue A, Dauber S, and Morganstern H (2010) Validation of a contemplation ladder in an adult substance use disorder sample. *Psychology of Addictive Behaviors* 24: 137–144.

Horan B, Smith M, Gardner EL, Lepore M, Ashby CR (1997) Nicotine produces conditioned place preference in Lewis, but not Fischer 344 rats. *Synapse* 26: 93–94.

Imber SD, Miller AE, Faillace LA, and Liberman B (1971) Temporal processes in alcoholism. *Quarterly Journal of Studies on Alcohol* 32: 304–309.

Jimura K, Myerson J, Hilgard J, Braver TS, and Green L (2009) Are people really more patient than other animals? Evidence from human discounting of real liquid rewards. *Psychonomic Bulletin and Review* 16: 1071–5.

Jimura K, Myerson J, Hilgard J, Keighley J, Braver TS, and Green L (2011) Domain independence and stability in young and older adults' discounting of delayed rewards. *Behavioural Processes* 87: 253–259.

Johnson MW and Bickel WK (2002) Within-subject comparison of real and hypothetical money rewards in delay discounting. *Journal of the Experimental Analysis of Behavior* 77: 129–146.

Johnson MW and Bickel WK (2008) An algorithm for identifying nonsystematic delay-discounting data. *Experimental and Clinical Psychopharmacology* 16: 264–274.

Johnson MW, Bickel WK, Baker F, Moore BA, Badger GJ, and Budney AJ (2010) Delay discounting in current and former marijuana-dependent individuals. *Experimental and Clinical Psychopharmacology* 18: 99–107.

Kelley TL (1939) The selection of upper and lower groups for the validation of test items. *Journal of Educational Psychology* 30: 17–24.

Keough KA, Zimbardo PG, and Boyd JN (1999) Who's smoking, drinking, and doing drugs? Time perspective as a predictor of substance use. *Basic and Applied Social Psychology* 21: 149–164.

Killeen PR (2009) An additive-utility model of delay discounting. *Psychological Review* 116: 602–619.

Kirby KN and Maraković NN (1995) Modeling myopic decisions: Evidence for hyperbolic delay-discounting within Subjects and Amounts. *Organizational Behavior and Human Decision Processes* 64: 22–30.

Kirby KN and Maraković NN (1996) Delay-discounting probabilistic rewards: Rates decrease as amounts increase. *Psychonomic Bulletin and Review* 3: 100–104.

Kirby KN, Petry NM, and Bickel WK (1999) Heroin addicts have higher discount rates for delayed rewards than non-drug-using controls. *Journal of Experimental Psychology: General* 128: 78–87.

Kobayashi S and Schultz W (2008) Influence of reward delays on responses of dopamine neurons. *Journal of Neuroscience* 28: 7837–46.

Koffarnus MN and Woods JH (2011) Individual difference in discount rate are associated with demand for self-administered cocaine, but not sucrose. *Addiction Biology* (epub ahead of print).

Kosten TA and Ambrosio E (2002) HPA axis function and drug addictive behaviors: insights from studies with Lewis and Fischer 344 inbred rats. *Psychoneuroendocrinology* 27, 35–69.

Kosten TA, Miserendino MJ, Chi S, and Nestler EJ (1994) Fischer and Lewis rat strains show differential cocaine effects in conditioned place preference and behavioral sensitization but not in locomotor activity conditioned taste aversion. *Journal of Pharmacology and Experimental Therapeutics* 269: 137–144.

Kosten TA, Miserendino MJ, Haile CN, DeCaprio JL, Jatlow PI, and Nestler EJ (1997) Acquisition and maintenance of intravenous cocaine self-administration in Lewis and Fischer 344 inbred rats strains. *Brain Research* 778: 418–429.

Kosten TA, Zhang XY, and Haile CN (2007) Strain differences in maintenance of cocaineself-administration and their relationship to novelty activity responses. *Behavioral Neuroscience* 121: 380–88.

Krishnan-Sarin S, Reynolds B, Duhig AM, Smith A, Liss T, McFetridge A, Cavallo DA, Carroll KM, and Potenza MN (2007) Behavioral impulsivity predicts treatment outcome in a smoking cessation program for adolescent smokers. *Drug and Alcohol Dependence* 88: 79–82.

Lagorio CH and Madden GJ (2005) Delay discounting of real and hypothetical rewards III: steady-state assessments, forced-choice trials, and all real rewards. *Behavioural Processes* 69: 173–187.

Loewenstein G (1988) Frames of mind in intertemporal choice. *Management Science* 34: 200–214.

Loewenstein G and Thaler RH (1989) Anomalies: Intertemporal choice. *Journal of Economic Perspectives* 3: 181–193.

Logue AW, Tobin J, Chelonis JJ, Wang RY, Geary N, and Schachter S (1992) Cocaine decreases self-control in rats: A preliminary report. *Psychopharmacology* 109: 245–247.

MacKillop J and Kahler CW (2009) Delayed reward discounting predicts treatment response for heavy drinkers receiving smoking cessation treatment. *Drug and Alcohol Dependence* 104: 197–203.

MacKillop J, Amlung MT, Few LR, Ray LA, Sweet LH, and Munafò MR (2011) Delayed reward discounting and addictive behavior: A meta-analysis. *Psychopharmacology* 216: 305–21.

Madden GJ (2000) A behavioral economics primer. In WK Bickel and RE Vuchinich (eds), *Reframing Health Behavior Change with Behavioral Economics* (pp. 3–26). Mahwah, NJ: Lawrence Erlbaum Associates Publishers.

Madden GJ, Begotka AM, Raiff BR, and Kastern LL (2003) Delay discounting of real and hypothetical rewards. *Experimental and Clinical Psychopharmacology* 11: 139–145.

Madden GJ and Johnson PS (2010) A delay-discounting primer. In GJ Madden and WK Bickel (eds), *Impulsivity: The Behavioral and Neurological Science of Discounting* (pp. 1–37). Washington, DC: American Psychological Association.

Madden GJ, Johnson PS, Brewer AT, and Pinkston JW (2010) Effects of Pramipexole on impulsive choice in male Wistar rats. *Experimental and Clinical Psychopharmacology* 18: 267–276.

Madden GJ, Petry NM, Badger GJ, and Bickel WK (1997) Impulsive and self-control choices in opioid-dependent patients and non-drug using control participants: Drug and monetary rewards. *Experimental and Clinical Psychopharmacology* 5: 256–262.

Madden GJ, Raiff BR, Lagorio CH, Begotka AM, Mueller AM, Hehli DJ, and Wegener AA (2004) Delay discounting of potentially real and hypothetical rewards II: Between- and within-subject comparisons. *Experimental and Clinical Psychoparmacology* 12: 251–261.

Madden GJ, Smith NG, Brewer AT, Pinkston J, and Johnson PS (2008) Steady-state assessment of impulsive choice in Lewis and Fischer 344 rats: Between-condition delay-manipulation. *Journal of the Experimental Analysis of Behavior* 90: 333–344.

Manganiello JA (1978) Opiate addiction: A study identifying three systematically related psychological correlates. *International Journal of the Addictions* 13: 839–847.

Martín S, García-Lecumberri C, Crespo J, Ferrado S, Izenwasser GI, and Elmer E (1997) Genetic differences in food and morphine operant reinforced behavior in four inbred rat strains. *NIDA Research Monograph* 179: 197.

Martín S, Manzanares J, Corchero J, García-Lecumberri C, Crespo J, Fuentes JA, and Ambrosio E (1999) Differential basal proenkephalin gene expression in dorsal striatum and nucleus accumbens, and vulnerability to morphine self-administration in Fischer 344 and Lewis rats. *Brain Research* 821: 350–355.

Marusich JA and Bardo MT (2009) Differences in impulsivity on a delay discounting task predict self-administration of a low unit dose of methylphenidate in rats. *Behavioural Pharmacology* 20: 447–454.

Marusich JA, Darna M, Charnigo RJ, Dwoskin LP, and Bardo MT (2011) A multivariate assessment of individual differences in sensation seeking and impulsivity as predictors of amphetamine self-administration and prefrontal dopamine function in rats. *Experimental and Clinical Psychopharmacology* 19: 275–284.

Mazur JE (1987) An adjusting procedure for studying delayed reinforcement. In ML Commons, JE Mazur, JA Nevin, and H Rachlin (eds), *Qualitative Analyses of Behavior: The Effect of Delay and of Intervening Events on Reinforcement Value* (pp. 55–73). Hillsdale, NJ: Erlbaum.

Mazur JE (1997) Choice, delay, probability, and conditioned reinforcement. *Animal Learning and Behavior* 25 (2): 131–147.

Mazur JE (2000) Tradeoffs among delay, rate, and amount of reinforcement. *Behavioural Processes* 49: 1–10.

Mazur JE and Logue AW (1978) Choice in a "self-control" paradigm: Effects of a fading procedure. *Journal of the Experimental Analysis of Behavior* 30: 11–17.

McBride WJ, Chernet E, Russell RN, Chamberlain JK, Lumeng L, and Li TK (1997) Regional CNS densities of serotonin and dopamine receptors in high alcohol-drinking (HAD) and low alcohol-drinking (LAD) rats. *Alcohol* 14: 603–609.

McCabe GP (1980) Use of the 27% rule in experimental design. *Communications in Statistics* A9: 765–776.

McClure SM, Ericson KM, Laibson DI, Loewenstein G, and Cohen JD (2007) Time discounting for primary rewards. *Journal of Neuroscience* 27: 5796–5804.

McKay JR, Franklin TR, Patapis N, and Lynch KG (2006) Conceptual, methodological, and analytical issues in the study of relapse. *Clinical Psychology Review* 26: 109–127.

Mendez IA, Simon HW, Hart N, Mitchell MR, Nation JR, Wellman PJ, and Setlow B (2010) Self-administered cocaine causes long-lasting increases in impulsive choice in a delay discounting task. *Behavioral Neuroscience* 124: 470–477.

Mischel W, Shoda Y, and Peake PK (1988) The nature of adolescent competencies predicted by preschool delay of gratification. *Journal of Personality and Social Psychology* 54: 687–696.

Mischel W, Shoda Y, and Rodriguez ML (1989) Delay of gratification in children. *Science* 244: 933–938.

Mitchell MR, Mendez IA, Vokes CM, Damborsky JC, Winzer-Serhan UH, and Setlow B (2012) Effects of developmental nicotine exposure in rats on decision-making in adulthood. *Behavioural Pharmacology* 23: 34–42.

Mitchell SH, Reeves JM, Li N, and Phillips TJ (2006) Delay discounting predicts behavioral sensitization to ethanol in outbred WSC mice. *Alcoholism: Clinical and Experimental Research* 30: 429–437.

Mitchell SH and Wilson VB (2010) The subjective value of delayed and probabilistic outcomes: Outcome size matters for gains but not for losses. *Behavioural Processes* 83: 36–40.

Murphy JG, Vuchinich RE, and Simpson CA (2001) Delayed reward and cost discounting. *Psychological Record* 51 (4): 571–588.

Myerson J, Green L, and Warusawitharana M (2001) Area under the curve as a measure of discounting. *Journal of the Experimental Analysis of Behavior* 76: 235–243.

Nevin JA and Grace RC (2005) Resistance to extinction in the steady state and in transition. *Journal of Experimental Psychology: Animal Behavior Processes* 31: 199–212.

Nicola SM and Deadwyler SA (2000) Firing rate of nucleus accumbens neurons is dopamine-dependent and reflects the timing of cocaine-seeking behavior in rats on a progressive ratio schedule of reinforcement. *Journal of Neuroscience* 20: 5526–5537.

Nicoll RA (1989) Introduction to the pharmacology of CNS drugs. In BG Katzung (ed.), *Basic and Clinical Pharmacology* (4th edn, p. 257). San Mateo, CA: Appleton & Lange.

Oberlin BG and Grahame NJ (2009) High-alcohol preferring mice are more impulsive than low-alcohol preferring mice as measured in the delay discounting task. *Alcoholism: Clinical and Experimental Research* 33: 1294–1303.

Oberlin BG, Bristow RE, Heighton ME, and Grahame NJ (2010) Pharmacologic dissociation between impulsivity and alcohol drinking in high alcohol preferring mice. *Alcoholism: Clinical and Experimental Research* 64: 1363–1375.

Odum AL, Madden GJ, and Bickel WK (2002) Discounting of delayed health gains and losses by current, never- and ex-smokers of cigarettes. *Nicotine and Tobacco Research* 4: 295–303.

Ohmura Y, Takahashi T, and Kitamura N (2005) Discounting delayed and probabilistic monetary gains and losses by smokers of cigarettes. *Psychopharmacology* (Berlin) 182: 508–515.

Ostaszewski P, Green L, and Myerson J (1998) Effects of inflation on the subjective value of delayed and probabilistic rewards. *Psychonomic Bulletin and Review* 5: 324–333.

Paine TA, Dringenberg HC, and Olmstead MC (2003) Effects of chronic cocaine on impulsivity: Relation to cortical serotonin mechanisms. *Behavioural Brain Research* 147: 135–147.

Perry JL and Carroll ME (2008) The role of impulsive behavior in drug abuse. *Psychopharmacology* 200: 1–26.

Perry JL, Larson EB, German JP, Madden GJ, and Carroll ME (2005) Impulsivity (delay discounting) as a predictor of acquisition of IV cocaine self-administration in female rats. *Psychopharmacology* 178: 193–201.

Perry JL, Morgan AD, Anker JJ, Dess NK, and Carroll ME (2006) Escalation of i.v. cocaine self-administration and reinstatement of cocaine-seeking behavior in rats bred for high and low saccharin intake. *Psychopharmacology* 186: 235–245.

Perry JL, Nelson SE, and Carroll ME (2008a) Impulsive choice as a predictor of acquisition of i.v. cocaine self-administration and reinstatement of cocaine-seeking behavior in male and female rats. *Experimental and Clinical Psychopharmacology* 16: 165–177.

Perry JL, Nelson SE, Anderson MM, Morgan AD, and Carroll ME (2007) Impulsivity (delay discounting) for food and cocaine in male and female rats selectively bred for high and low saccharin intake. *Pharmacology Biochemistry and Behavior* 86: 822–837.

Peters CC and Van Voorhis WR (1940) *Statistical procedures and their mathematical bases.* McGraw-Hill, New York, New York.

Petry NM (2001) Delay discounting of money and alcohol in actively using alcoholics, currently abstinent alcoholics, and controls. *Psychopharmacology* 15: 243–250.

Petry NM, Bickel WK and Arnett M (1998) Shortened time horizons and insensitivity to future consequences in heroin addicts. *Addiction* 93: 729–738.

Piazza PV, Deminére JM and Simon H (1989) Factors that predict individual susceptibility to amphetamine self-administration. *Science* 245: 1511–1513.

Pinkston JW and Lamb RJ (2011) Delay discounting in C57BL/6J and DBA/2J mice: Adolescent-limited and life-persistent patterns of impulsivity. *Behavioral Neuroscience* 125: 194–201.

Poulos CX, Le AD, and Parker JL (1995) Impulsivity predicts individual susceptibility to high levels of alcohol self-administration. *Behavioural Pharmacology* 6: 810–814.

Preacher KJ, Rucker DD, MacCallum RC, and Nicewander WA (2005) Use of the extreme groups approach: A critical reexamination and new recommendations. *Psychological Methods* 10: 178–192.

Pupe S, Brys I, Asherton PJE, and Bizarro L (2011) Prenatal alcohol exposure did not affect impulsivity in rats that performed delay or probability discounting tasks. *Psychology and Neuroscience* 4: 123–130.

Rachlin H and Green L (1972) Commitment, choice and self-control. *Journal of the Experimental Analysis of Behavior* 17: 15–22.

Rachlin H, Raineri A, and Cross D (1991) Subjective probability and delay. *Journal of the Experimental Analysis of Behavior* 55: 233–244.

Reynolds B, Richards JB, Horn K, and Karraker K (2004) Delay discounting and probability discounting as related to cigarette smoking status in adults. *Behavioural Processes* 65: 35–42.

Richards JB, Mitchell SH, de Wit H, and Seiden LS (1997) Determination of discount functions in rats with an adjusting-amount procedure. *Journal of the Experimental Analysis of Behavior* 67: 353–366.

Richards JB, Sabol KE, and de Wit H (1999) Effects of methamphetamine on the adjusting amount procedure, a model of impulsive behavior in rats. *Psychopharmacology* 46: 432–439.

Richter CP and Campbell KH (1940) Alcohol taste thresholds and concentrations of solution preferred by rats. *Science* 91: 507–508.

Ritz MC, Lamb RJ, Goldberg SR, and Kuhar MJ (1987) Cocaine receptors on dopamine transporter are related to self-administration of cocaine. *Science* 237: 1219–1222.

Rodzon K, Berry MS, and Odum AL (2011) Within-subject comparison of degree of delay discounting using titrating and fixed sequence procedures. *Behavioural Processes* 86: 164–167.

Roesch MR, Takahashi Y, Gugsa N, Bissonnette GB, and Schoenbaum G (2007) Previous cocaine exposure makes rats hypersensitive to both delay and reward magnitude. *Journal of Neuroscience* 27: 245–250.

Romer D, Duckworth AL, Sznitman S, and Park S (2010) Can adolescents learn self-control? Delay of gratification in the development of control over risk taking. *Prevention Science* 11: 319–330.

Roos P (1964) Time reference inventory. Mimeo, Austin State School, Austin, TX.

Roos P and Albers R (1965) Performance of alcoholics and normal on a measure of temporal orientation. *Journal of Clinical Psychology* 21: 34–36.

Rosenthal R (1979) The file drawer problem and tolerance for null results. *Psychological Bulletin* 86: 638–641.

Rossow I (2008) Alcohol consumption and discounting. *Addiction Research and Theory* 16: 572–584.

Sattler JM and Pflugrath JF (1970) Future-time perspectives in alcoholics and normals. *Quarterly Journal on Studies of Alcohol* 31: 839–850.

Schippers MC, Binnekade R, Schoffelmeer AN, and De Vries TJ (2011) Unidirectional relationship between heroin self-administration and impulsive decision-making in rats. *Psychopharmacology* (epub ahead of print).

Schweitzer JB and Sulzer-Azaroff B (1988) Self-control: Teaching tolerance for delay in impulsive children. *Journal of the Experimental Analysis of Behavior* 50: 173–186.

Setlow B, Mendez IA, Mitchell MR, and Simon NW (2009) Effects of chronic administration of drugs of abuse on impulsive choice (delay discounting) in animal models. *Behavioural Pharmacology* 20: 380–389.

Shelley MK (1993) Outcome signs, question frames, and discount rates. *Management Science* 39: 806–815.

Simon NW, LaSarge CL, Montgomery KS, Williams MT, Mendez IA, Setlow B, and Bizon JL (2008) Good things come to those who wait: Attenuated discounting of delayed rewards in aged Fischer 344 rats. *Neurobiology of Aging* 31: 853–862.

Simon NW, Mendez IA, and Setlow B (2007) Cocaine exposure causes long-term increases in impulsive choice. *Behavioral Neuroscience* 121: 543–549.

Smart RG (1968) Future time perspectives in alcoholics and social drinkers. *Journal of Abnormal Psychology* 73: 81–83.

Stanis JJ, Burns RM, Sherrill LK, and Gulley JM (2008) Disparate cocaine-induced locomotion as a predictor of choice behavior in rats trained in a delay-discounting task. *Drug and Alcohol Dependence* 98: 54–62.

Stein JS, Pinkston J, Brewer AT, Francisco MT, and Madden GJ (2012) Delay discounting in Lewis and Fischer 344 rats: Steady-state and rapid-determination adjusting-amount procedures. *Journal of the Experimental Analysis of Behavior* 97: 305-321.

Sun H, Cocker PJ, Zeeb FD, and Winstanley CA (2012) Chronic atomoxetine treatment during adolescence decreases impulsive choice, but not impulsive action, in adult rats and alters markers of synaptic plasticity in the orbitofrontal cortex. *Psychopharmacology* 219: 285–301.

Suzuki T, George FR, and Meisch RA (1988) Differential establishment and maintenance of oral ethanol reinforced behavior in Lewis and Fischer 344 inbred rat strains. *Journal of Pharmacology and Experimental Therapeutics* 245: 164–170.

Suzuki T, Otani K, Koike Y, and Misawa M (1988) Genetic differences in preferences for morphine and codeine in Lewis and Fischer 344 inbred rat strains. *Japanese Journal of Pharmacology* 47: 425–431.

Sweitzer MM (2008) Individual differences in delay discounting and nicotine self-administration in rats. Master's thesis, University of Akron.

Thanos PK, Taintor N, Rivera SN, Umegaki H, Ikari H, Roth G, Ingram DK, Hitzemann R, Fowler JS, Gatley J, Wang GJ, and Volkow BD (2004) DRD2 gene transfer into the nucleus accumbens of the alcohol preferring (P) and non preferring (NP) rats attenuates alcohol drinking. *Alcoholism: Clinical and Experimental Research* 28: 720–728.

Thanos PK, Michaelides M, Umegaki H, and Volkow ND (2008) D2R DNA transfer into the nucleus accumbens attenuates cocaine self-administration in rats. *Synapse* 62: 481–486.

Thanos PK, Volkow ND, Freimuth P, Umegaki H, Ikari H, Roth G, Ingram DK, and Hitzemann R (2001) Overexpression of dopamine D2 receptors reduces alcohol self-administration. *Journal of Neurochemistry* 78: 1094–1103.

Tomie A, Aguado AS, Pohorecky LA, and Benjamin D (1998) Ethanol induces impulsive-like responding in a delay-of-reward operant choice procedure: Impulsivity predicts autoshaping. *Psychopharmacology* 139: 376–382.

Volkow ND, Ding Y, Fowler J, and Wang G (1996) Cocaine addiction: Hypothesis derived from imaging studies with PET. *Journal of Addictive Diseases* 15: 55–71.

Vuchinich RE and Simpson CA (1998) Hyperbolic temporal discounting in social drinkers and problem drinkers. *Experimental and Clinical Psychopharmacology* 6: 292–305.

Wade TR, de Wit H, and Richards JB (2000) Effects of dopaminergic drugs on delayed reward as a measure of impulsive behavior in rats. *Psychopharmacology* 150: 90–101.

Washio Y, Higgins ST, Heil SH, McKerchar TL, Badger GJ, Skelly JM, and Dantona RL (2011) Delay discounting is associated with treatment response among cocaine-dependent outpatients. *Experimental and Clinical Psychopharmacology* 19: 243–248.

Wilhelm CJ and Mitchell SH (2008) Rats bred for high alcohol drinking are more sensitive to delayed and probabilistic outcomes. *Genes, Brain and Behavior* 7: 705–13.

Wilhelm CJ and Mitchell SH (2009) Strain differences in delay discounting using inbred rats. *Genes, Brain and Behavior* 8: 426–34.

Wilhelm CJ, Reeves JM, Phillips TJ, and Mitchell SH (2007) Mouse lines selected for alcohol consumption differ on certain measures of impulsivity. *Alcoholism: Clinical and Experimental Research* 31: 1839–1845.

Winstanley CA (2010) The neural and neurochemical basis of delay discounting. In GJ Madden and WK Bickel (eds), *Impulsivity: The Behavioral and Neurological Science of Discounting* (pp. 95–121). Washington, DC: American Psychological Association.

Winstanley CA, LaPlant Q, Theobald DE, Green TA, Bachtell RK, Perrotti LI, DiLeone RJ, Russo SJ, Garth WJ, Self DW, and Nestler EJ (2007) DeltaFosB induction in orbitofrontal cortex mediates tolerance to cocaine-induced cognitive dysfunction. *Journal of Neuroscience* 27: 10497–10507.

Yates JR, Marusich JA, Gipson CD, Beckmann JS, and Bardo MT (2011) High impulsivity in rats predicts amphetamine conditioned place preference. *Pharmacology Biochemistry and Behavior* 100: 370–376.

Yoon JH, Higgins ST, Heil SH, Sugarbaker RJ, Thomas CS, and Badger GJ (2007) Delay discounting predicts postpartum relapse to cigarette smoking among pregnant women. *Experimental and Clinical Psychopharmacology* 15: 176–186.

Zimbardo PG and Boyd JN (1999) Putting time in perspective: A valid, reliable individual-differences metric. *Journal of Personality and Social Psychology* 77: 1271–1288.

8

Assessment of Risk Taking in Addiction Research

Jennifer Dahne, Jessica M. Richards,
Monique Ernst, Laura MacPherson, and
Carl W. Lejuez

1 Introduction

In their seminal work, Jessor and Jessor (1977) defined risk taking as "behavior that is socially defined as a problem, a source of concern, or as undesirable by the norms of conventional society and the institutions of adult authority, and its occurrence usually elicits some kind of social control response" (p. 33). Focusing more explicitly on the potential consequences or outcomes of such behavior, risk taking has also been conceptualized as behavior that involves some potential for harm or negative consequence to the individual, but that may also result in a positive outcome or reward (Byrnes, Miller, and Schafer, 1999; Leigh, 1999). Further, the propensity to take risks exists on a continuum, with some risk taking being adaptive, and only more extreme levels being maladaptive (e.g., Lejuez et al., 2002).

Substance users frequently are considered to be risk-takers. In line with the definitions provided above, substance use includes short-term benefits balanced by potential consequences associated with obtaining substances, including social, emotional, and occupational problems associated with continued use (DSM-IV; American Psychiatric Association [APA], 2000). Given the frequent imbalance of losses versus gains associated with substance use, it is important to consider the directional relationship between substance use and risk taking. First, a preexisting risk-taking disposition may predispose individuals to gravitate toward substance use. It is well accepted that traits such as impulsivity have a biological basis (Cloninger, 1987), and these biologically based factors render an individual vulnerable to substance use as well as to other behavioral problems (Krueger et al., 2002; Lejuez et al., 2010). Second, contextual factors associated with the use of different drug classes may in part account for the behavioral variations across individuals using different types of substance. Variability in drug choice provides different opportunities for, and reinforcement of, impulsive and risky behaviors. An example of this is the strong association of crack cocaine use

The Wiley-Blackwell Handbook of Addiction Psychopharmacology, First Edition. Edited by James MacKillop and Harriet de Wit.
© 2013 John Wiley & Sons, Ltd. Published 2013 by John Wiley & Sons, Ltd.

and involvement in the sex-for-crack market (Baseman, Ross, and Williams, 1999; Ross *et al.*, 1999; Ross *et al.*, 2002). Finally, the long-term effects of substance use, including selective neural changes and consequent impairment in decision making, may lead to further risk taking and substance use. Thus, a willingness to take risks may lead to initiation of substance use, while continued use may increase riskiness and the progression to further use in a cyclical manner.

Given the dynamic relationship between substance use and risk taking, well-developed behavioral methodologies to study risk taking are crucial. Toward this goal, the current chapter will outline existing standardized and validated behavioral measures for assessing risk taking, including Slovic's Devil Task, the Balloon Analogue Risk Task, the Angling Risk Task, the Columbia Card Task, the Wheel of Fortune Task, the Iowa Gambling Task, and the Rogers Decision Making Task. As available theory, description, and data permit, each section will include a task description, discussion of its reliability, convergent/discriminant validity, criterion validity, genetic/neurobehavioral data, and methodological considerations for using the task.

2   Behavioral Tasks for Measuring Risk Taking

2.1   Slovic's Devil Task

One of the first well-characterized behavioral measures of risk taking was Slovic's Devil Task (1966). Although it has not been used to assess risk taking related to substance use in the extant literature, a review of the Devil Task is important for its historical significance and connection to current and commonly used risk-taking tasks.

As described by Slovic (1966), the Devil Task seated participants before a panel of ten small knife switches and the participants were told that nine of the switches were "safe" and that the tenth was a "disaster" switch, with it being impossible to distinguish which was the disaster switch prior to choosing it. Each participant was informed that a switch could only be pulled once (i.e., sampling without replacement), thus the likelihood of pulling the disaster switch increased with each subsequent trial. The participant was then asked to pull one of the switches and, if the participant chose a safe switch, he/she was allowed to place one spoonful of candies into a glass bowl. The participant then had to decide either to pull another switch or to stop and keep the candy he/she had already won. If the participant decided to continue but subsequently pulled the disaster switch, a buzzer sounded and the participant lost all the candy he/she had already earned. In the event that the participant pulled nine safe switches in a row, he/she was automatically forced to stop and take his/her nine spoonfuls of candy, as the only remaining switch necessarily was the "disaster" switch. Because both the probability and magnitude of one's potential loss increases with the number of switches pulled, stopping performance on the task can be considered an index of risk-taking tendencies (Slovic, 1966). Modified versions of the task include a version with ten wooden boxes, where one box contains a devil (Hoffrage, Weber, Hertwig, and Chase, 2003), as well as a computerized version of the Devil Task using boxes (Eisenegger *et al.*, 2010).

2.1.1   Reliability.   Reliability data are not available for the Devil Task.

2.1.2   Convergent/discriminant validity.   Convergent and discriminant validity data are not available for the Devil Task.

2.1.3   Criterion validity.   The Devil Task has been used to understand risk-taking behavior. For instance, gender differences have been reported, with boys taking more risks on the task than girls; however, developmental changes in risk taking have not been seen (Montgomery and Landers, 1974; Slovic, 1966). The task also discriminates between children who do and do not cross the street dangerously (Hoffrage, Weber, Hertwig, and Chase, 2003).

2.1.4   Neurobehavioral and genetic data.   Eisenegger and colleagues (2010) administered either 300 mg of L-dihydroxyphenylalanine (L-DOPA) or placebo to healthy subjects who were genotyped for the variable number of tandem repeats polymorphism in exon 3 of the dopamine receptor D4 gene (*DRD4* VNTR). Participants then completed the computerized variant of the Devil Task 60 minutes after L-DOPA/placebo administration. Riskiness on the Devil Task was related to presence of the 7-repeat allele of *DRD4*, such that individuals who had the 7-repeat allele displayed riskier behavior on the task in response to L-DOPA administration.

Büchel and colleagues (2011) examined the neural correlates of the effect of post-decisional information on subsequent risk taking on a modified version of the Devil Task. In the modified task, after the participant decided to end the round and collect earnings, the position of the devil was revealed, showing how far he/she could have gambled without losing. A large missed opportunity was defined as ending the round more than two boxes before reaching the devil. Results indicated that participants were more risky (i.e., opened more boxes) on trials after a large missed opportunity as compared to trials following a small missed opportunity. Corresponding fMRI data indicated that larger missed opportunities were associated with greater deactivation in a lateral region of the ventral striatum. Moreover, greater deactivation in the ventral tegmental area, anterior insula, and ventral striatum predicted greater risk taking on the next round of the task. Thus, deactivation in these dopaminergic regions may provide one neural mechanism by which missed opportunities impact future decision making.

2.1.5   Methodological considerations.   As discussed above, the Devil Task is most notable for its historical significance. Despite its limited use, the task possesses multiple features that make it a useful measure for studying risk taking. For example, the Devil Task discriminates between risk-takers without involving learning (Hoffrage, Weber, Hertwig, and Chase, 2003), suggesting that the task could be a useful vehicle for examining contextual influences on risk taking. Because the task has clear face validity, it is probably useful without extensive modification across developmental stages, and the short administration time makes it ideal for examining the impact of experimental manipulations such as stress or drug/alcohol administration on task performance.

2.2   Balloon Analogue Risk Task (BART)

Expanding on the basic framework of the Devil Task, Lejuez and colleagues developed the Balloon Analogue Risk Task (Lejuez *et al.*, 2002). The BART is a computerized measure that models real-world risk behavior by balancing the potential for reward and harm (Leigh, 1999; Lejuez *et al.*, 2002). In the task, the participant is presented with a balloon and asked to pump the balloon by clicking a button on the screen. With each click, the balloon inflates 0.3 cm and money is added to the participant's temporary winnings; however, balloons also have explosion points. The explosion point can be varied both across and within studies. Lejuez *et al.* (2002) used three different balloon colors, with each color associated with a range of 1–8, 1–32, or 1–128 pumps, respectively. The probability that a balloon would explode was arranged by constructing an array of N numbers. The number 1 was designated as indicating a balloon explosion. On each pump of the balloon, a number was selected without replacement from the array. The balloon exploded if the number 1 was selected. For example, for the blue balloon ranging from 1 to 128, the probability that a balloon would explode on the first pump was $1/128$. If the balloon did not explode on the first pump, the probability that the balloon would explode was $1/127$ on the second pump, $1/126$ on the third pump, and so on up until the 128th pump, at which the probability of an explosion was $1/1$ (i.e., 100%). According to this algorithm, the average break point is the midpoint of the range, in this case 64 pumps. Before the balloon pops, the participant can press "Collect $$$" which saves his or her earnings to a permanent bank. If the balloon pops before the participant collects the money, all earnings for that balloon are lost, and the next balloon is presented. Thus, each pump confers greater risk, but also greater potential reward.

The primary BART score is the adjusted average number of pumps on unexploded balloons (Bornovalova *et al.*, 2005; Lejuez *et al.*, 2002), with higher scores indicative of greater risk-taking propensity. In the original version of the task, each pump was worth $0.05 and there were 30 total balloons of each explosion range. Participants were given no information about the break points and the absence of this information allowed for the examination of participants' initial responses to the task and to changes as they experienced the contingencies related to payout collections and balloon explosions. Results of the original study also established that relationships between key outcome variables and BART scores were most evident at the largest balloon range of 1–128, with only this explosion range largely used in subsequent studies.

The BART has also been modified into a youth version (BART-Y; Lejuez *et al.*, 2007) in which balloon pumps produce points represented visually in a meter, with the points exchangeable for prizes at the conclusion of the task. The original version of the BART employs money as a reward for the task, a reward which may not be appropriate for adolescents for a variety of reasons (e.g., ethical concerns, saliency of the reward). Reliability and validity data on the BART-Y appear similar to the original BART.

2.2.1   Reliability.   Reliability of the BART has been established across a range of samples. Split-third reliability has been examined by comparing scores across the first, middle, and final block of 10 balloons (the task is typically arranged to ensure identical average explosions points across the different blocks). The reliability estimates indicate strong correlations (> 0.7) among the blocks (Lejuez *et al.*, 2003; Lejuez *et al.*, 2002). Adult participants tend to demonstrate modest increases in risk taking across the blocks (typically between one and three pumps; Lejuez *et al.*, 2003; Lejuez *et al.*, 2002), while scores tend to decrease from the first to the third block of balloons among adolescents (Lejuez *et al.*, 2007; MacPherson *et al.*, 2010a). Data also indicate test–retest reliability across multiple administrations in the same session among young adults, with modest yet significant increases across administrations (T2–T1Δ = 2.2 adjusted average pumps, T3–T1Δ = 2.3 adjusted average pumps) and reasonably robust correlations among administrations (T1/T2 r = 0.79, T1/T3 r = 0.62, T2/T3 r = 0.82; Lejuez *et al.*, 2003). Extended test–retest reliability has been indicated with the task presented twice across a 2-week period, with a nonsignificant increase across administrations (T2–T1Δ = 1.2 adjusted average pumps) and a reasonably robust test–retest correlation (T1/T2 r = 0.77; White, Lejuez, and de Wit, 2008).

2.2.2   Convergent/divergent validity.   It is notable that relationships between performance on the BART and self-report measures of disinhibition are inconsistent. The initial study indicated modestly robust relationships with both sensation seeking and impulsivity (i.e., $\geq$ 0.3; Lejuez *et al.*, 2002). However, more recent work, often using lower payouts (from 5 cents per pump to 1 or 2 cents or even hypothetical reward), suggest significant but considerably more modest relationships with sensation seeking and often no relationship with impulsivity (Bornovalova *et al.*, 2005; Lejuez *et al.*, 2007; Meda *et al.*, 2009).

2.2.3   Criterion validity.   Within adolescent studies, BART score is related to self-reported engagement in real-world risk-taking behaviors including substance use and delinquency/safety behaviors from middle adolescents to young adults in community samples (e.g., Aklin *et al.*, 2005; Fernie, Cole, Goudie, and Field, 2010; Lejuez *et al.*, 2002; Lejuez, Aklin, Zvolensky, and Pedulla, 2003; Lejuez *et al.*, 2007) as well as studies comparing clinical and nonclinical samples (e.g., Bornovolova *et al.*, 2005; Crowley *et al.*, 2006; Lejuez *et al.*, 2004). Additionally, BART-Y score was shown to vary with alcohol use across 3 years among early to middle adolescents (MacPherson *et al.*, 2010a). Thus, BART performance appears to be related to early engagement in substance use as well as to risk behaviors related to substance use. Consideration of moderators in the relationship between BART score and risk behavior may also be important. In one study, BART-Y score was prospectively related to number of risk-taking behaviors in the past year, but only for adolescents with low distress tolerance, even after controlling for gender and sensation seeking (MacPherson *et al.*, 2010b).

2.2.4   Neurobehavioral and genetic data.   Examining the effects of a functional polymorphism in the regulatory region (5-HTTLPR) of the human 5-HT transporter (5-HTT) gene on risk taking, Crisan and colleagues (2009) found that carriers of the short (*s*) compared to the long (*l*) repeats had significantly lower levels of risk taking on the BART. Within neuroimaging, Rao and colleagues (2008) created a version of the BART in which both active and passive modes of the task were administered. In the active mode, participants had the choice to discontinue inflating the balloon at any time, while in the passive mode, participants had no choice and the computer randomly determined the end size and corresponding monetary reward outcome for each balloon. Voluntary risk in the active mode as compared to involuntary risk in the passive mode was associated with increased activation in mesolimbic and frontal regions, including the midbrain, ventral and dorsal striatum, anterior insula, dorsal lateral prefrontal cortex, and anterior cingulate/medial frontal cortex, in addition to activation in visual pathways.

2.2.5 Methodological considerations.   Studies have varied the number of balloon trials on the BART, but the most common method includes 30 trials. In studies using 30 balloons, the score across all balloons is typically more reliable than any block of 10 balloons. However under time constraints, using fewer balloons may be preferable. Research indicates that correlations with the total score are acceptable for the first 10 balloons (~0.6) and are good for balloons 11–20 (~0.8) with little change for balloons 21–30 (~0.8) (Lejuez *et al.*, 2003; Lejuez *et al.*, 2002). Thus, an argument can be made for any choice between 10 and 30 balloons to manage cost and time.

One useful feature of the BART is the ability to examine a magnitude effect as it relates to the reward level for each pump. In one study, Bornovalova and colleagues manipulated the magnitude of reward/loss value, examining differences in BART score at 1, 5, and 25 cents per pump, as a function of trait impulsivity and sensation seeking. As the magnitude of monetary reward/loss value increased, risk taking on the task decreased. However, when examined separately among individuals with high impulsivity/sensation seeking as compared to individuals low in these traits, the negative relationship between reward/loss magnitude and riskiness was driven by those low in impulsivity/sensation seeking. Conversely, individuals high in impulsivity/sensation seeking showed little change in riskiness as reward/loss magnitude increased. These findings illustrate that higher reward/loss magnitudes convey less risk taking on the task, particularly for individuals low in impulsivity-related traits. Supporting this conclusion, similar relationships have been found with delay discounting, where rewards were discounted less due to delay when they were of larger magnitude (Baker, Johnson, and Bickel, 2003; MacKillop *et al.*, 2010). These findings suggest that researchers should consider the absolute magnitude value of reinforcers that are employed in behavioral risk-taking paradigms when interpreting results.

2.2.6 Dissociating distinct processes contributing to risk taking.   For the BART, it is well documented that participants are extremely risk averse. Past studies with the BART have shown that participants typically exhibit adjusted scores between 26 and 35 pumps, with few scoring at or above 64 pumps, the optimal number of pumps to maximize earnings (Lejuez *et al.*, 2003; Lejuez *et al.*, 2002). A concern about this level of pumping is that because risk behavior only is less productive above the average of 64 pumps, the most risky individuals also are making the most overall profit on the task. It is unclear why this low level of pumping occurs. One hypothesis is that the low pumping behavior might be the result of insufficient experience with the BART. However, several studies and some mathematical modeling work suggest that additional trials beyond 30 result in little increase in pumping rates (Lejuez *et al.*, 2002; Wallsten, Pleskac, and Lejuez, 2005).

To further address this issue, Pleskac, Wallsten, Wang, and Lejuez (2008) considered three manipulations to the task to address underperformance directly: (1) modifying instructions to inform participants that the expected-value maximizing strategy is 64 pumps, (2) providing event feedback on all trials indicating where the previous balloon was set to explode, and (3) adding an additional task version that allowed participants to type in the number of pumps instead of making each individual pump. These modifications produced a sample average target score of 61, which approached the expected-value maximizing strategy of 64 pumps. In fact, 29 out of 75 (39%) of the participants had mean target scores greater than 64, and thus earned less than their counterparts who were closer to the average of 64 pumps. The obvious limitation of this work was the manipulation of all three variables together, leaving little opportunity to determine the unique contribution of each.

2.3   Angling Risk Task (ART)

Following from the efforts to better understand the factors influencing risk taking on the BART, Pleskac (2008) developed the ART. In the ART, participants fish in a tournament for H rounds or trips (typically 30) in a pond that has 1 blue fish and $n - 1$ red fish. With each cast of a computerized fishing rod, the participant hooks a fish (each fish is equally likely to be caught). If it is red, then the participant earns $0.05 and can cast again. If it is blue, the round ends and the money earned on that round is lost. Laws of the game change, such that sometimes the rule is "catch 'n' keep" (sampled without replacement) and the red fish can be placed in the cooler on the right of the screen, reducing the total number of red fish in the pond by 1. However, sometimes the law is "catch 'n' release" (sampled with replacement) and the red fish is placed back into the pond. This change in the laws allowed Pleskac to manipulate subjects' mental model of the task. Different levels of learning can be manipulated by changing the weather conditions of the fishing tournament. For example, the tournament can take place on a sunny day, allowing participants to see the number of fish in the pond and eliminating the need to learn their distribution. In contrast, the tournament can take place on a cloudy day, concealing the fish in the pond, which in turn forces participants to learn about how many potential fish are in the pond. This cloudy condition is conceptually closer to the standard BART task. Pleskac (2008) found that the decision-making process, specifically how sensitive participants were to changes in payoffs, and not the learning process, accounted for differences between drug users and non-users. In fact, the learning process required during the cloudy conditions reduced the task's sensitivity in identifying drug use. There is limited reliability and validity data for the ART, but ongoing studies are currently addressing these key issues.

2.4   Columbia Card Task (CCT)

Whereas the ART provides a comparison of risk taking when one is and is not aware of the probabilities of positive and negative outcomes, the Columbia Card Task (CCT) developed by Figner, Mackinlay, Wilkening, and Weber (2009) provides a more isolated comparison of manual and automatic responding. Specifically, the CCT was developed to contrast risk taking motivated by spontaneous, automatic motivational-affective system as compared to more deliberative, effortful cognitive control systems (e.g., Cohen, 2005; McClure, Laibson, Loewenstein, and Cohen, 2004). To tease apart the relative contribution of the affective and cognitive control systems, Figner, Mackinlay, Wilkening, and Weber (2009) created two versions of the CCT: a "hot" version and a "cold" version. In the "hot" version, participants are permitted to make stepwise, incremental decisions in turning over cards and are provided with immediate feedback about whether the card was a gain or a loss card. After each gain card, participants can make the decision to either turn over another card, or terminate the trial and collect all gains from that round. Once a loss card is selected, the loss amount is subtracted from the participant's score and the trial ends. In the "cold" version of the task, participants must select the total number of cards that they would like to turn over on that trial, but cannot select which cards to turn over. In this version, participants do not receive any feedback about the consequences of their decision until the end of the task. Clearly, a strength of this task is the ability to parse the relative contributions of affective versus cognitive control processes (Figner and Weber, 2011), which will be especially useful as the task is applied more directly to substance use in future studies. To date, reliability and validity data are limited.

2.5   Wheel of Fortune (WOF)

The Wheel of Fortune (Ernst *et al.*, 2004) is a computerized, two-choice neuroimaging task involving probabilistic monetary outcomes. The two most common versions of the task comprise (a) "win–no win," in which subjects can only win or not win; and (b) "lose–no lose," in which subjects can only lose or not lose. Subjects are instructed to try to win as much money as possible. Both versions of the task are identical in most aspects. In the win–no win task, subjects are asked to select one of two options based on the likelihood of a gain and the magnitude of that gain. Four types of conditions are used to elicit behaviors of various degrees of risk seeking and risk avoiding. Subjects choose between two options, each with an assigned probability of winning a certain amount of money. If the computer randomly selects the same option as the subject, the subject wins the designated amount of money; if the computer randomly selects the other option, the subject wins nothing. For probabilities of winning/losing and possible amounts won/lost, see Table 8.1.

Each of the four monetary conditions is displayed as a two-slice Wheel of Fortune, with each slice representing a distinct option. Subjects are told to select one of the slices

Table 8.1   Reward/loss probabilities and magnitude of reward/loss for the WOF task

Contrast	Option 1	Option 2
1	10%/$4.00	90%/$0.50
2	30%/$2.00	70%/$1.00
3	50%/$4.00	50%/$4.00
4	50%/$0.50	50%/$0.50

by its color (blue or magenta). The area of the slice matches the likelihood of winning (e.g., 10%) an explicit amount of money (e.g., $4.00). Each trial is composed of three phases: a selection phase, an anticipation phase, and a feedback phase. During the selection phase, participants view a wheel and are asked to select either the blue or the magenta slice by pressing a button corresponding to where the color is located (right or left). In the anticipation phase, subjects continue to view the wheel while a 5-point rating scale appears on the screen to prompt them to rate their level of confidence in winning (1 unsure, 5 sure; button press). In the feedback phase, subjects are shown the dollar amount won ($0 if not won), the cumulative dollar amount won, and a 5-point rating scale along which they are asked to rate how they felt (1 neutral and 5 best for favorable outcomes, and 1 neutral to 5 worst for unfavorable outcomes). The lose–no lose condition is identical to the win–no win in all aspects except that: (1) "lose" replaces "win" and "no lose" replaces "no win;" and (2) subjects start with an endowment of US$75.00.

2.5.1 Reliability. As is common with many neuroimaging tasks, there has been little data examining reliability for the WOF.

2.5.2 Convergent/divergent validity. Several behavioral components of the WOF task can be examined, including reaction time and choice of the high- or low-risk option. Rao and colleagues (2011) utilized a laboratory version of the WOF that focused on behavioral responses and did not collect neuroimaging data, and compared it with the Behavioral Inhibition System (BIS) and Behavioral Activation System (BAS) scales, as well as the Junior Temperament and Character Inventory (JTCI). Results indicated that participants who made the more risky, low-probability, choice with greater frequency on the win–no win version had significantly higher scores on drive and fun-seeking scales of the BAS and reward-dependence scale of the JTCI.

2.5.3 Criterion validity. When choosing between high- and low-risk options, mal-treated children with depressive disorders more frequently select safe over risky choices than do controls (Guyer *et al.*, 2006). Relating to substance use, Rao and colleagues (2011) found that greater frequency of low-probability (high-risk) choices on the win–no win version of the WOF predicted substance-related problems, including drug involvement and related psychiatric and psychosocial problems. However, low-probability (low-risk) choice on the lose–no lose version of the task did not predict substance-related problems.

2.5.4 Neurobehavioral and genetic data. Although the WOF is typically used in a neuroimaging context, only one study to date has examined neural functioning during the WOF among substance users. Addicott and colleagues (2011) examined the effects of nicotine abstinence on brain function in adult smokers in a within-subject design using the WOF under two conditions: smoking abstinence and smoking-satiated. Breaking results down by phases of the task, during reward selection, participants exhibited slower reaction times and had greater neural activation in the postcentral gyrus, insula, and frontal and parietal cortices during smoking abstinence than in the smoking-satiated condition. These differences in activation between conditions suggest that abstinence is associated with increased cognitive effort, a finding that has been seen across nicotine withdrawal studies (e.g., Cole *et al.*, 2010; Evans and Drobes, 2009; Heishma, Taylor, and Henningfield, 1994). Reward anticipation was associated with greater activity in the left insular cortex, right frontal pole, and right paracingulate cortex during the abstinent condition and with greater activity in the left precentral gyrus and right putamen during the satiated condition. During the outcome phase, participants displayed greater activation in the paracingulate cortex when receiving rewards as compared to no rewards under the satiated versus the abstinent condition.

While the WOF has not yet been studied extensively in substance users beyond the work reviewed above, results of neuroimaging studies using the WOF indicate regions of brain activation that may be promising for future research with this population. As one example, researchers have examined differences in task-induced neural activation between adolescents and adults during specific phases of the task, including the selection and feedback phases (Ernst *et al.*, 2005; Eshel *et al.*, 2007). Beginning with the feedback phase, adolescents evidenced enhanced activation in the left nucleus accumbens and reduced activation in the left amygdala compared to adults (Ernst *et al.*, 2005). Moreover, adolescents also reported significantly greater intensity of positive emotions upon winning the rewards relative to adults. When examining responses to reward omissions specifically, adults demonstrated greater reductions in amygdala activation in response to reward omission than adolescents. The authors suggest the pattern of increased reward functioning (i.e., enhanced activation in the nucleus accumbens) and reduced recruitment of regions implicated in threat (i.e., the amygdala) may reflect one neural mechanism underlying adolescents' increased vulnerability to risk taking, including substance use, relative to adults.

Using data from the same sample, an additional study compared BOLD activation during the selection phase of the WOF between adults and adolescents, with results revealing greater activation in the orbital frontal cortex/ventrolateral prefrontal cortex and dorsal anterior cingulate cortex in adults than adolescents when making risky selections (Eshel *et al.*, 2007). Further, reduced activity in these areas predicted greater risk-taking performance in adolescents. Thus, during risky decision making, adolescents may engage prefrontal regulatory structures to a lesser extent than adults. These results are promising for future use of this task in substance users, considering that substance users may have different neural responses to both the selection and receipt of rewards, potentially playing a role in a reciprocal relationship between neural functioning and substance use.

2.5.5 Methodological considerations. As is often the case when developing paradigms for fMRI, it is important to consider the cost–benefit ratio of manipulating the duration of the task. Extending the task allows researchers to collect more data over repeated trials and increase statistical power; however, increased data quantity may come at the expense of data quality, as participants may become fatigued or disengaged during a long scan. The very nature of the WOF task in particular may complicate this issue further. Each trial is necessarily relatively long due to the temporal dissociation necessary between each task phase to differentiate the neural processes underlying the three stages of decision making (i.e., selection, anticipation, and feedback phases), yielding approximately 11 seconds total for each trial. This long trial duration limits the number of trials that can be administered while keeping the total task duration to a manageable length. Thus, researchers have utilized versions of the WOF of varying task lengths, with each run lasting approximately 7 to 9 minutes (e.g., Ernst *et al.*, 2004; Ernst *et al.*, 2005; Hardin, Pine, and Ernst, 2009). Varying the number of runs can yield total task times of approximately 18 to 36 minutes, during which 92 to 184 trials can be administered, providing an adequate level of statistical power to detect significant effects. Consequently, researchers have the option of adjusting the task duration to accommodate a variety of research designs; however, no fewer than two task runs are recommended.

2.5.6 Individual difference factors influencing task reliability and validity. An issue specific to any task of decision making is related to individual variability in the type and frequency of options selected. That is, some individuals may never select a specific option (e.g., the most risky option), or they may select some options too few times to yield a reliable BOLD signal. It is difficult to design a decision-making task ensuring that all options will be selected an adequate number of times by every participant. As such, researchers should consider the possibility of data loss due to insufficient option selection, and plan to recruit enough participants to account for this issue.

Another issue to consider is the possibility that the same outcome may not be considered similarly rewarding across populations of interest, thus confounding the effects of group status on neural functioning with the effects of reward appraisal and salience. Monetary outcomes have typically been used across fMRI tasks designed to assess reward-related decision making. However, it is not completely clear if a particular monetary outcome (e.g., winning $1.00) is of equivalent value for adults as compared to adolescents. Indeed, Ernst and colleagues (2005) reported that adolescents self-reported significantly greater intensity of positive affect upon winning monetary rewards relative to adults, suggesting developmental differences in the subjective value of monetary rewards. Specific to substance use, there is reason to believe that substance users may devalue monetary rewards relative to non-substance-using populations (e.g., Hommer, Bjork, and Gilman, 2011). As such, the reward values that are used in the WOF and other reward-based decision-making tasks should be piloted outside of the scanner on samples recruited from relevant participant populations before implementing the task in the fMRI.

2.5.7 Reward magnitude and probability. The WOF task manipulates two distinct parameters of choice; namely, the magnitude of reward, and the probability of receiving the reward. It is important, however, to display both parameters with a similar visual salience in order to permit a fair evaluation of relative sensitivity to these two parameters. Of interest to this particular issue, Smith and colleagues (2009) specifically modified the WOF to examine neural responses to variable reward magnitudes and differing probabilities of reward. The researchers visually presented these manipulations in precisely the same way in order to control for potential differences in salience across presentation types. Results indicated that selection of high, relative to low, reward magnitude increased activity in the insula, amygdala, middle and posterior cingulate cortex, and basal ganglia, while selection of low-probability, as opposed to high-probability, reward increased activity in anterior cingulate cortex, as did selection of risky, relative to safe, reward. The authors suggest that decision making without conflict (i.e., those based solely on reward magnitude) activates structures that code reward values and those implicated in motivational and perceptual information for behavioral responses. Conversely, decision making under conflict (i.e., when probability and risk are manipulated) activates areas involved in conflict monitoring. Given that decision making under conflict did not activate areas believed to be involved in the encoding of reward values, conflict seems to alter the pattern of neural responses to rewards and should be considered as a factor to either assess directly, or control for (i.e., remove probability manipulations) if researchers are solely interested in the effects of rewards on decision making.

2.5.8   Effects of contextual valence.   Finally, an issue to consider when assessing how people respond to the outcomes of their risky decisions is that the emotional significance of (and, by extension, the neural response to) a particular outcome may depend in part on the context in which it is experienced. Hardin, Pine, and Ernst (2009) assessed the effect of context on neural functioning during the WOF by directly comparing BOLD responses to the feedback phase of the win–no win version versus the lose–no lose version in a sample of healthy adults. The researchers found unique patterns of neural activation in response to decision outcomes, with the intensity of activation in some regions showing sensitivity to the contextual valence in which the outcome was experienced. Specifically, the nucleus accumbens and orbitofrontal cortex coded the most extreme outcomes in each context, with exaggerated activation in response to favorable outcomes in the positive (i.e., win–no win) context. Conversely, the amygdala and insula also coded highly salient outcomes, but showed potentiated responses to unfavorable outcomes in the negative (i.e., lose–no lose) context. Finally, the medial prefrontal cortex only coded favorable outcomes within the positive context, and showed wide inter-individual variability in activation in the negative context. These findings suggest that the neural processes involved in responding to decision outcomes are highly sensitive to the context in which the outcomes are received.

2.6   Iowa Gambling Task (IGT)

The Iowa Gambling Task (Bechara, Damasio, Damasio, and Anderson, 1994) is a decision-making task originally developed to examine decisional processes associated with neuropsychological impairment (e.g., Bechara, Damasio, Damasio, and Anderson, 1994; Rogers *et al.*, 1999a). At the beginning of the task, the participant is given $2,000, is provided with four decks of cards on the computer screen, and is instructed to maximize earnings over the course of 100 decision-making trials. As described by Bechara *et al.* (2001), the decks are labelled A, B, C, and D at the top end of each deck. All cards are identical, and each card is associated with real or hypothetical payoffs or losses. Accordingly, 10 draws from decks A and B (the "disadvantageous" decks) lead to a net loss of $250, while 10 draws from decks C and D (the "advantageous" decks) lead to a net gain of $250 (Bechara, Damasio, Damasio, and Anderson, 1994; Buelow and Suhr, 2009). For a description of average payouts and net gains/losses, see Table 8.2.

Table 8.2 Average pay and net amount won/lost for the IGT

Deck	A	B	C	D
Average pay	$100	$100	$50	$50
Net of 10 draws	−$250	−$250	+$250	+250

During each trial, the participant clicks on a card from one of the four decks. Once the card is selected, the computer makes a sound similar to that of a slot machine. The selected card appears as either red or black, indicating whether money was lost or gained, and the value of the reward or loss appears at the top of the screen. Following this feedback, the card disappears and the participant selects another card. Each deck of cards is programmed to have 60 cards (30 red and 30 black), although the participant is unaware of how many cards of each type are in each deck. Losses are equally frequent in each deck. The most widely reported measure of risky decision making on the IGT is the number or percentage of disadvantageous choices over 100 trials, with larger values representing greater riskiness. The percentage of disadvantageous choices is also commonly reported in blocks of 20 trials.

2.6.1 Reliability. There has not been extensive testing of IGT reliability, quite possibly because the task objective is to learn the rules of the task, suggesting that participants who have learned the task rules would behave differently on later as compared to earlier trials. For this reason, reliability may be poorer in nonclinical participants who "figure out" the task in the first administration, and show greater reductions in the rate of disadvantageous choices in subsequent administrations as compared to clinically impaired participants (Bechara, personal communication). As an example of this within substance users, Verdejo-Garcia and colleagues (2007) administered the IGT on two different occasions to abstinent users of marijuana or cocaine and healthy controls. Results indicated that both cocaine users and marijuana users performed worse than controls on the total IGT net score (total score across sessions 1 and 2). Furthermore, all groups exhibited between-session learning, but the rate of learning differed between groups such that cocaine users exhibited less learning than marijuana users and marijuana users exhibited less learning than controls. In studies that examined reliability, college student smokers displayed modest test–retest stability over the course of three administrations in a single testing session ($r = 0.57$–0.59; Lejuez *et al.*, 2003). In cocaine-dependent patients, Monterosso and colleagues (2001) found that the split-half reliability for total number of good decks chosen was $r = 0.80$, while the split-half reliability of good-decks chosen on the second half of the task was $r = 0.92$.

2.6.2 Convergent/discriminant validity. The IGT has been associated with rate of delay discounting ($r = 0.29$–0.37) but not with behavioral measures of impulsive disinhibition or impulsive inattention (Stanford *et al.*, 2009; Monterosso *et al.*, 2001). In a nonclinical sample, Franken and Muris (2005) examined the relationship between IGT performance and impulsivity as measured by the Dickman Impulsivity

Inventory (DII) and found no significant relationship between IGT performance and DII score, though the relationship between the functional impulsivity subscale of the DII and IGT performance trended toward significance. The relationship between IGT performance and related constructs of Behavioral Inhibition and Behavioral Activation as measured by the Behavioral Inhibition/Behavioral Activation Scale (BIS/BAS) remains unclear. While Suhr and Tsanadis (2007) found that individuals who scored highest on the Fun Seeking subscale of the BAS performed worst on the IGT, Franken and Muris (2005) found that good performance on the IGT was positively related to the BAS Sensitivity to Reward subscale, but not to the Fun Seeking subscale. Both studies found no significant relationship between BIS and IGT performance. Van Honk *et al.* (2002) found that individuals with a combination of high BAS and low BIS performed significantly worse on the IGT than individuals with low BAS and high BIS.

2.6.3 Criterion validity.
While the IGT was originally developed to assess neuropsychological impairment (e.g., Bechara, Damasio, Damasio, and Anderson, 1994; Rogers *et al.*, 1999b), more recent research has focused on differentiating typologies of individuals who engage in substance abuse. Several studies have provided evidence that adult drug abusers may be more risky than nondrug abusers, with drug abusers choosing the "bad" decks on the IGT at a significantly higher frequency than control participants (Bechara *et al.*, 2001; Grant, Contoreggi, and London, 2000; Petry, 2001; Petry, Bickel, and Arnett, 1998). These findings encompass individuals with alcohol dependence, methamphetamine dependence, heroin dependence, and cocaine dependence.

2.6.4 Neurobehavioral and genetic data.
Extending the line of IGT research to a neuroimaging context with adult substance users, Bolla *et al.* (2003) tested whether 25-day-abstinent cocaine abusers show alterations in normalized cerebral blood flow in the OFC using PET with ^{15}O during the IGT. Participants completed a control task as well, which allowed control for the sensorimotor aspects of the IGT, but did not involve decision making in order to isolate decision making as the process of interest. Cocaine abusers displayed nonsignificant inferior performance on the task as compared to controls. However, cocaine abusers did show significantly different patterns of prefrontal neural activation in response to decision making in the IGT, including greater activation in the right OFC, as well as reduced activation in the right dorsolateral prefrontal cortex and left medial prefrontal cortex compared to controls. In the genetics literature, He and colleagues (2010) found that the 5-HTTLPR polymorphism was significantly related to performance on the IGT such that, after controlling for intelligence and memory abilities, subjects homozygous for the *s* allele had lower IGT scores than *l* carriers in the first 40 trials of the IGT task. Moreover, the effects of 5-HTTLPR were stronger for males than for females.

2.6.5 Methodological considerations.
For the IGT, IQ is significantly positively related to the percentage of good decks chosen and negatively related to the percentage of bad decks chosen (Cauffman *et al.*, 2010). This relationship often makes it difficult to determine if differences between impaired clinical groups and healthy

controls are due to the clinical condition itself or associated lower levels of intelligence. Although there are likely to be IGT differences between those with low and high IQ, the task may be most useful for differentiating poor decision making and judgment when comparing groups of individuals that both hold intact memory, intelligence, and other cognitive functioning (Bechara, personal communication).

Another consideration when implementing the IGT is that much of the literature on the task has used little to no incentive for performance. Incentivizing makes a difference in task performance, especially when considering substance-using groups. Vadhan and colleagues (2009) compared performance on the IGT between cocaine-dependent individuals and non-using controls under two counterbalanced conditions: hypothetical earnings and losses versus cash earnings and losses. Under the hypothetical payment condition, cocaine abusers selected a greater proportion of cards from disadvantageous decks than advantageous decks, but took a similar amount of time to complete the task, relative to control participants. However, under the cash payment condition, no group differences were seen for card selection, and cocaine abusers took more time than controls to complete the task. Although this is only one study and it by no means suggests that the task cannot be effectively used without tangible incentives, it does suggest the importance of considering population-specific factors (e.g., sensitivity to instructional versus consequential control) when conducting neurobehavioral research in substance users.

Most research using the IGT institutes 100 trials of the task. Inconsistencies have arisen for combining data across trials during analysis. While number of bad decks chosen has been frequently used, alternative approaches have been implemented as well. For example, recent studies have examined how performance on the IGT changes over the course of the task using multilevel modeling (Cauffman *et al.*, 2010; Zermatten *et al.*, 2005). Using this data analytic strategy, Cauffman and colleagues (2010) found that, while younger individuals tended to make more disadvantageous choices on the IGT as compared to older individuals, this imbalance tapers off around 14 years of age.

Given that the goal of the task is to measure switching from the disadvantageous to the advantageous decks, it is not surprising that repeated administrations of the IGT have been found to lead to marked practice effects from one administration to the next in neurologically healthy participants (Buelow and Suhr, 2009; Lejuez *et al.*, 2003). Currently, it is less clear if the same marked effects occur with more impaired participants (Bechara, personal communication). Future work with both neurologically healthy and impaired participants will be important to develop a clear understanding of practice effects on the task, and the conditions under which the task can and cannot be used effectively in a repeated measures design.

2.7 Rogers Decision Making Task (RDMT)

A task that is similar in many ways to the IGT, but which is less focused on learning a specific dichotomy of disadvantageous and advantageous responses, is the Rogers Decision Making Task (Rogers *et al.*, 1999b). In the RDMT, subjects are presented with a display of a mixture of 10 red and blue boxes, and must decide whether they think a yellow token is hidden under a red box or a blue box. This is a relatively simple probabilistic decision, and the ratio of red to blue boxes (9:1, 8:2, 7:3, 6:4) varies from trial to trial in a randomized manner. Token location is pre-specified and pseudo-randomized; hence the probability of the subject choosing correctly is independent on each trial. Because of this independence between trials, the RDMT addresses the learning issues of the IGT. The subject indicates his/her decision by touching a response panel marked either "red" or "blue." After making this initial choice, the subject attempts to increase their score by placing a bet (5, 25, 50, 75 or 95% of the points available) on their confidence in their decision being correct. Each bet is displayed for a period of 5 seconds before being replaced by the next, and subjects must touch the box when they feel the displayed amount is an appropriate bet. Following bet selection, the token location is revealed. Correct choices increase the points total by the amount bet, while incorrect choices decrease the points total by the amount bet. Good decision making on the task consists of choosing the favorite consistently, and without long deliberation (Monterosso *et al.*, 2001). Similar results found with the IGT have been found with the RDMT. Specifically, chronic amphetamine abusers showed riskier decisions (correlated with years of abuse) than chronic opiate users or healthy controls who were given a tryptophan-depleting amino acid to reduce central 5-hydroxytryptamine (5-HT; serotonin) activity. Moreover, both chronic opiate users and amphetamine users deliberated for significantly longer on the task (Rogers *et al.*, 1999a). This pattern in amphetamine abusers is similar to that seen in patients with damage to the orbitofrontal PFC.

3   Future Directions

Researchers have an array of laboratory risk-taking tasks from which to choose when studying the role of risk taking and related processes within the field of substance use. The abundance of behavioral tasks developed to assess these processes is an asset to the field, given the theoretical and empirical relevance of risk taking to substance use, abuse, and dependence. Much has been learned about the processes underlying substance use and addictive behavior by employing behavioral analogues of risk taking; however, clear gaps remain in the extant literature. We now highlight two specific gaps that provide important future directions that can be pursued by utilizing behavioral risk-taking tasks in the study of substance use and risk taking.

3.1   Tasks to assess risk taking motivated by non-appetitive processes

Within the extant literature, the focus among available tasks is largely on appetitive stimuli (i.e., risk behavior resulting in some tangible reward). Within the existing tasks, the WOF task includes a version where one can pass on trials focused on potential losses as opposed to gains (Roy *et al.*, 2011). Additionally, a variant of the IGT has been developed (IGT-Variant Task (EFGH); Bechara, Tranel, and Damasio, 2000) in which the advantageous decks include high immediate losses but even higher future rewards, and the disadvantageous decks include small immediate losses, but even smaller future rewards. Within the field of substance use, performance on the

EFGH version of the IGT has been associated with real-world indicators of addiction severity, including psychiatric, employment, alcohol, and legal problems, among a sample of treatment-seeking substance-dependent individuals (Verdejo-Garcia, Bechara, Recknor, and Perez-Garcia, 2006).

Although these tasks examine risk behavior where the negative consequences are highlighted, the focus is on being less risky and avoiding a risk-related punisher. What was not previously available is a task that focuses on increased risk behavior motivated by avoiding negative stimuli (i.e., negative reinforcement). To address this issue, the Maryland Resource for the Behavioral Utilization of the Reinforcement of Negative Stimuli (MRBURNS) is a modified version of the positive reinforcement-based BART (MacPherson *et al.*, 2012) developed to measure negative reinforcement mechanisms underlying risk taking. In contrast to the BART, where a participant inflates a balloon to earn money, the MRBURNS involves a participant inflating a balloon to limit the duration of exposure to an aversive event, which is 19.2 seconds of 85 decibels (dB) white noise with an intermittent boat horn effect to limit habituation. MRBURNS uses pre-selection of the inflation value at the start of a balloon, as is used for the automatic version of the BART. Based on the number selected at the start of the balloon, the aversive noise duration is reduced by 0.15 seconds for each pump. The primary index of risk taking on the MRBURNS is average number of pumps. As with the BART, each balloon has an explosion point. To replicate the way that consequences of negative reinforcement responses occur in real-world settings, the consequence for a balloon exploding is a reduction in the probability that a participant will win a lottery at the end of the task. Specifically, the participant begins with a guaranteed win of the lottery, but the likelihood of winning is reduced with each exploded balloon. This choice in the design of the task was made to ensure a focus on explosions as opportunity costs.

The MRBURNS was recently validated in a sample of 18–19-year-old college students who reported having ever had a period of regular alcohol use (MacPherson *et al.*, 2012). The MRBURNS evidenced good psychometric properties, including high internal reliability, as evidenced by robust correlations across both halves of the task ($r = 0.90$) and across three different monetary lottery values ($r = 0.69$–0.88), convergent validity, as evidenced by positive correlations ($r = 0.22$–0.33) between average number of pumps and negative urgency, difficulties with emotion regulation, and depression and anxiety-related symptoms, and discriminant validity, as indicated by non-significant correlations ($r = 0.05$–0.15) between average pumps on the MRBURNS and performance on the original BART and self-reported sensation seeking and impulsivity. Moreover, engagement in negative reinforcement-based risk taking on the MRBURNS (i.e., higher average number of pumps to reduce the duration of the aversive noise) was positively correlated with number of alcohol-related problems ($r = 0.21$), as well as self-reported negative reinforcement-based alcohol use motives ($r = 0.28$–0.29). As such, this initial study demonstrates that MRBURNS may be a novel, effective behavioral analogue of negative reinforcement processes underlying risk taking. Additional research is needed to examine the extent to which performance on the MRBURNS can predict substance use outcomes across drug classes, and within more severe clinical samples.

3.2   Using performance on behavioral risk-taking tasks as a proxy for risky behavior

A relative advantage of behavioral measures over self-report measures of risk taking is that they can be administered repeatedly over time and in different contexts to assess changes in performance as a function of a particular experimental manipulation. A growing body of risk-taking research has utilized behavioral risk-taking tasks, including the BART in particular, as a proxy for risk taking. For instance, Lighthall, Mather, and Gorlick (2009) examined sex differences in risk taking on the BART as a function of a stress induction. Results indicated that stress increased risk taking among men, but decreased risk taking among women. Other recent studies show the influence of a variety of contextual factors, such as peer pressure and framing of gains versus losses, suggesting the viability of this type of research for answering important questions about the contextual determinants of risk behavior (e.g., Reynolds, 2011). However, it is important to note that not all contextual factors have been shown to produce expected changes on these tasks. For example, psychoactive drug challenges have not always shown a clear impact on risk behavior task performance (Hamidovic, Kang, and de Wit, 2008; Reynolds, Richards, Dassinger, and de Wit, 2004; van Eimeren *et al.*, 2009; for an exception, see White, Lejuez, and de Wit, 2007); however, more research is required to fully understand how these tasks can be used to study acute pharmacological effects.

4   Conclusions

In conclusion, a number of behavioral measures of risk taking are available for investigating the role of risk taking in addictive behavior. Overall, these behavioral paradigms have provided new opportunities and insights within the field of substance use and addiction. However, there are clear opportunities for expanding our knowledge base of the relationship between risk taking and substance use, across the spectrum from initiation to clinical outcomes. In the future, it will be important to investigate potential moderators in order to expand beyond what is globally related to risk taking and move toward a higher level of predictive specificity. Additionally, it is largely unclear how performance on behavioral assessments is related across task type and, in some cases, how individual processes within single tasks are related. Thus, considerably more work is needed to determine the extent to which these assessments capture important and unique aspects of real-world risk behavior, but the prospect for important advances in this area is high.

References

Addicott MA, Baranger DAA, Kozink RV, Smoski MJ, Dichter GS, and McClernon FJ (2011) Smoking withdrawal is associated with increases in brain activation during decision making and reward anticipation: A preliminary study. *Psychopharmacology*. doi: 10.1007/s00213-011-2404-3.

Aklin WM, Lejuez C, Zvolensky MJ, Kahler CW, and Gwadz M (2005) Evaluation of behavioral measures of risk taking propensity with inner city adolescents. *Behaviour Research and Therapy* 43: 215–228.

American Psychiatric Association (2000) *Diagnostic and Statistical Manual of Mental Disorders* (4th edn, rev.). Washington, DC: American Psychiatric Association.

Baker F, Johnson MW, and Bickel WK (2003) Delay discounting in current and never-before cigarette smokers: Similarities and differences across commodity, sign, and magnitude. *Journal of Abnormal Psychology* 112: 382–392.

Baseman J, Ross M, and Williams M (1999) Sale of sex for drugs and drugs for sex: An economic context of sexual risk behavior for STDs. *Sexually Transmitted Diseases* 26: 444–449.

Bechara A, Damasio AR, Damasio H, and Anderson SW (1994) Insensitivity to future consequences following damage to human prefrontal cortex 1. *Cognition* 50: 7–15.

Bechara A, Dolan S, Denburg N, Hindes A, Anderson SW, and Nathan PE (2001) Decision making deficits, linked to a dysfunctional ventromedial prefrontal cortex, revealed in alcohol and stimulant abusers 1. *Neuropsychologia* 39: 376–389.

Bechara A, Tranel D, and Damasio H (2000) Characterization of the decision making deficit of patients with ventromedial prefrontal cortex lesions. *Brain* 123: 2189–2202.

Bolla K, Eldreth DA, London ED, Kiehl KA, Mouratidis M, Contoreggi C, Matochik JA, Kurian V, Cadet JL, and Kimes AS (2003) Orbitofrontal cortex dysfunction in abstinent cocaine abusers performing a decision making task. *Neuroimage* 19: 1085–1094.

Bornovalova MA, Daughters SB, Hernandez GD, Richards JB, and Lejuez C (2005) Differences in impulsivity and risk-taking propensity between primary users of crack cocaine and primary users of heroin in a residential substance-use program. *Experimental and Clinical Psychopharmacology* 13: 311–318.

Büchel C, Brassen S, Yacubian J, Kalisch R, and Sommer T (2011) Ventral striatal signal changes represent missed opportunities and predict future choice. *NeuroImage* 57: 1124–1130.

Buelow MT and Suhr JA (2009) Construct validity of the Iowa gambling task. *Neuropsychology Review* 19: 102–114.

Byrnes JP, Miller DC, and Schafer WD (1999) Gender differences in risk taking: A meta-analysis. *Psychological Bulletin* 125: 367–383.

Cauffman E, Shulman EP, Steinberg L, Claus E, Banich MT, Graham S, and Woolard J (2010) Age differences in affective decision making as indexed by performance on the Iowa Gambling Task. *Developmental Psychology* 46: 193–207.

Cloninger CR (1987) Neurogenetic adaptive mechanisms in alcoholism. *Science* 236: 410–416.

Cohen JD (2005) The vulcanization of the human brain: A neural perspective on interactions between cognition and emotion. *Journal of Economic Perspectives* 19: 3–24.

Cole DM, Beckmann CF, Long CJ, Matthews PM, Durcan MJ, and Beaver JD (2010) Nicotine replacement in abstinent smokers improves cognitive withdrawal symptoms with modulation of resting brain network dynamics. *NeuroImage* 52: 590–599.

Crisan LG, Pan S, Vulturar R, Heilman RM, Szekely R, Drug B, Drago N, and Miu AC (2009) Genetic contributions of the serotonin transporter to social learning of fear and economic decision making. *Social Cognitive and Affect Neuroscience* 4: 399–408.

Crowley TJ, Raymond KM, Mikulich-Gilbertson SK, Thompson LL, and Lejuez CW (2006) A risk-taking "set" in a novel task among adolescents with serious conduct and substance problems. *Journal of the American Academy of Child Adolescent Psychiatry* 45: 175–183.

Eisenegger C, Knoch D, Ebstein RP, Gianotti LRR, Sándor PS, and Fehr E (2010) Dopamine receptor D4 polymorphism predicts the effect of L-DOPA on gambling behavior. *Biological Psychiatry* 67: 702–706.

Ernst M, Dickstein DP, Munson S, Eshel N, Pradella A, Jazbec S, Pine DS, and Leibenluft E (2004) Reward-related processes in pediatric bipolar disorder: A pilot study. *Journal of Affect Disorders* 82: S89–S101.

Ernst M, Nelson EE, Jazbec S, McClure EB, Monk CS, Leibenluft E, Blair J, and Pine DS (2005) Amygdala and nucleus accumbens in responses to receipt and omission of gains in adults and adolescents. *NeuroImage* 25: 1279–1291.

Eshel N, Nelson EE, Blair RJ, Pine DS, and Ernst M (2007) Neural substrates of choice selection in adults and adolescents: Development of the ventrolateral prefrontal and anterior cingulate cortices. *Neuropsychologia* 45: 1270–1279.

Eshel N, Nelson EE, Blair RJ, Pine DS, Ernst M, and Paulus MP (2005) Neurobiology of decision making: A selective review from a neurocognitive and clinical perspective. *Biological Psychiatry* 58: 597–604.

Evans DE and Drobes DJ (2009) Nicotine self medication of cognitive attentional processing. *Addiction Biology* 14: 32–42.

Fernie G, Cole JC, Goudie AJ, and Field M (2010) Risk-taking but not response inhibition or delay discounting predict alcohol consumption in social drinkers. *Drug and Alcohol Dependence* 112: 54–61.

Figner B and Weber EU (2011) Who takes risks when and why? Determinants of risk taking. *Current Directions in Psychological Science* 20: 211–216.

Figner B, Mackinlay RJ, Wilkening F, and Weber EU (2009) Affective and deliberative processes in risky choice: Age differences in risk taking in the Columbia Card Task. *Journal of Experimental Psychology: Learning, Memory, and Cognition* 35: 709.

Franken IHA and Muris P (2005) Individual differences in decision-making. *Personality and Individual Differences* 39: 991–998.

Grant S, Contoreggi C, and London ED (2000) Drug abusers show impaired performance in a laboratory test of decision making 1. *Neuropsychologia* 38: 1180–1187.

Guyer AE, Kaufman J, Hodgdon HB, Masten CL, Jazbec S, Pine DS, and Ernst M (2006) Behavioral alterations in reward system function: The role of childhood maltreatment and psychopathology. *Journal of the American Academy of Child and Adolescent Psychiatry* 45: 1059–1067.

Hamidovic A, Kang UJ, and de Wit H (2008) Effects of low to moderate acute doses of pramipexole on impulsivity and cognition in healthy volunteers. *Journal of Clinical Psychopharmacology* 28(1): 45–51.

Hardin MG, Pine DS, and Ernst M (2009) The influence of context valence in the neural coding of monetary outcomes. *NeuroImage* 48: 249–257.

He Q, Xue G, Chen C, Lu Z, Dong Q, Lei X, Ding N, Li J, and Li H (2010) Serotonin transporter gene-linked polymorphic region (5-HTTLPR) influences decision making under ambiguity and risk in a large Chinese sample. *Neuropharmacology* 59: 518–526.

Heishma SJ, Taylor RC, and Henningfield JE (1994) Nicotine and smoking: A review of effects on human performance. *Experimental and Clinical Psychopharmacology* 2: 345–395.

Hoffrage U, Weber A, Hertwig R, and Chase VM (2003) How to keep children safe in traffic: Find the daredevils early. *Journal of Experimental Psychology: Applied* 9: 249–260.

Hommer DW, Bjork JM, and Gilman JM (2011) Imaging brain response to reward in addictive disorders. *Annals of the New York Academy of Sciences* 1216: 50–61.

Jessor R and Jessor SL (1977) *Problem Behavior and Psychosocial Development: A Longitudinal Study of Youth.* New York: Academic Press.

Krueger RF, Hicks BM, Patrick CJ, Carlson SR, Iacono WG, and McGue M (2002) Etiologic connections among substance dependence, antisocial behavior and personality: Modeling the externalizing spectrum. *Journal of Abnormal Psychology* 111: 411–424.

Leigh BC (1999) Peril, chance, adventure: Concepts of risk, alcohol use and risky behavior in young adults. *Addiction* 94: 371–383.

Lejuez CW, Aklin W, Daughters S, Zvolensky M, Kahler C, and Gwadz M (2007) Reliability and validity of the youth version of the Balloon Analogue Risk Task (BART-Y) in the assessment of risk-taking behavior among inner-city adolescents. *Journal of Clinical Child and Adolescent Psychology* 36: 106–111.

Lejuez CW, Aklin WM, Jones HA, Richards JB, Strong DR, Kahler CW, and Read JP (2003) The balloon analogue risk task (BART) differentiates smokers and nonsmokers. *Experimental and Clinical Psychopharmacology* 11: 26–33.

Lejuez CW, Aklin WM, Zvolensky MJ, and Pedulla CM (2003) Evaluation of the Balloon Analogue Risk Task (BART) as a predictor of adolescent real-world risk-taking behaviours. *Journal of Adolescence* 26: 475–479.

Lejuez, CW, Magidson, JF, Mitchell, SH, Sinha, R, Stevens, MC, and DeWit, H (2010) Behavioral and biological indicators of impulsivity in the development of alcohol use, problems, and disorders. *Alcoholism: Clinical and Experimental Research* 34: 1334–1345.

Lejuez CW, Read JP, Kahler CW, Richards JB, Ramsey SE, Stuart GL, Strong DR, and Brown RA (2002) Evaluation of a behavioral measure of risk taking: The Balloon Analogue Risk Task (BART). *Journal of Experimental Psychology: Applied* 8: 75–84.

Lejuez CW, Simmons BL, Aklin WM, Daughters SB, and Dvir S (2004) Risk-taking propensity and risky sexual behavior of individuals in residential substance use treatment. *Addictive Behaviors* 29: 1643–1647.

Lighthall NR, Mather M, and Gorlick MA (2009) Acute stress increases sex differences in risk seeking in the Balloon Analogue Risk Task. *PLoS One* 4: e6002.

MacKillop J, Miranda Jr R, Monti PM, Ray LA, Murphy JG, Rohsenow DJ, McGeary JE, Swift RM, Tidey JW, and Gwaltney CJ (2010) Alcohol demand, delayed reward discounting, and craving in relation to drinking and alcohol use disorders. *Journal of Abnormal Psychology* 119: 106–114.

MacPherson L, Calvin NT, Richards JM, Guller L, and Lejuez CW (2012) Development and preliminary validation of a behavioral task of negative reinforcement underlying risk-taking and its relation to problem alcohol use in college freshmen, *Alcoholism: Clinical and Experimental Research* 36: 426-433.

MacPherson L, Magidson JF, Reynolds EK, Kahler CW, and Lejuez C (2010a) Changes in sensation seeking and risk taking propensity predict increases in alcohol use among early adolescents. *Alcoholism: Clinical and Experimental Research* 34: 1400–1408.

MacPherson L, Reynolds EK, Daughters SB, Wang F, Cassidy J, Mayes LC, and Lejuez C (2010b) Positive and negative reinforcement underlying risk behavior in early adolescents. *Prevention Science* 11: 331–342.

McClure SM, Laibson DI, Loewenstein G, and Cohen JD (2004) Separate neural systems value immediate and delayed monetary rewards. *Science* 306: 503–507.

Meda SA, Stevens MC, Potenza MN, Pittman B, Gueorguieva R, Andrews MM, Thomas AD, Muska C, Hylton JL, and Pearlson GD (2009) Investigating the behavioral and self-report constructs of impulsivity domains using principal component analysis. *Behavioural Pharmacology* 20: 390–399.

Monterosso J, Ehrman R, Napier KL, O'Brien CP, and Childress AR (2001) Three decision making tasks in cocaine dependent patients: Do they measure the same construct? *Addiction* 96: 1825–1837.

Montgomery GT and Landers WF (1974) Transmission of risk-taking through modeling at two age levels. *Psychological Reports* 34: 1187–1196.

Petry NM (2001) Substance abuse, pathological gambling, and impulsiveness. *Drug and Alcohol Dependence* 63: 29–38.

Petry NM, Bickel WK, and Arnett M (1998) Shortened time horizons and insensitivity to future consequences in heroin addicts. *Addiction* 93: 729–738.

Pleskac TJ (2008) Decision making and learning while taking sequential risks. *Journal of Experimental Psychology: Learning, Memory, and Cognition* 34: 167–185.

Pleskac TJ, Wallsten TS, Wang P, and Lejuez C (2008) Development of an automatic response mode to improve the clinical utility of sequential risk-taking tasks. *Experimental and Clinical Psychopharmacology* 16: 555–564.

Rao H, Korczykowski M, Pluta J, Hoang A, and Detre JA (2008) Neural correlates of voluntary and involuntary risk taking in the human brain: An fMRI study of the Balloon Analog Risk Task (BART). *NeuroImage* 42: 902–910.

Rao U, Sidhartha T, Harker KR, Bidesi AS, Chen LA, and Ernst M (2011) Relationship between adolescent risk preferences on a laboratory task and behavioral measures of risk-taking. *Journal of Adolescent Health* 48: 151–158.

Reynolds B, Richards JB, Dassinger M, and de Wit H (2004) Therapeutic doses of diazepam do not alter impulsive behavior in humans. *Pharmacolology Biochemistry and Behavior* 79: 17–24.

Reynolds EK (2011) Analogue study of peer influence on risk-taking behavior in older adolescents, Dissertation, University of Maryland, College Park.

Rogers R, Everitt B, Baldacchino A, Blackshaw A, Swainson R, Wynne K, Baker N, Hunter J, Carthy T and Booker E (1999a) Dissociable deficits in the decision making cognition of chronic amphetamine abusers, opiate abusers, patients with focal damage to prefrontal cortex, and tryptophan-depleted normal volunteers: Evidence for monoaminergic mechanisms. *Neuropsychopharmacology* 20: 322–339.

Rogers RD, Owen AM, Middleton HC, Williams EJ, Pickard JD, Sahakian BJ, and Robbins TW (1999b) Choosing between small, likely rewards and large, unlikely rewards activates inferior and orbital prefrontal cortex. *Journal of Neuroscience* 19: 9029–9038.

Ross MW, Hwang LY, Leonard L, Teng M, and Duncan L (1999) Sexual behaviour, STDs and drug use in a crack house population. *International Journal of STD and AIDS* 10: 224–230.

Ross MW, Hwang LY, Zack C, Bull L, and Williams ML (2002) Sexual risk behaviours and STIs in drug abuse treatment populations whose drug of choice is crack cocaine. *International Journal of STD and AIDS* 13: 769–774.

Roy AK, Gotimer K, Kelly AMC, Castellanos FX, Milham MP, and Ernst M (2011) Uncovering putative neural markers of risk avoidance. *Neuropsychologia* 49: 937–944.

Slovic P (1966) Risk-taking in children: Age and sex differences. *Child Development* 37: 169–176.

Smith BW, Mitchell DGV, Hardin MG, Jazbec S, Fridberg D, Blair RJR, and Ernst M (2009) Neural substrates of reward magnitude, probability, and risk during a wheel of fortune decision making task. *NeuroImage* 44: 600–609.

Stanford MS, Mathias CW, Dougherty DM, Lake SL, Anderson NE, and Patton JH (2009) Fifty years of the Barratt Impulsiveness Scale: An update and review. *Personality and Individual Differerences* 47: 385–395.

Suhr JA and Tsanadis J (2007) Affect and personality correlates of the Iowa Gambling Task. *Personality and Individual Differences* 43: 27–36.

Vadhan NP, Hart CL, Haney M, van Gorp WG, and Foltin RW (2009) Decision making in long-term cocaine users: Effects of a cash monetary contingency on Gambling Task performance. *Drug and Alcohol Dependence* 102: 95–101.

van Honk J, Hermans EJ, Putman P, Montagne B, and Schutter DJLG (2002) Defective somatic markers in sub-clinical psychopathy. *NeuroReport* 13: 1025.

van Eimeren T, Ballanger B, Pellecchia G, Miyasaki JM, Lang AE, and Strafella AP (2009) Dopamine agonists diminish value sensitivity of the orbitofrontal cortex: A trigger for pathological gambling in Parkinson's Disease? *Neuropsychopharmacology* 34: 2758–2766.

Verdejo-Garcia A, Bechara A, Recknor EC, and Perez-Garcia M (2006) Decision making and the Iowa Gambling Task: Ecological validity in individuals with substance dependence. *Psychologica Belgica* 46: 55–78.

Verdejo-Garcia A, Benbrook A, Funderburk F, David P, Cadet JL, and Bolla KI (2007) The differential relationship between cocaine use and marijuana use on decision-making performance over repeat testing with the Iowa Gambling Task. *Drug and Alcohol Dependence* 90: 2–11.

Wallsten TS, Pleskac TJ, and Lejuez C (2005) Modeling behavior in a clinically diagnostic sequential risk-taking task. *Psychological Review* 112: 862–880.

White TL, Lejuez C, and de Wit H (2007) Personality and gender differences in effects of d-amphetamine on risk taking. *Experimental and Clinical Psychopharmacology* 15: 599–609.

White TL, Lejuez C, and de Wit H (2008) Test-retest characteristics of the Balloon Analogue Risk Task (BART). *Experimental and Clinical Psychopharmacology* 16: 565–570.

Zermatten A, Van der Linden M, d'Acremont M, Jermann F, and Bechara A (2005) Impulsivity and decision making. *Journal of Nervous and Mental Disease* 193: 647–650.

9

Distress Tolerance

Jessica F. Magidson, Bina Ali, Alyson Listhaus, and Stacey B. Daughters

1 Introduction

Negative reinforcement models of addiction posit that the motivational basis for substance use is the reduction or avoidance of negative affective states (Baker *et al.*, 2004). More specifically, abstinence from substance use creates physical and psychological withdrawal states that contribute to overall negative affect, including feelings of irritability, anxiety, stress, and depression (Baker *et al.*, 2004). Substance use provides perceived and/or actual relief from negative affective states, thereby reinforcing this behavior and increasing the likelihood of substance use in the future. It has also been suggested that negative reinforcement processes underlie the initiation of substance use, as individuals are seeking to reduce negative affective states (Eissenberg, 2004). Taken together, a fundamental component of negative reinforcement models is that intra-individual differences in wanting to reduce or avoid negative affective states are a principal motive in the development and maintenance of substance use.

1.1 Distress tolerance

Early empirical support for negative reinforcement models of addiction relied heavily on animal models (see Shaham, Erb, and Stewart, 2000, for a review), yet recent work focusing on the concept of distress tolerance has bridged this knowledge to human models. Distress tolerance is most often defined as an individual's self-reported perceived ability to experience and endure negative emotional states (e.g., Simons and Gaher, 2005), or the behavioral ability to persist in goal-directed activity while experiencing affective distress (e.g., Daughters *et al.*, 2005a). There is also a behavioral physical dimension, defining distress tolerance as the capacity to tolerate aversive physiological states (e.g., Bernstein, Trafton, Ilgen, and Zvolensky, 2008). The distress tolerance assessment paradigms are unique in that they (a) measure a self-report or

The Wiley-Blackwell Handbook of Addiction Psychopharmacology, First Edition. Edited by James MacKillop and Harriet de Wit.
© 2013 John Wiley & Sons, Ltd. Published 2013 by John Wiley & Sons, Ltd.

behavioral response to physical and psychological distress as highlighted in negative reinforcement models (Baker *et al.*, 2004; Mello and Mendelson, 1970; Parrott, 1999; Wikler, 1977; Zinser, Baker, Sherman, and Cannon, 1992); and (b) help bridge the knowledge gleaned from patterns of animal drug reinstatement to human models of addiction.

Despite its utility as an index of negative reinforcement behavior, the measurement of distress tolerance has not been an easy or well-agreed-upon pursuit. Some researchers have relied more heavily on self-reported distress tolerance while others have focused on behavioral measurement approaches. There are also multiple variations within both self-report and behavioral assessment approaches. Moreover, evidence has pointed to the fact that these methods are often more unrelated than related to each other and may be predictive of distinct outcomes (McHugh *et al.*, 2010). Consequently, a focus on methods is timely. Improving our understanding of the assessment of distress tolerance has the potential to increase methodological rigor and precision as well as ultimately to increase the clinical utility of this construct.

The aim of this chapter is to provide a comprehensive overview of methods to measure distress tolerance across varying approaches and perspectives. Our hope is that through a comprehensive review of assessment methods, and how these methods link to distinct aspects of substance use, we will provide a strong sense of the multiple dimensions of this construct. The ultimate aim is not to identify a single "best" method to assess distress tolerance, but rather to provide sufficient evidence to demonstrate how specific methods of measuring distress tolerance are differentially related to substance use outcomes and highlight specific areas for future research.

2   Empirical Relevance of Distress Tolerance to Substance Abuse Research

Empirical evidence indicates that distress tolerance is associated with multiple stages of substance use, including initiation, continuation and frequency of use, and relapse. In adolescence, low distress tolerance is associated with higher rates of alcohol use in early adolescence (Daughters *et al.*, 2009; MacPherson *et al.*, 2010). Into adulthood, low distress tolerance is associated with greater frequency of substance use, in studies examining cigarette smoking (Marshall *et al.*, 2008; Quinn, Brandon, and Copeland, 1996), problematic alcohol use (Howell *et al.*, 2010; Simons and Gaher, 2005), and illicit drug use (O'Cleirigh, Ironson, and Smits, 2007; Quinn, Brandon, and Copeland, 1996).

At more clinical levels of substance use, low distress tolerance is associated with early relapse (Abrantes *et al.*, 2008; Brown, Lejuez, Kahler, and Strong, 2002; Brown *et al.*, 2009) and 12-month relapse status among cigarette smokers (Brandon *et al.*, 2003). Further, a laboratory study demonstrated decreases in distress tolerance over a 12-hour smoking deprivation period, suggesting a critical role of distress tolerance in early smoking abstinence (Bernstein, Trafton, Ilgen, and Zvolensky, 2008). Regarding other forms of substance use, low distress tolerance is associated with a shorter duration of most recent drug abstinence attempt among adult illicit substance users (Daughters *et al.*, 2005b), as well as early dropout from residential substance abuse treatment

(Daughters *et al.*, 2005a). In addition to actual engagement in substance use, low distress tolerance is associated with greater self-reported coping motives for alcohol, marijuana, and cocaine use (Howell *et al.*, 2010; Simons and Gaher, 2005; O'Cleirigh, Ironson, and Smits, 2007; Zvolensky *et al.*, 2009).

Despite clear evidence for a relationship between distress tolerance and multiple substance use outcomes, more nuanced relationships exist when the focus turns to assessment. In the aforementioned studies, ten different approaches were used to measure distress tolerance, ranging in focus from self-report to behavioral, and physical to psychological distress. Indeed, distinct patterns emerge when close attention is paid to how each measurement approach differentially predicts substance use variables. In the next section, we provide an overview of the empirically supported methods to assess distress tolerance, with a summary of how these distinct methods relate to specific substance use outcomes.

3   Standardized and Validated Methods and Methodological Recommendations

As indicated above, a wide range of methods exist to assess distress tolerance, and these can be categorized according to two distinct domains: self-report versus behavioral measures; and within behavioral approaches, both physical and psychological measures.

3.1   Self-report assessment of distress tolerance

3.1.1   Distress Tolerance Scale.   The Distress Tolerance Scale (DTS; Simons and Gaher, 2005) is a 14-item self-report measure that assesses one's perceived ability to withstand negative emotional states. The DTS has four subscales, comprising (1) ability to *tolerate* emotional distress (e.g., "I can't handle feeling distressed or upset"); (2) subjective *appraisal* of distress (e.g., "My feelings of distress or being upset are not acceptable"); (3) *absorption* of attention by negative emotions (e.g., "When I feel distressed or upset, I cannot help but concentrate on how bad the distress actually feels"); and (4) *regulation* efforts to alleviate distress (e.g., "When I feel distressed or upset, I must do something about it immediately"). Items are rated on a 5-point Likert scale ranging from "strongly agree" to "strongly disagree," with higher scores indicating higher levels of distress tolerance. Internal consistency for the total scale ranges from 0.82 to 0.93 across studies, and the subscales have also demonstrated good internal consistency across studies ($\alpha = 0.72–0.73$ for tolerate; $\alpha = 0.82–0.84$ for appraisal; $\alpha = 0.88–0.78$ for absorption; $\alpha = 0.70–0.74$ for regulation) (Buckner, Keough, and Schmidt, 2007; O'Cleirigh, Ironson, and Smits, 2007; Simons and Gaher, 2005; Zvolensky *et al.*, 2009).

3.1.2   Discomfort Intolerance Scale.   The Discomfort Intolerance Scale (DIS; Schmidt, Richey, and Fitzpatrick, 2006) is a 5-item self-report measure developed to assess "discomfort intolerance," defined as the capacity to withstand uncomfortable but non-painful bodily sensations (Schmidt, Richey, Cromer, and Buckner, 2007;

Schmidt, Richey, and Fitzpatrick, 2006). The DIS aims to measure the degree to which an individual believes he/she can tolerate uncomfortable physical sensations. The DIS comprises an overall discomfort intolerance scale as well as two subscales: (1) intolerance of discomfort or pain (e.g., "I can tolerate a great deal of physical discomfort" [reverse scored]) and (2) avoidance of physical discomfort (e.g., "I take extreme measures to avoid feeling physically uncomfortable"). Items are rated on a 0–6-point Likert scale based upon the degree to which the statement is applicable, ranging from "not at all like me" to "extremely like me," with higher scores indicating lower levels of discomfort tolerance. Internal consistency for the overall scale ranges from 0.70 to 0.72 across studies (Buckner, Keough, and Schmidt, 2007; Schmidt, Richey, and Fitzpatrick, 2006), and the two factors have also demonstrated good internal consistency across studies ($\alpha = 0.91$ for intolerance; $\alpha = 0.72$ for avoidance; Leyro, Zvolensky, Vujanovic, and Bernstein, 2008; Schmidt, Richey, Cromer, and Buckner, 2007).

3.1.3 Frustration–Discomfort Scale. The Frustration–Discomfort Scale (FDS; Harrington, 2005) is a 28-item self-report measure comprised of four seven-item subscales, with the first two being particularly relevant to the measurement of distress tolerance: (1) discomfort intolerance (demands that life should be easy, comfortable, and free of hassle [$\alpha = 0.88$]); (2) emotional intolerance (beliefs regarding uncertainty, controllability, and aversiveness of emotion [$\alpha = 0.87$]); (3) entitlement (demands for immediate gratification [$\alpha = 0.85$]); and (4) achievement-frustration (experiencing difficulties when seeking a specified goal [$\alpha = 0.84$]). Examples of items from the first two subscales most relevant to distress tolerance are "I can't stand having to persist at unpleasant tasks" (discomfort intolerance) and "I can't bear disturbing feelings" (emotional intolerance). Items are rated on a 5-point Likert scale ranging from "absent" to "very strong," with higher scores on the discomfort and emotional intolerance subscales indicating lower levels of discomfort/emotional tolerance. Of note, factor analysis has indicated a four-factor multidimensional model without a higher order (global frustration) tolerance factor (Harrington, 2005). The FDS has been shown to have excellent internal consistency for the full scale ($\alpha = 0.94$; Harrington, 2005) and good internal consistency for the four subscales (ranging from 0.84 to 0.88; Harrington, 2005; 2006).

3.1.4 Relationship between self-report measures and substance use. In sum, three distinct self-report measures exist to measure distress tolerance, with each capturing distinct aspects of the construct. The DTS, measuring the appraisal, tolerance, and regulation of emotional distress, is associated with substance use motives and substance use coping (Howell *et al.*, 2010; O'Cleirigh, Ironson, and Smits, 2007; Potter *et al.*, 2011; Simons and Gaher, 2005; Zvolensky *et al.*, 2009), as well as the development of alcohol and cannabis problems (Buckner, Keough, and Schmidt, 2007; Simons and Gaher, 2005). There have been mixed findings regarding the relationship between the DTS and alcohol use frequency, with some studies demonstrating a significant relationship between low distress tolerance on the DTS and increased self-reported frequency of alcohol and cannabis use (Buckner, Keough, and Schmidt,

2007; O'Cleirigh, Ironson, and Smits, 2007), while other studies demonstrate no relationship between the DTS and alcohol use frequency (Simons and Gaher, 2005).

Regarding cigarette-smoking outcomes, low distress tolerance measured using the DTS is associated with a greater number of smoking years and greater levels of nicotine dependence, but not daily smoking rate in daily smokers (Leyro *et al.*, 2011). In the same study, low distress tolerance was associated with increased endorsement of negative reinforcement as a result of smoking (e.g., "When I'm angry a cigarette can calm me down;" "Smoking reduces my anger"). Additionally, low distress tolerance on the DTS is associated with greater smoking reinforcement as indexed by higher rates of smoking following mood induction after overnight smoking abstinence (Perkins *et al.*, 2010).

Intolerance of uncomfortable bodily sensations measured using the DIS is associated with motives to use both tobacco (Leyro, Zvolensky, Vujanovic, and Bernstein, 2008) and alcohol (Howell *et al.*, 2010), including social enhancement motives and habitual reasons, and for negative affect reduction. The DIS is also related to substance use-related consequences and problems across cigarette smoking (Leyro, Zvolensky, Vujanovic, and Bernstein, 2008), alcohol use (Howell *et al.*, 2010), and cannabis use (Buckner, Keough, and Schmidt, 2007), as well as self-reported frequency of cigarette smoking (Marshall *et al.*, 2008) and alcohol use (Howell *et al.*, 2010).

There are no known studies to date which have examined the FDS in substance use research (cf. Ko *et al.*, 2008, who found a relationship between higher FDS discomfort intolerance subscale scores and greater levels of internet addiction); however, the overlap of this measure with the other measures of distress tolerance suggest its potential usefulness in this context.

3.2 Behavioral assessment of distress tolerance

Behavioral measures of distress tolerance include both physical and psychological distress tolerance. Each elicit physiological arousal and negative affect, and typically define distress tolerance continuously as persistence in seconds during the assessment task. A number of studies also define distress tolerance dichotomously as "quit" or "no quit," depending on whether or not the individual terminates the behavioral task.

3.2.1 *Physical distress tolerance*

3.2.1.1 THERMAL STRESS TASKS. The examination of the effects of thermal environmental conditions on humans has a longstanding empirical history (Blagden, 1775a; 1775b) and more recently has been applied to the measurement of distress tolerance specifically, capturing the capacity to endure stressful thermal conditions (Hancock, Ross, and Szalma, 2007). Three commonly utilized methods to measure thermal stress tolerance are the cold pressor task, full body cold and heat induced thermal stressors, and radiant heat stimulation.

The cold pressor task (CPT) involves placing an aversive but safe cold stimulus to the body in order to evoke distress (Burns, Bruehl, and Caceres, 2004; Hines and Brown, 1932; Neufeld and Thomas, 1977; Willoughby, Hailey, Mulkana, and Rowe, 2002).

Typically, the non-dominant hand and forearm are submerged in a bucket of ice water (typically 33 °F ± 1 °F), a stimulus that produces a gradual escalation of pain (Hines and Brown, 1932; Willoughby, Hailey, Mulkana, and Rowe, 2002). Participants are instructed to notify the experimenter when they begin to feel uncomfortable (i.e., one's "pain threshold"). They are then told to continue to keep their hand immersed in the cold water for as long as possible, but that they can remove their hand at any time. However, if the participant does not remove his/her hand typically before 5 minutes, the task is terminated to avoid potential harm (Hackett and Horan, 1980; Neufeld and Thomas, 1977; Willoughby, Hailey, Mulkana, and Rowe, 2002). Distress tolerance is typically measured as the time it takes for an individual to terminate the procedure by removing their hand (Burns, Bruehl, and Cacaeres, 2004; Hines and Brown, 1932). Endurance can also be calculated by subtracting one's "pain threshold" from their tolerance level to specify the period in which an individual persists in a state of pain/discomfort specifically (Neufeld and Thomas, 1977).

Thermal heat tolerance has been measured through full body heat induction consisting of an experimental procedure that exposes the whole body to extreme air temperatures over an extended period of time (see Hancock, Ross, and Szalma, 2007; Pilcher, Nadler, and Busch, 2002, for reviews). Although this has also been conducted for cold thermal stress conditions (i.e., temperatures less than 65 °F; Sharma and Panwar, 1987; Thomas, Ahlers, House, and Schrot, 1989; Van Orden, Benoit, and Osga, 1996), exposure to a heat thermal condition (i.e., temperatures of at least 70 °F; Hocking *et al.*, 2001; Hygge and Knez, 2001; Razmjou, 1996; Razmjou and Kjellberg, 1992) is more common. Thermal stressors of 90 °F or above (or 50 °F or below for cold thermal stressors) are most reliably and strongly correlated with poor cognitive-related task performances (Pilcher, Nadler, and Busch, 2002).

Radiant heat stimulation has also been used as a thermal heat stressor, which involves inducing cutaneous or skin surface pain, using extreme heat to measure distress. This is used to measure pain tolerance or get pain threshold ratings. Specifically, heat is often applied (e.g., through a light bulb) to the forehead (Kane, Nutter, and Weckowicz, 1971; Wolff and Jarvik, 1963), to the skin at one's wrist (Orbach *et al.*, 1996; Procacci, 1979), or to a finger of the dominant hand (Rhudy and Meagher, 2003). Participants are asked to report when they start to feel pain or notable bodily sensations in response to the heat (Kane, Nutter, and Weckowicz, 1971; Rhudy and Meagher, 2003), which is used as a measure of thermal heat tolerance. Although these methods have clear relevance to physical distress tolerance, thermal stressors are often utilized as more of an index of sensitivity to thermal heat or a measure of a pain threshold, rather than distress tolerance specifically. Findings in this area typically focus on the effects of negative mood in reducing pain tolerance following a mood induction (Zelman, Howland, Nichols, and Cleeland, 1991; Jones, Spindler, Jorgensen, and Zachariae, 2002; Schmidt and Cook, 1999; Uman, Stewart, Watt, and Johnson, 2006; Willoughby, Hailey, Mulkana, and Rowe, 2002). However, these methods have clear implications for distress tolerance assessment if a termination option is designated and distress tolerance is adequately defined.

3.2.1.2 BIOLOGICAL CHALLENGE TASKS. Physical distress tolerance has also been measured using biological challenges that manipulate oxygen and carbon dioxide

(CO_2) levels in a way that induces physiological activity associated with anxiety and arousal (Zvolensky and Eifert, 2000). The most common of these as applied to substance use research are breath holding (BH), the CO_2 challenge, and hyperventilation, which are all reviewed here. Across these tasks, measures of physiological arousal (e.g., heart and respiration rates; Marshall *et al.*, 2008) may be administered pre- and post- as manipulation check as well as to control for individual levels of arousal.

The breath holding (BH) challenge (Hajek, Belcher, and Stapleton, 1987) involves measuring the duration of breath holding as an index of distress tolerance. Specifically, participants are instructed to take a deep breath (sometimes following a period of normal breathing and a complete exhale) and hold it for as long as they can. They are asked to notify the experimenter when they begin to feel uncomfortable by holding up a sign that indicates they are feeling discomfort. However, as with the CPT, participants are instructed to continue holding their breath beyond that point of initial discomfort for as long as they can. Administration procedures may vary, for instance by repeating the BH challenge in a second trial after a brief rest period. Distress tolerance is typically defined as the maximum breath-holding duration (across trials when multiple trials are administered), or may also be measured as the latency in seconds between when the participant begins to feel uncomfortable and when they finally let out their breath (Brown, Lejuez, Kahler, and Strong, 2002; Hajek, 1991; Hajek, Belcher, and Stapleton, 1987; Zvolensky, Feldner, Eifert, and Brown, 2001).

A carbon dioxide (CO_2) challenge typically involves the inhalation of carbon dioxide-enriched air over a sequence of CO_2 presentations (e.g., 20% CO_2 enrichment; see Lejuez, Forsyth, and Eifert, 1998, for a review of devices and methods for administering CO_2-enriched air in experimental and clinical settings). Specifically, this may include multiple (typically two to three) trials separated by approximately 5 minutes, in which participants are presented with the carbon dioxide-enriched air for approximately 25 seconds (with the exception of the final trial). In the last trial, the participant determines the length of the final presentation. Specifically, once the final presentation of carbon dioxide-enriched air has begun, the participants can press a button on a computer keyboard to terminate the presentation at any time. If the participant does not press the button to end the task within a certain period of time (e.g., a maximum 30-second duration; Brown *et al.*, 2005), the presentation is automatically terminated. Distress tolerance is measured as the length of time before terminating the final trial (Brown *et al.*, 2005).

Hyperventilation as a measure of distress tolerance is conducted similarly to the carbon dioxide challenge, except voluntary hyperventilation is used instead of CO_2-enriched air delivery (Marshall *et al.*, 2008; Rosenthal, 1984). In this task, participants will typically sit alone in an experiment room while being guided through the hyperventilation procedure (typically audiotaped) and may be monitored by an experimenter (e.g., in an adjacent room using audiovisual equipment; Marshall *et al.*, 2008). The procedure typically involves an initial baseline adaptation period (e.g., 10 minutes), followed by a period of voluntary hyperventilation (e.g., 3 minutes), then a 10-minute recovery period. Next, participants have a final voluntary hyperventilation period (i.e., the "distressing" phase), in which participants are instructed to continue for as long as possible but can discontinue (i.e., stop the tape and breathe normally) at any time when they feel they can no longer continue. Participants are unaware that if they had not terminated (e.g., before 5 minutes), the procedure would have automatically ended. Lastly, participants typically have a final recovery period. The duration of time it takes for the participant to terminate the task (e.g., in seconds) during the final voluntary hyperventilation trial is typically used as the index of distress tolerance.

3.2.2 Psychological distress tolerance.   Early work measuring distress tolerance with behavioral assessment utilized two psychologically stressful tasks, including the Anagram Persistence Task (APT), in which participants were asked to solve a series of difficult anagrams, and the Mirror Tracing Persistence Task (MTPT), in which partic-ipants must trace difficult geometric shapes while looking at the shape only through a mirror with all aspects of the shaped reversed (Quinn, Brandon, and Copeland, 1996). Later, computerized behavioral measures of distress tolerance were developed, including the Paced Auditory Serial Addition Task (PASAT-C; Lejuez, Kahler, and Brown, 2003) and the computerized Mirror Tracing Persistence Task (MTPT-C; Strong *et al.*, 2003). Typically, a subjective distress scale is administered pre- and post-stress exposure as a stressor manipulation check, as well as to control for levels of subjective distress.

3.2.2.1 ANAGRAM PERSISTENCE TASK.   Anagram persistence tasks (APT) involve presenting participants with difficult anagrams, the formation of words by rearranging letters, to examine duration spent on unsolved anagrams (Eisenberger and Leonard, 1980). Specifically, participants are typically given a stack of numbered index cards (e.g., 11 cards; Brandon *et al.*, 2003; or 21 cards; Quinn, Brandon, and Copeland, 1996) with a different anagram printed on each card and an anagram solution sheet with the same number of lines. Participants attempt to solve each anagram trial in a row, with a mix (i.e., 2 to 5) of relatively easy-to-solve anagrams (e.g., CEABH = BEACH), with the remaining anagrams being extremely difficult to solve with very obscure words (e.g., LXYIK = KYLIK). Each trial is timed by an experimenter, and participants are instructed to notify the experimenter (e.g., by raising one's hand or verbally; Postman and Solomon, 1950) that they have reached a solution (to receive a point) or that they cannot solve the word and would like to move on (Eisenberger and Leonard, 1980). If the participant has not solved the anagram or moved on within 3 (Quinn, Brandon, and Copeland, 1996) to 4 minutes (Brandon *et al.*, 2003), the participant is told to move onto the next anagram. Of note, the points are assigned simply to track the number of anagrams accurately solved and not necessarily to be used as a reward for performance. The measure of distress tolerance in this task is typically calculated as the mean time spent on the difficult (unsolved) anagram trials before giving up and proceeding to the next anagram (Quinn, Brandon, and Copeland, 1996). Coefficient alpha reliability of this measure has been demonstrated to be high (i.e., calculated across six separate trials among smokers = 0.85; Brandon *et al.*, 2003).

3.2.2.2 MIRROR TRACING PERSISTENCE TASK (MTPT).   The Mirror Tracing Persistence Task involves hand tracing an outline of a geometric figure (e.g., a star), while observing one's own hand movements in a mirror (Matthews and Stoney, 1988; Quinn, Brandon, and Copeland, 1996). The MTPT has been shown to frustrate patients and to increase stress, pulse rate, and blood pressure (Matthews and Stoney, 1988; Tutoo, 1971). The MTPT task was designed to be analogous to the anagram task but to measure persistence using a motor as opposed to a cognitive task. Typically there are eight different mirror-tracing trials, with the first and last trials designed to be relatively easy to complete (i.e. simple line drawings), whereas the second to seventh trials are extremely difficult drawings to trace and are never successfully completed by participants. An experimenter records the time spent on each trial, and as with the APT, participants are instructed to move on if they successfully trace the current shape or give up. Participants are instructed to move onto the next trial after 5 minutes. The measure of distress tolerance using the MTPT typically is calculated as the mean time spent on all unsuccessfully completed trials. The coefficient alpha for this task has been shown to be 0.92 (Brandon *et al.*, 2003).

3.2.2.3   COMPUTERIZED MIRROR TRACING PERSISTENCE TASK.   The Mirror Tracing Persistence Task has also been revised into a computerized format (MTPC-C; Strong *et al.*, 2003) and resembles the original mirror tracing task, except it involves tracing geometric figures using a computer mouse (MTPC-C; Strong *et al.*, 2003). The MTPT-C has been shown to increase self-reported affective distress, including feelings of anger, frustration, irritability, and anxiety (e.g., Bornovalova *et al.*, 2008; Daughters *et al.*, 2005a; Daughters *et al.*, 2005b). Specifically, participants are instructed to trace a dot along lines of various shapes (e.g., a star) using the computer mouse, which is programmed to move the dot in the reverse direction such that when a participant moves the computer mouse down and to the left, the dot on the computer screen moves up and to the right. If a participant moves the dot outside the perimeter of the star or stops moving the mouse for more than 2 seconds, a loud buzzer sounds and the dot returns to the starting position. There are three rounds of the MTPT-C, with each shape presented progressing in difficulty. The first two rounds last 1 minute each, while the third round can last up to 7 minutes. In the third round, participants are told they have the option to terminate the task at any time by pressing any key on the computer (e.g., the space bar), but also that how well they do on the task will affect their monetary reward. Distress tolerance is measured by the latency in seconds to task termination during the final level of the task, or dichotomously as low (i.e., those who terminate the task) or high (i.e., those who persist the entire duration of the task). Additionally, the number of errors per second (i.e., the number of times the participant has to return to the starting position divided by the task time) can be recorded to control for effects of skill on persistence.

3.2.2.4   COMPUTERIZED PACED AUDITORY SERIAL ADDITION TEST.   The Computerized Paced Auditory Serial Addition Test (PASAT-C; Lejuez, Kahler, and Brown, 2003) has repeatedly been used as a behavioral measure of psychological distress tolerance (Brown, Lejuez, Kahler, and Strong, 2002; Daughters *et al.*, 2005b; Bornovalova *et al.*, 2008; Daughters *et al.*, 2009a) and has been shown to reliably increase participant distress levels and physiological arousal, specifically skin conductance changes and heart rate response (Lejuez, Kahler, and Brown, 2003). For this task, single-digit numbers are displayed sequentially on a computer screen. Participants are instructed to add the current number on the screen to the previously presented number, and use the computer's mouse to click on the correct response (or indicate verbally; e.g., Daughters *et al.*, 2005b) before the subsequent number appears. When participants answer correctly, a pleasant bell is sounded and a point is added to their score. When they answer incorrectly or do not make a response before the subsequent number appears, no point is added and an aversive explosion sound is heard. Numbers range from 1 to 20 with no sum exceeding 20 to reduce the role of mathematical skill in task performance. More specifically, the task consists of three levels that increase in difficulty. In the first level, the latency between number presentations is titrated to the participant's ability level to control for the effects of skill on the task. This titration phase lasts 3 to 5 minutes and is followed by level 2, the stress phase (approximately 5 minutes). Following a brief resting period, level 3 is the distress tolerance phase and can last 7 to 10 minutes, with the option to terminate exposure to the task. Specifically, during this final level, participants are given the option to terminate the task at any time by clicking on a "Quit" button in the upper-left-hand corner of the screen. However, participants are told that their performance on the task determines the magnitude of their payment at the end of the session. If the participant does not elect to terminate the task, the task will automatically terminate after between 7 and 10 minutes (Brown, Lejuez, Kahler, and Strong, 2002; Daughters *et al.*, 2005b; Lejuez, Kahler, and Brown, 2003). Distress tolerance is measured as either the time in seconds until the task is terminated or categorically (i.e., quit versus no quit) during the final level of the task.

3.2.2.5 BEHAVIORAL INDICATOR OF RESILIENCY TO DISTRESS. The Behavioral Indicator of Resiliency to Distress (BIRD; Danielson, Daughters, Ruggiero, and Lejuez, 2006) is a child and adolescent computerized distress tolerance task that has demonstrated effectiveness in increasing distress among adolescents (e.g., Daughters *et al.*, 2009). Participants are shown ten numbered boxes (1–10) on a computer screen and are told that a green dot will appear above one of the boxes. They are instructed to use the computer's mouse to click on the numbered box under the green dot before the green dot moves to another box. If the participant successfully clicks on the box before the green dot disappears, they earn 1 point, release the bird from the cage in the upper-left-hand corner of the screen, and hear a pleasant chirping sound. However, if the participant is unsuccessful, they do not earn a point, the bird remains in the cage, and they hear an aversive loud noise. Similar to the PASAT-C, the BIRD has three levels that increase in difficulty. The first level (5 minutes) begins with a 5-second latency between dot presentations and the latency is subsequently titrated based upon the participants' performance to control for the effects of skill on the task. To increase task difficulty, the second level involves 4 minutes of the titrated latency from the previous round and then 1 minute in which this latency is reduced by half (i.e., stress latency). Following a brief resting period, the third level lasts for 5 minutes and utilizes the stress latency from the final minute of the second level. Therefore, during the second and third levels, the average latency between dot presentations is reduced beyond participants' individual skill level, resulting in constant forced failure and aversive auditory feedback. Further, participants are told that their performance on the task influences the amount of compensation received at the end of the session. Similar to the PASAT-C, distress tolerance in this task is measured either as time in seconds until task termination or categorically (i.e., quit versus no quit) during the final level of the task.

3.2.3 Relationship between behavioral measures and substance use. In sum, numerous physical- and psychological-based behavioral measures of distress tolerance have been developed, and each has demonstrated a distinct relationship with substance use outcomes. Regarding the physical-based distress tolerance measures, studies using BH and CO_2 challenges to index distress tolerance have demonstrated low distress tolerance to be associated with early lapse to smoking (i.e. failure to sustain a quit attempt of more than 24 hours; Brown, Lejuez, Kahler, and Strong, 2002), even after controlling for levels of nicotine dependence and history of major depressive disorder (Brown *et al.*, 2009). Abrantes *et al.* (2008) also found that individuals with low distress tolerance assessed using the CO_2 and BH challenges were more likely to relapse to cigarette smoking, report a greater urge to smoke on a pre-designated quit day, and experience greater negative affect on quit day (Abrantes *et al.*, 2008). Welch and McGee (2010) measured breath holding and smoking in a general population birth cohort (from age 21 to age 32) and found a significant positive cross-sectional relationship between breath-holding capacity and successfully quitting smoking at age 21 among males (compared to current or non-smokers, and all women). However, no prospective relationships were detected, such that breath-holding capacity was not related to whether or not someone had quit smoking by age 32, yet it was related to reduced smoking frequency over time (measured in pack years [20 cigarettes per day for a year]). Finally, Bernstein, Trafton, Ilgen, and Zvolensky (2008) demonstrated that cigarette smokers following a 12-hour smoking cessation period had significantly lower distress tolerance, as indexed by the BH challenge, compared to cigarette smokers who were smoking as usual, suggesting the potential context-dependent nature of distress tolerance and the importance of physical distress tolerance in the early periods of smoking abstinence.

The psychological behavioral measures have also been widely used in substance use research. Using the Anagram Persistence Task and the Mirror Tracing Task to measure psychological distress tolerance, Quinn, Brandon, and Copeland (1996) found that cigarette smokers have lower levels of distress tolerance than nonsmokers (even after controlling for negative affectivity and degree of abuse), and that a more severe history of any substance use (e.g., alcohol, cigarettes, and drugs) was also related to low distress tolerance. Meanwhile, Brandon *et al.* (2003) demonstrated mixed findings across the behavioral tasks, such that low distress tolerance as measured by persistence on the MTPT was associated with abstinence at 12 months after a smoking cessation attempt among adult smokers, but this relationship was not significant when using the Anagram Persistence Task to measure distress tolerance. Using the PASAT-C, Daughters *et al.* (2005b) demonstrated that low psychological distress tolerance was associated with a shorter duration of one's most recent drug and alcohol abstinence attempt among substance users in residential treatment, above and beyond levels of substance use and negative affect. Using the BIRD, low levels of distress tolerance have been associated with high rates of alcohol use among Caucasian adolescents (Daughters *et al.*, 2009).

Finally, a few studies have utilized a combination of physical- and psychological-based behavioral measures of distress tolerance in relation to substance use outcomes. Daughters *et al.* (2005a) examined both physical (BH and CPT) and psychological (MTPT-C and PASAT-C) distress tolerance as predictors of dropout from a residential substance abuse treatment center. Findings illustrated that, while both measures of psychological distress tolerance were significantly associated with premature dropout from the residential center, there was no relationship between either measure of physical distress tolerance and dropout. Another study utilized two psychological (PASAT-C and MTPT-C) and two physical (BH and CPT) behavioral distress tolerance measures to examine the relationship between distress tolerance and pre-treatment dropout among adult regular smokers with depressive symptoms who reported motivation to quit smoking in the next month. Findings demonstrated that low psychological distress tolerance was associated with dropout among women only, while low physical distress tolerance was associated with dropout among men only, and effects remained even after controlling for anxiety sensitivity and current depressive symptoms (MacPherson *et al.*, 2008). These findings are in line with other studies suggesting that gender differences in distress tolerance may exist, particularly in levels of physical distress tolerance (e.g., Brown, Lejuez, and Strong, 2002).

3.3 Summary and methodological recommendations

In sum, numerous self-report and behavioral methods have been developed to assess distinct aspects of distress tolerance, primarily categorized as either physical or psychological. Despite the seeming focus on methodology to assess distress tolerance, these methods are rarely integrated with each other; nor have recommendations been provided for how to effectively do so. In fact, the focus in this area has been more about the differences between these measures (i.e. self-report and behavioral), as previous work has acknowledged that these measures tend to be more discrepant than similar (McHugh *et al.*, 2010). Self-reports tend to be significantly correlated with each other (e.g., the DTS and DIS; $r = -0.25$, $p < 0.01$; McHugh *et al.*, 2010), and the same for behavioral measures (e.g., the MTPT-C and PASAT-C; $r = 0.26$, $p < 0.01$; McHugh *et al.*, 2010; $r = 0.38$, $p < 0.001$; Daughters *et al.*, 2005a), yet rarely are behavioral and self-report measures significantly associated with each other (e.g., $r = 0.07$–0.11; McHugh *et al.*, 2010). However, by focusing on these differences, as well as the distinctions in how these methods have been used in empirical substance use-related work, we can begin to formulate recommendations for how to capitalize on all existing methodology.

In sum, the *self-report* distress tolerance measures are more likely to be associated with *self-reported* substance use variables, such as motives and associated problems, whereas the *behavioral* distress tolerance measures are more likely to be associated with *behavioral* substance use outcomes, such as dropout of substance use treatment and relapse (see Tables 9.1 and 9.2 for a summary of studies examining distress tolerance and substance use outcomes). However, one variable where there does seem to be some overlap between self-report and behavioral measures is self-reported frequency of substance use. Although we maintain that further research is needed before drawing

Table 9.1 Self-report measures of distress tolerance and substance use outcomes

Study	Measure	Substance use outcome
Buckner, Keough, and Schmidt (2007)	DIS	Self-reported marijuana frequency
Howell *et al.* (2010)	DIS	Self-reported alcohol-related problems
Leyro, Zvolensky, Vujanovic, and Bernstein (2008)	DIS	Self-reported motives for cigarette smoking; self-reported negative reinforcement from smoking
Marshall *et al.* (2008)	DIS	Self-reported frequency of cigarette smoking
Buckner, Keough, and Schmidt (2007)	DTS	Self-reported alcohol quantity; self-reported alcohol and marijuana problems among depressed individuals
Howell *et al.* (2010)	DTS	Self-reported coping motives for alcohol use
Leyro *et al.* (2011)	DTS	Self-reported number of smoking years; self-reported nicotine dependence; self-reported negative reinforcement from smoking
O'Cleirigh, Ironson, and Smits (2007)	DTS	Self-reported substance use coping and self-reported frequency of alcohol and cocaine use among individuals with major life events
Perkins *et al.* (2010)	DTS	Smoking reinforcement (higher rates of smoking following mood induction after overnight abstinence)
Potter *et al.* (2011)	DTS	Self-reported marijuana use coping motives among individuals with post-traumatic stress
Simons and Gaher (2005)	DTS	Self-reported coping motives for alcohol and marijuana use; self-reported problematic alcohol use
Zvolensky *et al.* (2009)	DTS	Self-reported marijuana use conformity and coping

Note: DIS = Discomfort Intolerance Scale; DTS = Distress Tolerance Scale. No studies on substance use utilized the FDS.

these firm conclusions, extant literature does seem to support this pattern. If findings continue to replicate, this would support the notion that distinct measures of distress tolerance may be useful for predicting distinct indices of substance use. Once this is more firmly understood, research also must turn to identifying meaningful ways in which these methodologies may be integrated to provide a more comprehensive clinical assessment.

Additionally, a few measures have been developed recently that circumvent some of the noted limitations of the aforementioned assessment methodologies. We briefly review these newly developed measures before discussing the limitations and future directions of existing work. While we believe it is useful to introduce these recently developed measures to provide the most up-to-date methodology available to assess distress tolerance, we also acknowledge that each of these measures is only in its nascent stage and requires much further empirical attention to test and validate its ability to capture distress tolerance.

Table 9.2 Behavioral measures of distress tolerance and substance use outcomes

Study	Measure	Substance use outcomes
Brandon et al. (2003)	APT	Level of nicotine dependence as measured by the FTND
Quinn, Brandon, and Copeland (1996)	APT	Self-reported cigarette smoking status; self-reported drug and alcohol abuse
Abrantes et al. (2008)	BH	Carbon monoxide analysis showed lapse to cigarette smoking on the assigned quit day; self-reported urge to smoke after quitting
Brown, Lejuez, Kahler, and Strong (2002)	BH	Carbon monoxide analysis showed early lapse to smoking (i.e., failure to sustain a quit attempt of more than 24 hours)
Brown et al. (2009)	BH	Carbon monoxide analysis showed early lapse to smoking following an unaided quit attempt
MacPherson et al. (2008)	BH	Observed pre-treatment dropout among male smokers with depressive symptoms
Welch and McGee (2010)	BH	Self-reported successfully quitting smoking at age 21 among males; self-reported smoking frequency assessed at ages 18, 21, 26, and 32 (measured in pack years)
Daughters et al. (2009)	BIRD	Self-reported alcohol use among Caucasian adolescents
Abrantes et al. (2008)	CO_2	Carbon monoxide analysis showed lapse to cigarette smoking on the assigned quit day; self-reported urge to smoke after quitting
Brown, Lejuez, Kahler, and Strong (2002)	CO_2	Carbon monoxide analysis showed early lapse to smoking (i.e., failure to sustain a quit attempt of more than 24 hours)
Brown et al. (2009)	CO_2	Carbon monoxide analysis showed early lapse to smoking following an unaided quit attempt
MacPherson et al. (2008)	CPT	Observed pre-treatment dropout among male smokers with depressive symptoms
Brandon et al. (2003)	MTPT	Level of nicotine dependence (FTND); observed entry into smoking cessation treatment; sustained abstinence through a 1-year follow-up (assessed using self-report, timeline follow back, and carbon monoxide testing); self-reported 1-year smoking abstinence self-efficacy
Quinn, Brandon, and Copeland (1996)	MTPT	Self-reported cigarette smoking status; self-reported drug and alcohol abuse
Daughters et al. (2005a)	MTPT-C	Observed early dropout from a residential substance abuse treatment center (i.e., less than 30 days)
MacPherson et al. (2008)	MTPT-C	Observed pre-treatment dropout among female smokers with depressive symptoms
Brown, Lejuez, Kahler, and Strong (2002)	PASAT-C	Carbon monoxide analysis showed early lapse to smoking (i.e., failure to sustain a quit attempt of more than 24 hours)
Daughters et al. (2005b)	PASAT-C	Self-reported shorter duration of most recent drug and alcohol abstinence
Daughters et al. (2005a)	PASAT-C	Observed early dropout from a residential substance abuse treatment center (i.e., less than 30 days)
MacPherson et al. (2008)	PASAT-C	Observed pre-treatment dropout among smokers with depressive symptoms

Note: APT = Anagram Persistence Task; BH = Breath Holding Challenge; BIRD = Behavioral Indicator of Resiliency to Distress; CPT = Cold Pressor Task; CO_2 = Carbon Dioxide Challenge; MTPT = Mirror Tracing Persistence Task; MTPT-C = Computerized Mirror Tracing Persistence Task; PASAT-C = Paced Auditory Serial Addition Task.

3.4   Novel measures

3.4.1   Willing to Pay-Distress Intolerance.   The Willing to Pay-Distress Intolerance (WTP-DI; McHugh, Hearon, Halperin, and Otto, 2011) task, driven by the field of economics, assesses the proportion of monthly income an individual would be willing to pay to escape from distress (e.g., pain) and avoid a stimulus (e.g., being cold) following the induction of that distressing state. Specifically, the task was recently developed to circumvent existing limitations of self-report and behavioral assessment of distress tolerance as well as assessment of emotion regulation more generally. The task was derived from economic research using willingness to pay (WTP) methods more generally that require participants to evaluate the utility of goods, resources or services by indicating how much they would pay for a particular outcome of interest. As applied to distress tolerance specifically, the WTP-DI assesses how much a participant would be willing to pay to avoid distress following the induction of a distressing state. The measure is a forced-choice format in which participants select from several monetary values (expressed as 0% to >15% of one's monthly income to control for the impact of income on responding; Damschroder, Ubel, Riis, and Smith, 2007), with a focus on relative WTP values across participants. The measure was designed to be utilized following the induction of distress in order to evaluate an *in vivo*, contextual response to distress. Responses are recorded on a 0–6-point Likert scale ranging from 0% to >15% of monthly income (McHugh, Hearon, Halperin, and Otto, 2011).

The developers of the measure suggest that this method addresses the core limitations of both self-report and behavioral assessments of distress tolerance by removing demand characteristics inherent in behavioral assessment that may motivate continuation on a distressing task as well as incorporating a behavioral *in vivo* reaction to distress that is often lacking from self-report assessment. The measure was also meant to address a limitation of existing methods that assessments are overly specified regarding a domain of distress, whereas this measure has the potential to be applied across domains of distress (i.e., physical and psychological). The WTP-DI has moderate to strong correlations with both self-report (i.e., DTS, DIS, FDS) and physical behavioral measures of distress tolerance (i.e., CPT, BH). Further, individuals with a substance dependence diagnosis reported significantly higher WTP scores than an affective disorder comparison group (current unipolar mood or anxiety disorder, no history of substance use disorder) and a healthy control group, supporting the notion that individuals with substance dependence may have particularly low levels of distress tolerance as measured using the WTP (McHugh, Hearon, Halperin, and Otto, 2011).

3.4.2   Intolerance for Smoking Abstinence Discomfort.   The Intolerance for Smoking Abstinence Discomfort (Sirota *et al.*, 2010) is a recently developed self-report measure that aims to assess inability to deal with discomfort associated with smoking abstinence specifically. This measure's development is in line with recent suggestions in the field that distress tolerance may be conceptualized as domain specific or varying based on type of distress (McHugh *et al.*, 2010; McHugh, Hearon, Halperin, and Otto, 2011). The measure was developed among a sample of 300 regular smokers (10 or more cigarettes per day for at least the past year) and was created by analyzing shared variance among smoking abstinence discomfort (IDQ-S; $\alpha = 0.87$), general physical discomfort (IDQ-P; $\alpha = 0.87$), and general emotional discomfort (IDQ-E; $\alpha = 0.81$) scales. The final 17-item measure that was developed comprises two subscales: (1) withdrawal intolerance (consisting of 12 items involving intolerance of affective, cognitive, and physical symptoms for nicotine withdrawal) and (2) cognitive coping (consisting of 5 items reflecting various cognitive-focused ways of coping with withdrawal). Preliminary evidence supports construct and discriminant validity for this measure as well as significant associations with smoking use, dependence, motivation, and length of past smoking cessation attempt. Continued work is needed to develop the measure and examine relationships with smoking outcomes. If psychometric support continues to replicate, this measure may provide useful evidence to further test the domain specificity hypotheses related to how we conceptualize distress tolerance.

3.4.3   Negative reinforcement risk-propensity behavioral measure: Maryland Resource for the Behavioral Understanding of Reinforcement from Negative Stimuli.

The MRBURNS (MacPherson *et al.*, in press) is a computerized behavioral assessment that assesses an individual's ability to engage in risk behavior (i.e., pump a balloon) in order to reduce aversive stimuli (i.e., a loud noise). There are a total of 30 trials (i.e., 30 separate balloons), and for each trial, a balloon appears on the screen and the participant: (1) selects a number of pumps at the start of the balloon; (2) experiences an aversive noise for a duration of time based on the number of pumps (each pump reduces the duration of the aversive noise by 0.15 seconds from a starting point of 19.2 seconds); and (3) watches the balloon inflate, sees if it explodes, and if it does then loses a chance to win a lottery later in the session (six drawings for either $1, $3, or $9 at the end of the session).

The task was designed to mimic the consequences of negative reinforcement responses that occur in real-world settings, particularly among adolescents during early alcohol use initiation. For instance, beyond the immediate relief provided by the negative reinforcement in that moment (e.g., by drinking alcohol), this also comes with later negative consequences that tend to not be a reinstatement of an initial aversive stimulus (i.e. negative affective state), but rather some opportunity cost in the future (e.g., later escalation of use and related problems). This is captured by the MRBURNS task through including a loss of an opportunity to win a lottery at the end of the session when the balloons explode. Specifically, participants are told that they start off with a guaranteed win of the lottery, but the likelihood of winning reduces with each exploded balloon. This was specifically designed not to be an *increase* in the chance of winning when a balloon did not explode to ensure a focus on opportunity cost with the explosions. Although offering only preliminary support, existing data do suggest that MRBURNS has strong psychometric properties, including convergent and discriminant validity and reliability across task trials. Risk taking on MRBURNS was significantly related to alcohol-related problems among college students, yet not heavy episodic alcohol use, and negative-reinforcement-based but not positive-reinforcement-based drinking motives, suggesting its particular utility in measuring negative-reinforcement-based processes.

4 Limitations, Shortcomings, and Future Directions

There has been a burgeoning body of literature supporting the role of distress tolerance in many aspects of substance use behavior; however, this area is still in many ways in its very early stages. It will be important for future research to address how self-report and behavioral measures of distress tolerance relate to each other, given the noted lack of a significant correlation between these assessment methods (McHugh *et al.*, 2010). This discrepancy suggests that perhaps one's perceived capacity to withstand distress does not map perfectly onto one's actual ability to tolerate distress. It is unclear at this point whether we can view self-report and behavioral measures of distress tolerance as tapping the same construct, or whether these methods may indeed be getting at different aspects of a similar underlying vulnerability.

Although it has been suggested that a behavioral measure of distress tolerance may be more reliable, given that it involves real-time assessment of immediate escape from distress and long-term reward of compensation, whereas self-report measures contain inherent limitations of recall bias and inaccurate reporting, limitations have also been noted regarding the behavioral measures, specifically their ecological validity, given the focus on achievement-oriented stress tasks, as well as a lack of research examining motivation and cognition during the task. Despite limitations and noted differences, these measures may in fact just correlate with different aspects of behavior, with behavioral measures perhaps more useful in predicting real-world ability to maintain abstinence, while self-report is more highly correlated with an assessment of coping motives and problems.

Similarly, it is also uncertain how the two subcategories of physical versus psychological distress tolerance correlate with each other. Negative reinforcement theory acknowledges the role of substances in alleviating both physical and psychological distress (e.g., Baker *et al.*, 2004; Mello and Mendelson, 1970; Parrott, 1999; Wikler, 1977; Zinser, Baker, Sherman, and Cannon, 1992), yet it remains unclear whether the construct of distress tolerance should be unified to capture the tolerance of both physical and psychological distress or whether these are distinct capacities. Indeed, behavioral measures of physical distress tolerance are often significantly correlated with each other (e.g., the CPT and BH; $r = 0.27$, $p < 0.01$), yet uncorrelated with behavioral measures of psychological distress tolerance (e.g., the BH; $r = 0.09$ and 0.05 for PASAT-C and MTPT-C respectively, both ns; McHugh *et al.*, 2010). Further, there has been very limited, if any, research conducted on the relationship between physical distress tolerance and substance use frequency for substances other than smoking; existing work largely has been limited to assessing substance users in residential treatment following complete detoxification when physical distress tolerance may be less relevant without acute withdrawal symptoms. As such, continued research is needed to more fully understand the relationship between physical distress tolerance and illicit drug and alcohol use.

Overall, there has indeed been criticism that the current definition of distress tolerance may be too specific in nature by being overly divided into subcategories (e.g., psychological or physical; Bernstein, Zvolensky, Vujanovic, and Moos, 2009; Schmidt, Mitchell, Keough, and Riccardi, 2010), and rather, to unify these multiple dimensions, we may need a broader, nonspecific methodology to test distress tolerance. However, despite this criticism of the overly specific nature of the construct, self-report and behavioral assessments of distress tolerance have been noted to be limited by their *lack* of specificity (Leyro *et al.*, 2010; McHugh *et al.*, 2010), with limited psychometric support for some self-report measures and criticism of behavioral assessments as measuring persistence to maintain a behavior related to reward contingencies rather than distress tolerance, as investigators often utilize rewards for persistence (Cloninger, Przybeck, and Svrakic, 1991).

Beyond the noted limitations of existing methodology for assessing distress tolerance, other limitations in this area relate to study design issues, which inhibit a deeper understanding of the relationship between distress tolerance and substance use. For instance, the association between distress tolerance and substance use has been largely established through cross-sectional studies (cf. Welch and McGee, 2010), which cannot conclude a temporal relationship between substance use and distress tolerance. At this point, it remains unclear whether low distress tolerance is a risk factor for substance use, or is a result of substance use, or whether bidirectional influences may be driving this relationship. Additionally, without a longitudinal design, it remains difficult to ascertain how other factors, such as learning history, genetics, biology, environment, and trauma may also influence how distress tolerance impacts substance use (Bernstein, Trafton, Ilgen, and Zvolensky, 2008). Future research should incorporate longitudinal designs to provide greater insight into the directionality between distress tolerance and substance use.

Additionally, there is a noticeable lack of research examining biological and neural indicators of distress tolerance. Despite a strong body of support indicating that a dysregulated hypothalamic–pituitary–adrenal (HPA) axis response to stress is associated with poor substance use outcomes (Daughters, Richards, Gorka, and Sinha, 2009; Sinha, 2011), no work to date has examined the relationship between HPA axis response to stress, distress tolerance, and substance use outcomes. In regard to the neural indices of distress tolerance and substance use, converging evidence points to the complex interaction of the limbic system, associated with stress and emotion, with the prefrontal (PFC) and anterior cingulate (ACC) circuits associated with inhibitory control, decision making, and goal-directed activity. Specifically, reduced functioning in the PFC and ACC, or weak connectivity within the cortico-striatal-limbic circuit, limits inhibitory control and may lead to habitual and automatic responses in times of emotional distress (Li and Sinha, 2008). To this end, versions of the PASAT-C and MTPT-C have been modified for us in an MRI environment (Daughters, Ross, Richards, and Stein, 2011), and preliminary evidence indicates the ability of these tasks to induce stress and activate cortico-limbic circuits; however, further research is needed to establish the relationship between neural indices of distress tolerance and substance use outcomes. Taken together, there is a clear need to integrate neurobiological mechanisms into our understanding of distress tolerance.

4.1   Conclusion

In sum, our understanding of the relationship between distress tolerance and substance use outcomes has been dynamic and rapidly expanding in recent years, which is primarily a reflection of the newly developing methodologies to assess distress tolerance and how these tools have been applied to substance use. Although the rapidly expanding number of methodologies available to assess distress tolerance has numerous advantages, it also illustrates the complexities of the construct and elicits questions as how to best define it. However, despite the need for continued replication and expansion upon current work, there is a strong consensus that distress tolerance is a key intra-individual motivational factor underlying all aspects of substance use, including initiation, escalation, and relapse. It is the hope that this chapter, by addressing various perspectives and methodological approaches to distress tolerance in the context of substance use research, fosters future work that bridges rather than further divides existing methodology.

References

Abrantes AM, Strong DR, Lejuez CW, *et al.* (2008) The role of negative affect in risk for early lapse among low distress tolerance smokers. *Addictive Behaviors* 33(11): 1394–1401. doi: 10.1016/j.addbeh.2008.06.018.

Baker TB, Piper ME, McCarthy DE, Majeskie MR, and Fiore MC (2004) Addiction motivation reformulated: An affective processing model of negative reinforcement. *Psychological Review* 111: 33–51. doi: 10.1037/0033-295X.111.1.33.

Bernstein A, Trafton J, Ilgen M, and Zvolensky MJ (2008) An evaluation of the role of smoking context on a biobehavioral index of distress tolerance. *Addictive Behaviors* 33: 1409–1415. doi: 10.1016/j.addbeh.2008.06.003.

Bernstein A, Zvolensky MJ, Vujanovic AA, and Moos R (2009) Anxiety sensitivity, distress tolerance, and discomfort intolerance: A hierarchical model of affect sensitivity and tolerance. *Behavior Therapy* 40: 291–301.

Blagden C (1775a) Experiments and observations in an heated room. *Philosophical Transactions of the Royal Society* 65: 111–123. doi: 10.1098/rstl.1775.0013.

Blagden C (1775b) Further experiments and observations in an heated room. *Philosophical Transactions of the Royal Society* 65: 484–494. doi: 10.1098/rstl.1775.0048.

Bornovalova MA, Gratz KL, Daughters SB, *et al.* (2008) A multimodal assessment of the relationship between emotion dysregulation and borderline personality disorder among inner-city substance users in residential treatment. *Journal of Psychiatric Research* 42: 717–726. doi: 10.1016/j.jpsychires.2007.07.014.

Brandon TH, Herzog TA, Juliano LM, Irvin JE, Lazev AB, and Simmons VN (2003) Pretreatment task persistence predicts smoking cessation outcome. *Journal of Abnormal Psychology* 112: 448–456. doi: 10.1037/0021-843X.112.3.448.

Brown R, Lejuez C, Kahler C, and Strong D (2002) Distress tolerance and duration of past smoking cessation attempts. *Journal of Abnormal Psychology* 111: 180–185. doi: 10.1037//0021-843X.111.1.180.

Brown RA, Lejuez CW, Kahler CW, Strong DR, and Zvolensky MJ (2005) Distress tolerance and early smoking lapse (theory and clinical implications). *Clinical Psychology Review* 25: 713–733. doi: 10.1016/j.cpr.2005.05.003.

Brown RA, Lejuez CW, Strong DR, *et al.* (2009) A prospective examination of distress tolerance and early smoking lapse in self-quitters. *Nicotine and Tobacco Research* 11: 493–502. doi: 10.1093/ntr/ntp041.

Buckner JD, Keough ME, and Schmidt NB (2007) Problematic alcohol and cannabis use among young adults: The roles of depression on discomfort and distress tolerance. *Addictive Behaviors* 32: 1957–1963. doi: 10.1016/j.addbeh.2006.12.019.

Burns J, Bruehl S, and Caceres C (2004) Anger management style, blood pressure reactivity, and acute pain sensitivity: Evidence for "trait x situation" models. *Annals of Behavioral Medicine* 27: 195–204. doi: 10.1207/s15324796abm2703_7.

Cloninger CR, Przybeck TR, and Svrakic DM (1991) The tridimensional personality questionnaire: US normative data. *Psychological Reports* 69: 1047–1057.

Damschroder LJ, Ubel PA, Riis J, and Smith, DM (2007) An alternative approach for eliciting willingness-to-pay: A randomized internet trial. *Judgment and Decision Making* 2(2): 96–106.

Danielson CK, Daughters SB, Ruggiero K, and Lejuez CW (2006) The Behavioral Indicator of Resiliency to Distress (BIRD). Unpublished manual.

Daughters SB, Lejuez CW, Bornovalova MA, Kahler CW, Strong DR, and Brown RA (2005a) Distress tolerance as a predictor of early treatment dropout in a residential substance abuse treatment facility. *Journal of Abnormal Psychology* 114: 728–734. doi: 10.1037/0021-843X.114.4.729.

Daughters SB, Lejuez CW, Kahler CW, Strong DR, and Brown RA (2005b) Psychological distress tolerance and duration of most recent abstinence attempt among residential treatment-seeking substance abusers. *Psychology of Addictive Behaviors* 19: 208–211. doi: 10.1037/0893-164X.19.2.208.

Daughters SB, Reynolds EK, MacPherson L, Kahler CW, Danielson CK, Zvolensky M, and Lejuez CW (2009) Distress tolerance and early adolescent externalizing and internalizing symptoms: The moderating role of gender and ethnicity. *Behaviour Research and Therapy* 47(3): 198–205. doi: 10.1016/j.brat.2008.12.001.

Daughters SB, Richards JM, Gorka SM, and Sinha R (2009) HPA axis response to psychological stress and treatment retention in residential substance abuse treatment: A prospective study. *Drug and Alcohol Dependence* 105: 202–208. doi: 10.1016/j.drugalcdep.2009.06.026.

Daughters SB, Ross T, Richards JM, and Stein EA (2011) fMRI Compatible PASAT-C and Mirror Tracing Distress Tolerance Tasks. *Unpublished manual.*

Eisenberger R and Leonard JM (1980) Effects of conceptual task difficulty on generalized persistence. *American Journal of Psychology* 93: 285–298. doi: 10.2307/1422233.

Eissenberg T (2004) Measuring the emergence of tobacco dependence: The contribution of negative reinforcement models. *Addiction* 99(Suppl. 1): 5–29. doi: 10.1111/j.1360-0443.2004.00735.x.

Hackett G and Horan JJ (1980) Stress inoculation for pain: What's really going on? *Journal of Counseling Psychology* 27: 107–116. doi: 10.1037/0022-0167.27.2.107.

Hajek P (1991) Individual differences in difficulty quitting smoking. *British Journal of Addiction* 86: 555–558. doi: 10.1111/j.1360-0443.1991.tb01807.x.

Hajek P, Belcher M, and Stapleton J (1987) Breath-holding endurance as a predictor of success in smoking cessation. *Addictive Behaviors* 12: 285–288. doi: 10.1016/0306-4603(87)90041-4.

Hancock PA, Ross JM, and Szalma JL (2007) A meta-analysis of performance response under thermal stressors. *Human Factors* 49(5): 851–877.

Harrington N (2005) The frustration discomfort scale: Development and psychometric properties. *Clinical Psychology and Psychotherapy* 12: 374–387. doi: 10.1002/cpp.465.

Harrington N (2006) Frustration intolerance beliefs: Their relationship with depression, anxiety, and anger, in a clinical population. *Cognitive Therapy and Research* 30: 699–709. doi: 10.1007/s10608-006-9061-6.

Hines EA and Brown GE (1932) A standard stimulus for measuring vasomotor reactions: Its application in the study of hypertension. *Mayo Clinic Proceedings* 7: 332.

Hocking C, Silberstein RB, Lau WM, Stough C, and Roberts W (2001) Evaluation of cognitive performance in the heat by functional brain imaging and psychometric testing. *Comparative*

Biochemistry and Physiology – Part A Molecular and Integrative Physiology 128: 719–734. doi: 10.1016/S1095-6433(01)00278-1.

Howell A, Leyro T, Hogan J, Buckner J, and Zvolensky M (2010) Anxiety sensitivity, distress tolerance, and discomfort intolerance in relation to coping and conformity motives for alcohol use and alcohol use problems among young adult drinkers. *Addictive Behaviors* 35(12): 1144–1147. doi: 10.1016/j.addbeh.2010.07.003.

Hygge S and Knez I (2001) Effects of noise, heat and indoor lighting on cognitive performance and self-reported affect. *Journal of Environmental Psychology* 21: 291–299. doi: 10.1006/jevp.2001.0222.

Jones A, Spindler H, Jorgensen MM, and Zachariae R (2002) The effect of situation-evoked anxiety and gender on pain report using the cold pressor test. *Scandinavian Journal of Psychology* 43: 307–313. doi: 10.1111/1467-9450.00299.

Kane EM, Nutter RW, and Weckowicz TE (1971) Response to cutaneous pain in mental hospital patients. *Journal of Abnormal Psychology* 77: 52–60. doi: 10.1037/h0030502.

Ko C, Yen J, Yen C, Chen C, and Wang S (2008) The association between internet addiction and belief of frustration intolerance: The gender difference. *CyberPsychology and Behavior* 11: 273–278. doi: 10.1089/cpb.2007.0095.

Leyro TM, Bernstein A, Vujanovic AA, McLeish AC, and Zvolensky MJ (2011) Distress tolerance scale: A confirmatory factor analysis among daily cigarette smokers. *Journal of Psychopathology and Behavioral Assessment* 33: 47–57. doi: 10.1007/s10862-010-9197-2.

Lejuez CW, Forsyth JP, and Eifert GH (1998) Devices and methods for administering carbon dioxide-enriched air in experimental and clinical settings. *Journal of Behavior Therapy and Experimental Psychiatry* 29(3): 239–248. doi: 10.1016/S0005-7916(98)00018-4.

Lejuez CW, Kahler CW, and Brown RA (2003) A modified computer version of the Paced Auditory Serial Addition Task (PASAT) as a laboratory-based stressor. *Behavior Therapy* 26: 290–293.

Leyro TM, Zvolensky MJ, and Bernstein A (2010) Distress tolerance and psychopathological symptoms and disorders: A review of the empirical literature among adults. *Psychological Bulletin* 136: 576–600. doi: 10.1037/a0019712.

Leyro TM, Zvolensky MJ, Vujanovic AA, and Bernstein A (2008) Anxiety sensitivity and smoking motives and outcome expectancies among adult daily smokers: Replication and extension. *Nicotine and Tobacco Research* 10: 985–994. doi: 10.1080/14622200802097555.

Li CS and Sinha R (2008) Inhibitory control and emotional stress regulation: Neuroimaging evidence for frontal-limbic dysfunction in psycho-stimulant addiction. *Neuroscience and Biobehavioral Reviews* 32: 581–597. doi:10.1016/j.neubiorev.2007.10.003.

MacPherson L, Calvin NT, Richards JM, *et al.* (in press) Development and preliminary validation of a behavioral task of negative reinforcement underlying risk taking and its relation to problem alcohol use in college freshmen. *Alcoholism: Clinical and Experimental Research*

MacPherson L, Reynolds EK, Daughters SB, Wang F, Cassidy J, Mayes L, and Lejuez CW (2010) Positive and negative reinforcement underlying risk behavior in early adolescents. *Prevention Science* 11(3): 331–342. doi: 10.1007/s11121-010-0172-7.

MacPherson L, Stipelman BA, Duplinsky M, Brown RA, and Lejuez CW (2008) Distress tolerance and pre-smoking treatment attrition: Examination of moderating relationships. *Addictive Behaviors* 33: 1385–1393. doi: 10.1016/j.addbeh.2008.07.001.

Marshall EC, Zvolensky MJ, Vujanovic AA, Gregor K, Gibson LE, and Leyro TM (2008) Panic reactivity to voluntary hyperventilation challenge predicts distress tolerance to bodily sensations among daily cigarette smokers. *Experimental and Clinical Psychopharmacology* 16: 313–321. doi: 10.1037/a0012752.

Matthews KA and Stoney CM (1988) Influences of sex and age on cardiovascular responses during stress. *Psychosomatic Medicine* 50: 46–56.

McHugh RK, Daughters SB, Lejuez CW, Murray HW, Hearon BA, Gorka SM, and Otto MW (2010) Shared variance among self-report and behavioral measures of distress tolerance. *Cognitive Therapy and Research* 35(3): 266–275. doi: 10.1007/s10608-010-9295-1.

McHugh RK, Hearon BA, Halperin DM, and Otto MW (2011) A novel method for assessing distress intolerance: Adaptation of a measure of willingness to pay. *Journal of Behavior Therapy and Experimental Psychiatry* 42(4): 440–446.

Mello NK and Mendelson JH (1970) Experimentally induced intoxication in alcoholics: A comparison between programmed and spontaneous drinking. *Journal of Pharmacology and Experimental Therapeutics* 173: 101–116.

Neufeld RWJ and Thomas P (1977) Effects of perceived efficacy of a prophylactic controlling mechanism on self-control under pain stimulation. *Canadian Journal of Behavioural Science* 9: 224–232.

O'Cleirigh C, Ironson G, and Smits JAJ (2007) Does distress tolerance moderate the impact of major life events on psychosocial variables and behaviors important in the management of HIV? *Behavior Therapy* 38(3): 314–323. doi: 10.1016/j.beth.2006.11.001.

Orbach I, Palgi Y, Stein D, Har-Even D, Lotem-Peleg M, Asherov J, and Elizur A (1996) Tolerance for physical pain in suicidal subjects. *Death Studies* 20: 327–341.

Parrott AC (1999) Does cigarette smoking cause stress? *American Psychologist* 54: 817–820.

Perkins KA, Karelitz JL, Giedgowd GE, Conklin CA, and Sayette MA (2010) Differences in negative mood-induced smoking reinforcement due to distress tolerance, anxiety sensitivity and depression history. *Psychopharmacology* 210: 25–34. doi: 10.1007/s00213-010-1811-1.

Pilcher JJ, Nadler E, and Busch C (2002) Effects of hot and cold temperature exposure on performance: A meta-analytic review. *Ergon* 45: 682–698. doi: 10.1080/00140130210158419.

Postman L and Solomon RL (1950) Perceptual sensitivity to completed and incompleted tasks. *Journal of Personality* 18: 347–357. doi: 10.1111/j.1467-6494.1950.tb01256.x.

Potter CM, Vujanovic AA, Marshall-Berenz EC, Bernstein A, and Bonn-Miller MO (2011) Posttraumatic stress and marijuana use coping motives: The mediating role of distress tolerance. *Journal of Anxiety Disorders* 25: 437–443. doi: 10.1016/j.janxdis.2010.11.007.

Procacci P (1979) Methods for the study of pain threshold in man. In JJ Bonica, JC Leibskind, and DG Albe-Fessard (eds), *Advances in Pain Research and Therapy* (Vol. 3, pp. 781–970). New York: Raven Press.

Quinn EP, Brandon TH, and Copeland AL (1996) Is task persistence related to smoking and substance abuse? The application of learned industriousness theory to addictive behaviors. *Experimental and Clinical Psychopharmacology* 4: 186–190.

Razmjou S (1996) Mental workload in heat: Toward a framework for analyses of stress states. *Aviation, Space, and Environmental Medicine* 67: 530–538.

Razmjou S and Kjellberg A (1992) Sustained attention and serial responding in heat: Mental effort in the control of performance. *Aviation, Space, and Environmental Medicine* 63: 594–601.

Rhudy JL and Meagher MW (2003) Negative affect: Effects on an evaluative measure of human pain. *Pain* 104: 617–626. doi: 10.1016/S0304-3959(03)00119-2.

Rosenthal RR (1984) Simplified eucapnic voluntary hyperventilation challenge. *Journal of Allergy and Clinical Immunology* 73(5): 679. doi: 10.1016/0091-6749(84)90304-X.

Schmidt NB and Cook JH (1999) Effects of anxiety sensitivity on anxiety and pain during a cold pressor challenge in patients with panic disorder. *Behaviour Research and Therapy* 37: 313–323. doi: 10.1016/S0005-7967(98)00139-9.

Schmidt NB, Mitchell MA, Keough ME, and Riccardi CJ (2010) Anxiety and its disorders. In A Bernstein, MJ Zvolensky, and AA Vujanovic (eds), *Distress Tolerance* (pp. 105–125). New York: Guilford Press.

Schmidt NB, Richey JA, and Fitzpatrick KK (2006) Discomfort intolerance: Development of a construct and measure relevant to panic disorder. *Journal of Anxiety Disorders* 20: 263–280. doi: 10.1016/j.janxdis.2005.02.002.

Schmidt NB, Richey JA, Cromer KR, and Buckner JD (2007) Discomfort intolerance: Evaluation of a potential risk factor for anxiety psychopathology. *Behaviour Therapy* 38: 247–255. doi: 10.1016/j.beth.2006.08.004.

Shaham Y, Erb S, and Stewart J (2000) Stress-induced relapse to heroin and cocaine seeking rats: A review. *Brain Research Reviews* 33: 13–33. doi: 10.1016/S0165-0173(00)00024-2.

Sharma V and Panwar M (1987) Variations in mental performance under moderate cold stress. *International Journal of Biometeorology* 31(1): 85–91. doi: 10.1007/BF02192842.

Simons JS and Gaher RM (2005) The Distress Tolerance Scale: Development and validation of a self-report measure. *Motivation and Emotion* 29: 83–102. doi: 10.1007/s11031-005-7955-3.

Sinha R (2011) New findings on biological factors predicting addiction relapse vulnerability. *Current Psychiatry Reports* doi: 10.1007/s11920-011-0224-0.

Sirota AD, Rohsenow DJ, MacKinnon SV, Martin RA, Eaton CA, Kaplan GB, Monti PM, Tidey JW, and Swift RM (2010) Intolerance for smoking abstinence questionnaire: Psychometric properties and relationship to tobacco dependence and abstinence. *Addictive Behaviors* 35: 686–693. doi: 10.1016/j.addbeh.2010.02.014.

Strong DR, Lejuez CW, Daughters S, Marinello M, Kahler CW, and Brown RA (2003) The computerized mirror tracing task (Version 1). http://www.addiction.umd.edu/downloads.htm. Accessed July 18, 2011.

Thomas IR, Ahlers ST, House JF, and Schrot J (1989) Repeated exposure to moderate cold impairs matching-to-sample performance. *Aviation, Space, and Environmental Medicine* 60: 1063–1067.

Tutoo DN (1971) Psychodiagnostic applications of the mirror-tracing test. *Indian Educational Review* 6: 293–303. doi: 10.1037/1064-1297.4.2.186.

Uman LS, Stewart SH, Watt MC, and Johnson A (2006) Differences in high and low anxiety sensitive women's responses to a laboratory-based cold pressor task. *Cognitive Behaviour Therapy* 35(4): 189–197. doi: 10.1080/16506070600898512.

Van Orden K, Benoit S, and Osga G (1996) Effects of cold stress on the performance of a command and control task. *Human Factors* 38(1): 130–141. doi: 10.1518/001872096778940796.

Welch D and McGee R (2010) Breath holding predicts reduced smoking intake but not quitting. *The Open Addict Journal* 3: 39–42.

Wikler A (1977) The search for the psyche in the drug dependence. *Journal of Nervous and Mental Disease* 165: 29–40.

Willoughby SG, Hailey BJ, Mulkana S, and Rowe J (2002) The effect of laboratory-induced depressed mood state on responses to pain. *Behavioral Medicine* 28: 23–31. doi: 10.1080/08964280209596395.

Wolff BB and Jarvik ME (1963) Variations in cutaneous and deep somatic pain sensitivity. *Canadian Journal of Psychology* 17: 37–44. doi: 10.1037/h0083264.

Zelman D, Howland E, Nichols S, and Cleeland C (1991) The effects of induced mood on laboratory pain. *Pain* 46: 105–111. doi: 10.1016/0304-3959(91)90040-5.

Zinser MC, Baker TB, Sherman JE, and Cannon DS (1992) Relation between self reported affect and drug urges and cravings in continuing and withdrawing smokers. *Journal of Abnormal Psychology* 101: 617–629. doi: 10.1037//0021-843X.101.4.617.

Zvolensky MJ and Eifert GH (2000) A review of psychological factors/processes affecting anxious responding during voluntary hyperventilation and inhalations of carbon dioxide-enriched air. *Clinical Psychology Reviews* 21(3): 375–400. doi: 10.1016/S0272-7358(99)00053-7.

Zvolensky MJ, Feldner MT, Eifert GH, and Brown RA (2001) Affective style among smokers: Understanding anxiety sensitivity, emotional reactivity, and distress tolerance using biological challenge. *Addictive Behaviors* 26(6): 901–915. doi: 10.1016/S0306-4603(01)00242-8.

Zvolensky MJ, Marshall EC, Johnson K, Hogan J, Bernstein A, and Bonn-Miller MO (2009) Relations between anxiety sensitivity, distress tolerance, and fear reactivity to bodily sensations to coping and conformity marijuana use motives among young adult marijuana users. *Experimental and Clinical Psychopharmacology* 17: 31–42.

Part II

Proximal Determinants
of Drug Use

10

Measuring Direct Effects of Drugs of Abuse in Humans[1]
Harriet de Wit

1 Introduction

This chapter will review some of the methods used in drug challenge studies that investigate the direct effects of psychoactive drugs in human volunteers. Drug challenge studies provide a means to directly assess the physiological, subjective, and behavioral effects of acute doses of drugs, under controlled conditions. They are a mainstay of human psychopharmacology, allowing investigators to assess the pharmacological effects of a drug while controlling a multitude of variables that could influence drug responses, including expectancies, dose, absorption and other pharmacokinetic variables, purity of the compound, physical and psychological environment, circadian variables, and participant characteristics. For example, participant characteristics to be controlled include recent and lifetime drug use, psychiatric or medical conditions, sleep and dietary factors, weight, sex, race, menstrual cycle phase, and education or cognitive capacities. Drug challenge studies provide the opportunity to assess a rich array of outcome measures, described below. In this chapter we will first review some of the applications of drug challenge studies to scientific, regulatory and clinical questions. We will summarize important issues that arise in such studies, including questions about design, expectancies and blinding, ethics and safety, dosing, and subject sample selection and environmental testing conditions. Then we will review the primary outcome measures obtained in these studies, including subjective ratings of drug effects,

[1]The author is supported by DA02812. Matthew Kirkpatrick and Emma Childs provided constructive comments on earlier versions of this chapter.

The Wiley-Blackwell Handbook of Addiction Psychopharmacology, First Edition. Edited by James MacKillop and Harriet de Wit.
© 2013 John Wiley & Sons, Ltd. Published 2013 by John Wiley & Sons, Ltd.

simple physiological effects not covered in other chapters, and tasks designed to assess specific behavioral constructs. Readers will be referred to other sources for further methodological guidance for specific measures, and to selected empirical papers as examples of the application of the methods.

Drug challenge procedures, which examine the direct effects of acute doses of drugs under controlled conditions, are used to address various research questions, and the optimal procedures to be used depend on the goal of the study. One important function of drug challenge studies is to evaluate the likelihood that a new medication will be abused. Regulatory bodies such as the Food and Drug Administration in the United States use data from studies which assess potential for abuse of a new medication to make policy decisions about controlling access to the drug. The likelihood that a new drug will be misused or abused is based on its ability to produce feelings of euphoria or subjective effects similar to known drugs of abuse. Abuse potential studies follow strict procedures regarding subject samples, doses, and outcome measures, which are described in detail in recent reviews (Carter and Griffiths, 2009; FDA, n.d.).

Another purpose is to study why individuals differ in their response to drugs, and identify possible sources of these differences. Individuals vary markedly in their responses to drugs, for a variety of reasons including prior experiences (e.g., drug use history), physiological states, psychiatric symptomatology, and genetic factors. Drug challenge studies investigating individual differences in acute responses to drugs are critical to identify populations who are at risk for using the drug repeatedly, escalating their use, or being likely to experience adverse effects. For example, Schuckit *et al.* (2011) in an extensive series of studies demonstrated that individuals with a family history of alcoholism exhibit dampened subjective responses to alcohol, and that this response pattern is predictive of future risk for alcoholism (Schuckit *et al.*, 2011; Newlin and Renton, 2010; King, de Wit, McNamara, and Cao, 2011). Alcohol challenge studies of this kind may advance our understanding of the processes by which risk for alcohol dependence is transmitted across generations. Other sources of individual differences in responses to drugs include those of biological origin (e.g., genetics, pharmacokinetics, circulating hormone levels, age, or sex) and those related to experiential factors (e.g., expectancies, prior conditioning, and learning). Drug challenge studies are also used to study the mechanisms of action of the drugs, especially when combined with a receptor antagonist or other compound known to modify neuronal function (Wachtel, Ortengren, and de Wit, 2002; Enggasser and de Wit, 2001). For example, one study examined the role of dopamine in the euphorigenic effects of alcohol, by co-administering the dopamine antagonist haloperidol. Haloperidol dampened the stimulant-like and euphorigenic effects of ethanol in healthy young adults (Enggasser and de Wit, 2001). Finally, acute challenge studies using drugs with known mechanisms of action can provide information about the brain mechanisms involved in specific behaviors. For example, a study on the cognitive effects of nicotine, which has known actions on cholinergic systems, may shed light on the brain processes involved in cognition or memory (Wignall and de Wit, 2011).

2   Methodological Considerations

2.1   Selection of participants

A critical consideration in studies assessing effects of drugs of abuse is selection of the appropriate participant sample, to suit the goals of the study. The subjective, behavioral, and physiological effects of a particular drug depend on the drug use history of the individual, from individuals who have never used the drug to regular users, dependent individuals, or abstaining ex-users. For some purposes, relatively drug-naïve individuals are preferable, whereas for other purposes more experienced drug users are needed (Dlugos *et al.*, 2007; Griffiths, Bigelow, and Ator, 2003; Griffiths, Richards, McCann, and Jesse, 2006). For example, for studies designed to assess genetic variables involved in the pharmacological effect of a drug, relatively inexperienced users might be preferable to minimize the influence of expectancies or tolerance (Dlugos *et al.*, 2007). In another recent example, studies investigating the ability of psilocybin to produce mystical-type experiences were conducted using participants without prior use of hallucinogens, to minimize expectancy effects (Griffiths, Richards, McCann, and Jesse, 2006). Other studies more appropriately investigate the effects of a drug in experienced users. For example, experienced drug users are more appropriate for studies designed to test the abuse potential of a novel medication (Griffiths, Bigelow, and Ator, 2003; Sofuoglu, Poling, Mitchell, and Kosten, 2005; Tompkins *et al.*, 2010), because they are at the highest risk for misusing drugs and most likely to report euphorigenic effects, thus providing the most sensitive index of abuse potential.

The relationship between history of drug use and acute drug responses is complex: certain effects may increase with repeated use whereas other drug effects may diminish with use (King, de Wit, McNamara, and Cao, 2011; Kirk and de Wit, 1999). Few studies have systematically examined the effects of the same drugs at different phases of the addiction cycle. Although it would be ethically difficult for researchers to administer repeated doses of drugs with potential for abuse, it would be of considerable clinical interest to compare the acute effects of drugs after varying periods of exposure. An approach with less experimental control is to compare acute drug effects in early users and regular users, during withdrawal, or after varying periods of abstinence. Relatively few controlled studies have examined the effects of repeated use of drugs to determine which effects either increase or diminish with prolonged use (Strakowski, Sax, Setters, and Keck, 1996; Boileau *et al.*, 2006). Drug responses in relatively drug-naïve volunteers may provide important information about the likelihood of drug use initiation, whereas established drug users more closely model the motivational and clinical manifestations of the full disorder (de Wit and Phillips, 2012). However, drug responses in established drug users are often complicated by uncontrolled variables such tolerance or sensitization, learning and conditioning, neuroadaptations, or other consequences of extensive prior use of drugs or drug-use lifestyle. Moreover, there are ethical considerations in recruiting drug users who are seeking treatment or trying to abstain, because the drug challenge may precipitate craving or relapse. National Institute on Alcoholism and Alcohol Abuse (NIAAA) guidelines for alcohol challenge studies advise against administering ethanol to alcohol-dependent individuals who are seeking treatment.

2.2   Subject screening

For both scientific and safety reasons, careful screening of potential participants is essential. Depending on the drug and the purpose of the study, screening will include assessments of age, sex, weight, physical and psychiatric health, race, language fluency, education, night-shift work, and a thorough lifetime history of prior drug use, including both medical and recreational. For certain drugs further medical screening is recommended, such as an electrocardiogram for studies involving amphetamine, or liver function tests for studies involving alcohol.

2.3   Instructions to participants

Another key consideration in any human drug challenge study is the instructions provided to participants about the purpose of the study and the identity of the drugs to be administered. It is axiomatic that expectancies can profoundly affect responses to drugs (Rohsenow and Marlatt, 1981; Harrell and Juliano, 2009; Kirsch and Weixel, 1988; Stacy, Widaman, and Marlatt, 1990; Mitchell, Laurent, and de Wit, 1996) and therefore the information provided to participants in drug challenge studies must be carefully controlled. Usually, the pharmacological effects of a drug are of primary interest, and so expectancies need to be minimized or controlled. Thus, the drug is administered under double-blind conditions, which means that neither the experimenter nor the participant knows the identity of the drug at the time of drug administration. The order of drug and placebo administration is usually counterbalanced or randomized to avoid confounds related to order. For the purposes of consent, the drug or the class of drug must be revealed to the participant before the study begins and after completion of the study, but during the sessions themselves the expectancies can be carefully controlled. There are different ways to minimize expectancies. Some studies advise participants that they might get any of a number of different drug types (e.g., stimulant, sedative, antihistamine, placebo) even if they will only receive one active drug (Johanson and Preston, 1998). Although this method does involve mild deception, requiring approval by the ethics committee, the method is usually justified by benefits in experimental control. Capsules, beverages, or drug infusions are typically formulated to mask the contents of the mode of administration. Capsules are opaque and special methods may be used to verify that they are swallowed without chewing. Placebo beverages that are to be compared with alcohol beverages usually contain a small amount of alcohol to make them similar in smell or taste, and drug infusions are typically matched for other constituents such as glucose or saline.

Another strategy to control expectancies is to manipulate systematically the drug and the instructions in a four-group, between-subject balanced placebo design, in which some participants are told they will get drug or placebo and others actually receive drug or placebo (Rohsenow and Marlatt, 1981; Mitchell, Laurent, and de Wit, 1996). This has most commonly been done with alcohol, but there are also examples of balanced placebo studies with marijuana and amphetamine (Mitchell, Laurent, and de Wit, 1996; Metrik *et al.*, 2009). Another experimental approach is to include an active placebo: that is, a control drug that nonetheless has some psychoactive effects.

For example, in a study on the ability of psilocybin to induce spiritual-like experiences, Griffiths, Richards, McCann, and Jesse (2006) compared the effects of psilocybin to methylphenidate, a drug with detectable subjective effects but without the unique effects of psilocybin. This design feature reduced the chance that participants' expectancies of having a "spiritual" experience would account for the results. It is also possible that participants in a drug challenge study will distinguish active drug from placebo by sensory characteristics unrelated to the subjective or behavioral effects of primary interest. For example, a recent study investigating the effects of transdermal nicotine included a placebo patch with a small amount of capsaicin, to mimic the sensory effects of the nicotine patch. Thus, the placebo condition was manipulated to reduce participants' tendency to identify the active drug based on peripheral sensations (Wignall and de Wit, 2011). In studies involving drugs with different time course, or drugs administered by different routes of administration, there may be a need for "double-dummy" (e.g., two capsules or beverages), or even "triple-dummy" (i.e., three separate forms of drug administration) procedures to blind both the participants and experimenters to the active drug administration. Some studies explicitly examine the contribution of expectancies themselves to the drug response, including studies using the balanced placebo design or studies investigating the contribution of expectancies to clinical responses (Hughes *et al.*, 1989).

2.4 Ethical considerations

A key consideration in drug challenge studies with drugs of abuse is the ethics of exposing participants to the drug. Any study that involves administration of an abused drug to human volunteers necessarily exposes the participants to some risk. The degree of risk depends on factors such as the drug, dose, subject group, route of administration, inter-dose interval, and the facilities and medical resources available in the testing environment. These risks must be assessed carefully, and every effort made to minimize risk to participants, in accordance with the requirements of the local institutional review board. Participants must be carefully screened, provide voluntary informed consent, and fully understand the procedures and possible consequences of their participation. Data must be stored securely, and research personnel should be fully educated in human subjects research policies. Guidelines for ethical administration of alcohol to humans are available from the National Institute on Alcoholism and Alcohol Abuse (NIAAA, 2005) and guidelines on administration of drugs of abuse to human volunteers are available from the National Institute on Drug Abuse (NIDA, 2006). More specific guidelines for particular classes of drugs are available in the scientific literature (e.g., psilocybin; Johnson, Richards, and Griffiths, 2008). Local institutional review boards have the final authority for approving human subjects studies (IRB, 1993). In addition to the ethical constraints, certain legal limitations also apply to drug challenge studies. For example, according to US law, alcohol cannot be administered to participants under 21, although the minimum age for administering other psychoactive drugs is typically 18. Risk to participants can be minimized by testing in a safe and controlled environment, thoroughly screening participants for medical and psychiatric wellbeing before drug administration, and tests for pregnancy and other drug use before each administration. Finally, participants should be released from the laboratory only when the drug effects have declined to a safe level. With alcohol challenge studies the NIAAA recommends a certain breath alcohol level at which it is safe to release participants, whereas with other drugs the standard tests are usually performance or subjective ratings to determine a safe point at which to release participants.

2.5   Dose and route of administration

Another essential consideration in drug challenge studies is the dose and route of administration of drug. Selection of doses requires a balance between ethical and scientific considerations. Ethically, it is desirable to minimize both the dose administered and the frequency of dosing. However, from a scientific point of view, several doses from very low to as high as safely possible, in logarithmic units, is preferable, to provide a complete profile of the drug's effects. Inclusion of high doses is especially important in abuse liability assessments, because drug users typically use doses in excess of the prescribed doses of drugs. The route of administration used (e.g., oral, smoking, intranasal, transdermal, intravenous) depends on the drug, the drug-use histories of the participants, the purpose of the study, and the available level of medical support. For example, intravenous drug administration is desirable for studies requiring precision in plasma concentrations and eliminates pharmacokinetic variability related to absorption (e.g., ethanol; Childs, Connor, and de Wit, 2011; Ramchandani and O'Connor, 2006) or cannabis (D'Souza *et al.*, 2008). However, this route can only be safely conducted with proper medical support.

2.6   Contextual factors

A final consideration in testing the direct effects of psychoactive drugs is the physical or psychological context in which participants are tested. Subjects are usually confined to a laboratory for the duration of testing, for both safety and scientific control. Laboratory environments may be highly clinical (e.g., brain imaging contexts), or they may be naturalistic (e.g., furnished to resemble a bar or a living room). The laboratory setting may facilitate the somatic effects of a drug whereas the naturalistic context might facilitate pleasurable or intoxicating feelings (de Wit, Metz, Wagner, and Cooper, 1990). In most studies, participants are tested alone, but the presence of other people, either experimenters or other participants, may influence the outcome (see Chapter 19 in this volume; Doty and Wit, 1995). Laboratory environments may also include other activities such as movies or games, and they may vary in the time of day of testing, the demands that are made on participants, and the presence of other concurrent stimuli, such as pain (Zacny and Beckman, 2004; de Wit, Uhlenhuth, and Johnason, 1985). Finally, another series of studies demonstrate that the participants' activities during the sessions (i.e., requiring concentration or relaxation) also may influence their responses to a drug (Jones, Garrett, and Griffiths, 2001; Alessi, Roll, Reilly, and Johanson, 2002). All of these should be carefully considered in the context of the experimental question and balanced in terms of costs and benefits.

3   Dependent Measures

The dependent measures used in drug challenge studies will be summarized into three broad categories: (1) self-reported subjective effects, some of which are used as the first indicator of abuse potential; (2) physiological effects, which provide an important indicator of the safety profile of the drug; and (3) behavioral effects, including both beneficial and adverse consequences of use (e.g., cognitive enhancement, performance impairments or increased risk taking).

3.1   Self-reported subjective effects

Self-report ratings of drug effects and mood states are the primary outcome measure of most human psychopharmacology studies and provide a rich array of information about the quality, magnitude, and time course of a drug's effects. Some measures are used across a wide range of drugs, whereas other measures are specific to a particular type of drug. Which measures are selected depend on many factors, but most important are the goal of the study and the known sensitivity of the measure to the drug's effects. Standardized measures are in almost all cases preferable to novel measures, because they usually have established psychometric properties and because they permit comparisons to the published literature. Measures of drug-induced states should be obtained at the time of the drug effect ("right now") rather than retrospectively, because retrieval of the drug effect from memory adds unwanted variability, and because certain drugs specifically affect memory. Additionally, in order to control for the natural variability in mood states across experimental sessions, these measures should be administered both before drug administration (i.e., baseline) and repeatedly thereafter. The burden of self-report ratings should not be excessive, to maximize compliance in accurately reporting states. There is no perfect 'rule of thumb' for the appropriate duration of an assessment, but excessive length will certainly diminish the overall quality of the data. Finally, the language used in the questionnaires should match the reading and comprehension capacity of the participants.

3.1.1   *Measures used across drug classes*

3.1.1.1   DRUG EFFECT QUESTIONNAIRE.   The Drug Effect Questionnaire (DEQ; Fraser *et al.*, 1961) consists of four or five visual analog rating scales on which participants answer questions about the drug effect, from "not at all" to "very much." The questions are typically: "Feel drug" (do you feel a drug effect?), "Like drug" (do you like the effects you feel?), "High" (are you "high"?) and "More" (do you want more of the drug you just received?). Sometimes investigators also include a scale for "Dislike," because of the potential ambiguity in the "Like drug" question and because it is possible to both like and dislike current drug effects at the same time.

3.1.1.2   VISUAL ANALOG SCALE.   The Visual Analog Scale (VAS; Folstein and Luria, 1973) consists of lists of adjectives associated with a 100-mm line on which participants indicate whether each adjective describes their current state, again from "not at all" to "very much." The adjectives may describe either mood states (e.g., anxious, depressed), subjective drug effects (e.g., high, floating), or physiological effects (e.g., dry mouth). The specific adjectives included in a study would vary depending on the drug that is administered.

3.1.1.3 PROFILES OF MOOD STATES. Profiles of Mood States (POMS; McNair, Lorr, and Droppleman, 1971) was designed to assess psychiatric symptoms in patient populations, but it has been adapted to assess mood states, including those induced by drugs, in healthy volunteers. The standardized version of the POMS is the 65-item version consisting of bipolar scales (McNair, Lorr, and Droppleman, 1992). Another, non-validated 72-item version of the POMS is also widely used in acute drug challenge studies (Johanson and Uhlenhuth, 1980; de Wit and Griffiths, 1991; Foltin and Fischman, 1991). In the 72-item version, subjects indicate how they feel at the moment in relation to each adjective on a 5-point scale from "not at all" (0) to "extremely" (4). Eight clusters (scales) of items have been separated empirically using factor analysis (Anxiety, Depression, Anger, Vigor, Fatigue, Confusion, Friendliness, Elation). The value of each scale is determined by averaging the scores for the adjectives in that cluster.

3.1.1.4 ADDICTION RESEARCH CENTER INVENTORY. The 49-item Addiction Research Center Inventory (ARCI; Martin, Sloan, Sapira, and Jaskinski, 1971) is a true–false questionnaire designed to assess subjective responses to psychoactive drugs. It consists of drug-related scales that measure prototypic drug effects, including sedative-like (Pentobarbital–Chlorpromazine–Alcohol Group scale), stimulant-like (Amphetamine and Benzedrine Group scales), somatic and dysphoric (LSD scale), and euphorigenic (Morphine–Benzedrine Group scale). Sometimes a Marijuana scale is also included (Chait and Perry, 1994).

3.1.1.5 END OF SESSION QUESTIONNAIRE (ESQ). Typically, participants are queried about their responses to a drug at the end of a study session. They are asked to identify the substance they received (e.g., stimulant, sedative, alcohol, or placebo), and to rate on a 100-mm line how much they liked its effects, and sometimes also whether they would take the substance again.

3.1.1.6 POSITIVE AND NEGATIVE AFFECT SCHEDULE. The Positive and Negative Affect Schedule (PANAS; Watson, Clark, and Tellegen, 1988) is a 20-item adjective rating scale that assesses the participant's current affective state. The Positive Affect scale reflects the degree to which a person feels joyful, active, elated, or strong, and the Negative Affect scale reflects the degree to which a person experiences negative arousal, such as distress, hostility, anger, or anxiety. Each item is rated from "not at all" (0) to "extremely" (5).

3.1.2 Measures specific to drug classes. Specialized questionnaires assess the effects of specific types of drug.

3.1.2.1 BRIEF QUESTIONNAIRE ON SMOKING URGES. The Brief Questionnaire on Smoking Urges (BQSU; Cox, Tiffany, and Christen, 2001), a 10-item questionnaire, is a shortened version of the QSU (Tiffany and Drobes, 1991) designed to measure the primary intention and desire to smoke, anticipation of pleasure from smoking, and anticipation of relief from negative affect and nicotine withdrawal. The BQSU is a reliable measure of desire to smoke and consists of two factors related to the positive and negative reinforcing properties of smoking (Willner, Hardman, and Eaton, 1995).

3.1.2.2 HUGHES–HATSUKAMI NICOTINE WITHDRAWAL SCALE. The 11-item Hughes–Hatsukami Nicotine Withdrawal Scale (HHNWS; Hughes and Hatsukami, 1986) assesses DSM-related symptoms of nicotine withdrawal. Subjects rate, on a 5-point Likert scale, their symptoms of smoking abstinence (i.e., irritability, anxiety, difficulty concentrating, restlessness, etc.).

3.1.2.3 SMOKING QUESTIONNAIRE. This 10-item questionnaire, adapted from the Questionnaire of Smoking Urges (QSU; Tiffany and Drobes, 1991), also queries participants on the nature and magnitude of their smoking urges. Subjects circle a response from 1 (strongly disagree) to 7 (strongly agree) regarding their urge to smoke.

3.1.2.4 CIGARETTE EVALUATION QUESTIONNAIRE. The Cigarette Evaluation Questionnaire (CEQ; Westman, Levin, and Rose, 1992) is a self-report questionnaire assessing the reinforcing effects of smoking. It contains 11 items covering both the reinforcing and the aversive effects of smoking. There are subscales measuring "Smoking Satisfaction," "Psychological Reward," "Aversion," "Enjoyment of Respiratory Tract Sensations," and "Craving Reduction."

3.1.2.5 SUBJECTIVE HIGH ASSESSMENT SCALE. On this scale (Schuckit, 1984), subjects are asked to rate themselves from 0 (none) to 36 (extremely) on their present feelings of being "high," "intoxication," "sleepiness," "floating sensations," "nausea," and other descriptors.

3.1.2.6 ALCOHOL URGE QUESTIONNAIRE. The Alcohol Urge Questionnaire (AUQ) is composed of eight items related to urge to drink alcohol. Each item is rated on a 7-point Likert scale from "Strongly Disagree" to "Strongly Agree." The AUQ has high reliability in experimental studies of state levels of urge to drink (Bohn, Krahn, and Staehler, 1995; MacKillop, 2006).

3.1.2.7 BIPHASIC ALCOHOL EFFECTS SCALE. The Biphasic Alcohol Effects Scale (BAES; (Martin *et al.*, 1993) consists of 14 adjectives describing the stimulant-like (e.g., elated, energized) and sedative-like (e.g., down, heavy head) effects of alcohol. Participants indicate the extent to which they are feeling each adjective on an 11-point scale from "not at all" (0) to "extremely" (10), in relation to their responses to alcohol. There is also a brief version of this questionnaire (Rueger, McNamara, and King, 2009).

3.1.2.8   OPIATE CHECKLIST.   The Opiate Checklist (Preston, Bigelow, Bickel, and Liebson, 1989) consists of 32 adjectives on which the subject rates their current state on a 5-point scale from 0 to 4 (maximum effect). The list consists of subscales measuring both agonist opioid effects (e.g., flushing, itchy skin, sweating) and antagonist effects symptomatic of opioid withdrawal (e.g., watery eyes, runny nose, restless).

3.1.2.9   HALLUCINOGEN RATING SCALE.   The Hallucinogen Rating Scale (HRS; Strassman, Qualls, Uhlenhuth, and Kellner, 1994) is a 99-item questionnaire designed to detect the effects of hallucinogens (Tiffany and Drobes, 1991). It consists of six subscales assessing intensity, somaesthesia, affect, perception, cognition, and volition.

3.1.2.10   ALTERED STATES OF CONSCIOUSNESS SCALE.   The Altered States of Consciousness Scale (ASC; Dittrich, 1998) is a 72-item yes/no questionnaire designed to assess altered states of consciousness such as those produced by hallucinogens (Dittrich, 1998). It consists of three major scales: oceanic boundlessness, dread of ego dissolution (dysphoria), and visionary restructuralization (visual pseudo-hallucinations, illusions, and synesthesias).

3.2   Physiological effects

Physiological measures are obtained to monitor safety, to obtain objective measures of magnitude and time course of drug effects, and to characterize the quality and extent of a drug's effects. Physiological effects are valuable to provide objective measures of autonomic activity related to the drug, complementing measures of subjective effects. The selection of the physiological measures depends on the drug, the dose, and the goals of the study.

3.2.1   Heart rate.   Heart rate may be measured at regular intervals or continuously. The typical dependent measure is beats per minute, but additional informative measures include peak heart rate changes or heart rate variability calculated from interbeat intervals (Zanstra and Johnston, 2011; Thayer and Lane, 2009; Romanowicz *et al.*, 2011; Appelhans and Luecken, 2006).

3.2.2   Blood pressure.   Both systolic and diastolic blood pressure (SP and DP, respectively) are measured at regular intervals. The two measures can be combined into a commonly used, single measure of mean arterial pressure calculated as follows: $[(2 \times DP) + SP]/3$.

3.2.3   Temperature.   Peripheral or core body temperature provide a valuable objective measure of onset or time course of a drug's effects. In preclinical studies hyperthermia and hypothermia are used as indices of contextual conditioning (Siegel, 1978), raising the possibility that they could also be used for conditioning studies in humans.

3.3 Psychophysiological measures

A range of psychophysiological measures are available assess sympathetic and parasympathetic function and brain activity. Typical psychophysiological measures include skin conductance response (e.g., Bailey, Goedecker, and Tiffany, 2010), muscle activity (electromyography; e.g., Wardle and de Wit, 2011), changes in pupil diameter with drugs or with thought and emotion (pupillometry; e.g., Hou, Langley, Szabadi, and Bradshaw, 2007), eye tracking, saccadic eye movements and direction-of-gaze methods (Roche and King, 2010). These measures are often used in the context of responses to positive or negative emotional stimuli. For example, Wardle and de Wit (2011) recently studied the effects of amphetamine on facial muscle activity in response to emotional stimuli, and found that the effects of the drug on the electromygraphic measure of "smile" and "frown" muscles were more sensitive than subjective ratings, to detect drug effects on emotional responses. Measures of brain activity, including event-related potentials, electroencephalography, and functional magnetic resonance imaging, are described elsewhere in this volume.

4 Behavioral Measures

Many behavioral tasks have been used to assess specific dimensions of cognition and performance in acute drug studies. The optimal tasks are standardized and validated for reliability and to permit cross-study comparison, and there should be minimal learning across repeated administration of the task. Some tasks are also relatively long or demanding, introducing fatigue that may interact with the drug effect, influencing the outcome.

4.1 Measures of impulsive choice

Impulsive choice refers to decision making without consideration of the consequences. One common measure of impulsive choice is delay discounting, which assesses sensitivity to delayed consequences (i.e., rewards or punishments; Ainslie, 1975; Logue, 1988; Rachlin and Green, 1972). Greater impulsive choice is defined as preference for immediate, smaller rewards over larger more delayed rewards. Comparable, standardized tasks are available for use with both humans (Green *et al.*, 1996; Kirby and Marakovic, 1996; Rachlin, Raineri, and Cross, 1991; Richards, Zhang, Mitchell, and de Wit, 1999) and nonhumans (Mazur, 1987; Bradshaw and Szabadi, 1992; Richards, Mitchell, de Wit, and Seiden, 1997), providing an opportunity for valuable translational studies. In these procedures, human participants choose between immediate (smaller) and delayed (larger) monetary rewards, whereas laboratory animals choose between immediate or delayed water or food rewards. Both humans and nonhumans discount delayed rewards according to a hyperbolic function ($Value = A/(1 + kD)$ where A is the amount of the reward, D is the delay to reward, and k is a free parameter. The value of k provides a quantitative measure of impulsivity: larger values of k indicate more rapid devaluation of reinforcer value. Discounting measures effectively detect differences between individuals, including drug users and nonusers (Kirsch and Weixel, 1998; Strassman, Qualls, Uhlenhuth, and Kellner, 1994; Dittrich, 1998;

Zanstra and Johnston, 2011; Thayer and Lane, 2009; Ainslie, 1975; Green *et al.*, 1996), but they have been less successful in detecting state changes (e.g., after drug administration; see below).

4.1.1 Monetary Choice Questionnaire.

The Monetary Choice Questionnaire (Green *et al.*, 1996; Kirby, Petry, and Bickel, 1999) is a simple and brief questionnaire consisting of 27 hypothetical choices between delayed and immediate amounts of money. The delays range from 7 to 186 days, and the amount of delayed money can be set low ($25) or high ($485). It provides a measure of k, which reflects the degree of discounting, and has the advantage of being short (less than 5 minutes to administer). However, its sensitivity as a measure of state changes in impulsive behavior has not been established.

4.1.2 Adjusting Amount Delay Discounting.

Adjusting Amount Delay Discounting (AADD; Mitchell, Laurent, and de Wit, 1996; Rachlin, Raineri, and Cross, 1991; Crean, de Wit, and Richards, 2000; de Wit, Enggasser, and Richards, 2002; Bickel, Odum, and Madden, 1999) is a computerized procedure in which subjects repeatedly choose between immediate and delayed amounts of money. The delayed amount is $10 or $20, and the delays can vary from 1 to 365 days. Across successive trials, for each delay, the amount of the immediate reward is varied systematically until the subject reaches an immediate value that has the same value as the delayed amount ("indifference point"). After the subject has answered all the questions and reached their indifference points, one response is randomly selected by the experimenter to be reinforced (i.e., the subject receives the immediate or delayed reward for that trial, depending on their choice). The indifference points attained at each of the delays are plotted to form a discount function, which is derived through curve-fitting analyses, and a value for the parameter k. This task is well correlated with other discounting procedures (Epstein *et al.*, 2003).

4.1.3 Experiential Discounting Task.

The Experiential Discounting Task (EDT; Reynolds, Richards, and de Wit, 2006) also uses the adjusting amount procedure but it involves delays from only 0 to 60 seconds. Thus, subjects experience the delays as well as the delayed rewards *within* the session, making it particularly well suited to drug challenge studies. In addition, the money is delivered physically, in the form of a cash dispenser, as soon as it becomes available, making the rewards more salient. In the EDT task, subjects press a key to choose between an immediate certain, smaller reward, and a larger, probabilistic (0.35) delayed reward, delivered in 1–60 seconds. When a reward becomes available, the subject presses a second key to collect the money (this is likened to a "consummatory" response which may further increase the salience of the reward). After they make this response the money is delivered immediately through a cash dispenser. A running total of the earned money is also displayed on the screen. In one study (Reynolds, Richards, and de Wit, 2006) using the EDT, alcohol increased the tendency to discount delayed monetary rewards in social drinkers, supporting the idea that it may be a sensitive measure of state changes in discounting.

4.1.4   Two Choice Impulsivity Paradigm.   The Two Choice Impulsivity Paradigm (TCIP; NRLC, 2003a) is a discrete-choice paradigm for assessing tolerance for delayed rewards. Based on the delay of reward/gratification model of impulsivity, it examines the individual's preference for a smaller reward delivered after a short delay compared to a larger reward delivered after a longer delay. On each trial the participants are required to choose between two shapes (a circle that delivers 5 points after 5 seconds or a square that delivers 15 points obtainable after a 15-second delay). The total number of smaller–sooner reward choices made out of the 50 trials in the session is measured.

4.1.5   Balloon Analogue Risk Task.   The Balloon Analogue Risk Task (BART; Lejuez *et al.*, 2003) is a measure of risk taking in which participants make decisions between increasing payoff at the increasing risk of loss. It corresponds well with trait measure of real-life risk-taking behaviors (NRLC, 2003), although its sensitivity to state changes, such as those induced by drugs, is less clear (e.g., (McDonald, Schleifer, Richards, and de Wit, 2003; Acheson, Reynolds, Richards, and de Wit, 2006; Zacny and de Wit, 2009; Reynolds, Richards, and de Wit, 2006).

4.2   Measures of impulsive action

4.2.1   Stop Task.   The Stop Task (Logan, 1981; Logan, Schachar, and Tannock, 1997) is designed to measure behavioral inhibition, or the ability to inhibit prepotent behaviors. The task is based on a mathematical model known as the "race model," which describes the cognitive processes underlying the competing influences of executing and inhibiting responses. Subjects press a key as quickly as possible in response to a brief visual stimulus, but withhold the response when a tone is presented, very soon after the go signal. The procedure provides a measure of Go reaction time, and of the time to inhibit the response (Stop RT). The task distinguishes drug users from nonusers (Acheson, Reynolds, Richards, and de Wit, 2006) and it is also sensitive to the direct effects of drugs (Acheson, Reynolds, Richards, and de Wit, 2006; Zacny and de Wit, 2009; Logan, 1981).

4.2.2   Go–no-go tasks.   Go–no-go tasks (Newman, Widom, and Nathan, 1985) also assess the ability to inhibit an inappropriate response, but differ from the Stop Task in that the signal to inhibit occurs before the go signal, rather than after. This version of the task consists of repeated presentations of eight pairs of numbers, of which four are designated "correct" and four "incorrect." The subject's task is to respond to the correct numbers, and to withhold responses to the incorrect numbers. The outcome measures are errors of omission (withholding a response when a "correct" stimulus is presented), and errors of commission (i.e., responding to an "incorrect" stimulus). While nonspecific impairments such as inattention or fatigue are expected to influence both types of error, differentially high errors of commission are considered indicators of impulsive behavior.

4.2.3   GoStop Impulsivity Paradigm.   The GoStop Impulsivity Paradigm (GoStop; Newman, Widom, and Nathan, 1985) is a response inhibition paradigm developed to assess the capacity to inhibit/withhold an already initiated response. Five-digit numbers are presented on the screen for 500 milliseconds followed by a 1,500-millisecond inter-stimulus interval consisting of a blank screen. The paradigm consists of three trial types: nostop, stop, and novel trials. The nostop trial consists of a go signal – a number identical to the previous number presented in black. A stop trial consists of a stimulus that matches the previously presented number, but changes from black to red at a specified interval after go signal onset. A novel trial consists of a non-matching, randomly generated number (e.g., 48,953 . . . 36,214). Participants are required to respond, by clicking the left mouse button, to identically matching numbers while they are still on the screen (i.e. on nostop trials), but not respond to a number that turns red (i.e. on a stop trial) or to a non-matching number (i.e. a novel trial). The variable of interest is the proportion of inhibited responses to the total number of stop trials.

4.3   Time perception

Time perception is assessed using either time reproduction or time estimation (Lange *et al.*, 1995). In the time reproduction task, subjects are first asked to attend to the duration of an auditory stimulus of a certain duration (10, 30, or 60 seconds) and then 10 seconds later they are asked to reproduce the interval, by pressing a key once to begin and once to end the interval. Subjects are often required to perform a simple arithmetic task during the interval to prevent them from counting. In the time estimation task, subjects are asked to estimate the duration of several intervals, ranging from 10 to 80 seconds.

4.4   Attention

4.4.1   Attention Network Task.   The Attention Network Task (ANT; Fan *et al.*, 2002) measures three independent aspects of visual attention: alerting, orienting, and executive control, based on a theoretical schema of attention (Posner and Petersen, 1990).

4.4.2   Divided Attention Task.   The Divided Attention Task (DAT; Thornton *et al.*, 1986) is designed to assess changes in vigilance and inhibitory control, combining concurrent pursuit-tracking and vigilance tasks. Participants track a moving circle on the video screen using the mouse, and also signal when a small black square appears at any of the four corners of the screen. Accurate tracking of the moving stimulus increases its speed proportionately.

4.4.3   Rapid Information Processing Task.   The Rapid Information Processing Task (RIT; Wesnes and Warburton, 1983) is designed to assess changes in sustained concentration and inhibitory control. A series of digits is presented at the rate of 100 digits per minute, and subjects are instructed to press a response button as quickly as possible whenever they detect sequences of three consecutive odd or three consecutive even digits. A point is earned for each correct "hit" and a point is deducted for each "miss" or "false alarm."

4.5   Nonspecific performance

4.5.1   Digit Symbol Substitution Test.   The Digit Symbol Substitution Test (DSST; Wechsler, 1958) is commonly used to assess nonspecific impairments in psychomotor and cognitive performance. In this task, subjects are required to transpose symbols to correspond with digits in a 90-second timed task. It is sensitive to the effects of many psychoactive drugs, including both drugs that improve performance and drugs that impair performance (for a review, see Hindmarch, 1980).

4.6   Memory

Measures of memory are described more thoroughly in other chapters. Here we describe several tasks that are commonly included in drug challenge studies.

4.6.1   Digit Span.   Digit Span (Forward and Reverse; Wechsler, 1958) measures working memory, a general measure of attentional capacity, and cognitive functioning. Subjects are provided with an increasing number of single digits, which they are asked to recall. Typically, subjects can recall a series of seven or eight numbers. On the reverse digits task, subjects are required to repeat the list of numbers in reverse order.

4.6.2   Hopkins Verbal Memory Test.   The Hopkins Verbal Memory Test (Brandt, 1991) is comprised of 12 items organized into three semantic categories, and presented over three consecutive learning trials. The experimenter reads the list, and the subject repeats the words. Twenty minutes later, subjects are required to recall the words, and then to recognize them. Two distracters are interspersed within the 12 test items during subsequent recognition testing. This task measures working memory (total score on the three trials), new learning (slope from trial 1 to 3), and delayed recall (free recall after 20–25 minutes).

4.6.3   Repeated Acquisition Task.   The Repeated Acquisition Task (RA; Kelly, Foltin, Emurian, and Fischman, 1993) assesses drug-induced changes in learning and memory. Participants are instructed to learn a ten-response sequence of button presses. A points counter increases by 1 each time the ten-response sequence is correctly completed. The sequence remains the same within a session, but a new random sequence is generated in each administration of the task.

4.7   Commercially available packages containing multiple tasks

There are several commercially available packages consisting of multiple standardized tasks. One is the Automated Neuropsychological Assessment Metrics (ANAM-Version IV; Reeves *et al.*, 2006), which assesses several cognitive domains including attention, concentration, reaction time, memory, processing speed, and decision making. It can be used to assess neurocognitive function at a single time, or at repeated intervals. It includes 22 assessments that are sensitive to cognitive change after acute drug administration. Another is the CANTAB (Cambridge Neuropsychological Test Assessment Battery) Cambridge Cognition Ltd, which consists of tasks designed to measure visual memory, semantic or verbal memory, executive function, decision-making and response control, and attention. The CANTAB tests are sensitive to the effects of a wide variety of centrally acting drugs, and provide excellent qualitative and quantitative measures of drug-induced impairment or enhancement of performance. A third is a series of cognitive and behavioral tasks available from Inquisit (Millisecond Software). Although detailed discussion of these packages is beyond the scope of this chapter, they provide useful tools in studies investigating the cognitive and behavioral effects of addictive drugs.

5 Conclusions

This chapter has reviewed methods and general principles in assessing acute effects of drugs of abuse in humans. We have described a wide range of outcome measures that may be included in drug challenge studies, including subjective or self-report measures, behavioral or performance measures, and measures of physiological responses. We have described principles for selecting measures, selecting participants, and designing the studies, and we have emphasized the importance of ethical considerations including safety and confidentiality. We have also discussed the importance of instructions and blinding procedures, and considerations about dose and route of administration. There is a large and evolving published literature on drug challenge studies with addictive drugs, which we hope will improve our understanding of both the determinants and the consequences of drug use.

References

Acheson A, Reynolds B, Richards JB, and de Wit H (2006) Diazepam impairs behavioral inhibition but not delay discounting or risk taking in healthy adults. *Experimental and Clinical Psychopharmacology* 14(2): 190–198. PMID: 16756423.

Ainslie G (1975) Specious reward: A behavioral theory of impulsiveness and impulse control. *Psychological Bulletin* 82(4): 463–496.

Alessi SM, Roll JM, Reilly MP, and Johanson CE (2002) Establishment of a diazepam preference in human volunteers following a differential-conditioning history of placebo versus diazepam choice. *Exp Clin Psychopharmacol* 10(2): 77–83, discussion 101–3.

Appelhans BM and Luecken LJ (2006) Heart rate variability as an index of regulated emotional responding. *Review of General Psychology* 10(3): 229–240.

Bailey SR, Goedeker KC, and Tiffany ST (2010) The impact of cigarette deprivation and cigarette availability on cue-reactivity in smokers. *Addiction* 105(2): 364–372.

Bedi G, Phan KL, Angstadt M, and de Wit H (2009) Effects of MDMA on sociability and neural response to social threat and social reward. *Psychopharmacology* (Berlin) 207(1): 73–83. PMID: 19680634.

Bickel WK, Odum AL, and Madden GJ (1999) Impulsivity and cigarette smoking: Delay discounting in current, never, and ex-smokers. *Psychopharmacology* 146(4): 447–454.

Bohn MJ, Krahn DD, and Staehler BA (1995) Development and initial validation of a measure of drinking urges in abstinent alcoholics. *Alcoholism: Clinical and Experimental Research* 19, 600–606.

Boileau I, Dagher A, Leyton M, Gunn RN, Baker GB, Diksic M, and Benkelfat C (2006) Modeling sensitization to stimulants in humans: A [^{11}C]raclopride/PET study in healthy volunteers. *Archives of General Psychiatry* 63: 1386–1395.

Bradshaw CM and Szabadi E (1992) Choice between delayed reinforcers in a discrete-trials schedule: The effect of deprivation level. *Quarterly Journal of Experimental Psychology B* 44(1): 1–6.

Brandt D (1991) The Hopkins verbal learning test: Development of a new memory test with six equivalent forms. *The Clinical Neuropsychologist* 5(2): 125–142.

Carter LP and Griffiths RR (2009) Principles of laboratory assessment of drug use liability and implications for clinical development. *Drug and Alcohol Dependence* 105(Suppl. 1): 14–25.

Chait LD and Perry JL (1994) Acute and residual effects of alcohol and marijuana, alone and in combination on mood and performance. *Psychopharmacology* 115(3): 340–349.

Childs E, O'Connor S, and de Wit H (2011) Bidirectional interactions between acute psychosocial stress and acute IV alcohol. *Alcoholism: Clinical and Experimental Research* 35(10): 1794–1803.

Cox LS, Tiffany ST, and Christen AG (2001) Evaluation of the brief questionnaire of smoking urges (QSU-brief) in laboratory and clinical settings. *Nicotine and Tobacco Research* 3(1): 7–16.

Crean JP, de Wit H, and Richards JB (2000) Reward discounting as a measure of impulsive behavior in a psychiatric outpatient population. *Experimental and Clinical Psychopharmacology* 8(2): 155–162.

de Wit H and Griffiths RR (1991) Testing the abuse liability of anxiolytic and hypnotic drugs in humans. *Drug and Alcohol Dependence* 28(1): 83–111.

de Wit H, Enggasser JL, and Richards JB (2002) Acute administration of d-amphetamine decreases impulsivity in healthy volunteers. *Neuropsychopharmacology* 27(5): 813–825.

de Wit H, Metz J, Wagner N, and Cooper M (1990) Behavioral and subjective effects of ethanol: Relationship to cerebral metabolism using PET. *Alcoholism: Clinical and Experimental Research* 14(3): 482–489.

de Wit H and Phillips TJ (2012) Do initial responses to drugs predict future use or abuse? *Neuroscience and Biobehavioral Reviews* 36(6):1565–1576. Epub 2012 Apr 21.

de Wit H, Uhlenhuth EH, and Johanson CE (1985) Drug preference in normal volunteers: Effects of age and time of day. *Psychopharmacology* 87(2): 186–193.

Dittrich A (1998) The standardized psychometric assessment of altered states of consciousness (ASCs) in humans. *Pharmacopsychiatry* 31, 80–84.

Dlugos A, Freitag C, Hohoff C, McDonald J, Cook EH, Deckert J, and de Wit H (2007) Norepinephrine transporter gene variation modulates acute response to D-amphetamine. *Biological Psychiatry* 61(11): 1296–1305.

Doty P and Wit H (1995) Effect of setting on the reinforcing and subjective effects of ethanol in social drinkers. *Psychopharmacology* 118(1): 19–27.

D'Souza DC, Ranganathan M, Braley G, Gueorguieva R, Zimolo Z, Cooper T, Perry E, and Krystal J (2008) Blunted psychotomimetic and amnestic effects of delta-9-tetrahydrocannabinol in frequent users of cannabis. *Neuropsychopharmacology* 33(10): 2505–2516.

Enggasser JL and de Wit H (2001) Haloperidol reduces stimulant and reinforcing effects of ethanol in social drinkers. *Alcoholism: Clinical and Experimental Research* 25(10): 1448–1456.

Epstein LH, Richards JB, Saad FG, Paluch RA, Roemmich JN, and Lerman C (2003) Comparison between two measures of delay discounting in smokers. *Experimental and Clinical Psychopharmacology* 11(2): 131–138.

Fan J, McCandliss BD, Sommer T, Raz A, and Posner MI (2002) Testing the efficiency and independence of attentional networks. *Journal of Cognitive Neuroscience* 14(3): 340–347.

Folstein MF and Luria R (1973) Reliability, validity, and clinical application of the visual analogue mood scale. *Psychological Medicine* 3(4): 479.

Foltin RW and Fischman MW (1991) Assessment of abuse liability of stimulant drugs in humans: A methodological survey. *Drug and Alcohol Dependence* 28(1): 3–48.

Food and Drug Administration (FDA) Guidance, compliance, and regulatory information. (n.d.). http://www.fda.gov/drugs/guidancecomplianceregulatoryinformation/default. htm.

Fraser HR, Van Horn GG, Martin WR, Wolbach AB, and Isbell H (1961) Methods for evaluating addiction liability. (A) 'Attitude' of opiate addicts toward opiate-like drugs. (B) A short-term 'direct' addiction test. *Journal of Pharmacology and Experimental Therapeutics* 133, 371–387.

Green L, Myerson J, Lichtman D, Rosen S, and Fry A (1996) Temporal discounting in choice between delayed rewards. *Psychology and Aging* 11(1): 79–84.

Griffiths RR, Bigelow GE, and Ator NA (2003) Principles of initial experimental drug abuse liability assessment in humans. *Drug and Alcohol Dependence* 5;70(3 Suppl):S41–S54. Review.

Griffiths RR, Richards WA, McCann U, and Jesse R (2006) Psilocybin can occasion mystical-type experiences having substantial and sustained personal meaning and spiritual significance. *Psychopharmacology* 187(3): 268–283.

Harrell PT and Juliano LM (2009) Caffeine expectancies influence the subjective and behavioral effects of caffeine. *Psychopharmacology* 207(2): 335–342.

Hindmarch I (1980) Psychomotor function and psychoactive drugs. *British Journal of Clinical Pharmacology* 10(3): 189–209. PMID: 7002180

Hou RH, Langley RW, Szabadi E, and Bradshaw CM (2007) Comparison of diphenhydramine and modafinil on arousal and autonomic functions in healthy volunteers. *Journal of Psychopharmacology* 21(6): 567–578.

Hughes J and Hatsukami D (1986) Signs and symptoms of tobacco withdrawal. *Archives of General Psychiatry* 43(3): 289–294.

Hughes JR, Strickler G, King D, Higgins ST, Fenwick JW, Gulliver SB, and Mireault G (1989) Smoking history, instructions and the effects of nicotine: Two pilot studies. *Pharmacology Biochemistry and Behavior* 34(1): 149–155.

Institutional Review Board (IRB) (1993) Introduction. In *IRB Guidebook*. http://www.hhs .gov/ohrp/archive/irb/irb_introduction.htm.

Johanson C and Preston K (1998) The influence of an instruction on the stimulus effects of drugs in humans. *Experimental and Clinical Psychopharmacology* 6(4): 427–432.

Johanson CE and Uhlenhuth EH (1980) Drug preference and mood in humans: D-amphetamine. *Psychopharmacology* 71(3): 275–279.

Johnson M, Richards W, and Griffiths R (2008) Human hallucinogen research: Guidelines for safety. *Journal of Psychopharmacology* 22(6): 603–620.

Jones HE, Garrett BE, and Griffiths RR (2001) Reinforcing effects of oral cocaine: Contextual determinants. *Psychopharmacology* (Berlin) 154(2): 143–152.

Kelly TH, Foltin RW, Emurian CS, and Fischman MW (1993) Performance-based testing for drugs of abuse: Dose and time profiles of marijuana, amphetamine, alcohol, and diazepam. *Journal of Analytical Toxicology* 17(5): 264–272.

King AC, de Wit H, McNamara PJ, and Cao D (2011) Rewarding, stimulant, and sedative alcohol responses and relationship to future binge drinking. *Archives of General Psychiatry* 68(4): 389–399.

Kirby KN and Marakovic NN (1996) Delay-discounting probabilistic rewards: Rates decrease as amounts increase. *Psychonomic Bulletin and Review* 3: 100–104.

Kirby KN, Petry NM, and Bickel WK (1999) Heroin addicts have higher discount rates for delayed rewards than non-drug-using controls. *Journal of Experimental Psychology: General* 128(1): 78–87.

Kirk JM and de Wit H (1999) Responses to oral Δ9-tetrahydrocannabinol in frequent and infrequent marijuana users. *Pharmacology Biochemistry and Behavior* 63(1): 137–142.

Kirsch I and Weixel LJ (1988) Double-blind versus deceptive administration of a placebo. *Behavioral Neuroscience* 102(2): 319–323.

Lange KW, Tucha O, Steup A, Gsell W, and Naumann M (1995) Subjective time estimation in Parkinson's disease. *Journal of Neural Transmission Supplement* 46: 433–438.

Lejuez CW, Aklin WM, Jones HA, Richards JB, Strong DR, Kahler CW, and Read JP (2003) The Balloon Analogue Risk Task (BART) differentiates smokers and nonsmokers. *Experimental and Clinical Psychopharmacology* 11(1): 26–33.

Logan GD (1981) Attention, automaticity, and the ability to stop a speeded choice response. In J Long and AD Baddeley (eds), *Attention and Performance* (Vol. IX). Hillsdale, NJ: Lawrence Erlbaum Associates.

Logan GD, Schachar RJ, and Tannock R (1997) Impulsivity and inhibitory control. *Psychological Science* 8(1): 60–64.

Logue AW (1988) Research on self-control: An integrated framework. *Behavioral Brain Science* 11, 665–709.

MacKillop J (2006) Factor structure of the alcohol urge questionnaire under neutral conditions and during a cue-elicited urge state. *Alcoholism: Clinical and Experimental Research* 30, 1315–1321.

Martin CS, Earleywine M, Musty RE, Perrine MW, and Swift RM (1993) Development and validation of the biphasic alcohol effects scale. *Alcoholism: Clinical and Experimental Research* 17(1): 140–146.

Martin WR, Sloan JW, Sapira JD, and Jaskinski DR (1971) Physiologic, subjective and behavioral effects of amphetamine, methamphetamine, ephedrine, phenmetrazine and methylphenidate in man. *Clinical Pharmacology and Therapeutics* 12(2): 245–258.

Mazur JE (1987) An adjusting procedure for studying delayed reinforcement. In ML Commons, JE Mazur, JA Nevin, and H Rachlin (eds), *Quantitative Analysis of Behavior: Vol. 5. The Effect of Delay and Intervening Events on Reinforcement Value* (pp. 55–73). Hillsdale, NJ: Erlbaum.

McDonald J, Schleifer L, Richards JB, and de Wit H (2003) Effects of delta [9]-tetrahydrocannabinol on behavioral measures of impulsivity in humans. *Neuropsychopharmacology* 28, 1356–1365. PMID: 12784123.

McNair DM, Lorr M, and Droppleman LF (1971) Measures of impulsivity in cigarette smokers and nonsmokers. *Manual for the Profile of Mood States* 146: 455–464.

McNair DM, Lorr M, and Droppleman LF (1992) *Revised Manual for the Profile of Mood States*. San Diego, CA: Educational and Industrial Testing Service.

Metrik J, Rohsenow DJ, Monti PM, McGeary J, Cook TA, de Wit H, Haney M, and Kahler CW (2009) Effectiveness of a marijuana expectancy manipulation: Piloting the balanced-placebo design for marijuana. *Experimental and Clinical Psychopharmacology* 4: 217–225. PMID: 19653787.

Mitchell SH, Laurent CL, and de Wit H (1996) Interaction of expectancy and the pharmacological effects of d-amphetamine: Subjective effects and self-administration. *Psychopharmacology* 125(4): 371–378.

National Institute on Alcoholism and Alcohol Abuse (NIAAA) (2005) Recommended Council Guidelines on Ethyl Alcohol Administration in Human Experimentation. http://www.niaaa.nih.gov/Resources/ResearchResources/job22.htm.

National Institute on Drug Abuse (NIDA) (2006) NACDA Guidelines for Administration of Drugs to Human Subjects. http://www.nida.nih.gov/funding/hsguide.html.

Neurobehavioral Research Laboratory and Clinic (NRLC), University of Texas Health Science Center (2003) *Two Choice Impulsivity Paradigm (Version 1.0)* [computer program]. Houston, TX.

Newlin DB and Renton RM (2010) High risk groups often have higher levels of alcohol response than low risk: The other side of the coin. *Alcoholism: Clinical and Experimental Research* 34(2): 199–205. PMID: 19951303.

Newman JP, Widom CS, and Nathan S (1985) Passive avoidance in syndromes of disinhibition: Psychopathy and extraversion. *Journal of Personality and Social Psychology* 48(5): 1316–1327.

Posner MI and Petersen SE (1990) The attention systems of the human brain. *Annual Review of Neuroscience* 13: 25–42.

Preston KL, Bigelow GE, Bickel WK, and Liebson IA (1989) Drug discrimination in human postaddicts: Agonist–antagonist opioids. *Journal of Pharmacology and Experimental Therapeutics* 250(1): 184–196.

Rachlin H and Green L (1972) Commitment, choice and self-control. *Journal of the Experimental Analysis of Behavior* 17(1): 15–22.

Rachlin H, Raineri A, and Cross D (1991) Subjective probability and delay. *Journal of the Experimental Analysis of Behavior* 55(2): 233–244.

Ramchandani VA and O'Connor S (2006) Studying alcohol elimination using the alcohol clamp method. *Alcohol Research and Health* 29(4): 286–290.

Reeves DL, Bleiberg J, Roebuck-Spencer T, Cernich AN, Schwab K, Ivins B, Salazar A M, Harvey SC, Brown FH, Jr, and Warden D (2006) Reference values for performance on the automated neuropsychological assessment metrics V3.0 in an active duty military sample. *Military Medicine* 171(10): 982–994.

Reynolds B, Richards JB, and de Wit H (2006) Acute alcohol effects on laboratory measures of impulsive behavior in humans. *Pharmacology, Biochemistry, and Behavior* 83(2): 194–202.

Richards JB, Mitchell SH, de Wit H, and Seiden LS (1997) Determination of discount functions in rats with an adjusting-amount procedure. *Journal of the Experimental Analysis of Behavior* 67(3): 353–366.

Richards J, Zhang L, Mitchell SH, and de Wit H (1999) Discounting by delay and probability in a model of impulsive behavior: Effects of alcohol. *Journal of the Experimental Analysis of Behavior* 71(2): 121–143.

Roche DJ and King AC (2010) Alcohol impairment of saccadic and smooth pursuit eye movements: Impact of risk factors for alcohol dependence. *Psychopharmacology* (Berlin) 212(1): 33–34.

Rohsenow DJ and Marlatt GA (1981) The balanced placebo design: Methodological considerations. *Addictive Behaviors* 6(2): 107–122.

Romanowicz M, Schmidt JE, Bostwick JM, Mrazek DA, and Karpyak VM (2011) Changes in heart rate variability associated with acute alcohol consumption: Current knowledge and implications for practice and research. *Alcoholism: Clinical and Experimental Research* (in press).

Rueger SY, McNamara PJ, and King AC (2009) Expanding the utility of the Biphasic Alcohol Effects Scale (BAES) and initial psychometric support for the Brief-BAES (B-BAES). *Alcoholism: Clinical and Experimental Research* 33(5): 916–924.

Schuckit MA (1984) Subjective responses to alcohol in sons of alcoholics and control subjects. *Archives of General Psychiatry* 41, 879–884.

Schuckit MA, Smith TL, Trim RS. Allen RC, Fukukura T, Knight EE, Cesario EM, and Kreikebaum SA (2011) A prospective evaluation of how a low level of response to alcohol predicts later heavy drinking and alcohol problems. *The American Journal of Drug and Alcohol Abuse* [Epub ahead of print].

Siegel S (1978) Tolerance to the hyperthermic effect of morphine in the rat is a learned response. *Journal of Comparative Physiological Psychology* 92(6): 1137–1149. PMID: 755060.

Sofuoglu M, Poling J, Mitchell E, and Kosten TR (2005) Tiagabine affects the subjective responses to cocaine in humans. *Pharmacology Biochemistry and Behavior* 82(3): 569–573.

Stacy AW, Widaman KF, and Marlatt GA (1990) Expectancy models of alcohol use. *Journal of Personality and Social Psychology* 55(5): 918–928.

Strakowski SM, Sax KW, Setters MJ, and Keck PE, Jr (1996) Enhanced response to repeated d-amphetamine challenge: Evidence for behavioral sensitization in humans. *Biological Psychiatry* 40(9): 872–880.

Strassman RJ, Qualls CR, Uhlenhuth EH, and Kellner R (1994) Dose-response study of N, N-dimethyltryptamine in humans. II Subjective effects and preliminary results of a new rating scale. *Archives of General Psychiatry* (51): 98–108.

Thayer JF and Lane RD (2009) Claude Bernard and the heart–brain connection: Further elaboration of a model of neurovisceral integration. *Neuroscience and Biobehavioral Reviews* 33(2): 81–88.

Thornton JE, Taylor JL, Gibson EL, Miller TP, and Tinklenberg JR (1986) Microcomputerized testing of drug effects on divided attention. *Psychopharmacology Bulletin* 22(1): 73–75.

Tiffany ST and Drobes DJ (1991) The development and initial validation of a questionnaire on smoking urges. *British Journal of Addiction* 86(11): 1467–1476.

Tompkins DA, Lanier RK, Harrison JA, Strain EC, and Bigelow GE (2010) Human abuse liability assessment of oxycodone combined with ultra-low-dose naltrexone. *Psychopharmacology* 210(4): 471–480.

Wachtel SR, Ortengren A, and de Wit H (2002) The effects of acute haloperidol or risperidone on subjective responses to methamphetamine in healthy volunteers. *Drug and Alcohol Dependence* 68(1): 23–33.

Wardle MC and de Wit H (2011) Effects of amphetamine on responses to positive emotional stimuli. *Psychopharmacology* (in press).

Watson D, Clark LA, and Tellegen A (1988) Development and validation of brief measures of positive and negative affect: The PANAS scales. *Journal of Personality and Social Psychology* 54(6): 1063–1070.

Wechsler D (1958) *The Measurement and Appraisal of Adult Intelligence* (4th edn). Baltimore, MD: Williams & Wilkins Co.

Wesnes K and Warburton DM (1983) Effects of smoking on rapid information processing performance. *Neuropsychobiology* 9(4): 223–229.

Westman E, Levin E, and Rose J (1992) Smoking while wearing the nicotine patch: Is smoking satisfying or harmful? *Clinical Research* 40: 871.

Wignall N and de Wit H (2011) Effects of nicotine on cognition and behavioral inhibition in healthy nonsmokers. *Experimental Clinical Psychopharmacology* (in press).

Willner P, Hardman S, and Eaton G (1995) Subjective and behavioural evaluation of cigarette cravings. *Psychopharmacology* 118(2): 171–177.

280 *Harriet de Wit*

Zacny JP and Beckman NJ (2004) The effects of a cold-water stimulus on butorphanol effects in males and females. *Pharmacology Biochemistry and Behavior* 78(4): 653–659.

Zacny JP and de Wit H (2009) The prescription opioid, oxycodone, does not alter behavioral measures of impulsivity in healthy volunteers. *Pharmacology Biochemistry and Behavior* 94(1): 108–113.

Zanstra YD and Johnston DW (2011) Cardiovascular reactivity in real life settings: Measurement, mechanisms and meaning. *Biological Psychology* 86(2): 98–105.

11

The Role of Aftereffects and Withdrawal in Addiction[1]

Jon D. Kassel, Jennifer C. Veilleux, Adrienne J. Heinz, Ashley Braun, and Stephanie Weber

1 Introduction

Experimentation and limited use of drugs, both licit and illicit, are developmentally normative phenomena. Hence, many individuals, typically during their adolescent years, make the decision to self-administer drugs and alcohol. Indeed, in the case of alcohol, an overwhelming majority of people have tried it, most without having experienced notable adverse consequences. At the same time, for a relatively small proportion of individuals who choose to use drugs and/or alcohol, their use becomes abuse and sometimes even transitions into drug dependence or addiction (terms that, while arguably different, will be treated as synonymous throughout this chapter). And it is these individuals who are the focus of the current chapter. In this context, an important point that warrants deference up front is that addiction is a process, one that unfolds over time and is influenced by a host of pharmacological, psychological, biological, and even societal factors. Moreover, we would argue that there is still no real consensus as to precisely how *addiction* is, or should be, best operationalized. Historically, the notion of addiction is most often defined or understood in terms of the addict fundamentally displaying a loss of control over consumption. Although this idea certainly holds intuitive appeal and some degree of face validity, exactly how the construct of "loss of control" is best assessed remains open to debate and discussion, as are other factors that no doubt play a role in, and reflect the very nature of, drug dependence (e.g., tolerance, craving, withdrawal).

Within the field of behavioral pharmacology, emphasis has traditionally been placed on studying and measuring the acute effects of drugs on host of behavioral, affective, and physiological outcomes (see Chapter 1 of this volume). The idea here is that

[1] Preparation of this chapter was made possible, in part, by NIH Grant 1PO1CA98262 from the National Cancer Institute.

to best understand how and why some individuals become addicted to drugs, one needs to fully elucidate the array of effects that said drugs exert on the organism (as assessed in animal models of addiction, or in humans, the focus of this chapter). That is, delineation of reinforcing (or rewarding) processes and outcomes should go a long way toward helping the field better understand why some people go on to become addicted to drugs, while the majority of those who use drugs do not end up transitioning on to the deleterious phase of drug addiction. And the rather voluminous research across diverse drugs that has addressed these issues has, no doubt, been critical in shaping the field's understanding of drug addiction over the years, ultimately holding important implications for and shaping policy, intervention, and prevention efforts.

Although fostering an understanding of the acute effects of drugs clearly remains a very important research target, another aspect of drug dependence has also emerged as crucial. This is the notion of drug withdrawal, viewed by many as the *sine qua non* of addiction itself. Simply put, the idea here is that repeated exposure to most major substances with abuse liability results in dependence, itself an altered physiological state inferred from the emergence of a withdrawal syndrome following cessation of drug administration (Harris and Gewirtz, 2005; Koob and Le Moal, 2001). Thus, according to some, it is the emergence of the state of withdrawal itself that lies at the core of, and ultimately defines, addiction. To reframe this stance just slightly, it is not the acute effects of drugs themselves that result in addiction, but rather, the consequences of *not using drugs* (for whatever reasons) that ultimately determine an outcome of substance dependence.

Moreover, manifestation of withdrawal clearly influences a host of important behavioral outcomes, including relapse in those who had tried to cease their drug use. As we will discuss shortly, virtually all signs and symptoms of withdrawal (across all drugs of abuse) are inherently aversive. As such, individuals in the throes of withdrawal are often highly motivated to escape or avoid such unpleasant symptoms. And the clearest and most effective way to do so is to re-administer the very drug(s) on which they have become dependent.

Hence, drug withdrawal clearly emerges as a critical component – again, some would argue *the* defining component – of addiction. Consequently, we will review the literature with respect to the role played by withdrawal (and, in the case of alcohol, the aftereffect of *hangover*) in drug addiction. Toward these ends, we begin by operationalizing substance withdrawal, and reviewing examples of various withdrawal syndromes. Based on the notion that the primary reinforcing mechanism through which withdrawal exerts its motivational significance is negative reinforcement, we proceed to briefly consider and review several influential theoretical models that have spawned important research and clinical findings. We then turn to a review of methods through which withdrawal and a critical component of withdrawal – craving – have been assessed. We then consider some relatively novel and promising approaches to the measurement of withdrawal, including paradigms steeped in a behavioral economics perspective and those that assess withdrawal effects utilizing psychophysiological approaches. We conclude by offering methodological recommendations while addressing limitations and challenges facing the field of substance dependence with respect to the critical role played by withdrawal in promoting, maintaining, and ultimately defining addiction.

2   Withdrawal Defined

Attempts at understanding the nature, classification, and operationalization of drug withdrawal have a long, storied, and at times, controversial history. As arguably important as the construct of withdrawal is, simply put, there remains discussion, debate, and uncertainty regarding its essence and very nature. Nonetheless, tremendous strides have been made in recent years toward achieving consensus regarding how withdrawal is best understood and measured. Turning to perhaps the most influential nosological system currently employed by the field, the *Diagnostic and Statistical Manual of Mental Disorders* (American Psychiatric Association [APA], 2000), we begin by examining their stance on withdrawal: "The essential feature of Substance Withdrawal is the development of a substance-specific maladaptive behavioral change, with physiological and cognitive concomitants, that is due to the cessation of, or reduction in, heavy and prolonged substance use (Criterion A). The substance-specific syndrome causes clinically significant distress or impairment in social, occupational, or other important areas of functioning (Criterion B). The symptoms are not due to a general medical condition and are not better accounted for by another mental disorder (Criterion C)" (p. 201). The DSM-IV-TR goes on to observe that withdrawal is usually, though not always, associated with a diagnosis of Substance Dependence, and that most – indeed, perhaps all – individuals who experience withdrawal signs and symptoms also experience a craving to re-administer the substance in order to reduce the otherwise aversive symptoms.

So, in sum, repeated administration of drugs with abuse liability can and, in the majority of instances, will result in the appearance of a withdrawal syndrome specific to that class of drug. Such symptoms are almost always experienced as aversive, and hence, serve as cues to motivate further drug self-administration. Importantly, the DSM-IV-TR further asserts that such withdrawal symptoms, and the syndrome itself, will probably result in negative consequences to the individuals across a realm of important areas of functioning in their lives. The diagnosis of withdrawal is recognized for the following groups of substances: alcohol; amphetamines and other related substances; cocaine; nicotine; opioids; and sedatives, hypnotics, or anxiolytics (see Table 11.1). Whereas it has been argued that there are some withdrawal symptoms that are universal in nature, such that they cut across virtually all drug classes (e.g., negative affect), the signs and symptoms of withdrawal are thought to vary according to the substance used, with most symptoms being the opposite of those observed in intoxication with the same substance. Thus, for example, if nicotine is experienced by most smokers as calming and facilitating attentional processing and ability to concentrate, a common withdrawal profile among deprived smokers is increased irritability and difficulty concentrating. Furthermore, the dose and duration of use and other factors, such as the presence or absence of additional illnesses, can affect withdrawal symptoms. In general, withdrawal develops when doses are reduced or stopped, whereas signs and symptoms of intoxication generally improve (gradually in some cases) after dosing stops.

A perusal of the symptoms observed in Table 11.1 leads to several interesting observations. First, craving is not to be found among the accepted withdrawal symptoms in any of the drug classes. As we will discuss later, the construct of craving has proven

Table 11.1 Withdrawal symptoms by psychoactive drug

Alcohol	Amphetamine	Cocaine	Nicotine	Opioids	Sedatives, hypnotics, or anxiolytics
Autonomic hyperactivity	Fatigue	Fatigue	Dysphoric mood	Dysphoric mood	Autonomic hyperactivity
Hand tremor	Vivid unpleasant dreams	Vivid unpleasant dreams	Irritability, frustration, or anger	Muscle aches	Hand tremor
Insomnia	Insomnia or hypersomnia	Insomnia or hypersomnia	Insomnia	Insomnia	Insomnia
Nausea or vomiting	Increased appetite	Increased appetite	Increased appetite or weight gain	Nausea or vomiting	Nausea or vomiting
Hallucinations	Psychomotor retardation or agitation	Psychomotor retardation or agitation	Difficulty concentrating	Lacrimation or rhinorrhea	Hallucinations
Psychomotor agitation			Anxiety/restlessness	Yawning	Psychomotor agitation
Anxiety					Anxiety
Grandmal seizures			Decreased heart rate	Diarrhea	Grandmal seizures
				Fever	
				Papillary dilation, piloerection, or sweating	

contentious at times, with some arguing that it is merely an epiphenomenon with little explanatory power. Moreover, it has also been observed that, because individuals who may not meet criteria for substance dependence also report experiencing drug craving, it should not be considered a withdrawal symptom. At the same time, virtually all drug addicts report profound experiences of craving and, as such, its clinical utility and phenomenological validity cannot really be questioned. Second, there clearly is variability in withdrawal symptoms across different drug classes. Furthermore, there is strong reason to believe that there is a great deal of variability in the manifestation of withdrawal within drug classes as well (e.g., tobacco withdrawal; see Shiffman, West, and Gilbert, 2004). So to be clear, for example, not every cigarette smoker who quits or attempts to quit smoking will experience the same profile of symptoms. Individual differences and other contextual factors can influence the nature of the withdrawal symptoms experienced. Last, withdrawal symptoms can be broadly categorized into four different categories (while acknowledging up front that such categorical distinctions are fairly arbitrary and possess overlap): (1) psychological distress (e.g., dysphoric mood, anxiety), (2) physical symptoms (e.g., decreased heart rate, diarrhea), (3) cognitive disruptions (particularly for nicotine, though probably manifest for other drugs as well; e.g., difficulty concentrating), and (4) behavioral factors (e.g., increased likelihood of drug re-administration [relapse]).

2.1 Withdrawal in the context of substance dependence

Substance dependence can be viewed as falling under the larger rubric of addiction. Indeed, the terms are often used interchangeably (Koob and Le Moal, 1997). The American Psychiatric Association defines the term "substance dependence" as a maladaptive pattern of substance use leading to clinically significant impairment or distress (APA, 1994; see also Koob and Le Moal, 1997). It has been conceptualized as a disorder that progresses from impulsivity to compulsivity across a cycle of addiction comprised of three stages: preoccupation/anticipation (craving), binge/intoxication, and withdrawal/negative affect (Koob and Le Moal, 1997). Substance dependence has also frequently been defined by two major characteristics: a compulsion to take the drug with a narrowing of the behavioral repertoire toward excessive drug intake, and a loss of control in limiting intake (Koob, 2003; World Health Organization, 1990). Alcohol and nicotine dependence (the most widely used substances and, as a result, subject to the most empirical investigation), in particular, have proven to be complex addictions with both genetic and environmental influences (Grant *et al.*, 2004). Family history and genetic factors have been found to affect many aspects of smoking behavior, including the development of nicotine dependence (Bierut *et al.*, 2004). Many other factors including availability, history of drug use, stressful life events, and family history can contribute to the transition from substance use to substance dependence.

Of paramount importance to the critical transition from use to misuse to drug dependence is the anticipation of use (craving), coupled with an increase in the amount of the substance taken in order to reach a similar effect (tolerance) (Zilberman, Tavarez, and el-Guebaly, 2003). Most of the literature has focused on cognitive-behavioral aspects of craving, while also acknowledging that personality styles may also play an important role in explaining individual differences in craving, such as impulsivity (Verheul, Van den Brink, and Geerlings, 1999). Individual differences in affect regulation strategies or personality styles, conditionability, sensitivity to alcohol or other drugs' effects, and related dysregulations in distinct neural circuitries or neurotransmitter systems all appear to play roles in the exacerbation of craving and the formation of substance dependence (Anton, 1999; Verheul, Van den Brink, and Geerlings, 1999).

The escape and avoidance of negative affect (negative reinforcement model) is often the prepotent motive for addictive drug use (Baker *et al.*, 2004). A multitude of factors, such as stressful life situations, lack of effective coping styles, and other psychological conditions (e.g., depression) may result in an individual seeking drugs more and more to alleviate or avoid problems and negative emotional states (Baker *et al.*, 2007; Anton, 1999). There are clearly high comorbidity rates between substance dependence and other psychological disorders. For example, those with nicotine dependence manifest greatly increased risk for also experiencing alcohol and illicit drug disorders, anxiety, and major depression (Breslau, 1995).

Withdrawal emerges as a critical component within the development of substance dependence, and is believed to follow the binge/intoxication stage of addiction (Koob and Kreek, 2007). The neuroadaptive model of substance dependence suggests that the prolonged presence of the drug induces actual changes in brain-cell function. An escalation in drug intake with extended access to drug self-administration is characterized by a dysregulation of brain reward pathways (Koob and Kreek, 2007). This causes an increased tolerance to the substance and, when deprived of the drug, results in an urge to use more (Koob, 2003; Koob and Kreek, 2007). Furthermore, even after cessation of use, the adaptive changes generate memories of the drug's positive effects that can be activated when drug-related environmental stimuli are encountered, even after prolonged abstinence, thereby leading to relapse (Anton, 1999). Among alcohol-dependent individuals, one of the factors leading to excessive drinking is the use of alcohol to relieve or avoid withdrawal symptoms (US Department of Health and Human Services, 1990). In fact, after alcohol dependence has been established, alcohol withdrawal symptoms, particularly negative emotional states, can persist for months following the removal of alcohol (Roberts *et al.*, 2000). Withdrawal symptoms may also represent a long-lasting shift in affective tone as a result of chronic alcohol exposure (Roberts *et al.*, 2000).

2.2   Examples of withdrawal syndromes

2.2.1   Alcohol.   The alcohol withdrawal syndrome (AWS) follows cessation of, or reduction in, alcohol use that has been heavy or prolonged, and most often involves significant physical and psychological symptoms (APA, 2000). Though rates of alcohol withdrawal are low in the general population (<5%), up to 86% of those admitted to hospital or treatment settings for alcohol-related issues experience some symptoms (McKeon, Frye, and Delanty, 2008). For some individuals, symptom onset can occur in as little as 6 hours after peak intoxication (Trevisan, Boutros, Petrakis, and

Krystal, 1998). Because alcohol is a central nervous system (CNS) depressant, the AWS syndrome most often includes agitation and, as observed earlier, effects generally opposite in direction to its acute effects (Becker, 2008). Thus, in the initial stage of AWS, physical symptoms may include tremor, insomnia, restlessness, and nausea (Becker, 2000; Hall and Zador, 1997; Saitz, 1998). These symptoms often dissipate on their own with little to no treatment in mildly dependent individuals. In upwards of 10% of individuals, however, AWS progresses and symptoms worsen. More dependent individuals may experience fever as well as increased respiration, heart rate, blood pressure, and profuse sweating (Trevisan, Boutros, Petrakis, and Krystal, 1998). In the most dependent individuals, these symptoms can escalate to seizures and result in serious cardiac issues (Becker, 2000; Hall and Zador, 1997; Saitz, 1998).

Psychologically, while acute alcohol use can suppress anxiety, prolonged use actually appears to be anxiogenic. Further, alcohol-dependent individuals are at greater risk for self-harm, perhaps due to alcohol's reduction of behavioral inhibition. Therefore, anxiety and depression are particularly common within 12 to 48 hours of drinking cessation (Madden, 1993; Peyser, 1982). Sleep disturbance is also common among alcoholics (Smith, 1995), and these problems persist throughout the course of the AWS. Most notably, in severely dependent individuals, delirium tremens can develop within several days. These often include a combination of hallucinations, mental confusion, and disorientation. Hallucinations not associated with delirium tremens occur in 3–10% of those with severe AWS within 7 days of drinking cessation or reduction (Platz, Oberlaender, and Seidel, 1995). If left untreated, these symptoms can be fatal.

2.2.2 Nicotine.

2.2.2 Nicotine. Smoking cessation or reduction in cigarette smoking in nicotine-dependent individuals results in the nicotine withdrawal syndrome (NWS) (APA, 2000). About 50% of regular smokers who quit endorse some symptoms of NWS (Hughes, 2007a), and some show these signs as soon as 3 hours after last cigarette use (Hendricks, Ditre, Drobes, and Brandon, 2006). As a CNS stimulant, nicotine increases heart rate and blood pressure after acute use. Real-time assessment of NWS, therefore, has shown that smokers experience decreased blood pressure and heart rate within 4 hours of abstinence (Morrell, Cohen, and al'Absi, 2008). Other physical symptoms of withdrawal from nicotine are less substantiated, however, as studies have focused on, and have therefore been more sensitive to, different symptom clusters (e.g., subjective emotional factors; Hughes, 2007b). Generally, the NWS includes physical problems such as constipation, cough, dizziness, and mouth ulcers (Hajek, Gillison, and McRobbie, 2003; Ussher *et al.*, 2004; West, Hajek, and McNeill, 1991). Further, restlessness often peaks within 2 days of abstinence and can endure for several weeks (Hatsukami *et al.*, 1991; Hughes and Hatsukami, 1992; Jorenby *et al.*, 1996). It remains difficult, however, to disentangle physical restlessness from related cognitive and emotional constructs (e.g., impatience). Also worth considering is the question of whether all identified withdrawal symptoms really possess clinical utility (in terms of predicting meaningful behavioral outcomes like relapse). For example, even though we know that decreased heart rate is a near inevitable withdrawal sign for those quitting smoking, is assessment of this outcome clinically relevant? We will revisit this important idea later in this chapter.

Irritability and difficulty concentrating are among the most common psychological symptoms of drug abstinence in general and NWS in particular (Hughes, Higgins, and Hatsukami, 1990). Further, like alcohol, nicotine is thought to decrease anxiety (Kassel, Stroud, and Paronis, 2003), though its effects on depression are less clear. Therefore, withdrawal from nicotine often includes increased irritability, anxiety, and possibly depression, as well as a decrease in concentration. These effects are thought to emerge within 4 hours of abstinence and are often more predictive of overall subjective experience (e.g., distress) than are the physical symptoms (Morrell, Cohen, and al'Absi, 2008). Whereas sleep disturbance is also common, empirical data point to a specific problem with sleep fragmentation, or awakenings during the night and shifts in stages of sleep, as opposed to more global insomnia (Hughes, 2007c). These symptoms tend to resolve quickly, as real-time assessment suggests a return to baseline levels within 10 days (Shiffman *et al.*, 2006).

2.2.3   Cannabis.   More recently, researchers have focused their efforts on describing and validating a cannabis withdrawal syndrome (CWS), as there has long been debate over whether individuals can truly develop cannabis dependence (also noting that cannabis withdrawal is not included in the DSM-IV-TR; APA, 2000). Budney and colleagues performed an extensive literature review and concluded that CWS includes the following primary symptoms: decreased appetite or weight loss, anger or aggression, irritability, nervousness/anxiety, restlessness, and sleep difficulties. The reviewed studies provided some evidence pointing to chills, stomach pain, shakiness, sweating, and depressed mood as well, though these symptoms are less reliable (Budney, Hughes, Moore, and Vandry, 2004). According to survey-based studies, up to one-third of regular cannabis users endorse some withdrawal symptoms in their lifetime (Wiesbeck *et al.*, 1996; Young *et al.*, 2002). CWS usually emerges within 1 day of cessation or reduction of use and symptoms generally decrease over time. The emotional and behavioral nature of problems associated with withdrawal remains unclear (Budney and Hughes, 2006), however, and future research will probably concentrate on evaluating the clinical significance of the syndrome itself.

2.2.4   Other drugs of abuse.   Stimulants like cocaine and the amphetamines represent a highly addictive class of drugs with pronounced withdrawal symptoms. Among the most salient of these is the withdrawal syndrome associated with amphetamine, as recent reports indicate that it has emerged as the most commonly used illicit substance aside from cannabis (WHO, 2010). As in other models of withdrawal, amphetamine withdrawal syndrome (AmWS) is characterized by symptoms that oppose its acute effects and resolve relatively quickly (i.e., within 2 weeks; Zorick *et al.*, 2010). Methamphetamine users in early abstinence, for example, often experience dysphoria and anhedonia, probably as a result of changes in metabolic activity of the brain (Barr and Markou, 2005; London *et al.*, 2004). Other symptoms include fatigue, anxiety, irritability, depression, inability to concentrate, and sometimes suicidality (Barr and Markou, 2005; Barr, Markou, and Phillips, 2002).

Opiate withdrawal syndrome (OWS) also has a long history of description and study in the literature. The OWS can appear within 4 hours and last several days, depending on the specific drug and accompanying dose. OWS comprises several physical and psychological symptoms similar to the flu that follow a somewhat predictable time course (Farrell, 1994; Redmond and Krystal, 1984). During the first phase of abstinence, OWS is dominated by subjective distress, including intense craving, anxiety, and agitation, as well as increased sweating. As time passes, physical symptoms of increased heart rate and breathing, sweating, vomiting and diarrhea, and tremor, as well as restlessness and insomnia, become more prominent. The severity of both subjective and objective experience has prompted researchers to focus on assisted-withdrawal as a way of easing detoxification and increasing the odds of prolonged abstinence (Gowing and Ali, 2006).

2.3   Drug-precipitated withdrawal

Pharmacological methods of inducing withdrawal have focused on blocking the acute effects of various substances of abuse. For most of these drugs, the dominant psychoactive properties are mediated through the mesolimbic dopaminergic or "reward" pathway (Heilig *et al.*, 2010). For example, this system might be partly responsible for the positive reinforcement of alcohol use, though its precise role is unclear. It is plausible that prolonged alcohol consumption might increase dependence on the endogenous opioid system and therefore increase withdrawal symptoms after administration of an opiate antagonist (O'Malley, Krishnan-Sarin, Farren, and O'Connor, 2000). Naltrexone has emerged as a potential option for testing this notion, as it blocks the reinforcing effects of alcohol consumption (O'Brien, Volpicelli, and Volpicelli, 1996). Further, its adverse effects are similar to those of alcohol withdrawal: namely, nausea, headache, dizziness, fatigue, insomnia, vomiting, and anxiety (Croop, Faulkner, and Labriola, 1997). Due to its more common use as a treatment for alcohol dependence (Roozen *et al.*, 2006), more research is necessary to determine whether it is a viable pharmacological option in the study of alcohol withdrawal syndrome (AWS) as well. Its explicit connection to the dopamine system has also allowed researchers to reliably demonstrate that naltrexone can serve as a precipitant of withdrawal symptoms in opiate-dependent individuals, even after a prolonged period of abstinence (Crowley, Wagner, Zerbe, and Macdonald, 1985).

Nicotine has a different mechanism of action than alcohol, binding instead to nicotinic acetylcholine (nAch) receptors located throughout the brain. An nAch antagonist is necessary, therefore, to precipitate symptoms of nicotine withdrawal. Mecamylamine, initially introduced as a treatment for hypertension, has thus emerged as more relevant in the study of nicotine withdrawal and smoking cessation. More specifically, it has been shown to increase periods of continuous abstinence by blocking the positive (reinforcing) effects of cigarette smoking and nicotine (Rose, Behm, and Westman, 1998). Mecamylamine has also been studied in preclinical investigations of nicotine withdrawal, with acute administration having been shown to mimic the physical and psychological symptoms of nicotine withdrawal syndrome (NWS) in rats (e.g., O'Dell *et al.*, 2004; Wilmouth and Spear, 2006). More research will clearly be needed in order to determine whether mecamylamine can be used as a pharmacotherapeutic adjunct to the study of nicotine withdrawal and dependence, and as a potential aid in treating nicotine addiction.

3   Theoretical Considerations Relevant to Withdrawal: Negative Reinforcement

In the last several decades, multidisciplinary approaches to the study of addiction have served to revolutionize the medical community's conceptualization of addiction as a treatable brain disease rather than a byproduct of moral failure, character weakness, and poverty of spirit. Despite this paradigm shift, coupled with numerous concerted efforts to develop effective treatments for individuals suffering from addiction (e.g., O'Brien, 2008), relapse remains the modal outcome among those trying to quit. For instance, it is estimated that following a period of remittance (e.g., treatment, self-quitting), 92% of individuals who abuse alcohol will relapse within 1 year (Miller, Westerberg, Harris, and Tonigan, 1996), and 95 to 98% of smokers will relapse within 6 to 12 months (Hughes, Keely, and Naud, 2004). Accordingly, a number of mechanisms have been advanced in the literature to explain how and why individuals move from drug initiation to dependence to abstinence and back (i.e., recycling). Of these potential explanatory mechanisms, the phenomenon of withdrawal has been studied most extensively. Indeed, compelling and highly influential theoretical depictions suggest that the triggering and avoidance of withdrawal symptoms go a long way toward perpetuating the addiction cycle.

Despite strong intentions to reduce or abstain from substances, many individuals find themselves returning to use and sometimes doing so outside of conscious awareness (i.e., automaticity; see Tiffany, 1990). Moreover, the individual continues to use knowing that severe and even devastating consequences may follow (e.g., job loss, ruined relationships, compromised health). As discussed earlier, withdrawal processes may lend robust explanatory power for this seemingly irrational pattern of behavior. Withdrawal is commonly described as an aversive state characterized by negative affect and physical discomfort among other untoward symptoms. Over time, the user learns that symptom distress is best ameliorated by reinstatement of the substance. Correspondingly, drug-related cues become more salient with chronic use (e.g., Robinson and Berridge, 2003) and conditioned cues can trigger or exacerbate withdrawal symptoms (e.g., Baker *et al.*, 2004; Tiffany, 1990). As such, learning theory and concepts of operant conditioning and negative reinforcement (learning to repeat a behavior that results in escape from an aversive state) play critical roles in helping to elucidate the enigmatic qualities of addiction.

Steeped in the tenets of Skinner's theory of operant conditioning, negative reinforcement, as applied to substance use, specifies that individuals frequently use substances to obtain relief from distress. Correspondingly, to the extent that relief is obtained, the individual will probably perform the same behavior under similar circumstances in the future. This notion is well articulated in various influential conceptualizations of substance use, emotion regulation, and negative reinforcement, including the stress-coping (Wills and Shiffman, 1985), self-medication (Khantzian, 1997), and tension-reduction (Cappell and Herman, 1972) models. Importantly, positive reinforcement processes (e.g., using to enhance experience) are probably more salient in the initial stages of drug use, while negative reinforcement processes emerge as generally more prominent in the dependence stages (Koob and Le Moal, 2008). For instance, drinking alcohol to cope or to suppress negative emotion is a strong predictor of problematic drinking in young adults (Carey and Correia, 1997; Mohr *et al.*, 2005; Park, Armeli, and Tennen, 2004; Kassel, Jackson, and Unrod, 2000). Additionally, expectations for smoking to relieve negative affect have been shown to predict increased smoking behavior and nicotine dependence over time (Heinz, Kassel, Berbaum, and Memelstein, 2010). Together, then, the shift from initiation to maintenance is driven, in part, by promise of affective benefits. This motivational pattern proceeds to confer increased risk for heavy and problematic substance use, and ultimately, the transition to dependence.

Substantial associative learning is thought to occur during the active phases of substance use, whereby drug cues become conditioned to elicit compensatory or withdrawal responses (e.g., Tiffany, 2010). Returning to the Pavlovian traditions of classical conditioning, after an unconditioned stimulus (UCS; acute effect of a substance) is repeatedly paired with an unconditioned response (UCR; compensatory attempt to restore homeostasis), the link between them becomes deeply entrenched in memory. Ultimately, the substance becomes a conditioned stimulus (CS) and the body's natural response to restore homeostasis following substance use becomes the conditioned response (CR). Hence exposure to the substance, or even cues that are associated with the substance (e.g., cigarette lighter, driving in a car), can function to elicit the CR. Consequently, it is believed that the CR can be triggered even in the absence of actual substance use and that a central and critical manifestation of the CR is the emergence of withdrawal symptoms (e.g., negative affect).

As an individual's substance use increases in chronicity, learning and expectations for substance use to alleviate aversive withdrawal symptoms (i.e., negative reinforcement) become engrained in memory with a behavioral "script" emerging for use under such circumstances (see Tiffany, 1990). Over time, an individual's explicit awareness of their withdrawal symptoms declines and instead the behavioral script for use is activated almost automatically. Of course, the question emerges: "What triggers the script?" when the individual in not in a state of withdrawal or has been abstinent for an extended period of time. Here, we can invoke the principles of associative learning, whereby encounters with drug cues that were paired with withdrawal symptoms in the past can come to elicit conditioned withdrawal responses. Evidence from the laboratory indicates that attention becomes disproportionately biased toward drug cues as the individual enters into heavier use and dependence, and that such attentional biases persist well after cessation (e.g., Robbins and Ehrman, 2004). Increased awareness of, and attention to, drug cues previously associated with withdrawal probably impede efforts to modulate use because the withdrawal avoidance script is readily triggered.

One of the earliest and most prominent models of relapse, the withdrawal-relief model, espouses that conditioning factors trigger relapse to opiates more than the expectation of drug-induced euphoria (Wikler, 1965). More specifically, drug-related environmental stimuli (e.g., people or situations associated with past drug use) elicit seemingly involuntary reactions (i.e., withdrawal response) that make the individual more susceptible to relapse even when they are not acutely experiencing withdrawal. This model is thought to explain why addicts quickly develop a tolerance to the euphoric effects of morphine and describe opiate dependence as an aversive existence that motivates their desire to quit.

Baker and colleagues (2004) expand upon Wikler's "cue-based" conceptualization of drug addiction and posit that negative affect, and the need to alleviate it, serves as the motivationally prepotent element of drug taking. Although, as described earlier, there is notable individual heterogeneity in the experience of physical withdrawal symptoms, negative affect appears to be a universal component of withdrawal syndromes across virtually all drugs of abuse. The authors propose that the physical symptoms of withdrawal function as interoceptive cues or conditioned stimuli signaling impending negative affect. Accordingly, the intensity of negative affect (high, low), processed through the amygdala, is thought to determine an addict's level of cognitive control over addictive behavior. At low levels, NA is preconsciously detected and influences decisions to avoid withdrawal (i.e., to use the drug) in a habitual or automatized fashion. In other words, negative affect, in this context, does not need to be conscious because the body can subconsciously detect fluctuations in negative affect via interoceptive cues. However, as negative affect (typically associated with drug abstinence/withdrawal) increases, hot cognitive processing is triggered that hijacks normal cognitive self-regulatory capacity (cf. Mischel, Shoda, and Rodriguez, 1989). The influence of declarative knowledge (e.g., generating alternatives to drug use, employing coping tools) is therefore suppressed and the likelihood of a controlled response execution (e.g., using the drug) dramatically increases.

The role of withdrawal in the transition to problem use has also been compellingly captured by the opponent process model (Koob and Le Moal, 2001). Solomon and Corbit's (1974) original opponent process theory of motivation posited that motivational states are characterized by opposing underlying processes. According to Koob and Le Moal's (2001; 2008) influential theory, addiction is conceptualized as a cycle wherein positive and negative reinforcement processes are inherently linked to support homeostatic mechanisms that restore natural balance in the organism. More specifically, the central nervous system is thought to automatically modulate hedonic states (i.e., reduce the intensity of hedonic feelings) in order to promote homeostasis. During the a-process, the drug initially exerts a pleasurable, hedonic effect which then initiates a secondary compensatory reaction (the b-process) designed to bring the body back to homeostasis (i.e., tolerance). Over time, however, continued use causes tolerance to the hedonic effects of the drug (i.e., a-process weakens). Subsequently, the b-process becomes more pronounced but is rendered less effective at returning the individual to the normal homeostatic range of reward function. The domination of the a-process by the b-process is manifested in the form of withdrawal symptoms and is ultimately a consequence of decreased regulation of reward mechanisms in the brain. Indeed, the authors have identified several neurobiological mechanisms, specifically brain stress systems (e.g., corticotropin releasing factor [CRF] in the amygdala; Heilig and Koob, 2007), that change over the course of addiction to produce the opponent processes that sustain addiction.

Finally, the Incentive Sensitization theory of addiction posits that complex and persistent changes in the mesocorticolimbic systems of the brain, which mediate conditioned incentive motivational processes, induce pathological and compulsive addictive behaviors (Robinson and Berridge, 2003). More specifically, repeated drug exposure hypersensitizes parts of the brain associated with reward to the positive effects of drugs. In turn, and as discussed above, addicts' attentional processing becomes biased toward drugs and stimuli associated with drugs. The incentive salience then attributed to drugs (above and beyond other rewards) consequently promotes pathological motivation and compulsive "wanting" to seek and take drugs. Importantly, the incentive sensitization model also proposes a secondary reinforcement process (i.e., reinforcement-based learning over time; Epstein, Willner-Reid, and Preston, 2010), whereby prolonged drug use results in neural adaptations associated with sensitized response to drug cues (e.g., sensory aspects of drug exposure, environmental cues).

In a review of the relevant research prompted by the introduction of their theory, Robinson and Berridge (2008) point out the seemingly limited role of affective processes in addiction. They note that, although negative affect associated with withdrawal and short-term abstinence probably contributes to drug taking, affective influences do not necessarily explain why addicts, for example, continue to "want" drugs years after quitting. Clearly, whereas drugs of abuse do exert significant pleasurable effects upon initial use, over time, individuals seem to habituate to this primary reinforcing effect of the drug. Paradoxically, though, addicts demonstrate increased "wanting" of the drug over time, despite decreased "liking" of the drug. The initiation of cue-induced secondary reinforcement processes (e.g., drug cues paired with withdrawal symptoms) described in the model seem to go some way toward explaining the transition from use to addiction.

In summary, the motivational significance of withdrawal is powerful and serves to govern negative reinforcement mechanisms. Although there are numerous influential models attempting to describe and predict these important phenomena, we have only briefly touched upon a few. Nonetheless, it is also clear that whereas manifestations of withdrawal vary both within and across different classes of drugs, negative affect (and other aversive states) typically accompany the withdrawal syndrome and, hence, serve as potent stimuli in provoking subsequent drug self-administration.

4　Hangover

Whereas the focus of this chapter is drug withdrawal, viewed under the larger umbrella of drug aftereffects, we also want to acknowledge another clinically relevant aftereffect: hangover. It is probably fair to assert that the scientific community has not come to a precise, agreed definition of "hangover." Indeed, some have argued that the construct of hangover is really synonymous with withdrawal. Nonetheless, researchers generally agree that a hangover may include, but is not limited to, the following symptoms following an episode of heavy drinking: headache, poor sense of overall wellbeing, diarrhea, anorexia, tremulousness, fatigue, and nausea (Wiese, Shlipak, and Browner, 2000). The onset of these symptoms may vary from the time a person stops drinking and their blood alcohol content (BAC) begins to fall, up to 24 hours after drinking

(Swift and Davidson, 1998). Indeed, some research indicates that maximal hangover symptoms occur 12–14 hours after commencement of drinking, at which point almost all ethanol and acetaldehyde have been eliminated from the blood (Ylikahri, Huttunen, Eriksson, and Nikkla, 1974).

Anecdotal evidence suggests that in a hangover state, cognitive abilities, such as memory and coordination, are impaired, although research supporting this claim is sparse. In one study of 71 social drinkers, subjective reports were consistent with this hypothesis, but only modest differences (relative to a no-alcohol session) were found on objective measures of vigilance and reaction time (Finnigan, Schulze, Smallwood, and Helander, 2005). Likewise, in a different study, intoxication the night before testing did not appear to affect psychomotor performance (Finnigan, Hammersley, and Cooper, 1998). Other investigations have suggested that under some conditions (i.e., joint administration of ethanol and sugar), psychomotor performance is significantly impaired compared to no alcohol/sugar (Seppälä *et al.*, 1976). Mixed results have also been found with regard to hangover's effects on memory. Delayed recall has been shown to be impaired the morning after intoxication, but immediate recall and recognition were unaffected (Verster *et al.*, 2003). Correspondingly, other studies have found no memory deficits during hangover (Finnigan, Schulze, Smallwood, and Helander, 2005). In sum, whereas some studies have indicated deficits in memory and/or psychomotor abilities during hangover, these findings are limited and warrant further examination.

4.1   Other drugs

Research regarding hangover from substances other than alcohol is scant. Few studies have been conducted on the hangover effects from marijuana, and of the studies that have examined this phenomenon, sample sizes have generally been small (e.g., $n < 20$). Thus far, strong evidence for a marijuana hangover has not been established (Chait, 1990; Chait, Fischman, and Schuster, 1985). Some research has also investigated the possibility of hangover from hypnotics (see Walters and Lader, 1971, for review). Whereas psychological and behavioral impairment has been found 12–15 hours after hypnotic administration, these studies also restricted caffeine consumption. As such, caffeine withdrawal cannot be ruled out as having played a role in the findings (Walters and Lader, 1971).

4.2   Psychological and personality correlates of hangover

Several psychological and personality components have been associated with increased hangover frequency and severity. The MacAndrew Scale (MAC) of the Minnesota Multiphasic Personality Inventory (MMPI) is designed to discriminate between individuals with and without an alcohol use disorder. Higher scores on the MAC are significantly correlated with more severe hangovers (Earleywine, 1993a; 1993b). Other psychological and personality factors that have been shown to reliably predict hangover include guilt about drinking, neuroticism, being angry or depressed when drunk, and negative life events (Harburg, Davis, Cummings, and Gunn, 1981; Harburg *et al.*, 1993).

4.3   Hangover as marker for risk

Another reason to study hangover is its suggested utility as a marker for risk for an alcohol use disorder (AUD). The severity and frequency of hangover has been linked to family history of AUD, as well as predicting future diagnosis of an AUD (Piasecki, Sher, Slutske, and Jackson, 2005). In fact, individuals with a current AUD exhibited more severe hangover before being diagnosed with AUD compared to those without AUD (Piasecki, Sher, Slutske, and Jackson, 2005). Additionally, sons of alcoholics tend to report increased hangover symptoms compared to sons of non-alcoholics, suggesting a genetic link (Newlin and Pretorius, 1990; Span and Earleywine, 1999). Hence, the tendency to experience greater hangover symptoms may contribute to the development of dependence or abuse.

4.4   Hangover assessment

Although the deleterious effects of hangover on performance and other domains are well established anecdotally, comprehensive empirical assessment of hangover is a more recent development. The Hangover Symptoms Scale (HSS; Slutske, Piasecki, and Hunt-Carter, 2003) is a 13-item questionnaire that assesses frequency of hangover symptoms after drinking in the past 12 months. Individuals respond to items (e.g., felt very nauseous, was anxious) using a 5-point rating scale that ranges from "never" to "every time." The HSS has strong psychometric properties and scale scores have been found to correspond positively with several known risk factors for hangover (e.g., quantity and frequency of drinking, family history or alcohol-related problems). In order to measure the acute effects of hangover, Rohsenow and colleagues (2007) developed the Acute Hangover Scale (AHS) using a within-subjects design (alcohol versus placebo) controlled laboratory study. The AHS is comprised of nine items to which individuals respond using a 7-point scale with four anchor points (none, mild, moderate, incapacitating). Data suggest that the AHS is a reliable and valid tool for capturing the acute residual effects of alcohol in a laboratory setting. Currently, no measures have been created to assess the hangover symptoms associated with substances other than alcohol.

5   Measuring Withdrawal: Self-Report Questionnaires and Interviews (with a Focus on Alcohol and Nicotine)

For nicotine and alcohol, there are a variety of self-report and other-report measures available to assess withdrawal, primarily in the form of rating scales. Measures also exist for illegal drugs, including opiates (Bradley, Gossop, Phillips, and Legarda, 1987; Gossop, 1990), cocaine (Voris, Elder, and Sebastian, 1991), and amphetamines (Srisurapanont, Jarusuraisin, and Jittiwutikan, 1999). For each drug, scales measure similar although not entirely consistent sets of withdrawal symptoms (Patten and Martin, 1996a; Williams, Lewis, and MacBride, 2001), suggesting that researchers vary in their conceptions of which symptoms are most central to the withdrawal syndrome. Because of space limitations and the fact that alcohol and nicotine are the most widely used substances, we limit our discussion primarily to these two drugs in this section.

In the measurement realm, assessment needs differ by drug and by clinical utility. For illegal drugs and alcohol, where the withdrawal syndrome has potentially fatal medical implications, assessments of withdrawal are more often conducted using an observer report or clinical interview rather than via self-report alone. Patients under the influence of these drugs may be in respiratory distress or even incapable of speaking for themselves (e.g. unconscious, delirious), thus necessitating utilization of objective measures. Assessments of withdrawal in these settings have clinical utility, as withdrawal severity influences the type and amount of medication administered for patient stabilization (Wetterling *et al.*, 1997). For example, a patient undergoing detoxification for alcohol dependence may experience alcohol withdrawal-induced delirium, and a reliable and valid clinical instrument that could assist physicians in predicting delirium could inform psychopharmacological prescriptions during the detoxification period (Palmstierna, 2001). Hence, it is important for clinically useful measures to capture changes in withdrawal symptomatology and severity over the course of time (Gossop *et al.*, 2002), such that a measure should be quick to administer and amenable to repeated measurements (e.g., once an hour).

For assessment of alcohol withdrawal, there are several rating scales available that measure over 30 symptoms (Williams, Lewis, and MacBride, 2001), although it is worth noting that many of these measurement tools were developed for single studies and were never subjected to rigorous psychometric testing. The gold standard among measures of alcohol withdrawal is an observer-rated scale called the Clinical Institute of Withdrawal Assessment for Alcohol (CIWA-A; Shaw *et al.*, 1981), which was subsequently amended into the revised CIWA (CIWA-Ar; Sullivan *et al.*, 1989). This measure, which can be administered in under 2 minutes by a nurse, physician, or otherwise trained health professional, assesses the ten domains of sweating, anxiety, tremor, auditory disturbances, visual disturbances, agitation, nausea, tactile disturbances, headache, and orientation/confusion. Each item is rated on a severity index of 0 to 7, except for orientation/confusion, which is rated on a 0 to 4 scale. Developers of the CIWA-Ar suggest that a score of less than 10 indicates a withdrawal mild enough to be tolerated without pharmacological treatment (Sullivan *et al.*, 1989). The CWIA-A has also spawned multiple derivatives, including an 8-item version that incorporates pulse and merges the hallucination symptoms into one item (CIWA-AD; Sellers, Sullivan, Somer, Sykora, 1991), as well as other versions (Gray *et al.*, 2010; Metcalfe, Sobers, and Dewey, 1995; Wetterling *et al.*, 1997). The CIWA-A and its derivatives have been extensively evaluated in terms of reliability and validity (e.g., Pittman *et al.*, 2007; Reoux and Oreskovich, 2006; Williams, Lewis, and MacBride, 2001), and have been translated into other languages (e.g. Stuppaeck *et al.*, 1994).

Due to the altered status of many patients with severe alcohol withdrawal syndromes, whereby patients may hallucinate or manifest disorientation, observer reports emerge as a necessary component of withdrawal assessment, particularly in emergency departments and detoxification centers. However, observer ratings, such as the CIWA-A and its variations, have been criticized as including excessive observer bias and, thus, potentially relying too heavily on observable behaviors (Gossop *et al.*, 2002).

Many withdrawal symptoms, most notably those in the affective domain (e.g., anxiety, depression), may appear differently to an observer than to a patient in the throes of withdrawal. Thus, in this regard, self-report scales may provide a useful adjunct to clinician observer ratings. A relatively new and promising self-report scale is the Short Alcohol Withdrawal Scale (Gossop *et al.*, 2002), which asks patients/participants to identify their intensity of ten different symptoms (anxiety, sleep disturbance, memory complaints, nausea, restlessness, tremor/shaking, mental confusion, sweating, heart pounding, and a general sense of misery) on a 4-point scale (0 = None; 3 = Severe). The scale has been independently evaluated for psychometric properties and found to be both reliable and valid (Elholm *et al.*, 2010). Another self-report scale, the Alcohol Withdrawal Symptom Checklist (AWSC; Pittman *et al.*, 2007) has 14 items rated on a 5-point Likert-type scale: nervousness, sweats, tremors, nausea, vomiting, loss of appetite, irritability, muscle cramps, chill, headache, craving for alcohol, depression, asthenia, and sleep disturbance. These symptoms clustered into five factors – autonomic arousal, depression, nausea and vomiting, craving, and tension/anxiety – and corresponded well with the observer-rated CIWA-Ar (Pittman *et al.*, 2007).

In the realm of nicotine, there are several multi-item measures used to assess withdrawal symptoms, including the Cigarette Withdrawal Scale (CWS; Etter, 2005), the Minnesota Nicotine Withdrawal Scale (MNWS; Hughes and Hatsukami, 1986), the Mood and Physical Symptoms Scale (MPSS; West and Hajek, 2004), the Wisconsin Smoking Withdrawal Scale (WSWS; Welsch *et al.*, 1999), the Shiffman–Jarvik Smoking Withdrawal Questionnaire (Shiffman and Jarvik, 1976), and the Smoker Complaint Scale (SCS; Schneider and Jarvik, 1984). Some of the earlier measures, such as the Shiffman–Jarvik scale and the Smoker Complaint Scale, have been criticized for their psychometric limitations and lack of a theoretical foundation (Patten and Martin, 1996a).

Newer scales, including the MNWS (Hughes and Hatsukami, 1986), CWS (Etter, 2005), and WSWS (Welsch *et al.*, 1999), appear to map onto the diagnostic criteria for nicotine or tobacco withdrawal, and have been found to demonstrate sufficient reliability and validity. Both the CWS and the WSWS are multi-subscale measures, where the CWS has six subscales in addition to a total score, assessing the domains of depression–anxiety, craving, irritability–impatience, appetite–weight gain, insomnia, and difficulty concentrating. The WSWS has seven subscales: anger, anxiety, difficulty concentrating, craving, hunger, sadness, and sleep disturbances. Neither scale assesses the DSM-IV symptom of decreased heart rate or the ICD-10 symptoms of malaise/weakness, increased cough or mouth ulceration (Etter and Hughes, 2006). Both measures include a craving subscale, which is a symptom of withdrawal recognized by the ICD-10 but no longer included as a symptom in the DSM-IV. The MNWS (Hughes and Hatsukami, 1986) is brief, with only one item per withdrawal symptom, making it quick to administer, and popular enough that it has been translated into several languages (e.g. Yu *et al.*, 2010; Kim, Gulick, Kim, and Seo, 2007). A recent comparison of the CWS, WSWS, and MNWS found all three measures to yield adequate reliability, content, and construct validity (Etter and Hughes, 2006), with similar results found in a subsequent comparative study of the CWS, WSWS, MNWS, and MPSS (West, Ussher, Evans, and Rashid, 2006).

It should be also noted that other measures are often used in addition to or in conjunction with the above measures to assess withdrawal: namely, mood measures, including the Profile of Mood States (POMS; McNair, Lorr, and Droppleman, 1971), the Spielberger State Anxiety scale (Spielberger *et al.*, 1983), and the Positive and Negative Affect Schedule (PANAS; Watson, Clark, and Tellegen, 1988). These adjunct measures are oft-used and well-validated measures of current emotional experience, frequently administered in research studies assessing withdrawal due to the salient negative affect observed in most withdrawal syndromes (e.g. Baker *et al.*, 2004).

In addition to the withdrawal-specific measures mentioned above, withdrawal is also frequently assessed in the context of dependence, relegated to a few items on general dependence measures, such as the item "After not smoking for a while, I need to smoke to relieve feelings of restlessness and irritability" on the Drive subscale of the Nicotine Dependence Syndrome Scale (NDSS; Shiffman, Waters, and Hickox, 2004). When included on general dependence measures, withdrawal symptoms and severity of withdrawal response are considered indicators of high dependence levels. The distinction between withdrawal items on dependence measures and specific withdrawal measures is important because some physical acute aftereffects of drugs manifest as withdrawal symptoms even for people who may not be dependent (e.g., alcohol hangover). When assessed as a part of dependence, additional structured interview protocols are available for use, such as the Composite International Diagnostic Interview (CIDI; Kessler and Üstün, 2004) and the Alcohol Use Disorder and Associated Disabilities Interview Schedule-DSM-IV Version (AUDADIS-IV; Grant, Dawson, and Hasin, 2001).

6　Drug Craving

Withdrawal symptoms are considered to be a central component of the dependence syndrome because, as argued throughout this chapter, alleviation of withdrawal is a primary reinforcer that contributes to continued use. Unpleasant withdrawal symptoms are a major hurdle for individuals trying to quit using, and are thought to contribute to poor cessation outcomes (Piasecki, 2006). Along the path to abstinence, for example, over 90% of tobacco users who attempt to quit experience at least one lapse (Brandon, Vidrine, and Litvin, 2007), defined here as a single slip in return to use after a quit attempt. A single lapse often results in full-blown relapse, defined as a return to regular use, even if not at the same pre-quit levels (Brandon, Tiffany, Obremski, and Baker, 1990; Shadel *et al.*, 2011).

Theoretically, because withdrawal symptoms are unpleasant to experience (Hughes, 2007c), the strength of these symptoms should predict who will lapse during a cessation event, and/or who among lapsers will go on to a full-blown relapse. However, the relationship between withdrawal symptoms, including craving, and cessation outcomes appears complicated, such that although withdrawal severity predicts relapse in some cases (e.g. Allen, Bade, Hatsukami, and Center, 2008; Killen and Fortmann, 1997), relapse often occurs long after withdrawal symptoms have abated (Brandon, Tiffany, Obremski, and Baker, 1990). Moreover, although replacement therapies (e.g. methadone maintenance for opioid dependence, nicotine replacement therapy) have been shown to be efficacious for assisting with cessation (e.g. Stead *et al.*, 2008), there is inconsistent evidence supporting the notion that such pharmacotherapies aid in successful cessation by attenuating withdrawal severity (Shiffman, Ferguson, and Gwaltney, 2006). Stated differently, although it seems clear that addicted patients abstaining from nicotine, alcohol, or drugs of dependence will probably experience a withdrawal syndrome, the withdrawal period is not always causally explanatory for cessation outcome and success (Patten and Martin, 1996b; Piasecki *et al.*, 2000; Piasecki *et al.*, 2002).

Further complicating the picture, the role of craving has been contested as a component of withdrawal. Craving, often referred to as an "urge" or "desire to use," remains a symptom of withdrawal according to the ICD-10 but was removed from the DSM criteria for dependence with the publication of version IV (APA, 1994), reportedly because craving also occurs among continuing users and is thus not specific to the withdrawal syndrome (Etter, 2005). However, many researchers have advocated for including craving as a symptom of withdrawal (Hughes, 2007c; Patten and Martin, 1996a; West and Hajek, 2004; Williams, Lewis, and MacBride, 2001), and craving continues to be a subscale on many withdrawal measures (Etter, 2005; Hughes and Hatsukami, 1986; Welsch *et al.*, 1999). Importantly, individuals report high levels of craving during quit attempts, and attribute cessation failures to uncontrollable urges, suggesting that at least when taking subjective rationales into account, craving remains an important construct both clinically and empirically (see Kassel and Shiffman, 1992).

Within the nicotine/tobacco research area, craving is typically studied in two contexts. The first, cue-induced craving, also called cue-reactivity, is craving in response to presentation of the drug of interest or cues depicting indices of the drug or the drug-using environment. For example, a cue might involve a research participant holding a lit cigarette (e.g. Sayette *et al.*, 2001), viewing pictures or videos of people smoking (e.g. Conklin *et al.*, 2008; Shadel, Niaura and Abrams, 2001), or imagining a smoking scene (e.g. Conklin and Tiffany, 2001). Results typically find that craving increases in response to smoking cues when compared to neutral cues (e.g. Carter and Tiffany, 1999). Cue-reactive craving can be induced in continuing users, and is influenced by availability of cigarettes as well as deprivation (Wertz and Sayette, 2001; see also Chapter 20 in the current volume).

The second context in which craving is studied is abstinence-induced craving, otherwise described as craving in conjunction with withdrawal. For example, among regular smokers who smoke a pack of cigarettes per day, symptoms of withdrawal, including negative affect and craving, may begin to increase soon after the last cigarette is extinguished (i.e., within minutes; Baker *et al.*, 2004). Compared to cue-induced craving, "naturally" occurring withdrawal or abstinence-induced craving has garnered considerably more support in terms of predicting lapse/relapse (Perkins, 2009). In prospective within-subject studies, where participants were followed over time and reported levels of craving before, during, and after lapses, craving reports were higher immediately before a lapse than during or after (Allen, Bade, Hatsukami, and Center, 2008; Piasecki *et al.*, 2000), or compared to "temptation" settings where people were tempted to use but chose not to (Shiffman *et al.*, 1996). Also, at a nomothetic level, smokers with overall higher craving levels post-cessation were more likely to lapse than those with lower craving ratings (Killen and Fortmann, 1997). At the same time, collective research on withdrawal, craving, and relapse suggests that although heightened craving is probably one of many contributors to relapse, it cannot be viewed as a causal agent (Patten and Martin, 1996b).

7 Psychophysiological Assessment of Withdrawal: Startle Response

The acoustic startle reflex is one physiological method that has been used repeatedly in both animal and human studies as an index of drug withdrawal. The startle reflex occurs in both animals and humans in response to intense stimuli (e.g., loud noise) with rapid onset (Cook, Hawk, Davis, and Stevenson, 1991). Studies examining the psychophysiological responses to high-intensity acoustic startle stimuli have found that these stimuli elicit a startle response that is characterized by a reflexive eyeblink, an immediate heart rate acceleration, and an increase in skin conductance amplitude (e.g., Graham, 1979; Turpin, 1986).

In recent years, researchers have used the startle reflex to study emotion in a variety of ways. Often, this is done by pairing an acoustic startle probe with images varying in valence and arousal levels (Vrana, Spence, and Lang, 1988). A startle response that is larger in magnitude has been reliably linked to greater anxiety (Cook, Hawk, Davis, and Stevenson, 1991). Prepulse inhibition (PPI) occurs when a relatively weak acoustic probe is presented immediately before a larger probe and serves to inhibit the subsequent startle response (Blumenthal, Elden, and Flaten, 2004). Finally, in animals, high-intensity acoustic stimuli produce ultrasonic vocalizations (USV) that have been used as a measure of anxiety (Kaltwasser, 1991). Because anxiety is one possible symptom of withdrawal, these paradigms have been used more often in recent years to study anxiety (and overall negative affect) associated with withdrawal.

Various startle methodologies have been used in animals to model withdrawal from several different drugs. For instance, in rats, withdrawal from morphine (via a deprivation paradigm) resulted in significantly increased acoustic startle responses (Harris and Gerwitz, 2004). Diazepam-withdrawn rats produced increased startle-induced USVs (Vivian, Farrell, Sapperstein, and Miczek, 1994). Compared to non-withdrawn rats, alcohol-withdrawn rats exhibited increased startle reactivity and decreased PPI, suggesting possible hyperexcitability of the central nervous system (CNS) during alcohol withdrawal (Rassnick, Koob, and Geyer, 1992). Similar findings have been found with cocaine. Rats in withdrawal from cocaine exhibited increased startle and USV, indicative of heightened negative affect in the throes of the withdrawal state (Barros and Miczek, 1996; Mutschler and Miczek, 1998).

Studies of human withdrawal have also utilized various startle methodologies, including startle to one acoustic probe as well as PPI. Investigators have used the startle eyeblink response, skin conductance response (SCR), and heart rate response (HRR) to startling acoustic stimuli as measures of attention (for reviews, see Dawson, Schell, and Filion, 2000; Filion, Dawson, and Schell, 1998; Lang, Bradley, and Cuthbert, 1990). As decreased attentional capacity has been evidenced as one symptom of withdrawal, particularly with regards to nicotine, these psychophysiological methods have utility in studying withdrawal. Studies have shown that smokers deprived of nicotine have higher SCRs to aversive auditory stimuli compared to non-deprived smokers (Boyd and Maltzman, 1984) and nonsmokers (Knott, 1980; 1984).

Additionally, withdrawn smokers have been shown to display decreased PPI to acoustic startle compared to nonsmokers and non-withdrawn smokers (Della Casa, Hoefer, Weiner, and Feldon, 1998; Duncan *et al.*, 2001; Rissling, Dawson, Schell, and Nuechterlein, 2007; though see Hutchison, Niaura, and Swift, 2000). Smoking after withdrawal improved smokers' PPI to higher than that of nonsmokers (Duncan *et al.*, 2001). Kumari and Gray (1991) found that smokers with higher scores of nicotine dependence exhibited less PPI to an acoustic startle compared to smokers with lower nicotine dependence scores. Furthermore, and of important clinical relevance, startle patterns have successfully predicted quitting success. Specifically, in a sample of cigarette smokers, startle response was measured before quitting (baseline), 24 hours after quitting, and 1 month later (Postma *et al.*, 2001). Individuals who successfully quit smoking 1 month later displayed high startle amplitude at baseline and a significant drop in amplitude during withdrawal compared to the unsuccessful quit group.

In sum, investigators have used psychophysiological measures to study withdrawal in both animals and humans. This can be done in a variety of ways including using an acoustic startle probe, PPI, and UVS in animals. Overall, studies indicate that animals and humans in a state of withdrawal show increased startle reactivity, increased USV, and decreased PPI.

8   Behavioral Economic Approach to Measuring Withdrawal

The critical question, "Why do some individuals continue to use drugs while others quit?" speaks to the substantial individual heterogeneity that typifies the substance use trajectory. Although several factors are known to shape the etiological pathway to addiction (e.g., family history, comorbid psychopathology), no single model fully explains the variance in substance use behavior. Behavioral economics, an emerging field that represents an intersection of psychology and economics, aims to measure one's decision to allocate resources (e.g., money) to the consumption of a reinforcer (e.g., drug; Hursh, 1980). Tools derived from behavioral economic theories function to consolidate and convert the influence of these diverse underlying addictive processes (e.g., emotion regulation, withdrawal relief) into a common metric (i.e., financial valuation) that corresponds to actual substance use. Indeed, the point at which an individual will accept money over a substance, or the extent to which they discount larger future rewards (e.g., substances) over smaller immediate rewards, reliably distinguishes individuals with an addictive disorder from those who do not and corresponds with patterns of use (Heinz, Lilje, Kassel, and de Wit, in press; MacKillop *et al.*, 2011).

Visceral factors such as craving are thought to create an enhanced motivational state that increases the relative value of a drug (see Loewenstein, 1996). For instance, in a deprived state, relative to a non-deprived state, one would expect an individual to pay more money in exchange for the substance. Accordingly, the ability to quantify one's demand for a substance may offer a more reliable and objective marker of withdrawal. Available measures to assess demand for substances include, but are not limited to, purchase tasks, delayed discounting tasks, and substance versus money tasks (for descriptions see Heinz, Lilje, Kassel, and de Wit, in press). Craving, a commonly accepted index of withdrawal and deprivation, has also been associated with elevated scores on behavioral economic measures for alcohol (e.g., MacKillop *et al.*, 2010a; MacKillop *et al.*, 2010b; MacKillop, Menges, McGeary, and Lisman, 2007), opiates (Badger *et al.*, 2007), and cigarettes (Perkins *et al.*, 1994; Sayette *et al.*, 2001). Finally, laboratory studies employing deprivation conditions also report sensitivity of these tasks to cigarette (e.g., Field *et al.*, 2006; Mitchell, 2004) and opiate (Giordano, 2002) deprivation.

9   Conclusions and Recommendations

In the preceding paragraphs, we have reviewed the construct of drug withdrawal, its role in promoting dependence, theories purporting to explain its motivational significance, and various ways in which it can be assessed. We viewed withdrawal as a syndrome comprised of affective, cognitive, physical, and behavioral symptoms. It becomes manifest in the presence of drug reduction or cessation, and is almost always experienced as aversive by the drug-dependent individual. As such, withdrawal serves as a potent motivator in terms of maintaining or re-establishing drug use. Withdrawal symptoms vary across different drug classes, and probably even within the same drug class. Nonetheless, one critical aspect of withdrawal that seemingly cuts across all withdrawal syndromes is the expression of negative affect, itself a potent cue for drug self-administration.

Whereas tremendous progress has been made in recent years in better understanding, describing, and measuring withdrawal, there are still some notable limitations with respect to our fully comprehending withdrawal and all of its motivational ramifications. First, it should be noted that the time course of withdrawal – that is, the temporal unfolding of withdrawal over time – remains poorly understood. Anecdotally, many recovering addicts assert that they felt addicted from the very first time they self-administered their drug of choice. Yet the important question remains relatively unanswered, as to how long it takes for withdrawal signs and symptoms to become manifest, and why some people do successfully appear able to escape the clutches of substance dependence and withdrawal (see, e.g., discussion of tobacco [Kassel *et al.*, 1994] and heroin [Zinberg and Jacobson, 1976] chippers; individuals who use each respective drug regularly but do not progress to dependence). Recent evidence from our own lab (e.g., Kassel *et al.*, 2007) revealed that even among very young (mean age 15.7) and light smokers, craving was evident with only minimal deprivation and then abated completely after smoking a cigarette. Hence, consistent with other burgeoning data, it may be that nicotine dependence (and perhaps this holds true for other drugs of abuse as well) may develop more quickly than previously believed (DiFranza, Ursprung, and Biller, 2012).

Correspondingly, the question of how long it takes withdrawal to fully subside also awaits further empirical scrutiny. Such important issues are probably best addressed by longitudinal studies that provide an opportunity for repeated assessment of withdrawal symptoms over time. As one example of such a study, Shiffman *et al.* (2006) examined the natural history of nicotine withdrawal in a sample of over 200 cigarette smokers who attempted to quit smoking. Findings revealed that all withdrawal symptoms returned to baseline levels within 10 days of quitting. Importantly, this study assessed not only affective symptoms, but also sleep disturbance and cognitive performance. Hence, these findings suggest that the time course of nicotine withdrawal may be shorter than previously reported. More studies of this kind, implemented across different drug classes, are sorely needed in order to advance the field in this respect.

Second, and as alluded to above, assessment of withdrawal should, wherever possible, employ a multimodal perspective, drawing upon all critical domains of withdrawal (behavioral, cognitive, physiological, and affective). Whereas cognitive disruption is not listed in the DSM-IV-TR criteria for most withdrawal syndromes (except for nicotine), many researchers and clinicians alike observe such disruptions as a salient feature among individuals attempting to abstain from drugs (e.g., nicotine; Jacobsen *et al.*, 2005; opiates; Rapeli *et al.*, 2006). Similarly, objective biological measures should be utilized when feasible. Although such measures were given relatively little discussion deference in this chapter, a host of potential hormonal, neurochemical, and electrophysiological changes that may reflect withdrawal processes need to be the subject of future investigation.

At the same time, it is important to note that whichever measures are chosen for study, they should demonstrate some clinically meaningful link to behavior (e.g., relapse). Hence, even if a symptom proves valid and reliable (e.g., decreased heart rate in smokers trying to quit), if there is no link to important phenomenological or behavioral outcomes, then its utility as a study target must be called into question. As such, more research is clearly needed to better prospectively link withdrawal symptoms to both successful and failed cessation efforts. Those symptoms that prove significant in this regard can then serve as specific targets of intervention.

Last, we strongly believe that part of what holds the field back with respect to fully understanding the role of withdrawal in the scheme of dependence is the lack of cross-talk among those ensconced in different drug "camps." Hence, we are calling for more conversation and sharing of theoretical and empirical perspective among those who study opiates, nicotine, amphetamines, hypnotic sedatives, cannabis, and so on. It may be that each of these respective drug classes is unique regarding the role of withdrawal and dependence. However, we tend to believe that, in fact, there are more similarities than differences across these diverse classes of drugs, and that such conversations will go a long way toward elucidating the critically important processes governing withdrawal and addiction.

References

Allen SS, Bade T, Hatsukami D, and Center B (2008) Craving, withdrawal, smoking urges on days immediately prior to smoking relapse. *Nicotine and Tobacco Research* 10: 35–45.
American Psychiatric Association (APA) (1994) *Diagnostic and Statistical Manual of Mental Disorders* (4th edn). Washington, DC: American Psychiatric Association.

American Psychiatric Association (APA) (2000) *Diagnostic and Statistical Manual of Mental Disorders* (4th edn, text revision). Washington, DC: American Psychiatric Association.

Anton RF (1999) What is craving? Models and implications for treatment. *Alcohol Research and Health* 23: 165–173.

Badger GJ, Bickel WK, Giordano LA, Jacobs EA, Loewenstein G, and Marsch L (2007) Altered states: The impact of immediate craving on the valuation of current and future opioids. *Journal of Health Economics* 26: 865–876.

Baker TB, Piper ME, McCarthy DE, Bolt DM, Smith SS, Kim S, and Conti D (2007) Time to first cigarette in the morning as an index of ability to quit smoking: Implications for nicotine dependence. *Oxford Journals: Nicotine and Tobacco Research* 9: S555–S570.

Baker TB, Piper ME, McCarthy DE, Majeski MR, and Fiore MC (2004) Addiction motivation reformulated: An affective processing model of negative reinforcement. *Psychological Review* 111: 33–51.

Barr AM and Markou A (2005) Psychostimulant withdrawal as an inducing condition in animal models of depression. *Neuroscience and Biobehavioral Reviews* 29: 675–706.

Barr AM, Markou A, and Phillips AG (2002) A "crash" course on psychostimulant withdrawal as a model of depression. *Trends in Pharmacological Sciences* 23: 475–482.

Barros HMT and Miczek KA (1996) Withdrawal from oral cocaine in rats: Ultrasonic vocalizations and tactile startle. *Psychopharmacology* 125: 379–384.

Becker HC (2000) Animal models of alcohol withdrawal. *Alcohol Research and Health* 24: 105–113.

Becker HC (2008) Alcohol dependence, withdrawal, and relapse. *Alcohol Research and Health* 31: 348–361.

Bierut LJ, Rice JP, Goate A, Hinrichs AL, Saccone NL, Foround T, and Reich T (2004) A genomic scan for habitual smoking in families of alcoholics: Common and specific genetic factors in substance dependence. *American Journal of Medical Genetics* 124A: 19–27.

Blumenthal TD, Elden A, and Flaten MA (2004) A comparison of several methods used to quantify prepulse inhibition of eyeblink responding. *Psychophysiology* 41: 326–332.

Boyd GM and Maltzman I (1984) Effects of cigarette smoking on bilateral skin conductance. *Psychophysiology* 21: 334–341.

Bradley B, Gossop M, Phillips G, and Legarda J (1987) The development of an opiate withdrawal score (OWS). *British Journal of Addiction* 82: 1139–1142.

Brandon TH, Tiffany ST, Obremski KM, and Baker TB (1990) Postcessation cigarette use: The process of relapse. *Addictive Behaviors* 15: 105–114.

Brandon TH, Vidrine JI, and Litvin EB (2007) Relapse and relapse prevention. *Annual Reviews of Clinical Psychology* 3: 257–284.

Breslau N (1995) Psychiatric comorbidity of smoking and nicotine dependence. *Behavior Genetics* 25: 95–101.

Budney AJ and Hughes JR (2006) The cannabis withdrawal syndrome. *Current Opinion in Psychiatry* 19: 233–238.

Budney AJ, Hughes JR, Moore BA, and Vandrey R (2004) Review of the validity and significance of cannabis withdrawal syndrome. *American Journal of Psychiatry* 161: 1967–1977.

Cappell H and Herman CP (1972) Alcohol and tension reduction: A review. *Quarterly Journal of Studies on Alcohol* 33: 33–64.

Carey KB and Correia CJ (1997) Drinking motives predict alcohol-related problems in college students. *Journal of Studies on Alcohol* 58: 100–105.

Carter BL and Tiffany ST (2001) The cue-availability paradigm: The effects of cigarette availability on cue reactivity in smokers. *Experimental and Clinical Psychopharmacology* 9: 183–190.

Chait LD (1990) Subjective and behavioral effects of marijuana the morning after smoking. *Psychopharmacology* 100: 328–333.

Chait LD, Fischman MW, and Schuster CR (1985) Hangover effects the morning after marijuana smoking. *Drug and Alcohol Dependence*: 229–238.

Conklin CA and Tiffany ST (2001) The impact of imagining personalized versus standardized urge scenarios on cigarette craving and autonomic reactivity. *Experimental and Clinical Psychopharmacology* 9: 399–408.

Conklin CA, Robin N, Perkins KA, Salkeld RP, and McClernon FJ (2008) Proximal versus distal cues to smoke: The effects of environments on smokers' cue-reactivity. *Experimental and Clinical Psychopharmacology* 16: 207–214.

Cook EW, Hawk LW, Davis TL, and Stevenson VE (1991) Affective individual differences and startle reflex modulation. *Journal of Abnormal Psychology* 100: 5.

Croop RS, Faulkner EB, and Labriola DF (1997) The safety profile of naltrexone in the treatment of alcoholism. Results from a multicenter usage study. The naltrexone usage study group. *Archives of General Psychiatry* 54: 1130–1135.

Crowley TJ, Wagner JE, Zerbe G, and Macdonald M (1985) Naltrexone-induced dysphoria in former opioid addicts. *American Journal of Psychiatry* 142: 1081–1084.

Dawson ME, Schell AM, and Filion DL (2000) The electrodermal system. In JT Cacioppo, LG Tassinary, and GG Berntson (eds), *Handbook of Psychophysiology* (2nd edn, pp. 200–223). New York: Cambridge University Press.

Della Casa V, Hoefer I, Weiner I, and Feldon J (1998) The effects of smoking on acoustic prepulse inhibition in healthy men and women. *Psychopharmacology* 137: 362–368.

DiFranza JR, Ursprung WW, and Biller L (2012) The developmental sequence of tobacco withdrawal symptoms of wanting, craving and needing. *Pharmacology, Biochemistry, and Behavior* 100: 494–497.

Duncan E, Madonick S, Chakravorty S, Parwani A, Szilagyi S, Efferen T, . . . Rotrosen J (2001) Effects of smoking on acoustic startle and prepulse inhibition in humans. *Psychopharmacology* 156: 266–272.

Earleywine M (1993a) Hangover moderates the association between personality and drinking problems. *Addictive Behaviors* 18: 291–297.

Earleywine M (1993b) Personality risk for alcoholism covaries with hangover symptoms. *Addictive Behaviors* 18: 415–420.

Elholm B, Larsen K, Hornnes N, Zierau F, and Becker U (2010) A psychometric validation of the Short Alcohol Withdrawal Scale (SAWS). *Alcohol and Alcoholism* 45: 362–365.

Epstein DH, Willner-Reid J, and Preston KL (2010) Addiction and emotion: Theories, assessment techniques, and treatment implications. In JD Kassel (ed.), *Substance abuse and emotion* (pp. 259-280). Washington. DC: American Psychological Association.

Etter JF (2005) A self-administered questionnaire to measure cigarette withdrawal symptoms, the Cigarette Withdrawal Scale. *Nicotine and Tobacco Research* 7: 47–57.

Etter JF and Hughes JR (2006) A comparison of the psychometric properties of three cigarette withdrawal scales. *Addiction* 101: 362–372.

Farrell M (1994) Opiate withdrawal. *Addiction* 89: 1471–1475.

Field M, Santarcangelo M, Sumnall H, Goudie A, and Cole J (2006) Delay discounting and the behavioural economics of cigarette purchases in smokers: The effects of nicotine deprivation. *Psychopharmacology* 186: 255–63.

Filion DL, Dawson ME, and Schell AM (1998) The psychological significance of human startle eyeblink modification: A review. *Biological Psychology* 47: 1–43.

Finnigan F, Hammersley R, and Cooper T (1998) An examination of next-day hangover effects after a 100 mg/100 ml dose of alcohol in heavy social drinkers. *Addiction* 93: 1829–1838.

Finnigan F, Schulze D, Smallwood J, and Helander A (2005) The effects of self-administered alcohol-induced "hangover" in a naturalistic setting on psychomotor and cognitive performance and subjective state. *Addiction* 100: 1680–1689.

Giordano L.A, Bickel WK, Loewenstein G, Jacobs EA, Marsch L, and Badger GJ (2002) Mild opioid deprivation increases the degree that opioid-dependent outpatients discount delayed heroin and money. *Psychopharmacology* 163: 174–182.

Gossop M (1990) The development of a Short Opiate Withdrawal Scale (SOWS). *Addictive Behaviors* 15: 487–490.

Gossop M, Keaney F, Stewart D, Marshall EJ, and Strang J (2002) A Short Alcohol Withdrawal Scale (SAWS): Development and psychometric properties. *Addiction Biology* 7: 37–43.

Gowing LR and Ali RL (2006) The place of detoxification in treatment of opioid dependence. *Current Opinion in Psychiatry* 19: 266–270.

Graham FK (1979) Distinguishing among orienting, defense, and startle reflexes. In HD Kimmel, EH van Olst, and JF Orlebeke (eds), *The Orienting Reflex in Humans* (pp. 137–167). Hillsdale, NJ: Erlbaum.

Grant BF, Dawson DA, and Hasin DS (2001) *The Alcohol Use Disorder and Associated Disabilities Interview Schedule-DSM-IV Version.* Bethesda, MD: National Institute on Alcohol Abuse and Alcoholism.

Grant BF, Dawson DA, Stinson FS, Chou SP, Dufour MC, and Pickering RP (2004) The 12-month prevalence and trends in DSM-IV alcohol abuse and dependence: United States. *Drug and Alcohol Dependence* 74: 223–234.

Gray S, Borgundvaag B, Sirvastava A, Randall I, and Kahan M (2010) Feasibility and reliability of the SHOT: A short scale for measuring pretreatment severity of alcohol withdrawal in the emergency department. *Academic Emergency Medicine* 17: 1048–1054.

Hajek P, Gillison F, and McRobbie H (2003) Stopping smoking can cause constipation. *Addiction* 98: 1563–1567.

Hall W and Zador D (1997) The alcohol withdrawal syndrome. *Lancet* 349: 1897–1900.

Harburg E, Davis D, Cummings KM, and Gunn R (1981) Negative affect, alcohol consumption and hangover symptoms among normal drinkers in a small community. *Journal of Studies on Alcohol* 42: 998–1012.

Harburg E, Gunn R, Gleiberman L, DiFranceisco W, and Schork A (1993) Psychosocial factors, alcohol use, and hangover signs among social drinkers: A reappraisal. *Journal of Clinical Epidemiology* 46: 413–422.

Harris AC and Gewirtz JC (2004) Elevated startle during withdrawal from acute morphine: A model of opiate withdrawal and anxiety. *Psychopharmacology* 171: 140–147.

Harris AC and Gewirtz JC (2005) Acute opioid dependence: Characterizing the early adaptations underlying drug withdrawal. *Psychopharmacology* 178: 353–366.

Hatsukami D, McBride C, Pirie P, Hellerstedt W, and Lando H (1991) Effects of nicotine gum on prevalence and severity of withdrawal in female cigarette smokers. *Journal of Substance Abuse* 3: 427–440.

Heilig M, Thorsell A, Sommer WH, Hansson AC, Ramchandani VA, George DT, . . . Barr CS (2010) Translating the neuroscience of alcoholism into clinical treatments: From blocking the buzz to curing the blues. *Neuroscience and Biobehavioral Reviews* 35: 334–344.

Heinz AJ, Kassel JD, Berbaum M, and Mermelstein R (2010) Adolescents' expectancies for smoking to regulate affect predict smoking behavior and nicotine dependence over time. *Drug and Alcohol Dependence* 111: 128–135.

Heinz AJ, Lilje TC, Kassel JD, and de Wit H (in press) A review of behavioral economic approaches to quantifying reinforcement and demand for psychoactive substances in humans.

Hellig M and Koob GF (2007) A key role for corticotrophin-releasing factor in alcohol dependence. *TRENDS in Neuroscience* 30: 399–406.

Hendricks PS, Ditre JW, Drobes DJ, and Brandon TH (2006) The early time course of smoking withdrawal effects. *Psychopharmacology* 187: 385–396.

Hughes JR (2007a) Effects of abstinence from tobacco: Etiology, animal models, epidemiology, and significance: A subjective review. *Nicotine and Tobacco Research* 9: 329–339.

Hughes JR (2007b) Measurement of the effects of abstinence from tobacco: A qualitative review. *Psychology of Addictive Behaviors* 21: 127–137.

Hughes JR (2007c) Effects of abstinence from tobacco: Valid symptoms and time course. *Nicotine and Tobacco Research* 9: 315–327.

Hughes JR and Hatsukami DK (1986) Signs and symptoms of tobacco withdrawal. *Archives of General Psychiatry* 43: 289–294.

Hughes JR and Hatsukami DK (1992) The nicotine withdrawal syndrome: A brief review and update. *International Journal of Smoking Cessation* 19: 21–26.

Hughes JR, Higgins ST, and Hatsukami DK (1990) Effects of abstinence from tobacco: A critical review. In LT Kozlowski, HM Annis, HD Cappell, FB Glaser, MS Goodstadt, Y Israel, . . . ER Vingilis (eds.), *Research Advances in Drug and Alcohol Problems* (pp. 317–398). New York: Plenum Press.

Hughes JR, Keely J, and Naud S (2004) Shape of the relapse curve and long-term abstinence among untreated smokers. *Addiction* 99: 29–38.

Hursh SR (1980) Economic concepts for the analysis of behavior. *Journal of the Experimental Analysis of Behavior* 34: 219–238.

Hutchison KE, Niaura R, and Swift R (2000) The effects of smoking high nicotine cigarettes on prepulse inhibition, startle latency, and subjective responses. *Psychopharmacology* 150: 244–252.

Jacobsen LK, Krystal JH, Mencl WE, Westerveld M, and Pugh KR (2005) Effects of smoking and smoking abstinence on cognition in adolescent tobacco smokers. *Biological Psychiatry* 57: 56–66.

Jorenby DE, Hatsukami DK, Smith SS, Fiore MC, Allen S, Jensen J, and Baker TB (1996) Characterization of tobacco withdrawal symptoms: Transdermal nicotine reduces hunger and weight gain. *Psychopharmacology* 128: 130–138.

Kaltwasser T (1991) Acoustic startle induced ultrasonic vocalization in the rat: A novel animal model of anxiety? *Behavioural Brain Research* 43: 133–137.

Kassel JD and Shiffman S (1992) What can hunger teach us about drug craving? A comparative analysis of the two constructs. *Advances in Behaviour Research and Therapy* 14: 141–167.

Kassel JD, Evatt DP, Greenstein JE, Wardle MC, Yates MC, and Veilleux JC (2007) The acute effects of nicotine on positive and negative affect in adolescent smokers. *Journal of Abnormal Psychology* 116: 543–553.

Kassel JD, Jackson SI, and Unrod M (2000) Generalized expectancies for negative mood regulation and problem drinking among college students. *Journal of Studies on Alcohol* 61: 332–340.

Kassel JD, Shiffman S, Gnys M, Paty J, and Zettler-Segal M (1994) Psychosocial and personality differences in chippers and regular smokers. *Addictive Behaviors* 19: 565–575.

Kassel JD, Stroud LR, and Paronis CA (2003) Smoking, stress, and negative affect: Correlation, causation, and context across stages of smoking. *Psychological Bulletin* 129: 270–304.

Kessler RC and Üstün TB (2004) The World Mental Health (WMH) Survey Initiative Version of the World Health Organization (WHO) Composite International Diagnostic Interview (CIDI). *International Journal of Methods in Psychiatric Research* 13: 93–122.

Khantzian EJ (1997) The self-medication hypothesis of substance use disorders: A reconsideration and recent applications. *Harvard Review of Psychiatry* 4: 231–244.

Killen JD and Fortmann SP (1997) Craving is associated with smoking relapse: Findings from three prospective studies. *Experimental and Clinical Psychopharmacology* 5: 137–142.

Kim SS, Gulick EE, Kim S, and Seo H (2007) Psychometric properties of the Minnesota Nicotine Withdrawal Scale: A Korean version. *Journal of Nursing Measurement* 15: 121–132.

Knott VJ (1980) Reaction time, noise distraction and autonomic responsivity in smokers and non-smokers. *Perceptual and Motor Skills* 50: 1271–1280.

Knott VJ (1984) Electrodermal activity during aversive stimulation: Sex differences in smokers and non-smokers. *Addictive Behaviors* 9: 195–199.

Koob GF (2003) Neuroadaptive mechanisms of addiction: Studies on the extended amygdala. *European Neuropsychopharmacology* 13: 442–452.

Koob G and Kreek MJ (2007) Stress, dysregulation of drug reward pathways, and the transition to drug dependence. *American Journal of Psychiatry* 164: 1149–1159.

Koob GF and Le Moal M (1997) Drug abuse: Hedonic homeostatic dysregulation. *Science* 278: 52–58.

Koob GF and Le Moal M (2001) Drug addiction, dysregulation of reward, and allostasis. *Neuropsychopharmacology* 24: 97–129.

Koob and Le Moal (2008) Neurobiological mechanisms for opponent motivational processes in addiction. *Philosophical Transactions of the Royal Society of London. Series B, Biological Sciences* 363: 3113–3123.

Kumari V and Gray JA (1999) Smoking withdrawal, nicotine dependence and prepulse inhibition of the acoustic startle reflex. *Psychopharmacology* 141: 11–15.

Lang PJ, Bradley MM, and Cuthbert BN (1990) Emotion, attention, and the startle reflex. *Psychological Review* 97: 377–395.

Loewenstein G (1996) Out of control: Visceral influences on behavior. *Organizational behavior and human decision processes* 65: 272–92.

London ED, Simon SL, Berman SM, Mandelkern MA, Lichtman AM, Bramen J, . . . Ling W (2004) Mood disturbances and regional cerebral metabolic abnormalities in recently abstinent methamphetamine abusers. *Archives of General Psychiatry* 61: 73–84.

MacKillop J, Amlung MT, Few LR, Ray LA, Sweet LH, and Munafò MR (2011) Delayed reward discounting and addictive behavior: A meta-analysis. *Psychopharmacology* 216: 1–17.

MacKillop J, Menges DP, McGeary JE, and Lisman SA (2007) Effects of craving and DRD4 VNTR genotype on the relative value of alcohol: An initial human laboratory study. *Behavioral and Brain Functions* 3: 1–12.

MacKillop J, Miranda R, Jr, Monti PM, Ray LA, Murphy JG, Rohsenow DJ, . . . Gwaltney CJ (2010a) Alcohol demand, delayed reward discounting, and craving in relation to drinking and alcohol use disorders. *Journal of Abnormal Psychology* 119: 106–114.

MacKillop J, O'Hagen S, Lisman SA, Murphy JG, Ray LA, Tidey JW, . . . Monti PM (2010b) Behavioral economic analysis of cue-elicited craving for alcohol. *Addiction* 105: 1599–1607.

Madden JS (1993) Alcohol and depression. *British Journal of Hospital Medicine* 50: 261–264.

McKeon A, Frye MA, and Delanty N (2008) The alcohol withdrawal syndrome. *Journal of Neurology, Neurosurgery and Psychiatry* 79: 854–862.

McNair DM, Lorr M, and Droppleman LF (1971) *Profile of mood states.* San Diego, CA: Educational and Industrial Testing Service.

Metcalfe P, Sobers M, and Dewey M (1995) The Windsor clinical alcohol withdrawal assessment scale (WCAWAS): Investigating factors associated with complicated withdrawals. *Alcohol and Alcoholism* 30: 367–372.

Mischel W, Shoda Y, and Rodriguez ML (1989) Delay of gratification in children. *Science* 244: 933–938.

Miller WR, Westerberg VS, Harris RJ, and Tonigan JS (1996) What predicts relapse? Prospective testing of antecedent models. *Addiction* 91(Suppl.): S155–72.

Mitchell SH (2004) Effects of short-term nicotine deprivation on decision-making: Delay, uncertainty and effort discounting. *Nicotine and Tobacco Research* 6: 819–828.

Mohr CD, Armeli S, Tennen H, Temple M, Todd M, Clark J, *et al.* (2005) Moving beyond the keg party: A daily process study of college student drinking motivations. *Psychology of Addictive Behaviors* 19: 392–403.

Morrell HE, Cohen LM, and al'Absi M (2008) Physiological and psychological symptoms and predictors in early nicotine withdrawal. *Pharmacology, Biochemistry, and Behavior* 89: 272–278.

Mutschler NH and Miczek KA (1998) Withdrawal from IV cocaine "binges" in rats: Ultrasonic distress calls and startle. *Psychopharmacology* 135: 161–168.

Newlin DB and Pretorius MB (1990) Sons of alcoholics report greater hangover symptoms than sons of nonalcoholics: A pilot study. *Alcoholism: Clinical and Experimental Research* 14: 713–716.

O'Brien CP (2008) Evidence-based treatments of addiction. *Philosophical Transactions of the Royal Society B: Biological Sciences* 363: 3277–3288.

O'Brien CP, Volpicelli LA, and Volpicelli JR (1996) Naltrexone in the treatment of alcoholism: clinical review. *Alcohol* 13: 35–39.

O'Dell LE, Bruijnzeel AW, Ghozland S, Markou A, and Koob GF (2004) Nicotine withdrawal in adolescent and adult rats. *Annals of the New York Academy of Sciences* 1021: 167–174.

O'Malley SS, Krishnan-Sarin S, Farren C, and O'Connor PG (2000) Naltrexone-induced nausea in patients treated for alcohol dependence: Clinical predictors and evidence for opioid mediated effects. *Journal of Clinical Psychopharmacology* 20: 69–76.

Palmstierna T (2001) A model for predicting alcohol withdrawal delirium. *Psychiatric Services* 52: 820–823.

Park CL, Armeli S, and Tennen H (2004) The daily stress and coping process and alcohol use among college students. *Journal of Studies on Alcohol* 65: 126–135.

Patten CA and Martin JE (1996a) Measuring tobacco withdrawal: A review of self-report questionnaires. *Journal of Substance Abuse* 8: 93–113.

Patten CA and Martin JE (1996b) Does nicotine withdrawal affect smoking cessation? Clinical and theoretical issues. *Annals of Behavioral Medicine* 18: 190–200.

Perkins K (2009) Does smoking cue-induced craving tell us anything important about nicotine dependence? *Addiction* 104: 1610–1616.

Perkins KA, Epstein LH, Grobe J, and Fonte C (1994) Tobacco abstinence, smoking cues, and the reinforcing value of smoking. *Pharmacology Biochemistry and Behavior* 47: 107–112.

Peyser H (1982) Stress and alcohol. In L Goldberger and S Breznotz (eds), *Handbook of Stress: Theoretical and Clinical Aspects* (pp. 585-598). New York: Free Press.

Piasecki TM (2006) Relapse to smoking. *Clinical Psychology Review* 26: 196–215.

Piasecki TM, Jorenby DE, Smith SS, Fiore MC, and Baker TB (2002) Smoking withdrawal dynamics: II. Improved tests of withdrawal-relapse relations. *Journal of Abnormal Psychology* 112: 14–27.

Piasecki TM, Niaura R, Shadel WG, Abrams D, Goldstein M, *et al.* (2000) Smoking withdrawal dynamics in unaided quitters. *Journal of Abnormal Psychology* 109: 74–86.

Piasecki TM, Sher KJ, Slutske WS, and Jackson KM (2005) Hangover frequency and risk for alcohol use disorders: Evidence from a longitudinal high-risk study. *Journal of Abnormal Psychology* 114: 223.

Pittman B, Gueorguieva R, Krupitsky E, Rudenko AA, Flannery BA, and Krystal JH (2007) Multidimensionality of the Alcohol Withdrawal Symptom Checklist: A factor analysis of the Alcohol Withdrawal Symptom Checklist and CIWA-Ar. *Alcoholism: Clinical and Experimental Research* 31: 612–618.

Platz WE, Oberlaender FA, and Seidel ML (1995) The phenomenology of perceptual hallucinations in alcohol-induced delirium tremens. *Psychopathology* 28: 247–255.

Postma P, Kumari V, Sharma T, Hines M, and Gray JA (2001) Startle response during smoking and 24 h after withdrawal predicts successful smoking cessation. *Psychopharmacology* 156: 360–367.

Rapeli P, Kivisaari R, Autti T, Kahkonen S, Puuskari V, Jokela O, and Kalska H (2006) Cognitive function during early abstinence from opioid dependence: A comparison to age, gender, and verbal intelligence matched control. *BMC Psychiatry* 6: 9.

Rassnick S, Koob GF, and Geyer MA (1992) Responding to acoustic startle during chronic ethanol intoxication and withdrawal. *Psychopharmacology* 106: 351–358.

Redmond DE, Jr, and Krystal JH (1984) Multiple mechanisms of withdrawal from opioid drugs. *Annual Review of Neuroscience* 7: 443–478.

Reoux JP and Oreskovich MR (2006) A comparison of two versions of the clinical institute withdrawal assessment for alcohol: The CIWA-Ar and the CIWA-AD. *American Journal on Addictions* 15: 85–93.

Rissling AJ, Dawson ME, Schell AM, and Nuechterlein KH (2007) Effects of cigarette smoking on prepulse inhibition, its attentional modulation, and vigilance performance. *Psychophysiology* 44: 627–634.

Robbins SJ and Ehrman RN (2004) The role of attentional bias in substance abuse. *Behavioral and Cognitive Neuroscience Reviews* 3: 243–260.

Roberts AJ, Heyser CJ, Cole M, Griffin P, and Koob GF (2000) Excessive ethanol drinking following a history of dependence: Animal model of allostasis. *Neuropsychopharmacology* 22: 581–594.

Robinson TE and Berridge KC (2003) The neural basis of drug craving: An incentive-sensitization theory of addiction. *Brain Research Reviews* 18: 247–291.

Robinson TE and Berridge KC (2008) The incentive sensitization theory of addiction: Some current issues. *Philosophical Transactions of the Royal Society* 363: 3137–3146.

Rohsenow DJ, Howland J, Minsky SJ, Almeida A, and Roehrs TA (2007) The Acute Hangover Scale: A new measure of immediate hangover symptoms. *Addictive Behaviors* 32: 1314–1320.

Roozen HG, de Waart R, van der Windt DA, van den Brink W, de Jong CA, and Kerkhof AJ (2006) A systematic review of the effectiveness of naltrexone in the maintenance treatment of opioid and alcohol dependence. *European Neuropsychopharmacology: Journal of the European College of Neuropsychopharmacology* 16: 311–323.

Rose JE, Behm FM, and Westman EC (1998) Nicotine-mecamylamine treatment for smoking cessation: The role of pre-cessation therapy. *Experimental and Clinical Psychopharmacology* 6: 331–343.

Saitz R (1998) Introduction to alcohol withdrawal. *Alcohol Health and Research World* 22: 5–12.

Sayette MA, Martin CS, Wertz JM, Shiffman S, and Perrott MA (2001) A multi-dimensional analysis of cue-elicited craving in heavy smokers and tobacco chippers. *Addiction* 96: 1419–1432.

Schneider NG and Jarvik ME (1984) Time course of smoking withdrawal symptoms as a function of nicotine replacement. *Psychopharmacology* 82: 143–153.

Sellers EM, Sullivan JT, Somer G, and Sykora K (1991) Characterization of DSM-III-R criteria for uncomplicated alcohol withdrawal provides an empirical basis for DSM-IV. *Archives of General Psychiatry* 48: 442–447.

Seppälä T, Leino T, Linnoila M, Huttunen M, and YIikahri R (1976) Effects of hangover on psychomotor skills related to driving: Modification by fructose and glucose. *Acta Pharmacologica et Toxicologica* 38: 209–218.

Shadel WG, Martino S, Setodji CM, Cervone D, Witkiewitz K, *et al.* (2011) Lapse-induced surges in craving influence relapse in adult smokers: An experimental investigation. *Health Psychology*. Advance online publication. doi: 10.1037/a0023445.

Shadel WG, Niaura R, and Abrams DB (2001) Effect of different cue stimulus delivery channels on craving reactivity: Comparing in vivo and video cues in regular cigarette smokers. *Journal of Behavior Therapy and Experimental Psychiatry* 32: 203–209.

Shaw JM, Kolesar GS, Sellers SM, Kaplan HL, and Sandor P (1981) Development of optimal treatment tactics for alcohol withdrawal. I. Assessment and effectiveness of supportive care. *Journal of Clinical Psychopharmacology* 1: 382–387.

Shiffman S and Jarvik ME (1976) Smoking withdrawal symptoms in two weeks of abstinence. *Psychopharmacology* 61: 718–722.

Shiffman S, Engberg JB, Paty JA, Perz WG, Gnys M, *et al.* (1997) A day at a time: Predicting smoking lapse from daily urge. *Journal of Abnormal Psychology* 106: 104–116.

Shiffman S, Ferguson SG, and Gwaltney CJ (2006) Immediate hedonic response to smoking lapses: Relationship to smoking relapse, and effects of nicotine replacement therapy. *Psychopharmacology* 184: 608–618.

Shiffman S, Patten C, Gwaltney C, Paty J, Gnys M, Kassel J, Hickcox M, Waters A, and Balabanis M (2006) Natural history of nicotine withdrawal. *Addiction* 101: 1822–1832.

Shiffman S, Paty JA, Gnys M, Kassel JD, and Hickcox M (1996) First lapses to smoking: Within-subjects analysis of real-time reports. *Journal of Consulting and Clinical Psychology* 64: 366–379.

Shiffman S, Waters AJ, and Hickox M (2004) The Nicotine Dependence Syndrome Scale: A multidimensional measure of nicotine dependence. *Nicotine and Tobacco Research* 6: 327–348.

Shiffman S, West RJ, and Gilbert DG (2004) Recommendation for the assessment of tobacco craving and withdrawal in smoking cessation trials. *Nicotine and Tobacco Research* 6: 599–614.

Slutske WS, Piasecki TM, and Hunt-Carter EE (2003) Development and initial validation of the Hangover Symptoms Scale: Prevalence and correlates of hangover symptoms in college students. *Development* 27: 1442–1450.

Smith JW (1995) Medical manifestations of alcohol in the elderly. *International Journal of the Addictions* 30: 1749–1798.

Solomon RL and Corbit JD (1974) An opponent-process theory of motivation: I. Temporal dynamics of affect. *Psychological Review* 81: 119–145.

Span SA and Earleywine M (1999) Familial risk for alcoholism and hangover symptoms. *Addictive Behaviors* 24: 121–125.

Spielberger CD, Gorsuch RL, Lushene R, Vagg PR, and Jacobs GA (1983) *Manual for the State-Trait Anxiety Inventory (Form Y)*. Palo Alto, CA: Consulting Psychologists Press.

Srisurapanont M, Jarusuraisin N, and Jittiwutikan J (1999) Amphetamine withdrawal. I. Reliability, validity, and factor structure of a measure. *Australian and New Zealand Journal of Psychiatry* 33: 89–93.

Stead LF, Perera R, Bullen C, Mant D, and Lancaster T (2008) Nicotine replacement therapy for smoking cessation. *Cochrane Database of Systematic Reviews* 3: 1–123.

Stuppaeck CH, Barnas C, Falk M, Guenther M, Hummer H, *et al.* (1994) Assessment of the alcohol withdrawal syndrome – validity and reliability of the translated and modified Clinical Institute Withdrawal Assessment for Alcohol Scale (CIWA-A). *Addiction* 89: 1287–1292.

Sullivan JT, Sykora K, Scheiderman J, Naranjo CA, and Sellers SM (1989) Assessment of alcohol withdrawal: The revised clinical institute withdrawal assessment for alcohol scale (CIWA-Ar). *British Journal of Addiction* 84: 1353–7.

Swift R and Davidson D (1998) Alcohol hangover: Mechanisms and mediators. *Alcohol and Health Research World* 22: 54-60.

Tiffany ST (1990) A cognitive model of drug urges and drug-use behavior: Role of automatic and nonautomatic processes. *Psychological Review* 97: 147–168.

Tiffany ST (2010) Drug craving and affect. In JD Kassel (ed.), *New Frontiers in Research on Substance Abuse and Emotion*. Washington, DC: American Psychological Association.

Trevisan LA, Boutros N, Petrakis IL, and Krystal JH (1998) Complications of alcohol withdrawal: Pathophysiological insights. *Alcohol Health and Research World* 22: 61–66.

Turpin G (1986) Effects of stimulus intensity on autonomic responding: The problem of differentiating orienting and defense responses. *Psychophysiology* 23: 1–14.

Ussher M, West R, Evans P, Steptoe A, McEwen A, Clow A, and Hucklebridge F (2004) Acute reduction in secretory immunoglobulin A following smoking cessation. *Psychoneuroendocrinology* 29: 1335–1340.

US Department of Health and Human Services (1990) *Seventh Special Report to the US Congress on Alcohol and Health*. United States Department of Health and Human Services, Washington, DC.

Verheul R, Van Den Brink W, and Geerlings P (1999) A three-pathway psychobiological model of craving for alcohol. *Alcohol* 34: 197–222.

Verster JC, van Duin D, Volkerts ER, Schreuder AH, and Verbaten MN (2003) Alcohol hangover effects on memory functioning and vigilance performance after an evening of binge drinking. *Neuropsychopharmacology* 28: 740–746.

Vivian JA, Farrell WJ, Sapperstein SB, and Miczek KA (1994) Diazepam withdrawal: Effects of diazepam and gepirone on acoustic startle-induced 22 kHz ultrasonic vocalizations. *Psychopharmacology* 114: 101-108.

Voris J, Elder I, and Sebastian P (1991) A simple test of cocaine craving and related responses. *Journal of Clinical Psychology* 47: 320–323.

Vrana SR, Spence EL, and Lang PJ (1988) The startle probe response: A new measure of emotion? *Journal of Abnormal Psychology* 97: 487–491.

Walters AJ and Lader MH (1971) Hangover effect of hypnotics in man. *Nature* 229: 637–638.

Watson D, Clark LA, and Tellegen A (1988) Development and validation of brief measures of positive and negative affect: The PANAS scales. *Journal of Personality and Social Psychology* 54: 1063–1070.

Welsch SK, Smith SS, Wetter DW, Jorenby DeE, Fiore MC, and Baker TB (1999) Development and validation of the Wisconsin Smoking Withdrawal Scale. *Experimental and Clinical Psychopharmacology* 7: 354–361.

Wertz JM and Sayette MA (2001) A review of the effects of perceived drug use opportunity on self-reported urges. *Experimental and Clinical Psychopharmacology* 9: 3–13.

West R and Hajek P (2004) Evaluation of the Mood and Physical Symptoms Scale (MPSS) to assess cigarette withdrawal. *Psychopharmacology* (Berlin) 177: 195–199.

West R, Hajek P, and McNeill A (1991) Effect of buspirone on cigarette withdrawal symptoms and short-term abstinence rates in a smokers clinic. *Psychopharmacology* 104: 91–96.

West R, Ussher M, Evans M, and Rashid M (2006) Assessing DSM-IV nicotine withdrawal symptoms: A comparison and evaluation of five different scales. *Psychopharmacology* 184: 619–627.

Wetterling T, Kanitz R, Besters B, Fischer D, Zerfass B, *et al.* (1997) A new rating scale for the assessment of the alcohol-withdrawal syndrome (AWS scale). *Alcohol and Alcoholism* 32: 753–760.

Wiesbeck GA, Schuckit MA, Kalmijn JA, Tipp JE, Bucholz KK, and Smith TL (1996) An evaluation of the history of a marijuana withdrawal syndrome in a large population. *Addiction* 91: 1469–1478.

Wiese JG, Shlipak MG, and Browner WS (2000) The alcohol hangover. *Annals of Internal Medicine* 132: 897.

Wikler A (1965) Conditioning factors in opiate addictions and relapse. In DM Wilner and GG Kassebaum (eds), *Narcotics* (pp. 85–100). New York: McGraw-Hill.

Williams D, Lewis J, and McBride A (2001) A comparison of rating scales for the alcohol-withdrawal syndrome. *Alcohol and Alcoholism* 36: 104–108.

Wills TA and Shiffman S (1985) Coping and substance use: A conceptual framework. In S Shiffman and TA Wills (eds.), *Coping and Substance Use* (pp. 3–24). New York: Academic Press.

Wilmouth CE and Spear LP (2006) Withdrawal from chronic nicotine in adolescent and adult rats. *Pharmacology, Biochemistry, and Behavior* 85: 648–657.

World Health Organization (WHO) (1990) *International Statistical Classification of Diseases and Related Health Problems.* Geneva: World Health Organization.

World Health Organization (WHO) (2010) *World Drug Report, 2010: Executive Summary.* Vienna: World Health Organization.

Ylikahri RH, Huttunen MO, Eriksson CJ P, and Nikklä EA (1974) Metabolic studies on the pathogenesis of hangover. *European Journal of Clinical Investigation* 4: 93–100.

Young SE, Corley RP, Stallings MC, Rhee SH, Crowley TJ, and Hewitt JK (2002) Substance use, abuse and dependence in adolescence: Prevalence, symptom profiles and correlates. *Drug and Alcohol Dependence* 68: 309–322.

Yu X, Xiao D, Li B, Wang G, Chen J, *et al.* (2010) Evaluation of the Chinese versions of the Minnesota Nicotine Withdrawal Scale and the Questionnaire on Smoking Urges. *Nicotine and Tobacco Research* 12: 630–634.

Zilberman ML, Tavarez H, and El-Guebaly N (2003) Relationship between craving and personality in treatment-seeking women with substance-related disorders. *BMC Psychiatry* 3: 1–5.

Zinberg NE and Jacobson RC (1976) The natural history of "chipping." *American Journal of Psychiatry* 133: 37–40.

Zorick T, Nestor L, Miotto K, Sugar C, Hellemann G, Scanlon G, . . . London ED (2010) Withdrawal symptoms in abstinent methamphetamine-dependent subjects. *Addiction* 105: 1809–1818.

12

Drug Self-Administration Paradigms: Methods for Quantifying Motivation in Experimental Research[1]

James MacKillop and Cara Murphy

1 Introduction

This chapter provides a review of the diverse experimental methods for studying drug consumption under controlled laboratory conditions, or what are typically referred to as self-administration paradigms. These methods measure an individual's level of motivation for a given drug, making them fundamental tools for both etiological and clinical research in addiction psychopharmacology. Despite evolving diagnostic conceptions of substance use disorders, persistent overconsumption is an essential feature of drug addiction and, therefore, the chapter starts with a discussion of the importance of valid self-administration methods in addiction research. Next, the array of methods available to addictions researchers is reviewed. These methods range in setting from inpatient residential laboratories to outpatient laboratory protocols and, most recently, estimation tasks that can be administered in almost any environment. In addition, these methods include both explicit and implicit approaches, the former being face-valid paradigms measuring voluntary drug consumption and the latter being paradigms using an unrelated pretext to obliquely measure consumption. Many of the approaches discussed evolved from the domains of operant learning theory and behavioral economics. These paradigms examine drug consumption under conditions of cost, either behavioral or monetary, and will be reviewed with a detailed discussion of demand curve analysis, a comprehensive analytic approach to consumption at escalating costs. In light of the array of tools available, the advantages and disadvantages of each approach will be discussed throughout, including methodological recommendations. Almost all of the methods described involve the provision of controlled and illegal substances to human participants, including, in some instances, individuals with substance use disorders. Therefore, the ethical issues in using self-administration

[1]This chapter is supported by NIH grants K23 AA016936, K23 AA016936-S1, R21 AA017696.

paradigms are also considered. Finally, we conclude with a discussion of priorities for further development and refinement of self-administration paradigms in addiction psychopharmacology.

2   Relevance of Self-Administration Paradigms to Addiction Psychopharmacology

Psychoactive drug use has existed in human society for millennia, most frequently in the context of rituals and for recreation, but also in the form of a drug addiction for a proportion of individuals (e.g., Carr, 2011; Crocq, 2007; Hamarneh, 1972). Formal definitions of addiction, however, are relatively new and although the condition has presumably not fundamentally changed over time, the defining features of addictive behavior – the diagnostic symptoms – have evolved considerably. In the first edition of the *American Psychiatric Association's Diagnostic and Statistical Manual* (DSM; 1952), addiction was divided into alcoholism and drug addiction and defined as a form of personality disturbance, specifically, a subtype of sociopathic personality disturbance for individuals whose lifestyles were at variance with cultural norms. In DSM II (1968), alcoholism and drug addiction retained their designations as personality disorders, but became a separate category and included more specificity by pattern of drinking and drug type. In DSM III (1980), DSM-III-R (1987), and DSM-IV (1994), drug addiction was no longer considered a personality disorder and became a new category, Substance Use Disorders, with a syndromal diagnostic approach (diagnosis given based on a certain number of symptoms) and lower and higher severity diagnoses (Abuse and Dependence). The next incarnation, DSM 5, proposes to collapse the two diagnoses into a single diagnosis (Substance Use Disorder) that will include all the DSM-IV symptoms, with the exception of the symptom of legal problems, which will be dropped and replaced with a new symptom involving powerful cravings for a substance. These vicissitudes have been accompanied by considerable debate, especially with regard to the use of the term "dependence" versus "addiction" (O'Brien, 2011; O'Brien, Volkow, and Li, 2006).

   Despite this debate, one fundamental aspect of the phenomenology of drug addiction is immutable and uncontroversial: persistent and excessive drug consumption. Although many features of a person's drug consumption may be variably clinically informative, such as the extent to which a person experiences compulsions to use or the extent to which a person is affected by resulting negative consequences, the consumption behavior itself is an essential element that is always present. Thus, excessive consumption is a defining feature of addiction. By analogy, drug consumption is to addiction as avoidance is to anxiety disorders. Individuals with acrophobia, social anxiety disorder, panic disorder, and post-traumatic stress disorder all experience clinical impairment as a result of avoiding heights, social situations, interoceptive somatic cues, and memories of trauma, respectively, making avoidance a defining index of these disorders. In the same way, excessive consumption is pathognomonic of addiction. Importantly, the reverse of the preceding argument is also true. In the same way that excessive drug taking is a defining element of the problem, reducing consumption is a defining feature of all treatment strategies. Regardless of whether the treatment is abstinence-oriented or moderation-oriented, or whether the mechanism is pharmacological or behavioral, the goal is to eliminate or reduce consumption. Thus, with the ultimate goal of all treatment strategies to decrease excessive consumption, self-administration paradigms can provide methods for investigating novel treatments and can illuminate mechanisms underlying efficacious treatments. Beyond studying consumption of drugs of known abuse liability (i.e., potential for addiction), self-administration paradigms may also play a critical role in screening novel compounds and novel delivery methods for abuse liability. For example, analgesic medications often are relatively high in terms of abuse liability; therefore, when novel analgesic medications are developed in preclinical research, it is important to characterize their liability systematically, both in general and relative to other related compounds. Other pertinent examples include anxiolytic medications for treating anxiety disorders and psychostimulant medications for treating attention-deficit/hyperactivity disorder. Examining the voluntary self-administration of these compounds in the laboratory provides a window into the probability they will be sought out for recreational use and abuse. This, in turn, may inform the relative risk from a new drug and the level of regulation that is appropriate if it were to be available on the market. For example, in the United States, these data would inform the drug schedule to which a drug is assigned by the Drug Enforcement Administration, reflecting the balance of medicinal utility versus abuse liability, and these data would inform the medical regulation of the drug by the Food and Drug Administration. Equally, when new substances emerge in recreational drug use, self-administration paradigms can inform and contextualize their abuse liability (e.g., Johnson *et al.*, 2011). Thus, across these various domains, validated methods for characterizing self-directed consumption are essential in addiction psychopharmacology.

In addition to modeling a critical behavioral dimension of addictive disorders, self-administration paradigms are important because the behavior reflects motivational drive for the drug and is distinct from many of the other proximal motivational variables discussed in this volume. Unlike other variables, such as subjective craving or mood, which can co-occur at higher or lower levels, self-administration involves mutually exclusive outcomes. In other words, a person cannot choose both to use and not to use a drug simultaneously. Thus, necessarily, these approaches focus on the choices people make – to drink or not to drink; to smoke or not to smoke; to use cocaine or not to use cocaine. In the same way that consumption is a defining feature of addiction as a clinical condition, at a microcosmic level, choices to consume are the final common pathway to actual consumption and self-administration paradigms provide a window into those choices and the factors surrounding them.

Although ostensibly obvious, before proceeding, it is worthwhile to provide a precise definition of self-administration paradigms and distinguish to them from other methods discussed in this volume. In contrast to drug administration studies (Chapter 10), which are essential for characterizing drug effects with high internal validity (e.g., controlled dosing, controlled timing), a self-administration paradigm can be defined as an experimental protocol that measures whether and how much of a drug an individual chooses to consume. The emphasis is on the *self-* in self-administration, as individuals are autonomous and permitted to choose their preferred level of consumption. In this way, these approaches all putatively measure the individual's level of *motivation*, typically via their level of consumption, with greater consumption reflecting greater motivation for the drug and vice versa. Self-administration approaches are not intended to measure drug effects per se, as individuals will elect to use varying amounts of the drug and will do so over different time courses. Drug administration studies are superior for measuring direct drug effects, but, because participants are passive recipients of the drug, they are inferior for characterizing a person's level of motivation. In contrast, the focus of this chapter is on experimental methods for measuring *active* interactions between individuals and addictive drugs – whether people will choose to consume a drug, how much they will use, and how high the motivational incentive value of the drug is. Importantly, it would be a false dichotomy to separate drug administration and self-administration paradigms too distinctly, as the two can be profitably combined to characterize a person's preferences in the context of specific drug effects (e.g., Anton *et al.*, 2004; de Wit and Chutuape, 1993; O'Malley *et al.*, 2002). Nonetheless, the distinction between administration and self-administration is a critical one, as the latter are uniquely suited to measure individuals' choices and preferences for a given drug.

3   Standardized and Validated Self-Administration Paradigms

3.1   Settings and durations

Although the fundamental feature of self-administration paradigms is the assessment of an individual's preferred level of drug consumption, there is enormous variability among the approaches available. Two dimensions on which this variability takes place are the experimental context and the duration of the protocol. At one end of the spectrum is the inpatient residential laboratory, where individuals reside for days or even weeks at a time; intermediate on the spectrum are relatively time-limited outpatient laboratory approaches, often comprising a single or several extended laboratory sessions; at the other end of the spectrum are estimation self-administration measures that can be administered briefly.

In the first case, residential laboratory methods emerged from the mid-1960s as part of a growing movement to apply systematic research methods to the ostensibly "messy" behavioral disorders of alcohol and drug addiction along with growing frustration at the reliance on retrospective reports of behavior. Much of the early research using residential laboratories focused on alcoholism, and seminal studies from that time revealed that the drinking behavior of chronic alcoholics could be systematically characterized under controlled conditions (Mello and Mendelson, 1965; Nathan *et al.*, 1970). Moreover, residential laboratory studies revealed that drinking behavior was indeed sensitive to behavioral requirements and the presence of mutually exclusive alternative reinforcers such as social contact, recreational activities, and visitors (for a review, see Bigelow, 2001). There is considerable variation in residential laboratory procedures, but the core features are that individuals enroll in a study for a period that is typically 2 or more weeks in duration, during which all aspects of an individual's environment, including drug access, are under experimental control. A good example is the residential laboratory environment used by Foltin, Fischman, and colleagues in studies on marijuana and amphetamine (for a review, see Fischman, Kelly, and Foltin, 1990). In this case, the laboratory environment included three efficiency apartments, each occupied by a participant, a common social area, and a shared bathroom. Participants were awakened each day at 9 a.m. for an assessment; from 10 a.m. to 4.45 p.m., participants engaged in a "work day" involving low-demand tasks, and from 5 p.m. to 11.45 p.m., participants were able to engage in social activities or to remain in their rooms, with an enforced bedtime of midnight. The participants' general behavior was monitored continuously by audio and video, and coded for activity type, especially social behavior; "work" behavior was used to evaluate performance effects; participants' food and tobacco intake also were systematically monitored. Thus, the residential laboratory provides a comprehensive and semi-naturalistic backdrop for observing drug effects and self-administration.

The clear strength of the residential laboratory setting is the level of experimental control available. It effectively permits complete control of the antecedent conditions and consequences surrounding self-administration and largely permits excluding the role of extraneous variables. Equally clear, however, are the very high resource demand and the restrictions on sample size that such protocols entail. For this reason, a second category of self-administration approaches uses outpatient laboratory protocols. These approaches have developed more recently, in part to address scientific questions and in part because they are more feasible. These protocols usually require one or more extended sessions, lasting several hours in duration. They typically overlap with inpatient studies insofar as the protocol includes choices that determine whether and how much of the drug is available, and they often include semi-naturalistic conditions, such as a "Bar Lab" environment (e.g., Amlung *et al.*, 2012; Drobes, Anton, Thomas, and Voronin, 2003), but outpatient approaches provide a more circumscribed perspective on motivation.

In contrast to residential and outpatient settings, the third category of self-administration paradigms is unique in its absence of a specific setting and the elimination of a protracted duration of time. The most recent evolution in self-administration measures is the use of tasks assessing estimated consumption as a proxy for actual self-administration. These measures, often referred to as purchase tasks, overlap with the preceding measures in their focus on an individual's preferred level of consumption, but typically are not directly yoked to a consumption outcome, which is a limitation. However, unlike the inpatient and outpatient laboratory procedures, purchase tasks are temporally short, have higher-resolution measurement, and are able to be administered to groups of individuals at a time, permitting much larger sample sizes. As such, these measure permit characterization of individual variation in incentive value as measured by estimated self-administration, which is not possible in small sample sizes.

These are the three settings and durations for investigating drug self-administration – inpatient (residential), outpatient (time-limited), and unrestricted – and it is within these parameters that specific self-administration paradigms are implemented.

3.2   Self-administration paradigms

3.2.1   Unrestricted (ad libitum) *consumption.*   The simplest self-administration paradigm is unrestricted access to the drug, or *ad libitum* (free) consumption. This permits observation of unconstrained motivation for the drug and can be implemented in residential laboratory paradigms, outpatient laboratory paradigms, and estimated consumption paradigms. For example, in a residential laboratory study, Foltin and Fischman (1988) permitted participants to smoke up to five standardized marijuana cigarettes over the course of a day to examine patterns of preferences, finding clear behavioral patterns over the course of a day and significant effects on social behavior. As an example of an outpatient application of this approach, Rush *et al.* (2005) examined the effects of methylphenidate on cigarette consumption using a 4-hour *ad libitum* access period, finding a significant increase in consumption relative to placebo. In the case of estimation tasks, most use free consumption as a starting point before implementing consumption at a cost (e.g., MacKillop *et al.*, 2008; Murphy and MacKillop, 2006). The basic requirements of *ad libitum* self-administration are the substance itself and a neutral, comfortable, environment in which it can be consumed. Another important dimension is that the timing of the procedure must be equated regardless of consumption. That is, participants must be engaged in the protocol for equal periods, regardless of how much they consume. This is to avoid confounding consumption with protocol duration (i.e., the more individuals consumes, the longer they remain in the protocol), which unintentionally introduces a negative consequence for consuming the drug. Valid *ad libitum* self-administration essentially characterizes how much of the drug voluntarily is consumed with no consequences other than those of the drug itself, *paribus ceteris* (all other things being equal).

As many studies using self-administration methods are investigating the effects of experimental therapeutics, *ad libitum* self-administration paradigms are often transparent about the drug available (the participant is informed what the drug available is). However, the identity of the drug may be obscured to minimize the effects of expectancies; this is typically the case in the context of measuring abuse liability in which an alternative *ad libitum* choice procedure is commonly used. This two-part procedure includes sampling sessions for both a psychoactive drug of interest and placebo, which are clearly distinguished from each other (e.g., Drug A, Drug B), followed by self-administration sessions in which the participants may choose which drug they prefer (e.g., Johanson and Uhlenhuth, 1980a; 1980b; Roehrs *et al.*, 1997). For instance, in a nine-session outpatient study, Johanson and Uhlenhuth provided participants with d-amphetamine or a placebo during the first four sessions and then permitted free choice during the subsequent five sessions, finding a clear preference for amphetamine, which was selected approximately 80% of the time. To fully characterize abuse liability, *ad libitum* self-administration is typically accompanied by measures of subjective liking, pleasant and unpleasant effects on mood, side-effects, behavioral performance, and perceived similarity to other drugs to which the individual has had prior exposure (for a review, see Griffiths, Bigelow, and Ator, 2003).

Primarily, the dependent variables in *ad libitum* consumption are whether and how much the participant consumes, although this can be complemented with other behavioral dimensions, such as how quickly an individual begins consumption (e.g., MacKillop and Lisman, 2005) or, for smoked drugs, topographical indices such as number of puffs and inter-puff interval (e.g., MacKillop and Tidey, 2011a; Tidey, Rohsenow, Kaplan, and Swift, 2005). Advantages of *ad libitum* self-administration are its face validity as a measure of motivation and the ease of interpretation of the resulting data. In addition, *ad libitum* self-administration is often relatively easy to implement, simply requiring the drug and a comfortable controlled environment. However, assessments that are more sophisticated require specialized equipment, such as smoking topography devices. Another example is intravenous self-administration paradigms, which clearly require specialized equipment and facilities, and permit direct consumption of the drug in the absence of pharmacokinetic variability (e.g., Zimmermann *et al.*, 2009; Zimmermann *et al.*, 2008).

An advantage of *ad libitum* self-administration paradigms is their straightforward implementation and interpretation. The principal disadvantage is that they create an imperfect model of typical drug consumption insofar as these paradigms provide the preferred drug free, with no direct costs or other consequences for consumption. In daily life, drug use almost always reflects a tradeoff between a drug's positively and negatively reinforcing effects and the literal and figurative costs of using. When the drug is provided at no cost, participants may consume the drug readily simply because a commodity of value, the drug, is free. Thus, self-administration via *ad libitum* consumption does not model the weighing of benefits versus costs, the real-world tension in decision making about drug consumption, meaning that it provides a dimension of motivation, but one that is restricted to consumption in the absence of adverse consequences.

3.2.2 *Methods from operant learning theory and behavioral economics.*

The need to model motivation for drugs in the context of direct costs of consumption is the basis of operant behavioral and behavioral economic self-administration approaches. As noted above, drug use in everyday life involves tradeoffs between the experiential benefits of the drug itself and the costs, both financial and in relation to other outcomes such as physical health, relationships with others, and occupational success. Thus, valid experimental paradigms seek to model this response conflict, the cost–benefit ratio of drug consumption. This is the common feature of both operant and behavioral economic approaches – these paradigms examine consumption under conditions of either behavioral or financial cost. If an imposed cost eliminates or substantially reduces consumption, the participant's motivation can be inferred to be lower than the cost; alternatively, if consumption is unaffected by the cost, the participant's level of motivation can be inferred to be greater than the cost. As an analogy, in the same way that an object's physical momentum can be inferred based on the resistance needed to stop it, a person's motivation can be inferred based on the response cost required to stop it (Nevin and Grace, 2000).

The distinction between operant learning and behavioral economic approaches is necessarily blurry because one major focus of behavioral economics largely grew out of operant theory. Over the course of the latter half of the last century, it became increasingly clear that the experimental conditions with two or more reinforcement options were essentially microeconomies in which the subjects or participants operated within a fixed set of environmental conditions and allocated finite resources (e.g., time, behavior, money) to gain access to activities of variable value (e.g., eating, drinking, leisure). Thus, the expenditure of effort, money, or time in operant behavior was recognized as economic behavior at the level of the individual organism and highly amenable to importing analytic concepts from economics (e.g., Hursh, 1984). Fundamentally, operant learning and behavioral economics examine the transactions between individuals and their environments in terms of their response costs (i.e., costs of consumption), such as allocations of effort, money, time, or other resources. In light of this, it is somewhat arbitrary to distinguish between the two domains, but, for clarity, we will refer to self-adminisistration paradigms involving the allocation of effort as operant approaches and those involving the allocation of money as behavioral economic approaches.

Operant self-administration approaches for studying drug self-administration have been in use for over four decades (Bigelow, Cohen, Liebson, and Faillace, 1972; Mello and Mendelson, 1965; Nathan *et al.*, 1970) and are active in contemporary research (Comer, Walker, and Collins, 2005; Hart *et al.*, 2008). All operant paradigms involve the execution of behavioral responses on a manipulandum to gain access to the drug, although the type of response varies considerably. For example, studies have used an effortful plunger (Johnson and Bickel, 2006), space-bar presses (Willner, Hardman, and Eaton, 1995), mouse clicks (Comer, Walker, and Collins, 2005), and even bicycle riding (Jones and Prada, 1975). In each case, once a behavioral requirement is met, the individual receives a unit of the drug, meaning the cost is the effort required for a unit of drug. In terms of the reinforcement schedules, operant self-administration paradigms typically use fixed-ratio (Ferster and Skinner, 1957) or progressive-ratio (Hodos, 1961) schedules. A fixed-ratio schedule refers to equal units of effort being necessary to receive a unit of drug and provides an index of consumption under stable levels of response cost i.e., cost for consumption, removing the question of whether consumption is simply a function of free access to the drug. A progressive-ratio schedule refers to successively increasing response requirements. For example, the response requirement might escalate from two responses to 2,000 responses over an array of intervals to earn access to the drug. Across these intervals, the price that finally eliminates consumption reflects the individual's "breakpoint," and reveals how far a participant will go in order to keep consuming the drug. In addition, progressive-ratio schedules can be analyzed using demand curve analysis, described in detail below. A third option for operant schedules is a concurrent choice schedule that permits participants to allocate their effort to a drug reward or an active alternative reward (Hogarth, 2011; Johnson and Bickel, 2003). As effort allocated on the task is zero-sum (allocation to one outcome prevents allocation to the other outcome), proportion of choices reflects the individual's motivation for the drug reward.

Operant schedules can be implemented in inpatient or outpatient settings and serve as the basis for some estimation self-administration measures. Operant tasks have a number of advantages and disadvantages. Similar to *ad libitum* consumption, consumption under conditions of cost makes inferring an individual's motivation relatively easy – the harder individuals are willing to work, as reflected by operant output, the higher their motivation for the drug. Another advantage is that these approaches provide actual drug outcomes based on behavioral rewards, avoiding reliance on hypothetical behavior and further increasing their validity. A specific advantage of progressive-ratio schedules is that they permit demand curve analysis. There are, however, disadvantages also. Self-administration periods are often lengthy to accommodate a full array of consumption preferences or response requirements. In addition, outpatient protocols sometimes require several sessions to characterize multiple response requirements. These factors make them suboptimal for assessing state variables, such as craving or mood manipulations, which are known to be potent but transient influences (Madden and Zwaan, 2001; Staiger and White, 1991; Zwaan, Stanfield, and Madden, 2000). Also notable, although operant tasks model consumption under conditions of response cost, which parallels typical drug consumption, other clinical features of consumption are not modeled, such as preference reversals (i.e., using more than intended) or excessive time allocation (Hughes and Bickel, 1997). Related, a final disadvantage of operant tasks is that the operant responses are largely inconsistent with real-world drug-seeking behavior. In other words, most people do not pull plungers, tap space bars, or ride stationary bicycles for access to drugs. Certainly, effort is typically involved in drug acquisition in the "catch-as-catch-can" world of drug addiction, but the efforts are highly idiosyncratic and very different from the operant tasks commonly used. Moreover, the majority of drug acquisition is independent of behavioral efforts and, instead, involves the allocation of money as the operant behavior. This disconnect between the nature of the experimental operant behaviors and the typical instrumental behaviors that result in drug access somewhat undermines the ecological validity of these paradigms.

Behavioral economic self-administration paradigms address this latter issue by specifically using money as the response cost of consuming or not consuming the drug. The common feature of these approaches is that an amount of money is made available to the participant, sometimes referred to as the "tab" (as in a bar tab), and individuals may keep the money or choose to allocate portions of the money provided in exchange for the drug. In most cases, the duration of access is equated across individuals to remove any positive contingency (e.g., leaving early) from abstaining. Thus, individuals effectively select whether they will allocate their money for the drug or spend the session drug-free. Of note, some of these approaches are not explicitly identified in the literature as either operant or behavioral economic measures, having evolved atheoretically from a practical and clinical interest in modeling consumption in the context of consequences. Nonetheless, these approaches meet the fundamental criterion of operant and behavioral economic measures: that of studying consumption in the context of response cost.

Operant and behavioral economic paradigms have been applied in both residential and outpatient protocols to test basic behavioral hypotheses about addictive disorders and to help identify efficacious pharmacotherapies for improving treatment. For example, one early study using a residential protocol examined whether monetary incentives could be used to motivate alcoholics to drink moderately or to abstain from drinking altogether following a priming dose of alcohol (Cohen, Liebson, Faillace, and Speers, 1971). Similarly, Higgins, Bickel, and Hughes (1994) tested the hypothesis that cocaine consumption would be substantially affected by the amount of money required to obtain it in a multi-session outpatient protocol. As predicted, cocaine was preferred over placebo in *ad libitum* choice preference, but, more importantly, as more money had to be allocated to cocaine (instead of kept by the participant), consumption significantly decreased and ultimately was suppressed entirely.

In terms of medication development, a novel outpatient behavioral economic self-administration paradigm has been developed to model alcohol-related decision making. This outpatient paradigm administers a priming dose of alcohol and provides participants with a fixed amount of money that can be spent on alcohol to model the choices made after an initial lapse. Participants are given the option of choosing to drink up to four "mini-drinks" that are approximately half-sized standard drinks during two successive 90-minute time-periods (two rounds of choices). The availability of up to four drinks permits variability in the level of consumption elected. This approach has been profitably used to investigate the mechanisms of naltrexone (ReVia) (O'Malley et al., 2002), nalmefene (Drobes, Anton, Thomas, and Voronin, 2003), gabapentin (Myrick et al., 2007), aripiprazole (Voronin, Randall, Myrick, and Anton, 2008), varenicline (McKee et al., 2009), and transdermal nicotine (McKee et al., 2008). A similar paradigm has been developed for tobacco self-administration, but comprises both a delay period, in which participants can earn $5 for each 5-minute interval they are able to refrain from smoking, and a self-administration period, in which half-cigarettes or whole cigarettes are available for $1 each (Leeman, O'Malley, White, and McKee, 2010; McKee et al., 2006). The use of incentives for delaying access has also been used by itself in measuring motivation for tobacco (Sayette et al., 2001).

For all of the preceding paradigms, if an escalating response cost is implemented, a specific analytic strategy termed demand curve analysis may be applied to the resulting data (for a review, see Hursh, Galuska, Winger, and Woods, 2005). This is an example of behavioral economics importing concepts and methodologies from microeconomics to study individual consumption behavior. In economics, demand refers to the amount of a commodity consumed or sought at a given price and a demand curve refers to the relationship between consumption and price across two or more prices (at least two points are required to plot the curve). This curve may then be quantified using demand curve analysis, which provides a multidimensional characterization of the incentive value of the drug. For example, if a participant were permitted to earn cigarettes across several sessions using a progressive-ratio operant schedule with behavioral response requirements of 30, 60, 90, 180, 360, and 720 spacebar presses, the resulting decreases in consumption behavior across the response "prices" would constitute a demand curve and the slope of that curve would reflect the individual's motivation.

If examined across an array of prices, demand curves tend to have common features across commodities and a prototypic example is provided in Figure 12.1. At very low prices, demand is typically relatively insensitive to price increases, or *inelastic*, defined as the portion of the demand curve in which the negative proportionate slope is less than 1.00.[2] This is because negative slopes between 0.00 and 0.99 reflect lower proportionate decreases in consumption relative to increases in price (e.g., a slope of 0.50 reflects a 5% decrease in consumption as a result of a 10% increase in price). As prices increase, however, demand tends to become more sensitive to

---

[2] It is worth noting that that the slope is implicitly designated as negative because demand either stays the same or decreases in response to increases in price.

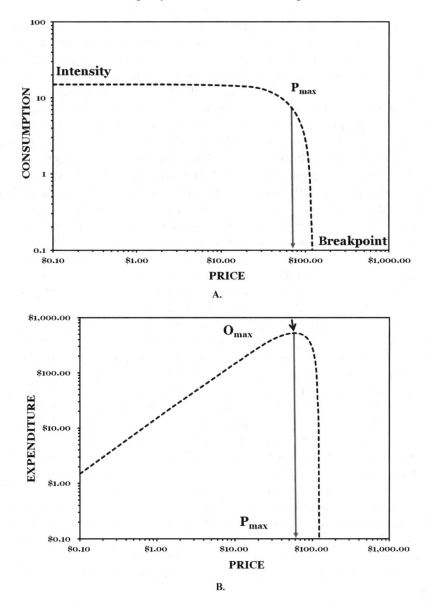

Figure 12.1 Prototypic demand and expenditure curves. Panel A provides the demand curve, with Intensity (i.e., consumption at minimal cost), P_{max} (i.e., the price at which demand becomes elastic), and Breakpoint (i.e., the price at which consumption is reduced to zero); elasticity is an overall property of the demand curve. Panel B provides the associated expenditure curve, with O_{max} reflecting the maximum expenditure on the commodity

increases in price, or *elastic*, defined as the portions of the demand curve in which the negative proportionate slope is equal to or greater than 1.00. This is for the same reason as the definition of inelasticity: negative proportionate slopes equal to or greater than 1.00 reflect equally proportionate or supraproportionate decreases in consumption relative to increases in price (e.g., a proportionate slope of 2.0 reflects a

20% decrease in consumption as a result of a 10% increase in price). Across the aggregated demand curve, elasticity refers to the overall price sensitivity of the individual to the costs of the drug, which can be modeled and quantified using nonlinear regression. Historically, this has been done using two-parameter models that examine the slope and acceleration of the demand curve (Hursh *et al.*, 1988; Hursh and Winger, 1995), but more recently, a single parameter model, termed "essential value," has been developed (Hursh and Silberberg, 2008). Essential value permits the assessment of relative decreases without undue influence of the commodity-specific units and provides a single index of price sensitivity that is much more interpretable than two parameters. Moreover, demand curve analysis provides several additional indices of incentive value based on other characteristics of the demand curve known as Intensity, Breakpoint, P_{max} (price maximum), and O_{max} (output maximum). Intensity is consumption at zero or very low response cost (the y-axis intercept), reflecting the initial level of consumption. Breakpoint is the price at which demand is completely suppressed to zero and reflects the furthest a person will go for the drug. P_{max}, or price maximum, is the point where demand becomes elastic and reflects how much of a price increase a person will accept before being affected by costs. Finally, O_{max}, or output maximum, is the maximum an individual will expend (in behavioral responses or money) on consumption of the drug. These indices of demand are also provided in Figure 12.1. Notably, P_{max} and O_{max} reflect two sides of the same coin: response output (expenditure) is maximized at the highest inelastic price, meaning that P_{max} is the price at which O_{max} is reached and vice versa. For example, if the maximum amount a person will spend on cigarettes per day is $10, and this reflects consumption of 10 cigarettes at a cost of $1 per cigarette, O_{max} is $10 and P_{max} is $1. However, that is not to say that these indices are redundant with one another; two individuals may have the same O_{max} but reach it at different levels of P_{max} (equal levels of expenditure but differing points of initial price sensitivity). Using the previous example, an O_{max} of $10 may be present at P_{max} values of $1 (10 cigarettes), $2 (5 cigarettes), or 50¢ (20 cigarettes). It is equally possible to have the same P_{max} but different levels of O_{max} (equal points where demand becomes elastic, but different maximum expenditure points). For example, two individuals could both spend the most money on cigarettes when the price is 50¢/cigarette, but one individual report smoking 20 at that price, resulting in an O_{max} of $10 whereas the other report smoking 15, resulting in an O_{max} of $7.50. Thus, the two are certainly related to each other, but are nonetheless distinct.

Taken together, demand curve analysis represents a powerful methodological approach for characterizing consumption data at multiple levels of response cost. It provides a multidimensional characterization of the drug's incentive value via the whole demand curve, with Intensity reflecting its starting point of unrestricted consumption, Breakpoint reflecting its end, and Elasticity, P_{max}, and O_{max} reflecting important characteristics of the intervening curve. More simply, demand curve analysis provides indices of drug consumption if price were no object (Intensity), maximum allocation of resources (O_{max}), the price limits before the costs outweigh the benefits (Breakpoint, P_{max}), and overall cost–benefit ratio (Elasticity). Of note, the low cost or zero cost prices effectively integrate *ad libitum* consumption into this approach, treating it as a starting point against which subsequent changes are assessed. Thus, although it is a somewhat more technically challenging analysis of consumption behavior, the approach can provide a comprehensive characterization of drug motivation.

Operant and behavioral economic self-administration approaches have both advantages and disadvantages. A clear advantage is their capacity to study consumption in a way that models the cost–benefit calculus that surrounds drug use in daily life. In the case of inpatient and comprehensive outpatient paradigms, an advantage is the ability of these approaches to conduct truly parametric studies, in which consumption can be analyzed at its maximal level, across multiple conditions, ultimately resulting in its elimination (e.g., Cohen, Liebson, Faillace, and Speers, 1971; Higgins, Bickel, and Hughes, 1994). Related to this, operant and behavioral economic approaches permit demand curve analysis in some cases, providing a multidimensional assessment of the incentive value of the drug that is arguably more valid than any single index designated as the primary measure. In addition, an advantage of these paradigms is that they can model some of the dynamic aspects of decision making in consumption, such as the self-administration model that combines an alcohol priming dose followed by alcohol availability in exchange for cash incentives.

However, these advantages come at costs: inpatient and comprehensive outpatient studies require a great deal of resources and, as a result, typically have very few conditions or participants. Outpatient single-session paradigms permit considerably more participants. For example, Drobes, Anton, Thomas, and Voronin (2003) enrolled 215 participants in a study examining the effects of two pharmacotherapies on alcohol self-administration, a number of subjects that would be unfeasible for an inpatient protocol or parametric outpatient protocol including sampling sessions and drug choice sessions at escalating levels of price. However, a disadvantage in such single-session studies is that the effects are limited to a single response cost and parametric findings are not available. In other words, in a "one-shot" outpatient paradigm, it is not clear what the effect of other responses might be or whether systematic modifications to response costs would bring the effects into sharper relief.

A further disadvantage of the preceding self-administration paradigms is they tend to be relatively long in duration and, using consumption as the dependent variable, they are largely limited in their ability to measure transient dynamic factors that influence self-administration. For example, an array of factors, such as subjective desire, positive and negative mood, and attentional bias putatively play roles in the decision to consume a substance, exerting transient but potentially very important influences on behavior. However, self-administration paradigms that can last in duration from an hour to several hours may be suboptimal for clarifying those influences. In understanding the dynamic processes at the initiation and progression of consumption, even the shortest operant and behavioral economic self-administration tasks that use direct consumption have a limited capacity for high-resolution data collection. A final disadvantage of most of the preceding paradigms is that, although they are frequently implemented in addiction psychopharmacology, their standardization is considerably lower and the basic validation properties are less studied compared to other methods in behavioral science. For example, in operant paradigms, there is heterogeneity in the behavioral response and reinforcement schedule used, and in behavioral economic paradigms, there is heterogeneity in the amounts of money used and the amounts of drug available. Thus, differences in findings across studies may be because of either actual differences in outcomes or subtle differences in methods that are nonetheless meaningful. Further, although all have face validity and ecological validity insofar as they measure the external behavior of interest (consumption), other aspects of validity, such as temporal stability and convergent/discriminant validity relative to level of addictive behavior, have largely not been studied. To an extent, this is understandable, given the resources involved, but this is nonetheless a disadvantage as such validation studies speak to the inherent validity of the paradigm. Moreover, they can directly improve an experimental paradigm or permit a clear judgment of quality among different options.

3.2.3 Estimation measures.   The third class of self-administration paradigms is a diverse group of measures that all use self-reported preferences to measure consumption. All of these measures are intended to be more efficient than the previously discussed inpatient or outpatient laboratory approaches and are relatively short in duration. They can be thought of as being behavioral economic approaches as they use money as a response cost; there are no estimated operant behavior estimation measures. Some of these are hybrids of laboratory behavioral economic paradigms in which a series of self-reported preferences are assessed and the participant receives one randomly selected choice. This putatively increases the validity of the procedure because participants understand that their choices are the basis for the amount of drug available, and the more choices they make for the drug (and the fewer for money), the more likely it is they will receive the drug. The distinction between the behavioral economic paradigms of the previous section and these measures is that, for the former, choices are directly equated with drug consumption (a unit of money reflects either a unit of consumption or an amount kept by the participant), but, for estimation measures, some or all of the preferences expressed are for hypothetical outcomes. More broadly, the differences in the dependent variables used in the different approaches clarify these terminological distinctions. In an *ad libitum* paradigm, the dependent variable is drug consumption. In operant and behavioral economic choice tasks, the dependent variable is the allocation of behavior or money for the drug, respectively. For estimation measures, the dependent variable is the pattern of self-reported consumption preferences.

The most widely used measure in this domain is the Multiple Choice Procedure (MCP; Griffiths, Troisi, Silverman, and Mumford, 1993) in which participants complete a series of choices in which they are asked to indicate their preferences for a fixed unit of a drug in comparison to an escalating amount of money. When there is a trivial response cost (i.e., the amount of money is zero or very low), preferences tend to be for the drug, but, as the amount of money available escalates, participants tend to switch their preference to the monetary reinforcer. This switch, the point at which preferences switch from the drug to money, is termed the *crossover point*, and is calculated as the mean of the adjacent amounts of money (i.e., the last price for which the drug is chosen and the first choice for which the money is chosen). Often, one randomly selected price on the MCP is picked and participants receive their corresponding drug or money (based on their indicated preference). The MCP can be used in the investigation of abuse liability, with participants exposed to a candidate drug and placebo, and then permitted to choose both between the two substances and also between each drug and money (Griffiths, Troisi, Silverman, and Mumford, 1993; Mumford, Rush, and Griffiths, 1995). For example, Mumford, Rush, and Griffiths (1995) compared a novel candidate anxiolytic, abecarnil, with alprazolam (Xanax), an established anxiolytic also known to have abuse liability, and placebo. Based on the MCP crossover points, placebo and abecarnil were equivalent and alprazolam had a significantly higher incentive value, suggesting that abecarnil had lower abuse potential than alprazolam. The MCP has also been used to study determinants of drug self-administration in drugs of established abuse liability (Jones, Garrett, and Griffiths, 1999; Sobel, Sigmon, and Griffiths, 2004). For example, an MCP was used to measure the incentive value of three doses of cocaine, three doses of nicotine, and placebo (Jones, Garrett, and Griffiths, 1999), finding that cocaine exhibited double the incentive value of nicotine at the highest doses.

Thus, the MCP represents an efficient method for collecting data on the incentive value of a drug in investigations that are similar to those using more extensive inpatient or outpatient paradigms. However, the MCP and other estimation methods can be used for quite different investigations also. The MCP has been applied in a clinical context to assess the incentive value of clinic privileges among patients in a methadone maintenance program (Kidorf, Stitzer, and Griffiths, 1995). The MCP has also been used to examine the relationship between level of drug involvement and incentive value. For example, alcohol crossover points have been found to be significantly positively associated with weekly levels of drinking, frequency of binge drinking, and negative consequences from drinking in young adults (Little and Correia, 2006). The psychometric properties of the MCP have been studied and it has been validated as being sensitive to reward magnitudes and delays in time (Benson, Little, Henslee, and Correia, 2009; Little and Correia, 2006). Finally, in a recent study, the MCP was used to examine dynamic effects of negative mood on the incentive value of alcohol. In that study, participants underwent either a negative mood or control induction (for a full discussion of these manipulations, see Chapter 15). The negative mood induction significantly increased the incentive value (as measured by the MCP) and significantly interacted with alcohol coping motives to further predict increases in incentive value (Rousseau, Irons, and Correia, 2011).

The second and more recent estimation method is the purchase task methodology. Purchase tasks assess a participant's estimated consumption of a standardized unit of a drug, first at zero cost or a very low price, then at escalating levels of price. These measures are analogues of operant progressive-ratio schedules but are behavioral economic measures insofar as they focus on costs as measured by prices per unit of drug. For example, a standard version of an Alcohol Purchase Task (APT) assesses consumption of standard alcoholic beverages (described for participants) on a typical day (Murphy and MacKillop, 2006). In addition, the instructional set includes other assumptions, such as no prior drinking, no other alcohol available, and no option to keep extra beverages for a future time (i.e., stockpiling). In addition to alcohol, purchase tasks have been developed for consumption of cigarettes (Jacobs and Bickel, 1999; MacKillop *et al.*, 2008), heroin (Jacobs and Bickel, 1999), and cocaine (Herin, Grabowski, and MacKillop, 2009). These tasks are typically administered as estimation tasks only, but can also be used as hybrid estimation-consumption tasks, with participants receiving one of their selected choices (Amlung *et al.*, 2011). In the latter case, self-administration choices pertain to a specific amount of money (e.g., a $15 "bar tab"), a specific number of drug units (e.g., eight alcoholic beverages), and specific periods for consumption and recovery. As with the earlier outpatient paradigms, regardless of the participants' choices the total duration of the study must be equated to avoid inadvertently adding a cost to consumption by requiring longer participation in the study.

Early validation studies on purchase tasks demonstrated that the data generated prototypic demand curves akin to those generated using operant schedules and amendable to demand curve analysis (Jacobs and Bickel, 1999; Murphy and MacKillop, 2006). Moreover, studies using an APT have shown that individual differences in the indices of alcohol demand are significantly associated with a person's level of alcohol consumption, alcohol-related consequences, and alcohol use disorder severity (MacKillop *et al.*, 2010a; Murphy and MacKillop, 2006; Murphy, MacKillop, Skidmore, and Pederson, 2009). Table 12.1 provides the zero-order and aggregated associations between alcohol demand and both level of drinking and alcohol problem severity. In both domains, high associations are evident between Intensity and the alcohol-related variables, with smaller magnitude associations evident for O_{max} and Breakpoint and negligible associations for P_{max}. In addition, as these demand indices putatively reflect the incentive value of alcohol, they are increasingly considered with other variables associated with addictive behavior. For example, there is initial evidence that higher incentive value of alcohol is associated with more impulsive discounting of delayed rewards (MacKillop *et al.*, 2010a), a behavioral economic index of impulsivity that has been consistently associated with addictive behavior (MacKillop *et al.*, 2011) (see also Chapter 7). In addition, higher demand for alcohol has been associated with personality traits such as sensation seeking (preferences for exciting novel experiences) and negative urgency (proneness to act out in response to negative emotions) (Skidmore and Murphy, 2011; Smith *et al.*, 2010). Indeed, indices of alcohol demand have been found to potentiate the associations between these impulsivity-related personality traits and both drinking level and alcohol problems (Smith *et al.*, 2010). Finally, demand indices from an APT have been incorporated into clinical and other applied domains. Higher demand for alcohol has been found to predict a diminished impact of a brief intervention (MacKillop and Murphy, 2007) and demand indices from an APT have also demonstrated the potent effect of academic demands on the incentive value of alcohol among college student drinkers (Skidmore and Murphy, 2011).

Parallel findings are largely present from studies using a Cigarette Purchase Task (CPT) to measure the incentive value of tobacco. Initial studies revealed highly orderly demand data (Jacobs and Bickel, 1999; MacKillop *et al.*, 2008) and that the demand indices were significantly associated with smoking rate and level of nicotine dependence (MacKillop *et al.*, 2008). These findings have subsequently been replicated in adolescent smokers (Murphy *et al.*, 2011) and nicotine-dependent adults, with and without schizophrenia (MacKillop and Tidey, 2011b). Table 12.1 also presents the associations between indices of tobacco demand and smoking-related variables, revealing substantial associations with Intensity and O_{max}, but smaller associations with P_{max} and Breakpoint. Furthermore, the incentive value of cigarettes has been inversely

Table 12.1 Associations between indices of demand and measures of substance consumption and problem severity. Published zero-order correlations (r) and aggregated effect sizes via random effects meta-analysis are provided. Dashes reflect instances in which certain indices were not reported. In addition, aggregations are not reported for elasticity as different derivations were used across studies.

Study	N	Sample	Assessment	Intensity	O_{max}	P_{max}	Breakpoint	Elasticity
			Alcohol					
MacKillop and Murphy (2007)	51	Young adult heavy drinkers	DDQ[a]	0.44	0.18	0.04	0.11	0.05
			RAPI[b]	0.18	-0.17	-0.19	0.08	0.00
MacKillop *et al.* (2010a)	61	Adult heavy drinkers	TLFB[a]	0.15	0.20	0.11	0.13	0.06
			SCID-AUD[b]	0.30	-0.05	-0.15	0.01	0.01
Murphy and MacKillop (2006)	267	Young adult drinkers	DDQ[a]	0.70	0.45	0.06	0.21	0.06
			RAPI[b]	0.48	0.24	-0.02	0.16	0.09
Murphy, MacKillop, Skidmore, and Pederson (2009)	38	Young adult drinkers	TLFB[a]	0.72	0.56	-0.07	0.14	-0.46
			YAAPST[b]	0.63	0.46	0.16	0.03	-0.32
Smith *et al.* (2010)	225	Young adult drinkers	DDQ[a]	0.57	0.39	–	–	–
			YAACQ[b]	0.40	0.29	–	–	–
			Consumption	0.55	0.22	0.05	0.18	–
			Problem severity	0.41	0.22	-0.05	0.12	–

Table 12.1 (*Continued*)

Study	N	Sample	Assessment	Intensity	O_{max}	P_{max}	Breakpoint	Elasticity
				Tobacco				
MacKillop et al. (2008)	33	Young adult smokers	C/D[a]	0.65	0.70	0.42	0.41	0.18
			FTND[a]	0.48	0.42	0.24	0.34	0.10
MacKillop and Tidey (2011)	35	Adult SCZ/non-SCZ smokers	C/D[a]	0.54	0.14	−0.09	−0.11	−0.15
			FTND[b]	0.34	0.35	0.13	0.09	−0.28
Few, Acker, Murphy, and MacKillop (2012)	11	Adult smokers	C/D[a]	0.66	0.88	–	−0.30	−0.85
			FTND[b]	0.56	0.53	–	−0.57	−0.33
Murphy et al. (2011)	138	Adolescent smokers	C/D[a]	0.30	0.34	0.09	0.21	−0.25
			FTND[b]	0.27	0.31	0.17	0.17	−0.24
			Consumption	0.51	0.54	0.14	0.13	–
			Problem severity	0.33	0.34	0.17	0.11	–

Notes: [a]consumption variable; [b]problem severity variable; DDQ = Drinking Days Questionnaire; RAPI = Rutgers Alcohol Problem Inventory; TLFB = Timeline Followback; SCID-AUD = Structured Clinical Interview for Diagnosis–Alcohol Use Disorders Severity; YAAPST = Young Adult Alcohol Problems Screening Test; YAACQ = Young Adult Alcohol Consequences Questionnaire; SCZ = Individuals with Schizophrenia; C/D = Cigarettes/Day; FTND = Fagerstrom Test of Nicotine Dependence.

associated with motivation to quit (Murphy *et al.*, 2011) and, using a smoking topography device in a human laboratory study, multiple demand indices were associated with the number of cigarettes consumed and the number of puffs/cigarette in an *ad libitum* paradigm (MacKillop and Tidey, 2011b). Interestingly, a recent clinical study compared the effects of buprorion (Zyban) and placebo using a CPT and did not find a significant effect of the drug per se, but did find that changes in the elasticity of demand over the course of treatment were predictive of subsequent outcome.

There is also an increasing application of purchase tasks as brief measures of incentive value in laboratory studies. This application of the purchase task approach configures the measures into a state format (e.g., "At the following prices, how many cigarettes would you smoke RIGHT NOW?"). In an initial study in smokers, Hitsman *et al.* (2008) found that an acute tyrosine/phenylalanine depletion to reduce dopaminergic neurotransmission acutely increased Intensity. Subsequently, toward improving the measurement of subjective craving for alcohol, an APT was used in a standard alcohol cue reactivity paradigm and revealed that alcohol cues significantly increased the incentive value of alcohol according to a number of indices and did so in ways that were independent of effects on subjective craving (MacKillop *et al.*, 2010b). Although only a small number of studies in this area have been conducted, like the MCP (Rousseau, Irons, and Correia, 2011), applying purchase tasks to assess dynamic changes in incentive value appears to have substantial promise.

The advantages of estimation measures are nearly the reverse of the advantages of inpatient operant paradigms at the other end of the spectrum. These measures are extremely efficient, both in terms of duration and in terms of the level of resolution for response requirements. As a result, they can be administered in diverse experimental settings and are integrated more easily into nontraditional experimental domains, such as clinical settings. The fact that both permit hybrid assessments that provide an actual drug outcome is a strength and there is evidence that performance for hypothetical outcomes corresponds to performance when one outcome is received (Amlung *et al.*, 2012; Benson, Little, Henslee, and Correia, 2009), providing further support for versions using hypothetical outcomes. Another advantage of these measures is that they have been subjected to more traditional psychometric validation and have been supported in terms of convergent validity and temporal reliability (e.g., Few, Acker, Murphy, and MacKillop, 2012; Murphy, MacKillop, Skidmore, and Pederson, 2009).

There are, however, disadvantages. For example, the open-response format has the potential for participants to report biologically implausible or very high-magnitude outlying responses. As such, data analysis of these measures requires careful consideration of data quality and outliers. In the case of the latter, a common method to avoid both excluding participants with outlying responses and including high-leverage data points that disproportionately influence the overall findings is recoding extreme values. Specifically, recoding outliers that exceed a criterion of Z-scores greater than 3.29 (99.95th percentile) or 4 (99.99th percentile) to the next non-outlying value or 1 unit above the next non-outlying value permits their inclusion but avoids excessive leverage (Tabachnick and Fidell, 2006). Equally, optimizing the prices for either the MCP or purchase tasks is an active research question and the translation of the measure from operant schedules resulted in early versions using prices that were not plausible for the marketplace (e.g., more than $1,000 for each unit of the drug; Jacobs and Bickel, 1999; MacKillop *et al.*, 2008; 2010a). In this case, careful consideration of the data is required and excluding responses above a certain price may be warranted as a preventive measure against outliers. Finally, a specific disadvantage of the MCP is that it does not permit volumetric assessment of consumption – the consumption option is a single unit of the drug (e.g., a drink, a cigarette) – which means the crossover value is the only dependent variable. In contrast, purchase tasks permit comprehensive demand curve analysis.

On balance, these estimation self-administration measures represent novel tools to complement the traditional inpatient and outpatient paradigms, but have both strengths and weaknesses to consider in their implementation.

3.2.4 Implicit self-administration paradigms. All of the preceding methods measure self-administration explicitly, but an alternative is the use of implicit measures of alcohol motivation. The critical distinction between the two is that, for explicit measures, the contingencies between choices and drug availability are clear and participants are aware that their consumption is a variable of interest, whereas, for implicit measures, participants engage in an activity that ostensibly has one purpose, but for which the real purpose is the assessment of consumption. The most common implicit method of studying alcohol self-administration is via a Taste-Rating Task paradigm (TRT; Marlatt, Demming, and Reid, 1973), in which participants are asked to sample varieties of a drug and to rate them. For example, a person may taste different types of beer and evaluate the qualitative characteristics (e.g., "sweet," "flavorful," "strong," "appetizing"). To capture volumetric consumption, participants are instructed to sample as much as they would like to arrive at their decisions, with the actual variable of interest being how much is consumed. Specifically, the amount freely consumed is assessed by subtracting the quantity remaining from the known pre-consumption amount. Of note, the TRT may appear to be a deceptive self-administration practice; however, participants are not instructed that consumption is not a behavior of interest and taste rating data are actually collected. As such, the TRT is an unobtrusive measure of self-administration in which measurement of the amount of drug consumed is not explicitly emphasized to the participant.

Primarily, the TRT has been used in alcohol research and has allowed several studies to disambiguate the quantity of alcohol consumed from various other factors. In an initial study using this approach, Marlatt, Demming, and Reid (1973) implemented a TRT in the context of a balanced-placebo design (see Chapter 17) and found that the only significant determinant of an individual's beverage consumption was the expectation of the content of the beverage. A TRT has been used to investigate alcohol consumption as a function of perceived helplessness (Noel and Lisman, 1980), temptation and preoccupation with alcohol (Collins, Gollnisch, and Izzo, 1996; Fillmore, 2001), tobacco deprivation (Colby *et al.*, 2004) and alcohol cues (Lau-Barraco and Dunn, 2008). A TRT has also been used to explore the influence of pharmacological interventions on alcohol motivation. Palfai, Davidson, and Swift (1999) examined the effect of naltrexone (ReVia) on craving and alcohol consumption using a TRT, finding a significant effect of naltrexone on urge to drink, but not on the amount of alcohol consumed during on the TRT.

One of the primary advantages of implicit self-administration measures is reducing experimental demand characteristics, or participants' reactions to what they believe is expected from them in a research protocol. This is particularly salient in addiction research because the behaviors under consideration are associated with social judgment and opprobrium, especially for individuals at high levels of use. For example, in an *ad libitum* alcohol consumption paradigm, where alcohol is free, participants may purposefully drink more alcohol because they infer that this is what they are expected to do under these conditions. Alternatively, inferring the same expectation, a participant may deliberately not drink to be oppositional (e.g., "I didn't drink any of the beer because I knew you wanted me to"). In both cases, the explicit nature of the task may communicate experimental expectations to the participant, erroneous or not, and, in turn, affect behavior. As a general recommendation, it is important to try to disabuse participants of experiment demand characteristics clearly and to the extent possible, and even to assess possible effects of demand characteristics during debriefing. Implicit self-administrations, however, go a step further by examining consumption under the pretext of an alternative activity.

A second advantage of implicit self-administration paradigms is that they provide a window into non-deliberative consumption. Even in the absence of any demand characteristics, all of the preceding self-administration paradigms include a degree of consideration and deliberation. Whether at no cost or in exchange for operant behaviors or financial costs, the participants are choosing how much they will consume and putatively weighing the pros and cons of the different options to some extent. In an implicit self-administration paradigm, however, individuals are engaged in an alternative task and their consumption may more accurately reflect preferences in the absence of conscious consideration of consumption. As alcohol, tobacco, and other drug use can be deeply instantiated habits, especially for those with substance use disorders, automatic behavior is putatively an important factor in maintaining addictive behavior (for a review, see Tiffany and Conklin, 2000), especially in contexts that do not pose specific reasons to deliberate. Thus, implicit self-administration paradigms may provide a window into more habit-driven consumption.

There are, however, disadvantages to the TRT approach. From a practical stand-point, the methodology is best suited for studying alcohol and is less applicable to other drugs. Sampling different beers or other alcoholic beverages is a credible pretext, akin to consumer research, but sampling different types of heroin or cocaine would presumably be less plausible and might actually elicit more demand characteristics out of suspicion about the procedure. In contrast, however, tobacco taste rating would be potentially plausible. A second disadvantage, similar to *ad libitum* paradigms, is that the TRT has no response cost, meaning it reflects consumption of a commodity of value in the absence of any objective negative consequences. More seriously, although the TRT may be sensitive to habitual behavior, it might also be sensitive to other extraneous factors, such as antagonistic or acquiescent personality traits. The general presumption of all taste testing is that consumption is not the objective of the activity. For example, it would be socially unacceptable to eat unlimited amounts of a promotional food at a tasting station at a grocery store, but no explicit prohibition is made. In this context, some individuals might be motivated to drink more, but not do so, and others might intentionally do so simply because they can. As such, performance on the TRT may not necessarily reflect the putative behavioral characteristic of motivation for alcohol. Alternative variables such as personality traits have not been examined in relation to the TRT, making this an open question. Moreover, as with a number of the behavioral paradigms reviewed, the TRT has not undergone extensive validation in relation to individual differences in alcohol involvement. For example, it has not been shown to correspond systematically with levels of alcohol problems. Such findings would be important for validating the TRT as an index of compulsive motivation, which is ultimately what these experimental approaches are attempting to model. Taken together, although the TRT has a number of strengths, it also has weaknesses and areas of ambiguity that should be considered in contemplating its implementation.

4   Ethical Issues in Drug Self-Administration Paradigms

As with all research involving human subjects and given the potential vulnerability of the participants in addiction psychopharmacology studies, there are several ethical considerations for implementing drug self-administration paradigms. Fundamentally, a balance must be achieved in which the potential knowledge to be gained outweighs potential risks to participants and others. The potential benefit from research that clarifies the etiology of addictive disorders and improves prevention and/or treatment is an important consideration given the enormity of the public health burden from addictive disorders (Mokdad, Marks, Stroup, and Gerberding, 2004). Conversely, providing access to drugs that are of known addictive potential and that, when consumed excessively or chronically, are of known negative health consequences, may pose a number of risks. For example, in an at-risk sample, could participation in a drug self-administration study further increase risk? In a clinical sample of individuals who are not seeking treatment, could participation exacerbate the condition? Finally, in a clinical sample of treatment-seeking or recovered individuals, could participation undermine successful resolution of these disorders? Furthermore, these questions and similar ones are charged because research on alcohol and drug addiction has a contentious history. For example, Jacob, Krahn, and Leonard (1991) conducted a study on parent–child interactions in which fathers with alcohol dependence were administered alcohol, stimulating considerable controversy and discussion (e.g., Stricker, 1991). These controversies may stem from assumptions about addictive disorders that originated in 12-step programs (Roizen, 1987). For example, the application of behavior therapy to moderation-oriented treatment for alcohol dependence provoked debate throughout the field and even accusations of scientific misconduct that were ultimately determined to be unsubstantiated (for a full review, see Roizen, 1987).

Although professional recommendations exist for ethical best practices when administering drugs, legal and illegal, to human subjects from the National Advisory Council on Alcohol Abuse and Alcoholism (NACAAA, 2005) and the National Advisory Council on Drug Abuse (NACDA, 2000), the primary focus is on drug challenge studies (passive administration), with little distinction for self-administration methods.

Here, however, the specific focus will be on self-administration methods, but many of the same recommendations apply. Both organizations endorse the general ethical practices in research outlined in the Belmont Report (1979), which, simply stated, requires that experiments ensure respect for persons (e.g., informed voluntary consent), beneficence (e.g., promote wellbeing and avoid harm), and justice (e.g., fairness and equality). In addition, both NACAAA and NACDA emphasize that, as with all studies with human participants, the ultimate determination of ethical acceptability comes from an investigator's Institutional Review Board.

The issues that are specific to drug self-administration research include promoting informed consent, avoiding coercion, maintaining safety, and determining the appropriate sample for a given study. To facilitate informed consent, it is important that participants be made fully aware of all the elements of the study, such as the opportunity to use a drug or a number of drugs, the duration of the protocol, and the study's benefits and risks (NACAAA, 2005; Tucker and Vuchinich, 2000). Avoiding coercion is a critical consideration and involves ensuring that no elements of the study, incentives or otherwise, are disproportionate and induce persons at risk for adverse outcomes to enroll. A practical recommendation in this area is to include eligibility screens that are temporally separate from enrollment in the study and the associated compensation (Tucker and Vuchinich, 2000). This ensures participants have time to consider their decisions and are not disproportionately influenced by immediate incentives. In terms of safety, minimizing inaccurate reporting about medical conditions, allergies, or other factors is essential. To minimize the risk of enrolling an inappropriate individual, two practical recommendations are to inform participants that accurate information is essential to avoid potentially adverse outcomes and to use objective measures, such as pregnancy tests, breathalyzers, drug tests, and other validated biomarkers. A further safety consideration is adequate recovery time for participants to return to safe levels of sobriety. For example, for alcohol, the breath alcohol recommendation is between 0.02 g% and 0.04 g% (NACAAA, 2005), which is 25% to 50% of the legal limit for intoxication in most US states. Protocols for procedures in case of emergencies during the administration sessions are also recommended.

The issue of study sample is a less clear area, but, nonetheless, a critical consideration in study design and potential ethical issues. There are some individuals for whom self-administration studies are categorically inappropriate, such as pregnant women, for whom no level of alcohol or other drug use is considered safe, whether or not it is voluntarily selected. Likewise, medically ill individuals, individuals taking medications with potential interactions, and the elderly are generally contraindicated (NACAAA, 2005; NACDA, 2000). The exception to this pertains to studies that are intended to specifically study drug use in a population defined by these characteristics, but would require thorough consideration of the ethical cost–benefit ratio.

In terms of drug-naïve individuals, although the use of self-administration paradigms would often be illogical for individuals with no prior experience and might also include unnecessary risk, individuals will be necessarily naïve to the drug for abuse liability studies using novel compounds. In terms of level of an addictive disorder, individuals may be classified based on severity: nonclinical (no symptoms), subclinical (some symptoms, no diagnosis), or clinical (positive for diagnosis). In addition, individuals may be designated as "at-risk" (e.g., children of alcoholics) or, among subclinical/clinical samples, by their treatment-seeking status (e.g., in treatment, seeking treatment, or recently completed treatment versus not actively seeking treatment). Determining the risk for individuals in these different categories is a study-by-study consideration. Preference for non-treatment-seeking individuals is recommended, as is providing treatment recommendations to these individuals following participation (e.g., brief intervention/feedback/resources) in an attempt to make research participation salutary (NACAAA, 2005; NACDA, 2000). However, enrolling treatment-seeking individuals in self-administration studies is increasingly and issue of debate. Clinical interventions are necessarily provided to individuals who are seeking treatment and operate in concert with existing levels of intrinsic motivation. Therefore, for studies seeking to inform interventions, it may make more sense to focus on individuals who are actively seeking treatment (Perkins, Stitzer, and Lerman, 2006). In any case, consideration of the potential of detrimental effects of study participation on the recovery process is recommended (NACAAA, 2005). Of course, individuals with a history of an addictive disorder who have achieved stable abstinence are not appropriate for self-administration paradigms in which direct access to the previously problematic drug, via sampling or no/low-cost conditions, might undermine success. Moreover, it is hard to envision a research question that responsibly seeks to study conditions in which successfully abstinent individuals resume drug taking, although this does not necessarily apply to the same extent with individuals who have achieved successful moderation. Typically, there are no concrete answers to these questions, as it is always a question of the experimental hypotheses and measures taken to minimize risk, but one universal recommendation is that the considerations be actively described in manuscripts and that journal editors permit adequate space for this information (Wood and Sher, 2000).

Importantly, these ethical questions are also fundamentally empirical questions. Consequently, addiction psychopharmacology may be best served if these issues are addressed from a data-driven approach. Goldman (2000) discussed the need to disambiguate strongly held cultural beliefs from scientific research and that a cost–benefit analysis cannot be conducted without high-quality research to guide ethical considerations. For example, in two alcohol self-administration studies of non-treatment-seeking individuals with alcohol dependence, follow-up analyses revealed a significant decrease in total number of drinking days and drinks per occasion and no significant increase in drinking among participants (Drobes and Anton, 2000; Sinha, Krishnan-Sarin, Farren, and O'Malley, 1999). Indeed, in one case, nearly two-thirds of participants reduced their drinking by 20% or more (Drobes and Anton, 2000). This suggests that research participation in self-administration protocols actually reduced subsequent drinking. Although these studies do not suggest administration of alcohol is a high risk or an exacerbation of drinking, is likely as Goldman (2000) noted, even when something is generally true, it is not possible that a finding will apply to every case. Thus, ethical guidelines, even when informed by empirical data, must consider the benefits and risks for each individual. More broadly, these studies demonstrate that these ethical considerations are not abstractions, but open questions that inform subsequent research.

5 Conclusions

A core feature of drug addiction is excessive consumption and experimentally characterizing individuals' motivation to use a substance via self-administration paradigms is critical in addiction psychopharmacology. This chapter has reviewed the methods that are currently available and in active use, and the diversity of approaches and variability is clearly substantial. Options range from inpatient protocols that intensively study small numbers of individuals over weeks at a time, to brief estimation methods that can be administered quickly and to large groups of individuals. Each of the approaches has advantages and disadvantages, and there are no categorical answers with regard to which paradigms are optimal. Ultimately, the paradigm(s) selected for a given study depend on the weighing of these pros and cons in the context of the aims of the study, its hypotheses, and potential research designs. However, an advantage of these various methods is that they permit investigations of a given question to employ different approaches. If a single overarching recommendation can be made for this area, it is for investigators to leverage these multiple methodologies, as a convergence of findings provides particularly strong evidence for conclusions. Moreover, if discrepancies exist, they may reveal nuances of the experimental question or be informative about the methodologies. As was noted on several occasions, continued progress in this area will depend on the ongoing refinement of these methods, in general and in relation to each other. As fundamental tools in addiction research, iterative optimization of these methods is essential for maximally understanding motivation in drug addiction.

References

American Psychiatric Association (1952) *Diagnostic and Statistical Manual of Mental Disorders.* Washington, DC: APA.

American Psychiatric Association (1968) *Diagnostic and Statistical Manual of Mental Disorders.* (2nd edn). Washington, DC: APA.

American Psychiatric Association (1980) *Diagnostic and Statistical Manual of Mental Disorders* (3rd edn). Washington, DC: APA.

American Psychiatric Association (1987) *Diagnostic and Statistical Manual of Mental Disorders* (3rd edn, rev.). Washington, DC: APA.

American Psychiatric Association (1994) *Diagnostic and Statistical Manual of Mental Disorders* (4th edn). Washington, DC: APA.

Amlung MT, Acker J, Stojek MK, Murphy JG, and MacKillop J (2012) Is talk "cheap"? An initial investigation of the equivalence of alcohol purchase task performance for hypothetical and actual rewards. *Alcoholism: Clinical And Experimental Research* 36: 716–724.

Anton RF, Drobes DJ, Voronin K, Durazo-Avizu R, and Moak D (2004) Naltrexone effects on alcohol consumption in a clinical laboratory paradigm: Temporal effects of drinking. *Psychopharmacology* (Berlin) 173: 32–40.

Benson TA, Little CS, Henslee AM, and Correia CJ (2009) Effects of reinforcer magnitude and alternative reinforcer delay on preference for alcohol during a multiple-choice procedure. *Drug and Alcohol Dependence* 100: 161–163.

Bigelow G (2001) An operant behavioral perspective on alcohol abuse and dependence. In N Heather, TJ Peters, and T Stockwell (eds), *International Handbook of Alcohol Dependence and Problems* (pp. 299–315). Chichester: JohnWiley & Sons, Ltd.

Bigelow G, Cohen M, Liebson I, and Faillace LA (1972) Abstinence or moderation? Choice by alcoholics. *Behavior Research and Therapy* 10: 209–214.

Carr GD (2011) Alcoholism: A modern look at an ancient illness. *Primary Care* 38: 9–21, v.

Cohen M, Liebson IA, Faillace LA, and Speers W (1971) Alcoholism: Controlled drinking and incentives for abstinence. *Psychological Reports* 28: 575–580.

Colby SM, Rohsenow DJ, Monti PM, Gwaltney CJ, Gulliver SB, Abrams DB, Niaura RS, and Sirota AD (2004) Effects of tobacco deprivation on alcohol cue reactivity and drinking among young adults. *Addictive Behaviors* 29: 879–892.

Collins RL, Gollnisch G, and Izzo CV (1996) Drinking restraint and alcohol-related outcomes: Exploring the contributions of beverage instructions, beverage content and self-monitoring. *Journal of Studies on Alcohol* 57: 563–571.

Comer SD, Walker EA, and Collins ED (2005) Buprenorphine/naloxone reduces the reinforcing and subjective effects of heroin in heroin-dependent volunteers. *Psychopharmacology* (Berlin) 181: 664–675.

Crocq MA (2007) Historical and cultural aspects of man's relationship with addictive drugs. *Dialogues in Clinical Neuroscience* 9: 355–361.

de Wit H and Chutuape MA (1993) Increased ethanol choice in social drinkers following ethanol preload. *Behavioural Pharmacology* 4: 29–36.

Drobes DJ and Anton RF (2000) Drinking in alcoholics following an alcohol challenge research protocol. *Journal of Studies on Alcohol* 61: 220–224.

Drobes DJ, Anton RF, Thomas SE, and Voronin K (2003) A clinical laboratory paradigm for evaluating medication effects on alcohol consumption: Naltrexone and nalmefene. *Neuropsychopharmacology* 28: 755–764.

Few LR, Acker J, Murphy CM, and MacKillop J (2012) Temporal stability of a cigarette purchase task: An initial study. *Nicotine and Tobacco Research* 14: 761–765.

Ferster CB and Skinner BF (1957) *Schedules of Reinforcement.* Acton, MA: Copley.

Fillmore MT (2001) Cognitive preoccupation with alcohol and binge drinking in college students: Alcohol-induced priming of the motivation to drink. *Psychology of Addictive Behaviors* 15: 325–332.

Fischman MW, Kelly TH, and Foltin RW (1990) Residential laboratory research: A multidimensional evaluation of the effects of drugs on behavior. *NIDA Research Monographs* 100: 113–128.

Foltin RW and Fischman MW (1988) Effects of smoked marijuana on human social behavior in small groups. *Pharmacology, Biochemistry and Behavior* 30: 539–541.

Goldman MS (2000) The culture of science and the ethics of alcohol administration in research. *Psychology of Addictive Behaviors* 14: 335–341.

Griffiths RR, Bigelow GE, and Ator NA (2003) Principles of initial experimental drug abuse liability assessment in humans. *Drug and Alcohol Dependence* 70: S41–54.

Griffiths RR, Troisi JR, Silverman K, and Mumford GK (1993) Multiple-choice procedure: An efficient approach for investigating drug reinforcement in humans. *Behavioural Pharmacology* 4: 3–13.

Hamarneh S (1972) Pharmacy in medieval Islam and the history of drug addiction. *Medical History* 16: 226–237.

Hart CL, Haney M, Vosburg SK, Rubin E, and Foltin RW (2008) Smoked cocaine self-administration is decreased by modafinil. *Neuropsychopharmacology* 33: 761–768.

Herin DV, Grabowski J, and MacKillop J (2009) Novel assessment of cocaine motivation using behavioral economics. Poster presented at the 48th Annual Meeting of the American College of Neuropsychopharmacology.

Higgins ST, Bickel WK, and Hughes JR (1994) Influence of an alternative reinforcer on human cocaine self-administration. *Life Sciences* 55: 179–187.

Hitsman B, MacKillop J, Lingford-Hughes A, Williams TM, Ahmad F, Adams S, Nutt DJ, and Munafo MR (2008) Effects of acute tyrosine/phenylalanine depletion on the selective processing of smoking-related cues and the relative value of cigarettes in smokers. *Psychopharmacology* (Berlin) 196: 611–621.

Hodos W (1961) Progressive ratio as a measure of reward strength. *Science* 134: 943–944.

Hogarth L (2011) The role of impulsivity in the aetiology of drug dependence: Reward sensitivity versus automaticity. *Psychopharmacology* (Berlin) 215: 567–580.

Hughes JR and Bickel WK (1997) Modeling drug dependence behaviors for animal and human studies. *Pharmacology Biochemistry and Behavior* 57: 413–417.

Hursh SR (1984) Behavioral economics. *Journal of the Experimental Analysis of Behavior* 42: 435–452.

Hursh SR and Silberberg A (2008) Economic demand and essential value. *Psychological Review* 115: 186–198.

Hursh SR and Winger G (1995) Normalized demand for drugs and other reinforcers. *Journal for the Experimental Analysis of Behavior* 64: 373–384.

Hursh SR, Galuska CM, Winger G, and Woods JH (2005) The economics of drug abuse: A quantitative assessment of drug demand. *Molecular Interventions* 5: 20–28.

Hursh SR, Raslear TG, Shurtleff D, Bauman R, and Simmons L (1988) A cost–benefit analysis of demand for food. *Journal for the Experimental Analysis of Behavior* 50: 419–440.

Jacob T, Krahn GL, and Leonard K (1991) Parent–child interactions in families with alcoholic fathers. *Journal of Consulting and Clinical Psychology* 59: 176–181; discussion 183.

Jacobs EA and Bickel WK (1999) Modeling drug consumption in the clinic using simulation procedures: Demand for heroin and cigarettes in opioid-dependent outpatients. *Experimental and Clinical Psychopharmacology* 7: 412–426.

Johanson CE and Uhlenhuth EH (1980a) Drug preference and mood in humans: d-amphetamine. *Psychopharmacology* (Berlin) 71: 275–279.

Johanson CE and Uhlenhuth EH (1980b) Drug preference and mood in humans: Diazepam. *Psychopharmacology* (Berlin) 71: 269–273.

Johnson MW and Bickel WK (2003) The behavioral economics of cigarette smoking: The concurrent presence of a substitute and an independent reinforcer. *Behavioural Pharmacology* 14: 137–144.

Johnson MW and Bickel WK (2006) Replacing relative reinforcing efficacy with behavioral economic demand curves. *Journal for the Experimental Analysis of Behavior* 85: 73–93.

Johnson MW, MacLean KA, Reissig CJ, Prisinzano TE, and Griffiths RR (2011) Human psychopharmacology and dose-effects of salvinorin A, a kappa opioid agonist hallucinogen present in the plant *Salvia divinorum*. *Drug and Alcohol Dependence* 115: 150–155.

Jones BE and Prada JA (1975) Drug-seeking behavior during methadone maintenance. *Psychopharmacologia* 41: 7–10.

Jones HE, Garrett BE, and Griffiths RR (1999) Subjective and physiological effects of intravenous nicotine and cocaine in cigarette smoking cocaine abusers. *Journal of Pharmacology and Experimental Therapeutics* 288: 188–197.

Kidorf M, Stitzer ML, and Griffiths RR (1995) Evaluating the reinforcement value of clinic-based privileges through a multiple choice procedure. *Drug and Alcohol Dependence* 39: 167–172.

Lau-Barraco C and Dunn ME (2008) Evaluation of a single-session expectancy challenge intervention to reduce alcohol use among college students. *Psychology of Addictive Behaviors* 22: 168–175.

Leeman RF, O'Malley SS, White MA, and McKee SA (2010) Nicotine and food deprivation decrease the ability to resist smoking. *Psychopharmacology* (Berlin) 212: 25–32.

Little C and Correia CJ (2006) Use of a multiple-choice procedure with college student drinkers. *Psychology of Addictive Behaviors* 20: 445–452.

MacKillop J and Lisman SA (2005) Reactivity to alcohol cues: Isolating the role of perceived availability. *Experimental and Clinical Psychopharmacology* 13: 229–237.

MacKillop J and Murphy JG (2007) A behavioral economic measure of demand for alcohol predicts brief intervention outcomes. *Drug and Alcohol Dependence* 89: 227–33.

MacKillop J and Tidey JW (2011) Cigarette demand and delayed reward discounting in nicotine-dependent individuals with schizophrenia and controls: An initial study. *Psychopharmacology* (Berlin) 216: 91–99.

MacKillop J, Amlung MT, Few LR, Ray LA, Sweet LH, and Munafo MR (2011) Delayed reward discounting and addictive behavior: A meta-analysis. *Psychopharmacology* (Berlin) 216: 305–321.

MacKillop J, Miranda J, R., Monti PM, Ray LA, Tidey JW, Rohsenow DJ, Gwaltney GJ, McGeary JE, and Swift RM (2010a) Alcohol demand, delayed reward discounting, and craving in relation to drinking and alcohol use disorders. *Journal of Abnormal Psychology* 119: 115–125.

MacKillop J, Murphy JG, Ray LA, Eisenberg DT, Lisman SA, Lum JK, and Wilson DS (2008) Further validation of a cigarette purchase task for assessing the relative reinforcing efficacy of nicotine in college smokers. *Experimental and Clinical Psychopharmacology* 16: 57–65.

MacKillop J, O'Hagen S, Lisman SA, Murphy JG, Ray LA, Tidey JW, McGeary JE, and Monti PM (2010b) Behavioral economic analysis of cue-elicited craving for alcohol. *Addiction* 105: 1599–1607.

Madden CJ and Zwaan RA (2001) The impact of smoking urges on working memory performance. *Experimental and Clinical Psychopharmacology* 9: 418–424.

Marlatt GA, Demming B, and Reid JB (1973) Loss of control drinking in alcoholics: An experimental analogue. *Journal of Abnormal Psychology* 81: 233–241.

McKee SA, Harrison ER, OMalley SS, Krishnan-Sarin S, Shi J, Tetrault JM, and . . . Balchunas E (2009) Varenicline reduces alcohol self-administration in heavy-drinking smokers. *Biological Psychiatry* 66: 185–190.

McKee SA, Krishnan-Sarin S, Shi J, Mase T, and O'Malley SS (2006) Modeling the effect of alcohol on smoking lapse behavior. *Psychopharmacology (Berl)* 189: 201–210.

McKee SA, O'Malley SS, Shi J, Mase T, and Krishnan-Sarin S (2008) Effect of transdermal nicotine replacement on alcohol responses and alcohol self-administration. *Psychopharmacology* 196: 189–200.

Mello NK and Mendelson JH (1965) Operant analysis of drinking patterns of chronic alcoholics. *Nature* 206: 43–46.

Mokdad AH, Marks JS, Stroup DF, and Gerberding JL (2004) Actual causes of death in the United States, 2000. *Journal of the American Medical Association* 291: 1238–1245.

Mumford GK, Rush CR, and Griffiths RR (1995) Abecarnil and alprazolam in humans: Behavioral, subjective and reinforcing effects. *Journal of Pharmacology and Experimental Therapeutics* 272: 570–580.

Murphy JG and MacKillop J (2006) Relative reinforcing efficacy of alcohol among college student drinkers. *Experimental and Clinical Psychopharmacology* 14: 219–227.

Murphy JG, MacKillop J, Skidmore JR, and Pederson AA (2009) Reliability and validity of a demand curve measure of alcohol reinforcement. *Experimental and Clinical Psychopharmacology* 17: 396–404.

Murphy JG, MacKillop J, Tidey JW, Brazil LA, and Colby SM (2011) Validity of a demand curve measure of nicotine reinforcement with adolescent smokers. *Drug and Alcohol Dependence* 113: 207–214.

Myrick H, Anton R, Voronin K, Wang W, and Henderson S (2007) A double-blind evaluation of gabapentin on alcohol effects and drinking in a clinical laboratory paradigm. *Alcoholism: Clinical and Experimental Research* 31: 221–227.

National Advisory Council on Alcohol Abuse and Alcoholism (NACAAA) (2005) Recommended Council Guidelines on Ethyl Alcohol Administration in Human Experimentation. Retrieved from: http://www.niaaa.nih.gov/research/guidelines-and-resources/administering-alcohol-human-studies#group.

National Advisory Council on Drug Abuse (NACDA) (2000) Guidelines for Administration of Drugs to Human Subjects. 2000. Retrieved from: http://www.drugabuse.gov/funding/clinical-research/nacda-guidelines-administration-drugs-to-human-subjects.

Nathan PE, Titler NA, Lowenstein LM, Solomon P, and Rossi AM (1970) Behavioral analysis of chronic alcoholism: Interaction of alcohol and human contact. *Archives of General Psychiatry* 22: 419–430.

Nevin JA and Grace RC (2000) Behavioral momentum and the law of effect. *The Behavioral and Brain Sciences* 23: 73–90; discussion 90–130.

Noel NE and Lisman SA (1980) Alcohol consumption by college women following exposure to unsolvable problems: Learning helplessness or stress induced drinking? *Behaviour Research and Therapy* 18: 429–440.

O'Brien C (2011) Addiction and dependence in DSM-V. *Addiction* 106: 866–867.

O'Brien CP, Volkow N, and Li TK (2006) What's in a word? Addiction versus dependence in DSM-V. *American Journal of Psychiatry* 163: 764–765.

Office for Protection from Research Risks. National Commission for the Protection of Human Subjects of Biomedical and Behavioral Research (1979) *The Belmont Report: Ethical Principles and Guidelines for the Protection of Human Subjects of Research* (GPO 887-809). Washington, DC: US Government Printing Office.

O'Malley SS, Krishnan-Sarin S, Farren C, Sinha R, and Kreek MJ (2002) Naltrexone decreases craving and alcohol self-administration in alcohol-dependent subjects and activates the hypothalamo-pituitary-adrenocortical axis. *Psychopharmacology* (Berlin) 160: 19–29.

Palfai T, Davidson D, and Swift R (1999) Influence of naltrexone on cue-elicited craving among hazardous drinkers: The moderational role of positive outcome expectancies. *Experimental and Clinical Psychopharmacology* 7: 266–273.

Perkins KA, Stitzer M, and Lerman C (2006) Medication screening for smoking cessation: A proposal for new methodologies. *Psychopharmacology* (Berlin) 184: 628–636.

Roehrs T, Pedrosi B, Rosenthal L, Zorick F, and Roth T (1997) Hypnotic self administration: Forced-choice versus single-choice. *Psychopharmacology* (Berlin) 133: 121–126.

Roizen R (1987) The great controlled-drinking controversy. In M Galanter (ed.) *Recent Developments in Alcoholism* (pp. 245–279). New York: Plenum.

Rousseau GS, Irons JG, and Correia CJ (2011) The reinforcing value of alcohol in a drinking to cope paradigm. *Drug and Alcohol Dependence* (in press).

Rush CR, Higgins ST, Vansickel AR, Stoops WW, Lile JA, and Glaser PE (2005) Methylphenidate increases cigarette smoking. *Psychopharmacology* (Berlin) 181: 781–789.

Sayette MA, Martin CS, Wertz JM, Shiffman S, and Perrott MA (2001) A multi-dimensional analysis of cue-elicited craving in heavy smokers and tobacco chippers. *Addiction* 96: 1419–1432.

Sinha R, Krishnan-Sarin S, Farren C, and O'Malley S (1999) Naturalistic follow-up of drinking behavior following participation in an alcohol administration study. *Journal of Substance Abuse Treatment* 17: 159–162.

Skidmore JR and Murphy JG (2011) The effect of drink price and next-day responsibilities on college student drinking: A behavioral economic analysis. *Psychology of Addictive Behaviors* 25: 57–68.

Smith AE, Martens MP, Murphy JG, Buscemi J, Yurasek AM, and Skidmore J (2010) Reinforcing efficacy moderates the relationship between impulsivity-related traits and alcohol use. *Experimental and Clinical Psychopharmacology* 18: 521–529.

Sobel BF, Sigmon SC, and Griffiths RR (2004) Transdermal nicotine maintenance attenuates the subjective and reinforcing effects of intravenous nicotine, but not cocaine or caffeine, in cigarette-smoking stimulant abusers. *Neuropsychopharmacology* 29: 991–1003.

Staiger PK and White JM (1991) Cue reactivity in alcohol abusers: Stimulus specificity and extinction of the responses. *Addictive Behaviors* 16: 211–221.

Stricker G (1991) Ethical concerns in alcohol research. *Journal of Consulting and Clinical Psychology* 59: 256–257.

Tabachnick BG and Fidell LS (2006) *Using Multivariate Statistics* (5th edn). Needham Heights, MA: Allyn H Bacon,

Tidey JW, Rohsenow DJ, Kaplan GB, and Swift RM (2005) Cigarette smoking topography in smokers with schizophrenia and matched non-psychiatric controls. *Drug and Alcohol Dependence* 80: 259–265.

Tiffany ST and Conklin CA (2000) A cognitive processing model of alcohol craving and compulsive alcohol use. *Addiction* 95 (Suppl. 2): S145–153.

Tucker JA and Vuchinich RE (2000) Creating a research context for reducing risk and obtaining informed consent in human alcohol studies. *Psychology of Addictive Behaviors* 14: 319–327.

Voronin K, Randall P, Myrick H, and Anton R (2008) Aripiprazole effects on alcohol consumption and subjective reports in a clinical laboratory paradigm: Possible influence of self-control. *Alcoholism: Clinical and Experimental Research* 32: 1954–1961.

Willner P, Hardman S, and Eaton G (1995) Subjective and behavioural evaluation of cigarette cravings. *Psychopharmacology* (Berlin) 118: 171–177.

Wood MD and Sher KJ (2000) Risks of alcohol consumption in laboratory studies involving human research participants. *Psychology of Addictive Behaviors* 14: 328–334.

Zimmermann US, Mick I, Laucht M, Vitvitskiy V, Plawecki MH, Mann KF, and O'Connor S (2009) Offspring of parents with an alcohol use disorder prefer higher levels of brain alcohol exposure in experiments involving computer-assisted self-infusion of ethanol (CASE). *Psychopharmacology* (Berlin) 202: 689–697.

Zimmermann US, Mick I, Vitvitskyi V, Plawecki MH, Mann KF, and O'Connor S (2008) Development and pilot validation of computer-assisted self-infusion of ethanol (CASE): A new method to study alcohol self-administration in humans. *Alcoholism-Clinical and Experimental Research* 32: 1321–1328.

Zwaan RA, Stanfield RA, and Madden CJ (2000) How persistent is the effect of smoking urges on cognitive performance? *Experimental and Clinical Psychopharmacology* 8: 518–523.

13

The Assessment of Craving in Addiction Research[1]

Lara A. Ray, Kelly E. Courtney, Guadalupe Bacio, and James MacKillop

1 Introduction

Although an association between addiction and craving has existed since antiquity, the relationship has only been the focus of scientific study over the past 60 years (Drummond, 2001). Craving for a drug is typically defined as a strong or persistent desire for the substance, and cravings putatively contribute to both the maintenance of ongoing drug use and success or failure in treatment. Clinically, craving itself is a symptom of substance dependence in the current version of the International Classification of Diseases (ICD-10; World Health Organization, 2010), and will be adopted as a new symptom in the next edition of the *Diagnostic and Statistical Manual of the American Psychiatric Association* (www.dsm-v.org). In treatment settings, moderate to intense cravings are reported by substantial proportions of patients (Oslin *et al.*, 2009; Yoon *et al.*, 2006) and its amelioration is a frequent treatment target (Pavlick, Hoffman, and Rosenberg, 2009).

However, the role of craving has also been a highly controversial topic in addiction research. Conceptually, craving as a determinant of substance use has been criticized for being tautological, reflecting circular reasoning (Mendelson and Mello, 1979). Empirically, the evidence that craving is a relapse precipitant is highly variable across studies (Hodgins, el-Guebaly, and Armstrong, 1995; Killen and Fortmann, 1997; Litman *et al.*, 1983; Ramo, Anderson, Tate, and Brown, 2005). Similarly, in human laboratory studies, associations with actual substance consumption have been mixed (for a review, see Tiffany and Conklin, 2000) and the evidence that craving in the laboratory is relevant to clinical outcomes is actively debated (Munafo and Hitsman, 2010;

[1]This chapter is supported by NIH grants K23 AA016936 (JM), R21 AA017696-01A1 (JM), R21 DA029831 (LR), and the UCLA Training Program in Translational Neuroscience of Drug Abuse 5 T32 DA024635 (KC).

Perkins, 2009). Thus, whether craving for a substance reflects a causative etiological process in addictive behavior or an epiphenomenon – a red herring – remains a vigorous area of research. Significant methodological limitations in the measurement of craving further complicate understanding its role in addiction. Craving is inherently a subjective experience and the operational definition of craving has been debated (Monti *et al.*, 2004). Both clinical and laboratory studies have been limited by the only recent development of well-validated measures of craving (Sayette *et al.*, 2000; Tiffany, Carter, and Singleton, 2000). Similarly, in early studies of post-treatment relapse, the use of retrospective reports may have been limited by the fact that craving episodes are generally poorly encoded in memory or may commonly take place in conjunction with other experiences that are more salient (Sayette *et al.*, 2000; Tiffany, Carter, and Singleton, 2000).

The assessment of craving has received a great deal of attention in the addiction literature over the past two decades and the evidence in support of craving as an important factor in addiction has been substantially accumulating. As examples, a longitudinal study of alcoholism course and chronicity found that craving was associated with the highest relative risk of all ICD-10 criteria for alcohol dependence (de Bruijn, van den Brink, de Graaf, and Vollebergh, 2005); craving has been consistently found to predict substance consumption in recent laboratory studies (e.g., Leeman, Corbin, and Fromme, 2009; Leeman, O'Malley, White, and McKee, 2010; MacKillop and Lisman, 2005; O'Malley *et al.*, 2002); and, in a recent nosological study on craving for tobacco (Shmulewitz *et al.*, 2011), craving complemented the other diagnostic symptoms in the unidimensional severity continuum that is prototypic across substances (Compton, Saha, Conway, and Grant, 2009; Kahler and Strong, 2006; Strong and Kahler, 2007). Furthermore, recent studies have advanced our understanding of craving in new and diverse domains. This includes investigations of the genetic bases of craving (e.g., Foroud *et al.*, 2007; Hutchison *et al.*, 2002), studies on promising medications for alcoholism (Hutchison *et al.*, 2006; Mason, Light, Williams, and Drobes, 2009; Miranda *et al.*, 2008; Ray, Chin, Heydari, and Miotto, in press) and neuroimaging studies (Brody *et al.*, 2002; Brody *et al.*, 2007; Filbey *et al.*, 2008a; Filbey *et al.*, 2008b).

Given how important valid assessments are in the study of craving, the objective of this chapter is to provide a systematic review of the instruments developed in this area. First, we provide a review of the standardized and validated methods used in the field. Here, an important distinction is between measures of *tonic* craving, referring to retrospective estimates of craving in general or over a specific time (e.g., preceding week), and *phasic* craving, referring to *in vivo* state reports (i.e., level of craving at a given moment). In the first case, tonic craving reflects a putatively stable overall level of craving a person typically experiences, whereas in the second case, phasic craving reflects dynamic changes in craving that can be elicited from a number of factors. For example, the cue reactivity paradigm (Chapter 14) is a gold-standard approach for examining craving elicited by environmental cues (Carter and Tiffany, 1999), such as the person's preferred alcoholic beverage, cigarettes, or other drug. To further illustrate this distinction with an analogy to food, tonic/phasic craving for a drug can be thought of as similar to hunger for food: a person could be assessed for how hungry they were in general over the last week (the tonic level of hunger) or how much hunger increased after a delicious meal was presented to them (a phasic increase in hunger). For both tonic and phasic craving, we focus on measures developed for the assessment of alcohol, cigarette, and illicit drug craving and discuss the psychometric properties of each scale. Of note, however, the focus is on measures for which the primary target is the measurement of craving, rather than those for which craving is assessed as an indicator of a more global construct (e.g., substance abuse/dependence). Second, we review alternatives to self-report assessments, such as psychophysiological indices, cognitive tasks, and behavioral economic measures of value. Third, we discuss special considerations in the assessment of craving, such as developmental factors (e.g., adolescents, older adults) and cultural factors (e.g., translation and validation to different languages and cultures). Finally, we conclude by discussing the limitations and priorities for future research and make recommendations and directions of future research. Recognizing the active debate with regard to craving as a scientific target, reliable and valid instruments for measuring craving are essential and this chapter is intended to be a resource for researchers and clinicians as a guide to the instruments that best fit the needs of their experimental and practice goals.

2   Instruments for the Assessment of Craving in Addiction

Selecting an appropriate measure of craving depends on numerous factors. Broadly speaking, the choice of craving assessment depends on the operational definition of craving, the drug of interest, the time frame over which craving will be assessed, the testing circumstances (including length of assessment), and the effect of interest (between-subject or within-subject effects). For example, the appropriateness of a craving scale often depends on the chosen time frame of assessment, with some scales being better at capturing phasic fluctuations in craving levels and others more appropriate for tonic craving measurement. Next we review the instruments developed for the assessment of alcohol, cigarette, and other drug craving, dividing the measures on the critical tonic/phasic distinction. For an overview of the measures described in this manuscript, including psychometric properties, please see Table 13.1.

2.1   Tonic craving measures

2.1.1   *Measures of alcohol craving*

2.1.1.1   OBSESSIVE-COMPULSIVE DRINKING SCALE.   The Obsessive-Compulsive Drinking Scale (OCDS; Anton, Moak, and Latham, 1995) is a multi-dimensional, self-report questionnaire consisting of 14 items rated on a Likert-type scale (range 0–4). It was developed to assess the obsessive and compulsive cognitive aspects of craving and heavy drinking in adult populations. The content domains (subscales) covered by this measure include obsessive and compulsive aspects of alcohol drinking. The OCDS takes approximately 5 minutes to complete, and can be scored using simple addition in under 1 minute. Adequate reliability estimates for this measure have been reported ($\alpha = 0.75$–0.89) in samples of individuals with alcohol dependence (Anton, Moak, and Latham, 1995; Bohn, Barton, and Barron, 1996; Connor, Jack, Feeney,

Table 13.1 Summary of assessment instruments

Authors (year)	Scale name	Drug assessed	Tonic/phasic	No. and type of items	No. and description of subscales	Reliability	Validity
Anton, Moak, and Latham (1995)	Obsessive-Compulsive Drinking Scale (OCDS)*†	Alcohol	Tonic	14: 5-point Likert-type	2: Obsessive and Compulsive	• α Total and subscales = 0.73–0.89 (sample = alc. dependents) • Test–retest r = 0.96 (24–48-hour interval)	• Convergent: YBOCS-hd, ADS, ASI, and alc. consumption (r = 0.83, 0.42, 0.48, and 0.60, respectively)
Bohn, Krahn, and Staehler (1995)	Alcohol Urge Questionnaire (AUQ)	Alcohol	Phasic	8: 7-point Likert-type	Total score only	• α Total = 0.91 (sample = alc. dependents) • Test–retest r = 0.82 (1 day) and r = 0.78 (1 week)	• Convergent: OCDS (r = 0.42), ADS (sR^2 = 0.22)
Collins and Lapp (1992)	Temptation and Restraint Inventory (TRI)	Alcohol	Tonic	15: 9-point Likert-type	2: Cognitive and Emotional Preoccupation (CEP) and Cognitive and Behavioral Concern (CBC)	• α factors = 0.76–0.91, α CEP = 0.91, α CBC = 0.79 (sample = mod. to excessive drinkers)	• Convergent: PAS (r = 0.76), DRIE (r = 0.70) • Discriminant: CEP and Self-Control factor of the Reasons for Limiting Drinking scale (r = –0.19) • Predictive: factors predict weekly alcohol consumption and alcohol-related problems (SMAST)

Reference	Scale	Substance	Type	Items/format	Subscales	Reliability	Validity
Cox, Tiffany, and Christen (2001)	Brief Questionnaire on Smoking Urges (QSU-Brief)	Cigarettes	Phasic	10: 7-point Likert-type	2: Intention, desire and positive outcomes, and relief from withdrawal and negative emotions and strong desire	α Total = 0.92, α subscales = 0.76–0.90 (sample = mod. to excessive drinkers); Test-retest Total and subscales r = 0.71 to 0.81 (7-week interval)	Predictive: lower levels of craving were predictive of an increased likelihood of cessation
Flannery, Volpicelli, and Pettinati (1999)	Penn Alcohol Craving Scale (PACS)*†	Alcohol	Tonic	5: 7-point Likert-type	Total score only	α Total = 0.92 (sample = alc. dependents)	Convergent: OCDS (r = 0.55) and AUQ (r = 0.39); Discriminant: DrInC (r = 0.04)
Franken, Hendriks, and van den Brink (2002)	Obsessive Compulsive Drug Use Scale (OCDUS)	Heroin	Tonic	12 (item 10 deleted): 5-point Likert-type	3: heroin thoughts and interference, desire and control, and resistance to thoughts and intention	α subscales = 0.89–91 (sample = Dutch detoxified heroin dependents); Test-retest ICC = 0.72–0.79 (2 days)	Convergent: Craving VAS (r = 0.76)
Halikas et al. (1991)	Minnesota Cocaine Craving Scale (MCCS)	Cocaine	Tonic	3: multiple formats	3 (no total): intensity of craving, frequency of episodes of craving, and duration of each episode of craving	α among 3 items = 0.83 (sample = cocaine dependents)	Construct: intensity subscale correlated with no. of days of cocaine use (r = 0.39), frequency (r = 0.45), and duration (r = 0.28)
Heishman, Singleton, and Liguori (2001)	Marijuana Craving Questionnaire (MCQ)†	Marijuana	Tonic	45: 7-point Likert-type	4: compulsivity, emotionality, expectancy, and purposefulness	α subscales = 0.55–0.82 (sample = marijuana smokers)	Convergent: subscales correlated single-item measures and visual analogue scales of craving; Construct: subscales correlated with history of marijuana use

(Continued)

Table 13.1 (*Continued*)

Authors (year)	Scale name	Drug assessed	Tonic/phasic	No. and type of items	No. and description of subscales	Reliability	Validity
Heishman *et al.* (2009)	Short Form–Marijuana Craving Questionnaire (MCQ-SF)	Marijuana	Tonic	12: 7-point Likert-type	4: compulsivity, emotionality, expectancy, and purposefulness	• α subscales = 0.61–0.84 (sample = marijuana smokers)	• Construct: all subscales increase as frequency and duration of craving episodes increase
Heishman, Singleton, and Moolchan (2003)	Tobacco Craving Questionnaire (TCQ)	Cigarettes	Tonic	47: 7-point Likert-type	4: expectancy, purposefulness, emotionality, and compulsivity	• α subscales = 0.48–0.82 (sample = polydrug smokers)	• Construct: increased subscale change scores as a function of craving intensity
Leonard, Harwood, and Blane (1988)	Preoccupation with Alcohol Scale (PAS)	Alcohol	Tonic	14: 7-point Likert-type	Total score only	• α Total = 0.89 (sample = male regular drinkers)	• Convergent: Quantity-Frequency Index (daily consumption; r = 0.49), ADS (r = 0.69), and SAI (r = 0.59)
Mol *et al.* (2003)	Benzodiazepine Craving Questionnaire (BCQ)	Benzodiazepines	Tonic	20: 7-point Likert-type	Total score only	• KR-20 Total = 0.94 (sample = Dutch current and former long term benzodiazepine users)	• Construct: higher BCQ for current (vs. past) benzodiazepine users
Ooteman *et al.* (2006)	Jellinek Alcohol Craving Questionnaire (JACQ)	Alcohol	Tonic	24: 5-point Likert-type	4: emotional urge, physical sensations, temptation to drink, and uncontrolled thoughts	• α JACQ-Now = 0.96, α JACQ-Past = 0.95 (sample = Dutch abstaining alc. dependents) • Test-retest JACQ-Past Total ICC = 0.87 and subscales ICC = 0.76–0.88	• Convergent: OCDS subscales (JACQ-Past r = 0.56–0.61 and Now r = 0.26–0.28), ACQ-NOW (JACQ-Now r = 0.77–0.87), and craving VAS (JACQ-now r = 0.79)

Study	Substance	Type	Items: Scale	Subscales	Reliability	Validity
Paliwal, Hyman, and Sinha (2008)	Cocaine	Tonic	10: 7-point Likert-type	Total score only	• α Total = 0.87 (sample = treatment-seeking cocaine dependents) • CCQ-Brief and CCQ-Now Total r = 0.87	• Convergent: CSSA cocaine craving (r = 0.46), craving frequency (r = 0.46), desire VAS (r = 0.47), and urge VAS (r = 0.49) • Predictive: total score predicted time to cocaine relapse assessed 90 days later
Raabe et al. (2005)	Alcohol	Tonic	30: 7-point Likert-type	2: urge and intention to drink alcohol, and positive and negative reinforcement	• α subscales = 0.93–0.96 (sample = German alc. abuse/dependents) • Test–retest Total and subscales r = 0.80–0.89	• Convergent: OCDS subscale ICCs = 0.57–0.67
Shiffman, Waters, and Hickcox (2004)	Cigarettes	Tonic	19: 5-point Likert-type	5: stereotypy, priority, tolerance, continuity, and drive	• α subscales = 0.55–0.84 (sample = daily smokers) • Test–retest r = 0.71–0.83	• Predictive: total score, and drive and priority subscales, predict urge intensity during the first 2 days of abstinence
Singleton, Tiffany, and Henningfield (1995)	Alcohol	Tonic	47: 7-point Likert-type	4: expectancy, purposefulness, emotionality, and compulsivity	• α subscales = 0.80–0.94 (sample = non-problem drinkers)	• Predictive: correctly classifying 78.3% of alcohol dependents and 84.6% of non-dependents • Construct: Lack of Control subscale predicted cue-elicited alcohol craving

(Continued)

Table 13.1 *(Continued)*

Authors (year)	Scale name	Drug assessed	Tonic/phasic	No. and type of items	No. and description of subscales	Reliability	Validity
Tiffany and Drobes (1991)	Questionnaire on Smoking Urges (QSU)†	Cigarettes	Tonic	32: 7-point Likert-type	2: intention, desire and positive outcomes, and relief from withdrawal and negative emotions and strong desire	• α subscales = 0.93–0.95 (sample = daily smokers)	• Predictive: positive factor predicted cigarette liking and progressive-ratio operant performance in nondeprived subjects, and negative factor predicted both cigarette liking and breaking point on the progressive-ratio schedule for the deprived subjects
Tiffany et al. (1993)	Heroin Craving Questionnaire (HCQ)	Heroin	Tonic	14 and 45: 7-point Likert-type	4: desire and intention, lack of control, positive and negative expectancies, general craving	• α HCQ-45 Total = 0.94 (sample = non-treatment-seeking heroin users) • HCQ-45 and HCQ-14 Total scores $r = 0.57$ (sample = opiate dependents)	• Convergent: desire subscale correlated with the craving and want items on a heroin craving VAS ($r = 0.54$ and 0.53), HCQ-14 total correlated with crave, want, and need VAS • Predictive: HCQ-45 total and desire subscale correlated with heroin-negative urines during treatment ($r = 0.22$–0.31)

*

Tiffany, Singleton, Haertzen, and Henningfield (1993)	Cocaine Craving Questionnaire (CCQ)	Cocaine	Tonic	45: 7-point Likert-type	4: desire and intention, lack of control, positive and negative expectancies, and general craving	α subscales CCQ-Gen and Now = 0.70–0.93 (sample = non-treatment-seeking, mostly male, cocaine users)	• Predictive: higher total scores on CCQ-Gen and CCQ-Now associated with lower confidence in ability to quit cocaine use, greater frequency of use over past 6 months, and frequency of cocaine use over the past 30 days (first three subscales only) • CCQ-Now total score associated with time to relapse assessed at a 90-day follow-up
Voris, Elder, and Sebastian (1991)	Voris Cocaine Craving Scale (VCCS)	Cocaine	Tonic	4: VAS	4 (no total): perceived craving, mood, energy, and health level	• Test–retest for craving item $r =$ 0.89 and 3 withdrawal related items $r = 0.51–0.78$ (2-day interval; sample of inpatient cocaine dependents)	• Convergent: VCCS craving item correlated with CCQ total ($r = -0.83$)

* A version of this instrument had been used and tested among adolescents. Refer to section 4.1 for details.
† Instrument is available in other languages. Refer to section 4.2 for details.

and Young, 2008). In addition, the test–retest reliability coefficient for the overall score was reportedly high ($r = 0.96$) for an assessment interval of 24–48 hours in a moderate size (Inpatient $n = 71$; Outpatient $n = 18$ outpatients) sample of alcohol drinkers (Anton, Moak, and Latham, 1995).

Adequate correlations between the interview version of the Yale–Brown Obsessive Compulsive Scale for heavy drinking interview (YBOCS-hd; Modell *et al.*, 1992) and the OCDS have been observed, suggestive of this scale's validity. In addition, the OCDS has shown good correlations with the Alcohol Dependence Scale ($r = 0.42$), the alcohol composite score of the Addiction Severity Index ($r = 0.48$) and alcohol consumption amount ($r = 0.60$) (Anton, Moak, and Latham, 1996). The OCDS may be a useful screening instrument for the presence of alcohol abuse and dependence, and may be used to differentiate between non-problematic drinkers and individuals who are alcohol dependent (Anton, 2000). It has also been used as an indicator of progress during alcohol treatment, with increasing scores predictive of relapse drinking (e.g. Roberts, Anton, Latham, and Moak, 1999). This questionnaire is recommended by the National Institute on Alcohol Abuse and Alcoholism (NIAAA), the American Psychological Association (APA), and the Treatment Improvement Protocol Series 28 (TIP 28). However, depending on how the measure is scored, the inclusion of alcohol consumption items in the OCDS can implicitly equate alcohol intake with the construct of craving. For this reason, it is important to focus on the scales and scoring procedure that avoid confounding consumption and craving.

2.1.1.2   PENN ALCOHOL CRAVING SCALE.   The Penn Alcohol Craving Scale (PACS; Flannery, Volpicelli, and Pettinati, 1999) is a unidimensional, five-item self-report questionnaire that is designed to measure alcohol craving over the past week or another chosen timeframe using a Likert-type scale (range 0–6). The items in this instrument assess the frequency, intensity, duration of thoughts about drinking, ability to resist drinking, and average rating of craving over the course of the past week, with all items loading onto a single craving factor. The PACS is appropriate for adults, takes only 1–2 minutes to complete and less than 1 minute to score. The PACS has been shown to exhibit high internal consistency ($\alpha = 0.92$) in a large ($N = 147$) alcohol-dependent sample (Flannery, Volpicelli, and Pettinati, 1999). In addition, the PACS was found to have moderate construct validity in this sample, significantly correlating with the OCDS ($r = 0.55$) and the Alcohol Urge Questionnaire (AUQ; $r = 0.39$). However, it was not shown to correlate with the Drinker's Inventory of Consequences (DrInC; $r = 0.04$), a measure of adverse consequences associated with alcohol abuse, which the scale authors propose as evidence of discriminant validity. Some support for the predictive utility of the PACS is also demonstrated in a subset of this sample ($n = 133$), where a logistic regression analysis of craving during the second week of the study predicted alcohol relapse during weeks 3 to 12 of the trial, and in a separate analysis of individuals with alcohol dependence ($n = 183$), where weekly PACS scores were found to predict the number of standard drinks in the subsequent treatment week, over and above that of AUQ scores and pretreatment drinking levels (Flannery, Poole, Gallop, and Volpicelli, 2003; Flannery, Volpicelli, and Pettinati, 1999). The PACS has been used broadly in pharmacotherapy and psychotherapy treatment studies to examine the relationship between self-reported alcohol craving and drinking outcomes, as well as to examine intervention effects on alcohol craving (e.g. Flannery, Poole, Gallop, and Volpicelli, 2003).

2.1.1.3 ALCOHOL CRAVING QUESTIONNAIRE.   The Alcohol Craving Questionnaire (ACQ-Now; Singleton, Tiffany, and Henningfield, 1995) is a multidimensional, 47-item self-report questionnaire designed to be used as a measure of acute alcohol craving, although its length makes its use as a phasic measurement tentative and precludes repeated administrations over brief intervals (hence its inclusion in this section). This measure assesses the individual's level of craving at the time of administration, with each item rated on a 7-point Likert-type scale. Adapted from the Cocaine Craving Questionnaire (CCQ), this instrument assesses craving across four domains (subscales): expectancy (anticipation of positive outcomes from drinking), purposefulness (intention to drink for positive outcomes), emotionality (anticipation of relief from withdrawal symptoms or negative mood), and compulsivity. The ACQ-Now is recommended by NIAAA, is appropriate for adult populations, and takes approximately 5–10 minutes to complete, and another 5 minutes to score. Reliability estimates for the ACQ-Now in a large ($N = 217$) sample of non-problem drinkers have been found to be generally high in terms of internal consistency ($\alpha = 0.80$–0.94) (Connolly *et al.*, 2009). The ACQ-Now exhibits good predictive validity, correctly classifying 78.3% of alcohol dependents and 84.6% of non-dependents (driven mostly by the Compulsiveness factor). In addition, the Lack of Control subscale was found to be the only predictor of cue-elicited alcohol craving in a study assessing social drinkers and alcohol dependents (Connolly *et al.*, 2009).

In addition to a 12-item short form of the instrument (ACQ-SF-R), a modified version of the ACQ-Now has been proposed (ACQ-R) which includes 30 of the original 47 items. Psychometric analyses of the ACQ-R in a large ($N = 243$) German sample of individuals with alcohol dependence or abuse has identified a two-factor structure, with 21 items loading onto an "urge and intention to drink alcohol" factor, and the remaining 9 items loading onto a "positive and negative reinforcement" factor. The reliability of this factor solution exhibited very high internal consistency for both factors ($\alpha = 0.93$–0.96), and the test–retest reliability ($N = 46$ subset of original sample) for the factors and overall ACQ-R score were also found to be high ($r = 0.80$–0.89). The ACQ-R was found to have moderate convergent validity, with intercorrelations between the ACQ-R and OCDS factors ranging from 0.57 to 0.67 (Raabe *et al.*, 2005).

2.1.1.4 TEMPTATION AND RESTRAINT INVENTORY.   The Temptation and Restraint Inventory (TRI) (Collins and Lapp, 1992) is a multidimensional, 15-item self-report questionnaire developed to measure drinking restraint (i.e., the preoccupation with controlling the amount of alcohol intake). Using a 9-point Likert-type scale (range 1–9), this instrument assesses five factors including: govern (difficulty controlling alcohol intake), restrict (attempts to limit drinking), emotion (negative affect as a reason for drinking), concern about drinking (plans to reduce drinking/worry about controlling drinking), and cognitive preoccupation (thoughts about drinking). Two higher-order factors are constructed from these factors: Cognitive and Emotional Preoccupation (CEP) and Cognitive and Behavioral Concern (CBC). The TRI is recommended by the NIAAA, appropriate for adults, and takes approximately 10 minutes to complete. The five factors assessed by this scale exhibit adequate levels of internal consistency ($\alpha = 0.76$–0.91) in a very large sample of moderate to excessive drinkers ($N = 323$). The CEP and CBC subscales also exhibit adequate internal consistency ($\alpha = 0.91$ and 0.79, respectively) in this sample (Collins and Lapp, 1992). Additionally, the CEP factor of the TRI was found to have high positive correlations with the Preoccupation with Alcohol Scale (PAS; $r = 0.76$) and the Drinking-Related Locus of Control scale (DRIE; $r = 0.70$), suggesting good convergent validity with each measure. Significant negative correlations between the CEP subscale and the Self-Control factor of the Reasons for Limiting Drinking scale ($r = -0.19$) suggests good discriminant validity as well. The TRI factors were found to predict weekly alcohol consumption and alcohol-related problems, as measured by the Short Michigan Alcoholism Screening Test (SMAST) in a large ($N = 296$) sample of heavy drinking adults (Collins, Koutsky, and Izzo, 2000). The TRI has also been psychometrically validated in young adult drinkers at various levels of risk (MacKillop, Lisman, and Weinstein, 2006), with CEP and CBC scores significantly associated with level of drinking and level of alcohol dependence.

2.1.1.5   JELLINEK ALCOHOL CRAVING QUESTIONNAIRE.   The Jellinek Alcohol Craving Questionnaire (JACQ; Ooteman *et al.*, 2006) is a multidimensional, 24-item self-report questionnaire developed for use in adult populations to assess alcohol craving. Using a 1–5 Likert-type rating scale, the items span across four domains within the craving construct: emotional urge, physical sensations, temptation to drink, and uncontrolled thoughts. The JACQ-Past version of the scale relates to the frequency of craving experiences, whereas the JACQ-Now version assesses the intensity of an acute craving experience. It has been purported by the scale authors to be the only measure to include a scale relating to the subjective assessment of psychophysiological symptoms (Ooteman *et al.*, 2006). Psychometric analyses of the JACQ in a moderately sized ($N = 251$ and 48) Dutch sample of abstaining alcohol-dependent individuals reveal very good internal consistency (JACQ-Now $\alpha = 0.96$ and JACQ-Past $\alpha = 0.95$), and high test–retest reliability for the JACQ-Past, with intraclass correlation coefficient estimates of the subscales ranging from 0.76 to 0.88 (overall $ICC = 0.87$). The JACQ-Now and JACQ-Past total scores were found to be low to moderately correlated with the OCDS subscales ($r = 0.56$–0.61 for the Past scale and 0.26–0.28 for the Now scale). In contrast to the OCDS, the ACQ-Now was found to be highly correlated with all subscales of JACQ-Now ($r = 0.77$–0.87). The JACQ-Now scale was found to correlate highly with mean craving scores of three visual analog scales ($r = 0.79$) (Ooteman *et al.*, 2006), suggesting the JACQ-Now is a potentially useful measure of phasic craving.

2.1.1.6   PREOCCUPATION WITH ALCOHOL SCALE.   The Preoccupation with Alcohol Scale (PAS; Leonard, Harwood, and Blane, 1988) is a unidimensional, 14-item self-report measure of alcohol preoccupation which includes questions that assess: excessive concern over the availability of alcohol, the active seeking out of heavy drinking, and increased thoughts and behaviors around alcohol. The items are rated on a 7-point Likert-type scale and are thought to load onto a single factor of preoccupation. The PAS revealed high internal consistency in two independent samples

($N = 67$ and 127) of male regular drinkers (both $\alpha = 0.89$). In addition, the PAS was moderately correlated with the Quantity-Frequency Index (a measure of average daily consumption; $r = 0.49$), to scores on the Alcohol Dependency Scale (ADS; $r = 0.69$), and to the global measure of Serious Alcohol-related negative Incidents (SAI; $r = 0.59$) in this sample, suggestive of the validity of this scale (Leonard, Harwood, and Blane, 1988).

2.1.2 Measures of cigarette craving

2.1.2.1 QUESTIONNAIRE ON SMOKING URGES. The Questionnaire on Smoking Urges (QSU; Tiffany and Drobes, 1991) is a multidimensional, Likert-type, self-report questionnaire developed to assess cravings elicited by abstinence from cigarette smoking in adult populations. The 32-items on this measure are rated on a scale of 1–7 and span four facets of craving: desire to smoke, anticipation of relief from nicotine withdrawal or from withdrawal-associated negative affect, anticipation of positive outcomes from smoking, and intention to smoke. Two subscales are derived from the items: intention, desire and positive outcomes; and relief from withdrawal and negative emotions and strong desire. The QSU has been estimated to have high internal consistency ($\alpha = 0.95$ and 0.93 for the first and second subscales, respectively) with a moderate intercorrelation of the subscales ($r = 0.71$) in a large ($N = 230$) sample of adult daily smokers (averaging 20 or more cigarettes daily) (Tiffany and Drobes, 1991). The predictive validity of this scale was addressed by Wilner and colleagues in a sample of daily smoking university students ($N = 40$; 10 or more cigarettes per day). The authors found differential predictive utility by the subscales of the QSU depending on the level of nicotine deprivation. For the nondeprived subjects, the first factor of the QSU served as a strong predictor of cigarette liking and progressive-ratio operant performance, whereas for the deprived subjects the second factor predicted both cigarette liking and the breakpoint on the progressive-ratio schedule (Willner, Hardman, and Eaton, 1995).

2.1.2.2 TOBACCO CRAVING QUESTIONNAIRE. Adapted from the ACQ, the Tobacco Craving Questionnaire (TCQ; Heishman, Singleton, and Moolchan, 2003) is a multidimensional, 47-item self-report measure developed for the assessment of tobacco craving in adult individuals not attempting to reduce or quit smoking. Each of the 47 items is rated on a 7-point Likert-type scale, which takes an average of 8 minutes to complete. Similar to the Cocaine Craving Questionnaire (CCQ) and ACQ, the items on the TCQ span five facets of nicotine craving: lack of control over use, desire to smoke, intention and planning to smoke cigarettes, the anticipation of relief from nicotine withdrawal symptoms or relief from negative mood, and the anticipation of positive outcomes from smoking. The items have been shown to cluster together to produce four clinically distinct subscales: expectancy (anticipation of positive outcomes from smoking), purposefulness (intention to smoke for positive outcomes), emotionality (anticipation of relief from withdrawal symptoms or negative mood), and compulsivity. In a large ($N = 213$) sample of polydrug using adult smokers (averaging 26 cigarettes daily), the TCQ was found to have low to high internal consistency across the subscales ($\alpha = 0.48–0.82$), with average inter-item correlations ranging from 0.19 to 0.49 (Heishman, Singleton, and Moolchan, 2003). The validity of the TCQ has been supported in an independent sample of adult cigarette smokers ($N = 48$; smoking 10 or more cigarettes daily). Participants undergoing an imagery-script procedure designed to induce craving exhibited increased TCQ change scores as a function of craving intensity for all subscales; however, responses on the expectancy and purposefulness subscales were found to be significant only in the high-craving condition relative to the no-craving condition in this sample (Singleton, Anderson, and Heishman, 2003).

2.1.3   *Measures of illicit drug craving*

2.1.3.1   COCAINE CRAVING QUESTIONNAIRE.   There are two versions of the Cocaine Craving Questionnaire (CCQ; Tiffany, Singleton, Haertzen, and Henning-field, 1993): CCQ-General and CCQ-Now. Each version is a multidimensional, 45-item, self-report measure of cocaine craving in adults. A 7-point Likert-type scale is used to rate each item, many of which were adapted from the QSU. The CCQ-Now assesses current craving for cocaine, whereas the CCQ-Gen assesses average craving over the preceding week. Like the ACQ-Now, the length of the CCQ-Now precludes repeated administrations over brief time periods and makes its utility as a phasic mea-surement of craving unclear. The items comprising both versions of the CCQ assess five facets of cocaine craving: lack of control over use, desire to use cocaine, inten-tion and planning to use cocaine, the anticipation of relief from cocaine withdrawal symptoms or relief from negative mood, and the anticipation of positive outcomes from cocaine use. The items have been shown to factor together to produce four subscales: desire and intention, lack of control, positive and negative expectancies, and a remaining factor representing general craving.

Initial psychometrics were estimated on a large ($N = 225$) sample of adult, non-treatment-seeking, mostly male, cocaine users. Internal consistency estimates of the CCQ-Gen and CCQ-Now factors were found to be high ($\alpha = 0.70–0.93$). Predictive validity was also assessed in this sample, with higher total scores on both versions found to be associated with lower confidence in ability to quit using cocaine and greater fre-quency of use over the past 6 months. In addition, the first three subscales were found to be associated with frequency of cocaine use over the past 30-day interval (Tiffany, Singleton, Haertzen, and Henningfield, 1993). Recent analyses on a large ($N = 132$) independent cocaine-dependent sample of mixed gender reveal the CCQ-Now total score was significantly associated with time to relapse assessed at 90-day follow-up, with the intent and plan to use cocaine and anticipation of positive outcome from using cocaine subscales driving the relationship (Paliwal, Hyman, and Sinha, 2008).

Since the CCQ takes approximately 15 minutes to administer, a ten-item ver-sion of the CCQ (CCQ-Brief) was developed to provide a shorter measure of acute cocaine craving. The ten items were extracted from the general craving factor of the CCQ-Now. The CCQ-Brief as a global measure of craving exhibited high internal consistency ($\alpha = 0.87$), was highly correlated with the CCQ-Now summary score ($r = 0.87$), and was moderately correlated with the Cocaine Selective Severity

Assessment (CSSA) cocaine craving ($r = 0.46$), craving frequency ($r = 0.46$), desire visual analog subscale ($r = 0.47$), and urge visual analog subscale ($r = 0.49$) in a large ($N = 123$) sample of treatment-seeking individuals with cocaine dependence. In addition, there was a significant association of the CCQ-Brief total score and time to cocaine relapse assessed 90 days later (Paliwal, Hyman, and Sinha, 2008), suggestive of the predictive utility of this scale.

2.1.3.2 MINNESOTA COCAINE CRAVING SCALE. The Minnesota Cocaine Craving Scale (MCCS; Halikas *et al.*, 1991) is a multidimensional, five-item, self-report questionnaire developed to assess past-week cocaine craving in adult populations. The items are rated in multiple formats (i.e., 100 mm visual analogue scale, multiple choice, and Likert-type rating) and measure three dimensions (subscales) of cocaine craving: intensity of craving, frequency of episodes of craving, and duration of each episode of craving. The three subscales were found to correlate moderately with each other (r = 0.59–0.64) in a small ($N = 35$) sample of inpatient individuals with cocaine dependence. The internal consistency of the items was found to be high ($\alpha = 0.83$) and craving assessed with the MCCS was found to be positively related to cocaine use, with the intensity subscale correlating with number of days of cocaine use ($r = 0.39$), frequency of use ($r = 0.45$), and duration of use ($r = 0.28$) (Halikas *et al.*, 1991).

2.1.3.3 VORIS COCAINE CRAVING SCALE. The Voris Cocaine Craving Scale (VCCS) (Voris, Elder, and Sebastian, 1991) is a multidimensional, four-item self-report visual analogue scale developed to assess four aspects of cocaine craving and withdrawal: perceived craving, mood, energy, and health level. The items are reverse coded such that a high score on each item is associated with less of the construct. Each item is scored separately and no total score can be derived from the VCCS. Test–retest reliability over a period of 2 days was high for the craving item ($r = 0.89$) and slightly lower for the withdrawal related items ($r = 0.51$–0.78) in a small ($N = 25$) sample of inpatient individuals with cocaine dependence. In a sample of 41 recently withdrawn cocaine-dependent patients (39 men and 2 women), the craving item of the VCCS was found to correlate highly with the Cocaine Craving Questionnaire (CCQ) total craving score ($r = 0.83$). Significant, yet somewhat lower correlations were also found for the mood and health items ($r = 0.43$ and 0.33, respectively) (Smelson, McGee-Caulfield, Bergstein, and Engelhart, 1999). However, the subscales of the VCCS failed to correlate with 30-day drug use in a large ($N = 247$) sample of treatment-seeking individuals with cocaine dependence (Sussner *et al.*, 2006).

2.1.3.4 OBSESSIVE COMPULSIVE DRUG USE SCALE. The Obsessive Compulsive Drug Use Scale (OCDUS) (Franken, Hendriks, and van den Brink, 2002) is a multidimensional, 12-item (with item 10 deleted, as advised by the scale authors), Likert-type self-report questionnaire adapted from the OCDS to assess general craving for heroin over the past week. Small modifications were made to the OCDS instrument to make the instrument applicable to heroin craving (including replacing the word "alcohol" by "heroin"). In addition, two questions from the OCDS that refer to the frequency of actual alcohol consumption were replaced by two items that refer to the frequency of urges and drive to use heroin, and the two items that refer to the interference of consumption with social life and leisure activities separately were combined into one item that refers to the interference heroin craving has on social life. This process resulted in three subscales that roughly correspond to the OCDS subscales: heroin thoughts and interference, desire and control, and resistance to thoughts and intention. Internal consistency of the thoughts, desire, and resistance subscales were found to be high ($\alpha = 0.90, 0.89, 0.91$, respectively) and test–retest reliability for the scales over a 2-day interval was good ($ICC = 0.79, 0.72$, and 0.79, respectively) in a large ($N = 102$) sample of detoxified (80% male) heroin-dependent patients. Convergent validity of the OCDUS was estimated to be adequate, as the OCDUS significantly correlated with a visual analogue scale of craving ($r = 0.76$) (Franken, Hendriks, and van den Brink, 2002).

2.1.3.5 HEROIN CRAVING QUESTIONNAIRE. Like the ACQ and CCQ, the Heroin Craving Questionnaire (HCQ; Tiffany *et al.*, 1993) is a multidimensional, self-report questionnaire designed to assess five theoretically distinct conceptualizations of craving in an adult population: desire to use heroin, purposefulness (intention to use heroin), expectancy (anticipation of positive outcome from heroin use), emotionality (anticipation of relief from withdrawal or dysphoria), and compulsivity. The items have been shown to factor together to produce four subscales: desire and intention, lack of control, positive and negative expectancies, and a remaining factor representing general craving. There are two versions of the HCQ: the HCQ-14 and HCQ-45. The HCQ-14 contains 14 items extracted from the 45-item version. The HCQ-45 takes approximately 15 minutes to administer. Responses to each item are recorded on a 7-point Likert-type scale. A total craving score can be derived by summing the individual items. The HCQ-45 total score was found to be highly reliable ($\alpha = 0.94$) in a sample (*n* not available) of non-treatment-seeking heroin users (Tiffany *et al.*, 1993).

Psychometric properties of the two versions of the HCQ were evaluated in a large sample of individuals with opiate dependence ($N = 101$). The single higher-order factors from both the 14- and 45-item HCQs were found to be highly correlated ($r = 0.57$). Concurrent validity was supported for the desire subscale of the HCQ, as this subscale was found to significantly correlate with the craving and want items on a heroin craving visual analogue scale ($r = 0.54$ and 0.53, respectively); however, no other subscales from the HCQ-45 demonstrated correlations above 0.5 (although they reached levels of significance in most cases). The total score from the 14-item HCQ demonstrated significant relationships with all three (crave, want, and need) visual analog craving scales (Heinz *et al.*, 2006). Some support of the predictive utility of this scale was observed in the sample of individuals with opiate dependence: small but statistically significant positive correlations were found between the total score and desire subscale of the HCQ-45, and the number of heroin-negative urines and percentage of heroin-negative urines during a 12-week treatment program ($r = 0.22$–0.31) (Heinz *et al.*, 2006).

2.1.3.6 MARIJUANA CRAVING QUESTIONNAIRE. The Marijuana Craving Questionnaire (MCQ; Heishman, Singleton, and Liguori, 2001) is a multidimensional, 45-item, self-report questionnaire that assesses marijuana craving in adult populations. Adapted from the CCQ, the MCQ contains items rated on a 7-point Likert-type scale that factor into four subscales of marijuana craving: compulsivity (inability to control marijuana use), emotionality (marijuana use in anticipation of relief from withdrawal or negative mood), expectancy (anticipation of positive outcomes from smoking marijuana), and purposefulness (intention and planning to use marijuana for positive outcomes). Psychometric properties of the MCQ were assessed in a large sample ($N = 217$) of current, non-treatment-seeking marijuana smokers (79% male). Internal consistency of the four subscales was found to be moderate to good, with the lowest reliability estimate found for the expectancy factor ($\alpha = 0.55$) and the highest for the compulsivity factor ($\alpha = 0.82$) (Heishman, Singleton, and Liguori, 2001). The MCQ subscales were found to be significantly correlated with history of marijuana use and a wide range of measures of craving, including single-item measures and visual analogue scales in this, as well as another sample of current marijuana smokers (Heishman, Singleton, and Liguori, 2001; Singleton *et al.*, 2002), suggestive of the convergent validity of this scale. A short form of the MCQ (MCQ-SF), consisting of three items from each of the four MCQ subscales, has also been developed. The MCQ-SF was found to measure the same four latent constructs as the MCQ in a very large ($N = 490$) sample of adult marijuana smokers, with similar internal consistency reliability estimates ($\alpha = 0.61–0.84$). Scores on all MCQ-SF subscales increased as a function of increasing frequency and duration of craving episodes, supporting the construct validity of this measure (Heishman, Singleton, and Liguori, 2009).

2.1.3.7 BENZODIAZEPINE CRAVING QUESTIONNAIRE. The Benzodiazepine Craving Questionnaire (BCQ; Mol *et al.*, 2003) is a unidimensional, 20-item self-report questionnaire that assesses benzodiazepine craving in adult populations. Adapted from the QSU and CCQ, the BCQ contains items rated on a 7-point Likert-type scale that spans the four domains assessed by the QSU: desire to use, anticipation of positive outcome from benzodiazepine use, anticipation of relief from withdrawal or withdrawal-associated negative affect, and intention to use. The scale authors included a fifth category, lack of control over use, as assessed in CCQ. Unlike the CCQ and QSU, analysis of the factor structure of the BCQ revealed a unidimensional scale in which the items could be ranked according to craving intensity, and thus a single total score derived from the item sum is advised for use as a measure of overall craving of benzodiazepines. Analysis of the subject discriminability (internal consistency) was found to be very high (KR-20 = 0.94; the Kuder–Richardson Formula 20 is a measure of internal consistency reliability equivalent to Cronbach's α for dichotomous items) in a Dutch sample of current and former long-term benzodiazepine users ($N = 113$) (Mol *et al.*, 2003). In addition, current benzodiazepine users scored significantly higher on the BCQ (i.e., reported more severe craving) than those who had quit by the time of assessment (Mol *et al.*, 2003), suggesting that the BCQ can differentiate between active and past users.

2.2 Phasic craving measures

2.2.1 Single-item phasic scales. Single-item scales are frequently used and provide some advantages to the assessment of phasic craving. Among these advantages are the face validity of the majority of these items and the ease of administration under various conditions, such as constrained laboratory settings where multiple-choice responses are difficult (e.g., in neuroimaging protocols) or ecological validity studies where respondents are less likely to complete lengthy questionnaires. The sensitivity to rapid fluctuations of craving states and the suitability for repeated and frequent administration make many single-item scales ideal for laboratory-based phasic assessments. Visual Analogue Scales (VASs) are commonly used single-item measures of phasic craving. Often employing a Likert-type rating scale, these scales are anchored by terms such as "none" or "0," and "extreme" or "100," with the respondent instructed to circle a numerical value or place a mark along a dimension to indicate the degree of acute craving.

However, several potential limitations must be considered before employing a single-item scale for the measurement of phasic craving. For example, single-item scales are inherently limited to assessing a single dimension of what some would argue is a multidimensional construct including cognitive, affective, physiological, and behavioral components (e.g. Tiffany and Drobes, 1991). However, others suggest this concern may be unfounded due to the high correlations observed between single-item and multi-item scales (Rosenberg, 2009). Operationalizing craving for respondents attempts to alleviate some of this concern, although doing so may lead to biased responses (Pickens and Johanson, 1992). In addition, the appropriate analysis of responses acquired on VASs is subject to debate. Although they are commonly treated as interval scales, some argue that the intervals between ratings on these scales differ as a function of location along the continuum (e.g., the interval between 20 and 30 may be meaningfully different from that between 90 and 100 on a 100-mm VAS) and thus should be transformed or analyzed as nonparametric data (Rosenberg, 2009). Other limitations include semantic issues, as some individuals may perceive the term "craving" to have pejorative connotations, and no nuances can be communicated using a single-item measure. As an example, the current assessment of craving for ICD-10 in the Semi-Structured Assessment for the Genetics of Alcoholism (SSAGA) (Bucholz *et al.*, 1994) consists of the following single item: "Did you ever want a drink so much that you could almost taste it?". While this item has been used in genetic studies of drug craving (Ehlers, Gizer, Vieten, and Wilhelmsen, 2010), it is unclear whether this single item fully captures the construct of craving. A final point is that single-item measures cannot be examined in terms of internal reliability, which makes them more psychometrically opaque than multi-item measures. Given that multi-item measures exist and even ad hoc multi-item measures address these issues, on balance, the benefits of multi-item measures generally justify the increased length, although some designs may preclude their use (e.g., neuroimaging paradigms).

2.2.2 Multi-item Phasic Scales.   As noted above, multi-item scales are putatively better able to capture the dimensional nature of the craving construct based on the increase in reliability, and thus power, achieved by increasing the total number of items. Caution must be employed when using these scales for the assessment of phasic craving, however, as they have the potential to induce responder reactivity depending on the length and repetition of assessment (Sayette *et al.*, 2000). In other words, individuals may report increases in craving as a result of being repeatedly asked to observe and report on their craving levels.

2.2.2.1 ALCOHOL URGE QUESTIONNAIRE. The Alcohol Urge Questionnaire (AUQ) (Bohn, Krahn, and Staehler, 1995) is a multidimensional, eight-item self-report measure of drinking urges developed for use in adult populations. Employing a seven-point Likert-type rating scale, the AUQ assesses desire to drink (four items), expectation of a positive effect from drinking (two items), and inability to avoid drinking if alcohol was available (two items), together loading on a single urge factor. Recommended by the TIP 28, the AUQ exhibited excellent internal consistency in a sample of 40 individuals with alcohol dependence. The test–retest reliability of this measure exhibited high reliability for a 1-day interval ($r = 0.82$), as well as a 1-week interval ($r = 0.78$). The AUQ also exhibited moderate concurrent validity in this sample, significantly correlating with the OCDS ($r = 0.42$). In addition, higher AUQ scores were related to higher alcohol dependence severity (measured by the ADS) and shorter duration of abstinence (Bohn, Krahn, and Staehler, 1995), suggestive of the construct validity of this measure. AUQ scores were found to increase in a sample of adult heavy drinkers following a standardized alcohol cue exposure, supporting the scale's utility in real-time laboratory urge assessment (MacKillop, 2006). The unidimensionality of the AUQ was confirmed both in a neutral craving state and in a high craving state (MacKillop, 2006).

2.2.2.2 BRIEF QUESTIONNAIRE ON SMOKING URGES. The Brief Questionnaire on Smoking Urges (QSU-Brief; Cox, Tiffany, and Christen, 2001) is a shortened version of the full-scale QSU, using ten items (some slightly reworded to reduce method variance) from two of the full-scale dimensions (desire to smoke and anticipation of relief from nicotine withdrawal), which can be completed in less than 2 minutes. The QSU-Brief uses a 100-point scale ranging from "strongly disagree" to "strongly agree" to rate each item. The QSU-Brief has similar psychometric properties as the full-length version, with high internal consistency ($\alpha = 0.76$–0.90 for the subscales and 0.92–0.93 for the total score across 3 weeks of assessment). Test–retest correlations between scores were also adequate, ranging from 0.71 to 0.81 for the subscales and total score across 7 weeks of testing. The predictive utility of this measure was also reported, where lower levels of craving were predictive of an increased likelihood of cessation in a very large sample ($N = 626$) of daily (≥ 10 cigarettes daily) smokers undergoing smoking cessation (Cappelleri *et al.*, 2007).

2.2.3 Magnitude estimation. Magnitude estimation is a method used to avoid problematic ceiling effects that often occur in studies where pre-manipulation craving responses approach the maximum values of the scale employed (e.g., studies requiring periods of abstinence prior to assessment). This method entails asking respondents to evaluate the degree of their craving level in relation to their previous craving rating. In practice, a magnitude estimate is achieved by first asking the responder to rate their craving on a given scale and subsequent ratings are then given as degrees of variation from this initial rating (e.g., if their initial craving level was given a value of 50 and the responder reports their craving in a subsequent condition to be double the initial level, it would be given a value of 100). The advantage of the magnitude estimation method is that the scale has no maximum endpoint, and thus no ceiling is ever reached. In most cases, standardized magnitude choices are not given to responders, leading to variability in individual interpretations of craving magnitudes; however, this limitation can be said of all self-report dimensional scales. Thus, training prior to assessment is advised when using a magnitude estimation approach. Additionally, statistical analysis of magnitude estimation scores must be carefully considered as these scores are rarely distributed normally and may not be applicable for interval-level analyses (Sayette *et al.*, 2000).

3   Additional Indices of Craving

Self-reports of subjective craving are commonly used in research and clinical practice. However, self-report instruments are subject to biases, such as recall bias (especially for measures of tonic craving) and social desirability bias (particularly important in clinical settings). In addition, individuals may vary in their interpretation of subjective craving items, which may also affect the reliability of self-report instruments. To address these concerns, a number of alternative indices of craving have been developed and validated in the literature. Next we review a series of such assessments with a focus on their psychometric properties. While these indices are typically embedded into an experimental manipulation, we describe such methods in brief, so as to maintain a focus on assessment issues.

3.1   Cognitive indices

Individuals who are in a craving state frequently show impaired cognitive processing. Eliciting craving through exposure to substance-related cues in laboratory studies has been found to impair working memory, a cognitive process related to effective decision making (Bechara and Martin, 2004), and affect an individual's temporal perception. For example, craving has been shown to both increase reaction time (Sayette *et al.*, 1994) and interfere with cognitive resource allocation (Sayette and Hufford, 1994). Further, while craving, individuals often overestimate the duration and intensity of their own future urges (Sayette, Loewenstein, Kirchner, and Travis, 2005).

Attention processes are also affected by drug craving. Attentional biases of substance-related stimuli develop through the repeated pairing of drug intake with the present contextual and interoceptive cues and, over repeated pairing, substance-related stimuli come to elicit or be associated with subjective craving (Field and Cox, 2008). Several tasks have been adapted to assess attentional bias of drug addiction in laboratory settings. This approach is based on the assumption that substance-related stimuli will capture the attention of individuals who are craving, resulting in less attention being allocated to secondary tasks. Studies that have used the Addictions Stroop Task (Cox, Fadardi, and Pothos, 2006), the Dot-Probe Task (Robbins and Ehrman, 2004), measures of eye tracking (Field, Eastwood, Bradley, and Mogg, 2006; Mogg, Bradley, Field, and De Houwer, 2003), and event-related potentials (Field, Munafò, and Franken, 2009) have demonstrated that individuals who use drugs display attentional bias for substance-related stimuli. A thorough review of these tasks is beyond the scope of this chapter; however, it is important to highlight that attentional bias elicited through these paradigms may be conceptualized as an indirect measure of craving, and that attentional bias of substance-related stimuli may elicit subjective craving or vice versa (Field, Munafò, and Franken, 2009). Nevertheless, craving seems to have an effect at different levels of attention as measured by these tasks. For example, the Addiction Stroop Task assesses the interference of substance-related stimuli in the ability to allocate attention to the task of naming the color of the presented substance-related word. Longer reaction times in the Addiction Stroop Task have been found to distinguish abusers and non-abusers of cannabis (Field, 2005), tobacco, and alcohol (Cox, Fadardi, and Pothos, 2006). The Dot-Probe Task indirectly assesses the maintenance of attention as individuals identify the location of a probe that follows the presentation of a substance-related stimulus and a control stimulus side by side. The faster reaction times to trials where the probe replaced a substance-related stimulus exhibited by abusers of alcohol (Townshend and Duka, 2001), nicotine (Ehrman *et al.*, 2002), and opiates (Lubman *et al.*, 2000) suggest these individuals maintain longer attention to substance-related stimuli compared to neutral stimuli. Tracking the fixation and eye movements as individuals are presented with a task such as the Dot-Probe provides a direct measure of initial orientation and maintenance of attention. For example, current smokers and heavy drinkers have been found to orient faster to and maintain longer attention on substance-related stimuli (Field *et al.*, 2011; Mogg, Bradley, Field, and De Houwer, 2003). Similarly, measuring event-related brain potentials (ERPs; e.g., P300, P3, late positive potential) as individuals are presented with substance-related stimuli has been used to more directly assess attention processing of substance-related stimuli. ERP studies with users of tobacco, opiates, and cocaine indicate that users display greater processing of substance-related cues (Franken *et al.*, 2008; Littel and Franken, 2007; Lubman, Allen, Peters, and Deakin, 2008).

3.2   Affective indices

Craving is often accompanied by automatic changes in affect. Laboratory studies have adapted measures used to study subjective emotional responses to assess affective indices of craving elicited in response to substance-related cues. The Facial Action Coding System (FACS) (Eckman and Friesen, 1978) and Facial electromyography (EMG) (Cacioppo, Petty, Losch, and Kim, 1986) are two methods often utilized to infer affective states from facial expressions upon cue exposure. In the FACS, recordings of participants' facial expressions are coded frame by frame, whereas the EMG detects key facial muscles subcutaneously (i.e., zygomaticus major and corrugators supercilii) in real time by way of electrodes placed directly on the face. Both approaches have shown that positive and negative affect are related to craving. For instance, using EMG, greater levels of dependence among individuals dependent on nicotine were associated with more prominent negative affect (Robinson *et al.*, 2011). Opportunity to smoke has been found to elicit affect in diverse ways; for example, when the delay was 15 seconds, smokers displayed positive affect; however, positive affect decreased among those delayed by 60 seconds (Sayette *et al.*, 2003). Further, drinking alcohol prior to smoking cue exposure has been shown to be associated with positive affect (Sayette *et al.*, 2005).

Subjective implicit affective associations with substance-related stimuli have also been used as an indicator of craving. The Implicit Association Test (IAT) (Greenwald, McGhee, and Schwartz, 1998) assesses the strength of the implicit associations between substance-related stimuli and an assigned positively or negatively paired word. Using this task, smokers have been shown to exhibit an implicit negative attitude toward smoking, but craving seems to be associated with less negative implicit attitudes toward smoking (Waters *et al.*, 2007). In studies of hazardous drinkers where alcohol-related words and neutral words were associated with approach and avoid cues, those with higher implicit approach attitudes reported stronger urges to drink, a greater number of drinks, and a greater number of binge episodes (Ostafin and Palfai, 2006; Palfai and Ostafin, 2003).

3.3   Psychophysiological indices

Craving may elicit psychophysiological changes as conditional responses to substance-related cues. Commonly studied psychophysiological indices in laboratory studies include heart rate, skin conductance, skin temperature, salivation, and startle–eye-blink response (for an extended review, see Chapter 21). It is not definite whether increased or decreased physiological cue reactivity is associated with craving or whether reactivity is universal across substances. For example, a meta-analysis found that increased heart rate was associated with craving in studies of alcohol, nicotine, and cocaine but not opiates; increased sweat gland activity was found in craving studies of alcohol, nicotine, opiates, and cocaine; and decreased skin conductance was reported only in studies of opiates and cocaine (Carter and Tiffany, 1999). Changes in salivation have also been associated with craving (Monti *et al.*, 1993); however, other studies have found positive, negative, and no relationships between craving and salivation (Coffey *et al.*, 1999; Field and Duka, 2001; MacKillop *et al.*, 2010b). Magnitude of the startle–eye-blink response to substance-related cues has also been used to assess craving indirectly. Startle response is an indicator of the positive or negative affective valence attributed to presented stimuli. It is not yet clear whether a potentiated or attenuated startle–eye-blink response is indicative of craving as studies have reported both findings. For instance, smoking cues have been found to elicit negative affect and a corresponding enhanced startle response (Elash, Tiffany, and Vrana, 1995). On the other hand, a study that compared alcohol-dependent individuals, social drinkers, and controls found that individuals who were dependent showed an inhibited startle response to alcohol cues (Grusser *et al.*, 2002). Assessing psychophysiological measures of craving is promising as these offer the advantage of being more automatic and less susceptible to the conscious processes associated with reporting subjective craving. Nevertheless, further research is needed to reliably establish the psychophysiological aspects of craving.

3.4   Behavioral economic measures

Behavioral economics is a hybrid field that integrates concepts from psychology and economics to understand decision making and the choices people make (MacKillop *et al.*, 2011). A behavioral economic approach has been extensively applied to the study of addictive behavior, including the measurement of craving. In this domain, behavioral economic measures quantify motivation using diverse methods, all of which have the common property of having one or more levels of *response cost*. In other words, drug consumption is made contingent on a tangible consequence (cf., *ad libitum* self-administration), such as effortful responses on a behavioral task or exchanging money for access to the drug (for a more detailed review, see Chapter 12), which putatively reflect how much the individual values the drug. Thus, a behavioral economic approach characterizes motivation using what are considered more objective indices of the relative value of the drug to the individual. Although much less widely used than self-report measures of craving, behavioral economic measures have been shown to complement subjective craving in studies using both tonic and phasic approaches (MacKillop, Menges, McGeary, and Lisman, 2007; MacKillop *et al.*, 2010a; MacKillop *et al.*, 2010b; Sayette *et al.*, 2001; Willner, Hardman, and Eaton, 1995).

3.5   Impulsivity

Impulsivity is a well-established risk factor for drug addiction, theorized to serve as both an antecedent and a consequence, but it can be challenging to concisely define as there are numerous different methods for measuring impulsivity (de Wit, 2009). Generally speaking, these can be divided into three domains: self-reported personality traits, behavioral tasks measuring delay discounting (i.e., how much a reward is discounted based on its delay in time, also referred to as capacity to delay gratification), and behavioral tasks measuring behavioral inhibition, or capacity to inhibit behavioral responses. Importantly, these domains are largely independent of one another (Cyders and Coskunpinar, 2011; Courtney *et al.*, 2012). Vis-à-vis craving, impulsivity is highly relevant to craving as it can be broadly defined as a person's proneness to respond to an impulse, with arising cravings being one such impulse. Thus, individuals who are higher in impulsivity may be more likely to act on cravings. Moreover, as states that are intrusive, powerfully felt, and cognitively demanding, the experience of craving may also potentiate how impulsive a person is. Although a full review is beyond the scope of this chapter (see Chapters 5, 6, and 7), there is evidence in support of these roles. For example, tonic levels of alcohol craving and delay discounting have been found to be significantly associated with one another (MacKillop *et al.*, 2010a) and personality measures of impulsivity are associated with cue-elicited craving and arousal (Doran, McChargue, and Spring, 2008; Doran, Spring, and McChargue, 2007). In addition, laboratory studies using withdrawal manipulations that induce craving also make delay discounting more impulsive (Field *et al.*, 2006; Giordano *et al.*, 2002; Mitchell, 2004). This is not always the case, however, as environmental drug cues, which are known to increase craving, have not been found to increase discounting (Field, Rush, Cole, and Goudie, 2007). However, a significant issue in this domain is that craving and impulsivity have only recently been studied together and most impulsivity measures are trait-level measures, both relatively lengthy in duration and designed for assessing relatively stable preferences. As phasic increases in craving are known to be an acute experiential state that decays relatively rapidly (MacKillop and Lisman, 2008; Madden and Zwaan, 2001; Staiger and White, 1991; Zwaan, Stanfield, and Madden, 2000), these measures may not be well suited for examining dynamic processes and, in turn, testing hypotheses about the relationship between craving and self-regulation. Careful consideration of these issues is important during study design and further progress in this area is one of the priorities we will address at the conclusion of the chapter.

3.6   Behavioral indices

In laboratory studies, latency to first substance self-administration serves as a possible indicator of craving. Participants are asked to refrain from using substances and are permitted to do so at differing time points. The mean duration time from the moment they are allowed to use the substance and self-administration serves as an indicator of motivation (MacKillop and Lisman, 2005). Speed of substance consumption has also been related to the participants' deprivation time prior to self-administration of the substance within laboratory paradigms (Rankin, Hodgson, and Stockwell, 1979). Smoking topography have also been used to index craving. Topography measures include number of cigarettes smoked, puff duration, puff volume, peak flow, time to peak, puff frequency, and strength and volume of inter-puff interval (Hogarth, Dickinson, and Duka, 2010; Kashinsky, Collins, and Brandon, 1995; Tidey, Rohsenow, Kaplan, and Swift, 2005). These indices are typically measured by the Clinical Research Support System (CRESS; Borgwaldt KC), which collects the data in real time and converts them to the topography indices.

3.7   Approach/avoidance motivation

In addition to measuring craving in the sense of capturing motivation to consume a drug, there is also increasing interest in capturing the ambivalence that often accompanies drug craving. This refers to ambivalence in a literal sense – a person being both drawn to the drug by desire for it and repelled by it by desire to abstain. Thus, approach and avoidance motivation can be simultaneously present and the latter is largely unmeasured in most assessments. Although only a small number of studies have been conducted in this domain to date, the presence of both approach and avoidance motives has been demonstrated to be present in the case of craving for cocaine (Avants, Margolin, Kosten, and Cooney, 1995), alcohol (Curtin *et al.*, 2005; McEvoy *et al.*, 2004; Smith-Hoerter, Stasiewicz, and Bradizza, 2004), and tobacco (Stritzke, Breiner, Curtin, and Lang, 2004).

4   Special Considerations

4.1   Developmental considerations

4.1.1   Adolescence.   Substance use typically begins in adolescence, and whereas most teens stop using substances as they transition to adulthood (Brown *et al.*, 2008), some escalate their use and ultimately become substance dependent. Developmentally appropriate measures of craving could potentially help distinguish adolescent users who use substances recreationally from heavy or dependent users. A limited number of self-report craving measures are available. For example, the Adolescent Obsessive-Compulsive Drinking Scale (A-OCDS) (Deas, Roberts, Randall, and Anton, 2001) is based on the adult OCDS and has been adapted to an adolescent sample, aged 14–20, and includes the same number of items as the adult version.

4.1.2 Older adults. Epidemiological findings indicate that older adults (65 and older) are less likely to use substances than their younger counterparts (Compton, Yonette, Frederick, and Bridget, 2007; Hasin, Stinson, Ogburn, and Grant, 2007), but do report higher rates of use of prescribed medications and medical comorbidities that may place them at greater risk for substance use (Lin *et al.*, 2011). Craving is assessed using the same instruments developed for adults. Whereas it is likely that these instruments are appropriate for this age group, there are no studies to suggest that these measures exhibit the same reliability and validity among older adults. Caution should be exerted when using these measures to assess craving among this age group.

4.2   Cultural considerations

The majority of assessment instruments have been developed and validated in the United States and western Europe. Most validation studies include ethnically homo-geneous samples, particularly those conducted among college students. Thus, it is critical to identify whether the craving instruments currently available are appropriate for use among non-English-speaking groups and ethnic minority groups. Neverthe-less several instruments have been translated into other languages, largely in countries other than the United States. However, it is important to exercise some caution in using these instruments. As highlighted by a recent study of lexicology, the concept of "craving" is very difficult to translate into other languages and a synonym is mostly absent from non-Western cultures (Hormes and Rozin, 2010). Thus, translating and adapting the concept of craving in the ways in which Western cultures assess this important indicator may not tap into the same concepts as originally intended.

The following measures have been translated and validated in the languages indi-cated: (a) the Obsessive Compulsive Drinking Scale has been translated and vali-dated into: Dutch (Schippers *et al.*, 1997), French (Chignon *et al.*, 1998), German (Mann and Ackerman, 2000), Italian (Janiri *et al.*, 2004), Japanese (Tatsuzawa *et al.*, 2002), and Spanish (Cordero *et al.*, 2009). The OCDS has also been translated into Hebrew and Swedish but it is unclear whether these instruments have been validated in these languages; (b) the Penn Alcohol Craving Scale has been translated and vali-dated to Korean (Kim *et al.*, 2008). The PACS has also been translated to Russian but it is unclear if it has been validated in this language; (c) the Jellinek Alcohol Craving Questionnaire-Now was developed and validated in a Dutch sample in the Netherlands (Ooteman *et al.*, 2006). The English version was provided by the developers but it is unclear whether it has been validated in a primarily English-speaking sample. This instrument has not been translated to other languages; (d) The Marijuana Craving Questionnaire has been translated into Portuguese and validated in a Brazilian sample (Pedroso, da Graça, and Araujo, 2009); and (e) The Questionnaire on Smoking Urges-Brief has been translated to Spanish and validated in a Spanish sample (Cepeda-Benito and Reig-Ferrer, 2004).

5   Limitations and Recommendations

The valid assessment of craving in addiction research has advanced enormously in the last two decades, but a number of limitations remain and point to priorities for future research. For example, at a narrow level, one clear limitation is that the majority of the measures reviewed remain incomplete with regard to psychometric validation. This may seem to be relatively prosaic, but fully clarifying the psychometric properties of a measure is nonetheless essential for improving measurement across studies. A second limitation is that of redundancy. Clearly there are several options in the various domains and few studies conduct head-to-head tests of different craving measures to establish which among them is superior or, if equal, which is more efficient. This issue will become even more pressing as craving is added to the DSM-V as a symptom of substance use disorders (www.dsm5.org) and there is an increasing need by clinicians for validated and standardized measures. Some of the scales have been tested in terms of classification on diagnostic status as reported above. Moreover, even in the absence of those data, there currently exist no clinical guidelines or "cut-off" severity scores to inform clinicians. If craving is to be an explicit focus of clinical diagnosis, the measures used to quantify craving must be fully characterized in terms and optimized for clinical use.

Beyond further validation of the existing measures, it should not be presumed that those measures are already optimal and cannot be improved upon. The domains included are often relatively narrow and a broader limitation is that current measures may not be capturing important nuances of the phenomenon of subjective desire. For example, mental imagery across sensory channels appears to be critical to the experience of craving (Kavanagh, Andrade, and May, 2005), across a range of substances, even food (May, Andrade, Panabokke, and Kavanagh, 2004; Smeets, Roefs, and Jansen, 2009). This line of work makes a compelling case for elaborated sensory imagery serving as a gateway to intense episodes of craving and the need for these elements to be captured in assessments. Similarly, it has long been recognized that, depending on the circumstances, craving can be affectively positive or negative (Baker, Morse, and Sherman, 1986) and may vary in the extent to which it is unpleasant. For example, intense urges for individuals who are actively in treatment and fighting to resist them may be very unpleasant, but for individuals who are not seeking treatment, anticipatory desire may be positive – a relishing of imminent consumption. This is provisionally supported by differences in affect accompanying craving across these different groups (MacKillop, 2006; Rohsenow, Monti, Abrams, Rubonis, 1992), but whether a craving is experienced as distressing is not directly captured in current phasic measures.

Finally, the preceding points pertain to limitations in the measurement of subjective desire, but another limitation is the need for continued progress to better understand craving beyond subjective self-report. There is a large literature documenting that individuals are by no means perfect at inferring the underlying motives for their actions via introspection (Wilson and Dunn, 2004). Therefore, a continuing priority will be applying diverse tools from cognitive science, behavioral economics, and other areas to fully characterize the multiple dimensions of acute motivation. Mixed and ambiguous findings will remain a likely outcome in future studies if there is not greater clarification of these other domains. However, it is often difficult to validate these indices as they are variably related to subjective craving and no biological gold standard of craving is available. For example, a recent fMRI-based investigation of craving for marijuana reported a null association between self-reported craving and BOLD signal response during a cue-exposure task in the scanner (Filbey *et al.*, 2009). These findings highlight the need for clearer consensus on what constitute the key elements of craving in addiction, which in turn can be used to refine the available assessment instruments.

These limitations provide priorities for the field and recommendations for current practices in experimental research. For researchers, the optimal selection of a measure of craving hinges upon a number of considerations, such as: the purpose of the assessment (e.g., clinical versus research), the time frame to be covered (e.g., tonic versus phasic), the patient population (e.g., social drinkers versus alcohol dependent; adults versus adolescents), substance of interest (e.g., alcohol, cocaine, cigarettes), and the experimental design (e.g., cue-exposure, neuroimaging task, medication study). For example, if the study is laboratory investigation of the effects of a manipulation on craving, it is important to identify high-quality phasic measures; however, if the study is a clinical trial and craving assessments will be taken weekly at office visits, a high-quality tonic measure will be necessary. In the first case, a tonic measure is unlikely to be sensitive to a laboratory manipulation, creating a false negative finding, and, in the second, phasic craving assessed during an office visit in a clinical setting may not be representative of the person's motivational state under naturalistic conditions since the last visit. With regard to quality of the measure, we recommend researchers select and implement the measures that have been most extensively psychometrically validated for the design being implemented. Moreover, even if the study's aims are not primarily that of validation, it is important to examine and report the properties of the measures (e.g., internal reliability) to contribute to the ongoing development of the measures. If, for example, an item on a multi-item measure was determined to be suboptimal (e.g., low item-total correlations) and the findings are in higher resolution by removing that item, 'tweaking' the measure by dropping the item and reporting the modified use of the measure would be warranted. Similarly, reporting both aggregate and item-level findings may be informative to the field, revealing which items are most sensitive across studies. In other words, we recommend a two-pronged approach to measure selection: researchers should select measures based on the strongest evidentiary and practical fit for a given study, but also use critical thinking in each investigation and use ongoing research as an opportunity to improve the measurement of craving.

Taken together, while a number of relatively high-quality measures of alcohol and other drug craving have been developed over the past two decades, the scientific study of the nature and role of craving in drug addiction remains very much a work-in-progress. For researchers who are actively using craving as a dependent variable, careful measure selection and an appreciation for the strengths and weaknesses of existing measures and, more generally, subjective self-report will be essential. Although limitations and challenges remain, they are by no means insurmountable, quite the opposite, and the prospect for continued progress via instrument refinement and innovation is very high. Ultimately, although the etiological, clinical, and translational relevance of craving remains high, its role in research and practice hinges on its valid assessment, making the importance of continued progress in this area essential.

References

Anton RF (2000) Obsessive-compulsive aspects of craving: Development of the Obsessive Compulsive Drinking Scale. *Addiction* 95: 211–217.

Anton R, Moak D, and Latham P (1995) The Obsessive Compulsive Drinking Scale: A self rated instrument for the quantification of thoughts about alcohol and drinking behaviour. *Alcoholism: Clinical and Experimental Research* 19: 92–99.

Anton RF, Moak DH, and Latham PK (1996) The Obsessive Compulsive Drinking Scale: A new method of assessing outcome in alcoholism treatment studies. *Archives of General Psychiatry* 53: 225–231.

Avants SK, Margolin A, Kosten TR, and Cooney NL (1995) Differences between responders and nonresponders to cocaine cues in the laboratory. *Addictive Behaviors* 20: 215–224.

Baker TB, Morse E, and Sherman JE (1986) The motivation to use drugs: A psychobiological analysis of urges. *Nebraska Symposium on Motivation* 34: 257–323.

Bechara A and Martin EM (2004) Impaired decision making related to working memory deficits in individuals with substance addictions. *Neuropsychology* 18: 152–162.

Bohn MJ, Barton BA, and Barron KE (1996) Psychometric properties and validity of the Obsessive-Compulsive Drinking Scale. *Alcoholism: Clinical and Experimental Research* 20: 817–823.

Bohn MJ, Krahn DD, and Staehler BA (1995) Development and initial validation of a measure of drinking urges in abstinent alcoholics. *Alcoholism: Clinical and Experimental Research* 19: 600–606.

Brody AL, Mandelkern MA, London ED, Childress AR, Lee GS, Bota RG, Ho ML, Saxena S, Baxter LR, Jr, Madsen D, and Jarvik ME (2002) Brain metabolic changes during cigarette craving. *Archives of General Psychiatry* 59: 1162–1172.

Brody AL, Mandelkern MA, Olmstead RE, Jou J, Tiongson E, Allen V, Scheibal D, London ED, Monterosso JR, Tiffany ST, Korb A, Gan JJ, and Cohen MS (2007) Neural substrates of resisting craving during cigarette cue exposure. *Biological Psychiatry* 62: 642–651.

Brown SA, McGue M, Maggs J, Schulenberg J, Hingson R, Swartzwelder S, Martin C, Chung T, Tapert S, Sher K, Winters K, Lowman C, and Murphy S (2008) A developmental perspective on alcohol and youths 16–20 years of age. *Pediatrics* 121: S290–S310.

Bucholz KK, Cadoret R, Cloninger CR, Dinwiddie SH, Hesselbrock VM, Nurnberger JI, Jr, Reich T, Schmidt I, and Schuckit MA (1994) A new, semi-structured psychiatric interview for use in genetic linkage studies: A report on the reliability of the SSAGA. *Journal of Studies on Alcohol* 55: 149–58.

Cacioppo JT, Petty RE, Losch ME, and Kim HS (1986) Electromyographic activity over facial muscle regions can differentiate the valence and intensity of affective reactions. *Journal of Personality and Social Psychology* 50: 260–268.

Cappelleri JC, Bushmakin AG, Baker CL, Merikle E, Olufade AO, and Gilbert DG (2007) Multivariate framework of the Brief Questionnaire of Smoking Urges. *Drug and Alcohol Dependence* 90: 234–242.

Carter BL and Tiffany ST (1999) Meta-analysis of cue-reactivity in addiction research. *Addiction* 94: 327–340.

Cepeda-Benito A and Reig-Ferrer A (2004) Development of a Brief Questionnaire of Smoking Urges – Spanish. *Psychological Assessment* 16: 402–407.

Chignon JM, Jacquesy L, Mennad M, Terki A, Huttin F, Martin P, and Chabannes JP (1998) Self-assessment questionnaire of alcoholic craving (ECCA Questionnaire: Behavior and cognition in relation to alcohol): French translation and validation of the Obsessive-Compulsive Drinking Scale. *Encephale* 24: 426–434.

Coffey SF, Saladin ME, Libet JM, Drobes DJ, and Dansky BS (1999) Differential urge and salivary responsivity to alcohol cues in alcohol-dependent patients: A comparison of traditional and stringent classification approaches. *Experimental and Clinical Psychopharmacology* 7: 464–472.

Collins RL and Lapp WM (1992) The Temptation and Restraint Inventory for measuring drinking restraint. *British Journal of Addiction* 87: 625–633.

Collins RL, Koutsky JR, and Izzo CV (2000) Temptation, restriction, and the regulation of alcohol intake: Validity and utility of the Temptation and Restraint Inventory. *Journal of Studies on Alcohol* 61: 766–773.

Compton WM, Saha TD, Conway KP, and Grant BF (2009) The role of cannabis use within a dimensional approach to cannabis use disorders. *Drug and Alcohol Dependence* 100: 221–227.

Compton WM, Yonette FT, Frederick SS, and Bridget FG (2007) Prevalence, correlates, disability, and comorbidity of DSM-IV drug abuse and dependence in the United States: Results from the National Epidemiologic Survey on Alcohol and Related Conditions. *Archives of General Psychiatry* 64: 566–576.

Connolly KM, Coffey SF, Baschnagel JS, Drobes DJ, and Saladin ME (2009) Evaluation of the Alcohol Craving Questionnaire-Now factor structures: Application of a cue reactivity paradigm. *Drug and Alcohol Dependence* 103: 84–91.

Connor JP, Jack A, Feeney GFX, and Young RM (2008) Validity of the Obsessive Compulsive Drinking Scale in a heavy drinking population. *Alcoholism: Clinical and Experimental Research* 32: 1067–1073.

Cordero M, Solis L, Cordero R, Torruco M, and Cruz-Fuentes C (2009) Factor structure and concurrent validity of the Obsessive Compulsive Drinking Scale in a group of alcohol-dependent subjects of Mexico City. *Alcoholism: Clinical and Experimental Research* 33: 1145–1150.

Courtney KE, Arellano R, Barkley-Levenson E, Galvan A, Poldrack RA, MacKillop J, Jentsch JD, and Ray LA (2012) The relationship between measures of impulsivity and alcohol misuse: An integrative structural equation modeling approach. *Alcoholism: Clinical and Experimental Research* 36: 923–931.

Cox LS, Tiffany ST, and Christen AG (2001) Evaluation of the Brief Questionnaire of Smoking Urges (QSU-brief) in laboratory and clinical settings. *Nicotine and Tobacco Research* 3: 7–16.

Cox MW, Fadardi SJ, and Pothos EM (2006) The Addiction-Stroop Test: Theoretical considerations and procedural recommendations. *Psychological Bulletin* 2006: 443–476.

Curtin JJ, Barnett NP, Colby SM, Rohsenow DJ, and Monti PM (2005) Cue reactivity in adolescents: Measurement of separate approach and avoidance reactions. *Journal of Studies on Alcohol* 66: 332–343.

Cyders MA and Coskunpinar A (2011) Measurement of constructs using self-report and behavioral lab tasks: Is there overlap in nomothetic span and construct representation for impulsivity? *Clinical Psychology Review* 31: 965–982.

de Bruijn C, van den Brink W, de Graaf R, and Vollebergh WA (2005) Alcohol abuse and dependence criteria as predictors of a chronic course of alcohol use disorders in the general population. *Alcohol andAlcoholism* 40: 441–446.

de Wit H (2009) Impulsivity as a determinant and consequence of drug use: A review of underlying processes. *Addict Biol* 14: 22–31.

Deas D, Roberts J, Randall CL, and Anton R (2001) Adolescent Obsessive-Compulsive Drinking Scale (A-OCSDS): An assessment tool for problem drinking. *Journal of National Medical Association* 93: 92–103.

Doran N, McChargue D, and Spring B (2008) Effect of impulsivity on cardiovascular and subjective reactivity to smoking cues. *Addictive Behaviors* 33: 167–172.

Doran N, Spring B, and McChargue D (2007) Effect of impulsivity on craving and behavioral reactivity to smoking cues. *Psychopharmacology (Berlin)* 194: 279–288.

Drummond DC (2001) Theories of drug craving, ancient and modern. *Addiction* 96: 33–46.

Eckman P and Friesen W (1978) *Facial Action Coding System*. Palo Alto, CA: Consulting Psychologists Press.

Ehlers CL, Gizer IR, Vieten C, and Wilhelmsen KC (2010) Linkage analyses of cannabis dependence, craving, and withdrawal in the San Francisco family study. *American Journal of Medical Genetics B: Neuropsychiatric Genetics* 153B: 802–811.

Ehrman RN, Robbins SJ, Bromwell MA, Lankford ME, Monterosso JR, and O'Brien CP (2002) Comparing attentional bias to smoking cues in current smokers, former smokers, and non-smokers using a dot-probe task. *Drug and Alcohol Dependence* 67: 185–191.

Elash CA, Tiffany ST, and Vrana SR (1995) Manipulation of smoking urges and affect through a brief-imagery procedure: Self-report, psychophysiological, and startle probe responses. *Experimental and Clinical Psychopharmacology* 3: 156–162.

Field M (2005) Cannabis "dependence" and attentional bias for cannabis-related words. *Behavioral Pharmacology* 16: 473–476.

Field M and Cox MW (2008) Attentional bias in addictive behaviors: A review of its development, causes, and consequences. *Drug and Alcohol Dependence* 97: 1–20.

Field M and Duka T (2001) Smoking expectancy mediates the conditioned responses to arbitrary smoking cues. *Behavioural Pharmacology* 12: 183–194.

Field M, Eastwood B, Bradley BP, and Mogg K (2006) Selective processing of cannabis cues in regular cannabis users. *Drug and Alcohol Dependence* 85: 75–82.

Field M, Hogarth L, Bleasdale D, Wright P, Fernie G, and Christiansen P (2011) Alcohol expectancy moderates attentional bias for alcohol cues in light drinkers *Addiction* 106: 1097–1103.

Field M, Munafò MR, and Franken IHA (2009) A meta-analytic investigation of the relationship between attentional bias and subjective craving in substance abuse. *Psychological Bulletin* 135: 589–607.

Field M, Rush M, Cole J, and Goudie A (2007) The smoking Stroop and delay discounting in smokers: Effects of environmental smoking cues. *J Psychopharmacol* 21: 603–610.

Field M, Santarcangelo M, Sumnall H, Goudie A, and Cole J (2006) Delay discounting and the behavioural economics of cigarette purchases in smokers: The effects of nicotine deprivation. *Psychopharmacology (Berlin)* 186: 255–263.

Filbey FM, Claus E, Audette AR, Niculescu M, Banich MT, Tanabe J, Du YP, and Hutchison KE (2008a) Exposure to the taste of alcohol elicits activation of the mesocorticolimbic neurocircuitry. *Neuropsychopharmacology* 33: 1391–1401.

Filbey FM, Ray L, Smolen A, Claus ED, Audette A, and Hutchison KE (2008b) Differential neural response to alcohol priming and alcohol taste cues is associated with DRD4 VNTR and OPRM1 genotypes. *Alcoholism: Clinical & Experimental Research* 32: 1113–1123.

Filbey FM, Schacht JP, Myers US, Chavez RS, and Hutchison KE (2009) Marijuana craving in the brain. *Proc Natl Acad Sci U S A* 106: 13016–13021.

Flannery BA, Poole SA, Gallop RJ, and Volpicelli JR (2003) Alcohol craving predicts drinking during treatment: An analysis of three assessment instruments. *Journal of Studies on Alcohol* 64: 120–126.

Flannery BA, Volpicelli JR, and Pettinati HM (1999) Psychometric properties of the Penn Alcohol Craving Scale. *Alcoholism: Clinical and Experimental Research* 23: 1289–1295.

Foroud T, Wetherill LF, Liang T, Dick DM, Hesselbrock V, Kramer J, Nurnberger J, Schuckit M, Carr L, Porjesz B, Xuei X, and Edenberg HJ (2007) Association of alcohol craving with alpha-synuclein (SNCA). *Alcoholism: Clinical & Experimental Research* 31: 537–545.

Franken IHA, Dietvorst RC, Hesselmans M, Franzek EJ, van de Wetering BJM, and Van Strien JW (2008) Cocaine craving is associated with electrophysiological brain responses to cocaine-related stimuli. *Addiction Biology* 13: 386–392.

Franken IHA, Hendriks VM, and van den Brink W (2002) Initial validation of two opiate craving questionnaires: The Obsessive Compulsive Drug Use Scale and the Desires for Drug Questionnaire. *Addictive Behaviors* 27: 675–685.

Giordano LA, Bickel WK, Loewenstein G, Jacobs EA, Marsch L, and Badger GJ (2002) Mild opioid deprivation increases the degree that opioid-dependent outpatients discount delayed heroin and money. *Psychopharmacology (Berlin)* 163: 174–182.

Greenwald AG, McGhee DE, and Schwartz JLK (1998) Measuring individual differences in implicit cognition: The Implicit Association Test. *Journal of Personality and Social Psychology* 74: 1464–1480.

Grusser SM, Heinz AR, Wessa M, Podschus J, and Flor H (2002) Stimulus-induced craving and startle potentiation in abstinent alcoholics and controls. *European Psychiatry* 17: 188–193.

Halikas JA, Kuhn KL, Crosby R, Carlson G, and Crea F (1991) The measurement of craving in cocaine patients using the Minnesota Cocaine Craving Scale. *Comprehensive Psychiatry* 32: 22–27.

Hasin DS, Stinson FS, Ogburn E, and Grant BF (2007) Prevalence, correlates, disability, and comorbidity of DSM-IV alcohol abuse and dependence in the United States: Results from the National Epidemiological Survey on Alcohol and Related Conditions. *Archives of General Psychiatry* 64: 830–842.

Heinz AJ, Epstein DH, Schroeder JR, Singleton EG, Heishman SJ, and Preston KL (2006) Heroin and cocaine craving and use during treatment: Measurement validation and potential relationships. *Journal of Substance Abuse Treatment* 31: 355–364.

Heishman SJ, Evans RJ, Singleton EG, Levin KH, Copersino ML, and Gorelick DA (2009) Reliability and validity of a short form of the Marijuana Craving Questionnaire. *Drug and Alcohol Dependence* 102: 35–40.

Heishman SJ, Singleton EG, and Liguori A (2001) Marijuana Craving Questionnaire: Development and initial validation of a self-report instrument. *Addiction* 96: 1023–1034.

Heishman SJ, Singleton EG, and Moolchan ET (2003) Tobacco Craving Questionnaire: Reliability and validity of a new multifactorial instrument. *Nicotine and Tobacco Research* 5: 645-654.

Hodgins DC, el-Guebaly N, and Armstrong S (1995) Prospective and retrospective reports of mood states before relapse to substance use. *Journal of Consulting and Clinical Psychology* 63: 400–407.

Hogarth L, Dickinson A, and Duka T (2010) The associative basis of cue-elicited drug taking in humans. *Psychopharmacology* 208: 337–351.

Hormes JM and Rozin P (2010) Does "craving" carve nature at the joints? Absence of a synonym for craving in many languages. *Addictive Behaviors* 32: 459–463.

Hutchison KE, McGeary J, Smolen A, Bryan A, and Swift RM (2002) The DRD4 VNTR polymorphism moderates craving after alcohol consumption. *Health Psychology* 21: 139–146.

Hutchison KE, Ray L, Sandman E, Rutter MC, Peters A, Davidson D, and Swift R (2006) The effect of olanzapine on craving and alcohol consumption. *Neuropsychopharmacology* 31: 1310–1317.

Janiri L, Calvosa F, Dario T, Pozzi G, Ruggeri A, Addolorato G, Di Giannantonio M, and De Risio S (2004) The Italian version of the Obsessive-Compulsive Drinking Scale: Validation, comparison with the other versions and difference between type1- and type2-like alcoholoics. *Drug and Alcohol Dependence* 74: 187–195.

Kahler CW and Strong DR (2006) A Rasch model analysis of DSM-IV alcohol abuse and dependence items in the National Epidemiological Survey on Alcohol and Related Conditions. *Alcoholism: Clinical & Experimental Research* 30: 1165–1175.

Kashinsky W, Collins BN, and Brandon TH (1995) A telemetric device for measuring smoking topography. *Behavior Research Methods, Instruments, and Computers* 27: 375–378.

Kavanagh DJ, Andrade J, and May J (2005) Imaginary relish and exquisite torture: The elaborated intrusion theory of desire. *Psychological Review* 112: 446–467.

Killen JD and Fortmann SP (1997) Craving is associated with smoking relapse: Findings from three prospective studies. *Experimental and Clinical Psychopharmacology* 5: 137–142.

Kim MJ, Kim SG, Kim HJ, Kim HC, Park JH, Park KS, Lee DK, Byun WT, and Kim CM (2008) A study of the realibility and validity of the Korean version of the Penn Alcohol Craving Scale for alcohol-dependent patients. *Psychiatry Investigations* 5: 175–178.

Leeman RF, Corbin WR, and Fromme K (2009) Craving predicts within session drinking behavior following placebo. *Pers Individ Dif* 46: 693–698.

Leeman RF, O'Malley SS, White MA, and McKee SA (2010) Nicotine and food deprivation decrease the ability to resist smoking. *Psychopharmacology (Berlin)* 212: 25–32.

Leonard KE, Harwood MK, and Blane HT (1988) The Preoccupation with Alcohol Scale: Development and validation. *Alcoholism: Clinical and Experimental Research* 12: 394–399.

Lin JC, Karno MP, Grella CE, Warda U, Liao DH, Hu P, and Moore AA (2011) Alcohol, tobacco, and nonmedical drug use disorders in US adults aged 65 and older: Data from the 2001–2002 National Epidemiologic Survey of Alcohol and Related Conditions. *American Journal of Geriatric Psychiatry* 19: 292–299.

Litman GK, Stapleton J, Oppenheim AN, Peleg M, and Jackson P (1983) Situations related to alcoholism relapse. *British Journal of Addiction* 78: 381–389.

Littel M and Franken IHA (2007) The effects of prolonged abstinence on the processing of smoking cues: An ERP study among smokers, ex-smokers and never-smokers. *Journal of Psychopharmacology* 21: 873–882.

Lubman DI, Allen NB, Peters LA, and Deakin JFW (2008) Electrophysiological evidence that drug cues have greater salience than other affective stimuli in opiate addiction. *Journal of Psychopharmacology* 22: 836–842.

Lubman DI, Peters LA, Mogg K, Bradley BP, and Deakin JFW (2000) Attentional bias for drug cues in opiate dependence. *Psychological Medicine* 30: 169–175.

MacKillop J (2006) Factor structure of the Alcohol Urge Questionnaire under neutral conditions and during a cue-elicited urge state. *Alcoholism: Clinical and Experimental Research* 30: 1315–1321.

MacKillop J and Lisman SA (2005) Reactivity to alcohol cues: Isolating the role of perceived availability. *Experimental and Clinical Psychopharmacology* 13: 229–237.

MacKillop J and Lisman SA (2008) Effects of a context shift and multiple context extinction on reactivity to alcohol cues. *Experimental and Clinical Psychopharmacology* 16: 322–331.

MacKillop J, Amlung MT, Murphy CM, Acker J, and Ray LA (2011) A behavioral economic approach to health behavior. In R DiClemente, LF Salazar, and RA Crosby (eds), *Theory and Practice for a New Public Health* (pp. 131–162). Burlington, MA: Jones and Bartlett.

MacKillop J, Lisman SA, and Weinstein A (2006) Psychometric validation of the Temptation and Restraint Inventory in two samples of drinkers. *Journal of Psychopathology and Behavioral Assessment* 28: 156–162.

MacKillop J, Menges DP, McGeary JE, and Lisman SA (2007) Effects of craving and DRD4 VNTR genotype on the relative value of alcohol: An initial human laboratory study. *Behavioral and Brain Functions* 3: 11.

MacKillop J, Miranda R, Jr, Monti PM, Ray LA, Murphy JG, Rohsenow DJ, McGeary JE, Swift RM, Tidey JW, and Gwaltney CJ (2010a) Alcohol demand, delayed reward discounting, and craving in relation to drinking and alcohol use disorders. *Journal of Abnormal Psychology* 119: 106–114.

MacKillop J, O'Hagen S, Lisman SA, Murphy JG, Ray LA, Tidey JW, McGeary JE, and Monti PM (2010b) Behavioral economic analysis of cue-elicited craving for alcohol. *Addiction* 105: 1599–1607.

Madden CJ and Zwaan RA (2001) The impact of smoking urges on working memory performance. *Experimental and Clinical Psychopharmacology* 9: 418–424.

Mann K and Ackerman K (2000) The OCDS-G: Psychometric characteristics of the German version of the Obsessive Drinking Scale. *Sucht* 46: 90–100.

Mason BJ, Light JM, Williams LD, and Drobes DJ (2009) Proof-of-concept human laboratory study for protracted abstinence in alcohol dependence: effects of gabapentin. *Addiction Biology* 14: 73–83.

May J, Andrade J, Panabokke N, and Kavanagh D (2004) Images of desire: Cognitive models of craving. *Memory* 12: 447–461.

McEvoy PM, Stritzke WG, French DJ, Lang AR, and Ketterman R (2004) Comparison of three models of alcohol craving in young adults: A cross-validation. *Addiction* 99: 482–497.

Mendelson JH and Mello NK (1979) One unanswered question about alcoholism. *British Journal of Addiction to Alcohol and Other Drugs* 74: 11–14.

Miranda R, Jr, MacKillop J, Monti PM, Rohsenow DJ, Tidey J, Gwaltney C, Swift R, Ray L, and McGeary J (2008) Effects of topiramate on urge to drink and the subjective effects of alcohol: A preliminary laboratory study. *Alcoholism: Clinical and Experimental Research* 32: 489–497.

Mitchell SH (2004) Effects of short-term nicotine deprivation on decision-making: Delay, uncertainty and effort discounting. *Nicotine Tob Res* 6: 819–828.

Modell JG, Glaser FB, Mountz JM, Schmaltz S, and Cyr L (1992) Obsessive and compulsive characteristics of alcohol abuse and dependence: Quantification by a newly developed questionnaire. *Alcoholism: Clinical and Experimental Research* 16: 266–271.

Mogg K, Bradley BP, Field M, and De Houwer J (2003) Eye movements to smoking-related pictures in smokers: Relationship between attentional biases and implicit and explicit measures of stimulus valence. *Addiction* 98: 825–836.

Mol AJJ, Voshaar RCO, Gorgels WJMJ, Breteler MHM, Van Balkom AJLM, Van De Lisdonk EH, Van Der Ven AHGS, and Zitman FG (2003) Development and psychometric evaluation of the Benzodiazepine Craving Questionnaire. *Addiction* 98: 1143–1152.

Monti PM, Rohsenow DJ, Rubonis AV, Niaura RS, Sirota AD, Colby SM, and Abrams DB (1993) Alcohol cue reactivity: Effects of detoxification and extended exposure. *Journal of Studies on Alcohol* 54: 235–245.

Monti PM, Tidey J, Czachowski CL, Grant KA, Rohsenow DJ, Sayette M, Maners N, and Pierre P (2004) Building bridges: The transdisciplinary study of craving from the animal laboratory to the lamppost. *Alcoholism: Clinical and Experimental Research* 28: 279–287.

Munafo MR and Hitsman B (2010) What's the matter with cue-induced craving? A commentary on Perkins. *Addiction* 105: 1860–1861.

O'Malley SS, Krishnan-Sarin S, Farren C, Sinha R, and Kreek MJ (2002) Naltrexone decreases craving and alcohol self-administration in alcohol-dependent subjects and activates the hypothalamo-pituitary-adrenocortical axis. *Psychopharmacology (Berlin)* 160: 19–29.

Ooteman W, Koeter MWJ, Vserheul R, Schippers GM, and van den Brink W (2006) Measuring craving: An attempt to connect subjective craving with cue reactivity. *Alcoholism: Clinical and Experimental Research* 30: 57–69.

Oslin DW, Cary M, Slaymaker V, Colleran C, and Blow FC (2009) Daily ratings measures of alcohol craving during an inpatient stay define subtypes of alcohol addiction that predict subsequent risk for resumption of drinking. *Drug and Alcohol Dependence* 103: 131–136.

Ostafin BD and Palfai TP (2006) Compelled to consume: The Implicit Association Test and automatic alcohol motivation. *Psychology of Addictive Behaviors* 20: 322–327.

Palfai TP and Ostafin BD (2003) Alcohol-related motivational tendencies in hazardous drinkers: Assessing implicit response tendencies using the modified-IAT. *Behavior Research and Therapy* 41: 1149–62.

Paliwal P, Hyman SM, and Sinha R (2008) Craving predicts time to cocaine relapse: Further validation of the Now and Brief versions of the Cocaine Craving Questionnaire. *Drug and Alcohol Dependence* 93: 252–259.

Pavlick M, Hoffman E, and Rosenberg H (2009) A nationwide survey of American alcohol and drug craving assessment and treatment strategies. *Addiction Research and Theory* 17: 591–600.

Pedroso RS, da Graça TdCM, and Araujo RB (2009) Marijuana Craving Questionnaire (MCQ-SF/Versão Brasil): Validação semântica./Marijuana Craving Questionnaire (MCQ-SF/Brazil Version): Semantic validation. *Jornal Brasileiro de Psiquiatria* 58: 218–222.

Perkins KA (2009) Does smoking cue-induced craving tell us anything important about nicotine dependence? *Addiction* 104: 1610–1616.

Pickens RW and Johanson C-E (1992) Craving: Consensus of status and agenda for future research. *Drug and Alcohol Dependence* 30: 127–131.

Raabe A, Grüsser SM, Wessa M, Podschus J, and Flor H (2005) The assessment of craving: Psychometric properties, factor structure and a revised version of the Alcohol Craving Questionnaire (ACQ). *Addiction* 100: 227–234.

Ramo DE, Anderson KG, Tate SR, and Brown SA (2005) Characteristics of relapse to substance use in comorbid adolescents. *Addictive Behaviors* 30: 1811–1823.

Rankin H, Hodgson R, and Stockwell T (1979) The concept of craving and its measurement. *Behaviour Research and Therapy* 17: 389–396.

Ray LA, Chin PF, Heydari A, and Miotto K (in press) A human laboratory study of the effects of quetiapine on subjective intoxication and alcohol craving. *Psychopharmacology (Berlin)*.

Robbins SJ and Ehrman RN (2004) The role of attentional bias in substance abuse. *Behavioral and Cognitive Neuroscience Reviews* 3: 243–260.

Roberts JS, Anton RF, Latham PK, and Moak DH (1999) Factor structure and predictive validity of the Obsessive Compulsive Drinking Scale. *Alcoholism: Clinical and Experimental Research* 23: 1484–1491.

Robinson JD, Lam CY, Carter BL, Minnix JA, Cui Y, Versace F, Wetter DW, and Cincipirini PM (2011) A multimodal approach to assessing the impact of nicotine dependence, nicotine abstinence, and craving on negative affect in smokers. *Experimental and Clinical Psychopharmacology* 19: 40–52.

Rohsenow DJ, Monti PM, Abrams DB, and Rubonis AV (1992) Cue elicited urge to drink and salivation in alcoholics: Relationship to individual differences. *Advances in Behaviour Research and Therapy* 14: 195–210.

Rosenberg H (2009) Clinical and laboratory assessment of the subjective experience of drug craving. *Clinical Psychology Review* 29: 519–534.

Sayette MA and Hufford MR (1994) Effects of cue exposure and deprivation on cognitive resources in smokers. *Journal of Abnormal Psychology* 103: 812–818.

Sayette MA, Loewenstein G, Kirchner TR, and Travis T (2005) Effects of smoking urge on temporal cognition. *Psychology of Addictive Behaviors* 19: 88–93.

Sayette MA, Martin CS, Wertz JM, Perrott MA, and Peters AR (2005) The effects of alcohol on cigarette craving in heavy smokers and tobacco chippers. *Psychology of Addictive Behaviors Behaviors* 19: 263–270.

Sayette MA, Martin CS, Wertz JM, Shiffman S, and Perrott MA (2001) A multi-dimensional analysis of cue-elicited craving in heavy smokers and tobacco chippers. *Addiction* 96: 1419–1432.

Sayette MA, Monti PM, Rohsenow DJ, Gulliver SB, Colby SM, Sirota AD, Niaura R, and Abrams DB (1994) The effects of cue exposure on reaction time in male alcoholics. *Journal of Studies on Alcohol* 55: 629–633.

Sayette MA, Shiffman S, Tiffany ST, Niaura RS, Martin CS, and Shadel WG (2000) The measurement of drug craving. *Addiction* 95: S189–S210.

Sayette MA, Wertz JM, Martin CS, Cohn JF, Perrott MA, and Hobel J (2003) Effects of smoking opportunity on cue-elicited urge: A facial coding analysis. *Experimental and Clinical Psychopharmacology* 11: 218–227.

Schippers GM, De Jong CAJ, Lehert P, Potgieter A, Deckers F, Casselman J, and Geerlings PJ (1997) The Obsessive Compulsive Drinking Scale: Translation into Dutch and possible modifications. *European Addiction Research* 3: 116–122.

Shiffman S, Waters AJ, and Hickcox M (2004) The Nicotine Dependence Syndrome Scale: A multidimensional measure of nicotine dependence. *Nicotine and Tobacco Research* 6: 327–348.

Shmulewitz D, Keyes KM, Wall MM, Aharonovich E, Aivadyan C, Greenstein E, Spivak B, Weizman A, Frisch A, Grant BF, and Hasin D (2011) Nicotine dependence, abuse and craving: Dimensionality in an Israeli sample. *Addiction* 106: 1675–1686.

Singleton EG, Anderson LM, and Heishman SJ (2003) Reliability and validity of the Tobacco Craving Questionnaire and validation of a craving-induction procedure using multiple measures of craving and mood. *Addiction* 98: 1537–1546.

Singleton EG, Tiffany ST, and Henningfield JE (1995) Development and validation of a new questionnaire to assess craving for alcohol. Proceeding of the 56th Annual Meeting, The College on Problems of Drug Dependence, Inc. Volume II: Abstracts. NIDA Research Monograph 153. Rockville, MD: National Institute on Drug Abuse.

Singleton EG, Trotman AJ-M, Zavahir M, Taylor RC, and Heishman SJ (2002) Determination of the reliability and validity of the marijuana craving questionnaire using imagery scripts. *Experimental and Clinical Psychopharmacology* 10: 47–53.

Smeets E, Roefs A, and Jansen A (2009) Experimentally induced chocolate craving leads to an attentional bias in increased distraction but not in speeded detection. *Appetite* 53: 370–375.

Smelson DA, McGee-Caulfield E, Bergstein P, and Engelhart C (1999) Initial validation of the Voris Cocaine Craving Scale: A preliminary report. *Journal of Clinical Psychology* 55: 135–139.

Smith-Hoerter K, Stasiewicz PR, and Bradizza CM (2004) Subjective reactions to alcohol cue exposure: A qualitative analysis of patients' self-reports. *Psychology of Addictive Behaviors* 18: 402–406.

Staiger PK and White JM (1991) Cue reactivity in alcohol abusers: Stimulus specificity and extinction of the responses. *Addictive Behaviors* 16: 211–221.

Stritzke WG, Breiner MJ, Curtin JJ, and Lang AR (2004) Assessment of substance cue reactivity: Advances in reliability, specificity, and validity. *Psychology of Addictive Behaviors* 18: 148–159.

Strong DR and Kahler CW (2007) Evaluation of the continuum of gambling problems using the DSM-IV. *Addiction* 102: 713–721.

Sussner BD, Smelson DA, Rodrigues S, Kline A, Losonczy M, and Ziedonis D (2006) The validity and reliability of a brief measure of cocaine craving. *Drug and Alcohol Dependence* 83: 233–237.

Tatsuzawa Y, Yoshimasu H, Moriyama Y, Furusawa T, and Yoshino A (2002) Validation study of the Japanese version of the Obsessive-Compulsive Drinking Scale. *Psychiatry and Clinical Neurosciences* 56: 91–95.

Tidey JW, Rohsenow DJ, Kaplan GB, and Swift RM (2005) Cigarette smoking topography in smokers with schizophrenia and matched non-psychiatric controls. *Drug and Alcohol Dependence* 80: 259–65.

Tiffany ST and Conklin CA (2000) A cognitive processing model of alcohol craving and compulsive alcohol use. *Addiction* 95(Suppl. 2): S145–S153.

Tiffany ST and Drobes DJ (1991) The development and initial validation of a questionnaire on smoking urges. *British Journal of Addiction* 86: 1467–1476.

Tiffany ST, Carter BL, and Singleton EG (2000) Challenges in the manipulation, assessment and interpretation of craving relevant variables. *Addiction* 95(Suppl. 2): S177–S187.

Tiffany S, Fields L, Singleton E, Haertzen C, and Henningsfield J (1993) The development of a heroin craving questionnaire [unpublished manuscript]. Purdue University.

Tiffany ST, Singleton E, Haertzen CA, and Henningfield JE (1993) The development of a cocaine craving questionnaire. *Drug and Alcohol Dependence* 34: 19–28.

Townshend JM and Duka T (2001) Attentional bias associated with alcohol cues: Differences between heavy and occasional social drinkers. *Psychopharmacology* 157: 67–74.

Voris J, Elder I, and Sebastian P (1991) A simple test of cocaine craving and related responses. *Journal of Clinical Psychology* 47: 320–323.

Waters AJ, Carter BL, Robinson JD, Wetter DW, Lam CY, and Cinciripini PM (2007) Implicit attitudes to smoking are associated with craving and dependence. *Drug and Alcohol Dependence* 91: 178–186.

Willner P, Hardman S, and Eaton G (1995) Subjective and behavioural evaluation of cigarette cravings. *Psychopharmacology (Berlin)* 118: 171–177.

Wilson TD and Dunn EW (2004) Self-knowledge: Its limits, value, and potential for improvement. *Annual Review of Psychology* 55: 493–518.

World Health Organization (2010) *ICD 10: International Statistical Classification of Diseases and Related Health Problems.* Geneva: World Health Organization.

Yoon G, Kim SW, Thuras P, Grant JE, and Westermeyer J (2006) Alcohol craving in outpatients with alcohol dependence: Rate and clinical correlates. *Journal of Studies on Alcohol* 67: 770–777.

Zwaan RA, Stanfield RA, and Madden CJ (2000) How persistent is the effect of smoking urges on cognitive performance? *Experimental and Clinical Psychopharmacology* 8: 518–523.

14

The Cue Reactivity Paradigm in Addiction Research

Elizabeth K. Reynolds and Peter M. Monti

1 Introduction

A significant amount of empirical literature has demonstrated that stimuli associated with drug administration (e.g., bottle of preferred alcohol, syringe, lighter, etc.) can elicit subjective reports of craving and patterns of physiological responding in persons who have drug use histories (Carter and Tiffany, 1999). This phenomenon, referred to as cue reactivity, is typically studied with a laboratory paradigm in which participants are systematically exposed to cues that elicit responses presumed to relate to the motivational processes involved in drug use (Watson *et al.*, 2010; Drobes, Saladin, and Tiffany, 2001; Drummond, Tiffany, Glautier, and Remington, 1995). Cue reactivity has been repeatedly shown among individuals dependent on a variety of drugs, including cocaine, alcohol, opiates, and nicotine (Carter and Tiffany, 1999).

A variety of cue presentation modes have been developed including *in vivo* (e.g., sitting in front of an open bottle of beer), imaginal (e.g., vividly imagining situations related to past drug use), audio (e.g., listening to a tape of someone describing drug use), video (e.g., watching a film of someone drinking), pictorial (e.g., viewing pictures of drug paraphernalia), and/or virtual reality (i.e., a computer-generated, three-dimensional world that changes in realistic ways in response to head, hand, and/or body motion) (Conklin, 2006). Typically, a variety of reactions to the drug-related stimuli are assessed, including self-reported craving responses, physiology (e.g., changes in heart rate, skin conductance, skin temperature, and salivation), lever pressing, and self-reported mood state. In addition, more recently, neuroimaging methods have been used to study regional changes in brain activity following cue exposure (e.g., Dagher *et al.*, 2009; Janes *et al.*, 2009; Yang *et al.*, 2009). Least studied are behavioral responses (Carter and Tiffany, 2001; Perkins, 2009), such as latency or amount of subsequent consumption, and only a small number of studies have been conducted demonstrating that the magnitude of cue reactivity predicts risk of relapse

The Wiley-Blackwell Handbook of Addiction Psychopharmacology, First Edition. Edited by James MacKillop and Harriet de Wit.
© 2013 John Wiley & Sons, Ltd. Published 2013 by John Wiley & Sons, Ltd.

prospectively (Abrams *et al.*, 1988; Braus *et al.*, 2001; Grusser *et al.*, 2004; Kosten *et al.*, 2006; Niaura, Abrams, DeMuth, and Pinto, 1989; Payne, Smith, Adams, and Diefenbach, 2006; Rohsenow *et al.*, 1994; Waters *et al.*, 2004).

Based on the paradigm's sound theoretical underpinnings and utility for studying addiction processes in the controlled laboratory setting, cue reactivity has become a frequently used method in addiction research for the last 20-plus years. In this chapter, we will review the empirical relevance of cue reactivity to substance abuse research, describe standardized and validated cue reactivity methods, as well as discuss limitations, shortcomings, and future directions for the field.

2   Empirical Relevance of Cue Reactivity to Substance Abuse Research

As previously stated, cue reactivity studies demonstrate that increases in self-reported craving and changes in autonomic functioning can be observed when drug users are exposed to drug-related stimuli compared with neutral stimuli (Carter and Tiffany, 1999). Cue reactivity effects are typically understood through consideration of basic classical conditioning: that is, repeated drinking or drug use in the presence of specific environmental stimuli, or cues, can lead to a set of conditioned responses when in the presence of those stimuli – cue reactivity (e.g., Abrams and Niaura, 1987; Carter and Tiffany, 1999; Drummond *et al.*, 1995; Monti, 2006). Within the framework of cue responses as a result of learning processes, drugs are unconditioned stimuli that lead to unconditioned responses. Over the course of drug use, various stimuli present at the time of drug administration (e.g., drug paraphernalia, environmental context) come to be reliably associated with drug use, a phenomenon that has been demonstrated in experimental work (e.g., Clements *et al.*, 1996; Field and Duka, 2002; Foltin and Haney, 2000; Glautier, Drummond, and Remington, 1994; Glautier, Bankart, and Williams, 2000; Lubman *et al.*, 2000). Ultimately, those stimuli become conditioned stimuli (i.e., cues) that can elicit conditioned responses. As a result, when an individual is exposed to those conditioned stimuli, either in the laboratory (e.g., Conklin and Tiffany, 2001) or in the real world (e.g., Shiffman *et al.*, 2002), changes in subjective measures (e.g., self-reported craving, mood alteration), physiology (e.g., heart rate, skin conductance, startle modulation), and/or behavior (e.g., drug seeking) are often observed (Conklin, 2006).

Presumably, these cue-specific reactions reflect motivational processes responsible for continuing drug use as well as the initiation of drug lapse and relapse (Childress *et al.*, 1992; O'Brien, Childress, Ehrmann, and Robbins, 1998). Thus, the utility of cue reactivity is based on the notion that drug craving is a critical factor in the maintenance of and relapse to addictive patterns of drug use (O'Brien, 2005). Of note, there has been some controversy surrounding this assertion. As noted by Perkins (2009), the limited clinically relevant research has not demonstrated a clear link between substance relapse risk and cue-elicited self-reported craving or physiological response. It is uncertain whether this lack of consistent findings is due to methodological limitations (e.g., craving measurement post-cue presentation, need for greater complexity in design/procedure), limitations of the global construct of subjective craving, or failure of the paradigm as an analogue of drug use motivational processes itself (Munafò and Hitsman, 2010).

In spite of the need for future research to better characterize the relationship between cue-elicited responses and clinical outcomes, cue reactivity remains a frequently used method within the addiction field. The main appeal of the cue reactivity paradigm is that it allows for the development of testable hypotheses with regard to addiction processes in a controlled laboratory setting and is grounded in widely studied general theories of human behavior (Drummond, 2000). In general, cue reactivity research within the field of addiction has focused on three main areas: basic phenomenology, evaluation of the efficacy of treatment programs, and tailoring interventions.

2.1   Basic phenomenology

A large majority of the cue reactivity literature has focused on describing the phenomenon of cue reactivity: that is, understanding the type of reactions, the reactors, and the characteristics of the eliciting cue. Of note, this will be discussed in more detail in section 3; yet, as a general overview, a variety of cue presentation modalities have been found to effectively elicit craving (*in vivo*, imaginal, audio, video, pictorial, and virtual reality; Erblich and Bovbjerg, 2004; Culbertson *et al.*, 2010; Litvin and Brandon, 2010) for a range of substances including alcohol, cocaine, heroin, marijuana, methamphetamine, and tobacco (Bauer and Kranzler, 1994; Carter and Tiffany, 1999; Conklin and Tiffany, 2001; Drobes and Tiffany, 1997; Lundahl and Johanson, 2011; Metrik *et al.*, 2009; Sell *et al.*, 2000; Singleton *et al.*, 2002; Sinha *et al.*, 2003; Streeter *et al.*, 2002; Stritzke, Breiner, Curtin, and Lang, 2004; Tolliver *et al.*, 2010). In addition to adults, the method has been used successfully with adolescents and young adults (Colby *et al.*, 2004; Curtin *et al.*, 2005; Gray, LaRowe, Watson, and Carpenter, 2010) as well as with social and dependent users (e.g., Sayette *et al.*, 2001; Vollstädt-Klein *et al.*, 2011; Watson *et al.*, 2010). Cue reactivity has also been found to be stable across sessions in both deprived and nondeprived users (Lee *et al.*, 2007; Miranda *et al.*, 2008b).

In terms of characterizing the cue-elicited responses, a highly cited meta-analysis of cue reactivity studies reported robust effects for self-report of craving in response to cues, and a somewhat smaller, though still meaningful effect size for physiological responses to cues (Carter and Tiffany, 1999). The autonomic profile of cue reactivity was found to be fairly similar across drugs of abuse and seemed to be characterized by increases in heart-rate and sweat-gland activity and decreases in peripheral temperature. When drug use measures are used in cue reactivity studies, the typical finding is a modest increase in drug-seeking or drug use behavior (e.g., Carter and Tiffany, 2001). In addition to self-report, physiological, and behavioral responses, other cue-elicited outcomes have been examined, including behavioral economic and brain responses. MacKillop and colleagues (2010) reported that alcohol versus neutral cues significantly increases multiple behavioral economic measures of the relative value of alcohol, including alcohol consumption under conditions of zero cost, maximum expenditure on alcohol, persistence in drinking to higher prices, and proportionate price insensitivity. Thus, drug cues appear to directly alter the incentive value of the drug. For brain responses, cue-induced activations have demonstrated consistency across different drugs, suggesting that craving and cue reactivity are processes general to addiction, rather than specific to the type of drug to which individuals are addicted. Although activations reported vary somewhat by cue type, severity of dependence, and individual difference variables, a number of regions have demonstrated activation in the majority of these studies. These regions include the amygdala, gyrus, ventral tegmental area, nucleus accumbens, anterior cingulate cortex, orbitofrontal cortex, dorsolateral prefrontal cortex, and insula (Dagher *et al.*, 2009; David *et al.*, 2005; Goldstein *et al.*, 2009; Janes *et al.*, 2009; Lee, Lim, Wiederhold, and Graham, 2005; McClernon, Hutchison, Rose, and Kozink, 2007; McClernon *et al.*, 2007; Schacht *et al.*, 2011; Tapert, Brown, Baratta, and Brown, 2004; Vollstädt-Klein *et al.*, 2010; Yang *et al.*, 2009).

2.2   Evaluation of the efficacy of treatment programs

In addition to basic phenomenology, the cue reactivity paradigm is commonly used to evaluate the efficacy of treatment, with the basic underlying hypothesis being that mitigation of cue-elicited increase in urge to use or withdrawal could be protective in high-risk situations. Simply, exposure to substance cues can simulate a high-risk situation for relapse (Monti *et al.*, 2000) and therefore is a useful paradigm for testing mechanisms of treatment effects on urge to use (Hersh, Bauer, and Kranzler, 1995; McCaul and Monti, 2003; Monti *et al.*, 1999; Robbins, Ehrman, Childress, and O'Brien, 1992; Rohsenow *et al.*, 2000). As such, cue reactivity as an outcome measure has been used quite frequently in medication studies (Hussain *et al.*, 2010; Hutchison *et al.*, 1999; Hutchison *et al.*, 2006; McGeary *et al.*, 2006; Miranda *et al.*, 2008a; Monti, Rohsenow, and Hutchison, 2000; Niaura *et al.*, 2005; Reid and Thakkar, 2009; Rohsenow *et al.*, 2007; Rohsenow *et al.*, 2008; Waters *et al.*, 2004).

For example, Monti, Rohsenow, and Hutchison (2000) conducted a study to investigate the effects of naltrexone on cue-elicited urge to drink among abstinent alcoholics in treatment. Alcohol-dependent subjects were randomized to 12 weeks of naltrexone or placebo after completing a partial hospital program. After 1 week on medication, all subjects participated in a cue reactivity assessment. Significantly fewer patients taking naltrexone reported any urge to drink during alcohol exposure than did those on placebo. Mean arterial pressure decreased significantly for those on placebo, but not for those on naltrexone, whereas cue-elicited decreases in heart rate were not affected by the medication. This study demonstrates how the cue reactivity methodology has utility for investigating hypothesized mediators of therapeutic effects of pharmacotherapies.

The utility of using the cue reactivity paradigm as an outcome for treatment studies is not exclusive to alcohol. For instance, a multi-center, randomized, placebo-controlled study was conducted with 296 smokers to evaluate the effectiveness of nicotine gum in relieving acute craving (Shiffman *et al.*, 2003). Participants received 3 days of either active or inactive nicotine gum. On the third day, participants were exposed to smoking cues and rated their cravings. Shiffman and colleagues (2003) found that active nicotine gum significantly reduced acute cravings following smoking cues compared to inactive gum. In another study with nicotine gum, 319 smokers were randomized to chew either a rapid-release nicotine gum or regular nicotine gum (Niaura *et al.*, 2005). Results showed that rapid-release formulation gum lowered cue-induced subjective ratings of tobacco craving more than a slower-release nicotine gum.

In sum, to the extent that treatments are designed with the purpose of diminishing craving, the cue reactivity methodology serves as a practical method to test the potential efficacy of treatments.

2.3   Tailoring interventions

As described above, assessing reactivity (craving and physiological responses) to drug cues has offered researchers and clinicians insight into potential relapse triggers and situations that lead to use, and thus cue exposure has been used in the context of a treatment approach to extinguish drug use. Typically, in cue exposure treatment, addicts are exposed to personally relevant drug cues (e.g., a pipe for marijuana, a pipe for crack, a preferred beverage for alcohol) either *in vivo* (handling drug paraphernalia) or imaginally (i.e., imagining being in a situation typical of past drug use). Repeated unreinforced exposure to stimuli previously associated with the substance use is presumed to extinguish the conditioned response (e.g., craving and drink seeking) to such cues. In other words, the repeated association of the drug with certain cues leads to the acquisition of conditioned responses, and the repeated exposure of the drug with response prevention, putatively leads to the extinction of those responses.

A series of case studies conducted in England provided preliminary evidence for the benefits of cue exposure for participants with a moderate drinking goal. These studies used priming doses of alcohol cues and then had participants practice resisting the urge to drink further. Outcomes including no drinking-related absences from work (Pickens, Bigelow, and Griffiths, 1973), reduced number of heavy drinking days (Hodgson and Rankin, 1976; Rankin, 1982), and complete abstinence during a 9-month follow-up (Blakely and Baker, 1980) were reported. More recently, there have been larger-scaled controlled studies of cue exposure. One such randomized controlled study involved 42 nondependent participants with a stated goal of moderation drinking (Sitharthan, Sitharthan, Hough, and Kavanagh, 1997). Participants were randomly assigned to either a cognitive behavior therapy or a modified cue exposure treatment group. Both interventions were conducted in six 90-minute group sessions over a 6-month period. Investigators found that over 6 months of follow-up, modified cue exposure treatment produced significantly greater decreases than cognitive behavior therapy in drinking frequency, amount per occasion, problems at work, legal trouble, and health problems, as well as reported dependence and impaired control over drinking.

This treatment approach has also been used with alcohol-dependent treatment-seekers. Drummond and Glautier (1994) evaluated the effectiveness of cue exposure treatment in comparison to a relaxation control treatment for 35 men who were alcohol dependent. During the 10-day treatment, the cue exposure group had 400 minutes of exposure to the sight and smell of their preferred drinks, while the relaxation control group had relaxation therapy, but spent an identical amount of time in the laboratory and had 20 minutes of exposure to alcohol cues. Experimenters found that the cue exposure group did not differ from the relaxation control group in terms of total abstinence. However, participants in the cue exposure group consumed less alcohol and took longer to relapse at the 6-month follow-up. Other cue exposure treatment work with alcoholics has shown promise. Rohsenow and colleagues (2001) found that compared to a meditation-relaxation control, patients who received cue exposure treatment had fewer heavy drinking days in the first 6 months following treatment. In the second 6 months, those who received cue exposure treatment continued to have fewer heavy drinking days among lapsers. In addition, the cue exposure treatment resulted in greater reductions in urge to drink on a measure of simulated high-risk situations and greater reports of use of coping strategies during the follow-up.

Although cue exposure treatment has shown some promise and been tested in clinical trials for alcohol, nicotine, cocaine, and opiate dependence (e.g., Dawe *et al.*, 1993; Drummond and Glautier, 1994; Niaura *et al.*, 1999; O'Brien, Childress, McLellan, and Ehrmann, 1990), critics have argued that research supporting this approach is scarce and that findings are inconsistent (Brandon, Piasecki, Quinn, and Baker, 1995; Conklin and Tiffany, 2002). Conklin and Tiffany (2002) stressed the need to identify the most relevant cues, environments, and/or contextual factors that serve to modulate craving and influence drug use. There has also been attention directed toward extinction learning; particularly that extinction-based efforts may poorly generalize beyond the setting in which they take place (Crombag, Bossert, Koya, and Shaham, 2008; MacKillop and Lisman, 2008). Therefore in order for cue exposure treatment to be effective, the treatment needs to maximize generalization of extinction (Conklin and Tiffany, 2002; Havermans and Jansen, 2003). While future research and treatment development is clearly needed, there remains cautious optimism with regard to the potential effectiveness of cue exposure treatment.

3   Standardized and Validated Cue Reactivity Methods

Cue exposure studies have a relatively standard procedure (Ferguson and Shiffman, 2009). First, subjects complete a series of baseline reports, ranging from subjective reports on their current state (e.g., substance craving) to physiological measurements (e.g., heart rate, skin conductance). Following this baseline assessment, subjects are exposed to either a neutral or substance-relevant stimulus through one of several possible cue presentation modes: imaginal (e.g., vividly imagining situations related to past drug use), audio (e.g., listening to a tape of someone describing drug use), video (e.g., watching a film of someone drinking), pictorial (e.g., viewing pictures of drug paraphernalia), and/or virtual reality (i.e., a computer-generated, three-dimensional world that changes in realistic ways in response to head and body motion) (Conklin, 2006). Following exposure, psychological and/or physiological measurements are repeated (post-exposure measurement).

The following is an example of an alcohol cue reactivity procedure from McGeary and colleagues (2006) based on Monti *et al.* (1999). Cue reactivity assessments take place between noon and 5 p.m. to reasonably control for time of day, which itself can serve as a cue (Monti, 2006). Breath alcohol level analysis is conducted to ensure that participants did not consume alcohol before the session. Participants are seated alone in a 5 feet by 6 feet sound-attenuated testing room equipped with a table and chair. One-way mirrors allow research staff to monitor participants' behavior. Participants receive instructions, a demonstration, and explanation of the questionnaire items. Participants are fitted with the blood pressure cuff on the nondominant arm and allowed to habituate to the inflation and deflation cycle (approximately every 40 seconds) of the blood pressure monitor during the instruction period. Trials are presented in the same order for all participants and instructions are audiotaped. A 3-minute relaxation period occurs first as a baseline, so that participants can habituate to the blood pressure cuff and baseline levels of urge and physiological measures can be collected. Next, a tray containing a glass half full of water and a commercially labeled bottle of water, both covered with an inverted pitcher, are placed in front of the participant. The experimenter removes the pitcher and leaves the room. The participant is instructed to begin to inhale the smell of the glass of water when s/he hears high tones and stop inhaling when s/he hears low tones. Participants are signaled to smell the beverage for 5 seconds per occasion, 13 times during the 3-minute trial. At the end of the trial, the participant is instructed to complete the questionnaires and the experimenter removes the tray, bottle, and glass. A second 3-minute relaxation period ensues. Then, a second 3-minute beverage trial commences, with the participant's preferred alcohol beverage prepared in his/her preferred way and a commercially labeled alcohol bottle replacing the water. Often, the alcoholic beverage exposure is repeated to determine whether participants habituate or become more sensitive to cues upon the second exposure (e.g., Rohsenow *et al.*, 2000). In addition to completing the questionnaires, during all trials, physiological assessments (e.g., diastolic blood pressure, systolic blood pressure, mean arterial pressure, and heart rate) are measured on average every 40 seconds.

With this procedure as the general foundation, there are a number of specific design considerations to take into account, including: necessity for neutral-control cue, cue presentation order, mode of cue presentation, substance factors, and type of reactivity measurement.

3.1 Neutral-control cue

The recommended approach in cue reactivity research is to use both drug-related and neutral control stimuli (e.g., pencil for smoking, water for alcohol; LaRowe, Saladin, Carpenter, and Upadhyaya, 2007; McGeary *et al.*, 2006) rather than solely comparing drug cue responses to a pre-stimulus baseline. This approach is utilized in order to aid cue specificity or the source of craving effects. Namely, when reactivity to drug cues is compared to pre-stimulus baseline conditions, it is thought that it is not possible to conclude that the changes from baseline can be attributed to the drug-salience of the cue (Carter and Tiffany, 1999). Yet, some studies have found that baseline levels of craving are similar to levels following a neutral cue (Doran, Cook, McChargue, and Spring, 2009; Rohsenow *et al.*, 2007; Sayette *et al.*, 2001), promoting the question of whether the neutral cue is indeed necessary (Hutchison *et al.*, 2002; Miranda *et al.*, 2008b). Nevertheless, other work has demonstrated that the neutral cue does produce significantly greater craving than baseline (e.g., Doran, Spring, and McChargue, 2007; Franklin *et al.*, 2007; LaRowe, Saladin, Carpenter, and Upadhyaya, 2007). Consequently, the control cue is still the most commonly used approach, particularly for nonverbal measures (e.g., cognitive measure, psychophysiological, neurobiological; Sayette, Griffin, and Sayers, 2010). Future work is needed to understand definitively how neutral cues compare to baseline and the extent to which this may be substance specific.

A related point is the suitability of the neutral cue condition (Tiffany and Wray, 2009). The growing consensus is that the neutral cue should have no psychoactive effects but be as similar as possible to the active substance (Stritzke, Breiner, Curtin, and Lang, 2004). Properties to consider include appearance, complexity, consumability, sensory properties, nutritional value, and desirability (Demmel and Schrenk, 2003; Newlin *et al.*, 1989; Payne *et al.*, 1992; Staiger and White, 1991).

3.2   Cue presentation order

With the inclusion of a neutral cue, a critical design consideration to address is whether to counterbalance the presentation order of the drug and neutral cues. As Sayette, Griffin, and Sayers (2010) describe, it has not been uncommon to counterbalance the presentation order. This decision seems to be based on the premise that a fixed order of neutral cue preceding drug cue would create the confound of presentation order and specifically that the drug cue effect cannot be disentangled from the order effect (therefore counterbalancing is used to control for the order effect). Yet, this decision whether to counterbalance is not as simple as it may seem. An important consideration to take into account is the possibility of carryover effects and specifically differential carryover effects across conditions. Explicitly, the concern is that exposure to the drug cue may bias response to the following neutral cue to a greater extent than the control cue biases the later presented drug cue. Thus, the initial drug cue may elevate craving and this craving may not dissipate completely before the neutral cue. In this set-up, the neutral or control cue becomes biased and this bias may vary by individual difference variables (e.g., heavy versus light user).

Initial evidence of carryover effects were reported in a seminal study conducted by Monti and colleagues (1987). In this study comparing alcoholics to non-alcoholics, counterbalancing the order of the stimuli masked the detection of between-group differences, thereby interfering with the determination of cue reactivity. This evidence of carryover effects has been replicated, with recent evidence demonstrating that cue-elicited urges do not always completely dissipate before the next cue presentation (Heishman, Singleton, and Moolchan, 2003; Heishman, Saha, and Singleton, 2004; Heishman, Lee, Taylor, and Singleton, 2010; Kavanagh, Andrade, and May, 2005; Paris *et al.*, 2011; Sayette, Loewenstein, Kirchner, and Travis, 2005). In contrast, there is no convincing evidence of commensurate carryover effects when neutral cues are presented first (Sayette, Griffin, and Sayers, 2010).

Sayette, Griffin, and Sayers (2010) have outlined a number of potential ways to handle the observed differential carryover effects. These potential approaches as well as their strengths and limitations are outlined in Table 14.1. With probable cons to each of the proposed methods, there is not a clearly preferable design choice. It is

Table 14.1 Pros and cons of approaches to cue presentation order

Approach	Pro	Con
Counterbalancing of cue order across multiple sessions	More time for carryover effects to dissipate compared to a single-session study	Possibility of drug cues in one session still impacting neutral cues in a subsequent session, necessity of multiple sessions and resulting potential for attrition, lack of clarity of required time between session
Insertion of neutral activities between cue exposures	Activity like watching a nature video provides a 'cleansing' effect	Increased time to complete protocol and consequently greater time since last drug use
Use of a between-subject design	Failsafe approach to prevent carryover effects as participants receive only one type of cue	Necessity for more participants, potential between group variability
Inclusion of order as a factor in all analyses	Controls for the order of cue presentation	Requires power to reliability assess interactions, complex interactions that are not easily understood
Inclusion of a baseline urge rating prior to each cue presentation	Possibility of covarying out residual effect	Assessment reactivity
Provision of drug and neutral cues in a fixed order	Avoidance of drug cue carryover effect	Potential impact of greater time since last drug use, only using one drug cue and one neutral cue may impact reliability
Removal of the neutral cue	Eliminates concern altogether if the baseline rating is similar to that produced by the neutral cue	Possibility that the neutral cue is a more robust control than the baseline measurement (i.e., higher craving with the neutral cue than at baseline)

critical for researchers utilizing the cue reactivity paradigm to take into account cue presentation order, carefully considering the strengths and weaknesses of the different means of addressing their design choice.

3.3 Mode of cue presentation

In considering the mode of cue presentation, it is first important to take into account the types of cue that exist and may elicit reactivity. Drummond (2000) has classified cue types into four categories: (1) exteroceptive; (2) interoceptive; (3) temporal; and (4) chained. Exteroceptive or external drug-related stimuli (e.g., sight, smell, and taste) are the most commonly studied in the laboratory and include people and places associated with drug use or drug paraphernalia such as needles, drug pipes, cocaine powder or beer cans, and *in vivo* exposure to the drug itself. Interoceptive refers to internal cues such as stress responses, negative affect, and withdrawal-related state (Childress *et al.*, 1994; Cooney *et al.*, 1997; Sinha and O'Malley, 1999; Sinha, Catapano, and O'Malley, 1999; Sinha, Fuse, Aubin, and O'Malley, 2000). The temporal category speaks to factors that are more proximal or distant to substance use as well as time of day: that is, the end of a work day may in and of itself serve as a cue. Chained relationships are included to capture the fact that substance use cues rarely occur in isolation: for example, the sight of a favorite drink may be linked to and thus more salient for an individual only in a certain context (e.g., in the evening, at a certain bar). Monti (2006) has emphasized the importance of contextual factors and these have been reviewed in a recent chapter (MacKillop and Monti, 2007). Drummond (2000) describes the possibility of a cue chain: "an office worker leaving work on a Friday evening, walks home on a route that passes his favourite pub, which he then enters, lights a cigarette and orders a beer" (p. S132). With this sequence, each environmental cue may increase the salience of the next.

These types of cue have been modeled in the laboratory through a number of different procedures including *in vivo*, imaginal, audio, video, pictorial, and virtual reality (Conklin, 2006). The central question in considering the mode of presentation has been which type of cue presentation mode is the most contextually realistic: that is, which approach most accurately represents real-world cue-exposures as well as what mode is suitable for the laboratory paradigm and its associated constraints (e.g., fMRI, psychophysiological assessments) (Tong, Bovbjerg, and Erblich, 2007).

A host of studies have been conducted to assess whether one type of cue modality is preferable to another. For example, Erblich and Bovbjerg (2004) conducted a study comparing *in vivo* and imaginal smoking cues. The rationale for the study was based on a conflict between opinion and empirical data. That is, it had been asserted that imaginal in contrast to *in vivo* would be a more valid laboratory model of cue-induced craving, as it allows the user to imagine idiographic cues and environmental contingencies (Tiffany, 1990). Yet, empirical work comparing the two modalities had found that craving reactions to *in vivo* and imaginal cues did not differ in magnitude (Burton and Tiffany, 1997; Drobes and Tiffany, 1997). To add clarity to this work, Erblich and Bovbjerg (2004) exposed 225 smokers to imaginal and *in vivo* smoking cues and measured craving reactions. Results indicated that both imaginal and *in vivo* smoking cues increased craving and that the magnitudes of imaginal and *in vivo* reactions were statistically comparable. In addition, results suggested that *in vivo*, but not imaginal, reactivity was related to duration of previous quit attempts, particularly in men.

Leading the effort to increase "real world" generalizability of cues, Conklin and colleagues (2008) have investigated cues and other stimuli with traditional cue-presentation methods. Using photographs to elicit smokers' cue reactivity, they found a significant effect of cue context (comparing smoking versus nonsmoking environments), demonstrating that pictures of smoking-related environments, completely devoid of cigarette cues (e.g., a bar scene without explicit cigarette cues), can elicit craving. They later compared photographs of three different smoking environments to photographs of explicit cues (e.g., cigarette in an ashtray) and found that smoking contexts elicited craving to smoke, but explicit cues led to significantly greater craving. They have built upon this work by developing a novel procedure for bringing smokers' real-world smoking and nonsmoking environments into the laboratory to compare them with standard (i.e., not personalized) environments (Conklin *et al.*, 2010). The procedure involves having participants use digital cameras to take pictures of the environments in which they do and do not smoke. In comparison to standard smoking cues, results demonstrated that personal environments led to a significantly larger smoking–nonsmoking difference in craving as well as enhanced stimuli vividness, relevance, positive affect, excitement, and heart rate changes from baseline.

A viable means to capture substance-using environments and model them in the laboratory is with virtual reality technology. In recent work, virtual reality has been used to elicit and assess cue reactivity in substance users (Baumann and Sayette, 2006; Bordnick *et al.*, 2005; Bordnick *et al.*, 2004; Traylor, Bordnick, and Carter, 2008). Virtual reality involves an immersive human–computer interaction with multi-sensory experiences that lead to a participant's feeling of presence in a three-dimensional virtual environment. Virtual reality allows researchers to present complex stimuli within contextually appropriate virtual environments to assess reactivity to more naturalistic cues while maintaining the control of a laboratory setting. Placing substance users in a virtual world, in an environment similar to that in which they are typically exposed to substance cues, may provide a more accurate picture of how cue reactivity manifests itself in the real world.

Most virtual reality studies have employed a method in which participants are presented with a sequence of virtual reality scenes, first neutral (a non-substance environment without cues) and later experimental (a substance environment with cues) with self-report of craving and physiological responding assessed after each scene. Cue reactivity studies using virtual reality have shown typical cue reactivity effects, with significant increases in self-reported craving, but mixed physiological findings among individuals dependent on various drugs of abuse, including alcohol (Bordnick *et al.*, 2008), cocaine (Saladin, Brady, Graap, and Rothbaum, 2006), marijuana (Gray, LaRowe, and Upadhyaya, 2008), and nicotine (Bordnick *et al.*, 2005; Bordnick *et al.*, 2004; Traylor, Bordnick, and Carter, 2008).

As previously stated, there are two central questions in considering the mode of cue presentation: (1) ecological validity and (2) suitability for the laboratory paradigm and associated constraints (e.g., fMRI, psychophysiological assessments) (Tong, Bovbjerg, and Erblich, 2007). Thus, although *in vivo* and virtual reality cues may increase the ecological validity of a cue manipulation, researchers have increasingly paired single-sensory modality cue presentations (e.g., visual) with physiological and fMRI assessments in order to better characterize the multidimensional (i.e., physiological, subjective) nature of craving. This decision is based on findings that physiological changes associated with cue manipulations can reflect processing demands of the situation unique to a given modality, rather than learned drug–stimulus associations (Tiffany, 1992). Such interactions and complexities are liable to produce inconsistent reactivity patterns. Accordingly, there are thought to be distinct advantages to presenting cues in a single modality that permits cue content and intensity to be systematically varied, controlled, and evaluated (Stritzke, Breiner, Curtin, and Lang, 2004).

In sum, there is great variability in the cue presentation mode. Regardless of cue modality, substance users tend to report an increased urge (Carter *et al.*, 2008). In designing a cue reactivity study, the critical question is what cue modality best fits the research question. The cue reactivity paradigm provides a window into the individual's typical life outside the laboratory, but does so to varying degrees, so the investigator must identify the study's priorities.

3.4   Substance factors

A critical component to consider in cue reactivity work is substance use factors; such factors include perceived availability of the substance, treatment status, and latency since last use. Research has demonstrated that when drugs are available for consumption during an experiment, drug users report significantly higher craving in response to drug cues than when drugs are not available for an extended period of time (Carter and Tiffany, 2001; Juliano and Brandon, 1998; Droungas, Ehrman, Childress, O'Brien, 1995); in addition to craving responses, this finding has also been shown with affective (Carter and Tiffany, 2001; Sayette *et al.*, 2003) and cognitive processes (Juliano and Brandon, 1998; Wertz and Sayette, 2001). Furthermore, physiological responses (e.g., heart rate, skin conductance) have been shown to be heightened with imminent drug use (Carter and Tiffany, 1999; Zinser, Fiore, Davidson, and Baker, 1999). These findings are similar to what has been observed with treatment-seekers versus non-treatment-seekers. That is, non-treatment-seekers who thus perceive that drug use will be available after the experiment have greater cue reactivity than those who are seeking or enrolled in treatment and thus may have limited drug availability and/or intent to use (Wertz and Sayette, 2001). It has been suggested that those seeking treatment may be motivated to maintain abstinence and thus may inhibit craving in response to drug cues (Wertz and Sayette, 2001).

Latency since last use is also a critical factor to consider. Research has demonstrated that deprivation prior to cue reactivity assessment can result in larger effects (e.g., Carter *et al.*, 2006) and has been supported by findings that smoking just prior to cue testing can diminish cue reactivity (Carpenter *et al.*, 2009). The critical component here is the potential effect of withdrawal: namely, that withdrawal may increase the reinforcement salience of cues (Cinciripini *et al.*, 2006).

In addition to considering the effect that deprivation from a substance has on cue reactivity to that substance, researchers have taken steps to understand the effects that deprivation from one substance has on another substance. For example, Palfai, Monti, Ostafin, and Hutchison (2000) examined the effects of tobacco deprivation in smokers who were also hazardous drinkers. Half of the 56 participants were deprived from smoking 6 hours prior to participating in a smoking cue reactivity protocol. Urges to smoke and drink, and alcohol consumption were assessed after smoking cue exposure. Results showed that smoking deprivation increased urges to drink and alcohol consumption. However, the smoking cues had little influence, leaving open the question as to what might have happened if alcohol cues had been used. A second study examined tobacco deprivation in alcohol-dependent smokers in early alcohol recovery (Cooney *et al.*, 2003). Using a within-subjects design, 40 participants completed an alcohol cue exposure assessment after either 34 hours of smoking deprivation or no deprivation. Smoking deprivation was associated with increased smoking urges but not with increased urge to drink. Most recently, Colby and colleagues (2004) investigated the effects of brief tobacco deprivation on alcohol cue-elicited urges to drink, corresponding psychophysiological reactions, and alcohol consumption among young adult moderate to heavy smokers and drinkers. Participants were either deprived of tobacco for 5 hours or not deprived and then exposed to *in vivo* alcohol or control beverage cues. Subsequently, participants engaged in a taste-rating task as an unobtrusive measure of alcohol consumption. Tobacco deprivation resulted in increased urge to smoke and decreased cardiovascular responses but did not increase alcohol urges or alcohol consumption. The researchers concluded that brief tobacco deprivation does not result in compensatory increases in alcohol consumption among young moderate to heavy drinkers. As treatments for polydrug abusers become more commonplace (e.g., Kahler *et al.*, 2008), cue reactivity assessment will necessarily become more complex and challenging.

In terms of addressing deprivation, researchers have tackled this concern by carefully assessing/controlling time since last use. For example, Colby and colleagues (2004) used the following procedures to ensure deprivation. Participants are instructed to abstain from alcohol, antihistamines, decongestants, and illicit drugs for at least 24 hours, to refrain from vigorous exercise for 4 hours, and to eat lunch and then fast 4 hours before the appointment. Half of the participants are also instructed to abstain from cigarettes and nicotine/tobacco products for 4 hours. All participants are asked to bring a pack of their usual cigarettes to the lab. Upon arrival at the lab, compliance with pre-experimental instructions is evaluated. Recent exposure to alcohol and tobacco consumption is evaluated using the blood alcohol level (BAL) and expired alveolar carbon monoxide (CO) level assessment. The participants are also asked to sign a compliance affidavit. Sessions are terminated if a participant has a positive BAL or does not sign the affidavit. Following compliance procedures and baseline questionnaires, the participants in the nondeprived conditions are instructed to smoke one cigarette to control time since the last cigarette and to ensure a lack of nicotine deprivation. Participants in the deprived conditions remained abstinent. CO is reassessed just prior to the onset of the laboratory protocol. In short, based on research demonstrating that deprivation can impact cue reactivity (e.g., Carter *et al.*, 2006; Carpenter, Schreiber, Church, and McDowella, 2009), it is necessary for researchers to take this variable into consideration when designing the cue paradigm. If deprivation effects are of concern, an approach such as that used by Colby and colleagues (2004) should be considered.

In sum, it is critical for cue reactivity researchers to take into account key substance use characteristics of the research sample, including abstinence/treatment status of the participants, latency since last use, and how the laboratory procedures influence perceived availability of the substance (Tiffany and Wray, 2009).

3.5   Type of reactivity measurement

A final component to consider is the type of outcome measurement to utilize: that is, how to best capture reactivity and demonstrate clinical predictive utility. As previously stated, a number of outcome measures have been used including self-report, physiological, lever pressing, behavioral economic, neurobiological, and behavioral, with the vast majority of studies focusing on self-report and physiological outcomes.

The seminal meta-analysis on cue reactivity (Carter and Tiffany, 1999) reported robust effects for self-report of craving in response to cues, and a somewhat smaller, though still meaningful effect size for physiological responses. Carter and Tiffany (1999) explained the finding by suggesting that physiological responding contains a great deal of noise as the assessed physiological processes (increased heart rate, sweat gland activity, and skin temperature) are probably engaged in many functions unrelated to manipulations of drug cues. Since this meta-analysis was conducted, a number of criticisms have been made against physiological assessment of craving (see Sayette *et al.*, 2000). Primary is the assertion that the physiological processes are not exclusive to motivation/craving for drug use as stated by Carter and Tiffany (1999) and that it is thus unclear what clinical and theoretical meaning should be assigned to observed changes in physiological processes. These criticisms have led to researchers selecting new physiological measures including evoked brain potentials and cue-modulated startle reflex which, for example, appear more closely connected to drinking and relapse than self-reported craving (Franken *et al.*, 2004). For instance, the startle modulation paradigm offers the advantages of being noninvasive, well characterized in human and animal models, and having an established neurophysiologic basis (Franken *et al.*, 2004 – see Chapter 21 in this volume for further discussion).

In terms of self-report, a commonly identified limitation is that many studies rely on a single-item craving measure. While there are many advantages of single-item scales (e.g., ease of administration and scoring, suitability for frequent and repeated measurement, sensitivity to rapid change, correlation with multi-item questionnaires) (Monti, 2006; Rosenberg, 2009), single-item measures have been criticized for failing to reflect the multidimensional nature of craving (e.g., Tiffany, 1992 – see Chapter 13 in this volume for further discussion). Thus it has been strongly recommended to utilize validated and reliable multi-item measures (cf., Perkins, 2009) that offer a more nuanced assessment of craving than the global "urge" or "craving."

In sum, the key component in considering outcome measures is focused on which criterion measures are representative of the drug-addiction construct, taking into account behavioral, emotion, cognitive, and motivational constructs.

4   Limitations, Shortcomings, and Future Directions for the Field

The cue reactivity paradigm has proven useful for investigating basic theoretical issues related to addictive behaviors (Drummond, Tiffany, Glautier, and Remington, 1995) and offers the advantages of being amenable to standardization and manipulation in the laboratory. As such, the paradigm has a rich history in the field of addiction. Yet, there exist a number of critical psychometric and methodological issues to be addressed for the paradigm to reach its full potential. Tiffany and Wray (2009) have identified a number of considerations, including characteristics of the predictor and criterion variables (e.g., reliability, stability, sensitivity, specificity), representativeness of the cue, nature of the paradigm (e.g., optimal number of cue trials, time between trials, and availability of the drug during the trials), mode of cue presentation, context in which the assessment takes place (i.e., natural environment, laboratory, clinic), timing in relation to where the participant is in a quit attempt (e.g., before, during, after), and key characteristics of the research sample (e.g., abstinence status, history of use, level of addiction). To these we would add age of the participants (i.e., adults versus adolescents); substance as interoceptive cue (e.g., alcohol challenge procedures); and the emerging role of ecological momentary assessment (EMA). While a number of these have been discussed at length previously in this chapter, we will take the time to further discuss a few with the focus being on future directions for the field.

4.1 Predictive validity of cue-specific craving

A major criticism of the cue reactivity paradigm is the lack of a clear link between relapse risk and cue-elicited responding and therefore clinical predictive utility (Perkins, 2009). This criticism is based on the fact that behavioral responses are the least studied outcome measure in cue reactivity research, with only a limited number of studies demonstrating a relation to risk of relapse prospectively (see Table 14.2). It is uncertain whether the inconsistent findings are due to methodological limitations (e.g., craving measurement post-cue presentation, need for greater complexity in design/procedure), limitations of the global construct of subjective craving, or failure of the paradigm as an analogue of drug use motivational processes itself (Munafò and Hitsman, 2010). As such, the field of addiction needs a clearer understanding of the associations between cue-specific craving and drug relapse in order to establish predictive validity.

4.2 Cue standardization

A second area for growth within cue reactivity research is in the reliability and validity of the utilized cues. The cue reactivity literature is littered with the use of inconsistent, unstandardized, and poorly controlled stimuli, which may, in part, compromise the comparability of findings across studies (e.g., Curtin *et al.*, 2005). Researchers (e.g., Grusser *et al.*, 2000; Wrase *et al.*, 2002) have highlighted the importance of stimuli standardization prior to creating a cue reactivity task in order to eliminate confounding differences, on features other than the cue-elicited effect of interest, between stimuli in the experimental and control conditions. For example, if alcohol cues were different from control cues in valence, differences in reactivity could not be ascribed to differential elicitation of urge or alcohol-related neural networks, but could simply be an artifact of stimulus affective tone. Furthermore, proper standardization of alcohol and control stimuli is imperative when using a methodology (e.g., neuroimaging) sensitive to stimuli differences (e.g., differential activation of visual cortex as a function of color) (Engel, Zhang, and Wandell, 1997). To standardize stimuli, ratings on such parameters of interest must be determined and compared (Wrase *et al.*, 2002). Efforts in this domain have been undertaken (Carter *et al.*, 2006; Pulido, 2010; Stritzke, Breiner, Curtin, and Lang, 2004) and continued work in this area will aid objectivity and rigor by minimizing the extent to which the stimuli of interest vary from the control conditions.

Table 14.2 Studies examining the predictive validity of cue-specific craving

Study	Drug type	Sample	Design	Predictor variable(s)	Main finding
Abrams *et al.* (1988)	Nicotine	48 chronic smokers	Pre-treatment cue reactivity assessment, provided treatment, followed for 6 months post-treatment; relapsers versus quitters compared.	Heart rate, galvanic skin conductance, self-reported urge, skill, anxiety	Relapsers had greater heart-rate reactivity and anxiety than the quitters after the cue exposure.
Braus *et al.* (2001)	Alcohol	4 abstinent alcoholics who fulfilled diagnostic criteria for alcohol dependence according to ICD 10 and 3 healthy control subjects	Alcoholics had been detoxified on a ward and were abstinent for at least 1 week before fMRI. Patients followed for 3 months.	Activation of the ventral putamen	Patients who displayed a strong cue-induced activation of the ventral putamen relapsed frequently and consumed high amounts of alcohol during the follow-up period.
Grusser *et al.* (2004)	Alcohol	10 abstinent alcoholics and control subjects	fMRI and visual alcohol-associated and control cues to assess brain activation. Patients were followed for 3 months.	Activation of the putamen, anterior cingulate and adjacent medial prefrontal cortex	Cue-induced activation of these brain areas was pronounced in the five alcoholics who subsequently relapsed during the observation period. Amount of subsequent alcohol intake was associated with the intensity of cue-induced brain activation but not the severity of alcohol craving, amount of previous alcohol intake, or duration of abstinence before scanning.

Study	Drug	Sample	Procedure	Measure	Results
Kosten *et al.* (2006)	Cocaine	17 cocaine-dependent patients	fMRI during a 2-week inpatient stay. The subjects then entered a 10-week outpatient placebo-controlled, double-blind randomized clinical trial where urine toxicologies were assessed three times weekly to calculate the treatment effectiveness score.	BOLD activation in the left precentral, superior temporal, and posterior cingulate cortices (PCC), and right middle temporal and lingual cortices	Worse treatment effectiveness score correlated with BOLD activation in these brain areas. The left PCC activation also distinguished eight relapsers from nine nonrelapsers.
Niaura, Abrams, DeMuth, and Pinto (1989)	Nicotine	54 adult smokers, who smoked 20 cigarettes per day or more	Prior to engaging in treatment for smoking cessation, subjects were tested for their responsiveness to cigarette smoking cues.	Heart rate	Smokers who relapsed by 3-months post-treatment were more likely to respond to smoking cues presented prior to treatment with a deceleratory change in heart rate.
Payne, Smith, Adams, and Diefenbach (2006)	Nicotine	62 smokers	Smokers participated in a smoking cue reactivity study, and subsequently enrolled in a smoking cessation program.	Heart rate	Mean heart rate during the cue presentation phase of the laboratory-based assessment predicted final session smoking rate and expired CO level.
Rohsenow *et al.* (1994)	Alcohol	45 alcoholic men admitted for detox to a treatment program	At admission, participants underwent a cue reactivity assessment protocol, received 3-month follow-up interviews.	Salivary reactivity	Greater salivary reactivity predicted greater frequency of drinking during follow-up.
Waters *et al.* (2004)	Nicotine	158 smokers	Cue-provoked craving ratings and reaction time responses were measured on first day of abstinence among 158 smokers who had been randomized to high-dose nicotine (35 mg) or placebo patch.	Self-reported smoking urge (on a 10-point, single-item scale)	Self-reported smoking urge response to holding an unlit cigarette predicted time to first lapse and 1-week abstinence in 81 subjects treated with nicotine patch but not in the 41 subjects quitting with placebo patch, and not in the entire sample as a whole.

4.3   Move toward ecological validity

While standardization of cues is important to reduce noise within the cue reactivity paradigm, this goal inherently requires balancing with real-world generalizability as cue reactivity is thought to be most relevant to the extent that substance users are actually exposed to relevant cues at vulnerable times (Shiffman, 2009). As previously described, Conklin and colleagues (2010) have conducted research with the goal of bringing the "real world" into the laboratory through the novel technique of having research participants take digital pictures of the environments in which they do and do not smoke. This work, maximizing the evocativeness of contextual cues, is critical for modeling addictive processes in the laboratory.

The development of personal cue methodology is particularly relevant and applicable to exposure or extinction-based treatments for addiction. As previously described, cue exposure treatment has been criticized due to the fact that extinction-based efforts poorly generalize beyond the setting in which they take place (cf., MacKillop and Lisman, 2008). This observation has been studied within animal models and termed "renewal effect," which refers to the recovery of an extinguished conditioned response as the result of a change in the context where that extinction took place (Crombag, Bossert, Koya, and Shaham, 2008). This effect thus limits the generalizability of extinction training (Conklin and Tiffany, 2002) and poses a challenge for cue exposure treatment. One means to address this challenge is through the use of personal cue methodology, which could potentially aid with reducing the impact of the renewal effect by exposing substance users to the environmental contexts where craving or urges to engage in a behavior are likely to take place. The potential opportunities to be gained from creative animal models have yet to be realized and this area clearly is in need of further development.

Another methodology that may be particularly useful for identifying the most relevant cues, environments, and/or contextual factors that serve to modulate craving and influence drug use is ecological momentary assessment (EMA). EMA involves real-time data collection in the natural environment (see Chapter 20 in this volume for further discussion). This approach captures a host of environmental and contextual factors (e.g., setting, mood, presence of others drinking). This method allows for the investigation of the subjective effects of substance use, along with their determinants (e.g., mood, setting, time of day) and consequences (e.g., quantity of additional substance consumed), as they occur in daily life. As such, EMA sidesteps possible biases introduced in artificial laboratory settings. Cue reactivity trials in natural settings allow for the gathering of real-time data such as craving levels, mood ratings, drug use behavior, temporal data, and contextual variables (Warthen and Tiffany, 2009; Wray, Godleski, and Tiffany, 2011), which are difficult if not impossible to stimulate in the laboratory (as is the case with adolescents, where EMA has recently been usefully employed; e.g., Monti *et al.*, 2010). EMA is an appropriate methodology to pair with cue reactivity paradigms and may greatly enhance our understanding of cue-elicited craving as well as enable us to study such phenomena in adolescents where alcohol administration would be prohibitive.

In sum, emerging novel methodologies such as digital personally relevant photos and EMA build on the classic cue reactivity paradigms and have the potential to increase the generalizability of findings to the natural environment of substance users of all ages.

4.4   Individual difference variables

In addition to methodological considerations within the cue reactivity paradigm, an additional consideration for future work is individual differences. Research in recent years has suggested that craving is highly variable from person to person. There is considerable variability in participant reactions to craving-related manipulations, with some participants not showing much of a response at all (Avants, Margolin, Kosten, and Cooney, 1995; Monti *et al.*, 1999; Rohsenow *et al.*, 1992; Shiffman *et al.*, 2003). These individuals who do not demonstrate any increase in the target variable from the baseline or neutral trials to drug trials have been labeled "non-reactors" or "non-responders" (e.g., Bradizza *et al.*, 1999). This "any increase" has been operationalized in different manners; some have defined this as any change (e.g., Bradizza *et al.*, 1999; MacKillop and Lisman, 2008; Monti *et al.*, 1993; Monti *et al.*, 1999; Rohsenow *et al.*, 1992) whereas others have specified an exact minimum change – for example, an increase of more than 1 point in average craving (e.g., Fonder *et al.*, 2005; Shiffman *et al.*, 2003; Tidey *et al.*, 2008).

Potential sources of variability include gender (Rubonis *et al.*, 1994), genetic factors (McGeary *et al.*, 2006), personality (Bradizza *et al.*, 1999; Litvin and Brandon, 2010), and substance use factors (e.g., lifetime alcohol use indices, parental drinking problems; Curtin *et al.*, 2005). Thus in moving forward, it is necessary for future work to first establish a clear and consistent definition of what constitutes a reaction and then to further develop the understanding of individual difference variables and how these factors may moderate cue reactivity. For example, existing research implicating genetic variation in the dopamine system serves as a foundation for a study examining all the functional polymorphisms of the dopamine system with accompanying laboratory paradigms (MacKillop and Monti, 2007). It will also be critical to consider moderation in the relation between reactivity and behavioral outcomes (e.g., lapse to use). It can be speculated that certain individual difference variables such as impulsivity (see Chapter 8, this volume) and distress tolerance (see Chapter 9, this volume) play a role. For example, those high in impulsivity (a preference for immediate rewards and a tendency to respond prematurely) may not be able to inhibit the urge to use following exposure to a conditioned cue. Likewise those with low distress tolerance may not be able to tolerate the physical and psychological sensations associated with craving and thus may seek a substance to alleviate the "distress." The examination of individual difference factors is fertile ground for future work.

5   Conclusion

Cue reactivity has become a frequently used method in addiction research. For nearly 25 years it has proven useful for investigating basic theoretical issues related to addictive behaviors (Drummond, Tiffany, Glautier, and Remington, 1995; Monti *et al.*,

1987) and it offers the advantages of being amenable to standardization and manipulation in the laboratory. In designing a cue reactivity paradigm there are a number of considerations to take into account, including the use and appropriateness of the neutral-control cue, cue presentation order, mode of cue presentation, substance use factors, and type of reactivity measurement. Moving forward, there are a number of factors that need further study in order to improve the paradigm's reliability and validity, including predictive validity of cue-specific craving, cue standardization, enhanced ecological validity, and consideration of individual difference variables.

References

Abrams DB and Niaura RS (1987) Social learning theory. In HT Blane and KE Leonard (eds), *Psychological Theories of Drinking and Alcoholism* (pp. 131–178). New York: Guilford Press.

Abrams DB, Monti PM, Carey KB, Pinto RP, and Jacobus SJ (1988) Reactivity to smoking cues and relapse: Two studies of discriminant validity. *Behaviour Research and Therapy* 26: 225–233. doi: 10.1016/0005-7967(88)90003-4.

Avants SK, Margolin A, Kosten TR, and Cooney NL (1995) Differences between responders and nonresponders to cocaine cues in the laboratory. *Addictive Behaviors* 20: 215–224. doi: 10.1016/0306-4603(94)00066-2.

Bauer LO and Kranzler HR (1994) Electroencephalographic activity and mood in cocaine-dependent outpatients: Effects of cocaine cue exposure. *Biological Psychiatry* 36: 189–197. doi: 10.1016/0306-4603(94)00066-2.

Baumann SB and Sayette MA (2006) Smoking cues in a virtual world provoke craving in cigarette smokers. *Psychology of Addictive Behaviors* 20: 484–489. doi: 10.1037/0893-164X.20.4.484.

Blakely R and Baker R (1980) An exposure approach to alcohol abuse. *Behaviour Research and Therapy* 18: 319–325.

Bordnick PS, Graap KM, Copp HL, Brooks J, and Ferrer M (2005) Virtual reality cue reactivity assessment in cigarette smokers. *Cyberpsychology, Behavior, and Social Networking* 8: 487–492. doi: 10.1007/s10484-005-6376-0.

Bordnick PS, Graap KM, Copp HL, Brooks J, Ferrer M, and Logue B (2004) Utilizing virtual reality to standardize nicotine craving research: A pilot study. *Addictive Behaviors* 29: 1889–1894. doi: 10.1016/j.addbeh.2004.06.008.

Bordnick PS, Traylor A, Copp HL, Graap KM, Carter BL, Ferrer M, and Walton AP (2008) Assessing reactivity to virtual reality alcohol based cues. *Addictive Behaviors* 33: 743–756. doi: 10.1016/j.addbeh.2004.06.008.

Bradizza CM, Gulliver SB, Stasiewicz PR, Torrisi R, Rohsenow DJ, and Monti PM (1999) Alcohol cue reactivity and private self-consciousness among male alcoholics. *Addictive Behaviors* 24: 543–549. doi: 10.1016/S0306-4603(98)00093-8.

Brandon TH, Piasecki TM, Quinn EP, and Baker TB (1995) Cue exposure treatment in nicotine dependence. In DC Drummond, ST Tiffany, S Glautier, and B Remington (eds), *Addictive Behaviour: Cue Exposure Theory and Practice* (pp. 211–227). Chichester: John Wiley & Sons, Ltd.

Braus DF, Wrase J, Grusser S, Hermann D, Ruf M, Flor H, Mann K, and Heinz A (2001) Alcohol-associated stimuli activate the ventral striatum in abstinent alcoholics. *Journal of Neural Transmission* 108: 887–894. doi: 10.1007/s007020170038.

Burton S and Tiffany S (1997) The effect of alcohol consumption on craving to smoke. *Addiction* 92: 15–26. doi: 10.1111/j.1360-0443.1997.tb03634.x.

Carpenter MJ, Saladin ME, DeSantis S, Gray KM, LaRowe SD, and Upadhyaya HP (2009) Laboratory-based, cue-elicited craving and cue reactivity as predictors of naturally occurring smoking behavior. *Addictive Behaviors* 34: 536–541. doi: 10.1016/j.addbeh.2009.03.022.

Carpenter KM, Schreiber TE, Church S, and McDowella D (2006) Drug Stroop performance: Relationships with primary substance of use and treatment outcome in a drug-dependent outpatient sample. *Addictive Behaviors* 31: 174–181. doi: 10.1016/j.addbeh.2005.04.012.

Carter BL and Tiffany ST (1999) Meta analysis of cue reactivity in addiction research. *Addiction* 92: 15–26. doi: 10.1046/j.1360-0443.1999.9433273.x.

Carter BL and Tiffany ST (2001) The cue-availability paradigm: The effects of cigarette availability on cue reactivity in smokers. *Experimental and Clinical Psychopharmacology* 9: 183–190. doi: 10.1037//1064-1297.9.2.183.

Carter BL, Bordnick P, Traylor A, Day SX, and Paris M (2008) Location and longing: The nicotine craving experience in virtual reality. *Drug and Alcohol Dependence* 95: 73–80. doi: 10.1016/j.drugalcdep.2007.12.010.

Carter BL, Robinson JD, Lam CY, Wetter DW, Tsan JY, Day SX, and Cinciripini PM (2006) A psychometric evaluation of cigarette stimuli used in a cue reactivity study. *Nicotine and Tobacco Research* 8: 361–369. doi: 10.1080/14622200600670215.

Carter BL and Tiffany ST (1999) Meta analysis of cue reactivity in addiction research. *Addiction* 92: 15–26. doi:10.1046/j.1360-0443.1999.9433273.x.

Carter BL and Tiffany ST (2001) The cue-availability paradigm: The effects of cigarette availability on cue reactivity in smokers. *Experimental and Clinical Psychopharmacology* 9: 183–190. doi:10.1037//1064-1297.9.2.183.

Childress AR, Ehrman R, McLellan AT, MacRae J, Natale M, and O'Brien CP (1994) Can induced moods trigger drug-related responses in opiate abuse patients? *Journal of Substance Abuse Treatment* 11: 17–23. doi: 10.1016/0740-5472(94)90060-4.

Childress AR, Ehrman R, Rohsenow DJ, Robbins SJ, and O'Brien CP (1992) Classically conditioned factors in drug dependence. In JH Lowinson, P Ruiz, and RB Millman (eds), *Substance Abuse: A Comprehensive Textbook* (pp. 55–69). Baltimore, MD: Williams & Wilkins.

Cinciripini PM, Robinson JD, Carter BL, Lam C, Wu X, de Moor CA, Baile WF, and Wetter DW (2006) The effects of smoking deprivation and nicotine administration on emotional reactivity. *Nicotine and Tobacco Research* 8: 379–392. doi: 10.1080/14622200600670272.

Clements K, Glautier S, Stolerman IP, White J-AW, and Taylor C (1996) Classical conditioning in humans: Nicotine as CS and alcohol as US. *Human Psychopharmacology: Clinical and Experimental* 11: 85–95. doi: 10.1002/(SICI)1099-1077(199603)11:2<85::AID-HUP756>3.3.CO;2-E.

Colby, SM, Rohsenow DJ, Monti PM, Gwaltney CJ, Gulliver SB, Abrams DB, Niaura RS, and Sirota AD (2004) Effects of tobacco deprivation on alcohol cue reactivity and drinking among young adults. *Addictive Behaviors* 29: 879–892. doi: 10.1016/j.addbeh.2004.03.002.

Conklin CA (2006) Environments as cues to smoke: Implication for human extinction-based research and treatment. *Experimental and Clinical Psychopharmacology* 14: 12–19. doi: 10.1037/1064-1297.14.1.12.

Conklin CA and Tiffany ST (2001) The impact of imagining personalized versus standardized urge scenarios on cigarette craving and autonomic reactivity. *Experimental and Clinical Psychopharmacology* 9: 399–408. doi: 10.1037//1064-1297.9.4.399.

Conklin CA and Tiffany ST (2002) Applying extinction research and theory to cue-exposure addiction treatment. *Addiction* 97: 155–167. doi: 10.1046/j.1360-0443.2002.00014.x.

Conklin CA, Perkins KA, Robin N, McClernon FJ, and Salkeld RP (2010) Bringing the real world into the laboratory: Personal smoking and nonsmoking environments. *Drug and Alcohol Dependence* 111: 58–63. doi: 10.1016/j.drugalcdep.2010.03.017.

Conklin CA, Robin N, Perkins KA, Salkeld RP, and McClernon FJ (2008) Proximal versus distal cues to smoke: The effects of environments on smokers' cue-reactivity. *Experimental and Clinical Psychopharmacology* 16: 207-214.doi: 10.1037/1064-1297.16.3.207

Cooney JL, Cooney NL, Pilkey DT, Kranzler HR, and Oncken CA (2003) Effects of nicotine deprivation on urges to drink and smoke in alcoholic smokers. *Addiction* 98: 913–921. doi: 10.1046/j.1360-0443.2003.00337.x.

Cooney NL, Litt MD, Morse PA, Bauer LO, and Gaupp L (1997) Alcohol cue reactivity, negative-mood reactivity, and relapse in treated alcoholic men. *Journal of Abnormal Psychology* 106: 243–250. doi: 10.1037/0021-843X.106.2.243.

Crombag HS, Bossert JM, Koya E, and Shaham Y (2008) Context-induced relapse to drug seeking: A review. *Philosophical Transactions of the Royal Society of London. Series B, Biological Sciences*. 363: 3233–3243. doi: 10.1098/rstb.2008.0090.

Culbertson C, Nicolas S, Zaharovits I, London ED, La Garza RD, Brody AL, and Newton, TF (2010) Methamphetamine craving induced in an online virtual reality environment. *Pharmacology Biochemistry and Behavior* 96: 454–460. doi: 10.1016/j.pbb.2010.07.005.

Curtin JJ, Barnett NP, Colby SM, Rohsenow DJ, and Monti PM (2005) Cue reactivity in adolescents: Measurement of separate approach and avoidance reactions. *Journal of Studies on Alcohol* 66: 332–343.

Dagher A, Tannenbaum B, Hayashi T, Pruessner JC, and McBride D (2009) An acute psychosocial stress enhances the neural response to smoking cues. *Brain Research* 1293: 40–48. doi: 10.1016/j.brainres.2009.07.048.

David SP, Munafò MR, Johansen-Berg H, Smith SM, Rogers RD, Matthews PM, and Walton RT (2005) Ventral striatum/nucleus accumbens activation to smoking-related pictorial cues in smokers and nonsmokers: A functional magnetic resonance imaging study. *Biological Psychiatry* 58: 488–494. doi: 10.1016/j.biopsych.2005.04.028.

Dawe S, Powell JH, Richards D, Gossop M, Strang J, and Gray JA (1993). Does post-withdrawal cue exposure improve outcome in opiate addiction? A controlled trial? *Addiction* 88: 1233–1245. doi: 10.1111/j.1360-0443.1993.tb02146.x.

Demmel R and Schrenk J (2003) Sensory evaluation of alcohol-related and neutral stimuli: Psychophysical assessment of stimulus intensity. *Addictive Behaviors* 28: 353–360. doi: 10.1016/S0306-4603(01)00228-3.

Doran N, Cook J, McChargue D, and Spring B (2009) Impulsivity and cigarette craving: Differences across subtypes. *Psychopharmacology* 207: 365–373. doi: 10.1007/s00213-009-1661-x.

Doran N, Spring B, and McChargue D (2007) Effect of impulsivity on craving and behavioral reactivity to smoking cues. *Psychopharmacology* 194: 279–288. doi: 10.1007/s00213-007-0832-x.

Drobes DJ and Tiffany ST (1997) Induction of smoking urge through imaginal and *in vivo* procedures: Physiological and self-report manifestations. *Journal of Abnormal Psychology* 106: 15–25. doi: 10.1037//0021-843X.106.1.15.

Drobes DJ, Saladin ME, and Tiffany ST (2001) Classical conditioning mechanisms in alcohol dependence. In N Heather, TJ Peters, and T Stockwell (eds), *International Handbook of Alcohol Dependence and Problems* (pp. 281–297). New York: John Wiley & Sons, Inc.

Droungas A, Ehrman RN, Childress AR, and O'Brien CP (1995) Effect of smoking cues and cigarette availability on craving and smoking behavior. *Addictive Behaviors* 20: 657–673. doi: 10.1016/0306-4603(95)00029-C.

Drummond DC (2000) What does cue-reactivity have to offer clinical research? *Addiction* 95: S129–S144. doi: 10.1046/j.1360-0443.95.8s2.2.x.

Drummond DC and Glautier ST (1994) A controlled trial of cue exposure treatment in alcohol dependence. *Journal of Consulting and Clinical Psychology* 62: 809–817. doi: 10.1037/0022-006X.62.4.809.

Drummond S, Tiffany ST, Glautier S, and Remington B (1995) Cue exposure in understanding and treating addictive behaviours. In DC Drummond, ST Tiffany, S Glautier, and B Remington (eds), *Addictive Behaviour: Cue Exposure Theory and Practice* (pp. 1–17). New York: John Wiley & Sons, Inc.

Engel S, Zhang X, and Wandell B (1997) Colour tuning in human visual cortex measured with functional magnetic resonance imaging. *Nature* 388: 68–71. doi: 10.1038/40398.

Erblich J and Bovbjerg DH (2004) *In vivo* versus imaginal smoking cue exposures: Is seeing believing? *Experimental and Clinical Psychopharmacology* 12: 208–215. doi: 10.1037/1064-1297.12.3.208.

Ferguson SG and Shiffman S (2009) The relevance and treatment of cue-induced cravings in tobacco dependence. *Journal of Substance Abuse Treatment* 36: 235–243. doi: 10.1016/j.jsat.2008.06.005.

Field M and Duka T (2002) Cues paired with a low dose of alcohol acquire conditioned incentive properties in social drinkers. *Psychopharmacology* 159: 325–334. doi: 10.1007/s00213-001-0923-z.

Foltin RW and Haney M (2000) Conditioned effects of environmental stimuli paired with smoked cocaine in humans. *Psychopharmacology* 149: 24–33. doi: 10.1007/s002139900340.

Fonder MA, Sacco KA, Termine A, Boland BS, Seyal AA, Dudas MM, and Vessicchio JC, George TP (2005) Smoking cue reactivity in schizophrenia: Effects of a nicotinic receptor antagonist. *Biological Psychiatry* 57: 802–808. doi: 10.1016/j.biopsych.2004.12.027.

Franken IHA, Hulstijn KP, Stam CJ, Hendriks VM, and van den Brink W (2004) Two new neurophysiological indices of cocaine craving: Evoked brain potentials and cue modulated startle reflex. *Journal of Psychopharmacology* 18: 544–552. doi: 10.1177/0269881104047282.

Franklin TR, Wang Z, Wang J, Sciortino N, Harper D, Li Y, Ehrman R, Kampman K, O'Brien CP, Detre JA, and Childress AR (2007) Limbic activation to cigarette smoking cues independent of nicotine withdrawal: A perfusion fMRI study. *Neuropsychopharmacology* 32: 2301–2309. doi: 10.1038/sj.npp.1301371.

Glautier S, Bankart J, and Williams A (2000) Flavour conditioning and alcohol: A multilevel model of individual differences. *Biological Psychiatry* 52: 17–36. doi: 10.1016/S0301-0511(99)00022-8.

Glautier S, Drummond C, and Remington B (1994) Alcohol as an unconditioned stimulus in human classical conditioning. *Psychopharmacology* 116: 360–368. doi: 10.1007/BF02245341.

Goldstein RZ, Tomasi D, Alia-Klein N, Carrillo JH, Maloney T, Woicik PA, Wang R, Telang F, and Volkow ND (2009) Dopaminergic response to drug words in cocaine addiction. *Journal of Neuroscience* 29: 6001–6006. doi: 10.1523/JNEUROSCI.4247-08.2009.

Gray KM, LaRowe SD, and Upadhyaya HP (2008) Cue reactivity in young marijuana smokers: A preliminary investigation. *Psychology of Addictive Behaviors* 22: 582–586. doi: 10.1037/a0012985.

Gray KM, LaRowe SD, Watson NL, and Carpenter MJ (2010) Reactivity to *in vivo* marijuana cues among cannabis-dependent adolescents. *Addictive Behaviors* 36: 140–143. doi: 10.1016/j.addbeh.2010.08.021.

Grusser SM, Wrase J, Klein S, Hermann D, Smolka MN, Ruf M, Weber-Fahr W, Flor H, Mann K, Braus DF, and Heinz A (2004) Cue-induced activation of the striatum and medial prefrontal cortex is associated with subsequent relapse in abstinent alcoholics. *Psychopharmacology* 175: 296–302. doi: 10.1007/s00213-004-1828-4.

Havermans RC and Jansen AT (2003) Increasing the efficacy of cue exposure treatment in preventing relapse of addictive behavior. *Addictive Behaviors* 28: 989–994. doi: 10.1016/S0306-4603(01)00289-1.

Heishman SJ, Lee DC, Taylor RC, and Singleton EG (2010) Prolonged duration of craving, mood, and autonomic responses elicited by cues and imagery in smokers: Effects of tobacco deprivation and sex. *Experimental and Clinical Psychopharmacology* 18: 245–256. doi: 10.1037/a0019401.

Heishman SJ, Saha S, and Singleton EG (2004) Imagery induced tobacco craving: Duration and lack of assessment reactivity bias. *Psychology of Addictive Behaviors* 18: 284–288. doi: 10.1037/0893-164X.18.3.284.

Heishman SJ, Singleton EG, and Moolchan ET (2003) Tobacco Craving Questionnaire: Reliability and validity of a new multi-factorial instrument. *Nicotine and Tobacco Research* 5: 645–654. doi: 10.1080/1462220031000158681.

Psychology of Addictive BehaviorsHersh D, Bauer LO, and Kranzler HR (1995) Carbamazepine and cocaine cue reactivity. *Drug and Alcohol Dependence* 39: 213–221. doi: 10.1016/0376-8716(95)01165-3.

Hodgson RJ and Rankin HJ (1976) Modification of excessive drinking by cue exposure. *Behaviour Research and Therapy* 14: 305–307. doi: 10.1016/0005-7967(76)90007-3.

Hussain S, Zawertailo L, Busto U, Zack M, Farvolden P, and Selby P (2010) The impact of chronic bupropion on plasma cotinine and on the subjective effects of adlib smoking: A randomized controlled trial in unmotivated smokers. *Addictive Behaviors* 35: 164–167. doi: 10.1016/j.addbeh.2009.09.004.

Hutchison KE, LaChance H, Niaura R, Bryan A, and Smolen A (2002) The DRD4 VNTR polymorphism influences reactivity to smoking cues. *Journal of Abnormal Psychology* 111: 134–143. doi: 10.1037//0021-843X.111.1.134.

Hutchison KE, Monti PM, Rohsenow DJ, Swift RM, Colby SM, Gnys M, Niaura RS, and Sirota AD (1999) Effects of naltrexone with nicotine replacement on smoking cue reactivity: Preliminary results. *Psychopharmacology* 142: 139–143. doi: 10.1007/s002130050872.

Hutchison KE, Ray L, Sandman, E, Rutter MC, Peters A, Davidson D, and Swift R (2006) The effect of olanzapine on craving and alcohol consumption. *Neuropsychopharmacology* 31: 1310–1317. doi: 10.1038/sj.npp.1300917.

Janes AC, Frederick B, Richardt S, Burbridge C, Merlo-Pich E, Renshaw PF, Evins AE, Fava M, and Kaufman MJ (2009) Brain fMRI reactivity to smoking-related images before and during extended smoking abstinence. *Experimental and Clinical Psychopharmacology* 17: 365–373. doi: 10.1037/a0017797.

Juliano LM and Brandon TH (1998) Reactivity to instructed smoking availability and environmental cues: Evidence with urge and reaction time. *Experimental and Clinical Psychopharmacology* 6: 45–53. doi: 10.1037//1064-1297.6.1.45.

Kahler CW, Metrik J, LaChance HR, Ramsey SE, Abrams DB, Monti PM, and Brown RA (2008) Addressing heavy drinking in smoking cessation treatment: A randomized clinical trial. *Journal of Consulting and Clinical Psychology* 76: 852–862. doi: 10.1037/a0012717.

Kavanagh DJ, Andrade J, and May J (2005) Imaginary relish and exquisite torture: The elaborated intrusion theory of desire. *Psychological Review* 112: 446–467. doi: 10.1037/0033-295X.112.2.446.

Kosten TR, Scanley BE, Tucker KA, Oliveto A, Prince C, Sinha R, Potenza MN, Skudlarski P, and Wexler BE (2006) Cue-induced brain activity changes and relapse in cocaine-dependent patients. *Neuropsychopharmacology* 31: 644–650. doi: 10.1038/sj.npp. 1300851.

LaRowe SD, Saladin ME, Carpenter MJ, and Upadhyaya HP (2007) Reactivity to nicotine cues over repeated cue reactivity sessions. *Addictive Behaviors* 32: 2888–2899. doi: 10.1016/j.addbeh.2007.04.025.

Lee DC, Myers CS, Taylor RC, Moolchan ET, and Heishman SJ (2007) Consistency and reliability of subjective responses to imagery-induced tobacco craving over multiple experimental sessions. *Addictive Behaviors* 32: 2130–2139. doi: 10.1016/j.addbeh.2007.01.029.

Lee J, Lim Y, Wiederhold BK, and Graham SJ (2005) A functional magnetic resonance imaging (fMRI) study of cue-induced smoking craving in virtual environments. *Applied Psychophysiology and Biofeedback* 30: 195–204. doi: 10.1007/s10484-005-6377-z.

Litvin EB and Brandon TH (2010) Testing the influence of external and internal cues on smoking motivation using a community sample. *Experimental and Clinical Psychopharmacology* 18: 61–70. doi: 10.1037/a0017414.

Lubman DI, Peters LA, Mogg K, Bradley BP, and Deakin JFW (2000) Attentional bias for drug cues in opiate dependence. *Psychological Medicine* 30: 169–175. doi: 10.1017/S0033291799001269.

Lundahl LH and Johanson CE (2011) Cue-induced craving for marijuana in cannabis-dependent adults. *Experimental and Clinical Psychopharmacology* 19: 224–230. doi: 10.1037/a0023030.

MacKillop J and Lisman SA (2008) Effects of a context shift and multiple context extinction on reactivity to alcohol cues. *Experimental and Clinical Psychopharmacology* 16: 322–331. doi: 10.1037/a0012686.

MacKillop J and Monti PM (2007) Advances in the scientific study of craving for alcohol and tobacco. In PM Miller and D Kavanagh (eds), *Translation of Addictions Science into Practice* (pp. 189–209). New York: Elsevier Science. doi: 10.1016/B978-008044927-2/50059-6.

MacKillop J, O'Hagen S, Lisman SA, Murphy JG, Ray LA, Tidey JW, McGeary JE, and Monti PM (2010) Behavioral economic analysis of cue-elicited craving for alcohol. *Addiction* 105: 1599–1607. doi: 10.1111/j.1360-0443.2010.03004.x.

McCaul ME and Monti PM (2003) Research priorities for alcoholism treatment. *Recent Developments in Alcoholism* 16: 405–414. doi: 10.1007/0-306-47939-7_27.

McClernon FJ, Hiott FB, Liu J, Salley AN, Behm FM, and Rose JE (2007) Selectively reduced responses to smoking cues in amygdala following extinction-based smoking cessation: Results of a preliminary functional magnetic resonance imaging study. *Addiction Biology* 12: 503–512. doi: 10.1111/j.1369-1600.2007.00075.x.

McClernon FJ, Hutchison KE, Rose JE, and Kozink RV (2007) DRD4 VNTR polymorphism is associated with transient fMRI-BOLD responses to smoking cues. *Psychopharmacology* 194: 433–441. doi: 10.1007/s00213-007-0860-6.

McGeary JE, Monti PM, Rohsenow DJ, Tidey J, Swift R, and Miranda R (2006) Genetic moderators of naltrexone's effects on alcohol cue reactivity. *Alcoholism, Clinical and Experimental Research* 30: 1288–1296. doi: 10.1111/j.1530-0277.2006.00156.x.

Metrik J, Rohsenow DJ, Monti PM, McGeary J, Cook T, deWit H, Haney M, and Kahler C (2009) Effectiveness of a marijuana expectancy manipulation: Piloting the balanced-placebo design for marijuana. *Experimental and Clinical Psychopharmacology* 17, 217–225. doi: 10.1037/a0016502.

Miranda R, MacKillop J, Monti PM, Rohsenow DJ, Tidey J, Gwaltney C, Swift R, Ray L, and McGeary J (2008a) Effects of topiramate on urge to drink and the subjective effects of alcohol: A preliminary laboratory study. *Alcoholism, Clinical and Experimental Research* 32: 489–497. doi: 10.1111/j.1530-0277.2007.00592.x.

Miranda R, Rohsenow DJ, Monti PM, Tidey J, and Ray L (2008b) Effects of repeated days of smoking cue exposure on urge to smoke and physiological reactivity. *Addictive Behaviors* 33: 347–353. doi: 10.1016/j.addbeh.2007.09.011.

Monti PM (2006) Translational research on craving: Promises, problems and potential. Invited plenary session presented at the Annual Meeting of the Research Society on Alcoholism, June, Baltimore, MD.

Monti PM, Binkoff JA, Abrams DB, Zwick WR, Nirenberg TD, and Liepman MR (1987) Reactivity of alcoholics and nonalcoholics to drinking cues. *Journal of Abnormal Psychology* 96: 122–126. doi: 10.1037//0021-843X.96.2.122.

Monti PM, Miranda R, Justus A, MacKillop J, Meehan J, Tidey J, and Swift R (2010) Biobehavioral mechanisms of topiramate and drinking in adolescents: Preliminary findings. Poster presented at the 49th American College of Neuro-psychopharmacology (ACNP) Annual Meeting, December, Miami Beach, FL.

Monti PM, Rohsenow DJ, and Hutchison KE (2000) Toward bridging the gap between biological, psychobiological and psychosocial models of alcohol craving. *Addiction* 95: 229S–236S. doi: 10.1046/j.1360-0443.95.8s2.11.x.

Monti PM, Rohsenow DJ, Hutchison KE, Swift RM, Mueller TI, Colby SM, Brown RA, Gulliver SB, Gordon A, and Abrams DB (1999) Naltrexone's effect on cue-elicited craving among alcoholics in treatment. *Alcoholism, Clinical and Experimental Research* 23: 1386–1394. doi: 10.1097/00000374-199908000-00013.

Monti PM, Rohsenow DJ, Rubonis AV, Niaura RS, Sirota AD, Colby SM, and Abrams DB (1993) Alcohol cue reactivity: Effects of detoxification and extended exposure. *Journal of Studies on Alcohol* 54: 235–245.

Munafò MR and Hitsman B (2010) What's the matter with cue-induced craving? A commentary on Perkins. *Addiction* 105: 1860–1861. doi: 10.1111/j.1360-0443.2010.03127.x.

Newlin DB, Hotchkiss B, Cox WM, Rauscher F, and Li TK (1989) Autonomic and subjective responses to alcohol stimuli with appropriate control stimuli. *Addictive Behaviors* 14: 625–630. doi: 10.1016/0306-4603(89)90004-X.

Niaura R, Abrams D, DeMuth B, and Pinto R (1989) Responses to smoking-related stimuli and early relapse to smoking. *Addictive Behaviors* 14: 419–428. doi: 10.1016/0306-4603(89)90029-4.

Niaura RS, Abrams DB, Shadel WG, Rohsenow DJ, Monti PM, and Sirota AD (1999) Cue exposure treatment for smoking relapse prevention: A controlled clinical trial. *Addiction* 94: 685–695. doi: 10.1046/j.1360-0443.1999.9456856.x.

Niaura R, Sayette M, Shiftman S, Glover ED, Nides M, Shelanski M, Shadel W, Koslo R, Robbins B, and Sorrentino J (2005) Comparative efficacy of rapid-release nicotine gum versus nicotine polacrilex gum in relieving smoking cue-provoked craving. *Addiction* 100: 1720–1730. doi: 10.1111/j.1360-0443.2005.01218.x.

O'Brien CP (2005) Anticraving medications for relapse prevention: A possible new class of psychoactive medications. *American Journal of Psychiatry* 162: 1423–1431. doi: 10.1176/appi.ajp.162.8.1423.

O'Brien CP, Childress AR, Ehrman R, and Robbins SJ (1998) Conditioning factors in drug abuse: Can they explain compulsion? *Psychopharmacology* 12: 15–22. doi: 10.1177/026988119801200103.

O'Brien CP, Childress AR, McLellan T, and Ehrmann R (1990) Integrating systematic cue-exposure with standard treatment in recovering drug dependent patients. *Addictive Behaviors* 15: 355–365. doi: 10.1016/0306-4603(90)90045-Y.

Palfai TP, Monti PM, Ostafin B, and Hutchison K (2000) Effects of nicotine deprivation on alcohol-related information processing and drinking behavior. *Journal of Abnormal Psychology* 109: 96–105. doi: 10.1037//0021-843X.109.1.96.

Paris MM, Carter BL, Traylor AC, Bordnick PS, Day SX, Armsworth MW, and Cinciripini PM (2011) Cue reactivity in virtual reality: The role of context. *Addictive Behaviors* 36: 696–699. doi: 10.1016/j.addbeh.2011.01.029.

Payne TJ, Rychtarik RG, Rappaport NB, Smith PO, Etscheidt M, Brown TA, and Johnson CA (1992) Reactivity to alcohol-relevant beverage and imaginal cues in alcoholics. *Addictive Behaviors* 17: 209–217. doi: 10.1016/0306-4603(92)90026-R.

Payne TJ, Smith PO, Adams SG, and Diefenbach L (2006) Pretreatment cue reactivity predicts end-of-treatment smoking. *Addictive Behaviors* 31: 702–710. doi: 10.1016/j.addbeh.2005.05.053.

Perkins KA (2009) Does smoking cue-induced craving tell us anything important about nicotine dependence? *Addiction* 104: 1610–1616. doi: 10.1111/j.1360-0443.2009.02550.x.

Pickens R, Bigelow GE, and Griffiths R (1973) An experimental approach to treating chronic alcoholism: A case study and one-year follow-up. *Behaviour Research and Therapy* 11: 321–325. doi: 10.1016/0005-7967(73)90010-7.

Pulido C, Brown SA, Cummins K, Paulus MP, and Tapert SF (2010) Alcohol cue reactivity task development. *Addictive Behaviors* 35: 84–90. doi: 10.1016/j.addbeh.2009.09.006.

Rankin HJ (1982) Cue exposure and response prevention in South London. In P Nathan and W Hay (eds), *Case Studies in the Behavioral Modification of Alcoholism* (pp. 227–248). New York: Plenum Press.

Reid MS and Thakkar V (2009) Valproate treatment and cocaine cue reactivity in cocaine dependent individuals. *Drug and Alcohol Dependence* 102: 144–150. doi: 10.1016/j.drugalcdep.2009.02.010.

Robbins SJ, Ehrman RN, Childress AR, and O'Brien CP (1992) Using cue reactivity to screen medications for cocaine abuse: A test of amantadine hydrochloride. *Addictive Behaviors* 17: 491–499. doi: 10.1016/0306-4603(92)90009-K.

Rohsenow DJ, Monti PM, Abrams D, Rubonis AV, Niaura RS, Sirota AD, and Colby SM (1992) Cue elicited urge to drink and salivation in alcoholics: Relationship to individual differences. *Advances in Behaviour Research and Therapy* 14: 195–210. doi: 10.1016/0146-6402(92)90008-C.

Rohsenow DJ, Monti PM, Hutchison KE, Swift RM, Colby SM, and Kaplan GB (2000) Naltrexone's effects on reactivity to alcohol cues among alcoholic men. *Journal of Abnormal Psychology* 109: 738–742. doi: 10.1037//0021-843X.109.4.738.

Rohsenow DJ, Monti PM, Hutchison KE, Swift RM, MacKinnon SV, Sirota AD, and Kaplan GB (2007) High-dose transdermal nicotine and naltrexone: Effects on nicotine withdrawal, urges, smoking, and effects of smoking. *Experimental and Clinical Psychopharmacology* 15: 81–92. doi: 10.1037/1064-1297.15.1.81.

Rohsenow DJ, Monti PM, Rubonis AV, Gulliver SB, Colby SM, Binkoff JA, and Abrams DB (2001) Cue exposure with coping skills training and communication skills training for alcohol dependence: Six and twelve month outcomes. *Addiction* 96: 1161–1174. doi: 10.1046/j.1360-0443.2001.96811619.x.

Rohsenow DJ, Monti PM, Rubonis AV, Sirota AD, Niaura RS, Colby SM, Wunschel SM, and Abrams DB (1994) Cue reactivity as a predictor of drinking among male alcoholics. *Journal of Consulting and Clinical Psychology* 62: 620–626. doi: 10.1037/0022-006X.62.3.620.

Rohsenow DJ, Tidey JW, Miranda R, McGeary JE, Swift RM, Hutchison KE, Sirota AD, and Monti PM (2008) Olanzapine reduces urge to smoke and nicotine withdrawal symptoms in community smokers. *Experimental and Clinical Psychopharmacology* 16: 215–222. doi: 10.1037/1064-1297.16.3.215.

Rosenberg H (2009) Clinical and laboratory assessment of the subjective experience of drug craving. *Clinical Psychology Review* 29: 519–534. doi: 10.1016/j.cpr.2009.06.002.

Rubonis AV, Colby SM, Monti PM, Rohsenow DJ, Gulliver SB, and Sirota AD (1994) Alcohol cue reactivity and mood induction in male and female alcoholics. *Journal of Studies on Alcohol* 55: 487–494. doi: 10.1016/S0306-4603(98)00093-8.

Saladin ME, Brady KT, Graap K, and Rothbaum BO (2006) A preliminary report on the use of virtual reality technology to elicit craving and cue reactivity in cocaine dependent individuals. *Addictive Behaviors* 31: 1881–1894. doi: 10.1016/j.addbeh.2006.01.004.

Sayette MA, Griffin KM, and Sayers WM (2010) Counterbalancing in smoking cue research: A critical analysis. *Nicotine and Tobacco Research* 12: 1068–1079. doi: 10.1093/ntr/ntq159.

Sayette MA, Loewenstein G, Kirchner TR, and Travis T (2005) Effects of smoking urge on temporal cognition. *Psychology of Addictive Behaviors* 19: 88–93. doi: 10.1037/0893-164X.19.1.88.

Sayette MA, Martin CS, Wertz JM, Shiffman S, and Perrott MA (2001) A multi-dimensional analysis of cue-elicited craving in heavy smokers and tobacco chippers. *Addiction* 96: 1419–1432. doi: 10.1046/j.1360-0443.2001.961014196.x.

Sayette MA, Shiffman S, Tiffany ST, Niaura RS, Martin CS, and Shadel WG (2000) The measurement of drug craving. *Addiction* 95: S189–S210. doi: 10.1046/j.1360-0443.95.8s2.8.x.

Sayette MA, Wertz JM, Martin CS, Cohn JF, Perrott MA, and Hobel J (2003) Effects of smoking opportunity on cue-elicited urge: A facial coding analysis. *Experimental and Clinical Psychopharmacology* 11: 218–227. doi: 10.1037/1064-1297.11.3.218.

Schacht JP, Anton RF, Randall PK, Li X, Henderson S, and Myrick H (2011) Stability of fMRI striatal response to alcohol cues: A hierarchical linear modeling approach. *NeuroImage* 56: 61–68. doi: 10.1016/j.neuroimage.2011.02.004.

Sell LA, Morris JS, Bearn J, Frackowiak RSJ, Friston KJ, and Dolan RJ (2000) Neural responses associated with cue evoked emotional states and heroin in opiate addicts. *Drug and Alcohol Dependence* 60: 207–216. doi: 10.1016/S0376-8716(99)00158-1.

Shiffman S (2009) Responses to smoking cues are relevant to smoking and relapse. *Addiction* 104: 1617–1618.

Shiffman S, Gwaltney CJ, Balabanis MH, Liu KS, Paty JA, Kassel JD, Hickcox M, and Gnys M (2002) Immediate antecedents of cigarette smoking: An analysis from ecological momentary assessment. *Journal of Abnormal Psychology* 111: 531–545. doi: 10.1037//0021-843X.111.4.531.

Shiffman S, Shadel WG, Niaura R, Khayrallah MA, Jorenby DE, Ryan CF, and Ferguson CL (2003) Efficacy of acute administration of nicotine gum in relief of cue-provoked cigarette craving. *Psychopharmacology* 166: 345–350.

Singleton EG, Trotman AJM, Zavahir M, Taylor RC, and Heishman SJ (2002) Determination of the reliability and validity of the Marijuana Craving Questionnaire using imagery scripts. *Experimental and Clinical Psychopharmacology* 10: 47–53. doi: 10.1037//1064-1297.10.1.47.

Sinha R and O'Malley SS (1999) Craving for alcohol: Findings from the clinic and the laboratory. *Alcohol and alcoholism* 34: 223–230. doi: 10.1093/alcalc/34.2.223.

Sinha R, Catapano D, and O'Malley SS (1999) Stress-induced craving and stress responses in cocaine dependent individuals. *Psychopharmacology* 142: 343–351. doi: 10.1007/s002130050898.

Sinha R, Fuse T, Aubin LR, and O'Malley SS (2000) Psychological stress, drug-related cues and cocaine craving. *Psychopharmacology* 152: 140–148. doi: 10.1007/s002130000499.

Sinha R, Talih M, Malison R, Cooney N, Anderson GM, and Kreek MJ (2003) Hypothalamic-pituitary-adrenal axis and sympatho-adreno-medullary responses during stress-induced and drug cue-induced cocaine craving states. *Psychopharmacology* 170: 62–72. doi: 10.1007/s00213-003-1525-8.

Sitharthan T, Sitharthan G, Hough MJ, and Kavanagh DJ (1997) Cue exposure in moderation drinking: A comparison with cognitive-behavioral therapy. *Journal of Consulting and
Clinical Psychology* 65: 878–882. doi: 10.1037//0022-006X.65.5.878.

Staiger PK and White JM (1991) Cue reactivity in alcohol abusers: Stimulus specificity
and extinction of the responses. *Addictive Behaviors* 16: 211–221. doi: 10.1016/0306-
4603(91)90014-9.

Streeter CC, Gulliver SB, Baker E, Blank SR, Meyer AA, Ciraulo DA, and Renshaw PF (2002)
Videotaped cue for urge to drink alcohol. *Alcoholism, Clinical and Experimental Research*
26: 627–634. doi: 10.1111/j.1530-0277.2002.tb02584.x.

Stritzke WGK, Breiner MJ, Curtin JJ, and Lang AR (2004) Assessment of substance cue
reactivity: Advances in reliability, specificity, and validity. *Psychology of Addictive Behaviors*
18: 148–159. doi: 10.1037/0893-164X.18.2.148.

Tapert SF, Brown GG, Baratta MV, and Brown SA (2004) fMRI BOLD response to alcohol stimuli in alcohol dependent young women. *Addictive Behaviors* 29: 33–50. doi:
10.1016/j.addbeh.2003.07.003.

Tidey JW, Rohsenow DJ, Kaplan GB, Swift RM, and Adolfo AB (2008) Effects of smoking abstinence, smoking cues and nicotine replacement in smokers with schizophrenia and controls.
Nicotine and Tobacco Research 10: 1047–1056. doi: 10.1080/14622200802097373.

Tiffany S (1990) A cognitive model of drug urges and drug-use behavior: Role of automatic
and nonautomatic processes. *Psychological Review* 97: 147–168. doi: 10.1037//0033-
295X.97.2.147.

Tiffany ST (1992) A critique of contemporary urge and craving research: Methodological,
psychometric, and theoretical issues. *Advances in Behaviour Research and Therapy* 14:
123–139. doi: 10.1016/0146-6402(92)90005-9.

Tiffany ST and Wray J (2009) The continuing conundrum of craving. *Addiction* 104: 1618–
1619. doi: 10.1111/j.1360-0443.2009.02588.x.

Tolliver BK, McRae-Clark AL, Saladin M, Price KL, Simpson AN, DeSantis SM, Baker NL,
and Brady KT (2010) Determinants of cue-elicited craving and physiologic reactivity in
methamphetamine-dependent subjects in the laboratory. *American Journal of Drug and
Alcohol Abuse* 36: 106-113. doi: 10.3109/00952991003686402.

Tong C, Bovbjerg DH, and Erblich J (2007) Smoking-related videos for use in cue-
induced craving paradigms. *Addictive Behaviors* 32: 3034–3044. doi: 10.1016/j.addbeh.
2007.07.010.

Traylor AC, Bordnick PS, and Carter BL (2008) Assessing craving in young adult smokers using virtual reality. *American Journal on Addictions* 17: 436–440. doi: 10.1080/
10550490802268876.

Vollstädt-Klein S, Kobiella A, Bühler M, Graf C, Feh C, Mann K, and Smolka MN (2011)
Severity of dependence modulates smokers' neuronal cue reactivity and cigarette craving
elicited by tobacco advertisement. *Addiction Biology* 16: 166–175. doi: 10.1111/j.1369-
1600.2010.00207.x.

Vollstädt-Klein S, Wichert S, Rabinstein J, Bühler M, Klein O, Ende G, Hermann D, and
Mann K (2010) Initial, habitual and compulsive alcohol use is characterized by a shift
of cue processing from ventral to dorsal striatum. *Addiction* 105: 1741–1749. doi:
10.1111/j.1360-0443.2010.03022.x.

Warthen MW and Tiffany ST (2009) Evaluation of cue reactivity in the natural environment of
smokers using ecological momentary assessment. *Experimental and Clinical Psychopharmacology* 17: 70–77. doi: 10.1037/a0015617.

Waters AJ, Shiffman S, Sayette MA, Paty JA, Gwaltney CJ, and Balabanis MH (2004) Cue-
provoked craving and nicotine replacement therapy in smoking cessation. *Journal of Consulting and Clinical Psychology* 72: 1136–1143. doi: 10.1037/0022-006X.72.6.1136.

Watson NL, Carpenter MJ, Saladin ME, Gray KM, and Upadhyaya HP (2010) Evidence for greater cue reactivity among low-dependent vs. high-dependent smokers. *Addictive Behaviors* 35: 673–677. doi: 10.1037//0893-164X.15.3.268.

Wertz JM and Sayette MA (2001) Effects of smoking opportunity on attentional bias in smokers. *Psychology of Addictive Behaviors* 15: 268–271.

Wrase J, Grüsser SM, Klein S, Diener C, Hermann D, Flor H, Mann K, Braus DF, and Heinz A (2002) Development of alcohol-associated cues and cue-induced brain activation in alcoholics. *European Psychiatry* 17: 287–291. doi: 10.1016/S0924-9338(02)00676-4.

Wray JM, Godleski SA, and Tiffany ST (2011) Cue-reactivity in the natural environment of cigarette smokers: The impact of photographic and *in vivo* smoking stimuli. *Psychology of Addictive Behaviors*. doi: 10.1037/a0023687.

Yang Z, Xie J, Shao YC, Xie CM, Fu LP, Li DJ, Fan M, Ma L, and Li SJ (2009) Dynamic neural responses to cue-reactivity paradigms in heroin-dependent users: An fMRI study. *Human Brain Mapping*, 30: 766–775. doi: 10.1002/hbm.20542.

Zinser MC, Fiore MC, Davidson RJ, and Baker TB (1999) Manipulating smoking motivation: Impact on an electrophysiological index of approach motivation. *Journal of Abnormal Psychology* 108: 240–254. doi: 10.1037//0021-843X.108.2.240.

15

Stress and Affective Inductions in Addiction Research

Suzanne Thomas and Amy Bacon

1 Introduction

That people take drugs and use alcohol to help alleviate stress or improve a bad mood is an assumed truth that seems too obvious to warrant scientific study. The very nature of drugs of abuse – all of which induce pleasure and other desirable affective states (Leshner and Koob, 1999) – seems to confirm that drugs and alcohol improve one's affect and would therefore be especially sought when the individual is stressed. Theories to explain substance use and addiction, including the self-medication hypothesis (Khantzian, 1985) and the tension reduction theory of alcohol use (Cappell and Herman, 1972; Conger, 1956), posit that drugs and alcohol are consumed in part because they are negatively reinforcing. Certainly, retrospective reports support that the desire to drink or use drugs increases under stress (Brown *et al.*, 1995; Fouquereau, Fernandez, Mullet, and Sorum, 2003). It is perplexing, then, that there is only modest scientific evidence that alcohol and drugs actually relieve stress (Kassel, Stroud, and Paronis, 2003; Sayette *et al.*, 2001), and as explained in the present chapter, prospective studies to examine whether stress increases urge to use drugs or alcohol are inconsistent.

Two research methods have been employed in prospective clinical studies to examine whether acute stress motivates substance use. Ecological momentary assessment (EMA) is an approach that captures participants' naturally occurring affective states and desire to use and/or actual use of substances in real time over several days or months (see Chapter 20). EMA allows investigators to determine temporal associations between events, and so is valuable for examining whether stress precedes incidences of increased substance use. Results from EMA studies are equivocal that substance use increases following stressful events or negative affective states (Helzer *et al.*, 2006; Park, Armeli, and Tennen, 2004; Shiffman *et al.*, 2002; Shiffman and Waters, 2004; Todd, Armeli, and Tennen, 2009).

The Wiley-Blackwell Handbook of Addiction Psychopharmacology, First Edition. Edited by James MacKillop and Harriet de Wit.
© 2013 John Wiley & Sons, Ltd. Published 2013 by John Wiley & Sons, Ltd.

Alternatively, the other method – applying a stressor in a clinical laboratory setting and measuring subsequent use or desire to use substances – affords the ability to employ true experimental methods to determine not just temporal relationships but actual causal connections between stress and increased motivation to use drugs or alcohol. In addition, data can (and should) be collected in clinical laboratory studies to confirm the internal validity of the experimental manipulation – that is, did the purported stressor actually induce a stress response?

In response to a stimulus that is perceived as a stressor (the threshold of which varies by individual), the hypothalamic–pituitary–adrenal (HPA) axis is activated, and corticotrophin releasing hormone (CRH) and vasopressin are released from the hypothalamus, resulting in corticotropin (ACTH) release from the pituitary gland, which stimulates the adrenal cortex to release cortisol. Cortisol then inhibits the release of CRH and ACTH in a negative feedback loop. In addition, the sympathetic nervous system is activated, which results in the release of noradrenaline and increased heart rate and blood pressure. Both the HPA axis and sympathetic nervous system work to increase arousal, preparedness, vigilance, and anxiety (see Kudielka and Kirschbaum, 2007), so confirmation of stress reactivity is afforded by clear biologic and physiologic sequelae. The most commonly used objective measures of stress reactivity are ACTH, cortisol, adrenaline metabolites, heart rate, blood pressure, and/or skin conductance, all of which are expected to increase following stress induction.

While objective indices of stress reactivity may or may not be included in a study, nearly every clinical laboratory study that involves stress induction as its primary manipulation includes a subjective (self-reported) measure of distress. Often this is a single-item question using a Likert scale or visual analog scale on which the participant rates his/her level of distress before and after exposure to the stressor. Even better is when studies include validated instruments of subjective distress, which allow results to be more easily compared across studies. Instruments that measure a host of emotions, such as the Positive and Negative Affect Schedule (PANAS) (Watson, Clark, and Tellegen, 1988) and the Differential Emotions Scale (Boyle, 1984; Izard, 1974) are especially valuable, as they provide a more comprehensive assessment of affect.

2   Applications to Addiction Research and Chapter Objectives

It is not simply to confirm that stress and negative affect increase motivation to use drugs that clinical laboratory studies are conducted; to the contrary, there are manifold applications. If a paradigm can be validated and replicated, it provides a tool that can be used to study important clinical questions and drive discoveries that will improve addiction treatment. For example, an effective paradigm can be used to test novel medications for addiction to determine, without the expense of a randomized clinical trial, whether a new treatment can reduce stress-induced drinking or drug use in addicted individuals (e.g., Drobes, Anton, Thomas, and Voronin, 2003). It may also be used clinically to assess relapse susceptibility in individuals in treatment (as suggested by Sinha, 2013). If amenable for use in neuroimaging scanners, the paradigm could show which brain areas are activated or suppressed during stress induction, so that new targets for treatments or prevention might be proposed. Finally, stress paradigms may be useful for understanding genetic contributions to variation in stress response and, in turn, vulnerability to drug addiction (e.g., Ray, 2011).

This chapter reviews the methods that have been most widely used in clinical laboratory studies to examine stress-induced motivation to consume drugs or alcohol. In the interest of clarity and brevity, the chapter is restricted in notable ways. First, only studies that employ stressors specifically to examine the effect on subsequent motivation to use drugs or alcohol are reviewed, which is a relatively small subset of studies that induce stress in clinical laboratory settings. Second, the term "stress induction" is used broadly (and admittedly indiscriminately) to reflect all forms of experimentally induced negative affect. As aptly argued by Kassel and colleagues (Kassel *et al.*, 2007), not all stress-induction methods induce the same kinds of negative emotions, and by definition, fear, anger, sadness, frustration, physical discomfort, pain, and embarrassment are not synonymous, yet as they are all associated with activation of the HPA axis and/or sympathetic nervous system, they are often combined in the literature, including in this chapter, under the catch-all term of "stress" or "negative affect." We elected to categorize stress-induction methods by how the manipulation is administered without regard to the primary negative emotion(s) that each procedure probably evokes. Stressors are presented as pharmacological, physical, or psychological in nature, with a final section on stressors that have been used in neuroimaging studies. Third, studies reviewed include both non-dependent and addicted participants and all drugs of abuse; results are described such that participants' dependent status and drug of abuse are included, but all studies conducted using a specific stressor are presented together. Finally, cue exposure, where an individual is exposed to the sight, smell, and/or taste of a specific drug, while potentially stress inducing and certainly urge inducing, is not considered a stress induction procedure in this review; cue exposure methods are well reviewed in Chapter 14. Some studies have combined a stressor with cue exposure (Coffey *et al.*, 2010; Stasiewicz *et al.*, 1997) to examine their integrated effect on craving; while certainly valuable and clinically relevant, these studies are excluded from this review.

3   Pharmacologic Stressors

Pharmacologic stressors are exogenous agents applied to activate or mimic activation of the HPA axis and/or sympathetic nervous system, including HPA axis peptides and serotonergic and adrenergic agents. Relatively few studies have been conducted that apply pharmacologic agents as stressors specifically to examine their effect on subsequent motivation to use drugs or alcohol. Most studies using pharmacologic stressors have been conducted to examine differences in HPA axis response between at-risk or currently dependent individuals and controls (Adinoff *et al.*, 2005; Anthenelli, Maxwell, Geracioti, and Haugher, 2001; Wand, Mangold, Ali, and Giggey, 1999).

3.1   Direct application of HPA axis peptides

A few studies have been conducted in which participants are administered HPA axis peptides, including ovine corticotopin releasing hormone (oCRH) (Back *et al.*,

2010; Moran-Santa Maria *et al.*, 2010) and cortisol (Elman *et al.*, 2003), to examine stress-induced craving. While there is compelling evidence that these agents induce HPA axis activity (increased ACTH and cortisol) and sympathetic activation (increased heart rate), evidence of self-reported "stress" following receipt of these agents is lacking or variable.

Regarding the effects on subsequent motivation for drugs, results are also mixed. Cortisol administration increased cocaine craving in cocaine-dependent individuals (Elman *et al.*, 2003), yet Back and Moran and colleagues (both studies used the same participants) found that less than half of their cocaine-dependent participants reported increased craving following oCRH administration (Back *et al.*, 2010; Moran-Santa Maria *et al.*, 2010).

3.2   Serotonergic agents

Serotonin regulates HPA axis function (Dinan, 1996), and so serotonergic agents have been studied as potential pharmacologic stressors. Meta-chlorophenylpiperazine (mCPP) is a central serotonergic agonist. Several investigators have applied mCPP in clinical laboratory studies to examine its ability to induce a stress response and elicit craving in individuals with alcohol dependence (George *et al.*, 1997; Krystal *et al.*, 1994; Umhau *et al.*, 2011). These studies included comprehensive assessments of the stress response with both objective (typically ACTH, cortisol, and heart rate) and subjective measures (self-reported distress, anxiety, nervousness, and other mood states), and assessed whether alcohol craving scores increased following drug infusion compared to placebo infusion.

Results consistently show that mCPP elicits HPA axis activation, as evidenced by increased ACTH and cortisol. The subjective effects of mCPP include nervousness and anxiety (Krystal *et al.*, 1994; Umhau *et al.*, 2011) but also effects that participants rated as "alcohol-like" (Krystal *et al.*, 1994), a finding consistent with animal drug-discrimination studies (Signs and Schechter, 1988). Studies also consistently show that mCPP increases alcohol craving in alcoholics (George *et al.*, 1997; Krystal *et al.*, 1994; Umhau *et al.*, 2011). The one study that included healthy controls and assessment of craving (self-reported "likelihood to drink") failed to show that mCPP increased urge for alcohol (George *et al.*, 1997).

Whether mCPP elicits craving in alcoholics because of its anxiogenic/stress-like effects or because it acts as an alcohol priming dose is a relevant question. George and colleagues suggest that it depends on the individual (George *et al.*, 1997). In participants with early-onset alcoholism, mCPP produced predominantly euphoric effects; for later-onset alcoholics (type I), mCPP produced predominantly negative effects, specifically anger and anxiety. Importantly, within type II and type I groups, degree of change in euphoria and anxiety, respectively, was positively correlated with self-reported increase in desire to drink. Thus, for early-onset alcoholics, mCPP may elicit craving by mimicking the effects of alcohol, and for later-onset alcoholics, it may elicit craving as a more conventional stressor, producing negative effects. Replication studies are needed to confirm this speculation.

Tryptophan depletion (TD) has also been used in clinical laboratory studies of stress-induced craving. Tryptophan is a precursor to serotonin; it can be depleted with oral administration of a tryptophan-free amino acid drink, thus antagonizing serotonin by reducing serotonin synthesis. Interestingly, some have hypothesized that TD would reduce craving and/or consumption compared to no treatment or trypto-phan enhancement (Leyton *et al.*, 2000; Petrakis *et al.*, 2002; Petrakis *et al.*, 2001); others proposed the opposite effect (Wedekind *et al.*, 2010). In studies conducted to date, including those testing male (Pihl, Young, Ervin, and Plotnick, 1987) and female (Leyton *et al.*, 2000) social drinkers and individuals with alcohol use disorders (Petrakis *et al.*, 2001; Wedekind *et al.*, 2010), there is no evidence that tryptophan depletion (compared to placebo or tryptophan supplementation) affects alcohol crav-ing or consumption. In cocaine-dependent participants, TD reduced cocaine craving (Satel *et al.*, 1995) and cocaine-related experience of "high" (Aronson *et al.*, 1995). The only study that showed positive effects of TD was in alcoholics with comorbid depression, where TD (compared to placebo control) increased urge to drink at 4 and 6 hours post-depletion (Pierucci-Lagha *et al.*, 2004). Clearly there is considerable ambiguity with regard to TD effects on motivation.

3.3 Adrenergic agents

Adrenaline is the primary neurohormone of the sympathetic nervous system. Yohim-bine blocks inhibitory alpha$_2$ adrenergic autoreceptors, thus promoting noradrenaline release from the locus coeruleus and stimulating release of adrenaline from the adrenal medulla. In addition, noradrenaline stimulates the hypothalamus to release CRH, thus activating the HPA axis (Kudielka and Kirschbaum, 2007). Preclinical data support that yohimbine is an effective stressor that reinstates alcohol seeking (Le *et al.*, 2005), and two studies have examined whether yohimbine's effects can be translated to alcohol-dependent humans (Krystal *et al.*, 1994; Umhau *et al.*, 2011). Both studies found that yohimbine increases ACTH, cortisol, and other objective measures of stress reactivity. However, evidence is equivocal whether yohimbine elicits subjective stress effects and whether it elicits craving in alcoholics. Interestingly, Krystal and colleagues found that while yohimbine increased feelings of nervousness, it did not increase alcohol craving; conversely, Umhau and colleagues found that yohimbine did not increase anxiety but did increase craving compared to placebo. Both studies included similar participants (inpatient alcoholics in early abstinence), and used identical doses of yohimbine (0.4 mg/kg), so there is not an obvious explanation for these discrepant results.

3.4 Summary of pharmacological stressors

The use of pharmacological agents as stressors for the purpose of studying stress-induced urge for drugs or alcohol is in its infancy, yet pharmacologic stress induction studies have particular value in that they afford the greatest opportunity for trans-lational research, where methods and results from preclinical studies can guide the methods and hypotheses of clinical laboratory studies (depending, obviously, on the safety of the drug of interest). To have value as an ecologically relevant model of stress-induced relapse, however, these studies must show that the agent induces negative affective states experienced in the real world, and also that the agent is not simply a priming dose or conditioned cue for drug use unrelated to subjective distress.

4 Physical Stressors

With the exception of pharmacologic stressors, all other stress induction methods utilize at least one of the five physical senses, so classifying a stressor as "physical" versus "psychological" is somewhat artificial. For the purpose of this review, if the stressor is applied through *only one* of the five senses *or* if it induces physical rather than psychic discomfiture, it is categorized as a physical stressor. Physical stressors are subcategorized here as tactile, auditory, or visual stressors; to our knowledge, no studies have been conducted using olfactory or gustatory stressors to study stress-induced urge for drugs or alcohol.

4.1 Tactile stressors

The Cold Pressor Task (CPT) is a standardized procedure in which the participant immerses his/her hand up to the wrist in a bath of cold water ($\sim$5 °C) for as long as tolerable and typically up to 60 seconds. Two studies have been conducted to examine whether the CPT enhances motivation to use substances of abuse, specifically cocaine (Back *et al.*, 2005) and alcohol (Brady *et al.*, 2006). Both studies tested individuals who met criteria for dependence, and both studies employed at least two objective measures (heart rate, skin conductance, ACTH, and/or cortisol) and one subjective measure of stress reactivity (self-reported distress and aversive states as measured on a 0–10-point scale) to assess stress reactivity prior to and following the CPT. Objective and subjective stress reactivity outcomes did not support that the CPT was an effective stressor, and the CPT did not induce urge or motivation to use alcohol or cocaine in either study.

Electric shocks have also been employed as stressors. McCarthy and colleagues (McCarthy, Gloria, and Curtin, 2009) delivered electric shocks of varying intensity to study participants (smokers and non-smokers) to examine the effect on attentional bias to smoking-related words, which has been used as an implicit measure of craving (Sayette *et al.*, 2000). The PANAS (Watson, Clark, and Tellegen, 1988) was used to measure negative affect. Results showed that although the shock condition induced negative affect, there was no effect of the stressor on attentional bias to smoking-related words, suggesting that it did not increase motivation to smoke.

Mulligan and colleagues used hyperventilation to induce distress (Mulligan and McKay, 2001). Internal validity of the manipulation was assessed only by heart rate (no subjective measures of distress), though the authors did not report whether heart rate was significantly increased by the challenge. Prior to and following hyperventilation, social drinkers were exposed to alcohol cues (beer and wine coolers), and urge for alcohol was assessed following each exposure period. The study design did not include a non-stressed control group, and only path analyses were reported in the results;

however, the reported means did not suggest that the hyperventilation challenge increased urge for alcohol.

4.2   Auditory stressors

Music has been used by several investigators to induce positive and negative mood and subsequently examine effects on motivation to consume alcohol in social drinkers (Birch *et al.*, 2004; Grant, Stewart, and Birch, 2007; Willner, Field, Pitts, and Reeve, 1998) and alcoholics (Jansma *et al.*, 2000). Induction of an affective state is confirmed in these studies by subjective indices only. Generally speaking, exposure to somber and festive music effectively induced the target mood, but results were mixed as to whether music-induced negative affect enhanced motivation to drink alcohol. In the only study conducted on alcohol-dependent subjects, somber music increased negative affect but did not increase desire to drink compared to exposure to a neutral mood condition (Jansma *et al.*, 2000). In the studies on social drinkers, music-induced negative mood increased motivation or urge to drink but only in subsets of participants – in coping-motivated drinkers (Birch *et al.*, 2004; Grant, Stewart, and Birch, 2007) and in individuals who were instructed to abstain from alcohol prior to the testing day (Willner, Field, Pitts, and Reeve, 1998).

4.3   Visual stressors

Fucito and Juliano (Fucito and Juliano, 2009) tested smokers in a challenge in which they watched a sad scene from a movie (a boy crying over his father's death) or control scene to induce neutral mood (a nature-related scene). Mood induction was assessed with Likert scales for target emotions (sad, unhappy, happy, joy); no objective measures for stress response were included. Following exposure to the scene, participants rated their urge to smoke and were permitted to smoke *ad libitum*. Although the sad film induced greater feelings of sadness than the neutral film, participants randomized to the sad condition did not report greater nicotine cravings, nor did they show greater smoking behaviors than controls. Only in a subset of smokers – those with preexisting depression – did the sad film increase smoking.

Static visual stimuli have also been used as visual stressors, including both pictures and words. Mason and colleagues (Mason, Light, Escher, and Drobes, 2008) showed non-treatment-seeking abstinent alcoholics negative pictures (e.g., scenes of serious physical injuries; dangerous weapons), positive pictures (e.g., adventurous sports scenes; intimate kissing) and neutral pictures (e.g., household objects) to determine whether the manipulation affected alcohol-cue induced craving (where participants viewed and sniffed their preferred alcoholic beverage following mood induction). The effect of exposure to the positive and negative images was determined by self-reported ratings of "strong emotions," both of which yielded higher ratings than neutral pictures. Participants reported higher alcohol craving following exposure to the positive but not to the negative images, so results did not support the hypothesis that negative mood potentiates alcohol craving. Zack and colleagues asked healthy participants to read a list of words conveying negative (e.g., anxious), neutral, or positive (e.g., happy) emotions and to derive synonyms for each (Zack *et al.*, 2006). Unfortunately, no data were collected to confirm whether the target mood was induced (and therefore, it is unknown whether the results were due to the manipulation), but participants who were randomized to the negative mood words consumed more beer in a covert taste task than those who read neutral or positive words.

4.4   Summary of physical stressors

While subjective measures generally support that physical stressors can induce a target emotion (sadness, distress, anxiety), objective confirmation of the internal validity of physical stressors is lacking, due either to lack of inclusion or to negative results when objective measures were collected. Most studies that have employed physical stressors have not found that motivation to use drugs or alcohol is increased; when positive results are found, the effect has generally been limited to a subset of participants, such as those with coping motives for drug use or subjects with preexisting depression. Because of their limited efficacy in inducing urge to use, difficulty in confirming stress reactivity with measures other than self-reported emotions, and debatable ecological relevance regarding precipitating substance use, physical stressors may not be optimal as an experimental manipulation in studies to examine the effect of stress on motivation to use drugs or alcohol.

5   Psychological Stressors

Psychological stressors use memories, cognitions, and threats to the self-esteem and self-perception to induce distress. Psychological stressors are the most widely used stressors in this area of study, as they have the greatest ability to induce ecologically relevant distress, and presumably the types of feeling that motivate individuals to seek and use alcohol or drugs.

5.1   Guided imagery

Guided imagery is the most commonly used psychological stressor in addiction research (for a review, see Sinha, 2011). Participants are instructed to imagine and re-experience emotion-laden events during the experimental procedure. Most of the studies using guided imagery use individualized guided imagery scripts, in which participants provide a detailed account of a personally experienced event, which is later presented via audio recording to the participant during the experimental setting. Most of these studies employ within-subjects designs, where each participant is exposed to stress-related and neutral scripts. The most rigorous of these studies include methods to train participants how to effectively generate an image and maintain it during the challenge session so that there is greater confidence in and calibration of the manipulation (Sinha, 2011).

Guided imagery stress induction is consistently effective in increasing subjective anxiety or distress, probably due to the fact that the script is personalized to the individual. Results are less consistent that guided imagery stressors activate objective markers of stress reactivity, with some finding evidence of physiological or neuroendocrine reactivity (Chaplin, Hong, Bergquist, and Sinha, 2008; Fox, Hong, Siedlarz, and Sinha, 2008; Fox *et al.*, 2005; Higley *et al.*, 2011; Sinha, Catapani, and O'Malley, 1999; Sinha *et al.*, 2009; Sinha, Fuse, Aubin, and O'Malley, 2000; Sinha *et al.*, 2003), and others not (Cooney *et al.*, 1997; Fox, Bergquist, Hong, and Sinha, 2007; Harris *et al.*, 2005).

Guided imagery stressors have been shown to increase craving in substance-dependent participants, including cocaine (Fox, Hong, Siedlarz, and Sinha, 2008; Fox *et al.*, 2005; Harris *et al.*, 2005; Sinha, Catapani, and O'Malley, 1999; Sinha, Fuse, Aubin, and O'Malley, 2000), nicotine (Colamussi, Bovbjerg, and Erblich, 2007), opiates (Childress, Ehrman, McLellan, and MacRae, 1994), and alcohol (Cooney *et al.*, 1997; Fox, Bergquist, Hong, and Sinha, 2007; Higley *et al.*, 2011; Rubonis, Colby, Monti, and Rohsenow, 1994; Sinha *et al.*, 2009). Studies have reported that guided imagery stressors can motivate desire to use in non-dependent individuals as well (Chaplin, Hong, Bergquist, and Sinha, 2008; Rousseau, Irons, and Correia, 2011). To our knowledge, no studies have yet examined whether guided imagery stressors induce alcohol or other drug consumption in the laboratory, though severity of stress-induced craving in the laboratory has been shown to be associated with time to relapse (Higley *et al.*, 2011; Sinha *et al.*, 2011).

5.2   Speech tasks

All other psychological stressors reviewed here involve experiential events, where the participant performs an activity that is presumed to be distressing. In speech tasks, participants are usually asked to prepare a self-disclosing speech or a speech on a controversial issue. The participant delivers the speech to a live audience, or the participant is instructed beforehand that his/her performance will be videotaped and then evaluated by others. In some studies, the speech is prepared but not delivered, in which case the stressor is the anticipation of delivering the speech.

The majority of the studies using speech tasks to study effects on motivation to use drugs or alcohol have studied non-dependent samples. These studies show that speech tasks consistently increase subjective reports of distress and anxiety, though objective measures to confirm stress induction are rarely collected, an unfortunate fact since speech tasks are amenable to objective confirmation (Dickerson and Kemeny, 2004).

Speech tasks have been shown to increase self-reported craving for alcohol (Field and Powell, 2007; Field and Quigley, 2009), cigarettes (Britt, Cohen, Collins, and Cohen, 2001; Juliano and Brandon, 2002), and marijuana (Buckner, Silgado, and Schmidt, 2011), though only in subpopulations (women and individuals with social anxiety disorder) for the latter. On actual consumption of drugs or alcohol, speech stressors have not been well studied, and results are mixed (Kidorf and Lang, 1999; McNair, 1996). In the only study conducted to date examining the influence of a speech stressor in dependent individuals, the task increased self-reported craving for cocaine, though to a lesser degree than the guided imagery task, which participants received on a different day (Sinha, Catapano, and O'Malley, 1999).

5.3 Social interaction tasks

While both speech and social interaction stressors involve the real or perceived threat of social evaluation, social interaction tasks typically include a dialogue, usually with a trained confederate whose goal is to make the interaction uncomfortable. In some methods, the discomfort is achieved because the confederate is instructed to remain silent, and so only the participant speaks (we categorize these as social interaction stressors rather than speech stressors, since the participant expects to engage in a reciprocal interaction). Various methods have been used for social interaction stressors, including talking to or the threat of having to impress members of the opposite sex (Higgins and Marlatt, 1975; Niaura, Shadel, Britt, and Abrams, 2002), receiving discouraging results from a bogus personality test prior to engaging in a social situation (Holroyd, 1978), receiving negative feedback about one's social skills from a confederate (Miller, Hersen, Eisler, and Hilsman, 1974), preparing for an interaction in which the topic is one's own susceptibility to anxiety (Samoluk and Stewart, 1996), and – a notably creative one – anticipating a second interaction with a child confederate trained to exhibit signs of conduct disorder and other externalizing behaviors (Lang, Pelham, Johnston, and Gelernter, 1989; Pelham *et al.*, 1997). These studies relied primarily on self-reported distress to confirm the validity of the stressor, all of which supported that the social interaction stressor increased anxiety; two studies also showed that the stressor increased heart rate (Miller, Hersen, Eisler, and Hilsman, 1974; Niaura, Shadel, Britt, and Abrams, 2002).

Results on alcohol- and drug-related outcomes are mixed, though generally positive. In social drinkers, several studies failed to find that social interaction tasks increased drinking (Holroyd, 1978; Miller, Hersen, Eisler, and Hilsman, 1974; Samoluk and Stewart, 1996), though Higgins and colleagues did find a positive effect (Higgins and Marlatt, 1975). The threat of dealing with an ill-behaved child increased alcohol consumption in both college students (Lang, Pelham, Johnston, and Gelernter, 1989) and parents (Pelham *et al.*, 1997). In dependent participants, social interaction tasks increased urge to smoke in smokers (Niaura, Shadel, Britt, and Abrams, 2002) and increased alcohol consumption in alcoholic patients (Miller, Hersen, Eisler, and Hilsman, 1974).

5.4 Mental arithmetic tasks

Using either standardized procedures (e.g., the Paced Auditory Serial Addition Test, PASAT) (Gronwall, 1977) or study-specific methods, mental arithmetic stressors require the participant to perform mathematic calculations, typically while being evaluated by one or more individuals, which adds an effective element of social evaluative threat (Dickerson and Kemeny, 2004). In general, these tasks elicit distress by frustrating the participant and/or inducing social evaluative anxiety.

Studies consistently show that mental arithmetic tasks are effective in inducing a stress response confirmed by both subjective and objective measures (cortisol, heart rate, and/or blood pressure), but results are less convincing that the stressor motivates drug/alcohol use, with positive effects on nicotine craving in smokers (Pomerleau and Pomerleau, 1987; Pomerleau, Pomerlau, McPhee, and Morrell, 1990), but no effect on cocaine craving (Back *et al.*, 2005) or on alcohol craving or consumption in dependent participants (Pratt and Davidson, 2009).

5.5 Trier Social Stress Test

Given the ability of speech tasks, social interaction tasks, and mental arithmetic tasks to induce distress, a stressor that incorporates all three of these tasks is likely to be especially potent. The Trier Social Stress Test (TSST) (Kirschbaum, Pirk, and Hellhammer, 1993) is a standardized experiential stressor, delivered in three sequential phases. The first phase is anticipation of events to follow, where the individual is instructed that s/he will have a few minutes to prepare for a mock job interview, during which the goal is to convince the audience "why you are the perfect candidate for the position." A countdown clock is activated and placed in front of the participant. Following the anticipation phase, the individual is escorted (without his/her prepared notes) to the interview room occupied by an audience of confederates instructed to be non-responsive. While the individual is expecting to have to deliver a speech, s/he also expects that the interviewers will actively participate in the interview, which they do only minimally. The third phase is a mental arithmetic task, where the individual performs serial subtraction (e.g., subtracting 13 from 1099) to the same audience, and each incorrect value is noted by one of the confederates who states, "That is incorrect; please start over from the top." Each of these three phases is 5 minutes long (though some have allotted 10 minutes to the anticipatory phase); thus, the TSST is typically a 15-minute stress induction procedure.

The TSST is considered the gold standard for psychological stressors inasmuch as it produces a robust stress response, measurable by objective and subjective indices (Dickerson and Kemeny, 2004). It elicits a 2- to 4-fold increase in cortisol levels (Kirschbaum, Strasburger, and Langkrar, 1993) and a predictable response curve for other measures of stress reactivity, including subjective distress, heart rate, blood pressure, and ACTH (Kirschbaum, Pirke, and Hellhammer, 1993a; Singh *et al.*, 1999). In all of the studies reviewed below, the TSST was confirmed as an effective stressor by both objective and subjective measures. Despite being an effective stressor, the TSST's effect on motivating drug use is less consistent. Among non-dependent users, the TSST induced desire for both alcohol and placebo drink equally (de Wit, Soderpalm, Nikolayev, and Young, 2003), and it failed to increase desire for more alcohol following an initial dose (Soderpalm and de Wit, 2002). Nesic and Duka found that the TSST increased craving and consumption in men but not women (Nesic and Duka, 2006).

Results are also mixed for studies conducted on dependent individuals. The TSST induced craving in daily (but not occasional) cigarette smokers (Buchmann *et al.*, 2010) and individuals dependent on marijuana (McRae-Clark *et al.*, 2011). It was ineffective in inducing craving in cocaine-dependent (Moran-Santa Maria *et al.*, 2010) and alcohol-dependent participants (Thomas *et al.*, 2011a). The TSST has also been examined for its ability to potentiate cue-elicited craving (craving following presentation of drug-related versus neutral cues) for both alcohol-dependent (Thomas *et al.*, 2011b) and marijuana-dependent participants (McRae-Clark *et al.*, 2011), but in both cases, the results were negative.

Interestingly, the TSST has been shown to induce greater alcohol consumption in the laboratory in both men and women with alcohol dependence (Thomas *et al.*, 2011a). Alcoholics who received the TSST were more likely than non-stressed counterparts to consume the maximum amount of alcohol available to them in an *ad libitum* drinking task, despite the lack of stress-induced craving (Thomas *et al.*, 2011a). No differences were detected in water consumption between the stressed and non-stressed groups, suggesting the effect was not due to non-specific increase in thirst.

5.6   Summary of psychological stressors

Psychological stressors are employed in clinical laboratory studies because they are presumed to have the greatest potential to conjure the complex emotions that may lead to drug or alcohol use or relapse. While psychological stressors generally have internal validity as determined by subjective reports of distress, if the goal is to understand the biological mechanisms by which acute stress motivates drug use, objective confirmation of a stress response through biological markers is an important addition in stress induction studies, including those that use psychological stressors. Psychological stressors increase craving more consistently than other types of stressor, but results are still mixed. The greatest support for positive effects come, not surprisingly, from studies in which dependent individuals are tested, regardless of the type of psychological stressor employed, though guided imagery stressors have received the greatest empirical support. Whether psychological stressors can increase substance use in the laboratory is not yet determined, as few studies have included actual consumption as an outcome. A summary of the outcomes from all three classes of stressors reviewed here – pharmacologic, physical, and psychological – is shown in Table 15.1.

6   Neuroimaging Studies of Stress Induction

There is growing interest in applying stress induction methods and neuroimaging techniques to examine brain areas that are activated by exposure to a stressor and how this activation is associated with increased motivation to use drugs or alcohol. Importantly, as the scanner itself may induce a stress response (Muehlhan, Lueken, Wittchen, and Kirschbaum, 2011), rigorous methodologic controls must be applied to avoid both timing confounds (for within-subjects designs) and masking of stressor effects (for between-groups designs).

A host of different stressors have been used in neuroimaging studies, including threat of electric shock (Duncan *et al.*, 2007), pharmacologic challenges (though not yet specifically for examining stress-related urge for drugs or alcohol) (Cameron, Zubieta, Grunhaus, and Minoshima, 2000; Lovallo, Robinson, Glahn, and Fox, 2010), and visual stimuli of angry or fearful faces (Cornelius, Aizenstein, and Hariri, 2010), though guided imagery and a scanner-friendly version of the TSST are increasingly likely to be employed in future neuroimaging studies in this area. Guided imagery is well suited for delivery in the scanner with little adjustment to its standard delivery. It has been widely employed in neuroimaging studies to examine its effects on stress

Table 15.1 Summary of evidence from clinical laboratory studies in which stressors are applied to examine the effects of stress induction on craving and substance use in non-dependent and dependent samples

Stressor applied in clinical laboratory		Stress confirmation		Stress-induced craving		Stress-induced use		References
		Obj.	Subj.	Non depend. Ss	Depend. Ss	Non depend. Ss	Depend. Ss	
Pharmacologic	Cortisol	+	–	0	+	0	0	Elman et al. (2003)
	OCRH	+	–	0	±	0	0	Back et al. (2010); Moran-Santa Maria et al. (2010)
	mCPP	+	+	0	+	0	0	George et al. (1997); Krystal et al. (1994); Signs and Schechter (1988); Umhau et al. (2011)
	Tryptophan depletion (TD)	0	0	–	±	–	–	Aronson et al. (1995); Leyton et al. (2000); Petrakis et al. (2001); Pierucci-Lagha et al. (2004); Pihl, Young, Ervin, and Plotnick (1987); Satel et al. (1995); Wedekind et al. (2010)
	Yohimbine	+	±	0	±	0	0	Krystal et al. (1994); Umhau et al. (2011)
Physical	Cold Pressor Task	–	–	0	–	0	0	Back et al. (2005); Brady et al. (2006)
	Electric shock	0	+	–	–	0	0	McCarthy, Gloria, and Curtin (2009)
	Hyperventilation	0	0	–	0	0	0	Mulligan and McKay (2001)
	Music (somber)	0	+	±	–	0	0	Birch et al. (2004); Grant, Stewart, and Birch (2007); Jansma et al. (2000); Willner, Field, Pitts, and Reeve (1998)
	Movie (sad scene)	0	+	0	–	0	±	Fucito and Juliano (2009)
	Static pictures (negative)	0	+	0	+	0	0	Mason, Light, Escher, and Drobes (2008)
	Word list (negative)	0	0	0	0	+	0	Zack et al. (2006)
Psychological	Guided imagery	±	+	+	+	0	0	Chaplin, Hong, Bergquist, and Sinha (2008); Cooney et al. (1997); Fox, Hong, Siedlarz, and Sinha (2008); Fox, Bergquist, Hong, and Sinha. (2007); Fox et al. (2005); Harris et al. (2005); Higley et al. (2011); Sinha, Catapano, and O'Malley (1999); Sinha et al. (2009); Sinha, Fuse, Aubin, and O'Malley (2000); Sinha et al. (2003); Rousseau, Irons, and Correia (2011)

(Continued)

Table 15.1 (*Continued*)

Stressor applied in clinical laboratory	Stress confirmation		Stress-induced craving		Stress-induced use		References
	Obj.	*Subj.*	*Non depend. Ss*	*Depend. Ss*	*Non depend. Ss*	*Depend. Ss*	
Speech	0	+	+	+	±	0	Britt, Cohen, Collins, and Cohen (2001); Buckner, Silgado, and Schmidt (2011); Field and Powell (2007); Field and Quigley (2009); Juliano and Brandon (2002); Kidorf and Lang (1999); McNair (1996); Sinha, Catapano, and O'Malley (1999)
Social interaction	+	+	0	+	±	+	Higgins and Marlatt (1975); Holroyd (1978); Lang, Pelham, Johnston, and Gelertner (1989); Miller, Hersen, Eisler, and Hilsman (1974); Niaura, Shadel, Britt, and Adams (2002); Pelham *et al.* (1997); Samoluk and Stewart (1996)
Mental arithmetic	+	+	0	±	0	−	Back *et al.* (2005); Pomerleau and Pomerleau (1987); Pomerleau, Pomerleau, McPhee, and Morrell (1990); Pratt and Davidson (2009)
Trier Social Stress Test	+	+	±	±	±	+	Buchmann *et al.* (2010); de Wit, Soderpalm, Nikolayev, and Young (2003); McRae-Clark *et al.* (2011); Moran-Santa Maria *et al.* (2010); Nesic and Duka (2006); Soderpalm and de Wit (2002); Thomas *et al.* (2011a; 2011b)

Note: + indicates that studies are generally supportive of the outcome noted in the column; ± = evidence is equivocal; − = negative results; 0 = studies are lacking. For stress confirmation, Obj. column reflects whether there is objective evidence of stress reactivity (e.g., elevations in heart rate, blood pressure, cortisol, and/or ACTH); Subj. reflects whether there is subjective evidence of stress reactivity (e.g., self-reported increase in negative affect or distress).

reactivity and craving (Sinha and Li, 2007, for a review). Stress-related scripts induced activation in areas of the brain associated with emotion regulation and motivation, specifically the hippocampus and anterior cingulate areas in healthy controls, but not in cocaine-dependent participants, despite inducing similar ratings of distress in these groups. In addition, activation in dependent subjects in the caudate and dorsal striatum was observed and was associated with stress-induced cocaine craving (see Sinha, 2011; Sinha and Li, 2007, for a review).

Not yet widely used in substance abuse research, the Montreal Imaging Stress Test (MIST) (Dedovic *et al.*, 2005) is an experiential stressor derived from the Trier Social Stress Task (Kirschbaum, Pirke, and Hellhammer, 1993). It reduces movement (which introduces noise variability) by removing the speech task, but maintains the important elements of uncontrollability and social evaluation to elicit a robust stress response (Dickerson and Kemeny, 2004). Briefly, the individual is instructed to solve difficult mental arithmetic problems presented by computer in the scanner after being told that most people correctly solve at least 85% of the problems. The amount of time the individual is given to solve each problem is adjusted (shortened) so that s/he has a failure rate much higher than s/he expects. Feedback of performance is provided on the screen to the participant; additionally, the experimenter verbally instructs the participant that s/he is performing below average and that it is important that s/he try harder to improve her/his performance, lest the experiment be compromised. Given these social evaluative and social threat pressures, it is not surprising that the MIST elicits a robust stress response. It increases cortisol (Dedovic *et al.*, 2005) and evokes differential brain activity compared to the control condition, a similar task without the time constraints and negative feedback (Dagher *et al.*, 2009; Dedovic *et al.*, 2005; Dedovic *et al.*, 2009; Pruessner, Cahampagne, Meaney, and Dagher, 2004).

Dagher and colleagues (2009) used the MIST to examine the effects of stress on brain activation following exposure to smoking cues in nicotine-dependent subjects. The MIST (versus no-stress control condition) increased nicotine-cue induced brain activation in areas of the brain that control attention and motivation, including the caudate, dorsomedial thalamus, and hippocampus, suggesting the neurobiological mechanisms by which stress may maintain addictive behavior and contribute to relapse.

7 Limitations, Shortcomings, and Future Directions

The equivocal results of the studies reviewed here suggest that clinical laboratory stressors are not equally effective at inducing ecologically relevant distress that is verifiable empirically, and even when they do, they may have no impact on urge to drink or use drugs. Thus, clinical laboratory studies do not provide a simple answer to the question of whether acute stress and/or negative affect motivate substance use. By their nature, clinical laboratory settings are imperfect approximations of the complex milieu of internal and external forces that drive motivation and behavior. Clinical laboratory studies emphasize experimental control over ecological relevance (i.e., internal validity over external validity), although the latter is certainly valued, and studies that attempt to maximize it are rewarded (i.e., as shown in the table, psychological stressors are generally more effective than physical stressors in inducing self-reported urge to drink or use drugs).

While clinical laboratory studies afford the ability to reveal causal connections between events, and so have been utilized to study whether stress motivates drug use, their greatest potential probably lies in developing clinical models that can be used to develop and test interventions. Thus, investigators should perhaps not look to these studies to answer the empirical question of whether stress induces drinking or drug use/relapse, but instead endeavor to develop the most consistent and valid model (that is, a tool) possible for a particular population, emotional state, and drug of interest. If a clinical model is developed that consistently shows anger-induced drinking in alcoholics, for example, it can then be used in studies to determine whether a pharmaceutical or behavioral intervention that reduces anger can reduce drinking in affected individuals. Certainly, such tools are critical for treatment and even prevention efforts, and there is ample opportunity to conduct studies that address research questions posed with this level of specificity.

Some shortcomings in studies conducted to date can help direct these efforts. While not all acute stressors used in clinical laboratory settings are amenable to confirmation with objective markers (Dickerson and Kemeny, 2004), and thus, the absence of objective measures of stress reactivity is not necessarily evidence that the stressor was ineffective, if only subjective indices are presented to confirm the validity of the stress induction procedure, the problem of demand bias plagues interpretation of results. Specifically, if a participant is presented with a stimulus that is presented as a "stressor," s/he may feel compelled to report feeling stressed, even if the stressor is ineffective. If at least one index of physiological stress reactivity is presented, the problem of demand bias (while not necessarily nullified) is at least tempered. An additional tack to reduce demand bias is to employ deception or an ambiguous experimental pretext regarding the nature of the stress provocation so that participants are not inadvertently encouraged to report the emotion of interest (see Thomas *et al.*, 2011b).

Regarding objective measures of stress reactivity, heart rate and blood pressure both index sympathetic arousal and can be collected inexpensively and non-invasively. Salivary cortisol is a cost-effective measure of HPA axis activity. Not only is it non-invasive, it provides an even more accurate measure of bioactive circulating cortisol than cortisol measured in serum (Gozansky, Lynn, Laudenslager, and Kohrt, 2005), and it is less susceptible to interference by oral contraceptives (Vining, McGinley, Maksvytis, and Ho, 1983).

Future studies should also include psychometrically validated instruments of subjective distress, as these will afford the opportunity to compare the relative effectiveness of different stress induction procedures across studies and aid in interpreting results. An ideal instrument would be sensitive to change in affective states and relatively quick to administer, and it would assess a range of positive and negative emotions. Two instruments are suggested that meet these criteria: the Positive and Negative Affect Schedule (Watson, Clark, and Tellegen, 1988) and the Differential Emotions Scale (Boyle, 1984; Izard, 1974). Both are short instruments (20 and 30 items, respectively) that capture both positive and negative mood states and are sensitive to fluctuations in affect. For studies that focus specifically on induction of anxiety, the State Trait Anxiety Inventory (Spielberger *et al.*, 1983) is a good choice. It is a 20-item instrument that captures severity of present state anxiety, but there is also a validated abbreviated 6-item version of the STAI (Marteau and Bekker, 1992). Including validated measures of affect does not preclude the use of study-specific questions, but greater gains will be made in the field if studies can be compared on standardized measures.

Similarly, as craving is a notoriously difficult construct to measure (Sayette *et al.*, 2000), investigators must thoughtfully select the instruments to be used to assess this outcome. Several validated instruments are available for assessing in the moment craving or urge (see Chapter 13 for guidance; see also Drobes and Thomas, 1999; Sayette, 1999, for reviews). Additionally, while craving has clinical relevance and is the best-studied outcome in this area for good reason, stress-induced craving is not ultimately the behavior of interest – stress-induced consumption is. Certainly, it is not always possible or ethical to assess consumption of drugs or alcohol in the laboratory in many studies, especially those assessing urge to use illicit drugs, and those in which participants include adolescents, treatment-seeking individuals, or individuals in recovery. However, if the study and participant population permit, the inclusion of actual consumption behavior as an outcome would be a real asset for developing a more behaviorally relevant clinical model of stress-induced substance use.

In summary, future investigators must be highly selective in every aspect of study design and methods. Investigators must carefully choose the best stressor for the research question with regard to its ability to evoke the emotion(s) of interest and its ability to be empirically confirmed, minimize demand bias in participants, determine how best to confirm the validity of the stressor, and incorporate the most sensitive measures of urge and/or actual substance use as outcomes. With these tenets as guides, we can design and conduct studies that contribute to an extant literature that advances our understanding of stress-induced substance use and yields clinically valuable tools that help improve prevention and treatment efforts.

References

Adinoff B, Krebaum SR, Chandler PA, Ye W, Brown MB, and Williams MJ (2005) Dissection of hypothalamic-pituitary-adrenal axis pathology in 1-month-abstinent alcohol-dependent men, part 2: response to ovine corticotropin-releasing factor and naloxone. *Alcoholism: Clinical and Experimental Research* 29: 528–537.

Anthenelli RM, Maxwell RA, Geracioti TD, Jr, and Hauger R (2001) Stress hormone dysregulation at rest and after serotonergic stimulation among alcohol-dependent men with extended abstinence and controls. *Alcoholism: Clinical and Experimental Research* 25: 692–703.

Aronson SC, Black JE, McDougle CJ, Scanley BE, Jatlow P, Kosten TR, Heninger GR, and Price LH (1995) Serotonergic mechanisms of cocaine effects in humans. *Psychopharmacology* 119: 179–185.

Back SE, Brady KT, Jackson JL, Salstrom S, and Zinzow H (2005) Gender differences in stress reactivity among cocaine-dependent individuals. *Psychopharmacology* 180: 169–176.

Back SE, Hartwell K, DeSantis SM, Saladin M, McRae-Clark AL, Price KL, Moran-Santa Maria MM, Baker NL, Spratt E, Kreek MJ, and Brady KT (2010) Reactivity to laboratory stress provocation predicts relapse to cocaine. *Drug and Alcohol Dependence* 106: 21–27.

Birch CD, Stewart SH, Wall A-M, McKee SA, Eisnor SJ, and Theakston JA (2004) Mood-induced increases in alcohol expectancy strength in internally motivated frinkers. *Psychology of Addictive Behaviors* 18: 231–238.

Boyle G (1984) Reliability and validity of Izard's differential emotions scale. *Personality and Individual Differences* 5: 747–750.

Brady KT, Back SE, Waldrop AE, McRae AL, Anton RF, Upadhyaya HP, Saladin ME, and Randall PK (2006) Cold pressor task reactivity: predictors of alcohol use among alcohol-dependent individuals with and without comorbid posttraumatic stress disorder. *Alcoholism: Clinical and Experimental Research* 30: 938–946.

Britt DM, Cohen LM, Collins FL, Jr, and Cohen ML (2001) Cigarette smoking and chewing gum: Response to a laboratory-induced stressor. *Health Psychology* 20: 361–368.

Brown SA, Vik PW, Patterson TL, Grant I, and Schuckit MA (1995) Stress, vulnerability and adult alcohol relapse. *Journal of Studies on Alcohol* 56: 538–545.

Buchmann AF, Laucht M, Schmid B, Wiedemann K, Mann K, and Zimmermann US (2010) Cigarette craving increases after a psychosocial stress test and is related to cortisol stress response but not to dependence scores in daily smokers. *Journal of Psychopharmacology* 24: 247–255.

Buckner JD, Silgado J, and Schmidt NB (2011) Marijuana craving during a public speaking challenge: Understanding marijuana use vulnerability among women and those with social anxiety disorder. *Journal of Behavior Therapy and Experimental Psychiatry* 42: 104–110.

Cameron OG, Zubieta JK, Grunhaus L, and Minoshima S (2000) Effects of yohimbine on cerebral blood flow, symptoms, and physiological functions in humans. *Psychosomatic Medicine* 62: 549–559.

Cappell H and Herman CP (1972) Alcohol and tension reduction: A review. *Quarterly Journal of Studies on Alcohol* 33: 33–64.

Chaplin TM, Hong K, Bergquist K, and Sinha R (2008) Gender differences in response to emotional stress: An assessment across subjective, behavioral, and physiological domains and relations to alcohol craving. *Alcoholism: Clinical and Experimental Research* 32: 1242–1250.

Childress AR, Ehrman R, McLellan AT, and MacRae J (1994) Can induced moods trigger drug-related responses in opiate abuse patients? *Journal of Substance Abuse Treatment* 11: 17–23.

Coffey SF, Schumacher JA, Stasiewicz PR, Henslee AM, Baillie LE, and Landy N (2010) Craving and physiological reactivity to trauma and alcohol cues in posttraumatic stress disorder and alcohol dependence. *Experimental and Clinical Psychopharmacology* 18: 340–349.

Colamussi L, Bovbjerg DH, and Erblich J (2007) Stress- and cue-induced cigarette craving: Effects of a family history of smoking. *Drug and Alcohol Dependence* 88: 251–258.

Conger JJ (1956) Alcoholism: theory, problem and challenge. II. Reinforcement theory and the dynamics of alcoholism. *Quarterly Journal of Studies on Alcohol* 17: 296–305.

Cooney NL, Litt MD, Morse PA, Bauer LO, and Gaupp L (1997) Alcohol cue reactivity, negative-mood reactivity, and relapse in treated alcoholic men. *Journal of Abnormal Psychology* 106: 243–250.

Cornelius JR, Aizenstein HJ, and Hariri AR (2010) Amygdala reactivity is inversely related to level of cannabis use in individuals with comorbid cannabis dependence and major depression. *Addictive Behaviors* 35: 644–646.

Dagher A, Tannenbaum B, Hayashi T, Pruessner JC, and McBride D (2009) An acute psychosocial stress enhances the neural response to smoking cues. *Brain Research* 1293: 40–48.

de Wit H, Soderpalm AHV, Nikolayev L, and Young E (2003) Effects of acute social stress on alcohol consumption in healthy subjects. *Alcoholism: Clinical and Experimental Research* 27: 1270–1277.

Dedovic K, Renwick R, Mahani NK, Engert V, Lupien SJ, and Pruessner JC (2005) The Montreal Imaging Stress Task: Using functional imaging to investigate the effects of perceiving and processing psychosocial stress in the human brain. *Journal of Psychiatry and Neuroscience* 30: 319–325.

Dedovic K, Rexroth M, Wolff E, Duchesne A, Scherling C, Beaudry T, Lue SD, Lord C, Engert V, and Pruessner JC (2009) Neural correlates of processing stressful information: An event-related fMRI study. *Brain Research* 1293: 49–60.

Dickerson SS and Kemeny ME (2004) Acute stressors and cortisol responses: A theoretical integration and synthesis of laboratory research. *Psychological Bulletin* 130: 355–391.

Dinan TG (1996) Serotonin and the regulation of hypothalamic–pituitary–adrenal axis function. *Life Sciences* 58: 1683–1694.

Drobes DJ and Thomas SE (1999) Assessing craving for alcohol. *Alc Res Health* 23: 179–186.

Drobes DJ, Anton RF, Thomas SE, and Voronin K (2003) A clinical laboratory paradigm for evaluating medication effects on alcohol consumption: Naltrexone and nalmefene. *Neuropsychopharmacology* 28: 755–764.

Duncan E, Boshoven W, Harenski K, Fiallos A, Tracy H, Jovanovic T, Hu X, Drexler K, and Kilts C (2007) An fMRI study of the interaction of stress and cocaine cues on cocaine craving in cocaine-dependent men. *The American Journal on Addictions* 16: 174–182.

Elman I, Lukas SE, Karlsgodt KH, Gasic GP, and Breiter HC (2003) Acute cortisol administration triggers craving in individuals with cocaine dependence. *Psychopharmacology Bulletin* 37: 84–89.

Field M and Powell H (2007) Stress increases attentional bias for alcohol cues in social drinkers who drink to cope. *Alcohol and Alcoholism* 42: 560–566.

Field M and Quigley M (2009) Mild stress increases attentional bias in social drinkers who drink to cope: A replication and extension. *Experimental and Clinical Psychopharmacology* 17: 312–319.

Fouquereau E, Fernandez A, Mullet E, and Sorum PC (2003) Stress and the urge to drink. *Addictive Behaviors* 28: 669–685.

Fox HC, Bergquist KL, Hong KI, and Sinha R (2007) Stress-induced and alcohol cue-induced craving in recently abstinent alcohol-dependent individuals. *Alcoholism: Clinical and Experimental Research* 31: 395–403.

Fox HC, Hong KI, Siedlarz K, and Sinha R (2008) Enhanced sensitivity to stress and drug/alcohol craving in abstinent cocaine-dependent individuals compared to social drinkers. *Neuropsychopharmacology* 33: 796–805.

Fox HC, Talih M, Malison R, Anderson GM, Kreek MJ, and Sinha R (2005) Frequency of recent cocaine and alcohol use affects drug craving and associated responses to stress and drug-related cues. *Psychoneuroendocrinology* 30: 880–891.

Fucito LM and Juliano LM (2009) Depression moderates smoking behavior in response to a sad mood induction. *Psychology of Addictive Behaviors* 23: 546–551.

George DT, Benkelfat C, Rawlings RR, Eckardt MJ, Phillips MJ, Nutt DJ, Wynne D, Murphy DL, and Linnoila M (1997) Behavioral and neuroendocrine responses to m-chlorophenylpiperazine in subtypes of alcoholics and in healthy comparison subjects. *American Journal of Psychiatry* 154: 81–87.

Gozansky WS, Lynn JS, Laudenslager ML, and Kohrt WM (2005) Salivary cortisol determined by enzyme immunoassay is preferable to serum total cortisol for assessment of dynamic hypothalamic–pituitary–adrenal axis activity. *Clinical Endocrinology* 63: 336–341.

Grant VV, Stewart SH, and Birch CD (2007) Impact of positive and anxious mood on implicit alcohol-related cognitions in internally motivated undergraduate drinkers. *Addictive Behaviors* 32: 2226–2237.

Gronwall DM (1977) Paced auditory serial-addition task: a measure of recovery from concussion. *Perceptual and Motor Skills* 44: 367–373.

Harris DS, Reus VI, Wolkowitz OM, Mendelson JE, and Jones RT (2005) Repeated psychological stress testing in stimulant-dependent patients. *Progress in Neuropsychopharmacology and Biological Psychiatry* 29: 669–677.

Helzer JE, Badger GJ, Searles JS, Rose GL, and Mongeon JA (2006) Stress and alcohol consumption in heavily drinking men: 2 years of daily data using interactive voice response. *Alcoholism: Clinical and Experimental Research* 30: 802–811.

Higgins RL and Marlatt GA (1975) Fear of interpersonal evaluation as a determinant of alcohol consumption in male social drinkers. *Psychology of Addictive Behaviors* 84: 644–651.

Higley AE, Crane NA, Spadoni AD, Quello SB, Goodell V, and Mason BJ (2011) Craving in response to stress induction in a human laboratory paradigm predicts treatment outcome in alcohol-dependent individuals. *Psychopharmacology* 218: 121–129.

Holroyd KA (1978) Effects of social anxiety and social evaluation on beer consumption and social interaction. *Journal of Studies on Alcohol* 39: 737–744.

Izard C (1974) The Differential Emotions Scale: A method of measuring the subjective experience of discrete emotions. Vanderbilt University, Nashville, TN.

Jansma A, Breteler MHM, Schippers GM, De Jong CAJ, and Van Der Staak CPF (2000) No effect of negative mood on the alcohol cue reactivity on in-patient alcoholics. *Addictive Behaviors* 25: 619–624.

Juliano LM and Brandon TH (2002) Effects of nicotine dose, instructional set, and outcome expectancies on the subjective effects of smoking in the presence of a stressor. *Journal of Abnormal Psychology* 111: 88–97.

Kassel JD, Stroud LR, and Paronis CA (2003) Smoking, stress, and negative affect: Correlation, causation, and context across stages of smoking. *Psychological Bulletin* 129: 270–304.

Kassel JD, Veilleux J, Wardle M, Yates M, Greenstein J, Evatt D, and Roesch L (2007) Negative affect and addiction. In M al' Absi (ed.), *Stress and Addiction: Biological and Psychological Mechanisms* (pp. 171–190). Burlington, MA: Academic Press.

Khantzian EJ (1985) The self-medication hypothesis of addictive disorders: Focus on heroin and cocaine dependence. *American Journal of Psychiatry* 142: 1259–1264.

Kidorf M and Lang AR (1999) Effects of social anxiety and alcohol expectancies on stress-induced drinking. *Psychology of Addictive Behaviors* 13: 134–142.

Kirschbaum C, Pirke KM, and Hellhammer DH (1993) The 'Trier Social Stress Test': A tool for investigating psychobiological stress responses in a laboratory setting. *Neuropsychobiology* 28: 76–81.

Kirschbaum C, Strasburger CJ, and Langkrar J (1993) Attenuated cortisol response to psychological stress but not to CRH or ergometry in young habitual smokers. *Pharmacology, Biochemistry and Behavior* 44: 527–531.

Krystal JH, Webb E, Cooney N, Kranzler HR, and Charney DS (1994) Specificity of ethanol-like effects elicited by serotonergic and noradrenergic mechanisms. *Archives of General Psychiatry* 51: 898–911.

Kudielka B and Kirschbaum C (2007) Biological basis of the stress response. In M al' Absi (ed.), *Stress and Addiction: Biological and Psychological Mechanisms* (pp. 3–22). Burlington, MA: Academic Press.

Lang AR, Pelham WE, Johnston C, and Gelernter S (1989) Levels of adult alcohol consumption induced by interactions with child confederates exhibiting normal versus externalizing behaviors. *Journal of Abnormal Psychology* 98: 294–299.

Le AD, Harding S, Juzytsch W, Funk D, and Shaham Y (2005) Role of alpha-2 adrenoceptors in stress-induced reinstatement of alcohol seeking and alcohol self-administration in rats. *Psychopharmacology* 179: 366–373.

Leshner AI and Koob GF (1999) Drugs of abuse and the brain. *Proceedings of the Association of American Physicians* 111: 99–108.

Leyton M, Young SN, Blier P, Baker GB, Pihl RO, and Benkelfat C (2000) Acute tyrosine depletion and alcohol ingestion in healthy women. *Alcoholism: Clinical and Experimental Research* 24: 459–464.

Lovallo WR, Robinson JL, Glahn DC, and Fox PT (2010) Acute effects of hydrocortisone on the human brain: An fMRI study. *Psychoneuroendocrinology* 35: 15–20.

Marteau TM and Bekker H (1992) The development of a six-item short-form of the state scale of the Spielberger State-Trait Anxiety Inventory (STAI). *British Journal of Clinical Psychology* 31(Pt 3): 301–306.

Mason BJ, Light JM, Escher T, and Drobes DJ (2008) Effect of positive and negative affective stimuli and beverage cues on measures of craving in non treatment-seeking alcoholics. *Psychopharmacology* 200: 141–150.

McCarthy DE, Gloria R, and Curtin JJ (2009) Attention bias in nicotine withdrawal and under stress. *Psychology of Addictive Behaviors* 23: 77–90.

McNair LD (1996) Alcohol use and stress in women: The role of prior vs. anticipated stressors. *Journal of Psychopathology and Behavioral Assessment* 18: 331–345.

McRae-Clark AL, Carter RE, Price KL, Baker NL, Thomas S, Saladin ME, Giarla K, Nicholas K, and Brady KT (2011) Stress- and cue-elicited craving and reactivity in marijuana-dependent individuals. *Psychopharmacology* 218: 49–58.

Miller PM, Hersen M, Eisler RM, and Hilsman G (1974) Effects of social stress on operant drinking of alcoholics and social drinkers. *Behaviour Research and Therapy* 12: 67–72.

Moran-Santa Maria MM, McRae-Clark AL, Back SE, DeSantis SM, Baker NL, Spratt EG, Simpson AN, and Brady KT (2010) Influence of cocaine dependence and early life stress on pituitary–adrenal axis responses to CRH and the Trier social stressor. *Psychoneuroendocrinology* 35: 1492–1500.

Muehlhan M, Lueken U, Wittchen HU, and Kirschbaum C (2011) The scanner as a stressor: Evidence from subjective and neuroendocrine stress parameters in the time course of a functional magnetic resonance imaging session. *International Journal of Psychophysiology* 79: 118–126.

Mulligan ME and McKay D (2001) Hyperventilation, anxiety sensitivity and the expectations for alcohol use. Subjective and physiological reactivity to alcohol cues. *Addictive Behaviors* 26: 375–383.

Nesic J and Duka T (2006) Gender specific effects of a mild stressor on alcohol cue reactivity in heavy social drinkers. *Pharmacology, Biochemistry and Behavior* 83: 239–248.

Niaura R, Shadel WG, Britt DM, and Abrams DB (2002) Response to social stress, urge to smoke, and smoking cessation. *Addictive Behaviors* 27: 241–250.

Park CL, Armeli S, and Tennen H (2004) The daily stress and coping process and alcohol use among college students. *Journal of Studies on Alcohol* 65: 126–135.

Pelham WE, Lang AR, Atkeson B, Murphy DA, Gnagy EM, Greiner AR, Vodde-Hamilton M, and Greenslade KE (1997) Effects of deviant child behavior on parental distress and alcohol consumption in laboratory interactions. *Journal of Abnormal Child Psychology* 25: 413–424.

Petrakis IL, Buonopane A, O'Malley S, Cermik O, Trevisan L, Boutros NN, Limoncelli D, and Krystal JH (2002) The effect of tryptophan depletion on alcohol self-administration in non-treatment-seeking alcoholic individuals. *Alcoholism: Clinical and Experimental Research* 26: 969–975.

Petrakis IL, Trevisan L, Boutros NN, Limoncelli D, Cooney NL, and Krystal JH (2001) Effect of tryptophan depletion on alcohol cue-induced craving in abstinent alcoholic patients. *Alcoholism: Clinical and Experimental Research* 25: 1151–1155.

Pierucci-Lagha A, Feinn R, Modesto-Lowe V, Swift R, Nellissery M, Covault J, and Kranzler HR (2004) Effects of rapid tryptophan depletion on mood and urge to drink in patients with co-morbid major depression and alcohol dependence. *Psychopharmacology* 171: 340–348.

Pihl RO, Young SN, Ervin FR, and Plotnick S (1987) Influence of tryptophan availability on selection of alcohol and water by men. *Journal of Studies on Alcohol* 48: 260–264.

Pomerleau CS and Pomerleau OF (1987) The effects of a psychological stressor on cigarette smoking and subsequent behavioral and physiological responses. *Psychophysiology* 24: 278–285.

Pomerleau CS, Pomerleau OF, McPhee K, and Morrell EM (1990) Discordance of physiological and biochemical response to smoking and to psychological stress. *British Journal of Addiction* 85: 1309–1316.

Pratt WM and Davidson D (2009) Role of the HPA axis and the A118G polymorphism of the mu-opioid receptor in stress-induced drinking behavior. *Alcohol and Alcoholism* 44: 358–365.

Pruessner JC, Champagne F, Meaney MJ, and Dagher A (2004) Dopamine release in response to a psychological stress in humans and its relationship to early life maternal care: A positron emission tomography study using [11C]raclopride. *Journal of Neuroscience* 24: 2825–2831.

Ray LA (2011) Stress-induced and cue-induced craving for alcohol in heavy drinkers: Preliminary evidence of genetic moderation by the OPRM1 and CRH-BP genes. *Alcoholism: Clinical and Experimental Research* 35(1): 166–174.

Rousseau GS, Irons JG, and Correia CJ (2011) The reinforcing value of alcohol in a drinking to cope paradigm. *Drug and Alcohol Dependence* 118: 1–4.

Rubonis AV, Colby SM, Monti PM, and Rohsenow DJ (1994) Alcohol cue reactivity and mood induction in male and female alcoholics. *Journal of Studies on Alcohol* 55: 487–494.

Samoluk SB and Stewart SH (1996) Anxiety sensitivity and anticipation of a self-disclosing interview as determinants of alcohol consumption. *Psychology of Addictive Behaviors* 10: 45–54.

Satel SL, Krystal JH, Delgado PL, Kosten TR, and Charney DS (1995) Tryptophan depletion and attenuation of cue-induced craving for cocaine. *American Journal of Psychiatry* 152: 778–83.

Sayette MA (1999) Does drinking reduce stress? *Alcohol Research & Health* 23: 250–255.

Sayette MA, Martin CS, Perrott MA, Wertz JM, and Hufford MR (2001) A test of the appraisal-disruption model of alcohol and stress. *Journal of Studies on Alcohol* 62: 247–256.

Sayette MA, Shiffman S, Tiffany ST, Niaura RS, Martin CS, and Shadel WG (2000) The measurement of drug craving. *Addiction* 95(Suppl. 2): S189–S210.

Shiffman S and Waters AJ (2004) Negative affect and smoking lapses: A prospective analysis. *Journal of Consulting and Clinical Psychology* 72: 192–201.

Shiffman S, Gwaltney CJ, Balabanis MH, Liu KS, Paty JA, Kassel JD, Hickcox M, and Gnys M (2002) Immediate antecedents of cigarette smoking: An analysis from ecological momentary assessment. *Journal of Abnormal Psychology* 111: 531–545.

Signs S and Schechter M (1988) The role of dopamine and serotonin receptors in the mediation of ethanol interoceptive cue. *Pharmacology, Biochemistry and Behavior* 30: 55–64.

Singh A, Petrides JS, Gold PW, Chrousos GP, and Deuster PA (1999) Differential hypothalamic–pituitary–adrenal axis reactivity to psychological and physical stress. *Journal of Clinical Endocrinology & Metabolism* 84: 1944–1948.

Sinha R (2013) Modeling relapse situations in the human laboratory. *Current Topics in Behavioral Neurosciences* 13: 379-402.

Sinha R and Li CS (2007) Imaging stress- and cue-induced drug and alcohol craving: Association with relapse and clinical implications. *Drug and Alcohol Review* 26: 25–31.

Sinha R, Catapano D, and O'Malley S (1999) Stress-induced craving and stress response in cocaine dependent individuals. *Psychopharmacology* 142: 343–351.

Sinha R, Fox HC, Hong KA, Bergquist K, Bhagwagar Z, and Siedlarz KM (2009) Enhanced negative emotion and alcohol craving, and altered physiological responses following stress and cue exposure in alcohol dependent individuals. *Neuropsychopharmacology* 34: 1198–1208.

Sinha R, Fox HC, Hong KI, Hansen J, Tuit K, and Kreek MJ (2011) Effects of adrenal sensitivity, stress- and cue-induced craving, and anxiety on subsequent alcohol relapse and treatment outcomes. *Archives of General Psychiatry* 68: 942–952.

Sinha R, Fuse T, Aubin LR, and O'Malley SS (2000) Psychological stress, drug-related cues and cocaine craving. *Psychopharmacology* 152: 140–148.

Sinha R, Talih M, Malison R, Cooney N, Anderson GM, and Kreek MJ (2003) Hypothalamic–pituitary–adrenal axis and sympatho-adreno-medullary responses during stress-induced and drug cue-induced cocaine craving states. *Psychopharmacology* 170: 62–72.

Soderpalm AHV and de Wit H (2002) Effects of stress and alcohol on subjective state in humans. *Alcoholism: Clinical and Experimental Research* 26: 818–826.

Spielberger CD, Gorsuch RL, Lushen R, Vagg PR, and Jacobs GA (1983) *Manual for the State-Trait Anxiety Inventory (form Y)*. Palo Alto, CA: Consulting Psychologists Press.

Stasiewicz PR, Gulliver SB, Bradizza CM, Rohsenow DJ, Torrisi R, and Monti PM (1997) Exposure to negative emotional cues and alcohol cue reactivity with alcoholics: A preliminary investigation. *Behaviour Research and Therapy* 35: 1143–1149.

Thomas SE, Bacon AK, Randall PK, Brady KT, and See RE (2011a) An acute psychosocial stressor increases drinking in non-treatment-seeking alcoholics. *Psychopharmacology* 218: 19–28.

Thomas SE, Randall PK, Brady K, See RE, and Drobes DJ (2011b) An acute psychosocial stressor does not potentiate alcohol cue reactivity in non-treatment-seeking alcoholics. *Alcoholism: Clinical and Experimental Research* 35: 464–473.

Todd M, Armeli S, and Tennen H (2009) Interpersonal problems and negative mood as predictors of within-day time to drinking. *Psychology of Addictive Behaviors* 23: 205–215.

Umhau JC, Schwandt ML, Usala J, Geyer C, Singley E, George DT, and Heilig M (2011) Pharmacologically induced alcohol craving in treatment seeking alcoholics correlates with alcoholism severity, but is insensitive to acamprosate. *Neuropsychopharmacology* 36: 1178–1186.

Vining RF, McGinley RA, Maksvytis JJ, and Ho KY (1983) Salivary cortisol: A better measure of adrenal cortical function than serum cortisol. *Annals of Clinical Biochemistry* 20(Pt 6): 329–335.

Wand GS, Mangold D, Ali M, and Giggey P (1999) Adrenocortical responses and family history of alcoholism. *Alcoholism: Clinical and Experimental Research* 23: 1185–1190.

Watson D, Clark LA, and Tellegen A (1988) Development and validation of brief measures of positive and negative affect: The PANAS scales. *Journal of Personality and Social Psychology* 54: 1063–1070.

Wedekind D, Herchenhein T, Kirchhainer J, Bandelow B, Falkai P, Engel K, Malchow B, and Havemann-Reinecke U (2010) Serotonergic function, substance craving, and psychopathology in detoxified alcohol-addicted males undergoing tryptophan depletion. *Journal of Psychiatric Research* 44: 1163–1169.

Willner P, Field M, Pitts K, and Reeve G (1998) Mood, cue and gender influences on motivation, craving and liking for alcohol in recreational drinkers. *Behavioural Pharmacology* 9: 631–642.

Zack M, Poulos CX, Fragopoulos F, Woodford TM, and MacLeod CM (2006) Negative affect words prime beer consumption in young drinkers. *Addictive Behaviors* 31: 169–173.

16

Substance Priming

Abigail K. Rose

1 Introduction

A factor believed to be important in substance administration is the "priming" effect. Priming refers to the process whereby initial administration of a substance can stimulate motivation to continue self-administration, perhaps to excessive levels. Anecdotal evidence suggests that an initial "slip drink" may precipitate full-blown relapse in individuals trying to abstain from drinking; however, priming is also observed in "social users." This is an important point: excessive and dependent substance use is always preceded by non-excessive and non-dependent substance use. The ability of initial substance use to motivate further administration may represent a key transitional stage in which risk of excessive and problematic use is high. Understanding how priming works, and who may be susceptible to substance priming, is therefore an important area of addiction research.

The priming effects of initial administration have been measured in a number of ways, including self-report (e.g., desire/craving; Rose and Duka, 2006; Rose and Grunsell, 2008), self-administration (e.g., *ad libitum* [ad lib] administration; Hodgson, Rankin, and Stockwell, 1979), and choice behavior (e.g., choosing alcohol over money; e.g., Chutuape, Mitchell, and de Wit, 1994). Other initial effects that may be involved in priming, such as automatic cognitive responses (e.g., attentional bias; Field, Mogg, and Bradley, 2005) and physiological responses (e.g., skin conductance; Laberg and Ellertsen, 1987), can also be measured. In addition, a number of neurotransmitters (e.g., dopamine) and brain regions (e.g., ventral tegmental area) have been associated with the ability of initial substance administration to motivate continued substance use (Stewart, 2008).

This chapter will provide an overview of how prominent addiction models account for priming effects and how research has supported these proposals, before reviewing the different methodologies used to investigate the priming effect. Although a full

The Wiley-Blackwell Handbook of Addiction Psychopharmacology, First Edition. Edited by James MacKillop and Harriet de Wit.

theoretical review is not possible, reviews are highlighted throughout the chapter for the interested reader. Given ethical and legal issues, the majority of human priming research has focused on alcohol priming; however, where appropriate, mention of other substances will be made (Newton, Mahoney, Kalechstein, and De La Garza, 2007).

2   Theoretical Models of Priming and Empirical Evidence

Given that priming is concerned with how an initial dose motivates further substance administration, that further administration is contingent on initial administration, and that the priming dose is likely to match further doses on several attributes (e.g., look, taste), conditioning and learning accounts of priming were quickly established. From these, a number of cognitive frameworks developed which focused on different processes, such as subjective effects and inhibitory control. The frameworks described are not mutually exclusive but emphasize different mechanisms, and it is important to note that the processes described below occur through interactions between brain regions, and it is this complex pattern of activity which produces substance-related behavior (i.e., seeking and administration) (see Everitt and Robbins, 2005; Everitt and Wolf, 2002; Wolf, 2002).

2.1   Learning theory

It was originally suggested that as dependence on a substance developed, withdrawal symptoms (unconditioned response) would be experienced, and cues (conditioned stimuli) associated with substance administration would come to elicit withdrawal-like responses (conditioned response). Accordingly, initial substance administration (e.g., non-contingent, priming doses) could trigger withdrawal symptoms (Ludwig, Wikler, and Stark, 1974), which could then prime the person to drink more in order to alleviate the negative state. Therefore, priming was placed within a framework of negative reinforcement (i.e., the increased probability of a behavior [e.g., substance administration] when that behavior removes a negative stimulus or state [e.g., withdrawal]). However, this account fails to explain why non-dependent individuals, who have no experience of withdrawal, demonstrate substance priming, or why dependent individuals fail to report withdrawal symptoms as a reason for substance use and relapse (e.g., Mcauliffe, 1982; Rose and Grunsell, 2008; Shaham *et al.*, 2003).

Rewarding stimuli are those which elicit approach behavior in the organism, while reinforcement is a process which strengthens the association between stimuli and responses (White, 1989). Thus competing theories postulate that priming may reflect the rewarding experience of initial substance administration. Stewart, de Wit, and Eikelboom's (1984) positive affective, motivational-incentive theory, suggests that substances produce positive effects via direct actions on the nervous system, and that these actions underlie motivation to continue substance use. Particularly in the short-term, sensitization to a substance's positive effects could result in a priming dose transiently motivating goal-directed substance behavior (Stewart and de Wit, 1987).

Goal-directed behavior suggests that priming activates positive expectancies regarding substance use (stimulus–outcome expectancy–response associations), and consequently, substance administration will reflect the current value of the substance (see de Wit and Dickinson, 2009). However, it is also possible that behavior may conform to stimulus–response associations in which, given a particular context (e.g., administering a substance), responses (e.g., continued substance use) occur regardless of potential outcomes (i.e., habitual behavior).

Devaluation paradigms, in which animals/humans are trained to make responses for particular rewarding outcomes before one of the outcomes is devalued, are used to assess whether behavior is goal directed or habit like. Hogarth, Dickinson, and Duka (2010) found evidence that smoking behavior was goal directed, as craving and smoking decreased as nicotine satiety increased. However, presentation of smoking cues abolished this satiety effect and smoking behavior occurred regardless of nicotine's incentive value (i.e., habit like). This research demonstrates the Pavlovian-to-Instrumental-Transfer (PIT) effect: that reward-related stimuli can elicit operant responding for that reward (stimulus-response–outcome associations). When a substance cue is presented in extinction (no response outcome), the behavioral response (substance seeking) is elicited, suggesting that the cue activates an expectancy of a specific outcome but not necessarily the current incentive value of that outcome. In other words, a priming dose may activate expectancies of further substance administration but not information on how rewarding, or unpleasant, the consequences of the substance administration will be. Most research investigates the impact of discrete exteroceptive cues on behavior; further research is needed to determine the effects of priming doses which are complex cues, including administration actions, sight, and pharmacological effects.

2.2 Subjective responses

The importance of the subjective responses to substances is associated with the previous section, which discussed reward and reinforcement. How a person perceives the effect of the substance is likely to have a significant impact on whether a person chooses to administer a substance.

Some research has found that risk for alcohol problems is related to a low level of response to acute administration: for example, in the offspring of alcoholics, alcohol administration (0.75–1.10 ml/kg) resulted in lower levels of response across a range of measures, including subjective intoxication, body sway, and neurochemical reactivity, compared with offspring of non-alcoholics (Schuckit, 1984; 1988). It is possible that the subjective effects of substance use feed back and regulate substance use behavior, but in some people, low response levels mean that administration continues unimpeded. Importantly, not all evidence supports the low level of response model; some research finds greater responses in those with, or at risk of, substance use disorders (see Newlin and Renton, 2010; Newlin and Thomson, 1990).

To understand such discrepancies, it is important to remember that alcohol administration produces two distinct stages: the first in which blood alcohol levels (BAL) increase (i.e., the ascending blood alcohol limb), and a second in which BALs decrease (i.e., the descending blood alcohol limb). Different subjective effects are associated with these two stages, with stimulant-like effects often occurring during the first stage and sedative-like effects usually occurring in the second stage. Although traditionally stimulant effects are often labeled as "positive" and sedative effects as "negative," some sedative effects (e.g., tension reduction) are positive and may be a goal of substance administration (Brown, 1985; Stockwell, Hodgson, and Rankin, 1982). Newlin and Thomson developed the "differentiator model," proposing that those at risk of alcohol use disorders are sensitive to alcohol's stimulant effects but tolerant to alcohol's sedative effects (see Newlin and Thomson, 1990).

King and colleagues (2002) found that, compared with placebo, alcohol consumption dose-dependently (0.4–0.8 g/kg, 2–4 units [unit information is based on a unit being 14 g alcohol, and a person weighing 70 kg]) increased stimulant-like effects during rising BALs and sedative effects during descending BALs. Self-reported measures of wanting also increased across alcohol dose during the ascending limb. Heavier drinkers were more sensitive to the stimulant effects and less sensitive to the sedative effects than light drinkers, and there was a tendency for heavier drinkers to report greater alcohol priming. Rose and Grunsell (2008) also found that binge drinkers reported lower sedative effects from an alcohol prime (0.6 g/kg, 3 units), and Corbin, Gearhardt, and Fromme (2008) found that the stimulant effects of an alcohol prime (dose achieved BAL of 0.06 g% [60 mg/dl]) positively related to higher levels of ad lib alcohol consumption. A recent study by King, de Wit, McNamara, and Cao (2011) corroborated the earlier findings; 0.4–0.8 g/kg of alcohol (2–4 units) resulted in heavier drinkers wanting more alcohol and reporting greater stimulant responses and lower sedative responses, compared with light drinkers. At a 2-year follow-up the priming responses and lower sedative responses to 0.8 g/kg of alcohol predicted drinking behavior trajectories in heavier drinkers.

2.3   Automatic processes and biases

The Cognitive Automaticity model proposes that, through repetition, neuronal pathways are strengthened and activation thresholds decrease, so that corresponding substance use behaviors can be easily triggered and become automatic: that is to say, effortless, fast, and less available to introspection (Tiffany, 1990; Tiffany and Conklin, 2000). A priming dose may activate automatic processes, leading to continued substance use, and so may be related to binge propensity. Even in an individual who has abstained for a prolonged period of time, administration of a priming dose (e.g., slip drink) may activate the automatic substance processes, which could supersede the non-automatic process of restraint (Tiffany, 1995).

There are a number of automatic processes which may be interrelated, including attentional bias and approach bias. Research shows that substance-related cues are able to grab and hold the attention of substance users (see Chapter 14), and this attentional bias may lead to substance cues having more influence on a person's behavior. A number of tasks, including the Addiction Stroop and Visual Probe, have demonstrated that users of alcohol, tobacco, cannabis, cocaine, and heroin display substance-related attentional biases (e.g., Field and Cox, 2008). Priming studies show that alcohol (0.3–0.6 g/kg, 1.5–3 units) increases attentional bias towards alcohol cues (Duka and Townshend, 2004; Rose and Duka, 2008); therefore, priming may involve increasing the salience of substance-related cues, and attentional focus on these cues may feedback onto behavior and support continued substance use (Weinstein and Cox, 2006). However, although one priming study found that a low dose of alcohol (0.3 g/kg, 1.5 units) increased attentional bias on a Visual Probe Task and self-reported craving for alcohol, these measures did not correlate with one another (Schoenmakers, Wiers, and Field, 2008).

The Implicit Association Task (IAT) can be used to measure individual differences in the associations held between substances and affective categories (e.g., positive or negative) and/or actions (e.g., approach or avoid). Participants learn to make particular responses to four categories of words or pictures (substance [e.g., beer], non-substance [e.g., tree], positive [e.g., fun], negative [e.g., angry]). On half of the trials, the response to the substance word is shared with the positive word (e.g., left response), and the non-substance word with the negative word (e.g., right response). On the other half of trials these associations are changed (i.e., the substance and negative words share the same response). It is assumed that participants will respond more quickly when the substance and positive words share a response if the participant holds more positive automatic alcohol associations. Using the IAT, Farris and Ostafin 2008 found that greater ad lib alcohol consumption was associated with quicker responding on alcohol-approach trials. However, as this was an ad lib paradigm, it is not clear whether these findings demonstrate an alcohol priming effect or whether naturally heavier drinkers have greater alcohol approach tendencies. Future research needs to assess more clearly the relationship between priming doses and implicit associations. An alternative approach task is the Stimulus–Response Compatibility Task, in which participants are required to rapidly categorize substance-related and neutral pictures by moving a manikin either towards (approach) or away from (avoid) the pictures. Substance use is positively associated with making faster substance approach responses, and this has been demonstrated in heavy drinkers, tobacco smokers, and cannabis users (Bradley, Field, Mogg, and De Houwer, 2004; Field and Cox, 2008; Field, Eastwood, Bradley, and Mogg, 2006; Mogg, Bradley, Field, and De Houwer, 2003).

The mechanisms underlying these biases have yet to be clarified; however, Wiers and colleagues (2007) suggest that over repeated substance exposure, the organism's appetitive approach system becomes sensitized while a regulatory executive system becomes attenuated. Priming doses would therefore activate the sensitized approach system and further inhibit the control system which could support substance use. There is tentative evidence to suggest that retraining avoidance, as opposed to approach, alcohol responses in alcohol-dependent patients results in better treatment outcomes (Wiers *et al.*, 2011); however, research is needed to determine whether a causal relationship exists between biases and priming effects.

2.4   Disinhibition

Some have proposed that acute substance administration can impair control, and that this effect may help explain why some people administer substances excessively: for example, the person who drinks to severe intoxication after intending to consume only a few drinks.

Impaired inhibitory control is known to be involved both as a risk for, and as a consequence of, substance use (see de Wit, 2009). Dispositional levels of impulsivity have also been found to correlate with self-reported desire following an alcohol prime (0.6 g/kg, 3 units) (Rose and Grunsell, 2008) and individuals with disorders of control may be more vulnerable to the disinhibiting effects of alcohol consumption (Weafer, Fillmore, and Milich, 2009).

Using cued go/no-go and stop signal tasks, some research has found that alcohol acutely increases inhibitory control failures (Fillmore and Rush, 2001; Marczinski and Fillmore, 2003) at doses which also produce priming effects (see Fillmore, 2003). When given the choice between earning alcohol or money, alcohol choice increased following a moderate dose of alcohol (0.55 g/kg, 2.75 units), compared with placebo, and this same dose increased impulsive responding on behavioral tasks of inhibition (Fillmore and Rush, 2001). Weafer and Fillmore (2008) found that 0.65 g/kg (3.25 units) of alcohol impaired inhibitory control on a cued go/no-go task and, importantly, the degree of impairment positively correlated with the amount of alcohol consumed in a separate alcohol taste test. In animal models, levels of impulsivity following placebo or alcohol (0.6, 0.9, 1.2, and 1.8 g/kg) increased dose-dependently, and these increases were observed 5, 15, 30, and 60, but not 120, minutes following substance administration (Poulos, Parker, and Le, 1998). Again, level of impulsive reactivity to alcohol was associated with ad lib alcohol consumption. These findings suggest that the disinhibiting effects of alcohol are directly related to alcohol priming, and individuals susceptible to the impulsive effects of alcohol may show greater alcohol priming. However, other research has found alcohol-induced disinhibition from an initial dose of alcohol (0.6 g/kg, 3 units) in the absence of a priming effect on craving (Rose and Duka, 2007; 2008).

Recently, it has been suggested that the impairing and rewarding effects of alcohol interact to produce priming. For example, acute alcohol consumption may make the incentive properties of drinking more salient, while the impaired control which accompanies drinking will allow processes of reward to go unimpeded (for a review see Field *et al.*, 2010). More research is needed to directly examine the role of substance's inhibitory effects (e.g., behavioral control, delayed discounting, interference inhibition) and priming.

3   Priming Methodology and Current Practices

The following provides an overview of the different methods used and indices taken when investigating substance priming (see Table 16.1). The discussion will focus on direct measures of priming: that is, motivation to continue substance use, rather than on the intoxicating effects of substance administration on cognitive mechanisms (see Chapter 1), which may or may not be relevant to substance priming. However, identifying the processes mediating the priming effect, and interactions between priming effects and other acute substance effects, is important and some studies which have attempted to do this have been discussed above (e.g., Rose and Duka, 2007; 2008; Rose and Grunsell, 2008; Weafer and Fillmore, 2008). Given the large number of potential processes mediating the priming effect, there is not yet enough priming-specific research focused on these mechanisms to evaluate meaningfully.

3.1   Experimental design

The priming paradigm provides the participant, or animal, with an initial substance dose and then assesses the effects of that dose at one, or multiple, later time points.

The effects of the substance dose(s) is usually compared with a placebo dose. This basic paradigm can be used in a number of ways: to assess the effects of the priming substance on motivation for that substance (e.g., does an initial cocaine dose increase further use or desire for cocaine?); to assess the priming effects of one substance on motivation for a different substance (e.g., does smoking prime drinking behavior?); to determine whether drugs can block substance priming (e.g., does naltrexone attenuate opiate priming?); and to investigate the cognitive mechanisms affected by the priming dose in order to understand how priming may work (e.g., does a priming dose of alcohol impair control?). In addition, the priming paradigm can be used to assess differences across participant populations (e.g., treatment/non-treatment seeking, light/moderate/heavy substance users, binge/non-binge drinkers) and to identify potential risk factors for, and protective factors against, strong priming effects (e.g., impulsive dispositions, functional genetic variants).

As priming is concerned with how initial administration "whets the appetite" and motivates further substance seeking and administration, early priming research tended to administer small substance doses; however, most recent priming research provides moderate doses of a substance (e.g., 0.5–0.6 g/kg, 2.5–3 units). This is based upon the finding that increased motivation for a substance tends to occur more robustly at moderate, compared with lower, doses, and across a wider range of substance-using populations (e.g. light–heavy, social–dependent drinkers).

3.2   Dependent variables

3.2.1   State measures of craving and desire.   de Wit and Chutuape (1993) found that self-reported desire for alcohol increased 30 and 60 minutes after a priming dose of 0.5 g/kg of alcohol but not 0.25 g/kg (2.5 and 1.25 units respectively) or placebo. Chutuape, Mitchell, and de Wit (1994) found an increase in desire 30 minutes following 0.25 g/kg, and 30 and 60 minutes after 0.5 g/kg of alcohol compared with placebo. In a series of studies, self-reported desire for alcohol increased 40–45 minutes (i.e. when BAL peaked) following 0.55 g/kg of alcohol (2.75 units), compared with placebo, and decreased during the descending blood alcohol curve (Fillmore, 2001; Fillmore and Rush, 2001). In addition, a low priming dose of 0.2 g/kg of alcohol (1 unit) increased self-reported desire in participants who also claimed to be cognitively preoccupied with alcohol (Fillmore, 2001), but this was not compared to a placebo dose. Several studies have found that increased desire in response to higher alcohol doses is accompanied by participants also reporting that they "liked the drug" and "felt high" (Chutuape, Mitchell, and de Wit, 1994; Fillmore, 2001; Fillmore and Rush, 2001).

Rose and Duka (2006) found that both choice behavior, using an imagery script, and self-reported desire for alcohol increased following 0.6 g/kg, but not 0.3 g/kg of alcohol (3 and 1.5 units respectively), in moderate–heavy social drinkers. The priming effects peaked 30 minutes after the end of the consumption phase before decreasing at 60 and 90 minutes, and this time effect has been confirmed by other work (e.g., Rose and Grunsell, 2008). In these studies, BALs peaked 30–40 minutes following initial administration (66–73 mg/dl). The evidence that priming occurs when BALs are peaking supports the suggestion that alcohol priming may involve the positive and stimulant subjective effects of consumption (King, de Wit, McNamara, and Cao, 2011;

Rose and Grunsell, 2008). BAL factors may also help explain differences across priming studies which use different dosing and different measurement times. For example, alcohol priming seems to be more robust at moderate alcohol doses; however, priming is also seen with low doses. For example, 0.3 g/kg (1.5 units) can prime self-reported desire 10 minutes following consumption compared with placebo (Schoenmakers, Wiers, and Field, 2008). It is possible that studies which wait for longer periods of time to assess priming (e.g., Rose and Duka, 2006) are missing the priming effects of lower doses. In addition, it would be laudable to assess priming effects after higher substance doses. Schoenmakers and Wiers (2010) conducted a pub-based field study to look at relationships between drinking factors and alcohol-related attentional bias. Although this method allows a large degree of variability in the quantity and attributes of the "priming" dose, they found that self-reported urge for alcohol was positively correlated with the number of drinks already consumed. These findings show that priming effects may exist throughout a typical substance administration session but research is needed to assess this.

3.2.2   *Behavioral measures (ad lib drinking, speed of drinking, operant and choice behavior, and pattern of responding)*

3.2.2.1   AD LIB DRINKING.   Providing the animal or participant with free, or relatively free, access to a substance(s) is the most direct measurement of priming. Walitzer and Sher (1990) gave sons of alcoholics and sons of non-alcoholics a low dose of alcohol (0.115 g/kg, 0.5 units), followed by the opportunity to consume either an alcoholic or a non-alcoholic drink. No differential priming effects were found based on risk category, but this may have been due to a ceiling effect: for instance, many of the subjects consumed alcohol and consumed the total amount on offer. This type of study is problematic when looking at a substance's ability to prime as there was no placebo condition to compare. Following consumption in the morning of placebo, 15 ml (approx. one-third of a unit) or 150 ml (approx. 3 units) of vodka, moderately and severely alcoholic participants were given the opportunity to consume further alcoholic drinks in the afternoon (Hodgson, Rankin, and Stockwell, 1979). Severely dependent drinkers consumed the most alcohol but this was independent of priming dose.

To avoid the ethical problems of providing large quantities of substance to administer, which is necessary for a true ad lib measure, a "taste test" is often used in alcohol administration research. The taste test provides a range of alcoholic drinks, or a mix of alcoholic and non-alcoholic drinks, and participants are told to consume as much as they like to ensure accurate beverage ratings (e.g., how pleasant the drink is). The total amount of alcohol, or the relative amount of alcohol to soft drink, is taken as the primary behavioral measure. In addition to ethical merits, the "taste test" procedure provides a good reason for giving participants beverages to drink, while concealing the aim of the study (e.g., to assess priming). Although some alcohol administration studies using taste tests have found differences across experimental manipulations (e.g. Jones, Cole, Goudie, and Field, 2011; Jones *et al.*, 2011), only a small number of priming studies have used this behavioral measure so more research is needed to clarify the validity of these methods. One priming study assigned male alcoholics and non-alcoholics to one of the four balanced placebo design conditions (told alcohol/given alcohol, told alcohol/given placebo, told placebo/given placebo, told placebo/given alcohol) (Marlatt, Demming, and Reid, 1973). Twenty minutes prior to a taste test, participants in the given alcohol conditions were primed with alcohol (approximately 1.3 units) and those in the given placebo conditions consumed a tonic water. Irrespective of what the 'priming' drinks actually contained, alcohol-dependent and non-dependent participants consumed more beverage during the taste test when they were told it was alcohol. In addition, by calculating the number of sips and total amount consumed, data showed that all participants gulped drinks when told alcohol but sipped drinks when told tonic water.

The balanced placebo design isolates the individual contributions of alcohol expectancies and pharmacology, and identifies the combined effects of expectancy and pharmacology on behavior. Although balanced placebo design studies have highlighted the importance of individual factors in determining substance behavior, there are a number of issues surrounding this paradigm, the most relevant being whether deception can be successful when providing alcohol at doses which robustly produce priming effects (Epps, Monk, Savage, and Marlatt, 1998; Sayette, Breslin, Wilson, and Rosenblum, 1994). Therefore, although the following section will highlight studies that have used the balanced placebo design, for a full discussion the interested reader should refer to reviews on this paradigm (e.g. Martin and Sayette, 1993).

3.2.2.2   SPEED OF DRINKING.   In Hodgson, Rankin, and Stockwell's (1979) study, discussed above, severely, but not moderately, dependent alcoholics consumed alcoholic drinks faster following the higher alcohol prime. Speed of consumption negatively correlated with self-reported desire in the severely dependent participants (i.e. the quicker the consumption, the greater the desire). In a priming study which provided access to several alcoholic (0.15–0.2 g/kg per drink, 0.75–1 units) and non-alcoholic drinks over a period of 1 hour and 40 minutes, social drinkers started drinking alcohol more quickly than soft drinks and speed of drinking correlated with urge for alcohol (Rose *et al.*, 2010).

3.2.2.3   OPERANT AND CHOICE BEHAVIOR, AND PATTERN OF RESPONDING.   In a group of alcoholics, moderate (0.6 g/kg, 3 units) and high (1.2 g/kg, 6 units) alcohol primes, compared with placebo, increased operant behavior (riding an exercise bike) for more alcohol (Ludwig, Wikler, and Stark, 1974). In social drinkers, alcohol (0.25, 0.5 g/kg: 1.25 and 2.5 units respectively), compared with placebo, dose-dependently increased choice behavior for alcohol over placebo plus money, 1 hour following the initial prime administration (de Wit and Chutuape, 1993). In a similar study, participants could respond for alcohol or money on an "Apple Picker" task 1 hour following consumption of placebo, 0.25, and 0.5 g/kg of alcohol (Chutuape, Mitchell and de Wit, 1994). Although the probability of earning alcohol remained stable, the probability of earning money changed across trials. Alcohol dose-dependently increased alcohol choice behavior but only when the probability of earning money was low.

An alcohol prime of 0.55 g/kg (2.75 units), compared with placebo, resulted in more people choosing to complete a stop signal task for an alcohol reward over a monetary reward 45 minutes after administration (Fillmore and Rush, 2001). Participants were given the option to play for alcohol or money five times, and alcohol preloads also increased the number of times alcohol was played for. However, these behavioral priming effects were only apparent when the monetary reward was low (5 cents), not high (50 cents).

3.3   Physiological measures

On the whole, acute substance administration can affect a number of physiological measures: for example, methamphetamine and alcohol can increase heart rate (Kirkpatrick *et al.*, 2011); however, few priming studies take physiological measures. Walitzer and Sher (1990) found that consumption of a small priming dose of alcohol (0.115 g/kg, 0.6 units) resulted in sons of alcoholics salivating more 5–22 minutes after consumption compared with sons of non-alcoholics. In addition, skin conductance increased while skin temperature decreased.

In comparison with placebo, following a low dose of alcohol (breath alcohol concentration: 50 mg% [50 mg/dl]), exposure to alcoholic odors, but not control odors, resulted in activation of the nucleus accumbens, medial and ventromedial frontal cortices, lateral orbitofrontal cortex, and precuneus/posterior cingulate regions (Bragulat *et al.*, 2008). In addition, the alcoholic odors triggered greater activation within the medial frontal cortex and right lateral orbitofrontal cortex. These findings suggest that initial alcohol priming may work by activating brain regions important in determining reward value and appetitive drive, perhaps by enhancing substance-related cue reactivity (Bragulat *et al.*, 2008).

Given that some research has found differences between physiological reactivity to acute substance administration based on factors which may also affect priming strength (e.g. familial risk for alcohol problems; Croissant, Rist, Demmel, and Olbrich, 2005), future research is needed to identify associations between different acute substance effects (e.g., behavioral, subjective, physiological) and the priming ability of that substance. Although not the primary focus of this chapter (see Chapter 21), physiological measures from cognitive neuroscience can also be applied in priming research (e.g., Bragulat *et al.*, 2008). Thus, the priming methodology can incorporate both measures of direct physiological effects (e.g., BAL) and physiological effects that can inform the functional mechanisms of priming doses (e.g., changes in brain activity).

3.4   Pharmacokinetics of alcohol

3.4.1   Gender issues.   As discussed, priming effects increase and decrease alongside blood substance levels, so it is important to measure blood substance levels when priming measures are taken. Particular differences between men and women may result in differences across blood substance levels: for example, men have a greater proportion of water in their bodies than women, while women have a greater proportion of fat;

in addition, metabolism can differ by gender (Baraona *et al.*, 2001; Thomasson, 1995). These differences have resulted in some priming studies giving different dose sizes to male and female participants (e.g. Fillmore, 2001). Mulvihill, Skilling, and Vogel-Sprott (1997) found that providing women with 87% of men's alcohol dose resulted in equal BALs across gender. This is an important consideration; however, it should be noted that studies which have provided the same dose to men and women have not reported differences in experimental measures across gender (e.g. Fillmore and Blackburn, 2002; Rose and Duka, 2006). However, it is not always clear from the original literature whether gender analysis has been performed. Future research should always explicitly state whether gender effects have been found, both in terms of experimental findings and in terms of the typical substance use habits of male and female participants.

3.4.2   Dose, speed, and method of administration.   The pharmacokinetics of alcohol can also differ across gender and participant populations, and can be affected by particular experimental methodologies, such as speed of administration. For instance, the faster the consumption, the quicker the ascending BAL, and the faster rising the BAL, the greater the acute effects of alcohol (Fillmore and Vogel-Sprott, 1998). Wherever possible, the BAL curve should be plotted at regular times following a priming dose (i.e., not just when priming assessments take place). Most priming research, especially earlier studies, include a specific g/kg dosing, which helps tailor the amount of substance given to the participant, rather than giving an arbitrarily chosen quantity (e.g., a small glass of wine or a standard bottle of beer), which could result in a wide range of pharmacokinetic differences across participants. However, the g/kg method still produces a large amount of variability: for example, a dose of 0.56 g/kg (2.8 units) resulted in a mean BAL of 57.40 mg/100 ml (57.4 mg/dl), with a wide range of 40.5–80.5 mg/100 ml (40.5–80.5 mg/dl) (Fillmore and Vogel-Sprott, 1998). Such variability has resulted in the majority of recent substance administration research providing tailored doses to achieve a target BAL (e.g., Ray and Hutchison, 2004). A major problem in priming research is the inconsistencies in reporting the details of alcohol administration: for example, the quantity of alcohol administered can be stated as g/kg, number of alcohol units (UK: 8 g, USA: 12/14 g), or number of alcoholic drinks (this can vary widely depending on the quantity of the drink and the volume of alcohol in the drink, but in the States a drink is usually referring to 1 unit). Alternatively, breath alcohol concentrations can be reported or converted to estimated blood alcohol levels. Again, how breath and blood alcohol concentrations are reported differ (e.g., mg%, mg/100 ml, g/dl). Although it is possible to convert measurements, some conversion formulas (e.g., estimating dose of alcohol given to produce a specific BAL, estimating BAL based on a specific dose of alcohol) require information that is often not reported (see Brick, 2006). Although the current chapter has provided more uniform detail, where possible, concerning the doses of alcohol given, future alcohol research should provide details of peak BALs, the time at which these BALs occurred (e.g., 30 minutes after drinking ended), and the approximate dose of alcohol needed to achieve these BALs in male and female participants.

3.5   Priming with other addictive substances

Most priming research has focused on alcohol for ethical and legal reasons but also, perhaps, because of the nature of drinking. Once drinking is initiated, some people respond with enhanced motivation to drink, but this pattern tends not to be seen with other legal substances: for example, a single cigarette is usually enough to sate nicotine craving (chain smoking does occur but this is usually due to other factors, such as stress). There has been some non-alcohol priming research, which is discussed below, but the equivocal results produced indicate that priming processes in non-alcohol substance administration are complex and require further attention.

Within cocaine research, a priming dose (40 mg, intravenous injection), compared to placebo, can increase substance wanting and craving 15 minutes after administration (Jaffe, Cascella, Kumor, and Sherer, 1989). Following a cocaine prime (0.4 mg/kg, smoked) or placebo, participants were able to complete sets of arithmetic questions in order to earn cocaine or monetary ($2) tokens an hour later (Dudish-Poulsen and Hatsukami, 1997). The cocaine prime resulted in increased heart rate, dystolic blood pressure, and self-reported craving immediately after the prime was administered. However, participants chose to earn cocaine tokens the majority of the time in both conditions, so no cocaine priming effect was found on behavioral measures. This latter finding could be due to several things: the placebo involved smoking a very small quantity of cocaine, which could have triggered a conditioned motivation to administer the substance; alternatively, a maximum of seven tokens could be earned and so this finding may represent a ceiling effect. Whatever the reason, the fact that priming was found by self-report but not behavioral measures illustrates an important point, that different types of measurement do not always co-occur and one is not necessarily dependent on the other (Carter and Tiffany, 1999). For example, an individual may crave heroin but work hard to resist administering any; alternatively, a person may smoke a cigarette even when they are not particularly in the mood to smoke. It is also the case that when several types of priming measure show an effect of initial dose (e.g., craving and consumption), this does not necessarily mean that these are related to one another.

Nicotine is a highly addictive substance and some animal models suggest that priming doses of nicotine (0.5 mg/kg) can re-establish conditioned place preferences for nicotine after successful extinction trials (Budzynska, Kruk, and Biala, 2009). In addition, exposure to nicotine following a quit attempt in humans increases the risk of full relapse. For example, after 3 days of abstinence participants trying to stop smoking were given either five cigarettes to smoke or nothing (Chornock, Stitzer, Gross, and Leischow, 1992). Within 48 hours, all participants given cigarettes had relapsed, while 16% of participants not given cigarettes remained abstinent until the end of the study (8 days). Perkins, Grobe, and Fonte (1997) asked participants to abstain from smoking from the night before testing. On arrival at the laboratory, participants smoked 0, 2, 6, or 12 (approximately 1 cigarette) puffs from a cigarette. During an additional session, participants could smoke normally the night before testing (i.e., no abstinence) and smoke one of their own brand of cigarettes on arrival at the experimental session. Immediately after the smoking manipulation, participants rated nicotine urge and how much they would pay for a cigarette, before completing a concurrent choice task for cigarettes and money. Responding for cigarettes was greater after 0 puffs relative to ad lib smoking, and marginally greater compared with 12 puffs. However, the 0, 2, and 6 puff conditions did not differ from one another. Self-reported nicotine craving and the amount willing to be paid for a cigarette decreased as prior exposure increased.

Within cannabis research, Curran and colleagues (2002) provided participants with capsules containing 0.0, 7.5, or 15 mg of D9-THC. Self-reports of liking and wanting more of the drug, and wanting to smoke a joint, were taken 1, 2, 4, 6, and 8 hours following capsule ingestion. Both of the active THC doses increased reports of liking the drug, compared with placebo, at most time points. However, wanting more of the drug was only greater 4 hours following THC administration, compared with placebo, while wanting to smoke a joint did not differ across conditions. Although research is needed to clarify differences between substances, existing evidence indicates that priming processes may not be a significant influencing factor in non-alcohol substance behavior.

3.6 Cross priming

Cross priming research is a specific type of priming research and, although not as prolifically tested as "within-substance" priming, shows that initial administration of one type of substance can prime motivation for other substances of addiction. In humans, alcohol (0.4–0.8 g/kg, 2–4 units) and d-amphetamine (0, 5, 15, 25 mg) dose-dependently increase urge to smoke tobacco and behavioral measures of smoking (Henningfield and Griffiths, 1981; King and Epstein, 2005), but smoking cannabis (THC concentration: 0, 1.29, 2.84, 4.00%) had no priming effects on tobacco smoking behavior (Nemeth-Coslett, Henningfield, O'Keeffe, and Griffiths, 1986). Diazepam, a benzodiazepine agonist, primed non-alcoholic beer consumption, decreased response latencies for alcohol-related but not non-alcohol-related words on a lexical salience task, and marginally increased self-reported desire for alcohol in male problem drinkers (Poulos and Zack, 2004). These findings occurred 1 hour after diazepam administration, when diazepam's subjective and behavioral effects were peaking.

3.7 Genetics

Although this chapter has focused on indices of priming effects, it is interesting to note that, as genetic research becomes more sophisticated, a number of potential functional genetic variants have been identified and associated with different responses to exteroceptive and interoceptive substance cues (e.g. McGeary et al., 2006). For example, carriers of the long variant of the exon 3 variable number of tandem repeats polymorphism in the dopamine D4 receptor gene (DRD4) have been reported to exhibit significantly greater priming-induced craving (Hutchison et al., 2002). In addition, a single nucleotide polymorphism in the μ-opioid gene OPRM1 (rs1799971) has been associated with greater priming-induced subjective effects of alcohol (Ray and Hutchison, 2004; Ray et al., 2010). Interestingly, in a functional magnetic resonance imaging study, these genetic loci have been differentially implicated in terms of craving, subjective effects, and brain activation (Filbey et al., 2008).

3.8   Treatment

Given the potential importance of priming in occurrences of relapse and excessive substance use, some studies have sought to determine whether potential pharmacotherapies for substance use disorders can block the priming effect. Drobes, Anton, Thomas, and Voronin (2003; 2004) conducted an alcohol priming experiment in which 0.4 g/kg (0.34 g/kg in women, 2 and 1.7 units respectively) of alcohol was given following 8 days of opiate antagonist medication (naltrexone [20–50 mg/day], nalmefene [20–50 mg/day]), or placebo. Self-reported urge and mood were measured 10, 20, 40 and 60 minutes following the prime and a 90-minute ad lib administration session followed at 50 minutes. During the ad lib session, up to four alcoholic drinks were available and for every drink not chosen, the participants received $2 as an incentive not to drink. Although dependent participants reported greater craving and stimulant effects, and consumed more alcohol overall, compared with non-dependent participants, opiate antagonists decreased self-reported craving and stimulation, and alcohol consumption in both groups. In a similar study, a 7-day medication regime (naltrexone [25–50 mg/day] or placebo) was followed by an experimental session in which dependent participants were primed with alcohol to achieve a BAL of 30 mg% (0.3 g/l) (Anton *et al.*, 2004). Participants then completed an immediate or 40-minute delayed ad lib drinking session, in which four alcoholic drinks were available. Naltrexone reduced alcohol consumption in the delayed, but not the immediate, priming assessment. As outlined before, alcohol priming peaks with BAL and so naltrexone may reduce the subjective responses which trigger the priming effect. Indeed, other studies have found that naltrexone reduces self-reported stimulation and "high" after alcohol consumption (King, Volpicelli, Frazer, and O'Brien, 1997; Swift *et al.*, 1994). In social drinkers, ratings of euphoria following an alcohol prime (males: 12 g of ethanol; females: 10.4 g; 0.86 and 0.74 units respectively) were found to be lower after a 6-day naltrexone regime (25–50 mg/day), compared with placebo, but this did not correspond to a decrease in operant responding for alcohol (Setiawan *et al.*, 2011). There are a number of human and animal studies which have assessed the impact of medications on substance priming (e.g., Le *et al.*, 1999; O'Malley *et al.*, 2002). However, these studies tend not to include placebo controls for the alcohol primes; therefore, although these studies are useful in identifying some of the pharmacological processes underlying priming, potential interactions between the medication and possible cognitive processes underlying priming (e.g., expectancy, placebo effects) cannot be tested.

4   Limitations, Shortcomings, and Future Recommendations

Substance priming research offers a real insight into how and why substance use is maintained and can help to identify why some people engage in excessive substance use. Throughout this chapter, potential research problems and improvements have been highlighted and, although the basic priming paradigm is sound, the following outlines some more recommendations for priming research.

4.1   Dose and priming thresholds

Laboratory studies should use a specific priming dose, rather than an ad lib priming session. This method provides important information concerning minimum dose requirements for priming effects within and across different substance populations (e.g., light and heavy drinkers). More naturalistic experiments (e.g., field studies) can be used to assess the impact of ad lib priming doses on substance-related behavior.

Studies should always include a substance and a placebo condition, and, where appropriate, a neutral condition (e.g., a soft drink condition in alcohol priming research). This allows identification of specific psychological effects associated with the belief that one has administered a substance, and isolates potential effects of general, non-substance administration.

For all substances of addiction, the magnitude of the initial dose will have an impact on the priming effect. In general, low initial doses support low, or zero, rates of responding for the substance, moderate doses support higher rates, while high doses can block responding altogether or increase responding to avoid substance administration (Henningfield, Cohen, and Heishman, 1991; Henningfield and Goldberg, 1983). This inverted U shape of responding suggests that there is a minimum threshold for priming effects to occur but that excessive initial doses may be toxic and abolish further administration (Henningfield, Cohen, and Heishman, 1991; Rose and Duka, 2006). It is likely that different "priming thresholds" exist for different populations and this may be one source of discrepancies across priming studies. For instance, lighter drinkers may be primed by lower doses of alcohol, compared with heavier drinkers who may require a greater initial dose to feel positive effects (Rose and Duka, 2006). However, some studies have found that operant behavior for access to morphine can be maintained by doses low enough not to yield subjective effects (3.75 mg) (Lamb *et al.*, 1991). Future research needs to determine what factors affect priming thresholds across substance populations, and these need to be taken into account when assessing priming in future research. Although it would be too time consuming to measure all possible doses, a range of doses should be tested, and by basing these on typical doses administered in real-world situations, the validity of laboratory-based priming studies would increase.

4.2   Time issues

A number of priming studies have highlighted that the blood substance level may be an important determinant of priming, so blood substance levels should be plotted at regular intervals. However, this may not always be appropriate and, in such cases, pilot work should be conducted to provide detailed blood substance curve plots for the experimental priming dose(s) in participants matching the experimental population. This will provide important information on the pharmacokinetics of the substance used and will help identify precisely how different methodologies, including active dose quantity (e.g., 0.5, 0.6 g/kg), preload quantity (e.g., 0.6 g/kg of alcohol mixed into a 250 or 500 ml beverage), different administration rates (e.g., 10 or 30 minutes), and different administration routes (e.g., oral or intravenous) impact on results and can be used to inform future research and identify possible sources of discrepancy across datasets.

In addition, matching blood substance plots with priming effects will help identify when, during a typical intake session, administration is at risk of becoming excessive through processes of priming. A laboratory study which attempted to better match how drinks are consumed in real-world situations, by providing multiple alcohol doses (five doses of 0.2g/kg, 1 unit each), found that self-reported urge for alcohol increased over the first half of the drinking session compared with placebo, and this effect was positively associated with feeling stimulated and typical drinking habits (Rose *et al.*, 2010). These procedures could also be used to assess at what time(s) during an administration session, different priming measures are associated and/or disassociated with one another. This type of research is needed to identify what mechanisms underlie substance use behavior at different points during an administration session. For example, although the positive subjective effects may motivate substance use during the early stages of administration, as more substance is administered, other processes may become important (e.g., impaired control; Field *et al.*, 2010).

It is also important to report at what time of day testing took place. Few studies do this but it is likely that priming effects will be more robust if assessed at times when the participant population would administer substances in real-world situations (e.g., alcohol in the afternoon and evening).

4.3   Procedures and measures

Given the finding that different types of priming measure can yield different results, multiple measures should be taken, including self-report and behavioral measures of motivation (e.g., ad lib administration, choice behavior). Particular behavioral measures (e.g., ad lib administration) increase the face validity of priming research and should be used whenever possible. However, there are potential confounds with offering ad lib administration at the end of an experimental condition: for instance, participants may want to administer a substance but choose not to in order to leave the laboratory and administer substances with friends. Although costly, to avoid this confound, some studies require participants to stay for several hours following the experiment, or overnight, irrespective of their administration behavior (e.g. de Wit and Chutuape, 1993). Alternatively, a taste test procedure of fixed duration (e.g., 15–30 minutes) can provide a measure of ad lib administration and may avoid some of these confounds, although it must be accepted that a taste test is not as strong in terms of face validity.

In some research, assumptions are made that different priming measures are associated with one another, or that if a substance has a particular cognitive effect (e.g., increased attentional bias), that this may be a priming mechanism. Although there are examples of studies in which priming measures are associated (e.g. Walitzer and Sher, 1990), some studies have failed to find such relationships (e.g., Perkins, Grobe, and Fonte, 1997), or have found that experimental manipulations affect some measures (e.g., substance administration) but not others (e.g., craving) (Nemeth-Coslett and Henningfield, 1986). In addition, some research has found cognitive effects (e.g., disinhibition) from substance administration but no direct effects on motivation to drink (e.g., craving) (Rose and Duka, 2007; 2008). It is possible that requiring the participant to focus on cognitively demanding tasks attenuates the priming effects of substance administration; therefore, priming measures should be taken just before tasks are completed. Comparing priming measures taken just before and after tasks will help identify potential effects of experimental demands on priming measures.

To reiterate, appropriate statistical analysis should always assess the degree of relationship between different types of measurement, direct measures of priming should always be incorporated into studies in which associations are made between substances' acute effects and motivation to engage in substance use behaviors, and, where possible, multiple-item measures should be used to cover different elements of motivation (Love, James, and Willner, 1998).

4.4 Multidisciplinary research

Priming research has already provided a good basis for understanding how acute substance effects influence substance-related behavior. However, there is still much we don't understand and the emergence of more sophisticated techniques gives an excellent opportunity for more multidisciplinary work. For example, there are relatively few placebo-controlled priming studies which have investigated the genetic basis of priming, or associated the neuropharmacological effects of substance administration with direct priming measures of motivation. It is also important to identify differences across substance populations (e.g., social and clinical populations). For example, as discussed earlier, substance-related behavior may become more habit like and there is some evidence that the part of the brain which subserves substance-related behavior shifts from prefrontal cortical regions to dorsal striatal regions (Everitt and Robbins, 2005). How and when such shifts occur needs to be identified in order to highlight potential windows of risk for substance use disorders.

5 Conclusions

Substance priming covers a wide range of subjective, behavioral, and neurochemical responses, and can be observed in social, hazardous, and dependent substance users. The state changes that occur during initial administration are likely to contribute to maintenance of substance use in a significant number of people. Priming, potentially, involves a wide range of processes including learning, cognitive and behavioral biases, and impaired inhibitory control, and, therefore, a more integrative theoretical approach would be useful to inform future priming research. Research is needed which systematically identifies potential priming processes and determines whether processes change dependent on factors such as blood substance levels and/or phase of administration session (e.g., at the beginning, middle, or end of a typical administration occasion). Once these aspects are better understood, future priming research will be able to more thoroughly test potential pharmacotherapies which target the priming effect, as well as informing psychosocial treatments aimed at educating individuals on

Table 16.1 Summary of measures commonly used in priming research to assess motivation for a substance

Measure	Construct measured	Description
Self-report measures		
Drug Visual Analogue Scales	Current subjective substance effects	Measures the subjective effects of a substance (e.g., feel the substance) and desire for a substance (e.g., want more of the substance). Can be used with all substances.
Alcohol Urge Questionnaire	Current urge for alcohol	Measures acute craving (3 factors: desire to drink, positive alcohol expectancies, inability to avoid drinking)
Desires for Alcohol Questionnaire	Current urge for alcohol	Measures acute craving (4 factors: intentions to drink alcohol, desires to consume alcohol, anticipation of positive outcomes from drinking, anticipation of relief of negative affect or alcohol withdrawal)
Desires for Alcohol Questionnaire (abbreviated)	Current urge for alcohol	Measures acute craving (4 factors: desires and intentions to drink, negative reinforcement, control over drinking, mild desires to drink)
Cocaine Craving Questionnaire – Now	Current urge for cocaine	Measures acute craving (5 factors: desire to use, anticipation of positive cocaine outcomes, anticipation of relief from withdrawal or relief from negative mood, intention to use cocaine, lack of control over use)
Behavioral measures		
Ad libitum administration	Administration behavior	Measures how much of a substance is administered and how quickly the substance is administered. Can be used to compare administration across substances. Sometimes measured using a "taste test" paradigm.
Operant choice (e.g., Apple Picker task)	Choice behavior	Measures preferences between two or more substances, or between a substance and money. Operant choice tasks can include various schedules of reinforcement (e.g., a fixed ratio of reinforcement for the primed substance and a variable ratio of reinforcement for the alternative reward).
Operant behavior	Motivation for substance	Measures how much effort a person is willing to expend to obtain a substance. Can be used to compare effort given across substances.

the cognitive and behavioral effects of substance use and retraining responses to substance administration. Lastly, the growing awareness of how individual factors (e.g., genetics) moderate the effects of substance administration is likely to prove important in identifying why discrepancies in priming research occur.

References

Anton RF, Drobes DJ, Voronin K, Durazo-Avizu R, and Moak D (2004) Naltrexone effects on alcohol consumption in a clinical laboratory paradigm: Temporal effects of drinking. *Psychopharmacology* (Berlin) 173 (1–2): 32–40.

Baraona E, Abittan CS, Dohmen K, Moretti M, Pozzato G, Chayes ZW, *et al.* (2001) Gender differences in pharmacokinetics of alcohol. *Alcoholism: Clinical and Experimental Research* 25 (4): 502–507.

Bradley B, Field M, Mogg K, and De Houwer J (2004) Attentional and evaluative biases for smoking cues in nicotine dependence: Component processes of biases in visual orienting. *Behavioural Pharmacology* 15 (1): 29–36.

Bragulat V, Dzemidzic M, Talavage T, Davidson D, O'Connor SJ, and Kareken DA (2008) Alcohol sensitizes cerebral responses to the odors of alcoholic drinks: An fMRI study. *Alcoholism: Clinical and Experimental Research* 32 (7): 1124–1134.

Brick J (2006) Standardization of alcohol calculations in research. *Alcoholism: Clinical and Experimental Research* 30 (8): 1276–1287.

Brown SA (1985) Expectancies versus background in the prediction of college drinking patterns. *Journal of Consulting and Clinical Psychology* 53 (1): 123–130.

Budzynska B, Kruk M, and Biala G (2009) Effects of the cannabinoid CB1 receptor antagonist AM 251 on the reinstatement of nicotine-conditioned place preference by drug priming in rats. *Pharmacological Reports* 61 (2): 304–310.

Carter BL and Tiffany ST (1999) Meta-analysis of cue-reactivity in addiction research. *Addiction* 94 (3): 327–340.

Chornock WM, Stitzer ML, Gross J, and Leischow S (1992) Experimental model of smoking re-exposure: Effects on relapse. *Psychopharmacology* (Berlin) 108 (4): 495–500.

Chutuape MA, Mitchell SH, and de Wit H (1994) Ethanol preloads increase ethanol preference under concurrent random-ratio schedules in social drinkers. *Experimental and Clinical Psychopharmcology* 2 (4): 310–318.

Corbin WR, Gearhardt A, and Fromme K (2008) Stimulant alcohol effects prime within session drinking behavior. *Psychopharmacology* (Berlin) 197 (2): 327–337.

Croissant B, Rist F, Demmel R, and Olbrich R (2005) Alcohol-induced heart rate response dampening during aversive and rewarding stress paradigms in subjects at risk for alcoholism. *International Journal of Psychophysiology* 61 (2): 253–61.

Curran HV, Brignell C, Fletcher S, Middleton P, and Henry J (2002) Cognitive and subjective dose–response effects of acute oral Delta(9)-tetrahydrocannabinol (THC) in infrequent cannabis users. *Psychopharmacology* (Berlin) 164 (1): 61–70.

de Wit H (2009) Impulsivity as a determinant and consequence of drug use: A review of underlying processes. *Addiction Biology* 14 (1): 22–31.

de Wit H and Chutuape MA (1993) Increased ethanol choice in social drinkers following ethanol preload. *Behavioural Pharmacology* 4 (1): 29–36.

de Wit S and Dickinson A (2009) Associative theories of goal-directed behaviour: A case for animal–human translational models. *Psychological Research* 73 (4): 463–476.

Drobes DJ, Anton RF, Thomas SE, and Voronin K (2003) A clinical laboratory paradigm for evaluating medication effects on alcohol consumption: Naltrexone and nalmefene. *Neuropsychopharmacology* 28 (4): 755–764.

Drobes DJ, Anton RF, Thomas SE, and Voronin K (2004) Effects of naltrexone and nalmefene on subjective response to alcohol among non-treatment-seeking alcoholics and social drinkers. *Alcoholism: Clinical and Experimental Research* 28 (9): 1362–1370.

Dudish-Poulsen SA and Hatsukami DK (1997) Dissociation between subjective and behavioral responses after cocaine stimuli presentations. *Drug and Alcohol Dependence* 47 (1): 1–9.

Duka T and Townshend JM (2004) The priming effect of alcohol pre-load on attentional bias to alcohol-related stimuli. *Psychopharmacology* (Berlin) 176 (3–4): 353–361.

Epps J, Monk C, Savage S, and Marlatt GA (1998) Improving credibility of instructions in the balanced placebo design: A misattribution manipulation. *Addictive Behaviors* 23 (4): 427–435.

Everitt BJ and Robbins TW (2005) Neural systems of reinforcement for drug addiction: From actions to habits to compulsion. *Nature Neuroscience* 8 (11): 1481–1489.

Everitt BJ and Wolf ME (2002) Psychomotor stimulant addiction: A neural systems perspective. *Journal of Neuroscience* 22 (9): 3312–3320.

Farris SR and Ostafin BD (2008) Alcohol consumption primes automatic alcohol-approach associations. *American Journal of Drug and Alcohol Abuse* 34 (6): 703–711.

Field M and Cox WM (2008) Attentional bias in addictive behaviors: A review of its development, causes, and consequences. *Drug and Alcohol Dependence* 97 (1–2): 1–20.

Field M, Eastwood B, Bradley BP, and Mogg K (2006) Selective processing of cannabis cues in regular cannabis users. *Drug and Alcohol Dependence* 85 (1): 75–82.

Field M, Mogg K, and Bradley BP (2005) Alcohol increases cognitive biases for smoking cues in smokers. *Psychopharmacology* (Berlin) 180 (1): 63–72.

Field M, Wiers RW, Christiansen P, Fillmore MT, and Verster JC (2010) Acute alcohol effects on inhibitory control and implicit cognition: Implications for loss of control over drinking. *Alcoholism: Clinical and Experimental Research* 34 (8): 1346–1352.

Filbey FM, Ray L, Smolen A, Claus ED, Audette A, and Hutchison KE (2008) Differential neural response to alcohol priming and alcohol taste cues is associated with DRD4 VNTR and OPRM1 genotypes. *Alcoholism: Clinical and Experimental Research* 32 (7): 1113–1123.

Fillmore MT (2001) Cognitive preoccupation with alcohol and binge drinking in college students: Alcohol-induced priming of the motivation to drink. *Psychology of Addictive Behaviors* 15 (4): 325–332.

Fillmore MT (2003) Drug abuse as a problem of impaired control: Current approaches and findings. *Behavioral and Cognitive Neuroscience* Reviews 2 (3): 179–197.

Fillmore MT and Blackburn J (2002) Compensating for alcohol-induced impairment: Alcohol expectancies and behavioral disinhibition. *Journal of Studies on Alcohol* 63 (2): 237–246.

Fillmore MT and Rush CR (2001) Alcohol effects on inhibitory and activational response strategies in the acquisition of alcohol and other reinforcers: Priming the motivation to drink. *Journal of Studies on Alcohol* 62 (5): 646–656.

Fillmore MT and Vogel-Sprott M (1998) Behavioral impairment under alcohol: Cognitive and pharmacokinetic factors. *Alcoholism: Clinical and Experimental Research* 22 (7): 1476–1482.

Henningfield JE and Goldberg SR (1983) Control of behavior by intravenous nicotine injections in human subjects. *Pharmacology, Biochemistry, and Behavior* 19 (6): 1021–1026.

Henningfield JE and Griffiths RR (1981) Cigarette smoking and subjective response: Effects of d-amphetamine. *Clinical and Pharmacological Therapeutics* 30 (4): 497–505.

Henningfield JE, Cohen C, and Heishman SJ (1991) Drug self-administration methods in abuse liability evaluation. *British Journal of Addiction* 86 (12): 1571–1577.

Hodgson R, Rankin H, and Stockwell T (1979) Alcohol dependence and the priming effect. *Behavioral Research and Therapy* 17 (4): 379–387.

Hogarth L, Dickinson A, and Duka T (2010) The associative basis of cue-elicited drug taking in humans. *Psychopharmacology* 208 (3): 337–351.

Hutchison KE, McGeary J, Smolen A, Bryan A, and Swift RM (2002) The DRD4 VNTR polymorphism moderates craving after alcohol consumption. *Health Psychology* 21 (2): 139–146.

Jaffe JH, Cascella, NG, Kumor KM, and Sherer MA (1989) Cocaine-induced cocaine craving. *Psychopharmacology* (Berlin) 97: 59–64.

Jones A, Cole J, Goudie A, and Field M (2011) Priming a restrained mental set reduces alcohol-seeking independently of mood. *Psychopharmacology* (Berlin). doi: 10.1007/s00213-011-2338-9.

Jones A, Guerrieri R, Fernie G, Cole J, Goudie A, and Field M (2011) The effects of priming restrained versus disinhibited behaviour on alcohol-seeking in social drinkers. *Drug and Alcohol Dependence* 113 (1): 55–61.

King AC, de Wit H, McNamara PJ, and Cao D (2011) Rewarding, stimulant, and sedative alcohol responses and relationship to future binge drinking. *Archives of General Psychiatry* 68 (4): 389–399.

King AC and Epstein AM (2005) Alcohol dose-dependent increases in smoking urge in light smokers. *Alcoholism: Clinical and Experimental Research* 29 (4): 547–552.

King AC, Houle T, de Wit H, Holdstock L, and Schuster A (2002) Biphasic alcohol response differs in heavy versus light drinkers. *Alcoholism: Clinical and Experimental Research* 26 (6): 827–835.

King AC, Volpicelli JR, Frazer A, and O'Brien CP (1997) Effect of naltrexone on subjective alcohol response in subjects at high and low risk for future alcohol dependence. *Psychopharmacology* (Berlin) 129 (1): 15–22.

Kirkpatrick MG, Gunderson EW, Levin FR, Foltin RW, and Hart CL (2011) Acute and residual interactive effects of repeated administrations of oral methamphetamine and alcohol in humans. *Psychopharmacology* (Berlin). doi: 10.1007/s00213-011-2390-5.

Laberg JC and Ellertsen B (1987) Psychophysiological indicators of craving in alcoholics: Effects of cue exposure. *British Journal on Addiction* 82 (12): 1341–1348.

Lamb RJ, Preston KL, Schindler CW, Meisch RA, Davis F, Katz JL *et al.* (1991) The reinforcing and subjective effects of morphine in post-addicts: A dose–response study. *Journal of Pharmacology and Experimental Therapeutics* 259 (3): 1165–1173.

Le AD, Poulos CX, Harding S, Watchus J, Juzytsch W, and Shaham Y (1999) Effects of naltrexone and fluoxetine on alcohol self-administration and reinstatement of alcohol seeking induced by priming injections of alcohol and exposure to stress. *Neuropsychopharmacology* 21 (3): 435–444.

Love A, James D, and Willner P (1998) A comparison of two alcohol craving questionnaires. *Addiction* 93 (7): 1091–1102.

Ludwig AM, Wikler A, and Stark LH (1974) The first drink: Psychobiological aspects of craving. *Archives of General Psychiatry* 30 (4): 539–547.

Marczinski CA and Fillmore MT (2003) Preresponse cues reduce the impairing effects of alcohol on the execution and suppression of responses. *Experimental and Clinical Psychopharmcologyacol* 11 (1): 110–117.

Marlatt GA, Demming B, and Reid JB (1973) Loss of control drinking in alcoholics: An experimental analogue. *Journal of Abnormal Psychology* 81: 223–241.

Martin CS and Sayette MA (1993) Experimental design in alcohol administration research: Limitations and alternatives in the manipulation of dosage-set. *Journal of Studies on Alcohol* 54 (6): 750–761.

Mcauliffe WE (1982) A test of Wikler theory of relapse: The frequency of relapse due to conditioned withdrawal sickness. *International Journal on Addiction* 17 (1): 19–33.

McGeary JE, Monti PM, Rohsenow DJ, Tidey J, Swift R, and Miranda R Jr (2006) Genetic moderators of naltrexone's effects on alcohol cue reactivity. *Alcoholism: Clinical and Experimental Research* 30 (8): 1288–1296.

Mogg K, Bradley BP, Field M, and De Houwer J (2003) Eye movements to smoking-related pictures in smokers: Relationship between attentional biases and implicit and explicit measures of stimulus valence. *Addiction* 98 (6): 825–836.

Mulvihill LE, Skilling TA, and Vogel-Sprott M (1997) Alcohol and the ability to inhibit behavior in men and women. *Journal of Studies on Alcohol* 58 (6): 600–605.

Nemeth-Coslett R and Henningfield JE (1986) Effects of nicotine chewing gum on cigarette smoking and subjective and physiologic effects. *Clinical Pharmacology and Therapeutics* 39 (6): 625–630.

Nemeth-Coslett R, Henningfield JE, O'Keeffe MK, and Griffiths RR (1986) Effects of marijuana smoking on subjective ratings and tobacco smoking. *Pharmacology, Biochemistry, and Behavior* 25 (3): 659–665.

Newlin DB and Renton RM (2010) High risk groups often have higher levels of alcohol response than low risk: The other side of the coin. *Alcoholism: Clinical and Experimental Research* 34 (2): 199–202.

Newlin DB and Thomson JB (1990) Alcohol challenge with sons of alcoholics: A critical-review and analysis. *Psychological Bulletin* 108 (3): 383–402.

Newton TF, Mahoney JJ, Kalechstein AD, and De La Garza R (2007) A qualitative and quantitative review of cocaine-induced craving: The phenomenon of priming. *Progress in Neuro-Psychophysiology* 31 (3): 593–599.

O'Malley SS, Krishnan-Sarin S, Farren C, Sinha R, and Kreek MJ (2002) Naltrexone decreases craving and alcohol self-administration in alcohol-dependent subjects and activates the hypothalamo–pituitary–adrenocortical axis. *Psychopharmacology* (Berlin) 160 (1): 19–29.

Perkins KA, Grobe J, and Fonte C (1997) Influence of acute smoking exposure on the subsequent reinforcing value of smoking. *Experimental and Clinical Psychopharmcology* 5 (3): 277–285.

Poulos CX and Zack M (2004) Low-dose diazepam primes motivation for alcohol and alcohol-related semantic networks in problem drinkers. *Behavioural Pharmacology* 15 (7): 503–512.

Poulos CX, Parker JL, and Le DA (1998) Increased impulsivity after injected alcohol predicts later alcohol consumption in rats: Evidence for "loss-of-control drinking" and marked individual differences. *Behavioral Neuroscience* 112 (5): 1247–1257.

Ray LA and Hutchison KE (2004) A polymorphism of the mu-opioid receptor gene (OPRM1) and sensitivity to the effects of alcohol in humans. *Alcoholism: Clinical and Experimental Research* 28 (12): 1789–1795.

Ray LA, Miranda R, Jr, Tidey JW, McGeary JE, MacKillop J, Gwaltney CJ, *et al.* (2010) Polymorphisms of the mu-opioid receptor and dopamine D4 receptor genes and subjective responses to alcohol in the natural environment. *Journal of Abnormal Psychology* 119 (1): 115–125.

Rose AK and Duka T (2006) Effects of dose and time on the ability of alcohol to prime social drinkers. *Behavioural Pharmacology* 17 (1): 61–70.

Rose AK and Duka T (2007) The influence of alcohol on basic motoric and cognitive disinhibition. *Alcohol and Alcoholism* 42 (6): 544–551.

Rose AK and Duka T (2008) Effects of alcohol on inhibitory processes. *Behavioural Pharmacology* 19 (4): 284–291.

Rose AK and Grunsell L (2008) The subjective, rather than the disinhibiting, effects of alcohol are related to binge drinking. *Alcoholism: Clinical and Experimental Research* 32 (6): 1096–1104.

Rose AK, Hobbs M, Klipp L, Bell S, Edwards K, O'Hara P, *et al.* (2010) Monitoring drinking behaviour and motivation to drink over successive doses of alcohol. *Behavioural Pharmacology* 21 (8): 710–718.

Sayette MA, Breslin FC, Wilson GT, and Rosenblum GD (1994) An evaluation of the balanced placebo design in alcohol administration research. *Addictive Behaviors* 19 (3): 333–342.

Schoenmakers TM and Wiers RW (2010) Craving and attentional bias respond differently to alcohol priming: A field study in the pub. *Eur Addict Res* 16 (1): 9–16.

Schoenmakers T, Wiers RW, and Field M (2008) Effects of a low dose of alcohol on cognitive biases and craving in heavy drinkers. *Psychopharmacology* (Berlin) 197 (1): 169–178.

Schuckit MA (1984) Subjective responses to alcohol in sons of alcoholics and control subjects. *Archives of General Psychiatry* 41 (9): 879–884.

Schuckit MA (1988) Reactions to alcohol in sons of alcoholics and controls. *Alcoholism: Clinical and Experimental Research* 12 (4): 465–470.

Setiawan E, Pihl RO, Cox SM, Gianoulakis C, Palmour RM, Benkelfat C, *et al.* (2011) The effect of naltrexone on alcohol's stimulant properties and self-administration behavior in social drinkers: Influence of gender and genotype. *Alcoholism: Clinical and Experimental Research* 35 (6): 1134–1141.

Shaham Y, Shalev U, Lu L, de Wit H, and Stewart J (2003) The reinstatement model of drug relapse: History, methodology and major findings. *Psychopharmacology* (Berlin) 168 (1–2): 3–20.

Stewart J (2008) Psychological and neural mechanisms of relapse. *Philosophical Transactions of the Royal Society, Part B* 363 (1507): 3147–3158.

Stewart J and de Wit H (1987) Reinstatement of drug-taking behaviour as a method of assessing incentive motivational properties of drugs. In MA Bozarth (ed.), *Methods of Assessing the Reinforcing Properties of Abused Drugs* (pp. 211–227). New York: Springer.

Stewart J, de Wit H, and Eikelboom R (1984) Role of unconditioned and conditioned drug effects in the self-administration of opiates and stimulants. *Psychological Review* 91: 251–268.

Stockwell T, Hodgson R, and Rankin H (1982) Tension reduction and the effects of prolonged alcohol-consumption. *British Journal of Addiction* 77 (1): 65–73.

Swift RM, Whelihan W, Kuznetsov O, Buongiorno G, and Hsuing H (1994) Naltrexone-induced alterations in human ethanol intoxication. *American Journal of Psychiatry* 151 (10): 1463–1467.

Thomasson HR (1995) Gender differences in alcohol metabolism: Physiological responses to ethanol. *Recent Developments in Alcoholism* 12: 163–179.

Tiffany ST (1990) A cognitive model of drug urges and drug-use behavior: Role of automatic and nonautomatic processes. *Psychological Review* 97 (2): 147–168.

Tiffany ST (1995) The role of cognitive factors in reactivity to drug cues. In DC Drummond, ST Tiffany, S Glautier, and B Remmington (eds), *Addictive Behaviour: Cue Exposure Theory and Practice* (pp. 137–165). Chichester: John Wiley & Sons, Ltd.

Tiffany ST and Conklin CA (2000) A cognitive processing model of alcohol craving and compulsive alcohol use. *Addiction* 95 (Suppl. 2): S145–S153.

Walitzer KS and Sher KJ (1990) Alcohol cue reactivity and ad lib drinking in young men at risk for alcoholism. *Addictive Behaviors* 15 (1): 29–46.

Weafer J and Fillmore MT (2008) Individual differences in acute alcohol impairment of inhibitory control predict *ad libitum* alcohol consumption. *Psychopharmacology* 201 (3): 315–324.

Weafer J, Fillmore MT, and Milich R (2009) Increased sensitivity to the disinhibiting effects of alcohol in adults with ADHD. *Experimental and Clinical Psychopharmacology* 17 (2): 113–121.

Weinstein A and Cox WM (2006) Cognitive processing of drug-related stimuli: The role of memory and attention. *Journal of Psychopharmacology* 20 (6): 850–859.

White NM (1989) Reward or reinforcement: What's the difference? *Neuroscience and Biobehavioral Reviews* 13 (2–3): 181–186.

Wiers RW, Bartholow, BD, van den Wildenberg E, Thush C, Engels RCME, Sher KJ, *et al.* (2007) Automatic and controlled processes and the development of addictive behaviors in adolescents: A review and a model. *Pharmacology, Biochemistry, and Behavior* 86 (2): 263–283.

Wiers RW, Eberl C, Rinck M, Becker ES, and Lindenmeyer J (2011) Retraining automatic action tendencies changes alcoholic patients' approach bias for alcohol and improves treatment outcome. *Psychological Science* 22 (4): 490–497.

Wolf ME (2002) Addiction: Making the connection between behavioral changes and neuronal plasticity in specific pathways. *Molecular Interventions* 2 (3): 146–157.

17

Understanding the Role of Substance Expectancies in Addiction

Jane Metrik and Damaris J. Rohsenow

1   Introduction: Theoretical Foundation and Definitions

Drug expectancies are cognitive representations of learning processes reflecting positive and negatively valenced effects of drug consumption. Acquired directly from drug use or indirectly by observation or vicarious learning, expectancies influence initiation and ongoing use of alcohol or drugs as well as relapse and cessation from use (Abrams and Niaura, 1987; Goldman, Brown, Christiansen, and Smith, 1991; Monti *et al.*, 2001; Marlatt and Donovan, 2005). Drug expectancies account for differences in drug response, explain commonly observed placebo effects, and explicitly and implicitly influence proximal drinking or drug use decisions as well as more global processes of initiation, maintenance, and cessation of drinking or drug use (Abrams and Niaura, 1987; Goldman, Brown, Christiansen, and Smith, 1991; Monti *et al.*, 2001; Reich, Below, Goldman, 2010). Substance expectancies have been conceptualized as stimulus versus outcome expectancies, and as explicit versus implicit outcome expectancies. Each of these aspects will be described, along with methodological issues in their assessment.

Any drug-taking situation (whether an alcohol beverage, drug, or medication) involves *stimulus expectancies* – expectations about the nature of the particular drug administered and expectancies about the effects or consequences associated with using the drug (i.e., response or outcome expectancies) according to social learning theory (Abrams and Niaura, 1987). Both types of expectancies are sequentially activated to influence outcomes (Kirsch and Sapirstein, 1999; Vogel-Sprott and Fillmore, 1999). In research, the belief that individuals have about the drug content (i.e., stimulus expectancy) may be experimentally manipulated via instructional set manipulation, as described below, in order to examine the pharmacologic versus placebo components of the drug response (Rohsenow and Marlatt, 1981). Stimulus expectancy activates participants' outcome expectancies about the effects that the drug is likely to have

The Wiley-Blackwell Handbook of Addiction Psychopharmacology, First Edition. Edited by James MacKillop and Harriet de Wit.
© 2013 John Wiley & Sons, Ltd. Published 2013 by John Wiley & Sons, Ltd.

on them, and these may add placebo effects (changes in mood, behavior) to any pharmacologic effects.

In the context of drug use expectancies, the term *outcome expectancies* refers most commonly to the expected effects of using the substance, but also refers to expected consequences of refraining from using the substance. While expected consequences could be both immediate and long-term ones, it is the short-term consequences (occurring within minutes or hours) that are considered to be the most relevant determinants of behavior; these are the outcomes usually assessed. In the broader sense, outcome expectancies can refer to the outcome of any behavior, such as the expected consequences of applying a coping skill, but this chapter will focus only on drug-related expectancies.

An individual's outcome expectancies for drug use include both *explicit expectancies*, expected effects that the person is able to verbalize, and *implicit expectancies*, expected effects that may be outside of awareness (Reich, Below, and Goldman, 2010). Explicit expectancies are considered to provide a conscious guide during decision making by activating learned schemas or memories about consequences that the person believes are likely to occur, and then weighing the pros and cons of each choice. Implicit expectancies are believed to affect behavior outside of conscious awareness. Together explicit and implicit expectancies are thought to represent associative memory links between alcohol or other substances and the behavioral, cognitive, and affective consequences of use that permit organisms to anticipate reward or punishment following behavioral actions (Reich, Below, and Goldman, 2010) as a basis for decision making.

2   Empirical Relevance of the Topic to Substance Abuse Research

2.1   Relevance of stimulus expectancies

2.1.1   Relevance of placebo designs.   The concept of stimulus expectancies derived originally from studies of placebo response. Placebos are routinely used as controls in clinical trials and in behavioral pharmacological studies. Because the pharmacological effects of a drug are confounded with effects of the expectancy about the acute effect of a drug, the pharmacologic effect is usually inferred by subtracting the placebo effect from the effect in the active condition. However, placebos in fact lead to robust effects that are often of comparable magnitude to the active medication or substance. Similar to the well-known placebo effects in depression, chronic medical conditions, and analgesia research (Benedetti *et al.*, 2005; Khan, Warner, and Brown, 2000; Khan, Redding, and Brown, 2008; Kirsch and Sapirstein, 1999), multiple studies with substance abusers find reduced substance use following treatment with placebo medications and demonstrate that placebos reproduce a significant majority of the improvement in active drugs. For example, placebo injectable naltrexone produced about 44% reduction from pretreatment drinking compared to a 63% reduction by 380 mg of naltrexone (Garbutt *et al.*, 2005). In a large-scale randomized alcoholism treatment clinical trial (the NIAAA COMBINE study), receiving placebo medication with medical management resulted in a higher percentage of days abstinent and lower relapse rates relative to behavioral therapy alone (Weiss *et al.*, 2008). Similarly, cocaine vaccine resulted in a significant reduction in cocaine's intoxicating effects after the first injection, despite the fact that antibody levels were low until the third vaccination, demonstrating a placebo response to the injection and other non-pharmacological procedures (Haney *et al.*, 2010).

A placebo effect is a psychobiological phenomenon occurring in the brain after the administration of an inert substance or of a sham treatment along with verbal suggestion and other cues of clinical benefit (Price, Finniss, and Benedetti, 2008). Placebo effect is defined as a change that occurs from the perception that an active substance or a therapeutic intervention was administered, but in the absence of a substance or intervention considered functional or effective (Kirsch and Sapirstein, 1999; Price, Finniss, and Benedetti, 2008) in terms of the outcome studied. These stimulus expectancies must be linked to outcome expectancies for the placebo effect to occur. Placebo effects of drugs are important determinants of behavioral and subjective responses to a drug independent of the pharmacological action of that drug (Vogel-Sprott and Fillmore, 1999). Placebos have been used both to study clinical interventions and to clarify the effects of psychoactive substances commonly abused.

2.1.2   Relevance of balanced-placebo designs.   The balanced-placebo design (BPD) was introduced to further eliminate confounds inherent in most placebo-controlled designs (Marlatt and Rohsenow, 1980). The standard placebo-controlled design did not clearly define the nature of the placebo effect due to ambiguous instructional set (i.e., subjects told they may or may not receive the active medication), so each condition probably had a mixture of people who did and did not believe they received the active substance. The BPD independently manipulates receipt of the active versus inert substance and the stimulus expectancy set (instructions plus contextual cues). Almost never used in intervention studies, the BPD is usually used to clarify the nature of pharmacologic versus expectancy effects of psychoactive substances in human laboratory investigations by disaggregating pharmacologic action from cognitive effects of stimulus expectancies.

The BPD method resulted in a rich line of experimental research on the behavioral effects of alcohol (Marlatt and Rohsenow, 1980; Hull and Bond, 1986; Testa *et al.*, 2006), tobacco (Juliano and Brandon, 2002; Perkins, Sayette, Conklin, and Caggiula, 2003; Perkins *et al.*, 2004; Kelemen and Kaighobadi, 2007), caffeine (Harrell and Juliano, 2009), and marijuana (Metrik *et al.*, 2009; Metrik *et al.*, 2011; Metrik et al., 2012). Neural mechanisms involved in alcohol, smoking, and drug stimulus expectancies have also been examined in studies that also utilized the BPD design (Gundersen *et al.*, 2008; Volkow *et al.*, 2003; Volkow *et al.*, 2006; Wilson, Sayette, Delgado, and Fiez, 2005).

In alcohol research, the bulk of studies have been consistent with the conclusions formed in early reviews: the effects of expectancy manipulations predominate over pharmacological effects for craving and consumption among alcohol-dependent individuals and for social and emotional behaviors (e.g., aggression, social anxiety, laughter to cartoons, and sexual arousal), while for memory and motor skills, alcohol consumption had a stronger effect than expectancy (Marlatt and Rohsenow, 1980; Hull and Bond, 1986). In nicotine research, instructional set manipulations using the BPD with denicotinized cigarettes have been shown to affect self-reported anxiety/tension, concentration, smoking urge, ratings of nicotine content, and reinforcing effects of smoking (Juliano and Brandon, 2002; Kelemen and Kaighobadi, 2007; Perkins, Sayette, Conklin, and Caggiula, 2003; Perkins *et al.*, 2004). In two BPD studies with marijuana, marijuana stimulus expectancy effects were found on smoking behavior, satisfaction, experiential delay discounting, subjective drug effects, and women's perceived likelihood of negative consequences of sexual risk behaviors, while pharmacologic effects were found on physiologic (heart rate) measures, subjective drug effects, cognitive tasks measuring impulsive disinhibition, and perceived positive consequences of risky sex (Metrik *et al.*, 2009; Metrik *et al.*, 2011; Metrik *et al.*, 2012). People in the latter study who both received and were told they received marijuana rated the likelihood of various risky behaviors more highly, suggesting recognition of the need to engage in compensatory behavior. Thus, BPD studies have yielded important information on the role that non-pharmacological factors play in the maintenance of alcohol abuse, smoking behavior, and marijuana use.

2.2   Relevance of explicit outcome expectancies

Explicit outcome expectancies represent a set of *if–then* probabilistic statements that are held in memory (e.g., I am more relaxed in social situations if I've been smoking marijuana) and that are activated by various drug-related cues (Reich, Below, and Goldman, 2010). In social learning theory (Bandura, 1986), outcome expectancies for substance use are a key determinant of behavior, conceptualized as the mediator through which learning and biology influence decisions. Drug use outcome expectancies can help to explain individual differences in drug seeking and in behavioral response to a drug or to a placebo, and predict substance use behavior (Rohsenow and Pinkston-Camp, in press). Individuals expecting more impairment from alcohol displayed poorer task performance under both alcohol and placebo administrations (Vogel-Sprott and Fillmore, 1999). Marijuana users who expected marijuana to cause more cognitive and behavioral impairment reported greater anxiety after smoking active marijuana but not after placebo (Metrik *et al.*, 2011). Expecting tobacco to result in negative affect reduction moderated the effect of instructional set (told tobacco versus told placebo) on anxiety among smokers (Juliano and Brandon, 2002). Using electronic diaries, positive expected effects of tobacco use on any one day predicted smoking behavior on the following day (Gwaltney, Shiffman, Balabanis, and Paty, 2005). More dependent smokers ascribed more importance to negative physical effects and to positive stimulating effects from smoking than did less dependent smokers (Rohsenow *et al.*, 2003). People reporting more positive effects in general from alcohol behaved less aggressively after provocation when they thought they had consumed alcohol versus tonic (Rohsenow and Bachorowski, 1984). Positive outcome expectancies exerted a significant effect on post-drinking perceptions and behavioral intentions of engaging in unsafe sexual behaviors (Fromme, Katz, and D'Amico, 1997). Patients who used more cocaine pretreatment expected less frequent positive effects and more frequent social withdrawal, consistent with clinical reports of effects of longer cocaine careers (Rohsenow, Sirota, Martin, and Monti, 2004).

Developmentally, expectancies are formed prior to any experience with alcohol or drugs (e.g., Christiansen, Goldman, and Brown, 1985; Miller, Smith, and Goldman, 1990) through vicarious processes, then gradually become more specific and include more anticipated positive effects from alcohol and drugs (Goldman, Darkes, and Del Boca, 1999). Greater positive outcome expectancies lead to earlier onset and heavier use (Dunn and Goldman, 1998). People with early-onset alcoholism expected more negative effects, aggression, and sexual enhancement than did late-onset alcoholics (Chen *et al.*, 2011). Drinking behavior, in turn, strengthens expectancies about alcohol's effects, which further contributes to alcohol use (Smith, Goldman, Greenbaum, and Christiansen, 1995; Sher, Wood, Wood, and Raskin, 1996). The effect of positive expectancies prior to the start of marijuana use on later marijuana use appear to be mediated by increasing intentions to use at an intermediate time (Malmberg *et al.*, 2012).

Cross-sectional studies, longitudinal studies, and experimental manipulations indicate that expectancies partially mediate the biopsychosocial risk for substance use (e.g., such as family history, dispositional factors, and environmental influences) and for alcohol or drug use behavior (see Goldman, Darkes, and Del Boca, 1999, for review). Much of the research on the mediating role of expectancies has been conducted in the context of the Acquired Preparedness Model, which integrates the influence of distal personality factors on more proximal substance use behaviors through social learning (Smith and Anderson, 2001; Anderson, Smith, and Fisher, 2003). For example, trait disinhibition has been shown to influence drinking behavior through its effect on positive and negative alcohol expectancies (McCarthy, Kroll, and Smith, 2001; McCarthy, Miller, Smith, and Smith,. 2001; Anderson, Smith, and Fisher, 2003) and on marijuana use through its effect on negative marijuana expectancies (Vangsness, Bry, and LaBouvie, 2005).

For expectancies concerning impairment, outcome expectancies can lead to behavioral effects in the opposite direction from the direction of the expected behavioral effect when people engage in compensatory behavior to counteract the expected effect. For example, energy drinks are marketed as beverages that will enhance energy and alertness, and promote partying and counteract alcohol's sedating and impairing effects, putatively so that people may drink more when combining alcohol with energy drinks (Howland *et al.*, 2011). Therefore, knowing the drug effect and the expectancy effects for these combinations is of particular relevance. Expecting strong impairment from alcohol led to a compensatory response that counteracted the effects of alcohol on impairment (Fillmore and Blackburn, 2002; Fillmore, Mulvihill, and Vogel-Sprott, 1994; Fillmore and Vogel-Sprott, 1996). Relative to expecting enhancement, expecting impairment from caffeine led to better performance after caffeine (Harrell and Juliano, 2009). When most participants expected that caffeine would increase the impairing effects of alcohol, caffeine actually decreased such impairing effects (Fillmore and Vogel-Sprott, 1995), but social drinkers who were led to expect that caffeine would counteract alcohol-induced impairment (peak breath alcohol of 0.08 g%) actually displayed greater alcohol-induced impairment (Fillmore, Roach, and Rice, 2002). Thus, the expectancies resulting from marketing of energy drinks are likely to actually increase the amount of impairment drinkers experience when combining these beverages (Howland *et al.*, 2011).

Some work has focused on specifically trying to modify expectancies. An experimental approach designed to change college students' alcohol outcome expectancies, the expectancy challenge paradigm in which the role of expectancies is demonstrated to the individual, has demonstrated concomitant reductions in alcohol expectancies and consumption up to 6 weeks after intervention (Darkes and Goldman, 1993; Darkes and Goldman, 1998; Dunn, Lau, Cruz, 2000; Wiers and Kummeling, 2004). However, in other studies short-term reductions in alcohol use were not associated with changes in drinking outcome expectancies, suggesting that modification of outcome expectancies may not be a prerequisite for behavioral changes (Brown, 1993; Jones, Corbin, and Fromme, 2001).

Expectancies have been used to predict likelihood of cessation. *Decisional balance*, a term from decision theories (Edwards, 1954), refers to the balance of positive (*pros*) versus negatively valenced effects (*cons*) expected to occur from a behavior or substance, a concept adopted by social learning theory to explain choices to engage in a behavior (Bandura, 1986). Although not usually covered in expectancies literature, the measures indeed assess expected effects of use or of changing use. Of particular interest is how this balance changes as people progress into behavior change. The perceived cons of smoking increased relative to the pros of smoking when moving from precontemplation to contemplating smoking cessation, just as the pros of quitting cocaine increased relative to the cons of quitting cocaine for those contemplating versus not yet contemplating cocaine cessation (Prochaska *et al.*, 1994). For individuals in action and maintenance of change, generally the expected pros of change remained higher than the cons of change (or cons of use remained higher than the pros of use) across stages. The implication is that clinical and prevention efforts should focus more on increasing awareness of negative effects of use rather than trying to counteract expected positive effects of substance use, since negative expectancies shift more and have a greater correlation with change.

Cessation expectancies represent cognitive processes underlying motivation to reduce or stop drinking or drug use. Expectations regarding the anticipated consequences of not using alcohol play a role in decisions to initiate drinking (Bekman *et al.*, 2011) as well as decisions to stop or reduce alcohol use (Metrik *et al.*, 2004). As drinking patterns escalate, people appear to expect more negative short-term consequences from choosing not to drink or limiting one's consumption (Metrik *et al.*, 2004). Cessation expectancies were negatively associated with positive alcohol use expectancies (Anderson *et al.*, 2011) and, when considered together, were uniquely associated with adolescent drinking behavior (Bekman *et al.*, 2011). Thus, cessation expectancies are useful in understanding recent onset of alcohol use, differences in the progression of adolescent alcohol experience, and efforts by individuals to cut down or stop drinking.

Expectancies have been investigated as predictors of likelihood of relapse in some studies. Among patients in treatment for cocaine, urges to use cocaine were greater for those who expected more positive effects (enhanced wellbeing, pain reduction, and sexual enhancement) from cocaine (Rohsenow, Sirota, Martin, and Monti, 2004). Among alcoholics in treatment for alcohol, four types of positive expected effect correlated with salivating more in the presence of alcohol cues (Rohsenow *et al.*, 1992), with such salivation having been found to be a risk factor for future relapse

(Rohsenow *et al.*, 1994). Alcohol-dependent patients who expected more positive effects of drinking reported less confidence about their ability to change their drinking (Brown, Carello, Vik, and Porter, 1998). Prospectively, cocaine-abusing patients who at admission expected more negative effects from cocaine used less cocaine during the 3 months following substance treatment (Rohsenow, Sirota, Martin, and Monti, 2004). Expecting negative effects from marijuana also prospectively predicted change in marijuana use in teens: teens who remained non-users and teens who ceased using marijuana both had reported more negative expected effects from marijuana use 2 years earlier compared to those who started or continued using (Aarons, Brown, Tice, and Coe, 2001). Among alcohol-dependent patients in treatment, negative but not positive alcohol expectancies at baseline predicted relapse to first drink (Jones and MacMahon, 1994). Thus, in general positive expectancies for alcohol or drug use are related to urges to use and self-confidence about change, but negative expectancies may have a stronger relationship to relapse.

For smoking, however, negative reinforcement expectancies were a better predictor of outcome. Expecting tension-reduction effects (a positively valued effect) predicted relapse after treatment (Shadel and Mermelstein, 1993). Similarly, expecting negative reinforcement from smoking (a positively valued effect) predicted less chance of success at end of treatment and at various times in the first 6 months, while the rated likelihood of most of the positive-reinforcement consequences had little predictive power and negative consequences only predicted 1-week outcomes (Copeland, Brandon, and Quinn, 1995; Wetter *et al.*, 1994). Knowing a person's expectancies about effects of a substance may improve ability to tailor behavioral treatments toward expectancies that are likely to increase relapse risk and tailor pharmacotherapies to address the desired effects.

2.3   Relevance of implicit outcome expectancies

More recently, implicit expectancies and related motivational and decision-making processes not accessible to consciousness have been investigated as a way to investigate expectancies without concerns about response bias distortions or conscious memory involvement. Much of the discourse on the distinction between explicit and implicit measures has centered on understanding the underlying mechanisms or memory processes (for a full model of these implicit motivational processes, see Curtin, McCarthy, Piper, and Baker, 2006). The premise is that once drug use is established, drug use motivation processes often occur automatically, without needing attention or much conscious awareness. Therefore, the user may remain unaware of having a motivation to use or of the situational stimuli that trigger that motivation as long as drug use behaviors are not blocked in some way (Curtin, McCarthy, Piper, and Baker, 2006). One aspect of these implicit processes is conditioned associations of drug use with positive appetitive effects, negative reinforcement effects, and unpleasant consequences, associations forming the basis of implicit expectancies about future effects. These become networks of associational structures in long-term memory (Moss and Albery, 2009) or are conceived of as involving propositional rule-based reasoning (Wiers and Stacy, 2010) or both in interplay (Moss and Albery, 2010). These expectancies may operate at an implicit level, since the conditioned associations or learned rules do not need to rise to the level of awareness. Stimuli associated with withdrawal, negative mood, or drug use can implicitly activate processing of drug information (Curtin, McCarthy, Piper, and Baker, 2006), including implicit expectancies about the effects of the drug in the situation.

Whether one or more memory components control the expression of explicit and implicit expectancies is subject to ongoing investigation in alcohol-related cognition research (see Reich, Below, and Goldman, 2010). A meta-analysis demonstrated a significant overlap between implicit and explicit measures ($r = 0.25$), with explicit expectancy measures accounting for more variance in drinking behavior relative to implicit expectancies ($r = 0.41$ and $r = 0.35$, respectively) but with each domain explaining unique variance in drinking outcomes. The degree of overlap is only about 6% of shared variance, however, and an emerging body of research suggests there are important differences between explicit expectancies and implicit associations. Specifically, under the circumstances in which executive control is weakened or impaired through acute intoxication, implicit associations are better predictors of behavior than the self-reported expectancies, while in people with good executive control or verbal abilities, alcohol-related behavior is predicted better by explicit expectancies (see review by Wiers and Stacy, 2010). Thus, assessing implicit expectancies may add to the predictive power provided by measures of explicit expectancies, particularly when poorer cognitive control is involved.

3 Standardized and Validated Methods

3.1 Placebo-controlled designs

3.1.1 Efficacy of placebos. The credibility of placebos for alcohol drinks was not generally assessed until the advent of the BPD when it was found that many common beverage/placebo combinations did not convince participants (Keane, Lisman, and Kreutzer, 1980; Rohsenow and Marlatt, 1981). Crucial to studying stimulus expectancy effects is the credibility of the expectancy manipulation, and this starts with using the beverages that participants cannot distinguish from each other at a greater than chance level. Studies devoted to finding effective placebo beverages concluded that the two combinations that were most effective were beer versus non-alcoholic beer, and a 1:5 ratio of high-quality vodka (80–100 proof) mixed with tonic versus pure tonic water, preferably with lime juice or a vodka "floater" – a very small amount of vodka added to the surface of the beverage for initial gustatory cues (Keane, Lisman, and Kreutzer, 1980; Marlatt, Demming, and Reid, 1973).

To determine whether the manipulation was successful, it is important to administer self-report credibility assessments at the end of the study. In alcohol research, a preferred way is to ask about not only what beverage participants believed they consumed but also the number of ounces of alcohol they believed was in the beverage, how intoxicated they felt, and what breath alcohol level (BrAC) they believed they attained, or similar questions. To decrease responding based on desire to please the investigator, credibility assessment questionnaires may be placed in a sealed envelope

	Told Drug	Told Placebo
Receive Drug	A	B
Receive Placebo	C	D

Figure 17.1 Balanced placebo design

that allegedly goes to a fictional departmental oversight committee. Similar procedures are used for other substances.

Placebos for tobacco cigarettes are now easily available through the purchase of denicotinized cigarettes. However, most denicotinized cigarettes still deliver a small amount of nicotine or have lower palatability than regular nicotine brands (Perkins, Sayette, Conklin, and Caggiula, 2003). *Quest* brand, which contains less than 0.05 mg nicotine per cigarette, has been successfully used by nicotine researchers (e.g., Kelemen and Kaighobadi, 2007; Juliano, Fucito, and Harrell, 2011). It is important to cover up brand information on the usual cigarettes and use the same cover-up on the placebo cigarette.

Placebo marijuana cigarettes (using marijuana with the tetrahydrocannabinol (THC) and other cannabinoids removed) along with matching marijuana cigarettes of an established THC content are available from the National Institute on Drug Abuse. However, since the placebo marijuana is often of a lighter color (Chait and Pierri, 1989), it is important to take steps to disguise, such as by closing off both ends of each cigarette (Metrik *et al.*, 2009).

3.1.2 Balanced placebo design methodology. Balanced placebo design (BPD) is a 2×2 factorial design that crosses the substance that is administered to the participant (drug or placebo) with instructions that are given to the participant about the drug content (drug or placebo). Thus, half of the participants are told they are receiving a drug, and half are told they are receiving no drug (i.e., instructional set manipulation). Half of the participants in each of those instructional conditions actually receive the drug and half do not. In this design, participants are randomly assigned to one of four conditions (see Figure 17.1). Under usual double-blind conditions, where participants are given no explicit instructions about the drug content, they may be left wondering what they are ingesting, which leads them to search for interoceptive cues (Rohsenow and Marlatt, 1981). This can increase accurate identification of the placebo versus the active drug, thus confounding pharmacologic effects with expectancy.

The following is a list of guidelines for alcohol BPD originally described in influential literature reviews (Rohsenow and Marlatt, 1981; Martin and Sayette, 1993) and corroborated with findings from a recent meta-analysis of alcohol placebo manipulations (Schlauch *et al.*, 2010).

(a) Present the alcoholic beverages in commercially labeled containers, pour from an unopened bottle, and mix the drink in front of subjects.
(b) Give false breath alcohol feedback using rigged equipment.

(c)   Minimize taste cues with alcohol floaters or sprays, chilling, flavoring, and/or mouthwash rinsing prior to placebo administration.
(d)   Deliver placebos in the context of a study that includes autonomic arousal tasks so that arousal can be attributed to the task rather than to drinking, if consistent with study aims.
(e)   Active alcohol condition drinks should have lower percentage of absolute alcohol per drink ($\leq$ 8–10% by volume).
(f)   Lower total alcohol doses result in less ability to distinguish alcohol from placebo (BrACs below 0.04–0.05 g% are recommended).
(g)   Use double-blind procedures; the staff member who prepares the content of the bottles should have no contact with participants.
(h)   To encourage belief in the instruction condition, use procedures to simulate randomizing participants to beverage condition in their presence (e.g., rigged coin toss).
(i)   Use a credible beverage/placebo combination, as described above (section 3.1.1).
(j)   Keep the participant seated until the last dependent measure is collected, since standing provides interoceptive sensations of intoxication.
(k)   Administer manipulation check measures. Giving them prior to the main task implementation lets the experimenter know beliefs at start of the tasks, but may cause introspection or raise suspicion that deception is involved, and this is avoided by giving the manipulation check just before debriefing.
(l)   Exclude participants' close friends or roommates; discourage talking about the deception to others.

Studies that utilized the above procedures showed equivalence between conditions in participant estimates of number of standard alcoholic beverages consumed, although most comparisons did not manage to equate conditions on self-reported subjective intoxication (Schlauch *et al.*, 2010). During debriefing, many people who said they felt somewhat intoxicated while saying they had no alcohol attributed the sensations to tonic water (unfamiliar to most), anxiety, or other causes. Although distraction from introspection with concurrent or demanding activities was recommended (Rohsenow and Marlatt, 1981), it was not found to influence the success of the manipulation checks in the meta-analysis. Additionally, studies conducted in a setting that maximized participant comfort, including positioning in an "easy chair" during the beverage consumption versus sitting on a less comfortable bar stool in a bar-lab, produced the largest effect sizes for both pharmacological and stimulus expectancy effects in another meta-analysis of alcohol challenge studies (McKay and Schare, 1999).

These guidelines have been adapted for other substances, such as tobacco and marijuana BPD studies. In nicotine research, a few puffs rather than a whole cigarette could be used in line with the recommended lower alcohol doses (Perkins, Sayette, Conklin, and Caggiula, 2003). In marijuana BPD research, lower THC doses have been successfully used, although doses higher than the 2.8% THC have not been tested in a BPD design (Metrik *et al.*, 2009; Metrik *et al.*, 2011). Importantly, conditioning patterns differ between alcohol and smoked drugs, such that drinking behavior is associated with both non-alcoholic and alcoholic beverages, whereas smoking behavior is invariably associated with the psychoactive effects of a given substance (Perkins,

Sayette, Conklin, and Caggiula, 2003). In the BPD, in order to reduce conditioned responses to marijuana, cigarettes in the two "told placebo" conditions (Metrik *et al.*, 2009; Metrik *et al.*, 2011) were rolled in an additional piece of purple cigarette paper with a grape aroma prior to the beginning of the experiment (Wachtel *et al.*, 2002). Furthermore, participants in the two "told THC" conditions in the marijuana BPD studies provided a saliva sample after they smoked, which they were told would be sent out for quantitative analysis to verify the amount of THC absorbed in the saliva, so as to increase the sense that they had received THC (Metrik *et al.*, 2009). For caffeine research, typically decaffeinated coffee is given with or without adding anhydrous caffeine solution or flattened tonic water (Harrell and Juliano, 2009). Those seeing the solution added are told they are receiving caffeine. For those expecting no caffeine, orange juice has been used as the beverage so that all receiving decaffeinated coffee are told it has caffeine and all those receiving orange juice are told it is just orange juice, regardless of actual caffeine content of the beverage (Schneider *et al.*, 2006). Since the procedures are newer for studies of tobacco, THC, and caffeine, cross-study evaluation of the efficacy of these manipulations is yet to be done. Within-study manipulation checks are vital.

3.1.3   Other design considerations.   Because the anti-placebo condition (i.e., told placebo/receive alcohol) often has reduced ability to successfully deceive participants (Martin and Sayette, 1993), some investigators prefer to use a three-cell design (alcohol, placebo, and no-beverage control conditions) (Martin and Sayette, 1993). This design, however, does not allow orthogonal comparisons of the impact of the instructional set versus pharmacology on the hypothesized outcomes and does not allow for a test of interaction between the pharmacologic and the instructional set main effects. Other alternatives to an alcohol BPD design are reviewed by Martin and Sayette (1993).

A practical consideration in the use of a BPD study is the choice of a between-subject versus a within-subject experimental design. A within-subjects design yields more statistical power, requires fewer subjects, and maximizes control of individual differences. However, it is usually not feasible in the context of a BPD study due to the carry-over conditioned learned effects or to participants thinking about the meaning of differences that could influence participants' responses in another BPD condition (Volkow *et al.*, 2006; Price, Finniss, and Benedetti, 2008). Alternatively, a mixed model design can add some within-subjects control by including repeated measures at baseline during non-drinking conditions and following alcohol administration whenever the use of repeated measures is appropriate (Stevens, 1992).

3.2   Assessing explicit expectancies

3.2.1   Methodological considerations.   Explicit expectancies are assessed by means of questionnaires, so the methodological issues have to do with thoughtful selection of one that is psychometrically sound, matches the population of interest, and has the degree of specificity that meets the researcher's question or clinician's needs. Psychometric development needs to include evidence of the underlying factor or component structure, internal consistency, reliability of the final scales, and evidence of construct validity. Temporal stability only has relevance to the extent that expectancies would have no reason to change over the time period (e.g., no intervention, short time period). Evidence of a higher-order factor/component structure is useful as it usually separates expectancies into desired and undesirable effects according to psychometric information rather than by investigator opinion.

3.2.1.1   Target Population Needs Consideration.   In general, the best measures are ones developed from people who used the substances frequently so have direct experiences as well as learning based on observation and instruction. For studies of college populations, the various measures developed on such populations may be most appropriate. For clinical use or for studies relevant to clinical populations, it is best if the measure was developed or at least validated using a clinical population of those who heavily use or are dependent on the substance, so that the measure will assess the expectancies actually held by the substance abusers. Furthermore, most measures developed on college populations are often too long or not very relevant to clinical populations. Ones developed for patient populations have often used item-selection methods to reduce the number of items needed to represent the expectancy domain.

3.2.1.2   The Specificity of the Items and Scales Needs to be Considered.   First, some of the measures intermix items asking about the effects on the respondent with items asking about beliefs about the substance's effects on people in general ("personal" versus "general" beliefs, per Rohsenow, 1983). In order to assess expectancies the respondent has for the effects of the substance on oneself, it is important to choose a measure where all items are phrased in the first person. For example, light versus heavy drinkers differ in expectancies for effects on themselves, as do women versus men when controlling statistically for heaviness of drinking, while expectancies about effects of alcohol on people in general resemble effects for heavy drinking men (Rohsenow, 1983). In clinical uses, this is an important consideration. Second, some expectancy measures only include expected positive (desired or liked) effects of a substance, while others include both positive and negative effects. When referring to expectancies as being positive or negative, these value determinations are usually made based on higher-order factor analyses or by directly asking participants to rate how much they like/dislike each effect, but sometimes are based on investigator judgment. It is preferable to base these judgments on some objective criterion rather than deciding whether "increased aggression" or "impairment," for example, are seen as positive or negative by respondents. Third, for some hypotheses it is only important to know about effects with positive valence, or about level of positive and negative expected effects, regardless of which specific expectancies are endorsed. In those cases, it may not be important to score individual expectancy factors but only to use the composite scores for positive or negatively valenced expectancies. In these cases, either using just the high-order factor scoring or using a brief expectancy measure of pros and cons (e.g., the six-item Smoking Decisional Balance Scale; Velicer, DiClemente, Prochaska, and Brandenburg, 1985) will provide the needed information. Fourth, how the items were generated is important, as specific expectancy domains need to reflect the pharmacodynamics of each substance measured as applied to the target population of interest. Some measures were created by altering an alcohol expectancy measure by simply changing the word "alcohol" to another substance. Such a measure may miss important expected effects for that particular substance, just as expectancies derived from non-clinical samples or college students may not sufficiently represent expectancies of clinical populations or of community adults. Fifth, to investigate situation-specific expectancies, it can be valuable to first use an open-ended assessment, as was done when alcohol-dependent individuals were asked what benefits alcohol would achieve for them during a relapse, resulting in interesting and useful information about goals that the alcoholics reported actually achieving by means of drinking (Connors, O'Farrell, and Pelcovits, 1988). Alternatively, it can be useful to use electronic diaries or smart telephone technology to ask some specific expectancy questions at various moments of the day to relate to substance use or craving events (Gwaltney, Shiffman, Balabanis, and Paty, 2005).

3.2.2 Overview of measures used.   This section is not intended to be a complete list of measures, but rather provides an overview of some of the principal assessments in light of the methodological considerations raised.

3.2.2.1   Measures of Alcohol Expectancies.   The alcohol expectancy measures were developed on university populations originally, with expansions to adolescents and some use in clinical settings. The expectancy domains covered originally included global positive effects, social and physical pleasure, sexual enhancement, power and aggression, social expressiveness, relaxation and tension reduction, cognitive and physical impairment, and careless unconcern (Alcohol Expectancies Questionnaire; Brown, Goldman, Inn, and Anderson, 1980; Brown, Christiansen, and Goldman, 1987; Alcohol Effects Questionnaire; Rohsenow, 1983). The Alcohol Effects Questionnaire–Self (Rohsenow, 1983) was designed to provide a condensed version of the Brown *et al.* (1980) Alcohol Expectancies Questionnaire but with all items reworded to apply to oneself (another version worded all items in the third person) and to include two domains of negative expectancies. Psychometric information is available for alcohol-dependent patients (Rohsenow, 1995) in addition to university students (Rohsenow, 1983). Expecting less relaxation from alcohol predicted worse treatment outcomes, showing the clinical value of one expectancy domain (Brown, 1985). A measure designed to cover negative expectancies more completely was developed (Negative Alcohol Expectancy Questionnaire; Jones and MacMahon, 1994) and found to predict relapse after alcohol treatment. Several other alcohol expectancy measures are similar to the Alcohol Expectancies Questionnaire in method of development but designed to expand the range of expectancies (e.g., Comprehensive Effects of Alcohol Questionnaire; Fromme, Stroot, and Kaplan, 1993). An adolescent version, the Alcohol Expectancies Questionnaire Adolescent Form (Christiansen, Goldman, and Inn, 1982), is phrased entirely in the third person but has been heuristic in understanding the development of expectancies across adolescence.

3.2.2.2   MEASURES OF TOBACCO USE EXPECTANCIES.   The first measure developed, the Smoking Consequences Questionnaire (Brandon and Baker, 1991), was psychometrically developed in college populations, where the smoking rate was half that in the general population. The items are worded for effects on oneself. Four reliable factors included negative consequences, negative reinforcement (reduction in negative affect), positive reinforcement (sensory satisfaction, boredom reduction), and appetite–weight control. While the questionnaire is widely used, having 80 items is not feasible in many patient populations and clinical settings, and the expectancies were less differentiated in this population of light smokers than using measures developed on more dependent adults. Also, responses rated the desirability of each effect if it were to occur, not how likely they believed it was to occur, so did not measure what expectancies they believed were true or probable. A revision was developed on older nicotine-dependent adults in smoking treatment that added likelihood ratings, with 55 items (Copeland, Brandon, and Quinn, 1995), showing eight factors when using the product of likelihood and desirability ratings, and ten factors when using likelihood ratings (Copeland, Brandon, and Quinn, 1995). For likelihood, negative consequence factors included negative physical feelings, negative social impression, and health risks; negative reinforcement included the scales of negative affect reduction, boredom reduction, and craving/addiction reduction; while the positive consequence factors included stimulation, taste/sensorimotor, manipulation, social facilitation, and weight control (Copeland, Brandon, and Quinn, 1995). The Smoking Effects Questionnaire for Adult Populations (Rohsenow *et al.*, 2003) was developed on community smokers, is worded for effects on oneself, and was reduced to 33 items with excellent reliability and validity of the six factors for easy use in busy clinical settings. Both true–false responses and ratings of the importance of the effect to the individual are included, with similar validity. Secondary factor analysis showed that the expectancy factors included three negatively valenced and four positively valenced scales (negative physical, negative psychosocial, health concerns; reduce negative affect, stimulation, positive social, and weight control). The Outcome Expectancy Scale (Godding and Glasgow, 1985) and several other minor measures had inadequate psychometric work, with no support for their validity.

3.2.2.3   MEASURES OF CAFFEINE EXPECTANCIES.   The 37-item Caffeine Expectancy Questionnaire (CEQ; Heinz, Kassel, and Smith, 2009) was developed on caffeine users, is worded in terms of effects on oneself, and uses 4-point ratings of agreement that the effect will occur. The CEQ has four factors assessing withdrawal symptoms, acute negative effects, positive mood effects (focusing on carefree, calming, outgoing, boredom relief), and positive effects (primarily energy and alertness). The measure has excellent psychometric properties and validity. There is little published work beyond the initial development of the CEQ.

3.2.2.4   MEASURES OF EXPECTANCIES FOR OTHER DRUGS.   All but one cocaine measure and the marijuana expectancy measure were developed on college populations, the majority with little or no experience using the substances, so they do not assess the expectancies held by users. The Cocaine Effect Expectancy Questionnaire (CEEQ; Schafer and Brown, 1991) was developed on college students, only 15% of whom had ever used cocaine, and thus reflects their beliefs derived from media and literature rather than from direct experience, and may not reflect the expectancies of clinical samples. At 71 items, it is also rather long for clinical purposes and thus was reduced to 24 items in later versions (Schafer and Fals-Stewart, 1993). Worded in terms of effects on oneself, five factors were found originally, but using more valid analytic methods it was later found to have three factors: positive effects, negative effects, and arousal (Schafer and Fals-Stewart, 1993). When the questionnaire was validated in a clinical treatment sample, users or frequent users endorsed fewer global positive effects and less expected arousal than less frequent users (Galen and Henderson, 1999), but the CEEQ scales were not related to lifetime cocaine use among users in another study (Lundahl and Lukas, 2007). When global positive and negative effects scales were compared to actual subjective response to a cocaine challenge, expecting positive effects was correlated with the experience of euphoria, "good" and "anxious," but expecting global negative effects correlated (against the hypothesis) with reporting greater "high," "stimulated," "desire to use cocaine," "happy," and "good" feelings after the cocaine challenge (Lundahl and Lukas, 2007). The factor structure was not confirmed among therapeutic community patients nor did the one supported scale with only four items remaining (Positive Effects) correlate with treatment participation (Schafer and Fals-Stewart, 1996). Thus, this measure is not well supported when used with populations of frequent cocaine users, possibly because it was developed on mostly non-users and a few non-dependent users.

The Cocaine Effects Questionnaire for Patient Populations (Rohsenow, Sirota, Martin, and Monti, 2004), on the other hand, was developed from cocaine-using substance-dependent patients in treatment. The items are worded in terms of effects on oneself, in plain language, with excellent reliability and validity. The seven factors load onto two higher-order components, showing five positive effects (enhanced well-being, sexual enhancement, social facilitation, pain reduction, increased aggression) and two negative effects (social withdrawal/distrust, increased tension). While a variety of positive and negative scales correlated with baseline substance use and dependence, it was the negative effects factor that predicted treatment success 3 months later. Thus, this measure developed on a patient population shows utility in clinical settings.

The Marijuana Effect Expectancy Questionnaire (MEEQ; Schafer and Brown, 1991) was developed on college students, 42% of whom had used marijuana, so the majority of the sample did not have direct personal experience with the substance and few had abuse or dependence. Worded in terms of effects on oneself, six factors were found including positive effects (relaxation/tension reduction, social/sexual facilitation, perceptual/cognitive enhancement) and three probably negatively valenced effect domains (cognitive and behavioral impairment, global negative effects, hunger and cravings for things). Among adolescents, the factor structure was supported and expectancies were associated with drug use patterns over 2 years (Aarons, Brown, Tice, and Coe, 2001).When MEEQ was validated in a clinical treatment sample, users or frequent users endorsed less expected arousal, relaxation, craving for food/things, and negative consequences than did those who did not use or infrequently used marijuana (Galen and Henderson, 1999). In a community sample of marijuana users, relaxation/tension reduction expectancies predicted frequency and severity of marijuana use; the latter was also predicted by global negative effects (Hayaki *et al.*, 2010).

The Stimulant Effect Expectancy Questionnaire was developed by adapting the Cocaine Effect Expectancy Questionnaire to ask about effects of stimulants more generally, so as to cover amphetamines (Aarons, Brown, Tice, and Coe, 2001). The psychometric qualities were good with adolescents, two of the five factors (global negative effects and anxiety) differentiated preference for stimulants versus marijuana or alcohol, and stimulant use was associated with expecting fewer global positive and negative effects and more anxiety compared to non-users (Aarons, Brown, Tice, and Coe, 2001). Since this measure was developed based on responses of mostly non-using university students and has been validated in non-clinical populations, it is probably most suitable for similar populations.

There are no psychometrically sound and clinically relevant opiate-specific measures of consequences or expectancies.

3.2.2.5 MEASURES OF EXPECTANCIES FOR ABSTINENCE. Measures to assess expectancies for effects of abstinence have been developed in a few cases. The Alcohol Cessation Expectancies Questionnaire (Metrik *et al.*, 2004) is a 23-item instrument developed to measure expectancies about cessation and/or reduction of alcohol use among young people. Two domains of cessation expectancies have been identified: anticipated global impact of not drinking and anticipated social impact of not drinking. This questionnaire was found to have high internal consistency and strong evidence for construct validity. Cessation expectancies prospectively predicted self-reported change efforts and associated reductions in drinking behavior over a year, controlling for alcohol involvement and related problems (Metrik, McCarthy, Frissell, and Brown, 2003; Metrik *et al.*, 2004). This measure has the greatest utility with individuals with more extensive drinking experience who may be experiencing alcohol problems and/or considering reductions in alcohol use. It was specifically developed with an adolescent sample to aid in studying cognitions involved in developmental progression into and out of youth alcohol involvement. Similar measures need to be adapted for use with adult clinical samples in order to study potential barriers to reducing heavy or dependent drinking and to identify barriers to treatment seeking.

The Smoking Abstinence Questionnaire was developed using community smokers, was phrased in terms of effects on oneself, provides 7-point ratings of likelihood of happening, and has modest to excellent reliability and excellent validity (Hendricks *et al.*, 2011). At 71 items it is rather long, but necessarily so, since it consists of ten factors. The factors concern withdrawal, social improvement, adverse outcomes, treatment effectiveness (likelihood that various treatments would work), common reasons for quitting (e.g., improved health), barriers to obtaining treatment, positive social support, optimistic outcomes (that quitting would be easy), effects on coffee use, and weight gain effects. This measure has not been reported as a predictor of treatment effects as yet.

The Nicotine and Other Substances Interaction Expectancies Questionnaire (NOSIE; Rohsenow, Colby, Martin, and Monti, 2005) and Barriers to Quitting Smoking in Substance Abuse Treatment (BQS-SAT; Asher *et al.*, 2003) were both developed on substance-dependent patients to assess expected negative effects of smoking and of smoking cessation on substance use and cessation, so as to identify barriers to address in smoking treatment. Both are brief and in simple language, are worded for effects on oneself, and are answered true–false with an adjunctive importance rating (BQS-SAT) or use 5-point ratings of strength of belief that the effect would occur (NOSIE). Both have excellent reliability and validity: the BQS-SAT was predictive of motivation to quit smoking (Martin *et al.*, 2006) and the NOSIE was used to predict smoking cessation success 1 month later (Rohsenow, Colby, Martin, and Monti, 2005). Both were used to provide corrective feedback in smoking treatment for substance-dependent patients (Rohsenow, Monti, Colby, and Martin, 2002).

A related construct, expected effects of changing (stopping or cutting down) a substance, is assessed by several of the Decisional Balance Scales), scored only for total positive or negative effects, rather than by specific expectancies (Prochaska *et al.*, 1994).

3.3 Assessing implicit expectancies

Implicit expectancies are usually assessed with variants of memory association measures, assessing either the associations among different words, or reaction time to different words or contextual stimuli.

3.3.1 Word association.   In a free-word association method, people quickly list the first word that comes to mind in response to a cue word or phrase, and investigators study how these words cluster that indicate associations with drinking (e.g., Stacy, Ames, and Grenard, 2006). Free associations ("first word it makes you think of") to "Alcohol makes me . . . " elicit explicit expectancies. Free associations to words representing possible immediate effects of drinking (e.g., party) provide a way to assess implicit expectancies by coding responses as alcohol-related or not (Stacy, Ames, and Grenard, 2006). This measure predicted alcohol or other drug use, even controlling for explicit expectancies (Rooke, Hine, and Thorsteinsson, 2008; Reich, Below, and Goldman, 2010), although an explicit measure accounted for more variance in drinking than this implicit task (Palfai and Wood, 2001).

3.3.2 The Implicit Association Test.   The Implicit Association Test (IAT; Wiers, Van Woerden, Smuldersm, and De Jong, 2002), the most common method used, is designed to determine implicit memory associations between words related to alcohol and to affect. Participants are asked to categorize a series of words appearing on a screen using two keys, one for "good" or "I like" or "energetic" paired with one target, and the other key being "bad" or "I dislike" or "relaxed" paired with another target, then switching the pairing of evaluation with target. The targets evaluated for alcohol associations are "alcohol" and "soda." For example, the right-hand key might be "good" and "alcohol" and later be changed to "bad" and "alcohol." The outcome measure is latency to respond when asked to sort a series of other words, with the idea being that greater association between the target beverage and affect results in faster responses. The result would be an index of the extent to which the individual associates alcohol with feeling good, bad, aroused, or sedated. In meta-analyses, this measure predicted alcohol or other drug use, even controlling for explicit expectancies, but explicit measures usually accounted for more variance (Rooke, Hine, and Thorsteinsson, 2008; Reich, Below, and Goldman, 2010).

3.3.3 The Extrinsic Affective Simon Task. The Extrinsic Affective Simon Task (EAST; De Houwer and De Bruycker, 2007), similar in concept to the IAT, asks people to pair alcohol words with affective categories while assessing latency to respond. It was designed to overcome the problem of requiring that people make distinctions between alcohol and soda for every word, since some words could apply equally to both (e.g., tasty). The EAST has stronger correlations with explicit measures than are found with the IAT, and high correlations were found between the EAST and drinking frequency, with the largest unique effect size of any of the implicit measures (Reich, Below, and Goldman, 2010).

3.3.4 Modified Stroop task. A modified Stroop task asks drinkers to name the color of the ink the word is printed in for a series of words that are either neutral or likely to be associated with drinking, smoking or drugs; after being primed with an alcohol beverage word, heavy drinkers have shown more interference in the task (speed and errors) than did light drinkers (Kramer and Goldman, 2003). This is taken to mean that the words that caused interference were effects implicitly associated with drinking, and that alcohol use may be mediated by these implicit expectancies. This can provide a way to determine the degree of association of all these other words with the concept of alcohol. Attentional bias provides a potential index of the incentive salience such that drug-related stimuli are particularly salient for individuals with heavy or problematic use and dependence. Similar implicit measures include attentional bias to tobacco and marijuana cues (Waters *et al.*, 2003; Powell, Tait, and Lessiter, 2002; Field, 2005). For example, there is evidence of cannabis-dependent individuals exhibiting significant attentional bias for marijuana-related words as measured by a modified Marijuana Stroop task (Field, 2005).

3.3.5 Expectancies Accessibility Task. An Expectancies Accessibility Task (Palfai and Wood, 2001; Read *et al.*, 2004) is a computerized way to measure the accessibility of alcohol or smoking outcomes expectancies in memory. This task requires participants to respond to a series of outcome expectancy phrases (e.g., "less anxious") preceded (for alcohol expectancies) by one of two stems, either "Alcohol makes me . . . " or "Television makes me . . . ." The expectancy accessibility score (difference in time to respond to alcohol-related versus neutral outcomes) indicates the ease and quickness with which alcohol expectancies are activated from memory in comparison to expectancies about a neutral control stimulus, with male heavy drinkers responding more quickly than male lighter drinkers (Read *et al.*, 2004). When used for smoking, this measure has been shown to be associated with cigarettes smoked per day above and beyond the effects of a questionnaire-based measure of expectancies, and predicted urge to smoke following exposure to a smoking cue even after controlling for the effects of smoking deprivation (Palfai *et al.*, 2000).

3.3.6 False memory paradigm. The Deese–Roediger–McDermott (DRM) false memory paradigm was adapted to assess alcohol expectancy memory associations (McEvoy, Nelson, and Komatsu, 1999). People study a list of words and are later asked to identify those that were on the list; false memory of semantically related words is believed to indicate that those words belong to dense networks of associations with the target words. It was adapted for alcohol by having people study words associated with alcohol expectancies while in a simulated bar, then other alcohol expectancy words were presented along with the original words and control words for the memory test (Reich, Goldman, and Noll, 2004). In multiple regression, people who usually drank more per occasion had more false memories of related alcohol expectancy words, even when controlling for a measure of explicit expectancies, but the explicit measure accounted for more variance.

3.3.7 Comparison of measures of implicit expectancies. Two meta-analyses (Reich, Below, and Goldman, 2010; Rooke, Hine, and Thorsteinsson, 2008) include studies that supported each of the above measures of implicit expectancies; each shows concurrent validity in relationship to drinking, construct validity in relationship to explicit expectancies, and discriminant validity by the relatively low amount of shared variance with explicit expectancies. When given in combination with implicit primes, the addition of such primes has increased alcohol consumed in studies of ad lib drinking in the lab (reviewed in Reich, Below, and Goldman, 2010). Most studies comparing implicit and explicit measures have been done with the IAT (nine) while only one or two studies are reported for each other measure (Reich, Below, and Goldman, 2010), so the IAT has the most consistent record of support for its validity.

There is less evidence for the reliability of the measures. Temporal stability (test–retest reliability) has generally been low, but best for the IAT at 1 month (Egloff, Schwerdtfeger, and Schmukle, 2005). Since expectancies are considered theoretically to be relatively stable after acquisition, outside of any intervention or preparation to change the behavior, test–retest reliability would be expected to be better than was found for the IAT. For most of the measures, internal consistency reliability does not apply, and within-subject comparisons of measures cannot easily be done without one measure priming the other and thus making the comparisons invalid (Reich, Below, and Goldman, 2010). Low reliability may be responsible for limiting the amount of correlation that it is possible to obtain between implicit and explicit measures or with drinking measures.

4 Limitations and Future Directions for the Field

4.1 Limitations

For studying stimulus expectancies, various limitations have been identified (Martin and Sayette, 1993). One limitation is that the ability to disguise whether the drink contains alcohol or not is not usually possible above about 0.07 g% breath alcohol level. Second, BPD studies of cocaine will be difficult to conduct until good placebos for intranasal or smoked routes of administration are available. Third, since people also see through the deception if they stand up, the deception cannot be maintained over longer periods of time. For studies of beverage placebos generally, a limitation of many studies outside the balanced placebo design literature is that the use of placebo beverages, such as whiskey with orange juice, has been found to be ineffective, and another limitation is failing to assess the effectiveness of the deception, leaving the studies confounded (problem identified by Rohsenow and Marlatt, 1981). However, the body of balanced placebo literature has added important information about the domains of behavior where expected effects may play as strong or stronger a role in behavior as pharmacologic effects. While stimulus expectancy designs have little clinical application, the results can be used clinically in helping people to understand that many of the social and emotional effects of alcohol may be generated from within oneself and can be obtained by other means.

For measures of outcome expectancies, several limitations can be identified. First, a number of measures that were derived based on beliefs of university students, mostly without any clinical problems and often with limited or no use history, have been applied in clinical populations without regard to the fact the expectancies of substance-dependent individuals might be broader or different in a number of ways. More measures derived from clinical populations are needed for clinical use. Second, several measures ask about the substance effects on people in general, yet conclusions are drawn that this indicates their beliefs about the substance effects on themselves, a conclusion not supported when disaggregated by Rohsenow (1983). Third, measures have still not been developed for several substances such as opiates and other street drugs. Fourth, measures of implicit expectancies seem to be weaker predictors of behavior than measures of explicit expectancies, at least in research to date. Also, while explicit expectancies can have utility in clinical practice in identifying effects that a patient needs to find alternative non-drug ways to achieve, as yet there are few clinical uses for implicit measures of expectancies. However, in understanding basic processes underlying substance use and abuse, implicit measures complement and add information beyond that which is identified by explicit measures of expectancies, and so may lead to further understanding and theoretical models of the cognitive underpinnings of substance use and abuse.

4.2   Future directions

The balanced placebo design has potential to yield information of high scientific value and significance to public health in future research. First, there is a paucity of addiction-related research on placebo mechanisms. With few notable exceptions (Gundersen *et al.*, 2008; Volkow *et al.*, 2003; Volkow *et al.*, 2006; Wilson, Sayette, Delgado, and Fiez, 2005), biobehavioral mechanisms that might account for the placebo effects with drugs of abuse have not been investigated. Second, combining the BPD design for an abused substance with the examination of candidate genes for this drug is likely to be useful due to increasing demand for narrow phenotypes (e.g., pharmacologic effect of a drug independent of the expectancy effects). Third, a BPD design is also useful when studying comorbid substance abuse or the interactive influence of drugs. For example, given the learned association between alcohol use and cigarette smoking

(Rohsenow *et al.*, 1997), the effects of alcohol use on craving for cigarettes may reflect expectancy processes as well as pharmacologic ones. BPD has been used to study pharmacologic versus expectancy effects of moderate alcohol doses on smoking urges (Sayette *et al.*, 2005) and on smokers' ability to resist initiating smoking when smoking abstinence was monetarily incentivized (Kahler *et al.*, 2012). Finally, the BPD methodology could be used to examine the neurobiological mechanisms underlying the placebo response following an expectancy manipulation using functional brain imaging. Evidence indicates that expectancy interacts with the same neurobiological systems as a given medication such as an analgesic, an anti-Parkinsonian drug, or an anti-depressant (Benedetti *et al.*, 2005).

Future work with outcome expectancies could include several aspects. First, measures of expectancies for other drugs need to be developed. This is particularly true for implicit expectancies, where the work has mainly involved alcohol. Second, more development of ways to understand the effects expected of one substance on the concurrent use of another substance would be of value, for better studying and understanding comorbid use and abuse. Third, the study of the expected effects of abstaining from a substance is in its infancy, yet could be clinically very useful. This should be extended to all substances that can be abused. Fourth, more work needs to be conducted in clinical populations, as so much of the existing work is on populations without clinical needs. This would extend our knowledge better from non-clinical to clinical populations. Studying change across stages of change, similar to the work of Prochaska and colleagues (1994), or across non-treatment seekers, treatment seekers, those in treatment, and those in lasting recovery would add information that might improve our understanding of factors associated with each of those stages. This could lead to improvements in treatment and relapse prevention approaches.

4.3   Conclusions

With improved knowledge of the unique contribution of non-pharmacological factors such as expectancy to treatment outcome, treatment providers can boost people's expectancies for the effect of a drug without the use of stronger doses. Specific instructions may enhance treatment effect (e.g., information that treatment is efficacious), reducing the risks of side-effects and lessening the costs of medical care (Stewart-Williams and Podd, 2004). An accurate description of powerful placebo effects and positive expectations from treatment would be an ethical and effective approach in clinical trials. An open-label randomized clinical trial without any deception or concealment demonstrated significant and clinically meaningful symptom improvement for patients receiving placebo relative to a no-treatment control group in patients with irritable bowel syndrome (Kaptchuk, Friedlander *et al.*, 2010). Better understanding of the effects people explicitly expect from alcohol, tobacco, and other substances could improve future prevention methods and treatment approaches, by better tailoring interventions to address the effects people seek and increasing awareness of effects people might prefer not to experience so as to moderate or curtail use.

References

Aarons GA, Brown SA, Tice E, and Coe MT (2001) Psychometric evaluation of the marijuana and stimulant effect expectancy questionnaires for adolescents. *Addict Behav* 26: 219–236. doi: 10.1016/S0306-4603(00)00103-9.

Abrams DB and Niaura RS (1987) Social learning theory. In HT Blane and KE Leonard (eds), *Psychological Theories of Drinking and Alcoholism* (pp. 131–178). New York: Guilford Press.

Anderson KG, Grunwald I, Bekman N, Brown SA and Grant A (2011) To drink or not to drink: Motives and expectancies for use and nonuse in adolescence. *Addict Behav* 36: 972–979. doi: 10.1016/j.addbeh.2011.05.009.

Anderson KG, Smith GT, and Fisher SF (2003) Women and acquired preparedness: Personality and learning implications for alcohol use. *J Stud Alcohol* 64: 384–392.

Asher MK, Martin RA, Rohsenow DJ, MacKinnon SV, Traficante R, and Monti PM (2003) Perceived barriers to quitting smoking among alcohol dependent patients in treatment. *J Subst Abuse Treat* 24: 169–174. doi: 10.1016/S0740-5472(02)00354-9.

Bandura A (1986) *Social Foundations of Thought and Action: A Social Cognitive Theory*. Englewood Cliffs, NJ: Prentice Hall.

Bekman NM, Anderson KG, Trim RS, Metrik J, Diulio AR, Myers MG, and Brown SA (2011) Thinking and drinking: Alcohol-related cognitions across stages of adolescent alcohol involvement. *Psychol Addict Behav* 25: 415–425. doi: 10.1037/a0023302.

Benedetti F, Mayberg HS, Wager TD, Stohler CS, and Zubieta JK (2005) Neurobiological mechanisms of the placebo effect. *J Neurosci* 25: 10390–10402. doi: 10.1523/JNEUROSCI.3458-05.2005.

Brandon TH and Baker TB (1991) The smoking consequences questionnaire: The subjected expected utility of smoking in college students. *Psychol Assessment* 3: 484–491. doi: 10.1037/1040-3590.3.3.484.

Brown SA (1985) Reinforcement expectancies and alcoholism treatment outcome after a one-year follow-up. *J Stud Alcohol* 46: 304–308.

Brown SA (1993) Drug effect expectancies and addictive behavior change. *Exp Clin Psychopharmacol* 1: 55–67. doi: 10.1037/1064-1297.1.1-4.55.

Brown SA, Carello PD, Vik PW, and Porter RJ (1998) Change in alcohol effect and self-efficacy expectancies during addiction treatment. *Subst Abuse* 19: 155–167. doi: 10.1080/08897079809511384.

Brown SA, Christiansen BA, and Goldman MS (1987) The Alcohol Expectancy Questionnaire: An instrument for the assessment of adolescent and adult alcohol expectancies. *J Stud Alcohol* 48: 483–491.

Brown SA, Goldman MS, Inn A, and Anderson LR (1980) Expectations of reinforcement from alcohol: Their domain and relation to drinking patterns. *J Cons Clin Psychol* 48: 419–426. doi: 10.1037/0022-006X.48.4.419.

Chait LD and Pierri J (1989) Some physical characteristics of NIDA marijuana cigarettes. *Addict Beh* 14: 61–67. doi: 10.1016/0306-4603(89)90017-8.

Chen Y-C, Prescott CA, Walsh D, Patterson DG, Riley BP, Kendler KS, and Kuo P-H (2011) Different phenotypic and genotypic presentations in alcohol dependence: Age matters. *J Stud Alc Drugs* 72: 752–762.

Christiansen BA, Goldman MS, and Brown SA (1985) The differential development of adolescent alcohol expectancies may predict adult alcoholism. *Addict Beh* 10: 299–306. doi: 10.1016/0306-4603(85)90011-5.

Christiansen BA, Goldman MS, and Inn A (1982) Development of alcohol-related expectancies in adolescents: Separating pharmacological from social learning influences. *J Cons Clin Psychol* 50: 336–344. doi: 10.1037/0022-006X.50.3.336.

Connors GJ, O'Farrell TJ, and Pelcovits MA (1988) Drinking outcome expectancies among male alcoholics during relapse situations. *Brit J Addict* 83: 561–566.

Copeland AL, Brandon TH, and Quinn EP (1995) The Smoking Consequences Questionnaire–Adult: Measurement of smoking outcome expectancies of experienced smokers. *Psychol Assessment* 7: 484–494. doi: 10.1037/1040-3590.7.4.484.

Curtin JJ, McCarthy DE, Piper ME, and Baker TB (2006) Implicit and explicit drug motivational processes: A model of boundary conditions. In RW Wiers and AW Stacy (eds), *The Handbook of Implicit Cognition and Addiction* (pp. 233–250). Thousand Oaks, CA: Sage.

Darkes J and Goldman MS (1993) Expectancy challenge and drinking reduction: Experimental evidence for a mediational process. *J Consult Clin Psychol* 61: 344–353. doi: 10.1037/0022-006X.61.2.344.

Darkes J and Goldman MS (1998) Expectancy challenge and drinking reduction: Process and structure in the alcohol expectancy network. *Exp Clin Psychopharmacol* 6: 64–76. doi: 10.1037/1064-1297.6.1.64.

De Houwer J and De Bruycker E (2007) The implicit association test outperforms the extrinsic affective Simon task as an implicit measure of inter-individual differences in attitudes. *Br J Soc Psychol* 46 (Pt 2): 401–421.

Dunn ME and Goldman MS (1998) Age and drinking-related differences in the memory organization of alcohol expectancies in 3rd-, 6th-, 9th-, and 12th-grade children. *J Consult Clin Psychol* 66: 579–585. doi: 10.1037/0022-006X.66.3.579.

Dunn ME, Lau HC, and Cruz IY (2000) Changes in activation of alcohol expectancies in memory in relation to changes in alcohol use after participation in an expectancy challenge program. *Exp Clin Psychopharmacol* 8: 566–575. doi: 10.1037/1064-1297.8.4.566.

Edwards W (1954) The theory of decision making. *Psychol Bull* 51: 380–417. doi: 10.1037/h0053870.

Egloff B, Schwerdtfeger A, and Schmukle SC (2005) Temporal stability and the Implicit Association Test–Anxiety. *J Pers Assess* 84: 82–88. doi: 10.1207/s15327752jpa8401_14.

Field M (2005) Cannabis "dependence" and attentional bias for cannabis-related words. *Behav Pharmacol* 16: 473–476.

Fillmore MT and Blackburn J (2002) Compensating for alcohol-induced impairment: Alcohol expectancies and behavioral disinhibition. *Journal of Studies on Alcohol* 63: 237–246.

Fillmore MT, Mulvihill LE, and Vogel-Sprott M (1994) The expected drug and its expected effect interact to determine placebo responses to alcohol and caffeine. *Psychopharmacology* 115: 383–388.

Fillmore MT, Roach E, and Rice J (2002) Does caffeine counteract alcohol-induced impairment? The ironic effects of expectancy. *Journal of Studies on Alcohol* 63: 745–754.

Fillmore MT and Vogel-Sprott M (1995) Behavioral effects of combining alcohol and caffeine: The contribution of drug-related expectancies. *Experimental and Clinical Psychopharmacology* 3: 33–38.

Fillmore MT and Vogel-Sprott M (1996) Evidence that expectancies mediate behavioral impairment under alcohol. *J Stud Alc* 57: 598–603.

Fromme K, Katz E, and D'Amico E (1997) Effects of alcohol intoxication on the perceived consequences of risk taking. *Exp Clin Psychopharmacol* 5: 14–23. doi: 10.1037/1064-1297.5.1.14.

Fromme K, Stroot E, and Kaplan D (1993) Comprehensive effects of alcohol: Development and psychometric assessment of a new alcohol expectancy questionnaire. *Psychol Assessment* 5: 19–26. doi: 10.1037/1040-3590.5.1.19.

Galen LW and Henderson MJ (1999) Validation of cocaine and marijuana effect expectancies in a treatment setting. *Addict Beh* 24: 719–724. doi: 10.1016/S0306-4603(98) 00110-5.

Garbutt JC, Kranzler HR, O'Malley SS, Gastfriend DR, Pettinati HM, Silverman BL, *et al.* (2005) Efficacy and tolerability of long-acting injectable naltrexone for alcohol dependence: A randomized controlled trial. *JAMA* 293: 1617–1625. doi: 10.1001/jama.293.13.1617.

Godding PR and Glasgow RE (1985) Self-efficacy and outcome expectations as predictors of controlled smoking status. *Cog Ther Res* 9: 583–590. doi:10.1007/BF01173011.

Goldman MS, Brown SA, Christiansen BA, and Smith GT (1991) Alcoholism and memory: Broadening the scope of alcohol-expectancy research. *Psychol Bull* 110: 137–146. doi: 10.1037/0033-2909.110.1.137.

Goldman MS, Darkes J, and Del Boca FK (1999) Expectancies mediation of biopsychosocial risk for alcohol use and alcoholism. In I Kirsch (ed.), *How Expectancies Shape Experience* (pp. 233–262). Washington, DC: American Psychological Association.

Gundersen H, Specht K, Gruner R, Ersland L, and Hugdahl K (2008) Separating the effects of alcohol and expectancy on brain activation: An fMRI working memory study. *Neuroimage* 42: 1587–1596. doi: 10.1016/j.neuroimage.2008.05.037.

Gwaltney CJ, Shiffman S, Balabanis MH, and Paty JA (2005) Dynamic self-efficacy and outcome expectancies: Prediction of smoking lapse and relapse. *J Abnorm Psychol* 114: 661–675. doi: 10.1037/0021-843X.114.4.661.

Haney M, Gunderson EW, Jiang H, Collins ED, and Foltin RW (2010) Cocaine-specific antibodies blunt the subjective effects of smoked cocaine in humans. *Biol Psychiatry* 67: 59–65. doi: 10.1016/j.biopsych.2009.08.031.

Harrell PT and Juliano LM (2009) Caffeine expectancies influence the subjective and behavioral effects of caffeine. *Psychopharmacology (Berlin)* 207: 335–342. doi: 10.1007/s00213-009-1658-5.

Hayaki J, Hagerty CE, Herman DS, de Dios MA, Anderson BJ, and Stein MD (2010) Expectancies and marijuana use frequency and severity among young females. *Addict Behav* 35: 995–1000. doi: 10.1016/j.addbeh.2010.06.017.

Heinz AJ, Kassel JD, and Smith EV (2009) Caffeine expectancy: Instrument development in the Rasch measurement framework. *Psychol Addict Behav* 23: 500–511 doi: 10.1037/a0016654.

Hendricks PS, Wood SB, Baker MR, Delucchi KL, and Hall SM (2011) The Smoking Abstinence Questionnaire: Measurement of smokers abstinence-related expectancies. *Addiction* 106: 716–728. doi: 10.1111/j.1360-0443.2010.03338.x.

Howland J, Rohsenow D, Calise TV, MacKillop J, and Metrik J (2011) Caffeinated alcoholic beverages: An emerging public health problem. *Am J Prev Med* 40: 268–271. doi: 10.1016/j.amepre.2010.10.026.

Hull JG and Bond CF (1986) Social and behavioral consequences of alcohol consumption and expectancy: A meta-analysis. *Psychol Bull* 99: 347–360. doi: 10.1037/0033-2909.99.3.347.

Jones BT and MacMahon J (1994) Negative alcohol expectancy predicts post-treatment abstinence survivorship: The whether, when and why of relapse to a first drink. *Addiction* 89: 1653–1665. doi:10.1111/j.1360-0443.1994.tb03766.x.

Jones BT, Corbin W, and Fromme K (2001) A review of expectancy theory and alcohol consumption. *Addiction* 96: 57–72. doi: 10.1080/09652140020016969.

Juliano LM and Brandon TH (2002) Effects of nicotine dose, instructional set, and outcome expectancies on the subjective effects of smoking in the presence of a stressor. *J Abnorm Psychol* 111: 88–97. doi: 10.1037/0021-843X.111.1.88.

Juliano LM, Fucito LM, and Harrell PT (2011) The influence of nicotine dose and nicotine dose expectancy on the cognitive and subjective effects of cigarette smoking. *Exp Clin Psychopharmacol*, 19: 105–115. doi: 10.1037/a0022937.

Kahler CW, Metrik J, Spillane NS, Leventhal AM, McKee SA, Tidey JW, McGeary JE, Knopik VS, and Rohsenow DJ (2012) Sex differences in stimulus expectancy and pharmacologic effects of a moderate dose of alcohol on smoking lapse risk in a laboratory analogue study. *Psychopharmacology* 222:71–80.

Kaptchuk TJ, Friedlander E, Kelley JM, Sanchez MN, Kokkotou E, Singer JP, *et al.* (2010) Placebos without deception: A randomized controlled trial in irritable bowel syndrome. *PLoS One* 5: e15591. doi: 10.1371/journal.pone.0015591.

Keane TM, Lisman, SA, and Kreutzer J (1980) Alcoholic beverages and their placebos: An empirical evaluation of expectancies. *Addict Beh* 5: 313–328. doi: 10.1016/0306-4603(80)90005-2.

Kelemen WL and Kaighobadi F (2007) Expectancy and pharmacology influence the subjective effects of nicotine in a balanced-placebo design. *Exp Clin Psychopharmacol* 15: 93–101. doi: 10.1037/1064-1297.15.1.93.

Khan A, Redding N, and Brown WA (2008) The persistence of the placebo response in antidepressant clinical trials. *J Psychiatr Res* 42: 791–796. doi: 10.1016/j.jpsychires.2007.10.004.

Khan A, Warner HA, and Brown WA (2000) Symptom reduction and suicide risk in patients treated with placebo in antidepressant clinical trials: An analysis of the Food and Drug Administration database. *Arch Gen Psychiatry* 57: 311–317.

Kirsch I and Sapirstein G (1999) Listening to Prozac but hearing placebo: A meta-analysis of antidepressant medications. In I Kirsch (ed.), *How Expectancies Shape Experience* (pp. 303–320). Washington, DC: American Psychological Association.

Kramer DA and Goldman MS (2003) Using a modified Stroop task to implicitly discern the cognitive organization of alcohol expectancies. *J Abnorm Psychol* 112: 171–175. doi: 10.1037/0021-843X.112.1.171.

Lundahl LH and Lukas SE (2007) Negative cocaine effect expectancies are associated with subjective response to cocaine challenge in recreational cocaine users. *Addict Beh* 32: 1262–1271. doi: 10.1016/j.addbeh.2006.09.001.

Malmberg M, Overbeek G, Vermulst AA, Monshouwer K, Vollebergh WAM, and Engels RC (2012) The theory of planned behavior: Precursors of marijuana use in early adolescence? *Drug Alcohol Depend* 123: 22-8.

Marlatt GA and Donovan DM (2005) *Relapse Prevention: Maintenance Strategies in the Treatment of Addictive Behaviors* (2nd edn). New York: Guilford Press.

Marlatt GA and Rohsenow DJ (1980) Cognitive processes in alcohol use: Expectancy and the balanced placebo design. In NK Mello (ed.), *Advances in Substance Abuse: Behavioral and Biological Research* (pp. 159–199). Greenwich, CT: JAI Press.

Marlatt GA, Demming B, and Reid JB (1973) Loss of control drinking in alcoholics: An experimental analogue. *J Abnorm Psychol* 81: 233–241. doi: 10.1037/h0034532.

Martin CS and Sayette MA (1993) Experimental design in alcohol administration research: Limitations and alternatives in the manipulation of dosage-set. *J Stud Alcohol* 54 (6): 750–761.

Martin RA, Rohsenow DJ, MacKinnon SV, Abrams DA, and Monti PM (2006) Correlates of motivation to quit smoking among alcohol dependent patients in residential treatment. *Drug Alcohol Depend* 83: 73–78. doi: 10.1016/j.drugalcdep.2005.10.013.

McCarthy DM, Kroll LS, and Smith GT (2001) Integrating disinhibition and learning risk for alcohol use. *Exp Clin Psychopharmacol*, 9: 389–398. doi: 10.1037/1064-1297.9.4.389.

McCarthy DM, Miller TL, Smith GT, and Smith JA (2001) Disinhibition and expectancy in risk for alcohol use: Comparing black and white college samples. *J Stud Alcohol* 62(3), 313–321.

McEvoy CL, Nelson DL, and Komatsu T (1999) What is the connection between true and false memories? The differential roles of iteritem associations in recall and recognition. *J Exp Psychol Learn* 25: 1177–1194. doi: 10.1037/0278-7393.25.5.1177.

McKay D and Schare ML (1999) The effects of alcohol and alcohol expectancies on subjective reports and physiological reactivity: A meta-analysis. *Addict Beh* 24: 633–647. doi: 10.1016/S0306-4603(99)00021-0.

Metrik J, Kahler CW, McGeary JE, Monti PM, and Rohsenow DJ (2011) Acute effects of marijuana smoking on negative and positive affect. *J Cogn Psychother* 25: 31–46. doi: 10.1891/0889-8391.25.1.31.

Metrik J, Kahler CW, Reynolds B, McGeary JE, Monti PM, Haney M, de Wit H, and Rohsenow DJ (2012) Balanced-placebo design with marijuana: pharmacologicaland expectancy effects on impulsivity and risk taking.*Psychopharmacology*, 223 (4), 489-499.

Metrik J, McCarthy, DM, Frissell KC, and Brown SA (2003) Predictive validity of adolescent alcohol cessation expectancies: A prospective analysis. *Alc Clin Exp Res* 27: 105A.

Metrik J, McCarthy DM, Frissell KC, MacPherson L, and Brown SA (2004) Adolescent alcohol reduction and cessation expectancies. *J Stud Alcohol* 65: 217–226.

Metrik J, Rohsenow DJ, Monti PM, McGeary J, Cook TA, de Wit H, *et al.* (2009) Effectiveness of a marijuana expectancy manipulation: Piloting the balanced-placebo design for marijuana. *Exp Clin Psychopharmacol* 17: 217–225. doi: 10.1037/a0016502.

Miller PM, Smith GT, and Goldman MS (1990) Emergence of alcohol expectancies in childhood: a possible critical period. *J Stud Alcohol* 51: 343–349.

Monti PM, Kadden R, Rohsenow DJ, Cooney N, and Abrams DB (2002) *Treating Alcohol Dependence: A Coping Skills Training Guide* (2nd edn). New York: Guilford Press.

Moss AC and Albery IP (2009) A dual-process model of the alcohol-behavior link for social drinking. *Psychol Bull* 135: 516–530. doi: 10.1037/a0015991.

Moss AC and Albery IP (2010) Are alcohol expectancies associations, propositions, or elephants? A reply to Weirs and Stacy (2010). *Psychol Bull* 136: 17–20. doi: 10.1037/a0018087.

Palfai TP and Wood MD (2001) Positive alcohol expectancies and drinking behavior: The influence of expectancy strength and memory accessibility. *Psychol Addict Behav* 15 (1): 60–67. doi: 10.1037/0893-164X.15.1.60.

Palfai TP, Monti PM, Ostafin B, and Hutchison K (2000) Effects of nicotine deprivation on alcohol-related information processing and drinking behavior. *J Abnorm Psychol* 109: 96–105.

Perkins K, Jacobs L, Ciccocioppo M, Conklin C, Sayette M, and Caggiula A (2004) The influence of instructions and nicotine dose on the subjective and reinforcing effects of smoking. *Exp Clin Psychopharm* 12: 91–101. doi: 10.1037/1064-1297.12.2.91.

Perkins K, Sayette M, Conklin C, and Caggiula A (2003) Placebo effects of tobacco smoking and other nicotine intake. *Nicotine Tob Res* 5 (5): 695–709. doi: 10.1080/1462220031000158636.

Powell J, Tait S, and Lessiter J (2002) Cigarette smoking and attention to signals of reward and threat in the Stroop paradigm. *Addiction* 97: 1163–1170.

Price DD, Finniss DG, and Benedetti F (2008) A comprehensive review of the placebo effect: Recent advances and current thought. *Annu Rev Psychol* 59: 565–590. doi: 10.1146/annurev.psych.59.113006.095941.

Prochaska JO, Velicer WF, Rossi JS, Goldstein MG, Marcus BH, Rakowski W, Fiore C, Harlow LL, Redding CA, Rosenbloom D, and Rossi SR (1994) Stages of change and decisional balance for 12 problem behaviors. *Health Psychol* 13: 39–46. doi: 10.1037/0278-6133.13.1.39.

Read JP, Wood MD, Lejuez CW, Palfai TP, and Slack M (2004) Gender, alcohol consumption, and differing alcohol expectancy dimensions in college drinkers. *Exp Clin Psychopharmacol* 12: 298–308. doi: 10.1037/1064-1297.12.4.298.

Reich RR, Below MC, and Goldman MS (2010) Explicit and implicit measures of expectancy and related alcohol cognitions: A meta-analytic comparison. *Psychol Addict Beh* 24: 13–25. doi: 10.1037/a0016556.

Reich RR, Goldman, MS, and Noll JA (2004) Using the false memory paradigm to test two key elements of alcohol expectancy theory. *Exp Clin Psychopharmacol* 12: 102–110. doi: 10.1037/1064-1297.12.2.102.

Rohsenow DJ (1983) Drinking habits and expectancies about alcohol's effects for self versus others. *J Cons Clin Psychol* 51: 752–756. doi: 10.1037/0022-006X.51.5.752.

Rohsenow DJ (1995) Alcohol Effects Questionnaire. In JP Allen and M Columbus (eds), *Assessing Alcohol Problems: A Guide for Clinicians and Researchers* (pp. 208–212). Rockville, MD: National Institute on Alcohol Abuse and Alcoholism.

Rohsenow DJ and Bachorowski J (1984) Effects of alcohol and expectancies on verbal aggression in men and women. *J Abnorm Psychol* 93: 418–432. doi: 10.1037/0021-843X.93.4.418.

Rohsenow DJ and Marlatt GA (1981) The balanced placebo design: Methodological considerations. *Addict Beh* 6: 107–122. doi: 10.1016/0306-4603(81)90003-4.

Rohsenow DJ and Pinkston-Camp MM (in press) Cognitive-behavioral approaches. In KJ Sher (ed.), *Oxford Handbook of Substance Use Disorders*.New York: Oxford University Press.

Rohsenow DJ, Abrams DB, Monti PM, Colby SM, Martin RA, and Niaura RS (2003) The Smoking Effects Questionnaire for adult populations: Development and psychometric properties. *Addict Beh* 28: 1257–1270. doi: 10.1016/S0306-4603(02)00254-X.

Rohsenow DJ, Colby SM, Martin RA, and Monti PM (2005) Nicotine and Other Substance Interaction Expectancies questionnaire: Relationship of expectancies to substance use. *Addict Beh* 30: 629–641. doi: 10.1016/j.addbeh.2005.01.001.

Rohsenow DJ, Monti PM, Abrams DB, Rubonis AV, Niaura RS, Sirota AD, and Colby SM (1992) Cue elicited urge to drink and salivation in alcoholics: Relationship to individual differences. *Adv Beh Res Ther* 14: 195–210. doi: 10.1016/0146-6402(92)90008-C.

Rohsenow DJ, Monti PM, Colby SM, and Martin RA (2002) Brief interventions for smoking cessation in alcoholic smokers. *Alcohol Clin Exp Res* 26: 1950–1951. doi:10.1111/j.1530-0277.2002.tb02515.x.

Rohsenow DJ, Monti PM, Colby SM, Gulliver SB, Sirota AD, Niaura RS, and Abrams DB (1997) Effects of alcohol cues on smoking urges and topography among alcoholic men. *Alcohol Clin Exp Res* 21 (1): 101–107.

Rohsenow DJ, Monti PM, Rubonis AV, Sirota AD, Niaura RS, Colby SM, Wunschel SM, and Abrams DB (1994) Cue reactivity as a predictor of drinking among male alcoholics. *J Cons Clin Psychol* 62: 620–626. doi: 10.1037/0022-006X.62.3.620.

Rohsenow DJ, Sirota AD, Martin RA, and Monti PM (2004) The Cocaine Effects Questionnaire for patient populations: Development and psychometric properties. *Addict Beh* 29: 537–553. doi: 10.1016/j.addbeh.2003.08.024.

Rooke SE, Hine DW, and Thorsteinsson EB (2008) Implicit cognition and substance use: A meta-analysis. *Addict Beh* 33: 1314–1328. doi: 10.1016/j.addbeh.2008.06.009.

Sayette MA, Martin CS, Wertz JM, Perrott MA, and Peters AR (2005) The effects of alcohol on cigarette craving in heavy smokers and tobacco chippers. *Psychol Addict Behav* 19 (3): 263–270. doi: 10.1037/0893-164X.19.3.263.

Schafer J and Brown SA (1991) Marijuana and cocaine effect expectancies and drug use patterns. *J Consult Clin Psych* 59: 558–565. doi: 10.1037/0022-006X.59.4.558.

Schafer J and Fals-Stewart W (1993) Effect expectancies for cocaine intoxication: Initial vs. descendent phases. *Addict Beh* 18: 171–177. doi: 10.1016/0306-4603(93)90047-D.

Schafer J and Fals-Stewart W (1996) Measuring cocaine effect expectancies among therapeutic community inpatients. *Addict Beh* 21: 205–210. doi: 10.1016/0306-4603(96)00046-9.

Schlauch RC, Waesche MC, Riccardi CJ, Donohue KF, Blagg CO, Christensen RL, et al. (2010) A meta-analysis of the effectiveness of placebo manipulations in alcohol-challenge studies. *Psychol Addict Behav* 24: 239–253. doi: 10.1037/a0017709.

Schneider R, Gruner M, Heiland A, et al. (2006) Effects of expectation and caffeine on arousal, well-being, and reaction time. *Int J Behav Med* 13: 330–339. doi: 10.1207/s15327558ijbm1304_8.

Shadel WG and Mermelstein RJ (1993) Cigarette smoking under stress: The role of coping expectancies among smokers in a clinic-based smoking cessation program. *Health Psychol* 12: 443–450. doi: 10.1037/0278-6133.12.6.443.

Sher KJ, Wood MD, Wood PK, and Raskin G (1996) Alcohol outcome expectancies and alcohol use: A latent variable cross-lagged panel study. *J Abnorm Psychol* 105: 561–574. doi: 10.1037/0021-843X.105.4.561.

Smith GT and Anderson KG (2001) Personality and learning factors combine to create risk for adolescent problem drinking: A model and suggestions for intervention. In PM Monti, SM Colby, and TA O'Leary (eds), *Adolescents, Alcohol, and Substance Abuse: Reaching Teens through Brief Interventions* (pp. 109–141). New York: Guilford Press. doi: 10.1037/0021-843X.104.1.32.

Smith GT, Goldman MS, Greenbaum PE, and Christiansen BA (1995) Expectancy for social facilitation from drinking: The divergent paths of high-expectancy and low-expectancy adolescents. *J Abnorm Psychol* 104: 32–40.

Stacy AW, Ames SL, and Grenard J (2006) Word association tests of associative memory and implicit processes: Theoretical and assessment issues. In RW Wiers and AW Stacy (eds), *The Handbook of Implicit Cognition and Addiction* (pp. 75–90). Thousand Oaks, CA: Sage.

Stevens J (1992) *Applied Multivariate Statistics for the Social Sciences* (2nd edn). Hillsdale, NJ: Lawrence Erlbaum Associates.

Stewart-Williams S and Podd J (2004) The placebo effect: Dissolving the expectancy versus conditioning debate. *Psychol Bull* 130: 324–340. doi: 10.1037/0033-2909.130.2.324.

Testa M, Fillmore MT, Norris J, Abbey A, Curtin JJ, Leonard KE, et al. (2006) Understanding alcohol expectancy effects: Revisiting the placebo condition. *Alcohol Clin Exp Res* 30: 339–348. doi: 10.1111/j.1530-0277.2006.00039.x.

Vangsness L, Bry BH, and LaBouvie EW (2005) Impulsivity, negative expectancies, and marijuana use: A test of the acquired preparedness model. *Addict Behav* 30: 1071–1076. doi: 10.1016/j.addbeh.2004.11.003.

Velicer WF, DiClemente CC, Prochaska JO, and Brandenburg N (1985) Decisional balance measure for predicting smoking status. *J Pers Soc Psychol* 48: 1279–1280. doi: 10.1037/0022-3514.48.5.1279.

Vogel-Sprott M and Fillmore MT (1999) Expectancy and behavioral effects of socially used drugs. In EI Kirsch (ed.), *How Expectancies Shape Experience* (pp. 215–232). Washington, DC: American Psychological Association.

Volkow ND, Wang GJ, Ma Y, Fowler JS, Wong C, Jayne M, et al. (2006) Effects of expectation on the brain metabolic responses to methylphenidate and to its placebo in non-drug abusing subjects. *Neuroimage* 32: 1782–1792. doi: 10.1016/j.neuroimage.2006.04.192.

Volkow ND, Wang GJ, Ma Y, Fowler JS, Zhu W, Maynard L, et al. (2003) Expectation enhances the regional brain metabolic and the reinforcing effects of stimulants in cocaine abusers. *J Neurosci* 23: 11461–11468.

Wachtel SR, ElSohly MA, Ross SA, Ambre J, and de Wit H (2002) Comparison of the subjective effects of delta-9-tetrahydrocannabinol and marijuana in humans. *Psychopharmacology* 161: 331–339.

Waters AJ, Shiffman S, Sayette MA, Paty JA, Gwaltney CJ, and Balabanis MH (2003) Attentional bias predicts outcome in smoking cessation. *Health Psychol* 22: 378–387. doi: 10.1037/0278-6133.22.4.378.

Weiss RD, O'Malley SS, Hosking JD, LoCastro JS, and Swift R (2008) Do patients with alcohol dependence respond to placebo? Results from the COMBINE Study. *J Stud Alcohol Drugs* 69: 878–884.

Wetter DW, Smith SS, Kenford SL, Jorenby DE, Fiore MC, Hurt RD, Offord KP, and Baker TB (1994) Smoking outcome expectancies: Factor structure, predictive validity, and discriminant validity. *J Abnorm Psychol* 103(4): 801–811.

Wiers RW and Kummeling RH (2004) An experimental test of an alcohol expectancy challenge in mixed gender groups of young heavy drinkers. *Addict Behav* 29: 215–220. doi: 10.1016/S0306-4603(03)00081-9.

Wiers RW and Stacy AW (2010) Are alcohol expectancies associations? Comment on Moss and Albery (2009). *Psychol Bull* 136: 12–16; discussion 17–20. doi: 10.1037/a0017769.

Wiers RW, Van Woerden N, Smuldersm FTY, and De Jong PJ (2002) Implicit and explicit alcohol-related cognitions in heavy and light drinkers. *J Abnorm Psychol* 111: 648–658. doi: 10.1037//0021-843X.111.4.648.

Wilson SJ, Sayette MA, Delgado MR, and Fiez JA (2005) Instructed smoking expectancy modulates cue-elicited neural activity: A preliminary study. *Nicotine Tob Res* 7: 637–645. doi: 10.1080/14622200500185520.

18

Implicit Cognition
Paul Christiansen and Matt Field

1 Introduction

The past two decades have seen huge growth in research investigating implicit cognitive processes in addiction. The impetus for this research stems from the observation that, in addiction, people deliberately engage in behaviors that cause great harm to their physical health, relationships, and academic and occupational achievement. Much human behavior can be viewed as the outcome of a reflective, rational decision-making process, in which people weigh the pros and cons of a given course of action before deciding how to act. Yet addiction is characterized by compulsive drug self-administration, even though addicts are aware of the harm that drug use is causing them and are often motivated to change their behavior. For addiction, rational decision making is lacking as an explanation for behavior.

Implicit cognition provides an alternative explanatory framework. Broadly defined, an implicit cognition approach assumes that behavior is influenced by "associations in memory that become spontaneously activated under various conditions . . . and channel behavior in ways that are not revealed through introspection, self-reflection, or causal attribution" (Stacy and Wiers, 2010: 552). Those authors provide an extensive discussion of what implicit cognition is, and what it is not, and we refer the reader to their excellent article rather than repeating their arguments here. However, what may be useful is to give examples of an "explicit" and "implicit" measure of alcohol-related cognitions. Most addiction researchers will be familiar with alcohol outcome expectancies (see Reich, Below, and Goldman, 2010, for a review), which are long-term memory structures in the form of explicit response–outcome contingencies: for example, "If I drink alcohol, I will feel more sociable." Outcome expectancies are usually assessed with questionnaires, in which participants indicate their degree of endorsement of statements such as this. Note that this form of assessment requires participants to introspect on their beliefs about alcohol and their past experiences with

The Wiley-Blackwell Handbook of Addiction Psychopharmacology, First Edition. Edited by James MacKillop and Harriet de Wit.
© 2013 John Wiley & Sons, Ltd. Published 2013 by John Wiley & Sons, Ltd.

it. Contrast this with an implicit association test (IAT). In this task, participants are required to rapidly categorize four types of words (related to alcohol, sodas [non-alcoholic drinks], positive words, and negative words), using only two response keys. The assumption that underlies the task is that if underlying associations between the concept "alcohol" and the concept "positive" are stronger than those between alcohol and the concept "negative," then participants should be faster to categorize the alcohol-related words when those words share a response key with positive words, rather than when alcohol words and negative words share a response key. Note that with this "implicit" measure, we can infer something about an individual's alcohol-related cognitions, but we did not ask them to introspect on their beliefs about alcohol, or past drinking experiences, in order to make this inference.

Despite their heterogeneity, all measures of "implicit cognition" have this one feature in common: they gauge automatic or spontaneous cognitions related to substances of abuse without relying on introspection, or effortful recall of previous experiences with the substance. Indeed, many researchers in the field now prefer to use the term "automatic" cognitive processes, as the term "implicit" has unwanted connotations of subliminal processing and lack of awareness. The implicit cognition approach suggests that addicts are not necessarily unaware of addiction-related stimuli, but they may be unaware of the *process* by which those stimuli influence their own behavior (Bargh and Morsella, 2008). Like other authors (De Houwer, Teige-Mocigemba, Spruyt, and Moors, 2009; Stacy and Wiers, 2010), we argue that it may be more useful to think of *spontaneous* and *automatic* processes – features of which include independence from current goals, being performed without intentions to act, lack of awareness of components of process (but not necessarily the whole process), efficiency and speed – rather than implicit or "subconscious" processes.

In this chapter, we provide a brief overview of the theoretical underpinnings of implicit cognition research, and the key findings from the past 20 years. We do not provide an exhaustive review; the interested reader is directed elsewhere for more comprehensive narrative reviews and meta-analyses (Field and Cox, 2008; Field, Munafò, and Franken, 2009; Roefs *et al.*, 2011; Rooke, Hine, and Thorsteinsson, 2008; Stacy and Wiers, 2010) or to an edited book devoted to the topic (Wiers and Stacy, 2006). The bulk of the current chapter comprises an extensive discussion of the methods used to explore implicit cognitive processes in addiction; here we identify pitfalls in the most commonly used methods, problems that arise when attempting to interpret seemingly straightforward findings, and recommendations for future research.

2 Empirical Relevance of the Topic to Substance Abuse Research

2.1 Theoretical background

Models of addiction based on neurobiological adaptations and cue reactivity converge with more general models of automaticity in cognition to provide a theoretical framework for the study of implicit cognitive processes in addiction. Firstly, the incentive sensitization theory (Robinson and Berridge, 1993; Robinson and Berridge, 2008) hypothesizes that addiction develops because chronic substance use leads to neurobiological adaptations which alter the motivational properties of drugs and drug-related cues. According to the theory, chronic drug use leads to sensitization of dopamine activity in the nucleus accumbens, resulting in aberrant incentive learning which causes drug-related cues to acquire abnormally high levels of "incentive salience." As a consequence, drug-related cues automatically command the attention and elicit behavioral approach, ultimately resulting in compulsive drug seeking.

The role of implicit cognitive processes in addiction has also been explained using memory network models that have been adopted from mainstream cognitive psychology (e.g., Anderson and Pirolli, 1984; Collins and Loftus, 1975). Generally, these models describe automatic retrieval of drug-related memories from the long-term associative store during exposure to affective triggers (e.g., negative mood) or environmental cues or contexts (e.g., the sight of a glass of beer, being in a bar) that have previously been associated with effects of the drug. This automatic retrieval of drug-related memories can, in turn, automatically initiate behavior aimed at obtaining and self-administering the drug. Similarly, Tiffany (1990) described an automaticity theory which argues that, after repeated drug self-administration when in the presence of drug-related cues (e.g., the sight of a lit cigarette), those cues are able to elicit drug-seeking behavior automatically, even in the absence of intentions to use the drug. In other words, while drug-related cues might initially elicit drug-related memories, which motivate drug-seeking behavior (stimulus–outcome–response, S–O–R learning), over time those stimuli are able to elicit drug-seeking behavior automatically, in the absence of retrieval of memories of drug effects (S–R learning). Although similar in some ways to incentive sensitization theory and memory network models, there are important differences. Tiffany's model suggests that habitual responses occur automatically after cue exposure (there is no motivational component), whereas the incentive sensitization theory posits that cues develop conditioned motivational properties (e.g., attentional bias, automatic cue approach) which then drive drug-seeking behavior.

Finally, dual process models (e.g., Wiers *et al.*, 2007; Deutsch and Strack, 2006) incorporate components of the previously described models, but they also permit more "rational" or controlled processes to influence drug-seeking behavior. These models suggest that drug use is initially the result of controlled processes (e.g., intentions to use the drug which arise from positive outcome expectancies). However, over time, chronic drug use strengthens automatic processes, making them a more powerful determinant of drug-seeking behavior, while simultaneously reducing the influence of controlled processes. When an experienced drug user makes a decision to abstain from drug use, automatic processes ("drink!") are in conflict with controlled processes ("don't drink!"). At this point, the relative strength of automatic and controlled processes dictates the behavioral outcome: powerful automatic appetitive cognitions and impaired ability to control behavior mean that the drug user will find it difficult to achieve abstinence.

Although the core theoretical underpinnings of these models are different, similar predictions about the contribution of implicit cognition to drug use can be made: (1) drug users will display automatic cognitive biases to drug-related cues, and drug-related memory distortions; (2) implicit or automatic drug-related cognitions should explain variance in drug use beyond that explained by explicit or controlled cognitive processes; and (3) manipulation of implicit or automatic drug-related cognitions should influence drug-seeking behavior.

2.2 Evidence for altered implicit cognitive processes in addiction

Although the evidence base is broad, research on implicit cognition has generally focused on biases in selective attention, automatic approach tendencies, and spontaneous memory associations. Regarding selective attention, it has been consistently demonstrated that drug-related words and pictures command the attention of smokers, heroin addicts, cocaine addicts, marijuana users, alcoholics, and heavy social drinkers (reviewed by Field and Cox, 2008). Word association and word production tasks reveal that substance abusers are biased to produce substance-related words in response to ambiguous primes (e.g., "draft," "weed"), and are likely to think of activities involving addictive substances when asked to think of the first thing that comes to mind in response to an ambiguous statement such as "having fun" (Stacy, 1994). The implicit association task (IAT) is another measure of spontaneous memory associations, which reveals that substance-related concepts are automatically associated with concepts such as positive valence, arousal, and behavioral approach in various populations, such as heavy drinkers, cocaine users, cannabis users, and tobacco smokers (reviewed by Roefs *et al.*, 2011; Stacy and Wiers, 2010). Finally, tasks that are conceptually related to the IAT reveal that substance-related cues elicit automatic approach tendencies in heavy drinkers, tobacco smokers, and cannabis users (reviewed by Stacy and Wiers, 2010).

Significantly, studies have shown that implicit measures such as these predict unique variance in individual differences in substance use, even after controlling for other important variables, including "controlled" processes such as alcohol outcome expectancies (Houben and Wiers, 2007; Houben and Wiers, 2008a; Ames and Stacy, 1998) and executive cognitive functioning (Fadardi and Cox, 2006). Similarly, Ames *et al.* (2007) found that word association tasks and implicit association tasks predicted unique variance in cannabis use in adolescents, even after controlling for working memory capacity and explicit cannabis outcome expectancies. However, in their meta-analysis of the contribution of implicit and explicit measures to alcohol consumption, Reich, Below, and Goldman (2010) found that although implicit and explicit measures (outcome expectancies) both predicted unique variance in alcohol consumption, there was a significant amount of overlap in the variance explained by the two constructs. In addition, the unique variance explained by explicit measures was significantly greater than that explained by implicit measures.

As well as predicting individual differences in drug use cross-sectionally, measures of implicit cognition also predict variance in prospective drug use. For example, Stacy (1997) found that performance on alcohol and cannabis word association tasks predicted use of both substances at 1-month follow-up, even after controlling for explicit measures. Kelly, Masterman, and Marlatt (2005) demonstrated that word association tasks predicted alcohol consumption at 6-month follow-up after controlling for demographic variables and previous alcohol consumption. Overall, these studies highlight that implicit cognitive processes are not merely a different way of measuring explicit cognitions such as outcome expectancies; they account for unique variance in individual differences in substance use both cross-sectionally and prospectively.

To test whether there is a causal relationship between implicit cognition and drug use, recent studies have attempted to manipulate implicit cognitive processes before examining the effects on craving and drug-seeking behavior in the laboratory. Field and Eastwood (2005) found that training an attentional bias for alcohol cues led to an increase in alcohol craving and alcohol consumption. Similarly, Wiers *et al.* (2010) trained heavy drinkers to automatically approach or avoid alcohol cues; those who were trained to approach alcohol cues consumed more beer in a laboratory taste test. However, there have been numerous failures to replicate the effects of attentional retraining on beer consumption in the laboratory (Field *et al.*, 2007; Schoenmakers *et al.*, 2007). Similarly, studies that manipulated attentional bias in smokers (Attwood *et al.*, 2008; Field, Duka, Tyler, and Schoenmakers, 2009; McHugh *et al.*, 2010) have not consistently demonstrated a causal effect of attentional retraining on craving or smoking behavior. These mixed results suggest that more research is required before a causal relationship between implicit cognitive processes and craving and substance use can be confirmed.

Some studies have investigated whether individual differences in implicit cognitions can predict the likelihood of addicts achieving abstinence after a quit attempt. Attentional bias has been shown to predict relapse in alcoholics, smokers, and heroin and cocaine addicts (Cox, Hogan, Kristian, and Race, 2002; Waters *et al.*, 2003; Carpenter, Schreiber, Church, and McDowell, 2006; Marissen *et al.*, 2006), which has prompted researchers to utilize modification of implicit cognitions as a treatment intervention (either as a standalone treatment, or as an adjunct to regular treatment). For example, Fadardi and Cox (2009) trained harmful drinkers to control their automatic distraction by alcohol-related cues (attentional bias). This intervention led to a reduction in alcohol use at 3-month follow-up, although unfortunately there was no comparison control group in this study. Schoenmakers *et al.* (2010) studied a different form of attentional bias modification in a sample of abstinent alcoholics, and found that those who were trained to direct their attention away from alcohol cues took longer to relapse than a control group, although groups did not differ in overall relapse rates at 3-month follow-up. Finally, Wiers *et al.* (2011) trained automatic avoidance tendencies in response to alcohol-related cues in inpatient alcoholics and found some suggestion of reduced relapse rates, compared to a control group, at 1-year follow-up. Collectively, these findings indicate that directly altering implicit cognitions may be a viable approach to the treatment of addictions. However, it is important to note that the available trials have shown small and inconsistent effects. Until large-scale randomized controlled trials are conducted, any conclusions about the efficacy of such treatments are tentative.

3   Standardized and Validated Methods Used in the Field, including Methodological Recommendations

As noted previously, a diversity of measures are used for measuring implicit cognition in addiction research and an overview of these approaches is provided in Table 18.1. The following sections discuss each approach.

Table 18.1   Summary of measures of implicit cognition

Measure	Construct measured	Dependent variable	Key feature(s)
Approach–avoidance task	Association strength	Reaction time	Physical approach–avoid responses, irrelevant-feature categorization
Attentional blink task	Attentional bias	Target words reported	Attentional bias to words
Attentional cueing task	Attentional bias	Reaction time	Attentional bias to single cue, variable SOA
Dual task paradigms	Attentional bias	Reaction time	Interference in performance produced by drug vs. neutral cues
Extrinsic Affective Simon Task	Association strength	Reaction time	Irrelevant-feature categorization, relative association strength
Flicker-induced change blindness	Attentional bias	Reaction time	Change detection
Implicit association test (bipolar)	Association strength	Reaction time	Relevant-feature categorization, relative association strength
Implicit association test (unipolar)	Association strength	Reaction time	Relevant-feature categorization, absolute association strength
Stimulus–response compatibility	Association strength	Reaction time	Symbolic approach–avoid responses, relevant-feature categorization
Stroop	Attentional bias	Reaction time/errors	Attentional bias to words, multiple formats
Visual probe	Attentional bias	Reaction time/eye movements	Attentional bias to competing cues, variable SOA
Word association:			
Cue-behavior	Association strength	Words produced (drug/neutral)	Ambiguous drug cue presented
Outcome-behavior	Association strength	Words produced (drug/neutral)	Ambiguous outcome presented
Drug cue	Association strength	Words produced (outcome)	Drug cue presented

3.1   Attentional bias measures

3.1.1 Addiction Stroop. In the addiction Stroop task, substance-related and matched neutral words are presented in colored font, and participants are required to rapidly identify the color in which words are printed, regardless of their semantic content. For example, if the word "Beer" is presented in red font, the correct response would be "red." Pictorial versions of the task, in which substance-related and matched neutral pictures are presented with colored borders, have also been used (e.g., Bruce and Jones, 2004; Hester, Dixon, and Garavan, 2006). Participants identify stimulus colors either verbally or with a forced-choice manual response, or a combination of the two. Cox, Fadardi, and Pothos (2006) identified a number of important moderators of the size of Stroop effects. Firstly, and perhaps surprisingly, effect sizes were negatively correlated with the total number of trials: that is, effect sizes were larger when a relatively small number of trials were used. This perhaps reflects habituation to the addiction-related stimuli over the course of extended testing periods, leading to a reduction in overall effect size. Larger effect sizes were also associated with increased consistency between substance-related and neutral word lists in terms of linguistic features such as word length, semantic relatedness, and frequency of occurrence in the language (i.e., good matching of word lists on these dimensions is important). It was also noted that combined vocal and manual measurement of color-naming produced larger effect sizes than vocal measurement alone, which was in turn preferable to manual measurement alone.

Cox, Fadardi, and Pothos (2006) identified two additional moderators which shed light on the cognitive mechanisms that underlie interference effects in the addiction Stroop. Firstly, effect sizes were larger with a card presentation format than a computer presentation format. With the card presentation format, a list of substance-related (or neutral) words is presented on a card, and participants must color-name each word on the card, before moving on to the next card containing neutral (or substance-related) words. With the computer presentation format, words are individually presented on a computer screen, and trials may be presented in a random order (i.e., substance-related and matched neutral words are intermixed), or in sub-blocks (i.e., all substance-related words are presented in one sub-block, and all neutral words are presented in a different sub-block). With studies that used a computerized presentation format, effect sizes were larger when a blocked rather than unblocked format was used, although this effect was only seen for the smoking Stroop, not the alcohol Stroop (but see Waters, Sayette, Franken, and Schwartz, 2005, for further demonstrations of larger effect sizes for Stroop interference with blocked presentations in various populations).

Why would Stroop effects be larger when addiction-related words are blocked together, rather than randomly intermixed with neutral words? Demonstrations of "carryover" effects in the addiction Stroop (Waters, Sayette, Franken, and Schwartz, 2005; Waters, Sayette, and Wertz, 2003) suggest one explanation. Waters, Sayette, Franken, and Schwartz (2005) and Waters, Sayette, and Wertz (2003) re-analyzed data from a number of addiction Stroop studies that used the computerized Stroop, and demonstrated that color-naming times for *neutral* words were slower on trials when those words were presented immediately after addiction-related words, compared to trials when they were presented immediately after another neutral word. Cane, Sharma, and Albery (2009) and Sharma and Money (2010) demonstrated that the carryover effects (from addiction-related words) led to slowed color naming of neutral words for up to three trials after presentation of an addiction-related word. Therefore, addiction-related words seem to slow color naming not only while those words are presented, but for several seconds afterwards. This explains why Stroop interference effects are larger when addiction-related words are blocked together: cumulative carryover effects substantially slow color-naming times for addiction words, and color-naming times for neutral words are not contaminated by previously presented addiction-related words. By contrast, when addiction-related and neutral words are intermixed within the same block, color-naming times for neutral words are contaminated by carryover effects, thereby obscuring overall differences in color-naming speed between addiction-related and neutral words.

The presence of carryover effects suggests that Stroop interference may not arise purely as a result of a bias in selective attention for addiction-related words. In a seminal paper, Algom, Chajut, and Lev (2004) demonstrated that threat-related words led to a *generic slowdown* in cognitive performance during performance of the emotional Stroop and related tasks; this generic slowdown could account for Stroop effects, without implying the presence of biased selective attention as the underlying mechanism. To our knowledge, no existing studies have explored generic slowdown as an explanation for addiction Stroop effects, and we highlight this as an important avenue for future research.

While it is plausible to speculate that the mechanisms that underlie Stroop effects for threatening information (including generic slowdown; see Algom, Chajut, and Lev, 2004) might also account for Stroop effects produced by addiction-related words, one important difference between the two types of stimulus is worthy of consideration. That is, threat-related words are negatively valenced, whereas it is generally assumed that addiction-related words are positively valenced due to their association with the appetitive nature of addictive drugs. Indeed, this assumption dominates interpretations of the addiction Stroop literature. But it is important to note that different sub-populations of substance abusers might perceive drug-related cues as appetitive (positively valenced) or aversive (negatively valenced). For example, the vast majority of alcohol Stroop research used community samples of heavy drinkers, and heavy drinkers recruited from university campuses. These individuals generally have no history of treatment for alcohol problems, and are not currently seeking treatment for alcohol problems. It is reasonable to assume that in such individuals, alcohol-related words have appetitive properties. But Stroop effects have also been demonstrated in alcohol-dependent individuals while they are undergoing treatment, or immediately after completion of a treatment program (e.g., Cox, Hogan, Kristian, and Race, 2002; Stormark, Laberg, Nordby, and Hugdahl, 2000). Given that these individuals are motivated to achieve and maintain abstinence from alcohol, it seems likely that alcohol-related words would be perceived as simultaneously appetitive (due to the high incentive value of alcohol) and aversive (as they represent a threat to achieving the goal of abstinence). We speculate that addiction Stroop effects might primarily reflect the appetitive nature of addiction-related words in non-dependent populations, but in individuals seeking treatment they might also reflect the aversive-nature of those words (see Breiner, Stritzke, and Lang, 1999).

To summarize, there are ambiguities about the cognitive and emotional processes that underlie Stroop interference produced by addiction-related words. As we discuss in the following section, studies that used other measures of attentional bias go some way toward resolving these ambiguities.

3.1.2 Attentional cueing tasks. The *visual probe task* and related attentional cueing tasks have been widely used to investigate attentional biases for addiction-related stimuli. In the visual probe task, a pair of stimuli (usually pictures, although words can be used) are presented on the left and right of a computer screen. After pictures are removed from view, a small visual probe (e.g., a dot or an arrow) is presented on either the left or the right of the screen, and participants must respond to the probe as quickly as possible by making a manual response. Based on research into spatial cueing of visual attention (Posner, Snyder, and Davidson, 1980), we expect more rapid responding to probes that replace an attended object rather than an unattended object. In the addiction-related visual probe task, probes replace addiction-related and neutral images with equal frequency; it is therefore possible to compare average reaction times to probes that replace addiction-related pictures (*congruent trials*) with reaction times to probes that replace control pictures (*incongruent trials*). As reviewed by Field and Cox (2008), a large body of evidence indicates that substance abusers, but not controls, are faster to respond to probes that replace addiction-related stimuli, which indicates an "attentional bias" for those stimuli.

Some investigators (e.g., Stormark, Field, Hugdahl, and Horowitz, 1997; Franken, Kroon, and Hendriks, 2000) have used a variant of the task in which only one stimulus is presented, and the probe location is either congruent or incongruent with the picture. Addiction-related and neutral pictures are presented on different trials. As with the visual probe task, attentional bias is inferred if participants are faster to respond to probes that replace addiction-related rather than neutral pictures. However, relatively few studies have used this form of attentional cueing task (the visual probe task is much more popular) and results obtained from the task tend to produce fairly small effect sizes when compared to the visual probe task. This may occur because the simple spatial cueing effect (i.e. the ability of any visual cue with an abrupt onset to attract attention to its location) is very powerful, and the enhancement of this basic perceptual effect by addiction-related stimuli is relatively small. However, no previous studies have directly compared the effect size of attentional bias indices derived from standard visual probe tasks and single cue variants, so this issue requires clarification in future research.

A common manipulation within attentional cueing tasks is to experimentally manipulate the stimulus onset asynchrony (SOA), which refers to the duration of picture presentation before visual probes are displayed. A straightforward observation is that results differ depending on the SOA used. For example, in an early study, Stormark, Field, Hugdahl, and Horowitz (1997) demonstrated that alcoholics showed attentional bias for alcohol cues presented for 100 milliseconds, but attentional *avoidance* when those same cues were presented for 500 milliseconds (see also Vollstädt-Klein *et al.*, 2009; Townshend and Duka, 2007; Noël *et al.*, 2006, for comparable findings). In other samples (e.g., non-dependent social drinkers, tobacco smokers, marijuana users, and ketamine users), the effect of SOA is inconsistent, with some studies reporting the predicted group differences in attentional bias at relatively short SOAs but not longer SOAs (e.g., Chanon, Sours, and Boettiger, 2010; Morgan, Rees, and Curran, 2008), and other studies reporting the opposite pattern (Field, Mogg, Zetteler, and Bradley, 2004; Field, Eastwood, Bradley, and Mogg, 2006; Bradley, Field, Healy, and Mogg, 2008).

Many investigators (see Field and Cox, 2008, for a review) have argued that attentional biases at "short" SOAs reflect a bias in initial orienting of attention, which is

presumed to be automatic, whereas biases at longer SOAs reflect a bias in the maintenance of attention, or delayed disengagement of attention. In alcoholics, the observed
attentional avoidance of alcohol-related stimuli at longer SOAs might reflect strategic
attempts to counteract automatic biases in the initial orienting of attention. Basic
research on the speed of attentional processing suggests that an attentional bias for
stimuli presented for anything up to 200 milliseconds may reflect a bias in the initial
orienting of attention, with longer durations (500–2,000 milliseconds and longer)
reflecting a bias in attentional disengagement. While distinctions between different
sub-components of selective attention are recognized in the literature (e.g., Cisler
and Koster, 2010; Posner and Petersen, 1990; Corbetta and Shulman, 2002), there
is some debate as to whether attentional cueing tasks can actually be used to distinguish between these different components, despite the superficial appeal of varying
the SOA in order to do so. In an important paper, Koster, Crombez, Verschuere,
and De Houwer (2004) used a visual probe task to investigate attentional biases
for threat-related information. On some trials, pairs of threat-related and matched
neutral images were presented side by side on the computer screen. On other trials,
two pairs of neutral pictures were presented. Using this elegant design, the authors
could examine whether threat-related cues led to a bias in the initial orienting of
attention by contrasting reaction times on congruent threat trials (threat–neutral
trials in which the probe appeared in the same location as the threat picture) and
neutral–neutral trials. They were also able to examine whether threat-related cues led
to slowed disengagement of attention by contrasting reaction times on incongruent
threat trials (threat–neutral trials in which the probe appeared in the opposite location
to the threat picture) and neutral–neutral trials. Koster, Crombez, Verschuere, and
De Houwer (2004) found that, at a 500-miilisecond SOA there was no evidence
that threat-related cues led to a bias in the initial orienting of attention; however,
robust delayed disengagement effects were found at the 500-millisecond SOA (see
also Fox, Russo, Bowles, and Dutton, 2001). However, Koster *et al.* (2006) did find
evidence of initial orienting of attention to threat cues, but only when those cues
were presented for 100 milliseconds. Other investigators have argued that even these
results are open to interpretation, and that additional control conditions are required
in order to demonstrate biases in initial orienting of attention (Mogg, Holmes,
Garner, and Bradley, 2008). Regardless, what is clear is that manipulation of the SOA
does not provide researchers with unambiguous measures of different components of
selective attention, unless neutral–neutral trials are included for additional contrasts.
Unfortunately, all of this work on modified visual probe tasks that included additional
control trials has been focused on attentional biases for threat-related information,
so it is unclear to what extent conclusions from these studies can be extrapolated to
studies of attentional biases in addiction. We encourage researchers to be mindful
of these issues and to include additional control conditions (e.g., Koster, Crombez,
Verschuere, and De Houwer 2004; Koster *et al.*, 2006; Mogg, Holmes, Garner, and
Bradley, 2008) in order to investigate the component processes of attentional biases
in addiction.

3.1.3   Other measures of attentional bias.   Space limitations preclude detailed discussion of other measures of attentional bias that have been used in addiction research,

but we briefly describe some alternative measures here. Firstly, eye movement monitoring during exposure to addiction-related cues, either during passive viewing (e.g., Rosse *et al.*, 1997) or while participants complete a visual probe task (e.g., Mogg, Bradley, Field, and De Houwer, 2003; Miller and Fillmore, 2010), provides a direct and unambiguous measure of biases in selective attention for drug-related cues. Eye movement monitoring can also be used to distinguish between early attentional processes (e.g., the latency to direct a fixation towards a drug-related cue) and later processes such as delayed disengagement or the maintenance of attention (as inferred from the average duration of fixations on addiction-related, as opposed to neutral, images). In the flicker-induced change blindness task (e.g., Jones, Jones, Blundell, and Bruce, 2002; Jones, Jones, Smith, and Copley, 2003), two similar but subtly different images are displayed in quick succession, so that the screen appears to "flicker". In a typical addiction-related version of the task, the images might depict an array of alcohol-related and alcohol-unrelated objects, with two of those objects rotated slightly in the different images. Attentional bias can be inferred if participants are quicker to detect an alcohol-related change rather than a change to a neutral, alcohol-unrelated object. In the attentional blink task (e.g., Tibboel, De Houwer, and Field, 2010; Brevers *et al.*, 2011), words are presented in a rapid serial visual presentation stream, and participants have to verbally report some of those words (e.g., those printed in green) at the end of each trial. The "attentional blink" refers to the observation that participants are often unable to report a target word that appears shortly after presentation of another target word. In other words, the attentional system appears to "blink," and if addiction-related words can "break through" this attentional blink, this is evidence of a bias in selective attention for addiction-related words (see Brevers *et al.*, 2011; Tibboel, De Houwer, and Field, 2010). In dual task paradigms, participants are required to respond rapidly to target stimuli (which are usually auditory) during exposure to drug-related or neutral stimuli (e.g., holding a lit cigarette or an alcoholic drink versus holding a pen). Findings typically indicate that reaction times are slower during drug cue exposure (see Field and Cox, 2008) but, as with the addiction Stroop task (see discussion above), it is unclear to what extent these effects can be attributed to a bias in selective attention, as opposed to a more generic cognitive slowdown produced by the cues, or to elevated craving as a consequence of drug cue exposure. Finally, electroencephalographic (EEG) activity while viewing drug-related versus neutral cues has recently been studied, and there is evidence that certain event-related potentials (ERPs), such as the P300, can be interpreted as evidence of engagement of attentional mechanisms. Therefore, more pronounced ERPs in response to drug-related versus neutral cues are evidence of an attentional bias for drug-related cues (e.g., Littel and Franken, 2007).

3.2 Implicit association tasks and related measures

3.2.1 The implicit association task. The implicit association task (IAT; Greenwald, McGhee, and Schwartz, 1998) is used to assess memory associations between different concepts. During the task, participants categorize four different types of words (although pictorial stimuli can be used), using only two response keys. For example, participants might be asked to rapidly categorize words related to alcohol, words related to soft drinks (sodas), positively valenced words, and negatively valenced words. In some blocks of the task, participants would use one key to categorize alcohol-related and positively valenced words, and the alternative key to categorize soda-related and negatively valenced words. In a different block of the task, stimulus–response assignments are varied, so that alcohol-related and negatively valenced words now share a response key, and soda-related and positively valenced words now share the other response key. The underlying rationale is that if participants' automatic alcohol associations are primarily positive, they should be faster to respond on the block where alcohol and positively valenced words share a response key, rather than the block where alcohol and negatively valenced words share a response key.

As reviewed elsewhere (Roefs *et al.*, 2011; Rooke, Hine, and Thorsteinsson, 2008; Stacy and Wiers, 2010), studies that used the IAT as described above generally found strong alcohol-negative associations (rather than the predicted alcohol-positive associations), regardless of whether participants were light drinkers, heavy drinkers, or alcohol dependent. However, negative associations tended to be slightly weaker in heavier drinkers (similar findings have been reported in cannabis users; Field, Mogg, and Bradley, 2004). Rather than take these findings at face value, it is important to remember that the standard version of the IAT provides only a *relative* index of the strength of associations between two constructs: alcohol-negative associations must be interpreted as greater *relative* to alcohol-positive associations, not as an *absolute* measure of association strength. Despite this, numerous studies have modified the attribute categories used in the IAT, focusing instead on concepts such as approach (versus avoidance) and arousal (versus sedation) rather than positive versus negative valence. Results from these studies demonstrate that, relative to light drinkers, heavy drinkers have stronger associations between alcohol and concepts related to approach and arousal, relative to concepts related to avoidance and sedation.

Because the standard IAT yields an overall index of the relative (rather than absolute) strength of associations, results can be difficult to interpret. For example, the observed stronger associations between alcohol and negatively valenced words might reflect strong negative associations with alcohol, or they may instead reflect very weak positive alcohol associations; with the standard IAT, it is impossible to tell. For this reason, numerous investigators have turned to a variant, the unipolar IAT. In this version of the task, associations between alcohol-related and positively valenced (versus neutral) words might be assessed in one block of the task, and associations between alcohol-related and negatively valenced (versus neutral) words are assessed in a different block. This provides a clearer measure of the strength of alcohol-positive and alcohol-negative associations, independently of each other. Studies that used unipolar IATs revealed that heavy drinkers and tobacco smokers had stronger positive *and* negative addiction-related associations compared to control subjects (McCarthy and Thompsen, 2006; Jajodia and Earlywine, 2003). Importantly, while negative associations were stronger than positive associations, the negative associations were unrelated to individual differences in smoking/drinking behavior, whereas the positive associations were significant predictors of individual differences in smoking/drinking behavior (see Stacy and Wiers, 2010). Various other manipulations of the addiction IAT seem to confirm this general picture. For example, "personalized" versions of the IAT (Olson and Fazio, 2004) seek to reduce the effects of cultural drug-related associations (which are often negative) on IAT performance. These tasks also reveal that only positive, but not negative associations are associated with individual differences in drinking and smoking behavior. Finally, figure–ground asymmetries may account for the counterintuitive strong alcohol-negative associations in all populations of drinkers: given that "alcohol" is a more salient category than "soda" (especially to a heavy drinker), and "negative" is a more salient category than "positive," individuals may be faster to respond on alcohol-positive rather than alcohol-negative blocks simply because the two most salient word categories share the same response key. Studies that have attempted to control for figure–ground asymmetries have demonstrated that this leads to a general reduction in the strength of negative alcohol associations (see Stacy and Wiers, 2010).

3.2.2 Irrelevant-feature association tasks (e.g., Extrinsic Affective Simon Task; EAST). In the alcohol IAT, the alcohol-relatedness of the stimuli that are presented is a *relevant feature* for task performance: on each trial, participants must decide whether the word that is presented is related to alcohol (versus soda), in order to select which response to make. This raises an interesting issue regarding interpretation of IAT effects: do effects arise because participants are reacting to the individual stimulus words that are used (e.g., "beer," "vodka," etc.), or because those words activate the broader category "alcohol" and it is this broader category that shows strong associations with positive valence, approach, and arousal (depending on the version of the IAT used)? As Simon and colleagues (e.g. Simon and Rudell, 1967) have demonstrated using so-called "Simon" tasks, task-irrelevant cues can influence responding to task-relevant stimuli. Variations of Simon tasks have been developed by addiction researchers to investigate how drug-related words and pictures can influence participants' responding even when those stimuli are not relevant for task performance, as in the Extrinsic Affective Simon Task (EAST; De Houwer, Crombez, Baeyens, and Hermans, 2001). In this task, positively and negatively valenced words must be categorized on the basis of their valence (positive or negative), but addiction-related and matched control stimuli must be matched on the basis of an *irrelevant feature*, such as the color in which the words are printed. Studies that used this task revealed that relatively strong alcohol-positive associations were associated with individual differences in drinking behavior; however, the reliability of the alcohol association measure was markedly lower than the reliability of conventional IATs (De Houwer and De Bruycker, 2007). Nonetheless, this paradigm demonstrates that meaningful implicit alcohol-positive associations can be detected even when participants do not have to encode the alcohol-stimuli on the basis of their alcohol-relatedness.

3.3   Automatic approach tendencies

As discussed previously, some investigators have used the IAT to demonstrate that heavy drinkers have implicit associations between alcohol and concepts related to approach, rather than avoidance (Ostafin and Palfai, 2006). A task known as the stimulus–response compatibility (SRC) task has been used to investigate associations between addiction-related stimuli and "approach," but the key difference from the IAT is that in the SRC task, participants must categorize addiction-related pictures by making a symbolic approach or avoidance movement, rather than by simultaneously categorizing addiction-related, control, approach and avoidance-related words. Like the IAT, the SRC task comprises two critical blocks of trials: in one block of the task ("approach block"), participants must categorize alcohol-related and matched control pictures by moving a manikin towards pictures that are alcohol-related, and away from pictures that are not related to alcohol. In a different block ("avoid block"), stimulus–response assignments are reversed, in that participants must now move the manikin away from pictures that are alcohol-related, and towards pictures that are not related to alcohol. Various studies have demonstrated that heavy drinkers, but not light drinkers, are faster to respond during the "approach" block compared to the "avoid" block (Christiansen, Cole, Goudie, and Field, 2012; Field, Kiernan, Eastwood, and Child, 2008; Field, Caren, Fernie, and De Houwer, 2011); comparable effects have been reported in tobacco smokers (versus non-smokers; Bradley, Field, Healy, and Mogg, 2008; Mogg, Bradley, Field, and De Houwer, 2003) and marijuana users (versus non-users; Field, Eastwood, Bradley, and Mogg, 2006). Overall, these studies suggest that addiction-related cues elicit an automatic approach tendency, as participants are faster to categorize those cues when required to make a symbolic approach movement, rather than an avoidance movement, in order to categorize the pictures.

As with studies that used the IAT, as discussed above, interpretation of results from the SRC task is not as straightforward as it may appear at first. Firstly, the task only provides an index of the strength of automatic approach tendencies *relative* to the strength of automatic avoidance tendencies; a large positive approach bias index might indicate strong approach associations, weak avoidance inclinations, or a combination of the two. Recently, Barkby, Dickson, Roper, Field (2012) administered the standard SRC task, with an additional control condition in which participants categorized pictures by moving the manikin sideways (left or right), to groups of inpatient alcoholics and matched controls. This additional control condition enabled us to calculate the speed of approach responses directed toward alcohol cues, relative to both the speed of avoidance and the speed of categorizing those pictures by making a neutral response that signified neither approach nor avoidance (i.e., moving sideways). Likewise, the speed of alcohol avoidance responses could be calculated relative to the speed of approach, and relative to the speed of neutral categorization. Importantly, we found no significant differences between alcoholics and controls on any of the approach or avoidance bias measures, which relates to a more general issue that is discussed in more detail in section 4. However, we did find that within the group of alcoholics, strong alcohol-approach tendencies (relative to both the speed of avoidance and the speed of neutral categorization) were associated with individual differences in drinking habits; however, avoidance tendencies (relative to the speed of neutral categorization) were unrelated to drinking habits. Although further research is required to replicate and clarify this finding, it does suggest that strengthened alcohol-approach tendencies as revealed by the conventional SRC task do reflect strengthened approach tendencies elicited by those cues, rather than weakened avoidance tendencies (but see Ostafin, Palfai, and Wechsler, 2003, for conflicting findings when using an approach–avoidance IAT).

The second issue with the SRC task is that the alcohol-relatedness of the pictures presented is again the *relevant feature* for categorization; depending on the task block, participants must approach (or avoid) pictures that are related to alcohol, and avoid (or approach) pictures that are related to the control category of pictures. Therefore, it is unclear if effects from the SRC task reflect rapid approach tendencies elicited by the alcohol pictures, or strong associations between the concept "alcohol" (which would be activated during the task as participants must think about whether pictures are alcohol-related, or belong to the control category) and the concept "approach." In a recent study (Field, Caren, Fernie, and De Houwer, 2011), participants completed a variant of the SRC task in which they categorized alcohol-related and matched control pictures by making a symbolic approach movement towards the pictures, but pictures were categorized on the basis of their spatial orientation: that is, whether the pictures were in portrait format, or landscape format. In this *irrelevant-feature* version of the task, termed the Simon task, heavy drinkers were equally fast to approach and avoid alcohol-related pictures, despite being faster to approach rather than avoid those same pictures during completion of a standard SRC task, in which the alcohol-relatedness of the pictures was the relevant feature. As with the EAST (versus IAT), the reliability of the approach bias index was also markedly inferior when the index was derived from the irrelevant-feature Simon task as compared to the relevant-feature SRC task. Overall, results from this study suggest that alcohol-related stimuli do not elicit an automatic approach tendency unless those stimuli are explicitly encoded on the basis of their alcohol-relatedness.

However, some recent studies that used a different version of an irrelevant-feature approach–avoidance task cast doubt on this conclusion. Wiers and colleagues (Wiers, Field, and Stacy, 2011; Wiers, Rinck, Dictus, and Van Den Wildenberg, 2009; Wiers *et al.*, 2010) describe the alcohol approach–avoidance task (AAT), in which participants categorize alcohol-related and matched neutral pictures on the basis of their spatial orientation by moving a joystick towards pictures that are tilted to the left (or right), and away from pictures that are tilted toward the right (or left). In order to create the sensations of approach and avoidance, pictures increased in size in response to the approach movement (pulling the joystick toward), and shrank in response to the avoidance movement (pushing the joystick away). Young adult heavy drinkers, compared to matched light drinkers, were faster to categorize the alcohol-related pictures by making the approach movement rather than the avoidance movement (Wiers, Rinck, Dictus, and Van Den Wildenberg, 2009). However, a subsequent study with adolescents found the opposite pattern of results (i.e., heavier drinkers were faster to avoid, rather than approach, the alcohol-related pictures; van Hemel-Ruiter, de Jong, and Wiers, 2011). In alcoholics, one study found that although alcoholics were faster to approach rather than avoid alcohol pictures, the same was true of control images (i.e. pictures of soft drinks), and indeed the speeded approach (relative to avoidance) was actually more pronounced for soft drinks than for alcohol cues, which raises questions about the specificity of the "approach bias" index derived from the AAT (i.e., is the effect specific to alcohol cues, or do alcoholics simply exhibit a generally stronger approach drive?). Overall, the AAT represents a novel approach to the assessment of automatic alcohol-approach tendencies, although current findings do not suggest that performance on this task is consistently related to heavy drinking. There is a small literature on approach and avoidance tendencies elicited by normatively valenced stimuli, and the emerging consensus is that while irrelevant-feature tasks might be suitable for capturing automatic approach and avoidance tendencies, the effects are larger and more consistent when relevant-feature tasks, such as the SRC task, are used (e.g., Krieglmeyer and Deutsch, 2010). It is too early to say whether this also applies to addiction-specific versions of these tasks, although the current data do suggest that effects are more reliable with the SRC task as opposed to the AAT. Future investigators should investigate whether certain methodological features of the AAT, such as the use of real (rather than symbolic) approach and avoidance movements, and the use of feedback to give the sensations of approach and avoidance, might contribute to the increased sensitivity, reliability, and validity of the AAT as compared to other feature-irrelevant Simon tasks (Field, Caren, Fernie, and De Houwer, 2011).

3.4   Word association/word production measures

Several different methodologies have been utilized to test implicit memory activation using words association and production tasks. The first two methods involve the presentation of ambiguous words or statements that could elicit drug-related or non-drug-related responses. In the cue-behavior version of the task, participants are required to state the first word that comes to mind in response to an ambiguous cue, such as a word, picture, or sentence. For example, the word "draft" might elicit the response "beer" or the word "army." In the outcome-behavior variant of the task, participants are required to think of the first action that comes to mind in response to a cue such as "having fun," which might elicit the response "drinking alcohol" or "watching movies." In both versions of the task, the dependent variable is the number or proportion of addiction-related associations that are spontaneously produced; as reviewed in the previous section, numerous studies have shown that these tasks are associated with individual differences in alcohol consumption and smoking behavior, and they predict prospective drug use even after statistically controlling for self-report measures (see Ames *et al.*, 2007; Rooke, Hine, and Thorsteinsson, 2008).

Alternatively, researchers have explored the types of feeling or behavioral outcome that are spontaneously produced in response to unambiguous addiction-related activities (e.g., "drinking beer"). In effect, these studies turn the methodology used in the previous studies on its head in order to examine if, for example, the prime "drinking beer" would generate the spontaneous response "having fun," rather than the other way around. Each prime can be presented once, so participants give the most salient association, or several times, which allows for multiple associations to be given. Such studies generally demonstrate that, as a whole, participants tend to generate more negatively valenced than positively valenced associates of tobacco smoking, marijuana use, and alcohol consumption. However, participants who were regular users of alcohol, tobacco, or marijuana generated a relatively higher proportion of positive associates (Benthin *et al.*, 1995).

Regarding methodological recommendations (see Wiers, Field and Stacy, 2011), the wording of task instructions in these types of task is crucial: participants must be instructed to respond with "the first thing that comes to mind," rather than being explicitly asked to recollect an outcome that they associate with "having fun" (for example). In addition, researchers who use these tasks go to great lengths to disguise the drug-related nature of the studies (e.g., asking participants about their substance use only *after* they have completed the memory association tests, and embedding addiction-related prime words within a much larger pool of neutral prime words). It also seems important to conduct extensive pilot work in order to select appropriate stimulus materials. In one of the first studies to use the outcome-behavior methodology, Stacy, Leigh, and Weingardt (1994) conducted a large pilot study to establish outcomes that were associated with drinking alcohol. This enabled them to identify which alcohol outcomes were most commonly reported (e.g., "more social"). In the subsequent experimental study, which involved participants recruited from the same population, a selection of high-frequency words/statements were presented. This study demonstrates that it is important to tailor the ambiguous word primes to the population under study. Indeed, word association tasks may be particularly sensitive to different cultures; researchers should be aware that many terms related to drugs may be colloquialisms that are used widely in some settings (e.g., rural Nebraska) but not others (e.g., inner-city London), and therefore they should tailor their ambiguous cues to suit the population assessed.

While these tasks are clearly indirect measures of addiction-related memory associations – as participants are not explicitly asked to think of words or activities that they associate with drinking or smoking, etc. – there is some debate as to what extent these tasks provide a measure of "implicit" processes. This issue is discussed at length by Stacy and Wiers (2010), but in essence a generally accepted definition of implicit memory is memory in the absence of deliberate or conscious recollection of a previous event. With word association and word production tasks such as those described above, activation or retrieval of associations is spontaneous, because participants are instructed not to attempt to recall previous events when generating responses, but rather to list the first word "that comes to mind." Therefore, on this basis, word association measures can be understood as tapping an implicit process. It may be useful to contrast these measures with more "explicit" versions of the same. For example, asking participants "what do you like to do on Friday nights?" would be a fairly explicit measure, but asking participants for the first action they think of in response to the prime "Friday night" leads to an implicit measure. Significantly, Ames *et al.* (2007) found that word association measures predicted unique variance in addictive behavior after controlling for a directly comparable explicit measure.

Some recent studies suggest that the predictive validity of word association measures can be improved by asking participants to code the alcohol (or drug) relatedness of their own responses, rather than requiring researchers to decide whether participants' spontaneous responses are drug-related or not. For example, the ambiguous prime "bottle" may elicit a spontaneous response such as "drinking," but it is difficult for a researcher to know if this response refers to drinking alcohol, or not. When participants code their own responses as alcohol- or drug-related (or not), the ability of these free association measures to predict individual differences in substance use is greater than when researchers code participants' responses (Frigon and Krank, 2009; Krank, Schoenfeld, and Frigon, 2010). Furthermore, this methodology may also have greater sensitivity to colloquialisms given as responses in word association tasks.

4 Limitations, Shortcomings, and Future Directions

Task-specific considerations and limitations were discussed in the previous section; in this final section, we discuss some more general issues that affect a variety of different measures. We also take a critical look at how far the field has come in its short history, and ask what it has to offer in the future.

The first general issue is the poor reliability of some measures. In their analysis of the internal reliability of measures of substance-related attentional bias, Ataya *et al.* (2012) found that the visual probe task had very poor internal reliability, and, although the Stroop task was marginally better, this was largely due to the acceptable reliability of the blocked format, with the unblocked format showing extremely poor reliability. Other studies have also shown that reliabilities of the interference index derived from the addiction Stroop range from low to moderate (Marissen *et al.*, 2006; Waters *et al.*, 2003) and addiction-related versions of attentional cueing tasks have very poor reliability (Spiegelhalder *et al.*, 2011), although eye movement measures have adequate reliability (Friese, Bargas-Avila, Hofmann, and Wiers, 2010). As a general observation, the absence of reliability data (e.g., internal consistency and test–retest) for addiction attentional bias studies is concerning: if the measures that have been widely used are unreliable, then replication of findings is likely to be difficult. With regard to association measures (e.g., IAT, EAST) and the related approach–avoidance tasks (e.g., SRC, AAT), there is emerging evidence that relevant-feature versions, in which participants must categorize stimuli on the basis of their drug-relatedness (e.g., IAT and SRC) are much more reliable than irrelevant-feature versions (e.g., EAST and AAT; De Houwer and De Bruycker, 2007; Stacy and Wiers, 2010; Field, Caren, Fernie, and De Houwer, 2011). At present, the only recommendation that can be offered is that investigators should use relevant-feature tasks wherever possible. This is not to say that irrelevant-feature tasks should be discarded, as they enable the investigation of important theoretical issues (e.g., the extent of automaticity of stimulus processing); rather, attempts should be made to improve the reliability of those measures.

The second general issue relates to the stimuli that are used in implicit cognition research, and it seems likely that this issue might be related to the potential poor reliability of the measures used. Most investigators use a standard set of stimuli (e.g., a standard set of alcohol-related words or pictures) for all participants. However, it is likely that individuals react more strongly to some stimuli than others. Consider a heavy drinker who drinks primarily beer (and perhaps s/he mainly sticks to a particular brand, such as Heineken), but rarely drinks wine or spirits. Theoretically, that participant should react very strongly to words such as "beer," "lager," or "Heineken" in modified Stroop tasks and implicit association tests, or to pictures of glasses of beer, or bottles of Heineken in visual probe tasks; their responding to words related to wine, spirits, or pictures depicting those drinks would be expected to be minimal. As a consequence, the overall index of attentional bias or association strength would be small (as it is derived from reactions to all alcohol-related stimuli), and the internal consistency of the index would be low. Having said this, there are clear advantages to using a standardized set of stimuli for all participants, as this ensures that results can be generalized to similar populations and other research groups can attempt to replicate the findings. To date, very little research has been conducted into the possible advantages and disadvantage of using individualized stimuli, although some recent studies do suggest advantages of taking this approach. For example, Houben and Wiers (2009) found that a single target IAT which assessed implicit attitudes toward beer predicted drinking behavior in a group of regular beer drinkers, whereas a standard alcohol IAT did not. In addition, Cox, Hogan, Kristian, and Race (2002) used personalized alcohol and "current concern" Stroop tests in a sample of treatment-seeking alcoholics. Participants who demonstrated greater attentional bias in the alcohol compared to the current concern Stroop had subsequently worse treatment outcomes, although as there was no standard Stroop comparison, no conclusions can be made about the advantages of this methodology. Personalized stimuli have also been shown to be efficacious when used in attentional retraining interventions for harmful drinkers, although again there was no comparison with standardized stimuli (Fadardi and Cox, 2009). We highlight this as an important avenue for future research. Finally, this issue is also probably related to the general superior reliability of relevant-feature association tasks, as discussed above. When participants are required to categorize stimuli on the basis of their substance-relatedness (as in the SRC task and the IAT), arguably the specific stimuli that are used are relatively unimportant, so long as they can easily be categorized as substance-related (or unrelated). But when participants are not required to think about the substance-relatedness of the stimuli that are used (as is the case in the EAST and AAT, but also all measures of attentional bias), then selection of appropriate stimuli, which may need to be tailored to individual participants, becomes a crucial issue.

One notable feature of the majority of implicit cognition research (which seems to apply to experimental psychopathology as a whole; i.e., it is not specific to addiction research) is that this research should tell us something about the psychology of *addiction*. However, most research participants are young adults who are generally not substance dependent (with an over-reliance on undergraduate students as participants). This would not be a problem in itself, but the minority of studies that have studied severely dependent samples certainly raises a number of issues. For example, studies that used the visual probe task to measure attentional bias revealed biases in delayed disengagement of attention from alcohol cues presented at SOAs of 500 milliseconds or above in heavy-drinking students (e.g., Field, Mogg, Zetteler, and Bradley, 2004), but alcoholic inpatients show attentional *avoidance* of alcohol stimuli presented for these durations (e.g., Noël *et al.*, 2006; Townshend and Duka, 2007; Stormark, Field, Hugdahl, and Horowitz, 1997; Vollstädt-Klein *et al.*, 2009). Thus, this is not just a quantitative difference, but an important qualitative difference between students (on whom the majority of research is based) and alcoholic inpatients (whose behavior we are ultimately trying to explain). Likewise, with implicit association tasks, most studies with non-clinical samples reveal positive correlations between implicit positive alcohol associations and individual differences in drinking behavior in student samples, but at present there are no published data demonstrating differential IAT performance in alcoholics versus light social drinkers. The picture for implicit measures of approach tendencies is no better: while heavy social drinkers show automatic approach tendencies elicited by alcohol cues, inpatient alcoholics either fail to show this difference (when compared to controls; Barkby, Dickson, Roper, and

Field, 2012), or they show the complete opposite: that is, alcohol cues elicit an automatic avoidance tendency (Spruyt *et al.*, 2012). There may be a ready explanation for some of these findings: for example, failures to show a difference between patients and controls on implicit measures might be attributed to poor reliability of the measures in severely dependent alcoholics. Nonetheless, we do encourage researchers to take stock of these findings. These findings do not in any way devalue the existing research, but they may suggest that implicit cognitive processes are useful for explaining heavy substance use in non-dependent populations, but once individuals become severely dependent, implicit processes might be less important determinants of substance use.

Next, we recommend that researchers take a step back and ask themselves the difficult question: do implicit measures really tell us very much more than we could have gleaned from self-report measures? The link between individual differences in implicit cognition and individual differences in substance use has been established beyond any doubt, in cross-sectional, prospective, and experimental manipulation studies (reviewed in section 2 of this chapter). Many researchers have shown that the predictive power of implicit measures is maintained even when statistically controlling for explicit (self-report) measures such as outcome expectancies (e.g., Ames *et al.*, 2007; Thush *et al.*, 2008), or general deficits in executive function (e.g., Fadardi and Cox, 2006). Other researchers are more skeptical about this conclusion: for example, Reich, Below, and Goldman (2010) demonstrated in a recent meta-analysis that, although implicit association measures and explicit outcome expectancy measures both accounted for unique variance in drinking behavior, the additional variance contributed by the implicit measures was small, with the majority of variance attributable to self-report measures. With regard to attentional bias, meta-analysis indicates a small but robust association between bias and the strength of subjective craving (Field, Munafò, and Franken, 2009). Although Marissen *et al.* (2006) reported that the longitudinal association between attentional bias and subsequent drug use remained statistically significant when individual differences in subjective craving were statistically controlled, longitudinal studies assessing implicit word associations have not controlled for subjective craving (e.g., Kelly, Masterman, and Marlatt, 2005; Stacy, 1997). This issue is of both practical as well as theoretical importance: given that implicit measures are generally more complicated and time consuming to administer than self-report measures, researchers may question including them in studies if their contribution to explaining individual differences in substance use is minimal once the contribution of self-report measures has been statistically controlled.

Other issues for future research include consideration of the context-specificity of implicit cognitions. Various researchers have speculated that addiction-related contexts might increase the strength of implicit cognitions, or improve their correlation with individual differences in substance use (Field, Schoenmakers, and Wiers, 2008; Stacy and Wiers, 2010). Much of the existing research has been conducted in laboratory settings, but recently developed technologies allow for the assessment of implicit cognitions in ecologically valid settings. For example, Houben and Wiers (2008b) found that an IAT completed in a laboratory had weaker associations with drinking behavior than an online IAT that participants completed at home. Other methods such as ecological momentary assessment (also known as experience sampling; Waters and Li, 2008; Waters, Miller, and Li, 2010) have also being utilized to investigate this issue, with encouraging results.

Our final point is that attempts to modify implicit cognitive processes in order to treat addiction have so far met with mixed success, or have yielded findings that are difficult to interpret (Schoenmakers *et al.*, 2010; Fadardi and Cox, 2009; Wiers *et al.*, 2011). We argue that it is important to clarify the cognitive and emotional mechanisms that underlie biases in implicit cognition, improve the reliability of implicit cognition tasks, and attempt to quantify the causal influence of implicit cognitive processes on drug-seeking behavior (after controlling for the influence of controlled processes). Clarification of these issues should lead to more effective interventions that target implicit cognitive processes.

References

Algom D, Chajut E, and Lev S (2004) A rational look at the emotional stroop phenomenon: A generic slowdown, not a stroop effect. *Journal of Experimental Psychology: General* 133: 323–338.

Ames SL and Stacy AW (1998) Implicit cognition in the prediction of substance use among drug offenders. *Psychology of Addictive Behaviors* 12: 272–281.

Ames SL, Grenard JL, Thush C, Sussman S, Wiers RW, and Stacy AW (2007) Comparison of indirect assessments of association as predictors of marijuana use among at-risk adolescents. *Experimental and Clinical Psychopharmacology* 15: 204–218.

Anderson JR and Pirolli PL (1984) Spread of activation. *Journal of Experimental Psychology: Learning, Memory, and Cognition* 10: 791–798.

Ataya AF, Adams S, Mullings E, Cooper RM, Attwood AS, and Mufano, MR (2012) Internal reliability of measures of substance-related cognitve bias. *Drug and Alcohol Dependence* 121: 148–151.

Attwood AS, O'Sullivan H, Leonards U, Mackintosh B, and Munafo MR (2008) Attentional bias training and cue reactivity in cigarette smokers. *Addiction* 103: 1875–1882.

Bargh JA and Morsella E (2008) The unconscious mind. *Perspectives on Psychological Science* 3: 73–79.

Barkby H, Dickson JM, Roper L, and Field M (2012) To approach or avoid alcohol? Automatic and self reported motivational tendencies in alcohol-dependence. *Alcoholism: Clinical and Experimental Research* 36: 361–368.

Benthin A, Slovic P, Moran P, Severson H, Mertz CK, and Gerrard M (1995) Adolescent health-threatening and health-enhancing behaviors: A study of word association and imagery. *Journal of Adolescent Health* 17: 143–152.

Bradley BP, Field M, Healy H, and Mogg K (2008) Do the affective properties of smoking-related cues influence attentional and approach biases in cigarette smokers? *Journal of Psychopharmacology* 22: 737–745.

Breiner MJ, Stritzke WGK, and Lang AR (1999) Approaching avoidance: A step essential to the understanding of craving. *Alcohol Research and Health* 23: 197–206.

Brevers D, Cleeremans A, Tibboel H, Bechara A, Kornreich C, Verbanck P, and Noël X (2011) Reduced attentional blink for gambling-related stimuli in problem gamblers. *Journal of Behavior Therapy and Experimental Psychiatry* 42: 265–269.

Bruce G and Jones BT (2004) A pictorial Stroop paradigm reveals an alcohol attentional bias in heavier compared to lighter social drinkers. *Journal of Psychopharmacology* 18: 527–533.

Cane JE, Sharma D, and Albery IP (2009) The addiction Stroop task: Examining the fast and slow effects of smoking and marijuana-related cues. *Journal of Psychopharmacology* 23: 510–519.

Carpenter KM, Schreiber E, Church S, and McDowell D (2006) Drug Stroop performance: Relationships with primary substance of use and treatment outcome in a drug-dependent outpatient sample. *Addictive Behaviors* 31: 174–181.

Chanon VW, Sours CR, and Boettiger CA (2010) Attentional bias toward cigarette cues in active smokers. *Psychopharmacology* 212: 309–320.

Christiansen P, Cole JC, Goudie AJ, and Field M (2012) Components of behavioural impulsivity and automatic cue approach predict unique variance in hazardous drinking. *Psychopharmacology* 219: 201–510.

Cisler JM and Koster EHW (2010) Mechanisms of attentional biases towards threat in anxiety disorders: An integrative review. *Clinical Psychology Review* 30: 203–216.

Collins AM and Loftus EF (1975) A spreading-activation theory of semantic processing. *Psychological Review* 82: 407–428.

Corbetta M and Shulman GL (2002) Control of goal-directed and stimulus-driven attention in the brain. *Nature Reviews Neuroscience* 3: 201–215.

Cox WM, Fadardi JS, and Pothos EM (2006) The Addiction-Stroop test: Theoretical considerations and procedural recommendations. *Psychological Bulletin* 132: 443–476.

Cox WM, Hogan LM, Kristian MR, and Race JH (2002) Alcohol attentional bias as a predictor of alcohol abusers' treatment outcome. *Drug and Alcohol Dependence* 68: 237–243.

De Houwer J and De Bruycker E (2007) The Implicit Association Test outperforms the Extrinsic Affective Simon Task as an implicit measure of inter-individual differences in attitudes. *British Journal of Social Psychology* 46: 401–421.

De Houwer J, Crombez G, Baeyens F, and Hermans D (2001) On the generality of the affective Simon effect. *Cognition and Emotion* 15: 189–206.

De Houwer J, Teige-Mocigemba S, Spruyt A, and Moors A (2009) Implicit measures: A normative analysis and review. *Psychological Bulletin* 135: 347–368.

Deutsch R and Strack F (2006) Duality models in social psychology: From dual processes to interacting systems. *Psychological Inquiry* 17: 166–172.

Fadardi JS and Cox WM (2006) Alcohol attentional bias: Drinking salience or cognitive impairment? *Psychopharmacology* 185: 169–178.

Fadardi JS and Cox WM (2009) Reversing the sequence: Reducing alcohol consumption by overcoming alcohol attentional bias. *Drug and Alcohol Dependence* 101: 137–145.

Field M and Cox WM (2008) Attentional bias in addictive behaviors: A review of its development, causes, and consequences. *Drug and Alcohol Dependence* 97: 1–20.

Field M and Eastwood B (2005) Experimental manipulation of attentional bias increases the motivation to drink alcohol. *Psychopharmacology* 183: 350–357.

Field M, Caren R, Fernie G, and De Houwer J (2011) Alcohol approach tendencies in heavy drinkers: Comparison of effects in a relevant stimulus response compatibility task and an approach/avoidance Simon task. *Psychology of Addictive Behaviors* 25: 697–701.

Field M, Duka T, Eastwood B, Child R, Santarcangelo M, and Gayton M (2007) Experimental manipulation of attentional biases in heavy drinkers: Do the effects generalise? *Psychopharmacology* 192: 593–608.

Field M, Duka T, Tyler E, and Schoenmakers T (2009) Attentional bias modification in tobacco smokers. *Nicotine and Tobacco Research* 11: 812–822.

Field M, Eastwood B, Bradley BP, and Mogg K (2006) Selective processing of cannabis cues in regular cannabis users. *Drug and Alcohol Dependence* 85: 75–82.

Field M, Kiernan A, Eastwood B, and Child R (2008) Rapid approach responses to alcohol cues in heavy drinkers. *Journal of Behavior Therapy and Experimental Psychiatry* 39: 209–218.

Field M, Mogg K, and Bradley BP (2004) Cognitive bias and drug craving in recreational cannabis users. *Drug and Alcohol Dependence* 74: 105–111.

Field M, Mogg K, Zetteler J, and Bradley BP (2004) Attentional biases for alcohol cues in heavy and light social drinkers: The roles of initial orienting and maintained attention. *Psychopharmacology* 176: 88–93.

Field M, Munafò MR, and Franken IHA (2009) A meta-analytic investigation of the relationship between attentional bias and subjective craving in substance abuse. *Psychological Bulletin* 135: 589–607.

Field M, Schoenmakers T, and Wiers RW (2008) Cognitive processes in alcohol binges: A review and research agenda. *Current Drug Abuse Reviews* 1: 263–279.

Fox E, Russo R, Bowles R, and Dutton K (2001) Do threatening stimuli draw or hold visual attention in subclinical anxiety? *Journal of Experimental Psychology: General* 130: 681–700.

Franken IHA, Kroon LY, and Hendriks VM (2000) Influence of individual differences in craving and obsessive cocaine thoughts on attentional processes in cocaine abuse patients. *Addictive Behaviors* 25: 99–102.

Friese M, Bargas-Avila J, Hofmann W, and Wiers RW (2010) Here's looking at you, Bud. *Social Psychological and Personality Science* 1: 143–151.

Frigon AP and Krank MD (2009) Self-coded indirect memory associations in a brief school-based intervention for substance use suspensions. *Psychology of Addictive Behaviors* 23: 736–742.

Greenwald AG, McGhee DE, and Schwartz JLK (1998) Measuring individual differences in implicit cognition: The implicit association test. *Journal of Personality and Social Psychology* 74: 1464–1480.

Hester R, Dixon V, and Garavan H (2006) A consistent attentional bias for drug-related material in active cocaine users across word and picture versions of the emotional Stroop task. *Drug and Alcohol Dependence* 81: 251–257.

Houben K and Wiers RW (2007) Are drinkers implicitly positive about drinking alcohol? Personalizing the alcohol-IAT to reduce negative extrapersonal contamination. *Alcohol and Alcoholism* 42: 301–307.

Houben K and Wiers RW (2008a) Implicitly positive about alcohol? Implicit positive associations predict drinking behavior. *Addictive Behaviors* 33: 979–986.

Houben K and Wiers RW (2008b) Measuring implicit alcohol associations via the internet: Validation of web-based implicit association tests. *Behavior Research Methods* 40: 1134–1143.

Houben K and Wiers RW (2009) Beer makes the heart grow fonder: Single-target implicit attitudes toward beer but not alcohol are related to drinking behaviour in regular beer drinkers. *Netherlands Journal of Psychology* 65: 10–21.

Jajodia A and Earleywine M (2003) Measuring alcohol expectancies with the implicit association test. *Psychology of Addictive Behaviors* 17 (2): 126–133.

Jones BC, Jones BT, Blundell L, and Bruce G (2002) Social users of alcohol and cannabis who detect substance-related changes in a change blindness paradigm report higher levels of use than those detecting substance-neutral changes. *Psychopharmacology* 165: 93–96.

Jones BT, Jones BC, Smith H, and Copley N (2003) A flicker paradigm for inducing change blindness reveals alcohol and cannabis information processing biases in social users. *Addiction* 98: 235–244.

Kelly AB, Masterman PW, and Marlatt GA (2005) Alcohol-related associative strength and drinking behaviours: Concurrent and prospective relationships. *Drug and Alcohol Review* 24: 489–498.

Koster EHW, Crombez G, Verschuere B, and De Houwer J (2004) Selective attention to threat in the dot probe paradigm: Differentiating vigilance and difficulty to disengage. *Behaviour Research and Therapy* 42: 1183–1192.

Koster EHW, Crombez G, Verschuere B, Van Damme S, and Wiersema JR (2006) Components of attentional bias to threat in high trait anxiety: Facilitated engagement, impaired disengagement, and attentional avoidance. *Behaviour Research and Therapy* 44: 1757–1771.

Krank MD, Schoenfeld T, and Frigon AP (2010) Self-coded indirect memory associations and alcohol and marijuana use in college students. *Behavior Research Methods* 42: 733–738.

Krieglmeyer R and Deutsch R (2010) Comparing measures of approach–avoidance behaviour: The manikin task vs. two versions of the joystick task. *Cognition and Emotion* 24: 810–828.

Littel M and Franken IHA (2007) The effects of prolonged abstinence on the processing of smoking cues: An ERP study among smokers, ex-smokers and never-smokers. *Journal of Psychopharmacology* 21: 873–882.

Marissen MAE, Franken IHA, Waters AJ, Blanken P, Van Den Brink W, and Hendriks VM (2006) Attentional bias predicts heroin relapse following treatment. *Addiction* 101: 1306–1312.

McCarthy DM and Thompsen DM (2006) Implicit and explicit measures of alcohol and smoking cognitions. *Psychology of Addictive Behaviors* 20 (4): 436–444.

McHugh RK, Murray HW, Hearon BA, Calkins AW, and Otto MW (2010) Attentional bias and craving in smokers: The impact of a single attentional training session. *Nicotine and Tobacco Research* 12: 1261–1264.

Miller MA and Fillmore MT (2010) The effect of image complexity on attentional bias towards alcohol-related images in adult drinkers. *Addiction* 105: 883–890.

Mogg K, Bradley BP, Field M, and De Houwer J (2003) Eye movements to smoking-related pictures in smokers: Relationship between attentional biases and implicit and explicit measures of stimulus valence. *Addiction* 98: 825–836.

Mogg K, Holmes A, Garner M, and Bradley BP (2008) Effects of threat cues on attentional shifting, disengagement and response slowing in anxious individuals. *Behaviour Research and Therapy* 46: 656–667.

Morgan CJA, Rees H, and Curran HV (2008) Attentional bias to incentive stimuli in frequent ketamine users. *Psychological Medicine* 38: 1331–1340.

Noël X, Colmant M, Van Der Linden M, Bechara A, Bullens Q, Hanak C, and Verbanck P (2006) Time course of attention for alcohol cues in abstinent alcoholic patients: The role of initial orienting. *Alcoholism: Clinical and Experimental Research* 30: 1871–1877.

Olson MA and Fazio RH (2004) Reducing the influence of extrapersonal associations on the implicit association test: Personalizing the IAT. *Journal of Personality and Social Psychology* 86: 653–667.

Ostafin BD and Palfai TP (2006) Compelled to consume: The implicit association test and automatic alcohol motivation. *Psychology of Addictive Behaviors* 20: 322–327.

Ostafin BD, Palfai TP, and Wechsler CE (2003) The accessibility of motivational tendencies toward alcohol: Approach, avoidance, and disinhibited drinking. *Experimental and Clinical Psychopharmacology* 11: 294–301.

Posner MI and Petersen SE (1990) The attention system of the human brain. *Annual Review of Neuroscience* 13: 25–42.

Posner MI, Snyder CR, and Davidson BJ (1980) Attention and the detection of signals. *Journal of Experimental Psychology: General* 109: 160–174.

Reich RR, Below MC, and Goldman MS (2010) Explicit and implicit measures of expectancy and related alcohol cognitions: A meta-analytic comparison. *Psychology of Addictive Behaviors* 24: 13–25.

Robinson TE and Berridge KC (1993) The neural basis of drug craving: An incentive-sensitization theory of addiction. *Brain Research Reviews* 18: 247–291.

Robinson TE and Berridge KC (2008) The incentive sensitization theory of addiction: Some current issues. *Philosophical Transactions of the Royal Society B: Biological Sciences* 363: 3137–3146.

Roefs A, Huijding J, Smulders FTY, MacLeod CM, de Jong PJ, Wiers RW, and Jansen ATM (2011) Implicit measures of association in psychopathology research. *Psychological Bulletin* 137: 149–193.

Rooke SE, Hine DW, and Thorsteinsson EB (2008) Implicit cognition and substance use: A meta-analysis. *Addictive Behaviors* 33: 1314–1328.

Rosse RB, Johri S, Kendrick K, Hess AL, Alim TN, Miller M, and Deutsch SI (1997) Preattentive and attentive eye movements during visual scanning of a cocaine cue: Correlation with intensity of cocaine cravings. *Journal of Neuropsychiatry and Clinical Neurosciences* 9: 91–93.

Schoenmakers TM, de Bruin M, Lux IFM, Goertz AG, Van Kerkhof DHAT, and Wiers RW (2010) Clinical effectiveness of attentional bias modification training in abstinent alcoholic patients. *Drug and Alcohol Dependence* 109: 30–36.

Schoenmakers T, Wiers RW, Jones BT, Bruce G, and Jansen ATM (2007) Attentional retraining decreases attentional bias in heavy drinkers without generalization. *Addiction* 102: 399–405.

Sharma D and Money S (2010) Carryover effects to addiction-associated stimuli in a group of marijuana and cocaine users. *Journal of Psychopharmacology* 24: 1309–1316.

Simon JR and Rudell AP (1967) Auditory S–R compatibility: The effect of an irrelevant cue on information processing. *Journal of Applied Psychology* 51: 300–304.

Spiegelhalder K, Jähne A, Kyle SD, Beil M, Doll C, Feige B, and Riemann D (2011) Is smoking-related attentional bias a useful marker for treatment effects? *Behavioral Medicine* 37: 26–34.

Spruyt A, De Houwer J, Tibboel H, Verschuere B, Crombez G, Verbanck P, Hanak C, Bervers D, and Noël X (2012) On the predictive validity of automatically activated approach/avoidance tendencies in abstaining alcohol-dependent patients. *Drug and Alcohol Dependence*, in press. doi: 10.1016/j.drugalcdep.06.019.

Stacy AW (1997) Memory activation and expectancy as prospective predictors of alcohol and marijuana use. *Journal of Abnormal Psychology* 106: 61–73.

Stacy AW and Wiers RW (2010) Implicit cognition and addiction: A tool for explaining paradoxical behavior. *Annual Review of Clinical Psychology* 6: 551–575.

Stacy AW, Leigh BC, and Weingardt KR (1994) Memory accessibility and association of alcohol use and its positive outcomes. *Experimental and Clinical Psychopharmacology* 2: 269–282.

Stormark KM, Field NP, Hugdahl K, and Horowitz M (1997) Selective processing of visual alcohol cues in abstinent alcoholics: An approach–avoidance conflict? *Addictive Behaviors* 22: 509–519.

Stormark KM, Laberg JC, Nordby H, and Hugdahl K (2000) Alcoholics' selective attention to alcohol stimuli: Automated processing? *Journal of Studies on Alcohol* 61: 18–23.

Thush C, Wiers RW, Ames SL, Grenard JL, Sussman S, and Stacy AW (2008) Interactions between implicit and explicit cognition and working memory capacity in the prediction of alcohol use in at-risk adolescents. *Drug and Alcohol Dependence* 94: 116–124.

Tibboel H, De Houwer J, and Field M (2010) Reduced attentional blink for alcohol-related stimuli in heavy social drinkers. *Journal of Psychopharmacology* 24: 1349–1356.

Tiffany ST (1990) A cognitive model of drug urges and drug-use behavior: Role of automatic and nonautomatic processes. *Psychological Review* 97: 147–168.

Townshend JM and Duka T (2007) Avoidance of alcohol-related stimuli in alcohol-dependent inpatients. *Alcoholism: Clinical and Experimental Research* 31: 1349–1357.

van Hemel-Ruiter ME, de Jong PJ, and Wiers RW (2011) Appetitive and regulatory processes in young adolescent drinkers. *Addictive Behaviors* 36: 18–26.

Vollstädt-Klein S, Loeber S, Von der Goltz C, Mann K, and Kiefer F (2009) Avoidance of alcohol-related stimuli increases during the early stage of abstinence in alcohol-dependent patients. *Alcohol and Alcoholism* 44: 458–463.

Waters AJ and Li Y (2008) Evaluating the utility of administering a reaction time task in an ecological momentary assessment study. *Psychopharmacology* 197: 25–35.

Waters AJ, Miller EK, and Li Y (2010) Administering the implicit association test in an ecological momentary assessment study. *Psychological Reports* 106: 31–43.

Waters AJ, Sayette MA, and Wertz JM (2003) Carry-over effects can modulate emotional Stroop effects. *Cognition and Emotion* 17: 501–509.

Waters AJ, Sayette MA, Franken IHA, and Schwartz JE (2005) Generalizability of carry-over effects in the emotional Stroop task. *Behaviour Research and Therapy* 43: 715–732.

Waters AJ, Shiffman S, Sayette MA, Paty JA, Gwaltney CJ, and Balabanis MH (2003) Attentional bias predicts outcome in smoking cessation. *Health Psychology* 22: 378–387.

Wiers RW and Stacy AW (2006) *Handbook on Implicit Cognition and Addiction*. Thousand Oaks, CA: Sage.

Wiers RW, Bartholow BD, van den Wildenberg E, Thush C, Engels RCME, Sher KJ, Grenard J, Ames SL, and Stacy AW (2007) Automatic and controlled processes and the development of addictive behaviors in adolescents: A review and a model. *Pharmacology Biochemistry and Behavior* 86: 263–283.

Wiers RW, Eberl C, Rinck M, Becker ES, and Lindenmeyer J (2011) Retraining automatic action tendencies changes alcoholic patients' approach bias for alcohol and improves treatment outcome. *Psychological Science* 22: 490–497.

Wiers RW, Field M, and Stacy AW (2011) Passion's slave? Cognitive processes in alcohol and drug abuse. In KJ Sher (ed.), *Oxford Handbook of Substance Use Disorders*. New York: Oxford University Press.

Wiers RW, Rinck M, Dictus M, and Van Den Wildenberg E (2009) Relatively strong automatic appetitive action-tendencies in male carriers of the OPRM1 G-allele. *Genes, Brain and Behavior* 8: 101–106.

Wiers RW, Rinck M, Kordts R, Houben K, and Strack F (2010) Retraining automatic action-tendencies to approach alcohol in hazardous drinkers. *Addiction* 105: 279–287.

19

Experimental Methods for Understanding the Role of Social Context in Drug Addiction

Matthew G. Kirkpatrick and Margaret C. Wardle

"I just wouldn't want to take ecstasy when I am not around friends or people that I know" – spoken by a potential research participant

1 Introduction

Most psychoactive drugs are used in social settings. For example, psychoactive drugs may enhance the social context, perhaps by increasing social interaction, and this enhancement may lead to a more pleasurable, euphorigenic drug experience. Yet, the vast majority of laboratory studies with these drugs are conducted under socially isolated conditions. The effects of drugs on social behavior may reveal some of the reasons why people take drugs, especially if they make social experiences more enjoyable. Equally, the question of whether, and how, social settings increase the "positive" effects of drugs or decrease their "negative" effects will help to understand the naturalistic reinforcing value of the drugs. These interactions, however, are highly complex, and perhaps for that reason have received less experimental attention than more basic questions regarding acute psychoactive effects or self-administration.

In this chapter, we will discuss methods for studying how social context affects drug use and, conversely, how drugs affect social behaviors. The chapter has three main goals. The first is to consider how the social context (defined here as the presence of more than one person during drug taking) affects the acute subjective, physiological, and behavioral effects of psychoactive drugs. We will review evidence that drugs facilitate social behaviors, and discuss methodologies for measuring these changes. We will review evidence that the social setting alters acute drug effects and examine methods used to study this, including use of group designs, selection of participants, and methods for analyzing complex group-interaction data. The second goal of the chapter is to examine how drugs influence social interaction. We will review evidence that psychoactive drugs affect social interaction and components of social behavior,

The Wiley-Blackwell Handbook of Addiction Psychopharmacology, First Edition. Edited by James MacKillop and Harriet de Wit.
© 2013 John Wiley & Sons, Ltd. Published 2013 by John Wiley & Sons, Ltd.

and discuss methods used to study this, including selection of tasks for eliciting and measuring social behaviors. In the third section, we will identify future directions of research, including the complex bidirectional interactions between acute drug effects and the social context. At the end of this chapter we will recommend several future directions and proposed methodologies suited to a systematic investigation of the possible bidirectional interactions between acute drug effects and the social context in which drugs are taken.

2   The Influence of Social Setting on Acute Drug Effects

Data from the relatively few studies that have examined the influence of the social setting on acute drug effects suggest that the presence of others enhances the acute effects of several drugs, including alcohol, sedatives, marijuana, and stimulants. The social contexts used in these studies include a variety of social settings, such as party- and bar-like settings or socially stressful settings. We will briefly describe and give examples of research that have used each of three major types of design to examine the impact of the social setting on drug responses: (1) designs comparing a social setting to an isolated setting; (2) designs manipulating structured social interactions; and (3) designs using a social stressor. Within each of these designs, the outcome measures include (1) euphorigenic effects, such as self-reported ratings of "I feel a good drug effect;" (2) physiological effects, such as heart rate and blood pressure; (3) reinforcing effects, such as choice to consume more of a drug within a single session or to self-administer a drug again at a subsequent session; and/or (4) behavioral effects, such as increased risk-taking behavior. In our description of the above study designs, we will briefly describe the dependent measures used to measure each of these effects (see also Chapter 1). We also recommend the best methodological practices to investigate the effects of the social context.

2.1   Designs comparing a social setting to an isolated setting

Studies that compare drug effects in social and isolated conditions extend our understanding of the effects of drugs in the natural setting. Whereas most drugs are used in social settings, the vast majority of human behavioral pharmacology studies are conducted under socially isolated conditions, providing a more controlled but also narrower perspective on the drugs' profile of effects. In this section we will describe some of the studies that have compared drug effects under social and isolated conditions, and review the methods used in these studies.

In one study, Pliner and Cappell (1974) investigated the effects of alcohol (0.5 g/kg or approximately 2.5 standard drinks) and placebo in social drinkers tested in a social setting compared to an isolated setting. The study consisted of four groups ($N = 15$ each): two placebo groups (one isolated and one social) and two alcohol groups (one isolated and one social). The social groups were tested in groups of three individuals who had no prior contact with each other. In both conditions (social or isolated), participants sat at a table before and after drug administration and performed a distractor task. They also completed mood scales before and after drug administration. These scales were based on the Clyde Mood Scale (a 7-point Likert scale; Clyde 1963) and were conceptually divided into two different psychological dimensions: social-affective (friendly, unhappy, aggressive, euphoric, bored) and physical symptoms (dizzy, clear-thinking, sleepy). In the social condition, alcohol produced increases in ratings of feeling friendly and euphoric and decreases in ratings of bored and unhappy compared to placebo. In the isolated condition, alcohol did not produce these effects, and instead increased ratings of aggressive and dizzy and decreased self-reported clarity of thinking. Although breath alcohol levels were the same, alcohol produced greater feelings of friendliness and euphoria and reduced feelings of boredom under social conditions.

Doty and de Wit (1995) conducted a similar study investigating the effects of alcohol (0.5 or 0.8 g/kg) under social versus isolated conditions. In this study, participants were divided into four groups: an isolated group receiving low-dose alcohol, an isolated group receiving high-dose alcohol, a social group receiving low-dose alcohol, and a social group receiving high-dose alcohol. Participants first completed sampling sessions during which they received placebo on two sessions and active alcohol on two sessions, and then on three subsequent choice sessions they were allowed to choose which beverage they preferred. During each sampling session, participants completed several subjective effects questionnaires (i.e., the DEQ, POMS, and ARCI). Consistent with the Pliner and Cappell (1974) study, alcohol produced primarily positive subjective effects (e.g., increased ratings of drug liking and euphoria) in the social setting, whereas in the isolated setting, it produced many negative effects (e.g., increased ratings of dysphoria). The Doty and de Wit study extended the finding to show that participants tested in the social setting also consumed more alcohol than those in the isolated condition.

Hart *et al.* (2005) assessed consumption of oral Δ^9-THC in regular marijuana users, in a residential inpatient laboratory where they were either alone or in a group. Participants lived together in groups of three to four, and were permitted to ingest the drug each day during a "work period," during which they completed several computerized cognitive/psychomotor task batteries in individual rooms without social contact, or during a "recreational period," during which they could socialize and watch movies, play videogames, or talk. Participants chose to self-administer more oral THC during the recreational period (i.e., the "social" setting) than during the work period (i.e., the "isolated" setting). Although several other factors could have influenced their choice of drug (e.g., time of day or drug-related performance impairments), these findings are generally consistent with the idea that social settings increase drug use.

Other studies have shown that the social context may influence drug-related behavioral effects, such as decision making, which are relevant to life in the natural ecology. For example, Sayette and colleagues (2004) studied decisions about risky choices in three-person groups who consumed either alcohol (0.82 g/kg) or a placebo beverage. After drinking, the participants made a group decision between a "less risky choice" (completing 30 minutes of paper questionnaires) and a "riskier choice" (completing no questionnaires or 60 minutes of questionnaires, determined by a coin toss). Compared to placebo, alcohol increased the number of times subjects chose the riskier choice, while in a subsequent study alcohol did not produce this effect when subjects were tested alone (Sayette *et al.*, 2011). Thus, it was the combination of social context and active drug that produced a significant change in behavior.

Other studies have detected no differences in drug effects between a social setting and an isolated setting. For example, Johanson and de Wit (1992) investigated the role of social setting in responses to a sedative, diazepam, but found that the effects of diazepam were similar whether subjects were tested alone or in a group. In another study, de Wit, Clark, and Brauer (1997) reported that social context increased heart rate and temperature to an acute oral dose of *d*-amphetamine in a social, compared to the isolated, condition, but the effects of the drug on subjective or reinforcing effects did not differ. The enhanced physiological response is consistent with preclinical findings of aggregate toxicity (i.e., an increased drug response in animals housed together: Gunn and Gurd, 1940; Greenblatt and Osterberg, 1961; Davis and Borne, 1984; Fantegrossi *et al.*, 2003). These findings indicate that the effects of social context depend on both the drug and the outcome measure examined. In some cases, drug effects are qualitatively different in social contexts, but, in others, the drug has effectively equivalent effects.

2.2   Designs manipulating structured social interactions

Several studies have investigated the effects of drugs in manipulated, structured social interactions using experimental confederates. Most of these studies have been conducted with alcohol, and most have examined alcohol consumption as the primary outcome measure. Early studies showed that alcohol consumption is influenced by the amount consumed by a drinking partner (Caudill and Marlatt, 1975; Cooper, Waterhouse, and Sobell, 1979; Watson and Sobell, 1982). That is, subjects consume more alcohol in the presence of a confederate who consumes more alcohol. Collins, Parks, and Marlatt (1985) extended this work, to show that the level of sociability of the partner also affected drinking. Confederates were trained to drink either "lightly" (i.e., 1–1.5 drinks in 30 minutes at a relatively slow rate) or "heavily" (i.e., 3.5–4 drinks in 30 minutes at a relatively fast rate), and to behave in either a sociable (i.e., they maintained a casual conversation, made frequent eye contact, and smiled) or an unsociable manner (i.e., they were unresponsive, made little eye contact, and did not smile). Subjects in the sociable groups modeled their drinking behavior after the confederates, drinking more alcohol in the heavy-drinking groups and less in the light-drinking groups. By contrast, in the unsociable groups, subjects did not model their drinking behavior after the confederates; subjects in these groups drank considerably more alcohol regardless of whether the confederates were light or heavy drinkers. Thus, both the level of alcohol consumption of others and the degree of sociability of drinking partners can influence alcohol consumption. Interestingly, Larsen and colleagues (2010) observed that individuals who carry the D4 receptor 7-repeat polymorphism were more likely to be influenced by a heavy-drinking confederate. Although these findings have not yet been replicated, this study is an example of a potentially promising direction of future research: elucidating the underlying mechanisms of individual differences in sensitivity to social influences on alcohol-drinking behavior.

The acute effects of marijuana intoxication are also influenced by the behavior of other individuals. For example, Carlin, Bakker, Halpern, and Post (1972) examined the acute effects of smoked marijuana under two different social conditions: one in which confederates were trained to act intoxicated and another in which confederates were trained to act sober. Subjects in the intoxicated-confederate group reported greater subjective feelings of marijuana intoxication and exhibited more cognitive performance disruptions compared to those in the sober-confederate group. It is notable that these findings are consistent with the early studies by Schacter and Singer (1962), who demonstrated that the psychological effects of epinephrine were readily modifiable by the social context in which subjects were tested. Thus, the perceived level of intoxication of other individuals can mediate the acute effects of psychoactive substances including epinephrine as well as marijuana and alcohol. It is likely that the same principle holds true for other psychoactive drugs.

2.3 Designs using a social stressor

Social settings may also negatively influence responses to drugs, when the settings are stressful or unpleasant. One way to examine this is to study the drug effect in a stressful social environment: for example, using a laboratory stress procedure such as the Trier Social Stress Task (TSST). In the TSST participants must give a 5-minute "job interview" speech to three confederates, and perform a 5-minute mental arithmetic task (Kirschbaum, Pirke, and Hellhammer, 1993). Stress induced by such tasks has been shown to alter acute responses to drugs and/or increase drug consumption. Several recent studies have shown that the TSST increases cigarette craving, CO boost, and subsequent pleasure from smoking the first cigarette (Childs and de Wit, 2010; Buchmann *et al.*, 2008; Colamussi, Bovbjerg, and Erblich, 2007; Erblich *et al.*, 2003). In other studies, the TSST decreased alcohol-related feelings of stimulation, increased alcohol-related feeling of sedation (Soderpalm and de Wit, 2002) and increased alcohol consumption (de Wit, Soderpalm, Nikolayev, and Young, 2003; Childs, O'Connor, and de Wit, 2011; Thomas *et al.*, 2011). Stress inductions are comprehensively discussed in Chapter 15 of this volume. Interestingly, Kirschbaum, Klauer, Filipp, and Hellhammer (1995) found that social support attenuated cortisol and subjective stress responses to the TSST, suggesting that social stress can be ameliorated by the presence of non-threatening individuals.

Taken together, there is some evidence that the direct effects of drugs are altered in the presence of stress. Whether this relationship holds with nonsocial stressors, or other forms of social stress, remains to be determined. It would also be of particular clinical interest to extend the findings of Kirschbaum, Klauer, Filipp, and Hellhammer (1995), to investigate the conditions under which social support ameliorates the effects of an acute stressor.

2.4 Methodological considerations and future directions

The existing data suggest that various social contexts modulate responses to psychoactive drugs. For future studies directly examining the effects of social context, several

methodological issues should be considered, including (1) the importance of controlling other variables in the social and isolated settings (e.g., physical environment,
concurrent activities); (2) the characteristics and state (e.g., intoxicated) of the co-
participants in a group; and (3) the statistical models used to assess interdependent
group interactions.

2.4.1   Design and procedural considerations.   In studies comparing responses to
drugs in isolated and social conditions, care should be taken to control variables,
other than the simple presence of absence of others, which might influence behavior.
This potential problem is illustrated in the Hart *et al.* (2005) study of the reinforcing
effects of oral THC, in which participants self-administered more THC during the
recreational, social period than during the isolated work period. However, the participants' choice could also have been influenced by the type of activities (i.e., relaxation
or work) or by the time of day (morning versus afternoon). For a clear investigation
of the role of social condition, the social and isolated conditions should be similar in
every other respect.

   Another important variable is the qualitative nature of the social or isolated environment. In "positive" settings, the compatibility or sociability of the participants may
alter the social setting. Further, some settings may be physically more or less conducive
to experiencing euphoria than other settings, especially in the isolated condition (e.g.,
a living-room-like environment versus a clinical hospital setting). Similarly the effects
of a "negative" social context depend on the nature of the negative experience, such
as the extent to which it is truly a social stressor. An alternative to the TSST for
inducing stress is the stress imagery task, in which participants develop personalized
scripts of a past stressful event to be read aloud later by the researcher. This may have
the advantage that it is adapted to the individual's experience (Harris *et al.*, 2005).

2.4.2   Participant considerations.   An important consideration in studies involving
more than one subject in a session is whether to administer an active drug to co-
participants during the same sessions, or whether to randomize the drug conditions
among subjects in a group. When subjects are tested in groups, they may be influenced
by the state of intoxication or sobriety of their co-participants, complicating the
analysis. One solution is to use a design that allows a direct comparison between
responses to a drug when the co-participants receive the active drug or placebo.

   It is also difficult to determine whether individual characteristics of co-participants
influence acute drug effects. Heterogeneity in age, race, and sex, as well as less easily
definable sociodemographic characteristics, may add uncontrolled variability. Assessing social-interactive compatibility of potential co-participants before the study may
help to identify truly incompatible strangers, who may not interact at all or even create
a negative environment. The extent to which co-participants know each other may
influence their responses to drugs, from strangers (i.e., previously unacquainted persons) to groups of friends. Interactions and interpersonal judgments among friends
may be more stable and less influenced by drug state than state changes with strangers.
Finally, researchers must determine whether it is preferable to retest the same group
of individuals (e.g., the same dyad) in repeated session designs, or whether to mix
participants. Increasing familiarity may influence the social manipulation.

2.4.3   Statistical considerations.   The dyadic and group designs needed to investigate these questions present some specific statistical considerations, which we will discuss briefly here (readers seeking more extensive discussion are directed to: Kenny *et al.*, 2002; Raudenbush and Bryk, 2002; Kenny, Kashy, and Cook, 2006). The most important statistical consideration is that measurements taken from members of the same group are not independent: that is, responses from two members of the same group are likely to be systematically more similar to (or more different from) each other than responses of two individuals from different groups. For example, a group may include one individual who displays a strong drug effect, thus increasing drug-related responses in others in the group, or an individual who dominates socially may repress social responses in others. It may be inappropriate to use the individual as the unit of analysis in an ANOVA or regression when the measures are related in this way, and more complex models of "contextual" group effects are recommended. Ignoring non-independence can result in either liberal or conservative bias in significance testing (for a discussion, see Kenny, Kashy, and Cook, 2006: 43). Some researchers have utilized statistics that attempt to determine whether non-independence is present to justify individual-level regression/ANOVA analyses, but small sample sizes may result in a non-significant test even when non-independence is actually present (Kenny *et al.*, 2002).

Fortunately, advances in statistical software have made procedures that correctly model both individual and group-level effects in grouped or "nested" designs widely available. Multilevel modeling (MLM), the procedure we recommend for handling group designs, is included in a number of statistical packages (e.g., SPSS, SAS, HLM, MLwiN, and R, among others). MLM is capable of estimating the effect of both categorical and continuous variables at both the individual level (e.g., assignment to either a speaker or listener role in a talking task, individual blood alcohol levels), and the group level (e.g., assignment of a group to alcohol or placebo manipulation, impact of the group's mean level of extraversion on drug effects). MLM techniques also handle missing observations and unequal group sizes gracefully.

There are several important details specific to individual designs in MLM that are beyond the scope of this chapter, including centering of variables, allowing estimates of parameters obtained at the individual level to vary at the group level, iterative estimation techniques, and concerns specific to individual statistics programs. For discussion of these in the specific context of dyadic and small group behavioral analyses we refer the reader to Kenny, Kashy, and Cook (2006) and Kenny *et al.* (2002), and for general information on MLM techniques we suggest Raudenbush and Bryk (2002). Given the widespread availability of MLM packages, "naïve" analyses that do not correctly account for non-independence no longer offer advantages in ease of use or availability, and their use with grouped data is highly discouraged.

3   Acute Drug Effects on Social Interaction

We have discussed evidence that social context affects drug responses. Conversely, drugs also have direct effects on social behavior. Several approaches have been taken to study effects of drugs on social behavior, which may be grouped into four broad categories: (1) components of social behavior – tasks that assess "building blocks" of social interactions, such as impression formation and recognition of facial emotions; (2) hypothetical social behaviors – tasks that examine social behavior through hypothetical vignettes; (3) structured social behavior – tasks that elicit single social behaviors of interest, such as speech, aggression, or cooperation, in a highly structured situation; and (4) unstructured social behavior – tasks that measure responses of more than one freely behaving participant in a semi-structured or unstructured situation. For each approach we will first describe the tasks used, then provide some illustrative examples of findings with drugs of abuse, and then summarize and discuss research considerations and future directions.

3.1   Components of social behavior

Social behavior is comprised of a complex interplay of perceptions, internal and overt reactions, interpretations and social motivations, any of which may be influenced by drugs and amenable to experimental study. Some of these components can be assessed in specific tasks that may not constitute social behavior per se, but capture key aspects of impression formation and communication that can strongly influence social behavior. The most commonly examined components of social interaction in behavioral pharmacology studies are "first impressions" of neutral faces, and responses to facial emotional expressions, discussed below.

3.1.1   Impression formation.   Drugs may alter "first impressions" of others, including traits such as attractiveness or trustworthiness, which may in turn influence social behavior. Impression formation studies typically use pictures of standardized faces with emotionally neutral expressions (e.g. Ebner, 2008; Oosterhof and Todorov, 2008), which subjects rate under the influence of a drug or placebo. The literature on "first impressions" and drugs of abuse has primarily focused on judgments of attractiveness, with findings that both alcohol (Jones, Jones, Thomas, and Piper, 2003; Parker, Penton-Voak, Attwood, and Munafò, 2008; Halsey, Huber, Bufton, and Little, 2010) and nicotine (Attwood, Penton-Voak, and Munafò, 2009) increase "first impression" ratings of attractiveness. This effect may contribute to the increased risky sexual activity observed under the influence of alcohol (Jones *et al.*, 2003). However, both the types of drug and the types of impression examined have been limited. Other "social" drugs such as MDMA that reportedly increase trust and bonding (Parrott, 2007) may do so in part by altering first impressions, so use of this paradigm with a wider variety of drugs is indicated. Further, future first impression studies with drugs of abuse could benefit from incorporating basic research on the neural underpinnings of social perception. Recent social neuroscience findings suggest two primary dimensions of face evaluation: "valence," which corresponds closely to attractiveness, and "dominance," which captures a set of traits that include aggression and confidence. These two types of judgment are represented in distinct brain regions, and stimuli sets have been constructed to specifically tap these two dimensions (Todorov, 2011). To date, no drug studies have examined dominance perceptions directly, and this may thus represent a promising future direction of research (e.g. Oosterhof and Todorov, 2008).

3.1.2 Emotion perception.   Several studies have shown that drugs of abuse also affect emotion perception, which is an integral part of social interaction. Studies of emotion perception have used as stimuli pictures of facial expressions associated with "basic" emotions, pictures of more complex "non-basic" emotions, emotional vocal samples, and videos of facial emotional expressions. The most commonly used of these types of stimulus are pictures of facial expressions associated with "basic" emotions (e.g. anger, fear, disgust, happiness and surprise; Ekman, 1992). Several standardized sets of these pictures have been developed (Pictures of Facial Affect: Ekman, 1993; Karolinska Directed Emotional Faces: Goeleven, De Raedt, Leyman, and Verschuere, 2008; NimStim Face Stimulus Set: Tottenham *et al.*, 2009; and others). Beyond prototypical "basic emotions," there is the Reading the Mind in the Eyes Task (RMET; Baron-Cohen *et al.*, 2001), which uses pictures of the eye area to convey a variety of "non-basic" emotional states, and has been previously studied with drugs of abuse (Bedi, Hyman, and de Wit, 2010). Less commonly, studies have used standardized auditory stimuli depicting emotional states (Baum and Nowicki, 1998; Golan, Baron-Cohen, Hill, and Rutherford, 2007), such as in Bedi, Hyman, and de Wit (2010). Finally, a few studies have used videos depicting faces that gradually transition from neutral to emotional expressions (Platt, Kamboj, Morgan, and Curran, 2010; Walter *et al.*, 2011), which may more realistically recreate typical experience and thus more effectively engage neural areas associated with face processing (LaBar, Crupain, Voyvodic, and McCarthy, 2003). The most common dependent variable used with these several types of stimulus has been accuracy of identification of the emotion. In an effort to increase sensitivity of this measure, some investigators use "morphed" picture stimuli (ambiguous stimuli representing intermediate stages between neutral and 100% emotion or between two different emotions; Attwood *et al.*, 2009a), brief presentation times, or psychophysical "threshold" procedures (e.g. Attwood *et al.*, 2009b). Other dependent variables used to assess the effects of drugs on emotion perception have included automatic direction of attention to emotional expressions, and brain activity in response to emotional expressions (Orozco, Wall, and Ehlers, 1999; Phan *et al.*, 2008; Bedi, Phan, Angstadt, and de Wit, 2009). Thus, several different types of stimulus are available for use in behavioral pharmacology studies of emotion perception with several possible outcome measures.

Examining the literature on emotion perception and drugs of abuse, initial studies on emotion perception were conducted primarily with alcohol, and focused on possible links between perceptions of anger and alcohol-induced aggression (Baribeau, Braun, and Dubé, 1986; Borrill, Rosen, and Summerfield, 1987). However, later studies examining alcohol and other abused drugs including THC and MDMA have found a pattern of results across both identification and brain activity variables more consistent with a general dampening of reactions to negative emotions than with increased aggression. In one investigation, alcohol intoxication increased the tendency to misidentify disgust as anger (Attwood *et al.*, 2009c) in male faces, which would be in line with increased aggression. However, in other subsequent studies, alcohol instead increased the threshold for identifying sadness (Attwood *et al.*, 2009a), decreased the threshold for identifying happiness (Kano *et al.*, 2003; Walter *et al.*, 2011), and decreased amygdala reactivity to negative emotional expressions (Sripada *et al.*, 2011), suggesting that alcohol may decrease negative and increase positive social reactions.

MDMA and THC have also produced effects consistent with increased social interaction. MDMA decreased accurate identification of negative emotions, decreased brain responses to negative emotional faces, and increased brain responses to positive emotional faces (Bedi, Phan, Angstadt, and de Wit, 2009; Bedi, Hyman, and de Wit, 2010). Similarly, THC also decreased amygdala reactivity to negative emotional faces (Phan *et al.*, 2008).

In summary, examining drug-related effects on emotion perceptions across several types of stimulus has generally indicated that several drugs alter emotion perception in ways that may promote social interaction. However, important considerations for future behavioral pharmacology research on emotion perception include that specific procedural variations with varying sensitivity may lead to different results across studies (cf. Kano *et al.*, 2003; Attwood *et al.*, 2009b), and that results are often significantly moderated by the match between the gender of the perceiver and the stimulus face (Orozco, Wall, and Ehlers, 1999; Attwood *et al.*, 2009a; Attwood *et al.*, 2009b), suggesting balancing stimuli and participants on gender is important. Further, although recent research suggests the existence of additional "self-conscious" basic emotions of pride and embarrassment, and there are validated picture sets representing these emotions (Tracy, Robins, and Scriber, 2009), to date no study has examined the effect of drugs of abuse on perceptions of these emotions, so this may be a future direction of this work.

3.2   Hypothetical social behavior

Another approach to studying the effects of drugs on social behavior has been to use hypothetical scenarios of social behaviors. Some types of social behavior are difficult to model in the laboratory (e.g. sexual behavior; Frohmader, Pitchers, Balfour, and Coolen, 2009), and instead researchers use hypothetical social situations, presented in written (Abbey, Buck, Zawacki, and Saenz, 2003; George *et al.*, 2009), audio (Cho and Span, 2010), or video form (MacDonald, MacDonald, Zanna, and Fong, 2000; Ebel-Lam, MacDonald, Zanna, and Fong, 2009). Typically, participants are asked to place themselves in the position of someone in the vignette, and then asked to report their intentions, with and without drug administration. For example, participants may be asked to report whether they would be likely to use a condom or to engage in risky sex in a particular situation, or they may provide self-reported or psychophysiological measures of arousal in response to a vignette. The majority of the literature utilizing this technique examines the impact of alcohol on sexual behavior. In one particular example illustrating this technique (Noel, Maisto, Johnson, and Jackson, 2009), young adult heterosexual males were administered a placebo, low or moderate dose alcoholic beverage. Participants then watched a video of a "date rape" scenario where forced sex appeared a likely outcome. This video contained either "anti-force cues" (e.g. the female character wearing a rape crisis center t-shirt), or no anti-force cues. Participants were asked to report both on what the male character in the video should do, and what they themselves would do in this situation. Researchers found that alcohol increased the endorsement of forced sex, regardless of the presence of anti-force cues. There are several published reviews of this type of literature on alcohol and sexual risk, but in brief, administration of alcohol consistently increases risky sexual decision making in hypothetical scenario laboratory models (see George and Stoner, 2000; and Hendershot and George, 2007).

These techniques have good face validity, as they correspond to findings about alcohol and risky sex obtained using survey and non-experimental techniques (George and Stoner, 2000). However, research considerations include that the vignettes used have varied across laboratories, and the cost of constructing and validating new vignettes may be high (especially for immersive techniques like video). This approach would benefit from construction of readily available standardized materials, similar to the face sets mentioned above. Further, this research could be extended to drugs other than alcohol that are also associated with risky sexual behavior (Frohmader, Pitchers, Balfour, and Coolen, 2009), and might also be productively utilized with other difficult-to-model behaviors, such as coercive aggression (see section 3.3.3).

3.3   Structured social behavior

Effects of drugs on social behavior have also been examined in highly structured social situations. In these structured techniques, participants often (although not always) interact with confederates rather than other freely behaving participants. Behaviors that have been modeled include decisions to socially interact with others, verbal behavior, aggressive behavior and cooperative/pro-social behavior.

3.3.1   Choosing to interact with others.   Drugs can alter the desire to be social and the value placed on socialization. In several studies assessing the acute effects of drugs on social choice (Higgins, Hughes, and Bickel, 1989), participants tested alone were asked to choose whether or not they wished to converse with another subject via a headset. Sometimes there was a monetary cost to the participant to activate the headset, providing a well-calibrated scale to measure the value of interaction. In the limited literature using this type of task, alcohol (in alcohol-dependent individuals) and amphetamine and secobarbitol (in normal volunteers) increased social choices (Griffiths, Bigelow, and Liebson, 1975; Heishman and Stitzer, 1989), and amphetamine did so even when the social option resulted in loss of a monetary reward (Higgins, Hughes, and Bickel, 1989). However, marijuana had no effect on choice behavior (Heishman and Stitzer, 1989).

In summary, in procedures examining the effect of drugs on the value of social interaction, many (but not all) of the abused drugs studied have increased the value of social interaction. However, the use of this technique has been limited to a small number of studies, and thus future directions could include use of this procedure with other potentially "pro-social" drugs of abuse, such as MDMA, or drugs such as nicotine that are hypothesized to enhance the value of co-occurring positive reinforcers such as socialization (Caggiula *et al.*, 2009).

3.3.2   Verbal behavior.   Another approach to assessing effects of drugs on social behavior has been to examine specific aspects of speech, including quantity, content, and organization. Studies examining the effect of drugs on speech have used monologues, recordings of "coincidental" speech (see below for definition), and interactive speech tasks in which participants speak with confederates or other participants to obtain speech samples. In the monologue design, subjects speak into a microphone for as much or as little time as they wish, with no other people present. Although this might not be on its face a measure of "social" behavior, parallel drug effects have been observed on monologue speech and "social" speech (speech with other participants) for several drugs (Stitzer, Griffiths, and Liebson, 1978; Higgins and Stitzer, 1988; 1989), suggesting monologues may proxy social speech, without the potentially confounding effects of a speech partner. In designs examining "coincidental" speech, no speech-eliciting task is used; instead, any speech directed at the experimenter during the session is simply recorded (e.g. Stitzer, McCaul, Bigelow, and Liebson, 1984). This type of task may capture variation in "urge to talk" better than tasks with higher demands, but may also produce wide variations in amount of speech obtained (Wardle, Cederbaum, and de Wit, 2011). In interactive speech designs with confederates, participants speak about a specific topic to an experimenter or confederate, such as describing a movie, speaking to "impress" an opposite-sex confederate, or answering a set of "disclosing" questions (Wilson, Perold, and Abrams, 1981; Schippers, De Boer, Van der Staak, and Cox, 1997; Monahan and Lannutti, 2000; Marrone, Pardo, Krauss, and Hart, 2010). Responses of the confederate/experimenter are generally very limited to aid in standardization, although some studies have attempted to standardize fairly complex roles (such as flirtatious interactions; Monahan and Lannutti, 2000). Finally some studies use a more complex interactive design in which two or more participants are assigned a task designed to promote talking, allowing bidirectional interactions and contributions. For example, participants may discuss a film, make up a collective story, or complete mock-psychiatric interviews (Janowsky *et al.*, 1979; Babor *et al.*, 1983; Lindfors and Lindman, 1987; Janowsky, 2003). These provide the most naturalistic social conversations, but also may introduce greater variation and difficulties in quantification. Dependent measures used with these speech designs have included amount of speech (e.g. length of utterances, number of words, or number of syllables, measured either automatically or manually; Stitzer, McCaul, Bigelow, and Liebson, 1984), speech organization (e.g. number of disjunctive pauses, observer ratings; Marrone, Pardo, Krauss, and Hart, 2010), speech content (e.g. ratings of degree of self-disclosure, aggression, or sexual content; Babor *et al.*, 1983; Lindfors and Lindman, 1987; Monahan and Lannutti, 2000), and perceptions of the quality of the speech and interaction as rated by participants, partners, or observers (Janowsky *et al.*, 1979; Janowsky, 2003).

Given the diversity of designs and dependent measures, this research area does not produce a ready synthesis of findings, but below we provide examples of use of each of the major dependent variables with drugs of abuse. Examining amount of speech, ethanol and secobarbitol increased the amount of time spent talking in both monologue and interactive speech tasks (Stitzer, Griffiths, and Liebson, 1978; Stitzer, Griffiths, Bigelow, and Liebson, 1981; Higgins and Stitzer, 1989), while hydromorphone increased coincidental speech directed at the examiner (Stitzer, McCaul, Bigelow, and Liebson, 1984). In contrast, chlorpromazine decreased speech time in an interactive task (Stitzer, Griffiths, Bigelow, and Liebson, 1981). Examining speech organization, methamphetamine increased speech fluency, whereas MDMA, which is pharmacologically similar, decreased speech fluency (as measured by disfluencies and filled pauses; Marrone, Pardo, Krauss, and Hart, 2010). In the area of speech content, alcohol disinhibited aggressive speech content and increased self-disclosure (Babor *et al.*, 1983; Monahan and Lannutti, 2000). Examining interaction quality, when amphetamine was given to interviewees in a mock-psychiatric interview, it increased interviewees' perceptions of the interviewers' regard for them (Janowsky, 2003). In contrast, THC given to interviewers decreased interviewees' perceptions of interviewer skill in a similar task (Janowsky *et al.*, 1979). Even this brief sampling of findings in this area shows, first, that drugs of abuse affect several different aspects of speech, and second, that these effects may be specific to drug type, design and dependent variable measured.

In summary, there are a number of designs for eliciting speech, and dependent variables for measuring speech, that are sensitive to drug effects. The primary research consideration in this area is the standardization of measures used to assess drug effects on speech. Until now, the measures used have varied across laboratories and there is little information on their reliability, stability, and validity. For example, speech samples have varied from 5 minutes to hours, introducing an important source of variability. There have been recent attempts to begin to standardize brief speech tasks for use in behavioral pharmacology (Wardle, Cederbaum, and de Wit, 2011). Similarly, varying strategies have been used to conduct content analysis, although there are commercially available programs for conducting content analysis that automatically analyze transcripts and produce word counts for a wide variety of content areas (Pennebaker, Booth, and Francis, 2007). Although some research questions may still require *de novo* coding systems, broader use of standardized programs can provide more readily comparable coding systems across studies and research areas.

3.3.3 Aggressive behavior. Among the best-documented effects of drugs on social behavior is their effect on aggressive social behaviors (Bushman and Cooper, 1990; Chermack and Giancola, 1997). Study designs examining aggression usually measure reactive aggression, or aggression in reaction to frustration or provocation using either the Taylor Aggression Paradigm or the Point Subtraction Aggression Paradigm. In the Taylor paradigm, participants are told that they are playing a competitive reaction time game with another player (actually a confederate), and whichever player loses will receive a shock at a level chosen by their opponent. The intensity of shock chosen by the participant is the measure of aggression. In the Point Subtraction paradigm, participants can push one button to earn money, or another button to subtract money from another player. That other player (actually a confederate) can also deduct points from their score (and does so at several predetermined points during the experiment). Aggression is measured as the number of presses on the participant's subtraction button. There are several reviews of these paradigms (Tedeschi and Quigley, 1996; Giancola and Chermack, 1998; Tedeschi and Quigley, 2000; Ritter and Eslea, 2005) and their sensitivity to alcohol in particular (Bushman and Cooper, 1990; Chermack and Giancola, 1997).

Research in this area has typically focused on the effects of alcohol, although some other drugs have been examined. In brief, alcohol consistently increases aggressive behavior (Bushman and Cooper, 1990; Chermack and Giancola, 1997), while the effects of marijuana, amphetamine, and diazepam have been more inconsistent (Salzman, Van Der Kolk, and Shader, 1976; Cherek, Steinberg, Kelly, and Robinson, 1987; Cherek, Steinberg, Kelly, and Sebastian, 1989; Cherek *et al.*, 1990). Although early research on alcohol and aggression focused primarily on main effects of alcohol, recently there has been more interest in examining moderating variables that determine in whom and under what circumstances alcohol intoxication leads to aggression (Giancola, 2008). Among individual difference variables that have been related to aggressive behavior, one of the best explored is executive functioning, which has been the subject of a series of recent studies (Giancola, 2004; Giancola, Godlaski, and Roth, 2011; Giancola, Parrott, and Roth, 2006; Godlaski and Giancola, 2009). Executive functioning is typically defined as the higher-order cognitive abilities involved in planning and regulation of goal-directed behavior (subsuming attentional control, inhibition, cognitive flexibility, and abstract reasoning; Giancola, 2000). Alcohol is known to disrupt executive functioning, and lowered executive functioning is related to aggressive behavior, as executive functioning normally serves to inhibit impulsive aggressive behavior (Giancola, 2000). Thus, individuals with lower executive functioning capacity when sober may be particularly aggressive under the influence of alcohol, as alcohol further reduces their level of control over aggressive impulses. This hypothesis has been supported in several studies to date (Giancola, 2004; Giancola, Godlaski, and Roth, 2011; Giancola, Parrott, and Roth, 2006; Godlaski and Giancola, 2009). In addition to the question of who is more susceptible to alcohol-induced aggression, progress has also been made on circumstances that inhibit versus encourage alcohol-induced aggression. This line of research has benefited from the Alcohol Myopia theory advanced by Steele and colleagues (Steele and Josephs, 1990). The Alcohol Myopia model proposes that intoxication impairs attentional capacity, limiting the attention of intoxicated individuals to only the most salient cues in the environment, and thus increasing the influence of those cues on behavior. This theory may explain both the main effects of alcohol on aggression (if provoking cues are assumed to be generally more salient than cues inhibiting aggression), and suggests that refocusing the attention of intoxicated individuals away from provoking cues may successfully reduce intoxicated aggression. This later type of intervention to reduce intoxicated aggression has been successfully demonstrated in two laboratory studies to date, one of which provided a cognitive distractor task, and one of which incorporated extremely salient anti-aggression cues into the environment (Giancola, Duke, and Ritz, 2011; Giancola, Josephs, Dewall, and Gunn, 2009). Thus, the social environment in which alcohol is consumed may be particularly important to whether intoxicated aggression is expressed.

In summary, the area of aggression boasts both a well-validated set of tasks tapping reactive aggression, and a consistent body of literature on the effects of alcohol on these tasks. However, although tasks assessing reactive aggression have been relatively well standardized and validated, proactive aggression (e.g., bullying, aggression for coercive purposes), and covert aggression (indirect or disguised aggression) are less well studied. These are important forms of aggression that may also be influenced by drugs of abuse, yet they may be difficult to elicit in the lab. Development of paradigms examining these alternate forms of aggression would be a valuable future direction.

3.3.4 Cooperation and pro-social behavior. Another way in which drugs may affect social behavior is to enhance cooperative or pro-social behavior (Boys, Marsden, and Strang, 2001). Indeed, some drugs, such as MDMA, are specifically prized for pro-social "empathogenic" effects (Parrott, 2001). Yet, there has been comparatively little research on pro-social behaviors such as cooperation, social bonding, and helpfulness. The most common research design in the wider field of cooperative behavior and trust has been the use of paradigms from game theory, such as the Prisoner's Dilemma, Trust Game, Dictator Game, etc. (Lane and Gowin, 2009), which quantify strategic interaction among individuals. In the Prisoner's Dilemma, participants are told they are playing with another participant, and that each participant may choose either a cooperative or non-cooperative option. If both choose the cooperative option, they both earn a small amount of money. If both choose the non-cooperative option, they both lose money. If one chooses the cooperative and one the non-cooperative, the non-cooperator earns a large amount of money. Trust is measured based on number of cooperative choices, with the other participant often, although not always, being a confederate. Other games have different structures but share the trait of money allocation to an unknown co-participant as a measure of trust (e.g. Baumgartner *et al.*, 2008). There is also an operant monetary cooperation game, similar to the Point Subtraction Aggression Paradigm, in which presses on a "cooperate" button measure cooperation (Spiga, Bennett, Cherek, and Grabowski, 1994), and there have also been some reports on non-monetary cooperative games, such as the "Tangrams" game, in which a pair of participants combine a set of puzzle pieces into configurations matching as many target shapes as possible within 10 minutes, and cooperation is measured through coded behaviors such as making suggestions, and non-cooperative behaviors through behaviors such as grasping pieces with intent of arriving at a unilateral solution (Tse and Bond, 2006). Last, there is a large body of literature in social psychology on helping, including a number of frequently used experimental measures of helpfulness, such as asking participants to voluntarily perform an additional boring task with no additional compensation, supposedly to help someone else (usually a member of the research team).

The designs described above are widely used in social psychology, but there are comparatively few examples in the literature of their use with drugs of abuse. Classic trust games like the Prisoner's Dilemma have been examined with non-abused drugs such as oxytocin and selective-serotonin reuptake inhibitors (SSRIs; Tse and Bond, 2006; Baumgartner *et al.*, 2008), but only minimally with abused drugs (Hurst, Radlow, Chubb, and Bagley, 1969). Two studies have examined nicotine and alcohol in operant cooperation games, and found that both drugs increase cooperative responding (Spiga, Bennett, Cherek, and Grabowski, 1994; Spiga, Bennett, Scmidtz, and Cherek, 1994). In another study, Steele, Critchlow, and Liu (1985) found that under high conflict (high pressure to help but also high inhibiting motives), alcohol increased helpfulness on a laboratory task, while having no effect under low-conflict conditions.

In summary, these techniques for the study of social cooperation have considerable potential for research on drugs of abuse, but until now they have not been widely used in this domain. Rather most of the research that can be used as models has been conducted with non-abused drugs such as SSRIs.

3.3.5   Other social behaviors.   Several other methods have been used to study the effects of drugs on social behavior, including procedures to assess sexual intention and measures of loneliness or social exclusion. One series of studies showed that alcohol increased perception of sexual behavior in a confederate (Abbey, Zawacki, and McAuslan, 2000; Abbey, Zawacki, and Buck, 2005), but this type of design has not been tested with other drugs (Frohmader, Pitchers, Balfour, and Coolen, 2009). Social exclusion has been assessed using the Cyberball paradigm, which simulates being left out of a virtual game of catch, prompting lowered mood and feelings of social rejection. This has been used to test the effects of oxytocin, which increases willingness to re-engage with the rejecting players in the game (Alvares, Hickie, and Guastella, 2010). It remains to be determined whether similar effects occur with MDMA, which increases oxytocin release in the brain (Thompson *et al.*, 2007). Thus, examining the basic research literature on other specific social behaviors of interest may yield yet more new designs adaptable for use in behavioral pharmacology studies.

3.3.6   General methodological considerations with structured tasks.   There are a few methodological concerns shared by most (although not all) of the structured behavior paradigms presented above, including use of deception and establishment of basic reliability and stability. As noted above, a number of these paradigms are adapted from social psychological research, which tends to utilize high-throughput, between-subjects designs, in contrast to the within-subject, placebo-controlled multiple-dose designs preferred in behavioral pharmacology. Thus the effect of multiple exposures to many of these tasks is unknown, a particular concern in tasks that require maintenance of a deception. The test–retest reliability and stability of most of the paradigms presented above are also not well understood, indicating that some basic methodological research is still necessary to use of most of these tasks in repeated-measures behavioral pharmacology research.

3.4   Unstructured/semi-structured tasks involving multiple participants

Finally, effects of drugs on social behavior have also been studied by recording and coding unstructured and semi-structured interactions between multiple participants. This approach has been taken in residential laboratories, where participant behavior can be observed over longer periods of time (Babor, Mendelson, Uhly, and Kuehnle, 1978), and also in bar-like settings (Samson and Fromme, 1984). The participants' time may be semi-structured with discussion topics, or time may be set aside for dyadic interaction, or specific behaviors may be assessed during "free" times. Dependent variables have included amount of talking (Ward, Kelly, Foltin, and Fischman, 1997), measured either automatically or manually, interpersonal distance between participants (Rachlinski, Foltin, and Fischman, 1989), time spent in interactive versus "coactive" activities (such as watching a movie; Foltin and Fischman, 1988) and "role behavior" (e.g. dominance, task orientation; Babor, Mendelson, Gallant, and Kuehnle, 1978).

These studies have used a variety of outcomes and addressed a range of research questions, which makes integration of the research findings using these designs difficult. Rather than covering each of the previously used designs individually, we will highlight how some of the methodological challenges in these unstructured tasks can be addressed with careful experimental designs, using Kirchner and colleagues (2006) as an example. In their study, previously unacquainted small groups of male participants were observed while consuming either alcoholic or placebo beverages. No explicit talking task was provided. This study examined the effect of alcohol on both the overall level of positive emotional expression and speech, and the coordination of emotional expression and speech (as an indicator of group cohesion). This study used previously developed well-validated coding systems to measure emotional expression (the FACS system; Ekman and Rosenberg, 1997) and turn taking in speech (Grouptalk; Dabbs, Ruback, and Leonard, 1987). The authors found increased coordination of smiling and speech over time in groups consuming alcohol.

Unstructured tasks like the one in this study may provide the most face valid samples of participant behavior, but also provide the most challenging data to quantify. Often drug abuse researchers may benefit from using measures derived from other areas of research (e.g. measures of emotional expression standardized in basic emotions research), as these researchers did. This study also highlights the important future direction of going beyond simple amount of behavior to the study of group dynamics and coordination. In summary, carefully designed studies using unstructured interactions have significant and largely untapped potential for revealing social effects of drugs that emerge only in the context of group interactions.

3.5 Summary

Effects of drugs on social behavior have been studied using a variety of methods, ranging from examining isolated "building blocks" of social interaction, to full-fledged examinations of spontaneous group interactions and dynamics. Several drugs of abuse may increase the attractiveness of others, increase perception of positive emotion in others, increase talkativeness, or increase coordination of group interactions in ways that might promote more pleasurable social interactions. However, drugs vary in their effects, and the same drug may have both positive and negative effects. Other drugs increase aggression, and decrease communicativeness, while alcohol has demonstrated both some potentially pro-social (increased attractiveness, increased desire for interaction, and increased talkativeness) and anti-social (increased aggression) effects. Future research in this area should focus on a few key questions. First, the tasks and outcome variables should be standardized, and incorporate already developed and standardized sophisticated coding systems taken from basic research on social interaction, empathy, and emotion. Second, the social context in which the drugs are taken should be carefully controlled. As noted in section 1, drug effects on various behaviors may be different in group versus isolated conditions or positive versus negative social situations, and although all of these tasks nominally examine "social" behavior, comparatively few designs actually involve free interactions between participants. Thus, this is a major future direction for research. Third, the role of drugs' social effects in their rewarding or reinforcing effects should be explored (as further addressed in section 4).

4   Bidirectional Interactions between Acute Drug Effects and Social Context

The studies summarized in section 1 provide evidence that the social context influences acute subjective, physiological, and behavioral drug effects. However, less is known about why the social context has this effect. It is likely that there is a bidirectional interaction between acute drug effects on social behavior and the social context under which these drugs are taken. That is, it is possible that the social context magnifies the acute drug response because drugs of abuse enhance social interaction. For example, alcohol may be more enjoyable in a group setting because alcohol enhances the attractiveness of others and increases talkativeness, leading to a more enjoyable experience overall. Of course, for the most part this is speculative; there is little empirical evidence concerning bidirectional interactions between acute drug effects and social interaction. Thus, in the following section we provide recommendations for study designs and social behavior tasks that seem particularly well suited to providing insight into how the social context may modulate acute drug effects.

4.1   Designing studies to examine bidirectional interactions

When studying bidirectional interactions between the social context and drugs effects, we first recommend designs that directly compare a social setting to a non-social setting. As noted previously, whereas drugs are most often used in social settings, the majority of human behavioral pharmacology studies are conducted under socially isolated conditions. Use of this design allows causal conclusions about the role of the social environment in drug effects, and combining the use of this design with explicit measurement of aspects of the social environment will allow stronger conclusions about which aspects of the environment influence drug effects.

Regarding the choice of these measures of the social environment, as we have reviewed, there are many explicit measures of aspects of the social environment (such as positive social interactions) that could mediate effects of the environment on acute experience of the drug. Some of these designs may be directly incorporated into a group study, while others would need to be measured with participants in isolation and then examined as mediators of drug effects in social groups. The components of social interaction measures are examples of tasks that would need to be measured in isolation, but might be used as mediators. For example, researchers could examine whether alcohol's effects on detection of happy facial expressions, measured in isolation, mediate alcohol-related increases in elation in a group situation. The hypothetical measures might be taken in isolation for use as mediators, or might be given to a group of participants, for example, if the effects of group decision making under intoxication were of interest. Of the structured tasks that we reviewed, some are amenable to direct use in dyadic and group designs, such as the Prisoner's Dilemma, which has been used both with confederates and with two experimental participants. Other of the structured paradigms may be more difficult to adapt to group testing situations, including reactive aggression paradigms, in which aggression is "provoked" at regular intervals by the confederate. Without this regularity of behavior in the confederate, these designs may produce unacceptable variability. However, it may be possible to adapt these tasks for use in group designs, with appropriate pre-testing and standardization. The unstructured social tasks are obviously already suitable for group designs, and may be enriched by incorporating standardized, easily replicable systems for coding behavior.

Given the use of the designs and measures noted above, the final link in the measurement of bidirectional interactions between social environments and drug effects is to directly examine whether alterations in social behaviors mediate acute drug effects. For example, in the Doty and de Wit (1995) study, both the isolated and grouped participants could have completed a "first impression" task in which they rated the attractiveness of standardized faces. We would expect that increases in the attractiveness of others would be related to enjoyment of the effects of alcohol in the grouped condition, but not in the isolated setting, thus suggesting one possible mechanism for the increase in enjoyment of alcohol in the group condition. Multilevel modeling analyses of the type recommended in section 1 can accommodate testing mediating variables of this type at both individual and group levels. Such studies may show that the effects of drugs on social behavior are partly responsible for their positive acute effects, indicating mechanisms of drug reinforcement not observable in isolated participants.

5   Conclusions

In conclusion, the examination of the influence of social context in acute drug effects is an area of behavioral pharmacology research that is both understudied, and has potentially large implications for drug use and abuse. Although we have focused on acute drug effects, social context and behavior may affect a wide range of drug-related behaviors, including cue-reactivity, relapse, and risk taking, each of which may be modeled in the laboratory, and each of which has been studied in group settings in only a few instances to date. Group settings much more closely approximate the conditions typically present in the real world when individuals are using, abusing or relapsing to drugs, and thus have the potential to generate important insights into this behavior. Throughout this chapter we have emphasized that careful equating of social and non-social conditions, selection of validated and standardized measures, use of appropriate statistical techniques, and explicit investigation of possible bidirectional effects of social context and drug effects will maximize the contribution of such research to our understanding of drug use, abuse, and dependence.

References

Abbey A, Buck PO, Zawacki T, and Saenz C (2003) Alcohol's effects on perceptions of a potential date rape. *Journal of Studies on Alcohol and Drugs* 64: 669–677.

Abbey A, Zawacki T, and Buck PO (2005) The effects of past sexual assault perpetration and alcohol consumption on men's reactions to women's mixed signals. *Journal of Social and Clinical Psychology* 24: 129–155.

Abbey A, Zawacki T, and McAuslan P (2000) Alcohol's effects on sexual perception. *Journal of Studies on Alcohol and Drugs* 61: 688–697.

Alvares GA, Hickie IB, and Guastella AJ (2010) Acute effects of intranasal oxytocin on subjective and behavioral responses to social rejection. *Experimental and Clinical Psychopharmacology* 18: 316–321.

Attwood AS, Ataya AF, Benton CP, Penton-Voak IS, and Munafò MR (2009a) Effects of alcohol consumption and alcohol expectancy on the categorisation of perceptual cues of emotional expression. *Psychopharmacology* 204: 327–334.

Attwood AS, Ohlson C, Benton C, Penton-Voak IS, and Munafò MR (2009b) Effects of acute alcohol consumption on processing of perceptual cues of emotional expression. *Journal of Psychopharmacology* (Oxford) 23: 23–30.

Attwood AS, Penton-Voak IS, and Munafò MR (2009) Effects of acute nicotine administration on ratings of attractiveness of facial cues. *Nicotine and Tobacco Research* 11: 44–48.

Babor TF, Mendelson JH, Gallant D, and Kuehnle JC (1978) Interpersonal behavior in group discussion during marijuana intoxication. *International Journal of the Addictions* 13: 89–102.

Babor TF, Mendelson JH, Uhly B, and Kuehnle JC (1978) Social effects of marihuana use in a recreational setting. *International Journal of the Addictions* 13: 947–959.

Babor TF, Berglas S, Mendelson JH, Ellingboe J, and Miller K (1983) Alcohol, affect, and the disinhibition of verbal behavior. *Psychopharmacology* (Berlin) 80: 53–60.

Baribeau JM, Braun CM, and Dubé R (1986) Effects of alcohol intoxication on visuospatial and verbal-contextual tests of emotion discrimination in familial risk for alcoholism. *Alcoholism: Clinical and Experimental Research* 10: 496–499.

Baron-Cohen S, Wheelwright S, Hill J, Raste Y, and Plumb I (2001) The "Reading the mind in the eyes" Test revised version: A study with normal adults, and adults with Asperger syndrome or high-functioning autism. *Journal of Child Psychology and Psychiatry* 42: 241–251.

Baum KM and Nowicki S, Jr (1998) Perception of emotion: Measuring decoding accuracy of adult prosodic cues varying in intensity. *Journal of Nonverbal Behavior* 22: 89–107.

Baumgartner T, Heinrichs M, Vonlanthen A, Fischbacher U, and Fehr E (2008) Oxytocin shapes the neural circuitry of trust and trust adaptation in humans. *Neuron* 58: 639–650.

Bedi G, Hyman D, and de Wit H (2010) Is ecstasy an "empathogen"? Effects of ± 3,4-methylenedioxymethamphetamine on prosocial feelings and identification of emotional states in others. *Biological Psychiatry* 68: 1134–1140.

Bedi G, Phan KL, Angstadt M, and de Wit H (2009) Effects of MDMA on sociability and neural response to social threat and social reward. *Psychopharmacology* (Berlin) 207: 73–83.

Borrill JA, Rosen BK, and Summerfield AB (1987) The influence of alcohol on judgement of facial expressions of emotion. *British Journal of Medical Psychology* 60: 71–77.

Boys A, Marsden J, and Strang J (2001) Understanding reasons for drug use amongst young people: A functional perspective. *Health Education Research* 16: 457.

Buchmann AF, Laucht M, Schmid B, Wiedemann K, Mann K, and Zimmermann US (2010) Cigarette craving increases after a psychosocial stress test and is related to cortisol stress response but not to dependence scores in daily smokers. *Journal of Psychopharmacology* 24: 247–255.

Bushman BJ and Cooper HM (1990) Effects of alcohol on human aggression: An intergrative research review. *Psychological Bulletin* 107: 341–354.

Caggiula AR, Donny EC, Palmatier MI, Liu X, Chaudhri N, Sved AF, and Bevins RA (2009) The role of nicotine in smoking: A dual-reinforcement model. In RA Bevins and AR Caggiula (eds), *The Motivational Impact of Nicotine and Its Role in Tobacco Use* (pp. 91–109). New York: Springer Science and Business Media.

Carlin AS, Bakker CB, Halpern L, and Post RD (1972) Social facilitation of marijuana intoxication: Impact of social set and pharmacological activity. *Journal of Abnormal Psychology* 80 (2): 132–140.

Caudill BD and Marlatt GA (1975) Modeling influences in social drinking: An experimental analogue. *Journal of Consulting and Clinical Psychology* 43 (3): 405–415.

Cherek DR, Steinberg JL, Kelly TH, and Robinson D (1987) Effects of d-amphetamine on aggressive responding of normal male subjects. *Psychiatry Research* 21: 257–265.

Cherek DR, Steinberg JL, Kelly TH, and Sebastian CS (1989) Effects of d-amphetamine on human aggressive responding maintained by avoidance of provocation. *Pharmacology Biochemistry and Behavior* 34: 65–71.

Cherek DR, Steinberg JL, Kelly TH, Robinson DE, *et al.* (1990) Effects of acute administration of diazepam and d-amphetamine on aggressive and escape responding of normal male subjects. *Psychopharmacology* (Berlin) 100: 173–181.

Chermack ST and Giancola PR (1997) The relation between alcohol and aggression: An integrated biopsychosocial conceptualization. *Clinical Psychology Review* 17: 621–649.

Childs E and de Wit H (2010) Effects of acute psychosocial stress on cigarette craving and smoking. *Nicotine and Tobacco Research* 12(4): 449–453.

Childs E, O'Connor S, and de Wit H (2011) Bidirectional interactions between acute psychosocial stress and acute intravenous alcohol in healthy men. *Alcoholism: Clinical and Experimental Research* (in press).

Cho Y-H and Span SA (2010) The effect of alcohol on sexual risk-taking among young men and women. *Addictive Behaviors* 35: 779–785.

Clyde DJ (1963) *Manual for the Clyde Mood Scale*. Coral Gables, FL: University of Miami, Biometric Laboratory.

Colamussi L, Bovbjerg DH, and Erblich J (2007) Stress- and cue-induced cigarette craving: Effects of a family history of smoking. *Drug and Alcohol Dependence* 88(2–3): 251–258.

Collins RL, Parks GA, and Marlatt GA (1985) Social determinants of alcohol consumption: The effects of social interaction and model status on the self-administration of alcohol. *Journal of Consulting and Clinical Psychology* 53(2): 189–200.

Cooper AM, Waterhouse GJ, and Sobell MB (1979) Influence of gender on drinking in a modeling situation. *Journal of Studies on Alcohol and Drugs* 40(7): 562–570.

Dabbs JM, Jr, and Ruback RB (1987) Dimensions of group process: Amount and structure of vocal interaction. In L Berkowitz (ed.), *Advances in Experimental Social Psychology* (pp. 123–169). San Diego, CA: Academic Press.

Davis WM and Borne RF (1984) Pharmacologic investigation of compounds related to 3,4-methylenedioxyamphetamine (MDA) *Substance and Alcohol Actions/Misuse* 5 (2): 105–110.

de Wit H, Clark M, and Brauer LH (1997) Effects of d-amphetamine in grouped versus isolated humans. *Pharmacology Biochemistry and Behavior* 57 (1–2): 333–340.

de Wit H, Soderpalm AH, Nikolayev L, and Young E (2003) Effects of acute social stress on alcohol consumption in healthy subjects. *Alcoholism: Clinical and Experimental Research* 27 (8): 1270–1277.

Doty P and de Wit H (1995) Effect of setting on the reinforcing and subjective effects of ethanol in social drinkers. *Psychopharmacology* (Berlin) 118 (1): 19–27.

Ebel-Lam AP, MacDonald TK, Zanna MP, and Fong GT (2009) An experimental investigation of the interactive effects of alcohol and sexual arousal on intentions to have unprotected sex. *Basic and Applied Social Psychology* 31: 226–233.

Ebner NC (2008) Age of face matters: Age-group differences in ratings of young and old faces. *Behavior Research Methods* 40: 130–136.

Ekman P (1992) An argument for basic emotions. *Cognition and Emotion* 6: 169–200.

Ekman P (1993) *Pictures of Facial Affect*. Oakland, CA: Author.

Ekman P and Rosenberg EL (1997) *What the Face Reveals: Basic and Applied Studies of Spontaneous Expression Using the Facial Action Coding System (FACS)*. New York: Oxford University Press.

Erblich J, Boyarsky Y, Spring B, Niaura R, and Bovbjerg DH (2003) A family history of smoking predicts heightened levels of stress-induced cigarette craving. *Addiction* 98 (5): 657–664.

Fantegrossi WE, Godlewski T, Karabenick RL, Stephens JM, Ullrich T, Rice KC, *et al.* (2003) Pharmacological characterization of the effects of 3,4-methylenedioxymethamphetamine ("ecstasy") and its enantiomers on lethality, core temperature, and locomotor activity in singly housed and crowded mice. *Psychopharmacology* (Berlin) 166 (3): 202–211.

Foltin RW and Fischman MW (1988) Effects of smoked marijuana on human social behavior in small groups. *Pharmacology Biochemistry and Behavior* 30: 539–541.

Frohmader KS, Pitchers KK, Balfour ME, and Coolen LM (2009) Mixing pleasures: Review of the effects of drugs on sex behavior in humans and animal models. *Hormones and Behavior* 58: 149–162.

George WH and Stoner SA (2000) Understanding acute alcohol effects on sexual behavior. *Annual Review of Sex Research* 11: 92–124.

George WH, Davis KC, Norris J, Heiman JR, Stoner SA, Schacht RL, Hendershot CS, and Kajumulo KF (2009) Indirect effects of acute alcohol intoxication on sexual risk-taking: The roles of subjective and physiological sexual arousal. *Archives of Sexual Behavior* 38: 498–513.

Giancola PR (2000) Executive functioning: A conceptual framework for alcohol-related aggression. *Experimental and Clinical Psychopharmacology* 8: 576–597.

Giancola PR (2004) Executive functioning and alcohol-related aggression. *Journal of Abnormal Psychology* 113: 541–555.

Giancola PR (2008) Current status and directions for future research on alcohol-related aggression. In BP Reimann (ed.), *Personality and Social Psychology Research* (pp. 7–11). New York, NY: Nova Science Publishers, Inc.

Giancola PR and Chermack ST (1998) Construct validity of laboratory aggression paradigms: A response to Tedeschi and Quigley (1996). *Aggression and Violent Behavior* 3: 237–253.

Giancola PR, Duke AA, and Ritz KZ (2011) Alcohol, violence, and the alcohol myopia model: Preliminary findings and implications for prevention. *Addictive Behaviors* 36: 1019–1022.

Giancola PR, Godlaski AJ, and Roth RM (2011) Identifying component-processes of executive functioning that serve as risk factors for the alcohol–aggression relation. *Psychology of Addictive Behaviors* 26: 201–211.

Giancola PR, Josephs RA, Dewall CN, and Gunn RL (2009) Applying the attention-allocation model to the explanation of alcohol-related aggression: Implications for prevention. *Substance Use and Misuse* 44: 1263–1279.

Giancola PR, Parrott DJ, and Roth RM (2006) The influence of difficult temperament on alcohol-related aggression: Better accounted for by executive functioning? *Addictive Behaviors* 31: 2169–2187.

Godlaski AJ and Giancola PR (2009) Executive functioning, irritability, and alcohol-related aggression. *Psychology of Addictive Behaviors* 23: 391–403.

Goeleven E, De Raedt R, Leyman L, and Verschuere B (2008) The Karolinska directed emotional faces: A validation study. *Cognition and Emotion* 22: 1094–1118.

Golan O, Baron-Cohen S, Hill JJ, and Rutherford MD (2007) The "Reading the Mind in the Voice" Test-Revised: A study of complex emotion recognition in adults with and without autism spectrum conditions. *Journal of Autism and Developmental Disorders* 37: 1096–1106.

Greenblatt EN and Osterberg AC (1961) Correlations of activating and lethal effects of excitatory drugs in grouped and isolated mice. *Journal of Pharmacology and Experimental Therapeutics* 131: 115–119.

Griffiths R, Bigelow G, and Liebson I (1975) Effect of ethanol self-administration on choice behavior: Money vs. socializing. *Pharmacology Biochemistry and Behavior* 3: 443–446.

Gunn JA and Gurd MR (1940) The action of some amines related to adrenaline: Cyclohexylalkylamines. *Journal of Physiology* 97 (4): 453–470.

Halsey LG, Huber JW, Bufton RDJ, and Little AC (2010) An explanation for enhanced perceptions of attractiveness after alcohol consumption. *Alcohol* 44: 307–313.

Harris DS, Reus VI, Wolkowitz OM, Mendelson JE, and Jones RT (2005) Repeated psychological stress testing in stimulant-dependent patients. *Progress in Neuropsychopharmacology and Biological Psychiatry* 29 (5): 669–677.

Hart CL, Haney M, Vosburg SK, Comer SD, and Foltin RW (2005) Reinforcing effects of oral Delta9-THC in male marijuana smokers in a laboratory choice procedure. *Psychopharmacology* (Berlin) 181 (2): 237–243.

Heishman SJ and Stitzer ML (1989) Effect of d-amphetamine, secobarbital, and marijuana on choice behavior: Social versus nonsocial options. *Psychopharmacology* (Berlin) 99: 156–162.

Hendershot C and George W (2007) Alcohol and sexuality research in the AIDS era: Trends in publication activity, target populations and research design. *AIDS and Behavior* 11: 217–226.

Higgins ST and Stitzer ML (1988) Effects of alcohol on speaking in isolated humans. *Psychopharmacology* (Berlin) 95: 189–194.

Higgins ST and Stitzer ML (1989) Monologue speech: Effects of d-amphetamine, secobarbital and diazepam. *Pharmacology Biochemistry and Behavior* 34: 609–618.

Higgins ST, Hughes JR, and Bickel WK (1989) Effects of d-amphetamine on choice of social versus monetary reinforcement: A discrete-trial test. *Pharmacology Biochemistry and Behavior* 34: 297–301.

Hurst PM, Radlow R, Chubb NC, and Bagley SK (1969) Drug effects upon choice behavior in mixed motive games. *Behavorial Science* 14: 443–452.

Janowsky DS (2003) Depression and dysphoria effects on the interpersonal perception of negative and positive moods and caring relationships: Effects of antidepressants, amphetamine, and methylphenidate. *Current Psychiatry Reports* 5: 451–459.

Janowsky DS, Clopton P, Leichner PP, Abrams AA, Judd LL, and Pechnick R (1979) Interpersonal effects of marijuana: A model for the study of interpersonal psychopharmacology. *Archives of General Psychiatry* 36: 781–785.

Johanson CE and de Wit H (1992) Lack of effect of social context on the reinforcing effects of diazepam in humans. *Pharmacology Biochemistry and Behavior* 43 (2): 463–469.

Jones BT, Jones BC, Thomas AP, and Piper J (2003) Alcohol consumption increases attractiveness ratings of opposite-sex faces: A possible third route to risky sex. *Addiction* 98: 1069–1075.

Kano M, Gyoba J, Kamachi M, Mochizuki H, Hongo M, and Yanai K (2003) Low doses of alcohol have a selective effect on the recognition of happy facial expressions. *Human Psychopharmacology: Clinical and Experimental* 18: 131–139.

Kenny DA, Kashy DA, and Cook WL (2006) *Dyadic Data Analysis*. New York: Guilford Press.

Kenny DA, Mannetti L, Pierro A, Livi S, and Kashy DA (2002) The statistical analysis of data from small groups. *Journal of Personality and Social Psychology* 83: 126–137.

Kirchner TR, Sayette MA, Cohn JF, Moreland RL, and Levine JM (2006) Effects of alcohol on group formation among male social drinkers. *Journal of Studies on Alcohol and Drugs* 67: 785–793.

Kirschbaum C, Klauer T, Filipp SH, and Hellhammer DH (1995) Sex-specific effects of social support on cortisol and subjective responses to acute psychological stress. *Psychosomatic Medicine* 57 (1): 23–31.

Kirschbaum C, Pirke KM, and Hellhammer DH (1993) The "Trier Social Stress Test": A tool for investigating psychobiological stress responses in a laboratory setting. *Neuropsychobiology* 28 (1–2): 76–81.

LaBar KS, Crupain MJ, Voyvodic JT, and McCarthy G (2003) Dynamic perception of facial affect and identity in the human brain. *Cerebral Cortex* 13: 1023–1033.

Lane SD and Gowin JL (2009) GABAergic modulation of human social interaction in a prisoner's dilemma model by acute administration of alprazolam. *Behavioural Pharmacology* 20: 657–661.

Larsen H, van der Zwaluw CS, Overbeek G, Granic I, Franke B, and Engels RC (2010) A variable-number-of-tandem-repeats ploymorphism in the dopamine D4 receptor gene affects social adaptation of alcohol use: Investigation of a gene-environment interaction. *Psychological Science* 21: 1064–1068.

Lindfors B and Lindman R (1987) Alcohol and previous acquaintance: Mood and social interactions in small groups. *Scandinavian Journal of Psychology* 28: 211–219.

MacDonald TK, MacDonald G, Zanna MP, and Fong G (2000) Alcohol, sexual arousal, and intentions to use condoms in young men: Applying alcohol myopia theory to risky sexual behavior. *Health Psychology* 19: 290–298.

Marrone GF, Pardo JS, Krauss RM, and Hart CL (2010) Amphetamine analogs methamphetamine and 3,4-methylenedioxymethamphetamine (MDMA) differentially affect speech. *Psychopharmacology* (Berlin) 208: 169–177.

Monahan JL and Lannutti PJ (2000) Alcohol as social lubricant: Alcohol myopia theory, social self-esteem, and social interaction. *Human Communication Research* 26: 175–202.

Noel NE, Maisto SA, Johnson JD, and Jackson LA, Jr (2009) The effects of alcohol and cue salience on young men's acceptance of sexual aggression. *Addictive Behaviors* 34: 386–394.

Oosterhof NN and Todorov A (2008) The functional basis of face evaluation. *Proceedings of the National Academy of Sciences* 105: 11087–11092.

Orozco S, Wall TL, and Ehlers CL (1999) Influence of alcohol on electrophysiological responses to facial stimuli. *Alcohol* 18: 11–16.

Parker LLC, Penton-Voak IS, Attwood AS, and Munafò MR (2008) Effects of acute alcohol consumption on ratings of attractiveness of facial stimuli: Evidence of long-term encoding. *Alcohol* 43: 636–640.

Parrott AC (2001) Human psychopharmacology of Ecstasy (MDMA): A review of 15 years of empirical research. *Human Psychopharmacology: Clinical and Experimental* 16: 557–577.

Parrott AC (2007) The psychotherapeutic potential of MDMA (3,4-methylenedioxymethamphetamine): An evidence-based review. *Psychopharmacology* (Berlin) 191: 181–193.

Pennebaker JW, Booth RJ, and Francis ME (2007) *Linguistic Inquiry and Word Count*. Available at: http://homepage.psy.utexas.edu/homepage/faculty/pennebaker/reprints/LIWC2007_OperatorManual.pdf.

Phan KL, Angstadt M, Golden J, Onyewuenyi I, Popovska A, and de Wit H (2008) Cannabinoid modulation of amygdala reactivity to social signals of threat in humans. *Journal of Neuroscience* 28: 2313–2319.

Platt B, Kamboj S, Morgan CJA, and Curran HV (2010) Processing dynamic facial affect in frequent cannabis-users: Evidence of deficits in the speed of identifying emotional expressions. *Drug and Alcohol Dependence* 112: 27–32.

Pliner P and Cappell H (1974) Modification of affective consequences of alcohol: A comparison of social and solitary drinking. *Journal of Abnormal Psychology* 83 (4): 418–425.

Rachlinski JJ, Foltin RW, and Fischman MW (1989) The effects of smoked marijuana on interpersonal distances in small groups. *Drug and Alcohol Dependence* 24: 183–186.

Raudenbush SW and Bryk AS (2002) Hierarchical Linear Models: Applications and Data Analysis Methods. London: Sage.

Ritter D and Eslea M (2005) Hot sauce, toy guns, and graffiti: A critical account of current laboratory aggression paradigms. *Aggressive Behavior* 31: 407–419.

Salzman C, Van Der Kolk B, and Shader R (1976) Marijuana and hostility in a small-group setting. *American Journal of Psychiatry* 133: 1029–1033.

Samson HH and Fromme K (1984) Social drinking in a simulated tavern: An experimental analysis. *Drug and Alcohol Dependence* 14: 141–163.

Sayette MA, Dimoff JD, Levine JM, Moreland RL, and Votruba-Drzal E (2011) The effects of alcohol and dosage-set on risk-seeking behavior in groups and individuals. *Psychology of Addictive Behaviors* (in press).

Sayette MA, Kirchner TR, Moreland RL, Levine JM, and Travis T (2004) Effects of alcohol on risk-seeking behavior: A group-level analysis. *Psychology of Addictive Behaviors* 18 (2): 190–193.

Schachter S and Singer J (1962) Cognitive, social, and physiological determinants of emotional state. *Psychological Review* 69: 379–399.

Schippers GM, De Boer MC, Van der Staak CPF, and Cox WM (1997) Effects of alcohol and expectancy on self-disclosure and anxiety in male and female social drinkers. *Addictive Behaviors* 22: 305–314.

Soderpalm AH and de Wit H (2002) Effects of stress and alcohol on subjective state in humans. *Alcoholism: Clinical and Experimental Research* 26 (6): 818–826.

Spiga R, Bennett RH, Schmitz JM, and Cherek DR (1994) Effects of nicotine on cooperative responding among abstinent male smokers. *Behavioural Pharmacology* 5: 337–343.

Spiga R, Bennett RH, Cherek DR, and Grabowski J (1994) Effects of ethanol on human free-operant cooperative responding. *Drug and Alcohol Dependence* 34: 139–147.

Sripada CS, Angstadt M, McNamara P, King AC, and Phan KL (2011) Effects of alcohol on brain responses to social signals of threat in humans. *Neuroimage* 55: 371–380.

Steele CM, Critchlow B, and Liu TJ (1985) Alcohol and social behavior: II. The helpful drunkard. *Journal of Personality and Social Psychology* 48: 35–46.

Steele CM and Josephs RA (1990) Alcohol myopia: Its prized and dangerous effects. *American Psychologist* 45: 921–933.

Stitzer ML, Griffiths RR, and Liebson I (1978) Effects of d-amphetamine on speaking in isolated humans. *Pharmacology Biochemistry and Behavior* 9: 57–63.

Stitzer ML, Griffiths RR, Bigelow GE, and Liebson I (1981) Human social conversation: Effects of ethanol, secobarbital and chlorpromazine. *Pharmacology Biochemistry and Behavior* 14: 353–360.

Stitzer ML, McCaul ME, Bigelow GE, and Liebson IA (1984) Hydromorphone effects on human conversational speech. *Psychopharmacology* (Berlin) 84: 402–404.

Tedeschi JT and Quigley BM (1996) Limitations of laboratory paradigms for studying aggression. *Aggression and Violent Behavior* 1: 163–177.

Tedeschi JT and Quigley BM (2000) A further comment on the construct validity of laboratory aggression paradigms: A response to Giancola and Chermack. *Aggression and Violent Behavior* 5: 127–136.

Thomas SE, Bacon AK, Randall PK, Brady KT, and See RE (2011) An acute psychosocial stressor increases drinking in non-treatment-seeking alcoholics. *Psychopharmacology* (Berlin) (in press).

Thompson MR, Callaghan P, Hunt GE, Cornish J, and McGregor IS (2007) A role for oxytocin and 5-HT1A receptors in the prosocial effects of 3, 4 methylenedioxymethamphetamine ("ecstasy"). *Neuroscience* 146: 509–514.

Todorov A (2011) Evaluating faces on social dimensions. In A Todorov, ST Fiske and DA Prentice (eds.), *Social Neuroscience: Toward Understanding the Underpinnings of the Social Mind* (pp. 54–76). New York: Oxford University Press.

Tottenham N, Tanaka JW, Leon AC, McCarry T, Nurse M, Hare TA, Marcus DJ, Westerlund A, Casey BJ, and Nelson C (2009) The NimStim set of facial expressions: Judgments from untrained research participants. *Psychiatry Research* 168: 242–249.

Tracy JL, Robins RW, and Schriber RA (2009) Development of a FACS-verified set of basic and self-conscious emotion expressions. *Emotion* 9: 554–559.

Tse WS and Bond AJ (2006) Noradrenaline might enhance assertive human social behaviours: An investigation in a flatmate relationship. *Pharmacopsychiatry* 39: 175–179.

Walter NT, Mutic S, Markett S, Montag C, Klein AM, and Reuter M (2011) The influence of alcohol intake and alcohol expectations on the recognition of emotions. *Alcohol* (in press).

Ward AS, Kelly TH, Foltin RW, and Fischman MW (1997) Effects of d-amphetamine on task performance and social behavior of humans in a residential laboratory. *Experimental and Clinical Psychopharmacology* 5: 130–136.

Wardle M, Cederbaum K, and de Wit H (2011) Quantifying talk: Developing reliable measures of verbal productivity. *Behavior Research Methods* 43: 168–178.

Watson DW and Sobell MB (1982) Social influences on alcohol consumption by black and white males. *Addictive Behaviors* 7(1): 87–91.

Wilson GT, Perold EA, and Abrams DB (1981) The effects of expectations of self-intoxication and partner's drinking on anxiety in dyadic social interaction. *Cognitive Therapy and Research* 5: 251–264.

20

Ecological Momentary Assessment[1]

Thomas R. Kirchner and Saul Shiffman

1 Introduction

Ecological Momentary Assessment (EMA) is a method for collecting data in real time and in real-world settings. EMA is particularly well suited for studying substance use, because use patterns are highly complex and related to contextual factors like mood, setting, and cues. This chapter addresses the application of EMA to substance use research, outlining principles of EMA design and analysis, and illustrating them with examples from the literature. The chapter considers the way technological innovations are facilitating the rapid evolution of EMA systems, and provides recommendations on current best practices. It reviews data on methodological issues such as compliance and reactivity, and looks forward to the way emerging technologies will enable increasingly unobtrusive assessment of both individual- and systems-level processes over time and space. EMA methods reveal substance use patterns not captured by questionnaires or retrospective data, and hold great promise for substance use research and treatment.

Accurate measurement, including the antecedents and effects that emerge as a consequence of substance ingestion, is a central focus of research on substance use and misuse. Yet while use patterns and the effects are heavily influenced by proximal internal states and environmental factors, most substance use research occurs in laboratory or clinic settings; in other words, outside the subject's natural environment. Ecological Momentary Assessment (EMA; Shiffman, 2007; Shiffman, Stone, and Hufford, 2008; Stone and Shiffman, 1994) aims to assess the ebb and flow of life, moment to moment, as a way of faithfully capturing the dynamics of behavior and experience

[1] This work was supported by National Institutes of Health, National Institute on Drug Abuse Grants RC1-DA028710 (PI: Kirchner) and R01-DA020742 (PI: Shiffman). Saul Shiffman is cofounder of invivodata, which provides electronic diaries for research, and serves as consultant to GlaxoSmithKline Consumer Healthcare exclusively regarding matters related to smoking cessation and also is developing new nicotine medications.

over time and across real-world settings. The application of EMA methods to studies of substance use is the focus of this chapter.

EMA methodology draws from a number of related approaches that share common elements. These include diary methods (Verbrugge, 1980), self-monitoring and functional analysis (McFall, 1977), experience sampling (Hektner, Schmidt, and Csikszentmihalyi, 2007; de Vries, 1992), social interaction and network analysis ("Studying Social Interaction with the Rochester Interaction Record," 1991), ambulatory physiological monitoring (e.g., Kamarck et al., 1998), and a broad array of monitoring approaches enabled by the recent development of sophisticated electronic sensors (Intille, 2007), including the concept of a "quantified self" for personal informatics. Spanning these methodological traditions are a broad range of data collection tools, including paper-and-pencil diaries, beepers, programmable watches, palmtop computers, automated telephone survey software, cellular telephones, GPS devices and other instruments for unobtrusive data collection. Processing and analysis of the "intensive" longitudinal data these methods provide is also a foundational cornerstone on which EMA science depends. EMA is thus an umbrella concept that provides a common framework for each of these complementary methodological traditions.

1.1 EMA principles

EMA methods are designed to collect data about behavior, thoughts, feelings, and physiological states over time, when and where they occur in the real world. This is accomplished with repeated assessments via a wide range of mobile data collection devices. The design, measurement schedule, assessment content, and mobile technology depends primarily on the goals of the research.

1.1.1 Momentary assessment. Momentary assessment close to the time of experience is a fundamental characteristic of EMA methodology. Measurement in the moment allows researchers to avoid the well-documented inaccuracies of autobiographical memory (i.e., subjective memories of a person's own experience; Bradburn, Rips, and Shevell, 1987; Hammersley, 1994; Shiffman *et al.*, 1997; Tourangeau, 2000). Beyond inaccuracy, retrospective measures are particularly problematic because they can introduce significant bias, and preclude prospective evaluation of the link between variables of interest and clinical outcomes like drug use. For example, knowledge of one's ultimate success or failure with abstinence from a drug can easily bias retrospective judgments about the circumstances that precipitated the result (Ross, 1989; Shiffman *et al.*, 1997). Thus, it should hardly be surprising when a retrospective study finds that those who have already relapsed recall concluding that the causes of the lapse were internal and unchanging. Only momentary assessment makes it possible to avoid retrospective biases, and identify prospective associations between fleeting real-world experiences and later outcomes.

1.1.2 Recurrent assessment. Dynamic behaviors that vary over time are prime targets for EMA research. When the target of assessment varies over time, these variations must be captured with recurrent assessments. Because the frequency and duration of behavioral variations varies widely, the intensity and associated "resolution" of measurements should coincide. For this reason, assessment protocols reported in the literature range greatly, from 65 assessments per day for 2 days (Shapiro, Jamner, Davtdov, and James, 2002), to daily assessment for as long as a year (Jamison *et al.*, 2001). EMA-based statistical analyses leverage the temporal resolution afforded by recurrent assessments to focus on within-subject changes in behavior and experience over time and across contexts.

1.1.3 Ecologic validity. Substance use and misuse occurs in real-world settings, characterized by multi-tiered influences that cannot be fully replicated in a research laboratory. Even if they could be modeled in the lab, researchers seldom have a priori information about what aspects of the social, physical, and subjective environment are more or less influential. EMA methodology allows us to study these phenomena in subjects' natural environments, not only to test hypothesized associations, but also to uncover unanticipated ones. The result is that empirical findings will then be generalizable to real-world substance use, enabling researchers and treatment providers to better understand the linkages between substance ingestion and the events, environments, and internal states that actually maintain use.

2 Empirical Relevance of EMA to Substance Abuse Research

EMA methods are well suited for study of substance use and misuse, because substance use itself is a discrete, episodic behavior that is influenced by proximal and environmental factors, and whose natural progression follows highly complex patterns over periods of daily life. Momentary data collection in the natural environment allows for assessment of temporally dynamic behavioral, psychological, and physiological processes (Smyth and Stone, 2003). Constructs emphasized in theories of drug abuse also lend themselves to EMA assessment. The immediate situation in which substance use occurs is thought to be especially important, and beyond the immediate situation, broader dynamic background influences in the person's life (e.g., stress, social support), as well as the acute effects of drugs (e.g., euphoria) loom large as factors driving substance use.

Another advantage to studying substance use in real-world settings is that the factors that influence substance are difficult to approximate and measure in the laboratory. This is magnified when studying illicit substance use, as laboratory environments are not conducive to eliciting such behavior. Situational patterns of substance use have traditionally been assessed through global reports on questionnaires ("Do you smoke more when stressed?"), yet data on use patterns suggest that questionnaires do not capture variations across settings and are thus less informative than field-based EMA. Correlations between EMA-assessed patterns and questionnaire-reported patterns are low, even when identical items were used in both assessments (e.g., Otsuki, Tinsley, Chao, and Unger, 2008; Shiffman, 1993). These discrepancies have clinical implications, as EMA measures have been found to prospectively predict outcomes like relapse better than traditional baseline questionnaires (Kirchner, Shiffman, and Wileyto, 2011; Shiffman, 2007; Shiffman *et al.*, 1997). Substance use antecedents and effects must be studied in the real world if we are to successfully account for complex interactions with time and socio-environmental context (Bolger, Davis, and Rafaeli, 2003; Moskowitz and Young, 2006).

3   EMA Sampling Design

Whatever the traditional design of an EMA study, at the level of comparison groups, procedures, etc., the EMA researcher must also consider the EMA sampling design. EMA sampling design focuses on the way assessments are distributed over time and space. Since EMA is based on repeated sampling over time, recognizing that momentary circumstances heavily influence the data, it is crucial to carefully consider the timing and context of assessments.

3.1   Event-based assessment

Event-based sampling schemes focus on discrete events of interest, rather than attempting to characterize subjects' ongoing daily experience. Event-based sampling is almost always included in studies of substance use, since substance use itself is usually *the* event of interest. Although event-based monitoring can be automated in some circumstances (see section 4.3), users are most often required to self-initiate an entry when the target event occurs. Event-based monitoring requires cooperation, and compliance with this instruction can be hard to verify (see section 8.4). It is also important that researchers and subjects agree on a clear definition of the event (e.g., whether a candy bar is a "snack" or a "meal;" whether a single puff of another's cigarette counts as "smoking"). Events may be very simple and objective – smoking one cigarette or drinking one beer – or may be complex or subjective – experiencing a "strong" temptation to smoke, or feeling intoxicated. For some research questions, a daily record of event frequency may be best: one may be interested in how many events there have been (e.g., to see if frequency of use has decreased with treatment), while the timing or context of the events within each day is not of interest. For other projects it is important to consider more fine-grained characteristics of the events – their spacing over time, the situational context, and their association with other dynamic factors.

3.2   Time-based assessment

Time-based sampling schemes are designed to characterize experience more broadly and inclusively, without a predefined focus on a particular event or set of co-occuring events. Most phenomena, including all subjective reports, have to be sampled intermittently on some schedule, because continuous quantification is impossible or at least impractical. However, an increasing array of phenomena can be captured continuously by automated sensors – e.g., physical movement, through actigraphy (see section 4.3).

The frequency of time-based assessments is based on considerations of how rapidly the target phenomenon is expected to vary, and how the data will be analyzed (Collins *et al.*, 2002). Assessment intensity in EMA studies of substance use has varied greatly, ranging from 3 assessments per day to 50 or more (Delfino, Jamner, and Whalen, 2001). It is imperative to consider participant burden, incentives, and compliance, especially when planning an intensive protocol.

One approach to time-based scheduling of assessments is to fix them over time, either by precise temporal intervals (e.g., every 30 minutes), or by milestone events (e.g., meals), or by phases of the day (e.g., morning, evening). The most basic kind of time-based protocol administers pre-scheduled assessments at regular time intervals. For example, National Cancer Institute, 2009 scheduled assessments every 30 minutes over an intensive 2-week period to capture within-subject trajectories of a broad set of variables including mood, health behavior, and social interactions. A limitation of this approach is that participants will often begin to anticipate assessments, which might affect their responses, especially if the assessment schedule becomes entrained to a natural rhythm in the person's life. Milestone events like meals or phases of the day offer an alternative, although when assessment always occurs in connection with particular milestone events, the data are unlikely to represent broader experience outside those events. Another challenge is that scheduling assessments during phases of the day (e.g., "evening") allows subjects to decide when to complete assessments, and thus risks introducing bias, as some subjects may systematically choose to complete their assessments when things are calm, while others tend to make their entries when they are feeling stressed.

When representative experience sampling is paramount, randomly scheduled assessments are an effective alternative to a fixed-interval approach, although technological and logistical requirements render this a more challenging solution. Like drawing a simple random sample from a population of people, sampling moments at random ensures that the data accurately represent the distribution of measured phenomenon within each person's daily experience. As in population sampling, a random time-based assessment protocol can be modified to maximize efficiency. For example, the randomized schedule can be stratified across time bins to ensure even coverage of the day (e.g., Armeli, Todd, and Mohr, 2005, sampled at random within blocks of 10:00–11:30, 15:00–16:30, and 20:00–21:30), and certain parts of the day can be over-sampled if theory warrants (Shiffman *et al.*, 2000).

Time-based assessment schedules require the use of cues, reminders, or "prompts" to trigger each assessment. When cooperation is high it can sometimes be left to the subject to recognize naturally occurring cues, like a milestone (e.g., a meal), a socially recognized interval (e.g., morning), or a particular time by the clock (e.g., record at 1 p.m.). Randomly scheduled assessments require cues that act like an alarm – alerting the user that it is time to make an entry. Investigators have used Personal Digital Assistants (PDAs, palmtop computers), programmed watches, beepers, and cell phones for this purpose. As discussed in section 6 of this chapter, as portable devices such as phones become more widespread, it will probably become easier to implement signaling on subjects' own devices, and to use "server-side" software to administer the schedules and prompt a variety of different devices, without programming each separately.

3.2.1   Time-based coverage protocols.   Time-based "coverage" schemes are used to capture summary data over all instances of a phenomenon of interest across the entire day (Shiffman, Stone, and Hufford, 2008). Subjects might be asked a few times each day, for example, how many drinks they have had since the previous assessment. Unlike momentary assessment approaches, coverage-based assessments do not focus on "real time," relying instead on retrospective recall over some predefined time interval. Coverage strategies can be an effective way to capture information about substance use (e.g., Armeli *et al.*, 2007; Todd, 2004). They provide a more comprehensive assessment than a sampling regimen that only assesses a subset of all experiences. In addition, for assessment of frequent drug-use episodes (e.g., smoking), a coverage scheme can reduce subject burden, since each episode need not be entered separately.

Coverage strategies have important limitations, the first of which is the substantial retrospective bias they can introduce. The coverage approach assumes that subjects can recreate an accurate timeline of prior assessments and intermediate events and experinces. To the contrary, research suggests that people are particularly poor at keeping track of time and identifying when events took place (Sudman and Bradburn, 1973). Instead, they often 'remember' events as having happened more recently than is accurate, resulting in double-counting of events. Research also indicates that people are not very good at summarizing their experiences over time, often over-weighting events associated with heightened affect, such that summary reports discount routine, ambient states while exaggerating salient affective peaks.

3.2.2   Daily diaries.   The promise of a particular type of fixed, daily coverage strategy, the *daily diary*, was recognized early (Roghmann and Haggerty, 1972), and has been used frequently in substance use research (Armeli, Todd, Conner, and Tennen, 2008; Mohr *et al.*, 2008; Park, Tudiver, Schultz, and Campbell, 2004; Toll, Cooney, McKee, and O'Malley, 2006). By definition, daily diaries have limited temporal resolution, restricting study to between-day phenomena. Depending on the target behavior, daily time resolution is often insufficient for studies of substance use and misuse. This is because proximal within-day factors, such as exposure to drug cues, have been shown to play an important predictive role. For example, Shiffman and Waters (2004) found that while daily measures of mood did not predict lapses to smoking after quitting, momentary measures of mood in the hours leading up to a lapse were significantly associated with relapse risk. Thus, day-level data may miss important sources of dynamic variation that drive substance use. Moreover, given that biases due to heuristic recall strategies are known to operate over short timeframes, daily recall of drug or alcohol consumption is likely subject to bias. When subjects are asked to summarize an entire day's experience, accurate recall is likely to stretch the capabilities of autobiographical memory. Recall bias may also be enhanced by affective circumstances at the time of data entry, especially when affect at the time of entry differs from affect at the time of a reported event, similar to what has been described as the "cold-to-hot" empathy gap (Loewenstein, 1999; Sayette *et al.*, 2000). In other words, past experiences may be particularly hard to recall accurately if the subject's affective state at the time of recall is different from their state at the time of the target event.

4 EMA Content

4.1 Self-reported survey assessment

Most EMA studies use psychometric self-report scales like those used in non-EMA laboratory-based assessment batteries. EMA self-report is not restricted to psychometrically validated questionnaires, which tend to be longer than is ideal for recurrent EMA, but adapting items for mobile administration is non-trivial (Dillman, Smyth, and Christian, 2009). A noteworthy challenge to adapting preexisting baseline measures for EMA is their length, which threatens to undermine the hallmark advantages of the EMA approach, including momomentary data collection that captures real-world phenomenon without inadvertently interfering with or altering it via overly burdensome response requirements. For this reason, researchers should carefully consider abbreviated or single-item scales for certain constructs, some of which (e.g., craving measures) have been found to perform as well as their more detailed and lengthy counterparts (Sayette *et al.*, 2000). Another approach being tested to shorten assessments is to use the statistical framework of Item Response Theory as a foundation for adaptive testing, which allows a startegically selected subset of items to achieve a full assessment (Kamarck *et al.*, 2010).

Most modern EMA systems support sophisticated management of survey administration (e.g., branching logic and skip patterns, testing data for validity of the responses, etc.). This is a major advantage over standard battery assessments as well as paper diaries, as subjects often violate skip patterns and enter invalid answers (Quinn, Goka, and Richardson, 2003). Other assessment modes such as phone-based interactive voice response (IVR) or SMS require that content is adapted to some degree. For instance, short message service (SMS) items should be restricted to 140 characters, while IVR questions must be restructured to avoid serial lists, as IVR systems present content aurally and serially, which can challenge subjects' cognitive capacity (e.g., forgetting the first response option by the time they get to the seventh).

Regardless of the mobile assessment mode, meta-analysis suggests that written measures presented on-screen are psychometrically equivalent to their paper versions (Gwaltney, Shields, and Shiffman, 2008), indicating that empirically validated self-report measures provide useful guidelines for survey construction. Moreover, there is evidence that self-administered telephone or otherwise mobile assessments mitigate "social desirability" effects and self-presentational concerns, such that drug use prevalence rates are higher and probably more accurate when assessed in the absense of an interviewer, survey administrator, or family member (Currivan, Nyman, Turner, and Biener, 2004; Tourangeau and Yan, 2007).

4.2 Cognitive and 'personality' measures

While EMA studies tend to rely on simple self-report, the EMA approach can incorporate a variety of other measures, particularly with the use of palmtop computers and, increasingly, "smart" phones capable of sophisticated stimulus presentation and response assessment. For example, mobile devices have been used to implement cognitive performance tests that assess both response accuracy and reaction time. In one early study of this kind (Shiffman, Paty, Kassel, and Gnys, 1995), tobacco abstinence was found to impair cognitive performance among heavy daily smokers, but not among light "casual" smokers who are not dependent.

More complex tasks can also be administered. Waters and Li (2008) have implemented several "emotional Stroop" tasks via PDA. Emotional Stroop tasks and other assessments of attentional bias measure the degree to which a topic, such as drug craving or anxiety, captures the subject's attention, to a degree that interferes with cognitive performance. Franken (2011) has used such momentary measures of attentional bias to predict relapse in opiate addicts. Others have extended EMA to assessment of cue reactivity, which is usually assessed in the laboratory (Carter and Tiffany, 2001; Kerst, 2011; Warthen and Tiffany, 2009), by using a PDA to present smokers with smoking-related and neutral photos. Warthen and Tiffany (2009) showed reliable effects on craving, which could allow assessment of reactivity under various contexts. McCarthy (2011) has implemented assessments of impulsiveness on mobile devices, and shown that these "traits," usually considered stable characteristics of individuals, change over the course of smoking cessation. Thus, an increasing array of mobile devices can be used to present a variety of stimuli as part of a cognitive processing assessment.

4.3   Electronic sensors

Electronic sensors on mobile devices available to consumers on the mass market are becoming increasingly sophisticated, capable of passively gathering data via photograph and video, ambient light, audio, temperature, physical location, and direction of travel. In particular, accelerometers have proven useful for what is often called *activity recognition*, and refinements of this technology show promise for passive detection of drug-use behaviors, with cigarette smoking as an early model (Varkey and Pompili, 2009). A range of even more sophisticated measures can also be incorporated via multiple accelerometers and other add-on wearable sensors, although these applications or more logisitically challenging and currently restricted to small-scale laboratory-based projects (Tapia, Intille, Lopez, and Larson, 2006). Recent applications with relevance here have shown promise for remote detection of alcohol ingestion (Kumar, al'Absi, and Ali, 2010; Venugopal *et al.*, 2008) and cocaine ingestion (Boyer, 2011). This work will continue to advance via sensors that gather physiological data (e.g., ambulatory heart rate and blood pressure; Liebo *et al.*, 2011), although a remaining barrier is the sheer volume of data they produce, which can challenge currently available storage capacity. On the other hand, patch-based sensors, including those that are designed to attach to the skin in a way that is flat, durable, and almost invisible (Kim *et al.*, 2011), will soon make integration of physiological measures alongside more standard phone-based sensors more logisically and financially feasible.

5   Ecological Momentary Intervention

Self-monitoring and functional analysis are core components of cognitive-behavioral therapy (CBT), with a strong empirical basis extending back to the rise of the cognitive revolution in psychology (Nelson, 1977; Sieck and McFall, 1976). The idea is that changing dysfunctional behavior patterns begins with systematic documentation of the affective, cognitive, and contextual factors associated with maintenance of the behavior. The individual is then empowered to disrupt or separate the link between these maintenance factors and the target behavior. Self-monitoring was quickly recognized as a particularly important component of treatment for substance misuse (e.g., Abrams and Wilson, 1979; Fremouw and Brown, 1980; Sobell, Sobell, and Sheahan, 1976), and features prominently in influential CBT-based models of relapse prevention (e.g., Marlatt, 1985). Leveraged for the purpose of self-monitoring, EMA methodology provides a natural extension for the implementation of this well-established approach to understanding and intervening upon dysfunctional substance use patterns.

Merely performing a self-monitoring regimen can positively affect unwanted behavior, perhaps by heightening awareness of deeply ingrained, habitual patterns that have previously gone unnoticed. In this regard, traditional "limitations" of the EMA approach like reactivity (see section 8.3) can be reconceptualized as positive evidence for the potential power of ecological momentary interventions. Extending simple event monitoring, there is evidence that a scheduled gradual reduction of a target behavior can be accomplished with guidance from a mobile device (Cinciripini *et al.*, 1997; Riley, Jerome, Behar, and Weil, 2002; Riley, Pici, Forman, and Behar, 2003). For example, Riley, Jerome, Behar, and Weil (2002) had subjects record all smoking episodes and then allow an automated reduction algorithm to take control of their smoking, signaling them when to smoke, and gradually increasing the interval between cigarettes.

Going beyond simple monitoring and reduction strategies, collection of richer data via EMA methods may provide richer adjuncts to treatment (Backinger and Augustson, 2011; Carter, Day, Cinciripini, and Wetter, 2007). EMA can provide valid and up-to-date assessments of the antecedents of substance use, which provides a natural link to treatment based on stimulus control or self-control methods: The patient can be guided to avoid triggering stimuli, or prepare coping strategies for use when encountering high-risk situations. For example, Kerst (2011) and others are using mobile devices to administer attentional retraining interventions meant to counter the attentional bias that seems to make users vulnerable to relapse. Further, real-time interventions seem to have great potential – for example, a mobile system can track trends in the data (e.g., craving rising, affect getting worse, exposure to drug stimuli) and warn patients when they are at risk and/or suggest a productive course of action. Thus, EMA-based treatment could provide on-the-spot intervention just when it is needed, any time of the day or night.

The promise of EMA for intervention is being rapidly advanced by the development of dozens of mobile applications by academic, advocacy, and industry groups. As of 2009 there were almost 50 mobile smoking cessation support apps available for download on the iPhone alone, although not all of these include EMA or tracking features (Abroms, Padmanabhan, Thaweethai, and Phillips, 2011). Social service organizations are making a significant contribution to development, perhaps best represented by the smoking cessation applications developed by the Lance Armstrong Foundation ("MyQuit Coach") and the American Legacy Foundation ("Become An EX Mobile"). Despite the flurry of mobile application development, current focus is almost exclusively on design and content issues, with very few published papers reporting effects on behavioral outcomes. One recent exception is a paper on a smoking cessation trial in which a PDA provided female quitters with extensive directions for smoking reduction and cues for coping, as well as assessing the outcomes (Wetter *et al.*, 2011). The project found that the mobile cessation support tools provided no advantage relative to usual care, although post hoc analyses suggested that subgroups who used the mobile support tools more than others had a lower likelihood of relapse. More encouraging results were presented at an invited symposium on mobile interventions at the 2011 annual meeting of the American Psychological Association, where mobile applications were presented that have yielded improved abstinence from opioids (Acosta, Marsch, and Grabinski, 2011), cocaine (Boyer, 2011), and cigarette smoking (Kirchner, 2011). Studies that have used scheduled and on-demand SMS (mobile phone text) messages to improve success at smoking cessation (Berkman, Falk, and Lieberman, 2011; Free *et al.*, 2011; Rodgers *et al.*, 2005) also suggest that mobile interventions can be effective. Thus the promise of EMA-based interventions for treatment of substance use remains high, but as yet unfulfilled.

6 Methodological Recommendations

Technological and methodologic advances are rapidly transforming the EMA landscape. The researcher must make a range of decisions about hardware, software, and other logistical factors that go well beyond sampling protocol design, or development and delivery of content. In this section we provide recommendations on hardware and software, as well as management of subjects and data.

6.1 Device ergonomics

Collection of EMA data requires a mobile device that can be carried in the field. This can be as simple as paper and pencil or as high-tech as a tablet computer. Portability is an essential feature, as subjects are usually expected to carry the device at all times, so that data are captured at representative moments. Cellular telephones provide an ideal solution, especially as cell-phone costs decline and penetration approaches 100% (Cellular Telephone Industry Association, 2011). Most importantly, most people already carry a cell-phone with them at all times, and cell-phones are increasingly capable of powerful computational processing. The growing dominance of cell-phones for mobile data collection notwithstanding, cost considerations can be a challenge, especially if the researcher does not require subjects to use their own phone and cellular service plan. When subjects' phones are used, privacy concerns become an important consideration.

6.2 EMA software

For an EMA study, software often matters more than hardware, and requires careful consideration. A variety of software and services are available, both from commercial sources and via open source or freeware (e.g., Borriello *et al.*, 2009; Le, Choi, and

Beal, 2006). As technology advances, the range of considerations is increasing, including whether the application runs "natively" on the device, whether it requires an active wireless data connection, or whether it runs natively but can "push" or "pull" data in the event that a wireless connection becomes available. The task of programming for an EMA study for a specific protocol, even re-programming freeware packages, should not be underestimated. Minor software errors can be disastrous, and limited functionality can substantially affect the scientific value of the data. Developing customized software is even more challenging, and investigators are well advised to use existing software or services with dedicated support. Even established systems are often device or platform dependent, limiting their use by a more general user base and thus limiting the ability to disseminate an application at scale. All of this has led to calls for the development of a more standardized mobile application archetechture that is "open" for use both across platforms and by the public, characteristics that made the internet an unrivaled platform for development (e.g., Estrin and Sim, 2010). At present the technological burden associated with EMA studies remains a substantial barrier to adoption.

6.3   Dynamic timing protocols

Managing the schedule of assessments (e.g., determining when a time-based assessment is to be made) is among the most complex aspects of any EMA protocol. Timing protocols that are integrated into the data-recording device are currently most common, although an emerging solution is the use of web-based systems that trigger assessments remotely, such as via SMS prompts. Compliance with timing protocols can be improved when they incorporate features that reduce participant burden, such as the ability to delay or "snooze" for a brief period and the ability to put the timing protocol to "sleep" at night, and when they can adapt to each person's real-world schedule, even as it changes over time (e.g., weekdays versus weekends; Shiffman *et al.*, 2002).

6.4   Data acquisition

The current gold standard for mobile data acquisition are systems that periodically upload data wirelessly to a central web-based data server, but that do not require an active wireless data connection for actual EMA entries (as is required by web-based survey applications like "Survey Monkey"). This avoids systematic missing data when participants do not have access to an active wireless data connection, while preserving the considerable benefits of remote continuous data collection. Remote data collection allows ongoing compliance and data-flow assessment that empower the researcher to identify problems and intervene as they occur, dramatically improving the quality and temporal precision of the data. Moreover, remote server-based systems often allow the researcher to adjust content and protocols as needed by pushing revised content and/or algorithms to all devices. It is also noteworthy that that such server-side systems also enable mixed-mode data entry options, allowing users to seamlessly complete the same survey items via IVR, SMS, email, mobile-web form, or mobile "App."

6.5   Administrative considerations

Implementation of an EMA requires significant resources and administrative effort related to managing both participants and the troves of data they produce. Training of subjects on the protocol, the assessment, and the device(s) used is an essential aspect of EMA studies, although using participants' own phones can ease this burden. Monitoring and supporting hardware and software problems as they occur in the field often requires full-time support or a professional support service. Managing real-time data on compliance and response anomolies, along with the inflow of assessment data, is also demanding. EMA studies often yield huge datasets with hundreds of thousands, and sometimes millions, of observations. These datasets include those records that do not have self-report data at all, but record other transactions of some importance (e.g., records of missed assessment prompts). Furthermore, preparation of datasets for particular analytic approaches usually requires substantial processing (e.g., finding observations preceding or succeeding events of interest). Data management capacity for maintaining databases and producing analytical datasets is an essential resource for EMA research. EMA studies can produce rich datasets, but realizing the value of these data demands a substantial commitment of resources and expertise.

7   Analytical Recommendations

Review of the EMA literature reveals a great deal of diversity and creativity regarding statistical analyses used to address questions of interest. Indeed, the analytic latitude provided by complex longitudinal data sets is precisely what attracts many methodologists to EMA research, while it scares away many others. Unlike traditional "repeated measures" designs, the assessment occasions in EMA datasets are often very numerous. Individuals typically vary in the number of assessments, and the assessments may not be evenly spaced in time, making both traditional between-subjects analyses and traditional repeated-measures approaches poor fits. As a starting point, the analysis of EMA data must take into account the nesting of multiple observations within each subject and the autocorrelation among observations.

A key issue that we will emphasize here is the way the analysis represents or deals with time – whether the passage of time is ignored (e.g., when collections of events are analyzed in a time-independent way in case-cross-over designs), becomes the dependent variable (e.g., in time-to-event analyses), or is treated as a dimension along which other factors vary (e.g., as time-varying covariates). It is beyond the scope of this chapter to address statistical approaches in detail, and we recommend other sources for this purpose (Schwartz and Stone, 1998; Singer and Willet, 2003; Walls and Schafer, 2006). The scope of possible analyses is very broad: Walls and Schafer (2006) introduce a very wide array of methods, many probably unfamiliar to substance use researchers.

7.1   The case-cross-over design

The *case-cross-over* design, combining event and time-based assessments (or, less often, two kinds of event), offers a powerful way to assess situational correlates of substance use. Without a contrasting set of data from situations that were *not* associated with substance use, data on substance use occasions can be misleading, much as epidemiological data about the correlates of a disease require data from both diseased and non-diseased individuals to construct a case-control design (Paty, Kassel, and Shiffman, 1992). A number of studies have combined event-based data and time-based data in a case-control (cases = drug events, controls = time-based non-drug) or case-cross-over design (Carter *et al.*, 2008; Delfino, Jamner, and Whalen, 2001; Moghaddam and Ferguson, 2007; Shiffman *et al.*, 2002; Shiffman, Ferguson, and Gwaltney, 2006; Shiffman, Paty, Gwaltney, and Dang, 2004). These case-cross-over design applications ignore time. That is, consistent with the case-control approach, they compare one collection of case observations (substance use events) with controls (time-based assessments), without any reference to their temporal ordering. The approach is essentially cross-sectional. But, given that EMA data are naturally ordered in time, they provide a platform for prospective analyses of substance use, and analyses that very much take time and temporal ordering into account.

7.2   Time-to-event analyses

Survival or time-to-event analyses estimate the risk of substance use occurring, over time, by attending to how much time passes until a substance use event occurs, modeling this as a function of covariate predictors. The time-to-event approach treats substance use differently from the traditional longitudinal approach. In the time-to-event approach, substance use is a discrete "binary" event that either occurs or not (regardless of quantity), whereas the time-block approach usually looks at the quantity of substance use, but ignores timing within blocks. However, it is possible to analyze a discrete outcome in the fixed-block approach, as in Delfino, Jamner, and Whalen's (2001) analysis of how mood at a particular assessment affected the probability (not quantity) of use in the next assessment. Conversely, one can bring quantity of use into the definition of events, as in Shiffman, Ferguson, and Gwaltney's (2006) analysis of "relapse," which was defined as smoking at least 5 cigarettes per day, for 3 consecutive days. A key difference is that, in the time-to-event approach, time is (relatively) continuous, while in the block approach time is discreet (i.e., baseline, follow-up). The time-to-event approach explicitly examines the passage of time without an event as an indicator of the risk of an event. This risk-over-time can be modeled from static predictors at the beginning of an interval (as exemplified in Todd *et al.*'s (2009) use of morning mood to predict onset of drinking for the rest of the day), or can vary dynamically over the interval (as exemplified by their cumulative mood index, which changed over days leading up to initiation of drinking). Time-to-event models can also handle large numbers of recurrent events, enabling analysis of the way factors associated with each successive use episode prospectively influence the timing of future events (e.g., Kirchner, Shiffman, and Wileyto, 2011; Wileyto *et al.*, 2005). EMA data provide multiple ways to examine influences over time, and thereby challenge the investigator to formulate clear theory-based models of how the variables in the analysis influence each other over time.

7.3   Trajectory of antecedents analyses

Another approach that has been used to prospectively assess antecedents of substance use events has been to examine the trajectory of responses during a period leading up to substance use. For example, to demonstrate that smoking lapses attributed to distress really were preceded by distress, Shiffman and Waters (2004) examined trends in negative affect in the hours preceding subjects' first lapses, and found significant increases in negative affect over the preceding 6 hours. Examination of a prior (non-lapse) day revealed no similar trend in affect, suggesting that the observed time-trends were not spurious variation. Similarly, Epstein *et al.* (2009) found that episodes of cocaine use in treated users were preceded by steeply rising likelihood of seeing the drug, and by increasing positive and negative mood indicators in the 5 hours preceding use. Increasing negative mood preceded episodes of craving for heroin, but, surprisingly, not heroin use itself. In a separate control analysis, Epstein *et al.* showed that the observed trends were not seen in the hours preceding a non-use control observation. These analyses do not "predict" the episode of use, as they are deliberately selected retrospectively from the period preceding a known episode of use, but they interpret the observed trends in relation to the target episode, and allow the sort of strong inferences that become possible when temporal ordering is established. Thus, the trajectory of experience, documented by time-based assessments preceding significant episodes, can be the focus of informative prospective analyses.

7.4   Individual differences

The discussion of EMA studies of substance use has emphasized within-subject effects, which are EMA's greatest strength. But EMA studies can also be used to examine between-subject effects, particularly in interaction with within-subject effects. Increasingly well-established statistical methods such as latent class growth mixture modeling (Muthén and Muthén, 2000) are able to simultaneously model within- and between-subject variance in a longitudinal response trajectory. For example, Muthén and Muthén (2000) found that longitudinal trajectories of heavy drinking among young adults could be better understood when classified into four between-subject classes of normative versus non-normative drinking progression. Other examples of individual difference moderators of within-subject associations with substance use abound. Beckham *et al.* (2008) showed that the association between stress and smoking was stronger in subjects with post-traumatic stress disorder. Shiffman and Paty (2006) showed that the association between drinking and smoking was stronger among non-dependent smokers (versus heavier, dependent smokers). This analysis also illustrated the use of within-subjects regression analyses to ideographically assess the strength of association between smoking and situational antecedents for each subject, as indexed by statistics analogous to R^2, abstracting from associations with particular stimuli to demonstrate greater stimulus control among the non-dependent smokers. EMA data can allow for strong inferences about within-subjects effects, which can, in turn, be tested for between-group differences.

7.5   Outcome analyses

EMA methods have unique advantages for process analyses, so it is not surprising that most of the studies reviewed have been observational studies with a process focus. Because substance use outcomes are usually quite complex, unfolding dynamically over extended periods of time (Brandon, Vidrine, and Litvin, 2007; Miller, Westerberg, Harris, and Tonigan, 1996), EMA methods can also be useful for outcome analyses. During the substance use cessation process some quitters experience rapidly occurring lapses, while others experience isolated lapses (e.g., Conklin *et al.*, 2005; Hoeppner *et al.*, 2008; Kirchner, Shiffman, and Wileyto, 2011). Analyses of these patterns has revealed, for instance, that factors that help maintain abstinence may not be the same as factors that promote recovery following a lapse (Swan and Denk, 1987; Wileyto *et al.*, 2005). As discussed above, time-based EMA monitoring has also been used to examine the effects of treatment on symptoms, such as craving and withdrawal, which are often regarded as outcomes in themselves. For example, a series of papers by Piasecki *et al.* (2003a; 2003b; 2003c) assessed dynamic patterns of withdrawal symptoms during smoking cessation, revealing a complex association between individual differences, treatment assignment, withdrawal, and outcomes. Emerging longitudinal analysis approaches will only increase our ability to leverage the richness of EMA data to understand the complex interplay between substance use interventions and behavior change processes.

8 Limitations

EMA may be particularly well suited to substance use research, but substance use research raises particular challenges for EMA methods, including statistical inference.

8.1 Cooperation of substance users

Application of EMA to studying substance use and abuse poses special challenges. Substance use may be illegal or, even if legal, frowned upon. Further, substance users and abusers often suffer from multiple personal and social pathologies, and are not considered particularly cooperative or conscientious subjects. The demonstrations of feasibility now making their way into the literature will probably encourage greater use of EMA methods among illicit drug users.

8.2 Reporting while intoxicated

A further challenge in collecting data about episodes of psychotropic substance use is the concern that subjects' intoxication might make it difficult for subjects to complete data entry or to do so in a valid way. The question of whether perceptions are blurred or biased by intoxication with alcohol or other drugs remains. This question is not unique to EMA, but also arises in laboratory studies where subjects are studied in intoxicated states, which could affect their response to psychometric scales, or even their ability to record their responses accurately.

Intoxication may not only impair subjects' ability to report EMA data but also their willingness to do so. Intoxication itself, and the settings and psychological states associated with it, may undermine subjects' motivation to engage in this instrumental task. Thus, some of the states and behaviors that may be of most interest to researchers (e.g., the peak of a drinking binge) may be rendered invisible in the data.

8.3 Reactivity

One concern that applies to all EMA studies is reactivity, which occurs when research methods affect the behavior under study. EMA for event recording of substance use episodes has particular reactive potential, especially when subjects are cutting down or otherwise attempting to change their behavior. Research has shown that self-monitoring of behavior is most reactive when subjects are motivated to change their behavior (McFall, 1977). Reactivity is also maximized when subjects are asked to record undesirable target events before they are completed (Rozensky, 1974), probably because this gives subjects a chance to reconsider the behavior. Thus, when substance use is considered undesirable, the threat of reactivity is heightened (which suggests that event recording could be scheduled to occur after an episode to minimize reactivity; see Shiffman, Paty, and Kassel, 1996). However, it is noteworthy that studies that have explored reactivity have generally failed to find substantial reactivity due to EMA (Hufford and Shiffman, 2002; Shiffman *et al.*, 2000).

8.4 Compliance

The burden of participating in EMA research is high. Subjects are expected to carry an assessment device, respond to randomly scheduled prompts and assessments, and record target behaviors. It can be tempting for researchers to err on the side of more data, but as the sampling rate and burden increase, compliance will suffer, possibly resulting in subject selection bias (Csikszentmihalyi and Larson, 1987). "Livability" features (Hufford and Shiffman, 2002) that allow subjects to more easily incorporate the EMA protocol into their daily lives can reduce burden, and this is an advantage of cell-phone-based systems. There is also a risk of perpetuating a "digital divide," since not everyone will be at the same proficiency level when it comes to new technical devices (Bolger, Davis, and Rafaeli, 2003), making proper training imperative to EMA research using electronic devices. Compliance is critical; when subjects choose when they do or do not record substance use or do or do not respond to time-based assessment prompts, they are systematically altering the results. This can produce a dataset that has a systematically "informative" pattern of "missingness," meaning that subsequent analyses cannot assume missing data are randomly distributed, and are subject to substantial bias that may or may not be corrected via multiple imputation or related techniques.

8.4.1 Compliance with recording of substance use. Assessing compliance with recording of substance use events is more challenging than assessing compliance with prompted assessments, because in the absence of specialized sensors we have no way of knowing how many events there truly were or when they occurred. Supplementing an event-based recording protocol with time-based prompting or a coverage protocol offers an opportunity to retrospectively confirm the absence of use events, but this is not an ideal corrective solution. Although we lack a true "gold standard" measure against which subject reports can be compared, substance use lends itself to objective verification more than other behaviors studied with EMA, because it leaves biological traces. Several studies have related EMA data on use to biochemical markers (Shiffman, 2009). While analyses of biochemical markers are informative, most markers are too limited to verify or contradict consumption of a particular amount of drug or its timing, due to the imprecision of current biochemical measures. The development of devices capable of recording biomarkers nearly in real time (see section 4.3; e.g., ethanol sensors on the skin; Venugopal *et al.*, 2008) will improve our ability to deal with this problem, making objective verification of EMA event recordings possible.

9   Future Directions

Although growing rapidly, the use of EMA in drug use research is still in its infancy. As EMA technologies and methodologies get both more powerful and easier to use, it is likely they will be applied with increasing frequency and sophistication. EMA data hold great promise for providing new and deeper insights into drug use and abuse, particular linking drug use to particular times and places, cues and triggers, feelings and cognitions.

The increasing sophistication and ubiquity of cell-phones heralds the day when EMA will no longer require a separate device; it will just run on the subject's cell-phone, and link to the investigator through the internet. As developers continue to produce smaller, more energy efficient, better-connected, more instrumented, easier to use, and more universal devices, EMA applications will become more sophisticated and capable while simultaneously becoming less of a burden on participants.

Data collection based on subjective report will continue to be a research tool for the foreseeable future. Research that helps define the circumstances under which recall yields reliable and valid data would help recall find its proper role, as would research on assessment methods that may minimize the distortions introduced by introspection.

EMA approaches are just beginning to be applied to intervention. Such ecological momentary interventions (EMI) will certainly improve, such that smart algorithms track behavior, thoughts, and feelings, and deliver an intervention ideally suited for the immediate circumstance, including contact with a human counselor when a crisis intervention is needed. Development of such protocols will raise many questions about how to assess the client's needs, how to select the right intervention, and how to learn what works and what doesn't. Such highly fluid and customized interventions will also be a challenge to evaluate.

9.1   Unobtrusive assessment

We are already seeing the rapid proliferation of small, smart, communicative sensors that track subject movement, physical and physiological state, and drug intake – all without requiring active response from the subject (section 4.3). Technology evolution will be the easy part: the challenge will be to securely store and meaningfully integrate the mass of multi-channel data. New statistical and conceptual models, and development of new analytics and theories to explain substance use across multiple levels – from cells to systems – will be required.

A particularly promising methodological development will be integration of EMA within geographic information systems (GIS) for the purpose of geospatially explicit EMA (GEMA). Mobile location tracking links individual behavior unfolding over time with a huge amount of ecological data. Among many applications, this can be used to assess the prospective association between ecological circumstances and EMA reports without the need for self-reported contextual assessments. When self-reported assessments do occur, they can be linked, or "tagged," to the individual's current location, making it possible to weight the influence of that location when the person returns in the future, even during the majority of occasions wherein they return but do not happen to make an EMA entry. Momentary mobile assessment linked to GIS is being pioneered in the area of environmental epidemiology, primarily to understand individual exposure to air pollution (Gulliver and Briggs, 2005; Nikzad *et al.*, 2012; Nuckols, Ward, and Jarup, 2004). We consider extension of these methods to the study of substance use a natural extension.

Geographic information systems make it possible to overlay individual-level EMA data with additional layers of rich socio-contextual information. The location of retail outlets and social clubs, combined with information about local policies on smoke-free air, alcoholic beverage sales, crime incidents (including drug-related crimes), and local economic conditions together provide a picture of each subject's immediate eco-logical context that cannot be captured with subjective report. An increasing number of studies are finding that the geospatial density of retail outlets selling tobacco (e.g., Andrew Peterson *et al.*, 2010; Ogneva-Himmelberger, Ross, Burdick, and Simpson, 2010; Peterson, Lowe, and Reid, 2005; Reid, Peterson, Lowe, and Hughey, 2005; Yu *et al.*, 2010) and alcohol products (Berke *et al.*, 2010; Kavanagh *et al.*, 2011; Matthews, McCarthy, and Rafail, 2011) is closely associated with a range of neighbor-hood factors that are linked to substance use and health. In two noteworthy examples, researchers found that the proximity of smokers' residence to tobacco outlets affected their likelihood of quitting, such that closer proximity led to lower abstinence rates (Paul *et al.*, 2010; Reitzel *et al.*, 2011). In another, geospatial analysis revealed that neighborhood factors had a large effect on New York City residents' participation rates in a city-wide smoking cessation program (Kirchner *et al.*, 2012). Ongoing work our group is conducting in Washington DC (Kirchner, 2011) demonstrates the way EMA can be integrated with GIS more directly, with DC residents who are trying to quit smoking recording EMA responses on phones that track their movements with GPS and thereby link their individual-level data to a GIS database across both time and space. Similar ongoing work is being conducted by Kenzie Preston and her colleagues, focused on illicit drug users in Baltimore. Approaches that use GPS to link individuals to the community-level geospatial ecology that surrounds them hold great promise for unraveling the multifaceted complexities affecting addicitve behavior.

10   Conclusions

EMA methods, which focus on studying real-world behavior when and where it occurs, are well-suited to studying substance use in all its phases: initiation, ongoing use, cessation and relapse. EMA studies have contributed detailed analyses of the relationship of mood to substance use, and of the details of relapse process, that would not have been possible with other methods. As EMA methods are further developed and more broadly applied, they are likely to offer even more detailed insight into substance use and abuse, perhaps laying foundations for new treatment paradigms. Further, the application of EMA approaches to on-the-spot intervention with substance users holds the potential to revolutionize treatment delivery.

References

Abrams DB and Wilson GT (1979) Effects of alcohol on social anxiety in women: Cognitive versus physiological processes. *Journal of Abnormal Psychology* 88: 161–173.

Abroms LC, Padmanabhan N, Thaweethai L, and Phillips T (2011) Iphone apps for smoking cessation: A content analysis. *American Journal of Preventive Medicine* 40: 279–285.

Acosta MC, Marsch LA, and Grabinski BA (2011) Development and evaluation of a mobile-based psychosocial intervention for substance use disorders. In an invited symposium on "Innovation and Opportunities in Mobile Interventions for Addictions" (B Moore, chair) at the American Psychological Association 119th Annual Meeting, Washington, DC.

Andrew Peterson N, Yu D, Morton CM, Reid RJ, Sheffer MA, and Schneider JE (2010) Tobacco outlet density and demographics at the tract level of analysis in New Jersey: A statewide analysis. *Drugs: Education, Prevention and Policy* 18 (1): 47–52.

Armeli S, Dehart T, Tennen H, Todd M, and Affleck G (2007) Daily interpersonal stress and the stressor-vulnerability model of alcohol use. *Journal of Social and Clinical Psychology* 26: 896–921.

Armeli S, Todd M, and Mohr C (2005) A daily process approach to individual differences in stress-related alcohol use. *Journal of Personality* 73: 1657–1686.

Armeli S, Todd M, Conner TS, and Tennen H (2008) Drinking to cope with negative moods and the immediacy of drinking within the weekly cycle among college students. *Journal of Studies on Alcohol and Drugs* 69: 313–322.

Backinger CL and Augustson EM (2011) Where there's an app, there's a way? *American Journal of Preventive Medicine* 40: 390–391.

Beckham JC, Wiley MT, Miller SC, Dennis MF, Wilson SM, McClernon FJ, and Calhoun PS (2008) Ad lib smoking in post-traumatic stress disorder: An electronic diary study. *Nicotine and Tobacco Research* 10: 1149–1157.

Berke EM, Tanski SE, Demidenko E, Alford-Teaster J, Shi X, and Sargent JD (2010) Alcohol retail density and demographic predictors of health disparities: A geographic analysis. *American Journal of Public Health* 100: 1967–1971.

Berkman ET, Falk EB, and Lieberman MD (2011) In the trenches of real-world self-control: Neural correlates of breaking the link between craving and smoking. *Psychol Sci* (in press).

Bolger N, Davis A, and Rafaeli E (2003) Diary methods: Capturing life as it is lived. *Annual Review of Psychology* 54: 579–616.

Borriello G, Anokwa Y, Brunette W, Hartung C, and Lerer A (2009) Modular open-source tools for mobile data collection. Presented at the 1st Annual Health Summit, Washington, DC.

Boyer EW (2011) Mobile technologies to promote adherence to behavioral therapies in veterans with comorbid PTSD and substance dependence. In an invited symposium on "Innovation and Opportunities in Mobile Interventions for Addictions" (B Moore, chair) at the American Psychological Association 119th Annual Meeting, Washington, DC.

Bradburn NM, Rips LJ, and Shevell SK (1987) Answering autobiographical questions: The impact of memory and inference on surveys. *Science* 236: 157–161.

Brandon TH, Vidrine JI, and Litvin EB (2007) Relapse and relapse prevention. *Annual Review of Clinical Psychology* 3: 257–284.

Carter BL and Tiffany ST (2001) The cue-availability paradigm: The effects of cigarette availability on cue reactivity in smokers. *Experimental and Clinical Psychopharmacology* 9: 183–190.

Carter BL, Day SX, Cinciripini PM, and Wetter DW (2007) Momentary health interventions: Where are we and where are we going? In AAEA Stone (ed.), *The Science of Real-Time Data Capture: Self-Reports in Health Research* (pp. 289–307). New York: Oxford University Press.

Carter BL, Lam CY, Robinson JD, Paris MM, Waters AJ, Wetter DW, and Cinciripini PM (2008) Real-time craving and mood assessments before and after smoking. *Nicotine and Tobacco Research* 10: 1165–1169.

Cellular Telephone Industry Association (CITA) (2011) Wireless Substitution Report. International Association for the Wireless Telecommunications Industry. http://www.ctia.org/advocacy/research/index.cfm/aid/10316.

Cinciripini PM, Hecht SS, Henningfield JE, Manley MW, and Kramer BS (1997) Tobacco addiction: Implications for treatment and cancer prevention. *Journal of the National Cancer Institute* 89: 1852–1867.

Collins KS, Hughes DL, Doty MM, Ives BL, Edwards JN, and Tenney K (2002) *Diverse Communities, Common Concerns – Assessing Health Care Quality for Minority Americans: Findings from the Commonwealth Fund 2001 Health Care Quality Survey*. New York: Commonwealth Fund.

Conklin CA, Perkins KA, Sheidow AJ, Jones BL, Levine MD, and Marcus MD (2005) The return to smoking: 1-year relapse trajectories among female smokers. *Nicotine and Tobacco Research* 7: 533–540.

Csikszentmihalyi M and Larson R (1987) Validity and reliability of the experience: Sampling method. *Journal of Nervous and Mental Disease* 175: 509–513.

Currivan DB, Nyman AL, Turner CF, and Biener L (2004) Does telephone audio computer-assisted self-interviewing improve the accuracy of prevalence estimates of youth smoking? *Public Opinion Quarterly* 68: 542–564.

Delfino RJ, Jamner LD, and Whalen CK (2001) Temporal analysis of the relationship of smoking behavior and urges to mood states in men versus women. *Nicotine and Tobacco Research* 3: 235–248.

de Vries M (1992) *The Experience of Psychopathology: Investigating Mental Disorders in their Natural Settings*. Cambridge: Cambridge University Press.

Dillman DA, Smyth JD, and Christian LM (2009) *Internet, Mail, and Mixed-Mode Surveys: The Tailored Design Method*. Hoboken, NJ: John Wiley and Sons, Inc.

Epstein DH, Willner-Reid J, Vahabzadeh M, Mezghanni M, Lin JL, and Preston KL (2009) Real-time electronic diary reports of cue exposure and mood in the hours before cocaine and heroin craving and use. *Archives of General Psychiatry* 66: 88–94.

Estrin D and Sim I (2010) Health care delivery. Open health architecture: An engine for health care innovation. *Science* 330: 759–760.

Franken IMA (2011) Implicit cognitions measured on a PDA during opiate detoxification. In an invited symposium on "Cognition and Addiction – Using PDAs to Predict and Prevent" (A Waters, chair) at the American Psychological Association 119th Annual Meeting, Washington, DC.

Free C, Knight R, Robertson S, Whittaker R, Edwards P, Zhou W, ... Roberts I (2011) Smoking cessation support delivered via mobile phone text messaging (txt2stop): A single-blind, randomised trial. *Lancet* 378: 49–55.

Fremouw WJ and Brown JP (1980) The reactivity of addictive behaviors to self-monitoring: A functional analysis. *Addictive Behaviors* 5: 209–217.

Gulliver J and Briggs DJ (2005) Time–space modeling of journey-time exposure to traffic-related air pollution using GIS. *Environmental Research* 97: 10–25.

Gwaltney CJ, Shields AS, and Shiffman S (2008) Equivalence of electronic and paper-and-pencil administration of patient reported outcome measures: A meta-analytic review. *Value in Health* 11: 322–333.

Hammersley R (1994) A digest of memory phenomena for addiction research. *Addiction* 89: 283–293.

Hektner JM, Schmidt JA, and Csikszentmihalyi M (2007) *Experience Sampling Method: Measuring the Quality of Everyday Life.* Thousand Oaks, CA: Sage.

Hoeppner BB, Goodwin MS, Velicer WF, Mooney ME, and Hatsukami DK (2008) Detecting longitudinal patterns of daily smoking following drastic cigarette reduction. *Addictive Behaviors* 33: 623–639.

Hufford MR and Shiffman SS (2002) Methodological issues affecting the value of patient-reported outcomes data. *Expert Review of Pharmacoeconomics and Health Outcomes* 2: 119–128.

Intille SS (2007) Technological innovations enabling automatic, context-sensitive ecological momentary assessment. In AA Stone, S Shiffman, A Atienza, and L Nebeling (eds), *Science of Real-Time Data Capture: Self-Reports in Health Research* (pp. 308–337). New York: Oxford University Press.

Jamison RN, Raymond SA, Levine JG, Slawsby EA, Nedeljkovic SS, and Katz NP (2001) Electronic diaries for monitoring chronic pain: One-year validation study. *Pain* 91: 277–285.

Kamarck TW, Shiffman S, Smithline L, Goodie JL, Paty J, Gnys M, and Jong JY-K (1998) Effects of task strain, social conflict, and emotional activation on ambulatory cardiovascular activity: Daily life consequences of recurring stress in a multiethnic adult sample. *Health Psychology* 17: 17–29.

Kamarck TW, Siewiorek D, Smailagic A, Shiffman S, and Stone A (2010) Developing ema-based self-report assessment of psychosocial stress. Part of invited symposium on "Psychosocial Stress as an Environmental Exposure: New Field Assessment Approaches and their Implications for Studies of Health and Disease." Presented at Annual Meeting of the American Psychosomatic Society, Portland, OR.

Kavanagh AM, Kelly MT, Krnjacki L, Thornton L, Jolley D, Subramanian SV, . . . Bentley RJ (2011) Access to alcohol outlets and harmful alcohol consumption: A multi-level study in Melbourne, Australia. *Addiction* (in press).

Kerst WA (2011) Cognitive retraining can be administered on a PDA in an ecological momentary assessment study. In an invited symposium on "Cognition and Addiction: Using PDAs to Predict and Prevent" (A Waters, chair) at the American Psychological Association 119th Annual Meeting, Washington, DC.

Kim DH, Lu N, Ma R, Kim YS, Kim RH, Wang S, . . . Rogers JA (2011) Epidermal electronics. *Science* 333: 838–843.

Kirchner TR (2011) Web-based mobile support for the DC tobacco quitline. In an invited symposium on "Innovation and Opportunities in Mobile Interventions for Addictions" (B Moore, chair) at the American Psychological Association 119th Annual Meeting, Washington, DC.

Kirchner TR, Shiffman S, and Wileyto EP (2011) Relapse dynamics during smoking cessation: Recurrent abstinence violation effects and lapse-relapse progression. *Journal of Abnormal Psychology* (in press). doi: 10.1037/a0024451.

Kirchner TR, Cantrell J, Anesetti-Rothermel A, Pearson J, Cha S, Kreslake J, Ganz O, Tacelosky M, Abrams D, and Vallone D (2012) Individual mobility patterns and real-time geo-spatial exposure to point-of-sale tobacco marketing. In Proceedings of ACM Wireless Health (Peer-reviewed Acceptance Rate = 20%): ACM, NY: New York.

Kumar S, al'Absi M, and Ali A (2010) Autosense: A wireless sensor system to quantify psychosocial stress and addictive substances in natural environments. New Frontiers in Measurement: Phenotypes, Endophenotypes, and Envirotypes for Genetic and Behavioral Studies of Nicotine Dependence. Presented at the Society for Research on Nicotine and Tobacco 16th Annual Meeting, Baltimore, MD.

Le B, Choi HN, and Beal DJ (2006) Pocket-sized psychology studies: Exploring daily diary software for palm pilots. *Behavior Research Methods* 38: 325–332.

Liebo MJ, Israel RL, Lillie EO, Smith MR, Rubenson DS, and Topol EJ (2011) Is pocket mobile echocardiography the next-generation stethoscope? A cross-sectional comparison of rapidly acquired images with standard transthoracic echocardiography. *Annals of Internal Medicine* 155: 33–38.

Loewenstein G (1999) A visceral account of addiction. In J Elster and OJ Skog (eds), *Getting Hooked: Rationality and Addiction* (pp. 235–264). Cambridge: Cambridge University Press.

Marlatt GA (1985) Relapse prevention: Theoretical rationale and overview of the model. In GA Marlatt and JR Gordon (eds), *Relapse Prevention: Maintenance Strategies in the Treatment of Addictive Behaviors* (pp. 3–70). New York: Guilford Press.

Matthews SA, McCarthy JD, and Rafail PS (2011) Using ZIP code business patterns data to measure alcohol outlet density. *Addictive Behaviors* 36: 777–780.

McCarthy DE (2011) Measures of impulsive choice and impulsive behavior during an attempt to stop smoking. In an invited symposium on "Cognition and Addiction: Using PDAs to Predict and Prevent" (A Waters, chair) at the American Psychological Association 119th Annual Meeting, Washington, DC.

McFall RM (1977) Parameters of self-monitoring. In RB Stuart (ed.), *Behavioral Self-Management: Strategies, Techniques, and Outcome* (pp. 196–214). New York: Brunner/Mazel.

Miller WR, Westerberg VS, Harris RJ, and Tonigan JS (1996) What predicts relapse? Prospective testing of antecedent models. *Addiction* 91: 155–172.

Moghaddam NG and Ferguson E (2007) Smoking, mood regulation, and personality: An event-sampling exploration of potential models and moderation. *Journal of Personality* 75: 451–478.

Mohr CD, Brannan D, Mohr J, Armeli S, and Tennen H (2008) Evidence for positive mood buffering among college student drinkers. *Personality and Social Psychology Bulletin* 34: 1249–1259.

Moskowitz DS and Young SN (2006) Ecological momentary assessment: What it is and why it is a method of the future in clinical psychopharmacology. *Journal of Psychiatry and Neuroscience* 31: 13–20.

Muthén B and Muthén LK (2000) Integrating person-centered and variable-centered analyses: Growth mixture modeling with latent trajectory classes. *Alcohol Clin Exp Res* 24: 882–891.

National Cancer Institute. Phenotypes and Endophenotypes: Foundations for Genetic Studies of Nicotine Use and Dependence. Tobacco Control Monograph No. 20. Bethesda, MD: U.S. Department of Health and Human Services, National Institutes of Health, National Cancer Institute. NIH Publication No. 09-6366, August 2009.

Nelson RO (1977) Assessment and therapeutic functions of self-monitoring. *Progress in Behavior Modification* 5: 263–308.

Nikzad N, Verma N, Ziftci C, Bales E, Quick N, Zappi P, Patrick K, Dasgupta S, Krueger I, Rosing TS, and Griswold W (2012) *CitiSense: Improving Geospatial Environmental Assessment of Air Quality Using a Wireless Personal Exposure Monitoring System.* In

Proceedings of ACM Wireless Health (Peer-reviewed Acceptance Rate = 20%): ACM, NY: New York.

Nuckols JR, Ward MH, and Jarup L (2004) Using geographic information systems for exposure assessment in environmental epidemiology studies. *Environmental Health Perspectives* 112: 1007–1015.

Ogneva-Himmelberger Y, Ross L, Burdick W, and Simpson SA (2010) Using geographic information systems to compare the density of stores selling tobacco and alcohol: Youth making an argument for increased regulation of the tobacco permitting process in Worcester, Massachusetts, USA. *Tobacco Control* 19: 475–480.

Otsuki M, Tinsley BJ, Chao RK, and Unger JB (2008) An ecological perspective on smoking among Asian American college students: The roles of social smoking and smoking motives. *Psychology of Addictive Behavior* 22: 514–523.

Park E, Tudiver F, Schultz JK, and Campbell T (2004) Does enhancing partner support and interaction improve smoking cessation? *Annals of Family Medicine* 2: 170–174.

Paty JA, Kassel JD, and Shiffman S (1992) Assessing stimulus control of smoking: The importance of base rates. In H De Vries (ed.), *The Experience of Psychopathology* (pp. 347–352). Cambridge: Cambridge University Press.

Paul CL, Mee KJ, Judd TM, Walsh RA, Tang A, Penman A, and Girgis A (2010) Anywhere, anytime: Retail access to tobacco in New South Wales and its potential impact on consumption and quitting. *Social Science and Medicine* 71: 799–806.

Peterson NA, Lowe JB, and Reid RJ (2005) Tobacco outlet density, cigarette smoking prevalence, and demographics at the county level of analysis. *Substance Use and Abuse* 40: 1627–1635.

Piasecki TM, Jorenby DE, Smith SS, Fiore MC, and Baker TB (2003a) Smoking withdrawal dynamics: I. Abstinence distress in lapsers and abstainers. *Journal of Abnormal Psychology* 112: 3–13.

Piasecki TM, Jorenby DE, Smith SS, Fiore MC, and Baker TB (2003b) Smoking withdrawal dynamics: III. Correlates of withdrawal heterogeneity. *Experimental and Clinical Psychopharmacology* 11: 276–285.

Piasecki TM, Jorenby DE, Smith SS, Fiore MC, and Baker TB (2003c) Smoking withdrawal dynamics II: Improved tests of withdrawal–relapse relations. *Journal of Abnormal Psychology* 112: 14–27.

Quinn P, Goka J, and Richardson H (2003) Assessment of an electronic daily diary in patients with overactive bladder. *British Journal of Urology* 91: 647–652.

Reid RJ, Peterson NA, Lowe JB, and Hughey J (2005) Tobacco outlet density and smoking prevalence: Does racial concentration matter? *Drugs: Education, Prevention, and Policy* 12: 233–238.

Reis HT and Wheeler L (1991) Studying social interaction with the rochester interaction record. *Advances in Experimental Social Psychology* 24: 269–317.

Reitzel LR, Cromley EK, Li Y, Cao Y, Dela Mater R, Mazas CA, . . . Wetter DW (2011) The effect of tobacco outlet density and proximity on smoking cessation. *American Journal of Preventive Medicine* 101: 315–320.

Riley WT, Jerome A, Behar A, and Weil J (2002) Computer and manual self-help behavioral strategies for smoking reduction: Initial feasibility and one year follow-up. *Nicotine and Tobacco Research* 4: S183–S188.

Riley WT, Pici M, Forman VL, and Behar A (2003) Computerized dosing of nicotine inhalers: Effects on use and quit rates. Paper presented at the 9th Annual meeting of the Society for Research on Nicotine and Tobacco, New Orleans, LA.

Rodgers A, Corbett T, Bramley D, Riddell T, Wills M, Lin RB, and Jones M (2005) Do u smoke after txt? Results of a randomised trial of smoking cessation using mobile phone text messaging. *Tobacco Control* 14: 255–261.

Roghmann KJ and Haggerty RJ (1972) The diary as a research instrument in the study of health and illness behavior: Experiences with a random sample of young families. *Med Care* 10 (2): 143–163.

Ross M (1989) Relation of implicit theories to the construction of personal histories. *Psychol Rev* 96: 341–357.

Rozensky RH (1974) The effect of timing of self-monitoring behavior on reducing cigarette consumption. *Journal of Behavior Therapy and Experimental Psychiatry* 5: 301–303.

Sayette MA, Shiffman S, Tiffany ST, Niaura RS, Martin CS, and Shadel WG (2000) The measurement of drug craving. *Addiction* 95: S189–S210.

Schwartz JE and Stone AA (1998) Strategies for analyzing ecological momentary assessment data. *Health Psychology* 17 (1), 6–16.

Shapiro D, Jamner LD, Davtdov DM, and James W (2002) Situations and moods associated with smoking in everyday life. *Psychology of Addictive Behavior* 16: 342–345.

Shiffman S (1993) Smoking cessation treatment: Any progress? *Journal of Consulting and Clinical Psychology* 61: 718–722.

Shiffman S (2007) Designing protocols for ecological momentary assessment. In AA Stone, S Shiffman, A Atienza, and L Nebeling (eds), *The Science of Real-Time Data Capture: Self-Reports in Health Research* (pp. 27–53). New York: Oxford University Press.

Shiffman S (2009) How many cigarettes did you smoke? Assessing cigarette consumption by global report, time-line follow-back, and ecological momentary assessment. *Health Psychology* 28: 519–526.

Shiffman S, Dresler CM, Hajek P, Gilburt SJ, Targett DA, and Strahs KR (2002) Efficacy of a nicotine lozenge for smoking cessation. *Archives of Internal Medicine* 162: 1267–1276.

Shiffman S, Ferguson SG, and Gwaltney CJ (2006) Immediate hedonic response to smoking lapses: Relationship to smoking relapse, and effects of nicotine replacement therapy. *Psychopharmacology (Berlin)* 184: 608–614.

Shiffman S, Hickcox M, Paty JA, Gnys M, Richards T, and Kassel JD (1997) Individual differences in the context of smoking lapse episodes. *Addictive Behaviors* 22: 797–811.

Shiffman S, Johnston JA, Khayrallah M, Elash CA, Gwaltney CJ, Paty JA, ... DeVeaugh-Geiss J (2000) The effect of bupropion on nicotine craving and withdrawal. *Psychopharmacology (Berlin)* 148: 33–40.

Shiffman S, Paty JA, Gnys M, Kassel JD, and Elash C (1995) Nicotine withdrawal in chippers and regular smokers: Subjective and cognitive effects. *Health Psychology* 14: 301–309.

Shiffman S, Paty JA, Gnys M, Kassel JD, and Hickcox M (1996) First lapses to smoking: Within-subjects analyses of real-time reports. *Journal of Consulting and Clinical Psychology* 64: 366–379.

Shiffman S, Paty JA, Gwaltney CJ, and Dang Q (2004) Immediate antecedents of cigarette smoking: An analysis of unrestricted smoking patterns. *Journal of Abnormal Psychology* 113: 166–171.

Shiffman S and Paty JA (2006). Smoking patterns of non-dependent smokers: Contrasting chippers and dependent smokers. *Journal of Abnormal Psychology* 115: 509–523.

Shiffman S, Stone AA, and Hufford M (2008) Ecological momentary assessment. *Annual Review of Clinical Psychology* 4: 1–32.

Shiffman S and Waters AJ (2004) Negative affect and smoking lapses: A prospective analysis. *Journal of Consulting and Clinical Psychology* 72 (2): 192–201.

Sieck WA and McFall RM (1976) Some determinants of self-monitoring effects. *Journal of Consulting and Clinical Psychology* 44: 958–965.

Singer JD and Willett JB (2003) Applied longitudinal data analysis: Modeling change and event occurrence. Oxford University Press, USA.

Smyth JM and Stone AA (2003) Ecological momentary assessment research in behavioral medicine. *Journal of Happiness Studies* 4: 35–52.

Sobell MB, Sobell LC, and Sheahan DB (1976) Functional analysis of drinking problems as an aid in developing individual treatment strategies. *Addictive Behaviors* 1 (2): 127–132.

Stone AA and Shiffman S (1994) Ecological momentary assessment (EMA) in behavioral medicine. *Annals of Behavioral Medicine* 16: 199–202.

Sudman S and Bradburn NM (1973) Effects of time and memory factors on response in surveys. *Journal of the American Statistical Association* 68: 805–815.

Swan GE and Denk CE (1987) Dynamic models for the maintenance of smoking cessation: Event history analysis of late relapse. *Journal of Behavioral Medicine* 10: 527–554.

Tapia E, Intille S, Lopez L, and Larson K (2006) The design of a portable kit of wireless sensors for naturalistic data collection. In KP Fishkin, B Schiele, P Nixon, A Quigley (eds), PERVASIVE 2006. LNCS, vol. 3968 (pp. 117–134). Heidelberg: Springer.

Todd M (2004) Daily processes in stress and smoking: Effects of negative events, nicotine dependence, and gender. *Psychology of Addictive Behavior* 18: 31–39.

Todd M, Armeli S, and Tennen H (2009) Interpersonal problems and negative mood as predictors of within-day time to drinking. *Psychology of Addictive Behavior* 23 (2): 205–215.

Toll BA, Cooney NL, McKee SA, and O'Malley SS (2006) Correspondence between interactive voice response (IVR) and timeline followback (TLFB) reports of drinking behavior. *Addictive Behaviors* 31: 726–731.

Tourangeau R (2000) Remembering what happened: Memory errors and survey reports. In AA Stone, CA Bachrach, JB Jobe, HS Kurtzman, and VS Cain (eds), *The Science of Self Report: Implications for Research and Practice* (pp. 29–48). Mahwah, NJ: Lawrence Erlbaum Associates.

Tourangeau R and Yan T (2007) Sensitive questions in surveys. *Psychological Bulletin* 133: 859–883.

Varkey J and Pompili D (2009) Movement recognition using body area networks. *Proc. of IEEE Global Telecommunications Conference (GLOBECOM)*, Honolulu, HW, USA.

Venugopal M, Feuvrel KE, Mongin D, Bambot S, Faupel M, Panangadan A, . . . Pidva R (2008) Clinical evaluation of a novel interstitial fluid sensor system for remote continuous alcohol monitoring. *Sensors Journal, IEEE* 8: 71–80.

Verbrugge LM (1980) Health diaries. *Medical Care* 18: 73–95.

Walls TA and Schafer JL (2006) *Models for Intensive Longitudinal Data.* New York: Oxford University Press.

Warthen M and Tiffany ST (2009) Evaluation of cue reactivity in the natural environment of smokers using ecological momentary assessment. *Experimental and Clinical Psychopharmacology* 17: 70–77.

Waters AJ and Li Y (2008) Evaluating the utility of administering a reaction time task in an ecological momentary assessment study. *Psychopharmacology (Berlin)* 197: 25–35.

Wetter DW, McClure JB, Cofta-Woerpel L, Costello TJ, Reitzel LR, Businelle MS, and Cinciripini PM (2011) A randomized clinical trial of a palmtop computer-delivered treatment for smoking relapse prevention among women. *Psychology of Addictive Behavior* 25: 365–71.

Wileyto EP, Patterson F, Niaura R, Epstein LH, Brown RA, Audrain-McGovern J, . . . Lerman C (2005) Recurrent event analysis of lapse and recovery in a smoking cessation clinical trial using bupropion. *Nicotine Tob Res* 7: 257–268.

Yu D, Peterson NA, Sheffer MA, Reid RJ, and Schnieder JE (2010) Tobacco outlet density and demographics: Analysing the relationships with a spatial regression approach. *Public Health* 124: 412–416.

Part III

Insights from Cognitive Science

21

Startle Reflex and Psychophysiology

Jeffrey C. Meehan and Robert Miranda, Jr

1 Introduction

Psychophysiological research is predicated on the idea that psychologically relevant events activate detectable biological processes in ways that can elucidate how biological and psychological processes are related to a behavior of interest. As such, psychophysiological methods allow for novel ways to explore hypotheses regarding the nature of addiction. The hope is that a better understanding of the psychophysiological correlates of substance use and addiction will enable refinement of the theoretical models, highlight potential targets for treatment, or provide innovative ways by which treatment progress can be monitored.

A variety of psychophysiological methodologies have been used successfully to link biological processes with psychological and behavioral outcomes, and many of these are reviewed in this book. In this chapter we review current practices and thinking relating to several commonly used psychophysiological methods. In addition, we review challenges and limitations of these techniques as scientific tools and discuss potential future directions for the field. But first, we briefly review some of the empirical literature to illustrate the relevance and value of incorporating these methods into research on addictive behaviors. A comprehensive review of empirical findings is beyond the scope of this chapter, however, and the reader is referred to previous reviews for more detailed discussions of the empirical literature (e.g., Braff, Geyer, and Swerdlow, 2001; Grillon and Baas, 2003).

2 Empirical Relevance to Substance Abuse Research

Much of addiction research has focused on psychological variables, such as personality, subjective reports of craving, emotional states, and expectancies; or behavioral

The Wiley-Blackwell Handbook of Addiction Psychopharmacology, First Edition. Edited by James MacKillop and Harriet de Wit.
© 2013 John Wiley & Sons, Ltd. Published 2013 by John Wiley & Sons, Ltd.

variables, such as amount of the drug consumed, pattern of use, and real-life consequences of substance misuse, such as work, relationship, and legal problems. These variables have limitations, however, as they are almost all verbally mediated and can be heavily influenced by demand characteristics, and many require participants to accurately describe thoughts, emotional states, or behavior from the past, a task that may be difficult given the limitations of human memory (Hammersley, 1994; Schacter, 1999). Additionally, these methods may not adequately assess the cognitive or emotional processes underlying substance misuse because this kind of information may not be consciously accessible and, more generally, the limits of introspection are well documented (Wilson and Dunn, 2004).

Psychophysiological methods help address these limitations and have several advantages. Most are largely free from voluntary control. It may be that automatic processes not amenable to self-report are important and distinct indicators of how motivational states are related to drug use behavior (Tiffany, 1990; Tiffany and Conklin, 2000; see Chapter 18 in this volume). Some psychophysiological methods also have the benefit of allowing for moment-by-moment assessments. Continuous assessments using verbally mediated methods have a relatively coarser time scale, are often cognitively demanding to participants, and can be difficult to integrate with other experimental procedures. Finally, and perhaps most importantly, psychophysiological methods often have well-delineated neurological pathways that help anchor the physiology to the anatomy and test/inform neurobiological models of addiction (Boucsein, 1992; Davis, 1986; Randall, 1984).

The methods reviewed in this chapter are the startle reflex, heart rate, and skin conductance, while others, such as electrophysiology, functional magnetic resonance (fMRI) imaging, positron emission tomography (PET), and magnetic resonance spectroscopy (MRS) are addressed in other chapters. While these techniques were selected because they are the most commonly used biologically related methods in addiction research, there are others that may be worth considering depending on the research questions involved, including body temperature (Carter and Tiffany, 1999), blood pressure (de Wit, Söderpalm, Nikolayev, and Young, 2003), respiration (Ooteman *et al.*, 2006), facial muscle electromyography (Drobes and Tiffany, 1997), salivation (Rohsenow *et al.*, 1994), cortisol (Söderpalm and de Wit, 2002), and pupillometrics (Rubin *et al.*, 1980). On the whole, different methods have somewhat specific advantages and drawbacks, and selection of the optimum technique is chiefly determined by the nature of the research question. Still, the methods described in this chapter have the advantage of being comparatively not burdensome to participants, non-invasive, inexpensive, and more transportable. Also, these methodologies are amenable for use with a range of emotion-inducing stimuli and can readily accommodate an array of cues.

2.1   The startle reflex

The startle reflex is a cascade of involuntary activations of predominantly flexor muscle groups in response to a sudden and intense external stimulus. It is universal across species, which renders it a unique translational tool for bridging preclinical and clinical research and for understanding the neurobiology of emotional and attention processes (Grillon and Baas, 2003). In humans, the startle reflex – which can be similarly elicited by acoustic, cutaneous, and photic stimulation (Landis and Hunt, 1939) – is manifest as a rapid muscular response that begins in the head and neck and quickly progresses downward through the extremities. The eye blink electromyogram (EMG) is a robust index of the auditory startle reflex in humans and is commonly used in psychophysiological research. Eye blink EMG has the advantage of being one of the earliest detectable components of the startle reflex, with a short latency (20–50 milliseconds; Berg and Balaban, 1999) and a wide range of amplitudes, enhancing the ease with which experimentally induced changes can be detected.

Plasticity of the startle reflex has been well documented and several characteristics of this reflex have been studied in relation to addiction, including the basal or "resting" startle response, prepulse inhibition, and affective modulation of the response. The *basal startle response* is a basic measure of sensitivity to startle-evoking stimuli in the absence of any other experimental manipulation. Interest in this measure is driven by the idea that variability in basal startle reactivity reflects inherent or acquired individual differences in central nervous system functioning (Grillon and Baas, 2003), which may be sensitive to the pharmacological effects of drugs of abuse. Higher resting responsiveness to startle probes is associated with increased arousal or vigilance and has been theorized to be central to certain anxiety disorders, such as post-traumatic stress disorder (Orr, Metgzer, Miller, and Kaloupek, 2004). Lower resting startle is believed to be indicative of low or under arousal, and possibly associated with emotional detachment (Herpertz *et al.*, 2001).

Drug users and those at risk for developing alcohol and drug problems tend to exhibit diminished basal responsiveness compared to controls, although there are differences in this pattern depending on the type of drug abused, the pattern of use, as well as the presence and length of withdrawal (e.g., Corcoran *et al.*, 2011; Hogle, Kaye, and Curtin, 2010; Postma *et al.*, 2001; Quednow *et al.*, 2004; van Goozen *et al.*, 2004; Walter *et al.*, 2011b; Zimmermann, Spring, Wittchen, and Holsboer, 2004). Others have studied the effects of acute drug administration on basal startle reactivity and found alcohol blunts startle reactivity in rodents (e.g., Brunell and Spear, 2006; Jones *et al.*, 2000; Pohorecky, Cagan, and Jaffe, 1976; Rassnick, Koob, and Geyer, 1992) and humans (Curtin, Lang, Patrick, and Stritzke, 1998; Grillon, Sinha, and O'Malley, 1994; Hutchison *et al.*, 2003; Stritzke, Patrick, and Lang, 1995). The magnitude of this reduction can be 50% or more compared to when sober (Curtin, Lang, Patrick, and Stritzke, 1998; Moberg and Curtin, 2009; Stritzke, Patrick, and Lang, 1995) and the extent of this attenuation appears to be associated with vulnerability factors for developing problems with alcohol, such as familial alcoholism and frequency of drinking during young adulthood (Grillon, Sinha, Ameli, and O'Malley, 2000; Hutchison *et al.*, 2003).

In contrast to intoxication, studies generally show that alcohol withdrawal potentiates startle reactivity following both acute and chronic alcohol exposure. This effect has been observed in rodents (e.g., Brunell and Spear, 2006; Rassnick, Koob, and Geyer, 1992; Slawecki and Ehlers, 2005) and humans (e.g., Grillon, Sinha, and O'Malley, 1994; Krystal *et al.*, 1997). Recent data, however, suggest that genetic factors may moderate this effect (e.g., Chester and Barrenha, 2007). Fewer studies have tested the effects of other drugs of abuse on baseline startle reactivity, but results generally show that drugs that stimulate brain activity potentiate startle while drugs that suppress activity attenuate startle (Bell *et al.*, 2003; Duncan *et al.*, 2001; Hong, Wonodi, Lewis, and Thaker, 2008); however, these effects may be age-dependent (Brunell and Spear, 2006; Marable and Maurissen, 2004).

Prepulse inhibition (PPI) of the startle reflex is another characteristic of startle reactivity that has been widely studied in the context of myriad forms of psychopathology, including substance use disorders. This psychomotor index is purported to assess an individual's capacity to disregard or "gate" insignificant or less salient sensory inputs from their environment while selectively focusing on more salient elements (see Braff, Geyer, and Swerdlow, 2001). Experimentally, PPI involves the presentation of a relatively weak sensory stimulus shortly before a startle probe (typically 30 to 500 milliseconds; Graham, 1975). In other words, this lower-level primer (prepulse) stimulus informs the individual of the imminent stimulus and in turn reliably attenuates the magnitude of the subsequent startle reflex. Disruptions in this "sensorimotor gating" are thought to inundate higher-order cognitive processes with irrelevant information and are associated with heightened distractibility, cognitive fragmentation, and behavioral disorganization (see Braff *et al.*, 2001a; Braff, Geyer, and Swerdlow, 2001; and Swerdlow *et al.*, 2008). Decreased PPI has been observed in individuals with a variety of psychiatric disorders, including obsessive-compulsive disorder (Hoenig *et al.*, 2005), schizotypal personality disorder (Cadenhead, Geyer, and Braff, 1993), and most notably schizophrenia (see Swerdlow *et al.*, 2008).

Addiction researchers have examined PPI to study the effects of nicotine, alcohol, and other pharmacological agents on sensorimotor gating in humans and animal models. This interest stems, in part, from the fact that brain mechanisms governing PPI are well characterized and involve several neurotransmitter systems thought to be disrupted in individuals with substance use disorders (e.g., dopamine, serotonin, *N*-methyl-D-apartate [NMDA], γ-aminobutyric acid). Administration of dopamine receptor agonists (e.g., amphetamine, apomorephine, quinpirole) reduces PPI in humans (Kumari *et al.*, 1998; Hutchison and Swift, 1999) and rats (Swerdlow, Braff, Masten, and Geyer, 1990), and this effect is reversed by the dopamine receptor antagonist haloperidol (Mansbach, Geyer, and Braff, 1988) and the α-adrenergic antagonist idazoxam (Larrauri and Levin, 2011). Similar disruptions in PPI were found with NMDA receptor antagonists, such as dizocilpine or phencyclidine (PCP), in both rodents (Mansbach and Geyer, 1989) and monkeys (Linn and Javitt, 2001). These effects, however, were not reversed by haloperidol (Keith, Mansbach, and Geyer, 1991), which suggests that NMDA-receptor antagonist disruptions in PPI are not mediated by the mesolimbic dopamine system. Of note, it remains unclear whether long-term exposure to these drugs produces lasting disruptions in PPI. Studies have found evidence for sensitization, tolerance, and no long-term effect (e.g., Culm and Hammer, 2004; Efferen *et al.*, 2000; Li, He, and Chen, 2011; Martin-Iverson, 1999; Schulz, Fendt, Pedersen, and Koch, 2001; Schwabe, Brosda, Wegener, and Koch, 2005).

Acute administration of nicotine, on the other hand, generally potentiates PPI in rodents (Acri, Grunberg, and Morse, 1991; Acri, Morse, Popke, and Grunberg, 1994; Spielewoy and Markou, 2004) and humans (Della Casa, Hofer, Weiner, and

Feldon, 1998; Duncan *et al.*, 2001; Kumari, Checkley, and Gray, 1996), and smokers exhibit decreases in PPI during nicotine withdrawal (Kumari and Gray, 1999). Of note, non-smokers show similar effects of nicotine on PPI, thereby discounting the possibility that nicotine's effects on PPI depend on withdrawal (Duncan *et al.*, 2001; Kumari, Cotter, Checkley, and Gray, 1997; Postma *et al.*, 2006). Although it has been proposed that nicotinic facilitation of PPI may be mediated by nicotine acetylcholine receptors (Schreiber, Dalmus, and De Vry, 2002; Suemaru *et al.*, 2004), some studies did not find nicotine to enhance PPI (e.g., Faraday, O'Donoghue, and Grunberg, 1999; Mirza, Misra, and Bright, 2000) even after smoking high-nicotine-content cigarettes (Hutchison, Niaura, and Swift, 2000). Nonetheless, emerging evidence suggests that nicotine transiently improves PPI in patients with schizophrenia, which may explain the disproportionately high rates of cigarette use in this population (e.g., George *et al.*, 2006; Hong, Wonodi, Lewis, and Thaker, 2008).

The effects of acute administration of cannabinoid antagonists on PPI also have been studied and findings are mixed. In rats, cannabinoid antagonists have been shown to potentiate PPI (Stanley-Cary, Harris, and Martin-Iverson, 2002), reduce PPI (Schneider and Koch, 2002), or have no effect on PPI (Mansbach, Rovetti, Winston, and Lowe, 1996). Although to our knowledge studies of acute administration of cannabinoid receptor antagonists, such as oral delta-9-tetrahydrocannabinol (THC), have not been done in humans, the enduring effects of prolonged cannabis use have been examined. Studies of chronic cannabis users generally show that they exhibit comparable patterns of PPI to healthy controls, suggesting that cannabis use is not associated with persistent disruptions in sensorimotor gating (Kedzior and Martin-Iverson, 2006; 2007; Mathias *et al.*, 2011; Quednow *et al.*, 2004). Many of these same studies, however, found that cannabis users exhibit schizophrenia-like disturbances in PPI when instructed to attend to the prepulse auditory stimulus (Kedzior and Martin-Iverson, 2006; 2007; Scholes and Martin-Iverson, 2009; Scholes-Balog and Martin-Iverson, 2011). These findings suggest that, while chronic cannabis users have intact sensorimotor gating processes at a basic level, they exhibit compromised attentional control under certain conditions (Scholes-Balog and Martin-Iverson, 2011).

Finally, several studies have examined the effects of alcohol on PPI. Using an animal model, Jones and colleagues (2000) found that acute administration of ethanol disrupted PPI in ethanol-preferring but not non-preferring rats. In humans, results of an initial study were equivocal (Weiss, Lorang, Bloom, and Koob, 1993) while subsequent studies found alcohol-induced disruption of PPI (Grillon, Sinha, Ameli, and O'Malley, 2000; Hutchison *et al.*, 1997; 2003), although this disruption was restricted to those with a family history of alcoholism in one study (Grillon, Sinha, Ameli, and O'Malley, 2000).

Affective modulation of startle is the third and most recent characteristic of the startle reflex studied in the context of addictive behaviors. It is well documented that the core startle response can be altered by emotion-laden stimuli; contractions of the eye blink reflex are enhanced by unpleasant stimuli and diminished by pleasant ones. According to a two-factor model of emotion, wherein emotions are conceptualized as action dispositions that prime an organism to avoid harm and attain rewards, modulation of the startle response is postulated to vary as a function of activated motivational systems of the brain (Bradley and Lang, 2000). Activation of the behavioral inhibition system prepares an organism to respond defensively and, consequently, protective reflex responses (such as the eye blink) are potentiated. Alternatively, when the behavioral activation system is primed and dominant, an organism is prepared to respond appetitively and reflexive responses to aversive stimuli are attenuated (Bradley and Lang, 2000). Startle responses to auditory probes are increased by presenting an aversive conditioned stimulus (Brown, Kalish, and Farber, 1951), viewing emotionally negative photographs and film clips (Jansen and Frijda, 1994; Lang, Bradley, and Cuthbert, 1990), and imagining emotionally negative scenes (Witvliet and Vrana, 1995). In contrast, pleasant pictures reliably reduce startle magnitudes (Bradley, Cuthbert, and Lang, 1999; Cuthbert, Bradley, and Lang, 1996). Affective modulation of startle is robust to repetition, maintaining itself within and between days, although overall startle magnitude may decline over time (Cuthbert, Bradley, and Lang, 1996; Lang, Bradley, and Cuthbert, 1998).

Addiction researchers have studied affective modulation of the startle reflex to test the effects of alcohol and other drugs on emotional processing. Although there is good evidence that acute alcohol administration substantially blunts the basal startle reflex, as discussed above, the typical pattern of affective modulation remains intact even with acute intoxication (Grillon, Sinha, and O'Malley, 1994; Zimmermann, Spring, Wittchen, and Holsboer, 2004). Researchers used the emotion-modulated startle reflex to probe emotional processes in individuals with a variety of substance use disorders as well as those vulnerable for developing these conditions, typically based on their family history of alcohol or other drug problems. Overall, substance abusers typically show similar patterns of affective modulation of startle to pleasant and unpleasant cues as controls (Franken *et al.*, 2004; Miranda, Meyerson, Myers, and Lovallo, 2003; Mucha, Geier, Stuhlinger, and Mundle, 2000). Such findings are not ubiquitous across all groups, however, as comorbid psychopathology may be an important individual difference variable to consider. For example, Miranda, Meyerson, Myers, and Lovallo (2003) found that alcohol-dependent individuals with antisocial personality disorder demonstrated blunted affective modulation of startle, while those with alcohol dependence alone showed a normal pattern. Of note, however, others have not found this pattern of results. For example, heroin-dependent individuals showed normal affective modulation of startle regardless of whether they were diagnosed with antisocial personality disorder (Walter *et al.*, 2011a).

Studies also have examined affective modulation of the startle reflex among non-dependent individuals to test whether differences observed among some substance abusers are detectable prior to the onset of problematic use and to explore whether such disruptions mark risk for developing dependence. Miranda, Meyerson, Buchanan, and Lovallo (2002) tested affective modulation of the startle reflex among young adults at low and high risk for alcohol dependence based on their family history. Results found that, while the low-risk group showed the normal response pattern, high-risk participants lacked the normal startle potentiation to the unpleasant pictures. These findings suggest impairment in motivational systems involved with responsiveness to unpleasant or aversive stimuli. The fact that such abnormalities are not consistently found in individuals with alcohol dependence highlights the need for additional research in this area.

Addiction researchers also have tested affective modulation of the startle reflex using drug-related cues (e.g., photographs, paraphernalia; Mucha, Geier, Stuhlinger, and Mundle, 2000). This integration of drug cues coincides with most theories of addiction, which posit that over time cues associated with drug use (e.g., bottle of preferred alcoholic beverage, pack of preferred cigarettes, etc.) become conditioned stimuli that evoke craving and motivational/reward systems in the brain (see Chapter 14 in this volume). The degree to which an individual finds such cues appetitive or aversive may depend, however, on the level of use, presence of dependence, length of abstinence, accessibility of the substance, current intoxication, and other individual difference variables.

Studies have tested several of these hypotheses in a variety samples, including individuals with alcohol dependence, non-dependent social drinkers, and light and heavy cigarette smokers. Results typically show that drug cues attenuate the startle response among treatment- and non-treatment-seeking individuals with substance dependence, producing appetitive effects similar to those of pleasant stimuli (Geier, Mucha, and Pauli, 2000; Heinz *et al.*, 2003; Loeber *et al.*, 2007; Nees, Diener, Smolka, and Flor, 2011; Walter *et al.*, 2011a; but see Lubman *et al.*, 2009). This pattern of appetitive reactivity was found among recently abstinent alcoholics (Grüsser *et al.*, 2002; Mucha, Geier, Stuhlinger, and Mundle, 2000) – even when participants subjectively rated the cues as unpleasant – as well as during nicotine withdrawal (Cinciripini *et al.*, 2006). But not all studies found this effect. For example, abstinent alcoholics had potentiated startle reactivity to alcohol cues during the first 2 weeks of withdrawal but not in later weeks, suggesting that alcohol is aversive during early withdrawal (Saladin, Drobes, Coffey, and Libet, 2002). Moreover, some studies have found no modulation of startle by drug cues (Franken *et al.*, 2004; Orain-Pelissolo, Grillon, Perez-Diaz, and Jouvent, 2004), and findings among non-dependent individuals also have been mixed (Drobes, Carter, and Goldman, 2009; Geier, Mucha, and Pauli, 2000). In addition, alcohol-dependent inpatients show diminished startle to alcohol cues if they reported being in a positive mood when drinking, suggesting that the emotional correlates of substance use may be important (Heinz *et al.*, 2003).

2.2 Heart rate

Emotionally relevant stimuli have acute effects on cardiac reactivity. These effects, which typically include an initial brief deceleration in heart rate in response to a novel stimulus followed by increases, are essential mechanisms by which the body prepares itself to approach appetitive stimuli or to engage or flee from threats. The initial deceleration is part of an orienting response to a new stimulus, while subsequent heart rate acceleration – which is often uneven and followed by a smaller deceleration appearing in the upward slope of the heart rate recovery (Bradley, 2000) – is thought to measure arousal (Bradley, 2000; Graham and Clifton, 1966; Stekelenburg and van Boxtel, 2002).

Within the addiction field, heart rate has been largely studied in the context of laboratory-based cue reactivity assessments. Cue reactivity involves experimentally exposing individuals to specific drug cues (e.g., bottle of preferred alcoholic beverage, cigarettes, photographs of preferred substance) while recording a variety of subjective (e.g., craving, mood) and physiological responses that are presumed to relate to the motivational processes involved in addiction (e.g., Watson *et al.*, 2010). This reactivity has been well documented in response to most major drugs of abuse, including alcohol, nicotine, cocaine, and opiates (Carter and Tiffany, 1999 – see Chapter 14 in this volume for further discussion).

In practice, assessment of heart rate within the cue reactivity paradigm typically involves measurement during a pre-cue exposure baseline period followed by exposure to drug-related stimuli in subsequent trials. During each trial, heart rate is assessed in real time and aggregated within the epochs of interest (e.g., baseline, neutral, drug cue). An initial meta-analysis of cue reactivity paradigms showed that substance abusers generally exhibited increased heart rate when exposed to drug-relevant stimuli, although the magnitude of this effect was reported to be modest ($d = 0.26$; Carter and Tiffany, 1999). Moreover, there is considerable variability in this effect across studies, types of drug, and modality of cue presentation (e.g., *in vivo*, imagery, photography). For instance, although most studies have found that social and heavy drinkers exhibit changes in heart rate in response to alcohol-related cues (e.g., Cassisi, Delehant, Tsoutsouris, and Levin, 1998; Kaplan *et al.*, 1985; Stormark *et al.*, 1995), studies of heart rate responses to smoking cues have produced mixed results. Some investigators reported increases in heart rate during exposure to cigarette cues (e.g., Abrams *et al.*, 1988; Drobes and Tiffany, 1997; Cepeda-Benito and Tiffany, 1996; Miranda *et al.*, 2008) while others found decreases (Niaura *et al.*, 1989) or no effect (e.g., LaRowe, Saladin, Carpenter, and Upadhyaya, 2007; Tidey, Rohsenow, Kaplan, and Swift, 2005; Tong, Bovbjerg, and Erblich, 2007). Similar inconsistencies exist among methamphetamine, opiate, and cannabis cue reactivity studies. One study found no effect of multimodal cue exposure (i.e., *in vivo*, photographs, video) on heart rate among participants with methamphetamine dependence (Price *et al.*, 2010), while another study found that individuals with methamphetamine dependence exhibited increased heart rate while viewing drug-related photographs and videos, but not after exposure to paraphernalia (Tolliver *et al.*, 2010). In terms of opiates, early studies did not find effects of heroin-related cues on heart rate (see Carter and Tiffany, 1999), while more recent research shows that heroin-related cues increase heart rate in abstinent heroin abusers (e.g., Ren *et al.*, 2009; Yu *et al.*, 2007). Finally, several studies have shown that exposure to cannabis-related cues elicit subjective craving in adults and adolescents (Haughey *et al.*, 2008; Singleton *et al.*, 2002; Wölfling, Flor, and Grüsser, 2008) but only three studies have tested the effects of cannabis-cue exposure on heart rate and all found no effect (Gray, LaRowe, and Upadhyaya, 2008, Gray, LaRowe, Watson, and Carpenter, 2011; Lundahl and Johanson, 2011; Nickerson *et al.*, 2011).

In addition to cue reactivity research, investigators have studied the effects of acute drug intake on cardiac reactivity. For example, studies have shown that alcohol intoxication is associated with changes in heart rate (Romanowicz *et al.*, 2011), and that these changes may be more pronounced among individuals at risk for developing alcohol problems (Brunelle *et al.*, 2004; Conrod, Pihl, and Vassileva, 1998), suggesting that greater reactivity to alcohol's stimulant properties, as indexed by cardiac reactivity, may be associated with liability for addiction. In addition, heart rate has been used to test the effects of acute drug ingestion on stress reactivity. For instance, acute cocaine and nicotine administration have potent cardiovascular effects and both potentiate heart rate responses during stress induction experiments (Benowitz, Jacob,

Jones, and Rosenberg, 1982; Hicks, Ogden, and Vamer, 2003; Perkins, Grobe, Fonte, and Breus, 1992).

2.3   Skin conductance

Accrine sweat glands cover much of the human body and are principally involved with regulating body temperature, but are also responsive to changes in emotional states via activation of the sympathetic nervous system (Venables and Christie, 1980). Their action can be readily studied because sweat is a good conductor of electricity, and as sweat glands saturate, the skin becomes a more efficient electrical conductor. When applying a constant voltage to an electrode, an increase in electrical current commensurate to an increase in sweat gland activity can be detected by another electrode on the skin. Skin conductance responses measure this change in current (Dawson, Schell, and Filion, 2007).

Skin conductance is positively associated with the intensity of a presented stimulus and conceptualized as a measure of overall arousal. For example, words with greater intensity produce larger responses (Manning and Melchiori, 1974), as do stimulating pictures irrespective of perceived valence (Amrhein, Mühlberger, Pauli, and Wiedemann, 2004; Bernat, Patrick, Benning, and Tellegen, 2006; Codispoti, Bradley, and Lang, 2001; Winton, Putnam, and Krauss, 1984). Imagery of arousing events also produces larger responses (Miller *et al.*, 1987; van Oyen, Witvliet and Vrana, 1995), and anticipation of an arousing positive or negative stimulus produces larger responses than anticipation of neutral stimuli (Sabatinelli, Bradley, Cuthbert, and Lang, 1996). Although skin conductance is most closely linked to arousal and is usually interpreted that way, stimulus valence may affect skin conductance responses. Some researchers have reported dissociations in the skin conductance responses induced by positive versus negative slides, with response magnitude being larger and recovery being longer for positive slides, especially on repeated presentations (e.g., Bradley, 2000). Therefore, it may be that skin conductance reactivity is more sensitive to stimulus intensity for positive stimuli but that negative stimuli produce similar skin conductance responses, regardless of intensity (Lithari *et al.*, 2010).

Across many substances, elevated skin conductance responses have been consistently associated with substance abusers' exposure to cues related to their drug of abuse ($d = 0.40$; see Carter and Tiffany, 1999, for a review). For example, Kaplan *et al.* (1985) found that, compared to controls, inpatient alcoholics showed significantly greater skin conductance increases in response to smelling and holding their preferred alcoholic beverage. The magnitude of this skin conductance response was positively associated with the number of heavy drinking days in the past month among those with alcohol dependence. Skin conductance was also positively correlated with self-reported craving for alcohol among alcoholics but not controls. More recently, patients with methamphetamine dependence showed increases in skin conductance in response to several types of drug cue (photographs, video, *in vivo*; Tolliver *et al.*, 2010). Similar results were found with adolescent cannabis users, where different types of cannabis cue (imagery, video, *in vivo*) provoked significantly larger skin conductance responses, compared to neutral stimuli (Gray, LaRowe, and Upadhyaya, 2008;

Gray, LaRowe, Watson, and Carpenter, 2011). Recent findings, however, suggest that drug-related cues are not ubiquitous with regard to their ability to elicit skin conductance responses. Nees, Diener, Smolka, and Flor (2011) found that pictures depicting the beginning of a drinking episode (e.g., containers of alcoholic beverages) evoked increases in skin conductance but this effect was not observed for post-consumption cues (e.g., empty bottles). Finally, some evidence shows that acute administration of psychoactive substances can alter skin conductance levels. For example, alcohol intake appears to diminish skin conductance responses among non-dependent drinkers (Sher *et al.*, 2007; Stritzke, Patrick, and Lang, 1995). Taken together, research shows that drug users generally exhibit increased arousal in response to drug cues. This effect may be limited to moderate to heavy users, however, as some studies show that light users do not exhibit this response (Cassisi, Delehant, Tsoutsouris, and Levin, 1998).

3   Standardized and Validated Methods

3.1   General considerations: stimuli, habituation, extraneous factors, and sampling rate

Affect-inducing stimuli are available in almost all sensory modalities, but visual cues are the most commonly used with psychophysiological assessments. For example, studies of affective modulation of startle typically use stimuli from the International Affective Picture System – a large, highly varied set of color photographs depicting a range of subjects (e.g., Lang, Bradley, and Cuthbert, 2008). These photographs were mapped onto a grid of perceived valence and arousal, which allows researchers to select subsets of photographs for specific studies (Bradley, 2000). When selecting subsets, it is important to match positive and negative photographs on arousal intensity so that valence can be studied in isolation; neutral photographs are selected to be intermediate in valence and low in arousal. Perceived arousal and valence in a given sample is verified using the Self Assessment Manikin (Lang, 1980), a visual analogue scale that assesses subjective affective valence and arousal for each photograph. Drug cues, in contrast, are not usually from standardized stimulus sets but are often unique to each research laboratory. A detailed discussion of drug cues is provided in Chapter 14 in this volume.

Habituation is a common factor inherent in most psychophysiological measures (Hogle, Kaye, and Curtin, 2010). Over time, physiological responding to stimuli diminishes as procedures become less novel. For instance, habituation of the startle reflex to startle elicitors is quite noticeable and occurs within a test session and across sessions separated by days (Ornitz and Guthrie, 1989). Although not regularly done, this habituation can be modeled in the analyses. Using varying stimulus probes may reverse some of the effects of habituation, and engaging participants in a task during the startle protocol can attenuate habituation (Carlsen *et al.*, 2003).

In addition to issues with habituation, comparative differences in EMG and other physiological responses tend to be fairly small. It is therefore imperative that steps are taken to minimize noise that will obscure the effects of interest. Additionally, many researchers are interested in experimentally induced changes in psychophysiological measures. Therefore, it is important to obtain an accurate baseline for comparison;

extraneous factors that may affect physiological activity should be carefully controlled to the extent possible. To that end, participants should be allowed time to habituate to the testing environment and apparatus before data recording occurs. And when recruiting a drug-using sample, care should be taken to ensure participants are neither impaired from drug use nor in withdrawal, unless these states are of experimental interest. Moreover, substance users also can have haphazard sleep schedules and significant sleep deprivation, which can substantially influence physiological responding and attention to stimuli. Actions should be taken to minimize the influence of these factors.

Finally, computational power has increased so considerably that psychophysiological measurement can achieve a high degree of temporal detail. Sampling at 1,000 Hz or more has become the standard in much research, and although lower sampling rates can be used successfully, an increasing amount of variability and failure to resolve inflections in the data curve will occur (Task Force of the European Society of Cardiology and the North American Society of Pacing and Electrophysiology, 1996).

3.2 Startle reflex: procedural considerations

Almost any sudden stimulus of sufficient magnitude can elicit a startle response. Some options include air puff-induced startle, glabellar tap, electrical stimulation, visual flash, and electrical shock (for review, see Blumenthal *et al.*, 2005). For a variety of reasons, including ease of experimental design and control, auditory stimuli are the most frequently used in human startle research and thus will be the only method discussed here. A survey of the addiction literature reveals that white noise bursts are the most commonly used type of startle probe with humans. Although these probes are highly effective at eliciting the startle reflex when presented with intensities ranging from 85 to 115 dB (usually for 50 milliseconds' duration with an instantaneous rise time), care must be taken to ensure the headphones or speakers used can produce an instantaneous burst of white noise without distortion (Berg and Balaban, 1999; Blumenthal *et al.*, 2005).

Startle probes in studies of PPI are typically more intense (100–116 dB) to ensure differentiation between the probe and prepulse stimulus. Lead stimuli in PPI studies, like startle probes, can be presented in many different modalities, but white noise bursts are the most commonly used. Timing of the lead stimulus is important, as maximum PPI occurs around 100–150 milliseconds (Graham, 1975; Norris and Blumenthal, 1996). Shorter inter-stimulus intervals produce less effective startle inhibition, and longer ones, particularly after 500–800 milliseconds, can facilitate startle (Hoffman and Searle, 1968; Graham, 1975). Additionally, some startle protocols deliver a constant white noise background during the procedure, ostensibly to eliminate the effects of background noise in the laboratory (Braff *et al.*, 2001a). This is especially true of PPI studies, where the lead stimulus is often an increase in white noise intensity above this background. Background noise may weaken PPI responses, however, in undesirable ways (Blumenthal, Noto, Fox, and Franklin, 2006). Consequently, it may be preferable to use noise-canceling headphones. In any case, frequent calibration auditory equipment is important for maintaining stimulus consistency.

Tight experimental control of other aspects of the environment is recommended, as startle is affected by many environmental factors. For example, the startle reflex is increased by unpleasant odors, heat, and darkness in humans (Crombez, Baeyens, Vansteenwegen, and Eelen, 1997; Ehrlichman, Brown, Zhu, and Warrenburg, 1995; Grillon, Pellowski, Merikangas, and Davis, 1997). Lastly, in affective modulation studies, stimuli are typically presented 2.5–8 seconds before startle probes, with variability in this delay to reduce predictability. Affective modulation of startle increases steadily as the stimulus–startle interval increases to about 3 seconds and then asymptotes (Bradley, Cuthbert, and Lang, 1999).

To capture electrical impulses from the orbicularis oculi muscle, which controls the eye blink component of the startle reflex, miniature Ag–AgCl electrodes are the standard. Skin preparation of the electrode placement site by light cleaning and abrasion is suggested, as this improves EMG signal quality (Berg and Balaban, 1999). Typically, one Ag–AgCl miniature electrode is attached directly below the horizontal center of the lower eyelid, another is attached 1–2 cm laterally from the first, and a third, which serves as an isolated ground, is attached to an electrically inactive site such as the mastoid process, forehead, or temple (Blumenthal *et al.*, 2005). EMG signals tend to be small, and filtering is an important consideration. Motion artifacts, for example, produce low-frequency noise, while electromagnetic noise, such as from the instrumentation, can produce high-frequency noise (Blumenthal *et al.*, 2005). The specific frequencies filtered out vary considerably across studies, with some using EMG data across a wide range (1–1, 500 Hz; Krystal *et al.*, 1997). Because EMG signals are strongest in the frequencies between 78 and 100 Hz, the best results will be obtained by sampling this range and some of the adjoining higher and lower frequencies, with suggested guidelines being to sample from 28 to 500Hz (van Boxtel, Boelhouwer, and Bos, 1998).

EMG signals have components that are above and below zero. As such, signals are rectified to absolute values and these data are then smoothed to reduce or eliminate multiple spikes in the EMG waveform. Researchers have flexibility in the amount of smoothing done to the rectified signal, by using different time constants. Shorter time constants (1 millisecond) produce only minor smoothing effects, while longer time constants (100 milliseconds) substantially alter the EMG waveform (Berg and Balaban, 1999). Although whether startle data should be smoothed is somewhat controversial, generally there is a high correlation between smoothed and unsmoothed EMG data on measures such as response magnitude and area under the curve. Nonetheless, some researchers recommend using raw EMG data for certain variables, such as startle onset latency, duration, and amplitude (Blumenthal *et al.*, 2005) and it is also important to keep in mind that when using smoothed EMG data the size of the amplitude and area under the curve is substantially reduced (Blumenthal, 1994; 1998). Yet smoothing can produce data that are more easily aggregated and analyzed, which makes it easier to detect the EMG peaks (Berg and Balaban, 1999). A second filtering technique is the identification and elimination of invalid eye blinks. For instance, reflexive eye blinks physiologically cannot occur sooner than 20 milliseconds or later than 80–150 milliseconds after startle probes. Therefore, responses that occur outside these parameters are often eliminated (Blumenthal, Elden, and Flaten, 2004; Graham, 1975).

The characteristic of the startle reflex most commonly studied is amplitude, recorded as the largest electrical voltage detected on a startle response curve. When reporting amplitude scores, it is important to outline all the data reduction procedures used (e.g., conversion factors, time constants for smoothing, etc.) in order to facilitate meaningful comparisons across studies (Berg and Balaban, 1999). Studies have also examined the latency between the startle probe and the inflection point in the EMG curve that corresponds to the onset of the startle response (Curtin, Lang, Patrick, and Stritzke, 1998; Vrana, Spence, and Lang, 1988). The duration of the startle response itself can also be calculated, but this has rarely been done. It is also possible to calculate the overall magnitude of a startle response by calculating the area under the startle response curve. In its simplest formulation, this is the EMG amplitude multiplied by the startle response duration (e.g., Bakker *et al.*, 2009; Frauscher *et al.*, 2007). Finally, inter-individual variability in startle response amplitudes can be significant. As such, many researchers utilize *t*-score and *z*-score transformations to allow for better comparison of startle across participants, especially when differences between groups are of interest (e.g., Miranda, Meyerson, Buchanan, and Lovallo, 2002; Miranda, Meyerson, Myers, and Lovallo, 2003; Patrick, Bradley, and Lang, 1993).

3.3 Heart rate: procedural considerations

Acquisition of heart rate or pulse is one of the most straightforward of all psycho-physiological methods and requires relatively simple and affordable equipment. There are several ways to acquire the heart rate signal, with three of the most popular being electrodes, sphygmomanometers, and photoplethysmographs (for a detailed review of heart rate methods, see Mulder, 1992; Porges and Byrne, 1992). When electrodes are used, placement on either the chest or an arm–leg combination is most customary (Jennings *et al.*, 1981). Electrode placement sites must be thoroughly cleaned and the junction between the electrode and the chest covered with a skin gel to enhance conduction of the cardio-electric signal. Ag–AgCl electrodes are the standard, given their conductive properties. Alternatively, sphygmomanometers are typically employed as blood pressure cuffs on the arm and detect heart rate by measuring rhythmic oscillations in blood pressure. Although these are fairly unobtrusive and can be especially advantageous when blood pressure is measured in addition to heart rate, they do constrain participants' use of one arm. The third approach uses the photoplethysmograph, which works by shining an infrared light into the skin and measuring the amount of light that either passes through the body to a sensor on the other side of a body part or that is reflected back to the sensor. Photoplethysmographs work because the skin is richly supplied with blood from capillaries; increased blood flow associated with a heartbeat absorbs more of this infrared light, resulting in less light reaching the device sensor. They are the easiest to employ of the three methods, but are fairly sensitive to movement artifact (Nakajima, Tamura, and Miike, 1996) and heart pulse peaks may be more difficult to detect with this method (Jennings *et al.*, 1981).

Quantification of heart rate is usually determined through an evaluation of interbeat intervals (IBIs). While some heart rate monitors calculate heart rate automatically, heart rate data can be analyzed with algorithms that calculate IBIs as the time between the start of the descending portions of adjacent heartbeat curves. Typically, heart rate data are aggregated across time to obtain more stable estimates of heart rate and heart rate change, although heart rate responsiveness curves can be created out of the IBIs present immediately after stimulus presentation. Generally speaking, heart rate has been the cardiac variable of interest in most addiction research, but newer methods examining other aspects of heart rate, such as heart rate variability, may be useful (see Romanowicz *et al.*, 2011; Vaschillo *et al.*, 2008).

As with the other methods, artifact is a significant processing challenge with heart rate data. There are many sources of artifact and, because neither human coders nor computerized analysis programs are infallible, elimination of invalid heart rate readings is often done through a combination of computerized data editors and visual inspection (Friesen *et al.*, 1990). There is no consensus on how to properly account for artifact or other heart rate data problems. IBIs that correspond to heart rate values that are clearly out of range (<30 bpm or >220 bpm) are usually eliminated, although interpolation of the data can be performed (Berntson *et al.*, 1997). Addressing these artifacts is critical, because misspecification of even one heart beat in a 2-minute span can conceal effects related to typical experimental manipulations (Berntson and Stowell, 1998).

3.4   Skin conductance: procedural considerations

Unlike heart rate monitors, equipment for skin conductance is primarily used in research settings, although there is a market for using skin conductance in biofeedback applications. Ag–AgCl electrodes are most commonly used in skin conductance research. The usual placement of the two skin conductance electrodes is on the volar side of the distal or medial phalanges of the middle and index fingers of a participant's non-dominant hand, with electrodes on the distal phalanges showing greater reactivity and thus being the preferable site for electrode placement (Scerbo *et al.*, 1992). There are other possibilities if placement on the hands is not possible, including on the palms or ankles.

Of prime concern for measuring skin conductance is the choice of electrode gel or paste that is used in the electrodes; for the best results the saline content of this material should closely mimic that of human sweat. When regular electrolyte gel is used, rather than a skin conductance gel, erroneous skin conductance results are often obtained (Sher *et al.*, 2007). Of note, cleaning or otherwise preparing the skin at the electrode site can diminish skin conductance levels by stripping away conductive salts; even so, it is preferred that all participants undergo a standard hand-washing procedure before electrode placement to standardize the procedure (e.g., Venables and Christie, 1973).

Skin conductance is of low frequency, so a low-pass filter with a cut-off around 1–2.5 Hz and a high-pass filter of 0.05–0.5 Hz (if one is used at all) is often employed to eliminate extraneous noise (Figner and Murphy, 2011; for a more detailed review, see Boucsein, 1992). The most commonly analyzed skin conductance variable in the addiction literatures is the magnitude of the skin conductance response (SCR), usually computed as a difference score between the skin conductance level (SCL) immediately preceding the SCR and the highest level of conductance in the SCR (Venables and Christie, 1980). Other variables that can be computed include the time after presentation of the stimulus before the start of the SCR (onset time), the time from SCR onset to peak in SCR magnitude (rise time), and the amount of time it takes for a decrease by 50% of the SCR magnitude amount of time (half recovery time; Dawson, Schell, and Filion, 2007).

There is a substantial delay between the presentation of a stimulus and the skin conductance response. SCRs are relatively slow to develop, with an onset of 1–4 seconds after stimulus presentation and a rise time to peak of about 1–3 seconds (Dawson, Schell, and Filion, 2007). This necessitates a fairly large temporal window to analyze for SCR peaks (1–7 seconds; Amrhein, Mühlberger, Pauli, and Wiedemann, 2004). In addition, there can be substantial variability in the time course of a skin conductance response (Dawson, Schell, and Filion, 2007). Moreover, unlike heart rate electrophysiology, there tends to be some drift over time in skin conductance levels and this drifting should be corrected for proper analysis. This can be effectively ignored by measuring SCRs from the point of deflection to the peak, by using transformation algorithms, or by using a 0.5 Hz high pass filter (Figner and Murphy, 2011). Establishing the useful variability of each participant's skin conductance responses can be done in a number of ways, such as a range correction procedure (Lykken and Venables, 1971) or standardizing each individual's SCRs (Ben-Shakhar, 1985). SCRs tend to have a non-normal distribution, so data transformation is often performed with logarithmic or square root transformations (Dawson, Schell, and Filion, 2007).

4 Limitations, Shortcomings and Future Directions

Addiction researchers have made considerable progress using psychophysiological methods to advance our understanding of addiction. Further refinement of the experimental methods, however, including a move toward more consistent procedures and analysis, would help organize this somewhat variable literature. Each of the methodologies reviewed in this chapter has limitations and shortcomings. For instance, unlike most other psychophysiological methods, an advantage of cardiovascular variables (e.g., heart rate) is that they can be continuously assessed in naturalistic settings outside the laboratory using ambulatory sensors. This technique has long been used in medical research and clinical assessment, particularly for hypertension (Pickering, Shimbo, and Haas, 2006) and some psychiatric disorders (Beckham *et al.*, 2000; Muraoka, Carlson, and Chemtob, 1998; Shear *et al.*, 1992; White and Baker, 1987), yet it remains largely unused in addiction studies. In comparison to heart rate, skin conductance tends to show more obvious responses to stimuli and serves as a more direct measure of sympathetic nervous system activity (Dawson, Schell, and Filion, 2007). But progression of skin conductance is comparatively slow and therefore not ideal for investigating rapidly occurring reactivity processes. Similarly, recovery of an SCR can be quite long, so ample time between stimulus exposures is necessary to prevent the second response in a series from contamination by recovery from the first (Grings and Schell, 1969). Conversely, the startle reflex is ideal for capturing momentary changes in reactivity, as it has a rapid onset and recovery and is readily influenced by shifting environmental stimuli. Another important advantage of the startle methodology is its ability to bridge preclinical and clinical research. This unique translational quality makes it an exemplary tool for investigating the pharmacological effects of drugs of abuse as well as for studying medications for treating addiction (see Grillon and Baas, 2003).

Yet despite the appeal of psychophysiological methods, addiction researchers have defensibly questioned their value on several grounds, including the often-poor concordance between subjective reports and physiological reactivity, the high degree of variability in findings across studies and laboratories, and the dearth of theoretical models to guide hypotheses regarding the directionality of expected response patterns (e.g., Carter and Tiffany, 1999; Sayette *et al.*, 2000). To address these concerns, we believe researchers must first confront some key questions that to date remain unanswered. We need a more complete understanding of the individual difference factors that underlie person-to-person variability in psychophysiological reactivity. Elucidating these factors may help explain inconsistencies in the literature. In addition, greater attention should be allocated to understanding how developmental factors affect psychophysiological processes. Addiction and substance use more broadly evolve and change over the lifespan. Mapping the psychophysiological correlates of substance use across development would inform theoretical models of addiction. Finally, and perhaps most importantly, we need a better understanding of whether and how psychophysiological measures correspond with and predict behavior, such as drug use and relapse. Forthcoming results in these areas will help address important criticisms of psychophysiological measures, advance multidimensional models of addiction, and help with the interpretation and integration of research in the field. We close by reviewing our recommendations for future work in more detail.

4.1   Individual difference variables

As reviewed here, there is often a high degree of variability in findings across studies of the same phenomenon (e.g., heart rate responses during cue reactivity). Although some differences are certainly attributable to variations in the methodological approaches employed, there is now convincing evidence that individual difference factors contribute greatly to how people respond physiologically to environmental stimuli and, by extension, to experimental tasks in the laboratory. For instance, a growing body of research indicates that genetic factors play an influential role in person-to-person variability in the startle reflex, including basal reactivity, PPI, and affective modulation. These effects have been observed in both psychiatric samples and healthy controls (e.g., Armbruster *et al.*, 2010; Bräuer *et al.*, 2009; Larson, Taubitz, and Robinson, 2010; Montag *et al.*, 2008; Pauli *et al.*, 2010; Quednow *et al.*, 2010). Furthermore, a recent study found that smokers homogeneous for the long allele of the polymorphic region *5-HTTLPR*, which codes for the serotonin transporter, showed greater suppression of the startle response across all valence categories following nicotine administration, as compared to placebo, than nonhomogeneous controls (Minnix *et al.*, 2011). The authors note that these findings suggest nicotine may be a more potent activator of appetitive mechanisms in certain individuals based on their genotype. In addition to genetic influences, there is evidence that phase of the menstrual cycle and use of oral contraceptives affect affective modulation of the startle reflex in women (Bannbers, Kask, Wikström, and Poromaa, 2010; Jovanovic *et al.*, 2004). Lastly, most studies examine psychophysiological reactivity in select types of substance abuser (e.g., alcoholics, smokers, cocaine abusers) as a unitary group, disregarding convincing evidence that these individuals constitute a largely heterogeneous population with differing etiological pathways, patterns of co-occurring drug use, and comorbid psychopathologies. There is little comparative study across the various drugs of abuse and it is unclear how much commonality exists in psychophysiological reactivity across these substances. Elucidating relevant individual differences in psychophysiological reactivity should be a major focus of future work.

4.2   Developmental factors

Psychophysiological studies of addiction have to a great extent focused almost exclusively on adults, with research on adolescents being comparatively sparse. The onset of drug use typically occurs during adolescence, however, and understanding the neurobiology of addiction processes during the early stages of pathology would probably improve prevention efforts and treatment outcomes. Indeed, limited theory and empirical data exist regarding the developmental course of psychophysiological effects or what they mean in relation to the addictive process. For example, little is known about how reactivity to drug cues changes over the course of addiction development (experimentation to more regular substance use and acquisition of abuse and dependence) and how this process compares to less problematic use and termination of drug use in other drug initiators. Moreover, animal models and emerging human studies indicate that adolescents may differ from adults on psychophysiological measures. For instance, research generally shows that startle reactivity increases throughout pubertal development and into adulthood (e.g., Bakshi and Geyer, 1999; Pian, Criado, and Ehlers, 2008; Sheets, Dean, and Reiter, 1988). But at least two reports found increased startle magnitude in adolescents relative to adults (Bell *et al.*, 2003; Elmer *et al.*, 2004). Differences between adolescents and adults have been reported for PPI in animal models as well (e.g., Brunell and Spear, 2006; Pian, Criado, and Ehlers, 2008), but these differences may be moderated by genetic factors (e.g., Pietropaolo and Crusio, 2009). Of note, several animal studies showed that alcohol differentially affected PPI in adolescents and adults, such that alcohol dose-dependently increased PPI in adolescents but not adults (Pian, Criado, and Ehlers, 2008; Slawecki and Ehlers, 2005). The authors interpret these findings as suggestive of greater ethanol-induced neurotoxicity in frontal cortical regions in adolescents. Paradoxical effects were observed, however, after amphetamine administration, such that PPI was disrupted in adult but not adolescent rats – alcohol did not affect PPI in either age cohort in this study (Brunell and Spear, 2006). Meanwhile, others have shown that chronic treatment with a synthetic cannabinoid agonist produced lasting reductions in PPI among peripubertal but not adult rats, and this effect was reversed by the dopamine antagonist haloperidol, suggesting that adolescence is a vulnerable period for the effects of cannabinoids (Schneider and Koch, 2003). Additional work is needed to elucidate whether and how developmental factors influence physiological reactivity to emotional stimuli and whether associations between patterns of reactivity and behavioral outcomes change across the lifespan (for further discussion, see Spear, 2009).

4.3   Predictive validity

Finally, there is a dearth of research on whether psychophysiological reactivity predicts patterns of future drug use and risk for relapse, although emerging research shows promise. For instance, Loeber and colleagues (2007) found that larger attenuation of startle to alcohol cues predicted the quantity alcohol consumed post-treatment. Similarly, smokers highly motivated to quit smoking showed larger startle responses to tobacco cues than those less motivated to quit, suggesting greater aversive reactions to the cues (Muñoz *et al.*, 2011). In another study of smokers trying to quit, those who relapsed were more likely to have lower basal startle reactivity before quitting and no change after quitting (Postma *et al.*, 2001). The strength of nicotine withdrawal symptoms was positively associated with an increased startle response, but only for unpredictable startle probes (Hogle, Kaye, Curtin, 2010). Lastly, Lubman *et al.* (2009) found that heroin users, as compared to healthy controls, had attenuated startle reactivity to opiate-related pictures and rated them as more pleasant; subjective ratings, but not startle responses, were a robust predictor of heroin use at follow-up. Other examples of this type of work have been reported for heart rate. Heart rate responses to systematic presentations of drug cues predicted treatment outcomes among cigarette smokers (Abrams *et al.*, 1988; Niaura *et al.*, 1992; Payne, Smith, Adams, and Diefenbach, 2006). But the direction of this association is inconsistent and other studies have not found this effect (Niaura *et al.*, 1989; Shadel *et al.*, 1998).

On the whole, this work suggests that psychophysiological methods may prove to be useful prognostic indicators of recovery and risk for relapse. But research in this area is sparse. The field needs additional research to uncover whether and how different types of psychophysiological measure are associated with drug use and relapse. Progress in this area will depend on the integration of findings across samples and modes of psychophysiological assessments.

References

Abrams DB, Monti PM, Carey KB, Pinto RP, and Jacobus SI (1988) Reactivity to smoking cues and relapse: Two studies of discriminant validity. *Behaviour Research and Therapy* 26: 225–233.

Acri JB, Grunberg NE, and Morse DE (1991) Effects of nicotine on the acoustic startle reflex amplitude in rats. *Psychopharmacology* 104: 244–248.

Acri JB, Morse DE, Popke EJ, and Grunberg NE (1994) Nicotine increases sensory gating measured as inhibition of the acoustic startle reflex in rats. *Psychopharmacology* 114: 369–374.

Amrhein C, Mühlberger A, Pauli P, and Wiedemann G (2004) Modulation of event-related brain potentials during affective picture processing: A complement to startle reflex and skin conductance response? *International Journal of Psychophysiology* 54: 231–240.

Armbruster D, Mueller A, Strobel A, Kirschbaum C, Lesch KP, and Brocke B (2010) Influence of functional tryptophan hydroxylase 2 gene variation and sex on the startle response in children, young adults, and older adults. *Biological Psychology* 83: 214–221.

Bakker MJ, Tijssen MA, van der Meer JN, Koelman JH, and Boer F (2009) Increased whole-body auditory startle reflex and autonomic reactivity in children with anxiety disorders. *Journal of Psychiatry and Neuroscience* 34: 314–322.

Bakshi VP and Geyer MA (1999) Ontogeny of isolation rearing-induced deficits in sensorimotor gating in rats. *Physiology and Behavior* 67: 385–392.

Bannbers E, Kask K, Wikström J, and Poromaa IS (2010) Lower levels of prepulse inhibition in luteal phase cycling women in comparison with postmenopausal women. *Psychoneuroendocrinology* 35: 422–429.

Beckham JC, Feldman ME, Barefoot JC, Fairbank JA, Helms MJ, Haney TL, Hertzberg MA, Moore SD, and Davidson JR (2000) Ambulatory cardiovascular activity in Vietnam combat veterans with and without posttraumatic stress disorder. *Journal of Consulting and Clinical Psychology* 68: 269–276.

Bell R, Rodd Z, Hsu C, Lumneg L, Murphy J, and McBride W (2003) Amphetamine-modified acoustic startle responding and prepulse inhibition in adult and adolescent alcohol-preferring and nonpreferring rats. *Pharmacology Biochemistry and Behavior* 75: 163–171.

Ben-Shakhar G (1985) Standardization within individuals: A simple method to neutralize individual differences in skin conductance. *Psychopysiology* 22: 292–299.

Benowitz NL, Jacob P, Jones RT, and Rosenberg J (1982) Interindividual variability in the metabolism and cardiovascular effects of nicotine in man. *Journal of Pharmacology and Experimental Therapeutics* 221: 368–372.

Berg WK and Balaban MT (1999) Startle elicitation: Stimulus parameters, recording techniques, and quantification. In ME Dawson, AM Schell, and A Böhmelt A (eds), *Startle Modification: Implications for Neuroscience, Cognitive Science, and Clinical Science* (pp. 21–50). Cambridge: Cambridge University Press.

Bernat E, Patrick CJ, Benning SD, and Tellegen A (2006) Effects of picture content and intensity on affective physiological response. *Psychophysiology* 43: 93–103.

Berntson GG and Stowell JR (1998) ECG artifacts and heart period variability: Don't miss a beat! *Psychophysiology* 35: 127–132.

Berntson GG, Bigger JT Jr, Eckberg DL, Grossman P, Kaufmann PG, Malik M, Nagaraja HN, Porges SW, Saul JP, Stone PH, and van der Molen MW (1997) Heart rate variability: Origins, methods, and interpretive caveats. *Psychophysiology* 34: 623–648.

Blumenthal TD (1994) Signal attenuation as a function of integrator time constant and signal duration. *Psychophysiology* 31: 201–203.

Blumenthal TD (1998) Comparing several measures of human startle eyeblink EMG response magnitude. *Journal of Psychophysiology* 12: 159–171.

Blumenthal TD, Cuthbert BN, Filion DL, Hackley S, Lipp OV, and van Boxtel A (2005) Committee report: Guidelines for human startle eyeblink electromyographic studies. *Psychophysiology* 42: 1–15.

Blumenthal TD, Elden A, and Flaten MA (2004) A comparison of several methods used to quantify prepulse inhibition of eyeblink responding. *Psychophysiology* 41: 326–332.

Blumenthal TD, Noto JV, Fox MA, and Franklin JC (2006) Background noise decreases both prepulse elicitation and inhibition of acoustic startle blink responding. *Biological Psychology* 72: 173–179.

Boucsein W (1992) *Electrodermal Activity*. New York: Plenum.

Bradley MM (2000) Emotion and motivation. In JT Cacioppo, LG Tassinary, and HG Berntson (eds), *Handbook of Psychophysiology* (2nd edn, pp. 602–642). Cambridge: Cambridge University Press.

Bradley MM and Lang PJ (2000) Measuring emotion: Behavior, feeling, and physiology. In RD Lane and L Nadel (eds), *Cognitive Neuroscience of Emotion* (pp. 242–276). New York: Oxford University Press.

Bradley MM, Cuthbert BN, and Lang PJ (1999) Affect and the startle reflex. In MEDawson, AM Schell, and A Böhmelt (eds), *Startle Modification: Implications for Neuroscience, Cognitive Science, and Clinical Science* (pp. 157–183). Cambridge: Cambridge University Press.

Braff DL, Geyer MA, and Swerdlow NR (2001) Human studies of prepulse inhibition of startle: Normal subjects, patient groups, and pharmacological studies. *Psychopharmacology* (Berlin) 156: 234–258.

Braff D, Geyer M, Light G, Sprock J, Perry W, Cadenhead K, and Swerdlow N (2001) Impact of prepulse characteristics on the detection of sensorimotor gating deficits in schizophrenia. *Schizophrenia Research* 49: 171–178.

Bräuer D, Stobel A, Hensch T, Diers K, Lesch KP, and Brocke B (2009) Genetic variation of serotonin receptor function affects prepulse inhibition of the startle. *Journal of Neural Transmission* 116: 607–613.

Brown JS, Kalish HI, and Farber IE (1951) Conditioned fear as revealed by magnitude of startle response to an auditory stimulus. *Journal of Experimental Psychology* 41: 317–328.

Brunell SC and Spear LP (2006) Effects of acute ethanol or amphetamine administration of the acoustic startle response and prepulse inhibition in adolescent and adult rats. *Psychopharmacology* 186: 579–586.

Brunelle C, Assaad JM, Barrett SP, Avila C, Conrod PJ, Tremblay RE, and Pihl RO (2004) Heightened heart rate response to alcohol intoxication is associated with a reward-seeking personality profile. *Alcoholism: Clinical and Experimental Research* 28: 394–401.

Cadenhead KS, Geyer MA, and Braff DL (1993) Impaired startle prepulse inhibition and habituation in patients with schizotypal personality disorder. *American Journal of Psychiatry* 150: 1862–1867.

Carlsen AN, Chua R, Inglis JT, Sanderson DJ, and Franks IM (2003) Startle response is dishabituated during a reaction time task. *Experimental Brain Research* 152: 510–518.

Carter BL and Tiffany ST (1999) Meta-analysis of cue-reactivity in addiction research. *Addiction* 94: 327–340.

Cassisi JE, Delehant M, Tsoutsouris JS, and Levin J (1998) Psychophysiological reactivity to alcohol advertising in light and moderate social drinkers. *Addictive Behaviors* 23: 267–274.

Cepeda-Benito A and Tiffany ST (1996) The use of a dual-task procedure for the assessment of cognitive effort associated with cigarette craving. *Psychopharmacology* (Berlin) 127: 155–163.

Chester JA and Barrenha GD (2007) Acoustic startle at baseline and during acute alcohol withdrawal in replicate mouse lines selectively bred for high or low alcohol preference. *Alcoholism: Clinical and Experimental Research* 31: 1633–1644.

Cinciripini PM, Robinson JD, Carter BL, Lam C, Wu X, de Moor CA, Baile WF, and Wetter DW (2006) The effects of smoking deprivation and nicotine administration on emotional reactivity. *Nicotine and Tobacco Research* 8: 379–392.

Codispoti M, Bradley MM, and Lang PJ (2001) Affective reactions to briefly presented pictures. *Psychophysiology* 38: 474–478.

Conrod PJ, Pihl RO, and Vassileva J (1998) Differential sensitivity to alcohol reinforcement in groups of men at risk for distinct alcoholism subtypes. *Alcoholism: Clinical and Experimental Research* 22: 585–597.

Corcoran S, Norrholm SD, Cuthbert B, Sternberg M, Hollis J, and Duncan E (2011) Acoustic startle reduction in cocaine dependence persists for 1 year of abstinence. *Psychopharmacology* (Berlin) 215: 93–103.

Crombez G, Baeyens F, Vansteenwegen D, and Eelen P (1997) Startle intensification during painful heat. *European Journal of Pain (London)* 1: 87–94.

Culm KE and Hammer RP (2004) Recovery of sensorimotor gating without G protein adaptation after repeated D2-like dopamine receptor agonist treatment in rats. *Journal of Pharmacology and Experimental Therapeutics* 308: 487–494.

Curtin JJ, Lang AR, Patrick CJ, and Stritzke WG (1998) Alcohol and fear-potentiated startle: The role of competing cognitive demands in the stress-reducing effects of intoxication. *Journal of Abnormal Psychology* 107: 547–557.

Cuthbert BN, Bradley MM, and Lang PJ (1996) Probing picture perception: Activation and emotion. *Psychophysiology* 33: 103–111.

Davis M (1986) Pharmacological and anatomical analysis of fear conditioning using the fear-potentiated startle paradigm. *Behavioral Neuroscience* 100: 814–824.

Dawson ME, Schell AM, and Filion DL (2007) The electrodermal system. In JT Cacioppo, LG Tassinary, and GG Berntson GG (eds), *Handbook of Psychophysiology* (3rd edn, pp. 159–181). New York: Cambridge University Press.

de Wit H, Söderpalm AH, Nikolayev L, and Young E (2003) Effects of acute social stress on alcohol consumption in healthy subjects. *Alcoholism: Clinical and Experimental Research* 27: 1270–1277.

Della Casa V, Hofer I, Weiner I, and Feldon J (1998) The effects of smoking on acoustic prepulse inhibition in healthy men and women. *Psychopharmacology* 137: 362–368.

Drobes DJ and Tiffany ST (1997) Induction of smoking urge through imaginal and *in vivo* procedures: Physiological and self-report manifestations. *Journal of Abnormal Psychology* 106: 15–25.

Drobes DJ, Carter AC, and Goldman MS (2009) Alcohol expectancies and reactivity to alcohol-related and affective cues. *Experimental and Clinical Psychopharmacology* 17: 1–9.

Duncan E, Madonick S, Chakravorty S, Parwani A, Szilagyi S, Efferen T, Gonzenbach S, Angrist B, and Rotrosen J (2001) Effects of smoking on acoustic startle and prepulse inhibition in humans. *Psychopharmacology* (Berlin) 156: 266–272.

Efferen TR, Duncan EJ, Szilagyi S, Chakravorty S, Adams JU, Gonzenbach S, Angrist B, Butler PD, and Rotrosen J (2000) Diminished acoustic startle in chronic cocaine users. *Neuropsychopharmacology* 22: 89–96.

Ehrlichman H, Brown S, Zhu J, and Warrenburg S (1995) Startle reflex modulation during exposure to pleasant and unpleasant odors. *Psychophysiology* 32: 150–154.

Elmer GI, Sydnor J, Guard H, Hercher E, and Vogel MW (2004) Altered prepulse inhibition in rats treated prenatally with the anitmitotic Ara-C: An animal model for sensorimotor gating deficits in schizophrenia. *Psychopharmacology* 174: 177–189.

Faraday MM, O'Donoghue VA, and Grunberg NE (1999) Effects of nicotine and stress on startle amplitude and sensory gating depend on rat strain and sex. *Pharmacology Biochemistry and Behavior* 2: 273–284.

Figner B and Murphy RO (2011) Using skin conductance in judgment and decision making research. In M Schulte-Mecklenbeck, A Kuehberger, and R Ranyard R (eds), *A Handbook of Processing Tracing Methods for Decision Research* (pp. 163–184). New York: Psychology Press.

Franken IH, Hulstijn KP, Stam CJ, Hendriks VM, and van den Brink W (2004) Two new neurophysiological indices of cocaine craving: Evoked brain potentials and cue modulated startle reflex. *Journal of Psychopharmacology* 18: 544–552.

Frauscher B, Löscher W, Högl B, Poewe W, and Kofler M (2007) Auditory startle reaction is disinhibited in idiopathic restless legs syndrome. *Sleep* 30: 489–493.

Friesen GM, Jannett TC, Jadallah MA, Yates SL, Quint SR, and Nagle HT (1990) A comparison of the noise sensitivity of nine QRS detection algorithms. *IEEE Transactions on Bio-Medical Engineering* 37: 85–98.

Geier A, Mucha RF, and Pauli P (2000) Appetitive nature of drug cues confirmed with physiological measures in a model using pictures of smoking. *Psychopharmacology* (Berlin) 150: 283–291.

George TP, Termine A, Sacco KA, Allen TM, Teutenauer E, Vessicchio JC, and Duncan EJ (2006) A preliminary study of the effects of cigarette smoking on prepulse inhibition in schizophrenia: Involvement of nicotinic receptor mechanisms. *Schizophrenia Research* 87: 307–315.

Graham FK (1975) The more or less startling effects of weak prestimuli. *Psychophysiology* 12: 238–248.

Graham FK and Clifton RK (1966) Heart-rate change as a component of the orienting response. *Psychological Bulletin* 65: 305–320.

Gray, KM, LaRowe SD, and Upadhyaya HP (2008) Cue reactivity in young marijuana smokers: A preliminary investigation. *Psychology of Addictive Behaviors* 22: 582–586.

Gray KM, LaRowe SD, Watson NL, and Carpenter MJ (2011) Reactivity to *in vivo* marijuana cues among cannabis-dependent adolescents. *Addictive Behaviors* 36: 140–143.

Grillon C and Baas J (2003) A review of the modulation of the startle reflex by affective states and its application in psychiatry. *Clinical Neurophysiology* 114: 1557–1579.

Grillon C, Pellowski M, Merikangas KR, and Davis M (1997) Darkness facilitates the acoustic startle reflex in humans. *Biological Psychiatry* 15: 453–460.

Grillon C, Sinha R, and O'Malley SS (1994) Effects of ethanol on the acoustic startle reflex in humans. *Psychopharmacology* (Berlin) 114: 167–171.

Grillon C, Sinha R, Ameli R, and O'Malley SS (2000) Effects of alcohol on baseline startle and prepulse inhibition in young men at risk for alcoholism and/or anxiety disorders. *Journal of Studies on Alcohol and Drugs* 61: 46–54.

Grings WW and Schell AM (1969) Magnitude of electrodermal response to a standard stimulus as a function of intensity and proximity of a prior stimulus. *Journal of Comparative and Physiological Psychology* 67: 77–82.

Grüsser SM, Heinz A, Raabe A, Wessa M, Podschus J, and Flor H (2002) Stimulus-induced craving and startle potentiation in abstinent alcoholics and controls. *European Psychiatry* 17: 188–193.

Hammersley R (1994) A digest of memory phenomena for addiction research. *Addiction* 89: 283–293.

Haughey HM, Marshall E, Schact JP, Louis A, and Hutchison KE (2008) Marijuana withdrawal and craving: Influence of cannabinoid receptor 1 (CNR1) and fatty acid amide hydrolase (FAAH) genes. *Addiction* 103: 1678–1686.

Heinz A, Löber S, Georgi A, Wrase J, Hermann D, Rey ER, Wellek S, and Mann K (2003) Reward craving and withdrawal relief craving: Assessment of different motivational pathways to alcohol intake. *Alcohol and Alcoholism* 38: 35–39.

Herpertz SC, Werth U, Lukas G, Qunaibi M, Schuerkens A, Kunert HJ, Freese R, Flesch M, Mueller-Isberner R, Osterheider M, and Sass H (2001) Emotion in criminal offenders with psychopathy and borderline personality disorder. *Archives of General Psychiatry* 58: 737–745.

Hicks AR, Ogden BA, and Vamer KJ (2003) Cardiovascular responses elicited during binge administration of cocaine. *Physiology and Behavior* 80: 115–122.

Hoenig K, Hochrein A, Quednow BB, Maier W, and Wagner M (2005) Impaired prepulse inhibition of acoustic startle in obsessive-compulsive disorder. *Biological Psychiatry* 15: 1153–1158.

Hoffman HS and Searle JL (1968) Acoustic and temporal factors in the evocation of startle. *Journal of the Acoustical Society of America* 43: 269–282.

Hogle JM, Kaye JT, and Curtin JJ (2010) Nicotine withdrawal increases threat-induced anxiety but not fear: Neuroadaptation in human addiction. *Biological Psychiatry* 68: 719–725.

Hong LE, Wonodi I, Lewis J, and Thaker GK (2008) Nicotine effect on prepulse inhibition and prepulse facilitation in schizophrenia patients. *Neuropsychopharmacology* 33: 2167–2174.

Hutchison KE and Swift R (1999) Effect of d-amphetamine on prepulse inhibition of the startle reflex in humans. *Psychopharmacology* (Berlin) 143: 394–400.

Hutchison KE, McGeary J, Wooden A, Blumenthal T, and Ito T (2003) Startle magnitude and prepulse inhibition: Effects of alcohol and attention. *Psychopharmacology* (Berlin) 167: 235–241.

Hutchison KE, Niaura R, and Swift R (2000) The effects of smoking high nicotine cigarettes on prepulse inhibition, startle latency, and subjective responses. *Psychopharmacology* (Berlin) 150: 244–252.

Hutchison KE, Rohsenow D, Monti D, Palfai T, and Swift R (1997) Prepulse inhibition of the startle reflex: Preliminary study of the effects of a low dose of alcohol in humans. *Alcoholism: Clinical and Experimental Research* 21: 1312–1319.

Jansen DM and Frijda NH (1994) Modulation of the acoustic startle response by film-induced fear and sex arousal. *Psychophysiology* 31: 565–571.

Jennings JR, Berg WK, Hutcheson JS, Obrist P, Porges S, and Turpin G (1981) Committee report: Publication guidelines for heart rate studies in man. *Psychophysiology* 18: 226–231.

Jones A, McBride W, Murphy J, Lumeng L, Li T-K, Shekhar A, and McKinzie D (2000) Effects of ethanol on startle responding in alcohol-preferring and non-preferring rats. *Pharmacology Biochemistry and Behavior* 67: 313–318.

Jovanovic T, Szilagyi S, Charkrovorty S, Fiallos AM, Lewison BJ, Parwani A, Schwartz MP, Gonzenbach S, Rotrosen JP, and Duncan EJ (2004) Menstrual cycle phase effects on prepulse inhibition of acoustic startle. *Psychophysiology* 41: 401–406.

Kaplan RF, Cooney NL, Baker LH, Gillepsie RA, Meyer RE, and Pomerleau OF (1985) Reactivity to alcohol-related cues: Physiological and subjective responses in alcoholics and nonproblem drinkers. *Journal of Studies on Alcohol and Drugs* 46: 267–272.

Kedzior KK and Martin-Iverson MT (2006) Chronic cannabis use is associated with attention-modulated reduction in prepulse inhibition of the startle reflex in healthy humans. *Journal of Psychopharmacology* 20: 471–484.

Kedzior KK and Martin-Iverson MT (2007) Attention-dependent reduction in prepulse inhibition of the startle reflex in cannabis users and schizophrenia patients – a pilot study. *European Journal of Pharmacology* 560: 176–182.

Keith VA, Mansbach RS, and Geyer MA (1991) Failure of haloperidol to block the effects of phencyclidine and dizocilpine on prepulse inhibition of startle. *Biological Psychiatry* 30: 557–566.

Krystal JH, Webb E, Grillon C, Cooney N, Casal L, Morgan CA, 3rd, Southwick SM, Davis M, and Charney DS (1997) Evidence of acoustic startle hyperreflexia in recently detoxified early onset male alcoholics: Modulation by yohimbine and m-chlorophenylpiperazine (mCPP). *Psychopharmacology* (Berlin) 131: 207–215.

Kumari V and Gray JA (1999) Smoking withdrawal, nicotine dependence and prepulse inhibition of the acoustic startle reflex. *Psychopharmacology* 141: 11–15.

Kumari V, Checkley SA, and Gray JA (1996) Effect of cigarette smoking on prepulse inhibition of the acoustic startle reflex in healthy male smokers. *Psychopharmacology* (Berlin) 128: 54–60.

Kumari V, Cotter PA, Checkley SA, and Gray JA (1997) Effect of acute subcutaneous nicotine on prepulse inhibition of the acoustic startle reflex in healthy male non-smokers. *Psychopharmacology* (Berlin) 128: 54–60.

Kumari V, Mulligan OF, Cotter PA, Poon L, Toone BK, Checkley SA, and Gray JA (1998) Effects of single oral administrations of haloperidol and *d*-amphetamine on prepulse inhibition of the acoustic startle reflex in healthy male volunteers. *Behavioural Pharmacology* 9: 567–576.

Landis C and Hunt WA (1939) *The Startle Pattern*. New York: Farrar and Rinehart.

Lang PJ (1980) Behavioral treatment and bio-behavioral assessment: Computer applications. In JB Sidowsky, JH Johnson, and EA Williams (eds), *Technology in Mental Health Care Delivery Systems* (pp. 119–137). Norwood, NJ: Ablex.

Lang PJ, Bradley MM, and Cuthbert BN (1990) Emotion, attention, and the startle reflex. *Psychological Review* 97: 377–395.

Lang PJ, Bradley MM, and Cuthbert BN (1998) Emotion and motivation: Measuring affective perception. *Journal of Clinical Neurophysiology* 15: 397–408.

Lang PJ, Bradley MM, and Cuthbert BN (2008) International affective picture system (IAPS): Affective ratings of pictures and instruction manual. Technical Report A-8. University of Florida, Gainesville, FL.

LaRowe SD, Saladin ME, Carpenter MJ, and Upadhyaya HP (2007) Reactivity to nicotine cues over repeated cue reactivity sessions. *Addictive Behaviors* 32: 2888–2899.

Larrauri JA and Levin ED (2011) The α2-adrenergic antagonist idazoxan counteracts prepulse inhibition deficits caused by amphetamine or dizocilpine in rats. *Psychopharmacology*. doi: 10.1007/s00213-011-2377-2.

Larson CL, Taubitz LE, and Robinson JS (2010) MAOA T941G polymorphism and the time course of emotional recovery following unpleasant pictures. *Psychophysiology* 47: 857–862.

Li M, He W, and Chen J (2011) Time course of prepulse inhibition disruption induced by dopamine agonists and NMDA antagonists: Effects of drug administration regimen. *Pharmacology Biochemistry and Behavior* 99: 509–518.

Linn GS and Javitt DC (2001) Phencyclidine (PCP) induced deficits of prepulse inhibition in monkeys. *NeuroReport* 12: 117–120.

Lithari C, Frantzidis CA, Papadelis C, Vivas AB, Klados MA, Kourtidou-Papadeli C, Pappas C, Ioannides AA, and Bamidis PD (2010) Are females more responsive to emotional stimuli? A neurophysiological study across arousal and valence dimensions. *Brain Topography* 23: 27–40.

Loeber S, Croissant B, Nakovics H, Zimmer A, Georgi A, Klein S, Diener C, Heinz A, Mann K, and Flor H (2007) The startle reflex in alcohol-dependent patients: Changes after cognitive-behavioral therapy and predictive validity for drinking behavior. A pilot study. *Psychotherapy and Psychosomatics* 76: 385–390.

Lubman DI, Yücel M, Kettle JW, Scaffidi A, Mackenzie T, Simmons JG, and Allen NB (2009) Responsiveness to drug cues and natural rewards in opiate addiction: Associations with later heroin use. *Archives of General Psychiatry* 66: 205–212.

Lundahl LH and Johanson CE (2011) Cue-induced craving for marijuana in cannabis-dependent adults. *Experimental and Clinical Psychopharmacology* 19: 224–230.

Lykken DT and Venables PH (1971) Direct measurement of skin conductance: A proposal for standardization. *Psychophysiology* 8: 656–672.

Manning SK and Melchiori MP (1974) Words that upset urban college students: Measured with GSRS and rating scales. *Journal of Social Psychology* 94: 305–306.

Mansbach RS and Geyer MA (1989) Effects of phencyclidine and phencyclidine biologs on sensorimotor gating in the rat. *Neuropsychopharmacology* 2: 299–308.

Mansbach RS, Geyer MA, and Braff DL (1988) Dopaminergic stimulation disrupts sensorimotor gating in the rat. *Neuropsychopharmacology* 94: 507–514.

Mansbach RS, Rovetti CC, Winston EN, and Lowe JA (1996) Effects of the cannabinoid CB1 receptor antagonist SR141716A on the behavior of pigeons and rats. *Psychopharmacology* 124: 315–322.

Marable BR and Maurissen JP (2004) Validation of an auditory startle response system using chemicals or parametric modulation as positive controls. *Neurotoxicology and Teratology* 26: 231–237.

Martin-Iverson MT (1999) Does sensitization occur to prepulse inhibition of the startle reflex effects of repeated apomorphine treatments in rats? *Psychopharmacology* 13: 261–273.

Mathias CW, Blumenthal TD, Dawes MA, Liguori A, Richard DM, Bray B, Tong W, and Dougherty DM (2011) Failure to sustain prepulse inhibition in adolescent marijuana users. *Drug and Alcohol Dependence* 116: 110–116.

Miller GA, Levin DN, Kozak MJ, Cook EW III, McLean A Jr, and Lang PJ (1987) Individual differences in imagery and the psychophysiology of emotion. *Cognition and Emotion* 1: 367-390.

Minnix JA, Robinson JD, Lam CY, Carter BL, Foreman JE, Vandenbergh DJ, Tomlinson GE, Wetter DW, and Cinciripini PM (2011) The serotonin transporter gene and startle response during nicotine deprivation. *Biological Psychology* 86: 1–8.

Miranda RJr, Meyerson LA, Buchanan TW, and Lovallo WR (2002) Altered emotion-modulated startle in young adults with a family history of alcoholism. *Alcoholism: Clinical and Experimental Research* 26: 441–448.

Miranda R Jr, Meyerson LA, Myers RR, and Lovallo WR (2003) Altered affective modulation of the startle reflex in alcoholics with antisocial personality disorder. *Alcoholism: Clinical and Experimental Research* 27: 1901–1911.

Miranda R, Jr, Rohsenow DJ, Monti PM, Tidey J, and Ray L (2008) Effects of repeated days of smoking cue exposure on urge to smoke and physiological reactivity. *Addictive Behaviors* 33: 347–353.

Mirza NR, Misra A, and Bright JL (2000) Different outcomes after acute and chronic treatment with nicotine in pre-pulse inhibition in Lister hooded rats. *European Journal of Pharmacology* 407: 73–81.

Moberg CA and Curtin JJ (2009) Alcohol selectively reduces anxiety but not fear: Startle response during unpredictable versus predictable threat. *Journal of Abnormal Psychology* 118: 335–347.

Montag C, Buckholtz JW, Hartmann P, Merz M, Burk C, and Reuter M (2008) COMT genetic variation affects fear processing: Psychophysiological evidence. *Behavioral Neuroscience* 122: 901–909.

Mucha RF, Geier A, Stuhlinger M, and Mundle G (2000) Appetitive effects of drug cues modeled by pictures of the intake ritual: Generality of cue-modulated startle examined with inpatient alcoholics. *Psychopharmacology* (Berlin) 151: 428–432.

Mulder LJ (1992) Measurement and analysis methods of heart rate and respiration for use in applied environments. *Biological Psychology* 34: 205–236.

Muñoz MA, Idrissi S, Sánchez-Barrera MB, Fernández MC, and Vila J (2011) Motivation to quit smoking and startle modulation in female smokers: Context specificity of smoking cue reactivity. *Psychopharmacology* (Berlin) (in press). doi: 10.1007/s0021301123340.

Muraoka MY, Carlson JG, and Chemtob CM (1998) Twenty-four-hour ambulatory blood pressure and heart rate monitoring in combat-related posttraumatic stress disorder. *Journal of Traumatic Stress* 11: 473–484.

Nakajima K, Tamura T, and Miike H (1996) Monitoring of heart and respiratory rates by photoplethysmography using a digital filtering technique. *Medical Engineering and Physics* 18: 365–372.

Nees F, Diener C, Smolka MN, and Flor H (2011) The role of context in the processing of alcohol-relevant cues. *Addiction Biology* (in press). doi: 10/1111/j13691600201100347.

Niaura R, Abrams D, Demuth B, Pinto R, and Monti P (1989) Responses to smoking-related stimuli and early relapse to smoking. *Addictive Behaviors* 14: 419–428.

Niaura R, Abrams DB, Pedraza M, Monti PM, and Rohsenow DJ (1992) Smokers' reactions to interpersonal interaction and presentation of smoking cues. *Addictive Behaviors* 17: 557–566.

Nickerson LD, Ravichandran C, Lundahl LH, Rodolico J, Dunlap S, Trksak GH, and Lukas SE (2011) Cue reactivity in cannabis-dependent adolescents. *Psychology of Addictive Behaviors* 25: 168–173.

Norris CM and Blumenthal TD (1996) A relationship between inhibition of the acoustic startle response and the protection of prepulse processing. *Psychobiology* 24: 160–168.

Ooteman W, Koeter MW, Vserheul R, Schippers GM, and van den Brink W (2006) Measuring craving: An attempt to connect subjective craving and cue reactivity. *Alcoholism: Clinical and Experimental Research* 30: 57–69.

Orain-Pelissolo S, Grillon C, Perez-Diaz F, and Jouvent R (2004) Lack of startle modulation by smoking cues in smokers. *Psychopharmacology* (Berlin) 173: 160–166.

Ornitz EM and Guthrie D (1989) Long-term habituation and sensitization of the acoustic startle response in the normal adult human. *Psychophysiology* 26: 166–173.

Orr SP, Metzger LJ, Miller MW, and Kaloupek DG (2004) Psychophysiological assessment of posttraumatic stress disorder. In JPWilson and TMKeane (eds), *Assessing Psychological Trauma and PTSD* (2nd edn, pp. 289–343). New York: Guilford.

Patrick CJ, Bradley MM, and Lang PJ (1993) Emotion in the criminal psychopath: Startle reflex modulation. *Journal of Abnormal Psychology* 102: 82–92.

Pauli P, Conzelmann A, Mucha RF, Weyers P, Baehne CG, Fallgatter AJ, Jacob CP, and Lesch KP (2010) Affect-modulated startle reflex and dopamine D4 receptor gene variation. *Psychophysiology* 47: 25–33.

Payne TJ, Smith PO, Adams SG, and Diefenbach L (2006) Pretreatment cue reactivity predicts end-of-treatment smoking. *Addictive Behaviors* 31: 702–710.

Perkins KA, Grobe JE, Fonte C, and Breus M (1992) "Paradoxical" effects of smoking on subjective stress versus cardiovascular arousal in males and females. *Pharmacology Biochemistry and Behavior* 42: 301–311.

Pian JP, Criado JR, and Ehlers CL (2008) Differential effects of acute alcohol on prepulse inhibition and event-related potentials in adolescent and adult Wistar rats. *Alcoholism: Clinical and Experimental Research* 32: 2062–2073.

Pickering TG, Shimbo D, and Haas D (2006) Ambulatory blood-pressure monitoring. *The New England Journal of Medicine* 354: 2368–2374.

Pietropaolo S and Crusio WE (2009) Strain-dependent changes in acoustic startle response and its plasticity across adolescents in mice. *Behavior Genetics* 39: 623–631.

Pohorecky LA, Cagan M, and Jaffe LS (1976) The startle response in rats: Effect of ethanol. *Pharmacology Biochemistry and Behavior* 4: 311–316.

Porges SW and Byrne EA (1992) Research methods for measurement of heart rate and respiration. *Biological Psychology* 34: 93–130.

Postma P, Gray JA, Sharma T, Geyer M, Mehrotra R, Das M, Zachariah E, Hines M, Williams SCR, and Kumari V (2006) A behavioural and functional neuroimaging investigation into the effects of nicotine on sensorimotor gating in healthy subjects and persons with schizophrenia. *Psychopharmacology* 184: 589–599.

Postma P, Kumari V, Sharma T, Hines M, and Gray JA (2001) Startle response during smoking and 24h after withdrawal predicts successful smoking cessation. *Psychopharmacology* (Berlin) 156: 360–367.

Price KL, Saladin ME, Baker NL, Tolliver BK, DeSantis SM, McRae-Clark AL, and Brady KT (2010) Extinction of drug cue reactivity in methamphetamine-dependent individuals. *Behaviour Research and Therapy* 48: 860–865.

Quednow BB, Kühn KU, Hoenig K, Maier W, and Wagner M (2004) Prepulse inhibition and habituation of acoustic startle response in male MDMA ("ecstasy") users, cannabis users, and healthy controls. *Neuropsychopharmacology* 29: 982–990.

Quednow BB, Wagner M, Mössner R, Maier W, and Kühn KU (2010) Sensorimotor gating in schizophrenia patients depends on catechol o-methyl-transferase val met polymorphism. *Schizophrenia Bulletin* 36: 341–346.

Randall WC (1984) *Nervous Control of Cardiovascular Function*. New York: Oxford University Press.

Rassnick S, Koob GF, and Geyer MA (1992) Responding to acoustic startle during chronic alcohol intoxication and withdrawal. *Psychopharmacology* 106: 351–358.

Ren ZY, Zhang XL, Liu Y, Zhao LY, Shi J, Bao Y, Zhang XY, Kosten TR, and Lu L (2009) Diurnal variation in cue-induced responses among protracted abstinent heroin users. *Pharmacology Biochemistry and Behavior* 91: 468–472.

Rhosenow DJ, Monti PM, Rubonis AV, Sirota AD, Niaura RS, Colby SM, Wunschel SM, and Abrams DB (1994) Cue reactivity as a predictor of drinking among male alcoholics. *Journal of Consulting and Clinical Psychology* 62: 620–626.

Romanowicz M, Schmidt JE, Bostwick JM, Mrazek DA, and Karpyak VM (2011) Changes in heart rate variability associated with acute alcohol consumption: Current knowledge and implications for practice and research. *Alcoholism: Clinical and Experimental Research* 35: 1092–1105.

Rubin LS, Gottheil E, Roberts A, Alterman A, and Holstine J (1980) Effects of alcohol on autonomic reactivity in alcoholics. Pupillometric studies III. *Journal of Studies on Alcohol and Drugs* 41: 611–622.

Sabatinelli D, Bradley MM, Cuthbert BN, and Lang PJ (1996) Wait and see: Aversion and activation in anticipation and perception. *Psychophysiology* 33: S72.

Saladin ME, Drobes DJ, Coffey SF, and Libet JM (2002) The human startle reflex and alcohol cue reactivity: Effects of early versus late abstinence. *Psychology of Addictive Behaviors* 16: 98–105.

Sayette MA, Shiffman S, Tiffany ST, Niaura RS, Martin CS, and Shadel WG (2000) The measurement of drug craving. *Addiction* 95: S189–S210.

Scerbo A, Freedman LW, Raine A, Dawson ME, and Venables PH (1992) A major effect of recording site on measurement of electrodermal activity. *Psychophysiology* 29: 241–246.

Schacter DL (1999) The seven sins of memory: Insights from psychology and cognitive neuroscience. *American Psychologist* 54: 182–203.

Schneider M and Koch M (2002) The cannabinoid agonist WIN 55,212-2 reduces sensorimotor gating and recognition memory in rats. *Behavioural Pharmacology* 13: 29–37.

Schneider M and Koch M (2003) Chronic pubertal, but not adult chronic cannabinoid treatment impairs sensorimotor gating, recognition memory, and the performance in a progressive ratio task in adult rats. *Neuropsychopharmacology* 28: 1760–1769.

Scholes KE and Martin-Iverson MT (2009) Alterations to pre-pulse inhibition (PPI) in chronic cannabis users are secondary to sustained attention deficits. *Psychopharmacology* (Berlin) 207: 469–484.

Scholes-Balog KE and Martin-Iverson MT (2011) Cannabis use and sensorimotor gating in patients with schizophrenia and healthy controls. *Human Psychopharmacology Clinical and Experimental* 26: 373–385.

Schreiber R, Dalmus M, and De Vry J (2002) Effects of alpha 4/beta 2-and alpha 7-nicotine acetylcholine receptor agonists on prepulse inhibition of the acoustic startle response in rats and mice. *Psychopharmacology* (Berlin) 159: 248–257.

Schulz B, Fendt M, Pedersen V, and Koch M (2001) Sensitization of prepulse inhibition deficits by repeated administration of dizocilpine. *Psychopharmacology* (Berlin) 156: 177–181.

Schwabe K, Brosda J, Wegener N, and Koch M (2005) Clozapine enhances disruption of prepulse inhibition after sub-chronic dizocilpine- or phencyclidine-treatment in Wistar rats. *Pharmacology Biochemistry and Behavior* 80: 213–219.

Shadel WG, Niaura R, Abrams DB, Goldstein MG, Rohsenow DJ, Sirota AD, and Monti PM (1998) Scripted imagery manipulations and smoking cue reactivity in a clinical sample of self-quitters. *Experimental and Clinical Psychopharmacology* 6: 179–186.

Shear MK, Polan JJ, Harshfield GA, Pickering T, Mann J, Frances A, and James G (1992) Ambulatory monitoring of blood pressure and heart rate in panic patients. *Journal of Anxiety Disorders* 6: 213–221.

Sheets LP, Dean KF, and Reiter LW (1988) Ontogeny of the acoustic startle response and sensitization to background noise in the rat. *Behavioral Neuroscience* 102: 706–713.

Sher KJ, Bartholow BD, Peuser K, Erickson DJ, and Wood MD (2007) Stress-response-dampening effects of alcohol: Attention as a mediator and moderator. *Journal of Abnormal Psychology* 116: 362–377.

Singleton EG, Trotman AJ, Zavahir M, Taylor RC, and Heishman SJ (2002) Determination of the reliability and validity of the Marijuana Craving Questionnaire using imagery scripts. *Experimental and Clinical Psychopharmacology* 10: 47–53.

Slawecki CJ and Ehlers CL (2005) Enhanced prepulse inhibition following adolescent ethanol exposure in Sprague-Dawley rats. *Alcoholism: Clinical and Experimental Research* 29: 1829–1836.

Söderpalm AH and de Wit H (2002) Effects of stress and alcohol on subjective state in humans. *Alcoholism: Clinical and Experimental Research* 26: 818–826.

Spear LP (2009) Heightened stress responsivity and emotional reactivity during pubertal maturation: Implications for psychopathology. *Development and Psychopathology* 21: 87–97.

Spielewoy C and Markou A (2004) Strain-specificity in nicotine attenuation of phencyclidine-induced disruption of prepulse inhibition in mice: Relevance to smoking in schizophrenia patients. *Behavior Genetics* 34: 343–354.

Stanley-Cary CC, Harris C, and Martin-Iverson MT (2002) Differing effects of cannabinoid agonist, CP 55,940, in an alcohol or Tween 80 solvent, on prepulse inhibition of the acoustic startle reflex in the rat. *Behavioural Pharmacology* 13: 15–28.

Stekelenburg JJ and van Boxtel A (2002) Pericranial muscular, respiratory, and heart rate components of the orienting response. *Psychophysiology* 39: 707–722.

Stormark KM, Laberg JC, Bjerland T, Nordby H, and Hugdahl K (1995) Autonomic cued reactivity in alcoholics: The effect of olfactory stimuli. *Addictive Behaviors* 20: 571–584.

Stritzke WG, Patrick CJ, and Lang AR (1995) Alcohol and human emotion: A multidimensional analysis incorporating startle-probe methodology. *Journal of Abnormal Psychology* 104: 114–122.

Suemaru K, Yasuda K, Umeda K, Araki H, Shibata K, Choshi T, *et al.* (2004) Nicotine blocks apomorphine-induced disruption of prepulse inhibition of the acoustic startle in rats: Possible involvement of central nicotinic alpha7 receptors. *British Journal of Pharmacology* 142: 843–850.

Swerdlow NR, Braff DL, Masten VL, and Geyer MA (1990) Schizophrenic-like sensorimotor gating abnormalities in rats following dopamine infusion into the nucleus accumbens. *Psychopharmacology* (Berlin) 101: 414–420.

Swerdlow NR, Weber M, Qu Y, Light GA, and Braff DL (2008) Realistic expectations of prepulse inhibition in translational models of schizophrenia research. *Psychopharmacology* 199: 331–388.

Task Force of the European Society of Cardiology and the North American Society of Pacing and Electrophysiology (1996) Heart rate variability: Standards of measurement, physiological interpretation and clinical use. *Circulation* 93: 1043–1065.

Tidey JW, Rohsenow DJ, Kaplan GB, and Swift RM (2005) Subjective and physiological responses to smoking cues in smokers with schizophrenia. *Nicotine and Tobacco Research* 7: 421–429.

Tiffany ST (1990) A cognitive model of drug urges and drug-use behavior: Role of automatic and nonautomatic processes. *Psychological Review* 97: 147–168.

Tiffany ST and Conklin CA (2000) A cognitive processing model of alcohol craving and compulsive alcohol use. *Addiction* 95: S145–S153.

Tolliver BK, McRae-Clark AL, Saladin M, Price KL, Simpson AN, DeSantis SM, Baker NL, and Brady KT (2010) Determinants of cue-elicited craving and physiologic reactivity in methamphetamine-dependent subjects in the laboratory. *American Journal of Drug and Alcohol Abuse* 36: 106–113.

Tong C, Bovbjerg DH, and Erblich J (2007) Smoking-related videos for use in cue-induced craving paradigms. *Addictive Behaviors* 32: 3034–3044.

van Boxtel A, Boelhouwer AJ, and Bos AR (1998) Optimal EMG signal bandwidth and inter-electrode distance for the recording of acoustic, electrocutaneous, and photic blink reflexes. *Psychophysiology* 35: 690–697.

van Goozen SH, Snoek H, Matthys W, van Rossum I, and van Engeland H (2004) Evidence of fearlessness in behaviourally disordered children: A study on startle reflex modulation. *The Journal of Child Psychology and Psychiatry* 45: 884–892.

van Oyen, Witvliet C, and Vrana SR (1995) Psychophysiological responses as indices of affective dimensions. *Psychophysiology* 32: 436–443.

Vaschillo EG, Bates ME, Vaschillo B, Lehrer P, Udo T, Mun EY, and Ray S (2008) Heart rate variability response to alcohol, placebo, and emotional picture cue challenges: Effects of 0.1-Hz stimulation. *Psychophysiology* 45: 847–858.

Venables PH and Christie MJ (1973) Mechanisms, instrumentation, recording techniques, and quantification of responses. In WF Prokasky and DC Raskin (eds), *Electrodermal Activity in Psychological Research* (pp. 1–124). New York: Academic Press.

Venables PH and Christie MJ (1980) Electrodermal activity. In I Martin and PH Venables (eds), *Techniques in Psychophysiology* (pp. 3–67). Chichester: John Wiley & Sons, Ltd.

Vrana SR, Spence EL, and Lang PJ (1988) The startle probe response: A new measure of emotion? *Journal of Abnormal Psychology* 97: 487–491.

Walter M, Degen B, Treugut C, Albrich J, Oppel M, Schulz A, Schächinger H, Dürsteler-Macfarland KM, and Wiesbeck GA (2011a) Affective reactivity in heroin-dependent patients with antisocial personality disorder. *Psychiatry Research* 187: 210–213.

Walter M, Wiesbeck GA, Degen B, Albrich J, Oppel M, Schulz A, Schächinger H, and Dürsteler-MacFarland KM (2011b) Heroin reduces startle and cortisol response in opioid-maintained heroin-dependent patients. *Addiction Biology* 16: 145–151.

Watson NL, Carpenter MJ, Saladin ME, Gray KM, and Upadhyaya HP (2010) Evidence for greater cue reactivity among low-dependent vs. high-dependent smokers. *Addictive Behaviors* 35: 673–677.

Weiss F, Lorang MT, Bloom FE, and Koob GF (1993) Oral alcohol self-administration stimulates dopamine release in the rat nucleus accumbens: Genetic and motivational determinants. *Journal of Pharmacology and Experimental Therapeutics* 267: 250–258.

White WB and Baker LH (1987) Ambulatory blood pressure monitoring in patients with panic disorder. *Archives of Internal Medicine* 147: 1973–1975.

Wilson TD and Dunn EW (2004) Self-knowledge: Its limits, value, and potential for improvement. *Annual Review of Psychology* 55: 493–518.

Winton WM, Putnam LE, and Krauss RM (1984) Facial and autonomic manifestations of the dimensional structure of emotion. *Journal of Experimental Social Psychology* 20: 195–216.

Witvliet CV and Vrana SR (1995) Psychophysiological responses as indices of affective dimensions. *Psychophysiology* 32: 436–443.

Wölfling K, Flor H, and Grüsser SM (2008) Psychophysiological responses to drug-associated stimuli in chronic heavy cannabis use. *European Journal of Neuroscience* 27: 976–983.

Yu J, Zhang S, Epstein DH, Fang Y, Shi J, Qin H, Yao S, Le Foll B, and Lu L (2007) Gender and stimulus difference in cue-induced responses in abstinent heroid users. *Pharmacology Biochemistry and Behavior* 86: 485–492.

Zimmermann U, Spring K, Wittchen HU, and Holsboer F (2004) Effects of ethanol administration and induction of anxiety-related affective states on the acoustic startle reflex in sons of alcohol-dependent fathers. *Alcoholism: Clinical and Experimental Research* 28: 424–432.

22

Using Quantitative EEG and EEG Tomography to Understand Drug Abuse: A Quantum Leap in New Methods and Benefits

David G. Gilbert and Herman A. Diggs

1 Introduction

The electroencephalogram (EEG) has an important past and a more important future in substance abuse research due to major recent developments in EEG technology and experimental paradigms during the past decade. This current renaissance of EEG technology includes validated three-dimensional quantification of electrical activity in different brain structures, analysis of event-related brain-wave oscillations (proven to be predictive of drug-related vulnerability and effects), and capacity to characterize brain functioning in a manner not provided by other imaging techniques. Additionally, the affordability of EEG enables researchers to run more subjects and sessions than is generally feasible with other brain imaging techniques, which allows the study of individual differences and multiple assessments across time (e.g., prior to and at various points after drug withdrawal or treatment initiation). These paradigms provide an opportunity for substance abuse researchers to characterize drug effects across situational and trait-related factors that influence substance use and abuse. The new developments in EEG technology build on the old strengths of EEG, including the millisecond quantification of brain activity, and portability across a variety of research contexts – a combination that no other brain imaging modality can provide. One of the major foci of this chapter is a description of these methods and the knowledge that they can generate concerning drug use and dependence.

During recent years there has been growing recognition that drug-related research will greatly benefit from: (1) methodological upgrading of drug-related EEG studies (use of state-of-the-art EEG methods) and (2) use of brain/neuroscience theory-based models that include the characterization of neuronal networks (Galderisi and Sannita, 2006). Thus, a major focus of this chapter is on state-of-the-art methods including: (1) the empirical relevance of EEG to substance abuse research, (2) new and traditional standardized and validated methods used in the field, (3) methodological recommendations, and (4) limitations, challenges, and future directions.

The Wiley-Blackwell Handbook of Addiction Psychopharmacology, First Edition. Edited by James MacKillop and Harriet de Wit.
© 2013 John Wiley & Sons, Ltd. Published 2013 by John Wiley & Sons, Ltd.

2   Empirical Relevance of EEG to Substance Abuse Research

This section reviews: (1) the biological basis of EEG and its brain activity-marker utility, (2) validation and benefits of EEG, and (3) an overview of situational (state and contextual) and trait moderation of drug effects on EEG. Then, general recording and analysis methods are described, followed by summaries of validated drug-related experimental paradigms and findings.

2.1   The neurophysiological bases of EEG

Knowledge of the neurophysiological basis of EEG comes primarily from human and subhuman animal intracranial recordings, brain-lesions, neurochemical abnormalities, and acute drug administration studies (reviewed by Jerbi *et al.*, 2009; Knight, 1990; Lanre-Amos and Kocsis, 2010). EEG measured at scalp sites reflects rhythmic oscillations (ranging from 0.1 to 150 + cycles/sec [Hz]) of large ensembles of synchronous postsynaptic dendritic activation and deactivation of 10,000 or more closely situated neurons, primarily vertically aligned pyramidal cells in the cortex (see Davidson, Jackson, and Larson, 2000). However, there are exceptions to the rule that cortical pyramidal cells are the primary source of the EEG signal of interest. For example, brainstem auditory evoked response (BAER) assessed by averaging 1,000–1,500 trials can accurately detect the firing of deep activity (far-field potentials) of the auditory nerve and brainstem auditory structures, including the thalamus (Gobbelé, Buchner, Scherg, and Curio, 1999; Ponton, Moore, and Eggermont, 1996). Given the history of advances in EEG technology, it would not be unreasonable to predict that additional EEG indices of subcortical deep structures will be forthcoming. Detailed discussions of the neurophysiological etiology of the EEG can be found in Nunez and Srinivasan (2006) and Niedermeyer and Lopes da Silva (1993).

EEG at a given scalp site is typically assessed as the difference in voltage between the active sites electrodes and a reference (details in section 3.1.5). The EEG is a time series of varying voltages (Figure 22.1) composed of multiple overlapping sine waves of various frequencies and amplitudes. The relative "strength" (or power) of various frequencies (e.g., delta = 1–4 Hz, theta = 4–8 Hz, alpha = 8–13 Hz, beta = 13–30 Hz, gamma = 30–150 Hz, and ultra-high frequency = up to 1,000 Hz) are common dependent variables in EEG (Klostermann, 2005; Lopes da Silva, Gomez, Velis, and Kalitzin, 2005).

2.1.1   EEG frequency domain.   The most prominent features of EEG waveforms are momentary oscillations at different frequencies. These oscillations reflect synchronized neural network information processing in different brain areas responsible for cognition, affect, and behavior. It has been shown that neurons working in synchrony generate EEG oscillations that can be reliably measured with scalp electrodes (Pfurtscheller and Lopes da Silva, 1999) that reflect relative increases and decreases in excitatory and inhibitory activation occurring at specific frequencies of the EEG cycle. These oscillations can be characterized during spontaneous EEG as well as during task-specific paradigms. Situations that require a high degree of visual attention

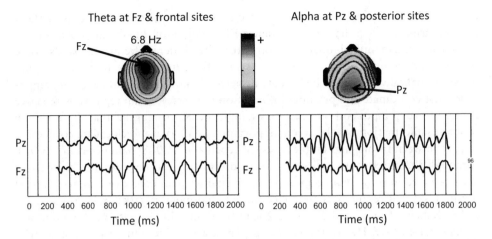

Figure 22.1 Topographical maps and associated theta and alpha EEG activity at frontal and parietal sites. Theta is dominant at frontal midline sites (e.g., Fz) while alpha is dominant a posterior sites (e.g., Pz). Refer to Plate 1 for the colored version of this figure

promote activation of attentional networks and associated EEG involving frontal, parietal, and (frequently) insular cortices (Sridharan, Levitin, and Menon, 2008), whereas situations with minimal cognitive load allow the activation of various resting or default networks (Sridharan, Levitin, and Menon, 2008) and associated EEG patterns. There many different cognition-, affect-, and behavior-related neural networks whose relative activations generate different EEG frequency patterns across different brain structures (Csicsvari, Jamieson, Wise, and Buzsaki, 2003) and whose occurrence is a function of situational and trait factors, including impulsivity, depression, and disposition to drug abuse (Bauer, 2001a; Coan and Allen, 2003a; 2003b; Davidson, 1995; Napflin, Wildi, and Sarnthein, 2007).

EEG patterns across brain sites and across time reflect complex interactions among external situational factors, top-down global neural networks, and bottom-up local circuits, including those modulated by drugs (Nunez and Srinivasan, 2006). Thus, while thalamic and septohippocampal nuclei, which have extensive projections to cortical centers (Klimesch, 1999; McKormick and Bal, 1997) frequently play important modulatory and component roles in the generation of many EEG oscillations, it is probably inappropriate to infer that the thalamus or other single brain structures are EEG *pacemakers* independent of other brain structures and input from the external environment (Nunez and Srinivasan, 2006). The finding that cooling the thalamus slows scalp EEG alpha oscillations (Andersen and Andersson, 1968) is a demonstration of the modulatory role of subcortical activity. Delta oscillations have also been recorded in thalamic neurons that project to various regions of the cortex (McCormick and Pape, 1990), yet cortico-cortical interactions also play a major causal role in the generation of delta, especially delta associated with decision making and after target stimuli (Devrim, Demiralp, Ademoglu, and Kurt, 1999). Beta frequency activity frequently is an index of increased GABAergic inhibitory activity (Lopes da Silva, 2002). Most generally, EEG can be viewed as waves of cortical excitation and inhibitions that help coordinate communication between different areas of the brain. It is at these neurotransmission loci that drugs influence EEG, cognition, affect, and behavior.

Research has identified functional correlates of the different frequency bands, some of which are summarized in Table 22.1. Slow frequency (delta, theta, and alpha) waves are typically generated by broadly dispersed brain sources and have high amplitudes that coordinate and promote information flow across brain regions by selective gating of neural input and output. For example, evidence suggests that theta activity promotes information flow between hippocampal/temporal and cingulate cortices, as well as between frontal and limbic areas (Mitchell *et al.*, 2008; Sammer *et al.*, 2007). Although theta frequently reflects states of drowsiness and response inhibition, it is also increased in some brain regions (e.g., frontal scalp and anterior cingulate gyrus) during tasks that require intense concentration and memory tasks (Scheeringa *et al.*, 2008; Kahana, Seelig, and Madsen, 2001). Greater EEG activity in the alpha frequency band (8–13 Hz) is frequently associated with relaxation/less mental activity (Knott, Bakish, Lusk, and Barkely, 1997) and decreased visual information processing (Pfurtscheller and Lopes da Silva, 1999). However, paradoxically, as reviewed in subsequent sections, alpha power is decreased, not increased, by anxiolytic medications during standard relaxing conditions (reviewed by Saletu, Anderer, and Saletu-Zyhlarz, 2010). The higher-frequency beta and gamma waves are coherent over more limited brain areas and may reflect suppression of lower frequencies and a state of high neuronal excitability (Fries, Nikolic, and Singer, 2007). Beta is commonly thought to be an arousal response of the cortex, whereas gamma may serve as a basic mechanism for feature binding (Singer, 1999). Gamma also frequently co-occurs (cross-coupling) with theta waves in a systematic manner. This suggests that low-frequency waves reflect oscillations in neuronal excitability that promote communication among neural networks at the gamma frequency (Crick and Koch, 1990; Mitchell, McNaughton, Flanagan, and Kirk, 2008). The EEG power profile across different EEG bands is strongly influenced by situational/state and individual difference factors including previous drug use, and genotype and task- and drug-related effects vary across scalp locations and brain structure (Jensen and Tesche, 2002; Jokisch and Jensen, 2007).

2.1.2 Overview of neurophysiological basis of information processing by event-related potentials (ERPs) and event-related oscillations (EROs). ERPs are event time-locked and wave phase-locked time-varying scalp electromagnetic fields composed of various EEG oscillations. In relationship to stimulus-independent, spontaneous EEG (5–100 μV amplitude), ERPs have small amplitudes ranging from 2 to 20 μV. Thus, the identification of ERPs requires enhancement of the signal-to-noise ratio, usually by averaging across multiple trials (recent advances in technology now allow accurate identification of single-trial ERPS – see section 3.1). The neurophysiological basis of ERPs is the same as that for spontaneous EEG, as the ERP simply reflects EEG activity that is time locked to an event (stimulus or participant response). EROs (event-related oscillations – wave synchronizations and desynchronizations) are time locked, but not phase locked. Thus, EROs can frequently be easily detected with single trials, though averaging across trials increases the reliability of these signals.

The ERP varies somewhat across event sensory modalities (e.g., visual versus auditory) and intensity, but ERPs all consist of a series of waves that are labeled based on

Table 22.1 EEG band power and coherence: neurophysiological and psychological states

Band (Hz)	Location	Psychological states	Neurophysiology
Delta – Δ 1–2/4	• Cortico-cortical interactions • Frontal and limbic cortex • Thalamus	• Adults slow stages 3 and 4 of sleep • Continuous attention tasks (Kirmizi-Alsan et al., 2006) • EROs in delta range = related to signal detection/decision making	• BOLD: Positive correlation in cortical areas (Dang-Vu et al., 2008; Tyvaert et al., 2008) • Dopaminergic activity associated with reduction of (Alper, 1999; Dimpfel, 2008) • Neurons inhibited by GABA • Sleep-inducing peptide promotes
Theta – θ 3/4–8	• Diffuse type θ vs. task-related frontal θ • Anterior cingulate in memory tasks (Onton, Delorme, and Makeig, 2005)	• Drowsiness and frontal idling • Response inhibition (Kirmizi-Alsan et al., 2006) • Short-term memory (Vertes, 2005) • Hippocampal readiness to process stimuli (Buzsáki, 2002) • Increase with high memory loads (Gevins, Smith, McEvoy, and Yu, 1997; Jensen and Tesche, 2002)	• BOLD: Negatively correlated with brain default mode network structures (Scheeringa et al., 2008) • Different generators and functions in different brain areas (Kahana, Seelig, and Madsen, 2001) • Subcortical and frontolimbic pathology • High coherence in alcoholics and high-risk offspring at posterior sites (Chorlian et al., 2007)
Alpha – α 8–13 α_1 8–10 α_2 11–13	• Posterior (esp. occipital) regions • Thalamus • Anterior cortex typically lower amplitude	• Relaxed, idling state • Lack of visual information processing (occipital), REM sleep • Inhibitory control in different brain locations (Klimesch, Sauseng, and Hanslmayr, 2007; Coan and Allen 2003a) • Active suppression of sensory input	• BOLD: Positive correlation with thalamic activity and negative correlation with occipital, parietal and frontal cortical activity (Laufs et al., 2006; Tyvaert et al., 2008); blood flow correlates with alpha frequency (Jann et al., 2010) • Generators in occipital and/or thalamus • Cooling thalamus reduces alpha frequency • High coherence = low level of stimulation

(Continued)

Table 22.1 (*Continued*)

Band (Hz)	Location	Psychological states	Neurophysiology
Beta – β 13–30 β₁ 13–15 β₂ 16–25 β₃ 25–30	• Frontally dominant in many conditions • Somatosensory and motor cortex	• Alert/working • Active, busy or active concentration • Increased when movement has to be resisted or suppressed (Baker, 2007) • Suppression of slower rhythms	• BOLD: Positive correlation with posterior cingulate, precuneus, temporoparietal, dorsomedial prefrontal cortex (Laufs *et al.*, 2003) • Beta power reflects a balance of excitatory pyramidal cells and inhibitory GABA[A] interneurons (Krystal *et al.*, 2006) • Greater beta power appears to reflect greater GABA activity (Lopes da Silva, 2002)
Gamma – γ 30–100 and ultra-high	• Somato-sensory cortex • Visual cortex	• During cross-modal sensory and memory processing (Herrmann, Munk, and Engel, 2004; Kanayama, Sato, and Ohira, 2007) • Feature binding • Conscious attention	• BOLD: Positively correlated with superior temporal gyrus activation (Lachaux *et al.*, 2007) • Decrease with cognitive decline • Co-occurs with θ "carrier" waves (Kendrick *et al.*, 2011)

Note: The locations and states are simply representative of some of the more common findings and locations. For example, alpha oscillations occur throughout the cortex, but typically have greater amplitude in posterior (occipital and parietal) cortex.

their voltage polarity (positive or negative) and post-event onset time at which they peak. These waves reflect various combinations of phase resetting and locking by the event and, in some cases, transient, event-related increases in synchronization of EEG oscillations at certain frequencies. Thus, it is important to note that although events used in ERP and ERO studies frequently decrease (desynchronize) ongoing alpha or other waves, some stimuli can enhance (synchronize) ongoing waveforms in some contexts (Pfurtscheller and Lopes da Silva, 1999). General reviews of ERPs, EROs, and associated experimental paradigms are available (e.g., Handy, 2009; Olofsson, Nordin, Sequeira, and Polich, 2008). Section 4.2 reviews ERP and ERO experimental findings and paradigms that appear among the most promising for drug-dependence research.

2.2   Situational (state and contextual) and trait moderation of EEG

The effects of the behavioral and psychological effects of drugs and drug withdrawal cannot be accurately characterized independently of drug dose, the situation (state and contextual), and inter-individual trait characteristics of the individual (Janke, 1983; Perkins, 1999). Thus, it is important to characterize the moderating effects of situational and trait factors, as well as dose-response relationships in EEG studies (Bauer, 2001a; Gilbert, 1979; 1997; Janke, 1983). Given that the reinforcing effects of drug use reflect in large part the interaction of situational factors with genetic, temperamental, and drug history traits (Eysenck, 1983; Pergadia *et al.*, 2006), there is a need for experimental paradigms that manipulate these factors, while controlling other influential situational variables (reviewed by Pivik *et al.*, 1993).

2.3   Relevance of EEG to drug dependence research

Better than other commonly used functional brain imaging techniques, EEG can be used to identify the rapidly changing sequences of brain neurotransmission-related information processing associated with drug-related cognition, affect, and behavior. As reviewed below, when combined with of neuroscience methods, the uniquely high temporal resolution of EEG, new time-frequency analyses, and high-density 3-D EEG tomography have catalyzed new and exciting research findings and opportunities to explore drug dependence.

3   Standardized and Validated Methods and Recommendations

3.1   Fundamentals of laboratory setup, acquisition, and analysis

Numerous software and hardware packages are available to acquire and process EEG. Although each of these systems has its distinct advantages and the guiding principles of EEG analysis depend largely on the paradigm of interest, there are general guidelines that remain relevant across manufacturer and paradigm. Electrode placement, participant interaction, acquisition procedures, processing, and analysis of the EEG data are the primary skills that must be mastered by any researcher interested in the encephalographic correlates of substance abuse (Usakli, 2010; see IPEG, 1982, 1987, 1990, and 1998 for EEG guidelines of the International Pharmaco EEG Society [IPEG]).

3.1.1   Electrode location and placement.   Through the 1970s, EEG was rarely collected from more than 32 electrodes, and many published studies assessing psychological processes used as few than eight. Today, high-density (HD) EEG caps and nets with as many as 512 electrodes are used for EEG acquisition. The standard for electrode placement in EEG research has been the International 10–20 electrode placement system (Jasper, 1958). While slight modifications of the 10–20 placement system are used with 64 or fewer electrodes, there are a number of different electrode placement systems available when the number of electrodes exceeds 64 (although most closely correspond to the 10–20 electrode positions). Precise positioning of electrodes requires placement based on proportional distances between specified (fiducial) points on the skull. The standard fiducial points for EEG, MRI, and fMRI are the nasion, inion, and pre-auricular points (defined as the bridge of the nose, an occipital skull bump, and immediately anterior of the ear opening, respectively) (Atcherson, Gould, Pousson, and Prout, 2007). By using fiducial points and relative distances from these points for electrode placement, the relationship of each electrode to brain areas can be accurately estimated (Towle *et al.*, 1993).

Accurate electrode placement in terms of fiducial points is especially important for tomographical (3D) EEG studies, as the 3D coordinates of electrode positions are used to develop digitized head models for source localization. Although most software packages provide or allow the incorporation of spherical or standard (average) head models generated using a specific electrode configuration, more precise procedures for specifying electrode location are available and beneficial in characterizing neural source localization (Luu, Poulsen, and Tucker, 2009). Koessler *et al.* (2007) provide an excellent review of the manual, electromagnetic, ultrasound, MRI volume localization, and photogrammetry procedures used to calculate 3D coordinates of electrodes. These procedures generate head models based on individual subjects' anatomy and electrode locations, thus providing more precise spatial characterization of the EEG signal for source localization.

3.1.2   Electrodes and electrolytes.   Silver/silver-chloride (Ag/AgCl) electrodes have become the standard in the field, as they are more electrically stable (do not form chemical reactions with electrolytes) and thereby exhibit less low-frequency (DC) drift relative to other electrode types (Tallgren, Vanhatalo, Kaila, and Voipio, 2005). In most cases, electrodes are recessed in a plastic or rubber housing about 2–5 mm above the scalp. An electrolyte (electrically conductive gel, paste, or solution) fills the electrode housing and helps promote a stable electrical contact between the scalp and electrode. The nature of the electrolyte depends on the nature of the housing and is typically recommended by the manufacturer of commercial EEG caps/nets. Electrodes that require saline solution hydration are quicker to apply and use in short-duration recording sessions but require frequent reapplication of the aqueous electrolyte to the sponges to keep impedance at an acceptable level. Aqueous electrolytes are also more prone to electrolyte bridging (shorting) between electrodes – a major problem with HD recordings because of the distortion of the EEG signals.

3.1.3   EEG sampling rate, filtering, and electrode number.   EEG sampling rate typically occurs between 250 and 1,000 Hz and must be at least twice as fast as the highest frequency (including high-frequency EMG and noise) that occurs in the sampled signal. Voltage signals at frequencies higher than half of the sampling rate (the Nyquist frequency) are mischaracterized as lower frequencies (aliasing). Thus, commercial EEG systems include low-pass filters that greatly attenuate signals greater than half of the sampling rate and thus minimize the likelihood of such aliasing. Generally, 250–500 Hz sampling rates are adequate for the majority of EEG substance abuse studies because this rate allows the assessment of frequencies through high gamma.

Electromagnetic force (EMF) generated by electrical wiring and equipment generates 50 or 60 Hz noise and many types of equipment (e.g., CRT monitors) generate high-frequency artifacts. While modern equipment does not require the degree of EMF shielding that was needed by older equipment, electrical sources near the subject can introduce artifactual voltage signals that overcome the filtering capacity of the equipment and may create aliasing. Thus, it may be important to keep computer monitors, power lines, and other equipment at distances greater than 1 meter from the participant.

In ERP studies, using a 0.01 or 0.05 Hz HP filter only minimally attenuates late slow wave ERP components such as the P300 and CNV, but using HP filters greater than 0.1 Hz causes reductions in the amplitude of components. Choice of filtering parameters should be informed by published studies using similar methods. Studies of the frequency domain commonly use HP filters from 0.1 to 1 Hz.

Electrode number/density requirements depend largely on the goals of the research: 128 or more electrodes appear to provide substantially more precise tomographic source characterization of smaller and deeper source signals (Srinivasan, Tucker, and Murias, 1998). However, in some cases a much smaller number may be adequate if the literature suggests that fewer electrodes are adequately sensitive for the task at hand (e.g., P50 suppression or simple P3 tasks).

3.1.4   Steps to maximize EEG data quality prior to and while recording.   Recording of quality EEG data requires: (1) training the participant to perform the task while minimizing artifact-generating behavior (e.g., muscle tension, movement) that contaminates the EEG signal; (2) prompting the participant to provide quality data immediately prior to each recording; (3) considering and standardizing situational factors that might influence the participant's attentional and emotional state; and (4) low scalp impedance at each electrode.

Orientation (practice) sessions are highly recommended for several reasons. First, a practice session prior to the experimental session(s) allows the experimenter to focus on teaching the participant how to reliably provide low-artifact, high-quality EEG data. Allowing the participant to view their EEG in real time while they perform a sequence of artifact-generating movements (e.g. head movement, eye blinks, squinting, and tensing muscles) can be very useful in helping make participants aware of how slight changes in their behavior can greatly harm or benefit the quality of the EEG recording. Orientation and practice sessions including such biofeedback should also include the proposed experimental tasks because tasks generally produce additional artifacts (e.g., facial muscle tension during demanding visual tasks). Orientation sessions and task practice also promote adaptation to the novelty of an experimental EEG session.

It is important to devote a few minutes to monitor the EEG tracings immediately before initiation of recording so that subject-generated and other artifacts can be reduced. Also, it is generally wise to prompt the participant to behave in a manner that will provide maximal EEG quality and validity. It is important to assure that the participant is in a comfortable position, the room temperature is controlled, and the recording room is sound attenuated, possibly with background white noise if sound attenuation is less than ideal. It is highly recommended that the experimenter ask open-ended questions such as "What about your position is least comfortable?" and "How else could we make you more comfortable?". Systematic use of such open-ended questions frequently produces far fewer muscle artifacts.

Finally, impedances at each electrode site needs to be reduced (generally to below 50 K ohm with modern systems and 5 K with older systems). Abrasion of the skin beneath the electrode using a blunt needle or similar sterile instrument can help quickly reduce high impedances to acceptable levels. Parting of hair and firmly seating the electrode against the scalp is critical to assure stable impedances and to prevent electrolyte from leaking out under the electrode housing that may cause bridging between electrodes.

3.1.5   Choice of reference.   Voltage recordings, including EEG, are bipolar in nature and represent the difference between the electrode and reference. Many researchers choose to report their results using multiple reference montages (e.g., linked mastoids and average reference) to reduce the probability of skewed results based solely on choice of reference site (Scherg, Ille, Bornfleth, and Berg, 2002). Current source density or Laplacian waveforms are also advocated by many EEG researchers, although they have their own challenges and limitations (see Murray, Brunet, and Michel, 2008; Saron, Schroeder, Foxe, and Vaughan, 2001). Some modern analyses (e.g. LORETA and other tomographic current source localizations) provide reference-independent measures based on current rather than voltage (Michel *et al.*, 2004).

3.1.6   Epoching (data segmenting).   After the raw EEG data have been filtered, the next step is to select epochs of time that will subsequently be used for data analysis. Longer epochs increase the frequency resolution but make inclusion of artifact within an epoch more likely and make the rejection of a specific epoch more costly. Once continuous data have been epoched, artifacts should be identified and bad epochs (those with excessive artifact) may be deleted with automatic bad-epoch identification programs based on statistical or amplitude thresholding, or may be rejected manually. Automatic identification programs allow researchers to set parameters of deviant variance on which to identify and reject bad epochs, but may introduce bias into the dataset and severely limit the number of epochs available for later analyses (Kaiser and Sterman, 2001).

3.1.7   Artifact attenuation.   All EEG contains some artifact. While highly effective artifact attenuation procedures are now available (for an empirical review of artifact detection, see Delorme, Sejnowski, and Makeig, 2007), it is important to extensively assess the effects of artifact-reduction procedures on specific datasets in order to assure that the procedures are not systematically biasing or distorting the data. EMG artifact overlaps with beta and gamma frequency bands, eye blinks and eye movement generate large artifacts in the middle and low frequency ranges (delta through alpha), and the electrocardiogram (ECG) signal that is common in HD recordings includes both high- and low-frequency activity. While it is possible to delete eye-blink or movement-related EMG contaminated epochs, ECG and chronic EMG associated with tension require attenuation by mathematical algorithms. A familiarity with the strengths and drawbacks of these approaches is fundamental for unbiased EEG analysis. The following overview notes many of the major artifact rejection procedures used in the field.

Blind source separation (BSS) canonical correlations assume that muscle activity sources will have lower autocorrelation in comparison to brain activity sources. Automatic BSS programs for EMG artifact reduction are available and may provide more objective artifact reduction techniques than manual independent components analysis (ICA) component rejection (De Clercq *et al.*, 2006; James and Gibson, 2003; Vergult *et al.*, 2007). Many common software packages provide BSS procedures, including EEGLAB (see Delorme *et al.*, 2007, for a review). Alternative regression-based myogenic correction techniques for EMG attenuation are also available but are not recommended for most analyses (see McMenamin *et al.*, 2009, for review).

A number of techniques have been developed to attenuate eye-blink and electrooculographic (EOG) artifacts contained in raw EEG (Croft *et al.*, 2005; Hoffman and Falkenstein, 2008; Ille, Berg, and Scherg, 2002; Joyce, Gorodnitsky and Kutas, 2004; Picton *et al.*, 2000). Statistical regression-based methods (Gratton, Coles, and Donchin, 1983; Schlogl *et al.*, 2007) aim to subtract blink-related artifacts from the true EEG by assuming the signal from electrodes above and below one or both eyes, and ICA attempts to isolate eye blinks components for rejection (Jung *et al.*, 2000; Vigario, 1997). While some have found better results with ICA-based techniques (Hoffman and Falkenstein, 2008; Joyce, Gorodnitsky and Kutas, 2004), others have found that regressive techniques may perform just as well or better than ICA for EOG attenuation (Schlógl, Ziehe, Müller, 2009; Klados, Papadelis, Lithari, and Bamidis, 2009). Lindsen and Bhattacharya (2010) combined ICA with empirical mode decomposition to isolate eye blinks and found that this technique may result in a smaller loss of true EEG signal than pure regressive or ICA-based approaches. Wallstrom *et al.* (2004) provide a review of the strengths of both regression and component-based approaches for ocular artifact removal.

The heartbeat-generated ECG artifact frequency spectrum overlaps with theta, alpha, and beta, making it particularly problematic for frequency-domain analyses in studies where drugs and other procedures influence heart rate. ICA is the most commonly used method for removing ECG artifact (Devuyst *et al.*, 2008; Urrestarazu *et al.*, 2004). Other effective ECG artifact approaches have utilized the energy interval histogram (Park, Jeong, and Park, 2002) or wavelet-transform methods (Jiang *et al.*, 2007).

Semi-automatic artifact identification and artifact-attenuation procedures based on ICA components have become standard in the field and automatic ICA correction techniques based on wavelet analysis are also now available (Delorme, Sejnowski, and Makeig, 2007; Ghandeharion and Erfanian, 2010; Mammone, La Foresta, and Morabito, 2011; Nolan, Whelan, and Reilly, 2010; Viola *et al.*, 2009). Although these automatic procedures have a high degree of overlap with manual artifact correction procedures for eye blinks and EMG, they may not perform as well for the correction of ECG artifacts (Viola *et al.*, 2009). Any of the aforementioned artifact-attenuation procedures should be used only after testing with the specific dataset to be analyzed. ICA-based artifact attenuation techniques have emerged as the most common method for preprocessing EEG data, and a sound understanding of these techniques is fundamental to EEG signal processing.

3.1.8 Channel interpolation.   Bad (noisy, offline) electrode sites should be replaced by imputation/interpolation. Interpolations for faulty electrodes should be based on raw data (continuous or epoched) with either linked mastoid or central reference. An average reference should not be used during interpolation because of the influence of the bad sites on the generated average (Ferree, 2000). Spherical spline interpolation and nearest neighbor interpolation are commonly used (Perrin, Pernier, Bertrand, and Echallier, 1989; Soong, Lind, Shaw, and Coles, 1993; Soufflet *et al.*, 1991). In general, spherical spline interpolations perform better than nearest neighbor interpolations when attempting to reconstitute EEG maps using cross-validation criteria (Michel *et al.*, 2004). Spherical splines may also perform better in situations where electrode bridging occurs in high-density nets (Greischar *et al.*, 2004). Spherical spline interpolation software is available in many EEG analysis packages, including EEGLAB.

3.1.9 EEG analysis: the frequency domain.   After artifact cleaning, the EEG can be characterized by plotting the amount of oscillatory activity at each of the frequencies of the EEG (primarily 1 to 70 Hz). The EEG spectrum is grouped into frequency bands (delta, theta, alpha, beta, and gamma) that are commonly subdivided into two or more sub-bands that reflect functionally different brain activity (see Table 22.1). Spectral analyses are typically conducted with the fast Fourier transform (FFT) (Cooley and Tukey, 1965). The EEG power spectral density is depicted visually with frequency on the horizontal axis and power (or power/Hz) on the vertical axis (Figure 22.2). The spectral density function reflects the mean power at each EEG frequency across a brief time window (typically 1–10 seconds). The frequency resolution generated by the FFT is the reciprocal of the epoch length ($1/T$). For example, epochs of 1-second duration will provide numeric values corresponding to mean power across 1-Hz-wide bins, whereas 10-second epochs will provide 0.1-Hz-wide bins. Thus, the identification of small changes in frequency requires longer-duration epochs. Because the FFT requires the number of data points in the epoch to be a power of 2, epochs typically consist of 256, 512, 1,024, or 2,048 data points. A 0.5-Hz frequency resolution would thus be generated by a sampling rate of 256 Hz for 2 seconds. EEG acquisition systems that sample at rates other than multiples of a power of 2 cannot generate data that will allow the FFTs to generate exactly 0.5-Hz wide bins. An approximation of 0.5-Hz-wide bins can be generated with 2,048-millisecond-duration epochs that generate

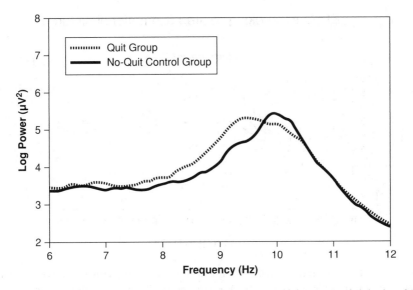

Figure 22.2 Slowing of dominant alpha frequency and centroid (mean) of alpha band in a group of tobacco smokers when abstinent versus a group of non-abstinent smokers (based on Gilbert *et al.*, 1999)

1,024 points/epoch when sampled at 500 Hz. In order to generate a more reliable assessment of the power of different frequencies, average FFT spectra are derived by taking the mean of typically from 15 to 100 individual epochs. Because power distributions tend to be skewed, it is appropriate to log transform (either natural or log base 10) the mean FFT power in each band to normalize the data. FFTs require a tapering function (e.g., a Hanning or Hamming window) that attenuates the value of data points at the beginning and end of epochs (Heinzel, Rudiger, and Schilling, 2002). Given the importance of accurate characterization of drug-related effects on EEG frequency, it is recommended that in most cases spontaneous EEG epoching be at least 2 seconds in duration. Use of 4-second epochs provides better resolution (0.25 Hz) and greater sensitivity to changes in dominant and centroid frequencies in different EEG bands. Epochs longer than 4 seconds are more likely to include artifacts that may limit any potential additional benefits of greater frequency resolution.

Degree of correspondence between EEG oscillations at different electrode sites is provided by coherence analysis. Coherence analysis quantifies the correlations in the frequency domain between two simultaneously measured EEG sites and corresponds to the squared correlation coefficient of simultaneous frequency consistency between signals (values range from 0 to 1). Coherence refers to a constant phase difference in two or more waves across time. The waves are incoherent if the crests and troughs are randomly related across time. Coherence analysis provides a means to investigate cortical interactions (e.g., connectivity between cortical regions) and has been used to examine the effects of drug administration on connectivity between cortical regions of interest (Alonso *et al.*, 2010; Sampaio *et al.*, 2007).

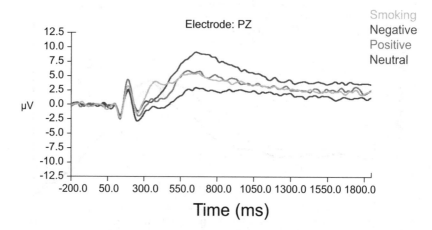

Figure 22.3 ERPs to smoking-related and emotionally valent pictures. N1 occurs about 100 milliseconds post picture onset, P170 occurs about 170 milliseconds post picture onset, and the late positive component (LPC) ranges from 400 milliseconds to more than 1,800 milliseconds in the case of the negative pictures. This LPC is largest in response to the negative pictures, and smallest in response to neutral pictures. Refer to Plate 2 for the colored version of this figure

3.1.10 EEG analysis: time domain – event-related potentials (ERPs). ERPs (Figure 22.3) and time-frequency profiles (see section 3.1.11) take advantage of EEG's exquisite temporal resolution. The term "time domain" refers to changes in degree of positive or negative voltage relative to pre-stimulus levels that occur within a brief time window after the onset of an experimenter-presented stimulus or (less frequently) a subjected-generated response. Changes in EEG voltage within these brief time windows are referred to as ERP components and are usually obtained by averaging voltage signals across a number of stimulus time-locked EEG epochs. For example, the P300 ERP peak voltage occurs at approximately 300 milliseconds after the onset of a target stimulus in some experimental paradigms. The latencies of an ERP component peak vary considerably based on the paradigm used and are the variable of interest. Many researchers use the polarity and ordinal position of the waveform instead of latency when defining components (e.g. P3 instead of P300). The temporospatial properties of ERPs provide measures of neural activity associated with a variety of psychological processes, including those related to substance abuse and dependence that are explored in detail in section 4.2.

Baseline correction (BC) is used to correct for the substantial variance in EEG voltage that occurs across time that is independent of brain processes (e.g., changes in electrolyte–electrode chemistry due to electrolyte drying, sweating). BC corrects for this variance by subtracting a voltage (usually the mean voltage across a 100–200-millisecond prestimulus baseline) from the voltage values during the post-event onset period (usually 400 to 3,000 milliseconds) for each epoch (Delorme and Makeig, 2004; Le Van Quyen *et al.*, 2001). BC with rapidly presented stimuli or for response-locked ERPs may require more sophisticated mathematical techniques (Lutkenhoner, 2010).

Because event or response-locked changes in the EEG generate only slight alterations in the ongoing EEG and each epoch contains stimulus-independent background EEG "noise," a number of individual ERP trials must be averaged to generate ERPs that have adequate signal to noise ratio. Mathematically, the remaining noise in an average ERP decreases as a square root of the function of the number ERP trials. Thus, many trials are necessary to obtain a reliable ERP if the signal is small relative to the background EEG "noise." Therefore, small ERP signals (e.g., the P50) require many more trials than large ERPs (e.g. P3). Single-trial ERPs can be obtained for large (e.g., P300) signals (Jung *et al.*, 2001).

Although average ERP peak amplitude is a common index in the ERP literature, this index can be problematic in drug-related research where drugs or drug deprivation frequently increases variability in individual ERP trial peak latency. Greater peak latency variability reduces mean peak amplitude (Luck, 2005). Thus, mean amplitude-based measures are recommended because they are superior to peak measures in most instances of latency variability. Peak amplitude measures, if desired, should include one of a number of mathematical approaches to correcting latency variability effects on amplitude (Luck, 2005).

3.1.11   EEG analysis: time-frequency domain – event-related oscillations (EROs). ERO analyses (see Figure 22.4) combine excellent temporal resolution characteristic of ERPs with the additional valuable information concerning event-related changes in the EEG power at different frequency at different points in time within the epoch. ERO patterns include event-related synchronization (increases in activity or magnitude within a band) and event-related desynchronizations (decreases in activity within a frequency band). ERO approaches typically use wavelet analyses, rather than FFT analyses, because wavelet analysis provides much more precise information about the onset and offset of EEG oscillations within frequency bands than do FFTs (Samar,

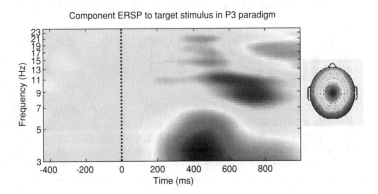

Figure 22.4   Event-related oscillation power as a function of oscillation frequency and time after the onset of target stimuli (time 0) in an oddball paradigm. Note the increase in delta and theta power from 250 to 580 milliseconds, corresponding to the P3b. Refer to Plate 3 for the colored version of this figure

Swartz, and Raghuveer, 1995). FFTs typically have a 1- or 2-second temporal resolution, roughly the same as fMRI. However, wavelet analysis provides resolution of the order of tens of milliseconds (Samar, Swartz, and Raghuveer, 1995), several hundred times more precise than fMRI and FFT approaches. Rennie, Robinson, and Wright (2002) provides an excellent review of the relation between EEG spectra and evoked potentials. There are a number of commercial as well as free-ware (e.g., EEGLAB) software packages that can be used to easily provide this important time–frequency information.

3.1.12 Scalp topography and tomographic (3D) source localization. Quantitative scalp topographical mapping and tomography provide researchers with important tools to visualize common EEG/ERP components or EEG frequency band-specific power among groups of electrode sites (topography) and brain structures (tomography). Topographical mapping in conjunction with ICA provides a summary of the distribution of brain electrical activity across the scalp, often color-coded to help identify patterns of activity of interest. Figure 22.5 presents surface EEG topographic activity at different points in time (from 200 to 386 milliseconds) after the onset of rare target oddball auditory stimuli that generate a P3 ERP. Smoking in this study tended to enhance P3b amplitude relative to abstinence at from 296 to 320 milliseconds post oddball onset. It is important to note that, although color scales may change across references sites used, the topographical profile of EEG is reference independent as long as the reference is correctly included in the model (Geselowitz, 1998). Topographic profiles may be particularly useful for quickly visualizing frequency effects of drug administration on broad areas of the cortex. There is also preliminary evidence that rapid changes in topographic profiles can be used to identify switching between brain operations performed by different neuronal assemblies, or operational synchrony (Fingelkurts *et al.*, 2007). Perhaps most importantly, topographic profiles of EEG can now inform subsequent source localization (tomography) efforts.

P3 in Oddball task when Smoking vs. 3-Days Post Quitting

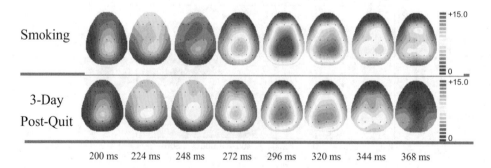

Figure 22.5 Mean P3b response topographies to target stimuli during an oddball paradigm in a group of smokers before and after quitting smoking. The onset of target stimuli = time 0. Red color reflects greater ERP amplitude, while blue reflects small amplitude. Refer to Plate 4 for the colored version of this figure

The fundamental challenge of EEG tomography is the electromagnetic inverse problem that states that the given electrical potential recorded at the scalp can be attributed to an infinite number of sources unless assumptions are made. A priori assumptions about neural sources allow the inverse problem to be solved to some degree (Fender, 1987). A number of different a priori algorithms have been proposed to allow source localization (see Baillet, Mosher, and Leahy, 2001; Xu, Xu, and He, 2004; Michel *et al.*, 2004, for reviews). The most commonly used models for EEG tomography are the weighted minimum norm which is used in low-resolution brain electromagnetic tomography (LORETA – http://www.uzh.ch/keyinst/loreta.htm), local autoregressive average (LAURA), and overdetermined dipolar models brain electrical source analysis (BESA – www.besa.de) (Pascual-Marqui, Esslen, Kochi, and Lehmann, 2002; Grave de Peralta, Murray, Gonzalez, and Andino, 2004; Scherg Pascual-Marqui, Esslen, Kochi, and Lehmann and Berg, 1993). LORETA and BESA are by far the most widely used and validated distributed source identification software packages. During the last decade an impressive correspondence of fMRI and LORETA (including s and e versions) and other source-localization procedures have been demonstrated (Corrigan *et al.*, 2009; Pascual-Marqui, Esslen, Kochi, and Lehmann, 2002). LORETA and most other modern source-localization programs work effectively in both the frequency and time domains, although most LORETA source-localization efforts have focused on the frequency domain (Thatcher, 2010).

4   Standardized and Validated EEG Methods for Drug Research

Knowledge of the basic constructs and experimental methods that best characterize drug-related neurophysiological and psychological processes can help the investigator select appropriate paradigms for answering research questions, as well as inform the creation of new tasks that are needed in the field. This section provides a brief review of pharmaco-EEG research, including the effects of different classes of drugs on spontaneous (S)-EEG spectral profiles. The majority of S-EEG studies have relied on simple quantitative descriptive accounts of drug effects and interpretations based on a small number of analyses and conceptualizations (Galderisi and Sannita, 2006). Thus, there is an imperative for research using more complex situation by trait designs combined with modern experimental paradigms in order to provide more information about drug effects on brain states and reactivity related to cognition, affect, and behavior. More complex paradigms are addressed in subsequent sections.

Different drug classes influence a variety of S-EEG and event-related EEG parameters. Saletu, Anderer, and Saletu-Zyhlarz (2010) review the direct effects of therapeutic drugs on S-EEG power and frequency, and Bauer (2001a) reviews EEG studies of substance abuse up to the point in time that high-density tomographic studies began their rapid expansion. Kenemans and Kähkäonen (2011) review ERP studies related to general psychopharmacology. Remaining chapter sections address constructs and methods not included in previous major reviews, including methods for assessing drug cue reactivity, emotional stimulus reactivity in substance abuse research, and best-practice guidelines, as they emphasize recently developed state-of-the-art methods and the moderation of drug effects by situational and trait factors.

4.1   Acute drug effects on spontaneous EEG (S-EEG)

This section provides a selective review of drug effects on EEG with the goal of providing insight into results and methods that have produced reliable effects and important knowledge of drug-related effects on brain processes.

4.1.1   Resting S-EEG power-spectral drug profiles.   To date, literature reviews on S-EEG profiles have focused almost exclusively on the indices reviewed by Saletu, Anderer, and Saletu-Zyhlarz (2010): (1) S-EEG power and centroid frequencies in different frequency bands, (2) total power across all EEG bands, (3) power in each band relative to the total power across all bands, (4) centroid frequency across all bands, and (5) LORETA-based assessment of brain current sources. During resting conditions, acute administration pharmaco-EEG studies show different psychotropic drug classes to have unique effects on S-EEG power spectrum patterns, as exemplified in Table 22.2. Psychomotor stimulants, heroin, THC/cannabis, anxiolytics, hypnotics, alcohol, antidepressants, and hallucinogens have distinct acute drug-response profiles. Stimulants decrease theta power and increase alpha frequency, while alcohol and opioids have the opposite effects – increasing theta power and decreasing alpha frequency. Benzodiazepines decrease theta power (like alcohol and opioids) but also substantially and reliably increase beta power and suppress alpha power while increasing alpha frequency. The beta-enhancing effects of benzodiazepines are thought to index GABAergic activation (Lopes da Silva, 2002). These complex drug profiles clearly indicate that a simplistic arousal or EEG activation model (e.g., assuming that alpha reflects relaxation while alpha desynchronization means brain activation or arousal) is not adequate to explain differences in drug effects. More complex conceptual models and experimental paradigms, such as those outlined in section 4.2, can help better characterize drug EEG and psychological effects.

Saletu, Anderer, and Saletu-Zyhlarz (2006) provide convincing evidence supporting the view that tomographic (3D, structure-specific) analysis of S-EEG provides important structure-specific information that is more theoretically meaningful than traditional topographic methods. For example, in addition to identifying brain areas not suggested by surface topographic approaches, the LORETA tomographic analyses closely matched findings of fMRI studies. Figure 22.6 presents LORETA images from our lab of theta-band EEG current density in response to pictures depicting smoking-related, emotionally positive, negative, or neutral content after 3 days of tobacco smoking abstinence in habitual smokers randomly assigned to either nicotine patch or placebo patch. It can be seen that the effects of drug treatment on theta-band current varied as a function of picture type and brain structure. Blue areas reflect relatively less brain reactivity (theta current) in the nicotine condition relative to the placebo condition during 2–3 seconds after the offset of the picture stimuli.

Table 22.2 Effects of acute drug relative to placebo on resting state spontaneous EEG power and frequency at time of maximum efficacy after administration

Drug		Delta	Theta	Alpha1	Alpha2	Beta1	Beta2	Beta3
(Meth)	Power		↓↓	?↓?	0	0	↓fm,C	0
amphetamine	Frequency		↓		↑↑		0	
Cocaine	Power	↓↓	↓↓	0	0		↑?	
	Frequency							
MDMA	Power		↓↓	↓↓	↓↓	?	?	?
	Frequency	0			↑↑		?	
Nicotine	Power	↓↓	↓↓	↓↓	↑ec/s	s	s	s
	Frequency		↓		↑			
Benzodiazepines	Power	↓	↓↓	↓↓	↓↓	↑	↑↑	↑↑
	Frequency		↓		↑↑		↑	
Opioids	Power	↑↑	↑↑	0	0		↑↑	↑↑
	Frequency							
THC	Power		↓↓	eu/s↑p	?eu/s↑p	?	?↓?	?
	Frequency							
Alcohol	Power	↑	↑↑	↑	↑	?	?	?
	Frequency	↓ or 0			↓↓		0	
Haldol	Power	↑	↑↑		↑		↑fm,c	
	Frequency		0		0		0	

Note: 0 = no effect; ? = unknown; s = state-dependent; ec = eyes closed; eu = euphoric state-related; f = frontal, fm = frontal midline; c = central; p = posterior; l = left-dominant, r = right-dominant. Methamphetamine: Reid *et al.* (2006). Cocaine: Herning *et al.* (1985); Reid *et al.* (2006). MDMA (Ecstasy): Lansbergen *et al.* (2011). Nicotine: Knott, Harr, Ilivitsky, and Mahoney (1998); Gilbert, Dibb, Plath, and Hiyane (2000). Benzodiazepines: Saletu, Anderer, and Saletu-Zyhlarz (2010). Opioids: Greenwald and Roehrs (2005). Marijuana/THC: Böcker *et al.* (2009); Lansbergen *et al.* (2011); Lukas, Mendelson, and Benedikt (1995); Zuurman *et al.* (2008; 2010). Alcohol: Lansbergen *et al.* (2011); Lukas and Mendelson (1988); Haldol: Saletu, Anderer, and Saletu-Zyhlarz (2010).

4.1.2 Trait-dependent S-EEG power-spectral drug sensitivity profiles. The moderation of drug S-EEG power-spectral signatures, including tomography, by temperamental and psychiatric traits has been assessed in a number of studies that generally support a key–lock relationship between drug effects on S-EEG and S-EEG spectral power signature of the disorder (Saletu, Anderer, and Saletu-Zyhlarz, 2010). The key–lock principle is a version of the self-medication hypothesis of substance use and states that individual differences in traits moderate the effects of psychoactive drugs (Eysenck, 1983; Janke, 1983; Lujic, Reuter, and Netter, 2005). These trait-dependent effects of drugs are likely to prove greater for brain areas associated with the trait or disorder (Eysenck, 1997; Gilbert, 1997; Saletu, Anderer, and Saletu-Zyhlarz, 2010). Saletu, Anderer, and Saletu-Zyhlarz (2010) provided evidence for this hypothesis by demonstrating that differences between a number of psychiatric disordered patients and non-psychiatric controls in S-EEG power and frequency are the opposite of the effects induced by drugs used to treat these disorders compared to placebos.

Nicotine-Placebo Cessation Day 3 Minus Pre-Quit Baseline Theta1

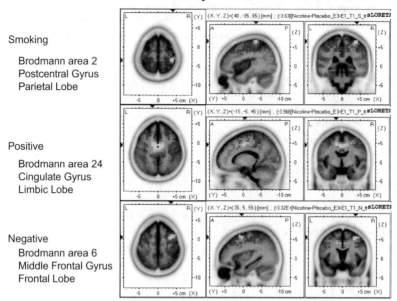

Smoking

Brodmann area 2
Postcentral Gyrus
Parietal Lobe

Positive

Brodmann area 24
Cingulate Gyrus
Limbic Lobe

Negative

Brodmann area 6
Middle Frontal Gyrus
Frontal Lobe

Figure 22.6   LORETA tomographic images of theta-band EEG current-density changes. The images reflect differences between nicotine and placebo conditions after 3 days of tobacco smoking abstinence. Refer to Plate 5 for the colored version of this figure

4.1.3   Situation-dependent S-EEG power-spectral drug profiles.   As expected by any measure of brain activity that reflects information processing states, resting S-EEG power-spectral signatures of drugs are moderated by situational factors including task demands and emotionally valent stimuli. For example, the effects of nicotine on cortical activation tend to be less when participants are under high degrees of stress (Gilbert, Estes, and Welser, 1997) and stressful stimuli have been found to modulate the effects of nicotine in a manner that depends on hemisphere and brain topography (Gilbert *et al.*, 2004a; Gilbert, Robinson, Chamberlin, and Spielberger, 1989). Recording with eyes open can result in different drug effects in some EEG frequency bands than eyes-closed recording (Gilbert, Dibb, Plath, and Hiyane, 2000). It is clear that drug effects on S-EEG typically vary as a function of environmental stress and task demands, genetically based personality traits, genotype, and brain site (Gilbert, Robinson, Chamberlin, and Spielberger, 1989; Gilbert *et al.*, 1999; 2004a; Knott, 1989; Saletu, Anderer, and Saletu-Zyhlarz, 2010). The acute effects of one drug on S-EEG are also frequently moderated by the effects of other drugs (Gilbert, Dibb, Plath, and Hiyane, 2000; Lansbergen *et al.*, 2011). It is important to note that, while the above evidence indicates that situational factors can moderate some of the EEG effects of drugs, few studies have examined the extent of such moderation and there is virtually no understanding of the complexities of state by drug interactions at the individual level. Systematic dose by situation by trait studies are needed to determine the moderating effects of contextual situations on drug use and the acute effects of drugs on EEG.

4.1.4   Dose, time, and baseline dependencies of S-EEG power-spectral profiles.   Because of the time and cost of doing large experimental studies in humans, surprisingly little work has been done on the dose, time, and baseline dependencies of S-EEG spectral profiles. Pre-drug baseline EEG state is rarely assessed as a potential moderator of drug effects, though Saletu, Anderer, and Saletu-Zyhlarz (2010) review studies of psychiatric populations in which drug effects tend to normalize patterns while having smaller effects in healthy controls, possibly due to ceiling effects.

4.1.5   Recommendations for S-EEG power-spectral drug sensitivity profiles.   (1) Given the reliability of drug-effect spectral profiles within the resting eye-closed context, S-EEG profiling should include total power across all bands, absolute and relative spectral power within each frequency band (delta through beta), as well as centroid frequency within bands and across all bands. (2) Source localization using LORETA or other validated distributed source analyses is also recommended. (3) Traditional power and frequency analyses should be expanded to include gamma and higher frequency to assess coherence/neural networks, microstates and related methods that can characterize dynamically changing brain information processing states. (4) Given the dependency of drug subjective and EEG effects on dose, time since administration, and trait and situational factors, each of these variables should be carefully controlled and where possible manipulated within or across groups. (5) Methods should be used that assure that subjects are not falling asleep during resting eye-closed conditions. (6) There is a great need for comparison of drug S-EEG effects during resting conditions (primarily reflecting various default network information processing) with drug effects on tasks known to characterize specific psychological and neurophysiological processes. Event-related EEG oscillation and ERP paradigms provide this complementary role for knowledge generation.

4.2   Paradigms for measuring drug effects using event-related EEG potentials and oscillations

Event-related potentials (ERPs) and, more generically, event-related oscillations (EROs) are uniquely capable of providing important insights into how drugs and drug-use dispositions influence time-locked brain activity in response to specific environmental stimuli or to behavioral responses. The rapidly changing pattern of EROs across the second or so after stimulus onset reflects the successive stages of information processing and the extent of processing of stimulus events, most of which occur outside the focus of attention (Muller-Gass and Campbell, 2002). Thus, EROs can provide precise temporal resolution of brain processes and sequential neural-network activation involved in a variety of processes related to drug effects and substance abuse. For example, in a study of the effects of nicotine on distraction in non-smokers, Knott *et al.* (2011) noted that different processing stages of automatic (involuntary) orienting of attention to distracter events in an auditory discrimination task (Schroger and Wolff, 1998) are marked by deviant stimulus-elicited ERP difference waveforms that reflect three stages of distracter processing: an initial mismatch negativity (100–250 milliseconds), attentional orienting toward the changed stimulus indexed at 300 milliseconds by a frontal P3a waveform, and a frontal reorienting negativity at 400–700 milliseconds indexing reallocating attention back to the original task.

Abused drugs have significant modulatory effects on multiple aspects of brain information processing, including automatic and controlled attention, attentional bias to affective and drug-related stimuli, conflict monitoring, response inhibition, affect modulation, and cue reactivity. The ERP and ERO paradigms described immediately below are validated means of assessing neural network activity reactivity to drug use-related states and traits. The sequence of tasks reviewed begins with paradigms designed to characterize lower-level relatively automatic stimulus filtering and information processing and then moves to paradigms that characterize more complex and top-down executive mechanisms.

4.2.1 Automatic stimulus gating (inhibition, filtering) – P50, N1 with rapidly repeated stimuli. Short inter-stimulus, interval auditory stimuli can be used to characterize EEG moderation by drug states and traits on automatic stimulus filtering/processing. A very brief (e.g., 100 μs) duration auditory click stimulus 500 milliseconds prior to the presentation of a subsequent click reduces the P50 amplitude (and associated gamma frequency oscillations) in response to the second click in the two-click pair. The P50 to the second click is larger in patients with lateral prefrontal cortical lesions but not with other cortical lesions, indicating that this suppression probably reflects inhibition of auditory cortex by frontal cortex (Millar *et al.*, 2011). Kenemans and Kähkäonen (2011) summarize evidence indicating that normal levels of P50 suppression require delicate prefrontal interactions of cholinergic, serotonergic, noradrenergic, and GABAergic transmission. Consistent with their inability to filter stimuli, schizophrenics have attenuated P50 suppression that can be acutely normalized by nicotine administration (Adler *et al.*, 1992; Millar *et al.*, 2011). The N1 component of the auditory ERP that occurs about 100 milliseconds after stimulus onset is also sensitive to stimulus repetition and has many characteristics in common with the P50 (Kenemans and Kähkäonen, 2011). EROs in the gamma range are major constituents of the P50 and may be particularly sensitive to deficits in sensory gating (Hall *et al.*, 2011) and to drug-related modulation of stimulus filtering.

4.2.2 Stimulus filtering by inhibition of response to excessively intense stimulation – the loudness-dependent auditory ERP (LDAERP) paradigm. LDAERPs provide a measure of stimulus filtering of high-intensity stimuli that is calculated by the slope of the increase in N1-P2 amplitude peak differences across progressively higher levels of auditory stimulation. Evidence supports the view that LDAERP slope reflects serotonergic activity such that low levels of activity are associated with greater slopes, while greater activity is associated with smaller increases in slope (reviewed by Kenemans and Kähkäonen, 2011; Nathan *et al.*, 2006). However, some acute drug administration studies have failed to support this relationship with serotonin and preliminary evidence suggests that other neurotransmitters may also modulate LDAERP slope. LDAERP slope (also referred to as augmenting versus reducing) has been related to individual differences in sensation seeking and related trait measures (e.g., novelty seeking) that are associated with vulnerability to drug use and dependence (Beauducel, Debener, Brocke, and Kayser, 2000; Zuckerman, 2005).

4.2.3 *Automatic deviance detection – mismatch negativity (MMN) and N400 paradigms.*

Automatic processing both extracts sensory information and promotes attention to changes in the stimulus environment (reviewed by Näätänen, 1992). The MMN paradigm is widely used to index automatic attention and is maximal at fronto-central sites, where it begins at about 100 milliseconds and lasts until about 250 milliseconds after the onset of an infrequent deviant stimulus embedded in a series of standard stimuli. The deviant stimulus can differ from the standards in one or more perceptual features (e.g., pitch, intensity, duration, location, or partial omission of a compound stimulus) (Näätänen, 1992). The MMN paradigm is appropriate for investigations of drug-related changes on distraction from a controlled attention task (e.g., maintaining vigilance or performing another task). An excellent review of drug-related MMN studies is provided by Kenemans and Kähkäonen (2011), who conclude that excitatory (glutamatergic) and inhibitory neurotransmitters (GABA) are involved in the generation of MMN and that alcohol generally reduces MMN. Unlike many ERPs, MMN is elicited regardless of whether the person is consciously paying attention to the stimuli and regardless of stimulus significance.

The N400 occurs in response to attended stimuli that deviate from the expected meaning, given the context. For example, the word "rock" would elicit an N400 in the context of the sentence "My favorite food is well-cooked rock." The N400 occurs from 250 to 500 milliseconds, and is typically maximal over centro-parietal sites. The N400 paradigm has potential as an index of a variety of drug-related processes including drug-cue salience and as a means of assessing individual differences in stimulus evaluation and drug-related effects. For example, in the sentence "I never have an urge to use marijuana," the word "marijuana" would be expected to elicit an N400 in marijuana users, but not in nonusers.

4.2.4 *Controlled/selective attention and distraction.*

Different aspects of selective attention can be assessed with different experimental paradigms. A number of paradigms commonly used in substance abuse research are reviewed below.

4.2.4.1 ATTENTION-RELATED EEG AND PROCESSING NEGATIVITY – NEGATIVE DIFFERENCE WAVE (ND).

Selective attention is frequently assessed by comparing ERPs to attended (relevant) stimuli with ERPs to irrelevant stimuli during an interval from about 100 to about 300 milliseconds after stimulus onset. The ERPs are more negative for attended than for ignored stimuli. Thus, the difference between these ERPs is referred to as a selection potential (S-ERP) and the difference or selection potentials are referred to as "processing negativity" or the negative difference (Nd) wave (Näätänen, 1982). Nd can be used as a general index of the orienting of attention to or distraction by a stimulus. Generally, Nd is enhanced by modest doses of psychomotor stimulants when the subject's goal is to attend to a stimulus (Iwanami *et al.*, 1993).

4.2.4.2 CONTINGENT NEGATIVE VARIATION AND STIMULUS-PRECEDING NEGATIVITY. Drugs, personality traits, distraction, and arousal state influence contingent negative variation (CNV) and stimulus-preceding negativity (SPN). These slow, negative-going brain voltage potentials index attentional allocation in anticipation of an emotional/motivationally significant stimulus (SPN; Parker and Gilbert, 2008) or in anticipation of an imperative stimulus instructing the subject to press a button or otherwise respond (CNV; Tecce, 1972; Tecce and Cattanach, 1993). In their review, Tecce and Cattanach (1993) concluded that the CNV reflects both attention and arousal, and that its amplitude is influenced by drugs, sleep deprivation, anxiety, and fear of failure. Gilbert *et al.* (2007) found that, relative to placebo, the nicotine patch increased the CNV between the second and third digits in 3-digit target sequences. SPN paradigms are presented in section 4.2.6 below in the discussion of drug cue reactivity.

4.2.5 Sustained attention and working memory EEG paradigms. Brain activity associated with vigilance, working memory (WM), and target detections during sustained attention tasks can be assessed with a number of tasks, three of which we describe below. The first of these tasks, the Mackworth Clock task, is a relatively pure index of vigilance/sustained attention that requires a button-press response to very brief pauses of a clock "second hand" that occurs on average once every 45–75 seconds. The second task, the N-back task, assesses executive attention working memory (Krieger *et al.*, 2005; Rose, Simonotto, and Ebmeier, 2006). Subjects press a button when the current stimulus (typically a number or letter) is the same as the one presented *n* trials earlier; where *n* is usually 1, 2, or 3. The n-back task requires information storage, updating, and manipulation, all of which are elements of working memory. Drug-related n-back tasks have used drug-related pictures or words to assess interference associated with drug-related stimuli in drug-dependent individuals (Evans, Craig, Oliver, and Drobes, 2011). The third task, the Rapid Visual Information Processing (RVIP) test, presents individual digits one at a time at a rate of about 100/minute and a key press is required whenever three odd or three even digits appear in sequence. The RVIP requires memory for the temporal structure of digits in which a target is likely to occur. Thus, the RVIP can assess short-term anticipation, something that the n-back and most other working memory and vigilance tasks cannot do.

S-EEG and ERO activity associated with the above three tasks has been systematically analyzed in a large number of studies, some of which have included drug manipulations. During n-back-like WM tasks, theta power increases at frontal-midline scalp and anterior cingulate locations while parietal alpha1 activity decreases (Gevins, Smith, McEvoy, and Yu, 1997; Klimesch, 1999). Given that both hypo- and hyper-frontal activity are associated with WM deficits and sustained attention, a clearer understanding of a drug's effects on WM and sustained attention will probably be found in investigations using a range of doses and a range of WM loads and task durations. Most well-designed studies have found stimulant drugs (e.g., nicotine, caffeine, amphetamine) to enhance RVIP Macworth Clock target detection and P3b amplitude in response to targets (Gilbert *et al.*, 2007; Pritchard, Sokhadze, and Houlihan, 2004), as well as to increase CNV amplitude between the second and third digits in

RVIP 3-digit target sequences (Gilbert *et al.*, 2007). S-EEG and associated power spectra can be assessed during the long inter-target intervals; and EROs and ERPs can be assessed in response to target digits. The S-EEG immediately prior to missed targets can be compared to the EEG prior to detections. EROs in response to targets can also be assessed in terms of hits and misses. As would be expected, a P3b and associated delta and theta synchronizations, along with alpha desynchronization, occur in response to the infrequent target stimuli.

4.2.6   Indices of stimulus salience (attentional bias) and cue reactivity.   Well-validated EEG indices of stimulus salience and cue reactivity include the P3 and late positive component (LPC), processing negativity (PN), and desynchronization of alpha and other power indices. Recently, LORETA analyses have characterized distributed current sources for cue and emotional stimulus reactivity in brain structures that correspond to those identified by fMRI studies (Gilbert *et al.*, 2009a; Meltzer, Negishi, Mayes, and Constable, 2007).

4.2.6.1   P3a and P3b as indices of novelty detection and memory updating. The 3-stimulus oddball is a common paradigm used to elicit both the P3a and P3b, using repeated random presentations of three types of stimulus (non-attended frequent stimuli, non-attended oddball, and attended target oddball). Little and Franken (2010) assessed implicit versus explicit selective attention to smoking cues in smokers using the smoking pictures as either rare targets or rare non-attended oddball stimuli in a 3-stimulus oddball paradigm. The P3a, or novelty P3, has a peak latency from 250 to 280 milliseconds after stimulus onset and reflects the involuntary orienting of attention to environmental changes that are not the conscious focus of attention (e.g. when told to ignore infrequent stimulus). The P3b occurs around 300–400 milliseconds with focused attention toward an infrequent stimulus. Scalp P3a peak amplitude occurs at frontal midline sites, whereas the P3b peak occurs over parietal midline sites (Polich, 2003). In their review of the literature, Polich and Criado (2006) note that substantial evidence supports the view that P3a and P3b reflect neural inhibitory processes that enhance attentional focus and thereby facilitate memory storage. Evidence provided by Polich *et al.* supports the view that P3a results from an early attention-related process related to changes detected in working memory, and that P3b results from change detection signals in temporal and parietal structures. fMRI studies have supported his position by showing that P3 activation is associated with activation of bilateral foci in the middle part of the superior temporal gyrus known to be associated with novelty detection (Opitz, Mecklinger, Friederici, and von Cramon, 1999). While the P3a provides an important tool for drug effects on novel stimuli, it is important to note that this ERP habituates quickly with repeated presentation of rare stimuli. Thus, caution should be exercised when measuring drug-related effects on P3 components across multiple assessments.

P3a amplitude may be attenuated with acute nicotine administration, suggesting attentional filtering mechanisms (Knott *et al.*, 2011). P3b amplitude (reflecting allocation of attentional resources to the processing of specific task-relevant stimuli) is generally increased and latency (reflecting speed of evaluation of task-relevant stimuli) is decreased with nicotine administration in smokers (Houlihan, Pritchard, and

Robinson, 1996; Knott, Kerr, Hooper, and Lusk-Mikkelsen, 1995). Many studies have found enhancement of P3 to drug-related stimuli (van de Laar, Licht, Franken, and Hendriks, 2004; Little and Franken, 2010; Nickerson *et al.*, 2011; Versace *et al.*, 2010).

4.2.6.2 DRUG-CUE AND EMOTIONAL DISTRACTOR-INDUCED P3 SUPPRESSION. Evidence and theory suggest, generally, that many abused drugs alter selective attentional bias to affective stimuli and drug-related cues, with possible impacts on affect regulation, craving, and patterns of reinforcement associated with smoking behavior and relapse in abstaining smokers. Several models of the role of drugs on attentional bias agree that dependence-promoting drugs enhance attention toward positive affect stimuli but differ regarding nicotine's expected attentional effects with negative-affect and smoking-related cues (e.g., Baker *et al.*, 2004; Gilbert, 1995; Robinson and Berridge, 1993; 2000). For example, the Incentive Sensitization model (Robinson and Berridge, 1993; 2000) poses that drugs that increase mesotelencephalic dopamine (most abused drugs) promote attentional bias to drug-related and reward-related cues and possibly to aversive stimuli as well. In contrast, the Situation by Trait Adaptive Response (STAR) model (Gilbert, 1997) predicts that such drugs bias attention away from negative affective stimuli and drug-related cues when highly salient positive stimuli are also present. Consistent with this hypothesis, emotional and smoking-related pictures have been found to reduce the amplitude of parietal P3 responses to target stimuli occurring 600 milliseconds after a distractor picture during a visual rapid information processing task and this P3 suppression was greater for emotionally negative pictures in nicotine-deprived as opposed to a non-deprived state (Gilbert *et al.*, 2007). Similarly, Engelmann, Gewirtz and Cuthbert (2011) found that P3 suppression was larger in abstinent smokers than in non-smokers and that abstinence-induced increases in cigarette craving were associated with P3 suppression during tobacco-related pictures.

4.2.6.3 LATE POSITIVE COMPONENT (LPC) AND DELTA-BAND EROs AS INDEX OF STIMULUS SALIENCE AND DRUG-CUE REACTIVITY. The LPC occurs beginning around 600 milliseconds post-stimulus onset and continues for several hundred milliseconds or more during tasks involving working memory and stimulus encoding (Azizian and Polich, 2007). Visual cues depicting motivationally relevant situations engage appetitive and defensive systems and elicit attentional allocation and enhancement of reward/threat processing and are associated with large and long-duration LPCs (Lang, Bradley, and Cuthbert, 1997). The LPC and associated delta-band EROs have been identified as large and reliable indexes of motivational–emotional significance of visual stimuli (Cuthbert *et al.*, 2000; Klados, Papadelis, Lythari, and Bamidis, 2008). LPC demonstrates elevated positivity to high-arousing, attention-grabbing stimuli regardless of affective valence (Cuthbert *et al.*, 2000). A number of studies have demonstrated enhanced incentive salience to drug-related cues in dependent populations, indicating that the LPC may be a particularly useful measure of motivational engagement/arousal in drug users (e.g., Little and Franken, 2010; Versace *et al.*, 2010). fMRI–ERP correlation analyses have identified a distributed network of brain regions in the lateral occipital, inferotemporal, and parietal visual area associated with the LPC (Sabatinelli, Lang, Keil, and Bradley, 2007).

4.2.6.4 EROs TO EMOTIONAL STIMULI AND DRUG CUES. ERO analyses can be performed on data collected using paradigms for classical ERP studies. Because the techniques for the assessment of EROs emerged only during the 1990s, ERO studies of responses to emotional stimuli and drug-related cues are less frequently used than ERP indices such as the LPC. However, there is reason to believe that they may be equally or more predictive of specific brain activity than ERPs because of the ability of ERD to detect both phase- and non-phase-locked, event-related brain responses (Klados *et al.*, 2009). A substantial portion of the variance in ERPs reflects EROs in the delta and theta frequencies (Basar-Eroglu, Basar, Demiralp, and Schurmann, 1992). Emotionally valent stimuli evoke hippocampal theta activity, suggesting this variant of theta is related to discrimination of emotional stimuli (Nishitani, 2003). Delta oscillations may be used as indexes of craving and motivational approach mechanisms in the ventral tegmentum and nucleus accumbens (Panksepp, 1998; Robinson and Berridge, 1993). Alpha oscillations have been linked with motor inhibition and are often negatively correlated with localized brain activity in frontal and parietal cortices (Laufs *et al.*, 2003; Pfurtscheller and Lopes da Silva, 1999). Time frequency and wavelet analyses allow precise temporal characterization of ERD/ERS, which may provide additional information on the neural response to emotionally salient and drug-related cures.

4.2.6.5 STIMULUS-PRECEDING NEGATIVITY (SPN). A promising, but rarely used approach is that of the SPN paradigm in which a brief cue (S_1) is followed from 1,000 to 10,000 milliseconds later by a motivationally or emotionally salient stimulus (S_2). S_1 is typically either symbolic (e.g., a letter or ideogram) or a very brief presentation of the longer-presented S_2 that in either case is the salient stimulus. During the S_1–S_2 interval, frontal scalp sites exhibit an increasingly more negative slow drift that terminates shortly after the onset of S_2. Modeling after a study by Costell, Lunde, Kopell, and Wittner (1972) that used erotic stimuli, Parker and Gilbert (2008) used smoking-related and IAPS affective and neutral pictures in an SPN paradigm where S_1 was presented on a computer monitor for 500 milliseconds, followed 3,500 milliseconds later by a 2,000 milliseconds re-presentation of the same picture. Smokers exhibited significantly greater mean SPN amplitudes in anticipation of smoking-related pictures relative to neutral pictures. Among non-smokers, the SPN was significantly smaller in anticipation of smoking pictures compared with neutral pictures. These findings are consistent with the incentive sensitization theory of addiction and other conditioning and cue-reactivity models.

4.2.6.6 FRONTAL EEG ALPHA POWER ASYMMETRY AND APPROACH MOTIVATION RESPONSE TO DRUG CUES. Zinser, Fiore, Davidson, and Baker (1999) exposed overnight abstinent and non-abstinent smokers to an *in vivo* smoking cue and found that, as hypothesized by Davidson's model of frontal EEG asymmetry and approach behavior (Davidson, 1995), greater left than right frontal EEG hemispheric activation (greater approach motivation) was observed in those smokers who were both deprived of smoking and exposed to the smoking cue. However, few studies have assessed the effects of SR stimuli exposure on EEG frequency. This effect may be further enhanced by deprivation in substance-dependent users, indicating an enhanced motivational approach reaction to drug cues (Zinser, Fiore, Davidson, and Baker, 1999).

4.2.6.7 SUMMARY OF EEG CUE REACTIVITY INDICES. A broad range of EEG techniques have been used to investigate craving and drug cue-reactivity in substance abusers. Methodologically this research has included adequate controls (at both the group and stimulus level), employed both abstinence and cue-elicited approaches, utilized a variety of cue types, and examined self-report correlates of brain responses. While additional research is needed, the results of these studies preliminarily suggest that drug-related cues are salient and approach motivating stimuli for drug users, and that cue-elicited craving correlates with brain responses in regions associated with emotion and reward (e.g., insula, orbitofrontal cortex, anterior cingulate cortex). Future research in this area should attempt to replicate findings using the same cue exposure methods across imaging techniques. Further, future studies should also evaluate the effects of longer-term abstinence on responses to drug cues by following abstaining drug users longitudinally. There is a need for studies that characterize functional EEG connectivity among brain regions associated with cue-reactivity, withdrawal symptoms, craving, relapse, and inhibitory control (e.g., the insula, anterior and posterior cingulate, and prefrontal cortices – see Garavan, 2010).

4.3   Drug abstinence effects and aftereffects

Several studies suggest that spontaneous EEG spectral power profile changes may be substantially less prone to bias and testing effects than self-report measures if a full-length practice session is used to adapt subjects to the EEG and related assessment procedures. An important early study of the effects of tobacco abstinence on EEG in nicotine-dependent individuals used hospitalized individuals to assure abstinence compliance (Pickworth, Herning, and Henningfield, 1989). EEG was assessed during a smoking baseline, then across 10 days of abstinence, and then after having resumed smoking. EEG delta and theta power increased across the 10 days of abstinence and then fell to baseline levels after resuming smoking. To provide an example of a well-controlled, randomized study of how drug-abstinence effects can be assessed without hospitalization with EEG and to note the benefits of such studies, we now summarize studies that assessed the effects of smoking abstinence on EEG, mood, and withdrawal symptoms (Gilbert *et al.*, 1998; 1999; 2004a; Gilbert *et al.*, 2009b). These studies used full-length EEG task-orientation and practice sessions (including EEG recordings with artifact minimization training) held prior to baseline sessions. The subjects participated in as many as four pre-quit baseline EEG sessions prior to subject randomization to an immediate-quit group or to a delayed-quit control group. After the baseline sessions, the quit group subjects quit smoking for a period of 31 or 45 days, depending on the study. The control group continued to smoke during the period that the immediate-quit group maintained abstinence and then quit immediately after the 31 or 45 abstinence period for the immediate quit group. Thus, the delayed- and immediate-quit groups performed the same tasks and same number and types of sessions during the abstinence periods, providing excellent controls given the randomized nature of the study. These randomized-quit-time (RQT) studies provided large financial incentives for biochemically verified abstinence and each study achieved 80% + abstinence and study completion. Two important findings of these RQT studies were: (1) the EEG measures (EEG slowing as indexed by quit-group increases in delta, theta, and alpha$_1$ power and lowered alpha centroid frequency) did not tend to return to delayed-quit group or baseline levels across time; and (2) unlike the stable EEG indices, self-reported mood and withdrawal symptom scores exhibited a dramatic testing effect – decreased indices of negative affect and withdrawal-related symptoms across time during the multiple pre-quit baseline period. This lack of stability of self-reported negative affect has been demonstrated in other populations (e.g., Sharpe and Gilbert, 1998).

Consistent with the above-described smoking abstinence findings showing abstinent smokers failing to return to baseline levels after 31 to 45 days, other important directions for withdrawal characterization studies are suggested by the work of Fingelkurts *et al.* (2007), who found that opioid withdrawal resulted in increased local and remote functional connectivity (network activations) at EEG alpha and beta frequencies. There is a need for studies to characterize associations functional EEG connectivities among brain regions associated with withdrawal symptoms, craving, and relapse (e.g., the insula, anterior and posterior cingulate, and prefrontal cortices – see Garavan, 2010).

4.4 Assessment of distal determinants of drug use

4.4.1 Genetics, EEG, and drug use disposition. Consistent with the above-described smoking abstinence findings showing abstinent smokers failing to return to baseline levels after 31 to 45 days, Porjesz and Begleiter (1996; 1998) summarize the large Collaborative Study on the Genetics of Alcoholism (COGA) data demonstrating that P3 amplitude remains low in alcoholics who have been abstinent for as long as 10 years and that the low P3 amplitude in alcoholic first-degree relatives is related to genetic rather than personal drinking history. COGA generated definitive evidence demonstrating the high heritability of brain oscillations (van Beijsterveld, Molenaar, de Geus, and Boomsma, 1996), which averaged 76% for delta (1.5–3.5 Hz), 89% for theta (4–7.5 Hz), 89% for alpha (8–12.5 Hz), and 86% for beta (13–25 Hz). Increased resting (eyes-closed) beta power is observed in abstinent alcoholics and high-risk children (Rangaswamy *et al.*, 2002; 2004). Other COGA evidence indicates that, compared to those with other genotypes, individuals with the rarer genotype of the GABRA2 gene have more beta-2 power and CNS disinhibition, which increases the risk for alcoholism, other forms of substance abuse, and impulsive, risky, and antisocial behavior (Porjesz, and Rangaswamy, 2007). Anokin, Golosheykin, and Heath (2008) provided additional evidence of the heritability of EEG-assessed frontal brain function related to action monitoring. Finally, Gilbert *et al.* (2004a) observed greater EEG deactivation during smoking abstinence in individuals with a dopamine D2 receptor A1 allele.

4.4.2   Disinhibition disorders, impulsivity, inhibitory control, and reward and punishment sensitivities.   A rapidly developing literature, including the above-noted COGA studies, characterizes EEG with state and trait disinhibition, impulsivity, and risky behavior. Error-related negativity (ERN) is a response-locked ERP occurring between 50 and 100 milliseconds after the commission of a response that the subject recognizes to be in error. The ERN indexes action outcomes that are associated with partial phase-locking of Fm theta-band activity. Error feedback elicits feedback-related negativity (FRN). After unfavorable feedback or monetary losses, FRN typically peaks at 250 to 300 milliseconds after feedback onset. Source localization studies show that ERN and FRN are generated in the anterior cingulate cortex (Holroyd, Nieuwenhuis, Yeung, and Cohen, 2003). Individuals high in negative affect-related traits exhibit larger ERN and FRN in response to errors than do those low in these traits (Hajcak, McDonald, and Simons, 2004; Luu, Collins, and Tucker, 2000). Wiswedea, Müntea, Goschked, and Rüsselera (2009) demonstrated that negatively valenced pictures immediately prior to performance errors were associated with larger ERN compared to trials preceded by neutral and pleasant pictures. These findings are consistent with our general recommendation that both situational and trait factors should be assessed and manipulated in drug-related studies of EEG. Given evidence (reviewed by Garavan, 2010) that the insula is associated with subjective awareness of felt body responses associated with negative feedback and studies suggesting that decreased insular cortical volume is associated with chronic drug abuse, drug researchers are encouraged to use tomographic approaches such as LORETA to characterize insular activity.

4.4.3   Neuroticism/negative affectivity and extraversion/positive affectivity.   Frontal EEG alpha power asymmetries have been associated with depressive affect, drug withdrawal, and drug response. Greater left than right alpha power has been associated with depressive affect and a greater disposition toward avoidance than approach behavior (Coan and Allen, 2003a; 2003b; Davidson, 1995). The spatial processing deficits of those high in depressive traits have been shown to be associated with decreased posterior RH activity (Henriques and Davidson, 1997; Rabe, Debener, Brocke, and Beauducel, 2005). Several studies have found that, compared to individuals low in such characteristics, individuals higher in negative affectivity and depressive traits respond to acute doses of nicotine and to nicotine abstinence as though nicotine reduces depression-related frontal alpha EEG asymmetry (Gilbert *et al.*, 1999; 2004a).

   Most psychoactive drugs alter heart rate. However, most studies in this area have not used ICA or other means to eliminate the ECG artifacts that are asymmetric to the left-lateralized location of the heart. There is greater left posterior and greater right anterior ECG artifact power (including in the alpha band) that might explain some of the observed differences between approach/avoidance states/traits and affectivity. High levels of approach level and task engagement are associated with higher heart rates and more ECG artifacts per unit time. Thus, drug-related and affective state and trait-related differences in heart rate can induce what appear to be EEG hemispheric asymmetries in EEG power spectra if these artifacts are not eliminated from the EEG signal. For this and many other reasons, it is important that investigators eliminate ECG artifacts from their EEG data.

4.4.4 Sex and racial influences.   Despite evidence that there may be important differences between males and females for a number of drug effects (Perkins *et al.*, 2001; Wetter *et al.*, 1999), few EEG or other imaging studies have been designed or powered to address this issue.

4.4.5 Developmental factors.   Any work with EEG or other brain imaging needs to consider developmental factors that influence EEG norms and brain functioning. It is well established that there are very large differences in both EEG spectral patterns and ERPs as a function of age (Courchesne, 1990; John *et al.*, 1980; Polich, 1997). However, very little is known about age-related differences in drug responses or the developmental course of EEG indices of drug abuse vulnerability.

5   Limitations, Challenges, and Future Directions for EEG Studies of Drug Abuse

5.1   Limitations of EEG studies

As currently conceived and assessed, the primary limitation of EEG is its modest ability to precisely determine the three-dimensional localization of EEG source generators (the inverse problem). The resolution of HD EEG tomography with current state-of-the-art software and hardware is in the range of 3–8 mm (Cohen *et al.*, 1990; Im *et al.*, 2007), whereas BOLD fMRI may provide sub-millimeter resolution for blood-flow changes that indirectly reflect neural activity (van der Zwaag *et al.*, 2009). However, EEG's spatial tomographic limitation is being addressed by several different means. First, using MRI spatial constraints may increase relative accuracy of localization (Liu, Ding, and He, 2006). Second, simultaneous EEG and fMRI is now becoming more common and may provide additional insight into the neural generators of EEG (Ullsperger and Debener, 2010). Simultaneous MEG/EEG acquisition may also lead to greater spatial resolution, especially when more accurate head models are included (Liu, Ding, and He, 2006). As the neural generators of EEG are characterized, subsequent EEG studies can assess the precise temporal processing associated with these spatial activations and provide a great deal of insight into the characterization of neural processing across both domains.

5.2   Future directions and opportunities of combined imaging techniques

Combining functional imaging techniques to investigate a single phenomenon can make up for the resolution limitations of a single technique while simultaneously providing convergent validity. Further, new techniques allowing for the simultaneous collection of EEG/ERPs during fMRI scans have been developed (though acquisition of both at different times but under the same conditions would still provide opportunities to complement the high spatial resolution of fMRI with the high temporal resolution of ERP). Research on cue-reactivity, cognitive performance, and emotional information processing would all potentially benefit from multimodal acquisition schemes.

6 Summary

EEG represents an important and still advancing set of methods for answering questions related to substance use and addiction. Characterization of the large individual differences in states and traits associated with drug abuse vulnerability will require continued expansion of studies along the lines of COGA and of those using random assignment to treatments and procedures designed to carefully characterize such effects and the time trajectories of drug and drug abstinence effects. Future EEG studies will greatly benefit from using the state-of-the-art EEG methods outlined in this chapter and by investigating areas including sex differences, comorbid psychiatric and substance abuse disorders, treatment effects, the genetic basis of drug dependence, the effects of drugs in non-users, and effects of differing durations of abstinence. Functional connectivity and neural network modeling are areas of rapid development in EEG neuroscience, but few studies have pursued this critically important approach in drug-dependence research. Work by Frank, Pizzagalli and colleagues (Frank and Fossella, 2011; Pizzagalli, Sherwood, Henriques, Davidson, 2005; Santesso *et al.*, 2009) on the effects of pharmacological manipulations (e.g., dopamine agonists and antagonists) on reinforcement learning and associated EEG tomography and topography in humans provides innovative and scientifically exciting approaches that characterize the spirit of much of the present chapter, including the importance of modeling interactions of situational factors (e.g., negative versus positive reinforcement) with theoretically related individual difference traits.

References

Adler L, Hoffer L, Griffith J, Waldo M, and Freedman R (1992) Normalization by nicotine of deficient auditory sensory gating in the relatives of schizophrenics. *Biological Psychiatry* 32: 607–616.

Alonso JF, Mananas MA, Rosero S, Hoyer D, Riba J, and Barbanoj MJ (2010) Drug effect on EEG connectivity assessed by linear and nonlinear couplings. *Human Brain Mapping* 31: 487–497.

Alper KR (1999) The EEG and cocaine sensitization: A hypothesis. *Journal of Neuropsychiatry and Clinical Neuroscience* 11: 209–221.

Andersen P and Andersson SA (1968) *Physiological Basis of the Alpha Rhythm*. New York: Century-Crofts.

Anokin AP, Golosheykin S, and Heath AC (2008) Heritability of frontal brain function related to action monitoring. *Psychophysiology* 45: 524–534.

Atcherson SR, Gould HJ, Pousson MA, and Prout TM (2007) Variability of electrode positions using electrode caps. *Brain Topography* 20: 105–111.

Azizian A and Polich J (2007) Evidence for attentional gradient in the serial position memory curve from ERPs. *Journal of Cognitive Neuroscience* 19: 2071–2081.

Baker SN (2007) Oscillatory interactions between sensorimotor cortex and the periphery. *Current Opinion in Neurobiology* 17: 649–655.

Baker TB, Piper ME, McCarthy DE, Majeskie MR, and Fiore MC (2004). Addiction motivation reformulated: An affective processing model of negative reinforcement. *Psychological Review* 111: 33–51.

Baillet S, Mosher JC, and Leahy RM (2001) Electromagnetic brain mapping. *IEEE Signal Processing Magazine* 18: 14–30.

Basar-Eroglu C, Basar E, Demiralp T, and Schurmann M (1992) P300-response: Possible psychophysiological correlates in delta and theta frequency channels: A review. *International Journal of Psychophysiology* 13: 161–179.

Bauer LO (2001a) Electroencephalographic studies of substance use and abuse. In MJ Kaufman (ed.), *Brain Imaging and Substance Abuse: Research, Clinical and Forensic Applications* (pp. 77–112). Totowa, NJ: Humana Press.

Bauer LO (2001b) CNS recovery from cocaine, cocaine and alcohol, or opioid dependence: A P300 study. *Clinical Neurophysiology* 112: 1508–1515.

Beauducel A, Debener S, Brocke B and Kayser, J (2000) On the reliability of augmenting/reducing. *International Journal of Psychophysiology* 14: 226–240.

Böcker KBE, Hunault CC, Gerritsen J, Kruidenier M, Mensinga TT, and Kenemans JL (2009) Cannabinoid modulations of resting state EEG theta power and working memory are correlated in humans. *Journal of Cognitive Neuroscience* 22: 1906–1916.

Buzsáki G (2002) Theta oscillations in the hippocampus. *Neuron* 33: 325–340.

Chorlian DB, Tang Y, Rangaswamy M, O'Connor S, Rohrbaugh J, Taylor R, and Porjesz B (2007) Heritability of EEG coherence in a large sib-pair population. *Biological Psychology* 75: 260–266.

Coan JA and Allen JJ (2003a) The state and trait nature of frontal EEG asymmetry in emotion. In K Hugdahl and RJ Davidson (eds.), *The Asymmetrical Brain* (pp. 565–615). Cambridge, MA: MIT Press.

Coan JA and Allen JJ (2003b) Frontal EEG asymmetry and the behavioral activation and inhibition systems. *Psychophysiology.* 40: 106–114.

Cohen D, Cuffin BN, Yunokuchi K, Maniewski R, Purcell C, Cosgrove GR, Ives J, and Kennedy J (1990) MEG versus EEG localization test using implanted sources in the human brain. *Annals of Neurology* 28: 811–817.

Cooley JM and Tukey JW (1965) An algorithm for the machine calculation of complex Fourier series. *Mathematics of Computation* 19: 297–301.

Corrigan NM, Richards T, Webb SJ, Murias M, Merkle K, Kleinhans NM, Johnson LC, Poliakov A, Aylward E, and Dawson G (2009) An investigation of the relationship between fMRI and ERP source localized measurements of brain activity during face processing. *Brain Topography* 22: 83–96.

Costell RM, Lunde DT, Kopell BS, and Wittner WK (1972) Contingent negative variation as an indicator of sexual object preference. *Science* 177: 718–720.

Courchesne E (1990) Chronology of postnatal human development: Event related potential, positron emission tomography, myelinogenesis, and synaptogenesis studies. In JW Rohrbaugh (ed.), *Event Related Potentials of the Brain* (pp. 210–241). New York: Oxford Press.

Crick F and Koch C (1990) Towards a neurobiological theory of consciousness. Seminars in the *Neurosciences* 2: 263–275.

Croft R, Chandler J, Barry R, Cooper N, and Clarke A (2005) EOG correction: A comparison of four methods. *Psychophysiology* 42: 16–24.

Csicsvari J, Jamieson B, Wise KD, and Buzsaki G (2003) Mechanisms of gamma oscillations in the hippocampus of the behaving rat. *Neuron* 37: 311–322.

Cuthbert BN, Schupp HT, Bradley MM, Birbaumer N, and Lang PJ (2000) Brain potentials in affective picture processing: Covariation with autonomic arousal and affective report. *Biological Psychology* 52: 95–111.

Dang-Vu TT, Schabus M, Desseilles M, Albouy G, Boly M, *et al.* (2008) Spontaneous neural activity during human slow wave sleep. *Proceedings of the National Academy of Science, USA* 105: 15160–15165.

Davidson JR, Jackson DC, and Larson CL (2000) Human electroencephalography. In JT Cacioppo, LG Tassinary and GG Bernston (eds), *Handbook of Psychophysiology* (2nd edn, pp. 27–52). Cambridge: Cambridge University Press.

Davidson RJ (1995) Cerebral asymmetry, emotion, and affective style. In RJ Davidson and K Hugdahl (eds), *Brain Asymmetry* (pp. 361–387). Cambridge, MA: MIT Press.

De Clercq W, Vergult A, Vanrumste B, Van Paesschen W, and Van Huffel S (2006) Canonical correlation analysis applied to remove muscle artifacts from the encephalogram. *IEEE Transactions on Biomedical Engineering* 53: 2583–2587.

Delorme A and Makeig S (2004) EEGLAB: An open source toolbox for analysis of single-trial EEG dynamics including independent component analysis. *Journal of Neuroscience Methods* 134: 9–21.

Delorme A, Palmer J, Oostenveld R, Onton J, and Makeig S (2007) Comparing results of algorithms implementing blind source separation of EEG data. Unpublished manuscript available at http://sccn.ucsd.edu/mediawiki/images/2/22/Delorme_unpub.pdf.

Delorme A, Sejnowski T, and Makeig S (2007) Enhanced detection of artifacts in EEG data using higher-order statistics and independent component analysis. *NeuroImage* 34: 1443–1449.

Devrim M, Demiralp T, Ademoglu A, and Kurt A (1999) A model for P300 generation based on responses to near-threshold visual stimuli. *Cognitive Brain Research* 8: 37–43.

Devuyst S, Dutoit T, Stenuit P, Kerkhofs M, and Stanus E (2008) Cancelling ECG artifacts in EEG using a modified independent component analysis approach. *EURASIP Journal on Advances in Signal Processing* 45: 1–13.

Dimpfel W (2008) Pharmacological modulation of dopaminergic brain activity and its reflection in spectral frequencies of the rat electropharmacogram. *Neuropsychobiology* 58: 178–186.

Engelmann JM, Gewirtz, JC and Cuthbert BN (2011) Emotional reactivity to emotional and smoking cues during smoking abstinence: Potentiated startle and P300 suppression. *Psychophysiology* 48: 1656–1668.

Evans DE, Craig C, Oliver JA, and Drobes DJ (2011) The Smoking N-Back: A measure of biased cue processing at varying levels of cognitive load. *Nicotine and Tobacco Research* 13: 88–93.

Eysenck HJ (1983) Psychopharmacology and personality. In W Janke (ed.), *Response Variability to Psychotropic Drugs* (pp. 127–154). New York: Pergamon Press.

Eysenck HJ (1997) Addiction, personality, and motivation. *Human Psychopharmacology: Clinical and Experimental* 12: S79–S87.

Fender DH (1987) Source localization of brain electrical activity. In AS Gevins and A Remond (eds), *Methods of Analysis of Brain Electrical and Magnetic Signals* (pp. 355–403). Amsterdam: Elsevier.

Ferree TC (2000) Spline interpolation of the scalp EEG. *Technical report*, Electrical Geodesics, Inc., Eugene, Oregon.

Fingelkurts AAA, Fingelkurts AAA, Kivisaari R, Autti T, Borisov S, Puuskari V, Jokela O, and Kähkönen S (2007) Opioid withdrawal results in an increased local and remote functional connectivity at EEG alpha and beta frequency bands. *Neuroscience Research* 58: 40–49.

Frank MJ and Fossella JA (2011) Neurogenetics and pharmacology of learning, motivation and cognition. *Neuropsychopharmacology Reviews* 36: 133–152.

Fries P, Nikolic D, and Singer W (2007) The gamma cycle. *TINS* 30 (7): 309–316.

Galderisi S and Sannita WG (2006). Pharmaco-EEG: A history of progress and a missed opportunity. *Clinical EEG and Neuroscience* 37: 61–65.

Garavan H (2010) Insula and drug cravings. *Brain Structure and Function* 214: 593–601.

Geselowitz DB (1998) The zero of potential. *IEEE Engineering in Medicine and Biology* 17: 128–132.

Gevins A, Smith ME, McEvoy L, and Yu D (1997) High-resolution EEG mapping of cortical activation related to working memory: Effects of task difficulty, type of processing, and practice. *Cerebral Cortex* 7: 374–385.

Ghandeharion H and Erfanian A (2010) A fully automatic ocular artifact suppression from EEG data using higher order statistics: Improved performance by wavelet analysis. *Medical Engineering and Physics* 32: 720–729.

Gilbert DG (1979) Paradoxical tranquilizing and emotion-reducing effects of nicotine. *Psychological Bulletin* 86: 643–661.

Gilbert DG (1995) *Smoking: Individual Differences, Psychopathology, and Emotion.* Washington, DC: Taylor and Francis.

Gilbert DG (1997) The situation x trait adaptive response (STAR) model of substance use and craving. *Human Psychopharmacology: Clinical and Experimental* 12: S89–S102.

Gilbert DG, Dibb WD, Plath LC, and Hiyane SG (2000) Effects of nicotine and caffeine, separately and in combination on EEG topography, mood, heart rate, cortisol, and vigilance. *Psychophysiology* 37: 583–595.

Gilbert DG, Estes SL, and Welser R (1997) Does noise stress modulate effects of smoking/nicotine? Mood, vigilance, and EEG responses. *Psychopharmacology* (Berlin) 129: 382–389.

Gilbert DG, McClernon FJ, Rabinovich NE, Dibb WD, Plath LC, Hiyane S, *et al.* (1999) EEG, physiology, and task-related mood fail to resolve across 31 days of smoking abstinence: Relations to depressive traits, nicotine exposure, and dependence. *Experimental and Clinical Psychopharmacology* 7: 427–443.

Gilbert DG, McClernon FJ, Rabinovich NE, Plath LC, Jensen RA, and Meliska CJ (1998) Effects of smoking abstinence on mood and craving in men: Influences of negative-affect-related personality traits, habitual nicotine intake and repeated measurements. *Personality and Individual Differences* 25: 399–423.

Gilbert DG, McClernon FJ, Rabinovich NE, Sugai C, Plath LC, Asgaard G, *et al.* (2004a) Effects of quitting smoking on EEG activation and attention last for more than 31 days and are more severe with stress, dependence, DRD2 A1 allele, and depressive traits. *Nicotine and Tobacco Research* 6: 249–267.

Gilbert DG, Robinson JH, Chamberlin CL, and Spielberger CD (1989) Effects of smoking/nicotine on anxiety, heart rate, and lateralization of EEG during a stressful movie. *Psychophysiology* 26: 311–320.

Gilbert DG, Sugai C, Murali S, Kreke E, and Rabinovich NE (2009a) Differential and similar effects of nicotine and bupropion on brain reactivity to smoking-related and emotional pictures. Paper presented by first author as part of Symposium on ERPs. The 49th Annual Meeting of the Society for Psychological Research, Berlin.

Gilbert DG, Sugai C, Zuo Y, Eau Claire N, McClernon FJ, Rabinovich NE, Markus T, Asgaard G, and Radtke R (2004b) Effects of nicotine on brain responses to emotional pictures. *Nicotine and Tobacco Research* 6: 985–996.

Gilbert DG, Sugai C, Zuo Y, Rabinovich NE, McClernon F J, and Froeliger B (2007) Brain indices of nicotine's effects on attentional bias to smoking and emotional pictures and to task-relevant targets. *Nicotine and Tobacco Research* 9: 351–363.

Gilbert DG, Zuo Y, Rabinovich NE, Riise H, Needham R, and Huggenvik JI (2009b) Neurotransmission-related genetic polymorphisms, negative affectivity traits, and gender predict tobacco abstinence symptoms across 44 days with and without nicotine patch. *Journal of Abnormal Psychology* 118: 322–334.

Gobbelé R, Buchner H, Scherg M, and Curio G (1999) Stability of high-frequency (600 Hz) components in human somatosensory evoked potentials under variation of stimulus rate – evidence for a thalamic origin. *Clinical Neurophysiology* 110: 1659–1663.

Gratton G, Coles M, and Donchin E (1983) A new method for off-line removal of ocular artifact. *Electroencephalography and Clinical Neurophysiology* 55: 468–484.

Grave de Peralta R, Murray M, Gonzalez M, and Andino SL (2004) Improving the performance of linear inverse solutions by inverting the resolution matrix. *IEEE Transaction on Biomedical Engineering* 42: 216–225.

Greenwald MK and Roehrs TA (2005) Mu-opioid self-administration vs. passive administration in heroin abusers produces differential EEG activation. *Neuropsychopharmacology* 30: 212–221.

Greischar LL, Burghy CA, van Reekum CM, Jackson DC, Pizzagalli DA, and Mueller C (2004) Effects of electrode density and electrolyte spreading in dense array electroencephalographic recording. *Clinical Neurophysiology* 115: 710–720.

Hall M-H, Taylor G, Salisbury DF, and Levy DL (2011) Sensory gating event-related potentials and oscillations in schizophrenia patients and their unaffected relatives. *Schizophrenia Bulletin* 37: 1187–1199.

Hajcak G, McDonald N, and Simons RF (2004) Error-related psychophysiology and negative affect. *Brain and Cognition* 56: 189–197.

Handy TC (2009) Brain *Signal Analysis: Advances in Neuroelectric and Neuromagnetic Methods.* Cambridge, MA: MIT Press.

Heinzel G, Rudiger A, and Schilling R (2002) *Spectrum and Spectral Density Estimation by Discrete Fourier Transform (DFT), including a Comprehensive List of Window Functions and Some New Flat-Top Windows.* Hanover: Max Plank Institute für Gravitationsphysik (Albert-Einstein-Institut).

Henriques JB and Davidson RJ (1997) Regional brain electrical asymmetries discriminate between depressed and nondepressed subjects during cognitive task performance. *Biological Psychiatry* 42: 1039–1050.

Herning RI, Jones RT, Hooker WD, Mendelson J and Blackwell L (1985) Cocaine increases EEG beta: A replication and extension of Hans Berger's historic experiments. *Electroencephalography and Clinical Neurophysiology* 60: 470–477.

Herrmann CS, Munk MHJ, and Engel AK (2004) Cognitive functions of gamma-band activity: Memory match and utilization. *Trends in Cognitive Sciences* 8 (8): 347–355.

Hoffmann S and Falkenstein M (2008) The correction of eye blink artifacts in the EEG: A comparison of two prominent methods. *PLoS ONE* 3: e3004.

Holroyd CB, Nieuwenhuis S, Yeung N, and Cohen JD (2003) Errors in reward prediction are reflected in the event-related brain potential. *NeuroReport* 14: 2481–2484.

Houlihan ME, Pritchard WS, and Robinson JH (1996) Faster P300 latency after smoking in visual but not auditory oddball tasks. *Psychopharmacology* 123: 231–238.

Ille N, Berg P, and Scherg M (2002) Artifact correction of the ongoing EEG using spatial filters based on artifact and brain signal topographies. *Clinical Neurophysiology* 19: 113–124.

Im C-H, Gururajan A, Zhang N, Chen W and He B (2007) Spatial resolution of EEG cortical source imaging revealed by localization of retinotopic organization in human primary visual cortex. *Journal of Neuroscience Methods* 161: 142–154.

IPEG (1982) 1982 Guidelines for pharmaco-EEG studies in man. http://www.internationalpharmacoeeggroup.org/contents.htm.

IPEG (1987) Recommendations for standardization of data acquisition and signal analysis in pharmaco-electroencephalography. http://www.internationalpharmacoeeggroup.org/contents.htm.

IPEG (1990) Recommendations for EEG and evoked potential mapping. http://www.internationalpharmacoeeggroup.org/contents.htm.

IPEG (1998) IPEG guideline on statistical design and analysis for pharmacodynamic trials. http://www.internationalpharmacoeeggroup.org/contents.htm.

Iwanami A, Suga I, Kato N, Nakatani Y, and Kaneko T (1993) Event-related potentials in methamphetamine psychosis during an auditory discrimination task: A preliminary report. *European Archives of Psychiatry and Clinical Neuroscience* 242: 203–208.

James CJ and Gibson OJ (2003) Temporally constrained ICA: An application to artifact rejection in electromagnetic brain signal Analysis. *IEEE Transactions on Biomedical Engineering* 50: 1108–16.

Janke W (1983) Response variability to psychotropic drugs: Overview of the main approaches to differential pharmaco-psychology. In W Janke (ed.), *Response Variability to Psychotropic Drugs* (pp. 33–65). New York: Pergamon Press.

Jann K, Loenig T, Dierks T, Boesch C, and Federspiel A (2010) Association of individual resting state EEG alpha frequency and cerebral blood flow. *NeuroImage* 51: 365–372.

Jasper HH (1958) The ten twenty electrode system of the international federation. *Electroencephalography and Clinical Neurophysiology* 10: 371–375.

Jensen O and Tesche CD (2002) Frontal theta activity in humans increases with memory load in a working memory task. *European Journal of Neuroscience* 15: 1395–1399.

Jerbi K, Ossandón T, Hamamé CM, Senova S, Dalal SS, Jung J, Minotti L, Bertrand O, Berthoz A, Kahane P, and Lachaux JP (2009) Task-related gamma-band dynamics from an intracerebral perspective: review and implications for surface EEG and MEG. *Human Brain Mapping* 30: 1758–1771.

Jiang JA, Chao CF, Chiu MJ, Lee RG, Tseng CL and Lin R (2007) An automatic analysis method for detecting and eliminating ECG artifacts in EEG. *Computers in Biology and Medicine* 37, 1660–1671.

John ER, Ahn H, Prichep LS, *et al.* (1980) Developmental equations for the electroencephalogram. *Science* 210: 1255–1258.

Jokisch D and Jensen O (2007) Modulation of gamma and alpha activity during a working memory task engaging the dorsal or ventral stream. *Journal of Neuroscience* 27: 3244–3251.

Joyce CA, Gorodnitsky IF, and Kutas M (2004) Automatic removal of eye movement and blink artifacts from EEG data using blind component separation. *Psychophysiology* 41: 313–325.

Jung TP, Makeig S, Westerfield M, Townsend J, Courchesne E, and Sejnowski TJ (2000) Removal of eye activity artifacts from visual event-related potentials in normal and clinical subjects. *Clinical Neurophysiology* 111: 1745–1758.

Jung TP, Makeig S, Westerfield M, Townsend J, Courchesne E, and Sejnowski TJ (2001) Analysis and visualization of single-trial event-related potentials. *Human Brain Mapping* 14: 166–185.

Kahana MJ, Seelig D, and Madsen JR (2001) Theta returns. *Current Opinion in Neurobiology* 11: 739–744.

Kaiser DA and Sterman MB (2001) Automatic artifact detection, overlapping windows and state transitions. *Journal of Neurotherapy* 4: 85–92.

Kanayama N, Sato A, and Ohira H (2007) Crossmodal effect with rubber hand illusion and gamma-band activity. *Psychophysiology* 44: 392–402.

Kendrick KM, Zhan Y, Fischer H, Nicol AU, Zhang X, and Feng J (2011) Learning alters theta amplitude, theta-gamma coupling and neuronal synchronization in inferotemporal cortex. *BMC Neuroscience* 12: 55.

Kenemans JL and Kähkäonen S (2011) How human electrophysiology informs psychopharmacology: From bottom-up driven processing to top-down control. *Neuropsychopharmacology* 36: 26–51. doi:10.1038/npp.2010.157.

Kirmizi-Alsan E, Bayraktaroglu Z, Gurvit H, Keskin YH, Emre M, and Demiralp T (2006) Comparative analysis of event-related potentials during Go/NoGo and CPT: Decomposition of electrophysiological markers of response inhibition and sustained attention. *Brain Research* 1104: 114–128.

Klados MA, Frantzidis CA, Vivas AB, Papadelis CL, Lithari CD, Pappas C, and Bamidis PD (2009) A framework combining delta event-related oscillations (EROs) and synchronisation effects (ERD/ERS) to study emotional processing. *Computational Intelligence and Neuroscience*, Article ID 549419.

Klados MA, Papadelis C, Lythari C, and Bamidis PD (2008) The removal of ocular artifacts from EEG signals: A comparison of performances for different methods. *Proceedings of the 4th European Conference of the International Federation for Medical and Biological Engineering* 1259–1263: Antwerp, Belgium.

Klimesch W (1999) EEG alpha and theta oscillations reflect cognitive and memory performance: A review and analysis. *Brain Research Reviews* 29: 169–195.

Klimesch W, Sauseng P, and Hanslmayr S (2007) EEG alpha oscillations: The inhibition-timing hypothesis. *Brain Research Reviews* 53: 63–88.

Klostermann F (2005) 500–1000 Hz responses in the somatosensory system: Approaching generators and function. *Journal of Clinical EEG and Neuroscience* 1: 293–305.

Knight RT (1990) Neural mechanisms of event-related potentials from lesion studies. In JW Rohrbaugh, R Parasuraman, and R Johnson, Jr (eds), *Event Related Brain Potentials* (pp. 3–18). New York: Oxford University Press.

Knott VJ (1989) Brain electrical imaging the dose-response effects of cigarette smoking. *Neuropsychobiology* 22: 236–242.

Knott V, Bakish D, Lusk S, and Barkely J (1997) Relaxation-induced EEG alterations in panic disorder patients. *Journal of Anxiety Disorders* 11: 365–376.

Knott VJ, Harr A, Ilivitsky V, and Mahoney C (1998) The cholinergic basis of the smoking-induced EEG activation profile. *Neuropsychobiology* 38: 97–107.

Knott V, Heenan A, Shah D, Bolton K, Fisher D, and Villeneuve C (2011) Electrophysiological evidence of nicotine's distracter-filtering properties in non-smokers. *Journal of Psychopharmacology* 25: 239–248.

Knott VJ, Kerr C, Hooper C, and Lusk-Mikkelsen S (1995) Cigarette smoking and event-related brain electrical potential (ERP) topographies associated with attentional-distractive processes. In EF Domino (ed.), *Brain Imaging of Nicotine and Tobacco Smoking* (pp. 191–221). Ann Arbor: NPP Books.

Koessler L, Maillard L, Benhadid A, Vignal JP, Braun M, and Vespignani H (2007) Spatial localization of EEG electrodes. *Clinical Neurophysiology* 37: 97–102.

Krieger S, Lis S, Janik H, Cetin T, Gallhofer B, *et al.* (2005) Executive function and cognitive subprocesses in first-episode, drug-naive schizophrenia: An analysis of N-back performance. *American Journal of Psychiatry* 162: 1206–1208.

Krystal JH, Staley J, Mason G, JH Petrakis IL, Kaufman J, Harris RA, Gelernter J, and Lappalainen J (2006) γ-Aminobutyric acid type A receptors and alcoholism intoxication, dependence, vulnerability, and treatment. *Archives of General Psychiatry* 63: 957–968.

Lachaux JP, Fonlupt P, Kahane P, Minotti L, Hoffmann D, Bertrand O, and Baciu M (2007) Relationship between task-related gamma oscillations and BOLD signal: New insights from combined fMRI and intracranial EEG. *Human Brain Mapping* 28: 1368–1375.

Lang PJ, Bradley MM, and Cuthbert BN (1997) Motivated attention: Affect, activation, and action. In PJ. Lang, RF Simons, and MT Balaban (eds), *Attention and Orienting: Sensory and Motivational Processes* (pp. 97–135). Mahwah, NJ: Lawrence Erlbaum Associates.

Lanre-Amos T and Kocsis B (2010) Hippocampal oscillations in the rodent model of schizophrenia induced by amygdala GABA receptor blockade. *Frontiers in Psychiatry* 1: 1–11.

Lansbergen MM, Dumont GJH, van Gerven JMA, Buitelaar JK, and Jan Verkes R (2011) Acute effects of MDMA (3,4-methylenedioxymethamphetamine) on EEG oscillations: Alone and in combination with ethanol or THC (delta-9-tetrahydrocannabinol). *Psychopharmacology* 213: 745–756.

Laufs H, Holt JL, Elfont R, Krams M, Paul JS, Krakow K, and Kleinschmidt A (2006) Where the BOLD signal goes when alpha EEG leaves. *NeuroImage* 31: 1408–1418.

Laufs HH, Krakowm K, Sterzer P, Eger E, Beyerle A, Salek-Haddadi A, and Kleinschmidt A (2003) Electroencephalographic signatures of attentional and cognitive default modes in spontaneous brain activity fluctuations at rest. *Proceedings of the National Academy of Sciences USA* 19: 11053–11058.

Le Van Quyen M, Foucher J, Lachaux J, Rodriguez E, Lutz A, Martinerie J, and Varela FJ (2001) Comparison of Hilbert transform and wavelet methods for the analysis of neuronal synchrony. *Journal of Neuroscience Methods* 111: 83–98.

Lindsen JP and Bhattacharya J (2010) Correction of blink artifacts using independent component analysis and empirical mode decomposition. *Psychophysiology* 47: 955–960.

Little M and Franken IHA (2010) Implicit and explicit selective attention to smoking cues in smokers indexed by brain potentials. *Journal of Psychopharmacology* 25: 503–513.

Liu Z, Ding L, and He B (2006) Integration of EEG/MEG with MRI and fMRI in functional neuroimaging. *IEEE Engineering in Medicine and Biology Magazine* 25: 46–53.

Lopes da Silva F (2002) Pharmaco-EEG: From cellular to the network level. EEG beta spectral power as a biomarker for GABAergic inhibition and its role in the assessment of AEDs. *Methods and Findings in Experimental and Clinical Pharmacology* 24 (Suppl. D): 3.

Lopes da Silva FH, Gomez JP, Velis DN, and Kalitzin S (2005) Phase clustering of high frequency EEG: MEG components. *Journal of Clinical EEG and Neuroscience* 36: 306–310.

Luck SJ (2005) *An Introduction to the Event-Related Potential Technique*. Cambridge, MA: MIT Press.

Lujic C, Reuter M, and Netter P (2005) Psychobiological theories of smoking and smoking motivation. *European Psychologist* 10: 1–24.

Lukas SE and Mendelson JH (1988) Electroencephalographic activity and plasma ACTH during ethanol-induced euphoria. *Biological Psychiatry* 23: 141–148.

Lukas SE, Mendelson JH, and Benedikt R (1995) Electroencephalographic correlates of marihuana-induced euphoria. *Drug and Alcohol Dependence* 37: 131–140.

Lutkenhoner B (2010) Baseline correction of overlapping event-related responses using a linear deconvolution technique. *Neuroimage* 52: 86–96.

Luu P, Collins P, and Tucker D (2000) Mood, personality, and self-monitoring: Negative affect and emotionality in relation to frontal lobe mechanisms of error monitoring. *Journal of Experimental Psychology: General* 129: 43–60.

Luu P, Poulsen C, and Tucker DM (2009) Neurophysiological measures of brain activity: Going from the scalp to the brain. In DD Schmorrow (ed.), *Augmented Cognition* (pp. 488–494). Berlin: Springer-Verlag.

Mammone N, La Foresta F, and Morabito F (2011) Automatic artifact rejection from multichannel scalp EEG by wavelet ICA. *IEEE Sensors Journal* 99: 10.1109/JSEN. 2011.2115236.

McCormick DA and Bal T (1997) Sleep and arousal: Thalamocortical mechanisms. *Annual Review of Neuroscience* 20: 185–215.

McCormick DA and Pape HC (1990) Properties of a hyperpolarization-activated cation current and its role in rhythmic oscillation in thalamic relay neurons. *Journal of Physiology* 431: 291–318.

McMenamin BW, Shackman AJ, Maxwell JS, Greischar LL, and Davidson RJ (2009) Validation of regression-based myogenic correction techniques for scalp and source-localized EEG. *Psychophysiology* 46: 578–592.

Meltzer JA, Negishi M, Mayes LC, and Constable TR (2007) Individual differences in EEG theta and alpha dynamics during working memory correlate with fMRI responses across subjects. *Clinical Neurophysiology* 118: 2419–2436.

Michel CM, Murray MM, Lantz G, Gonzalez S, Spinelli L, and Grave de Peralta R (2004) EEG source imaging. *Clinical Neurophysiology* 115: 219–222.

Millar A, Smith D, Choueiry J, Fisher D, Albert P, and Knott V (2011) The moderating role of the dopamine transporter gene on P50 sensory gaiting and its modulation by nicotine. *Neuroscience* 180: 148–156.

Mitchell DJ, McNaughton N, Flanagan D, and Kirk IJ (2008) Frontal-midline theta from the perspective of hippocampal "theta." *Progress in Neurobiology* 86 (3): 156–185.

Muller-Gass A and Campbell K (2002) Event-related potential measures of the inhibition of information processing: I. Selective attention in the waking state. *International Journal of Psychophysiology* 46: 177–195.

Murray MM, Brunet D, and Michel CM (2008) Topographic ERP analyses: A step-by-step tutorial review. *Brain Topography* 20: 249–264.

Näätänen R (1982) Processing negativity: An evoked-potential reflection of selective attention. *Psychological Bulletin* 92: 605–640.

Näätänen R (1992) *Attention and Brain Function*. Hillsdale, NJ: Lawrence Erlbaum Associates.

Napflin M, Wildi M, and Sarnthein J (2007) Test–retest reliability of resting EEG spectra validates a statistical signature of persons. *Clinical Neurophysiology* 118: 2519–2524.

Nathan PJ, Segrave R, Phan KL, O'Neill B, and Croft RJ (2006) Direct evidence that acutely enhancing serotonin with the selective serotonin reuptake inhibitor citalopram modulates the loudness dependence of the auditory evoked potential (LDAEP) marker of central serotonin function. *Human Psychopharmacology* 21: 47–52.

Nickerson LD, Ravichandran C, Lundahl LH, Rodolico J, Dunlap S, Trksak GH, and Lukas SE (2011) Cue reactivity in cannabis-dependent adolescents. *Psychology of Addictive Behavior* 25: 168–173.

Niedermeyer E and Lopes da Silva F (1993) *Electroencephalography: Basic Principles, Clinical Applications, and Related Fields*. Baltimore: Williams & Wilkins.

Nishitani N (2003) Dynamics of cognitive processing in the human hippocampus by neuro-magnetic and neurochemical assessments. *NeuroImage* 20: 561–571.

Nolan H, Whelan R, and Reilly R (2010) FASTER: Fully automated statistical thresholding for EEG artifact rejection. *Journal of Neuroscience Methods* 192: 152–162.

Nunez PL and Srinivasan R (2006) *Electric Fields of the Brain: The Neurophysics of EEG* (2nd edn). New York: Oxford University Press.

Olofsson JK, Nordin S, Sequeira H, and Polich J (2008) Affective picture processing: An integrative review of ERP findings. *Biological Psychology* 77: 247–265.

Onton J, Delorme A, and Makeig S (2005) Frontal midline EEG dynamics during working memory. *NeuroImage* 27: 341–356.

Opitz B, Mecklinger A, Friederici AD, and von Cramon DY (1999) the functional neu-roanatomy of novelty processing: Integrating ERP and fMRI results. *Cerebral Cortex* 9: 379–391.

Panksepp J (1998) *Affective Neuroscience: The Foundation of Human and Animal Emotions*. New York: Oxford University Press.

Park H, Jeong D, and Park K (2002) Automated detection and elimination of periodic ECG artifacts in EEG using the energy interval histogram method. *IEEE Transactions on Biomedical Engineering* 49: 49–65.

Parker AB and Gilbert DG (2008) Brain activity during anticipation of smoking-related and emotionally positive pictures in smokers and nonsmokers: A new measure of cue reactivity. *Nicotine and Tobacco Research* 10: 1627–1631.

Pascual-Marqui RD, Esslen M, Kochi K, and Lehmann D (2002) Functional imaging with low-resolution brain electromagnetic tomography (LORETA): A review. *Methods and Findings in Experimental and Clinical Pharmacology* 24 (Suppl. C): 91–95.

Pergadia ML, Heath AC, Agrawal A, Bucholz KK, Martin NG, and Madden PA (2006) The implications of simultaneous smoking initiation for inferences about the genetics of smoking behavior from twin data. *Behavior Genetics* 36 (4): 567–576.

Perkins KA (1999) Baseline-dependency of nicotine effects: A review. *Behavioural Pharmacology* 10: 597–615.

Perkins KA, Gerlach D, Vender J, Grobe J, Meeker J, and Hutchison S (2001) Sex differences in the subjective and reinforcing effects of visual and olfactory cigarette smoke stimuli. *Nicotine and Tobacco Research* 3: 141–150.

Perrin F, Pernier J, Bertrand O, and Echallier JF (1989) Spherical splines for scalp potential and current density mapping. *Electroencephalography and Clinical Neurophysiology* 72: 184–187.

Pfurtscheller G and Lopes da Silva FH (1999) Event-related EEG/MEG synchronization and desynchronization: Basic principles. *Clinical Neurophysiology* 110: 1842–1857.

Pickworth WB, Herning RI, and Henningfield JE (1989) Spontaneous EEG changes during tobacco abstinence and nicotine substitution in human volunteers. *Journal of Pharmacology and Experimental Therapeutics* 251: 976–982.

Picton TW, van Roon P, Armilio ML, Berg P, Ille N, and Scherg M (2000) The correction of ocular artifacts: A topographic perspective. *Clinical Neurophysiology* 111: 53–65.

Pivik RT, Broughton RJ, Coppola R, *et al.* (1993) Guidelines for the recording and quantitative analysis of electroencephalographic activity in research contexts. *Psychophysiology* 30: 547–558.

Pizzagalli DA, Sherwood RJ, Henriques JB, and Davidson RJ (2005) Frontal brain asymmetry and reward responsiveness: A source localization study. *Psychological Science* 16: 805–813.

Polich J (1997) EEG and ERP assessment of normal aging. *Electroencephalography and Clinical Neurophysiology* 104: 244–256.

Polich J (2003) Overview of P3a and P3b. In J Polich (ed.), *Detection of Change: Event-Related Potential and fMRI Findings* (pp. 83–98). Boston: Kluwer Academic Press.

Polich J and Criado JR (2006) Neuropsychology and neuropharmacology of P3a and P3b. *International Journal of Psychophysiology* 60: 172–185.

Ponton CW, Moore JK, and Eggermont JJ (1996) Auditory brain stem response generation by parallel pathways: Differential maturation of axonal conduction time and synaptic transmission. *Ear and Hearing* 17: 402–410.

Porjesz B and Begleiter H (1996) Effects of alcohol on electrophysiological activity of the brain. In H Begleiter and B Kissin (eds), *Alcohol and Alcoholism*, Vol. 2: *The Pharmacology of Alcohol and Alcohol Dependence* (pp. 207–247). New York: Oxford University Press.

Porjesz B and Begleiter H (1998) Genetic basis of the event–related potentials and their relationship to alcoholism and alcohol use. *Journal of Clinical Neurophysiology* 15: 44–57.

Porjesz B and Rangaswamy M (2007) Neurophysiological endophenotypes, CNS disinhibition, and risk for alcohol dependence and related disorders. *Scientific World Journal* 7: 131–141.

Pritchard WS, Sokhadze E, and Houlihan ME (2004) Effects of nicotine on event-related potentials (ERPs): A review. *Nicotine and Tobacco Research* 6: 961–984.

Rabe R, Debener S, Brocke B, and Beauducel A (2005) Depressive mood and posterior cortical activity during performance of neuropsychological verbal and spatial tasks. *Personality and Individual Differences* 39: 601–611.

Rangaswamy M, Porjesz B, Chorlian DB, Wang K, Jones KA, Bauer LO, Rohrbaugh J, O'Connor SJ, Kuperman S, Reich T, and Begleiter H (2002) Beta power in the EEG of alcoholics. *Biological Psychiatry* 52: 831–842.

Rangaswamy M, Porjesz B, Chorlian DB, Wang K, Jones KA, Kuperman S, Rohrbaugh J, O'Connor SJ, Bauer LO, Reich T, and Begleiter H (2004) Resting EEG in offspring of male alcoholics: Beta frequencies. *International Journal of Psychophysiology* 51: 239–251.

Reid MS, Flammino F, Howard B, Nilsen D, and Prichep LS (2006) Topographic imaging of quantitative EEG in response to smoked cocaine self-administration in humans. *Neuropsychopharmacology* 31: 872–884.

Rennie CJ, Robinson PA, and Wright JJ (2002) Unified neurophysical model of EEG spectra and evoked potentials. *Biological Cybernetics* 86: 457– 471.

Robinson TE and Berridge KC (1993) The neural basis of drug craving: An incentive-sensitization theory of addiction. *Brain Research Reviews* 18: 247–291.

Robinson T and Berridge K (2000) The psychology and neurobiology of addiction: An incentive-sensitization view. *Addiction* 95: 91–117.

Rose EJ, Simonotto E, and Ebmeier KP (2006) Limbic over-reactivity in depression during preserved performance on the n-back task. *NeuroImage* 29: 209–215.

Sabatinelli D, Lang PJ, Keil A, and Bradley MM (2007) Emotional perception: Correlation of functional MRI and event related potentials. *Cerebral Cortex* 17: 1085–1091.

Saletu B, Anderer P, and Saletu-Zyhlarz GM (2006) EEG topography and tomography (LORETA) in the classification and evaluation of the pharmacodynamics of psychotropic drugs. *Clinical EEG and Neuroscience* 37 (2): 66–80.

Saletu B, Anderer P, and Saletu-Zyhlarz GM (2010) EEG mapping and tomography in drug evaluation. *Medicographia* 32: 190–200.

Samar VJ, Swartz KP, and Raghuveer MR (1995) Multiresolution analysis of event-related potentials by wavelet decomposition. *Brain and Cognition* 27: 398–438.

Sammer G, Blecker C, Gebhardt H, Bischoff M, Stark R, Morgen K, and Vaitl D (2007) Relationship between regional hemodynamic activity and simultaneously recorded EEG-theta associated with mental arithmetic-induced workload. *Human Brain Mapping* 28: 793–803.

Sampaio I, Puga F, Veiga H, Cagy M, Piedade R, and Ribeiro P (2007) Influence of bromazepam on cortical interhemispheric coherence. *Arquivos de Neuro-Psiquiatria* 65: 77–81.

Santesso DL, Evins AE, Frank MJ, Schetter EC, Bogdan R, and Pizzagalli DA (2009) Single dose of a dopamine agonist impairs reinforcement learning in humans: Evidence from event-related potentials and computational modeling of striatal-cortical function. *Human Brain Mapping* 30 (7): 1963–1976.

Saron CD, Schroeder CE, Foxe JJ, and Vaughan HG (2001) Visual activation of frontal cortex: Segregation from occipital activity. *Cognitive Brain Research* 12: 75–88.

Scheeringa R, Bastiaansen MC, M Petersson KM, Oostenveld R, Norris DG and Hagoort, P (2008) Frontal theta EEG activity correlates negatively with the default mode network in resting state. *International Journal of Psychophysiology* 67: 242–251.

Scherg M and Berg P (1993) *Brain Electrical Source Analysis (Ver. 2.0)*. Herndon, VA: NeuroScan.

Scherg M, Ille N, Bornfleth H, and Berg P (2002) Advanced tools for digital EEG review: Virtual source montages, whole-head mapping, correlation, and phase analysis. *Clinical Neurophysiology* 19: 91–112.

Schlogl A, Keinrath C, Zimmermann D, Scherer R, Leeb R, and Pfurtscheller G (2007) A fully automated correction method of EOG artifacts in EEG recordings. *Clinical Neurophysiology* 118: 98–104.

Schlógl A, Ziehe A, and Müller K (2009) Automated ocular artifact removal: Comparing regression and component-based methods. *Nature Precedings* 4: 1–24.

Schröger E and Wolff C (1998) Behavioral and electrophysiological effects of task-irrelevant sound change: A new distraction paradigm. *Cognitive Brain Research* 7: 71–87.

Sharpe JP and Gilbert DG (1998) Effects of repeated administration of the Beck Depression Inventory and other measures of negative mood states. *Personality and Individual Differences* 24: 457–463.

Singer (1999) Striving for coherence. *Nature* 39: 391–393.

Soong A, Lind J, Shaw G, and Koles Z (1993) Systematic comparisons of interpolation techniques in topographic brain mapping. *Electroencephalography and Clinical Neurophysiology* 87: 185–195.

Soufflet L, Toussaint M, Luthringer R, Gresser J, Minot R, and Macher JP (1991) A statistical evaluation of the main interpolation methods applied to 3-dimensional EEG mapping. *Electroencephalography and Clinical Neurophysiology* 79: 393–402.

Sridharan D, Levitin DJ, and Menon V (2008) A critical role for the right fronto-insular cortex in switching between central-executive and default-mode networks. *PNSA* 105: 12569–12574.

Srinivasan R, Tucker DM, and Murias M (1998) Estimating the spatial Nyquist of the human EEG. *Behavior Research Methods, Instruments and Computers* 30: 8–19.

Tallgren P, Vanhatalo S, Kaila K, and Voipio J (2005) Evaluation of commercially available electrodes and gels for recording of slow EEG potentials. *Clinical Neurophysiology* 116: 799–806.

Tecce JJ (1972). Contingent negative variation (CNV) and psychological processes in man. *Psychological Bulletin* 77: 73–108.

Tecce JJ and Cattanach L (1993) Contingent negative variation: CNV. In E Niedermeyer and F Lopes da Silva (eds), *Electroencephalography: Basic Principles, Clinical Applications, and Related Fields* (3rd edn, pp. 887–910). Baltimore: Williams & Wilkins.

Thatcher RW (2010) Validity and reliability of quantitative electroencephalography. *Journal of Neurotherapy* 14: 122–152.

Towle VL, Bolanos J, Suarez D, Tan K, Grzeszczuk R, Levin DN, Cakmur R, Frank SA, and Spire JP (1993) The spatial location of EEG electrodes: Locating the best-fitting sphere relative to cortical anatomy. *Electroencephalography and Clinical Neurophysiology* 86: 1–6.

Tyvaert L, Levan P, Grova C, Dubeau F, and Gotman J (2008) Effects of fluctuating physiological rhythms during prolonged EEG-fMRI studies. *Clinical Neurophysiology* 119: 2762–2774.

Ullsperger M and Debener S (2010) *Simultaneous EEG and fMRI Recording, Analysis, and Application*. New York: Oxford University Press.

Urrestarazu E, Iriarte J, Alegre M, Valencia M, Viteri C, and Artieda J (2004) Independent component analysis removing artifacts in ictal recordings. *Epilepsia* 45: 1071–1078.

Usakli AB (2010) Improvement of EEG signal acquisition: An electrical aspect for state of the art of front end. *Computational Intelligence and Neuroscience*, Article ID 630649: 1–7.

van Beijsterveldt CEM, Molenaar PCM, de Geus EJ, and Boomsma DI (1996) Heritability of human brain functioning as assessed by electroencephalography. *American Journal of Human Genetics* 58: 562–573.

van de Laar MC, Licht R, Franken IHA, and Hendriks VM (2004) Event-related potentials indicate motivational relevance of cocaine cues in abstinent cocaine addicts. *Psychopharmacology* (Berlin) 177: 121–129.

van der Zwaag W, Francis S, Head K, Peters A, Gowland P, Morris P, and Bowtell R (2009) fMRI at 1.5, 3 and 7 T: Characterising BOLD signal changes. *NeuroImage* 47: 1425–1434.

Vergult A, De Clercq W, Palmini A, Vanrumste B, Dupont P, Van Huffel S, and Van Paesschen W (2007) Improving the interpretation of ictal scalp EEG: BSS-CCA algorithm for muscle artifact removal. *Epilepsia* 48: 950–958.

Versace F, Robinson JD, Lam CY, Minnis JA, Brown VL, Carter BL, Wetter DA, and Cinciripini PM (2010) Cigarette cues capture smokers' attention: Evidence from event-related potentials. *Psychophysiology* 47: 435–441.

Vertes RP (2005) Hippocampal theta rhythm: A tag for short-term memory. *Hippocampus* 15: 923–935.

Vigário R (1997) Extraction of ocular artifacts from EEG using independent component analysis. *Electroencephalography and Clinical Neurophysiology* 103: 395–404.

Viola FC, Thorne J, Edmonds B, Schneider T, Eichele T, and Debener S (2009) Semi-automatic identification of independent components representing EEG artifact. *Clinical Neurophysiology* 120: 868–877.

Wallstrom GL, Kass RE, Miller A, Cohn JF, and Fox NA (2004) Automatic correction of ocular artifacts in the EEG: A comparison of regression based and component-based methods. *International Journal of Psychophysiology* 53: 105–119.

Wetter DW, Fiore MC, Young TB, McClure JB, de Moor CA, and Baker TB (1999) Gender differences in response to nicotine replacement therapy: Objective and subjective indexes of tobacco withdrawal. *Experimental and Clinical Psychopharmacology* 7: 135–144.

Wiswedea D, Müntea TF, Goschked T, and Rüsselera J (2009) Modulation of the error-related negativity by induction of short-term negative affect. *Neuropsychologia* 47: 83–90.

Xu X, Xu B, and He B (2004) An alternative subspace approach to EEG dipole source localization. *Physics in Medicine and Biology* 49: 327–343.

Zinser MC, Fiore MC, Davidson RJ, and Baker TB (1999) Manipulating smoking motivation: Impact on an electrophysiological index of approach motivation. *Journal of Abnormal Psychology* 108: 240–254.

Zuckerman M (2005) *Psychobiology of Personality* (2nd edn). New York: Cambridge University Press.

Zuurman L, Roy C, Schoemaker RC, Amatsaleh A, Guimaeres L, Pinquier JL, *et al.* (2010) Inhibition of THC-induced effects on the central nervous system and heart rate by a novel r antagonist AVE1625. *Journal of Psychopharmacology* 24: 363–371.

Zuurman L, Roy C, Schoemaker RC, Hazekamp A, den Hartigh J, Bender JC, *et al.* (2008) Effect of intrapulmonary tetrahydrocannabinol administration in humans. *Journal of Psychopharmacology* 22: 707–716.

23

Functional Magnetic Resonance Imaging in Addiction Research

Lawrence H. Sweet, Michael T. Amlung, and
James MacKillop

1   Introduction

Functional magnetic resonance imaging (FMRI) is a noninvasive neuroimaging technique that enables quantification of brain function over time with an unprecedented balance of temporal and spatial resolution. Although clinical applications exist, FMRI is primarily used in research settings to quantify changes in neuronal activity in brain systems associated with targeted cognitive, behavioral, or emotional challenges. The relative advantages of FMRI and the proliferation of MRI scanners have made it the method of choice for a wide range of research applications in human cognitive, affective, and clinical neurosciences.

Inherently transdisciplinary and translational, FMRI incorporates different methodologies and theoretical perspectives. At its core, FMRI examines stimulus–response relationships, where the quantified brain responses are evaluated in the context of a wide range of controlled challenges (i.e., FMRI paradigms). In most areas of FMRI research, including addictions, these are supplemented with careful behavioral assessments. Versatility in scientific approach is a major strength when employed to address questions about how the (dys)function of neural circuits relates to complex behaviors, such as the factors involved in addiction and its treatment.

Quantification of both brain and behavioral responses to targeted FMRI paradigms that challenge specific neural networks presents extraordinary opportunities to test diverse theoretical models of addiction. Moreover, FMRI enables novel a priori and exploratory approaches to reveal yet uncharted neural markers and mechanisms of addiction. For instance, FMRI offers addiction researchers the opportunity to objectively assess neural signatures of subjective states, such as craving, withdrawal, effort, and associated emotional states. As occurred previously with the advent of psychophysiological assessments and early functional neuroimaging techniques, today

---

The Wiley-Blackwell Handbook of Addiction Psychopharmacology, First Edition. Edited by
James MacKillop and Harriet de Wit.
© 2013 John Wiley & Sons, Ltd. Published 2013 by John Wiley & Sons, Ltd.

FMRI offers a set of objective methods that complement current approaches used to examine addiction.

With rapidly advancing methodology and broadening research applications, it has become critical that addiction scientists and clinicians understand the potential strengths and limitations of FMRI. The goal of this chapter is to provide an overview of the application of FMRI to addiction research. First, we review the conceptual basis and empirical findings from applications of FMRI in addiction research. Then, toward informing future FMRI research, we provide a critical overview of FMRI methodology, from study and paradigm design to data analysis. Finally, as the FMRI methods reflect a work-in-progress, we conclude by discussing challenges and future directions.

2   Applications to Addictions Research

2.1   Conceptual basis

The conceptual basis for applying FMRI methodologies to understand addiction is twofold. First, it permits neurocognitive characterization of processes that are known to be implicated in addictive behavior. Second, innovations in FMRI permit characterization of novel and heretofore unobservable brain characteristics that are relevant to addiction. In the following sections, we review the insights from FMRI applications in several different domains. Much of this work uses cross-sectional between-subjects designs to infer ways in which individuals with substance use disorders differ from control participants. This is a classic experimental psychopathology design, but does not permit inferring causality; observed differences may reflect effects of persistent drug use and/or preexisting differences that contribute to the development of addictive behavior. Ultimately, however, the goal of FMRI studies is to contribute across the research enterprise. The approach may be used to inform etiology and progression in longitudinal designs. Additionally, individual brain activation profiles in response to specific paradigms may contribute to diagnosis and predicting treatment responses. Finally, FMRI may serve as a platform for understanding genetic influences on addictive behavior, using individual variation in neurocognitive activity as novel phenotypes. As we review below, initial progress has been made in each of these areas.

2.2   Cognitive paradigms

An array of cognitive factors have been implicated in addictive behavior, such as executive function or working memory (see Chapter 2 in this volume), and many of the measures used in those domains have been translated into FMRI paradigms. In turn, studies using these paradigms have provided significant insights into differences in cognitive processing in individuals with addictive disorders, providing potential clues about neurocognitive factors that may reflect either etiological vulnerabilities or the long-term consequences of persistent drug misuse. A full review of the studies in this broad domain is beyond the scope of this chapter, but the findings pertaining to one paradigm in particular, the Iowa Gambling Task (IGT; Bechara, Damasio, Damasio, and Anderson, 1994), are both relevant and illustrative.

The IGT is a neuropsychological measure of executive functioning that assesses advantageous versus disadvantageous decision making in a card selection task over 100 trials. The task uses four decks, two of which have "disadvantageous" aggregate patterns (higher-magnitude gains, but also higher-magnitude losses that result in a net loss), and two of which have "advantageous" aggregate patterns (smaller-magnitude gains and losses that result in a net gain). Over the 100 trials, participants typically sample from all four decks at first and then migrate their choices to the advantageous decks once the contingencies are learned. However, individuals with lesions in the ventromedial prefrontal cortex do not learn the contingencies and perform significantly more poorly, even when they are aware of the contingencies (Bechara, Damasio, Tranel, and Damasio, 1997; Bechara, Tranel, and Damasio, 2000). Moreover, similar deficits have been found in an array of different substance-dependent samples compared to control groups (Bechara *et al.*, 2001; Bechara, Dolan, and Hindes, 2002; Dolan, Bechara, and Nathan, 2008; Miranda *et al.*, 2009; van der Plas *et al.*, 2009; Xiao *et al.*, 2008).

Importantly, brain activity during the IGT can be examined using functional brain imaging and can inform these behavioral findings. Initial work in this area used positron emission tomography (PET) in cocaine (e.g., Bolla *et al.*, 2003) and marijuana abusers (e.g., Bolla, Eldreth, Matochik, and Cadet, 2005). To date, two studies have used FMRI in the context of substance abuse. Tanabe and colleagues (2007) investigated IGT performance in substance-dependent individuals with or without comorbid pathological gambling and found that the substance-dependent groups showed decreased activation in several regions of medial and lateral frontal cortex. Interestingly, the individuals with comorbid gambling problems had activity levels that were intermediate to controls and non-gambling substance users. More recently, chronic marijuana users have been found to have decreased neural responses to losses in anterior cingulate cortex, medial frontal cortex, cerebellum, and regions of parietal and occipital cortex compared to controls (Wesley, Hanlon, and Porrino, 2011).

2.3   Cue reactivity paradigms

Individuals with substance use disorders are known to be particularly vulnerable to substance misuse in the presence of stimuli associated with previous drug use episodes (MacKillop and Monti, 2007). Over time, environmental contexts and physical stimuli associated with drug use putatively become conditioned stimuli that are imbued with increased incentive salience (Robinson and Berridge, 2001). Subsequent exposure to these stimuli evokes acute increases in subjective craving, psychophysiological arousal, and the relative value of the drug (MacKillop, 2006; MacKillop *et al.*, 2010a; Sayette *et al.*, 2001), as well as significant changes in affect and cognition (Rohsenow *et al.*, 1992; Sayette, Schooler, and Reichle, 2010; Wertz and Sayette, 2001). These associations are the basis of cue reactivity paradigms that are frequently employed to investigate responses to drug-related stimuli (e.g., Monti *et al.*, 1987). In the context of neuroimaging, a long line of research has investigated the neural response to drug-related cues across a range of addicted samples (for reviews, see Naqvi and Bechara, 2009; Wilson, Sayette, and Fiez, 2004). The substantial breadth of this work allows for comparison of neural activation across studies. For instance, a qualitative meta-analysis by Wilson *et al.* (2004) emphasized the importance of anterior cingulate, dorsolateral prefrontal, and orbitofrontal cortices, as well as the amygdala, in processing cues. Naqvi and Bechara (2009) have focused on the insula as an important neural substrate of drug craving and Yalachkov, Kaiser, and Naumer (2010) recently proposed an expanded craving network to include sensory and motor brain regions.

While qualitative reviews of the neuroimaging literature are an important first step in characterizing commonalities across studies, quantitative coordinate-based approaches such as activation likelihood estimation (ALE; e.g., Laird *et al.*, 2005) can be used to examine statistically significant convergence across studies. Two separate ALE meta-analyses of cue reactivity studies have now been published (Chase, Eickhoff, Laird, and Hogarth, 2011; Kuhn and Gallinat, 2011). Taken together, these analyses found significant overlap in ventral striatum, amygdala, anterior cingulate, and orbitofrontal cortex. Treatment status also appears to be an important factor in which areas are active. For instance, prefrontal cortex activation is observed predominantly in non-treatment-seeking individuals (Chase, Eickhoff, Laird, and Hogarth, 2011; Wilson, Sayette, and Fiez, 2004), while amygdala activation was more likely to be found in treatment-seekers (Chase, Eickhoff, Laird, and Hogarth, 2011). An ALE analysis approach has also been used to identify brain regions that are consistently correlated with self-reported craving, including ventral striatum, ventral pallidum, anterior cingulate, and prefrontal cortex (Chase, Eickhoff, Laird, and Hogarth, 2011; Kuhn and Gallinat, 2011). Together, these regions have been hypothesized to constitute a core neural network for drug-related craving (Kuhn and Gallinat, 2011).

More recent work in this area has progressed beyond simply characterizing the neural correlates of cue reactivity to investigating its genetic basis and translational significance in the context of substance abuse treatment. For instance, elevated blood oxygen level dependent (BOLD) response to smoking cues in several regions, including the amygdala, insula, and anterior cingulate, among others, predicted smoking lapse in a nicotine-dependent sample (Janes *et al.*, 2010). Stronger activation in striatum and medial prefrontal cortex has also been shown to predict relapse in alcohol-dependent patients (Grusser *et al.*, 2004). This preliminary evidence suggests that neural activation to cues could potentially be used to prospectively screen individuals who are particularly relapse-prone to aid personalized treatment. Other studies have investigated whether a variety of treatments alter cue-elicited brain activation (e.g., Hermann *et al.*, 2006; Myrick *et al.*, 2008; Schneider *et al.*, 2001; Vollstädt-Klein *et al.*, 2006). For example, cue-exposure-based extinction training was accompanied by a decrease in the BOLD signal in anterior cingulate, insula and ventral striatum (Vollstädt-Klein *et al.*, 2006). In the case of alcoholism pharmacotherapies, amisulpride has been found to block cue-induced BOLD response in thalamus in alcohol-dependent participants (Hermann *et al.*, 2006). Similarly, the combination of alcohol, naltrexone, and ondansetron showed significantly decreased ventral striatal activation to alcohol cues (Myrick *et al.*, 2008), as did aripiprazole (Myrick *et al.*, 2010). Taken together, these findings highlight particularly promising applications of the cue reactivity paradigm. Continued translational research in this area may lead to the development of more effective treatment interventions for substance use disorders.

2.4   Behavioral inhibition paradigms

A substantial body of research has implicated impairments in behavioral inhibition with drug addiction (see Fillmore, 2003). Inhibitory processing can be easily assessed via a variety of behavioral paradigms, including the go/no-go and stop-signal tasks. Both tasks utilize rapid, serial presentation of response execution and response inhibition cues to assess the relative contribution of response activation and response suppression. One advantage of these paradigms is the relative ease with which they can be administered in the MRI environment using event-related FMRI to investigate the neural correlates of inhibitory control in healthy and substance use disorder samples (e.g., Fu *et al.*, 2008; Garavan, Kaufman, and Hester, 2009; Hester, Nestor, and Garavan, 2009; Hester and Garavan, 2004; Li *et al.*, 2009; Nestor *et al.*, 2011). In terms of healthy adults, a recent ALE analysis of 11 go/no-go FMRI studies revealed a number of common regions across studies that included the pre-supplementary motor area prefrontal cortex, insula, and inferior parietal lobe, among others, and activity was largely lateralized on the right side of the brain (Simmonds, Pekar, and Mostofsky, 2008). In studies investigating addictive behavior, Li *et al.* (2009) observed that patients with alcohol dependence showed decreased activity in regions of dorsolateral prefrontal cortex during stop-signal performance, and substance-dependent individuals also show dysfunction in motor regions, insular cortex, striatum, and amygdala (e.g., Fu *et al.*, 2008; Hester, Nestor, and Garavan, 2009; Kaufman, Ross, Stein, and Garavan, 2003; Li *et al.*, 2009; Yan and Li, 2000). Perhaps the most consistent finding across studies, however, is dysfunction in medial prefrontal areas involved in inhibition, action selection, and error monitoring. Specifically, studies with cocaine (Hester and Garavan, 2004; Kaufman, Ross, Stein, and Garavan, 2003), opiates (Forman *et al.*, 2004; Fu *et al.*, 2008), and marijuana (Hester, Nestor, and Garavan, 2009) have all reported some degree of dysfunction in anterior cingulate cortex during inhibitory control. Taken together, these results suggest a central role for this region in impaired inhibitory processing in individuals with substance use disorders.

Recent data suggest that successful abstinence from drugs may be associated with increased top-down prefrontal control of behavior (Nestor *et al.*, 2011). In this study, current smokers showed decreased prefrontal cortex activation during trials requiring response inhibition relative to controls, but ex-smokers actually had elevated activity relative to both controls and smokers. Acute nicotine withdrawal has also been shown to be associated with compensatory neural activation in inferior frontal cortex during response inhibition (Kozink, Kollins, and McClernon, 2010). Another particularly promising application of inhibitory paradigms involves studying the effects of acute drug consumption on behavior and corresponding neural activity (e.g., Anderson *et al.*, 2011; Garavan, Kaufman, and Hester, 2008). Increased response time and inhibitory errors following alcohol consumption were accompanied by decreased activity in anterior cingulate cortex, prefrontal cortex, parietal cortex, and insula (Anderson *et al.*, 2011). On the other hand, cocaine administration has been shown to actually improve inhibitory performance in cocaine-dependent individuals and is acutely associated with increased activation in dorsolateral, inferior, and medial frontal cortices (Garavan, Kaufman, and Hester, 2008). Finally, this approach can be used to examine individuals who are at-risk for developing addictive disorders. In a recent study of at-risk youth, adolescents with decreased inhibitory-related activation in regions of frontal cortex, cingulate gyrus, and striatum, among others, were more likely to transition into heavy alcohol use at follow-up (Norman *et al.*, 2011). Although this work requires replication, it nonetheless suggests that inefficient neural processing during development may place individuals at greater risk for subsequent substance misuse. Taken together, these findings provide evidence for altered neural processing during inhibitory control in SUDs and illustrate the diverse applications of go/no-go FMRI applications.

2.5   Neuroeconomic paradigms

Neuroeconomics refers to the integration of methods and concepts from psychology, economics, and cognitive neuroscience to understand the multifarious factors that influence preferences, values, and choices (Glimcher and Rustichini, 2004; Loewenstein, Rick, and Cohen, 2008). The most widely used tool in neuroeconomics is FMRI and it has been applied to understand both basic decision making in healthy individuals and the dysregulated decision making that is present in individuals with substance use disorders. Most relevant to addictive behavior, a number of studies have used FMRI to understand delay discounting, a behavioral economic index of impulsivity that reflects relative preference for small immediate rewards compared to larger delayed rewards (i.e., capacity to delay gratification) (for a full review, see Chapter 7). This form of impulsivity is typically studied using decision-making tasks that pit "smaller-sooner" rewards against "larger-later" rewards that are available at different future timepoints (e.g., "Would you prefer $60 today or $100 in 3 months' time?").

A number of FMRI studies of delay discounting have identified several common brain regions that are recruited during this type of decision making (Bickel, Pitcock, Yi, and Angtuaco, 2009; Kable and Glimcher, 2007; McClure, Laibson, Loewenstein, and Cohen, 2004). Specifically, a recent activation likelihood estimation (ALE) analysis integrating findings from 13 studies found 25 regions of common activation, including cortical structures (e.g., medial and inferior PFC, the anterior insular cortex, the posterior parietal cortex and posterior cingulate) and subcortical structures (e.g., ventral striatum, midbrain) (Carter, Meyer, and Huettel, 2010). The role of these areas has recently been supported by a study that examined age-related differences in discounting and found that the lower levels of impulsivity observed in older participants were a function of increasing activation in the ventromedial PFC and decreasing activation in the ventral striatum, insula, and anterior cingulate, among others (Christakou, Brammer, and Rubia, 2011). Considered together, the regions of activation are theorized to reflect a neurocognitive "tug-of-war" between cortical circuits that are responsible for self-control and subcortical circuits that are responsible for motivational drive (Bickel *et al.*, 2007; McClure, Laibson, Loewenstein, and Cohen, 2004). In other words, the observed selection of the smaller immediate reward or larger delayed reward is putatively determined by the relative balance between the drive and control systems (metaphorically, the gas pedal and the brakes). However, this dual process account is by no means fully accepted and alternative single-process accounts are arguably better supported (Kable and Glimcher, 2007; Monterosso and Luo, 2010).

Much of this work has been conducted in healthy samples, but a small number of studies have used neuroeconomics to investigate addictive behavior. Using a paradigm that focused on easy and difficult discounting choices, Monterosso *et al.* (2007) found that, when making easy choices, stimulant-dependent individuals exhibited a smaller difference in activity between "easy" and "hard" choices in prefrontal and parietal cortex relative to control participants. The stimuli presented and difficulty designation were determined by pre-scan decision-making assessment. Parallels to these findings were evident in a second study of discounting in stimulant-dependent individuals that revealed a smaller difference between easy and hard choices for activity in the dorsolateral PFC, precuneus, and ventral striatum (Hoffman *et al.*, 2008). This was attributed to evidence that the clinical group exhibited greater activation during the easy trials. Most recently, a study comparing three groups of HIV+ individuals who either had current, past or no history of cocaine dependence found similar patterns (Meade *et al.*, 2011). Compared to individuals with no history, actively cocaine-dependent participants exhibited generally less frontoparietal activity during all active stimuli compared to control stimuli, and, within active stimuli, exhibited smaller differences in activity in the anterior cingulate, precentral gyrus, and areas within the PFC. Taking these findings together, it appears that stimulant-dependent individuals require greater cognitive effort to engage in these types of decision and do not exhibit commensurate increases in activity for hard choices, perhaps reflecting a cognitive asymptote.

In terms of other types of drug addiction, two studies have been conducted on individuals with varying levels of alcohol problems. Comparing alcohol-dependent individuals and controls, Boettiger *et al.* (2009) found differential activation in the prefrontal cortex and posterior parietal cortex, among other regions. Differences with controls were particularly notable in terms of greater dorsolateral PFC activity, but attenuated lateral orbitofrontal cortex activity. Most recently, Claus, Kiehl, and Hutchison (2011) examined discounting using FMRI in a large sample of treatment-seeking and non-treatment-seeking hazardous drinkers ($N = 151$). This study found that impulsive choices were characterized by activity in the inferior frontal gyrus, orbitofrontal gyrus, and middle temporal gyrus, whereas non-impulsive choices were characterized by activity in the insula, anterior cingulate, and precuneus; and severity of alcohol involvement was also significantly correlated with activity in a number of these regions. Interestingly, more severe problems with alcohol appeared to be associated with greater cognitive resource allocation to successfully delay gratification, akin to stimulant-dependent individuals. To date, only one study (to our knowledge) has examined discounting and nicotine dependence. Using a within-subjects design and choices for both monetary and cigarette rewards, delay discounting in nicotine dependent adults was found to recruit similar brain regions to those previously noted, with significant correlations between activity in the ventral striatum, temporoparietal cortex, medial frontal gyrus, and middle frontal gyrus and behavioral discounting performance (MacKillop *et al.*, in press). Interestingly, however, when divided by commodity, a different profile of activity was present between discounting of money and cigarette rewards, suggesting that domain-general rewards may not be optimal assays to understand decision making in the context of addictive commodities or the trade-offs between addictive commodities and non-addictive commodities (i.e., cross-commodity discounting; Bickel *et al.*, 2011).

Taken together, although only a small number of studies have been conducted, the findings to date suggest that individuals with substance use disorders exhibit meaningful differences in cortical and subcortical regions responsible for balancing motivation for short-term gratification versus long-term positive outcomes. However, caution must be applied interpreting these findings, as the studies are cross-sectional and it is not clear whether the differences necessarily reflect etiological causes of addictive behavior, the consequences of long-term drug use, or both. Future work in this area using longitudinal designs has the potential to directly address this issue and, more generally, these studies illustrate that the promise of applying a neuroeconomic approach to addiction research is very high.

2.6   Imaging genetics

A final profitable application of FMRI to addiction research is in the identification and elucidation of novel phenotypes for genetic influences on addiction. As a result of only modest success clarifying the genetic basis for clinical diagnosis as a phenotype, there is increasing interest in mechanistic phenotypes that are putatively more closely connected to specific sources of genetic variation, or what are referred to as interme-diate phenotypes or endophenotypes (Flint and Munafo, 2007; Goldman and Ducci, 2007; Gottesman and Gould, 2003; MacKillop *et al.*, 2010b). In this domain, FMRI is a powerful tool for potentially revealing brain activation patterns that reflect genetic influences as novel phenotypes, but also are highly informative mechanistically as they provide specific regional localization of genetic influences (Green *et al.*, 2008).

Several recent studies illustrate the promise in this area. For example, using the cue reactivity paradigm, polymorphisms in the dopamine D_4 receptor gene (*DRD4*) are associated with elevated neural response in orbitofrontal cortex, anterior cingulate cortex, and striatum (Filbey *et al.*, 2008) whereas polymorphisms in the gene respon-sible for GABA-A receptor's α_2 subunit are associated with elevated response in medial prefrontal cortex (Kareken *et al.*, 2010). Similarly, using a neuroeconomic approach, Boettiger *et al.* (2007) found significant differences in discounting decision making and brain activity in the dorsal PFC and posterior parietal cortex based on the *COMT* val158met polymorphism; the *COMT* gene encodes catechol-O-methyltransferase enzyme, which is partially responsible for the breakdown of dopamine in the synapse. In addition to measured genetic factors, FMRI studies can also investigate oblique genetic risk by examining individuals with a positive family history. For example, response inhibition and decision making have been targeted as important behavioral phenotypes in studies of family-history positive individuals (e.g., Acheson *et al.*, 2009). Although only a small number of studies have been conducted using an imaging genet-ics approach in addiction, the potential is very high.

3   FMRI Methods

Now firmly established as a valuable technique to examine a wide range of brain func-tions, FMRI actually represents an extremely versatile set of approaches with enormous untapped potential. These approaches have been evolving at a rapid pace over the past

20 years, yielding a handful of frequently used experimental design types and analysis approaches. Despite these commonalities, data acquisition parameters, processing pipelines, and reporting styles vary considerably across neuroimaging laboratories. Moreover, there have been only limited efforts to standardize FMRI paradigms and develop norms for brain and behavioral responses. While these methodological deviations can complicate replication and efforts to implement multisite studies, they pose the greatest problem when their significance is not understood. Therefore it is critical that FMRI researchers and consumers of this research consider these factors. This section presents a discussion of the strengths and weaknesses of FMRI, followed by an overview of conventional and less conventional approaches that have recently been used.

3.1   Advantages and disadvantages

Prior to the development of FMRI for human research just 20 years ago (Bandettini *et al.*, 1992; Kwong *et al.*, 1992; Ogowa *et al.*, 1992), electroencephalography (EEG) and radiological techniques, such as positron emission tomography (PET), were the most common functional neuroimaging methods available. While EEG has outstanding temporal resolution, localization of signal source is relatively difficult, especially in subcortical brain regions. Radiological methods rely on the detection of the binding of radioactive contrast agents that are typically administered through intravenous infusion. These techniques offer the spatial and temporal resolution needed to examine neural responses to functional challenges; however, they are limited in design sophistication due to the use of these radioactive tracers and the timeframe during which they are taken up in the tissue. Blood oxygen level dependent (BOLD) FMRI, on the other hand, relies on endogenous contrast created by changes in the ratio of oxygenated to deoxygenated hemoglobin that are induced by the increased neural activity. Although the details of this mechanism remain under investigation, it has been demonstrated that this hemodynamic response is coupled linearly and additively to the underlying function of the adjacent neurons (Dale and Buckner, 1997; Menon *et al.*, 1995; Buxton and Frank, 1997). The functional neuroimaging methods most frequently used today offer some overlap in the information they provide; however, they each offer advantages and disadvantages and also provide unique information. Table 23.1 summarizes key advantages and limitations of common functional neuroimaging techniques.

There are several advantages of BOLD FMRI. These include an excellent balance of spatial resolution, temporal sampling, experimental design flexibility, and the availability of scanner facilities. As typically performed, BOLD FMRI offers the advantages of investigating concurrent relationships between brain responses, behavioral and subjective responses, and structural morphometry as observed on routinely acquired high-resolution T1-weighted images. Moreover, any of the other numerous MRI scan sequences available (e.g., fluid attenuated inversion recovery, arterial spin labeling, diffusion tensor imaging, spectroscopy, angiography) may be used to acquire supplemental data during the FMRI session with only relatively little additional inconvenience to the research participant (i.e., additional time). Specific brain systems are

Table 23.1 Functional neuroimaging techniques

	Typical units of resolution	Relative cost	Advantages	Disadvantages
SPECT	cm	High	Absolute measures, targets specific molecules, out of scanner paradigms possible	Radioactive tracers, invasive, experimental design limitations, cyclotron availability
PET	mm	Higher		
EEG	low	Low	Non-invasive, flexible designs (availability of EEG)	Spatial resolution, especially subcortical structures (availability of MEG)
MEG	mm	Higher		
BOLD FMRI	mm	High	Non-invasive, availability, multi-sequence imaging, flexible designs	Movement and susceptibility artifact, noise, confined space, strong magnetic field and radio waves, hemodynamic lag
NIRS	low	Low	Non-invasive, portable, flexible	Limited to small areas of cortex

Notes: SPECT = single photon emission computed tomography, PET = positron emission tomography, EEG = electroencephalography, MEG = magnetoencephalography, BOLD = blood oxygen dependent, FMRI = functional magnetic resonance imaging, NIRS = near infrared spectroscopy, min = minutes, sec = seconds, ms = milliseconds.

targeted using carefully designed experimental stimulation, yet information about collateral neural systems may also be quantified during the same FMRI paradigm. This provides both specific information about the targeted functional challenge and more holistic assessments of global shifts in brain function. Since FMRI also usually includes acquisition of behavioral data, the observed brain responses are placed in the context of brain-behavioral relationships that serve as an internal validity check and one of the bases for generalizability of results.

BOLD FMRI is non-invasive, repeatable, and less expensive than PET, allowing more design flexibility. While typical FMRI spatial resolution is 3–5 mm^3 for whole-brain studies with typical temporal resolution of 2–4 seconds, spatial resolution <1 mm^3 or temporal resolution below 1 second can be achieved. A good balance of spatial and temporal resolution is chosen based upon the study question, with a trade-off between these two parameters and the extent of brain coverage. Thus, relatively small regions of interest (ROIs) and transient cognitive processes can be reliably observed using FMRI. FMRI designs have been constantly evolving and provide greater flexibility than other functional neuroimaging approaches, especially after the introduction of rapid event-related designs in the late 1990s (e.g., Buckner *et al.*, 1996; Josephs, Turner, and Friston, 1997; Zahran, Aguire, and D'Esposito, 1997). Finally, FMRI has the advantage of the proliferation of MRI systems in medium to large-sized medical settings and commercial facilities. All standard clinical MRI scanners are technically capable of running FMRI sequences; however, an additional contract with the scanner manufacturer is usually necessary to permit the use of this capability, and such facilities may often not be equipped with stimulus presentation and response collection devices needed to run FMRI experiments.

3.2   Experimental design

The relative nature of FMRI effects and a low signal to noise ratio are the two basic characteristics of FMRI that fundamentally drive experimental design. Other critical factors to consider in any FMRI design are the nature of construct to be assessed and the timeframe during which associated brain activity is expected to occur, potential limitations on how the stimuli must be presented, expected effect sizes of contrasts of these conditions, sampling rate (temporal resolution), and the time allotted for the experiment. Design choice has a major impact on length of the experiment and the data analysis strategies that will be employed.

In the first case, it is important to note that FMRI effects are always relative. Unlike functional imaging using radiological tracers and other rare MRI perfusion methods (e.g., arterial spin labeling; Wong, Buxton, Frank, 1998), BOLD FMRI does not provide an absolute measure of the hemodynamic responses associated with brain activity. Changes in oxyhemoglobin to deoxyhemoglobin ratios resulting from underlying neural activity are monitored over time and examined for relationships to the time course of carefully designed stimulus presentations within a given FMRI paradigm. Ultimately, these changes are expressed in terms of change relative to a resting baseline or an active control baseline. Therefore, results of experiments must be interpreted in the context of the baseline used.

A second characteristic of FMRI that fundamentally affects experimental design is a low signal to noise ratio during data acquisition because of high variability in FMRI data. In order to improve reliability, FMRI paradigms must be designed to repeatedly sample the paradigm's contrasts of interest. That is, the experimental condition(s) are compared to an appropriate baseline or control condition in the FMRI paradigm. For example, a blocked design experiment might include six cycles of repeated experimental and control blocks and event-related designs might include 30 trials per condition. A single block or event is insufficient to provide a reliable measure of any condition. The actual number of blocks or trials needed to overcome low signal to noise depends on several factors related to the scanner, optimization of acquisition parameters, and the expected effect sizes in the FMRI paradigm. This may also be determined through published research using the planned FMRI paradigm and pilot studies on the planned MRI scanner. Methods have been developed to estimate the sufficient number of stimulus presentations prior to data acquisition based on these factors (Wager and Nichols, 2003; Kao, Mandal, Lazar, and Stufken, 2009) and using simulation options provided by data analysis software (e.g., Ward, 2000).

FMRI experimental design can be categorized into blocked or event-related designs, or a combination of the two, which is often called a mixed design. Each design has strengths and weaknesses compared to the others; however, the decision about which design to use is ultimately determined by the particular constructs to be assessed and the broader research question. The design type employed must allow both controlled stimulation of the brain systems under study and quantification of neural responses in the timeframe during which the construct of interest manifests as a discernible BOLD signal.

Blocked paradigms are used to present either sustained or repeated stimulation of the same experimental condition. Blocks of an experimental condition are alternated with blocks of other experimental conditions, an active control condition, or rest. Blocked experiments are ideal for brain responses that occur during a 20–40-second timeframe or cognitive or emotional sets that are maintained by repeated stimulation (e.g., Skudlarski, Constable, and Gore, 1999; Bandettini and Cox, 2000; Turner *et al.*, 1998). Block lengths are designed to capture these processes of interest while avoiding subjective threats to internal validity (e.g., boredom) and the confounding effects of psychological processes. Examples include acute craving responses to stimuli (e.g., Schneider *et al.*, 2001; Due, Huettel, Hall and Rubin, 2002), or sustained cognitive sets such as working memory buffering and maintenance (e.g., Kumari *et al.*, 2003; Sweet *et al.*, 2008). Blocked design experiments benefit from increased statistical power because the images acquired during these time courses efficiently sample discrete sets of sustained stimulation that are clearly classified by experimental condition and more easily distinguished from noise (Bandettini and Cox, 2000). This is due in part to the overlapping, linear, and additive nature of the BOLD response to repeated individual events (Dale and Buckner, 1997). Therefore, blocked experiments are often much shorter than event-related experiments. One criticism of blocked design experiments is the likelihood that sustained presentation of any stimulus (including control tasks and resting baselines) might be confounded by within-block variations in brain activity. For example, individual factors, such as daydreaming and task-independent thought, and paradigm-specific factors, such as habituation, fatigue and boredom, might be important sources of uncontrolled within-block variation. Attempts to control this are traditionally addressed by repeated sampling of blocks, counterbalancing of blocks, the use of appropriate block lengths, and mixed designs. While some investigators quantify these within-block dynamics post hoc to rule out confounding influences, others have intentionally examined within-block dynamics (Cohen *et al.*, 1997; Holt *et al.*, 2005; Paskavitz *et al.*, 2010; Sweet *et al.*, 2012).

Event-related experiments are designed to present individual stimuli (events) alternated by variable length (i.e., jittered) interstimulus intervals, which serve as the baseline for contrasts with each condition. Event types correspond to a particular experimental or control condition. In contrast to blocked design experiments, responses to a class of stimulus-events are specifically modeled, and these events may be sorted into conditions based on the participant's performance (e.g., choices). Numerous stimuli are presented for each condition, either randomized or intentionally placed in systematic relationships to other events. Event-related designs are used when the goal is to resolve the brain response of each type of stimulus, or if the experiment requires randomization at the individual stimulus level. Therefore, event-related designs require more complicated design and data analysis strategies than blocked designs. These designs also require more time compared to blocked designs.

Prior to the development of rapid event-related methods, event-related experiments used long interstimulus intervals to accommodate the time course of the BOLD hemodynamic response, which is delayed by 5 seconds, takes 5–10 seconds to peak, and returns to baseline after approximately 20 seconds (Bandettini and Cox, 2000). These experiments were long and exacerbated common threats to internal validity, such as boredom, sleeping, mind-wandering, and head movement. Rapid event-related designs used pseudorandom jitter coupled with complex linear modeling to measure the resulting delayed and overlapping BOLD responses. This was a major advance, as the much shorter interstimulus intervals mitigated these threats and enabled substantially more design versatility, making it feasible to examine a broad new range of cognitive functions not possible with slow event-related or blocked designs.

A key consideration in event-related designs is the time of repetition (TR; the time it takes to acquire one brain volume). Since event presentations are short in duration, greater sampling rates (temporal resolution) facilitate better resolution of hemodynamic response function for a particular event type. Considering the inherent trade-off between temporal and spatial resolution on any MR scanner, investigators using event-related designs must more carefully weigh these factors.

Mixed designs employ both blocked and event-related strategies, such that particular event types distributed within larger blocks may be examined. Therefore, a design challenge is ensuring that there will be enough event types embedded within the blocks to generate reliable effects. Whether the focus is blocks, events, or both, the common goal is to determine the strength of relationships between the temporal courses of the presented stimulus conditions and the associated brain activity. Ultimately, the decision about which design to use is determined by scientific and practical considerations about how to elicit the targeted brain response and the temporal nature of the neural process that has been provoked.

3.3   Quantification of brain response

3.3.1   Data acquisition and quantification of individual effects.   BOLD FMRI employs a T2* contrast that is capable of detecting changes in the electromagnetic properties of oxyhemoglobin and deoxyhemoglobin, and specifically changes in their ratio in cerebral capillaries. Images are acquired in multiple slices in one plane (i.e., axial, sagittal, or coronal) in sufficient numbers and thickness either to sample the whole brain or to encompass ROIs. One complete acquisition of all slices is called a repetition and the duration is called the TR. For example, whole-brain coverage might be accomplished by acquiring 48 3-mm thick axial slices during each 3-second TR. The basic unit of data sampling is the voxel, a three-dimensional pixel. The size of the voxel is determined by the slice-thickness and the in-plane spatial resolution, which varies, but is often between 3 mm^2 and 4 mm^2 in recent FMRI research. Specific scanning parameters depend upon the scanner equipment, experimental design, and decisions about the balance of temporal and spatial resolution.

The resulting datasets from each imaging run are sometimes called 3D + time data, since the three-dimensional brain volumes that were acquired during each TR are arranged in temporal order into one file. Several preprocessing procedures are completed on each individual's 3D + time dataset to improve data quality before analyses are begun. These steps often include slice time corrections to compensate for the between-slice differences in acquisition time, registration of the 3D + time series of brain volumes to compensate for movement, temporal filtering to improve reliability, and 3D spatial blurring to improve reliability and reduce the effects of normal individual variation in anatomy and localization of brain functions.

To determine the individual brain response during the FMRI paradigm, the observed raw BOLD signal over time from each voxel is converted to a standardized metric to allow comparison across groups of participants or across within-group factors. This involves contrasting the individual's observed BOLD signal during an experimental condition with the observed signal during a control task or resting baseline. Specifically, the General Linear Model (GLM) is usually used to determine how closely each voxel's BOLD signal time course (i.e., dependent variable) is synchronized with the time course of the presented experimental conditions (i.e., independent variables) and covariates of the stimulation paradigm. Therefore, voxel-wise GLM analyses assign a value to each voxel for each condition of the FMRI paradigm after controlling other known sources of variance (e.g., observed head movement). Each value corresponds to the variance in that voxel's BOLD signal over time that is associated with each experimental condition versus an appropriate baseline.

Group-level statistical tests may be performed once task-related effects are calculated per voxel for each individual. Although group-level analysis is usually the goal of FMRI research, these values, often called parameter estimates or beta weights, can be assigned a statistical value-based effect size and multiple comparisons correction to determine individual significance thresholds. Therefore individual activation maps may be thresholded individually if the goal is to make inferences at the individual level. Examples of this include clinical applications, such as presurgical mapping, and volumetric analyses, where *volumes* of significant brain response are summarized for group-level analyses. That is, these thresholded maps may be used to quantify the volume of significant activity per person for group-level ROI analyses. Although ROI analyses can be conducted on regional volumetric measures or by summarizing regional parameter estimates without spatial standardization across participants, it is common practice to spatially transform individual activation maps into standard stereotaxic space (e.g., Talairach and Tournoux, 1988; Mazziotta *et al.*, 1995) before group-level analyses. It is also most common to leave the parameter estimates unthresholded for use as the dependent measure in group-level analyses.

3.3.2   Group-level analyses.   The two most common methods used to examine group-level effects are voxel-wise and ROI analyses. These are overlapping techniques that inform each other, and they are frequently employed together in a given data-processing stream. For instance, voxel-wise analysis may be used to empirically define clusters of significant group-level activation to serve as regions in ROI analyses. Conversely, meaningful regional definitions are needed to evaluate the results of voxel-wise analyses.

In group-level voxel-wise analyses, the stereotaxically standardized individual brain maps are examined for group-level effects in each voxel. The unit of analysis is the voxel and the dependent measure for each test is usually the parameter estimate resulting from the GLM for each contrast of interest (e.g., the beta value representing the effect of drug cues versus neutral cues). The statistical test used in these analyses depends upon the purpose of the resulting group summary activation map. If the objective is to identify clusters of significant brain activity associated with a paradigm within a single group, the spatially standardized results of the individual activation maps may be contrasted with a hypothetical mean of zero using a voxel-wise one-sample t-test. This approach assumes the null hypothesis that the experimental and baseline conditions do not differ. If the goal is to examine the effects of group, experimental condition, or their interaction, conventional statistical tests, such as independent samples t-tests, paired samples t-tests, or ANOVAs, may be performed for each brain voxel across groups, conditions, or both.

Each of these voxel-wise approaches results in an intensity value, such as a mean difference, and statistical metric per brain voxel that can be thresholded and corrected for multiple comparisons, and a cluster size threshold is usually applied. Whether individual or group-level summary maps are examined, the term "activation" is used to denote clusters of voxels in which the association of the BOLD signal to the task condition exceeds a significance threshold. Deactivation denotes significant decreases in activity relative to a resting or active control baseline. In between-group or within-group voxel-wise contrasts, clusters of thresholded voxels represent regions of significant group or condition effects. In each of these analyses, clusters of thresholded voxels reveal where the strongest effects have survived after the stringent Type I Error correction needed for voxel-wise analyses has been applied (see the discussion on statistical power in section 3.3.3).

Voxel-wise approaches are ideal for exploratory research, where the objectives are identification of clusters that exhibit the greatest effect of the FMRI paradigm, or the greatest between-group or within-group effects. These methods have been used for localization of brain responses to FMRI paradigms and for the identification of regions in which groups or experimental conditions significantly differ. However, they have important limitations when used in hypothesis testing, since a refutable hypothesis about brain activity requires a precise prediction about spatial location and extent. That is, the voxel is usually not a theoretically meaningful spatial unit when testing hypotheses about a particular brain function. While clusters of significant response that result from voxel-wise analyses may overlap regions of anatomical and functional significance, without pre-defined ROIs it is difficult to posit a refutable a-priori hypothesis. For example, if an ROI is specified a priori, and a resulting cluster of significant activity includes 50% of the voxels in that ROI, it also includes 50% that are not, and compelling arguments might be equally made for and against support of the hypothesis.

In ROI analyses, paradigm-related effects from individual GLM analyses are summarized per ROI in order to test study hypotheses at the group level. ROIs are theoretically meaningful spatial boundaries within which to test hypotheses about groups or within-group effects. Examples of ROIs are anatomical, histological, (e.g., precentral gyrus, Brodmann Area 3), and functionally defined (e.g., Broca's Area, Wernicke's Area) areas, including clusters of significant activity reported in previous literature and regions defined empirically within the same study. For example, ROIs may be identified from group activation maps by selecting a conjunction or disjunction of the significant clusters of activity. Metrics such as the means, medians, and variance of the betas or other descriptive statistics resulting from the individual GLMs may be used. Since these measures involve one metric per ROI per person, ROI analyses allow straightforward hypothesis testing using standard statistical packages and methods, including important covariate analyses (e.g., age, performance level, dependence severity, withdrawal and craving levels).

3.3.3 *Power analysis and error correction strategies.*

Statistical power is a very significant issue for FMRI research, both because there are important considerations for determining the sample size necessary to detect significant effects and, in analyzing datasets comprising thousands upon thousands of observations, statistical power must be carefully considered to balance Type 1 error (α; false positives) and Type 2 errors (β; false negatives). Thus, power considerations play a critical role during both study design and data analysis. In addition, there are several further complicating factors. For example, greater inter-subject variability arises from variation in participant brain characteristics from person to person, and greater intra-subject variability may arise from small amounts of movement, signal drift, or other extraneous factors during the assessment. As noted above, data acquisition and analysis approaches vary across research groups, making comparability across studies challenging. Finally, MRI scans are relatively expensive, often introducing practical constraints on sample sizes. Although it is beyond the scope of this chapter to fully review statistical power, we will provide an overview of the issues involved during both study design and data analysis (for a complete discussion, see Lazar, 2008).

Selecting a sample size that will permit valid hypothesis testing is an essential step in study design. For power analyses, FMRI research is no different to other approaches in the sense that effect size and sample size are typically inversely related. Equally, other standard practices also apply. For example, a first step always is to survey the literature to identify the sample sizes that have previously been reported in studies using the intended paradigm (or a similar one). Summarizing the range of sample sizes that have been able to characterize meaningful changes in neurocognitive activity in previous relevant investigations can clearly inform sample size. For entirely novel paradigms, attempts should be made to identify paradigms that share important characteristics, such as event-related or block designs. In both cases, reviewing other paradigm parameters, such as number of stimuli, duration of runs, and number of TRs, can further identify parameters that have previously been used successfully. Finally, paradigm pilot testing of candidate stimuli can establish the exact or probable number of stimuli that will be generated.

This preceding 'due diligence' is important for leveraging previous work in the field to ascertain estimated effect sizes. In addition, simulation methods can be used to esti- mate statistical power at varying levels of effect size (magnitude of percentage signal change), α level (Type 1 error rate) and inter-subject variability toward identifying the appropriate sample size. Desmond and Glover (2002) provide a very thorough exam- ple of this approach, using simulation data to generate power estimates for different magnitudes of effect size under varying conditions of inter-subject variability and α levels, which were then cross-validated using empirical data. Importantly, however, the power curves generated are applicable to other studies using similar event-related designs. Power estimates based on Desmond and Glover (2002) are provided in Table 23.2 and reveal the highly varying levels of power depending on the effect size and sample size, even with the presumption of fixed inter-subject variability. Taken together, there are no easy 'rules of thumb' to conducting power analyses for FMRI studies as person-, group-, task-, and scanner-level factors have important influences on variability and, as a result, power. However, assiduous consideration of previous studies and simulation data can provide a data-driven basis for sample size selection.

Table 23.2 FMRI power estimates at three levels of two-tailed α (Type 1 error – false positive) and three magnitudes of effect size (BOLD % signal change). These estimates are adapted from Desmond and Glover (2002), with intra-subject variability (σ_W) = 0.75%, inter-subject variability (σ_B) = 0.5%, and 100 events/condition. Dashes reflect unavailable data

	$\alpha = 0.05$			$\alpha = 0.002$			$\alpha = 0.000002$		
Cell N	0.25%	0.50%	0.75%	0.25%	0.50%	0.75%	0.25%	0.50%	0.75%
10	28%	74%	97%	<5%	21%	60%	–	<5%	<5%
15	43%	91%	>99%	6%	54%	92%	–	<5%	11%
20	54%	97%	>99%	14%	76%	99%	–	6%	39%
25	63%	>99%	>99%	18%	91%	>99%	–	18%	68%
30	72%	>99%	>99%	25%	95%	>99%	–	38%	87%
35	80%	>99%	>99%	36%	>99%	>99%	–	52%	96%
40	87%	>99%	>99%	39%	>99%	>99%	–	69%	99%
45	95%	>99%	>99%	47%	>99%	>99%	–	80%	>99%
50	>99%	>99%	>99%	59%	>99%	>99%	–	94%	>99%

At the other end of the spectrum, the second major domain in which statistical power is an important consideration is the use of error correction strategies during data analysis. In this case, the issue is that of multiplicity, or, beyond a study's a-priori analyses, the problem of many simultaneous comparisons that inflates Type I error. The conventional Type I error rate of 0.05 reflects a false positive rate of five for every 100 independent tests and, as FMRI analyses commonly involve tens of thousands of voxels, it is a statistical certainty that false positives will emerge by chance alone. Thus, rather than being a concern about being underpowered to detect a specific effect, this is the problem of an overabundance of power and ostensibly significant effects occurring by chance.

There are several strategies for addressing this issue, all of which seek to identify the most appropriate α level in light of the many tests. The most stringent of these is a Bonferroni correction, which adjusts the overall familywise error rate (FWER; total error rate across voxels) by simply dividing the α level by the number of tests. Using the previous example, if 100 tests were conducted, a Bonferroni-adjusted α level would be 0.0005 (0.05 divided by 100, or an estimated false positive rate of 1 in 10,000). However, the Bonferroni correction is largely accepted as being excessively conservative in FMRI research because it assumes independence, which is not the case. Voxels are arbitrary units that are not mapped onto brain function and brain activity is frequently interrelated across voxels, reflecting the underlying brain activity. Moreover, this physiological reality is further reflected in FMRI data via the Gaussian smoothing of the data during data preprocessing to reflect these relationships. In light of this, it is largely accepted that a Bonferroni correction is inappropriate for FMRI and there are several alternatives that use different strategies to identify more appropriate significance thresholds.

The first method that is commonly used is an adaptation of the Bonferroni FWER correction, termed the false discovery rate (FDR), which is a "step-up" procedure to control the proportion of false positives among the statistically significant tests (i.e., significant voxels that are only significant by chance). First introduced in FMRI research by Genovese, Lazar, and Nichols (2002), an FDR correction applies the methodology of Benjamini and Hochberg (1995) in which p values are ordered in ascending order and the p for a given voxel is based on its position in the order, the total number in the order, and the investigator-determined FDR, denoted as q. This permits an escalating FDR that is less conservative than an FWER Bonferroni correction. Another approach that is commonly used is the use of clustering to reduce the FWER. The statistical basis for this is that false positive voxels putatively occur at random and the probability of multiple false positives randomly occurring adjacent to one another is both of even lower likelihood and quantitatively discernible. In reverse, the rationale is that adjacent active voxels putatively reflect true positive activity. For example, in a three-dimensional space comprising 50,000 voxels, the probability of 20 independent voxels occurring by chance at all is much higher than occurring by chance *and* being located adjacent to one another. Based on this, adjusted FWER can be generated for clusters of a given size, which is considerably more powerful. An early study on clustering by Forman *et al.* (1995) suggested that 10 voxel clusters at $\alpha = 0.05$ and 7–9 voxels at $\alpha = 0.02$–0.03 are appropriate, but programs such as AlphaSim (Ward, 2000) are available to permit dataset-specific cluster thresholding.

As with sample size selection, there is no unambiguously optimal strategy in false positive thresholding in FMRI research. Moreover, it is important to recognize that Type 1 and Type 2 error rates are reciprocally related, meaning that minimizing the number of false positive voxels increases the probability of false negative voxels, and brain regions that may be important in a given neurocognitive process may not be detected. Thus, our recommendation is thoughtful consideration of these different approaches and a balanced analytic strategy that balances Type 1 and Type 2 error rates. Moreover, it is important to return to the earlier point that these methods largely apply to exploratory analyses in FMRI, not a-priori hypothesis testing. If specific ROIs are identified and are putatively independent of each other, it is reasonable to use conventional statistical thresholds to test the hypothesis. If many a-priori tests are conducted, some level of error correction may be appropriate, but, fundamentally, it is important to consider these are approaches for handling large numbers of atheoretical tests that, when aggregated, create a high risk for false positives. Optimally, a data analysis plan should comprise both a-priori and exploratory a-posteriori strategies that maximize the characterization of actual brain activity while minimizing error from false positives and false negatives.

3.4   Innovations

FMRI has remained at the forefront of neuroscience research since its first demonstrations in humans in 1992 (Bandettini *et al.*, 1992; Kwong *et al.*, 1992; Ogowa *et al.*, 1992). Like PET before it, FMRI complemented existing assessment modalities, providing a method for direct and objective observation of brain functions, from basic perception to higher-order cognition. However, BOLD FMRI stood out among the existing functional neuroimaging techniques because it was non-invasive, provided more design versatility, and was capable of greater spatial and temporal resolution. Consequently, FMRI provided greater specificity in terms of processing domains that could be challenged and brain systems that could be examined. These advantages and the increased availability, lower cost, introduction of higher field strength systems, and significant methodological advances have since kept FMRI on the cutting edge. Constantly developing methodological advances and their application in innovative research have gone well beyond the conventional approaches described in previous sections. Many of these novel approaches focus on the identification of altered neural function that is not apparent in behavioral and subjective assessments.

One of these strategies is the a-priori prediction of compensatory overactivation among patients and at-risk groups. Compensatory overactivation refers to greater activity in brain regions associated with a behavioral challenge or recruitment of regions that are not usually associated with the task in order to maintain performance levels. During cognitive FMRI paradigms that provide an objective behavioral measure of performance level, it can be determined if research participants vary their level of processing effort to meet a performance criterion. Therefore, it is critical to evaluate observed overactivation in the context of behavioral performance levels, and also other factors that might result in the need for participants to exert greater effort to maintain performance levels (e.g., withdrawal states or fragmented sleep). Similarly, addiction studies have demonstrated overactivation of limbic and subcortical neurocircuitry in response to cues designed to elicit craving and reward (Schneider *et al.*, 2001; Due, Huettel, Hall, and Rubin, 2002). In the context of corroborating subjective reports of increased craving and reward, these findings are interpreted in a straightforward manner as endogenous markers of increased craving or reward. In this context it is possible that limbic overactivation might be modulated by cortical systems to meet social norms, for example. The degree to which this modulation is present and success-ful may be represented in inhibitory control systems as compensatory overactivation. Several research groups have demonstrated overactivation of expected brain regions, recruitment of unexpected regions, or both, among patients and groups at risk for cognitive and emotional/motivational problems (Bookheimer *et al.*, 2000; Staffen *et al.*, 2002; Sweet *et al.*, 2006; Haley *et al.*, 2008; Johansen-Berg *et al.*, 2002; Cabeza, Andersen, Locantore, and McIntosh, 2002; Due, Huettel, Hall, and Rubin, 2002; Schneider *et al.*, 2001; Breiter *et al.*, 1996). Overall, these findings suggest that additional neural resources may be recruited to maintain task performance or emo-tional/motivational homeostasis, and the degree of this compensatory activity might be used as an objective index of subjective factors such as effort, difficulty, or control of impulses. They also highlight the utility of examining multiple brain systems, despite the use of an FMRI paradigm that is targeted to a particular cognitive or emotional construct.

Other methods have been developed to examine indirect effects on other net-works, in addition to the quantification of effects in brain regions thought to be directly associated with the processing demands of the FMRI paradigm presented. One of these relates to suppression of baseline resting state processing during exter-nally focused demanding tasks, which presents as relative deactivation on brain maps of task-associated effects. The study of deactivation and resting state networks, such as the default network (DN) in particular, has been a recent development in our understanding of effortful processes. The DN is a system of brain regions that is most active when there are no external cognitive demands and least active when external cognitive demands exist. It is distributed bilaterally and is comprised of the posterior cingulate, precuneus, medial frontal gyrus, and regions of the inferior pari-etal lobes and anterior and medial temporal lobes (Buckner, Andrews-Hanna, and Schacter, 2008; Broyd *et al.*, 2010). It has been proposed that the DN is related to one's internal stream of consciousness and that this may serve as an imagery simula-tor for creative thinking (Buckner, Andrews-Hanna, and Schacter, 2008). Consistent positive relationships to several internal thought processes have been observed, such as stimulus-independent thoughts, mind wandering, imagining the future, and self-referential thought (McKiernan *et al.*, 2003; Ramnani and Owen, 2004; Mason *et al.*, 2007). The exact processes mediated by the DN are under investigation. However, relative deactivation of the DN during active cognitive challenges appears to repre-sent a shift in cognitive focus from task-unrelated cognitive processes associated with the DN to the FMRI paradigm, such that the DN processes present at baseline are relatively suppressed or abandoned during the more difficult condition (Hahn *et al.*, 2007; Sweet *et al.*, 2008). For instance, there is converging evidence that attenuation of baseline DN activity during difficult working memory processing may be a more sensitive index of effort than performance accuracy (Sweet *et al.*, 2008; 2010a; 2010b;

Paskavitz, Sweet, and Samuel, 2004). Greater relative abandonment of DN activity in the context of normal behavioral performance has been observed in Multiple Sclerosis patients (Paskavitz, Sweet, and Samuel, 2004), among smokers during nicotine withdrawal (Sweet *et al.*, 2010a), in obstructive sleep apnea patients after withdrawal of positive airway pressure treatment (i.e., fragmented sleep induction; Sweet *et al.*, 2010b), and in healthy participants during increased phonological interference (Sweet *et al.*, 2008). These findings suggest that the degree of suppression of DN processing may be an objective index of effort and focus that may serve as an endophenotypic marker of brain dysfunction, even before behavioral signs manifest.

Over the past decade, functional connectivity has become a widely used method to examine the coherence and disorganization resting state networks, such as the DN (e.g., Greicius, Krasnow, Reiss, and Menon, 2003), and networks associated with active tasks (e.g., Honey *et al.*, 2002; Janes *et al.*, 2010). Resting state functional connectivity is not FMRI in the traditional sense because the goal is not to quantify brain response to an FMRI challenge. In fact, the resting state cognitive functions under investigation are typically neither provoked nor experimentally controlled, and a baseline control period is not used to determine relative increases or decreases in activity. Rather, the change in observed brain activity is quantified relative to the activity of another brain region over time. The goal is to quantify the degree to which brain regions covary over time. This approach has provided strong support for the existence of several coherent resting state networks (Broyd *et al.*, 2009; Buckner, Andrews-Hanna, and Schacter, 2008; Deco and Corbetta, 2011), and evidence that this coherence may vary as a function age and neuropsychiatric status (Li *et al.*, 2000; Garrity *et al.*, 2007; Buckner *et al.* 2005; Kennedy, Redcay, and Courchesne, 2006). Functional connectivity methods have yielded sensitive markers of neuropsychiatric disease risk and severity, and hold great potential for the study of addictions. Several studies have demonstrated changes in functional organization in substance-dependent samples (Ma *et al.*, 2010; Lui *et al.*, 2009; Janes *et al.*, 2010), and one reported weaker functional connectivity between the insula ACC, and DLPFC during a smoking cue paradigm in smokers who lapsed following cessation treatment (Janes *et al.*, 2010).

Another useful approach for addictions research is a variation of the mixed design: that is, to examine within-block changes during sustained cognitive or motivational challenges. As noted above, blocked designs are optimized to utilize repeated and prolonged stimulus presentations in several blocks to improve reliability. However, mixed designs with sufficient statistical power may be employed to examine within-block dynamics. Often considered a potential confound in FMRI designs, when properly powered and modeled, within-block variation in brain response has important implications in addictions research. Such designs allow assessment of key addictions constructs such as distress tolerance (e.g., cognitive persistence), habituation, satiation, effort, and cognitive focus over time. For instance, several behavioral studies have found that distress tolerance can be used to predict quitting rates and relapse following treatment for substance dependence (Brown, Lejuez, Kahler, and Strong, 2002; Brown *et al.*, 2005; Brown *et al.*, 2009). One potential method for examining cognitive distress tolerance (i.e., cognitive persistence), defined as the ability to maintain performance during a difficult sustained challenge, is to quantify changes in brain activity and cognitive performance observed within blocks of the sustained challenge. For example, it has been shown that during blocks of a difficult verbal working memory task, brain response increased as performance decreased over time (Paskavitz *et al.*, 2010). The rate of these changes in brain activity may prove useful as measures of persistence, effort, focus, and onset of fatigue. Another recent application of this method is quantification of reactivity and habituation in studies of emotion, craving, and reward (Holt *et al.*, 2005; Tana, Montin, Cerutti, and Bianchi, 2010; Sweet *et al.*, 2012).

4　Challenges and Future Directions

4.1　Challenges

Despite methodological advantages and its demonstrated utility in addictions research, there are also limitations to BOLD FMRI. BOLD FMRI effects are relative in nature because raw BOLD signals are not directly contrasted between groups, or even between different scans of the same individual. The effects of interests represent interactions of brain activity during the paradigm's experimental condition versus a baseline, across the between-group factors (e.g., smokers versus nonsmokers) or within-group factors (e.g., satiated versus withdrawal). Therefore, activity associated with the paradigm's baseline is not specifically controlled between imaging sessions or across groups. Measurement error is attenuated across sessions by the use of the same relative contrast of experimental condition and baseline; however, baseline differences that might vary as a function of the between-group or within-group factors of interest are not. Unfortunately, without additional and infrequently used scanning techniques such as ASL, it is not possible to determine if groups are truly equated on the baseline.

Due to low effect sizes and low signal-to-noise ratios BOLD FMRI employs repeated sampling to improve statistical power. Brain response to FMRI paradigms may be as high as a 10% signal change relative to baseline during robust paradigms, such as visual stimulation, but the change in BOLD response is typically much smaller and variance is high. Several factors contribute to measurement error, including the scanner, acquisition parameters, susceptibility artifact, and head movement. Engineering support may be needed to optimize the scanner equipment and software, and to identify the parameters that produce the best results for each FMRI paradigm. A major source of noise in BOLD FMRI is distortion in regions of rapid transitions between space, bone, and parenchyma (i.e., susceptibility artifact). It is a particular problem in orbitofrontal regions near the nasal sinuses and inferior temporal regions. It is noteworthy that the brain regions encompassed by this artifact are of particular interest to addictions researchers (e.g., orbitofrontal and ventromedial frontal cortices, ventral striatum). Specialized imaging sequences (e.g., spiral readout) and shimming procedures have been employed to attenuate susceptibility artifact (Glover and Lee, 1995; Du *et al.*, 2007; Constable and Spencer, 1999; Hsu and Glover, 2005). Although these methods improve signal in susceptibility regions, they are technically more complicated, take more time to implement, and can introduce other artifacts (Constable and Spencer, 1999; Delattre *et al.*, 2010; Block and Frahm, 2005; Glover, 2011).

Head movement is another major source of noise in FMRI. It is possible to attenuate this artifact, but impossible to prevent it. Depending upon the spatial resolution of the scan, head movement of only 3 mm may be enough to shift data sampling completely from an original voxel to an adjacent voxel. Movement is particularly problematic if it is correlated with any of the conditions of the FMRI paradigm, such as movement associated with button pressing or changes in respiration. Numerous devices have been used to attenuate movement, including vacuum pillows, bite bars, molded face masks, foam wedges, and straps. Careful participant screening, training, and practice are also essential. Approaches used to attenuate movement artifact during data analyses include frequency filtering, removal of linear drift, removal of the effects of physiological processes (e.g., pulse and respiration), volume registration, and statistically controlling the effects of movement (i.e., observed rotation and displacement) in the individual GLM analyses. There are numerous techniques and several software packages available to implement each of these steps, but how these steps are implemented varies considerably across laboratories, including whether or not to implement some of them at all. For example, statistically controlling movement or physiological processes in the GLM analyses could remove variance of interest if these factors are associated with one of the experimental conditions (Iacovella and Hasson, 2011; Gopinath *et al.*, 2009).

The indirect assessment of neural function using cerebrovascular response might also be considered a limitation of BOLD FMRI. Despite evidence that neural function and the hemodynamic response are linearly coupled, the cerebrovascular response begins approximately 5 seconds after the stimulus is presented (Dale and Buckner, 1997). Despite rapid whole-brain data acquisition and excellent methods available to model overlapping responses, the actual BOLD signal is delayed at different rates across individuals and brain regions (Handwerker, Ollinger, and D'Esposito, 2004). Moreover, the assumption that neural and hemodynamic function is tightly coupled may not be supported in some clinical and aging populations (Huettel, Singerman, and McCarthy, 2001; Rombouts *et al.*, 2005; Ford *et al.*, 2005). With the finding that the BOLD response is altered among older healthy adults (Huettel, Singerman, and McCarthy, 2001; Taoka *et al.*, 1998; D'Esposito, Zarahn, Aguirre, and Rypma, 1999) and FMRI responses are attenuated in cardiovascular disease patients (Haley *et al.*, 2007; Irani *et al.*, 2009), it is crucial to understand how hemodynamic mechanisms change in older adults and patients with compromised cerebrovascular systems.

Physiological effects of drugs and medications pose unique problems for addictions researchers. While it has been reported that some drugs have no significant physiological effects on the BOLD signal (e.g., Jacobsen, 2002; Gollub *et al.*, 1998), this potential confound needs to be investigated across drugs and medications under study, as well as medications used to treat the disorders under investigation. Similarly, the cognitive, emotional, and motivational effects of such psychoactive substances, and withdrawal from them in dependent samples, are potential confounding factors if they are not explicitly controlled in the FMRI paradigm.

FMRI investigators must be particularly sensitive to participant safety and comfort. MR contraindications include some surgical implants, some injuries involving metal, pregnancy (for research purposes), and claustrophobia. Women are typically excluded from research if they test positive for pregnancy and participants endorsing possible injuries involving metal, particularly to the eyes, are usually excluded from research. Also, patients who require oxygen tanks, wheelchairs, and other assistive devices require special provisions for assessment in the scanner. Patients with claustrophobia cannot be administered anxiolytic medication due to confounding effects on the cognitive and emotional processes under investigation. Safety is also a special consideration with cognitively impaired participants (e.g., intoxication, withdrawal, dementia), who may be unable to follow instructions or may forget to disclose important information. Other comfort issues include screening for body morphometry (size and shape), the loud scanner noise produced by the scanner during BOLD sequences, and ability to lie still during the exam, which may last more than an hour. Scanner noise may make verbal responding impossible, and may require more sophisticated responding and stimulus presentation paradigms. Such participant comfort issues have implications beyond comfort per se, as participants who are distracted or cannot lie still during the exam may not yield reliable data.

Other technical issues include stimulus presentation, response collection, generalizability of results, and the expense and expertise required to implement such multidisciplinary research projects. All equipment must be MRI-compatible (safe and functional in a strong magnetic field) and capable of presenting stimuli to participants who are lying with their head in the center of a narrow MRI bore (i.e., an approximately 55-cm diameter, 2-m long tube). Generalizability of findings may be a problem across FMRI laboratories because acquisition equipment and parameters, preprocessing methods, statistical analyses, thresholding of significant effects, and technology differ across sites and studies. Finally, clinical FMRI research requires a sophisticated infrastructure and considerable expertise. It depends upon specialized equipment and highly trained personnel from several different disciplines, such as clinicians, radiologists, engineers, physicists, statisticians, neuroscientists, programmers, computer technologists, and scanner technologists.

4.2   Future directions

Only two decades since endogenous BOLD FMRI contrast was first demonstrated in humans during visual stimulation and motor performance (Bandettini *et al.*, 1992; Kwong *et al.*, 1992; Ogawa *et al.*, 1992), it has become firmly established as the method of choice for a wide variety of functional neuroimaging research questions in cognitive, affective, and clinical neurosciences. FMRI has proven very useful in localization of basic and higher-order neural functions, and in the investigation of altered brain function. The capacity for excellent temporal *and* spatial resolution, research design versatility, and rapidly growing logistical feasibility are key advantages of FMRI. These methodological advantages have facilitated major contributions to many fields of inquiry, including addictions research. FMRI also has great potential to make further contributions specifically to addictions research. It offers new methods to objectively assess constructs that have been traditionally assessed via subjective reports; to evaluate neural mechanisms and models of addiction; and to discover novel markers of risk. FMRI enables direct examination of specific neural systems associated with dependence risk, dependence severity, and relapse risk, and has the advantage of avoiding response bias and other measurement error associated with behavioral assessments. The increased sensitivity and specificity provided by the results of traditional FMRI analyses of targeted challenges, combined with constantly emerging novel neuroimaging methods will continue to yield substantial improvements in our understanding of addiction and its treatment. For instance, since FMRI complements other common approaches in addictions research, it is likely to improve assessment accuracy and consequently improve our ability to predict and evaluate treatment outcomes. Clinical applications of FMRI are likely to become more common in the near future, leading to refinement of individual assessment approaches and the tailoring of treatments. This will require standardization of FMRI paradigms and publication of norms for both behavioral and brain responses. Such clinical utility of FMRI assessments may prove economical in the near future, given constantly emerging advances in technical approaches, lowering of scanner costs, and the proliferation of transdisciplinary expertise.

References

Acheson A, Robinson JL, Glahn DC, Lovallo WR, and Fox PT (2009) Differential activation of the anterior cingulate cortex and caudate nucleus during a gambling simulation in persons with a family history of alcoholism: Studies from the Oklahoma Family Health Patterns Project. *Drug and Alcohol Dependence* 100 (1–2): 17–23.

Anderson BM, Stevens MC, Meda SA, Jordan K, Calhoun VD, and Pearlson GD (2011) Functional imaging of cognitive control during acute alcohol intoxication. *Alcoholism: Clinical and Experimental Research* 35 (1): 156–165.

Bandettini PA, Wong EC, Hinks RS, Tikofsky RS, and Hyde JS (1992) Time course EPI of human brain function during task activation. *Magnetic Resonance in Medicine* 25 (2): 390–397.

Bandettini PA and Cox RW (2000) Event-related FMRI contrast when using constant interstimulus interval: theory and experiment. *Magnetic Resonance in Medicine* 43 (4): 540–548.

Bechara A, Damasio AR, Damasio H, and Anderson SW (1994) Insensitivity to future consequences following damage to human prefrontal cortex. *Cognition* 50: 7–15.

Bechara A, Damasio H, Tranel D, and Damasio AR (1997) Deciding advantageously before knowing the advantageous strategy. *Science* 275: 1293–1295.

Bechara A, Dolan S, and Hindes A (2002) Decision-making and addiction (part II): Myopia for the future or hypersensitivity to reward? *Neuropsychologia* 40: 1690–1705.

Bechara A, Dolan S, Denburg N, Hindes A, Anderson SW, and Nathan PE. (2001) Decision-making deficits, linked to a dysfunctional ventromedial prefrontal cortex, revealed in alcohol and stimulant abusers. *Neuropsychologia* 39: 376–389.

Bechara A, Tranel D, and Damasio H (2000) Characterization of the decision-making deficit of patients with ventromedial prefrontal cortex lesions. *Brain: A Journal of Neurology* 123 (Pt 11): 2189–2202.

Benjamini Y and Hochberg Y (1995) Controlling the false discovery rate: A practical and powerful approach to multiple testing. *Journal of the Royal Statistical Society: Series B (Statistical Methodology)* 57: 289–300.

Bickel WK, Landes RD, Christensen DR, Jackson L, Jones BA, *et al.* (2011) Single- and cross-commodity discounting among cocaine addicts: The commodity and its temporal location determine discounting rate. *Psychopharmacology* (Berlin) 217: 177–187.

Bickel WK, Miller ML, Yi R, Kowal BP, Lindquist DM, and Pitcock JA (2007) Behavioral and neuroeconomics of drug addiction: Competing neural systems and temporal discounting processes. *Drug and Alcohol Dependence* 90 (Suppl. 1): S85–S91.

Bickel WK, Pitcock JA, Yi R, and Angtuaco EJ (2009) Congruence of BOLD response across intertemporal choice conditions: Fictive and real money gains and losses. *Journal of Neuroscience* 29: 8839–8846.

Block KT and Frahm J (2005) Spiral imaging: A critical appraisal. *Journal of Magnetic Resonance Imaging* 21 (6): 657–668.

Boettiger CA, Kelley EA, Mitchell JM, D'Esposito M, and Fields HL (2009) Now or later? An FMRI study of the effects of endogenous opioid blockade on a decision-making network. *Pharmacology Biochemistry and Behavior* 93: 291–299.

Boettiger CA, Mitchell JM, Tavares VC, Robertson M, Joslyn G, *et al.* (2007) Immediate reward bias in humans: Fronto-parietal networks and a role for the catechol-O-methyltransferase 158(Val/Val) genotype. *Journal of Neuroscience* 27 (52): 14383–14391.

Bolla KI, Eldreth DA, London ED, Kiehl KA, Mouratidis M, Contoreggi C, *et al.* (2003) Orbitofrontal cortex dysfunction in abstinent cocaine abusers performing a decision-making task. *NeuroImage* 19 (3): 1085–1094.

Bolla KI, Eldreth DA, Matochik JA, and Cadet JL (2005) Neural substrates of faulty decision-making in abstinent marijuana users. *NeuroImage* 26 (2): 480–492.

Bookheimer SY, Strojwas MH, Cohen MS, Saunders AM, Pericak-Vance MA, *et al.* (2000) Patterns of brain activation in people at risk for Alzheimer's disease. *New England Journal of Medicine* 343: 450–456.

Breiter HC, Gollub RL, Weisskoff RM, Kennedy DN, Makris N, *et al.* (1997) Acute effects of cocaine on human brain activity and emotion. *Neuron* 19 (3): 591–611.

Breiter HC, Rauch SL, Kwong KK, Baker JR, Weisskoff RM, Kennedy DN, Kendrick AD, Davis TL, Jiang A, Cohen MS, Stern CE, Belliveau JW, Baer L, O'Sullivan RL, Savage CR, Jenike MA, and Rosen BR (1996) Functional magnetic resonance imaging of symptom provocation in obsessive-compulsive disorder. *Archives of General Psychiatry* 53 (7): 595–606.

Brown RA, Lejuez CW, Kahler CW, and Strong DR (2002) Distress tolerance and duration of past smoking cessation attempts. *Journal of Abnormal Psychology* 111 (1): 180–185.

Brown RA, Lejuez CW, Kahler CW, Strong DR, and Zvolensky MJ (2005) Distress tolerance and early smoking lapse. *Clinical Psychology Review* 25 (6): 713–733.

Brown RA, Lejuez CW, Strong DR, Kahler CW, Zvolensky MJ, *et al.* (2009) A prospective examination of distress tolerance and early smoking lapse in adult self-quitters. *Nicotine and Tobacco Research* 11 (5): 493–502.

Broyd SJ, Demanuele C, Debener S, Helps SK, James CJ, and Sonuga-Barke EJ (2009) Default-mode brain dysfunction in mental disorders: A systematic review. *Neuroscience and Biobehavioral Reviews* 33 (3): 279–296.

Buckner RL, Andrews-Hanna JR, and Schacter DL (2008) The brain's default network: Anatomy, function, and relevance to disease. *Annals of the New York Academy of Sciences* 1124: 1–38.

Buckner RL, Bandettini PA, O'Craven KM, Savoy RL, Petersen SE, *et al.* (1996) Detection of cortical activation during averaged single trials of a cognitive task using functional magnetic resonance imaging. *Proceedings of the National Academy of Sciences USA* 93 (25): 14878–14883.

Buckner RL, Snyder AZ, Shannon BJ, LaRossa G, Sachs R, *et al.* (2005) Molecular, structural, and functional characterization of Alzheimer's disease: Evidence for a relationship between default activity, amyloid, and memory. *Journal of Neuroscience* 25: 7709–7717.

Buxton RB and Frank LR (1997) A model for the coupling between cerebral blood flow and oxygen metabolism during neural stimulation. *Journal of Cerebral Blood Flow and Metabolism* 17 (1): 64–72.

Cabeza R, Anderson ND, Locantore JK, and McIntosh AR (2002) Aging gracefully: Compensatory brain activity in high-performing older adults. *NeuroImage* 17 (3): 1394–1402.

Carter RM, Meyer JR, and Huettel SA (2010) Functional neuroimaging of intertemporal choice models: A review. *Journal of Neuroscience, Psychology, and Economics* 3: 27–45.

Chase HW, Eickhoff SB, Laird AR, and Hogarth L (2011) The neural basis of drug stimulus and craving: An Activation Likelihood Estimation meta-analysis. *Biological Psychiatry* 70 (8): 785–793.

Christakou A, Brammer M, and Rubia K (2011) Maturation of limbic corticostriatal activation and connectivity associated with developmental changes in temporal discounting. *NeuroImage* 54: 1344–1354.

Claus ED, Kiehl KA, and Hutchison KE (2011) Neural and behavioral mechanisms of impulsive choice in alcohol use disorder. *Alcoholism: Clinical and Experimental Reseach* 35: 1209–1219.

Cohen, JD, Perlstein , WM, Braver TS, *et al.* (1997) Temporal dynamics of brain activation during a working memory task. *Nature* 386: 604–607.

Constable RT and Spencer DD (1999) Composite image formation in z-shimmed functional MR imaging. *Magnetic Resonance in Medicine* 42 (1): 110–117.

Dale AM and Buckner RL (1997) Selective averaging of rapidly presented individual trials using FMRI. *Human Brain Mapping* 5: 329–340.

Deco G and Corbetta M (2011) The dynamical balance of the brain at rest. *Neuroscientist* 17 (1): 107–23.

Delattre BM, Heidemann RM, Crowe LA, Vallée JP, and Hyacinthe JN (2010) Spiral demystified. *Magnetic Resonance Imaging* 28 (6): 862–881.

Desmond JE and Glover GH (2002) Estimating sample size in functional MRI (FMRI) neuroimaging studies: Statistical power analyses. *Journal of Neuroscience Methods* 118: 115–128.

D'Esposito M, Zarahn E, Aguirre GK, and Rypma B (1999) The effect of normal aging on the coupling of neural activity to the bold hemodynamic response. *NeuroImage* 10(1): 6–14.

Dolan SL, Bechara A, and Nathan PE (2008) Executive dysfunction as a risk marker for substance abuse: The role of impulsive personality traits. *Behavioral Sciences and the Law* 26: 799–822.

Du YP, Dalwani M, Wylie K, Claus E, and Tregellas JR (2007) Reducing susceptibility artifacts in fMRI using volume-selective z-shim compensation. *Magnetic Resonance in Medicine* 57 (2): 396–404.

Due DL, Huettel SA, Hall WG, and Rubin DC (2002) Activation in mesolimbic and visuospatial neural circuits elicited by smoking cues: Evidence from functional magnetic resonance imaging. *American Journal of Psychiatry* 159 (6): 954–960.

Filbey FM, Ray L, Smolen A, Claus ED, Audette A, and Hutchinson KE (2008) Differential neural response to alcohol priming and alcohol taste cues is associated with DRD4 VNTR and OPRM1 genotypes. *Alcoholism: Clinical and Experimental Research* 32 (7): 1113–1123.

Fillmore MT (2003) Drug abuse as a problem of impaired control: Current approaches and findings. *Behavioral and Cognitive Neuroscience Reviews* 2: 1–19.

Flint J and Munafo MR (2007) The endophenotype concept in psychiatric genetics. *Psychological Medicine* 37: 163–180.

Ford JM, Johnson MB, Whitfield SL, Faustman WO, and Mathalon DH (2005) Delayed hemodynamic responses in schizophrenia. *NeuroImage* 26 (3): 922–931.

Forman SD, Cohen JD, Fitzgerald M, Eddy WF, Mintun MA, and Noll DC (1995) Improved assessment of significant activation in functional magnetic resonance imaging (FMRI): Use of a cluster-size threshold. *Magnetic Resonance in Medicine* 33: 636–647.

Forman SD, Dougherty GG, Casey BJ, Siegle GJ, Braver TS, *et al.* (2004) Opiate addicts lack error-dependent activation of rostral anterior cingulate. *Biological Psychiatry* 55 (5): 531–537.

Fu LP, Bi GH, Zou ZT, Wang Y, Ye EM, *et al.* (2008) Impaired response inhibition function in abstinent heroin dependents: An fMRI study. *Neuroscience Letters* 438 (3): 322–326.

Garavan H, Kaufman JN, and Hester R (2008) Acute effects of cocaine on the neurobiology of cognitive control. *Philosophical Transactions of the Royal Society B: Biological Sciences*, 363: 3267–3276.

Garrity AG, Pearlson GD, McKiernan K, Lloyd D, Kiehl KA, and Calhoun VD (2007) Aberrant "default mode" functional connectivity in schizophrenia. *American Journal of Psychiatry* 164, 450–457.

Genovese CR, Lazar NA, and Nichols T (2002) Thresholding of statistical maps in functional neuroimaging using the false discovery rate. *NeuroImage* 15: 870–878.

Glimcher PW and Rustichini A (2004) Neuroeconomics: The consilience of brain and decision. *Science* 306: 447–452.

Glover GH (2011) Spiral imaging in fMRI. *NeuroImage* [Epub ahead of print].

Glover GH and Lee AT (1995) Motion artifacts in FMRI: Comparison of 2DFT with PR and spiral scan methods. *Magnetic Resonance in Medicine* 33: 624–635.

Goldman D and Ducci F (2007) Deconstruction of vulnerability to complex diseases: Enhanced effect sizes and power of intermediate phenotypes. *Scientific World Journal* 7: 124–130.

Gollub RL, Breiter HC, Kantor H, Kennedy D, Gastfriend D, *et al.* (1998) Cocaine decreases cortical cerebral blood flow but does not obscure regional activation in functional magnetic resonance imaging in human subjects. *Journal of Cerebral Blood Flow and Metabolism* 18 (7): 724–734.

Gopinath K, Crosson B, McGregor K, Peck K, Chang YL, *et al.* (2009) Selective detrending method for reducing task-correlated motion artifact during speech in event-related FMRI. *Human Brain Mapping* 30 (4): 1105–1119.

Gottesman, II and Gould TD (2003) The endophenotype concept in psychiatry: Etymology and strategic intentions. *American Journal of Psychiatry* 160: 636–645.

Green AE, Munafo MR, Deyoung CG, Fossella JA, Fan J, and Gray JR (2008) Using genetic data in cognitive neuroscience: From growing pains to genuine insights. *Nature Reviews Neuroscience* 9: 710–720.

Greicius MD and Menon V (2004) Default-mode activity during a passive sensory task: Uncoupled from deactivation but impacting activation. *Journal of Cognitive Neuroscience* 16: 1484–1492.

Greicius MD, Krasnow B, Reiss AL, and Menon V (2003) Functional connectivity in the resting brain: A network analysis of the default mode hypothesis. *Proceedings of the National Academy of Sciences USA* 100 (1): 253–258.

Grusser SM, Wrase J, Klein S, Hermann D, Smoka MN, *et al.* (2004) Cue-induced activation of the striatum and medial prefrontal cortex is associated with subsequent relapse in abstinent alcoholics. *Psychopharmacology* 175 (3): 296–302.

Hahn B, Ross TJ, Yang YH, Kim I, Huestis MA, and Stein EA (2007) Nicotine enhances visuospatial attention by deactivating areas of the resting brain default network. *Journal of Neuroscience* 27: 3477–3489.

Haley AP, Gunstad J, Cohen RA, Jerskey BA, Mulligan R, and Sweet LH (2008) Neural correlates of visuospatial working memory in healthy young adults at risk for hypertension. *Brain Imaging and Behavior* 2: 192–199.

Haley AP, Sweet LH, Gunstad J, Forman DE, Poppas A, *et al.* (2007) Verbal working memory and atherosclerosis in patients with cardiovascular disease: An fMRI study. *Journal of Neuroimaging* 17 (3): 227–233.

Handwerker DA, Ollinger JM, and D'Esposito M. (2004) Variation of BOLD hemodynamic responses across subjects and brain regions and their effects on statistical analyses. *NeuroImage* 21 (4): 1639–1651.

Hermann D, Smolka MN, Wrase J, Klein S, Nikitopoulos J, *et al.* (2006) Blockade of cue-induced brain activation of abstinent alcoholics by a single administration of amisulpride as measured with fMRI. *Alcoholism: Clinical and Experimental Research* 30 (8): 1349–1354.

Hester R and Garavan H (2004) Executive dysfunction in cocaine addiction: Evidence for discordant frontal, cingulate, and cerebellar activity. *Journal of Neuroscience* 24 (49): 11017–11022.

Hester R, Nestor L, and Garavan H (2009) Impaired error awareness and anterior cingulate cortex hypoactivity in chronic cannabis users. *Neuropsychopharmacology* 34 (11): 2450–2458.

Hoffman WF, Schwartz DL, Huckans MS, McFarland BH, Meiri G, *et al.* (2008) Cortical activation during delay discounting in abstinent methamphetamine dependent individuals. *Psychopharmacology* (Berlin) 201: 183–193.

Holt DJ, Weiss AP, Rauch SL, Wright CI, Zalesak M, *et al.* (2005) Sustained activation of the hippocampus in response to fearful faces in schizophrenia. *Biological Psychiatry* 57 (9): 1011–1019.

Honey GD, Fu CH, Kim J, Brammer MJ, Croudace TJ, *et al.* (2002) Effects of verbal working memory load on corticocortical connectivity modeled by path analysis of functional magnetic resonance imaging data. *NeuroImage* 17 (2): 573–582.

Hsu JJ and Glover GH (2005) Mitigation of susceptibility-induced signal loss in neuroimaging using localized shim coils. *Magnetic Resonance in Medicine* 53 (2): 243–248. Erratum in: *Magnetic Resonance in Medicine* (2005) 53 (4): 992.

Huettel SA, Singerman JD, and McCarthy G (2001) The effects of aging upon the hemodynamic response measured by functional MRI. *NeuroImage* 13 (1): 161–175.

Iacovella V and Hasson U. (2011) The relationship between BOLD signal and autonomic nervous system functions: Implications for processing of "physiological noise." *Magnetic Resonance Imaging* 29 (10): 1338–1345.

Irani F, Sweet LH, Haley AP, Gunstad JJ, Jerskey BA, *et al.* (2009) An fMRI study of verbal working memory, cardiac output and ejection fraction in elderly patients with cardiovascular disease. *Brain Imaging and Behavior* 3 (4): 350–357.

Jacobsen LK, Gore JC, Skudlarski P, Lacadie CM, Jatlow P, and Krystal JH (2002) Impact of intravenous nicotine on BOLD signal response to photic stimulation. *Magnetic Resonance Imaging* 20(2): 141–145.

Janes AC, Pizzagalli DA, Richardt S, deB Frederick B, Chuzi S, *et al.* (2010) Brain reactivity to smoking cues prior to smoking cessation predicts ability to maintain tobacco abstinence. *Biological Psychiatry* 67 (8): 722–729.

Johansen-Berg H, Rushworth MF, Bogdanovic MD, Kischka U, Wimalaratna S, and Matthews PM (2002) The role of ipsilateral premotor cortex in hand movement after stroke. *Proceedings of the National Academy of Sciences USA* 99 (22): 14518–14523.

Josephs O, Turner R, and Friston K (1997) Event-related FMRI. *Human Brain Mapping* 5: 243–248.

Kable JW and Glimcher PW (2007) The neural correlates of subjective value during intertemporal choice. *Nature Neuroscience* 10: 1625–1633.

Kao MH, Mandal A, Lazar N, and Stufken J (2009) Multi-objective optimal experimental designs for event-related fMRI studies. *NeuroImage* 44: 849–856.

Kareken DA, Liang T, Wetherill L, Dzemidzic M, Bragulat V, *et al.* (2010) A polymorphism in GABRA2 is associated with the medial frontal response to alcohol cues in an fMRI study. *Alcoholism: Clinical and Experimental Research* 34 (12): 2169–2178.

Kaufman JN, Ross TJ, Stein EA, and Garavan H (2003) Cingulate hypoactivity in cocaine users during a GO-NOGO task as revealed by event0related functional magnetic resonance imaging. *Journal of Neuroscience* 23 (21): 7839–7843.

Kennedy DP, Redcay E, and Courchesne E (2006) Failing to deactivate: Resting functional abnormalities in autism. *Proceedings of the National Academy of Sciences USA* 103: 8275–8280.

Kozink RV, Kollins SH, and McClernon FJ (2010) Smoking withdrawal modulates right inferior frontal cortex but not presupplementary motor area activation during inhibitor control. *Neuropsychopharmacology* 35: 2600–2606.

Kuhn S and Gallinat J (2011) Common biology of craving across legal and illegal drugs: A quantitative meta-analysis of cue-reactivity brain response. *European Journal of Neuroscience* 33 (7): 1318–1326.

Kumari V, Gray JA, Ffytche DH, Mitterschiffthaler MT, Das M, *et al.* (2003) Cognitive effects of nicotine in humans: An FMRI study. *NeuroImage* 19 (3): 1002–1013.

Kwong KK, Belliveau JW, Chesler DA, Goldberg IE, Weisskoff RM, *et al.* (1992) Dynamic magnetic resonance imaging of human brain activity during primary sensory stimulation. *Proceedings of the National Academy of Sciences USA* 89 (12): 5675–5679.

Laird AR, Fox PM, Price CJ, Glahn DC, Uecker AM, *et al.* (2005) ALE meta-analysis: Controlling the false discovery rate and performing statistical contrasts. *Human Brain Mapping* 25 (1): 155–164.

Lazar NA (2008) *The Statistical Analysis of Functional MRI Data*. New York: Springer.

Li CSR, Luo X, Yan P, Bergquist K, and Sinha R (2009) Altered impulse control in alcohol dependence: Neural measures of stop signal performance. *Alcoholism: Clinical and Experimental Research* 33: 740–750.

Li SJ, Biswal B, Li Z, Risinger R, Rainey C, *et al.* (2000) Cocaine administration decreases functional connectivity in human primary visual and motor cortex as detected by functional MRI. *Magnetic Resonance in Medicine* 43 (1): 45–51.

Liu J, Liang J, Qin W, Tian J, Yuan K, *et al.* (2009) Dysfunctional connectivity patterns in chronic heroin users: An fMRI study. *Neuroscience Letters* 460(1): 72–77.

Loewenstein G, Rick S, and Cohen JD (2008) Neuroeconomics. *Annual Review of Psychology* 59: 647–672.

Ma N, Liu Y, Li N, Wang CX, Zhang H, *et al.* (2010) Addiction related alteration in resting-state brain connectivity. *NeuroImage* 49 (1): 738–744.

MacKillop J. (2006) Factor structure of the alcohol urge questionnaire under neutral conditions and during a cue-elicited urge state. *Alcoholism: Clinical and Experimental Research* 30: 1315–1321.

MacKillop J and Monti PM (2007) Advances in the scientific study of craving for alcohol and tobacco: From scientific study to clinical practice. In PM Miller and DJ Kavanagh (eds), *Translation of Addictions Sciences into Practice*. Amsterdam: Elsevier.

MacKillop J, Amlung MT, Wier L, David SP, Ray LA, Bickel WK, and Sweet LH (in press) The neuroeconomics of nicotine dependence: A preliminary study of delay discounting of monetary and cigarette rewards in smokers using FMRI. *Psychiatry Research: Neuroimaging.*

MacKillop J, Obasi E, Amlung MT, McGeary JE, and Knopik VS (2010b) The role of genetics in nicotine dependence: Mapping the pathways from genome to syndrome. *Current Cardiovascular Risk Reports* 4: 446–453.

MacKillop J, O'Hagen S, Lisman SA, Murphy JG, Ray LA, *et al.* (2010a) Behavioral economic analysis of cue-elicited craving for alcohol. *Addiction* 105: 1599–1607.

Mason MF, Norton MI, Van Horn JD, Wegner DM, Grafton ST, and Macrae CN (2007) Wandering minds: The default network and stimulus-independent thought. *Science* 315 (5810): 393–395.

Mazziotta JC, Toga AW, Evans A, Fox P and Lancaster J (1995) A probabilistic atlas of the human brain: Theory and rationale for its development. *NeuroImage* 2: 89–101.

McClure SM, Laibson DI, Loewenstein G, and Cohen JD (2004) Separate neural systems value immediate and delayed monetary rewards. *Science* 306: 503–507.

McKiernan KA, Kaufman JN, Kucera-Thompson J, and Binder JR (2003) A parametric manipulation of factors affecting task-induced deactivation in functional neuroimaging. *Journal of Cognitive Neuroscience* 15: 394–408.

Meade CS, Lowen SB, MacLean RR, Key MD, and Lukas SE (2011) FMRI brain activation during a delay discounting task in HIV-positive adults with and without cocaine dependence. *Psychiatry Research* 192: 167–175.

Menon RS, Ogawa S, Hu X, Strupp JP, Anderson P and Ugurbil K (1995) BOLD based functional MRI at 4 Tesla includes capillary bed contribution: Echo-planar imaging correlates with previous optical imaging using intrinsic signals. *Magnetic Resonance in Medicine* 33 (3): 453–459.

Miranda R, Jr., MacKillop J, Meyerson LA, Justus A, and Lovallo WR (2009) Influence of antisocial and psychopathic traits on decision-making biases in alcoholics. *Alcoholism: Clinical and Experimental Research* 33: 817–825.

Monterosso J and Luo S (2010) An argument against dual valuation system competition: Cognitive capacities supporting future orientation mediate rather than compete with visceral motivations. *Journal of Neuroscience, Psychology and Economics* 3: 1–14.

Monterosso JR, Ainslie G, Xu J, Cordova X, Domier CP, and London ED (2007) Frontoparietal cortical activity of methamphetamine-dependent and comparison subjects performing a delay discounting task. *Human Brain Mapping* 28: 383–393.

Monti PM, Binkoff JA, Abrams DB, Zwick WR, Nirenberg TD, and Liepman, MR (1987) Reactivity of alcoholics and nonalcoholics to drinking cues. *Journal of Abnormal Psychology* 96 (2): 122–126.

Myrick H, Anton RF, Li X, Henderson S, Randall PK, and Voronin K (2008) Effect of naltrexone and ondansetron on alcohol cue-induced activation of the ventral striatum in alcohol-dependent people. *Archives of General Psychiatry* 65 (4): 466–475.

Myrick H, Li X, Randall PK, Henderson S, Voronin K, and Anton RF (2010) The effect of aripiprazole on cue-induced brain activation and drinking parameters in alcoholics. *Journal of Clinical Psychopharmacology* 30: 365–372.

Naqvi NH and Bechara A. (2009) The hidden island of addiction: The insula. *Trends in Neurosciences* 32 (1): 56–67.

Nestor L, McCabe E, Jones J, Clancy L, and Garavan H (2011) Differences in "bottom-up" and "top-down" neural activity in current and former cigarette smokers: Evidence for neural substrates which may promote nicotine abstinence through increased cognitive control. *NeuroImage* 56 (4): 2258–2275.

Norman AL, Pulido C, Squeglia LM, Spadoni AD, Paulus MP, and Tapert SF (2011) Neural activation during inhibition predicts initiation of substance use in adolescence. *Drug and Alcohol Dependence* 119 (3): 216–223.

Ogawa S, Tank DW, Menon R, Ellermann JM, Kim SG, *et al.* (1992) Intrinsic signal changes accompanying sensory stimulation: Functional brain mapping with magnetic resonance imaging. *Proceedings of the National Academy of Sciences USA* 89 (13): 5951–5955.

Paskavitz J, Sweet LH, Wellen J, Helmer K, and Cohen R (2010) Recruitment and stabilization of brain activation within a working memory task: an FMRI study. *Brain Imaging and Behavior* 4 (1): 5–21.

Paskavitz J, Sweet LH, and Samuel J (2008) Deactivations during working memory distinguishes multiple sclerosis patients from controls. *NeuroImage* 41 (S1), S5.

Ramnani N and Owen AM (2004) Anterior prefrontal cortex: Insights into function from anatomy and neuroimaging. *Nature Reviews Neuroscience* 5 (3): 184–194.

Robinson TE and Berridge KC (2001) Incentive-sensitization and addiction. *Addiction* 96 (1): 103–114.

Rohsenow DJ, Monti PM, Abrams DB, Rubonis AV, Niaura RS, *et al.* (1992) Cue elicited urge to drink and salivation in alcoholics: Relationship to individual differences. *Advances in Behavior Research and Therapy* 14: 195–210.

Rombouts SA, Goekoop R, Stam CJ, Barkhof F, and Scheltens P (2005) Delayed rather than decreased BOLD response as a marker for early Alzheimer's disease. *NeuroImage* 26 (4): 1078–1085.

Sayette MA, Martin CS, Wertz JM, Shiffman S, and Perrott MA (2001) A multi-dimensional analysis of cue-elicited craving in heavy smokers and tobacco chippers. *Addiction* 96: 1419–1432.

Sayette MA, Schooler JW, and Reichle ED (2010) Out for a smoke: The impact of cigarette craving on zoning out during reading. *Psychological Science* 21: 26–30.

Schneider F, Habel U, Wagner M, Franke P, Salloum JB, *et al.* (2001) Subcortical correlates of craving in recently abstinent alcoholic patients. *American Journal of Psychiatry* 158 (7): 1075–1083.

Simmonds DJ, Pekar JJ, and Mostofsky SH (2008) Meta-analysis of Go/No-go tasks demonstrating that fMRI activation associated with response inhibition is task-dependent. *Neuropsychologia* 46 (1): 224–232.

Skudlarski P, Constable RT, and Gore JC (1999) ROC analysis of statistical methods used in functional MRI: Individual subjects. *NeuroImage* 9 (3): 311–329.

Staffen W, Mair A, Zauner H, Unterrainer J, Niederhofer H, *et al.* (2002) Cognitive function and FMRI in patients with multiple sclerosis: Evidence for compensatory cortical activation during an attention task. *Brain* 125 (6): 1275–1282.

Sweet LH, Hassenstab JJ, McCaffery JM, Raynor HA, Bond DS, Demos KE, Haley AP, Cohen RA, Del Parigi A, and Wing RR (2012) Brain response to food stimulation in obese, normal weight, and successful weight loss maintainers. *Obesity* (Silver Spring). May 9. doi: 10.1038/oby.2012.125 [Epub ahead of print].

Sweet LH, Jerskey BA, and Aloia MS (2010a) Withdrawal of positive airway pressure treatment and default network response to a verbal working memory challenge in obstructive sleep apnea. *Brain Imaging and Behavior* 4 (2): 155–163.

Sweet LH, Mulligan RC, Finnerty C, Jerskey BA, Cohen R, and Niaura R (2010b) Effects of nicotine withdrawal on verbal working memory. *Psychiatry Research: Neuroimaging* 183 (1): 69–74.

Sweet LH, Paskavitz JF, Haley AP, Gunstad JJ, Mulligan RC, *et al.* (2008) Imaging phonological similarity effects on verbal working memory. *Neuropsychologia* 46 (4): 1114–1123.

Sweet L, Rao S, Primeau P, Durgerian S, and Cohen R (2006) FMRI response to increased verbal working memory demands among patients with multiple sclerosis. *Human Brain Mapping* 27 (1): 28–36.

Talairach J and Tournoux P (1988) *Co-planar Stereotaxic Atlas of the Human Brain: 3-Dimensional Proportional System – an Approach to Cerebral Imaging.* New York: Thieme Medical Publishers

Tana MG, Montin E, Cerutti S, and Bianchi AM (2010) Exploring cortical attentional system by using fMRI during a Continuous Performance Test. *Computational Intelligence and Neuroscience* 2010: ID 329213.

Tanabe J, Thompson L, Claus E, Dalwani M, Hutchinson K, and Banich MT (2007) Prefrontal cortext activity is reduced in gambling and nongambling substance users during decision-making. *Human Brain Mapping* 28: 1276–1286.

Taoka T, Iwasaki S, Uchida H, Fukusumi A, and Nakagawa H (1998) Age correlation of the time lag in signal change on EPI-FMRI. *Journal of Computer Assisted Tomography* 22 (4): 514–517.

Turner R, Howseman A, Rees GE, Josephs O, and Friston K (1998) Functional magnetic resonance imaging of the human brain: Data acquisition and analysis. *Experimental Brain Research* 123 (1–2): 5–12.

van der Plas EA, Crone EA, van den Wildenberg WP, Tranel D, and Bechara A (2009) Executive control deficits in substance-dependent individuals: A comparison of alcohol, cocaine, and methamphetamine and of men and women. *Journal of Clinical and Experimental Neuropsychology* 31: 706–719.

Vollstädt-Klein S, Loeber S, Kirsch M, Bach P, Richter A *et al.* (2011) Effects of cue-exposure treatment on neural cue reactivity in alcohol dependence: A randomized trial. *Biological Psychiatry* 69 (11): 1060–1066.

Wager TD and Nichols TE (2003) Optimization of experimental design in fMRI: A general framework using a genetic algorithm. *NeuroImage* 18 (2): 293–309.

Ward BD (2000) Simultaneous inference for FMRI data. Analysis of Functional Images (AFNI) Documentation, http://afni.nimh.nih.gov/pub/dist/doc/program_help/AlphaSim.html.

Wertz JM and Sayette MA (2001) Effects of smoking opportunity on attentional bias in smokers. *Psychology of Addictive Behaviors* 15: 268–271.

Wesley MJ, Hanlon CA, and Porrino LJ (2011) Poor decision-making by chronic marijuana users is associated with decreased functional responsiveness to negative consequences. *Psychiatry Research* 191 (1): 51–59.

Wilson SJ, Sayette MA, and Fiez JA (2004) Prefrontal responses to drug cues: A neurocognitive analysis. *Nature Neuroscience* 7 (3), 211–214.

Wong EC, Buxton RB, and Frank LR (1998) A theoretical and experimental comparison of continuous and pulsed arterial spin labeling techniques for quantitative perfusion imaging. *Magnetic Resonance in Medicine* 40(3): 348–355.

Xiao L, Bechara A, Cen S, Grenard JL, Stacy AW, *et al.* (2008) Affective decision-making deficits, linked to a dysfunctional ventromedial prefrontal cortex, revealed in 10th-grade Chinese adolescent smokers. *Nicotine and Tobacco Research* 10: 1085–1097.

Yalachkov Y, Kaiser J, and Naumer MJ (2010) Sensory and motor aspects of addiction. *Behavioural Brain Research* 207 (2): 215–222.

Yan P and Li CSR (2009) Decreased amygdala activation during risk taking in non-dependent habitual alcohol users: A preliminary fMRI study of the stop signal task. *American Journal of Drug and Alcohol Abuse* 35 (5): 284–289.

Zahran E, Aguire G, and D'Esposito M (1997) A trial-based experimental design for FMRI. *NeuroImage* 6: 122–138.

24

The Role of Positron Emission Imaging (PET) in Understanding Addiction

Dean F. Wong, James Robert Brašić,
Emily Gean, and Ayon Nandi

1 Introduction

Since the early 1980s, it has been possible to image dopamine in the living human brain (Wagner, 1986), normal aging (Wong, 2008), neuropsychiatric conditions (Wong *et al.*, 1986), and opiate receptors (Sadzot, Mayberg, and Frost, 1990). A fundamental component of understanding the pathology of drug addiction is the neurochemistry of the brain in normal and addicted states. Historically, human neurochemical investigation was limited to postmortem analysis, but, with positron emission tomography (PET) and single photon emission computed tomography (SPECT) radiolabeled drugs, it is now possible to study many sites where drugs of addiction first begin to act.

PET is an imaging tool (see Figure 24.1) that uses radioactive ligands to track targeted biological events in living humans. Radioactive neurotransmitter agonists are often used to estimate the amount of endogenous neuroreceptor binding. In addiction research, the most widely examined neuroreceptors are the dopamine D2 receptors of the striatum. The striatal dopaminergic system underlies rewards, from drugs and alcohol (Volkow *et al.*, 2007a), to video games (Koepp *et al.*, 1998), food (Volkow *et al.*, 2008a), and sex (Melis and Argiolas, 1995). Specifically, rewards (e.g., food, drugs, and sex) increase intrasynaptic dopamine in the ventral striatum.

In drug addiction, however, the dopamine release in the ventral striatum in response to rewards is attenuated, as are reported feelings of euphoria. This blunted dopamine release is accompanied by an increased dopamine release in the dorsal striatum in response to cues associated with the substance, such as drug paraphernalia. Activity in frontal brain regions – namely, the orbitofrontal cortex, which is involved in salience attribution, the anterior cingulate gyrus, which is involved in inhibitory control, and the dorsolateral prefrontal cortex, which is involved

The Wiley-Blackwell Handbook of Addiction Psychopharmacology, First Edition. Edited by James MacKillop and Harriet de Wit.
© 2013 John Wiley & Sons, Ltd. Published 2013 by John Wiley & Sons, Ltd.

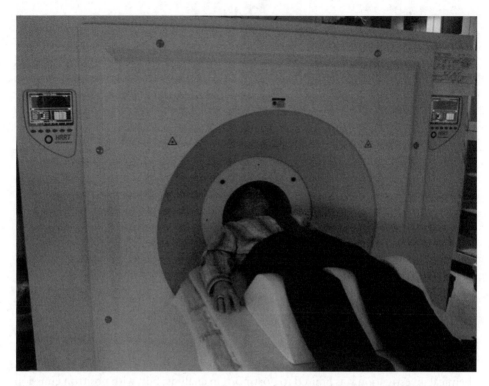

Figure 24.1   This high resolution research tomography (HRRT) (Siemens Medical Solutions USA, Inc., Malvern, PA) scanner obtains positron emission tomography (PET) images of the brain with a resolution approaching 2 mm (Sossi *et al.*, 2005). (Photo provided courtesy of Jeffrey Galecki, Division of Nuclear Medicine, The Russell H. Morgan Department of Radiology and Radiological Science, The Johns Hopkins University School of Medicine, Baltimore, Maryland). Refer to Plate 6 for the colored version of this figure

in decision making – also decreases in addicts. Thus, addicts have a heightened expectation, or craving, for drugs, but experience blunted pleasurable effects of the drug itself, contributing to the development of a strong motivation to seek out drugs, and a lack of interest in any other previously reinforcing activities (Volkow and Fowler, 2000).

PET imaging of the dopaminergic system has been crucial in uncovering these findings in that it allows the *in vivo* measurement of activity of targeted receptors in humans. Functional magnetic resonance imaging (fMRI), a popular imaging tool in psychological research, does not allow for this specificity. Ultimately, addiction research using PET can help inform treatment. The existing findings suggest that addiction treatment goals may include decreasing the reward value of drugs and increasing the reward value of healthful rewards, weakening conditioned drug behaviors, and strengthening frontal inhibitory and executive control (Volkow *et al.*, 2007a). In this chapter, we present an overview of findings in addiction research using PET, and a methodological guide for conducting research in the field.

2   History of Positron Emission Tomography (PET) Imaging in Drug Abuse Research

In 1988, Volkow and co-workers demonstrated that drug abuse patients had abnormal cerebral blood flow, as measured with 2-deoxy-2-[^{18}F]fluoro-D-glucose positron emission tomography (FDG PET) (Volkow, *et al.*, 1988a). Δ^9-tetrahydrocannibinol (THC) administration in normal subjects showed an increase in metabolism in the cerebellum (Volkow *et al.*, 1991). People with cocaine abuse had lower metabolic activity in frontal regions, which persisted after 3–4 months of detoxification (Volkow *et al.*, 1992b), and, when tested within 1 week of withdrawal, people with cocaine abuse had higher levels of global brain metabolism and higher regional metabolism in the basal ganglia and orbitofrontal cortex (Volkow *et al.*, 1990a).

There were also abnormalities in brain metabolism in alcoholics. FDG PET on people with alcoholism had decreased brain glucose metabolism (Wang *et al.*, 1993). Blood flow and metabolism analyses using SPECT and PET revealed decreased blood flow and metabolism in the frontal cortex of a person with chronic alcoholism without evidence of neurological or neuropsychological impairment (Wang *et al.*, 1992). FDG PET showed that ethanol inhibits cortical and cerebellar glucose metabolism in both controls and people with alcoholism, but more so in people with alcoholism (Volkow *et al.*, 1990b). After 6 to 32 days of alcohol discontinuation, whole-brain metabolism of people with alcoholism was lower than in control subjects, with the most dramatic differences in the left parietal and right frontal cortices (Volkow *et al.*, 1992a).

Blood flow measurements with [^{15}O]-labeled water showed that high doses of alcohol reduced blood flow to the cerebellum, right temporal, and prefrontal cortex (Volkow *et al.*, 1988b). [^{15}O]-labeled water for cerebral blood flow (CBF) in people with chronic cocaine use decreased relative CBF in prefrontal cortex, even after 10 days of cocaine withdrawal (Volkow *et al.*, 1988a).

PET has also revealed differences in receptor binding in people with drug abuse versus controls. Measurement of cocaine binding with [^{11}C]cocaine showed the highest binding in the corpus striatum 4–10 minutes after injection, and it reached half of the peak value at 25 minutes (Fowler *et al.*, 1989). Cocaethylene, a metabolite of cocaine found in postmortem brains of individuals who have taken both cocaine and alcohol, was suspected to underlie the increased toxicity of cocaine plus alcohol use. Uptake and clearance from brain of [^{11}C]cocaine and cocaethylene was similar, however, indicating that the increased toxicity is due to the independent effects of the two substances, and not their interaction (Fowler *et al.*, 1992). Chronic cocaine abusers, detoxified for 1 week or less, had lower postsynaptic dopamine receptor binding in the striatum, as measured with [^{18}F]-N-methylspiperone (NMSP) PET (Volkow *et al.*, 1990a). Affinity for the dopamine D2 receptor, as measured with NMSP PET, decreased with amphetamine administration (Dewey *et al.*, 1991). A cocaine analog with affinity for the dopamine transporter (DAT) inhibited [^{11}C]cocaine binding, which lasted 2–3 days in the baboon brain (Volkow *et al.*, 1995).

The relationship of dopamine and drug addiction has been established. Subjects with cocaine addiction showed reduced dopamine release in the striatum in response to administration of intravenous methylphenidate, which caused an increase in synaptic dopamine, like cocaine (Volkow *et al.*, 1997b), and [^{11}C]cocaine PET showed

DAT blockade of 60–77% of receptors at commonly used doses of cocaine, with corresponding subjective reports of positive feelings (Volkow *et al.*, 1997a).

3 Empirical Relevance of PET Imaging to Substance Abuse Research

PET makes it possible to visualize the brains of living human beings by tracking radioactive compounds (i.e., radiotracers) targeted for specific biological functions (Wong and Brašić, 2001). A radiotracer is produced in the laboratory by attaching a radioactive atom or molecule to a compound of interest and is then injected into the patient's bloodstream, from which it can be taken up into the brain. The distribution of the radiotracer within the brain can be measured over time to obtain information about the targeted physiological process. Information on the process being studied can be obtained by tracking the radioactive molecule using a measuring device called a positron emission tomography (PET) scanner (Figure 24.1). Then, using sophisticated computer software, investigators can generate three-dimensional images of the structures where the radiotracer is found.

For PET imaging, investigators need radiotracers that can cross the blood–brain barrier, distribute proportionally with the blood flow through the brain (i.e., regional cerebral blood flow [rCBF]), and remain in the brain long enough to permit imaging. PET tracers typically are analogues to naturally occurring molecules in the brain, except that the radiotracers contain a radioactive atom.

The radioactive atoms most commonly used in PET for studying addiction are radioactive fluorine (^{18}F), carbon (^{11}C), and oxygen (^{15}O).

4 Effects of Chronic Drug Use on Neurotransmitters

4.1 Overview of neuronal communication

Drugs' effects on the brain are mediated by numerous neurotransmitters and their highly complex interactions. In general, the pleasurable psychological experiences associated with drug consumption appear to be mediated by dopamine, noradrenalin, and the endogenous opioids and their receptors, whereas the unpleasant psychological effects of drugs and alcohol appear to be facilitated by serotonin and its receptors (Basavarajappa and Hungund, 2002). Other neurotransmitters commonly affected by drugs and alcohol are glutamate and GABA.

4.2 Drug and alcohol effects on inhibitory neurotransmitters

Drugs and alcohol are thought to influence the inhibitory neurotransmitter GABA (Korpi, Gründer, and Lüddens, 2002; Nevo and Hamon, 1995). Alcohol and drugs appear to enhance the inhibitory actions of GABA (Nevo and Hamon, 1995), which may contribute to both the acute and the chronic effects of drugs and alcohol and to the phenomena of dependence, tolerance, and withdrawal (Nevo and Hamon, 1995).

Chronic alcohol and drug consumption leads to a decline in the number of GABA receptors in the brain and reduces GABA's ability to bind to its receptors, thereby allowing the body to compensate for the drug- and alcohol-induced enhancement of GABA's actions. These effects are a part of the changes in brain function that lead to tolerance and dependence on the drugs or alcohol (Nevo and Hamon, 1995). When drugs or alcohol are withheld, however, and their stimulating effect on GABA is eliminated, the body suddenly has too few GABA receptors to balance the actions of the excitatory neurotransmitters. As a result, the brain experiences an excess of excitatory nerve signals, or rebound hyperexcitability, which may contribute to the physical and psychological manifestations of drug and alcohol withdrawal (Nevo and Hamon, 1995). The benzodiazepine, lorazepam, which facilitates GABA transmission, decreased whole-brain metabolism in cocaine users compared to controls, with the largest differences in the striatum, thalamus, and parietal cortex (Volkow *et al.*, 1998).

4.3   Drug and alcohol effects on excitatory neurotransmitters

Drug and alcohol use appears to influence the transmission of signals mediated by many excitatory neurotransmitters, most prominently glutamate, dopamine, and serotonin (Nevo and Hamon, 1995).

4.3.1   Glutamate.   Glutamate, an excitatory neurotransmitter, exerts its effects by interacting with several types of receptor, including one called the *N*-methyl-D-aspartate (NMDA) receptor. Currently, several radioligands are available to study metabotropic glutamate receptors (mGluRs), such as [^{18}F]FPEB1 (Hamill *et al.*, 2005) and [^{11}C]ABP6882 (Ametamey *et al.*, 2006), both of which label mGluR subtype 5 (mGluR5). Currently, ligands for other subtypes (e.g., mGluR1, mGluR2, and mGluR3) are still being developed for imaging in humans.

The glutamate system has several known roles in drug addiction. Glutamatergic transmission is a mediator of synaptic plasticity as well as extinction of learning. Therefore, modulating glutamate transmission may affect extinction of drug addiction "learning" (Cleva *et al.*, 2010). For example, D-cycloserine (an NDMA partial agonist) has been shown to facilitate conditioned fear responses (Vervliet, 2008; Davis and Gould, 2008) and decrease drug-seeking behavior in animal models (Botreau, Paolone, and Stewart, 2006; Thanos *et al.*, 2009). Alcohol acts on these NMDA receptors, inhibiting their functions and thereby diminishing glutamate-mediated neurotransmission. Since NMDA receptors may play a role in memory formation, prenatal, acute, and chronic drug and/or alcohol exposure may hinder the person's ability to learn and to retain new material (Nevo and Hamon, 1995).

2-Methyl-6-(phenylethynyl)pyridine hydrochloride (MPEP) (Tocris Bioscience, 2012a) and 3-((2-methyl-1,3-thiazol-4-yl)ethynyl)pyridine hydrochloride (MTEP) (Tocris Bioscience, 2012b) (allosteric modulators of mGluRs) both prevent reinstatement of cocaine self-administration in animal models (Iso *et al.*, 2006). mGluR5 receptors have also been linked to depression and drug abuse. Specifically, mGluR5 positive allosteric modulators (PAMs) have been shown to aid in extinction of drug-seeking behavior and reduce cognitive defects related to drug abuse (Cleva and Olive,

2011). Agonists to mGluR2/3 reduce rewarding effects of drug cues (Moussawi and Kalivas, 2010). Grueter and colleagues (2006) showed that mGluR5 activation induced long-term depression (LTD) in the hippocampus and that this LTD is disrupted by repeated exposure to cocaine.

Acute administration of stimulants (cocaine and amphetamine) increases glutamate release in limbic structures, nucleus accumbens, and prefrontal cortex, but not in the striatum, and the increase in glutamate release in nucleus accumbens is probably mediated by dopamine (Reid, Hsu, and Berger, 1997). The decrease in dopamine D2 availability in chronic drug use is associated with decreased frontal activity, via the glutamatergic pathway (Volkow *et al.*, 1993).

4.3.2 Dopamine. In contrast to its dampening effects on the activity of the glutamate system, acute drug and alcohol consumption enhances the excitatory effect of dopamine (Nevo and Hamon, 1995). Correspondingly, acute withdrawal from drugs and alcohol reduces dopamine's excitatory effect. Studies with PET have confirmed that dopamine and its actions in the brain are involved in the subjective experience of reward (Koob and Weiss, 1992).

Anatomically, the reward system, the mesolimbic dopaminergic system, is located deep in the brain in a region called the ventral striatum, with nerve fibers projecting to an area known as the nucleus accumbens and subsequently to higher regions of the brain. Alcohol and other drugs, as well as food or sex, can trigger the release of dopamine in this reward system and reinforce the subjective pleasurable experiences associated with alcohol, drugs, or the other stimuli that are a component of the reward process. PET studies have allowed researchers to directly investigate the role of dopamine and the reward system in drug and alcohol consumption in humans (Oswald *et al.*, 2005; Volkow *et al.*, 2007a). These studies have found that the dopamine-dependent reward system plays an important role in the initiation of alcohol and drug use but is less important in people who are already alcohol or drug dependent (Volkow *et al.*, 2002; Volkow and Fowler, 2000). Individuals dependent on alcohol (see Figure 24.2) (Wong *et al.*, 2003) and other substances have lower densities of D2 receptors than do normal controls (Volkow *et al.*, 2009).

When drugs or alcohol induce the release of dopamine in the nucleus accumbens, nerve signals are sent to the cortex, where they are registered as "experience" and memories of the rewarding effects of alcohol, such as its taste or the feelings of relaxation after drinking. Once registered, these memories can stimulate further drug intake, completing the reward system. Because memories of the rewarding effects of drugs and alcohol also include the environment in which drinking or drug taking occurred, even sights or smells related to that environment can subsequently trigger the reward system. Indeed, several studies have suggested that alcoholics and drug abusers are predisposed to relapse and that environmental stimuli related to drugs and alcohol can trigger the impulse to take drugs or alcohol (Flannery *et al.*, 2001). Animal studies have confirmed that the nucleus accumbens is involved in the rewarding aspects of drug and alcohol consumption and may also mediate the stimulatory effects of environmental cues associated with past drug and alcohol consumption (Katner and Weiss, 1999). Another study using SPECT found that alcoholics ingesting a sip of alcohol during brain imaging showed enhanced neuronal activity in a certain region

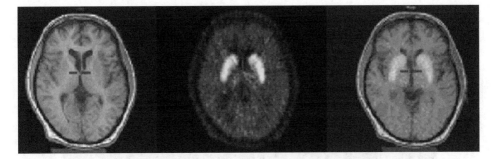

Figure 24.2 Pictures of the same level of the brain of a 40-year-old male alcoholic. Left: image obtained by magnetic resonance imaging (MRI). Center: view obtained by positron emission tomography (PET) after the administration of the agent [^{11}C]raclopride, which binds to the dopamine receptor. Right: image resulting from the simultaneous combination of MRI and PET. Each picture shows the front of the brain at the top, the back of the brain at the bottom, the left side of the brain at the left, and the right side at the right of the picture. The cross in the images is in the midline between the bodies of the putamena on either side. The MRI image clearly shows the anatomic structures. The PET image demonstrates that both the putamen and the caudate have high densities of dopamine receptors, as indicated by the brighter regions. However, the borders of these anatomical structures are blurred on the PET image, making them appear as a single structure. Superimposing the MRI and PET images yields an image that facilitates the identification of the distinct borders of anatomical structures such as the putamen and the caudate. In contrast to healthy normal adults, the density of dopamine receptors is reduced in this man with alcohol dependence. (Reproduced with permission from Wong *et al.*, 2003; http://pubs.niaaa.nih.gov/publications/arh27-2/161-173.htm, accessed November 8, 2012). Refer to Plate 7 for the colored version of this figure

of the ventral striatum (i.e., a part of the basal ganglia) that correlated highly with their increase in craving (Modell, Mountz, and Beresford, 1990). Because alcohol and drug consumption increases dopamine release preferentially in the ventral striatum, these findings support the view that dopamine activation is a common property of alcohol and drugs and contributes to their reinforcing effects.

The mesolimbic dopamine system is also influenced by stress. Stressful situations increase the release of glucocorticoids, most prominently, cortisol. Glucocorticoids can increase mesolimbic dopamine release (Piazza and Le Moal, 1996; Biron, Dauphin, and Di Paolo, 1992; Fahlke *et al.*, 1994; Piazza *et al.*, 1994). The stress-induced increase in dopamine release may make a person more sensitive to the rewarding effects of alcohol and drugs, which may represent one of the pathways leading to drug abuse and dependence (Deroche *et al.*, 1995; Piazza *et al.*, 1990; Kalivas and Stewart, 1991). Researchers have utilized PET to study the relationship between cortisol release and amphetamine-induced dopamine release (see Figure 24.3) (Wong *et al.*, 2003; Oswald *et al.*, 2007). These preliminary studies, which suggest a high correlation between cortisol release and dopamine release, may open the way for future studies of these relationships in alcoholics and drug abusers and their relatives. Alcoholics appear to have an abnormal hormonal response to stress, which may also be present in the offspring of alcoholics who are not as yet heavy drinkers (Wand *et al.*, 1998).

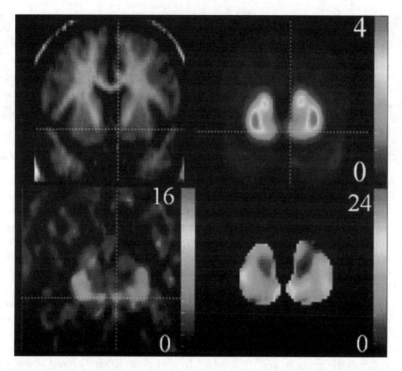

Figure 24.3 Amphetamine-induced dopamine release in the ventral striatum. The upper-left image demonstrates a coronal section of magnetic resonance imaging (MRI) of an adult human participant (Zhou *et al.*, 2003). The lower-left image demonstrates the increased uptake of [^{11}C]raclopride in a coronal section of an adult human participant (Zhou *et al.*, 2003). The upper-right image demonstrates a coronal section with the nondisplaceable binding potential (BP$_{ND}$) (Innis *et al.*, 2007) with dynamic positron emission tomography (PET) when [^{11}C]raclopride is injected intravenously into a human adult participant 5 minutes after the intravenous administration of 10 ml 0.9% NaCl to simulate the resting tonic state (Zhou *et al.*, 2003). The lower-right image demonstrates a coronal section of dopamine release in an adult human participant (Zhou *et al.*, 2003), where

$$\text{dopamine release} = \frac{\text{BP}_{ND\ saline} - \text{BP}_{ND\ amphetamine}}{\text{BP}_{ND\ saline}}.$$

Refer to Plate 8 for the colored version of this figure

PET studies have revealed that substance abuse is associated with changes in dopamine transporters (DATs) (see Figures 24.4 and 24.5) (McCann *et al.*, 2008). Specifically, DAT availability, measured with [^{11}C]PE21, was 20% lower in dorsal striatum, ventral striatum, midbrain, middle cingulate, and thalamus in drug users compared with controls (Leroy *et al.*, 2012). Decreases in striatal DAT BP were associated with deficits in memory in abstinent methamphetamine users (McCann *et al.*, 2008). Former heroin users both on methadone maintenance and after prolonged abstinences demonstrate reductions in DAT uptake as measured with [^{11}C] 2-beta-carbomethoxy-3-beta-(4-fluorophenyl)tropane ([^{11}C] CFT), also known as [^{11}C]WIN35,428 (Shi *et al.*, 2008). The rate of occupancy of DAT has also been

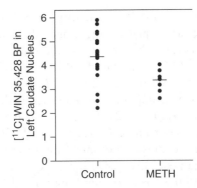

Figure 24.4 The nondisplaceable binding potential (BP_{ND}) (Innis *et al.*, 2007) in the left caudate nucleus estimated by dynamic positron emission tomography (PET) for 90 minutes after the intravenous administration of [^{11}C]WIN35,428 in healthy normal adult control participants (Control) and adults who use methamphetamine (METH) (McCann *et al.*, 2008). This estimate of the density of the dopamine transporter (DAT) demonstrates a reduction in those with methamphetamine use (McCann *et al.*, 2008). (Reproduced from UD McCann, H Kuwabara, A Kumar, M Palermo, R Abbey, J Brašić, W Ye, M Alexander, DF Dannals, DF Wong, and GA Ricaurte (2008) Persistent cognitive and dopamine transporter deficits in abstinent methamphetamine users. *Synapse* 62 (2): 95, figure 2. Copyright 2007 Wiley-Liss, Inc. This material is reproduced with permission of John Wiley & Sons, Inc.)

shown to have an important role in methylphenidate addiction, as measured with PET (Spencer *et al.*, 2006). Imaging studies with SPECT have demonstrated an increase in striatal dopamine in acutely abstinent cocaine-abusing subjects compared to control subjects (Malison *et al.*, 1998a), and mazindol blocks DATs in cocaine-dependent subjects, but to a very limited degree at tolerable doses (Malison *et al.*, 1998b).

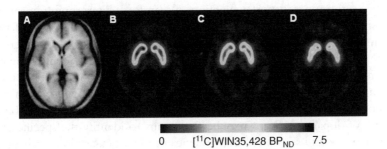

0   [^{11}C]WIN35,428 BP_{ND} 7.5

Figure 24.5 Transaxial representations at the level of the striatum of (A) magnetic resonance imaging (MRI) of a healthy adult and average nondisplaceable binding potentials (BP_{ND}) (Innis *et al.*, 2007) estimated from dynamic positron emission tomography (PET) after the intravenous administration of [^{11}C]WIN35,428 to healthy adults (B), adults with methamphetamine use (C), and adults with Parkinson's disease (D). (Reproduced from UD McCann, H Kuwabara, A Kumar, M Palermo, R Abbey, J Brašić, W Ye, M Alexander, DF Dannals, DF Wong, and GA Ricaurte (2008) Persistent cognitive and dopamine transporter deficits in abstinent methamphetamine users. *Synapse* 62 (2): 96, figure 3. Copyright 2007 Wiley-Liss, Inc. This material is reproduced with permission of John Wiley & Sons, Inc.). Refer to Plate 9 for the colored version of this figure

4.3.3 Serotonin.   Serotonin, another excitatory neurotransmitter involved in the brain's reward system, appears to play an important role in addiction. Animal studies have demonstrated that acute alcohol administration resulted in enhanced serotonin release (Yoshimoto *et al.*, 2000), and withdrawal from alcohol was associated with reduced serotonin release (De Witte *et al.*, 2003). Moreover, studies have found that excessive drug and alcohol consumption was associated with impaired serotonin and dopamine activity (Berggren *et al.*, 2002). The reduction in serotonin is hypothesized to lead to the reduction in dopamine (Berggren *et al.*, 2002). Finally, there is a genetic defect in the gene encoding a serotonin transporter in some people who were particularly sensitive to the toxic effects of chronic excessive alcohol consumption on the brain (Heinz *et al.*, 2000). The serotonin transporter located in the pre-synaptic neuron originally producing serotonin, removes serotonin from the synaptic cleft, the space between neurons, to stop the effect of serotonin on the post-synaptic neuron that is stimulated by serotonin. Individuals with cocaine dependence have increased serotonin transporter binding, as measured with $[^{123}I]\beta-CIT$ SPECT during acute cocaine abstinence (Jacobsen *et al.*, 2000). Further, cocaine users whose serotonin levels were depleted with tryptophan experienced increased striatal dopamine release and intensity of craving in response to cocaine, suggesting that low levels of serotonin may be one factor in addiction susceptibility (Cox *et al.*, 2011). Thus, individuals with abnormal serotonin transporter function may be particularly susceptible to the reduced excitatory effect of heavy substance use. The reduced effect of serotonin probably leads to reduced effects of dopamine. Thus, drug addicts with abnormal serotonin transporter function probably need to consume greater amounts of the substance to attain the pleasurable feelings associated with drug and alcohol consumption (Heinz *et al.*, 2000; Volkow *et al.*, 2007a).

A goal of research on serotonin and other neurotransmitters in substance addiction is to identify distinct biological subtypes of drug addiction and their biological markers. For example, a biological subtype of drug addiction may be characterized by defective serotonin transporter function. A scan for the serotonin transporter may then constitute the tool to obtain a biological marker of the deficiency of the serotonin transporter. Repeating the scan after the administration of a treatment for the deficiency of the serotonin transporter may then be a means to identify the effect of the treatment. Future studies of the effects of chronic drug and alcohol consumption on the serotonin system may clarify the role of serotonin and dopamine in the subtypes of alcoholism. Deficiencies of serotonin in substance abuse probably lead to deficiencies of dopamine. Scans may be the means to identify the specific chemical, such as dopamine and serotonin, that is deficient in particular biological subtypes of drug abuse, and the means to monitor the effects of potential therapies targeted for the specific deficiency of the biological subtype (Wong *et al.*, 2002).

4.3.4 Endogenous opioids.   Endogenous opioids are molecules produced in the body that resemble opium. They probably reinforce the effects of alcohol and play a role in the pleasurable effects of both acute and chronic alcohol consumption, but the specific role of endogenous opioids in alcohol abuse and dependence remains to be clarified (Nevo and Hamon, 1995). Endogenous opioids apparently function like excitatory neurotransmitters to stimulate neurons. Alcohol influences one of the opioid receptors – the mu receptor – in the brain. For example, chronically heavy drinkers have elevated numbers of mu receptors in neurons both in the outer layer of the brain and in structures deep in the center of the brain. In addition, studies have found that a medication called naltrexone that inhibits opiate receptors in the brain is an effective treatment for alcoholism (Romach *et al.*, 2002; Terenius, 1996), particularly for people with a family history of alcoholism or with a strong craving for alcohol (Monterosso *et al.*, 2001). Alcoholics carrying a specific variant of the mu receptor have a lower relapse rate after treatment with naltrexone than do those carrying other receptor variants (Oslin *et al.*, 2003). Alcoholics with a particular genetic makeup are particularly likely to benefit from treatment with naltrexone. PET technology measurements of the density and the distribution of mu opiate receptors in the brain may help identify alcoholics who may benefit from interventions, such as naltrexone, that affect these receptors.

4.3.5 Cannabinoids. Cannabinoids are a group of substances that are related structurally to Δ^9-tetrahydrocannibinol (THC) and interact with cannabinoid receptors. Two main subtypes of cannabinoid receptors have been identified (Howlett *et al.*, 2002): CB1 and CB2. While THC is itself a psychoactive compound, the rewarding effects of nicotine, alcohol, opioids, and other drugs involve the release of endocannabinoids (Maldonado, Valverde, and Berrendero, 2006).

PET studies have revealed that subjects administered oral THC have decreased cortical [^{11}C]raclopride binding potential (BP) (Innis *et al.*, 2007) in the right middle frontal gyrus, left superior frontal gyrus, and left superior temporal gyrus, and this decreased frontal BP (Innis *et al.*, 2007) correlated with catechol-O-methyl transferase (COMT) val108 status (Stokes *et al.*, 2011b). Further, resting global, prefrontal, and anterior cingulate cortex (ACC) blood flow are lower in cannabis users than controls, and chronic cannabis users have impairments in time estimation, attention, working memory, cognitive flexibility, decision making and psychomotor speed (Martín-Santos *et al.*, 2010).

Currently, there are several potential radiotracers in development for labeling of CB1, including 1-(2,4-dichlorophenyl)-4-cyano-5-(4-[^{11}C]methoxyphenyl)-N-(piperidin-1-yl)-1*H*-pyrazole-3-carboxamide ([^{11}C]JHU75528) (Fan *et al.*, 2006; Horti *et al.*, 2006), also known as [^{11}C]OMAR (Wong *et al.*, 2010). [^{11}C]OMAR has been tested in controls and in schizophrenic subjects, but there are many lines of evidence that suggest the CB1 is also involved in drug addiction (Solinas *et al.*, 2007).

In a preclinical model, a synthetic cannabinoid agonist was shown to provoke relapse after prolonged withdrawal periods (De Vries *et al.*, 2002). De Vries and colleagues (2002) also showed that a selective cannabinoid antagonist reduced relapse in response to cocaine cues. Rimonabant, a CB1 antagonist, attenuates or blocks cue-induced reinstatement of the seeking of cocaine, nicotine, heroin, methamphetamine, and alcohol in rodents (De Vries and Schoffelmeer, 2005; Fattore, Fadda, and Fratta, 2007). Rimonabant also decreased the dopamine release and rewarding effects of THC (Le Foll and Goldberg, 2005). Rimonabant, a CB1 antagonist, decreased the dopamine release and rewarding effects of THC (Le Foll and Goldberg, 2005).

4.3.6 Nicotine. The cerebral nicotinic acetylcholine receptor (nAChR) subtype α4β2 is the most abundant and there are several radiolabelled compounds for this receptor (Gao *et al.*, 2009). 2-[^{18}F]fluoro-2-deoxy-D-glucose (2-[^{18}F]FDG) PET shows that heavy smokers have greater increases in glucose metabolism during neutral versus cue scans in the perigenual anterior cingulate gyrus. Reports of craving are correlated with metabolism in the orbitofrontal cortex, dorsolateral prefrontal cortex, anterior insula, and right sensorimotor cortex (Brody *et al.*, 2002).

The tracer (S)-5-[(^{123})I]iodo-3-(2-azetidinylmethoxy)pyridine ([^{123}I]5-IA), which binds to the nicotinic acetylcholine receptor containing the beta2*subunit β$_2$*-nAChR, has been shown to be safe and effective using SPECT in humans (Brašić *et al.*, 2009). After smoking to satiety, smokers exhibited β$_2$*-nAChR receptor occupancy ranging from 55 to 80% (Esterlis *et al.*, 2010). The nondisplaceable binding in thalamus was approximately 20% of total binding (Esterlis *et al.*, 2010). β$_2$*-nAChR availability in the thalamus, and parietal, frontal, anterior cingulate, temporal, and occipital cortices has been correlated with pain sensitivity in smokers after 7–13 days of nicotine abstinence. The magnitude of the change in pain sensitivity from the first test to the second was correlated with β$_2$*-nAChR availability in thalamus, cerebellum, striatum, parietal, anterior cingulate, temporal, and occipital cortices (Cosgrove *et al.*, 2010).

Smokers exhibited greater α4β2* nAChR density than nonsmokers through tomography with 2-[^{18}]fluoro-3-(2(S)-azetidinylmethoxy)pyridine (2-[^{18}]FA), a PET tracer with high affinity for α4β2* nAChRs (Mukhin *et al.*, 2008). When 2-[^{18}F]FA PET imaging is performed within a few hours of the subjects having smoked, there are fewer available α4β2* nAChR receptors than in nonsmoking controls, suggesting that the nicotine from the cigarette smoke binds to the α4β2* nAChR receptors (Brašić *et al.*, 2012). 2-[^{18}]FA PET binding of α4β2* nAChR has also shown to be predictive of development of Alzheimer's Disease (AD); mild cognitive impairment was associated with reduction in α4β2* nAChR compared to controls, but only in those patients who later developed AD (Kendziorra *et al.*, 2011). (-)-2-(6-(18)F-fluoro-2,3'-bipyridin-5'-yl)-7-methyl-7-azabicyclo[2.2.1]heptane ([^{18}F]AZAN), a recently developed nAChR tracer, is probably a better alternative to 2-[^{18}]FA since it has greater BP values and faster brain kinetics (Horti *et al.*, 2010).

5 What PET Has Taught Us about Substance Abuse Susceptibility

Drug addicts have decreased D2 receptor availability in the striatum and frontal regions, including the orbitofrontal cortex, which is implicated in compulsive behaviors in obsessive compulsive disorder. In the presence of drugs or drug cues, however, there is an increase in activity in these regions. Decreased D2 receptors in striatum may be a risk factor for addiction. Methamphetamine users have been shown to have lower D2 receptor availability than controls, and those who relapse have lower D2 receptor availability in the striatum, but those who completed detoxification did not

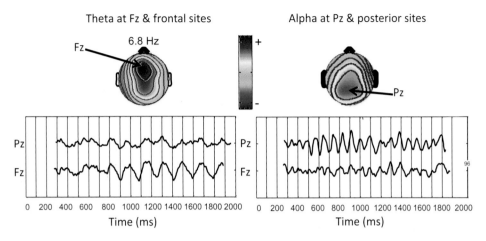

Plate 1 (Figure 22.1) Topographical maps and associated theta and alpha EEG activity at frontal and parietal sites. Theta is dominant at frontal midline sites (e.g., Fz) while alpha is dominant a posterior sites (e.g., Pz)

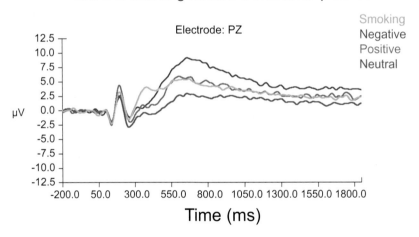

Plate 2 (Figure 22.3) ERPs to smoking-related and emotionally valent pictures. N1 occurs about 100 milliseconds post picture onset, P170 occurs about 170 milliseconds post picture onset, and the late positive component (LPC) ranges from 400 milliseconds to more than 1,800 milliseconds in the case of the negative pictures. This LPC is largest in response to the negative pictures, and smallest in response to neutral pictures

The Wiley-Blackwell Handbook of Addiction Psychopharmacology, First Edition. Edited by James MacKillop and Harriet de Wit.
© 2013 John Wiley & Sons, Ltd. Published 2013 by John Wiley & Sons, Ltd.

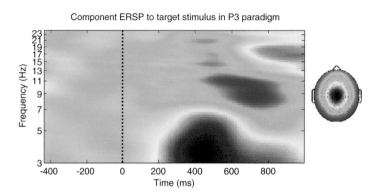

Component ERSP to target stimulus in P3 paradigm

Plate 3 (Figure 22.4) Event-related oscillation power as a function of oscillation frequency and time after the onset of target stimuli (time 0) in an oddball paradigm. Note the increase in delta and theta power from 250 to 580 milliseconds, corresponding to the P3b

P3 in Oddball task when Smoking vs. 3-Days Post Quitting

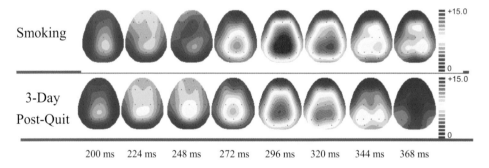

Smoking

3-Day Post-Quit

200 ms 224 ms 248 ms 272 ms 296 ms 320 ms 344 ms 368 ms

Plate 4 (Figure 22.5) Mean P3b response topographies to target stimuli during an oddball paradigm in a group of smokers before and after quitting smoking. The onset of target stimuli = time 0. Red color reflects greater ERP amplitude, while blue reflects small amplitude

Nicotine-Placebo Cessation Day 3 Minus Pre-Quit Baseline Theta1

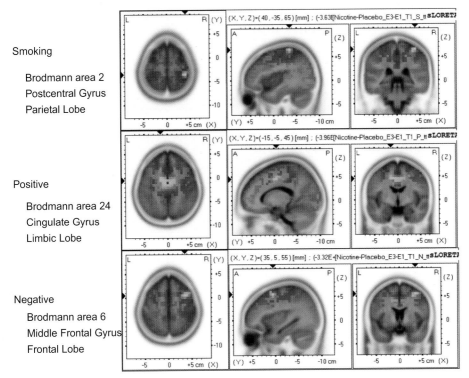

Plate 5 (Figure 22.6) LORETA tomographic images of theta-band EEG current-density changes. The images reflect differences between nicotine and placebo conditions after 3 days of tobacco smoking abstinence

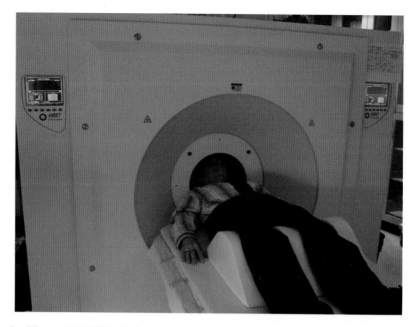

Plate 6 (Figure 24.1) This high resolution research tomography (HRRT) (Siemens Medical Solutions USA, Inc., Malvern, PA) scanner obtains positron emission tomography (PET) images of the brain with a resolution approaching 2 mm (Sossi *et al.*, 2005). (Photo provided courtesy of Jeffrey Galecki, Division of Nuclear Medicine, The Russell H. Morgan Department of Radiology and Radiological Science, The Johns Hopkins University School of Medicine, Baltimore, Maryland)

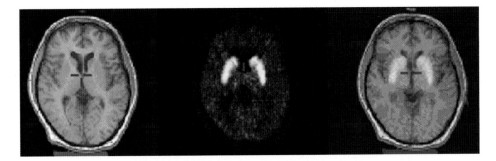

Plate 7 (Figure 24.2) Pictures of the same level of the brain of a 40-year-old male alcoholic. Left: image obtained by magnetic resonance imaging (MRI). Center: view obtained by positron emission tomography (PET) after the administration of the agent [^{11}C]raclopride, which binds to the dopamine receptor. Right: image resulting from the simultaneous combination of MRI and PET. Each picture shows the front of the brain at the top, the back of the brain at the bottom, the left side of the brain at the left, and the right side at the right of the picture. The cross in the images is in the midline between the bodies of the putamena on either side. The MRI image clearly shows the anatomic structures. The PET image demonstrates that both the putamen and the caudate have high densities of dopamine receptors, as indicated by the yellow. However, the borders of these anatomical structures are blurred on the PET image, making them appear as a single structure. Superimposing the MRI and PET images yields an image that facilitates the identification of the distinct borders of anatomical structures such as the putamen and the caudate. In contrast to healthy normal adults, the density of dopamine receptors is reduced in this man with alcohol dependence. (Reproduced with permission from Wong *et al.*, 2003; http://pubs.niaaa.nih.gov/publications/arh27-2/161-173.htm)

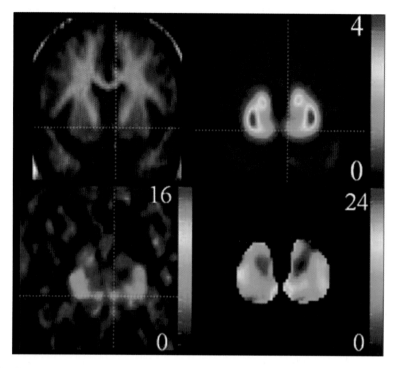

Plate 8 (Figure 24.3) Amphetamine-induced dopamine release in the ventral striatum. The upper-left image demonstrates a coronal section of magnetic resonance imaging (MRI) of an adult human participant (Zhou *et al.*, 2003). The lower-left image demonstrates the increased uptake of [^{11}C]raclopride in a coronal section of an adult human participant (Zhou *et al.*, 2003). The upper-right image demonstrates a coronal section with the nondisplaceable binding potential (BP$_{ND}$) (Innis *et al.*, 2007) with dynamic positron emission tomography (PET) when [^{11}C]raclopride is injected intravenously into a human adult participant 5 minutes after the intravenous administration of 10 ml 0.9% NaCl to simulate the resting tonic state (Zhou *et al.*, 2003). The lower-right image demonstrates a coronal section of dopamine release in an adult human participant (Zhou *et al.*, 2003), where

$$\text{dopamine release} = \frac{\text{BP}_{\text{ND saline}} - \text{BP}_{\text{ND amphetamine}}}{\text{BP}_{\text{ND saline}}}$$

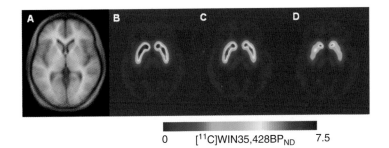

0       $[^{11}C]WIN35,428BP_{ND}$ 7.5

Plate 9 (Figure 24.5) Transaxial representations at the level of the striatum of (A) magnetic resonance imaging (MRI) of a healthy adult and average nondisplaceable binding potentials (BP_{ND}) (Innis *et al.*, 2007) estimated from dynamic positron emission tomography (PET) after the intravenous administration of $[^{11}C]WIN35,428$ to healthy adults (B), adults with methamphetamine use (C), and adults with Parkinson's disease (D). (Reproduced from UD McCann, H Kuwabara, A Kumar, M Palermo, R Abbey, J Brašić, W Ye, M Alexander, DF Dannals, DF Wong, and GA Ricaurte (2008) Persistent cognitive and dopamine transporter deficits in abstinent methamphetamine users. *Synapse* 62 (2): 96, figure 3. Copyright 2007 Wiley-Liss, Inc. This material is reproduced with permission of John Wiley & Sons, Inc.)

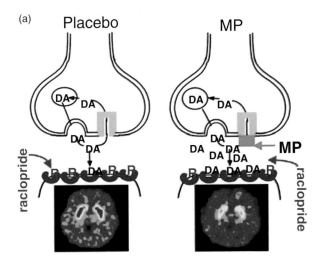

Plate 10 (Figure 24.6) Illustration of $[^{11}C]$raclopride positron emission tomography to estimate the density of dopamine D_2 receptors after the administration of a placebo (left) and methylphenidate (MP) (right). Many dopamine D_2 receptors are already occupied by MP so few are available for $[^{11}C]$raclopride (right). (Reprinted from ND Volkow, JS Fowler, and G-J Wang (2004) The addicted human brain viewed in the light of imaging studies: Brain circuits and treatment strategies. *Neuropharmacology* 47 (suppl. 1): 3–13. Copyright (2004), with permission from Elsevier)

have different D2 availability than controls (Wang *et al.*, 2011). It is possible that relatively low levels of D2 receptor availability may make individuals vulnerable to developing addictions.

Another predisposing factor may be an individual's degree of impulsivity. People with low impulsivity have more dopamine release during low or moderate stress than do highly impulsive people. Further, high-impulsivity individuals experience more intense pleasure with amphetamine. Together, this suggests that low-impulsivity people are more likely to receive adequate levels of dopamine from relatively low-risk stimuli, whereas high-impulsivity individuals require much more stressful or risky situations to elicit levels of dopamine that provide enough pleasure (Oswald *et al.*, 2007). In support of this, cortisol levels are positively associated with amphetamine-induced dopamine release in the ventral striatum and dorsal putamen, and higher cortisol response is associated with reports of more intense pleasurable effects of the drug (Oswald *et al.*, 2005). In addition, males experience more positive effects of amphetamine than do females (Munro *et al.*, 2006).

PET studies have helped researchers assess risk factors for alcoholism. In nonalcoholics, certain sedatives (i.e., benzodiazepines) produce a temporary impairment in coordination and cognition and a decrease in brain glucose metabolism similar to the effects of alcohol consumption. In alcoholics, however, some regions in the frontal lobe respond to benzodiazepines less strongly than they do in nonalcoholics (Gilman *et al.*, 1996). Alcoholics may have a diminished capacity to dampen excessive neuronal activity and therefore may be less able to inhibit behavior.

6   The Powerful Role of Learning in Addiction

When an organism receives a burst of dopamine in the striatum in response to a reward, such as drugs or alcohol, food, or sex, the stimuli around them, such as drug paraphernalia, the smell of the food, or the appearance of a mate, may become associated with the pleasure of the reward. These cues that are present just prior to the delivery of the reward serve as predictors and come to elicit the dopamine release themselves. Thus, cues associated with drug and alcohol consumption play a powerful role in drug-seeking behavior.

PET studies have revealed that there is an increase in D2 receptor occupancy, and accompanying experience of craving, in the putamen of drug users presented with drug-related cues (Wong *et al.*, 2006). Dopamine release alone is not sufficient to elicit craving. Craving is elicited in the presence of methylphenidate only if drug craving cues are also given (Volkow *et al.*, 2008b). In a study by Yoder and colleagues (2009), subjects were given either cues associated with alcohol or neutral cues associated with an electrolyte solution, followed by an injection of either the placebo or alcohol. Subjects who received the alcohol cues followed by the electrolyte solution had decreased striatal dopamine concentration compared to baseline, while subjects who were presented with cues predicting the electrolyte solution followed by an injection of alcohol, had increased striatal dopamine concentration.

7   Using PET to Measure the Effects of Substances of Abuse

PET imaging has been used extensively to study the changes in dopamine transmission, and receptor/transporter levels. The serotonin system has also been studied extensively.

Table 24.1 gives examples of PET measurements of characteristics of neurotransmitters in healthy adults and patients with substance abuse and dependence and other neuropsychiatric disorders. Table 24.2 provides a list of common PET tracers used to study functions and neurotransmitters systems in drug addiction.

8   Types of PET Studies

1) Receptor/transporter density
   a. Simply takes baseline measurements of receptor or transporter density in various subject pools.
2) Challenge studies:
   a. Pharmacological: uses a stimulant like amphetamine or phentermine (George *et al.*, 2012) to induce release of neurotransmitter. The difference in radiotracer occupancy between baseline and post-drug scans directly related to the amount of neurotransmitter released (see Figure 24.6) (Volkow *et al.*, 2004a; Laruelle and Huang, 2001; Oswald *et al.*, 2005).
   b. Non-pharmacological: Koepp and colleagues (1998) showed that a non-pharmacological challenge can also elicit a measurable dopamine release. The paper reported changes in [^{11}C]raclopride binding while the subjects were playing a video game. In drug addiction research, "cues" are used to elicit craving, for example, in cocaine abuse (Wong *et al.*, 2006; Volkow *et al.*, 2008b).
   c. Cue-induced craving: Specific visual images combined with personalized scripts (Sinha, 2009) are now being used to elicit craving in drug abusers, and with PET, one can measure the release of dopamine in response to different types of cue in different situations.

9   PET Studies of Brain Glucose Metabolism and Blood Flow

9.1   Glucose metabolism

The brain needs a continuous supply of glucose, whose breakdown provides most of the energy the cells need for their diverse functions. Brain regions that are more active require more glucose and lower-than-normal glucose metabolism suggests reduced brain activity. PET studies can help researchers identify active brain regions by administering radioactively labeled glucose ([^{18}F]FDG) and measuring its distribution in the brain. Brain glucose metabolism detectable with PET occurs mainly in the gray matter whose volume can vary substantially among subjects. Chronic alcoholics frequently have smaller gray matter volumes than nonalcoholics (Sullivan *et al.*, 2000). Glucose

Table 24.1 Characterization of neurotransmitters in healthy adults and people with substance abuse and dependence and other neuropsychiatric disorders

Target investigated	Drug used	Finding	Reference
D2 dopamine (DA) receptors	Cocaine	↓ Acute withdrawal	Volkow *et al.* (1993)
		↓ Detoxified	Volkow *et al.* (1993; 1996a)
	Alcohol	↓ Acute withdrawal	Rominger *et al.* (2011); Hietala *et al.* (1994)
		↓ Detoxified	Volkow *et al.* (2002)
	Methamphetamine	↓ Detoxified	Volkow *et al.* (2001)
	Nicotine	0 Detoxified	Fehr *et al.* (2008)
	Cannabis	0 Detoxified	Sevy *et al.* (2008)
	Heroin	↓ Active user	Wang *et al.* (1997)
DA transporters	Cocaine	↑ Acute withdrawal	Malison *et al.* (1998a)
		0 Detoxified	Volkow *et al.* (1996b)
	Alcohol	↓ Acute withdrawal	Laine *et al.* (1999)
		0 Detoxified	Volkow *et al.* (1996c)
	Methamphetamine	↓ Detoxified	Chang *et al.* (2007)
	Cigarettes	↓ Active user	Yang *et al.* (1999)
Vesicular monoamine transporters-2	Methamphetamine	↓ Detoxified	Chang *et al.* (2007)
Metabolism monoamine oxidase type B (MAOB)	Cigarettes	↓ Active user	Fowler *et al.* (1999)
Synthesis (dopa decarboxylase)	Alcohol	0 Detoxified	Heinz *et al.* (2005)
Dopamine release	Cocaine	↑ Active user	Schlaepfer *et al.* (1997)
		↓ Detoxified	Volkow *et al.* (1997a)
	Alcohol	↓ Detoxified	Volkow *et al.* (2007b)
	Methylphenidate in cocaine abusers	increased dopamine in striatum, but only induced craving when cocaine cues present	Volkow *et al.* (2008b)
GABA transmission	Cocaine	↓ Active user	Volkow *et al.* (1998)
Metabolism in orbitofrontal cortex	Cocaine	↑ Early withdrawal	Volkow *et al.* (1993)
	Cocaine	↓ Protracted withdrawal	Volkow *et al.* (1992b)

Table 24.1 (*Continued*)

Target investigated	Drug used	Finding	Reference
Pharmacokinetics of cocaine vs. methylphenidate	Cocaine	Fast uptake in striatum; slower clearance from brain	Volkow *et al.* (1995)
	Methylphenidate	Fast uptake in striatum; faster clearance from brain	Volkow *et al.* (1995)
Mu-opioid receptor	Alcohol	↑ Active user	Weerts *et al.* (2011)
Delta-opioid receptor	Alcohol	↑ Recent alcohol drinking in alcohol-dependent subjects	Weerts *et al.* (2011)

Source: Reproduced with permission from Volkow *et al.* (2009). Copyright 2009 Elsevier.

Table 24.2 PET Tracers used in studies of drug addiction

Blood flow	$[^{15}O]H_2O$	*Blood flow*
Metabolism	$[^{18}F]FDG$	*Glucose metabolism*
Dopamine (DA) system	$[^{18}F]Flourodopa$	*DA synthesis*
Dopamine receptors and transporters	$[^{11}C]$Raclopride	D_2 antagonist
	$[^{18}F]$Fallypride	Dopamine transporter (DAT)
	$[^{11}C]$WIN 35, 428	D_1 antagonist
	$[^{11}C]$Sch23390	D_1 antagonist
	$[^{11}C]$NNC-112*	$D_{2/3}$ agonist
	$[^{11}C]$PHNO*	D_2 agonist
	$[^{11}C]$MNPA*	$D_{2/3}$ agonist (Tsukada et al., 2011)
Opiates	$[^{11}C]$carfentanil	Mu opiate antagonist
	$[^{11}C]$naltrendole	Delta opiate antagonist
	$[^{11}C]$diprenorphine	Non-selective opiate antagonist
Nicotinic cholinergic	2-$[^{18}F]$FA $[^{123}I]$5-IA	$\alpha 4 \beta 2$ agonist
	$[^{11}C]$nicotine (R and S)	$\alpha 4 \beta 2$ agonist
	$[^{18}F]$AZAN	nAChR
		nAChR
Glutamate	$[^{11}C]$FPEP	mGluR5
	$[^{11}C]$ABP	mGluR5
Serotonin	$[^{11}C]$MDL100,907	5-HT$_{2A}$ antagonist
	$[^{11}C]$McNeil5652	5-HTT
	$[^{11}C]$DASB	5-HTT
Cannabinoid receptors	$[^{11}C]$OMAR	CB1 antagonist

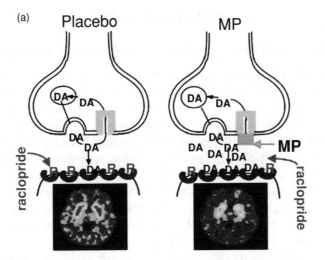

Figure 24.6   Illustration of [^{11}C]raclopride positron emission tomography to estimate the density of dopamine D_2 receptors after the administration of a placebo (left) and methylphenidate (MP) (right). Many dopamine D_2 receptors are already occupied by MP so few are available for [^{11}C]raclopride (right). (Reprinted from ND Volkow, JS Fowler, and G-J Wang (2004) The addicted human brain viewed in the light of imaging studies: Brain circuits and treatment strategies. *Neuropharmacology* 47 (suppl. 1): 3–13. Copyright (2004), with permission from Elsevier). Refer to Plate 10 for the colored version of this figure

metabolism must be expressed in terms of the gray matter volume of a specific region, which can be determined by structural imaging techniques such as MRI.

PET studies have shown that glucose metabolism in alcoholics is decreased in the entire brain (Volkow *et al.*, 1992a), but most dramatically in the frontal lobes and cerebellum. However, functioning in people with alcohol dependence is complicated by the alcohol-induced damage to other organs (e.g., the liver and the stomach). For example, people with liver cirrhosis resulting from chronic alcohol consumption exhibit decreased glucose utilization by gray matter in the frontal and temporal lobes and the basal ganglia (Kato, *et al.*, 2000).

9.2   Regional blood flow

Glucose is brought to the brain via the bloodstream; accordingly, the rates of regional cerebral blood flow (rCBF) are regulated depending on the changing demands of these areas. To detect changes in rCBF, investigators inject a radiotracer (typically, radioactively labeled water ([^{15}O]H_2O)) into the bloodstream and measure its deposition in the brain tissue. [^{15}O]H_2O has a short half-life of 2 minutes and can therefore be injected repeatedly while the subjects perform various motor, sensory, or cognitive tasks under different conditions. This approach can also be used to track the effects of acute alcohol ingestion on regional blood flow over a period of time (Sullivan *et al.*, 2000).

10 PET Analytic Methods

10.1 Developing models for interpreting PET analyses

The data obtained in drug abusers and alcoholics with functional imaging techniques such as PET typically must undergo a set of processing steps to yield information that is useful to researchers. Researchers must develop mathematical representations (i.e., kinetic models) of physiological processes such as the metabolism of neurotransmitters or their receptors with which they can develop a mathematical equation describing the tissue-response curve expected in the measurements. The tissue-response curve plots the radioactivity of specific parts of the brain before, during, and after the injection of the radioisotope, and correlates with the amount of the chemical identified by the radioisotope in the regions of the brain. By performing the scans on groups of people with and without substance abuse, the increases and decreases of chemicals in the brains of substance abusers can be identified.

To develop appropriate models and provide a basis for interpreting the measured behavior of the tracer, it is important to know how fast and to what extent the tracer is transported from the site of the injection in the bloodstream to the tissue being analyzed (e.g., a specific brain region). The basic steps of this transport are as follows:

- The tracer is transported by the blood to the small blood vessels (i.e., capillaries) in the brain.
- The tracer moves across the capillary wall into the synapses, the fluid-filled spaces, between the brain cells.
- The tracer crosses the membrane surrounding the cells or binds to neurotransmitter receptors in the synaptic clefts between neurons.
- If it enters the cells, the tracer participates in various biochemical reactions.

PET can follow the progress of the tracer by measuring the amounts of radioactivity in different areas of the brain as well as the tracer concentrations in the blood. To interpret the data obtained in this way, investigators can use a variety of mathematical or statistical modeling methods (e.g., the compartment model, graphical model, and tissue input graphical model approaches).

10.2 Correction of partial volume errors

PET images are blurred because of the limited resolution of the PET scanners. One consequence of this is an apparent loss of radioactivity signals from the region of interest into and out of the adjacent tissues and these effects are known as "partial volume errors," and are more pronounced in alcohol-related brain shrinkage where loss of signal due to partial volume errors could be confounded with an actual loss of tissue function (Rousset, Ma, and Evans, 1998).

To correct for partial volume errors, both an MRI scan and a PET scan of a patient's brain are conducted and then combined. Computer simulations are then used to mimic the effect of limited spatial resolution to characterize the partial volume effects for each brain region (Rousset, Ma, and Evans, 1998), and investigators can then apply correction factors to obtain more accurate estimates of the actual regional activity (e.g., regional blood flow or glucose metabolism).

11   Limitations, Challenges, and Future Directions for the Field

Despite the unique advantages of addiction research in PET, there are limitations and challenges that must be addressed; these include limitations of the PET procedure in general, in PET imaging of D2 receptors, and in conducting addiction research specifically.

One major limitation of PET research in general is the cost. The expense of the procedure limits the sample size and requires that researchers pay very close attention to the details of the procedure to ensure that each scan goes smoothly. Another challenge is the requirement that subjects stay as still as possible during the scans. Head movements introduce noise in the data. Remaining still for over an hour, the typical scan length for [^{11}C]raclopride, may be particularly difficult for neurological and psychiatric patient populations. Methods for limiting noise from head movement include the use of motion-tracking devices and motion correction algorithms (Rahmim, Rousset, and Zaidi, 2007).

Imaging D2 dopamine receptors, in particular, comes with its own challenges, one of which is the short half-life of [^{11}C], which necessitates that a cyclotron be on-site for synthesis of the radiotracer (Wong and Brašić, 2001). Another challenge is the question of the validity of the measurement process when quantifying D2 receptor occupancy in the presence of amphetamine. It is assumed that, with D2 agonist administration, [^{11}C]raclopride is measuring competition between endogenous and radioligand binding to D2 receptors, but other processes may be involved. Pure competition of receptor binding is suspect because increases in extracellular dopamine and behavioral effects of the agonist last 2 hours, while the accompanying decrease in D2 receptor binding potential lasts 4–24 hours. It has been proposed that this temporal discrepancy may be due to variability in receptor affinity. Specifically, it has been shown that D2 receptor agonists cause receptor internalization, a process during which a portion of the receptors are drawn into the cell membrane. While surface and internalized receptors retain high affinity, the affinity of the internalized receptors is reduced (Wong, Brašić, and Cascella, 2011). The binding potential is thus probably decreased, not only as a result of increase in intrasynaptic DA, but also as the affinity is reduced due to receptor internalization (Guo *et al.*, 2010; Laruelle and Huang, 2001).

Other variables affecting D2 receptor binding include gender, age, menstrual cycle status, type of drug of abuse, and smoking status. Males have greater release of DA in the ventral striatum with amphetamine and report more intense positive effects than do females (Munro *et al.*, 2006). D2 receptor binding, however, declines with age, and the pattern of decline differs between males and females; while young males have more dopamine binding than do young females, the levels decrease exponentially with age, while in females, the reduction is linear (Wong *et al.*, 1984). Further, the striatal dopamine transporter (DAT) binding is higher in young to middle-aged (younger than 60 years) women than men, but this effect disappears in the elderly (60 years and older) (Wong *et al.*, 2012). The DAT is involved in the reuptake of DA into the presynaptic cells. Therefore, high levels of the DAT translate to higher levels of intrasynaptic DA and, thus, higher levels of DA binding. Women's DA binding also differs from that of men in that it fluctuates with their menstrual cycle, with binding lows during the follicular phase and highs in the periovulatory and luteal phases (Wong *et al.*, 1988).

In addition to factors such as age and gender, a history of and the current use of substances influence dopamine binding. While a range of addictive substances taken chronically affect the D2 receptors, history of cannabis use is not associated with differences in D2/D3 receptors (Stokes *et al.*, 2011a). The current use of substances is also an important variable. Smoking causes a release of DA (Brody *et al.*, 2004). Therefore, when designing addiction studies, it is important to take this into account; subjects should abstain from smoking prior to the scans for at least 72 hours, and researchers should measure the amount of nicotine present at the time of the scan (using an expired breath CO meter, for example) and correlate with measures of receptor binding (Fowler *et al.*, 1999; Montgomery *et al.*, 2007). Finally, when using drug cues to elicit craving, it is important that the cues are tailored to the individual. An established method for eliciting drug craving uses individualized scripts that are then read to the subjects during the scans (Sinha, 2009).

Moving forward, the future of addiction research in PET will benefit from the use of radiotracers that bind to cortical dopamine receptors, specifically, high-affinity radiotracers that bind to extrastriatal low-density cortical dopamine D2 receptor populations: namely, $[^{11}C]$FLB 457, $[^{123}I]$epidepride, and $[^{18}F]$fallypride (Olsson, Halldin, and Farde, 2004; Riccardi *et al.*, 2008). In addiction, D2 receptors of the prefrontal cortex implicated in response inhibition and salience attribution become inhibited, resulting in an excessive focus on drugs and drug-related cues, decreased sensitivity to non-drug reinforcers, and compromised ability to inhibit detrimental behaviors (Volkow *et al.*, 1997c; Goldstein and Volkow, 2011; Febo *et al.*, 2009). Thus, to understand the complicated mechanisms of addiction, it is necessary to examine the entire cortico-limbic pathway in humans, *in vivo*.

In addition to dopaminergic pathways, it is important to also understand how other neurotransmitter systems interact in addiction. For example, ketamine, a glutamate receptor antagonist, used as an anesthetic and also as a recreational drug (Morgan and Curran, 2012), increases cortical D2/D3 binding, suggesting an important glutamate–dopamine interaction (Aalto *et al.*, 2005). A new cannabinoid CB 1 receptor PET tracer, $[^{11}C]$OMAR, is also a potentially promising tool for addiction research (Wong *et al.*, 2010).

Addiction is a complicated disease that requires a multidisciplinary approach. PET is one of the tools that has the potential to greatly facilitate progress in this area.

12   The Future of PET Studies in Substance Abuse

Although researchers have been employing PET and other functional imaging techniques in the analysis of drug- and alcohol-induced changes in brain functioning, the potential of these approaches has not yet been realized. For example, it might be useful to correlate functional imaging data with information on demographic traits of the subjects (Brašić, 2003), including ethnicity (Brašić, 2003), as well as with behavioral measures (Brašić *et al.*, 2009; 2012), including questionnaires addressing psychological traits and the desire for drugs and alcohol. Demographic (Brašić, 2003; 2004) and psychological traits (Brašić *et al.*, 2009; 2012) may identify biological subtypes of drug abuse and alcoholism detected by PET. Questionnaires to identify behavioral data may be developed to function as biological markers of the presence of distinct biological variants of drug abuse and alcoholism to identify the effects of potential therapeutic interventions targeted to the distinct variant (Wong *et al.*, 2003).

Several other approaches are promising means to understand addiction through the application of PET as follows:

- Characterization of neurochemical processes with craving for drugs and alcohol, including (1) the production, the release (Figure 24.6) (Volkow, Fowler, and Wang, 2004; Volkow *et al.*, 2004), and the transport of neurotransmitters and (2) changes in receptor concentrations.
- Elucidation of the pathophysiology of addiction in specific brain regions by PET and SPECT.
- Monitoring the effects of behavioral and pharmacological interventions on relevant brain regions by PET and SPECT.
- Characterization of neurochemical processes associated with abuse and dependence.
- Investigation of dysfunction of neurotransmission of dopamine, serotonin, acetylcholine, and opiates.
- Identification of neurological circuits' contribution to the cognitive deficits with acute drug and alcohol intake.
- Elucidation of pathways through which functional deficits in specific neurological circuits and resulting cognitive deficits contribute to reward, reinforcement and reinstatement.
- Analyses of neurobiological markers of vulnerability to alcohol and drug abuse.
- Utilization of multiple modality imaging, including functional magnetic resonance imaging (fMRI), diffusion tensor imaging (DTI), and magnetic resonance spectroscopy (MRS), to generate a spectrum or a fingerprint of substance abuse (Wong, Tauscher, and Gründer, 2009).
- Identification of neural circuits that play a role in the cognitive deficits associated with acute alcohol intake; elucidation of the pathways through which functional deficits in specific neural circuits and the resulting cognitive deficits may contribute to excessive drug and alcohol intake.
- Analyses of neurobiological markers of vulnerability to drug and alcohol abuse.
- Combination with structural imaging techniques (e.g., computed tomography [CT] or MRI) to obtain a fused image automatically.
- Development of new pharmaceutical agents to prevent and treat drug abuse and alcoholism (Wong, Potter, and Brašić, 2002).

References

Aalto S, Ihalainen J, Hirvonen J, *et al.* (2005) Cortical glutamate–dopamine interaction and ketamine-induced psychotic symptoms in man. *Psychopharmacology (Berlin)* 182: 375–383.

Ametamey SM, Kessler LJ, Honer M, *et al.* (2006) Radiosynthesis and preclinical evaluation of 11C-ABP688 as a probe for imaging the metabotropic glutamate receptor subtype 5. *Journal of Nuclear Medicine* 47: 698–705.

Basavarajappa BS and Hungund BL (2002) Neuromodulatory role of the endocannabinoid signaling system in alcoholism: An overview. *Prostaglandins, Leukotrienes, and Essential Fatty Acids* 66: 287–299.

Berggren U, Eriksson M, Fahlke C, *et al.* (2002) Is long-term heavy alcohol consumption toxic for brain serotonergic neurons? Relationship between years of excessive alcohol consumption and serotonergic neurotransmission. *Drug and Alcohol Dependence* 65: 159–165.

Biron D, Dauphin C, and Di Paolo T (1992) Effects of adrenalectomy and glucocorticoids on rat brain dopamine receptors. *Neuroendocrinology* 55 (4): 468–476.

Botreau F, Paolone G, and Stewart J (2006) d-Cycloserine facilitates extinction of a cocaine-induced conditioned place preference. *Behavioural Brain Research* 172: 173–178.

Brašić JR (2003) Documentation of demographic data. *Psychological Reports* 93: 151–152.

Brašić JR (2004) Documentation of ethnicity. *Psychological Reports* 95: 859–861.

Brašić JR, Cascella N, Kumar A, *et al.* (2012) Positron emission tomography experience with 2-[^{18}F]fluoro-3-(2(S)-azetidinylmethoxy)pyridine (2-[^{18}F]FA) in the living human brain of smokers with paranoid schizophrenia. *Synapse* 66: 352–368.

Brašić JR, Zhou Y, Musachio JL, *et al.* (2009) Single photon emission computed tomography experience with (S)-5-[(^{123})I]iodo-3-(2-azetidinylmethoxy)pyridine in the living human brain of smokers and nonsmokers. *Synapse* 63: 339–358.

Brody AL, Mandelkern MA, London ED, *et al.* (2002) Brain metabolic changes during cigarette craving. *Archives of General Psychiatry* 59: 1162–1172.

Brody AL, Olmstead RE, London ED, *et al.* (2004) Smoking-induced ventral striatum dopamine release. *American Journal of Psychiatry* 161: 1211–1218.

Chang L, Alicata D, Ernst T, *et al.* (2007) Structural and metabolic brain changes in the striatum associated with methamphetamine abuse. *Addiction* 102 (Suppl. 1): 16–32.

Cleva RM and Olive MF (2011) Positive allosteric modulators of type 5 metabotropic glutamate receptors (mGluR5) and their therapeutic potential for the treatment of CNS disorders. *Molecules* 16: 2097–2106.

Cleva RM, Gass JT, Widholm JJ, *et al.* (2010) Glutamatergic targets for enhancing extinction learning in drug addiction. *Current Neuropharmacology* 8: 394–408.

Cosgrove KP, Esterlis I, McKee S, *et al.* (2010) Beta2* nicotinic acetylcholine receptors modulate pain sensitivity in acutely abstinent tobacco smokers. *Nicotine and Tobacco Research* 12: 535–539.

Cox SM, Benkelfat C, Dagher A, *et al.* (2011) Effects of lowered serotonin transmission on cocaine-induced striatal dopamine response: PET [^{11}C]raclopride study in humans. *British Journal of Psychiatry* 199: 391–397.

Davis JA and Gould TJ (2008) Associative learning, the hippocampus, and nicotine addiction. *Current Drug Abuse Reviews* 1: 9–19.

De Vries TJ and Schoffelmeer AN (2005) Cannabinoid CB1 receptors control conditioned drug seeking. *Trends in Pharmacological Sciences* 2005 26 (8): 420–426.

De Vries TJ, Schoffelmeer AN, Binnekade R, *et al.* (2002) Relapse to cocaine- and heroin-seeking behavior mediated by dopamine D2 receptors is time-dependent and associated with behavioral sensitization. *Neuropsychopharmacology* 26: 18–26.

De Witte P, Pinto E, Ansseau M, *et al.* (2003) Alcohol and withdrawal: From animal research to clinical issues. *Neuroscience and Biobehavioral Reviews* 27: 189–197.

Deroche V, Marinelli M, Maccari S, *et al.* (1995) Stress-induced sensitization and glucocorticoids. I. Sensitization of dopamine-dependent locomotor effects of amphetamine and morphine depends on stress-induced corticosterone secretion. *Journal of Neuroscience* 15: 7181–7188.

Dewey SL, Logan J, Wolf AP, *et al.* (1991) Amphetamine induced decreases in (^{18}F)-N-methylspiroperidol binding in the baboon brain using positron emission tomography (PET). *Synapse* 7: 324–327.

Esterlis I, Cosgrove KP, Batis JC, *et al.* (2010) Quantification of smoking-induced occupancy of beta2-nicotinic acetylcholine receptors: Estimation of nondisplaceable binding. *Journal of Nuclear Medicine* 51: 1226–1233.

Fahlke C, Engel JA, Eriksson CJ, *et al.* (1994) Involvement of corticosterone in the modulation of ethanol consumption in the rat. *Alcohol* 11: 195–202.

Fan H, Ravert HT, Holt DP, Dannals RF, and Horti AG (2006) Synthesis of 1-(2,4-dichlorophenyl)-4-cyano-5-(4-[^{11}C]methoxyphenyl)-N-(piperidin-1-yl)-1H-pyrazole-3-carboxamide ([^{11}C]JHU75528) and 1-(2-bromophenyl)-4-cyano-5-(4-[^{11}C]methoxyphenyl)-N-(piperidin-1-yl)-1H-pyrazole-3-carboxamide ([^{11}C]JHU75575) as potential radioligands for PET imaging of cerebral cannabinoid receptor. *Journal of Labelled Compounds and Radiopharmaceuticals* 49: 1021–1036.

Fattore L, Fadda P, and Fratta W (2007) Endocannabinoid regulation of relapse mechanisms. *Pharmacological Research* 56: 418–427.

Febo M, Akbarian S, Schroeder FA, *et al.* (2009) Cocaine-induced metabolic activation in cortico-limbic circuitry is increased after exposure to the histone deacetylase inhibitor, sodium butyrate. *Neuroscience Letters* 465: 267–271.

Fehr C, Yakushev I, Hohmann N, *et al.* (2008) Association of low striatal dopamine D2 receptor availability with nicotine dependence similar to that seen with other drugs of abuse. *American Journal of Psychiatry* 165: 507–514.

Flannery BA, Roberts AJ, Cooney N, *et al.* (2001) The role of craving in alcohol use, dependence, and treatment. *Alcoholism: Clinical and Experimental Research* 25: 299–308.

Fowler JS, Volkow ND, MacGregor RR, *et al.* (1992) Comparative PET studies of the kinetics and distribution of cocaine and cocaethylene in baboon brain. *Synapse* 12: 220–227.

Fowler JS, Volkow ND, Wolf AP, *et al.* (1989) Mapping cocaine binding sites in human and baboon brain in vivo. *Synapse* 4: 371–377.

Fowler JS, Wang GJ, Volkow ND, *et al.* (1999) Smoking a single cigarette does not produce a measurable reduction in brain MAO B in non-smokers. *Nicotine and Tobacco Research* 1: 325–329.

Gao Y, Ravert HT, Kuwabara H, *et al.* (2009) Synthesis and biological evaluation of novel carbon-11 labeled pyridyl ethers: candidate ligands for in vivo imaging of alpha4beta2 nicotinic acetylcholine receptors (alpha4beta2-nAChRs) in the brain with positron emission tomography. *Bioorganic and Medical Chemistry* 17: 4367–4377.

George N, Brašić JR, Alexander M, *et al.* (2012) Differentiation of dopaminergic from noradrenergic neurobehavioral effects of stimulants. http://www.nrm12.org/upldrctry/NRM12_All_Abstracts.pdf. Late Breaking Poster Presentation No: LB03. Accessed online on November 8, 2012 [abstract].

Gilman S, Koeppe RA, Junck L, *et al.* (1996) Benzodiazepine receptor binding in the cerebellum in multiple system atrophy and olivopontocerebellar atrophy studied with positron emission tomography. *Advances in Neurology* 69: 459–466.

Goldstein RZ and Volkow ND (2011) Dysfunction of the prefrontal cortex in addiction: Neuroimaging findings and clinical implications. *Nature Reviews Neuroscience* 12: 652–669.

Grueter BA, Gosnell HB, Olsen CM, *et al.* (2006) Extracellular-signal regulated kinase 1-dependent metabotropic glutamate receptor 5-induced long-term depression in the bed nucleus of the stria terminalis is disrupted by cocaine administration. *Journal of Neuroscience* 26: 3210–3219.

Guo N, Guo A, Kralikova M, *et al.* (2010) Impact of D2 receptor internalization on binding affinity of neuroimaging radiotracers. *Neuropsychopharmacology* 35 (3): 806–817.

Hamill TG, Krause S, Ryan C, *et al.* (2005) Synthesis, characterization, and first successful monkey imaging studies of metabotropic glutamate receptor subtype 5 (mGluR5) PET radiotracers. *Synapse* 56: 205–216.

Heinz A, Jones DW, Mazzanti C, *et al.* (2000) A relationship between serotonin transporter genotype and *in vivo* protein expression and alcohol neurotoxicity. *Biological Psychiatry* 47: 643–649.

Heinz A, Siessmeier T, Wrase J, *et al.* (2005) Correlation of alcohol craving with striatal dopamine synthesis capacity and D2/3 receptor availability: A combined [^{18}F]DOPA and [^{18}F]DMFP PET study in detoxified alcoholic patients. *American Journal of Psychiatry* 162 (8): 1515–1520.

Hietala J, West C, Syvälahti E, *et al.* (1994) Striatal D2 dopamine receptor binding characteristics *in vivo* in patients with alcohol dependence. *Psychopharmacology (Berlin)* 116: 285–290.

Horti AG, Fan H, Kuwabara H, *et al.* (2006) ^{11}C-JHU75528: A radiotracer for PET imaging of CB1 cannabinoid receptors. *Journal of Nuclear Medicine* 47: 1689–1696.

Horti AG, Gao Y, Kuwabara H, *et al.* (2010) Development of radioligands with optimized imaging properties for quantification of nicotinic acetylcholine receptors by positron emission tomography. *Life Sciences* 86: 575–584.

Howlett AC, Barth F, Bonner TI, *et al.* (2002) International Union of Pharmacology. XXVII. Classification of cannabinoid receptors. *Pharmacological Reviews* 54: 161–202.

Innis RB, Cunningham VJ, Delforge J, *et al.* (2007) Consensus nomenclature for *in vivo* imaging of reversibly binding radioligands. *Journal of Cerebral Blood Flow and Metabolism* 27: 1533–1539.

Iso Y, Grajkowska E, Wroblewski JT, *et al.* (2006) Synthesis and structure–activity relationships of 3-[(2-methyl-1,3-thiazol-4-yl)ethynyl]pyridine analogues as potent, noncompetitive metabotropic glutamate receptor subtype 5 antagonists; search for cocaine medications. *Journal of Medical Chemistry* 49: 1080–1100.

Jacobsen LK, Staley JK, Malison RT, *et al.* (2000) Elevated central serotonin transporter binding availability in acutely abstinent cocaine-dependent patients. *American Journal of Psychiatry* 157: 1134–1140.

Kalivas PW and Stewart J (1991) Dopamine transmission in the initiation and expression of drug- and stress-induced sensitization of motor activity. *Brain Research Reviews* 16: 223–244.

Katner SN and Weiss F (1999) Ethanol-associated olfactory stimuli reinstate ethanol-seeking behavior after extinction and modify extracellular dopamine levels in the nucleus accumbens. *Alcoholism: Clinical and Experimental Research* 23: 1751–1760.

Kato A, Suzuki K, Kaneta H, *et al.* (2000) Regional differences in cerebral glucose metabolism in cirrhotic patients with subclinical hepatic encephalopathy using positron emission tomography. *Hepatology Research* 17: 237–245.

Kendziorra K, Wolf H, Meyer PM, *et al.* (2011) Decreased cerebral $\alpha 4\beta 2$* nicotinic acetylcholine receptor availability in patients with mild cognitive impairment and Alzheimer's disease assessed with positron emission tomography. *European Journal of Nuclear Medicine and Molecular Imaging* 38: 515–525.

Koepp MJ, Gunn RN, Lawrence AD, *et al.* (1998) Evidence for striatal dopamine release during a video game. *Nature* 393: 266–268.

Koob GF and Weiss F (1992) Neuropharmacology of cocaine and ethanol dependence. *Recent Developments in Alcoholism* 10: 201–233.

Korpi ER, Gründer G, and Lüddens H (2002) Drug interactions at GABA(A) receptors. *Progress in Neurobiology* 67: 113–159.

Laine TP, Ahonen A, Räsänen P, *et al.* (1999) Dopamine transporter availability and depressive symptoms during alcohol withdrawal. *Psychiatry Research* 90: 153–157.

Laruelle M and Huang Y (2001) Vulnerability of positron emission tomography radiotracers to endogenous competition: New insights. *Quarterly Journal of Nuclear Medicine* 45: 124–138.

Le Foll B and Goldberg SR (2005) Cannabinoid CB1 receptor antagonists as promising new medications for drug dependence. *Journal of Pharmacology and Experimental Therapeutics* 312: 875–883.

Leroy C, Karila L, Martinot JL, *et al.* (2012) Striatal and extrastriatal dopamine transporter in cannabis and tobacco addiction: A high-resolution PET study. *Addiction Biology* 17: 981–990.

Maldonado R, Valverde O, and Berrendero F (2006) Involvement of the endocannabinoid system in drug addiction. *Trends in Neurosciences* 29: 225–232.

Malison RT, Best SE, van Dyck CH, *et al.* (1998a) Elevated striatal dopamine transporters during acute cocaine abstinence as measured by [^{123}I] beta-CIT SPECT. *American Journal of Psychiatry* 155: 832–834.

Malison RT, McCance E, Carpenter LL, *et al.* (1998b) [^{123}I]beta-CIT SPECT imaging of dopamine transporter availability after mazindol administration in human cocaine addicts. *Psychopharmacology (Berlin)* 137: 321–325.

Martín-Santos R, Fagundo AB, Crippa JA. et al. (2010) Neuroimaging in cannabis use: A systematic review of the literature. *Psychological Medicine* 40: 383–398.

McCann UD, Kuwabara H, Kumar A, *et al.* (2008) Persistent cognitive and dopamine transporter deficits in abstinent methamphetamine users. *Synapse* 62: 91–100.

Melis MR and Argiolas A (1995) Dopamine and sexual behavior. *Neuroscience and Biobehavioral Reviews* 19: 19–38.

Modell JG, Mountz JM, and Beresford TP (1990) Basal ganglia/limbic striatal and thalamocortical involvement in craving and loss of control in alcoholism. *Journal of Neuropsychiatry and Clinical Neuroscience* 2: 123–144.

Monterosso JR, Flannery BA, Pettinati HM, *et al.* (2001) Predicting treatment response to naltrexone: The influence of craving and family history. *American Journal on Addictions* 10: 258–268.

Montgomery AJ, Lingford-Hughes AR, Egerton A, *et al.* (2007) The effect of nicotine on striatal dopamine release in man: A [^{11}C]raclopride PET study. *Synapse* 61: 637–645.

Morgan CJ and Curran HV; Independent Scientific Committee on Drugs (2012) Ketamine use: A review. *Addiction* 107: 27–38.

Moussawi K and Kalivas PW (2010) Group II metabotropic glutamate receptors (mGlu2/3) in drug addiction. *European Journal of Pharmacology* 639: 115–122.

Mukhin AG, Kimes AS, Chefer SI, *et al.* (2008) Greater nicotinic acetylcholine receptor density in smokers than in nonsmokers: A PET study with 2-^{18}F-FA-85380. *Journal of Nuclear Medicine* 49: 1628–1635.

Munro CA, McCaul ME, Wong DF, *et al.* (2006) Sex differences in striatal dopamine release in healthy adults. *Biological Psychiatry* 59: 966–974.

Nevo I and Hamon M (1995) Neurotransmitter and neuromodulatory mechanisms involved in alcohol abuse and alcoholism. *Neurochemistry International* 26: 305–342.

Olsson H, Halldin C, and Farde L (2004) Differentiation of extrastriatal dopamine D2 receptor density and affinity in the human brain using PET. *NeuroImage* 22: 794–803.

Oslin DW, Berrettini W, Kranzler HR, *et al.* (2003) A functional polymorphism of the mu-opioid receptor gene is associated with naltrexone response in alcohol-dependent patients. *Neuropsychopharmacology* 28: 1546–1552.

Oswald LM, Wong DF, McCaul M, *et al.* (2005) Relationships among ventral striatal dopamine release, cortisol secretion, and subjective responses to amphetamine. *Neuropsychopharmacology* 30: 821–832.

Oswald LM, Wong DF, Zhou Y, *et al.* (2007) Impulsivity and chronic stress are associated with amphetamine-induced striatal dopamine release. *NeuroImage* 36: 153–166.

Piazza PV and Le Moal ML (1996) Pathophysiological basis of vulnerability to drug abuse: Role of an interaction between stress, glucocorticoids, and dopaminergic neurons. *Annual Review of Pharmacology and Toxicology* 36: 359–378.

Piazza PV, Deminiere JM, le Moal M, *et al.* (1990) Stress- and pharmacologically-induced behavioral sensitization increases vulnerability to acquisition of amphetamine self-administration. *Brain Research* 514: 22–26.

Piazza PV, Marinelli M, Jodogne C, *et al.* (1994) Inhibition of corticosterone synthesis by Metyrapone decreases cocaine-induced locomotion and relapse of cocaine self-administration. *Brain Research* 658: 259–264.

Rahmim AR, Rousset O, and Zaidi H (2007) Strategies for motion tracking and correction in PET. *PET Clinics* 2: 251–266.

Reid MS, Hsu K Jr, and Berger SP (1997) Cocaine and amphetamine preferentially stimulate glutamate release in the limbic system: Studies on the involvement of dopamine. *Synapse* 27: 95–105.

Riccardi P, Baldwin R, Salomon R, *et al.* (2008) Estimation of baseline dopamine D2 receptor occupancy in striatum and extrastriatal regions in humans with positron emission tomography with [^{18}F] fallypride. *Biological Psychiatry* 63: 241–244.

Romach MK, Sellers EM, Somer GR, *et al.* (2002) Naltrexone in the treatment of alcohol dependence: A Canadian trial. *Canadian Journal of Clinical Pharmacology* 9: 130–136.

Rominger A, Cumming P, Xiong G, *et al.* (2011) [^{18}F]fallypride PET measurement of striatal and extrastriatal dopamine $D_{2/3}$ receptor availability in recently abstinent alcoholics. *Addiction Biology* 17 (2): 490–503.

Rousset OG, Ma Y, and Evans AC (1998) Correction for partial volume effects in PET: Principle and validation. *Journal of Nuclear Medicine* 39: 904–911.

Sadzot B, Mayberg HS, and Frost JJ (1990) Detection and quantification of opiate receptors in man by positron emission tomography: Potential applications to the study of pain. *Neurophysiogie Clinique* 20: 323–334.

Schlaepfer TE, Pearlson GD, Wong DF, *et al.* (1997) PET study of competition between intravenous cocaine and [^{11}C]raclopride at dopamine receptors in human subjects. *American Journal of Psychiatry* 154: 1209–1213.

Sevy S, Smith GS, Ma Y, *et al.* (2008) Cerebral glucose metabolism and D_2/D_3 receptor availability in young adults with cannabis dependence measured with positron emission tomography. *Psychopharmacology (Berlin)* 197: 549–556.

Shi J, Zhao LY, Copersino ML, *et al.* (2008) PET imaging of dopamine transporter and drug craving during methadone maintenance treatment and after prolonged abstinence in heroin users. *European Journal of Pharmacology* 579: 160–166.

Sinha R (2009) Modeling stress and drug craving in the laboratory: Implications for addiction treatment development. *Addiction Biology* 14 (1): 84–98.

Solinas M, Yasar S, and Goldberg SR (2007) Endocannabinoid system involvement in brain reward processes related to drug abuse. *Pharmacological Research* 56: 393–405.

Sossi V, de Jong HW, Barker WC, *et al.* (2005) The Second Generation HRRT – a Multi-Centre Scanner Performance Investigation. *2005 IEEE Nuclear Science Symposium Conference Record*: 2195–2199.

Spencer TJ, Biederman J, Ciccone PE, *et al.* (2006) PET study examining pharmacokinetics, detection and likeability, and dopamine transporter receptor occupancy of short- and long-acting oral methylphenidate. *American Journal of Psychiatry* 163: 387–395.

Stokes PR, Egerton A, Watson B, *et al.* (2011a) History of cannabis use is not associated with alterations in striatal dopamine D2/D3 receptor availability. *Journal of Psychopharmacology* 26 (1): 144–149.

Stokes PR, Rhodes RA, Grasby PM, *et al.* (2011b) The effects of the COMT Val108/158Met polymorphism on BOLD activation during working memory, planning, and response inhibition: A role for the posterior cingulate cortex? *Neuropsychopharmacology* 36: 763–771.

Sullivan EV, Deshmukh A, Desmond JE, *et al.* (2000) Contribution of alcohol abuse to cerebellar volume deficits in men with schizophrenia. *Archives of General Psychiatry* 57 (9): 894–902.

Terenius L (1996) Alcohol addiction (alcoholism) and the opioid system. *Alcohol* 13: 31–34.

Thanos PK, Bermeo C, Wang GJ, *et al.* (2009) D-cycloserine accelerates the extinction of cocaine-induced conditioned place preference in C57bL/c mice. *Behavioural Brain Research* 199: 345–349.

Tocris Bioscience (2012a) MPEP hydrochloride. http://www.tocris.com/dispprod.php?ItemId=1328. Accessed online on May 16, 2012.

Tocris Bioscience (2012b) MTEP hydrochloride. http://www.tocris.com/dispprod.php?ItemId=5408. Accessed online on May 16, 2012.

Tsukada H, Ohba H, Nishiyama S, Ishiyama, and Kakiuchi T (2011) Differential effects of stress on [^{11}C]raclopride and [^{11}C]MNPA binding to striatal D$_2$/D$_3$ dopamine receptors: A PET study in conscious monkeys. *Synapse* 65: 84–89.

Vervliet B (2008) Learning and memory in conditioned fear extinction: Effects of D-cycloserine. *Acta Psychologica (Amsterdam)* 127: 601–613.

Volkow ND and Fowler JS (2000) Addiction, a disease of compulsion and drive: Involvement of the orbitofrontal cortex. *Cereberbral Cortex* 10: 318–325.

Volkow ND, Chang L, Wang GJ, *et al.* (2001) Low level of brain dopamine D$_2$ receptors in methamphetamine abusers: Association with metabolism in the orbitofrontal cortex. *American Journal of Psychiatry* 158: 2015–2021.

Volkow ND, Fowler JS, and Wang, GJ (2004) The addicted human brain viewed in the light of imaging studies: Brain circuits and treatment strategies. *Neuropharmacology* 47 (Suppl. 1): 3–13.

Volkow ND, Fowler JS, Logan J, *et al.* (1995) Carbon-11-cocaine binding compared at sub-pharmacological and pharmacological doses: A PET study. *Journal of Nuclear Medicine* 36: 1289–1297.

Volkow ND, Fowler JS, Wang GJ, *et al.* (1993) Decreased dopamine D$_2$ receptor availability is associated with reduced frontal metabolism in cocaine abusers. *Synapse* 14: 169–177.

Volkow ND, Fowler JS, Wang GJ, *et al.* (2004) Dopamine in drug abuse and addiction: Results from imaging studies and treatment implications. *Molecular Psychiatry* 9: 557–569.

Volkow ND, Fowler JS, Wang GJ, *et al.* (2007a) Dopamine in drug abuse and addiction: Results of imaging studies and treatment implications. *Archives of Neurology* 64: 1575–1579.

Volkow ND, Fowler JS, Wang GJ, *et al.* (2009) Imaging dopamine's role in drug abuse and addiction. *Neuropharmacology* 56 (Suppl. 1): 3–8.

Volkow ND, Fowler JS, Wolf AP, *et al.* (1990a) Effects of chronic cocaine abuse on postsynaptic dopamine receptors. *American Journal of Psychiatry* 147: 719–724.

Volkow, ND, Gatley SJ, Fowler JS, *et al.* (1996b) Cocaine doses equivalent to those abused by humans occupy most of the dopamine transporters. *Synapse* 24 (4): 399–402.

Volkow ND, Gillespie H, Mullani N, *et al.* (1991) Cerebellar metabolic activation by delta-9-tetrahydrocannabinol in human brain: A study with positron emission tomography and ^{18}F-2-fluoro-2-deoxyglucose. *Psychiatry Research* 40: 69–78.

Volkow ND, Hitzemann R, Wang GJ, *et al.* (1992a) Decreased brain metabolism in neurologically intact healthy alcoholics. *American Journal of Psychiatry* 149: 1016–1022.

Volkow ND, Hitzemann R, Wang GJ, *et al.* (1992b) Long-term frontal brain metabolic changes in cocaine abusers. *Synapse* 11: 184–190.

Volkow ND, Hitzemann R, Wolf AP, *et al.* (1990b) Acute effects of ethanol on regional brain glucose metabolism and transport. *Psychiatry Research* 35: 39–48.

Volkow ND, Mullani N, Gould KL, *et al.* (1988a) Cerebral blood flow in chronic cocaine users: A study with positron emission tomography. *British Journal of Psychiatry* 152: 641–648.

Volkow ND, Mullani N, Gould L, *et al.* (1988b) Effects of acute alcohol intoxication on cerebral blood flow measured with PET. *Psychiatry Research* 24: 201–209.

Volkow ND, Wang GJ, Fischman MW, *et al.* (1997a) Relationship between subjective effects of cocaine and dopamine transporter occupancy. *Nature* 386: 827–830.

Volkow ND, Wang GJ, Fowler JS, *et al.* (1996a) Cocaine uptake is decreased in the brain of detoxified cocaine abusers. *Neuropsychopharmacology* 14 (3): 159–168.

Volkow ND, Wang GJ, Fowler, JS, *et al.* (1996c) Decreases in dopamine receptors but not in dopamine transporters in alcoholics. *Alcoholism: Clinical and Experimental Research* 20 (9): 1594–1598.

Volkow ND, Wang GJ, Fowler JS, *et al.* (1997b) Decreased striatal dopaminergic responsiveness in detoxified cocaine-dependent subjects. *Nature* 386: 830–833.

Volkow ND, Wang GJ, and Fowler JS (1997c) Imaging studies of cocaine in the human brain and studies of the cocaine addict. *Annals of the New York Academy of Sciences* 820: 41–54.

Volkow ND, Wang GJ, Fowler JS, *et al.* (1998) Enhanced sensitivity to benzodiazepines in active cocaine-abusing subjects: A PET study. *American Journal of Psychiatry* 155: 200–206.

Volkow ND, Wang GJ, Fowler JS, *et al.* (2008a) Overlapping neuronal circuits in addiction and obesity: Evidence of systems pathology. *Philosophical Transactions of the Royal Society B: Biological Sciences* 363: 3191–3200.

Volkow ND, Wang GJ, Maynard L, *et al.* (2002) Effects of alcohol detoxification on dopamine D2 receptors in alcoholics: A preliminary study. *Psychiatry Research* 116: 163–172.

Volkow ND, Wang GJ, Telang F, *et al.* (2007b) Profound decreases in dopamine release in striatum in detoxified alcoholics: Possible orbitofrontal involvement. *Journal of Neuroscience* 27 (46): 12700–12706.

Volkow ND, Wang GJ, Telang F, *et al.* (2008b) Dopamine increases in striatum do not elicit craving in cocaine abusers unless they are coupled with cocaine cues. *NeuroImage* 39: 1266–1273.

Wagner HN, Jr (1986) Quantitative imaging of neuroreceptors in the living human brain. *Seminars in Nuclear Medicine* 16: 51–62.

Wand GS, Mangold D, El Deiry S, *et al.* (1998) Family history of alcoholism and hypothalamic opioidergic activity. *Archives of General Psychiatry* 55: 1114–1119.

Wang GJ, Smith L, Volkow ND, *et al.* (2011) Decreased dopamine activity predicts relapse in methamphetamine abusers. *Molecular Psychiatry*, July 12. doi: 10.1038/mp.2011.86 [Epub ahead of print].

Wang GJ, Volkow ND, Fowler JS, *et al.* (1997) Dopamine D$_2$ receptor availability in opiate-dependent subjects before and after naloxone-precipitated withdrawal. *Neuropsychopharmacology* 16 (2):174–182.

Wang GJ, Volkow ND, Hitzemann R, *et al.* (1992) Brain imaging of an alcoholic with MRI, SPECT, and PET. *American Journal of Physiologic Imaging* 7 (3–4): 194–198.

Wang GJ, Volkow ND, Roque CT, *et al.* (1993) Functional importance of ventricular enlargement and cortical atrophy in healthy subjects and alcoholics as assessed with PET, MR imaging, and neuropsychologic testing. *Radiology* 186: 59–65.

Weerts EM, Wand GS, Kuwabara H, *et al.* (2011) Positron emission tomography imaging of mu- and delta-opioid receptor binding in alcohol-dependent and healthy control subjects. *Alcoholism: Clinical and Experimental Research* 35: 2162–2173.

Wong DF (2008) Is getting older all that rewarding? *Proceedings of the National Academy of Sciences U.S.A.* 105: 14751–14752.

Wong DF and Brašić JR (2001) *In vivo* imaging of neurotransmitter systems in neuropsychiatry. *Clinical Neuroscience Research* 1: 35–45.

Wong DF, Brašić JR, and Cascella N (2011) Neuroreceptor imaging of schizophrenia. In ME Shenton and BI Turetsky (eds), *Understanding Neuropsychiatric Disorders: Insights from Neuroimaging* (pp. 78–87). Cambridge: Cambridge University Press.

Wong DF, Broussolle EP, Wand G, *et al.* (1988) *In vivo* measurement of dopamine receptors in human brain by positron emission tomography: Age and sex differences. *Annals of the New York Academy of Sciences* 515: 203–214.

Wong D, Kuwabara H, Horti AG, *et al.* (2010) Quantification of cerebral cannabinoid receptors subtype 1 (CB1) in healthy subjects and schizophrenia by the novel PET radioligand [^{11}C]OMAR. *NeuroImage* 52: 1505–1513.

Wong DF, Kuwabara H, Schretlen DJ, *et al.* (2006) Increased occupancy of dopamine receptors in human striatum during cue-elicited cocaine craving. *Neuropsychopharmacology* 31: 2716–2727.

Wong DF, Maini A, Rousset OG, *et al.* (2003) Positron emission tomography: A tool for identifying the effects of alcohol dependence on the brain. *Alcohol Research and Health* 27: 161–173; http://www.ncbi.nlm.nih.gov/pubmed/15303627. Accessed on November, 8, 2012.

Wong DF, Potter WZ, and Brašić JR (2002) Proof of concept: Functional models for drug development in humans. In KL Davis, D Charney, JT Coyle, and C Nemeroff (eds), *Neuropsychopharmacology: The Fifth Generation of Progress* (pp. 457–473). Baltimore, MD: Lippincott Williams & Wilkins.

Wong DF, Tauscher J, and Gründer G (2009) The role of imaging in proof of concept for CNS drug discovery and development. *Neuropsychopharmacology* 34: 187–203.

Wong DF, Wagner HN, Jr, Dannals RF, *et al.* (1984) Effects of age on dopamine and serotonin receptors measured by positron tomography in the living human brain. *Science* 226 (4681): 1393–1396.

Wong DF, Wagner HN, Jr, Tune LE, *et al.* (1986) Positron emission tomography reveals elevated D$_2$ dopamine receptors in drug-naive schizophrenics. *Science* 234: 1558–1563.

Wong KK, Müller ML, Kuwabara H, *et al.* (2012) Gender differences in nigrostriatal dopaminergic innervation are present at young-to-middle but not at older age in normal adults. *Journal of Clinical Neuroscience* 19: 183–184.

Yang P, Wentzlaff KA, Katzmann JA, *et al.* (1999) Alpha1-antitrypsin deficiency allele carriers among lung cancer patients. *Cancer Epidemiology, Biomarkers, and Prevention* 8: 461–465.

Yoder KK, Morris ED, Constantinescu CC, *et al.* (2009) When what you see isn't what you get: Alcohol cues, alcohol administration, prediction error, and human striatal dopamine. *Alcoholism: Clinical and Experimental Research* 33: 139–149.

Yoshimoto K, Ueda S, Kato B, *et al.* (2000) Alcohol enhances characteristic releases of dopamine and serotonin in the central nucleus of the amygdala. *Neurochemistry International* 37: 369–376.

Zhou Y, Maini A, Brasic JR, *et al.* (2003) Detection of physiological effects of pharmacological challenges in human dynamic PET studies by parametric imaging and statistical moment analysis. *Journal of Nuclear Medicine* 44 (5 suppl.): 14P [abstract].

25

Application of Magnetic Resonance Spectroscopic Imaging to Addiction Research[1]

Sujung Yoon, In Kyoon Lyoo, and Perry F. Renshaw

1 Introduction

With increasing acceptance of addiction as a brain disease (Leshner, 1997), remarkable advances in research methodologies have taken place over the past few decades and our understanding of addiction has been greatly enhanced. Among several quantitative and qualitative approaches implemented in the field of addiction research, neuroimaging techniques are important and unique in that they can noninvasively provide not only *in vivo* evidence regarding each drug's neurobiological effects on the brain but also direct information on the brain mechanisms of susceptibility to drug abuse (Fowler, Volkow, Kassed, and Chang, 2007; Licata and Renshaw, 2010). Magnetic resonance spectroscopy (MRS), which measures concentrations of neurochemical metabolites within the brain, is a particularly useful noninvasive neuroimaging technique that provides insights into biochemical changes during or after drug exposure (Licata and Renshaw, 2010). Since proton MRS methodology was first implemented in a study of alcohol-dependent patients (Martin *et al.*, 1995), the applications of MRS in addiction research have significantly expanded.

This chapter focuses on the application of MRS methodologies and their relevance to addiction research. Specifically, we will introduce the significant features and characteristics of currently available MRS techniques and summarize empirical findings. We will also outline the limitations of current MRS approaches and highlight potential future research directions to provide an enhanced understanding of brain mechanisms that underlie addiction.

[1] This work was supported by National Institute on Drug Abuse Grants R01 DA024070 (to Drs Lyoo and Renshaw) and K05 DA031247 (to Dr Renshaw).

The Wiley-Blackwell Handbook of Addiction Psychopharmacology, First Edition. Edited by James MacKillop and Harriet de Wit.
© 2013 John Wiley & Sons, Ltd. Published 2013 by John Wiley & Sons, Ltd.

2   Methodological Aspects of Magnetic Resonance Spectroscopic Imaging

2.1   Proton (^{1}H) magnetic resonance spectroscopic imaging

The most widely used nucleus for MRS studies on drug abuse is hydrogen nucleus, which includes a single proton. This is mainly because of the high MR signal sensitivity of the ^{1}H nucleus and the high natural abundance of the ^{1}H nucleus. Further, the fact that standard radio-frequency coils developed for acquisition of clinical and diagnostic MR images are also adequate for ^{1}H MRS also enables its wide availability. In contrast, MRS using other nuclei, for example ^{31}P or ^{13}C may require special MRI coils which are tuned to each nucleus and expensive scanner components. Since hydrogen exists in most metabolites, ^{1}H MRS has been regarded as the most powerful and sensitive tool to enable non-invasive *in vivo* measurement of a wide range of neurobiologically important metabolites of the brain. Peaks of several major neurochemical metabolites can be detected and quantified by using water- and lipid-suppressed localized proton (^{1}H) spectra (Figure 25.1A) (Licata and Renshaw, 2010). The most prominent resonances are N-acetylaspartate (NAA), choline-containing compounds (Cho), myo-inositol (mI) and creatine/phosphocreatine (Cr). A handful of amino acids, including glutamate, γ-aminobutyric acid (GABA), glutamine, and lactate, are also detectable using proton MRS methods.

The resonance from NAA, which occurs at 2.02 parts per million (PPM), contributes to the largest signal in the water-suppressed proton spectrum (Urenjak, Williams, Gadian, and Noble, 1993; Stork and Renshaw, 2005). The exact function of NAA in the brain remains unclear. Nevertheless, since NAA is primarily localized within neurons (Ross and Bluml, 2001), its concentration is thought to reflect neuronal density and viability. Reductions in NAA levels have been associated with

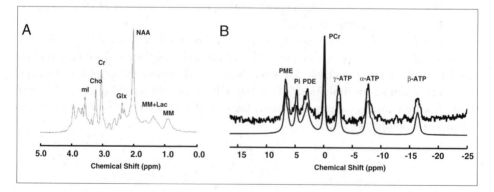

Figure 25.1   Sample magnetic resonance spectroscopy spectra from ^{1}H MRS (A) and ^{31}P MRS (B) at 3T

Abbreviations: Cho, choline/phosphocholine; Cr, creatine/phosphocreatine; Glx, glutamate/glutamine; Lac, lactate; mI, myo-inositol; MM, macromolecules; NAA, N-acetylaspartate; PME, phosphomonoesters; PDE, phosphodiesters; Pi, inorganic phosphate; PCr, phosphocreatine; ATP, adenosine triphosphate

potential neuronal injury or loss (Brooks, Friedman, and Gasparovic, 2001; Chen, Charles, Barboriak, and Doraiswamy, 2000; Demougeot, Marie, Giroud, and Beley, 2004). Based on the role of NAA levels as a neuronal marker, a considerable number of ^{1}H MRS studies on drug abuse have interpreted findings of reduced NAA levels as *in vivo* evidence for drug-induced neurotoxicity (Licata and Renshaw, 2010). The reversibility of changes in NAA levels with prolonged abstinence has also been accentuated by ^{1}H MRS studies of drug abuse populations. In addition, changes in NAA concentration may also arise from alterations in mitochondrial oxidative phosphorylation. This possibility has recently received attention based on reports of several psychiatric disorders where mitochondrial dysfunction plays an important role (reviewed in Stork and Renshaw, 2005). Given that the synthesis of NAA is an energy-dependent step that occurs primarily in the mitochondria (Truckenmiller, Namboodiri, Brownstein, and Neale, 1985; Patel and Clark, 1979), changes in NAA levels in drug abusers might also be viewed being consistent with drug-induced mitochondrial dysfunction.

The main components that contribute to the Cho peak detected at 3.23 ppm are soluble membrane phospholipid metabolites including phosphocholine and glycerophosphocholine. Less than 5% of the Cho signal arises from free choline and acetylcholine (Miller *et al.*, 1996). Because phosphocholine and glycerophosphocholine are involved in the synthesis and degradation of the cell membrane, respectively (Brenner *et al.*, 1993), altered Cho signal primarily appears to reflect changes in membrane phospholipid metabolism (Govindaraju, Young, and Maudsley, 2000). Although results remain inconsistent, several ^{1}H MRS studies have reported on potential relationships between drug abuse and Cho level changes which could suggest that altered membrane turnover may be implicated in the neurochemical mechanisms underlying substance abuse.

Since mI is most highly concentrated in glial cells, the proton resonances of mI at 3.56 ppm have commonly been regarded as a marker reflecting glial contents (Brand, Richter-Landsberg, and Leibfritz, 1993). For example, increased mI signal may represent glial proliferation. In addition, mI functions as a precursor for the synthesis of phosphatidylinositol, which is a component of phospholipid membranes, as well as a substrate for the phosphoinositide second-messenger system (Ross and Bluml, 2001; Kato, Inubushi, and Kato, 1998). Osmoregulation and storage of glucose have also been suggested as major roles of mI (Ross, 1991). Many, but not all, ^{1}H MRS studies have reported elevation of mI levels that may indicate abnormal phospholipid metabolism and intracellular signaling systems in drug abusers (reviewed below).

Although the resonance of Cr in the ^{1}H spectrum has been regarded to be relatively constant in the normal brain (Pouwels and Frahm, 1998), and therefore is suitable for use as an internal reference to normalize the metabolite peaks (Bonavita, Di Salle, and Tedeschi, 1999), recent studies have demonstrated that cerebral Cr levels may be altered in several pathological conditions (Marshall *et al.*, 1996). The Cr peak generally reflects the total cellular creatine stores, namely the sum of creatine and phosphocreatine from both sides of the creatine kinase reaction (Sauter and Rudin, 1993).

The spectral resonances of glutamate and glutamine, which are closely related to each other, considerably overlap and hard to resolve separately, particularly at lower field strength (Ross and Bluml, 2001). Likewise, the resonance of GABA is also difficult to measure owing not only to overlapping resonances with those of Cr and macromolecules (Behar, Rothman, Spencer, and Petroff, 1994; Kish, Perry, and Hansen, 1979) but also to its low concentration of approximately 1 mM (Du *et al.*, 2004). Therefore, the measurement of GABA often requires selective acquisition methodologies as well as specific editing techniques (Ke *et al.*, 2000; Sanacora *et al.*, 1999). Changes in the 'Glx' signal, arising from the combined resonance of glutamate, glutamine, and GABA, are assumed to reflect alterations in gluta-mate/glutamine/GABA cycle (Stork and Renshaw, 2005). Since GABA receptors are major targets for the action of alcohol in the brain, efforts to measure *in vivo* brain levels of GABA non-invasively began in the late 1990s (Behar *et al.*, 1999). Altered Glx resonance intensities have also been reported in alcoholics as well as in other drug abusers, and this may support an important role of amino acid neurotransmission in the pathophysiological mechanisms underlying addiction.

2.2   Phosphorus (^{31}P) magnetic resonance spectroscopic imaging

Data from ^{31}P MRS, which detects a total of seven peaks from phosphorus containing compounds, including phosphomonoesters (PME), phosphodiesters (PDE), phos-phocreatine (PCr), inorganic phosphate and nucleoside triphosphate (NTP), may provide information on membrane phospholipid metabolism (PME and PDE) and tissue bioenergetics (PCr, inorganic phosphate, and NTP) (Figure 25.1B) (Agarwal *et al.*, 2010; Moore, Frederick, and Renshaw, 1999).

While the PME resonance reflects the level of precursors of phospholipids, including phosphocholine and phosphoethanolamine, the PDE resonance arises from more mobile phospholipids and reflects the products of phospholipid breakdown, including glycerophosphocholine and glycerophosphoethanolamine (Buchli, Duc, Martin, and Boesiger, 1994). Changes in PME and PDE are generally attributed to alterations of membrane integrity in both neuronal and non-neuronal tissues (Moore, Frederick, and Renshaw, 1999).

Resonances reflecting high-phosphate energy metabolism include PCr, inorganic phosphate, and α-, β-, γ-nucleoside triphosphate (Moore, Frederick, and Renshaw, 1999). PCr is a high-energy phosphate formed from ATP and creatine by creatine kinase and functions as a buffer to maintain constant tissue levels of ATP (Erecinska and Silver, 1989).

Although increasing preclinical evidence has implicated drug-induced changes not only in phospholipid membrane metabolism but also in brain bioenergetics (Hoek and Rubin, 1990; Song *et al.*, 2010; Cunha-Oliveira, Rego, and Oliveira, 2008), only a few studies, to date, have adopted ^{31}P MRS methodology to explore the involvement of these neurochemical mechanisms in the pathophysiology of drug abuse.

2.3   Carbon (^{13}C) magnetic resonance spectroscopic imaging

More recently, *in vivo* quantitative assessment of the glutamate–glutamine cycle as well as glucose oxidation has been made possible with the development of local-ized ^{13}C MRS techniques (Rothman, Behar, Hyder, and Shulman, 2003). After the injection or ingestion of ^{13}C-labeled precursors, the rate of appearance of labeled products may be measured to determine rates of oxidation and neurotransmitter metabolism (Mason *et al.*, 1995; Mason, Rothman, Behar, and Shulman, 1992). In the glutamate–glutamine cycle, glutamate, which is released from nerve terminals, is transported into adjacent glial cells and subsequently converted to glutamine (Rothman, Behar, Hyder, and Shulman, 2003). Glial cells release glutamine, which is then absorbed via presynaptic terminals by neurons (Rothman, Behar, Hyder, and Shulman, 2003). In neurons, glutamine is subsequently metabolized into glutamate by glutaminase and then the cycle is completed (Rothman, Behar, Hyder, and Shulman, 2003). Measurement of ^{13}C label tracking within the glutamate–glutamine cycle provides information on neuronal–glial interactions that are closely related to glutamatergic neurotransmission (Rothman *et al.*, 1999; Rothman *et al.*, 2002). Although several methodological and technical considerations have significantly limited the implementation of ^{13}C MRS techniques in human addiction research (Mason *et al.*, 1995; Rothman, Behar, Hyder, and Shulman, 2003), future studies using these methods would provide unique insights into the contribution of glial–neuronal energy metabolism to the pathophysiology of addiction.

3 Understanding of Addiction: Current Empirical Evidence from Studies Using MRS Methodology

3.1 Alcohol

Functional and structural alterations observed in neuroimaging studies (see Table 25.1) support the conclusion that chronic exposure to alcohol results in neurotoxic effects on the brain (Buhler and Mann, 2011; Sullivan and Pfefferbaum, 2005). Mounting evidence at the neuropathological level indicates that binge alcohol exposure appears to produce cell death as well as degeneration of axons and dendrites in several brain regions, although it remains unclear whether these neurotoxic effects are permanent or reversible (Obernier, Bouldin, and Crews, 2002; Nixon and Crews, 2004). Consistent with these preclinical findings, rigorous analyses of alcohol-dependent patients using several imaging techniques have noted volume reductions as well as functional deficits in the cortical, subcortical, and cerebellar brain regions (Buhler and Mann, 2011; Sullivan and Pfefferbaum, 2005). Cognitive and emotional disturbances corresponding to these brain regional deficits have also been observed in studies of alcohol dependence, supporting the clinical relevance of alcohol-induced neurotoxic effects on the brain (Raimo and Schuckit, 1998; Oscar-Berman and Marinkovic, 2007). Since the early 1990s, several research groups have devoted themselves to the characterization of neurochemical alterations related to chronic alcohol consumption and its clinical implications using MRS (Mason *et al.*, 2005; Meyerhoff and Durazzo, 2008).

Among neurochemical metabolites that can be detected in ^{1}H spectra, changes in NAA levels have received attention mainly as an indicator of alcohol-induced neurotoxicity (Jagannathan, Desai, and Raghunathan, 1996; Bendszus *et al.*, 2001;

Table 25.1 Published MRS research in patients with alcohol dependence

Study	Subjects	Gender (M/F)	Mean age (SD)[1]	Patients' characteristics	Imaging methods	Regions examined/ Voxel size	Results on metabolites[2]	Clinical correlations
^{1}H MRS studies focusing on NAA, Cho, and mI changes related to alcohol dependence								
Martin et al. (1995)	10 patients 9 controls	6/4 6/3	19–73 (range) 20–60 (range)	• 10 current AUD	• 1.5T • single voxel • PRESS	• superior cerebellar vermis • 8 cm³	• increased Cho/NAA ratio after a 1 month of abstinence	• a negative correlation between cerebellar Cho/NAA ratio and CNS impairment
Jagannathan, Desai, and Raghunathan (1996)	10 patients 27 controls	NA NA	46 44	• 10 current AUD	• 1.5T • single voxel • STEAM	• frontal lobe/ cerebellum/ thalamus • NA	• ↓ NAA/Cho ratios and NAA/Cr ratios in frontal lobe, cerebellum, and thalamus	• not examined
Schweinsburg et al. (2000)	9 patients 5 controls	9/0 5/0	47 (7) 45 (8)	• 9 current AUD (4 recently detoxified and 5 long-term abstinent patients)	• 1.5T • single voxel	• frontal GM/ frontal WM/ thalamus • 8 cm³/8 cm³/ 3.4 cm³	• ↑ mI in frontal GM and thalamus in recently detoxified patients	• not examined
Bendszus et al. (2001)	17 patients 12 controls	11/6 7/5	41 (8) 43 (8)	• 17 current AUD	• 1.5 T • single voxel • PRESS	• midfrontal lobe/left cerebellum • 24 cm³/8 cm³	• ↓ NAA/Cr ratios in midfrontal lobe and cerebellum • ↓ Cho/Cr ratio in cerebellum • increased NAA/Cr ratios in midfrontal lobe and cerebellum after a 1 month of abstinence • increased Cho/Cr ratios in cerebellum after a 1 month of abstinence	• a significant correlation between increased NAA/Cr ratio in midfrontal lobe and improved performance on verbal learning with abstinence

Study	Patients/controls	Gender (M/F)	Age mean (SD)	Sample	Method	Region	Findings	Correlations
Schweinsburg et al. (2001)	37 patients 15 controls	34/3 14/1	40 (10) 38 (8)	• 37 current AUD	• 1.5T • single voxel • PRESS	• right frontal WM/right parietal WM • 8 cm³	• ↓ NAA levels in frontal WM • ↑ mI level in frontal and parietal WM	• a negative correlation between frontal NAA levels and illness duration
Parks et al. (2002)	31 patients 12 controls	27/4 5/7	47 (10) 35 (8)	• 31 current AUD (8 early relapse/12 late relapse/11 non-relapse)	• 1.5 T • single voxel • PRESS	• right anterior frontal lobe/anterior cerebellar vermis • 8 cm³	• ↓ NAA and Cho levels in cerebellum increased cerebellar NAA level after 3 months of abstinence	• not examined
Schweinsburg et al. (2003)	25 patients 25 controls	17/8 13/12	36M/43F 39M/36F	• 25 current AUD	• 1.5 T • single voxel • PRESS	• frontal GM/frontal WM • 8 cm³	• ↓ NAA levels in frontal WM • ↓ NAA levels in frontal GM in female patients, not in male patients	• not examined
Bloomer, Langleben, and Meyerhoff (2004)	12 patients 10 controls	12/0 10/0	47 (5) 45 (7)	• 12 current AUD	• 1.5 T • single voxel • PRESS	• brainstem • bilateral hippocampi/mesial temporal lobe • 70 cm³	• ↓ NAA/Cr ratio in brainstem • ↓ Cho/Cr ratio in brainstem	• not examined
Durazzo, Gazdzinski, Banys, and Meyerhoff (2004)	24 patients 26 controls	24/0 21/5	50 (7) 48 (5)	• 24 current AUD (10 nonsmokers and 14 smokers)	• 1.5T • multislice	• covering major lobes	• ↓ NAA levels in frontal GM and WM • ↓ Cho levels in frontal GM/WM, parietal GM/WM, and thalamus	• associations between smoking history and lower NAA levels in frontal WM/midbrain as well as lower Cho level in midbrain

(*Continued*)

Table 25.1 (Continued)

Study	Subjects	Gender (M/F)	Mean age (SD)[1]	Patients' characteristics	Imaging methods	Regions examined/ Voxel size	Results on metabolites[2]	Clinical correlations
Meyerhoff et al. (2004)	46 patients 52 controls	38/8 32/20	41 (9) 41 (9)	• 46 current AUD	• 1.5T • multislice	• covering major lobes	• ↓ NAA levels in frontal WM • ↑ Cr levels in parietal GM	• positive correlation between frontal WM NAA levels and executive/working memory function
Ende et al. (2005)	33 patients 30 controls	21/12 20/10	46 (9) 44 (10)	• 33 current AUD (followed up after 3 and 6 months of abstinence)	• 1.5T • multislice	• frontal lobe (frontal WM/ DLPFC/ACC) • cerebellum (vermis/dentate nucleus/ cerebellar cortex)	• ↓ Cho level in frontal WM and cerebellar cortex • increased Cho level in all regions after 3 months of abstinence	• no associations between changes in metabolite levels and abstinence duration
Durazzo et al. (2006)	26 patients 29 controls	24/2 24/5	50 (10) 49 (5)	• 26 current AUD (17 nonsmokers and 19 smokers/ 25 followed up after 1 month of abstinence)	• 1.5T • multislice	• covering major lobes	• ↓ NAA levels in parietal WM • ↓ Cho levels in parietal WM • Increased frontal NAA and frontoparietal Cho levels after 1 month of abstinence	• significant correlations between increased NAA and Cho levels *and* improved working memory and visuospatial learning with abstinence, respectively
Bartsch et al. (2007)	15 patients 10 controls	10/5 6/4	42 (8) 47 (7)	• 15 current AUD (follow up after the short-term abstinence)	• 1.5 T • single voxel • PRESS	• left cerebellum/ midfrontal lobe • 8 cm³ (cerebellum)/ 24 cm³ (frontal lobe)	• Increased NAA levels of midfrontal lobe and Cho levels of cerebellum after the short-term abstinence in patients	• significant correlations between increased midfrontal NAA level and improved attention with abstinence

Study	Sample	Sex (M/F)	Age	Subjects	Field/Technique	Coverage	Findings	Correlations
Durazzo, Gazdzinski, Yeh, and Meyerhoff (2008)	70 patients	67/3	28–66 (range)	• 70 current AUD (26 abstainers and 44 resumers followed up after 6–12 months)	• 1.5T • multislice	• covering major lobes	• ↓ NAA levels of frontal GM, temporal GM, frontal WM in resumers relative to abstainers • ↓ Cho levels of frontal GM in resumers relative to abstainers	• in resumers, negative correlations between NAA levels in frontal WM and temporal GM and drinking days at follow-up
Wang et al. (2009)	48 patients 26 controls	46/2 25/1	50 (9) 48 (7)	• 54 current AUD (22 nonsmokers and 26 smokers)	• 1.5T • multislice	• covering major lobes	• ↓ NAA levels of frontal WM in smoking, but not in nonsmoking patients • no difference in in Cho, Cr, and mI levels of frontal WM between groups	• not examined
Gazdzinski, Durazzo, Mon, and Meyerhoff (2010)	54 patients	54/0	28–66 (range)	• 54 current AUD	• 1.5T • multislice	• covering major lobes	• not examined	• negative correlations between several metabolite levels including NAA, Cho, Cr, mI in the frontal lobe, subcortical nuclei, and cerebellar vermis and BMI

(Continued)

Table 25.1 (*Continued*)

Study	Subjects	Gender (M/F)	Mean age (SD)[1]	Patients' characteristics	Imaging methods	Regions examined/ Voxel size	Results on metabolites[2]	Clinical correlations
Gazdzinski et al. (2010)	36 patients 22 control	33/3 20/2	50 (10) 48 (8)	• 36 current AUD (16 nonsmokers and 20 smokers)	• 1.5T • multislice	• covering major lobar white matter	• ↓ NAA level of frontal WM in smoking patients • ↓ NAA level of parietal WM in nonsmoking patients • no changes in NAA, Cho, mI levels with 1 month of abstinence • no difference in Cho, Cr, and mI levels of WM between groups	• not examined
^{1}H MRS studies focusing on glutamate, glutamine, and GABA changes related to alcohol dependence								
Modi et al. (2011)	9 patients 13 controls	9/0 13/0	41 (8) 47 (6)	• 9 current AUD	• 1.5 T • single voxel • PRESS	• left occipital lobe • 3.4 cm³	• ↑ Cho/Cr ratio • no difference in NAA/Cr ratio	• not examined
Behar et al. (1999)	5 patients 5 hepatic encephalopathy 10 controls	NA NA NA	46 (11) 40 (6) 35 (7)	• 5 current AUD • 5 hepatic encephalopathy	• 1.5 T • single voxel	• occipital lobe • 13.5 cm³	• ↓ GABA levels in alcohol-dependent patients • ↓ GABA levels in patients with hepatic encephalopathy	• not examined

Study	Patients/Controls	Sex ratio	Age	Sample	Acquisition	Location/Voxel	Findings	Correlations
Miese et al. (2006)	26 patients 19 cirrhosis 18 controls	18/8 14/5 8/10	54 (13) 61 (12) 56 (14)	• 26 current AUD (with cirrhosis) • 19 nonalcoholic cirrhosis	• 1.5 T • single voxel	• basal ganglia/occipital WM • 8 cm³	• ↑ Glx/Cr ratios in the basal ganglia and occipital WM • ↓ mI/Cr ratios in the basal ganglia and occipital WM • ↓ Cho/Cr ratios in the basal ganglia	• no specific clinical correlations with metabolite ratios
Mason et al. (2006)	12 patients 8 controls	12/0 8/0	39 (8) 39 (9)	• 12 current AUD (5 nonsmokers and 7 smokers)	• 2.1T spectrometer • J-editing sequence	• occipital lobe • 13.5 mm³	• Decreased GABA levels in nonsmoking patients with 1 month of abstinence • no difference in NAA, Cho, glutamate/glutamine, and GABA levels	• not examined
Lee et al. (2007)	13 patients 18 controls	13/0 18/0	34 (6) 33 (1)	• 13 current AUD	• 1.5 T • single voxel • PRESS	• ACC/Insula • 4 cm³	• ↑ glutamate/Cr ratio in ACC • ↓ Cho levels in ACC • ↓ Cr levels in ACC • no difference in NAA and mI levels in ACC	• a positive correlation between glutamate levels in ACC and memory retention ability • a positive correlation between glutamate levels in ACC and alcohol consumption amount
Thoma et al. (2011)	13 patients 17 controls	10/3 9/8	35 (7) 32 (8)	• 7 current AUD • 6 AUD in remission	• 3 T • single voxel • PRESS	• ACC • 12 cm³	• ↓ glutamate levels • ↑ glutamine levels • no difference in NAA, Cho, Cr, and mI levels	• a negative correlation between glutamate levels and scale scores on quantifying alcohol use consequence • a positive correlation between glutamine levels and scale scores on quantifying alcohol use consequence

(Continued)

Table 25.1 (*Continued*)

Study	Subjects	Gender (M/F)	Mean age (SD)[1]	Patients' characteristics	Imaging methods	Regions examined/ Voxel size	Results on metabolites[2]	Clinical correlations
^{1}H MRS studies focusing on medication effects on metabolite changes related to alcohol dependence								
Umhau *et al.* (2010)	15 with ACAMP 18 with placebo	9/6 10/8	33 (1) 34 (1)	• 33 current AUD • 4 weeks of treatment with ACAMP or placebo	• 3 T • single voxel • PRESS	• ACC • 15.6 cm³	• decreased glutamate/Cr ratio with ACAMP treatment • no changes of NAA/Cr and Cho/Cr in both treatment groups	• not examined
^{31}P MRS studies focusing on phospholipid metabolism related to alcohol dependence								
Meyerhoff *et al.* (1995)	47 patients 49 controls	47/0 49/0		• 47 current AUD (32 HIV-positive/15 HIV-negative)		• GM/WM	• ↓ PDE and PCr levels in WM • ↓ PDE in GM in HIV seropositive patients relative to HIV seronegative controls	• not examined
Estilaei *et al.* (2001)	13 patients 17 control	13/0 17/0	44 (9) 37 (10)	• 13 current AUD	• 1.5T • single voxel • ISIS	• centrum semiovale • 158 cm³	• no differences in PME, PDE, PCr, γ-ATP, and Pi levels	• not examined

[1]years (SD)

[2]All results presented in Table 25.1 are those of patients with alcohol use disorders relative to comparison subjects except where indicated otherwise. Only positive findings are presented in this table.

Abbreviations: ACAMP, acamprosate; ACC, anterior cingulate cortex; ATP, adenosine triphosphate; AUD, alcohol use disorder; Cho, choline-containing compound; CNS, central nervous system; Cr, creatine and phosphocreatine; DLPFC, dorsolateral prefrontal cortex; GABA, γ-aminobutyric acid; Glx, glutamine + glutamate; GM, gray matter; HIV, human immunodeficiency virus; MRS, magnetic resonance spectroscopy; mI, myo-inositol; NA, not available; NAA, N-acetylaspartate; PCr, phosphocreatine; PDE, phosphodiester; PI, inorganic phosphate; PRESS, point resolved spectroscopy; SD, standard deviation; STEAM, stimulated echo acquisition mode; T, tesla; WM, white matter.

Schweinsburg *et al.*, 2001; Schweinsburg *et al.*, 2003; Parks *et al.*, 2002; Bloomer, Langleben, and Meyerhoff, 2004; Durazzo, Gazdzinski, Banys, and Meyerhoff, 2004; Durazzo *et al.*, 2006; Durazzo, Gazdzinski, Yeh, and Meyerhoff, 2008; Meyerhoff *et al.*, 2004; Wang *et al.*, 2009; Gazdzinski *et al.*, 2010) as NAA is identified as a neuronal marker (Ross and Bluml, 2001). The clinical relevance of NAA-level reductions in alcoholic patients has been supported by its correlation with poor cognitive performance (Meyerhoff *et al.*, 2004) as well as by its potential to predict treatment outcome (Durazzo, Gazdzinski, Yeh, and Meyerhoff, 2008). Reduced NAA levels, as putative evidence for neuronal dysfunction, have been noted in the alcoholic brains, primarily in the frontal gray/white matter (Jagannathan, Desai, and Raghunathan, 1996; Bendszus *et al.*, 2001; Schweinsburg *et al.*, 2001; Schweinsburg *et al.*, 2003; Durazzo, Gazdzinski, Banys, and Meyerhoff, 2004; Meyerhoff *et al.*, 2004; Durazzo, Gazdzinski, Yeh, and Meyerhoff, 2008; Wang *et al.*, 2009; Gazdzinski *et al.*, 2010), the cerebellum (Jagannathan, Desai, and Raghunathan, 1996; Bendszus *et al.*, 2001; Parks *et al.*, 2002; Bloomer, Langleben, and Meyerhoff, 2004), and less frequently in other areas including the parietal/temporal lobes (Durazzo *et al.*, 2006; Durazzo, Gazdzinski, Yeh, and Meyerhoff, 2008) and the thalamus (Jagannathan, Desai, and Raghunathan, 1996). These findings of frontal lobar and cerebellar involvement indirectly support the regional vulnerability of the brain to alcohol-induced neurotoxicity, which is generally consistent with previous preclinical and human neuroimaging studies (Sullivan, 2003; Kril, Halliday, Svoboda, and Cartwright, 1997; Buhler and Mann, 2011; Sullivan and Pfefferbaum, 2005).

Several clinical and demographic factors may play a role in accelerating or attenuating chronic alcohol-induced alterations in NAA levels. Smoking, which is frequently comorbid with alcohol dependence, is likely to exacerbate chronic alcohol-induced neuronal injury (Penland, Hoplight, Obernier, and Crews, 2001). A series of ^{1}H MRS studies by Meyerhoff *et al.* have demonstrated NAA level reductions, as well as a predominant involvement in the frontal lobe, in smoking and alcohol-dependent patients relative to nonsmoking patients (Durazzo, Gazdzinski, Banys, and Meyerhoff, 2004; Durazzo *et al.*, 2006; Wang *et al.*, 2009; Gazdzinski *et al.*, 2010). Further, comorbid smoking may impede a potential metabolic recovery from chronic alcohol-induced neuronal injury following abstinence (Durrazo *et al.*, 2006). These findings may underlie the cumulative adverse effects of both nicotine and alcohol on the brain at a metabolic level.

Gender has also been considered to modulate the effects of chronic alcohol use on the brain (Hommer, Momenan, Kaiser, and Rawlings, 2001). While frontal white matter is likely to be equally affected by chronic alcohol consumption in both male and female alcoholics, Schweinsburg *et al.* (2003) reported a greater reduction in NAA levels within frontal gray matter in female patients compared to their male counterparts, indicating a gender-specific vulnerability of women to alcohol-induced gray matter injury, particularly in the frontal lobe, regardless of alcohol use status.

Cho, as an indicator of cell membrane turnover (Govindaraju, Young, and Maudsley, 2000), is the second most frequently affected metabolite in alcohol-dependent patients (Martin *et al.*, 1995; Bendszus *et al.*, 2001; Parks *et al.*, 2002; Bloomer, Langleben, and Meyerhoff, 2004; Durazzo, Gazdzinski, Banys, and Meyerhoff, 2004; Ende *et al.*, 2005; Durazzo *et al.*, 2006; Durazzo, Gazdzinski, Yeh, and Meyerhoff,

2008; Modi *et al.*, 2011). Reduced Cho levels have been noted in several brain regions of alcoholic patients including the cerebellum and the fronto-parietal lobes (Bendszus *et al.*, 2001; Parks *et al.*, 2002; Bloomer, Langleben, and Meyerhoff, 2004; Durazzo, Gazdzinski, Banys, and Meyerhoff, 2004; Ende *et al.*, 2005; Durazzo *et al.*, 2006; Durazzo, Gazdzinski, Yeh, and Meyerhoff, 2008). Potential mechanisms at a molecular level, such as altered membrane phospholipid constituents or myelin abnormalities, could account for chronic alcohol use-related changes in Cho levels.

A few studies have reported elevated mI levels, particularly in recently detoxified alcoholic patients, rather than in long-term abstinent patients (Schweinsburg *et al.*, 2000). Given the role of mI in osmoregulation and its increase in hyperosmolar states (Ross, 1991), the finding of elevated mI levels could be understood in terms of the brain's attempt to stabilize intracellular environments in acute alcohol-induced hyperosmolarity (Schweinsburg *et al.*, 2000; Snyder, Williams, Zink, and Reilly, 1992). Glial proliferation commonly accompanying alcohol-induced neurotoxicity might also underlie the changes in mI levels in alcoholic patients (Schweinsburg *et al.*, 2000).

Long-standing research efforts have also been made to determine whether alcohol-induced cerebral metabolic disturbances are reversible with abstinence from alcohol. If these disturbances are indeed reversible, research over extended periods of abstinence would be required to observe normalization of alcohol-induced metabolic disturbances. Recent animal studies using the binge-drinking model have argued in favor of the potential reversibility of alcohol-induced metabolite changes (Zahr *et al.*, 2010). Corroborating this preclinical evidence, most, but not all, longitudinal studies of alcohol-dependent patients have reported at least partial normalization of reduced metabolite levels of NAA as well as those of Cho in both the frontal and cerebellar regions after a month of abstinence from alcohol (Martin *et al.*, 1995; Bendszus *et al.*, 2001; Parks *et al.*, 2002; Ende *et al.*, 2005; Durazzo *et al.*, 2006; Bartsch *et al.*, 2007). These findings also appear to be compatible with ongoing neuroimaging studies that demonstrate the recovery of volume reductions in the cortical as well as subcortical brain structures during abstinence (Carlen *et al.*, 1978; Pfefferbaum *et al.*, 1995; Buhler and Mann, 2011; Sullivan and Pfefferbaum, 2005). Furthermore, the extent of reversal of metabolite abnormalities may occasionally be associated with improved cognitive performance following abstinence (Bendszus *et al.*, 2001; Durazzo *et al.*, 2006; Bartsch *et al.*, 2007). Taken together, although continued alcohol exposure may lead to permanent metabolic changes in the brain, current evidence supports the capability of the brain to recover from alcohol-induced neurotoxicity when abstinence can be maintained.

More recent efforts have been directed to probe the roles of glutamatergic and GABAergic neurotransmission in the pathophysiology of alcohol dependence. Because the $GABA_A$ receptor is a major target of alcohol intoxication (Buck, 1996; Green and Grant, 1998; Grobin, Matthews, Devaud, and Morrow, 1998) and GABAergic adaptation is responsible for alcohol tolerance, withdrawal, and dependence (Buck and Harris, 1990; Ticku, 1990), *in vivo* and non-invasive measurement of GABA levels may extend the scope of our understanding of alcohol dependence. Owing to the development of selective acquisition and processing, alternative ^1H MRS techniques have been recently implemented to enable the quantification of brain GABA levels (Ke *et al.*, 2000; Sanacora *et al.*, 1999). Despite the importance of these observations, there have been few ^{1}H MRS studies to date exploring GABA levels in alcohol-dependent patients and the findings are rather disparate (Behar *et al.*, 1999; Mason *et al.*, 2006). Occipital GABA levels were reduced in recently detoxified alcohol-dependent patients (Behar *et al.*, 1999) and this finding may be consistent with clinical studies showing low-plasma GABA levels during early abstinence (Adinoff, Kramer, and Petty, 1995). Although small sample sizes may limit the inferences that can be made, recent evidence has suggested that abstinence-related reductions in GABA level may be interrupted by smoking (Mason *et al.*, 2006). Further research is warranted to replicate these findings as well as to characterize potential mechanisms underlying alterations in alcohol-induced GABAergic neurotransmission.

Since not only GABA systems but also the glutamate-glutamine cycle play a crucial role in moderating alcohol withdrawal and craving, Glx, which arises from the combined resonances of glutamate, glutamine, and GABA, is expected to be a major neurometabolic indicator of interest in alcohol dependence. Increased extracellular glutamate levels with repeated exposure to alcohol intoxication and withdrawal have also been noted in animal studies (Dahchour and DeWitte, 2003; Michaelis *et al.*, 1990). Although the finding that remitted alcoholics for at least 1 year demonstrated lower glutamate and higher glutamine levels in the frontal lobe suggests prolonged perturbations in the glutamate–glutamine cycle in chronic alcohol dependence (Thoma *et al.*, 2011), increased Glx levels have been found in the basal ganglia (Miese *et al.*, 2006) as well as in the frontal lobe (Lee *et al.*, 2007) of recently abstinent patients. Interestingly, 4 weeks of treatment with acamprosate significantly suppressed frontal glutamate/Cr ratios in alcohol-dependent patients relative to their placebo counterparts (Umhau *et al.*, 2010). Taken these findings together, ^{1}H MRS appears to be a useful translational tool that can be applied to measure glutamatergic and GABAergic neurotransmission for monitoring not only alcohol withdrawal symptoms but also responses to pharmacotherapies.

3.2   Amphetamine

3.2.1   Methamphetamine.   Methamphetamine (MA) (see Table 25.2) is known to be a highly addictive psychostimulant drug, and chronic exposure to MA leads to extensive neural damage (Barr *et al.*, 2006). Although they remain to be fully understood, several cellular mechanisms by which MA exerts its toxic effects on the brain have been proposed to date, including oxidative stress (Frost and Cadet, 2000; Tata and Yamamoto, 2007), mitochondrial damage (Tata and Yamamoto, 2007), pro-inflammatory immune reaction (Itzhak and Achat-Mendes, 2004), and glutamate-related excitotoxicity (Frost and Cadet, 2000; Tata and Yamamoto, 2007). At a macroscopic level, neurotoxic effects of chronic MA use have been examined mostly using *in vivo* neuroimaging techniques and manifest as structural, functional, and metabolic alterations particularly in the fronto-striato-limbic areas (Berman *et al.*, 2008; Baicy and London, 2007; Chang, Alicata, Ernst, and Volkow, 2007).

Because the dopaminergic circuit in the fronto-striatal region is a major target of MA action (Chang, Alicata, Ernst, and Volkow, 2007), the frontal cortex and the basal ganglia have been regarded as being particularly vulnerable to the neurotoxic effects of chronic MA use. Therefore these regions have primarily been focused in

Table 25.2 Published ^{1}H MRS research in patients with methamphetamine dependence

Study	Subjects	Gender (M/F)[1]	Mean age (SD)[1]	Patients' characteristics	Imaging methods	Regions examined/ Voxel size	Results on metabolites[2]	Clinical correlations
^{1}H MRS studies focusing on NAA, Cho, and mI changes related to methamphetamine dependence								
Ernst, Chang, Leonido-Yee, and Speck (2000)	26 patients 24 controls	13/13 12/12	33 (8) 30 (5)	• 26 MA dependence	• 1.5 T • single voxel • PRESS	• ACC/frontal WM/basal ganglia • 3–5 cm³	• ↓ NAA levels in frontal WM and basal ganglia • ↓ Cr levels in basal ganglia • ↑ Cho and mI levels in ACC	• a negative correlation between NAA levels in frontal WM and cumulative MA dose
Sekine et al. (2002)	13 patients 11 controls	8/5 7/4	26 (4) 26 (2)	• 13 MA dependence	• 1.5 T • single voxel • PRESS	• basal ganglia • 8 cm²	• ↓ Cr/Cho ratios in bilateral basal ganglia	• a negative correlation between Cr/Cho ratios in basal ganglia and illness duration • a positive correlation between Cr/Cho ratios in basal ganglia and severity of psychotic symptoms
Nordahl et al. (2002)	9 patients 9 controls	9/0 9/0	33 (6) 33 (7)	• 9 MA dependence	• 1.5 T • single voxel • PRESS	• ACC/ occipital cortex • 4 cm³	• ↓ NAA/Cr ratios in ACC • ↑ Cho/Cr ratios in ACC	• no specific clinical correlations with metabolite ratios
Nordahl et al. (2005)	24 patients 16 controls	9/15 5/8	37 (2) 34 (2)	• 24 MA dependence (8 with long-term and 16 with short-term abstinence)	• 1.5 T • single voxel • PRESS	• ACC/ occipital cortex • 4 cm³	• ↓ NAA/Cr ratios in ACC • ↑ Cho/NAA ratios in short-term, but not in long-term abstinent patients	• a positive correlation between ACC NAA/Cr ratios and illness duration • a negative correlation between ACC Cho/NAA ratios and illness duration • a negative correlation between ACC Cho/NAA and Cho/Cr ratios and the duration of abstinence

Study	Sample size	Sex (M/F)	Age	Sample	Method	Region / voxel size	Findings	Correlations / effects
Chang, Ernst, Speck, and Grob (2005)	60 patients / 83 controls	38/22 / 23/16	36 (7) / 36 (9)	• 60 MA dependence (24 HIV-positive and 36 HIV-negative)	• 1.5 T • single voxel • PRESS	• ACC/frontal WM/basal ganglia • 3–5 cm³	• ↓ NAA levels of frontal WM and basal ganglia in HIV-negative patients • ↑ Cho and mI levels of ACC in HIV-negative patients	• additive effects of HIV positive status on NAA level reductions in ACC, frontal WM, basal ganglia, Cr level reduction in basal ganglia, and mI level elevation in frontal WM
Salo et al. (2007)	36 patients / 16 controls	13/23 / 8/8	37 (2) / 32 (2)	• 36 MA dependence	• 1.5 T • single voxel • PRESS	• ACC/occipital cortex • 4 cm³	• ↓ NAA/Cr ratios in ACC • ↑ Cho/NAA ratios in ACC	• a positive correlation between NAA/Cr ratios in ACC and attention control
Sung et al. (2007)	30 patients / 20 controls	25/5 / 15/5	35 (5) / 33 (6)	• 30 MA dependence (9 with ≤ 100 grams and 21 with >100 grams of cumulative MA dose)	• 3 T • single voxel • PRESS	• frontal GM/WM • 3.4 cm³	• ↑ mI levels in frontal WM • ↓ NAA levels in frontal GM in patients with large cumulative MA dose	• negative correlations between NAA levels in frontal GM/WM and cumulative MA dose • a positive correlation between NAA levels in frontal GM and the duration of abstinence
Salo et al. (2011)	47 patients / 24 controls	19/28 / 12/12	36 (8) / 32 (8)	• 47 MA dependence (17 with long-term and 30 with short-term abstinence)	• 1.5 T • single voxel • PRESS	• ACC/occipital cortex • 4 cm³	• ↓ NAA/Cr and ↑ Cho/NAA ratios of ACC in short-term abstinent patients • no differences in metabolites ratios in long-term abstinent patients	• a positive correlation between NAA/Cr ratios in ACC and the duration of abstinence • a negative correlation between Cho/NAA ratio in ACC and the duration of abstinence
Cloak et al. (2011)	54 patients / 53 controls	20/34 / 23/30	18 (1) / 18 (1)	• 54 MA dependence (periadolescent age: 13–23 years)	• 3 T • single voxel • PRESS	• ACC/frontal WM/basal ganglia/thalamus • 5–9 cm³	• no difference in metabolite levels between groups	• a drug by age by sex interaction effect on Cho levels in ACC (absence of age appropriate increase in ACC Cho level in male patients)

(Continued)

Table 25.2 (Continued)

Study	Subjects	Gender (M/F)	Mean age (SD)[1]	Patients' characteristics	Imaging methods	Regions examined/Voxel size	Results on metabolites[2]	Clinical correlations
^{1}H MRS studies focusing on glutamate, glutamine, and GABA changes related to methamphetamine dependence								
Ernst and Chang (2008)	25 patients 28 controls	11/14 14/14	32 (7) 33 (9)	• 25 MA dependence (16 with ≤ 1 month of abstinence) • 12 rescanned 5 months later	• 1.5 T • single voxel • PRESS	• ACC/ frontal WM/ basal ganglia • 5–6 cm³	• no difference in metabolite levels between groups • ↓ Glx levels of frontal GM in patients with ≤ 1 month of abstinence • ↓ Glx levels of frontal GM in patients with craving symptoms	• positive correlations between Glx levels in frontal GM/WM and the duration of abstinence • a negative correlation between changes in Glx levels in frontal GM and the duration of abstinence at a trend level
Sialasuta et al. (2010)	18 patients 22 controls	11/7 12/10	35 (9) 32 (10)	• 18 MA dependence	• 3 T • single voxel • PRESS	• right frontal WM/ occipital cortex • 8 cm³	• ↑ glutamate levels in frontal WM • ↓ NAA levels in frontal WM	• a negative correlation between glutamate levels in frontal WM and the duration of abstinence
^{1}H MRS studies focusing on medication effects on metabolite changes related to methamphetamine dependence								
Yoon et al. (2010)	16 with CDP-choline 15 with placebo	12/4 11/4	39 (4) 38 (4)	• 31 MA dependence • 4 weeks of treatment with CDP-choline or placebo	• 3 T • single voxel • PRESS	• ACC • 3.4 cm³	• increased NAA levels with CDP-choline treatment • increased Cho levels with CDP-choline treatment	• a positive correlation between changes in NAA levels and negative urine results

[1]years (SD)

[2]All results presented in Table 25.2 are those of patients with methamphetamine dependence relative to comparison subjects except where indicated otherwise. Only positive findings are presented in this table.

Abbreviations: ACC, anterior cingulate cortex; CDP-choline, cytidine-5'-diphosphate choline; Cho, choline-containing compound; Cr, creatine and phospho-creatine; GABA, γ-aminobutyric acid; Glx, glutamine + glutamate; GM, gray matter; HIV, human immunodeficiency virus; MA, methamphetamine; mI, myo-inositol; MRS, magnetic resonance spectroscopy; NAA, N-acetylaspartate; PRESS, point resolved spectroscopy; SD, standard deviation; T, tesla; WM, white matter.

MRS studies to investigating neural metabolic alterations in MA-dependent patients. Since Ernst, Chang, Leonido-Yee, and Speck (2000) first reported chronic MA use-related neurometabolite abnormalities using ^{1}H MRS, several other research groups have replicated the findings of lower NAA levels (Nordahl *et al.*, 2002; Nordahl *et al.*, 2005; Chang, Ernst, Speck, and Grob, 2005; Salo *et al.*, 2007; Sung *et al.*, 2007; Salo *et al.*, 2011), higher Cho levels (Nordahl *et al.*, 2002; Nordahl *et al.*, 2005; Chang, Ernst, Speck, and Grob, 2005; Salo *et al.*, 2007), higher mI levels (Sung *et al.*, 2007), and lower Cr levels (Sekine *et al.*, 2002) in MA-dependent patients relative to control subjects.

Reduced NAA levels reflecting neuronal density decrement, injury, or loss have been most frequently observed in the basal ganglia (Ernst, Chang, Leonido-Yee, and Speck, 2000; Chang, Ernst, Speck, and Grob, 2005), frontal gray matter (Nordahl *et al.*, 2002; Nordahl *et al.*, 2005; Salo *et al.*, 2007; Sung *et al.*, 2007; Salo *et al.*, 2011), and, to a lesser extent, in the frontal white matter (Ernst, Chang, Leonido-Yee, and Speck, 2000; Chang, Ernst, Speck, and Grob, 2005). Chronic MA use appears to decrease NAA levels in the frontal area in a dose-dependent manner. For example, a greater cumulative lifetime dose of MA was correlated with lower NAA levels in the frontal gray and white matter (Ernst, Chang, Leonido-Yee, and Speck, 2000; Sung *et al.*, 2007). Moreover, longer durations of MA use have also been associated with further reductions in NAA levels (Nordahl *et al.*, 2005; Salo *et al.*, 2011). Together with the quantitative and/or cumulative effects that MA use could exert on the brain, brain capacity for recovery from MA-induced neurotoxicity following abstinence has been an important issue addressed in [1] H MRS research on MA dependence. Although there is a paucity of longitudinal data regarding neurometabolic changes in MA-dependent patients, several, but not all, cross-sectional studies have reported a positive correlation between the duration of abstinence and NAA levels in the frontal cortex (Sung *et al.*, 2007; Salo *et al.*, 2011). Conversely, the findings of Nordahl *et al.* (2005) suggested that differences between MA-dependent individuals with short-term and long-term abstinence may lie in Cho/NAA ratios, but not in NAA/Cr ratios. In a subsequent study by the same group, however, frontal NAA/Cr ratios as well as Cho/NAA ratio reductions were similarly associated with the duration of abstinence (Salo *et al.*, 2011). Taken together, these findings suggest the reversibility of MA-induced neurotoxicity following a history of substantial abstinence from MA. However, considering the disparity between findings, it remains an important issue that needs to be confirmed in longitudinal studies of MA-dependent individuals with larger sample sizes.

Mitochondrial dysfunction and neuronal energy impairment have been proposed as a central pathophysiological mechanism for MA-induced neurotoxicity (Frost and Cadet, 2000; Tata and Yamamoto, 2007). Considering that NAA levels reflect mitochondrial function, not only the reduced Cr levels reported in early ^{1}H MRS studies on MA dependence (Ernst, Chang, Leonido-Yee, and Speck, 2000), but also the most replicated finding of reduced NAA levels are consistent with the preclinical evidence of neuronal energy impairment associated with chronic MA use. In an effort to discover novel therapeutics for MA dependence, a recent clinical trial has examined the effects of cytidine-5'-diphosphate choline (CDP-choline), which exerts its role in not only restoring membrane phospholipid metabolism but also increasing cerebral energy metabolism, on neurochemical changes in MA-dependent subjects

(Yoon *et al.*, 2010). Four weeks of CDP-choline treatment significantly increased NAA as well as Cho levels in MA-dependent individuals relative to placebo treatment (Yoon *et al.*, 2010). Further, increases in NAA levels induced by CDP-choline treatment were correlated with a reduction in MA use during the treatment period (Yoon *et al.*, 2010).

Alterations in other neurometabolites including Cho, mI and Cr have also been implicated in the neural processes associated with chronic MA use. A series of studies by Nordahl and colleagues have clarified the role of Cho metabolites in MA use-related neural changes (Nordahl *et al.*, 2002; Nordahl *et al.*, 2005; Salo *et al.*, 2007; Salo *et al.*, 2011). They interpreted elevations of Cho levels in early remission to reflect a period of recovery from MA-induced insults through sequential processes, including the release of choline-containing compounds in response to acute damage to membranes, reactive gliosis, and membrane biosynthesis (Nordahl *et al.*, 2005). The fact that Cho level alterations have primarily been shown in short-term, rather than in long-term, abstinent MA-dependent individuals (Salo *et al.*, 2011) supports these speculations regarding cellular level changes. Consistent with these findings on Cho levels, elevations of mI levels, also considered as a glial marker, in the frontal white matter of MA-dependent individuals, could be viewed as evidence for glial proliferation in response to MA-induced neuronal injury (Sung *et al.*, 2007).

Studies on the clinical relevance of altered neurometabolite levels in MA-dependent patients have focused on neurocognitive deficits and psychiatric symptoms that often accompany MA dependence (Salo *et al.*, 2007; Sekine *et al.*, 2002). Reduced frontal NAA/Cr ratios have been associated with poor performance on attention control in MA-dependent patients (Salo *et al.*, 2007), while reductions in Cr/Cho ratios in the bilateral basal ganglia were related to the severity of residual psychiatric symptoms (Sekine *et al.*, 2002).

As a growing number of women of childbearing age as well as adolescents are becoming addicted to MA (Wouldes, LaGasse, Sheridan, and Lester, 2004; Rawson, Gonzales, McCann, and Ling, 2007), studies on the effects of chronic MA use on the developing brain may have important clinical implications. Smith *et al.* (2001) initially reported that children who were prenatally exposed to MA exhibited higher Cr levels in the striatum. In their following study on children with a larger sample size as well as a narrower age range, prenatally MA-exposed children showed not only higher Cr levels but also higher NAA and Glx levels in the frontal white matter (Chang *et al.*, 2009). The findings of higher metabolite levels could be understood from a developmental perspective, for example, as an accelerated growth pattern in children who were exposed to MA *in utero* (Chang *et al.*, 2009). There is only one ^{1}H MRS study to date on adolescent MA abusers. Cloak *et al.* (2011) found that male adolescent MA abusers did not exhibit normal age-appropriate increases in Cho levels in the frontal gray matter which may occur during normal brain metabolic development. Further longitudinal studies, which can prove the effects of MA on brain maturation trajectories, will be necessary.

More recently, there have been increased efforts directed to clarify the role of glutamate–glutamine cycle changes in the pathophysiology of MA dependence with evolving ^{1}H as well as ^{13}C MRS methods to enable *in vivo* measurement of brain glutamate and glutamine. Ernst and Chang (2008) first reported that Glx levels in the frontal gray matter were lowest in early abstinence from MA and were subsequently normalized with continuing abstinence. Another line of research using both ^{1}H and ^{13}C MRS methods to evaluate MA users by Sailasuta and colleagues exhibited not only increased glutamate levels in the frontal cortex (Sailasuta, Abulseoud, Harris, and Ross, 2010) but also severe reductions in glial TCA cycle rate and then accumulation of frontal glutamate (Sailasuta *et al.*, 2010). The causes and effects of chronic MA use-associated glial dysfunction as well as abnormalities in glutamatergic function remain to be further resolved by future studies.

3.2.2   3,4-methylenediocymethamphetamine.   A considerable body of evidence from animal studies including rodents and nonhuman primates has suggested that use of 3,4-methylenediocymethamphetamine (MDMA) may produce long-lasting or even permanent brain damages, particularly to serotonin neurotransmission systems (Green *et al.*, 2003; Morton, 2005; Lyles and Cadet, 2003). Based on these non-human basic findings, research efforts to seek the human relevance of MDMA-induced neurotoxicity have been made with the use of *in vivo* neuroimaging modalities (Cowan, 2007; Cowan, Roberts, and Joers, 2008; Gouzoulis-Mayfrank and Daumann, 2006; Reneman *et al.*, 2001a). Although existing data from nuclear imaging studies demonstrating reduced 5-HTT-ligand binding support, to some extent, findings from animal models of MDMA toxicity, published human neuroimaging studies using MRS methodologies to date do not seem to indicate a consistent pattern of region-specific alterations in neurometabolite levels (Cowan, 2007; Cowan, Roberts, and Joers, 2008; Gouzoulis-Mayfrank and Daumann, 2006; Reneman *et al.*, 2001b) (see Table 25.3).

As in the case of chronic MA use, altered NAA and mI levels reflecting neuronal loss as well as glial proliferation could initially be expected in chronic MDMA users. A few studies, including the first MRS report on MDMA abusers in 1999 (Chang *et al.*, 1999), have revealed reduced NAA/Cr ratios in the frontal gray matter (Reneman, Majoie, Flick, and den Heeten, 2002) as well as elevated mI levels in the parietal white matter (Chang *et al.*, 1999) and the basal ganglia (Liu *et al.*, 2011). These metabolic alterations occurred in a dose-dependent manner, for example having an association with cumulative MDMA dose (Reneman, Majoie, Flick, and den Heeten, 2002; Chang *et al.*, 1999; Liu *et al.*, 2011). However, several other studies published so far have not found any differences in metabolite levels not only in the cortex (Reneman *et al.*, 2001b; Daumann *et al.*, 2004; de Win *et al.*, 2007; de Win *et al.*, 2008a; de Win *et al.*, 2008b) but also in the subcortical structure, such as the hippocampus (Obergriesser, Ende, Braus, and Henn, 2001; Daumann *et al.*, 2004). Although other imaging modalities examining cerebral blood flow or white matter microstructure have detected regional involvement of the thalamus in new MDMA users, a series of recent longitudinal studies using multimodal designs by de Win *et al.* (2007; 2008a; 2008b) have not supported concerns regarding extensive neurometabolic abnormalities in incidental MDMA users. These investigators reported that there were no interval changes in metabolite levels in new MDMA users at not only 8 months (de Win *et al.*, 2007) but also 17 months (de Win *et al.*, 2008a) after the first MDMA use.

Table 25.3 Published ^{1}H MRS research in patients with 3,4-methylenediocymethamphetamine (MDMA) dependence

Study	Subjects	Gender (M/F)	Mean age (SD)[1]	Patients' characteristics	Imaging methods	Regions examined/ Voxel size	Results on metabolites[2]	Clinical correlations
Chang, Ernst, Grob, and Poland (1999)	21 patients 37 controls	15/6 22/15	43 (15) 38 (15)	• 21 MDMA dependence	• 1.5T • single voxel • PRESS	• frontal GM/parietal WM/occipital GM • 3–5 cm²	• ↑ mI levels and mI/Cr ratios in right parietal WM	• positive correlations between mI levels in the parietal WM as well as the occipital GM and NAA/Cho ratios in and cumulative MDMA dose
Obergriesser, Ende, Braus, and Henn (2001)	5 patients 5 control	NA NA	26 (3) 27 (3)	• 5 MDMA dependence	• 1.5T • single voxel • PRESS	• hippocampus • 4 cm²	• no differences in metabolite levels	• not examined
Reneman et al. (2001b)	8 patients 7 control	8/0 7/0	NA NA	• 8 MDMA dependence	• 1.5T • single voxel • PRESS	• frontal GM/ temporoparietal GM/occipital GM • 4.5 cm²	• no differences in metabolite ratios	• a positive correlation between NAA levels in frontal GM and delayed memory function
Reneman, Majoie, Flick, and den Heeten (2002)	15 patients 12 control	NA NA	27 (5) 27(4)	• 15 MDMA dependence	• 1.5T • single voxel • PRESS	• frontal GM/ temporoparietal GM/occipital GM • 4.5 cm²	• ↓ NAA/Cr and NAA/Cho ratios in frontal GM	• negative correlations between NAA/Cr and NAA/Cho ratios in frontal GM and cumulative MDMA dose
Daumann et al. (2004)	13 patients 13 control	3-Oct 3-Oct	27 (4) 26 (3)	• 13 MDMA dependence	• 1.5T • single voxel • PRESS	• frontal/occipital cortices (8 cm³) • hippocampus (7.9 cm³)	• no differences in metabolite ratios	• not examined

Study	Groups	Sex ratio, Age[1] years (SD)	Subjects	Method	Voxel location / size	Findings	Correlations
de Win et al. (2007)	30 prospective MDMA users	12/18 22 (32)	• 30 MDMA users (MDMA naive at baseline and follow-up after 8 months)	• 1.5T • single voxel • PRESS	• frontal GM/ frontoparietal GM/occipital GM • 6.5 cm³	• no changes in metabolite levels from baseline in prospective MDMA users	• not examined
de Win et al. (2008a)	59 prospective MDMA users 56 controls	23/34 22 (3) 23/33 22 (2)	• 59 MDMA users (MDMA naive at baseline and follow-up after 17 months)	• 1.5 T • single voxel • PRESS	• frontal GM/ frontoparietal GM/occipital GM • 6.5 cm³	• no changes in metabolite levels from baseline in prospective MDMA users	• not examined
de Win et al. (2008b)	33 MDMA users 38 non-MDMA substance users	44/27 23 (4)	• 33 MDMA dependence comorbid with other substance dependence • 38 substance dependence other than MDMA	• 1.5 T • single voxel • PRESS	• frontal GM/ frontoparietal GM/occipital GM • 6.5 cm³	• no differences in metabolite levels in polysubstance abusers according to MDMA use	• not examined
Liu et al. (2011)	31 patients 33 controls	24/7 25 (4) 17/16 24 (4)	• 31 MDMA dependence	• 3 T • single voxel • PRESS	• frontal GM/ basal ganglia • 8 cm³	• ↑ mI levels in the basal ganglia	• a positive correlation between Cho levels in the right basal ganglia and cumulative MDMA dose

[1] years (SD)

[2] All results presented in Table 25.3 are those of patients with MDMA dependence relative to comparison subjects except where indicated otherwise. Only positive findings are presented in this table.

Abbreviations: Cho, choline-containing compound; Cr, creatine and phosphocreatine; GM, gray matter; MDMA, 3,4-Methylenedioxymethamphetamine; mI, myo-inositol; MRS, magnetic resonance spectroscopy; NA, not available; NAA, N-acetylaspartate; PRESS, point resolved spectroscopy; SD, standard deviation; T, tesla; WM, white matter.

These conflicting results may be, in part, attributed to methodological issues including MDMA-specific sample characteristics (Cowan, 2007). For instance, highly prevalent concomitant polysubstance use in MDMA users (Pedersen and Skrondal, 1999; Scholey *et al.*, 2004) as well as unknown and even mixed purity of ecstasy pills sold as MDMA (Cole *et al.*, 2002; Parrott, 2004; Tanner-Smith, 2006) may be regarded as a challenging issue to determine MDMA-specific neurotoxic effects on the brain (Cowan, 2007).

Taken together, unambiguous MDMA-induced neurotoxic effects on the human brain metabolite levels have not yet been proven, although they remain plausible (Cowan, 2007; Cowan, Roberts, and Joers, 2008; Gouzoulis-Mayfrank and Daumann, 2006; Reneman *et al.*, 2001b). Existing data may critically require more sensitive methodologies to allow subtle changes in brain metabolism produced by a recreational dose of MDMA use as well as more sophisticated research strategies using a prospective design with larger cohorts of MDMA users without the comorbidity of polysubstance abuse.

3.3   Cannabis

Cannabis, or marijuana (see Table 25.4), is known to be the most commonly used illegal drug in most countries (Hall and Degenhardt, 2009). There have long been advocates for the medical use of cannabis for the relief of chronic pain or spasticity (Moore *et al.*, 2007; Hall and Degenhardt, 2009). However, global increases in the recreational use of cannabis, particularly by adolescents or young adults, are now deemed a major public health problem (Hall and Degenhardt, 2009). Although there is actually some debate over the topic (Tarter *et al.*, 2006), cannabis use generally starts early, and cannabis may sometimes act as a gateway drug to increase future risks of more deleterious drug use (Kandel, 1975; Kandel and Faust, 1975; Lessem *et al.*, 2006). A recent meta-analysis has also warned concerning the risk of cannabis use in the development of psychosis (Moore *et al.*, 2007). Further, recent preclinical findings add new evidence in support of cannabis-induced neuronal injury (Chan, Hinds, Impey, and Storm, 1998; Landfield, Cadwallader, and Vinsant, 1988). Overall, the human brain effects of chronic cannabis use appear to have been underestimated to date.

Since Chang, Cloak, Yakupov, and Ernst (2006) first reported chronic cannabis use-related neurometabolic abnormalities, the efforts of a small handful of groups have been devoted to documenting possible neurotoxic effects of cannabis on the brain metabolite levels. NAA is the most affected metabolite in chronic cannabis users. For instance, several ^{1}H MRS studies have reported reduced NAA levels not only in the basal ganglia (Chang, Cloak, Yakupov, and Ernst, 2006) but also in the wide range of the frontal lobe including the anterior cingulate and dorsolateral prefrontal cortices (Hermann *et al.*, 2007; Prescot, Locatelli, Renshaw, and Yurgelun-Todd, 2011). Regions showing cannabis-related neuronal loss as evidenced by reductions in the level of this neuronal marker may well be compatible with the brain areas which appear to be frequently affected in people with schizophrenia (Bertolino *et al.*, 2003; Molina *et al.*, 2005). These findings contribute to *in vivo* human evidence suggesting that chronic cannabis use increases the risk for future psychosis (Moore *et al.*, 2007) as well as aggravation of psychotic symptoms in schizophrenic patients (Hall, Degenhardt, and

Table 25.4 Published ^{1}H MRS research in patients with cannabis dependence

Study	Subjects	Gender (M/F)	Mean age (SD)[1]	Patients' characteristics	Imaging methods	Regions examined/Voxel size	Results on metabolites[2]	Clinical correlations
Chang, Cloak, Yakupov, and Ernst (2006)	45 patients 21 HIV-positive patients 30 controls	38/7 17/4 24/6	39 (2) 44 (3) 42 (2)	• 45 cannabis dependence (21 HIV positive and 24 HIV negative)	• 4T • single voxel • PRESS	• thalamus/basal ganglia/frontal WM/cerebellar vermis/parietal WM/occipital GM • 3–5 cm³	• ↓ NAA, Cho, glutamate levels in the basal ganglia (independent of HIV effects) • ↑ Cr levels in the thalamus (independent of HIV effects)	• a positive correlation between glutamate levels in the frontal WM and the duration of cannabis use
Hermann et al. (2007)	13 patients 13 controls	13/0 13/0	22 (2) 23 (2)	• 13 cannabis dependence	• 1.5 T • MRSI	• basal ganglia, thalamus/DLPFC/frontal WM/hippocampus/VTA/ACC/PCC	• ↓ NAA/Cr ratios in the DLPFC	• a positive correlation between NAA/Cr ratios in the basal ganglia and cannabidiol
Silveri et al. (2011)	15 patients 11 controls	15/0 11/0	21 (3) 25 (5)	• 15 cannabis dependence	• 4T • CSI • PRESS	• basal ganglia/thalamus/temporal and parietal lobes/occipital GM/occipital WM	• ↓ global mI/Cr ratios • altered distribution of mI/Cr between GM and WM (absence of higher mI/Cr in WM than GM)	• associations between more negative mI/Cr slope and a greater frequency of cannabis use and an earlier onset age
Prescot, Locatelli, Renshaw, and Yurgelun-Todd (2011)	17 patients 17 controls	15/2 8/9	18 (1) 16 (2)	• 17 cannabis dependence	• 3 T • single voxel • PRESS	• ACC • 22.5 cm³	• ↓ NAA, glutamate, Cr, and mI levels in the ACC	• no specific clinical correlations with metabolite levels

[1]years (SD)

[2]All results presented in Table 25.4 are those of patients with cannabis dependence relative to comparison subjects except where indicated otherwise. Only positive findings are presented in this table.

Abbreviations: ACC, anterior cingulate cortex; Cho, choline-containing compound; Cr, creatine and phosphocreatine; CSI, Chemical Shift Imaging; DLPFC, dorsolateral prefrontal cortex; GM, gray matter; HIV, human immunodeficiency virus; mI, myo-inositol; MRS, magnetic resonance spectroscopy; MRSI, Magnetic Resonance Spectroscopic Imaging; NA, not available; NAA, N-acetylaspartate; PCC, posterior cingulate cortex; PRESS, point resolved spectroscopy; SD, standard deviation; T, tesla; VTA, ventral tegmental area; WM, white matter.

Teesson, 2004). The most recent study that reported neurometabolic abnormalities of the midfrontal cortex in adolescent users also underscores the cannabis-induced neurotoxicity even in the early stage of drug use (Prescot, Locatelli, Renshaw, and Yurgelun-Todd, 2011).

Along with reduced mI levels in several brain regions (Silveri *et al.*, 2011), alterations of glutamate levels, predominantly decreases, suggest glial dysfunction in cannabis-dependent individuals that may decrease glutamate reuptake or undermine reshuttling of glutamine to neurons (Chang, Cloak, Yakupov, and Ernst, 2006; Prescot, Locatelli, Renshaw, and Yurgelun-Todd, 2011). Further studies of the role of glutamatergic and GABAergic neurotransmission using alternative ^{1}H MRS or ^{13}C MRS methodologies which could improve the *in vivo* quantitative assessment of glutamate, glutamine, and GABA will be required in order to prove the clinical implications of these findings.

Although much more human research is necessary to provide convincing conclusions, currently available ^{1}H MRS findings on cannabis abusers appears to support the neurotoxic effects of cannabis suggested by preclinical studies.

3.4   Cocaine

Cocaine (Table 25.5), a potent CNS stimulant, exerts neurotoxic effects that are manifested as neurological, psychiatric, and neuropsychological impairments, particularly in the brains of chronic users (Mody *et al.*, 1988; Lowenstein *et al.*, 1987; Levine *et al.*, 1990; O'Malley, Adamse, Heaton, and Gawin, 1992). Preclinical and clinical studies have provided convincing evidence that chronic cocaine use may frequently bring about fatal as well as non-fatal cerebrovascular events (Kaufman *et al.*, 1998; Buttner, 2011). Among several molecular and cellular mechanisms that have been proposed thus far, cerebral vasoconstriction either by cocaine or by its metabolites may be primarily responsible for cocaine-induced ischemic infarction or hemorrhage (Kaufman *et al.*, 1998; Buttner, 2011).

Although MRS findings in cocaine dependence so far do not attest to a consistent pattern of cocaine-induced biochemical alteration, reduced NAA levels and elevated mI and Cr levels, primarily in the frontal and subcortial areas that could reflect neuronal damage, as well as increased inflammation or glial cell activities in those regions, are the most replicated findings in chronic cocaine abusers (Chang *et al.*, 1997; Chang, Ernst, Strickland, and Mehringer, 1999; Li, Wang, Pankiewicz, and Stein, 1999; Meyerhoff and Bloomer, 1999; O'Neill, Cardenas, and Meyerhoff, 2001). Further, altered Cr and mI levels have been associated with greater as well as longer use of cocaine (Chang *et al.*, 1997).

Sexual dimorphism is an important issue that has frequently been of consequence in addiction research (Levin *et al.*, 1994; Weiss *et al.*, 1997; Kosten, Gawin, Kosten, and Rounsaville, 1993). Chang *et al.* (1999), in their ^{1}H-MRS study with the largest sample size of cocaine abusers reported to date, not only replicated their original findings of increased Cr and mI levels in cocaine-dependent individuals (Chang *et al.*, 1997) but also noted gender-specific effects of cocaine on neurochemical alterations. Consistent with the clinical observations of fewer frontal perfusion deficits as well as

Table 25.5 Published ^{1}H MRS research in patients with cocaine dependence

Study	Subjects	Gender (M/F)	Mean age (SD)[1]	Patients' characteristics	Imaging methods	Regions examined/ Voxel size	Results on metabolites[2]	Clinical correlations
^{1}H MRS studies focusing on NAA, Cho, and mI changes related to cocaine dependence								
Chang et al. (1997)	26 patients 26 controls	26/0 26/0	33 (8) 32 (9)	• 26 cocaine dependence (6 comorbid with polysubstance abuse)	• 1.5T • single voxel • PRESS	• temporoparietal subcortical WM/occipital GM • 7–15 cm^3	• ↑ Cr level and ↑ mI levels in the subcortical WM	• positive correlations between Cr and mI levels in the subcortical WM and the frequency/ duration of cocaine use
Li, Wang, Pankiewicz, and Stein (1999)	21 patients 13 controls	16/5 7/6	35 (5) 25(4)	• 21 cocaine dependence	• 1.5T • single voxel • PRESS	• basal ganglia (6 cm^3)/thalamus (4.5 cm^3)	• ↓ NAA levels in the thalamus	• not examined
Chang, Ernst, Grob, and Poland (1999)	64 patients 58 controls	34/30 29/29	32 (4) 32 (5)	• 64 cocaine dependence	• 1.5T • single voxel • PRESS	• frontal GM/ frontal WM • 3–5 cm^3	• ↓ NAA levels and ↑ mI levels in the frontal GM • ↓ NAA/Cr ratios and ↑ mI levels/ mI/Cr ratios in the frontal WM • ↑ Cr levels in the frontal GM in male patients (a significant interaction effect) • ↑ mI levels in the frontal GM in female patients (a significant interaction effect)	• no clinical correlations between cumulative cocaine dose and metabolite levels
Meyerhoff and Bloomer (1999)	22 patients 11 controls	19/3 9/2	41 (6) 37 (9)	• 22 cocaine dependence • (15 comorbid with alcohol dependence)	• 1.5T • multislice	• covering major lobes	• ↓ NAA levels in the dorsolateral prefrontal cortex and ↑ Cho levels in the frontal WM in cocaine-dependent patients comorbid alcohol dependence	• a positive correlation between Cho levels in the WM and the duration of cocaine use

(Continued)

Table 25.5 (Continued)

Study	Subjects	Gender (M/F)[1]	Mean age (SD)	Patients' characteristics	Imaging methods	Regions examined/ Voxel size	Results on metabolites[2]	Clinical correlations
O'Neill, Cardenas, and Meyerhoff (2001)	37 patients, 13 controls	30/7, 11/2	43 (3), 36 (8)	• 8 cocaine dependence, 12 alcohol dependence • 17 cocaine and alcohol dependence	• 1.5T • multislice	• covering major lobes	• ↑ Cr levels in the parietal WM in cocaine-dependent relative to non-cocaine-dependent patients	• no specific clinical correlations with metabolite levels
[1] H MRS studies focusing on glutamate, glutamine, and GABA changes related to cocaine dependence								
Ke et al. (2004)	35 patients, 20 controls	26/9, 7/13	43 (7), 39 (8)	• 35 cocaine dependence (23 comorbid with alcohol dependence)	• 1.5T • single voxel	• left frontal cortex • 18.75 cm³	• ↓ GABA levels in the prefrontal cortex • ↓ GABA levels in cocaine-dependent patients either without or with comorbidity of alcohol dependence	• a negative correlation between GABA levels and the duration of cocaine use
Yang et al. (2009)	14 patients, 14 controls	10/4, 7/7	37 (5), 34 (9)	• 14 cocaine dependence	• 3T • single voxel • PRESS	• ACC • 8 cm³	• ↓ glutamate/Cr ratios in the ACC	• a positive correlation between glutamate/Cr ratios and the duration of cocaine use
[1] H MRS studies focusing on medication effects on metabolite changes related to cocaine dependence								
Streeter et al. (2005)	9 with pramipexole, 9 with venlafaxine, 10 with placebo	7/2, 8/1, 7/3	45 (8), 48 (7), 47 (8)	• 28 cocaine dependence • 8 weeks of treatment with pramipexole, venlafaxine, or placebo	• 1.5T • single voxel	• left frontal cortex • 18.75 cm³	• increased GABA levels with pramipexole treatment relative to placebo treatment	• no specific clinical correlations with changes in metabolite levels

[1] years (SD)

[2] All results presented in Table 25.5 are those of patients with cocaine dependence relative to comparison subjects except where indicated otherwise. Only positive findings are presented in this table.

Abbreviations: ACC, anterior cingulate cortex; Cho, choline-containing compound; Cr, creatine and phosphocreatine; GM, gray matter; mI, myo-inositol; MRS, magnetic resonance spectroscopy; NA, not available; NAA, N-acetylaspartate; PRESS, point resolved spectroscopy; SD, standard deviation; T, tesla; WM, white matter.

better treatment outcomes in cocaine-dependent women (Levin *et al.*, 1994; Weiss *et al.*, 1997; Kosten, Gawin, Kosten, and Rounsaville, 1993), alterations in NAA and mI levels were more prominent in male cocaine-dependent subjects than in females. Although the underlying mechanisms remain unclear, the authors suggested that hormonal differences may play a potential protective role in cocaine-induced neural injury (Chang *et al.*, 1999).

Inasmuch as accompanying alcohol-related problems are frequently found in cocaine-dependent individuals (Grant and Harford, 1990) and alcohol misuse also produces a wide range of neurometabolic alterations (reviewed in this chapter), it would be worthwhile to examine independent as well as interactive effects of both cocaine and alcohol, on neurochemical metabolite levels. Existing data have suggested that NAA levels may be comparably reduced with a similar regional pattern both in individuals dependent only on cocaine and in those dependent on alcohol and cocaine (Meyerhoff and Bloomer, 1999; O'Neill, Cardenas, and Meyerhoff, 2001).

In contrast to the effects of chronic cocaine use, acute neurometabolic changes after an experimental infusion of cocaine present a dissimilar pattern (Christensen *et al.*, 2000). A cocaine infusion may immediately increase, rather than decrease, NAA and Cho levels in the basal ganglia in a dose-dependent manner in comparison with a placebo infusion. These changes in metabolites are suggested to be partly attributed to cocaine-administration induced osmotic stress and intracellular water content (Christensen *et al.*, 2000). As suggested by the authors, these findings could be consistent with the inhibition of the $Na+/K+$-adenosinetriphosphatase by cocaine through its indirect agonist actions on dopamine D1 receptor (Lien *et al.*, 1994; Bertorello, Hopfield, Aperia, and Greengard, 1990). The physiological and behavioral relevance of these acute cocaine infusion effects on brain neurochemical metabolite levels remain to be determined in future studies.

Until recently, only a handful of research groups have attempted to evaluate the role of glutamatergic and GABAergic neurotransmission in cocaine dependence (Hetherington, Newcomer, and Pan, 1998; Ke *et al.*, 2004; Yang *et al.*, 2009). Along with preclinical evidence suggesting the involvement of the GABAergic system in cocaine self-administration (McFarland and Kalivas, 2001; McFarland, Lapish, and Kalivas, 2003), findings of reduced frontal (Ke *et al.*, 2004) and occipital (Hetherington, Newcomer, and Pan, 1998) GABA levels in cocaine-dependent subjects may have clinical implications. For example, agents that could increase GABA activity may serve as potential treatment options for cocaine dependence (Dewey *et al.*, 1998; Streeter *et al.*, 2005). In a preliminary study, a recent clinical trial on potential therapeutics that could alter prefrontal GABA abnormalities caused by chronic cocaine use has produced intriguing results (Streeter *et al.*, 2005). In this study, Streeter *et al.* (2005) did not find reduction in cocaine consumption in both pramipexole- and placebo-treated cocaine-dependent subjects that may be, in part, attributed to a small sample size as well as a relatively low dose of medication. However, 8 weeks of pramipexole treatment significantly increased prefrontal GABA levels in cocaine-dependent individuals relative to placebo treatments (Streeter *et al.*, 2005).

There has been only one published human ^{1}H MRS study to report cocaine-related alterations in glutamate levels (Yang *et al.*, 2009). Yang *et al.* (2009) reported lower prefrontal glutamate levels in cocaine-dependent patients. However, reflecting another challenging finding in this study, a rather counterintuitive correlation between longer cocaine use and increased prefrontal glutamate levels suggests that replication in a larger group of cocaine-dependent individuals may be warranted.

3.5   Opioids

Opioids (Table 25.6) have a long history of being used as potent analgesics or sedatives. However, because of their high potential for abuse, clinical applications of certain types of opioids, especially heroin, have been limited (Raehal and Bohn, 2005). Further, opioids are known to be among the leading substances that substantially increase mortality in drug abusers (Buttner, 2011). Macroscopic effects on the brain, including neurovascular abnormalities, leukoencephaopathty, atrophy, and infection, have been found in opioid abusers, indicative of acute and chronic opioid effects (reviewed in Borne *et al.*, 2005). More recently, a prefrontal predominance of neuropathological changes, such as white matter hyperintensity and reduced gray matter density, has been reported in opioid-dependent individuals using T2-weighted MRI and voxel-based morphometry, respectively (Lyoo *et al.*, 2004; Lyoo *et al.*, 2006).

Nevertheless, only a few MRS studies have been undertaken in opioid-dependent individuals so far and very limited findings on changes in neurochemical levels have been available in the research of opioid dependence (Haselhorst *et al.*, 2002; Silveri *et al.*, 2004; Yucel *et al.*, 2007). In alignment with other structural and functional neuroimaging studies on opioid dependence, prefrontal neuronal loss as evidenced by reduced NAA levels has been found in two ^{1}H MRS studies of opioid abusers (Haselhorst *et al.*, 2002; Yucel *et al.*, 2007). Nonspecific reduction in prefrontal Glx levels caused by chronic opioid use has been demonstrated as well (Yucel *et al.*, 2007).

Cerebral bioenergetics and phospholipid metabolism may be altered in opioid abusers, particularly during the first month of methadone substitution treatment (Silveri *et al.*, 2004). Silveri *et al.* (2004) have reported reduced PCr and elevated PDE levels in opioid abusers who recently started methadone therapy. These neurometabolic alterations became prominent after approximately 4 weeks of methadone treatment. Although the pharmacologic actions may be shared by opioid and methadone, these findings suggest the recovery of cerebral oxygenation in opioid abusers shortly after methadone treatment, which is consistent with the clinical observation of neurocognitive improvement in opioid abusers after 2 months of methadone treatment (Gruber *et al.*, 1998).

Even though the number of studies using MRS techniques has been greatly increasing in addiction research, comparatively little is known regarding the acute and chronic effects of opioid use on the brain metabolism. Thus, further investigations implementing several MRS technologies would be of interest.

4   Understanding of Addiction: Limitations and Future Applications of MRS Methodology

MRS has enabled *in vivo* quantitative as well as qualitative neurochemical assessments of the human brain and its utility has long been proved in addressing a number of

Table 25.6 Published MRS research in patients with opioid dependence

Study[1]	Subjects	Gender (M/F)	Mean age (SD)[1]	Patients characteristics	Imaging methods	Regions examined/ Voxel size	Results on metabolites[2]	Clinical correlations
1H MRS studies on opioid dependence								
Haselhorst *et al.* (2002)	12 patients 12 controls	10/2 10/2	36 (5) matched	• 12 opioid dependence (12 methadone substitution treatment)	• 1.5 T • single voxel PRESS	• frontal GM/ frontal WM • 8 cm³	• ↓ NAA levels in the frontal GM	• not examined
Yucel *et al.* (2007)	24 patients 24 controls	13/11 13/11	30 (7) 30 (6)	• 24 opioid dependence (10 methadone and 14 buprenorphine substitution treatment)	• 3 T • single voxel PRESS	• dorsal ACC • 6.5 cm³	• ↓ NAA levels and ↓ Glx levels in the dorsal ACC	• not examined
31P MRS studies on opioid dependence								
Silveri *et al.* (2004)	43 patients 15 controls	23/20 8/7	38 (2) 39 (2)	• 43 opioid dependence (43 methadone substitution treatment)	• 1.5 T • spin echo sequence	• regions encompassing the frontal cortex and the basal ganglia	• ↓ PCr levels and ↑ PDE levels	• no specific clinical correlations with brain metabolite levels

[1] years (SD)

[2] All results presented in Table 25.6 are those of patients with opioid dependence relative to comparison subjects except where indicated otherwise. Only positive findings are presented in this table.

Abbreviations: ACC, anterior cingulate cortex; Cho, choline-containing compound; Cr, creatine and phosphocreatine; Glx, glutamine + glutamate; GM, gray matter; mI, myo-inositol; MRS, magnetic resonance spectroscopy; NAA, N-acetylaspartate; PCr, phosphocreatine; PDE, phosphodiester; PRESS, point resolved spectroscopy; SD, standard deviation; T, tesla; WM, white matter.

fundamental questions in addiction research. However, there may also be methodology- and sample-specific considerations that should be taken into account in interpreting the results and planning future research.

In this chapter, we have reviewed a number of MRS studies for neurometabolite quantification and localization in each patient group dependent on different classes of substance. Although there are some different features of brain localization across substance dependence, reduced NAA levels are universally observed in most types of drug addiction. Considering the role of NAA as a neuronal marker, it may be supposed that chronic as well as addictive use of all kinds of substances may potentially render the human brain more vulnerable to their neurotoxic effects. According to brain-regional specificity in the actions of each substance as well as the distributions of target receptors, the brain areas more affected by chronic substance use seem to be different. Although it seems to be oversimplified, similar overlapping patterns in alterations of other metabolites including mI and Cho representing glial content and membrane phospholipid turnover, respectively, have also been suggested across different classes of substance dependence. It is possible that the human brain could evolve to efficiently react to a range of potential insults such as drug exposure by increasing gliosis and/membrane biosynthesis.

In addition to identifying clinically relevant changes in neurometabolite levels, both ^{1}H and ^{31}P MRS have been proved to be useful tools in addiction research for assessing the efficacy of treatment as well as the trajectories of neurometabolite change during ongoing drug use or abstinence. The levels of NAA, as a neuronal marker, may not only predict future abstinence and the prognosis of patients with alcohol dependence (Durazzo, Gazdzinski, Yeh, and Meyerloff, 2008) but also indicate the medication response in CDP choline-treated MA-dependent individuals (Yoon *et al.*, 2010). Brain bioenergetic improvements by the first month of the switch from heroin to methadone have efficiently assessed by ^{31}P MRS (Silveri *et al.*, 2004). As in Streeter *et al.* (2005), ^{1}H MRS could be applied to assess treatment efficacy of compounds that target amino acid metabolism by tracking relevant brain amino acid levels. Future clinical trials that incorporate MRS findings as outcome measures will be necessary to verify their value as biomarkers for treatment efficacy in drug abuse.

All the findings of MRS studies in drug abusers not only have provided insight into the neurobiochemical consequences of chronic drug use but also have greatly extended our understanding of the neurobiological bases of drug addiction. To some degree, however, it remains challenging to determine drug class-specific neurochemical alterations using currently available MRS techniques. Drug sample characteristics – for example, a high rate of codependency on several substances as well as frequent co-morbidity of other psychiatric disorders – may also limit efforts to determine drug class-specific chemical signatures (Grant and Harford, 1990; Pedersen and Skrondal, 1999; Scholey *et al.*, 2004; Najt, Fusar-Poli, and Brambilla, 2011). Ongoing advances in acquisition, processing, and quantification of spectra may enable us to assess a more extensive range of neurometabolites and amino acids in the near future, thereby allowing so-called "neurochemical sampling" of each drug dependence on the basis of distributions of neurochemical metabolites. In this regard, a recent approach using a relatively novel water suppression technique, Presaturation Utilizing Relaxation Gradients and Echoes (PURGE), has suggested the potential to detect level of MDMA or its metabolites using ^{1}H MRS methodology (Liu, Decatur, Proni, and Champeil, 2010).

Currently available MRS research has focused on the direct, primarily neurotoxic, effects of each class of substance on neurochemical metabolism rather than on the brain metabolic mechanisms of vulnerability to the development of drug abuse. Fewer research efforts have been made on proving the neurochemical capability to recover from drug abuse. Special endeavors on the application of unique research strategies, which will evolve gradually toward longitudinal follow-up of high-risk groups for drug abuse as well as combine genetic approaches, may yield important insights into the neurochemical vulnerability to drug abuse. A recent study has suggested a potential relevance of MRS findings as endophenotypes in imaging genomic studies of alcohol dependence (Meyerhoff and Durazzo, 2008). Clinical application as well as extensive utilization of this information will provide an important clue to the genetic relevance of MRS findings, thereby facilitating the multidimensional understanding of risk for drug abuse.

When interpreting and comparing results across MRS studies on substance dependence, several potential confounding factors should be taken into consideration. As reviewed in this chapter, several factors at a subject level, including not only demographic characteristics (for instance, age and sex) but also drug use patterns (lifetime cumulative dose, duration of abstinence, mode of intake, and presence of co-dependence on other drugs), may have various additive as well as interactive effects on neurometabolite levels in drug abusers. Along with those of other comorbid psychiatric disorders, the brain effects of HIV infection, which may frequently accompany intravenous drug use, have been well recognized (Meyerhoff *et al.*, 1995; Chang, Ernst, Speck, and Grob, 2005; Chang, Cloak, Yakupov, and Ernst, 2006). The fact that most studies have obtained drug use-related histories on the basis of patient self-report is also one of the challenging problems in MRS studies of illegal substance abuse (Neale and Robertson, 2003). Underestimation as well as inaccuracy of information regarding drug use patterns should be taken into consideration as well.

When used in combination with other imaging modalities, MRS technology may overcome its technical limitations in terms of temporal and spatial resolution. Although the application of multimodal imaging approaches including MRS to addiction research is in its early stage, diffusion tensor imaging as well as functional MRI analyses have increasingly been employed along with ^{1}H MRS methodology in alcohol- (Gazdzinski, Durazzo, Mon, and Meyerhoff, 2010; Gazdzinski *et al.*, 2010), MDMA- (de Win *et al.*, 2007; de Win *et al.*, 2008a; de Win *et al.*, 2008b), and opioid-dependent (Yucel *et al.*, 2007) individuals. Multinuclear MRS of ^{1}H and ^{31}P may be used to help elucidate the mechanisms of drug-induced membrane phospholipid and cerebral bioenergetic metabolism (Renshaw *et al.*, 2001a; Lyoo *et al.*, 2003; Thatcher *et al.*, 2002).

In conclusion, MRS techniques have been established to be very useful tools to directly measure metabolite concentrations in the human brain *in vivo*. MRS has been extensively used in addiction research, as it allows the demonstration of substance-specific alterations in brain neurochemical metabolites, tracking the disease course of each substance dependence, and assessing the potential treatment efficacy in substance abusers. The MRS results to date also provide valuable insights into our understanding of the clinical relevance of neurometabolic changes induced by chronic drug use as well as the regional specificity of each drug's neurotoxic effects. Findings on the dynamic changes in brain neurometabolites in response to chronic drug use could be employed in patient monitoring as well as in medication development strategies. Although there have been only few cases of direct clinical applications of MRS in the field of addiction so far, ongoing and future studies to expand the use of MRS findings as a potential surrogate biomarker that can help medication development for drug abuse are likely to have unique clinical benefits.

References

Adinoff B, Kramer GL, and Petty F (1995) Levels of gamma-aminobutyric acid in cerebrospinal fluid and plasma during alcohol withdrawal. *Psychiatry Research* 59: 137–144.

Agarwal N, Sung YH, Jensen JE, daCunha G, Harper D, *et al.* (2010) Short-term administration of uridine increases brain membrane phospholipid precursors in healthy adults: A 31-phosphorus magnetic resonance spectroscopy study at 4T. *Bipolar Disorders* 12: 825–833.

Baicy K and London ED (2007) Corticolimbic dysregulation and chronic methamphetamine abuse. *Addiction* 102 (Suppl. 1): 5–15.

Barr AM, Panenka WJ, MacEwan GW, Thornton AE, Lang DJ, *et al.* (2006) The need for speed: An update on methamphetamine addiction. *Journal of Psychiatry and Neuroscience* 31: 301–313.

Bartsch AJ, Homola G, Biller A, Smith SM, Weijers H-G, *et al.* (2007) Manifestations of early brain recovery associated with abstinence from alcoholism. *Brain* 130: 36–47.

Behar KL, Rothman DL, Petersen KF, Hooten M, Delaney R, *et al.* (1999) Preliminary evidence of low cortical GABA levels in localized 1H-MR spectra of alcohol-dependent and hepatic encephalopathy patients. *American Journal of Psychiatry* 156: 952–954.

Behar KL, Rothman DL, Spencer DD, and Petroff OA (1994) Analysis of macromolecule resonances in 1H NMR spectra of human brain. *Magnetic Resonance in Medicine* 32: 294–302.

Bendszus M, Weijers H-G, Wiesbeck G, Warmuth-Metz M, Bartsch AJ, *et al.* (2001) Sequential MR imaging and proton MR spectroscopy in patients who underwent recent detoxification for chronic alcoholism: Correlation with clinical and neuropsychological data. *American Journal of Neuroradiology* 22: 1926–1932.

Berman S, O'Neill J, Fears S, Bartzokis G, and London ED (2008) Abuse of amphetamines and structural abnormalities in the brain. *Annals of the New York Academy of Sciences* 1141: 195–220.

Bertolino A, Sciota D, Brudaglio F, Altamura M, Blasi G, *et al.* (2003) Working memory deficits and levels of N-acetylaspartate in patients with schizophreniform disorder. *American Journal of Psychiatry* 160: 483–489.

Bertorello AM, Hopfield JF, Aperia A, and Greengard P (1990) Inhibition by dopamine of (Na(+) + K+)ATPase activity in neostriatal neurons through D1 and D2 dopamine receptor synergism. *Nature* 347: 386–388.

Bloomer CW, Langleben DD, and Meyerhoff DJ (2004) Magnetic resonance detects brainstem changes in chronic, active heavy drinkers. *Psychiatry Research* 132: 209–218.

Bonavita S, Di Salle F, and Tedeschi G (1999) Proton MRS in neurological disorders. *European Journal of Radiology* 30: 125–131.

Borne J, Riascos R, Cuellar H, Vargas D, and Rojas R (2005) Neuroimaging in drug and substance abuse part II: opioids and solvents. *Topics in Magnetic Resonance Imaging* 16: 239–245.

Brand A, Richter-Landsberg C, and Leibfritz D (1993) Multinuclear NMR studies on the energy metabolism of glial and neuronal cells. *Developmental Neuroscience* 15: 289–298.

Brenner RE, Munro PM, Williams SC, Bell JD, Barker GJ, *et al.* (1993) The proton NMR spectrum in acute EAE: The significance of the change in the Cho:Cr ratio. *Magnetic Resonance in Medicine* 29: 737–745.

Brooks WM, Friedman SD, and Gasparovic C (2001) Magnetic resonance spectroscopy in traumatic brain injury. *Journal of Head Trauma Rehabilitation* 16: 149–164.

Buchli R, Duc CO, Martin E, and Boesiger P (1994) Assessment of absolute metabolite concentrations in human tissue by 31P MRS in vivo. Part I: Cerebrum, cerebellum, cerebral gray and white matter. *Magnetic Resonance in Medicine* 32: 447–452.

Buck KJ (1996) Molecular genetic analysis of the role of GABAergic systems in the behavioral and cellular actions of alcohol. *Behavior Genetics* 26: 313–323.

Buck KJ and Harris RA (1990) Benzodiazepine agonist and inverse agonist actions on GABAA receptor-operated chloride channels. II. Chronic effects of ethanol. *Journal of Pharmacology and Experimental Therapeutics* 253: 713–719.

Buhler M and Mann K (2011) Alcohol and the human brain: A systematic review of different neuroimaging methods. *Alcoholism: Clinical and Experimental Research* (in press).

Buttner A (2011) Review: The neuropathology of drug abuse. *Neuropathology and Applied Neurobiology* 37: 118–134.

Carlen PL, Wortzman G, Holgate RC, Wilkinson DA, and Rankin JC (1978) Reversible cerebral atrophy in recently abstinent chronic alcoholics measured by computed tomography scans. *Science* 200: 1076–1078.

Chan GC, Hinds TR, Impey S, and Storm DR (1998) Hippocampal neurotoxicity of Delta9-tetrahydrocannabinol. *Journal of Neuroscience* 18: 5322–5332.

Chang L, Alicata D, Ernst T, and Volkow N (2007) Structural and metabolic brain changes in the striatum associated with methamphetamine abuse. *Addiction* 102: 16–32.

Chang L, Cloak C, Jiang CS, Farnham S, Tokeshi B, *et al.* (2009) Altered neurometabolites and motor integration in children exposed to methamphetamine in utero. *NeuroImage* 48: 391–397.

Chang L, Cloak C, Yakupov R, and Ernst T (2006) Combined and independent effects of chronic marijuana use and HIV on brain metabolites. *Journal of Neuroimmune Pharmacology* 1: 65–76.

Chang L, Ernst T, Grob CS, and Poland RE (1999) Cerebral 1H MRS alterations in recreational 3,4-methylenedioxymethamphetamine (MDMA, "ecstasy") users. *Journal of Magnetic Resonance Imaging* 10: 521–526.

Chang L, Ernst T, Speck O, and Grob CS (2005) Additive effects of HIV and chronic methamphetamine use on brain metabolite abnormalities. *American Journal of Psychiatry* 162: 361–369.

Chang L, Ernst T, Strickland T, and Mehringer CM (1999) Gender effects on persistent cerebral metabolite changes in the frontal lobes of abstinent cocaine users. *American Journal of Psychiatry* 156: 716–722.

Chang L, Mehringer CM, Ernst T, Melchor R, Myers H, *et al.* (1997) Neurochemical alterations in asymptomatic abstinent cocaine users: A proton magnetic resonance spectroscopy study. *Biological Psychiatry* 42: 1105–1114.

Chen JG, Charles HC, Barboriak DP, and Doraiswamy PM (2000) Magnetic resonance spectroscopy in Alzheimer's disease: Focus on N-acetylaspartate. *Acta Neurologica Scandinavica. Supplementum* 176: 20–26.

Christensen JD, Kaufman MJ, Frederick Bd, Rose SL, Moore CM, *et al.* (2000) Proton magnetic resonance spectroscopy of human basal ganglia: Response to cocaine administration. *Biological Psychiatry* 48: 685–692.

Cloak CC, Alicata D, Chang L, Andrews-Shigaki B, and Ernst T (2011) Age and sex effects levels of choline compounds in the anterior cingulate cortex of adolescent methamphetamine users. *Drug and Alcohol Dependence* (in press).

Cole JC, Bailey M, Sumnall HR, Wagstaff GF, and King LA (2002) The content of ecstasy tablets: Implications for the study of their long-term effects. *Addiction* 97: 1531–1536.

Cowan R (2007) Neuroimaging research in human MDMA users: A review. *Psychopharmacology* 189: 539–556.

Cowan RL, Roberts DM, and Joers JM (2008) Neuroimaging in human MDMA (ecstasy) users. *Annals of the New York Academy of Sciences* 1139: 291–298.

Cunha-Oliveira T, Rego AC, and Oliveira CR (2008) Cellular and molecular mechanisms involved in the neurotoxicity of opioid and psychostimulant drugs. *Brain Research Reviews* 58: 192–208.

Dahchour A and De Witte P (2003) Effects of acamprosate on excitatory amino acids during multiple ethanol withdrawal periods. *Alcoholism: Clinical and Experimental Research* 27: 465–470.

Daumann J, Fischermann T, Pilatus U, Thron A, Moeller-Hartmann W, *et al.* (2004) Proton magnetic resonance spectroscopy in ecstasy (MDMA) users. *Neuroscience Letters* 362: 113–116.

de Win MML, Jager G, Booij J, Reneman L, Schilt T, *et al.* (2008a) Sustained effects of ecstasy on the human brain: A prospective neuroimaging study in novel users. *Brain* 131: 2936–2945.

de Win MML, Jager G, Booij J, Reneman L, Schilt T, *et al.* (2008b) Neurotoxic effects of ecstasy on the thalamus. *British Journal of Psychiatry* 193: 289–296.

de Win MML, Reneman L, Jager G, Vlieger E-JP, Olabarriaga SD, *et al.* (2007) A prospective cohort study on sustained effects of low-dose ecstasy use on the brain in new ecstasy users. *Neuropsychopharmacology* 32: 458–470.

Demougeot C, Marie C, Giroud M, and Beley A (2004) N-acetylaspartate: A literature review of animal research on brain ischaemia. *Journal of Neurochemistry* 90: 776–783.

Dewey SL, Morgan AE, Ashby CR, Jr., Horan B, Kushner SA, *et al.* (1998) A novel strategy for the treatment of cocaine addiction. *Synapse* 30: 119–129.

Du F, Chu WJ, Yang B, Den Hollander JA, and Ng TC (2004) *In vivo* GABA detection with improved selectivity and sensitivity by localized double quantum filter technique at 4.1T. *Magnetic Resonance Imaging* 22: 103–108.

Durazzo TC, Gazdzinski S, Banys P, and Meyerhoff DJ (2004) Cigarette smoking exacerbates chronic alcohol-induced brain damage: A preliminary metabolite imaging study. *Alcoholism: Clinical and Experimental Research* 28: 1849–1860.

Durazzo TC, Gazdzinski S, Rothlind JC, Banys P, and Meyerhoff DJ (2006) Brain metabolite concentrations and neurocognition during short-term recovery from alcohol dependence: Preliminary evidence of the effects of concurrent chronic cigarette smoking. *Alcoholism: Clinical and Experimental Research* 30: 539–551.

Durazzo TC, Gazdzinski S, Yeh P-H, and Meyerhoff DJ (2008) Combined neuroimaging, neurocognitive and psychiatric factors to predict alcohol consumption following treatment for alcohol dependence. *Alcohol and Alcoholism* 43: 683–691.

Ende G, Welzel H, Walter S, Weber-Fahr W, Diehl A, *et al.* (2005) Monitoring the effects of chronic alcohol consumption and abstinence on brain metabolism: A longitudinal proton magnetic resonance spectroscopy study. *Biological Psychiatry* 58: 974–980.

Erecinska M and Silver IA (1989) ATP and brain function. *Journal of Cerebral Blood Flow and Metabolism* 9: 2–19.

Ernst T and Chang L (2008) Adaptation of brain glutamate plus glutamine during abstinence from chronic methamphetamine use. *Journal of Neuroimmune Pharmacology* 3: 165–172.

Ernst T, Chang L, Leonido-Yee M, and Speck O (2000) Evidence for long-term neurotoxicity associated with methamphetamine abuse. *Neurology* 54: 1344–1349.

Estilaei MR, Matson GB, Payne GS, Leach MO, Fein G, *et al.* (2001) Effects of chronic alcohol consumption on the broad phospholipid signal in human brain: An *in vivo* 31P MRS study. *Alcoholism: Clinical and Experimental Research* 25: 89–97.

Fowler JS, Volkow ND, Kassed CA, and Chang L (2007) Imaging the addicted human brain. *Science Practice Perspectives* 3: 4–16.

Frost DO and Cadet JL (2000) Effects of methamphetamine-induced neurotoxicity on the development of neural circuitry: A hypothesis. *Brain Research Reviews* 34: 103–118.

Gazdzinski S, Durazzo TC, Mon A, and Meyerhoff DJ (2010) Body mass index is associated with brain metabolite levels in alcohol dependence: A multimodal magnetic resonance study. *Alcoholism: Clinical and Experimental Research* 34: 2089–2096.

Gazdzinski S, Durazzo TC, Mon A, Yeh P-H, and Meyerhoff DJ (2010) Cerebral white matter recovery in abstinent alcoholics: A multimodality magnetic resonance study. *Brain* 133: 1043–1053.

Gouzoulis-Mayfrank E and Daumann J (2006) Neurotoxicity of methylenedioxyamphetamines (MDMA; ecstasy) in humans: How strong is the evidence for persistent brain damage? *Addiction* 101: 348–361.

Govindaraju V, Young K, and Maudsley AA (2000) Proton NMR chemical shifts and coupling constants for brain metabolites. *NMR in Biomedicine* 13: 129–153.

Grant BF and Harford TC (1990) Concurrent and simultaneous use of alcohol with cocaine: Results of national survey. *Drug and Alcohol Dependence* 25: 97–104.

Green AR, Mechan AO, Elliott JM, O'Shea E, and Colado MI (2003) The pharmacology and clinical pharmacology of 3,4-methylenedioxymethamphetamine (MDMA, "ecstasy"). *Pharmacological Reviews* 55: 463–508.

Green KL and Grant KA (1998) Evidence for overshadowing by components of the heterogeneous discriminative stimulus effects of ethanol. *Drug and Alcohol Dependence* 52: 149–159.

Grobin AC, Matthews DB, Devaud LL, and Morrow AL (1998) The role of GABA(A) receptors in the acute and chronic effects of ethanol. *Psychopharmacology* (Berlin) 139: 2–19.

Gruber SA, Tzilos GK, Silveri MM, Pollack M, Renshaw PF, *et al.* (2006) Methadone maintenance improves cognitive performance after two months of treatment. *Experimental and Clinical Psychopharmacology* 14: 157–164.

Hall W and Degenhardt L (2009) Adverse health effects of non-medical cannabis use. *Lancet* 374: 1383–1391.

Hall W, Degenhardt L, and Teesson M (2004) Cannabis use and psychotic disorders: An update. *Drug and Alcohol Review* 23: 433–443.

Haselhorst R, Dursteler-MacFarland K, Scheffler K, Ladewig D, Muller-Spahn F, *et al.* (2002) Frontocortical N-acetylaspartate reduction associated with long-term IV heroin use. *Neurology* 58: 305–307.

Hermann D, Sartorius A, Welzel H, Walter S, Skopp G, *et al.* (2007) Dorsolateral prefrontal cortex N-acetylaspartate/total creatine (NAA/tCr) loss in male recreational cannabis users. *Biological Psychiatry* 61: 1281–1289.

Hetherington HP, Newcomer BR, and Pan JW (1998) Measurements of human cerebral GABA at 4.1 T using numerically optimized editing pulses. *Magnetic Resonance in Medicine* 39: 6–10.

Hoek JB and Rubin E (1990) Alcohol and membrane-associated signal transduction. *Alcohol and Alcoholism* 25: 143–156.

Hommer D, Momenan R, Kaiser E, and Rawlings R (2001) Evidence for a gender-related effect of alcoholism on brain volumes. *American Journal of Psychiatry* 158: 198–204.

Itzhak Y and Achat-Mendes C (2004) Methamphetamine and MDMA (ecstasy) neurotoxicity: 'Of mice and men'. *IUBMB Life* 56: 249–255.

Jagannathan NR, Desai NG, and Raghunathan P (1996) Brain metabolite changes in alcoholism: An in vivo proton magnetic resonance spectroscopy (MRS) study. *Magnetic Resonance Imaging* 14: 553–557.

Kandel D (1975) Stages in adolescent involvement in drug use. *Science* 190: 912–914.

Kandel D and Faust R (1975) Sequence and stages in patterns of adolescent drug use. *Archives of General Psychiatry* 32: 923–932.

Kato T, Inubushi T, and Kato N (1998) Magnetic resonance spectroscopy in affective disorders. *Journal of Neuropsychiatry and Clinical Neuroscience* 10: 133–147.

Kaufman MJ, Levin JM, Ross MH, Lange N, Rose SL, et al. (1998) Cocaine-induced cerebral vasoconstriction detected in humans with magnetic resonance angiography. *Journal of the American Medical Association* 279: 376–380.

Ke Y, Cohen BM, Bang JY, Yang M, and Renshaw PF (2000) Assessment of GABA concentration in human brain using two-dimensional proton magnetic resonance spectroscopy. *Psychiatry Research* 100: 169–178.

Ke Y, Streeter CC, Nassar LE, Sarid-Segal O, Hennen J, et al. (2004) Frontal lobe GABA levels in cocaine dependence: a two-dimensional, J-resolved magnetic resonance spectroscopy study. *Psychiatry Research: Neuroimaging* 130: 283–293.

Kish SJ, Perry TL, and Hansen S (1979) Regional distribution of homocarnosine, homocarnosine-carnosine synthetase and homocarnosinase in human brain. *Journal of Neurochemistry* 32: 1629–1636.

Kosten TA, Gawin FH, Kosten TR, and Rounsaville BJ (1993) Gender differences in cocaine use and treatment response. *Journal of Substance Abuse Treatment* 10: 63–66.

Kril JJ, Halliday GM, Svoboda MD, and Cartwright H (1997) The cerebral cortex is damaged in chronic alcoholics. *Neuroscience* 79: 983–998.

Landfield PW, Cadwallader LB, and Vinsant S (1988) Quantitative changes in hippocampal structure following long-term exposure to delta 9-tetrahydrocannabinol: Possible mediation by glucocorticoid systems. *Brain Research* 443: 47–62.

Lee E, Jang D-P, Kim J-J, An SK, Park S, et al. (2007) Alteration of brain metabolites in young alcoholics without structural changes. *NeuroReport* 18: 1511–1514. 1510.1097/WNR.1510b1013e3282ef7625.

Leshner AI (1997) Addiction is a brain disease, and it matters. *Science* 278: 45–47.

Lessem JM, Hopfer CJ, Haberstick BC, Timberlake D, Ehringer MA, et al. (2006) Relationship between adolescent marijuana use and young adult illicit drug use. *Behavior Genetics* 36: 498–506.

Levin JM, Holman BL, Mendelson JH, Teoh SK, Garada B, et al. (1994) Gender differences in cerebral perfusion in cocaine abuse: Technetium-99m-HMPAO SPECT study of drug-abusing women. *Journal of Nuclear Medicine* 35: 1902–1909.

Levine SR, Brust JC, Futrell N, Ho KL, Blake D, et al. (1990) Cerebrovascular complications of the use of the "crack" form of alkaloidal cocaine. *New England Journal of Medicine* 323: 699–704.

Li S-J, Wang Y, Pankiewicz J, and Stein EA (1999) Neurochemical adaptation to cocaine abuse: Reduction of N-acetyl aspartate in thalamus of human cocaine abusers. *Biological Psychiatry* 45: 1481–1487.

Licata SC and Renshaw PF (2010) Neurochemistry of drug action. *Annals of the New York Academy of Sciences* 1187: 148–171.

Lien R, Mishra OP, Graham E, Delivoria-Papadopoulos M, and Anday EK (1994) Alteration of brain cell membrane function following cocaine exposure in the fetal guinea pig. *Brain Research* 637: 249–254.

Liu H-S, Chou M-C, Chung H-W, Cho N-Y, Chiang S-W, *et al.* (2011) Potential long-term effects of MDMA on the basal ganglia–thalamocortical circuit: A proton MR spectroscopy and diffusion-tensor imaging study. *Radiology.*

Liu J, Decatur J, Proni G, and Champeil E (2010) Identification and quantitation of 3,4-methylenedioxy-N-methylamphetamine (MDMA, ecstasy) in human urine by 1H NMR spectroscopy: Application to five cases of intoxication. *Forensic Science International* 194: 103–107.

Lowenstein DH, Massa SM, Rowbotham MC, Collins SD, McKinney HE, *et al.* (1987) Acute neurologic and psychiatric complications associated with cocaine abuse. *American Journal of Medicine* 83: 841–846.

Lyles J and Cadet JL (2003) Methylenedioxymethamphetamine (MDMA, ecstasy) neurotoxicity: Cellular and molecular mechanisms. *Brain Research Reviews* 42: 155–168.

Lyoo IK, Kong SW, Sung SM, Hirashima F, Parow A, *et al.* (2003) Multinuclear magnetic resonance spectroscopy of high-energy phosphate metabolites in human brain following oral supplementation of creatine-monohydrate. *Psychiatry Research* 123: 87–100.

Lyoo IK, Pollack MH, Silveri MM, Ahn KH, Diaz CI, *et al.* (2006) Prefrontal and temporal gray matter density decreases in opiate dependence. *Psychopharmacology* (Berlin) 184: 139–144.

Lyoo IK, Streeter CC, Ahn KH, Lee HK, Pollack MH, *et al.* (2004) White matter hyperintensities in subjects with cocaine and opiate dependence and healthy comparison subjects. *Psychiatry Research* 131: 135–145.

Marshall I, Wardlaw J, Cannon J, Slattery J, and Sellar RJ (1996) Reproducibility of metabolite peak areas in 1H MRS of brain. *Magnetic Resonance Imaging* 14: 281–292.

Martin PR, Gibbs SJ, Nimmerrichter AA, Riddle WR, Welch LW, *et al.* (1995) Brain proton magnetic resonance spectroscopy studies in recently abstinent alcoholics. *Alcoholism: Clinical and Experimental Research* 19: 1078–1082.

Mason G, Bendszus M, Meyerhoff D, Hetherington H, Schweinsburg B, *et al.* (2005) Magnetic resonance spectroscopic studies of alcoholism: From heavy drinking to alcohol dependence and back again. *Alcoholism: Clinical and Experimental Research* 29: 150–158.

Mason GF, Gruetter R, Rothman DL, Behar KL, Shulman RG, *et al.* (1995) Simultaneous determination of the rates of the TCA cycle, glucose utilization, alpha-ketoglutarate/glutamate exchange, and glutamine synthesis in human brain by NMR. *Journal of Cerebral Blood Flow and Metabolism* 15: 12–25.

Mason GF, Petrakis IL, de Graaf RA, Gueorguieva R, Guidone E, *et al.* (2006) Cortical gamma-aminobutyric acid levels and the recovery from ethanol dependence: Preliminary evidence of modification by cigarette smoking. *Biological Psychiatry* 59: 85–93.

Mason GF, Rothman DL, Behar KL, and Shulman RG (1992) NMR determination of the TCA cycle rate and alpha-ketoglutarate/glutamate exchange rate in rat brain. *Journal of Cerebral Blood Flow and Metabolism* 12: 434–447.

McFarland K and Kalivas PW (2001) The circuitry mediating cocaine-induced reinstatement of drug-seeking behavior. *Journal of Neuroscience* 21: 8655–8663.

McFarland K, Lapish CC, and Kalivas PW (2003) Prefrontal glutamate release into the core of the nucleus accumbens mediates cocaine-induced reinstatement of drug-seeking behavior. *Journal of Neuroscience* 23: 3531–3537.

Meyerhoff DJ and Bloomer C (1999) Cortical metabolite alterations in abstinent cocaine and cocaine/alcohol-dependent. *Addiction Biology* 4: 405.

Meyerhoff DJ and Durazzo TC (2008) Proton magnetic resonance spectroscopy in alcohol use disorders: A potential new endophenotype? *Alcoholism: Clinical and Experimental Research* 32: 1146–1158.

Meyerhoff D, Blumenfeld R, Truran D, Lindgren J, Flenniken D, *et al.* (2004) Effects of heavy drinking, binge drinking, and family history of alcoholism on regional brain metabolites. *Alcoholism: Clinical and Experimental Research* 28: 650–661.

Meyerhoff DJ, MacKay S, Sappey-Marinier D, Deicken R, Calabrese G, *et al.* (1995) Effects of chronic alcohol abuse and HIV infection on brain phosphorus metabolites. *Alcoholism: Clinical and Experimental Research* 19: 685–692.

Michaelis EK, Freed WJ, Galton N, Foye J, Michaelis ML, *et al.* (1990) Glutamate receptor changes in brain synaptic membranes from human alcoholics. *Neurochemical Research* 15: 1055–1063.

Miese F, Kircheis G, Wittsack HJ, Wenserski F, Hemker J, *et al.* (2006) 1H-MR spectroscopy, magnetization transfer, and diffusion-weighted imaging in alcoholic and nonalcoholic patients with cirrhosis with hepatic encephalopathy. *American Journal of Neuroradiology* 27: 1019–1026.

Miller BL, Chang L, Booth R, Ernst T, Cornford M, *et al.* (1996) *In vivo* 1H MRS choline: Correlation with *in vitro* chemistry/histology. *Life Science* 58: 1929–1935.

Modi S, Bhattacharya M, Kumar P, Deshpande SN, Tripathi RP, *et al.* (2011) Brain metabolite changes in alcoholism: Localized proton magnetic resonance spectroscopy study of the occipital lobe. *European Journal of Radiology* 79: 96–100.

Mody CK, Miller BL, McIntyre HB, Cobb SK, and Goldberg MA (1988) Neurologic complications of cocaine abuse. *Neurology* 38: 1189–1193.

Molina V, Sanchez J, Reig S, Sanz J, Benito C, *et al.* (2005) N-acetyl-aspartate levels in the dorsolateral prefrontal cortex in the early years of schizophrenia are inversely related to disease duration. *Schizophrenia Research* 73: 209–219.

Moore CM, Frederick BB, and Renshaw PF (1999) Brain biochemistry using magnetic resonance spectroscopy: Relevance to psychiatric illness in the elderly. *Journal of Geriatric Psychiatry and Neurology* 12: 107–117.

Moore TH, Zammit S, Lingford-Hughes A, Barnes TR, Jones PB, *et al.* (2007) Cannabis use and risk of psychotic or affective mental health outcomes: A systematic review. *Lancet* 370: 319–328.

Morton J (2005) Ecstasy: Pharmacology and neurotoxicity. *Current Opinion in Pharmacology* 5: 79–86.

Najt P, Fusar-Poli P, and Brambilla P (2011) Co-occurring mental and substance abuse disorders: A review on the potential predictors and clinical outcomes. *Psychiatry Research* 186: 159–164.

Neale J and Robertson M (2003) Comparisons of self-report data and oral fluid testing in detecting drug use amongst new treatment clients. *Drug and Alcohol Dependence* 71: 57–64.

Nixon K and Crews FT (2004) Temporally specific burst in cell proliferation increases hippocampal neurogenesis in protracted abstinence from alcohol. *Journal of Neuroscience* 24: 9714–9722.

Nordahl TE, Salo R, Natsuaki Y, Galloway GP, Waters C, *et al.* (2005) Methamphetamine users in sustained abstinence: A proton magnetic resonance spectroscopy study. *Archives of General Psychiatry* 62: 444–452.

Nordahl TE, Salo R, Possin K, Gibson DR, Flynn N, *et al.* (2002) Low N-acetyl-aspartate and high choline in the anterior cingulum of recently abstinent methamphetamine-dependent subjects: A preliminary proton MRS study. *Psychiatry Research: Neuroimaging* 116: 43–52.

Obergriesser T, Ende G, Braus DF, and Henn FA (2001) Hippocampal 1H-MRSI in ecstasy users. *European Archives of Psychiatry and Clinical Neuroscience* 251: 114–116.

Obernier JA, Bouldin TW, and Crews FT (2002) Binge ethanol exposure in adult rats causes necrotic cell death. *Alcoholism: Clinical and Experimental Research* 26: 547–557.

O'Malley S, Adamse M, Heaton RK, and Gawin FH (1992) Neuropsychological impairment in chronic cocaine abusers. *American Journal of Drug and Alcohol Abuse* 18: 131–144.

O'Neill J, Cardenas VA, and Meyerhoff DJ (2001) Separate and interactive effects of cocaine and alcohol dependence on brain structures and metabolites: Quantitative MRI and proton MR spectroscopic imaging. *Addiction Biology* 6: 347–361.

Oscar-Berman M and Marinkovic K (2007) Alcohol: Effects on neurobehavioral functions and the brain. *Neuropsychology Review* 17: 239–257.

Parks MH, Dawant BM, Riddle WR, Hartmann SL, Dietrich MS, *et al.* (2002) Longitudinal brain metabolic characterization of chronic alcoholics with proton magnetic resonance spectroscopy. *Alcoholism: Clinical and Experimental Research* 26: 1368–1380.

Parrott AC (2004) Is ecstasy MDMA? A review of the proportion of ecstasy tablets containing MDMA, their dosage levels, and the changing perceptions of purity. *Psychopharmacology* (Berlin) 173: 234–241.

Patel TB and Clark JB (1979) Synthesis of N-acetyl-L-aspartate by rat brain mitochondria and its involvement in mitochondrial/cytosolic carbon transport. *Biochemical Journal* 184: 539–546.

Pedersen W and Skrondal A (1999) Ecstasy and new patterns of drug use: A normal population study. *Addiction* 94: 1695–1706.

Penland S, Hoplight B, Obernier J, and Crews FT (2001) Effects of nicotine on ethanol dependence and brain damage. *Alcohol* 24: 45–54.

Pfefferbaum A, Sullivan EV, Mathalon DH, Shear PK, Rosenbloom MJ, *et al.* (1995) Longitudinal changes in magnetic resonance imaging brain volumes in abstinent and relapsed alcoholics. *Alcoholism: Clinical and Experimental Research* 19: 1177–1191.

Pouwels PJ and Frahm J (1998) Regional metabolite concentrations in human brain as determined by quantitative localized proton MRS. *Magnetic Resonance in Medicine* 39: 53–60.

Prescot AP, Locatelli AE, Renshaw PF, and Yurgelun-Todd DA (2011) Neurochemical alterations in adolescent chronic marijuana smokers: A proton MRS study. *NeuroImage* 57: 69–75.

Raehal KM and Bohn LM (2005) Mu opioid receptor regulation and opiate responsiveness. *AAPS Journal* 7: E587–591.

Raimo EB and Schuckit MA (1998) Alcohol dependence and mood disorders. *Addictive Behaviors* 23: 933–946.

Rawson RA, Gonzales R, McCann M, and Ling W (2007) Use of methamphetamine by young people: Is there reason for concern? *Addiction* 102: 1021–1022.

Reneman L, Booij J, Majoie CBLM, Van den Brink W, and den Heeten GJ (2001a) Investigating the potential neurotoxicity of ecstasy (MDMA): An imaging approach. *Human Psychopharmacology: Clinical and Experimental* 16: 579–588.

Reneman L, Majoie CB, Flick H, and den Heeten GJ (2002) Reduced N-acetylaspartate levels in the frontal cortex of 3,4-methylenedioxymethamphetamine (ecstasy) users: Preliminary results. *American Journal of Neuroradiology* 23: 231–237.

Reneman L, Majoie CB, Schmand B, van den Brink W, and den Heeten GJ (2001b) Prefrontal N-acetylaspartate is strongly associated with memory performance in (abstinent) ecstasy users: Preliminary report. *Biological Psychiatry* 50: 550–554.

Renshaw PF, Parow AM, Hirashima F, Ke Y, Moore CM, *et al.* (2001) Multinuclear magnetic resonance spectroscopy studies of brain purines in major depression. *American Journal of Psychiatry* 158: 2048–2055.

Ross B and Bluml S (2001) Magnetic resonance spectroscopy of the human brain. *Anatomical Record* 265: 54–84.

Ross BD (1991) Biochemical considerations in 1H spectroscopy: Glutamate and glutamine; myo-inositol and related metabolites. *NMR Biomedicine* 4: 59–63.

Rothman DL, Behar KL, Hyder F, and Shulman RG (2003) *In vivo* NMR studies of the glutamate neurotransmitter flux and neuroenergetics: Implications for brain function. *Annual Review of Physiology* 65: 401–427.

Rothman DL, Hyder F, Sibson N, Behar KL, Mason GF, *et al.* (2002) *In vivo* magnetic resonance spectroscopy studies of the glutamate and GABA neurotransmitter cycles and functional neuroenergetics. In KL Davis , D Charney , JT Coyle , and C Nemeroff (eds), *Neuropsychopharmacology: The Fifth Generation of Progress* (pp. 315–342). Philadelphia: Lippincott Williams & Wilkins.

Rothman DL, Sibson NR, Hyder F, Shen J, Behar KL, *et al.* (1999) *In vivo* nuclear magnetic resonance spectroscopy studies of the relationship between the glutamate–glutamine neurotransmitter cycle and functional neuroenergetics. *Philosophical Transactions of the Royal Society B: Biological Sciences* 354: 1165–1177.

Sailasuta N, Abulseoud O, Harris KC, and Ross BD (2010) Glial dysfunction in abstinent methamphetamine abusers. *Journal of Cerebral Blood Flow and Metabolism* 30: 950–960.

Sailasuta N, Abulseoud O, Hernandez M, Haghani P, and Ross BD (2010) Metabolic abnormalities in abstinent methamphetamine dependent subjects. *Substance Abuse: Research and Treatment* 4: 9–20.

Salo R, Buonocore MH, Leamon M, Natsuaki Y, Waters C, *et al.* (2011) Extended findings of brain metabolite normalization in MA-dependent subjects across sustained abstinence: A proton MRS study. *Drug and Alcohol Dependence* 113: 133–138.

Salo R, Nordahl TE, Natsuaki Y, Leamon MH, Galloway GP, *et al.* (2007) Attentional control and brain metabolite levels in methamphetamine abusers. *Biological Psychiatry* 61: 1272–1280.

Sanacora G, Mason GF, Rothman DL, Behar KL, Hyder F, *et al.* (1999) Reduced cortical gamma-aminobutyric acid levels in depressed patients determined by proton magnetic resonance spectroscopy. *Archives of General Psychiatry* 56: 1043–1047.

Sauter A and Rudin M (1993) Determination of creatine kinase kinetic parameters in rat brain by NMR magnetization transfer: Correlation with brain function. *Journal of Biological Chemistry* 268: 13166–13171.

Scholey AB, Parrott AC, Buchanan T, Heffernan TM, Ling J, *et al.* (2004) Increased intensity of ecstasy and polydrug usage in the more experienced recreational ecstasy/MDMA users: A WWW study. *Addictive Behaviors* 29: 743–752.

Schweinsburg BC, Alhassoon OM, Taylor MJ, Gonzalez R, Videen JS, *et al.* (2003) Effects of alcoholism and gender on brain metabolism. *American Journal of Psychiatry* 160: 1180–1183.

Schweinsburg BC, Taylor MJ, Alhassoon OM, Videen JS, Brown GG, *et al.* (2001) Chemical pathology in brain white matter of recently detoxified alcoholics: A 1H magnetic resonance spectroscopy investigation of alcohol-associated frontal lobe injury. *Alcoholism: Clinical and Experimental Research* 25: 924–934.

Schweinsburg BC, Taylor MJ, Videen JS, Alhassoon OM, Patterson TL, *et al.* (2000) Elevated myo-inositol in gray matter of recently detoxified but not long-term abstinent alcoholics: A preliminary MR spectroscopy study. *Alcoholism: Clinical and Experimental Research* 24: 699–705.

Sekine Y, Minabe Y, Kawai M, Suzuki K, Iyo M, *et al.* (2002) Metabolite alterations in basal ganglia associated with methamphetamine-related psychiatric symptoms: A proton MRS study. *Neuropsychopharmacology* 27: 453–461.

Silveri MM, Jensen JE, Rosso IM, Sneider JT, and Yurgelun-Todd DA (2011) Preliminary evidence for white matter metabolite differences in marijuana-dependent young men using 2D J-resolved magnetic resonance spectroscopic imaging at 4 Tesla. *Psychiatry Research: Neuroimaging* 191: 201–211.

Silveri MM, Pollack MH, Diaz CI, Nassar LE, Mendelson JH, *et al.* (2004) Cerebral phosphorus metabolite and transverse relaxation time abnormalities in heroin-dependent subjects at onset of methadone maintenance treatment. *Psychiatry Research: Neuroimaging* 131: 217–226.

Smith LM, Chang L, Yonekura ML, Grob C, Osborn D, *et al.* (2001) Brain proton magnetic resonance spectroscopy in children exposed to methamphetamine in utero. *Neurology* 57: 255–260.

Snyder H, Williams D, Zink B, and Reilly K (1992) Accuracy of blood ethanol determination using serum osmolality. *Journal of Emergency Medicine* 10: 129–133.

Song BJ, Moon KH, Upreti VV, Eddington ND, and Lee IJ (2010) Mechanisms of MDMA (Ecstasy)-induced oxidative stress, mitochondrial dysfunction, and organ damage. *Current Pharmaceutical Biotechnology* 11: 434–443.

Stork C and Renshaw PF (2005) Mitochondrial dysfunction in bipolar disorder: Evidence from magnetic resonance spectroscopy research. *Molecular Psychiatry* 10: 900–919.

Streeter C, Hennen J, Ke Y, Jensen J, Sarid-Segal O, *et al.* (2005) Prefrontal GABA levels in cocaine-dependent subjects increase with pramipexole and venlafaxine treatment. *Psychopharmacology* 182: 516–526.

Sullivan EV (2003) Compromised pontocerebellar and cerebellothalamocortical systems: Speculations on their contributions to cognitive and motor impairment in nonamnesic alcoholism. *Alcoholism: Clinical and Experimental Research* 27: 1409–1419.

Sullivan EV and Pfefferbaum A (2005) Neurocircuitry in alcoholism: A substrate of disruption and repair. *Psychopharmacology* (Berlin) 180: 583–594.

Sung YH, Cho SC, Hwang J, Kim SJ, Kim H, *et al.* (2007) Relationship between N-acetyl-aspartate in gray and white matter of abstinent methamphetamine abusers and their history of drug abuse: A proton magnetic resonance spectroscopy study. *Drug and Alcohol Dependence* 88: 28–35.

Tanner-Smith EE (2006) Pharmacological content of tablets sold as "ecstasy": Results from an online testing service. *Drug and Alcohol Dependence* 83: 247–254.

Tarter RE, Vanyukov M, Kirisci L, Reynolds M, and Clark DB (2006) Predictors of marijuana use in adolescents before and after licit drug use: Examination of the gateway hypothesis. *American Journal of Psychiatry* 163: 2134–2140.

Tata DA and Yamamoto BK (2007) Interactions between methamphetamine and environmental stress: Role of oxidative stress, glutamate and mitochondrial dysfunction. *Addiction* 102 (Suppl. 1): 49–60.

Thatcher NM, Badar-Goffer RS, Ben-Yoseph O, McLean MA, Morris PG, *et al.* (2002) A comparison of some metabolic effects of N-methylaspartate stereoisomers, glutamate and depolarization: A multinuclear MRS study. *Neurochemical Research* 27: 51–58.

Thoma R, Mullins P, Ruhl D, Monnig M, Yeo RA, *et al.* (2011) Perturbation of the glutamate–glutamine system in alcohol dependence and remission. *Neuropsychopharmacology* 36: 1359–1365.

Ticku MK (1990) Alcohol and GABA-benzodiazepine receptor function. *Annals of Medicine* 22: 241–246.

Truckenmiller ME, Namboodiri MA, Brownstein MJ, and Neale JH (1985) N-Acetylation of L-aspartate in the nervous system: Differential distribution of a specific enzyme. *Journal of Neurochemistry* 45: 1658–1662.

Umhau JC, Momenan R, Schwandt ML, Singley E, Lifshitz M, *et al.* (2010) Effect of acamprosate on magnetic resonance spectroscopy measures of central glutamate in detoxified alcohol-dependent individuals: A randomized controlled experimental medicine study. *Archives of General Psychiatry* 67: 1069–1077.

Urenjak J, Williams SR, Gadian DG, and Noble M (1993) Proton nuclear magnetic resonance spectroscopy unambiguously identifies different neural cell types. *Journal of Neuroscience* 13: 981–989.

Wang JJ, Durazzo TC, Gazdzinski S, Yeh P-H, Mon A, *et al.* (2009) MRSI and DTI: A multimodal approach for improved detection of white matter abnormalities in alcohol and nicotine dependence. *NMR in Biomedicine* 22: 516–522.

Weiss RD, Martinez-Raga J, Griffin ML, Greenfield SF, and Hufford C (1997) Gender differences in cocaine dependent patients: A 6 month follow-up study. *Drug and Alcohol Dependence* 44: 35–40.

Wouldes T, LaGasse L, Sheridan J, and Lester B (2004) Maternal methamphetamine use during pregnancy and child outcome: What do we know? *New Zealand Medical Journal* 117: U1180.

Yang S, Salmeron BJ, Ross TJ, Xi Z-X, Stein EA, *et al.* (2009) Lower glutamate levels in rostral anterior cingulate of chronic cocaine users: A 1H-MRS study using TE-averaged PRESS at 3 T with an optimized quantification strategy. *Psychiatry Research: Neuroimaging* 174: 171–176.

Yoon SJ, Lyoo IK, Kim HJ, Kim T-S, Sung YH, *et al.* (2010) Neurochemical alterations in methamphetamine-dependent patients treated with cytidine-5[prime]-diphosphate choline: A longitudinal proton magnetic resonance spectroscopy study. *Neuropsychopharmacology* 35: 1165–1173.

Yucel M, Lubman DI, Harrison BJ, Fornito A, Allen NB, *et al.* (2007) A combined spectroscopic and functional MRI investigation of the dorsal anterior cingulate region in opiate addiction. *Molecular Psychiatry* 12: 691–702.

Zahr NM, Mayer D, Rohlfing T, Hasak MP, Hsu O, *et al.* (2010) Brain injury and recovery following binge ethanol: Evidence from *in vivo* magnetic resonance spectroscopy. *Biological Psychiatry* 67: 846–854.

Conclusions:
Consilience as the Future of
Addiction Psychopharmacology
James MacKillop and Harriet de Wit

The goal of this volume was to bring together the many diverse methodologies and technologies that are used to study addictive behavior. The assembled chapters provide a range of perspectives on addiction, from top-down approaches that frame addictive disorders across the lifespan to bottom-up approaches that focus on the micro-determinants or neurobiological substrates of addiction. The single theme that is common across them all is a focus on rigorous experimental methodology and empiricism. Recognizing that addictive behavior is complex and heterogeneous, a full understanding of the causes, consequences, and best interventions for addiction requires objective methods and thoughtful synthesis of empirical data.

Importantly, studies of addiction usually involve more than a single method, and the methods selected complement and enhance one another. Until recently, addiction researchers have operated within disciplinary "silos," which can lead to myopia for understanding the behavior. Now, it is recognized that the methods must be integrated methods across domains, and the benefits to the field will be exponential. For example, the cognitive neuroscience paradigms could complement standard baseline assessment of individual differences in longitudinal investigations. Or, elements of personality, executive functioning, or impulsivity could be further leveraged to better understand and investigate the role of craving or negative affect in drug taking. Greater transdisciplinary *consilience*, a fuller integration of perspectives and methods, is the clear direction forward for the future of addiction research.

The need for greater consilience in addiction research reflects the emphasis on translational research in behavioral and biomedical research in general (National Advisory Mental Health Council Behavioral Science Workgroup, 2000; Onken and Bootzin,

1998; Woolf, 2008). Translational research can refer to "bench-to-bedside" translation of basic research findings into clinical investigations and, ultimately, into novel treatments and standards of care (e.g., Gorini, Bell, and Mayfield, 2011; Paterson, 2011). However, translational research is also seen as recursive and reciprocal: basic science findings used to improve clinical science, and clinical science used to improve basic science. For example, behavioral research with nonhuman models may serve as a "forward translation" platform to identify candidates for medications, while on the other hand, etiological and clinical factors identified in patient samples (e.g., craving or high trait-level impulsivity) may suggest "back translation" of novel phenotypes for modeling in preclinical paradigms. This bidirectional relationship between different fields and methodologies is the essence of what we mean by defining greater consilience as the future of addiction research.

An important direction of current addiction research is to identify genetic factors related to the disorder. It is clear that genetic factors play an important role in addiction, but there is a wide gulf between ~50% heritability of these conditions and the specific genetic risk variants that have been identified, to date (Goldman, Oroszi, and Ducci, 2005; MacKillop *et al.*, 2010). In part, this is because clinical diagnosis is an imprecise phenotype. Instead, genetic influences are probably transmitted via intermediary effects on risk and protective variables, referred to as endophenotypes or intermediate phenotypes (Goldman and Ducci, 2007; Flint and Munafò, 2007). The methods used to study the genetic basis of addiction are extremely rapidly evolving, and as such beyond the scope of the current volume. Nevertheless, the methods discussed here include novel phenotypes that are well suited for mapping the pathways from genetic factors to risk for addiction itself. The cognitive neuroscience methodologies, especially, offer powerful tools to examine the phenotypic expression of genotypic variation in brain activity (e.g., Edenberg *et al.*, 2004; Filbey *et al.*, 2008; McClernon, Hutchison, Rose, and Kozink, 2007; for a review, see Green *et al.*, 2008). However, there is also promise for many of the other experimental domains reviewed, such as subjective intoxication (e.g., Dlugos *et al.*, 2010; Ray and Hutchison, 2004), cue reactivity (Hutchison *et al.*, 2002; van den Wildenberg *et al.*, 2007), aspects of impulsivity (e.g., Eisenberg *et al.*, 2007; Hamidovic *et al.*, 2009), and even developmental trajectories (e.g., Dick *et al.*, 2009). Although it is highly likely that each of these phenotypes in themselves will be complex, with variation reflecting the influences of tens, hundreds, or even thousands of loci, they may nonetheless be important mechanistic processes that add to our understanding of latent vulnerabilities to addiction.

Achieving consilience in addiction research will be no small feat. As reflected in the many domains represented here, the fields of psychopharmacology, behavioral science, cognitive neuroscience, and behavioral genetics must work together, and the theoretical perspectives and methodologies derived in these fields must be integrated. The alternative to not pursuing greater consilience in addiction research, however, is tacitly accepting the myopia of many narrow perspectives on a complex and highly heterogeneous disorder. This status quo will generate incremental progress, but a thoroughly integrative and transdisciplinary approach has the potential to generate categorically new insights that no single approach could ever achieve.

References

Dick DM, Latendresse SJ, Lansford JE, Budde JP, Goate A, Dodge KA, Pettit GS, and Bates JE (2009) Role of GABRA2 in trajectories of externalizing behavior across development and evidence of moderation by parental monitoring. *Archives of General Psychiatry* 66 (6): 649–657.

Dlugos AM, Hamidovic A, Hodgkinson CA, Goldman D, Palmer AA, and de Wit H (2010) More aroused, less fatigued: Fatty acid amide hydrolase gene polymorphisms influence acute response to amphetamine. *Neuropsychopharmacology* 35 (3): 613–22.

Edenberg HJ, Dick DM, Xuei X, Tian H, Almasy L, Bauer LO, Crowe RR, Goate A, Hesselbrock V, Jones K, Kwon J, Li TK, Nurnberger JI, Jr, O'Connor SJ, Reich T, Rice J, Schuckit MA, Porjesz B, Foroud T, and Begleiter H (2004) Variations in GABRA2, encoding the alpha 2 subunit of the GABA(A) receptor, are associated with alcohol dependence and with brain oscillations. *American Journal of Human Genetics* 74 (4): 705–714.

Eisenberg DT, MacKillop J, Modi M, Beauchemin J, Dang D, Lisman SA, Lum JK, and Wilson DS (2007) Examining impulsivity as an endophenotype using a behavioral approach: A DRD2 TaqI A and DRD4 48-bp VNTR association study. *Behavioral and Brain Functions* 3: 2.

Filbey FM, Ray L, Smolen A, Claus ED, Audette A, and Hutchison KE (2008) Differential neural response to alcohol priming and alcohol taste cues is associated with DRD4 VNTR and OPRM1 genotypes. *Alcoholism: Clinical and Experimental Research* 32 (7): 1113–1123.

Flint J and Munafò MR (2007) The endophenotype concept in psychiatric genetics. *Psychological Medicine* 37 (2): 163–180.

Goldman D and Ducci F (2007) Deconstruction of vulnerability to complex diseases: Enhanced effect sizes and power of intermediate phenotypes. *Scientific World Journal* 2 (7): 124–130.

Goldman D, Oroszi G and Ducci F (2005) The genetics of addictions: uncovering the genes. *Nature Reviews Genetics* 6 (7): 521–532.

Gorini G, Bell RL, and Mayfield RD (2011) Molecular targets of alcohol: Action translational research for pharmacotherapy development and screening. *Progress in Molecular Biology and Translational Science* 98: 293–347.

Green AE, Munafò MR, DeYoung CG, Fossella JA, Fan J, and Gray JR (2008) Using genetic data in cognitive neuroscience: From growing pains to genuine insights. *Nature Reviews Neuroscience* 9 (9): 710–720.

Hamidovic A, Dlugos A, Skol A, Palmer AA, and de Wit H (2009) Evaluation of genetic variability in the dopamine receptor D2 in relation to behavioral inhibition and impulsivity/sensation seeking: An exploratory study with d-amphetamine in healthy participants. *Experimental and Clinical Psychopharmacology* 17 (6): 374–383.

Hutchison KE, LaChance H, Niaura R, Bryan A, and Smolen A (2002) The DRD4 VNTR polymorphism influences reactivity to smoking cues. *Journal of Abnormal Psychology* 111 (1): 134–143.

MacKillop J, Obasi E, Amlung MT, McGeary JE, and Knopik VS (2010) The role of genetics in nicotine dependence: Mapping the pathways from genome to syndrome. *Current Cardiovascular Risk Reports* 4 (6): 446–453.

McClernon FJ, Hutchison KE, Rose JE, and Kozink RV (2007) DRD4 VNTR polymorphism is associated with transient fMRI-BOLD responses to smoking cues. *Psychopharmacology (Berlin)* 194 (4): 433–441.

National Advisory Mental Health Council Behavioral Science Workgroup (2000) *Translating Behavioral Science into Action*. Bethesda, MD: National Institute of Mental Health (NIMH).

Onken LS and Bootzin RR (1998) Behavioral therapy development and psychological science: If a tree falls in the wood and nobody hears it. *Behavior Therapy* 29: 539–544.

Paterson NE (2011) Translational research in addiction: Toward a framework for the development of novel therapeutics. *Biochemical Pharmacology* 81(12): 1388–1407.

Ray LA and Hutchison KE (2004) A polymorphism of the mu-opioid receptor gene (OPRM1) and sensitivity to the effects of alcohol in humans. *Alcoholism: Clinical and Experimental Research* 28 (12): 1789–1795.

van den Wildenberg E, Wiers RW, Dessers J, Janssen RG, Lambrichs EH, Smeets HJ, and van Breukelen GJ (2007) A functional polymorphism of the mu-opioid receptor gene (OPRM1) influences cue-induced craving for alcohol in male heavy drinkers. *Alcoholism: Clinical and Experimental Research* 31 (1): 1–10.

Woolf SH (2008) The meaning of translational research and why it matters. *Journal of the American Medical Association* 299: 211–213.

Index

The Wiley-Blackwell Handbook of Addiction Psychopharmacology, First Edition. Edited by
James MacKillop and Harriet de Wit.
© 2013 John Wiley & Sons, Ltd. Published 2013 by John Wiley & Sons, Ltd.

Index